The Complete Murders of the Black Museum
1835–1985

The Complete Murders of the Black Museum

the Black Museum

1835–1985

Gordon Honeycombe

This edition first published in 1995 by
Leopard Books
Random House, 20 Vauxhall Bridge Road, London SW1V 2SA

1 3 5 7 9 8 6 4 2

ISBN 0 7529 0001 3

Typeset in Sabon by
SX Composing Ltd, Rayleigh, Essex
Printed and bound in Great Britain by
Mackays of Chatham

The Murders of
the Black Museum
1870–1970

I do not now believe that any one of the hundreds of executions I carried out has in any way acted as a deterrent against future murder. Capital punishment, in my view, achieved nothing except revenge.

Albert Pierrepoint, 1974

Contents

Contents

NOTE:

The years given above refer to the year of the crime in which
the named victim was killed, not the year in which the
ensuing trial took place.

  In cases of multiple killing the victim listed is the one for whose
death the accused was tried. Neither Tratsart nor Merrett ever
came to trial.

Foreword

The Black Museum is now over a hundred years old. It came into being in 1875, when exhibits that had been acquired as evidence and produced in court in connection with various crimes were collected together and privately displayed in a cellar in 1 Palace Place, Old Scotland Yard, Whitehall. Ten years later the augmented collection was moved to a small back room on the second floor of the offices of the Convict Supervision Department. By then the objects on display, consisting mainly of weapons and all carefully labelled, numbered about 150.

In 1890, when the Metropolitan Police began moving into their impressive new headquarters at New Scotland Yard on the Victoria Embankment (designed by Norman Shaw RA), the museum went too. It was now called the Police Museum, its primary object being to provide some lessons in criminology for young policemen and its secondary one to act as a repository for artefacts associated with celebrated crimes and criminals. Privileged visitors, criminologists, lawyers, policemen and people working with the police were guided around the museum by the curator, who over the last century has always been a former policeman, with a special responsibility for the cataloguing, maintenance and display of the exhibits and for dealing with correspondence from criminologists all over the world.

In 1968, when the Metropolitan Police moved into their modern high-rise premises at 10 The Broadway, London SW1, the museum, now officially called the Crime Museum, occupied a large room on the second floor. Eleven years later, on the 150th anniversary of the founding of the Metropolitan Police force, it was decided to reassess, reorganize and modernize every aspect of the museum – as well as the three other Metropolitan Police museums: the Mounted Police Museum at Imber Court in Surrey; the Thames Museum at Wapping; and the Training Museum in Hendon Training School. The last had assumed completely the instructional role previously shared with the Crime Museum, which was now able to fulfil its entire function as a museum. Its original title was restored, and on 12 October 1981 the Black Museum, on the first floor of New Scotland Yard, was officially reopened by the Commissioner, Sir David McNee.

The Black Museum's historical collection of articles and exhibits is unique. It covers more than murder. Other sections deal with Forgeries, Espionage, Drugs, Offensive Weapons, Abortions, Gaming, Housebreaking, Bombs and Sieges, and Crime pre-1900. The museum also houses displays concentrating on particular crimes, such as the Great Train Robbery and the attempted kidnapping of Princess Anne, and possesses such peculiar exhibits as Mata Hari's visiting-card, a fake Cullinan diamond, a loving-cup skull with silver handles, two death masks of Heinrich Himmler, and thirty-two plaster casts of the heads of hanged criminals, men and women, executed in the first half of the nineteenth century at Newgate, Derby and York. The heads, still bearing the mark of the rope, are said to have been made to record the features of those who were executed. Many criminals then used aliases, and the only way of identifying them after death (before the use of photographs and finger-prints) was to keep these plaster likenesses. In addition, some if not all of the heads were probably made for doctors or phrenologists bent on proving theories about the physiognomy of criminal types by examining the bumps, shapes and all aspects of an actual criminal's head after its owner was dead and gone.

Visitors' books, also maintained in the museum, contain records of a different sort: the signatures of such notable persons as HM King George V, HRH Edward, Prince of Wales, Stanley Baldwin, Sir Arthur Sullivan, W. S. Gilbert, Captain Shaw of the London Fire Brigade, and William Marwood, executioner.

Some items discovered in the stock-taking of the museum in 1981 have still to be identified, and there is an undisplayed mass of other material (newspapers, cuttings, photographs, documents, letters and miscellaneous objects) relating to the exhibits on show and to other crimes. This material is kept under lock and key in cupboards below the showcases, mainly because space is restricted, but also because some of the items – for instance, the police photographs of Gordon Cummins's victims – are too obscene to be shown.

I first visited the Black Museum in 1979. It was a most interesting and very disturbing experience. There was a certain grim fascination in seeing the actual instruments and implements used by criminals, infamous or otherwise, and in seeing other more innocuous items given a sinister cast in the context of their use. But the effect of the exhibits on display was cumulatively shocking. They presented a dreadful picture of ruthlessness, greed, cruelty, lust, envy and hate, of man's inhumanity to man – and especially to women. There was nothing of kindness or consideration. There was no nobility, save that of the policemen murdered on duty. There was very little mercy. But the museum made me realize what a policeman must endure in the course of his duty: what sights he sees, what dangers he faces, what depraved and evil people he has to deal with so that others may live secure. The museum also made me curious to know more facts about the people whose stories were shadowed by the exhibits on display.

This book deals with a very few of the murders investigated by the officers of the Metropolitan Police between 1870 and 1970. This hundred-year period embraces many of the major murder cases in the history of Scotland Yard as well as the major advances in crime detection. The museum has some exhibits relating to murders before 1870 (notably a letter written by the poisoner William Palmer) and several associated with murders after 1970 (notably the murder of Lesley Whittle by Donald Neilson in 1975 and the multiple murders of Dennis Nilsen, convicted in 1983). But I felt that the grief suffered by families whose relatives had been murdered after 1970 was too recent to be revived by a detailed account. The murder that ends this book, that of Mrs McKay, seemed a fitting conclusion to the whole sequence, having been more publicized than most and being in many ways extraordinary. In fact if may have happened not in 1970 but at the end of 1969.

The accounts of these murders of the Black Museum have been dealt with as case histories, with an emphasis on factual, social and historical detail, and on the characters and backgrounds of both the victim and the killer. Principal sources are listed at the back of the book, but in the main statements and court proceedings have formed the basis for each story. No dialogue has been invented; it has been reproduced from statements and evidence given by the murderer as well as by witnesses and the police. What was said or alleged at the time by those most closely involved in a murder case may not always be true, but it is, I feel, of paramount importance in understanding the events that lead up to an act of murder and the complex motives and personalities of those most closely concerned. Like the superintendent or inspector in charge of a case I have tried to find out exactly what happened and why. It is my impression that the police officers investigating a murder ultimately have a clearer understanding of character, method and motive than some of the lawyers who take part in the ensuing trial. A court of law is seldom a place where the whole truth is told or revealed. It is in some respects a theatre of deception, with witnesses, defendants and barristers seeking to deceive the jury and each other. Even the judge, the arbitrator of truth, can mislead and be misled through ignorance or bias. But in a police station, although a suspect may lie as much as he or she likes, a truer picture of events and character is more likely to be attained in the end. Police reports concerning a murder and sent to a chief constable or commissioner are most sensible, lucid presentations of comment and fact. It is a pity they are not also available to the members of a jury in a court of law.

In working on this book I have been afforded the generous co-operation of New Scotland Yard. For this I am most grateful, and I would particularly like to thank the following for their individual assistance: Mr Peter Neivens; Patricia Plank and the staff of the Commissioner's Reference Library; the Museums' Co-ordinator, Paul Williams; and the Curator of the Black Museum, Bill Waddell.

Introduction

Murder is a very rare event in Britain. Its exceptional nature is in fact part of its fascination. More than ten times as many people are killed on the roads each year as are victims of a murderer.

In 1980, 564 cases of murder, manslaughter and infanticide, all now classed as homicide, were currently recorded in England and Wales. On the roads of Britain in 1979/80, 6,352 people were killed and 81,000 injured.

It must be said, however, that these figures for death on the roads were the lowest for thirty years and that the homicide figure was unnaturally high. Indeed the car-death figure, when compared with that of other decades and with the number of cars on the road, shows an astonishing decrease in fatalities. In 1931, for instance, when 1,104,000 cars and vans were on the roads, 6,691 people were killed and over 200,000 injured. Yet in 1979/80, with over 15 million cars on the road, the death-toll was much lower, as was the number of those injured. The worst year for road fatalities was significantly 1941, the second full year of the Second World War, when 9,169 people were killed. It is worth noting that deaths caused by reckless driving are not classified as homicide by the police, who recorded 235 such deaths on the roads in Britain in 1980.

The year 1980 was unusual in terms of homicide in that, of the 564 homicides currently recorded, 94 occurred in fires – 37 in a Soho club and 10 in a hostel in Kilburn. In addition 23 deaths that had occurred in fires in the Hull area between 1973 and 1978, when they were regarded as accidental, were recorded as homicides in 1980. This meant that the homicide figure for 1980, without the unusually high figure of deaths in fires, would have been under 450 – a great reduction on the 551 homicides recorded in 1979. Instead, with the figure of 94 deaths in fires included, the overall number of currently recorded homicides in 1980 (564) is the highest on record.

Although this figure is very small when compared with road fatalities and when seen against the total population of this country, it nonetheless shows a small increase in deaths by murder, manslaughter and infanticide. The figure, seen as a percentage per million of the population of England and Wales, is 11.5. In 1970, when 339 homicides were ultimately recorded, the percentage was 7.

Offences currently recorded by the police as homicide, seen against the number per million of the population, are as follows:

1970	339 :	7.0	1976	489 :	9.9
1971	407 :	8.3	1977	418 :	8.5
1972	409 :	8.3	1978	472 :	9.6
1973	391 :	8.0	1979	551 :	11.2
1974	526 :	10.7	1980	564 :	11.5
1975	444 :	9.0			

Peak years in homicide were 1974 and 1979. The table shows that there has been a general increase in homicide over the last decade – an increase that becomes more apparent when two decades are compared. There was a 55 per cent increase in homicides initially recorded in 1971–80 compared with 1961–70. However, it should be noted that in these two decades, offences of violence against the person increased by about 170 per cent, while serious offences of violence rose by about 60 per cent.

The incidence of murder in this country is small compared with that in America, where one murder is committed every 23 minutes or so. There are about 20,000 murders every year in the USA. The state with the highest figures for murder in 1979 was Florida, where 1,084 people were murdered – a high proportion of them from drug-related causes. This was an increase of 14.2 per cent on 1978.

There is no doubt that we live in an increasingly violent society, in which more violence is being committed by the young and in which more is directed against women and the elderly. In London in 1980 there were 13,984 incidents involving robbery, mugging and violent theft – an increase of 20 per cent on the previous year. Of the victims involved in these incidents, nearly 2,000 were over the age of sixty, and 3,387 were over fifty. And in the 584,137 serious offences recorded in London in 1980, 25 per cent of those arrested were aged between ten and sixteen.

Nonetheless, although there has been a vast increase in all types of crime since 1900, the comparative rise in murder has been very slight. There has, moreover, been little variation in the kinds and causes of murder. The commonest murders are still domestic ones – of a wife by her husband, of a woman by a lover, of a child by a parent. Of 456 murders examined in the period 1957–60 (70 per cent of those victims over the age of sixteen were women) the victim and the murderer were related in 53 per cent of all cases. In 27.9 per cent they were known to each other and 19.1 per cent were strangers. This is very similar to the Home Office statistical interpretation of the figures for homicide between 1970 and 1980: when about 50 per cent of the victims and killers were related, when over 30 per cent knew each other, and about 19 per cent were strangers. A notable feature of the Home Office statistics is that infants less than one year old, viewed as a percentage of that age-group in the population, were most at risk.

The survey of the 1957–60 murders, carried out by Terence Morris and Louis Blom-Cooper, also found that a very high percentage of the murderers had previous criminal records, usually for property offences, and that 70 per cent of the men convicted of capital murder in 1960 had previous convictions. It was also found that murderers were predominantly of the lower classes; that of these many had been in the services or were merchant seamen; that not a few were coloured; and that many murders were associated with heavy drinking.

Sir John MacDonnell wrote in 1905 that murder was 'an incident in miserable lives in which disputes, quarrels, angry words and blows are common'. This still applies – as the 1980 Home Office Criminal Statistics for England and Wales show when listing the apparent circumstances of homicides in 1970 and in 1980.

	1970	1980
Quarrel, revenge or loss of temper	173	239
In furtherance of theft or gain	34	56
Attributed to acts of terrorism	0	4
While resisting or avoiding arrest	0	2
Attributed to gang warfare or feud	4	5
The result of offences of arson	0	84
Homicide of women undergoing illegal abortion	4	0
Other circumstances, including sex attack	51	66
Not known, because:		
The suspect committed suicide	19	20
The suspect was mentally disturbed	34	39
Other reason	20	49
	339	564

Over the last decade the means by which murder is done has also varied very little, although, compared with the 1950s, there is less shooting or gas-poisoning, and a much reduced use of the blunt instrument – a reflection of changing social conditions. One constant has, however, been murder by strangulation or asphyxiation.

The Home office list of figures for offences currently recorded as homicide by apparent method of killing is as follows.

	1970	1980
Sharp instrument	107	160
Strangulation or asphyxiation	70	89
Hitting, kicking, etc.	57	94
Blunt instrument	43	61
Shooting	23	19

Drowning	12	14
Poison or other drugs	9	14
Burning	1	94
Explosion	0	0
Other	15	19
Not known	2	0
	339	564

Of some interest is the fact that suicide – there were 4,200 in Britain in 1979 – homicide and mental illness are connected and complementary. Between 1900 and 1949, 29 per cent of the persons suspected of murder committed suicide, a proportion that rose to 33 per cent in the next decade. Again, between 1900 and 1949, 21.4 per cent of the persons found guilty of murder were also adjudged to be insane or unfit to plead. This figure rose in the next decade to 26.5 per cent. It seems that a person suffering from morbid depression, frustration or anxiety, whose mental balance is disturbed, may, as that mental stress or illness increases, commit either suicide or murder. If it is murder, that person may recover as a result of such an act, or become insane. There also seems to be a case for viewing murder as an act of displaced self-destruction, when the disturbed person, unable to kill himself or herself, kills someone near them as a substitute. Some women, unable to kill themselves or a husband or a lover, direct their act of destruction against someone more vulnerable, a child, almost as a token sacrifice.

Another factor connected with the causes of murder is the actual or subconscious yearning of a nonentity for notoriety, a desire inflamed these days by the ease with which other nonentities achieve a spurious fame through appearing on television or from the inflated attentions of the press. People desire to be noticed, to be distinguished in some way by what they are or do. In some cases, where a person is totally undistinguished and untalented, desperate measures are taken to remedy the defect.

Bruce Lee, aged twenty – his real name was Peter Dinsdale – was convicted of killing people by setting fire to the houses in which they lived in and around Hull. Said to be suffering from a psychopathic personality disorder, he admitted in court to twenty-six cases of manslaughter on the grounds of diminished responsibility and to ten charges of arson. Some doubt has since been cast on these claims and the prosecution's case. He was committed on 20 January 1981 to a psychiatric institution in Liverpool for an indefinite period. His counsel, Mr Harry Ognall, QC, said at Dinsdale's trial: 'No words of mine could assist this crippled, solitary and profoundly disordered young man. This pathetic nobody has, by his deeds, achieved a notorious immortality.' Perhaps this was one of Dinsdale's unacknowledged desires.

It was certainly the aim of seventeen-year-old Marcus Serjeant, from Capel le Ferne in Kent, who on 13 June 1981 fired five blank shots at the

Queen as she rode down the Mall to the ceremony of Trooping the Colour in Horse Guards Parade. Tried under Section 2 of the Treason Act, he was sentenced to five years in jail. He claimed he had been influenced by the shooting of John Lennon and by the assassination attempt on President Reagan. To a friend he wrote: 'I am going to stun and mystify the whole world with nothing more than a gun ... I may in a dramatic moment become the most famous teenager in the whole world. I will remain famous for the rest of my life.'

Such a desire was probably not shared by Crippen, Christie or Haigh. But the last two certainly relished their notoriety, and they may have been subconsciously influenced by a desire to be different, to do something alien, at least to become notable by doing something notorious.

One interesting trait shared by many murderers is their use of pseudonyms. It appears that they assume false names not only to evade detection, but chiefly to invent for themselves new personas – as though they cannot bear what they are.

In most if not all premeditated murders the act of murder is not in fact the only solution to a particular emotional or mental problem. Yet it is the one way out that a potential murderer chooses. There are many and complex reasons for this, apart from the minor factors outlined above. There is supposedly an X factor, a chemical reason, strictly speaking an extra Y chromosome in the genetic structure of a few people that turns them into psychopaths if not into killers. There is undoubtedly a rage in the blood and in the mind that leads to murder, whatever its cause. But what the murderers in this book have in common – and most are to some degree amoral, vain, cunning, cruel, avaricious, selfish, stupid and bad – is that without exception they are, and behave like, fools.

There is one other factor that the case histories in this book reveal – the apparent significance of *place* in the perpetration of murder. This may only be an oddity. But in this connection it should be noted that of the thirty-seven women poisoners executed for murder between 1843 and 1955 (sixty-eight women were hanged in all in this period), twenty lived in towns and seventeen in the country. Of the *latter*, five lived in or near Boston in Lincolnshire and six in and around Ipswich in Suffolk. The Ipswich murders may have been imitative – they all occurred within a period of eight years – but the Boston murders were many years apart.

In considering the fifty murders described in this book, one wonders how great a part chance and coincidence played in the following facts: that Miss Holland and Mrs McKay were murdered within a few miles of each other – and near Bishop's Stortford, near where the poisoner George Chapman ran a pub and where Harry Roberts went to ground; that Mrs Deeming and Mr Maybrick died within a few miles of each other in Liverpool; that Frederick Deeming, Mrs Maybrick, Mahon, Armstrong, Kennedy and Wrenn at some time all lived in Liverpool; that Parker and Probert, Haigh, Thorne and Mahon killed within a twenty-mile radius of Lewes in Sussex (at Portslade, Crawley, Crowborough and Langney); that Mrs Pearcey and Samuel Furnace killed within a few hundred yards of each other in Camden

– a mile away from Crippen's house and two miles from where the Seddons lived; and that of thirty-nine murders detailed in this book and committed in the London area, only eight were committed south of the River Thames.

Why is it that so many victims and murderers in this book have visited and stayed at Bournemouth? The town has had some sensational murders, like that of Irene Wilkins in 1921 by Thomas Allaway, that of Mr Rattenbury by George Stoner in 1935, that of Walter Dinivan by Joseph Williams in 1939, and that of Doreen Marshall by Neville Heath in 1946. But Samuel Dougal, George Smith, Major Armstrong, the Thompsons, Ronald True, Emily Kaye, Frederick Browne, Neville Heath – and Montague Druitt – all stayed there within a few months of a murder. They did not choose other resorts nearer London for their visits, or any further away to the north. Why Bournemouth?

What is most odd, however, is the number of murderers – mass-murderers – who were born and brought up west and south of Leeds. Although Haigh was not born in Yorkshire, he was brought up from an early age in Outwood, south of Leeds. Christie was born and lived in a suburb of Halifax. The Black Panther, Donald Neilson (real name: Nappey) was born in Morley south of Leeds and lived in Bradford to the west; and the Yorkshire Ripper, Peter Sutcliffe, was born in Shipley and brought up in Bingley. To them can be added Peter Dinsdale, the killer-arsonist who came from Hull – to the east of Leeds but on the same latitude.

Finally, besides the mass-murderers, there are four other Yorkshiremen, who between them caused the deaths of over 600 men and women: James Berry, executioner, who was born in Heckmondwike, south-west of Leeds (between Christie and Haigh) and lived in Bradford; and the three Pierrepoints, Tom, Harry and Albert, all executioners, who came from Clayton, a western suburb of Bradford. The last two also lived in Huddersfield. Whoever said that God was a Yorkshireman was worshipping some strange gods indeed.

The Murders of
the Black Museum
1870–1970

CHAPTER 1

Charles Peace

The murder of Arthur Dyson, 1876

Murder is often compounded with theft and sex – which is to say that it frequently results from a compulsive desire to deprive, or a compulsion not to be deprived of one's desire. Fortunately, much thieving seems to be related to a low or inadequate sexual capability. But not always. A randy thief or robber has therefore more problems than his undersexed counterpart, problems that can lead to murder – as they did in the case of Charles Frederick Peace.

He was born in Sheffield on 14 May 1832, the son of a respected shoemaker; he was not a good scholar, but was very dexterous, making artistic shapes and objects out of bits of twisted paper. Apprenticed at a rolling-mill, he was badly injured when a piece of red-hot steel rammed his leg, leaving him with a limp. Later on his jaw was fractured, and this enabled him to alter his expression more or less at will. He took part in amateur theatricals, and he learned to play the violin with sufficient flair and skill to be billed at local concerts as 'The Modern Paganini'.

When he was about twenty, in search of other excitements and reluctant to earn a living, he began to thieve. He was not too successful at first, and between 1851 and 1866 was jailed for burglary four times, with sentences of one month, four, six and seven years. When he was not in jail he wandered from town to town. In 1859 he met and married Mrs Hannah Ward – she was a widow with a son called Willie – and returned to Sheffield in 1872. About three years later he set up shop in Darnall, then a village a few miles east of Sheffield, trading as a picture-framer and gilder. He was also a collector and seller of musical instruments and bric-à-brac.

In 1875 Peace was forty-three. He was, according to a Sheffield police description issued after the murder of Arthur Dyson: 'Very slightly built, height 5 feet 4 inches, hair grey; lacking one or more fingers of his left hand; cut marks on the back of both hands; cut marks on forehead; walks with his legs wide apart; speaks somewhat peculiarly, as though his tongue was too large for his mouth, and is a great boaster.' He looked about ten years older than his actual age, and apart from being plain ugly, he was as agile as a monkey and very strong. He was also utterly selfish, salacious, mendacious and shrewd.

Towards the end of 1875, or early in 1876, he became involved with his neighbours (next door but one) in Britannia Road, Darnall. Their name was Dyson. Arthur Dyson, very tall (6 ft 5 ins) and genteel, was a civil engineer, employed by railway companies. He had met his future wife, a young Irish girl called Katherine, when he was in America. She was tall, buxom and blooming, and fond of a drink. They married in Cleveland, Ohio, about 1866. Returning to England some seven years later, they lived for a time with Dyson's mother in Tinsley before coming to Darnall. It seems they often had rows.

Peace, commissioned by the Dysons to frame four pictures, including a portrait of Dyson's mother, became familiar with them and was soon enamoured of Mrs Dyson – 'If I make up my mind to a thing,' he once said, 'I am bound to have it.' She unwisely responded to his attentions. It seems they visited pubs, music-halls and fairs together and that their place of assignation was a garret in an empty house between their two homes. Peace took to calling on the Dysons at any time, including meal-times, until Mr Dyson put his foot down. But Mrs Dyson continued to associate with Peace, sending him notes informing him when her husband was out and likely to stay away.

In June 1876 Peace was forbidden by Arthur Dyson to call on his neighbours any more. Dyson wrote on a visiting-card, 'Charles Peace is requested not to interfere with my family,' and threw it into Peace's yard.

This was something Peace could not endure. He began to harass and threaten the Dysons. 'We couldn't get rid of him,' said Kate Dyson, talking later to the *Sheffield Independent*'s reporter. 'I can hardly describe all that he did to annoy us after he was informed that he was not wanted at our house. He would come and stand outside the window at night and look in, leering all the while . . . He had a way of creeping and crawling about, and of coming upon you suddenly unawares . . . He wanted me to leave my husband!'

On Saturday, 1 July 1876, Peace tripped up Mr Dyson in the street. That same evening he chanced to encounter Mrs Dyson outside her home in Britannia Road as she was complaining to three female neighbours about the assault. He demanded to know if they were talking about him; he was told they were. Asked by him to repeat what she had been saying, Kate Dyson did so, whereupon Peace pulled out a revolver and said: 'I will blow your bloody brains out and your husband's too!'

The following morning a magistrate's warrant was obtained for his arrest and he fled with his family to Hull, where Mrs Peace found employment as the supervisor of an eating-house.

For a time the Dysons were, it appears, undisturbed by their former neighbour. But on 26 October, still apprehensive about Peace's reappearance – or perhaps Arthur Dyson was still suspicious about his wife's association with Peace – the Dysons moved to the other side of Sheffield, to Banner Cross Terrace off Eccleshall Road. Their furniture went ahead of them in a wagon, and when they arrived at their new home that evening to take possession of it, Peace walked out of the front door and confronted them. After he and Dyson had exchanged some remarks

Peace said: 'You see, I am here to annoy you wherever you go.' Dyson reminded him that there was a warrant out for his arrest. Peace retorted that he cared nothing for the warrant, nor for the police. He then entered a grocer's called Gregory's, next door to the Dyson's house, to buy some tobacco.

A month later, on Wednesday, 29 November 1876, Peace was seen hanging about Banner Cross Terrace between 7 and 8 pm. He visited Gregory's, asking for Mr Gregory, who was out. He requested a woman in the street to take a message to Mrs Dyson, asking her to come and see him; the woman told him to deliver the message himself. He loitered for a while, and just before 8 pm accosted a labourer, Charles Brassington, outside the Banner Cross Hotel and began to malign the Dysons; Brassington moved away. Peace's behaviour may have been connected with the fact, as was later suggested in court, that he had had a rendezvous in the Stag Hotel the night before with Mrs Dyson and on the outcome of a murder trial in Manchester. But more of that later.

About 8 pm that evening, Kate Dyson put her little boy, aged five, to bed. She came downstairs to the back parlour, where her husband was seated in an armchair reading, and about ten past eight she put on her pattens, or clogs, took a lantern and, leaving the rear door open, went to the outside closet, which stood in a passage at the end of the terrace. It was a moonlit night. Peace later claimed that she left the house when he whistled for her.

Her closet visit concluded, she opened the door. Peace stood before her, gun in hand. 'Speak, or I'll fire,' he said, presumably meaning the opposite. She shrieked, slammed the door and locked it. Mr Dyson, alarmed, rushed out of the rear door of his house and around the corner of the building. As he did so his wife emerged from the closet. He pushed past her, pursuing Peace down the passage, across the forecourt, down some steps and on to the pavement. According to Mrs Dyson the two men never came to grips. According to Peace there was a struggle. He fired one shot, he said, to frighten Dyson. It missed. 'My blood was up,' said Peace. 'I knew if I was captured, it would mean transportation for life. That made me determined to get off.' He fired a second shot that struck Dyson in the forehead. The shots were fired in quick succession. Mr Dyson fell on to his back, and his wife screamed: 'Murder! You villain! You have shot my husband!'

Peace ran across the road, hopped over a garden wall and ran across a field. In doing so he dropped a small packet, containing more than twenty notes and letters and Dyson's card requesting Peace not to interfere. The notes, clearly written by a woman, said such things as: 'You can give me something as a keepsake if you like' – 'Will see you as soon as I possibly can' – 'You must not venture for he is watching' – 'Not today, anyhow he is not very well' – 'I will give you the wink when the coast is clear . . . Will sure tell you' – 'He is gone out, come now for I must have a drink' – 'Send me a drink, I am nearly dead' – 'Meet me in the Wicker, hope nothing will turn up to prevent it' – 'He is out now so be quick.'

Arthur Dyson was carried into the Gregory's house and then into his own home, where a surgeon, Mr Harrison found him propped up in a chair, a bullet-hole in his left temple, the bullet being in Dyson's brain. He died about half-past ten.

From then on Charlie Peace was really on the run, wanted for murder, with a reward on his head of £100. He disguised the missing two fingers on his left hand by fitting a tube over that arm, to which he appended an iron hook, so that he appeared to be minus a hand and arm. He acquired the nickname 'One-Armed Jemmy'. Burgling as he went, he travelled from town to town, from Sheffield to Bristol, to Oxford, to Derby, to Nottingham and Hull, where his disguise was so complete that his daughter, Jenny, failed to recognize him. During an attempted burglary in Hull in February 1877, he was surprised by the householder, a Mr Johnson, and fired two shots at him, both of which missed. From Hull, Peace went back to Nottingham, and there he met Susan Thompson, a widow aged about thirty, who was also known as Susan Bailey, or Grey. They lived together as man and wife, and Peace supported them by committing several burglaries locally, until one day the police called at his house. He escaped out of a back window and fled south to London, where he found lodgings in Lambeth. Here Susan joined him – and so, before long, did Hannah Ward and her son, whose presence, so the police later believed, 'protected his mother from sudden death'. For Hannah 'possessed the great secret of the Banner Cross murder' – which one day she divulged to Susan Thompson 'in a bad temper'. The two women, sworn on a bible to secrecy, managed to suppress their mutual animosity and 'act the part of friendship between themselves and the man'.

The Peace household now moved to Greenwich, before settling at 5 East Terrace, Evelina Road, Nunhead, near Peckham. Hannah Ward was installed in the basement with her son. Charlie occupied the other rooms with Susan Thompson – 'A dreadful woman for drink and snuff,' according to him – and they passed themselves off as Mr and Mrs Thompson. Before long she bore him a son.

The house was richly furnished, adorned with a quick turnover of other people's possessions and alive with dogs, cats, rabbits, canaries, parrots and cockatoos. As the women were always quarrelling it must have been quite a clamorous household. In the evenings Peace sometimes entertained friends and neighbours with musical soirées, at which he played a fiddle he had made himself, recited monologues and sang.

Meanwhile, he continued his trade, driving around South London by day in his pony and trap looking for likely 'cribs' to crack, and returning to them at night with his tools concealed in a violin case. He dressed well on these outings – 'The police never think of suspecting anyone who wears good clothes' – and looked quite different from his Sheffield self, having shaved off his beard, dyed his hair black and stained his face; he also wore spectacles. He became more successful, more daring than ever, and although his exploits attracted much attention in the papers, no one knew who he was. Every Sunday he and Mrs Thompson went to church.

It seems in the end that someone grassed on him, perhaps one or other of his women. Certainly the police were out in unusually large numbers in the early hours of Thursday, 10 October 1878, in the suburbs south-east of Greenwich Park. About 2 am PC Edward Robinson noticed a flickering light in the rear rooms of 2 St John's Park. He acquired the assistance of PC William Girling and Sergeant Charles Brown, and the latter went round to the front of the house and rang the door-bell, while the other two policemen hovered by the garden wall at the rear. They saw the roving light within the house go out and a figure make a swift exit from the dining-room window on to the lawn. PC Robinson gave chase, running across the moonlit garden, and was six yards away when Peace turned and shouted: 'Keep back, keep off, or by God, I'll shoot you!' PC Robinson said: 'You had better not.'

Peace fired three times, according to Robinson, narrowly missing the constable's head. He rushed at Peace, who fired a fourth shot that missed, and as they struggled – 'You bugger, I'll settle you this time!' exclaimed the burglar – a fifth shot entered Robinson's right arm above the elbow. Undaunted and no doubt now enraged, Robinson flung Peace on the ground, seized the revolver and hit Peace with it several times. 'You bugger!' said Peace, 'I'll give you something else!' and allegedly reached for some weapon in one of his pockets. But by then Girling, followed by Brown, had come to Robinson's assistance and Peace was overpowered.

While he was being searched, Peace made another attempt to escape and was incapacitated by a blow from Girling's truncheon. A spirit flask, a cheque-book and a letter-case, stolen from the house, were found in his possession, as well as a small crowbar, an auger, a jemmy, a gimlet, two chisels, a centre-bit and a hand-vice.

As Robinson was now feeling faint through loss of blood, the two other policemen took charge of the captive burglar. He was escorted to Park Row police station near the Royal Naval College at Greenwich and not far from the River Thames. There he was charged with burglary and with the wounding of PC Robinson with intent to murder. He gave his name as 'John Ward', and when asked where he lived replied: 'Find out!' Inspector John Bonney of Blackheath Road police station was put in charge of the case, and later that morning Peace was brought before Detective Inspector Henry Phillips, local head of the newly formed Criminal Investigation Department of Scotland Yard, the CID.

DI Phillips later wrote a full, vivid and as yet unpublished memoir of the case. Writing in 1899, he said that Peace's 'repulsive' appearance could be verified by the wax image of him in Madame Tussaud's – where it is to this day.

On the morning of 10 October 1878, Phillips and Bonney tried to elicit information from the bloody-minded burglar, who exclaimed: 'If you want to know where I live, find out! It's your business!' When he became insolent, Bonney threatened to thrash him – 'All to no purpose,' wrote Phillips.

So the two inspectors 'subjected him to a little trap, a trick not sanctioned by the Police Authorities ... After the prisoner was remanded he was put in one of the Police Cells alone. I then,' wrote Phillips, 'made up a man under my charge, and the Gaoler put him into the Cell with the prisoner. He was pushed in head foremost and very nearly fell on top of Mr Ward. The newcomer commenced by using abusive and threatening language towards the Police Gaoler. Mr Ward then offered a little sound advice for the benefit of his fellow prisoner. He said: "Young man, don't never kick up a row with the Police – it's a bad plan and you will always find they get the best of you."'

Unfortunately for Phillips, Peace revealed nothing about his own circumstances, other than that he had been brutally treated by the arresting policemen and charged with burglary.

Peace was then lodged in Newgate prison, where he was visited by Phillips more than once. Phillips wrote later: 'He was very talkative and boasted of his misdeeds as if they were something to be proud of,' and he concluded that although Peace could seem 'religious-minded' and a 'nice quiet old man', he was really 'a canting hypocrite'.

The following month, Peace was tried under the name 'John Ward' at the Central Criminal Court in the Old Bailey on 19 November 1878, charged with the attempted murder of Edward Robinson. The judge was Mr Justice Hawkins; Mr Pollard was the prosecutor and Mr Montague Williams spoke on the prisoner's behalf.

After a four-minute consultation the jury found Peace guilty. Asked by Mr Reed, the clerk of the court, if he had anything to say before judgement was pronounced, the prisoner made a lengthy, whining speech that apparently impressed most of his listeners, except the judge. Peace said: 'My Lord, I have not been fairly dealt with, and I swear before God I never had the intention to kill the policeman. All I meant was to frighten him in order that I might get away. If I had the intention to kill him I could easily have done it. But I never had the intention to kill him. I declare I did not fire five shots. I only fired four shots . . . If your Lordship will look at the pistol you will see that it goes off very easily, and the sixth barrel went off of its own accord after I was taken into custody at the station. At the time the fifth shot was fired the constable had hold of my arm and the pistol went off quite by accident. I really did not know the pistol was loaded, and I hope, my Lord, you will have mercy upon me. I feel that I have disgraced myself and am not fit to live or die. I am not prepared to meet my God, but I fear that my career has been made to appear much worse than it really is. Oh my Lord, do have mercy upon me, and I assure you that you shall never repent it. Give me one more chance of repenting and preparing myself to meet my God. As you hope for mercy yourself at the hands of the great God, do have mercy upon me, a most wretched miserable man – a man that am not fit to die. I am not fit to live, but with the help of my God, I will try to become a good man,' etc. Peace was sentenced to penal servitude for life.

The judge then called PC Robinson forward, commended his courageous conduct and recommended him for promotion and for a reward of £25. Robinson was duly promoted to sergeant, and for a time a waxwork of him stood in Madame Tussaud's beside that of Peace.

The prisoner was incarcerated in Pentonville prison, which in 1878, wrote Phillips, was 'a preparatory prison for all convicts sentenced to Penal Servitude. It was here they performed the first 9 months of their sentence, under what was known as the solitary system.'

By this time Peace's real identity had been established, as well as the fact that he was wanted for the murder of Arthur Dyson in Sheffield.

Some two weeks before the Old Bailey trial, while Peace was lodged in Newgate jail, he wrote a letter requesting a certain gentleman, a Mr Brion, to visit him. This Mr Brion did, and was tailed when he left the jail and returned to his home in Philip Road, Peckham Rye. Phillips and Bonney decided to call on him that same night, Saturday, 3 November, although they were 'in some sort of doubt as to who the man was' – he might have been an accomplice of Peace. 'However,' continued Phillips in his memoir, 'we took a straightforward course after inspecting the house in which Mr Brion resided, which appeared to be of a highly respectable appearance and not at all like the haunt of Burglars. We were fortunate in finding Mr Brion at home, and we were still more fortunate in finding we had met with a very respectable man, very willing to assist us in this interesting enquiry. Mr Brion, a map-maker, had apparently believed "Mr Thompson" to be equally respectable and had been as surprised as Mrs Brion to hear that their acquaintance was in Newgate. They had believed Peace's story that he was inventing "an unsinkable boat", and had taken out a patent. He had explained his night-time excursions by saying that he was testing his boat on the Thames at night so that no one else could observe him.'

The Brions were able to tell the two inspectors where Mr Thompson lived and with whom – Susan Thompson and Hannah Ward. But their house, said Mr Brion, had 'broken up', Mrs Ward having gone to the north of England and Mrs Thompson to Nottingham. However, the latter, who had been staying with the Brions, was expected back very soon. The policemen asked to be informed by telegram the moment she returned.

On Monday, 5 November, the telegram came from Mr Brion and the inspectors returned to Peckham. At the Brions' house they were introduced in the front parlour to Susan Thompson – 'a tall, angular-featured woman,' according to Phillips, 'with a certain amount of determination and reserve in her disposition.' She was 'the Key to the whole situation,' he said. 'But the Key was rusty at first and required some lubrication.' First persuasion was used, and then threats.

'After two hours,' wrote Phillips, 'we were well nigh tired of our work, which seemed so fruitless. We begged her to tell us who the man was. She refused pointblank. I had been successful in finding a small silver watch in a bedroom she occupied, and this was brought into use when terror was brought to the front. We told her we should arrest her for receiving the stolen watch. If ever there was an object for pity, she was during these hours. Mrs Brion implored her to tell all she knew. She said: "I cannot tell you. I have taken an oath not to tell you anything." The torment she was going through began to tell upon her. I pointed out the disgrace she would bring upon Mr Brion if she was arrested at his house. She looked at me with tears in her eyes and said: "I dare not tell you." I said: "You need not tell one word with your lips – write it." I pulled out my pocket book and handed her a pencil, and this is what she wrote: *I know that is name is not Ward is Charles Peace of Sheffield.'*

Phillips continued: 'The Key had opened the door and now her conscience was relieved as to the Oath. Information as to John Ward's antecedents began to flow freely. She said: "He is the greatest criminal that ever lived and so you will find out. He used to live at Darnall near Sheffield and is wanted for murder and there is a reward for his arrest."' Susan Thompson eventually received that reward – £100.

Inspector Bonney thought Peace was a most inappropriate name for a burglar and alleged murderer and doubted Mrs Thompson's story. But he and Phillips went off to report to the recently appointed Director of the CID, Mr Howard Vincent, who immediately, to their surprise, sent them north along with Mr Brion, 'at the Public Expense'. Phillips wrote: 'The Director knew nothing of red tape and waited on no occasion for Office rules to be complied with.'

It seems that Phillips had never been north of Finchley, and his experiences over the next few weeks, as well as Peace's character and crimes, left a lasting impression. Over twenty years later he wrote: 'We went by the Midland Railway, all the way in the dark. The Country looked very dismal, but was lighted up by various bonfires, it being the 5th November. At Trent we separated. Bonney with Brion went on to the town of Nottingham, while I kept on with the Express and soon found myself in Sheffield.

'It is a strange feeling of loneliness to be suddenly landed in a great City, having no knowledge of any person within its boundaries. After some enquiry I found myself at the Central Police Office. It was 9.45 pm and an Inspector was then parading the night duty men, very much after the system of the Metropolitan Police. I thought them a very fine body of men. I now introduced myself to the Inspector, and having told him I had come to Sheffield to make enquiries, something like the following conversation took place. "Is there a place near Sheffield known as Darnall?" "Yes, there is a village named Darnall near Attercliffe." "Have you ever heard of the name of Peace as a family living about Sheffield?" "Oh, yes. We have been looking for a man named Charles Peace for some time – he is wanted for a Murder at Banner Cross near here. But our Chief has received some information that he died in a Coal Pit in Derbyshire." I said: "What is your man like?" and at the same time said: "Has he lost some fingers?" "Yes," said he. Then I said: "My friend, you may depend upon it that Charles Peace did not die in a Coal Pit, but is at the present time in Newgate Prison awaiting trial for attempted murder." He said: "You had best see Chief Constable Jackson in the morning."

'I asked for a recommendation to some good hotel and I was taken to the Hen and Chickens, kept by one Tingle. Now Tingle was a man anybody could take to because he was homely, and after 5 minutes interview and a Chat, I felt I had known the man for a much longer time. Here I stayed then till after breakfast the 6th Nov, and upon going to the Central Police

Station I had an interview with Chief Constable Jackson (who died in 1898, 20 years after my first introduction to him). A finer stamp of a Police Officer I have never met. No formalities with him – common sense was his motto before all technicalities. He at first doubted if the man Ward in Newgate was Peace. He put several Photographs of Criminals before me and I was soon able to point out the one most resembling John Ward, and then he told me that was the portrait of Peace.

'However, in order to make matters perfectly clear on this point, he sent off a Police Officer to London, telegraphing to Mr Vincent, and by the time the Officer arrived at Scotland Yard, Home Office Authority had been obtained for the inspection of John Ward, who of course was identified as Charles Peace – much to the discomfort of that person. A telegram soon arrived in Sheffield notifying the result of the interview.'

DI Phillips then set out to find Hannah Ward, assisted by an inspector from Attercliffe 'a true type of Yorkshireman,' wrote Phillips. 'I had never got in contact with such men before. They seemed to have the Knack of making you feel you had known them for years.' They journeyed to Darnall – 'a wild barren-looking country, the more so in November' – and found where Hannah Ward, now aged fifty, was staying, in a cottage with her daughter (by Peace) and son-in-law.

Phillips wrote: 'As luck would have it she came to the door in answer to my Knock. I told her I wanted to know if she would give up the possession of the house at Nunhead, trying to make her believe that I was Agent for her Landlord. I got inside the house under this pretence and at once noticed a Clock on a Chest of drawers which answered the description of one stolen at Blackheath. The Inspector came up with the Village Constable and then Mrs Peace began to look rather discomfited. I at once arrested her upon the charge of receiving the Clock with a guilty knowledge, and I searched the house and found property consisting of valuable wearing apparel, such as a sealskin jacket, silver plate and various articles which looked quite out of place in a four-roomed Cottage, whose real occupant was a Collier. Having packed up this property, we set out for Sheffield with our Prisoner and a very heavy bundle of goods which were never expected to find the way back to their owners, but they did.'

On 9 November, having heard of Hannah's arrest, Peace wrote from Newgate to 'a gentleman in Sheffield', beseeching him to save Hannah – 'She is inesent, she knows nothing of my doings . . . It is me and not her.'

Hannah Ward appeared before the Sheffield magistrates, was remanded for a week, and some time before Christmas was taken by Phillips back to London on an overnight train and charged by him 'at Bow Street one Saturday morning about 4 am'. On 14 January 1879 she appeared at the Old Bailey before Mr Commissioner Kerr, charged with receiving stolen goods. She was discharged, however, on the grounds that she was Peace's wife although – this was never proved or established by a search of civil records (as could easily have been done) – and had acted under his authority.

Eight days after her case was dismissed, early on the morning of

Wednesday, 22 January, Peace was taken from Pentonville and, handcuffed and attended by two warders, was put on the 5.15 am express from London to Sheffield for the magistrate's hearing. It was very cold: up north there was snow on the ground. Peace was very troublesome, but 'all went well', wrote Phillips, until the train neared Sheffield. It passed through Worksop and going full speed reached the Yorkshire border, where the railway line ran parallel with a canal.

'Peace was well acquainted with the locality,' Phillips wrote. 'He expressed a wish to pass water, and for that purpose the window was lowered and he faced it. He was wearing handcuffs and with a chain 6 inches long, so that he had some use with his hands – and he immediately sprang through the window. One of the warders caught him by the left foot. There he held him suspended, of course with the head downwards. He kicked the warder with the right foot and struggled with all his might to get free. The Chief Warder was unable to render his colleague any assistance because the Warder's body occupied the whole of the space of the open window. He hastened to the opposite side of the Carriage and pulled the Cord to alarm the Guard, but the Cord would not act. But some gentlemen in the next compartment, seeing the state of affairs, assisted the efforts of the Warder to stop the train. All this time the struggle was going on between the Warder and the Convict, and eventually Peace succeeded in kicking off his shoe and, his head striking the footboard of the Carriage, he fell on the line.'

The train eventually came to halt before it reached Kiveton Park, and the two warders ran for over a mile back along the railway line and found their prisoner prostrate in the snow and apparently dead. To their relief he soon recovered consciousness, professing to be in great pain from the bloody wound in his head and dying from cold. A slow train heading for Sheffield chanced to appear and was stopped by the two warders. Peace was lifted up and placed in the guard's van. The train proceeded on its way, arriving in Sheffield at 9.20.

Meanwhile, 'an immense crowd had assembled to get sight of this great Criminal,' continued Phillips, 'and the excitement became intense when the 8.54 Express arrived without him. The Guard reported that Peace had escaped. The crowd were unbelieving and they suggested that the statement was a ruse to get the crowd away. But when they saw a sword and a rug and a bag belonging to the Warders brought from an empty carriage and handed to Inspector Bird, it was then generally believed that the statement was true and that Peace had escaped from Custody and that the Warders were on his track.

'At the Sheffield Police Court great preparations had been made for the reception of Charles Peace and the Court was crowded. All the persons required to be in attendance were present, except one, and that was the Prisoner. The Magistrate, Mr Welby, was there. Mr Pollard of the Treasury was ready with all his documents to carry out the Prosecution on behalf of the Crown, while Mr W. E. Clegg, a solicitor, was there to defend. Mr Jackson, Chief Constable of Sheffield, entered the Court in a state of some excitement and made the startling statement to the Bench that Peace had escaped from the Warders. The ordinary business of the Court proceeded, when it suddenly became known that Peace had been captured and was actually in Sheffield, although it was doubtful if he would be able to attend the Court that day in consequence of his injuries.

'On reaching the Police Station Peace was carried to a Cell, where he was seen by Dr Stewart, the Police Surgeon, and a Mr Hallam, a Surgeon of Sheffield. They found him suffering from a severe scalp wound and concussion of the brain. He appeared to be in an exhausted state and vomited freely, and it was with some difficulty that stimulants were administered to him. His wounds were carefully dressed, and he was laid in a bed in a Cell and covered with rugs. There the little old man lay, with his head peeping out of the rugs, guarded by 2 Officers. During the first hour he was frequently roused and he partook of some brandy. At first, force had to be used to get him to take it, but subsequently he drank without any trouble: at the same time he said he should prefer whisky if he was compelled to take spirit. When he was handled by his Police attendants, for the purpose of giving these stimulants, he ground his teeth, clenched his hands and appeared to be in a fit. But when extra force was used he obeyed the Officers. On one of these occasions a Police Officer who knew him well said: "Now, Charley, it's no use. Let's have none of your hanky-panky games here. You will have to take it." And he did take it – a Coward you see when subdued. He next complained of being cold and extra clothing was provided for him, the object of the Authorities being of course to bring him round as soon as possible so as to get him before the Magistrate. In a few days the Surgeon certified him as being fit to attend the Court.'

In fact the court went to him, and the magistrate's hearing was held on Friday, 24 January, by candlelight in the corridor outside his cell.

Swathed in rugs and bandages, he cursed, groaned, complained and endlessly interrupted. 'What are we here for. What is this?' he protested. The stipendiary replied: 'This is the preliminary enquiry which is being proceeded with after being adjourned.' Said Peace: 'I wish to God there was something across my shoulders – I'm very cold! It isn't justice. Oh dear. If I'd killed myself it'd be no matter. I ought to have a remand! I feel I want it, and I must have one!' The hearing was attended by Mrs Dyson, who had been brought back to England from America, whither she had gone after her husband's death. As the prosecution's principal witness she seemed to enjoy the drama of her situation and was evidently not put out by Peace's presence, appearance and his aspersions. When she took the oath without lifting her veil, he exclaimed: 'Will you be kind enough to take your veil off? You haven't kissed the book!' At one point he put his feet on the table. At the end of the hearing he was carried back into his cell blaspheming.

Committed for trial at Leeds Assizes, he was taken by train to Wakefield prison. A large crowd again assembled at Sheffield's railway station to witness his departure. Professing to be helpless, he was carried from the police van by prison warders. He looked pale and haggard, despite his brown complexion, which was heightened by the white bandage around his head. 'He wore his Convict suit,' wrote Phillips, 'and very comical he looked in the cap surmounting the bandage, and appeared as feeble as a Child.'

When he arrived at Wakefield, less sympathetic, or more astute officials compelled him to walk unaided to his cell. There he spent the next few days writing penitential and moralistic letters. One, on 26 January, was to Mrs Thompson.

'My dear Sue – This is a fearful affair which has befallen me, but I hope you will not foresake me, as you have been my bosom friend, and you have oftimes said you loved me, and would die for me. What I hope and trust you will do is to sell the goods I left you to raise money to engage a Barrister to save me from the perjury of that villainous woman Kate Dyson. It will have to be done at once . . . as the Assizes commence on January 28th. I hope you will not forget the love we have had for each other. Do your best for me. I should like you to write or come and see me if you can. I am very ill from the effects of the jump from the train. I tried to kill myself to save all further trouble and distress, and to be buried at Darnall. I remain your ever true lover till death.'

He signed himself 'John Thompson. Charles Peace.'

Sue Thompson replied – 'Dear Jack, I received your letter and am truly sorry to receive one from you from a Prison, and in regard to what you ask me I have parted with all the things in my possession. I sold some of the goods before Hannah and I went away and I shared with her the money that was in the house, and what I had, had to be sold for my subsistence as you well know. I had nothing to depend upon, and have not a friend of my own, but what have turned their backs upon me, my life is indeed most miserable. I have 2 friends who have not turned upon me for which I am most grateful. I am sorry you made such a rash attempt upon your life, for your sufferings are greater than they would have been . . . You are doing me a great injury by saying I have been out to work with you. Do not die with such a base falsehood upon your conscience, for you know I am young and have my home and character to redeem. I pity you and myself to think we should have met. In conclusion, I hope and trust you will be very penitent and that we shall meet in Heaven. Yours, etc. – Sue.'

On Tuesday, 4 February 1879, Charles Peace was put on trial at Leeds Assizes before Mr Justice Lopes. The prosecutor was Mr Campbell Foster, QC, and the accused was defended by Mr Frank Lockwood. The mayor, the sheriff, MPs and a peer were present, and the court was packed, many of the women being armed with opera glasses. Peace, wizened, but wiry and unshaven, his scarred head and hollow features bristling with thin grey hairs, sat in an armchair within a semi-circular spiked enclosure.

Mr Campbell Foster contended in his opening remarks that the shooting of Arthur Dyson was premeditated and committed 'with malice aforethought'.

The prosecution's chief witness, Mrs Dyson, although evidently embarrassed by the implications of some of the defence's questions in cross-examination, behaved with a degree of flippancy, even levity. When asked by Mr Lockwood how wide the passage was outside the closet, she replied: 'I don't know – I am not an architect.' Lockwood, bent on getting her to admit that Dyson and Peace had come to grips before the shots were fired, quoted what she had said before the magistrate – 'I cannot say, whether he, that is my husband, attempted to get hold of him or not.' She now declared: 'He never touched him. He did not get close enough.' She was obdurate, although badgered by Lockwood on this point for some time. She was shown her signed deposition and he read from it – 'I cannot say my husband did not get hold of him.' 'He did not try to get hold of him,' the witness responded. 'Do you remember saying what I have read?' demanded Mr Lockwood. Mrs Dyson: 'I said he did not try to get hold of him.' Lockwood: 'Do you remember saying the words I have repeated to you?' Mrs Dyson: 'Yes. I do remember saying it, but the word "try" is left out.' 'Do you remember?' 'I can't say I do.' 'Will you swear that you did not?' 'I won't swear I did *not*, because it is written down.' 'Will you swear your husband did not get hold of him?' 'I say he did not, because he was not near enough to him.' 'Did you give that as the reason when you were before the magistrate?' 'Yes. They did not press me so hard – not as hard as you!' There was laughter in court.

Mr Lockwood pressed on regardless, until the judge intervened: 'Whatever you said before the magistrate is correct?' 'Yes,' Mrs Dyson replied.

But Mr Lockwood would not let go. To his question 'Did this man touch him with his fist?' she replied: 'No, the *bullet* touched him.' More laughter.

Lockwood was more successful in implying that Mrs Dyson had had an association with Peace, that he gave her a ring, that she continued to meet him after her husband had expressed his dislike of Peace, and had been photographed with him at the Sheffield Summer Fair in 1876. She denied that letters and notes referring to assignations were in her handwriting. She was forced to admit, when confronted by witnesses, that she had gone with Peace to a pub called the Marquis of Waterford in Russell Street, Sheffield, to the Norfolk Dining Rooms in Exchange Street, and to the Star Music Hall. But she denied that she bought drink at the Halfway House in Peace's name, that she gave a man called Kirkham notes for Peace, that she was ever evicted from a pub for being drunk, and that she was with Peace in the Stag Hotel the night before her husband was killed.

Throughout Mrs Dyson's cross-examination Peace leaned forward, looking at her, occasionally summoning his solicitor and whispering to him.

Various witnesses corroborated the circumstances surrounding the shooting of Arthur Dyson, and then Mr Lockwood, in his speech for the defence, proposed that the shooting was accidental, that Peace's threats were meaningless and that the prosecution's principal witness was unreliable and her evidence tainted and uncorroborated. The prosecution, he said, had not established their charge. In conclusion, he urged the jury not to lay themselves open to the reproach that they had 'wrongfully taken away the life of a fellow man'.

The judge told the jury that the plea of provocation failed altogether 'where preconceived ill-will against the deceased was proved'.

The jury took fifteen minutes to reach a verdict of 'guilty of wilful murder' and Peace was sentenced to death. On being asked if he had anything to say before sentence was passed, he muttered: 'Will it be any use for me to say anything?'

Peace was removed to Armley jail in Leeds where, thoroughly penitent, he made a full confession of all his crimes to the Reverend J. H. Littlewood, vicar of Darnall. He revealed that four months *before* the killing of Arthur Dyson he had shot and killed a police constable in Manchester.

Two young Irish brothers called Habron had been accused of the constable's murder, and one had been sentenced to death. Their story was also told by Inspector Phillips in his 180-page memoir on Peace.

'About 1870, four young labourers named Habron left their village home in County Mayo and in a suburb of the City of Manchester they settled down. Thomas Habron went into the service of Mr Grealey, a Farmer. The others, William, John and Frank were engaged by Mr Francis Deakin, Farmer, and there the brothers remained without further notice until the summer of 1875. They bore excellent characters on the whole and regularly remitted a portion of their earnings to the old folks at home. All that stood to their disadvantage took the form of 3 summonses for drunkenness. Two were issued in July 1876 at the instance of a young Constable, Nicholas Cock, who however seems to have made a mistake and the summons were dismissed on the 1st August 1876. John and William went to a Beer House known as the Royal Oak where they were regular customers. John drank to his safe return, while William was heard to say: "Here's Damn the Bobbies," adding if the Bobby did him, he would do the Bobby. John, contending that the Constable had no right to summon him, said: "If he does, by God, we will shunt him!" The landlady said: "Why, Jack, what do you mean?" And the reply was: "We will shift him. We will get our Gaffer, Mr Deakin, to shift him."

'The night was a dark one, and the well-to-do neighbourhood of Whalley Range with the great houses and large gardens seemed more than ordinarily deserted, and while the 3 brothers slept as was their wont in the out-house in Mr Deakin's premises, the object of their spleen, Police Constable Cock, commenced his beat from Charlton Village along Chorley Lane to West Point, where he was due at midnight. In Charlton Lane he was met by a pedestrian, a Mr Simpson, and at West Point they were met by PC Beanland. Immediately after, the figure of a man was seen moving along in the shadow towards the garden of a house that had been in the occupation of a Mr Gratrix, and when Mr Simpson had said: "Goodnight, Beanland," he went into the garden where the mysterious figure had apparently disappeared and examined the door of the house. He had barely turned away again when 2 shots fired in rapid succession were heard. Hurriedly retracing their steps, Beanland and Simpson were horrified to find Constable Cock lying in the roadway, shot through the right breast. The sound of wheels was heard and a night-cart coming along, and on this rude vehicle the body of the insensible Policeman was conveyed to the nearest surgery. The wounded Constable did not live long.

'The local Superintendent immediately suspected the Habrons, and within an hour, in company with some Constables, had taken possession of the outhouse where the brothers slept. Promptly bidding the brothers to get out of bed, he instituted a rigorous search, ordering each man to put on the clothes he was wearing yesterday ... By 3 am the 3 Habrons were in the cells at Northumberland St Station.'

The charges against Frank Habron were dropped through lack of evidence. But John and William (the youngest brother) were sent for trial at Manchester Assizes on 27 November 1876.

The prosecution implied that Cock had been shot by one or other of the Habrons out of spite and in revenge. Various witnesses recalled various threats the brothers had made, that William had inspected a revolver in the ironmongers, and that John had said 'shoot him' not 'shift him'. *Two* men were alleged to have been seen lurking near the scene of the crime; one of them wore a coat and hat similar to those worn by William Habron. Although Mr Simpson described the mysterious figure he had seen as 'elderly and with a stooping gait', PC Beanland was positive that the man had walked erect and definitely resembled William Habron. Footprints found near the scene matched those made by the boots of the accused, and some percussion caps were found in a waistcoat pocket worn by William. Mr Deakin, convinced his employees were innocent, explained that he had given the waistcoat to the accused and had probably left the caps in the pocket himself.

On 28 November the jury, having consulted for two and a half hours, found John not guilty and William guilty, adding a recommendation for mercy 'on the grounds of his youth'. William was nineteen. Mr Justice Lindley, who had summed up in the prisoners' favour, observed in passing sentence that he did so in the execution of his duty.

Peace had watched the whole trial from the public gallery. He kept silent. 'What man would have done otherwise in my position?' he later demanded.

The following night in Sheffield, on 29 November, he shot and killed Arthur Dyson.

For three weeks William Habron was confined in the condemned cell. But on 19 December the Home Secretary, Mr Cross, granted a reprieve and the sentence was commuted to one of penal servitude for life. William Habron was sent to Portland prison as Convict 1547, where he remained for over two years – until Peace, now under sentence of death himself, chose to confess. He told the Reverend Littlewood that he thought it right 'in the sight of God and man to clear the young man'.

Peace's written confession, dated 17 February 1879 and reprinted in Phillips's memoir, said that all the witnesses who appeared for the prosecution perjured themselves, except one (presumably Mr Simpson). A detailed map, drawn by Peace, was included with the confession, indicating with dotted lines the movements of the main protagonists. Peace said that about midnight, as he entered Seymour Grove, he saw two policemen and two civilians standing near a ducking pond. He crossed the road, hurried away from them and slipped into the garden of a house by the gate. When Beanland followed him in and tried the front door, turning on his bull's-eye lantern, Peace returned to the road via the garden wall, crossing the road to the other side. Cock must have seen him, for he came down the road towards the burglar, shouting at him to stand where he was.

'This policeman was as determined a man as myself,' Peace admitted later, 'and after I had fired wide at him, I observed him seize his staff, which was in his pocket, and he was rushing at me and about to strike me. I then fired the second time. "Ah, you bugger," he said, and fell. I could not take as careful an aim as I would have done, and the ball, missing the arm, struck him in the breast. I got away, which is what I wanted.'

At the confession's end Peace wrote: 'As a proof of his [Habron's] inescence you will find that the ball that was taken from Cox's breast was one of Haley's No 9 Pinfire cartridges, and was fired out of my revolver now at the Leeds Town Hall.' He ended: 'What I have said is nothing but the truth and that is my dying words. I have done my duty and leave the rest to you.'

On 19 March 1879 William Habron was moved from Portland to Millbank and then set free with a full pardon. Mr Deakin was there to meet him, with the news that William's father had died six months earlier 'of a broken heart'. He was given £1000 in compensation 'to ease his pain and anguish'.

Years later Phillips wrote: 'No part of the case gave Bonney and myself so much satisfaction as the release of the Convict William Habron, an innocent man.'

Charles Peace was hanged at Armley jail in Leeds at 8 am on 25 February 1879.

His last days were spent in interminable letter-writing and prayer and the Christian exhortation of others. But his reprobate real self prevailed. Of his last breakfast he said: 'This is bloody rotten bacon!' And when a warder began banging on the door as Peace lingered overlong in the lavatory on the morning of his execution, he shouted: 'You're in a hell of a hurry! Are you going to be hanged or am I?' On the scaffold he refused to wear the white hood – 'Don't! I want to look' – and insisted on making a speech of forgiveness, repentance and trust in the Lord.

Four journalists who were present wrote down his last words, spoken as his resolution left him: 'I should like a drink. Have you a drink to give me?' As he spoke, Marwood, the executioner, released the trap-door. Peace fell; the vertebrae at the base of his head fractured and dislocated, and his spinal cord was severed. A doctor wrote on his death certificate: 'Hanging by virtue of a sentence of law.'

Peace wrote his own epitaph for the memorial card which he himself printed in jail: 'In memory of Charles Peace who was executed in Armley Prison, Tuesday, February 25th 1879. For that I done but never intended.'

In due course Inspector Phillips donated the tube that Peace had used to cover his arm, a crucible and a collapsible ladder to the Black Museum at Scotland Yard. A hundred years later, Phillips's very informative, hand-written memoir was in turn donated to the museum by lorry-driver Peter Coyle on behalf of Phillips's great-niece, Mrs Bell.

CHAPTER 2

'Jack the Ripper'

The Whitechapel murders, 1888

Fiction far outweighs fact in the volume of words used to describe the crimes, motives and character of 'Jack the Ripper'. The facts are few, almost as few as the five murders he is believed to have committed. The fictions stem from the fact – despite mountains of theory and speculation – that no one knows for certain who he was. No single writer, in the last fifty years, has been able to establish the identity of the Whitechapel murderer, as he was originally called. Significantly, the first full-length work on the subject, The Mystery of Jack the Ripper, was not published until more than a generation, forty-one years, after the murders. It was written by an Australian journalist, Leonard Matters. Since then, and despite confident claims by various writers that they have found The Answer, or The Final Solution, they have not. They fail to convince, to provide conclusive proof, their causes and case histories being spoiled by misconception, misreporting, error, and the perpetuation of earlier journalistic imaginings, assumptions and fancy unsupported by fact. The identity of the Whitechapel murderer is and will remain an enigma. He is not even definitely named in the so-called secret files of Scotland Yard.

Five murders are known to have been committed by the Ripper, but two others were once thought to have been his work as well. The first was of Emma Smith, an ageing prostitute, who lived at 18 George Street, Spitalfields. She was attacked in Osborn Street in the early hours of 3 April 1888. Her face and ear were cut, and some instrument, not a knife, had been thrust violently up her vagina. She said she had been assaulted by four men, but could or would not identify them. She died the next day in the London Hospital of peritonitis.

Four months later, at 3 am on 7 August, the body of Martha Tabram, aged thirty-five, was found on a staircase landing in George Yard Buildings in Commercial Street. Her throat and stomach had been stabbed or pierced thirty-nine times with something sharp like a bayonet. Earlier that night she and another prostitute had been seen in the company of two soldiers, who were arrested and paraded with others in front of the second prostitute. But she failed or refused to identify either her own or the other woman's partner.

It should be remembered that in 1888 the East End of London, a few square miles, was inhabited by about 900,000 people, virtual outcasts living in conditions of extreme depravity, poverty and filth. Fifty-five per cent of East End children died before they were five. Each squalid room in each rotting house was occupied by between five and seven persons – men, women and children. In Whitechapel, about 8,500 people crammed into 233 lodging-houses every night, paying as much as 4d for a bed. The parish of Whitechapel was infested altogether with about 80,000 artisans, labourers and derelicts, of whom the better-off – the poor as opposed to the very poor – earned about £1 a week. The more menial tasks yielded a shilling a day, women being paid less than men. People lived from day to day, earning or stealing what they could to eat and stay alive. Drunkenness and prostitution were rampant. The Metropolitan Police estimated that in October 1888 about 1,200 of the lowest sort of prostitute plied their trade in the dingy Whitechapel streets. Consequently women were assaulted and injured every night. Some were killed.

Twenty-four days after the death of Martha Tabram there occurred the first of the accepted Ripper killings. About 3.30 am on Friday, 31 August, Mary Ann Nichols, a forty-two-year-old prostitute, was murdered. She was found in Buck's Row, lying on her back, her skirt pushed up above her knees; her eyes were open. Her throat had been slashed twice, from left to right, the second eight-inch-long cut almost severing the head. Blood from the cut had been absorbed by her stained and shabby clothes: a brown ulster, a brown linsey frock, two petticoats, stays, and black wool stockings. She also wore a black straw bonnet. Her face was bruised. She was 5 ft 2 ins tall and had lost five of her front teeth. It was not until her body was removed to the mortuary by the old Montague Street workhouse that other injuries were revealed. Her stomach had been hacked open and slashed several times. Mary Ann Nichols, also known as Polly, had lodged at 18 Thrawl Street, Spitalfields, as well as at 56 Flower and Dean Street. She was last seen alive at 2.30 am on the corner of Osborn Street, staggering drunkenly down Whitechapel Road towards Buck's Row (now Durward Street).

Because she, Tabram and Smith were all murdered within 300 yards of each other and were prostitutes, a connection was made between them that now seems insubstantial. A man known to have ill-treated prostitutes and to have been seen with Nichols became a prime suspect. Known as Leather Apron, he was a Jewish bookmaker, John Pizer – also called Jack.

The next murder was eight days later. The body of Annie Chapman, aged forty-five, also known as Dark Annie, Annie Siffey or Sievey (she had lived with a man who made sieves), was found in the back yard of 29 Hanbury Street at 6 am on Saturday, 8 September. She lay on her back beside steps leading from a passage into the yard. Her knees were wide apart and her dirty black skirt pushed up over them. Her face was swollen and her chin and jaw were bruised; her tongue protruded from her mouth. Two deep and savage cuts had practically separated her head from her body. Her stomach had been torn open and pulled apart; sections of skin from the stomach lay on her left shoulder – on the right was another piece of skin and a mess of small intestines. It was later established that she had been disembowelled – her uterus, part of the vagina and the bladder had been carved out and taken away.

Slight bloodstains were discovered on the palings of a fence beside the body and specks of blood spattered the rear wall of the house above the prostrate corpse. Her rings were missing – they had been torn from her fingers. At her feet lay some pennies and two new farthings; a comb also lay by the body. Presumably this and the coins had been in the pocket under her skirt which had been ripped open. Other adjacent items – which probably had nothing to do with the murder – included part of an envelope stamped 28 August 1888 and bearing the crest of the Sussex Regiment on the back, as well as a piece of paper containing two pills and a leather apron soaked with water and about two feet from a tap.

Annie Chapman was a small, stout woman (5 ft) with dark hair, blue eyes, a thick nose and two teeth missing from her lower jaw. She had lodged at 35 Dorset Street, from where she had been evicted at 2 am because she lacked the few pennies for a bed. Drunk and ill, she had wandered off towards Brushfield Street. She was last seen alive at 5.30 am (a clock was striking the half hour) by a park-keeper's wife who was on her way to market. She saw Chapman standing outside 29 Hanbury Street, haggling with a foreign-looking man, aged about forty, who was shabbily but respectably dressed and wearing a deerstalker, probably brown. Number 29 was a lodging-house, occupied by seventeen people, none of whom heard anything untoward. But the street was not quiet: carts and workers were already moving up and down. Some people were going to work.

Several suspects were taken to Commercial Street police station for questioning on Sunday, 9 September, and in the early hours of Monday the 10th, John Pizer, Leather Apron, was found at 22 Mulberry Street and arrested. Witnesses said that two months earlier he had been ejected from 35 Dorset Street and that he wore a deerstalker hat. The police found five long-bladed knives in his lodgings, of a sort thought to have been used by the murderer. Pizer said that he used them in his bootmaking trade. He protested his innocence, and his story that he had been in hiding in the Mulberry Street house for four days, since Thursday, was backed up by his stepmother and brother who lived there. He also had an alibi for the night Mary Ann Nichols was murdered – he was in a lodging-house in Holloway Road.

At the inquest on Annie Chapman, the leather apron found in the back yard not far from her body was identified as the property of John Richardson, whose widowed mother lived in 29 Hanbury Street. She had washed the apron on Thursday, leaving it by the fence where it was found on Saturday by the police. Richardson had actually visited the house about 4.45 am on his way to work, to check that his mother's padlocked cellar (it had recently been robbed) was intact. In the dawn light he saw that it was and that the yard was empty.

Another yard was the scene of the murder of Elizabeth Stride, a forty-four-year-old Swedish prostitute, also known as Long Liz. She was killed about 1 am on Sunday, 30 September, a wet and windy night. Her body was discovered by a hawker, Louis Diemschutz, who worked as a steward in a Jewish Socialist Club that backed on to a yard in Berner Street. As he drove into the yard in a pony and trap, the horse shied to the left, doing so twice and drawing the hawker's attention to a heap of clothes on the ground. He poked at it with his whip and lit a match, which was snuffed out by the wind. But he had seen enough and fetched help from the club, where members were singing and dancing.

Long Liz lay on her muddy left side, her legs drawn up, right arm over her stomach, her left arm extended behind her back, the hand clutching a packet of cashew nuts. Her right hand was bloody, and her mouth was slightly open. The bow of a check silk scarf around her throat had pulled tight and had turned to the left of her neck. The scarf's lower edge was frayed, as if by a very sharp knife – which had also slit her throat from left to right, severing the windpipe. Bruises on her shoulders and chest indicated that she had been seized and forced down on to the ground before her throat had been cut. Her body was still warm. Evidently the murderer had been frightened off by the returning pony and trap. There were no other injuries or mutilations. It was noted at the mortuary that the dead woman had no teeth in her left lower jaw.

Like Nichols and Chapman, Stride was married but separated from her husband. Like them, she was something of an alcoholic. She had lived in Fashion Street with a labourer called Michael Kidney, who had then moved to 35 Dorset Street. But on the Tuesday before her death she had walked out, lodging instead at 32 Flower and Dean Street. On the Saturday night she had been seen by a labourer, William Marshall, at about 11.45 pm in Berner Street, talking to a mild-voiced, middle-aged, stout and decently dressed man, wearing a cutaway coat. He had looked like a clerk to Marshall: he wore no gloves, carried no stick or anything else in his hands, and on his head was 'a round cap with small peak to it' like a sailor's hat. He kissed Long Liz and he said: 'You would say anything but your prayers.' Then they walked down the street.

She was seen again in Berner Street at about 12.30 am by a policeman, PC Smith. He described Stride's companion as they stood and talked as 'of respectable appearance . . . He had a newspaper parcel in his hand.' The man was about 5 ft 7 ins in height, wore an overcoat and dark trousers and had a dark, hard felt deerstalker on his head. Smith gave the man's age as 'about twenty-eight'. The *Police Gazette* later expanded this to: 'complexion dark, small dark moustache; dress, black diagonal coat, hard felt hat, collar and tie.'

A third witness, a boxmaker, James Brown, crossed Berner Street about 12.45 am and noticed a couple standing by a wall. He heard the woman say: 'Not tonight. Some other night.' A glance revealed to him that the man was wearing a long dark coat. The *Gazette* elaborated Brown's description as follows: 'Age about thirty, height 5 ft 5 ins; complexion fair, hair dark, small brown moustache, full face, broad shoulders; dress, dark jacket and trousers, black cap with peak.'

Are Smith and Brown describing the same man? And was he the man who killed Elizabeth Stride at about 1 am and on being disturbed by the pony and trap fled westwards towards Aldgate?

Just after 1.30 am and half a mile to the west in Duke Street, three Jews, one of whom was a Mr Lawende, saw a man talking to a woman in Church Passage, which led into Mitre Square. She was wearing a black jacket and bonnet and was about three or four inches shorter than the man. He was later described in the *Police Gazette* as: 'Aged thirty, height 5 ft 7 ins, or 8 ins; complexion fair, moustache fair, medium build; dress: pepper and salt colour loose jacket, grey cloth cap with peak of some material, reddish neckerchief tied in knots; appearance of a sailor.' The woman was Catherine Eddowes, aged forty-three. Less than ten minutes later she was dead.

She had been married to a man called Conway, but for seven years she had lived at 6 Fashion Street with another man, John Kelly, and accordingly called herself Kate Kelly. That Saturday night she had been arrested in Aldgate about 8.30 pm: she was drunk and disorderly. Taken to Bishopsgate police station she had been left to sober up in a cell and was discharged at 1 am – at the same time as Elizabeth Stride's throat was cut in the yard of Berner Street. Eddowes walked off southwards, down Houndsditch towards Aldgate High Street and Mitre Square, as Stride's murderer hurried westwards towards her, his blood-lust unslaked.

At 1.45 am her body was discovered by the bull's-eye lamp of PC Watkins as he walked on his beat through the square. It lay on its back in a corner. 'I have been in the force a long while,' said Watkins, 'but I never saw such a sight.' The body had been ripped open, said Watkins, like a pig in the market. The left leg was extended and the right leg bent. The throat had been deeply slit and the face had been slashed and cut. There were also abrasions on both cheeks. Both sets of eyelids had been nicked and part of the nose and the right ear had been sliced off. The trunk had been torn apart from the sternum to the groin by a series of disjointed thrusts, the pointed knife that was employed being angled from right to left. The woman had been disembowelled – entrails had been thrown across her right shoulder. The uterus and the left kidney had been cut away and removed.

Police sketches and photographs of Catherine Eddowes's body greatly minimize the view that the murderer had some anatomical knowledge – or took 'at least five minutes' over his work. He clearly worked in a frenzy – cutting the throats of his victims, *ripping* their bodies and pulling out organs with neither care nor skill, and all in a couple of minutes at the most. He would have worked with speed, frantic with blood-lust and also fearful of being caught. He may have had a very rough knowledge of anatomy, sufficient for him knowingly to silence each victim by severing her windpipe, and he must have known what a womb looked like (he removed two) and have been able to distinguish such a comparatively small and obscure item among the mass of organs in the gut. But this does not mean that he had had any actual medical experience or had been a butcher, slaughterman, farmer or hunter of any sort.

The idea propounded at the time by some doctors, that the throats of the victims had been cut (the cause of death) as they lay on the ground, is in reality not very likely – unless the women were already unconscious, or dead. For despite their dirty clothes and drunken state, they are unlikely to have stretched out on the much dirtier, or muddy ground to have sex. This service would most likely have been provided standing up against a wall, with their backs to it – or facing it. And it is unlikely that the women were suffocated or strangled *before* their throats were cut. If they *had* been strangled, they would surely have fought for their lives. But in no case was there any sign of a struggle, nor were any bruises found on the women's necks where pressure in strangulation would have been applied. Despite the cut throats, some such marks, if they had been there, must have remained. There were, however, bruises and abrasions on the *faces* of the women, about the chin and jaw.

It seems likely that the murderer seized the women from behind, with his left arm or hand gripping face or chin and forcing it upwards, thereby stifling any cry and exposing the throat to the long-bladed knife in his right hand. He would then cut from left to right. In every case the drunken women were taken by surprise. Despite the fact that people were awake and within a few yards of the murders, there was evidently never any resistance or any sound.

Catherine Eddowes wore a black cloth jacket with an imitation fur collar; her black straw bonnet was trimmed with beads and velvet; her dark green dress was patterned with michaelmas daisies and lilies. In her pockets were a handkerchief, a comb, two clay pipes, a cigarette case, a matchbox containing some cotton, a ball of worsted, a mitten, a small tin box containing tea and sugar, five pieces of soap and a blunt table-knife. Around her neck was a ribbon and 'a piece of old white coarse apron', presumably in place of a scarf. The three previous victims had also worn scarves. Part of this blood-stained apron had been cut off, and was found at the bottom of some common stairs leading to 108–119 Wentworth Dwellings, Goulston Street (north-east of Mitre Square and on the way to Spitalfields) at 2.55 am.

PC Long, who noticed the bloody rag during his night patrol, stated that at 2.20 am it had not been there. Nor, he said, had a five-lined message written in chalk on a black-bricked wall in the passage – 'The Juwes are / The men that / Will not / be Blamed for nothing.' When the Commissioner of the Metropolitan Police, Sir Charles Warren, arrived in Goulston Street about 5 am, he ordered the words to be rubbed out – even before a daylight photograph could be taken of this possible clue. The words, however, were copied. Warren's action was explained by his concern to avoid the exacerbation of prevailing anti-semitic prejudice. For apart from the fact that some main suspects had been Jews, the last four women had been murdered in Jewish areas and near buildings occupied by Jews.

The 'double event' of the murders of Eddowes and Stride provided the press with even more sensational and lurid headlines and reports, and added further fuel to the clamour for the resignation of Sir Charles Warren and the Home Secretary. It was felt that not enough was being done to identify and apprehend the murderer, and the police were strongly criticized. Vigilance Committees were formed, petitions signed and demonstrations made. Thousands of letters about the murders and the murderer's identity were sent to the police and the press, exhibiting every kind of social, sexual and racial prejudice.

Meanwhile, in the East End, where large morbid crowds had gathered in the streets to view the murder scenes and indulge in rabid speculation, a 'terrible quiet' descended.

Then a letter and a postcard, received by the Central News Agency, were published with the permission of the police on 3 October. From now on the murderer had a name – Jack the Ripper.

The letter, addressed to *The Boss, Central News Office, London City,* was dated 25 September 1888 and posted in the East End on 27 September, the Thursday *before* the double murder in the early hours of Sunday, 30 September. It read:

Dear Boss
I keep on hearing the police have caught me but they wont fix me just yet. I have laughed when they look so clever and talk about being on the right track. That joke about Leather Apron gave me real fits. I am down on whores and I shant quit ripping them till I do get buckled. Grand work the last job was. I gave the lady no time to squeal . . . [This would be Annie Chapman] I love my work and want to start again. You will soon hear of me with my funny little games. I saved some of the proper *red* stuff in a ginger beer bottle over the last job to write with but it went thick like glue and I cant use it. Red ink is fit enough I hope *ha ha*. The next job I do I shall clip the ladys ears off and send to the police officers just for jolly wouldnt you. Keep this letter back till I do a bit more work, then give it out straight. My knife's nice and sharp I want to get to work right away if I get a chance. Good luck.

yours truly
Jack the Ripper

Dont mind me giving the trade name
wasnt good enough to post this before I got all
the red ink off my hands curse it. No luck yet.
They say I'm a doctor now *ha ha*.

This letter was followed a few days later by a postcard. It was postmarked 1 October – the Monday after the double murder and *not*, as many writers have said, on the same day – even 'a few hours after' the murders of Stride and Eddowes. The postcard was probably written at least 24 hours after the murders, and after details of them had been sensationally splashed in the Monday morning papers. It was addressed to: *Central News Office, London City, EC,* and it said:

I wasnt codding dear old Boss when I gave you the tip. youll hear about saucy Jackys work tomorrow double event this time number one squealed a bit couldnt finish straight off. had no time to get ears for police thanks for keeping last letter back till I got to work again.

Jack the Ripper

The postcard might have been written on Sunday the 30th, anything from twelve to twenty hours after the murders, which were within the few hours after midnight. It might have been written by someone in the locality who had heard of the 'double event', or indeed by a journalist, or by anyone connected with the police or medical investigations. In no way does the postcard betoken any foreknowledge of the murders.

Misconception and myth also cloud the next alleged communication from the murderer. Seventeen days after the murders of Stride and Eddowes, on Tuesday, 16 October, at either 5 pm or 8 pm (there were two postal deliveries in the evening in those days), a builder, Mr George Lusk, who was chairman of the Whitechapel Vigilance Committee and lived in Alderney Street, Mile End, received a small brown paper parcel, 3½ inches square. Within was a cardboard box that contained half a kidney. The postmark was indecipherable, although post office workers thought the parcel could have been posted in the Eastern or East Central areas. A brief letter came with the stinking kidney, with an address at the top – 'From hell'.

Sor I send you half the kidne I took from one women prasarved it for you tother piece I fried and ate it was very nise I may send you the bloody knif that took it out if you only wate a whil longer.

signed Catch me when you can
Mishter Lusk

The writer of this note is probably not the same man who penned the 'Jack the Ripper' epistles. Apart from the fact that the handwriting is different, the spelling of the Ripper letter and card are superior and written in quite a neat copperplate. A curious feature of the note to Mr Lusk is the oddly illiterate spelling – it seems deliberate. Words like 'half', 'piece', 'fried' and 'bloody' are properly spelt, yet 'kidne' 'prasarved' 'nise' 'knif' 'wate' and 'whil' are not, being given a sort of phonetic spelling which in three cases is merely attained by the omission of the last letters – 'kidne', 'knif' and 'whil'. Yet in the last two words, the silent letters 'k' and 'h' are included. There is also an obvious Irishness to the spelling of 'Sor' and 'Mishter'.

Mr Lusk had already been bothered by a prowler and other letters, and was at first inclined to dismiss the kidney as a disagreeable hoax. But friends advised him to submit the half kidney to the inspection of the police and doctors, and on 18 October Dr Openshaw, at the Pathological Museum, after examining the offensive organ, concluded that the kidney had come from a woman who drank, had Bright's Disease, and that it was part of a *left* kidney. He thought it had been removed within the last three weeks. It had also been preserved in spirits after its removal.

It has since been assumed that the kidney was the one missing from the body of drunken Catherine Eddowes. There is no proof of this. Eddowes was buried in the City of London cemetery at Ilford on 8 October, so there was no chance of direct verification or of comparing the alleged length of renal artery attached to the postal kidney and that still in the murdered woman. It is also virtually impossible – it would have been completely so in 1888 – to tell whether a kidney comes from a woman or a man. Moreover, Bright's Disease, which infected the kidney, is not necessarily caused by alcoholism, and the postal kidney had been put in spirits within a few hours of its removal – something the murderer of Eddowes would surely not have thought of or had time to do.

Assumptions and error have gilded the half-kidney since it was sent to Mr Lusk. The sender was most probably a morbid hoaxer, possibly a medical student or hospital worker, who must have been much gratified by the success of his little device. On 29 October another illiterate letter was sent, this time to Dr Openshaw –

Old boss you was rite it was the left kidny i was goin to hopperate agin clos to your ospitle just as i was goin to dror my nife along of er bloomin throte them cusses of coppers spoilt the game but i guess i wil be on the job soon and will send you another bit innerds Jack the ripper.

An interesting feature of all the letters quoted, one or two of which are thought by some to have been written by the actual Whitechapel murderer, is that the addresses were correct (and correctly *spelt*) and that none of them was addressed to the police – who in fact received thousands of letters. This is odd, for murderers with a literary leaning invariably feel bound to communicate with the police, and no one else – with the exception of Dr Cream, who wrote to everyone.

Sir Robert Anderson, who became head of the CID at the Yard in September 1888, said later: 'The "Jack the Ripper" letter which is preserved in the Police Museum at New Scotland Yard is the creation of an enterprising journalist.' And Sir Melville Macnaghten, who became an Assistant Chief Constable at the Yard in 1889 and head of the CID in 1903, wrote: 'In this ghastly production I have always thought I could discern the stained finger of the journalist – indeed, a year later I had shrewd suspicions as to the actual author! But whoever did pen the gruesome stuff, it is certain to my mind that it was not the mad miscreant who had committed the murders.'

The fifth and final murder generally attributed to the 'Ripper' happened forty days after the 'double event'. It was different in that the victim, a prostitute, was young and attractive, killed indoors and more horribly and extensively mutilated than any female murder victim before, or perhaps since.

Mary Jane Kelly, also known as Dark Mary, Mary Ann and Marie, aged twenty-four, was murdered in the early hours of Friday, 9 November, in a back room of 26 Dorset Street. Two women in nearby but separate rooms said they heard a woman cry 'Murder!' about 3.45 am. Mary Kelly's lodging, rented for four shillings a week, was Room 13 in the house and had its own entrance, a side-door opening into a passage called Miller's Court. Until 30 October she had shared the room with her common-law husband, Joseph Barnett. After a stormy row he left her, since when another prostitute had stayed with her occasionally.

Kelly's body was discovered about 10.45 am by her landlord's assistant, Thomas Bowyer, who had been sent to ask her for the thirty-five shillings she owed in rent. Getting no answer to his knocking – the door was locked – he peered through a broken window, removing rags that filled the gap and pulling aside a curtain to do so. The police were sent for, but as the Commissioner, Sir Charles Warren, had chosen to resign the day before, the police force were in some confusion and Kelly's room was not entered (at first by the window) until 1.30 pm.

The blood-stained room was sparsely furnished. Mary Kelly, wearing the remains of a chemise or slip, was lying on her back on a bed where she had been placed after the murderer cut her throat. By the light of a fire, fuelled by clothes and other items he found in the room (although Kelly's, folded on a chair, were not so used), he set to work mutilating her body, which was stabbed, slashed, skinned, gutted and ripped apart. Her nose and breasts were cut off and dumped on a table; entrails were extracted; some were removed; other parts lay on the bed. Mary Kelly was nearly three months pregnant.

The last person believed to have seen her alive was George Hutchinson, an unemployed labourer. He had known Kelly for three years. He met her in Thrawl Street, as he walked towards Flower and Dean Street about 2 am. She said: 'Hutchinson, will you lend me sixpence?' 'I can't,' he replied. 'I've spent all my money going down to Romford.' She shrugged. 'Good morning,' she said. 'I must go and find some money.' She walked off, and a man coming in the opposite direction accosted her – they both laughed. Hutchinson watched. He heard Kelly say: 'All right.' 'You'll be all right for what I've told you,' said the man. They walked towards Hutchinson and passed him – he was standing under a lamp outside a pub, the Queen's Head. The man lowered his head and his hat as he passed. But Hutchinson was later able to describe him as being about thirty-four, 5 ft 6 ins tall, dark-haired, with a small moustache curled up at the ends. He was dressed in a long dark coat, with a dark jacket and trousers; but his waistcoat was as pale as his face, and across it was a gold chain. He wore a white shirt, button boots with gaiters and his black tie had a horseshoe-shaped pin in it. He seemed quite respectable, and Jewish.

Hutchinson's description is very exact: it seems too good to be true. He goes on to say that he followed Kelly and her pick-up into Dorset Street, where they stood talking by Miller's Court for a couple of minutes. He heard Kelly say: 'All right, my dear. Come along – you'll be comfortable.' The man kissed her, and they went into Miller's Court. Hutchinson waited, but they failed to reappear.

Nothing is known about Hutchinson that might lend credence or otherwise to his statement. The man he saw need not have been Kelly's murderer – she was not killed until at least an hour and a half later. Unlike the dark gentleman who chatted quite carelessly outside Miller's Court, the murderer would have been very careful, one imagines, about *not* being seen with Mary Kelly and certainly not so near her room.

The rest is silence, apart from the clamour of speculation at the time, as well as more than a generation later, about the identity of the Whitechapel murderer.

Another heavy-drinking prostitute, Alice McKenzie, was murdered in Whitechapel, in Castle Alley, on 17 July 1889. She was found in the street with her throat cut (or rather, stabbed twice); her dress had been pushed above her knees, and there were cuts and scratches on her stomach. However, the death of 'Clay-pipe Alice' is not thought to have been the work of the Ripper, who is generally believed to have died soon after the murder of Mary Kelly.

Who was he? What happened to him? No one can say for certain. Sir Charles Warren is reported (by his grandson) to have believed the murderer 'to be a sex maniac who committed suicide after the Miller's Court murder – possibly the young doctor whose body was found in the Thames on December 31st 1888.' Sir Robert Anderson in his memoirs wrote: 'I am almost tempted to disclose the identity of the murderer . . . In saying that he was a Polish Jew, I am merely stating a definitely ascertained fact.' Sir Henry Smith, Acting Commissioner of the City Police at the time of the murders, thought the murderer must be the man described by Joseph Lawende. Chief Detective Inspector Abberline, who was the senior Yard detective investigating the murders, thought George Chapman (his real name was Severin Klosowski) was the killer. Chapman (a hairdresser's assistant in Whitechapel in 1888, when he was twenty-three) was ultimately hanged in 1903 for poisoning his three wives – another kind of murder altogether. Other police officers involved at the time, like Leeson and Dew, disagreed, writing in their autobiographies – 'Nobody will ever know' – 'I am as mystified now as I was then.'

One man, Sir Melville Macnaghten, wrote in February 1894 what must be the most sensible account of the murders. It was a hand-written seven-page memorandum deposited in the Ripper file to discredit and disprove a newspaper story that a deranged fetishist, Thomas Cutbush, was the Ripper. Cutbush was arrested in 1891 for maliciously wounding two women by stabbing them in the rear, found guilty but insane, and incarcerated in an asylum. Macnaghten states: 'The Whitechapel murderer had 5 victims – & 5 victims only.' They were: Nichols, Chapman, Stride, Eddowes and Kelly. He says:

It will be noticed that the fury of the mutilations *increased* in each case, and, seemingly, the appetite only became sharpened by indulgence. It seems, then, highly improbable that the murderer would have suddenly stopped in November '88, and been content to recommence operations by merely prodding a girl behind some 2 years and 4 months afterwards. A much more rational theory is that the murderer's brain gave way altogether after his awful glut in Miller's Court, and that he immediately committed suicide, or, as a possible alternative, was found to be so hopelessly mad by his relations, that he was by them confined in some asylum.

No one ever saw the Whitechapel Murderer, many homicidal maniacs were suspected, but no shadow of proof could be thrown on any one. I may mention the cases of 3 men, any one of whom would have been more likely than Cutbush to have committed this series of murders:

1. A Mr M. J. Druitt, said to be a doctor and of good family, who disappeared at the time of the Miller's Court murder, and whose body (which was said to have been upwards of a month in the water) was found in the Thames on 31st Dec. – or about 7 weeks after that murder. He was sexually insane and from private info I have little doubt but that his own family believed him to have been the murderer.

2. Kosminski, a Polish Jew and resident in Whitechapel. This man became insane owing to many years indulgence in solitary vices. He had a great hatred of women, especially of the prostitute class, and had strong homicidal tendencies: He was removed to a lunatic asylum about March 1889. There were many crimes connected with this man which made him a strong 'suspect'.

3. Michael Ostrog, a Russian doctor, and a convict, who was frequently detained in a lunatic asylum as a homicidal maniac. This man's antecedents were of the worst possible type, and his whereabouts at the time of the murders could never be ascertained.

Nothing more is known about Kosminski and Ostrog. Much more has since been revealed about Montague Druit.

Born on 15 August 1857 at Wimborne in Dorset, he was educated at Winchester College, where he was a prefect, played cricket for the First Eleven, was the best at playing fives, and won a scholarship to New College, Oxford. There he studied Classics and obtained a Third Class Honours degree in 1880. He may then have studied medicine for a year (he had a cousin who was a doctor) before switching to law, enrolling at the Inner Temple in May 1882. While he studied law, he taught at a crammer's school in Blackheath, where forty-two boys were boarders. He was called to the Bar in April 1885. His father died in September, after which Druitt rented chambers at 9 King's Bench Walk in the Temple. His career as a barrister was undistinguished and unrewarding; he continued to teach at the Blackheath school until he was sacked about 1 December 1888. The reason for the dismissal is not known: he may have shown homosexual tendencies or behaved unreasonably or oddly – the latter being not unlikely, as his mother had been certified as insane in July that year and put in a mental home in Chiswick. He apparently feared for his own sanity.

Last seen alive on Monday, 3 December 1888, he penned a note – 'Since Friday I felt I was going to be like Mother and the best thing was for me to die' – weighted the pockets of his overcoat with stones and jumped or waded into the River Thames. His body was found floating in the river near Chiswick on Monday, 31 December, four weeks after his disappearance. He was thirty-one. Was he the Ripper?

We know that he was a keen cricketer. A member of the MCC, for several years he played for Blackheath and also for teams in Dorset. The day after Mary Ann Nichols was murdered (about 3.30 am on Friday, 31 August), M. J. Druitt played cricket for Canford against Wimborne in Dorset (on Saturday, 1 September). Some *five hours* after the murder of Annie Chapman (about 5.45 am on Saturday, 8 September) Druitt was playing cricket for Blackheath in South London. Where was he, one wonders, on the night of 29/30 September and at dawn on Friday, 9 November? To the question, 'Could he have committed such atrocious crimes and then played cricket?' the answer must be 'Yes.'

Of all the suspects, Druitt seems the one most likely, from what we know, to have been the Whitechapel murderer. But as in every other case there is no definite, conclusive proof. Other theories, about doctors, butchers, Jews, freemasons, lodgers, other murderers and a member of the monarchy (the Duke of Clarence), may reasonably, if regretfully, be dismissed.

Of all the books written about the Whitechapel murders, the most useful are those by Donald Rumbelow, a police sergeant in the City, and Whittington-Egan (see the Bibliography).

One area of interest remains – the actual scenes of the murders and the addresses of the victims: Nichols, Chapman, Stride, Eddowes and Kelly.

Why Whitechapel – rather than other areas of prostitution? And why, when about 1,200 prostitutes are said to have worked in Whitechapel, did the five murdered women (although murdered some distance apart) all live within a few hundred yards of each other? It is conceivable that they not only visited the same pubs and touted for custom in the same streets, but actually knew each other, at least by sight. Annie Chapman lived in 35 Dorset Street – so did Jack Pizer and Michael Kidney, with whom Elizabeth Stride used to live. Mary Kelly lived in and was killed at the back of 26 Dorset Street. Nichols, Stride and Eddowes all lodged at one time or another in Flower and Dean Street – as the last two also did in Fashion Street. Is it coincidence that these five possible acquaintances were killed? Or was some other factor at work?

CHAPTER 3

Florence Maybrick

The murder of Mr Maybrick, 1889

Judges cannot ever be truly impartial, being inevitably led by their own opinions, background, education, sex and social position to exhibit an occasionally less than objective attitude to the accused, especially if the accused is a woman. Such bias was shown by the learned gentlemen who judged Edith Thompson, Alma Rattenbury, Ruth Ellis – and Florence Maybrick.

Miss Florence Elizabeth Chandler was an American, a Southern belle from Alabama, who at the age of eighteen married Mr James Maybrick in London on 27 July 1881. She was the daughter of a banker from Mobile, and she and her future husband met on the White Star liner *Baltic* when she was on a tour of Europe with her mother. He was a forty-two-year-old English cotton-broker, a frequent visitor to America. His two brothers disapproved of the match, believing that Florence was as flighty, as suspect, as her thrice-married mother, Baroness von Roques.

The Maybricks settled in Liverpool in 1884, eventually purchasing an imposing mansion, Battlecrease House (complete with modern flush toilets), in a southern suburb of the city called Aigburth. Living beyond their means, they were attended by four servants: a cook, two maids, and a nanny called Alice Yapp, who looked after the two young Maybrick children, a boy and a girl. Mrs Maybrick was given £7 a week by her husband to pay not only for the food and domestic requirements but also all the servants' wages. Naturally she was soon in debt.

James Maybrick was a boorish, irascible man, and a lifelong hypochondriac. Ever complaining of being out of sorts, of pains and numbness and problems with his liver and his nerves, he was a believer in homoeopathic medicines, and was forever swallowing pills and pick-me-ups to improve his health and sexual potency; the mixtures included strychnine and arsenic. 'I think I know a good deal of medicine,' he once told a doctor.

He maintained a mistress on the side, as Florence discovered by chance in 1887. The unhappy young wife found some consolation in the arms of one of her husband's Liverpool friends, a tall and handsome young bachelor, Mr Alfred Brierley, whom she met at a dance at Battlecrease House. In March 1889 the couple spent a weekend together in a London hotel – Mrs Maybrick made the arrangements. They planned to be there a week, but for some reason they left the hotel – Flatman's in Henrietta Street – on the Monday, when Brierley paid the bill; Mrs Maybrick spent the rest of the week with friends. She said later: 'Before we parted, he gave me to understand that he cared for somebody else and could not marry me, and that rather than face the disgrace of discovery he would blow his brains out. I then had such a revulsion of feeling I said we must end our intimacy at once.' She returned to Liverpool on Friday, 28 March.

The next day she went to Aintree with her husband for the Grand National. There she happened to meet Brierley, and despite her revulsion and her husband's wishes, she left his carriage and walked up the course with the young man. Maybrick was furious. She returned home on her own. He arrived ten minutes later. There was a row and at one point he punched her. Alice Yapp said later: 'I heard Mr Maybrick say to Mrs Maybrick: "This scandal will be all over the town tomorrow!" They then went down into the hall, and I heard Mr Maybrick say: "Florrie, I never thought you would come to this." . . . They then went into the vestibule, and I heard Mr Maybrick say: "If you once cross this threshold you shall never enter these doors again!"' Mrs Maybrick had in fact ordered a cab and threatened to walk out of the house, but Nanny Yapp intervened, reminding her of her children – 'I put my arm around her waist and took her upstairs. I made the bed for her that night and she slept in the dressing-room.'

On Sunday, Mr Maybrick made a new will, excluding his wife. She went to see the family doctor, Dr Hopper, who said later: 'She complained that she was very unwell, that she had been up all night . . . and she asked my advice. I saw that she had a black eye. She said that her husband had been very unkind to her . . . and he had beaten her . . . She said that she had a very strong feeling against him, and could not bear him to come near her.' She wanted a divorce. But the doctor was able to effect a reconciliation; she asked her husband's forgiveness for considerable debts she had incurred (£1,200) and he paid them off – presumably with difficulty, as he was in debt himself.

On 13 April, Mr Maybrick journeyed to London on business connected with his wife's debts and stayed with his bachelor brother, Michael, a singer and composer, in his flat in Wellington Mansions, Regent's Park. Using the pseudonym Stephen Adams, Michael composed such hymns as *The Holy City* and *Star of Bethlehem*. James Maybrick consulted Michael's doctor, complaining of pains in his head and numbness in his right leg. After an hour-long examination the doctor concluded there was very little wrong with him, apart from indigestion, and he prescribed an aperient, a tonic, and liver pills. Mr Maybrick returned to Liverpool on 22 April.

Soon after this, he met a friend of his in the Palatine Club, a former Mayor of Liverpool, Sir James Poole, who said later: 'Someone made the remark that it was becoming the common custom to take poisonous medicines. [Maybrick] had an impetuous way and he blurted out: "I take poisonous medicines." I said: "How horrid! Don't you know, my dear friend, that the more you take of these things the more you require, and you will go on till they carry you off?''' The previous year, in June, Mrs Maybrick had visited Dr Hopper. He said later: 'She told me that Mr Maybrick was in the habit of taking some very strong medicine which had a bad influence on him; for he always seemed worse after each dose. She wished me to see him about it, as he was very reticent in the matter.' There seems no doubt that he was an eater of arsenic, amongst other poisons, and three American witnesses at the trial vouched that he often took arsenic in a cup of beef tea, saying it was 'meat and liquor to him' and 'I take it when I can get it.' A chemist from Norfolk in Virginia attested to the fact that Mr Maybrick's consumption of '*liquor arsenicalis*' given in a tonic, increased over eighteen months by 75 per cent.

On or about Monday, 23 April, Mrs Maybrick bought one dozen fly-papers from a chemist in Aigburth. She told him that the flies were troublesome in her kitchen. Each paper contained about one grain of arsenic, although the experts at her trial disagreed about the actual amount, saying it depended on whether the arsenic was extracted by boiling the papers or by soaking them in cold water.

On or about that Monday, fly-papers were seen by the nanny and a maid soaking in a basin on the Maybricks' bedroom wash-stand. Mrs Maybrick later explained that the arsenic which she extracted from those fly-papers was for a cosmetic preparation, a face-wash, something she had used for years; she wanted to clear up some skin trouble before going to a ball. A hairdresser, Mr Bioletti, later agreed that there was 'an impression among ladies that it is good for the complexion'. It was also used, he said, as a depilatory.

The following Saturday, the 27th, Mr Maybrick felt funny and was sick. He went to the Wirrall Races in the afternoon, got wet in the rain, and later dined with friends; his hands were so unsteady that he upset some wine.

On Sunday morning the children's doctor, Dr Humphreys, was sent for. Mr Maybrick was in bed, complaining about pains in his chest and his heart, caused, he said, by a strong cup or tea. He was afraid of becoming paralysed. The doctor prescribed some diluted prussic acid, and forbade him to drink anything other than soda water and milk. Mrs Maybrick told the doctor that her husband had taken an overdose of strychnine. Two months earlier she had spoken to him about her husband's habit of dosing himself with strychnine and had written in some concern to his brother Michael, saying she had found a certain white powder which her husband habitually took. When Michael obliquely asked his brother about this, James Maybrick expostulated: 'Whoever told you that? It's a damned lie!'

Dr Humphreys saw his new patient again on 29 and 30 April, concluded he was a chronic dyspeptic and put him on a diet. On the night of 30 April Florence Maybrick went to a fancy-dress ball with her brother-in-law, Edwin, a bachelor cotton merchant, who was staying in Battlecrease House after a recent visit to America.

James Maybrick was back in his office on Wednesday, 1 May. Said Edwin: 'Mrs Maybrick gave me a parcel to take to his office ... It contained a brown jug in which there was some farinaceous food in liquid form [Barry's Revalenta]. My brother poured the liquid into a saucepan and heated it over the fire, and he then poured it into a basin and partook of it. He remarked: "The cook has put some of that damned sherry in it, and she *knows* I don't like it!"'

By Friday, Maybrick was ill again and Dr Humphreys was summoned about 10 am. He said: 'I found Mr Maybrick in the morning-room on the ground floor. He said he had not been so well since the day before, and he added that he did not think my medicine agreed with him. Mrs Maybrick was present and said: "You always say the same thing about anybody's medicine after two or three days."' Dr Humphreys' advice was 'to go on the same for two or three weeks.' He went away and was called back at midnight. In the interim Mr Maybrick had gone out and had a Turkish bath. He was now in bed; he had been sick twice and complained of gnawing pains in his legs.

On Saturday, his hands felt numb, and he was constantly sick; the doctor said he should 'abate his thirst by washing out with water or by sucking ice or a damp cloth.' On Sunday, his sore throat and foul tongue troubled him; Valentine's meat juice was prescribed as well as the prussic acid solution. Mrs Maybrick thought that a second opinion was unnecessary. She said: 'He has seen so many [doctors] and they have done him so little good.' She was in constant attendance on him day and night, sleeping in the dressing-room.

At 8.30 am on Monday, 6 May, Dr Humphreys was back. 'I told [him] to stop the Valentine's beef juice ... I was not surprised at it making Mr Maybrick sick, as it made many people sick.' Humphreys now prescribed some arsenic, Fowler's solution, which contained in all 1/25th of a grain, and that evening the patient was fed with Brand's beef tea, some chicken broth, Neave's food and some milk and water. He continued to vomit, and a blister was applied to his stomach. On Tuesday morning he seemed better and told Dr Humphreys: 'I am quite a different man today.' Nonetheless, a second opinion was now sought by Edwin Maybrick. His choice, Dr Carter, arrived about 5 pm. Carter's conclusion was that the patient was suffering from acute dyspepsia, resulting from 'indiscretion of food, or drink, or both.' He prescribed a careful diet and small doses of sedatives. Both Carter and Humphreys thought Maybrick would be well in a few days.

But on Wednesday, 8 May, there was a general turn for the worse. Two of the invalid's friends, Mrs Matilda Briggs and Mrs Martha Hughes (they were sisters) called at the house in the morning and were told by Nanny Yapp about the soaking fly-papers and other suspicious matters. Mrs Briggs took immediate action. She told the exhausted wife to send for a trained nurse. She spoke to Edwin. She also telegraphed Michael Maybrick in London – 'Come at once. Strange things going on here.'

The nurse arrived at 2.15 pm. About three o'clock, Mrs Maybrick came to the garden gate and gave Alice Yapp a letter to post. The young nanny was minding the Maybricks' three-year-old daughter and walked to the post office with the child. On the way there the letter, according to Alice, was dropped in the dirt, and needed a new envelope. At any rate, she read the letter, failed to post it and handed it over to Edwin about half-past five. The letter was addressed to A. Brierley, and had been written in reply to a somewhat frosty missive from him suggesting that he and Florence did not meet again until the autumn.

Mrs Maybrick wrote:

Dearest,

Since my return I have been nursing M day and night – *he is sick unto death*! . . . And now all depends upon how his strength will hold out . . . We are terribly anxious . . . But relieve your mind of *all fear of discovery* now and in the future. M has been delirious since Sunday and I know *he is perfectly ignorant of everything . . . and also that he has not been making any enquiries whatever!*

This was reported to Michael when he arrived from London that night. Edwin instructed the nurses to let no one else attend his sick brother, while Michael discussed the family's suspicions with Dr Humphreys.

The following day the patient was weaker, complaining of much pain in his rectum: he now had dirrhoea. His faeces and urine, a bottle of brandy and a bottle of Neave's food were all examined for arsenic. None was found.

That evening the cook (also called Humphreys) was followed downstairs by Mrs Maybrick, who said: 'I am blamed for all this.' 'In what way?' asked the cook. 'In not getting other nurses and doctors.' Mrs Maybrick went into the servant's hall and began to cry. She said her position in the house was not worth anything, that Michael Maybrick, who had always had a spite against her, had turned her out of the master's bedroom. The cook, who thought her mistress had been 'very kind' to Mr Maybrick and 'was doing her best under the circumstances', was much moved and said: 'I would rather be in my own shoes than yours.'

Nurse Gore came on duty at 11 pm and gave her charge some Valentine's meat juice, and noticed how Mrs Maybrick removed the bottle (which had been provided by Edwin) and took it into the dressing-room. She closed the door; a few minutes later she returned, placed the bottle in a surreptitious manner on a bedside table, and sent the nurse to fetch some ice. Mrs Maybrick later explained: 'After Nurse Gore had given my husband beef tea, I went and sat on the bed beside him. He complained to me of being very sick and very depressed and he implored me then to give him this powder, which he had referred to early in the evening, and which I had declined to give him. I was overwrought, terribly anxious, miserably unhappy, and his evident distress utterly unnerved me. He had told me that the powder would not harm him, and that I could put it in his food. I then consented . . .' But, she said, he never had any, as he was asleep when she returned to the bedroom. Later he was sick. The bottle was later found to contain half a grain of arsenic.

On Friday, 10 May, James Maybrick was much weaker, with a very faint but rapid pulse; he was very restless and his tongue was foul. He was given sulphonal, nitroglycerine, cocaine (for his throat) and some phosphoric acid (for his mouth). In the afternoon, Michael Maybrick caught Mrs Maybrick changing medicine from one bottle to another. 'Florrie! How dare you tamper with the medicine!' he cried. No arsenic was later found in the bottle which he removed. Later on that day, the duty nurse, Nurse Callery, was administering some medicine, assisted by Florrie, when the patient said: 'Don't give me the wrong medicine again!' That evening, according to Nurse Wilson, Mr Maybrick, who was now delirious, said to his wife: 'Oh, Bunny, Bunny, how could you do it? I did not think it of you.' 'You silly old darling,' said Mrs Maybrick. 'Don't trouble your head about things.' Later, Mrs Maybrick said her husband had been referring to a whispered conversation she had had with him, confessing to her affair with Brierley, assuring him it was over, and asking for his forgiveness.

On Saturday, 11 May, the doctors had a consultation after midday and concluded that their patient would never recover: his case was hopeless. His children were brought to him at 5 pm. James Maybrick died some three hours later. Florence Maybrick swooned and then retired to her bed in the dressing-room. She was more or less confined there by the dead man's brothers while a hasty search was made of the bedroom and the house by the servants, the nurses, the doctors, the brothers and Mrs Briggs.

A sealed packet with a red label saying *Arsenic – Poison –* 'for cats' had been added – was found in a trunk. Arsenic was later detected in an imperfectly cleaned jug of Barry's Revalenta, and in two ordinary medicine bottles. Several small bottles and a scrap of handkerchief were discovered in a chocolate box: the scrap had traces of arsenic. Three bottles found in a man's hat-box contained varying solutions of arsenic. In another hat-box was a glass and another handkerchief: both bore traces of milk and arsenic. More traces were found in the pocket of Mrs Maybrick's dressing-gown. There was enough arsenic in the house to poison fifty people.

On Monday, 13 May, a post-mortem was carried out by Doctors Carter, Humphreys and Barron. They concluded that death had been caused by some irritant poison acting on the stomach and bowels. But when the body was exhumed on 30 May, less than half a grain of arsenic (two grains would be fatal) was the total found in his liver, kidneys and intestines. There was none in his stomach, spleen, heart or lungs. There were, however, traces of strychnine, hyoscine, prussic acid and morphia.

In the meantime, Mrs Maybrick had been detained on suspicion of causing her husband's death. She had been removed to the hospital at Walton jail, after a magistrate formally opened the investigation in her bedroom, but not before a letter she wrote to Brierley – 'Appearances may be against me, but before God I swear I am innocent' – was intercepted by Mrs Briggs and given to the police.

When Mrs Maybrick appeared at the brief magisterial hearing on 13 June, she was hissed at by a large number of women as she left the court. She hoped her trial would take place in London. 'I shall receive an impartial verdict there,' she wrote to her mother, 'which I cannot expect from a jury in Liverpool, whose minds have come to a "moral conviction" . . . The tittle-tattle of servants, the public, friends and enemies, besides their personal feelings for Jim, must leave their traces and prejudice their minds, no matter what the defence is.' She was advised otherwise, and the trial began at Liverpool Summer Assizes on Wednesday, 31 July 1889.

There was an all-male Lancashire jury, including three plumbers and two farmers. Mrs Maybrick was defended by Sir Charles Russell, QC, MP, later the Lord Chief Justice. The medical experts agreed that Mr Maybrick had died of gastro-enteritis, but disputed whether this had been caused by arsenic, impure food or a chill. The defence claimed that there was an absence of most symptoms usually associated with arsenical poisoning, that the deceased had overdosed himself, and died of natural causes, that Mrs Maybrick had no need to adopt the clumsy and uncertain contrivance of soaking fly-papers (so openly) to get arsenic, when so much was available elsewhere in the house. She gave no evidence, but made an ill-advised statement, explaining her reasons for soaking the fly-papers and what she was doing with the meat-juice.

The summing-up of the judge, Mr Justice Stephen, who was himself a very sick man, lasted two days. It was a rambling peroration, not without some errors of fact, laying emphasis on the accused's admitted adultery with Brierley. The judge said: 'For a person to go on deliberately administering poison to a poor, helpless, sick man, upon whom she has already inflicted a dreadful injury – an injury fatal to married life – the person who could do such a thing must indeed be destitute of the least trace of feeling . . . Then you have to consider . . . the question of motives which might act upon this woman's mind. When you come to consider that, you must remember the intrigue which she carried on with this man Brierley, and the feelings – it seems horrible to comparatively ordinary innocent people – a horrible and incredible thought, that a woman should be plotting the death of her husband in order that she might be at liberty to follow her own degrading vices . . . There is no doubt that the propensities which lead persons to vices of that kind do kill all the more tender, all the more manly, or all the more womanly, feelings of the human mind.'

The jury, after an absence of three quarters of an hour, found Florence Maybrick guilty of murder. Before sentence of death was passed she said: 'With the exception of my intimacy with Mr Brierley, I am not guilty of this crime.'

The judge was booed as he left the court. Many meetings were held, letters were sent, petitions organized, and articles written (by doctors and lawyers) decrying the verdict – there was no appeal court then. Leading Americans, including the President, brought pressure to bear on the English authorities. The Home Secretary and the Lord Chancellor reviewed the case and interviewed the judge. Meanwhile, in Liverpool, Mrs Maybrick heard the gallows being erected in Walton jail.

Then, on 22 August, the Home Office announced that the sentence had been commuted to penal servitude for life, without 'the slightest reflection on the tribunal by which the prisoner was tried' and with 'the concurrence of the learned judge'. A message announcing the reprieve reached Walton jail at 1.30 am on 23 August, three days before the date set for Florence's execution.

Despite further efforts to obtain her release, Florence Maybrick remained in jail for fifteen years. The first nine months of her sentence were spent in solitary confinement; she was fed on bread and gruel, wore a brown dress marked with arrows and had to make at least five men's shirts a week.

Her imprisonment began in Woking jail and ended in Aylesbury. She was freed on 25 January 1904, when she went to France and visited her aged mother before returning to America, where she had not been for more than twenty years. For a time she was something of a celebrity and wrote a book called *My Fifteen Lost Years*. Soon after it was published, the Court of Criminal Appeal was established in 1907.

She died in squalor, surrounded by cats in a Connecticut cottage, on 23 October 1941. She was seventy-eight. It was fifty-two years since her husband's death and many years since the death of the judge, Mr Justice Stephen. He retired soon after the trial and died in a lunatic asylum.

CHAPTER 4

Mrs Pearcey
The murder of Mrs Hogg, 1890

Women rarely commit murder. Those who have done so have generally been poor, illiterate, aggressive if not volatile, mentally unstable, and poison their usual method of bringing death. More than half (thirty-seven) of the women hanged for murder (sixty-eight) between 1843 and 1956 were poisoners. The murders women commit are mostly domestic ones – of a child, husband or lover, and occur when the murderess can no longer endure the anguish of a relationship or a situation. Children have often been murdered by women in a kind of misdirection of their anguish – as a substitute for the husband or lover, or for the suicide of the murderess herself. A very few women have murdered for gain, to improve their economic or social conditions. Some murder out of spite. Associated causes of murder where women have been concerned are sexual frustration, nymphomania, lesbianism, post-natal depression, the menopause, alcoholism and feeble-mindedness. In the case of Mrs Pearcey, sexual jealousy has been mooted as the mainspring of the murders she committed. They are more likely to have arisen from circumstances similar to those described in Congreve's famous sentence: 'Heaven has no rage like love to hatred turned, nor hell a fury like a woman scorned.'

Mrs Pearcey was not in fact married. Her real and maiden name was Mary Eleanor Wheeler. But when she went to live with a man called Pearcey, she assumed the name and title of his wife, retaining both when, for reasons unknown, he left her. Male reporters later portrayed her as being tall and powerful, with striking almost masculine features, a full figure and fine eyes. A woman correspondent of the *Pall Mall Budget* described her as being 'a woman of about five feet six, neither slight nor stout. There is nothing of the murderess in her appearance; in fact, she is a mild, harmless-looking woman. Her colouring is delicate and her hands are small and shapely. But she has not a single good feature in her face. Her eyes are dark and bright . . . Her mouth is large and badly formed, and her chin is weak and retreating.'
Eleanor Pearcey's emotional instability and depressing loneliness – her nearest relatives were an aged mother and an older sister – seem to have led her into a series of affairs, further solaced by drink. In 1890, at the age of twenty-four, she was on her way to being a full-time courtesan. The three

rooms she occupied on the ground floor of 2 Priory Street, Kentish Town, were paid for by an admirer, Mr Crichton of Gravesend in Kent, who called on her once a week. The rooms were small but attractively furnished. On the left of the entrance hall of the house was her front parlour, in which there was an upright piano; folding doors opened on to a bedroom overlooking the yard at the rear. There was a tiny kitchen.

Another admirer was a furniture remover, Frank Samuel Hogg. Him she apparently loved; she used to put a light in her window to let him know when she was free. A feckless, sentimental and selfish man, who had known Eleanor Pearcey for some time, he was vain enough, it appears, to imagine that all women who looked on him loved him, and was pleased to be proved right. One conquest, however, turned out to be a careless triumph in more ways than one. She became pregnant, and such was the weight of her family's opinion, backed up by several large brothers, that Frank Hogg was persuaded to marry her. The marriage was not happy, and when his wife, Phoebe, a large, plain woman, duly produced a baby girl, also called Phoebe, this apparently so lowered her bearded husband's self-esteem and increased his self-pity that he used to speak of suicide to his young bosom-friend, Eleanor Pearcey. He would weep in her arms and bemoan his wretched state, adding his frustrations to hers. As an alternative to suicide he talked of emigration. Both were anathema to Mrs Pearcey.

Although she had known Phoebe Hogg before her marriage to Frank Hogg and had been friends with his sister Clara – the actual relationship between the three women appears to have been quite complex – Mrs Pearcey seems to have become increasingly jealous of Mrs Hogg and full of hate. Apparently Eleanor Pearcey felt that Frank was essential to her happiness and that the realization of his happiness must be her prime aim. She wished to be his wife, to have him all to herself.

In her letters she besought him not to kill himself, to go on living for her sake if not for his. She wrote:

> You ask me if I was cross with you for coming only such a little while. If you knew how lonely I am you wouldn't ask. I would be more than happy if I could see you for the same time each day, dear. You know I have a lot of time to spare and I cannot help thinking. I think and think until I get so dizzy that I don't know what to do with myself. If it wasn't for our love, dear, I don't know what I should really do, and I am always afraid you will take that away, and then I should quite give up in despair, for that is the only thing I care for on earth. I cannot live without it now. I have no right to it, but you gave it to me, and I can't give it up.

It must have seemed that her emotional dilemma could only be resolved by the destruction of Phoebe Hogg, and all Mrs Pearcey's passionate envy and frustration focused on the other, older woman, who had the benefit of Frank's company night and day.

Frank and Phoebe Hogg lived with his sister Clara and his mother in rooms at 141 Prince of Wales Road, Kentish Town. On Thursday, 23 October 1890, Mrs Hogg (now aged thirty-one) received a note from Mrs Pearcey inviting her to 2 Priory Street for tea. She showed the note to her sister. It said: 'Dearest, come round this afternoon and bring our little darling. Don't fail.' But Mrs Hogg was for some reason unable to go there that day. Her sister later told the police that Mrs Pearcey had once invited Phoebe to go with her to Southend and look over an empty house.

The next day, Friday the 24th, Eleanor Pearcey gave a small boy a penny to deliver a second note, and this time, without telling anyone where she was going, Phoebe Hogg left her house about 3.30 pm and set out, pushing her daughter in a bassinette or pram down Kentish Town Road and into Royal College Street towards the drab little road (now Ivor Street) where Mrs Pearcey lived. Mrs Hogg pulled the pram up the steps and parked it in the narrow entrance hall. She then followed the younger smaller woman either into the front parlour or into the pokey kitchen at the end of the hall. The baby girl may have remained in the pram.

It was in the kitchen that Phoebe Hogg was slaughtered, despatched with a poker and more than one knife. Her skull was fractured and her throat so severely cut that her head was almost severed from her body. It seems that Mrs Hogg was not easy to kill, that she struggled and fought for her life: the arms of both women were bruised. Two window panes were broken and the kitchen's walls and ceiling were spattered with blood. Mrs Pearcey's neighbours heard what they called 'banging and hammering' at about four o'clock. Another neighbour said she heard a child screaming – or what sounded like a child. But like most good neighbours they hesitated to intrude, readily assuming in a noisy neighbourhood, where cries and fights were not unknown, that the rumpus was in some way connected with workmen repairing a pub on the corner.

Afterwards Mrs Pearcey probably washed her hands and the weapons, took off and washed her top-skirt, tried to scrub out the bloodstains on a rug, on curtains and an apron. At some point she heaved the body of the murdered woman into the pram, possibly on top of the little girl. She covered them both with an antimacassar. About six o'clock Mr and Mrs Butler, who lived in the second-floor flat at the top of the stairs, returned separately to 2 Priory Street. Both knocked against the bassinette parked in the darkened hallway. Mrs Pearcey called out to each of them to take care.

Sometime after this, when it was quite dark, she put on her bonnet and went out, bumping the pram down the few steps at the front door on to the pavement and, turning right, wheeled her dreadful load away from the house into Chalk Farm Road, then up Adelaide Road and into Eton Avenue. Pushing the weighty pram before her, she sought some deserted place in the gas-lit streets where she might unburden herself, unobserved, of the pram and what it contained. The body of Mrs Hogg was deposited by a partly built house in Crossfield Road, near Swiss Cottage. The child was dumped on some waste land in Finchley Road.

By now the child was dead, having suffocated, it is said, in the pram – no signs of violence were found on her. On the other hand, the little girl may have been suffocated in the house, perhaps by a cushion. The child is unlikely to have remained silent if she was in the kitchen when her mother was murdered.

As if in a daze, as if tied to the now empty pram, Eleanor Pearcey walked on for over a mile through the quieter, richer streets around Abbey Road, finally abandoning the pram in Hamilton Terrace, between Maida Vale and St John's Wood. She then began the long walk home through the shadowed streets. In all, she walked about six miles that night.

Evidently the horror of her deeds was too much for her. She was seen about 8 pm by a friend – possibly before she started out on her terrible errand – standing on a pavement near her home staring vacantly about her, her face drawn and pale, her clothes much disordered and her hat askew. The friend, who had at first failed to recognize her, assumed that Mrs Pearcey was drunk and passed on without a word.

In any event, Eleanor Pearcey was apparently not at home later on that night. For about 10 pm Frank Hogg called on her. He had a latch-key and let himself in. No one answered his calls. Apart from a lamp in the bedroom, Mrs Pearcey's rooms were in darkness, he said later. He peered, he said, into the front parlour, saw nothing untoward and withdrew. But he left a note saying – 'Twenty-past ten. Cannot stay.'

Frank Hogg later alleged that he was unaware that his wife and Mrs Pearcey were on friendly terms. It seems that after calling at the house in Priory Street on his way home from work about ten o'clock, he walked on to Prince of Wales Road, where his wife's absence had apparently caused no alarm. It was assumed in the Hogg household that Phoebe had gone to visit her sick father in Rickmansworth. Nonetheless, Frank Hogg sat up until 2 am awaiting her return.

On Saturday morning he left home soon after six o'clock and went to work – he was employed in the furniture-moving business by his brother. He came home for breakfast about 8 am. About the same time the Hoggs' landlady, Mrs Styles, who had heard rumours of a murder in Hampstead, said to Clara Hogg: 'Have you heard of this dreadful murder?' 'What do you mean?' asked Clara, adding – 'Tell me all about it. My sister-in-law has not been home all night. You gave me quite a turn. We have been enquiring in all directions and can't find a trace of her.' Clara went out to buy a morning paper and read that the body of a woman, brutally murdered, had been found by a police constable in Hampstead on Friday night. She talked to her brother and he set off for Rickmansworth to see if his wife was there. She decided to visit Mrs Pearcey.

Eleanor Pearcey was at home, and the two women conversed in the front parlour. Clara Hogg asked Mrs Pearcey if she had seen or heard of Phoebe. Mrs Pearcey said 'No.' Clara rephrased the question and Mrs Pearcey then replied: 'Well, as you press me, I will tell you. Phoebe wished me particularly not to say anything, and that is why I said "No". She did come round at five o'clock. She asked me to mind the baby for a little while, and I refused. She also asked me to lend her some money. I could not lend her any, as I only had 1s 1½d in my purse.' Phoebe, said Mrs Pearcey, then left the house. Clara Hogg was puzzled: she thought it most unlikely that her sister-in-law, who had a horror of being in debt, would ask for a loan, even a small one. However, she made no comment, only remarking that she intended to visit the Hampstead police station and to ask to see the body of the woman who had been murdered the night before, in case it was Phoebe. She asked Mrs Pearcey to accompany her, for moral support.

For some reason Mrs Pearcey agreed – she could, after all, have invented some excuse. But her part in the murder of Mrs Hogg had probably been blotted out of her mind. DI Thomas Bannister took the two women to the Hampstead mortuary, where they were both shown the body of Mrs Hogg. The baby's body was not found until the morning of the following day.

Eleanor Pearcey said she was unable to recognize the unwashed, bloody mask of the woman on the mortuary table. 'That's not her,' she said. 'It's not her. It's not her! Let's go away!' She became hysterical. Clara said: 'That's her clothing.' But she could not identify the features. DI Bannister took the two women out of the room and said to Clara: 'Surely if she is a relative and you have been living together, you can form a reliable opinion as to whether it is the person or not.' Both women were brought back to look at the body. Clara was still doubtful, and when she attempted to touch the corpse's clothing, Mrs Pearcey screamed – 'Oh, don't touch her!' – and tried to pull Clara away. 'Don't drag me!' scolded Clara. A doctor in attendance at the mortuary was then asked by Bannister to wash the face of the corpse. When this was done, Clara said: 'Oh, that's her – Don't drag me!' she added again.

Detective Murray then took both women to see the bassinette, which Clara Hogg identified. Sergeant Beard was sent to accompany the women back to 141 Prince of Wales Road, where Frank Hogg and Mrs Styles were questioned. He was searched and in a pocket his key to 2 Priory Street was found. All three women and the unhappy husband were asked to come to Hampstead police station for further questioning, and Mrs Pearcey was detained there. DI Bannister, mystified and made suspicious by her excessive and odd reaction in the mortuary, asked if one or two of his men could inspect her apartment. She agreed and said: 'I would like to go with them.'

About 3 pm she returned to Priory Street with Sergeants Nursey and Parsons. They examined her rooms. One of the sergeants then went out to send a telegram to DI Bannister. The other sergeant stayed and engaged Mrs Pearcey in conversation in the front parlour, where she played the piano and sang. She also talked about her 'poor dear dead Phoebe' whom she loved so much, and about the 'dear baby, who was just beginning to prattle, oh so prettily.'

On receiving the telegram, DI Bannister went straight to 2 Priory Street. He spoke to Mrs Pearcey, questioned her as well as her neighbours and searched her rooms with one of his sergeants; she appeared to him to be distraught and her speech was somewhat incoherent. In the blood-stained kitchen he found two carving-knives, their handles similarly stained; a recently washed apron and skirt were also discovered, as well as a stained rug, smelling strongly of paraffin as if an attempt had been made to clean it. The curtains were missing – they and a bloody tablecloth were found in an outhouse. In the fender of the kitchen grate was a long, heavy poker with a ring handle: it was smeared with matted hair and blood.

Bannister took the knives and the poker into the parlour, where Mrs Pearcey was now whistling and affecting indifference. Asked what she had been doing with the poker, she responded: 'Killing mice, killing mice!'

She could offer no sensible explanation for the bloodstained rooms. Bannister said to her: 'Mrs Pearcey, I am going to arrest you for the murder of Mrs Hogg last night, also on suspicion of murdering the child, Phoebe Hogg.' Mrs Pearcey jumped up and said: 'You can arrest me if you like. I'm quite willing to go with you. But I think you have made a mistake.' He took her to Kentish Town police station. On the way she said: 'I wouldn't do such a thing. I wouldn't hurt anyone.'

In the police station she was charged and searched. When she removed her gloves, her hands were seen to have cuts on them. She wore two rings: one of brass, the other a broad gold wedding ring, which was later proved to have been removed from Phoebe Hogg's fingers. The search also revealed that Eleanor Pearcey's underclothes, unchanged for twenty-four hours, were saturated with blood. They were removed and she was supplied with workhouse garments.

Mrs Pearcey appeared at the Marylebone police court on 27 October charged with the murder of Mrs Hogg. She was sent for trial at the Central Criminal Court in the Old Bailey and appeared there, before Mr Justice Denman, on 1 December 1890. Mr Forrest Fulton and Mr C. F. Gill led for the Crown and the accused was defended by Mr Arthur Hutton. Still wearing her workhouse clothes, Mrs Pearcey gave no evidence and remained stonily impassive throughout the trial, seemingly indifferent to everything. The trial ended on its fourth day, when she was found guilty and sentenced to death.

Eleanor Pearcey was hanged at Newgate prison on Tuesday, 23 December 1890, on a bitterly cold and foggy morning. A crowd of about 300 people gathered outside the prison gates. A reporter in the *Pall Mall Budget* wrote: 'The bell of St Sepulchre's church commenced tolling at a quarter to eight, the tones ringing out sharply on the morning air. It had no effect upon the crowd, many of whom were women, and obscene and ribald jokes could be heard among every group, the females especially being fiercely denunciatory of the convict's conduct ... At one minute before eight o'clock a yell from the crowd proclaimed the fact that the black flag was hoisted, and directly after the crowd gave vent to their feelings in a loud cheer.

The day before her execution Mrs Pearcey was visited by her solicitor, Mr Palmer. She asked him to distribute certain trinkets as keepsakes to relatives and friends. She also asked him to put an advertisement in the Madrid papers, addressed to certain initials. Mr Palmer inquired if this had anything to do with her case. 'Never mind,' said Mrs Pearcey. He asked her: 'Do you admit the justice of the sentence?' 'No,' she replied. 'I do not. I know nothing about the crime.' 'Are you satisfied with what we have done for your defence and the efforts we have since made on your behalf?' 'I am perfectly satisfied,' she said. He continued: 'If you have any facts to reveal and will let me know them, even at this late hour, I will lay them before the Home Secretary in the hope of obtaining mercy.' 'I have nothing more to say,' she replied. 'Don't forget about those things. Goodbye.' She walked away across the yard to her cell.

She had repeatedly asked to see Frank Hogg, and permission had at last been given for him to visit her between two and four o'clock that Monday afternoon. Her expectation of seeing him again was great. But as time passed and he did not appear, she became 'nervous and impatient.' When she realized that he would never appear she was overcome, and lay on her bed, her hands over her face, sobbing. After a while she controlled herself and got to her feet, her face now quite calm and composed. She sat down at a table in the cell and began to read.

Her executioner was James Berry, then aged thirty-eight. In his autobiography he described her last hours.

The night before her execution was spent in the condemned cell, watched by three female warders, who stated that her fortitude was remarkable. When introduced to her, I said: 'Good morning, madam,' and she shook my proffered hand without any trace of emotion. She was certainly the most composed person in the whole party. Sir James Whitehead, the Sheriff of the County of London, asked her if she wished to make any statement, as her last opportunity for doing so was fast approaching, and after a moment's pause she said: 'My sentence is a just one, but a good deal of the evidence against me was false.' As the procession was formed and one of the female warders stepped to each side of the prisoner, she turned to them with a considerate desire to save them the pain of the death scene and said: 'You have no need to assist me, I can walk by myself.' One of the women said that she did not mind, but was ready and willing to accompany Mrs Pearcey, who answered: 'Oh, well, if you don't mind going with me, I am pleased.' She then kissed them all and quietly proceeded to her painless death.

She weighed nine stone and was given a six-foot drop. Reporters, who had been excluded from the execution by special order of the sheriff, were also refused permission to see the body, which was, however, viewed by the coroner's jury.

Her final message duly appeared in the papers. It was: 'Have not betrayed – Eleanor.'

After her death Frank Hogg sold several items and furnishings connected with the murder, including the poker and the pram, to Madame Tussaud's for a large fee, and for many years these objects and a waxwork of Mrs Pearcey were a popular attraction there.

CHAPTER 5

Dr Cream

The murder of Matilda Clover, 1891

There is a kind of crazy vanity in murderers that prompts some of them to put their heads in the lion's mouth. They go out of their way to meet and talk to the investigating police, and often pose as conscientious citizens eager to assist the police enquiries. In addition, such murderers sometimes cannot resist writing taunting letters to the police or notes containing useless information. One man who pushed this literary bent to extremes was Neill Cream.

About 7.30 pm on 13 October 1891, a young prostitute, Ellen Donworth, aged nineteen, was plying her trade along Waterloo Road when she staggered and collapsed on the pavement. A man called James Styles ran to her and half-carried her to her nearby lodgings in Duke Street, off Westminster Bridge Road. She was in agony, but she was able to gasp that a tall gentleman with cross-eyes and a silk hat had given her some 'white stuff' to drink from a bottle when she met him earlier that evening in the York Hotel in Waterloo Road. She died on the way to hospital. A post-mortem revealed strychnine in her stomach. A jeweller's traveller was later arrested in connection with her death but soon released.

The coroner officiating at her inquest, Mr G. P. Wyatt, received a letter on 19 October from 'G. O'Brian, Detective'. It said. 'I am writing to say that if you and your satellites fail to bring the murderer of Ellen Donworth, alias Linell . . . to justice, I am willing to give you such assistance as will bring the murderer to justice, provided your government is willing to pay me £300,000 for my services. No pay if not successful.'

Another letter, from 'H. Bayne, Barrister' was sent to Mr W. F. D. Smith, MP, a member of the newsagent family, W. H. Smith and Son Limited. The letter said that two incriminating letters from Ellen Donworth had been found in her possession and the writer offered his services as 'counsellor and legal adviser'.

A week after her death, on 20 October, the cries of another prostitute, twenty-six-year-old Matilda Clover, aroused the house of ill-fame in Lambeth Road run by Mother Phillips, in which she had a room. Matilda was also mother of a two-year-old boy. Writhing and screaming in agony she managed, before she died, to say that a man called Fred had given her some white pills. A servant-girl, Lucy Rose, recalled seeing this Fred, who was tall and moustached, aged about forty, and wore a tall silk-hat and a cape. Matilda's death was attributed to DTs caused by alcoholic poisoning – not unreasonably, as she drank heavily, morning, noon and night. She was buried in a pauper's grave in Tooting.

A month later, a distinguished doctor in Portman Square, Dr William Broadbent, was astonished to get a letter on 28 November 1891 from 'M. Malone' accusing him of the murder of Matilda Clover, who had been 'poisoned with strychnine', and threatening him with exposure unless he paid £2,500. In December, Countess Russell, a guest at the Savoy Hotel, received a blackmail note naming her husband as Matilda's murderer.

Then the poisoner's epistles and murderous activities suddenly ceased. He had fallen in love and had become engaged.

But several months later, on 12 April 1892, two more young prostitutes died in agony. They were Emma Shrivell and Alice Marsh, who both lived in second-floor rooms in 118 Stamford Street, a house of ill-fame kept by a woman called Vogt. Before they died the girls told a policeman that a doctor called Fred had visited them that night, and after a meal of bottled beer and tinned salmon he had given each of them three long thin pills. He was stoutish, dark, bald on top of his head, wore glasses, and was about 5 ft 8 ins or 9 ins. The policeman, PC Cumley, recalled seeing such a man leave the building at 1.45 am.

It was established later that both prostitutes had been poisoned with strychnine, and the newspapers speculated wildly about the identity of the Lambeth Poisoner. Could he be Jack the Ripper, whose activities had suddenly ceased in 1888?

'What a cold-blooded murder!' exclaimed Dr Neill (as Thomas Neill Cream called himself) when he read about the inquest on the two girls in a newspaper on Easter Sunday, 17 April. He told his landlady's daughter, Miss Sleaper, that he was determined to bring the miscreant to justice. A tall, bald, cross-eyed, broad-shouldered man, who wore tall hats and glasses specially made for him in Fleet Street, Dr Cream had rented a second-floor room in 103 Lambeth Palace Road since 9 April, after returning to London from Canada. He had stayed there before, between 7 October the previous year and January, when he took a trip to America. In December, he had become engaged to a girl called Laura Sabbatini, who lived with her mother in Berkhamsted. He made out a will in her favour. On Christmas day he had dined with the Sleapers in his lodgings, joining in their family entertainments, singing hymns in the evening and playing the zither. He was no trouble, going out at night alone to places of entertainment and debauchery.

In those days that area south of the River Thames between Westminster and Waterloo bridges was thronged with bars, theatres, prostitutes and other amusements. There was Astley's circus and playhouse; the Surrey, with its rowdy melodramas (gallery, 6d; pit, 1s); the Canterbury music-hall, with its picture gallery; and the Old Vic, which had, however, become respectable, with blameleass programmes and temperance bars, since Emma Cons became a director in 1880.

Cream was ready on his night-time jaunts, it seems, to converse with any man about plays or music, but his favourite topic was women, about whom he spoke quite crudely. He would describe his tastes and pleasures and exhibit a collection of indecent pictures which he carried about with him.

An article published in the *St James's Gazette* said he dressed with taste and care and was well informed. It continued: 'His very strong and protruding under-jaw was always at work chewing gum, tobacco or cigars . . . He never laughed or even smiled . . . He occasionally said "Ha-ha!" in a hard, stage-villain-like fashion, but no amount of good nature could construe it into an expression of gentility.' The article also referred to his 'never-ending talk about women' and referred to the fact that he swallowed pills which he said had aphrodisiac properties.

In the same lodging-house as Dr Cream was a young medical student from St Thomas's Hospital, Walter Harper. Cream told Miss Sleaper most forcibly that it was Harper who had killed the girls. The police had proof, he said, and the girls had been warned by letter. Miss Sleaper, a girl of spirit, replied that he must be mad. Unabashed, Cream wrote to young Harper's father, a doctor in Barnstaple, accusing his son of the murders and offering to exchange such evidence as he had for £1,500. He wrote: 'The publication of the evidence will ruin you and your family for ever, so that when you read it you will need no one to tell you that it will convict your son . . . If you do not answer at once, I am going to give evidence to the coroner at once.'

Cream was just as outspoken with a drinking acquaintance, an engineer named Haynes, who also happened to be a private enquiry agent. Haynes showed great interest in what Cream had to say, and in due course disclosed all he had discovered to Police Sergeant McIntyre of the CID. Sergeant McIntyre was also taken into Cream's confidence and shown a letter that had allegedly been received by the Stamford Street victims of the Lambeth Poisoner, warning them about a Dr Harper, who would serve them as he had served Matilda Clover and a certain Louise Harvey.

It was a fatal error. Dr Cream had indeed given Louise Harvey some pills to take the previous October. But she had only pretended to swallow them. She was very much alive, and willing to assist police enquiries.

She told the police how, on 25 or 26 October, she had met Cream in Regent Street about 12.30 at night, having seen him earlier that evening in the Alhambra Theatre at the back of the dress circle. She spent the night with him in a Soho hotel and met him again the following night on the Embankment, opposite Charing Cross underground station. 'Good evening. I'm late!' he said, giving her some roses and inviting her to take a glass of wine with him in a nearby pub, the Northumberland. The night before he had commented on some spots on her forehead and promised to provide her with a remedy for them. After they left the Northumberland he produced some pills which he said would effect a cure. They were walking along the Embankment. Something in his manner put her on her guard. He insisted she took the pills and she pretended to swallow them, putting her hand to her mouth. But when he happened to look away, she threw them over the Embankment wall into the River Thames. The solicitous doctor then bade her farewell. But before he left he gave her five shillings to go to a music-hall.

Oddly enough, she saw him again about three weeks later, in Piccadilly Circus. He failed to recognize her, and when she approached him he invited her to a bar in Air Street, to join him for a glass of wine. 'Don't you know me? Don't you remember me?' she asked. 'You promised to meet me one night outside the Oxford.' 'I don't remember you. Who are you?' 'Have you forgotten Lou Harvey?' she asked. He hurried away.

As described by Lou Harvey, Dr Cream was a 'bald and very hairy man; he had a dark ginger moustache, wore gold-rimmed glasses, was well-dressed, cross-eyed, and spoke with an odd accent.' It was what would now be called a transatlantic accent.

In fact, Thomas Neill Cream was Scottish, having been born in Glasgow on 27 May 1850, although he and his parents emigrated to Canada when he was thirteen. His father was the prosperous manager of a ship-building and lumber firm. Young Cream graduated as a doctor at McGill University, Montreal, in 1876. But thereafter he led an obsessional life of crime that included arson, abortion, blackmail, fraud, extortion, theft and attempted murder – each crime being often followed up by a demand for some kind of payment. Three women died under his care as a doctor. A fourth, whom he had tried to abort, he was forced by her father to marry. She died of consumption when he was completing his medical studies in Edinburgh, where he qualified as a physician and surgeon. While practising as a doctor of the 'quack' variety in Chicago he had an affair with a young woman, Mrs Julia Stott, and poisoned her elderly and epileptic husband – who was taking Dr Cream's medicinal cures, and whose life Dr Cream had thoughtfully tried to insure. Daniel Stott died on 14 July 1881 after imbibing one of Cream's remedies, given to him by his wife. Before absconding with Mrs Stott, Cream, wrote to the coroner and the District Attorney accusing a chemist of malpractice and implying that Mr Stott had not died of natural causes and should be exhumed. He was, and was found to have been poisoned with strychnine.

The couple were apprehended and Mrs Stott turned state's evidence. Cream was sentenced to life imprisonment in Joliet prison, Illinois. He was released, unexpectedly early, in July 1891. In the meantime his father had died, leaving him £116,000.

Cream left America, arriving in England on 1 October 1891, the month in which Ellen Donworth and Matilda Clover died and Louise Harvey escaped death. In December he became engaged to Miss Sabbatini. In January, he returned to America, and also visited Canada, where, in Quebec, he had 500 hand-outs printed (but never distributed) notifying the guests of the Metropole Hotel in London that one of the employees there had poisoned Ellen Donworth. Then on 9 April he returned to London: Emma Shrivell and Alice Marsh died three days later.

After Cream's conversation with Sergeant McIntyre, the police began a very cautious investigation. Louise Harvey was found and interviewed. Cream's lodgings were watched, and he himself shadowed. He told an acquaintance who pointed this out to him that the police were keeping an eye on young Harper. On 17 May another woman escaped poisoning when, in her room off Kennington Road, she wisely refused 'an American drink' which Cream prepared for her. On 26 May Inspector Tunbridge of the CID called on Cream in his rooms in Lambeth Palace Road. Cream complained about being followed by the police and showed Tunbridge a leather case containing, among other drugs, a bottle of strychnine pills, which he said could only be sold to chemists or doctors. The police toiled on. Next, on 27 May, Tunbridge went to Barnstaple and saw Dr Harper, who showed him the threatening letter which was clearly in Cream's handwriting. But it was not until 3 June that Cream was arrested at his lodgings, having just booked a passage to America. 'You have got the wrong man!' he exclaimed, 'Fire away!'

He was first charged at Bow Street with attempting to extort money from Dr Joseph Harper. The inquest on Matilda Clover (exhumed on 5 May) began on 22 June. Its conclusion was that Thomas Neill, as he was still being called, had administered poison to her with intent to destroy life. Now charged with her murder, he was put on trial at the Old Bailey before Mr Justice Hawkins on 17 October 1892. The Attorney-General, Sir Charles Russell, led for the Crown, and Mr Gerald Geoghegan appeared for the accused. Insolent and overbearing in court, Cream was convinced he would be acquitted. But the evidence was conclusive. After sentence of death was pronounced, he muttered: 'They will never hang me.'

He never slept the night before his execution, pacing up and down his cell or lying awake on his bed. White as a sheet and shaking, he was hanged at Newgate prison on 15 November 1892 at the age of forty-two. Madame Tussaud's bought his clothes and belongings for £200.

Although he made no confession, it is alleged that on the scaffold he said: 'I am Jack the – ' just before he fell – an impossibility, as at the time of the Whitechapel murders Cream was very definitely under lock and key in Joliet prison, Illinois.

CHAPTER 6

Frederick Deeming

The murder of Miss Mather, 1891

Barristers defending persons accused of murder quite often claim that the defendant is insane. How else can the accused's apparently normal behaviour before and after the horrible event be explained? Sometimes, indeed, more time is spent on discussing medical theories about mental states than on the actual circumstances of the murder. In these instances, the defence usually suffers from the difficulty that the defendant looks and sounds far from mad, and is on the contrary the very picture of an agreeable, even good-looking person, wrongfully accused and naturally aggrieved, even angry, at being so. Fifty years ago and more, juries appear not to have been too bothered with technicalities and took a simpler, black and white view of right and wrong. They were not too worried, it seems, whether the accused was mad or not, since oddness, eccentricity, and even abnormal behaviour were perhaps more usual – and more tolerated – than they are now. The question then was whether or not the accused had been satisfactorily proved to have done the deed – and if he had, he deserved to hang.

Frederick Bailey Deeming was certainly an unusual man, an adventurer in every way, engaging, larger than life, dedicated to enjoying himself and to avoiding work whenever possible. Other members of his family also seem to have been rather odd. According to Fred's older brother Edward, their father, a tinsmith, 'died an imbecile in Tranmere Workhouse, Birkenhead' and before this had tried four times to commit suicide by cutting his throat. Fred himself, born about 1842, was the youngest of seven children and spoiled by his mother. As a boy he was, according to Edward, 'hysterical and peculiar in his habits' and known as 'Mad Fred'. It seems he was supported by his parents for many years, only doing enough in the way of work to pay for his pleasures in Liverpool. It is said that when he was eighteen he became a steward on a liner and disappeared for several years. On his return he was, it seems, transformed, full of tales of adventure in the South African gold-fields, and flamboyantly attired. From then on he kept disappearing overseas and reappearing, bejewelled anew, with a new suit and a new lady-friend by his side. Women, it seems, were fascinated by him. But he never exploited them financially, acquiring his money instead through theft, extortion and fraud.

When his mother died in 1875, her youngest son (according to brother Edward) 'was greatly distressed and very ill, and subsequently went on several voyages, visiting, amongst other places, Calcutta, where he had a severe attack of brain-fever ... Afterwards his mind appeared to be affected [and] he did the most extraordinary things ... He represented himself as being a person of distinction and would dress in peculiar ways. Sometimes he insisted on going out of doors in the morning wearing an evening dress coat [and] on other occasions he would go out as if dressed for a funeral, wearing deep mourning. [He was] subject to delusions, and frequently, after his mother's death, declared that he had seen her vision, and that she had directed him to do certain things.'

His travels took him not only into Europe but to America, Australia, New Zealand and South Africa. At some point he married an English girl, of whom little is known except that she bore him four children, was abandoned in Australia (where she sang in the streets of Sydney to earn money) and again in South Africa. By 1890 Frederick Deeming was forty-eight or so, a large, muscular, hard-faced, handsome man with fair hair and moustache and light blue eyes. Early in 1890 he was in Antwerp, posing as Lord Dunn, and was accepted as such by the town's smart society. But some piece of embezzlement or other misdemeanour soon occasioned his departure and he returned to his home territory on Merseyside.

He took up residence at the Railway Hotel, Rainhill, a few miles south of St Helens and east of Liverpool. He informed people that he worked for the government and was an Inspector of Regiments. Such was his ostentatious style of living that the hotel proprietor ventured to suggest that his establishment was too humble, even inadequate to cater for such a guest. Deeming was gracious. He said he was in Rainhill to look for a modest but comfortable little house within convenient distance of Liverpool on behalf of a friend, Baron Brook. The proprietor was pleased to recommend a charming villa near Rainhill, which an acquaintance, Mrs Mather, wished to let furnished to a good tenant.

Supplied with a letter of introduction Deeming visited Mrs Mather that afternoon and viewed the property, Dinham Villa, which he pronounced to be entirely suitable and satisfactory. He was shown over the house by Mrs Mather's twenty-five-year-old daughter, Emily, a small (5 ft) brown-haired woman of slight build.

Captivated by Deeming's personality, persiflage and protestations, Mrs Mather let him move into the villa without paying any rent in advance. Believing her handsome tenant to be a single man, she was intrigued to hear that Baron Brook had insisted on being Deeming's best man when he married. To everyone's satisfaction the courtship of Emily Mather proceeded apace.

Before long, however, Deeming's wooing of Miss Mather was interrupted by the unexpected arrival – by cab and with little luggage – of his incorrigible wife and her four children. She had found her way back to England, to his brothers' families in Liverpool, and thence to Rainhill. She was determined to live with him as his wife.

Miss Mather heard about the new arrivals and wondered who they were. Deeming teased her, mocking her casual curiosity and revealing at last that the woman was not his wife but his sister. Her husband, he said, had recently obtained a lucrative position abroad, and she had come to holiday briefly with her brother to discuss some private financial matters which had to be settled before she left England.

From Deeming's point of view the sooner she went the better. Her presence and that of the children was inconvenient. When he quarrelled with her, the children cried – it was intolerable. People would soon find out who she really was and then his flourishing romance with Miss Mather would be ruined. As Mrs Deeming refused to leave him – and he was reluctant this time to leave her – something had to be done.

After some thought, he went to Mrs Mather and said that, with her permission, he proposed to make one or two alterations to the villa which would render the house more desirable to Baron Brook, who possessed a number of valuable carpets acquired in his travels. The floorboards at the villa were poorly laid, uneven, and let in the damp, and Deeming proposed at his own expense to cement the ground beneath the floorboards and then to re-lay them, so that they were flat and formed suitable surfaces for the Baron's carpets. Mrs Mather agreed.

Deeming then called on a local builder, buying a pickaxe and a large quantity of cement. He said his sister and her family had just left, and so, with the house to himself, he proposed to begin the alterations at once.

Over the next few days he cemented the ground-floor rooms himself with a local carpenter re-laying the floorboards. As soon as this was done he celebrated by giving a little party in the villa. There was dancing in the kitchen, light refreshments being served, in other rooms. The culmination of the party was the announcement of the engagement of Miss Mather and Mr Deeming – he had proposed that night and she had accepted. The healths of the happy couple were drunk and the merry guests danced happily over the now even floors – under which, encased in cement, lay the bodies of Mrs Deeming and her four children.

The Inspector of Regiments next announced that his duties required him to visit Australia. The wedding must therefore take place before he left. At the same time he revealed that Baron Brook had abandoned the idea of acquiring a house near Liverpool, and Mrs Mather was obliged to agree that it would be convenient if Deeming vacated the villa and stayed with her until he married her daughter. For some reason the marriage took place at Beverley in East Yorkshire.

Weeks later the couple, now known as Mr and Mrs Williams, set sail on the *Kaiser Wilhelm II*. They arrived in Australia, at Melbourne, in December 1891, and rented a small furnished house in Andrew Street, Windsor. Within a few days, on or about 20 December, Emily Mather was cemented in under the dining-room hearth and Mr Williams had disappeared.

The carelessness of a hurried repeat performance meant that, without the benefit of professional assistance, the floorboards were badly re-laid. The owner of the house was compelled to put the poor workmanship right, and in doing so uncovered part of a trussed naked body. The police were sent for. They eventually dug out the remains of Miss Mather, who had been hit on the head six times before her throat was cut.

Deeming was not traced until March 1892, by which time his real identity had been established. He was found in Western Australia, in Perth, where he had been making plans to marry yet again, in this case a certain Miss Rounsevell. Arrested by Detective Cawsey, Deeming was brought in the last week of March by train to Albany, a sea-port on the state's south coast. On the way the train stopped at York and a large hostile crowd demonstrated at the railway station. When the train pulled out Deeming had a fit – whether real or faked is not clear – writhing and kicking for about an hour. At Albany, where Deeming and his captors embarked on a steamer for the 1,500 mile journey to Melbourne, the prisoner shaved off his moustache, although he subsequently denied having done so. None the less, he was identified by several people when he was paraded before them in the yard of Melbourne jail.

He appeared at Melbourne's criminal court in the last week of April 1892, charged with the murder of Emily Mather. The judge was Mr Justice Hodges; the prosecutor was Mr Walsh; and the accused was defended by Mr Deakin.

Meanwhile, in England, Mrs Mather, informed of the method of her daughter's burial, had been horribly reminded of the cementing of the floors of Dinham Villa. When they were dug up the remains of Deeming's wife and four children were found where he had laid them.

In Melbourne, Deeming's trial aroused a great deal of local interest, and crowds mobbed the court-house every day. His defence was that he was insane. It was suggested that he suffered from epileptic fits. He was certainly infected with VD, and this may have impaired his mind, for he was moody and loquacious and fantasized about his past. He claimed that his dead mother had told him to kill Miss Mather and that he had sometimes been overwhelmed by an irresistible impulse to slaughter the current lady in his life. He was thoroughly examined by at least six doctors who were interested in the criminal mentality, and was even examined by an eye specialist, Dr Ruddal, who said the prisoner's eyes were perfectly normal. Dr Shields, a prison doctor, said of the accused: 'I have frequently conversed with him, but I cannot believe anything he says.' Asked by Dr Shields whether he had any standards of right and wrong, Deeming had replied that stealing for example was a matter of conscience. If a person in needy circumstances stole money from one who could well afford it, that was quite justifiable and proper. Murder, he said, was also permissible in certain circumstances – he had several times gone out with a revolver searching for the woman who had given him VD, intending to kill her. He believed in the extermination of such women. Mr Dick, Inspector-General of Lunatic Asylums in Victoria, examined the prisoner five times, testing his memory and inspecting his eyes, head and general appearance. He was unable to detect any signs of insanity and he concluded that Deeming was 'an instinctive criminal'. During the trial no doctor, not even those who spoke for the defence, would unequivocally say that Deeming was insane.

Towards the end of the trial, on Monday, 2 May, Deeming, with the judge's permission, made a speech – 'I wish to say a few words in my defence.'

He spoke for nearly an hour, rambling on without hesitation or nervousness, denying the accusations against him and making some of his own. He began: 'I have not had a fair trial. It is not the law that is trying me, but the press. The case was prejudiced even before my arrival by the exhibition of photographs in shop-windows, and it was by means of these that I was identified . . . If I could believe that I committed the murder, I would plead guilty rather than submit to the gaze of the people in this court – the ugliest race of people I have ever seen . . .' He ended: 'I am as innocent as a man can be. That is my comfort.' The Reuters' correspondent in the court wrote: 'While this extraordinary scene was being enacted, daylight faded into darkness. Gas and candles were lighted, and the whole scene was weird in the extreme. The judge then summed up.'

The all-male jury were out for just over an hour. To their verdict that Deeming was guilty they added a rider that he was *not* insane.

After sentence of death had been passed, Deeming thanked the judge, smiled at the jury, waved at friends and with his hands in his pockets disappeared from view.

In the three weeks before his execution Deeming wrote his autobiography, which was destroyed with all his papers after his death – his writings were said by the authorities to have been 'a compound of ribaldry and folly'. In prison, Deeming, who was alternately angry and depressed and at times incoherent, upbraided his solicitor, Mr Lyle, bewailed his fate, declared his innocence and said he would kill himself if he could. He also made a will leaving the little he had to Mr Lyle and Miss Rounsevell, whom his mother's spirit, he said, was nonetheless still urging him to kill.

A long and closely argued petition was prepared by Mr Lyle and sent to the Melbourne Executive, asking for further enquiries and medical examinations to be made as well as for a stay of execution. The petition was dismissed on 9 May.

Another petition was then sent to the Privy Council in England in a last attempt to have the case reconsidered. It included evidence from Edward Deeming and his wife concerning the prisoner's insanity. This petition was lodged at the Privy Council's office in Downing Street on 18 May, and the matter was discussed the following day with the Lord Chancellor in the chair. On the morning of Friday, 20 May, the Lords of the Judicial Committee of the Privy Council reported to Her Majesty, Queen Victoria, that the petition for special leave to appeal should be dismissed.

On Monday, 23 May 1892, just before ten o'clock, Frederick Deeming walked to his execution smoking a cigar. A large crowd of ticket-holding officials and pressmen were present, and in an attempt to remain incognito the hangman wore a false white beard while his assistant wore a false black one. Asked by the sheriff if he had anything to say, Deeming replied faintly: 'May the Lord receive my spirit.' The cap was put over his head and the entire burial service was read by a chaplain before the lever was pulled.

While he was in prison Deeming claimed to be Jack the Ripper – an impossibility, as he had been in jail at the time of the Whitechapel murders. None the less, after his execution a plaster death-mask was made of his head in case his claim was verified, and his brain and skull were studied by doctors interested in phrenology and the criminal mind. His body was also examined to determine whether there was evidence of physical degeneration, which would assist in identifying the 'criminal type'.

The head, sent to Scotland Yard, soon found a home in the Black Museum, where it was displayed for some time as the death-mask of Jack the Ripper – thus perpetuating yet another myth.

CHAPTER 7

Milsom and Fowler

The murder of Henry Smith, 1896

The phrase 'partners in crime' has a special meaning when that crime is murder. For there seems little doubt that the intense association of two persons, often criminally inclined, acts as a catalyst, so that one of them, becoming grossly exhibitionistic, kills a third person as a result. In this case, as in several others of a similar sort, the victim was old and feeble, and the attack both needlessly brutal as well as cowardly.

Henry Smith, aged seventy-nine and a widower, was a retired engineer who lived alone (although attended by servants) in Muswell Lodge, a decaying mansion at Tetherdown, off Fortis Green in North London. Wealthy Mr Smith was apprehensive about being robbed, and his gardener had obligingly set up mantraps and alarms in the grounds of the house, trip-wires that were supposed to trigger guns into firing a warning shot.

On the night of 13/14 February 1896, no gun-shot was heard, but on the morning of Friday the 14th, the gardener, Charles Webber, discovered the body of Mr Smith in his nightshirt, lying on the kitchen floor. There had been something of a struggle before the old man died from repeated blows on his head, twelve in all, probably delivered by two people. His arms had been tied to his body by strips of a tablecloth, part of which (with a towel) had been wrapped around his head. Pieces of rag had also been used as a gag. Two penknives, employed to rip the cloth, lay one on each side of the body.

Two penknives suggested two men, and from the start a pair of burglars was sought. It was evident they had tried to force the sitting-room and scullery windows with a jemmy before entering the house through a kitchen window. The noise of their entry had clearly awakened Mr Smith, who on coming downstairs to investigate had been bludgeoned to death in the kitchen. The safe in his bedroom had been opened and ransacked. But apart from the pair of penknives, the only clue was a toy lantern found near the body of Mr Smith.

Police investigations revealed that two men had been seen lurking in the neighbourhood of Muswell Lodge two days before the murder, and a detective who had been keeping a watchful eye on an ex-convict out on parole noticed that the man had vanished from his usual haunts. This was a large brute of a man, Henry Fowler, aged thirty-one, whose known partner in petty crime was a small, mean crook called Albert Milsom, aged thirty-three, who lived in Southern Street, King's Cross. Both were labourers by trade.

Their families were questioned, and the brother of Milsom's wife, a fifteen-year-old youth called Henry Miller – who used to call Fowler 'Bunny' – added certainty to suspicion when he positively identified the toy lantern. 'That's mine,' he said.

A warrant was obtained for the arrest of Milsom and Fowler, who in the meantime had disappeared. A postmark on a letter eventually led to their apprehension on Sunday, 12 April 1896, in Bath, in a shop in Monmouth Street. Fowler resisted arrest and was incapacitated by several blows to his head from a police revolver. In the intervening weeks he and Milsom had been to Liverpool, Manchester, Cardiff, London, Swindon and Bath, part of the time with a travelling show, in which they had purchased a partnership, calling themselves Taylor and Scott.

Milsom made a statement admitting the robbery but denying any involvement in the murder, which he said had been committed by Fowler while he, Milsom, was outside.

He told his brother, Fred: 'Fowler killed the old man. I begged and prayed of Fowler to save the old man's life, and I ran away and Fowler ran after me. Fowler fetched me back, and Fowler went and done the robbery.' He also told the police where in the grounds of Muswell Lodge the pair had buried their tools.

Fowler claimed that his partner, 'a dirty dog', had killed the old man. He said: 'He first put his foot on the old man's neck and made sure he was dead.'

Their three-day trial at the Old Bailey began on 19 May 1896, before Mr Justice Hawkins. Mr C. F. Gill and Horace Avory appeared for the Crown; Milsom was defended by Mr Hutton and Mr Rooth, and Fowler by Mr Woodfall and Mr Abinger. The evidence was overwhelming – a £10 note stolen from the Smith residence had also been found in Fowler's possession.

While the jury were out considering their verdict the two accused remained in the dock, and Fowler, determined that Milsom should die – if not hang – fell upon the other man. He almost succeeded in strangling Milsom before he was forcibly subdued by attendant warders and policemen. *The Times* correspondent wrote:

> The constables climbed into the dock from the body of the Court to aid the warders. In the course of the struggle part of the glass partition which is on one side of the dock was smashed. Meanwhile there was great excitement in the body of the Court and in the gallery, both of which were crowded to excess. The members of the bar present and the rest of the spectators rose in their places in order to obtain a better view of what was going on, many of them standing on the seats.

Sentenced to death on 21 May, they were hanged together in Newgate prison on 9 June 1896, sharing a triple execution with a Whitechapel murderer called Seaman. He was hanged between them.

This was the last triple execution that took place at Newgate prison. As the authorities believed that the three men who were to be hanged simultaneously might struggle and resist, four warders were in close attendance on the scaffold. One of them happened to obscure the figure of Warbrick, the assistant executioner, as he pinioned the feet of one of the doomed men. He was still doing so when the chief hangman, James Billington, pulled the lever opening the three trapdoors, catapulting his assistant into the pit. Warbrick, however, heard the bolt beneath him being drawn, and instinctively grabbed the legs of the man in front of him. He plunged head-first through the trap, but retained his hold, ending up swinging below the feet of the three dead men.

This scaffold, described by Billington's successor, Harry Pierrepoint, as 'the finest scaffold in the whole country, being fitted to hang three persons side by side' was moved to Pentonville prison in 1902, when Newgate prison was demolished. The first hanging at Pentonville took place on this scaffold on 30 September 1902, an event that was also marked by the discontinuance of the practice of flying a black flag when an execution occurred. Instead a bell was tolled.

In 1903 the number of people executed for murder in Britain rose to its highest level for over seventy years – twenty-seven people being hanged. This, however, was below the average for the years between 1811 and 1832, when about eighty people were hanged every year – and far less than the average rate of executions which, in the brief reign of Edward VI (1547–53) reached record heights, about 560 people being executed each year at Tyburn alone.

It was in 1903 that building on the site of the demolished Newgate prison began, concluding three years later. The new edifice, topped by a large bronze figure of Justice, was the imposing Central Criminal Court, known by the name of the street in which it stood, the Old Bailey.

CHAPTER 8

Mrs Dyer

The murder of Doris Marmon, 1896

Some sorts of murder in the nineteenth century arose out of the economic and social conditions peculiar to that age; they could never happen now, having been eliminated by social progress and improvements in housing, wages, hygiene and the status of women. Baby-farming was a peculiarity of late Victorian England, when unwanted or inconvenient babies and children, whether illegitimate or merely burdensome, were farmed out to women acting as foster-mothers who were paid to 'adopt' the infants or to look after them for months or years, Such a surrogate mother was Mrs Dyer, who killed at least seven children, and in her twenty years as a baby-farmer may have killed many more. Mrs Dyer also has the distinction of being the oldest woman to have been hanged in Britain between 1843 and 1955.

A native of Bristol, where she was born, brought up and married, Mrs Amelia Elizabeth Dyer was a member of the Salvation Army. She began acting as a midwife and foster-mother about 1875 if not before. In 1880 she was jailed for six weeks for running a baby-farm in Long Ashton, a village south-west of Bristol. Between 1891 and 1894 she was thrice admitted to lunatic asylums for a month or so – twice, it is said, because she had tried to commit suicide.

In June 1895 she left Barton Regis workhouse with an old woman called Granny Smith and went to Cardiff, where the pair lodged with Mrs Dyer's married daughter, Mrs Mary Ann (Polly) Palmer, for a few months. During this period Polly Palmer had a baby that died of 'convulsions and diarrhoea' and probably neglect. Her husband, Arthur, was twenty-five and unemployed. Mrs Dyer's husband, William, whom she had left many years earlier, worked in a Bristol vinegar factory.

In September 1895 the Palmers, Mrs Dyer and Granny Smith, evading creditors and the police, absconded from Cardiff and travelled east to Caversham, a village outside Reading. Here Mrs Dyer (using an assumed name) advertised her trade, and children for adoption or boarding began to arrive. She was assisted in this business by her daughter and presumably Granny Smith; Arthur Palmer remained out of work.

The ten-month-old baby daughter of a barmaid probably arrived first:

the mother, Elizabeth Goulding, paid Mrs Dyer £10. A nine-year-old boy, Willie Thornton, was next, followed by another baby and a girl aged four.

In January 1896 the Palmers moved to London, renting two rooms in Willesden for seven shillings a week and taking with them an infant called Harold, another of Mrs Dyer's charges. She herself moved from Piggott's Road to her third address in Caversham, Kensington Road; and using yet another alias, Mrs Thomas, carried on as before. The children she now acquired were Ellen Oliver, aged ten; Helena Fry, who was fifteen months old; and two illegitimate babies of servant girls.

On 30 March 1896 bargemen on the River Thames at Reading fished the body of a baby girl out of the water: she had been wrapped in a brown paper parcel and weighted with a brick. The infant (who was Helena Fry) had been strangled with a tape. On the brown paper was inscribed 'Mrs Thomas, Piggot's Road, Lower Caversham.' The next day, in Cheltenham, Mrs Dyer was paid £10 by Eleanor Marmon to take care of her illegitimate four-month-old daughter Doris. The day after that, at Paddington station in London, Mrs Dyer and her daughter Polly collected a baby boy, Harry Simmons, from a Mrs Sergeant, whose maid had given birth to him a year before and then disappeared. Mrs Sargeant was relieved no doubt to dispose of the baby to the kindly elderly woman whose advertisement in the *Weekly Dispatch* had caught her eye: 'Couple having no child would like the care of one or would adopt one. Terms £10.'

The following day, 2 April, Doris and Harry, who had been strangled, were dumped in a weighted carpet bag into the Thames. Two days later the police at last identified Mrs Thomas of Piggott's Road as Mrs Dyer of Kensington Road. She was arrested on 4 April.

At Reading police station she tried unsuccessfully to kill herself with a pair of scissors and then by choking herself with a bootlace. Her daughter Polly and her son-in-law, Arthur Palmer, were also arrested. 'What's Arthur here for?' asked Mrs Dyer. 'He's done nothing.' The two babies found in her house in Kensington Road were returned to their mothers and Willie Thornton and Ellen Oliver were eventually found other homes. A four-year-old boy who arrived after the arrests was sent away by Granny Smith.

The river was dragged for other bodies, and the decomposed corpse of a baby boy was recovered from the river on 8 April, as was another boy two days later. Neither was ever identified. On 10 April the carpet bag containing Doris Marmon and Harry Simmons was retrieved from the river-bed. Miss Goulding's baby was dredged up on 23 April and another unidentified baby boy a week later. The total had now reached seven.

Meanwhile, in Reading prison, Mrs Dyer tried to ease her mind and save her daughter and son-in-law by writing a letter to the Superintendent of Police.

I feel my days are numbered. But I do feel it is an awful thing, drawing innocent people into trouble. I do know I shall have to answer before my Maker in Heaven for the awful crimes I have committed, but as

God Almighty is my Judge in Heaven as on Earth, neither my daughter, Mary Ann Palmer, nor her husband, Arthur Ernest Palmer, I do most solemnly swear that neither of them had anything at all to do with it. They never knew I contemplated doing such a wicked thing until too late.

The matron at Reading prison, Ellen Gibbs, said to Mrs Dyer: 'By a letter like this, you plead guilty to everything.' 'I wish to,' remarked the prisoner. 'They cannot charge me with anything worse than I have done . . . Let it go.'

She never revealed how many children she had killed, merely saying later: 'You'll know all mine by the tape round their necks.'

The charges against Palmer and his wife were never proved, and Polly Palmer became the chief witness for the prosecution, giving evidence against her mother at the magistrates' hearing on 2 May and later at the Old Bailey trial. Mrs Palmer's story was that on 31 March her mother turned up in Willesden carrying a ham and a carpet bag and holding a baby, Doris Marmon, temporarily 'for a neighbour'. The baby must have been strangled, said Mrs Palmer, while she was out fetching some coal, for when she returned the baby had disappeared and Mrs Dyer was shoving the carpet bag under the sofa. Harry Simmons, she said, must have been killed (again in Willesden) the following night, before she, her mother and her husband went out to a music-hall. At any rate he had disappeared by the following morning – Mrs Dyer slept on a sofa in the living-room – although there was an odd parcel under the sofa beside the carpet bag. 'What will the neighbours think if they saw you come in with a baby and go away without it?' So said Polly, allegedly. To which her mother allegedly replied: 'You can very well think of some excuse.'

Later that day the Palmers accompanied Mrs Dyer to Paddington station. While Mrs Dyer went to buy some cakes to eat on the Reading train, Palmer held the now bulging carpet bag.

Mrs Amelia Dyer was charged with the murder of Doris Marmon and tried at the Old Bailey on 21 and 22 March 1896 before Mr Justice Hawkins. The trial began on the afternoon of the day on which Mr Justice Hawkins had sentenced to death Albert Milsom and Henry Fowler.

The Crown's case at Mrs Dyer's trial was put by Mr A. T. Lawrence and Mr Horace Avory. Mr Kapadia, who defended her, accepted that she was guilty but tried to prove that she was insane. Dr Logan of Gloucester Asylum said that in 1894 she had been violent and suffered from delusions: she heard voices and said birds talked to her. Dr Forbes Winslow, who saw her twice in Holloway prison, said she was suffering from delusional insanity, depression and melancholia. He did not believe she was shamming insanity. Two other doctors appearing for the prosecution said that her insanity was feigned. One of them, Dr Scott, the medical officer of Holloway, who had seen her daily, said he had discovered nothing in her which was inconsistent with her being a sane person, beyond her own statements. The jury took just five minutes to find her guilty and not insane.

Mrs Dyer, aged fifty-seven, a short, squat woman with thin white hair scraped into a bun behind her head, was hanged at Newgate prison on 10 June 1896.

Before she died she made a long statement explaining some of her actions and thoroughly exonerating her daughter and son-in-law. It ended: 'What was done I did do myself. My only wonder is I did not murder all in the house when I have had these awful temptations on me. Poor girl [Polly], it seems such a dreadful thing to think she should suffer all this through me. I hope and trust you will believe what I say, for it is perfectly correct, and I know she herself will speak the truth, and what she says I feel sure you can believe.'

The Reading baby-farmer evidently loved her own and only surviving child.

CHAPTER 9

Richard A. Prince

The murder of William Terris, 1897

Murderers often tend to play a part, to assume other names, achievements and emotions, to invent autobiographical details, to pose, pretend and lie. They would make, one imagines, good actors. On the other hand, only one actor is believed to have committed a murder. He was Richard Prince, whose ambitions were scorned, his affections spurned and his whole existence mocked. He was more than neurotic and just a little mad, and his victim was an actor like, but much better than, himself.

His real name was Richard Millar Archer. He also called himself William Archer and William Archer Flint. Short, dark, with a thin black moustache waxed at both ends, he was Scottish, having been born in 1858 on a farm on the Baldoran Estate just outside Dundee. His father was a ploughman. His mother, Margaret Archer, later attributed the fact that Richard was 'soft in the head' to the summer day when she left him as a baby out in a harvest-field in the sun. He was educated in Dundee, and as a lad was employed in a minor capacity at the Dundee Theatre for two years. In 1875, when he was seventeen, the Archers came temporarily to London, and the fantasies of the stage-struck youth must have been set alight by the glamorous world of gas-lit West End theatres, in which the idols of the stage, before films and television eclipsed their glory, declaimed and emoted to much effect and immense adulation. But before long the Archers were back in bleak Dundee.

Little is known of Prince's movements over the next twelve years. Presumably, like many young aspiring actors, he was more out of work than in, finding employment where and how he could. His native accent may have limited his chances on the London stage, although he probably modified and disguised it as best he could. What he was unable to alter was an increasingly theatrical manner, a slight squint and a villainous appearance which meant he was invariably cast as a 'heavy'.

However, in 1887 he was in London, employed as a 'super' or extra at the Adelphi Theatre in the Strand, appearing in *The Union Jack*. He stayed with the play on its provincial tour, and is also said to have toured in *Alone in London* and *The Harbour Lights* (in 1889). This was a revival of the play written by George R. Sims and Henry Pettit which in December 1885 had established the Adelphi as the home of popular melodrama. It had also established the romantic association of its two stars, Jessie Millward and William Terriss, which was also played out in private: she was his mistress.

William Terriss was one of the most popular actors at that time on the English stage. His real name was William Charles James Lewin; Terriss was his stage name. Popularly known as Breezy Bill, he was born in London on 20 February 1847, educated privately and at Christ's Hospital, and took up various occupations before he became a full-time actor. As a youth he joined the merchant navy for a few weeks (he liked the uniform), embarking as a cadet on a sea-ship at Gravesend and disembarking at Plymouth, having discovered a sailor's life was not for him. He also tried his hand at silver-mining and horse-breeding in America and at sheep-farming in Australia and the Falkland Islands, where his daughter, Ellaline Terriss, a future Gaiety Girl and wife of Seymour Hicks, was born. Her mother was Isabel Lewis, who on holiday in Margate had been captivated by the athletic figure of young William Lewin sporting in the sea. They were married in 1868 when he was twenty-one.

Before long the family left the Falklands and returned to England, and Terriss, who had dabbled in amateur theatricals, obtained his first notable professional engagement. In 1871 he was cast as Robin Hood in a Drury Lane extravaganza called *Rebecca*, which was based on Sir Walter Scott's *Ivanhoe*. The *Observer* critic, Clement Scott, said: 'It is really pleasant to find anyone determined to speak as ordinary people speak on the boards of the theatre, whereon strange tones and emphases prevail.'

Terriss's face, figure and voice being his fortune, he soon became successful, establishing his reputation as an actor with Henry Irving's company at the Lyceum Theatre. Aged thirty-one when he joined the company, Terriss gave several acclaimed performances: in *The Corsican Brothers*; as Squire Thornhill in *Olivia*, with Ellen Terry as Olivia and Irving as Dr Primrose; as Nemours in *Louis XI*; as the King in *Henry VIII*; and as Henry II, with Irving in the title role of Tennyson's play, *Becket*, which was given a royal command performance in Windsor Castle in 1893 before Queen Victoria. In 1895 Irving was knighted, the first actor to be so honoured.

Several years before this, in October 1882, Jessie Millward, then aged twenty-one had appeared as Hero in the Lyceum's production of *Much Ado about Nothing*; Terriss was Claudio. It was three years after this, in December 1885, that they made a name for themselves as a romantic team in *The Harbour Lights*, in which Terriss played Lt David Kingsley and Jessie Millward the lovely Lina. The end of Act III saw them both trapped by the rising tide below some cliffs, with Lina injured. As a wave dashes over them David cries: 'Oh God, the end has come! We are lost, Lina.' He tries to raise her. 'Lina, one effort! It is for our lives.' Slowly opening her eyes, she gazes up at him and says: 'Dave, *you* can climb. Go, and leave me.' 'No, Lina!' he exclaims. 'Not while God spares my reason and my life to battle for us *both*!' But just as they are about to be swept off the rocks by the sea, Tom and Jack enter in a boat and save them.

One critic said of Terriss's performance: 'He does not act, he *is* the frank, handsome sailor whose joyous laugh, bright eye and sturdy ringing voice bring life and hope to the darkest hour. The fine presence, boyish, handsome face and free, fearless gestures suit the role to perfection.'

From then on, Terriss and Miss Millward often appeared in the same productions, touring Britain and America. In London in the 1890s he used to dally with her in her flat off Oxford Circus, while his wife (they were both Catholics) kept up appearances and the family home in Bedford Park, West London.

It was in September 1894 that Terriss and Jessie Millward – he called her 'Sis' and she referred to him as 'my comrade' – embarked on the series of popular successes at the Adelphi that affirmed their national reputation, appearing in plays like *The Fatal Card, The Girl I Left Behind Me, One of the Best, Boys Together,* and *Black-eyed Susan.* He invariably played gallant sailors or soldiers. In *One of the Best* (1895) he was court-martialled and falsely convicted of espionage. As the drums rolled, the marks of his rank, his collar and cuffs, were torn from his uniform, his face the while depicting the agony he suffered. But when his medals were seized he cried out: 'Stay! You may take my name, my honour, my life – but you cannot take my Victoria Cross!'

Capitalizing on his manly mien and personality, Breezy Bill, now approaching fifty and wearing pince-nez in private, strode nightly about the stage, declaring his love for Queen, country and innocent womanhood, foiling the foe at every turn. The audience loved him. Admired and acclaimed, living up to his motto *Carpe Diem,* blessed with a wife, three children and a loving mistress, with good business sense and membership of the better London clubs, he seemed unassailably successful, without a care or enemy in the world.

The year 1897 was Queen Victoria's Diamond Jubilee. Terriss had turned fifty, though said to be younger, and Jessie Millward was thirty-six. Richard Prince, who gave his age as thirty-two, was now thirty-nine and in a dangerous, desperate plight.

Nothing is known about how Prince became acquainted with Terriss. It may have been during the run of *The Union Jack* in 1888. Perhaps Terriss gave the younger actor a walk-on job; it was not unusual for struggling actors to be encouraged or patronized by an established star. Perhaps there was some ground for the uncharitable rumours that were later circulated about their association. What is known is that Terriss, during the run of *The Harbour Lights,* caused Prince to be sacked after the swarthy Scot had made an offensive remark about him. Later on Terriss, out of generosity it is said, sent (or caused to be sent) small sums of money to Prince when he was out of work, via the Actors' Benevolent Fund, and he apparently used his influence to get the younger man on the provincial tours in which Prince occasionally appeared.

But the managers of these touring companies found him increasingly unemployable. One of them, Mr Ralph Croydon, a theatre manager in Newcastle, hired Prince towards the end of October 1897, at 25s a week, but soon sacked him, because in rehearsal he was 'absolutely incapable . . .

absurdly dramatic' and unable to remember the lines of quite a small part. 'Ah!' exclaimed Prince on hearing of his dismissal, 'I have *two* enemies now!' He informed the manager that the other was Terriss – 'the dirty dog'. 'You're mad!', said Mr Croydon. 'Yes,' said Prince. 'And the world will ring with my madness!' Another manager received a letter from Prince that said: 'You hell-hound! You Judas! You have got me out of my engagement by blackmailing me to get on yourself! You cur! I am not a woman, you hound! How dare you blackmail a Highlander!'

Abject but useless apologies would follow such outbursts, which were also heard in theatre dressing-rooms, where Prince was known as Mad Archer. He wearied company members with diatribes about the management and other actors, who he claimed had impeded or prevented his advancement. Prince was as rabid with his pen, sending effusive messages of congratulation and condolence to politicians and royal persons whenever the occasion, birthday or bereavement, arose. He also wrote poems and plays, one of which, *Countess Otto*, he sent to an up-and-coming young actor, Fred Terry. It was written in longhand in exercise-books. Terry made no immediate acknowledgement or return of the script and soon received the following postcard – 'Sir, please return play *Countess Otto* at once. If you are hard up for money will send it. Terriss, the Pope, and Scotland Yard. I will answer in a week – Richard A. Prince.'

Despite the consolation of Sunday services in Westminster Abbey, which he often attended, Prince's professional and private life must have been miserable. When 'resting', he was employed in an ironworks in Dundee, where the workmen 'used to torment him because he was soft'. He was 'very strange in his ways', according to a foreman, 'and very jealous'. Once in 1895, when his wretchedness or sense of drama got the better of him, Prince jumped in the Regent's Canal. His vanity probably kept him from killing himself. 'I am a member of the handsomest family in Scotland!' he would say.

But in November 1897, after being sacked by the Newcastle manager, his poverty was extreme. Existing on handouts from the Actors' Benevolent Fund which had been prompted by a letter from Terriss, Prince lived in a bed-sit near Victoria station, in Buckingham Palace Road. The rent was 4s a week which a sympathetic landlady, Mrs Darby, reduced to 3s. He had no luggage or possessions; his clothes, apart from those he wore, had been pawned. He fed on bread and milk. On 9 December he received what was to be his last payment (10s) from the Benevolent Fund.

On Monday, 13 December, he tried to get a complimentary seat for a show at the Vaudeville Theatre by showing his card at the box-office. It read: 'Richard Archer Prince, Adelphi Theatre'. Asked if he was employed there, he replied: 'No, I'm not. But I was. I suppose I should have written "Late Adelphi Theatre". But other people don't, so why should I?' No ticket was given him, and he became so abusive that he had to be removed from the theatre foyer. He said he would go to the Adelphi a few yards away and tell Mr Gatti how he had been treated. Mr Gatti owned both the Vaudeville and the Adelphi. Prince failed to see him, but at the stage door of the Adelphi he inquired as to when Mr Terriss arrived at the theatre and when he left.

That night or the next Miss Millward heard raised voices in Terriss's dressing-room; Prince was there. She asked Terriss later if anything was the matter; he was dismissive and said: 'This man's becoming a nuisance.'

On Wednesday she again visited his dressing-room, haunted by a feeling of impending ill – she had had a dreadful dream in which Terriss, dying, fell into her arms in some barren room. She asked for some remembrance of him. Amused, he gave her his watch and chain, with her picture in the lid. Another member of the Adelphi company who had a prophetic dream of death was Terriss's understudy, Mr Lane. Meanwhile the show went on. It was called *Secret Service*. Written by William Gillette, it was a four-act drama set during the American Civil War.

In another part of London Mrs Darby asked her poor Scottish lodger when he would be able to pay his overdue rent. He told her she would be paid when he received a certain letter; he would then be 'one way or the other'. Mrs Darby asked him what he meant. Prince replied: 'That is best known to God and man.'

The certain letter arrived on the morning of Thursday, 16 December. It informed him that the Benevolent Fund had terminated his grant. Penniless, starving and poorly clad under his slouch hat and cloak, he set off on foot towards the West End for the last time. In the Strand he happened to meet his step-sister and asked her for some money. She said she would rather see him dead in the gutter than give him anything. If she had, he said later, he would never have bent his steps towards the Adelphi Theatre.

He waited outside its warmth and glamour with a crazy resolve to kill.

Will Terriss spent the early part of that Thursday afternoon playing poker with Fred Terry in the Green Room Club. At four o'clock he and a friend, Harry Greaves, a surveyor, dined in Jessie Millward's flat in Princes Street, Hanover Square. The two men settled down to play chess after their meal, and at about seven o'clock Jessie Millward left them to finish a game while she went on ahead. 'I must get down to the theatre,' she said. 'I hate being rushed.' They followed soon afterwards, riding in a hansom cab to Maiden Lane, the narrow street that runs behind the Adelphi and the Vaudeville. They got out at the street-corner and walked the short distance towards the rear of the Adelphi. Its stage-door was then in Bull Inn Court.

There was another entrance, a pass-door, which also served as the royal box entrance. This was in Maiden Lane. It now serves as an exit-door of the present theatre, being marked, then and now, by the royal crest above the door. The present stage-door is right beside it. Terriss used this pass-door to avoid his fans, and Greaves accompanied him to the theatre probably in case a particular person should prove again to be a nuisance. The door was kept locked. In the dank, gas-lit street Terriss fumbled for his key.

As he inserted it in the lock and opened the door, a dark figure that had been lurking near Rule's Restaurant rushed across the street and with great force stuck a kitchen knife in Terriss's back. Another blow slashed Terriss's side as he turned. A third thrust penetrated his chest.

The attack was carried out in silence. Jessie Millward, in her dressing-room above the door, heard Terriss arrive and the door open – and then nothing.

Suddenly apprehensive, she ran down the stairs with her maid, Lottie, and saw Terriss leaning against the wall by the open door. 'Here are my keys, Lottie,' he said, quite calmly. 'Catch that man.' The maid ran outside. 'Sis,' he whispered, gazing at Jessie. 'Sis, I am stabbed.'

Although she tried to support him he collapsed, and they both fell on the bare boards of the hall at the foot of the stairs. 'Mr Terriss has met with an accident!' she cried. 'Send for a doctor!' She held him in her arms as shocked company members crowded around.

Doctors from the nearby Charing Cross Hospital soon arrived, as well as the police.

Out in Maiden Lane, Prince, who made no resistance, had been seized by Greaves and Lottie and was now handcuffed and in the charge of a uniformed constable; the knife was found in his pocket. He was reported to have said after the murder: 'I did it for revenge. He had kept me out of employment for ten years, and I had either to die in the street or kill him.' He was taken past Covent Garden to Bow Street police station, where five pawn tickets were found on him but no money.

Meanwhile, Terriss still lay on the floor of the little hall, supported by Jessie Millward, whose control was such she did not, or could not cry. Nothing could be done for him; he was dying and barely conscious. Once or twice he murmured: 'Sis . . . Sis . . .' Five or six minutes before the curtain was due to rise, he died.

The audience was already aware that something was amiss, as no orchestra had appeared, the footlights were not lit, and the sound of agitated voices could be heard behind the curtain. A minute or so before 8 pm the curtains parted and the shadowy figure of the ASM, Mr Budd, appeared. Lifting a hand for silence, he said: 'Ladies and gentlemen, I am deeply grieved and pained to announce to you that our beloved friend, Mr Terriss, has met with a serious, nay terrible, accident, which will make the performance of *Secret Service* this evening quite impossible. I will ask you to be good enough to pass into the street as quietly as possible, and it is hardly necessary to me to add that your money will be returned on application at the pay-boxes.' Those who went to the stage-door to enquire what had happened soon learned that William Terriss had been stabbed to death. Word quickly spread; crowds gathered, and within an hour special editions of the evening papers were on the streets with the news.

At Bow Street police station Prince was charged with murder, and having admitted the charge said: 'Can you give me something to eat?'

The following morning Bow Street court, opposite the Royal Opera House, Covent Garden, was crammed with theatre-goers, actors and actresses, who greeted Prince's appearance in the dock with loud sounds of disapprobation. But the villain of the piece was suitably unmoved and smiled disdainfully; indeed, he clearly relished his leading role in front of a full house, nodding, grimacing, smiling, stroking his moustache, twirling the ends, as he listened to the witnesses. Reporters described him as 'Mephistophelian'. The audience's loathing increased as the hearing proceeded, and when he was committed for trial – when he bowed and smiled – a torrent of shouts and yells accompanied his exit.

The funeral of William Terriss took place at 1 pm on 21 December, a bitterly cold and windy day. The funeral procession was half a mile long and took an hour to make the journey from the Terriss family home in Bedford Park to Brompton Cemetery; many thousands of people lined the route. Sir Henry Irving was the most celebrated of the mourners; he had been asked by the Queen to convey her condolences to Terriss's family. He also personally conveyed Jessie Millward to the funeral service; she had hardly slept or eaten since Terriss's death. Mrs Terriss did not attend the service, the family being represented by Terriss's two sons – his daughter, Ellaline, had just lost her first baby and was very ill in Eastbourne. It is said that ten thousand people gathered at the cemetery.

The Adelphi Theatre remained closed for over a week, reopening on Monday, 27 December, with Mr Herbert Waring in place of Terriss and May Whitty taking over Jessie Millward's role. For many months the stage-door in Bull Inn Court became a mistaken place of pilgrimage for morbid sensation-seekers and fans.

Richard Prince was tried at the Old Bailey on 13 January 1898 before Mr Justice Channell. The prosecutor was Mr C. F. Gill, assisted by Mr Horace Avory; Mr W. H. Sands represented the accused, who was swathed in an Inverness cape. The gas-lit courtroom was packed.

At the start, Prince pleaded 'Guilty with provocation' and was advised to change this plea. He said: 'I am guilty, but I have to ask a favour. I believe the law of England allows me a Queen's counsel. I have a counsel, but I should like a Queen's counsel to watch the case on my behalf. I have no friend, and my mother cannot help me with a penny for my defence.' His request was refused and he eventually accepted Mr Sands's advice and changed his plea to 'Not guilty'.

Prince again behaved with much theatricality, but the audience was this time more subdued. The defence was insanity, and his family and several Scottish neighbours and associates were produced to vouch for his strangeness. Two doctors spoke of his 'insane delusions' and said he was 'of unsound mind'. When his mother gave evidence, Prince was much amused and often laughed, loudly translating her Dundonian accent for the benefit of judge and jury. She said: 'He was born mad, and he grew up wi' passions that pit him wrang in his mind.'

The trial lasted one day. The jury retired at 6.35 pm and after a thirty-minute deliberation found the accused 'Guilty, but according to the medical evidence not responsible for his actions.' The judge consigned Prince to the criminal lunatic asylum at Broadmoor, to the prisoner's evident relief. He embarked on an oration of thanks, which was interrupted by the judge. Prince was removed from court.

In Broadmoor he was apparently happy, a leading light in the entertainments of the inmates. He conducted the prison orchestra, and declaimed Shakespeare in a garden courtyard, hanging his cloak on a tree. But was he really insane? Irving thought otherwise, and is reported to have said: 'They will find some excuse to get him off – mad, or something. Terriss was an actor . . .'

Secret Service ended its run at the Adelphi on 20 January, a week after the trial. The enterprising Gatti management transferred another play from Islington to the Adelphi. Preceded by a farce, *BB*, it opened at 8.30 pm on 21 January. The play was a drama about the assassination, by knife, of Jean Marat, and was called *Charlotte Corday*.

Some months before this, Terriss's wife, it is said, had happened to be reading the reviews of *Charlotte Corday* and had told her husband that she thought the part of Marat would suit him very well.

'Ah, no,' he replied. 'Horrible! I couldn't bear that scene with the knife!'

CHAPTER 10

Samuel Dougal

The murder of Miss Holland, 1899

The character of some murders is determined in part by the nature of society. As social conventions and inhibitions alter, so do kinds of murder, some vanishing, others developing. Murder in the course of a terrorist hijack or kidnapping has become a feature of the past decade. A feature of the late-Victorian and Edwardian eras was the number of single and susceptible women with money who were courted by unscrupulous but charming rogues, whose sole aim was to deprive the ladies of their savings and sometimes of their lives. The circumstances surrounding the murder of Miss Holland and the social situation of those involved belong to a different age, when manners made a man and might unmake a maid.

Miss Camille Cecile Holland was a little spinster lady of fifty-five in 1898 when she met Samuel Herbert Dougal, then aged fifty-two, either at the Earl's Court Exhibition or through an advertisement in some journal dealing with persons seeking friendship and/or matrimony.

Miss Holland, born in India, where her French mother had married a Liverpudlian, was brought up largely in England by an aunt who ran a girls' school. When Aunt Sarah retired Miss Holland became her companion and finally her heiress in 1893. She inherited about £6,000 in investments, a great deal of money then, as well as all her aunt's furniture and jewellery. Thus enriched and freed from family considerations – her only living relatives were two nephews and a niece – Miss Holland, then aged fifty, flowered, disguising the ravages of middle age by powdering her face, dying her hair red-gold and being most particular about her dress. She was not unattractive to gentlemen who appreciated her very Victorian accomplishments: she played the piano, composed sentimental songs (both words and music), painted sentimental water-colours – and, a good Catholic, regularly went to church. But it seems she retained her virtue, left intact for many years after an early object of her affections, a young naval officer and the brother of a school-friend, drowned. In fond memory of him she always wore his cornelian ring.

Yet something was missing from her life, something she needed so desperately that at the age of fifty-five she sacrificed her virtue and her Victorian propriety by going away with a most unsuitable middle-aged married man and living with him as his wife. It was not as if she were mindlessly besotted with him, although she romanticized their association to start with, referring to him as 'her sweetheart'. Before long she had realized just what a mercenary rogue he was – and yet she still went to live with him.

Samuel Herbert Dougal was a ruthless, amoral and utterly engaging beast. He possessed an animal vitality and magnetism that helped him to deprive women of their virtue and both men and women of their money. With few scruples he used his attractions and abilities to exploit others. His aim, it seems, was always enjoyment, whether as Jekyll or Hyde, and he had humours to match.

Born at Bow in the East End of London in May 1846, he was given a basic education and acquired a job as an apprentice in a civil engineering office. But this was far too humdrum for his extrovert, adventurous nature, and when his debts and dissipation and the strictures of father became intolerable he joined the army, enlisting at Chatham in the Royal Engineers on 6 March 1866. He remained with the RE for twenty-one years, serving in Ireland, Wales, and Nova Scotia, where he remained for ten years. He worked as a surveyor and a clerk, ending his service on 22 March 1887 as the chief clerk for the RE at Aldershot, with the rank of quartermaster-sergeant. His conduct and character were described as 'very good' and he was commended as being 'a very good clerk'.

His domestic life was not so good. In 1869, when he was twenty-three, he married a Miss Griffiths. She had four children and much unhappiness; apparently he drank and ill-treated her. They put up with each other for sixteen years until, towards the end of his ten years in Halifax, Nova Scotia, she suddenly fell ill, dying in agony within twelve hours. This was in June 1885.

Two months later, after a brief leave in England, he returned to Halifax with a second wife, who in October was also suddenly taken ill. Vomiting excessively, she died. Both wives were buried in Halifax within twenty-four hours of their deaths which, having occurred in military quarters, were not required to be entered in a civil register.

When his regiment returned to England early in 1887, the year of Queen Victoria's Golden Jubilee, he brought with him a young girl from Halifax, passing her off as his wife.

He was now forty. Evidently she believed that his intentions were honourable and included marriage. She had a baby, but was so abused and beaten by him that she returned with her child to Halifax, posing as a widow.

After leaving the army Dougal became in turn a salesman, storekeeper, the steward of two Conservative clubs, publican, surveyor and clerk, along the way acquiring as many women as jobs (if not more) to keep him company and in a manner to which he had not hitherto been accustomed – most notably a widow who bore him two children and absconded when his brutality became unbearable. For a time he ran a pub at Ware in Hertfordshire with the help of an elderly woman and her money. But not for long; both the pub and a house insured by Dougal caught fire. He applied for the insurance but was arrested instead and tried at St Albans in

December 1889. On being acquitted through lack of evidence he moved to Ireland, to Dublin, where he met Sarah White, eventually marrying her on 7 August 1892. She was his third wife and bore him two children.

Two years later he was back in London, wifeless but not a widower, seeking some other lady to support him. The unlucky woman this time was Miss Emily Booty, who met him as she emerged from a Camberwell bank. With her money they leased and furnished a house in Watlington, Oxfordshire, and at his invitation the third Mrs Dougal, more enduring than his other wives or women, brought her children to England and moved into Miss Booty's house. She suffered this and Dougal's behaviour for a few months, during which the youngest Dougal died of convulsions. But when she began packing her boxes Dougal became so threatening that she fled and went to the police. They searched *his* boxes and found within them some of Miss Booty's minor possessions: a linen-duster, two tea-cloths and four yards of dimity. Arrested and charged with larceny, Dougal appeared at Oxford Quarter Sessions in April 1895, where he defended himself so impressively that the jury, also impressed it seems by his fine army record, found him not guilty.

The jury at the Central Criminal Court in January 1896 were not so impressionable when he was charged with forging the signature of Lord Frankfort on a cheque in Dublin, and he was sentenced to twelve months' hard labour. This he served in the Cane Hill Lunatic Asylum, where he was taken from Pentonville prison suffering from acute melancholia after half-heartedly trying to hang himself in his cell.

He was pronounced sane and discharged in December 1896. By then he was fifty, and having served a prison sentence and lost his army pension as a result he found it difficult to get work. He was saved by his brother Henry, who provided him with some clerical work at Biggin Hill for over a year, during which time Mrs Dougal returned to him and then left again, retreating to Dublin with her surviving child, Olive, when her husband's immoral and immoderate behaviour became too much for her. It also became too much for Henry, who sacked his brother and in so doing sent him back to London and into the arms of Miss Holland.

They met in September 1898 when she was staying at 37 Elgin Crescent, Bayswater, in a boarding-house run by Mrs Florence Pollock, a widow. He visited Miss Holland there twice, posing as Captain Dougal, and once the middle-aged couple spent a weekend together at the Royal Hotel, Southend. Sometime in November Miss Holland's dressmaker, Annie Whiting, calling on her one morning before (as she thought) Miss Holland was due to go off to Brighton with her sweetheart, was told: 'We've parted. I've found out he doesn't want me, only my money. What do you think – he wants me to withdraw all my money and let him invest it in his name. But I won't do it – so we've entirely parted.' Commonsense had prevailed.

Yet so plausible and persuasive was her burly, bearded wooer, and his rude virility so bewitching, that on 2 December Dougal rented a furnished house, Parkmoor, at Hassocks near Brighton, at £6 a month. The money was Miss Holland's. Three days later she left Elgin Crescent and travelled to Brighton, ostensibly on her honeymoon. 'We were under the impression that Miss Holland was going away to be married,' remarked Mrs Pollock later. 'But some of my gentlemen thought not.'

The couple spent Christmas and New Year at Parkmoor, during which Dougal devised the scheme that would lead to Miss Holland's death. It is unlikely that he derived any satisfaction from the association, for his preference was for buxom girls. But he had to humour her, and possibly grimly amused himself in doing so.

It was doubtless on his persuasion that Miss Holland bought a farm for £1,550. A contract was drawn up in January 1899 by Dougal and an estate agent. It was in his name and he signed it. Then Miss Holland, showing unexpected wariness and independence, caused it to be destroyed and a new one to be made out in *her* name. This was signed on 19 January. A week later the couple moved to lodgings in Saffron Walden in Essex to be near their property – Coldhams Farm, Quendon near Clavering, soon to be renamed by Dougal as Moat House Farm, a name that would one day be notorious.

They remained at Saffron Walden for three months while the deeds and furnishing of the farm were finalized, occupying a bedroom and a sitting-room in 4 Market Row. Dougal used to frequent local hostelries, including those at Bishop's Stortford. It is more than likely that he met and socialized with the landlord of The Grapes there, one George Chapman, who was later to be hanged for the murder by poison of *his* three wives.

Miss Holland, posing as Mrs Dougal, became quite friendly with her landlady, Mrs Henrietta Wisken, who later described her as follows: 'The lady I knew as Mrs Dougal, when dressed, looked about fifty years of age, but when in bed ten or fifteen years older. She had golden hair, grey or blue eyes, powdered face. She was about 5 feet 2 or 3 inches in height, and had a good figure for an aged person. She had very small feet . . . also very small hands. She had a very nice set of teeth.'

Although Mrs Wisken believed that Mrs Dougal was well educated and a lady, she was not fooled by her guest's pretences; she knew that the other woman dyed her hair, and without comment pushed letters under the Dougals' bedroom door which were marked 'Miss C. C. Holland'. She liked Mrs Dougal and her little brown and white dog called Jacko, and was doubtless intrigued by the middle-aged lovers, who seemed devoted to each other. Although Mr Dougal would sometimes be detained overnight in London 'by business', he would dutifully send telegraph messages to this effect, and on his return would greet his spouse most warmly, assuaging her evident suspicions. 'I don't believe he need stay up at all,' she once said to Mrs Wisken. 'He could have come back if he'd wanted.' But on his return from Moat House Farm (where he was supervising the takeover of the property) he would ring the bell of his bicycle as he entered Market Row, and Miss Holland would leave her little sitting-room and go to the front door to let him in, when he would greet her with a kiss.

On 27 April she and Dougal left Saffron Walden in a pony and trap and were driven by an ancient farmworker, Henry Pilgrim, to Moat House Farm.

In three weeks' time Miss Holland was dead.

The small, neat farmhouse was surrounded by a wide moat and reached by a little bridge. Fir trees and apple trees screened it from view – unnecessarily, as it was isolated in some bleak countryside, at that time but sparsely peopled. The nearest house, Rickling Vicarage, was about half a mile away.

Two days after the couple moved in, a twenty-year-old girl, Lydia Faithful, previously engaged by Miss Holland as a domestic servant, arrived. She moved out a week later, perhaps driven away by the attentions of Dougal – as was the next maidservant, Florence Havies, aged nineteen, who was hired by Miss Holland at Bishop's Stortford on 9 May. She arrived on Saturday 13 May, and departed a week later – the day after her new mistress disappeared.

Florrie's story, as told to the court, of her own and Miss Holland's last days at Moat House Farm was as follows: 'The first night I slept in a little bedroom at the back of the house . . . The next morning I got up about six o'clock and commenced my duties. I was the only one up. About half an hour afterwards the prisoner came down alone and into the scullery where I was. He came up unawares and kissed me. I objected very much, and as soon as I saw Miss Holland I made a complaint to her.'

Miss Holland was even more upset and cried bitterly. She also begged the girl not to leave, probably anxious on her own account, even apprehensive, wondering how she could extricate herself from her uncomfortable situation. However, she was not too timid to upbraid Dougal for his conduct.

A few days later, on the evening of Tuesday 16 May, Florrie retired to bed about nine o'clock. She said: 'Miss Holland went to bed at the same time. The prisoner remained downstairs in the dining-room. Soon after, about ten minutes after, someone came to my door, I knew the voice . . . He called "Florrie" three times in an undertone, and pulled at the door with all his might.' The door had a bolt and he nearly pulled it off. 'I screamed for Mrs Dougal. Miss Holland came to my door and I had hysterics. After I came to I made a complaint to Miss Holland. She took me into the prisoner's bedroom. He was in bed and pretending to be asleep. Mrs Dougal said: "It's no use pretending to be asleep." In consequence of what happened Miss Holland and I slept together in the same bed that night. I had made up my mind to go home but yielding to pressure from Miss Holland I agreed to stay on.' Again, Miss Holland burst into tears and begged the girl not to leave her. Florrie felt oddly sorry for her. As she said later: 'She was so kind to me . . . I did not like to leave her alone.'

Reassured by each other's presence, the two women slept together in the spare bedroom on Wednesday and Thursday nights. During the day Florrie observed that no tradesmen or postmen called at the house, supplies being fetched by Dougal in the trap, and letters being taken by him off the postman at the outer gate.

On the early evening of Friday, 19 May, about half-past six, Miss Holland entered the kitchen where Florrie was at work: 'Do you mind if I go into the town to do a little shopping?' she asked. Replied Florrie: 'No. Not so long as Mr Dougal goes with you.' He would be doing so, said Miss Holland – he was driving the trap. She was wearing a dark dress with a bustle and a fall of lace at her throat; on her head was a white sailor hat with a veil. Before they left, Miss Holland called: 'Goodbye, Florrie. I shan't be long.'

Florrie watched her go down the path, across the little bridge and get into the trap with Dougal. She never saw her again.

It grew dark; night fell and there was still no sign of either Dougal or Miss Holland. Florrie must have become very worried. Then at last the trap returned. It was now about half-past eight.

Dougal entered the kitchen, alone. 'Where's the mistress?' Florrie exclaimed. He replied: 'Gone to London.' 'What!' cried Florrie, aghast. 'Gone to London and left me here all alone?' 'Yes,' said Dougal. 'But never mind, she's coming back, and I'm going to meet her.' He then went out to feed the pony, returning to the kitchen at about nine o'clock, remaining in the house for ten minutes or so. Then he went out again, saying he was going to meet Mrs Dougal at the station. He disappeared, but Florrie did not hear the trap depart. He was back half an hour later. He said: 'She hasn't come back. I suppose she'll come by that train something after ten o'clock.' A few minutes later he again left the house, saying he was going to meet the train. In half an hour he again returned. 'No, she hasn't come,' he said. 'I suppose she will come by the twelve o'clock train.' He disappeared yet again, not returning this time until a quarter to one. 'The mistress has not come,' he said. 'You had better go to bed.'

Florrie said later: 'I went up to the spare bedroom and stayed there, without undressing, for the rest of the night. I was awake and sat by the window all night' – ready to leap out should Dougal try to force the door. At 6.30 am he knocked at her door to wake her up. But she did not come downstairs until some farm labourers had arrived. He had made the breakfast: tea, bacon and eggs. He told her he had received a letter from Mrs Dougal, saying she had gone on holiday and that a woman friend would be coming to stay. Florrie paid little attention – she only wanted to leave. She was in fact waiting for her mother to arrive. The previous day she had sent her mother a note, which so alarmed Mrs Havies that as soon as she received it she hired a trap to get her from Newport to Moat House Farm.

On her arrival, she told Dougal what she thought of him and that she had come to take her daughter away. Dougal retorted that he had not harmed her, and relieved, no doubt, to get rid of the pair, put a month's wages for Florrie on the kitchen table and enough money for their return train fares to Waltham. They departed that morning and Dougal immediately telegraphed his real wife, telling her to come to Moat House Farm. That evening he and Pilgrim picked her up at Newport station.

He had written to her some time before this, suggesting that she take up residence in a cottage in the vicinity. Instead, she moved with her little daughter, Olive, into Moat House Farm, and was presented to the vicar of

Clavering and his wife as Dougal's widowed daughter – as she was to the next maidservant to arrive at the farm, Emma Burgess. Not as fearful as Florrie, Emma remained for just under a year, when an indisposition caused her temporary absence.

In the meantime, all pretence at Mrs Dougal's kinship was dropped and she became generally known as what she was, Dougal's wife. For a time, despite frequent quarrels, she made the most of her situation as mistress of Moat House Farm. She wore some of Miss Holland's clothes, altered by Emma, and told the vicar's wife that Miss Holland was away yachting.

At one point the little dog, Jacko, ran away, turning up six and a half miles away at Saffron Walden outside Mrs Wisken's house. She was delighted to see the dog and presumed she would soon be seeing his mistress, from whom she had heard nothing for over six months. No mistress appeared, and Mrs Wisken duly wrote to Moat House Farm, requesting some instructions concerning the dog. Dougal replied, and it was he who reappeared one night in Market Row to take the dog away. All Mrs Wisken's enquiries about Miss Holland were ignored.

Soon after Miss Holland's disappearance Dougal had begun to forge her simple signature on cheques and letters, and by stages over the next two years he acquired the rest of her capital, which he banked in his own name. By September 1901 he had accumulated £2,912 15s. He also transferred the ownership of Moat House Farm to himself.

Thus enriched and unthreatened he dropped the pretence of being a farmer, although he still kept some cows, chickens and pigs. He bought a car, the first ever seen in that part of the country, and pursued the convivial pleasures of a country gentleman – hunting, shooting, smoking, drinking and generally enjoying himself – on one occasion by giving naked girls bicycle lessons in a field behind the farmhouse.

Along the way he sired several children on servant-girls and other women, and at one time was pleasuring three sisters as well as their mother.

Naturally, rumours abounded in the neighbourhood about the goings-on at Moat House Farm, and in due course (January 1902) Mrs Dougal upped and left – in company with an engine-driver, George Killick. Divorce proceedings were instituted by Dougal in May and, the suit being undefended, he was given a decree nisi on 1 August 1902.

In September another servant-girl, Kate Cranwell, aged eighteen, went home to have a child. This time, however, there was a paternity suit, which he foolishly chose to contest, thus inviting the ire of the women in the case and the attention of the local law.

'You have had twelve months for forging cheques,' said Eliza Cranwell, who had gone with Dougal to Tenby to serve notice of divorce on his wife. 'You'll be hung next for killing that woman.'

Eliza, a dressmaker, was Kate's older sister. Another sister, Millie, aged sixteen, who for some months had been a servant at Moat House Farm at the same time as Kate, was taken away from the farm by Mrs Dougal when she left. A fourth sister, Georgina Cranwell, became Dougal's last female servitor, staying at the farm in the winter of 1902/3.

In January 1903, a month after the birth of Kate Cranwell's child, the matter of Miss Holland's disappearance aroused more concern than ever. Where was she? That was the question that now concerned the King's Proctor, whose representative was investigatlng whether or not the decree nisi should be made absolute. Miss Holland was missing, allegedly abroad. But many if not all of her personal possessions remained at Moat House Farm. Was the local rumour true that said Dougal had killed and buried her?

Fired by these enquiries and by his own suspicions, PC Drew wrote to his chief constable at the end of January 1903. His letter began: 'Sir, I have the honour to report, for your information that it is a talk in this Village Clavering about Mr Herbert Samuel Dougal . . .'

Official police enquiries were set in motion and Miss Holland's nephews, her bankers and solicitors were contacted. Superintendent Pryke visited Moat House Farm five days before the decree nisi was actually rescinded on 9 March. He and Dougal had a friendly talk concerning 'a scandal in the village' and the whereabouts of Miss Holland. Said Pryke: 'I thought he had told me the truth, and I shook hands with him on leaving.'

But the financial investigations of DI Bower of the CID at Scotland Yard, and DI Marden of the Essex Constabulary, gave them grounds for much unease, in particular a cheque dated 28 August 1902, made out to 'Mr J. Heath' and signed 'Camille C. Holland'. Her nephew, Mr Ernest Holland, said the signature was definitely not his aunt's.

Meanwhile Dougal had determined on flight. The day after Pryke's visit he withdrew £605 from his accounts and went up to London, where he stayed at the Central Hotel, Long Lane, returning to Moat House Farm a week later. He was only there for one night, his last in the place that had been his home for nearly four years.

On Friday, 13 March, he moved out with a pile of luggage, staying that night once again in the Central Hotel. Here he was joined on the Saturday by Georgina Cranwell, pregnant and also bearing a quantity of luggage which she left in the cloakroom of Liverpool Street station. She and Dougal then travelled on to Bournemouth for a weekend of pleasure, which included a steamer-trip to Swanage. They stayed at the Coburg Hotel. On Tuesday they returned to London, where Dougal remained while Georgina went back to Essex and Moat House Farm.

On Wednesday, 18 March at about 1.30 pm, he entered the Bank of England in the City and presented fourteen £10 notes, which he wanted changed into smaller currency. The cashier, William Lawrence, on glancing at the notes, realized that some bore numbers of notes that had been stopped. He told Dougal: 'I am sorry, but I shall have to ask you to accompany me to the secretary's office.' Dougal demanded: 'Why? Are the notes stopped?' 'Some of them are,' said Lawrence, adding that the other man would not be detained long. He asked Dougal to endorse one of the notes, and Dougal wrote: 'Sydney Domville, Upper Terrace, Bournemouth'.

As Dougal sat in the secretary's office, DI Henry Cox, on duty at the bank, was sent for. After a brief discussion with the secretary, Mr Dale, Cox approached Dougal and questioned him, concluding with a request that he come to the detectives' office in Old Jewry. 'Your name is Dougal,' said DI Cox. 'Yes,' admitted Dougal, and accompanied the inspector into the street, where he unexpectedly bolted, running towards Cheapside and then into Frederick's Place. It was a cul-de-sac.

There Cox collared the hapless Dougal. They both fell to the ground in the ensuing struggle, but with the assistance of a constable, Cox soon overpowered the older, overweight man.

When Dougal was searched there were found on him eighty-three £5 notes, eight £10 notes, £63 in gold, a £5 gold coin, seven rings (five of them made for a woman and one being Miss Holland's cornelian ring), five watches, several items of feminine jewellery, six moonstones, a walking-stick, a pipe and a cloakroom ticket.

He was charged with forgery of the cheque made out to Mr J. Heath and taken the following day to the police station at Saffron Walden. That day the search of Moat House Farm began.

The police moved in, led by DS Scott, who took up residence in the farmhouse. He and his helpers, having examined every inch of the house, began to dig, concentrating mainly on the moat, which was drained.

For five weeks they dug, until the farm looked like a battlefield. Little Jacko roamed about, deaf now and almost blind. Then Inspector Bower heard locally that Dougal had caused a drainage ditch to be filled in soon after his arrival at the farm; it had run from the horse-pond to the moat and was full of sewage and manure – 'black liquid filth', according to DS Scott. His men opened it up.

On the afternoon of Monday, 27 April – four years to the day since Miss Holland's arrival at Moat House Farm – a small boot was unearthed by a pitchfork. Inside was a skeletal foot.

Slowly, all that remained of Miss Holland's fully clothed corpse was revealed, partly preserved by blackthorn branches that had been laid on top of her. The remains were dug out in a slab, which was then placed on two chairs in a greenhouse. Mrs Wisken managed to identify the body, chiefly through its many garments, some of which she had stitched and altered herself.

On the day she died, Miss Holland had been wearing, apart from a dress, two pairs of combinations, steel-framed corsets, two underbodices, stockings, bloomers and two petticoats. She had been shot at close range. The bullet from a revolver that was proved to have belonged to Dougal was found inside the skull. It had entered the skull a few inches above and behind the right ear, and had been fired, according to the pathologist, Dr Pepper, 'by a person in a higher position than the deceased'. Evidently Dougal, from his seat in the trap, had leaned over and shot Miss Holland as she stood on the ground with her back to him.

Dougal was charged on Thursday, 30 April 1903 by DI Alfred Martin with 'wilfully, maliciously, feloniously, with malice aforethought' killing and slaying Miss Holland. He was charged in the dining-room of Moat

House Farm on a dismal, rainy day, the day on which the inquest was opened in the old barn.

Dougal was remanded several times, finally being committed for trial, protesting his innocence, on 29 May. In the interim he wrote several cheerfully chatty letters to the women in his life, including Mrs Dougal, who became a Roman Catholic and called herself Mary Magdalene.

The trial began in the Shire Hall at Chelmsford, Essex, on Monday, 22 June, before Mr Justice Wright. Leading counsel for the Crown was Mr C. F. Gill, KC, while the accused, who gave no evidence, was defended by Mr George Elliott.

At 4.50 pm on the following day, after an absence of seventy-five minutes, the jury found Dougal guilty and he was sentenced to death. To this he made no reply.

An appeal was later dismissed. He himself wrote to the Home Secretary, confessing now that he had indeed shot Miss Holland – by accident. His explanation was that on their return from Stansted, where they had done some shopping – 'stopping on the way at the Chequers public-house and had a glass of whisky each' – Miss Holland had seated herself on a box at the coach-house door while he stabled the horse. As she gazed at the starlit sky he picked up a loaded revolver 'lying on a shelf' and began unloading it; earlier that day he had done some shooting with it. The gun, he said, was in his left hand when she said: 'Come and look at the beautiful silvery moon.' He moved towards her and 'the revolver accidentally exploded'. Her head fell forward. He said: 'I hope you are not hurt, dear.' Thinking she had fainted he supported her, saying tenderly: 'Speak, Cecily dear.' Then, he said, he ran to the house for some brandy and was confronted by the maid, who asked him where her mistress was. He replied that she had gone to London. He then returned with the brandy, he said, and found that her pulse was still beating. 'I took off her hat and veil and could see no blood, and afterwards removed her cloak, and still saw no blood. At this time I became demented, not knowing what I did. I took her in my arms and carried her up into the fields where there was a breeze, thinking it would revive her . . . I went back indoors, and shortly returned to her and found her dead. I did not know what to do then. I carried her back towards the coach-house, and seeing the open ditch . . . I laid her on some straw in the ditch, and returned to the house again. I could not rest, so returned to where she was. I knelt down and kissed her, and placed a piece of lace over her face, and put some straw over her . . . Afterwards I placed a branch of a thorn-bush on the straw, so that the fowls could not scratch the straw off her body. After that I walked about the yard . . .' He could not sleep that night, he said, and the following morning Alfred Shaw, who had already begun filling in the ditch, continued doing so 'until the trench was level, taking about a fortnight'.

Dougal was hanged at Chelmsford prison on 8 July 1903 on a bright, sunny morning. He was fifty-seven. The executioner was James Billington. A zealous chaplain, determined to save the condemned man's soul on the scaffold, demanded of Dougal (by then hooded and haltered), 'Are you guilty or not guilty?' There was no response. Again the chaplain repeated the question. Dougal's hooded head half-turned and his voice said 'Guilty' as the lever was pulled.

The chaplain's explanation for his conduct, which was criticized by the papers and in parliament, was that Dougal had promised to confess before his execution but had failed to do so. 'My spiritual anxiety became intense,' said the chaplain. 'I prayed earnestly with him during the last quarter of an hour, during which he sobbed . . . I knew not what to do more, so under strong impulse, and quite on the inspiration of the moment, I made the strong appeal at the scaffold.'

Dougal's body was buried in Chelmsford prison. On Miss Holland's grave in Saffron Walden churchyard a cross was raised on which was carved the figure of an angel receiving a sweet young girl. The inscription said that she died, aged fifty-six, 'under distressing circumstances'. Little Jacko, who had finally found a home with Mrs Wisken, died a year later. He was stuffed and mounted in a glass case in Mrs Wisken's parlour.

CHAPTER 11

Alfred and Albert Stratton

The murders of Mr and Mrs Farrow, 1905

Petty crime was the background to murder in the case of the Stratton brothers, as it has been so often. But their trial is unique in that for the first time in a British court fingerprint evidence was used to obtain a conviction for murder.

Alfred Stratton, aged twenty-two, and Albert, twenty, lived in south-east London, at Deptford. Both had previous convictions for housebreaking and burglary. They got to hear or believed that an elderly local tradesman, Thomas Farrow, kept a cache of money in his chandler's store, which dealt in oil, paint, candles and soap, at 34 High Street, Deptford. He and his wife Ann, both in their sixties, lived above the shop, which was owned not by them but by an absentee landlord, Mr Chapman.

At about 7.30 am on Monday, 27 March 1905, their young assistant, a boy, arrived for work and found the shop door open. This was not unusual, for Mr Farrow often rose early to supply painters and decorators with materials on their way to work. But no one was in the shop and no one answered the assistant's call. On entering the back parlour, the boy found Mr Farrow dead on the floor and drenched in blood. His head had been badly battered. Mrs Farrow was discovered in a similar state in her bed, unconscious; she died in hospital three days later. Apparently the old man had come downstairs about 7 am in response to knocking at the shop door. Attacked by the men he let into the shop, he had managed to reach the parlour before being bludgeoned to death. His wife, awakened, and calling out anxiously, probably then had to be silenced. The cash-box, in which there were only a few pounds, had been broken open and was empty.

Two masks made from black silk stockings were found in the shop, as was a fingerprint on the cash-box's metal tray – the print of a bloody right thumb.

All those who were known to have touched the tray, including the victims, the shop-boy and a policeman, were fingerprinted. The thumb-print belonged to none of them.

Chief Inspector Fox, investigating the murder, thought the murderers must be local men – why had they worn masks unless they feared recognition? All the minor villains in the Deptford area were sought out and their alibis checked. The Stratton brothers, already known to the police, had disappeared, but Alfred's girlfriend was questioned. Disgruntled and afraid (she had a black-eye), she eventually admitted that the brothers had been out all night the previous Sunday, that Alfred had later destroyed the coat he had been wearing, and that he had dyed his brown shoes black. A milkman and his boy assistant revealed that they had seen two men leave the chandler's shop in a hurry about 7.15 am on Monday, leaving the door open.

The following Sunday Alfred was picked up in a public-house and Albert in lodgings in Stepney. They were brought to Tower Bridge police station. Both had their fingerprints taken, and Alfred's thumb-print was found to match the bloody print on the cash-box. There were eleven points of resemblance, it was said later in court.

The brothers' trial took place at the Central Criminal Court in the Old Bailey in May 1905, before Mr Justice Channell.

Inspector Collins, of the newly formed Fingerprint Branch at Scotland Yard, said that they now had about 85,000 sets of prints. Knowledgeably questioned by the prosecutor, Mr Richard Muir, who had studied the matter, Collins described how the system of fingerprint identification worked. As an example, the fingerprints of one of the jurymen were taken and examined by the rest of the jury. Mr H. G. Rooth, defending Alfred Stratton, said that the fingerprint system was 'unreliable' – it 'savoured more of the French courts than of English justice' – and this new-fangled evidence was contested by experts for the defence. The judge himself was dubious about the irrefutable nature of such evidence. But the jury had no doubts and found both brothers guilty. Each blamed the other for the murders.

They were hanged together.

Three years later, in 1908, the hanging of persons under the age of sixteen was abolished. Between 1908 and 1921 inclusive, a period of fourteen years, no woman was hanged, although fifty-one women were convicted of murder, sentenced to death and then reprieved.

CHAPTER 12

Dr Crippen

The murder of Cora Crippen, 1910

Very few doctors have been murderers but not a few may have committed murder without any suspicion being aroused. They have both the know-how and the wherewithal to bring about illness and death: the instruments, the dangerous drugs and poisons. They can pronounce with authority on the cause of death and sign certificates to this effect; they have also the necessary facility of viewing people as objects. The doctors who have killed (and have been detected) have largely been poisoners, as one would expect. Such a one was Dr Crippen, whose extraordinary story also illustrates the frequent connection between murder and dressing-up, playing a part, and the use of pseudonyms.

Hawley Harvey Crippen was born in Coldwater, Michigan in 1862, and acquired his medical training through the winning of diplomas in Cleveland, London and New York. But strictly speaking he never qualified or practised as a doctor. His father was a dry-goods merchant, called Myron Crippen. In 1887 young Crippen married Charlotte Bell, his first wife; they had a son, Otto. She died about 1890.

Two or three years later in Jersey City, he married Cora Turner, whom he first met when she was seventeen and living with another man, a stove manufacturer. Her real name was Kunigunde Mackamotzki, her father being a Russian Pole and her mother German. Crippen paid for Cora to train as an opera-singer, though to no avail, and when they settled in 1900 in London, where he became the manager of a patent medicine firm, she tried to succeed as a music-hall artiste, calllng herself Belle Elmore. She sang in various halls in London and elsewhere, going away for about two weeks at a time. Her singing voice, however, was as small as her talents, though her speaking voice was loud and clear with a sharp American twang. She herself was short and stout, and with her dark eyes and hair, bright jewels and colourful clothes, seemed like a plump bird of paradise. Her flamboyant appearance was at odds with her meanness, both of which were mildly tolerated by her husband.

Considerate and courteous, Crippen was a short (5 ft 3 ins) slightly feminine man, with thinning hair, a long and straggly sandy moustache, and prominent grey eyes behind gold-rimmed glasses, 'Somewhat slovenly in appearance,' said a later police description – 'Wears his hat at back of head. Very plausible and quiet spoken, remarkably cool and collected demeanour ... Throws his feet outward when walking.' He was known to his friends as 'Peter'.

He worked for a patent medicine company, Munyon's (who paid him £3 a week), and was a partner with Dr Rylance in Yale Tooth Specialists, situated in Albion House, New Oxford Street.

In September 1905, the Crippens moved to 39 Hilldrop Crescent, a semi-detached house which they rented at £52 10s a year. The crescent connected with Camden Road and was less than half a mile from Holloway prison. They occupied separate bedrooms, and had frequent rows. 'She went in and out just as she liked,' said Crippen, 'and did what she liked. It was of no interest to me ... I was rather a lonely man and rather miserable.' By this time Mrs Crippen had acquired many music-hall friends – although on her last appearance on stage, during an artistes' strike, at the Bedford and Euston Palace, she was hissed for being a blackleg. Thenceforth she enthusiastically embraced the office of honorary treasurer of the Music-Hall Ladies Guild. She also persuaded her husband to become a Roman Catholic. They entertained a lot at home, but their private lives were quite squalid, mainly spent in the dingy and disorderly basement kitchen. The grimy windows were never opened – she disliked fresh air – and her two cats were never let out. Her gentleman friends were let in, however, when Dr Crippen was at work. They gave her gifts and also, it seems, money.

Her husband had by now also found consolation, having fallen in love with the typist who had worked for him for more than seven years, Ethel le Neve, a boyishly attractive girl who was slightly taller than he.

By 1910 she had been his mistress for three years. She was twenty-seven; he forty-eight; Mrs Crippen was thirty-five.

Perhaps Ethel le Neve had by then become rather discontented, wishing to be more than a mistress. Certainly Mrs Crippen, aware of her husband's association with his typist, was threatening to leave, to go and live with one of her gentlemen and take all 'her' money with her. Most of their money, £600, was in fact banked in a joint deposit account, to which she had somehow contributed £330. Significantly, on 15 December 1909, she gave twelve months' notice of withdrawal of the whole amount, which would have been paid to her without question in December 1910.

Dr Crippen, on the other hand, was in some financial trouble. Entertaining Ethel must have been costly – they made love in hotels – and in November 1909 Munyon's stopped employing him as a manager and only paid him a commission on his sales. Even these payments came to an end on 31 January 1910.

That night the Crippens gave a small dinner-party for two retired music-hall artistes, Mr and Mrs Paul Martinetti. Dinner was served in the breakfast room, next to the kitchen. Later they went upstairs to the parlour where they played whist. The Martinettis – 'It was quite a nice evening and Belle was very jolly' – left at 1.30 am, saying goodbye on the gaslit front-door steps that led down to the dark cold street. 'Don't come down, Belle,' said Clara Martinetti, 'You'll catch a cold.'

When the guests had departed there was a marital row, Mrs Crippen accusing her husband of not having escorted old and ill Mr Martinetti upstairs to the lavatory, when he went there earlier that evening. 'She abused me,' said Crippen in his first statement to the police. 'She said: "This is the finish of it – I won't stand it any longer – I shall leave you tomorrow and you will never hear of me again!" She had said this so often, he continued, that 'I did not take much notice of it. But she did say one thing which she had never said before, viz, that I was to arrange to cover up any scandal with our mutual friends and the Guild, the best way I could.'

A fortnight before this on 17 January, Crippen had ordered five grains of a narcotic poison called hyoscine (for homoeopathic purposes) from a New Oxford Street chemist's, Lewis and Burrows. They had had none in stock, but had been able to deliver the crystals on 19 January. He had signed the poisons register.

The morning after the dinner, on Tuesday, 1 February, Crippen called at the Martinettis' flat in Shaftesbury Avenue to enquire about Mr Martinetti's health. 'How is Belle?' enquired Mrs Martinetti. 'Oh, she's all right,' was the reply. On 2 February and 9 February, Crippen pawned some of his wife's jewellery in Oxford Street for £195, more than he used to earn from Munyon's in a year.

On the afternoon of 2 February Mrs Crippen failed to appear for the usual meeting of the Music-Hall Ladies Guild, held every Wednesday at Albion House in a room loaned by Dr Crippen. Miss le Neve, however, appeared with two letters signed by Belle Elmore, but not in her handwriting, which said that she had been obliged to go to America because of a relative's illness and would have to resign from the Guild.

Crippen said later that Miss le Neve spent the night with him in 39 Hilldrop Crescent. She stayed other nights and he began giving her his wife's jewellery and clothes.

Belle's friends thought it odd when they did not hear from her – not a single letter or a postcard. They were amazed when on 20 February, at the dinner and ball organized by the Guild for their Benevolent Fund at the Criterion (each ticket cost half a guinea), they saw Dr Crippen with Miss le Neve, who was wearing a brooch that had belonged to Belle. Later they saw the typist wearing Belle's furs. Their anxious requests for news about Belle and her address were disposed of by Crippen, who said she was 'right up in the wilds of the mountains of California'. Later they were told that she was seriously ill with double pneumonia.

Meanwhile, on 12 March, Miss le Neve moved permanently into 39 Hilldrop Crescent, sometimes posing as the housekeeper, although she had now acquired a French maid.

Since the beginning of February she had in fact spent few nights in her own lodgings, and before she left them on 12 March she gave her landlady, Mrs Jackson, articles of clothing, including six coats, six skirts, five blouses, three nightgowns, stockings and hats, telling her that Mrs Crippen had gone to America. According to Mrs Jackson, Ethel le Neve had been much depressed and in tears in January – 'Very tired and strange,' said Mrs

Jackson. She enquired why. 'It's Miss Elmore,' Ethel had confessed. 'When I see them go away together it makes me realize what my position is . . . She's been threatening to go away . . . and when she does that the doctor's going to divorce her and marry me.' She was much more cheerful at the beginning of February, 'really happy'. When Mrs Jackson jokingly asked her if someone had died and left her money, Ethel answered that 'someone' had gone to America.

On Wednesday, 16 March Dr Crippen gave his landlord three months' notice of leaving the house.

On Thursday, 24 March, he and Ethel, calling themselves Mr and Mrs Crippen, went to Dieppe for five days over Easter. The same morning Mrs Martinetti received a telegram sent from Victoria Station – 'Belle died yesterday at six o'clock . . . Shall be away a week. Peter.' It is thought that during the crossing to France, Belle's head in a weighted handbag was dropped overboard.

During their absence a notice of her death appeared in *The Era* on 26 March. When the couple returned, Peter set about dealing with mourning friends, calls and letters of condolence. He said his wife had been cremated in America, and in May told people that he had her ashes at home.

Crippen must have felt, after three months had passed, that he and Ethel were secure. For on 18 June he arranged with his landlord to stay on at Hilldrop Crescent until 29 September. But ten days later Mr and Mrs Nash, who were friends of Belle and had recently returned from America where Mrs Nash had been touring the music-halls as Lil Hawthorne, called and questioned Crippen about his wife's demise. Dissatisfied with the little doctor's answers, Mr Nash communicated his unease on 30 June to a friend of his, Detective Superintendent Froest at Scotland Yard. Froest was in charge of the newly formed Serious Crimes squad.

Chief Inspector Walter Dew was asked to investigate further, and on Friday, 8 July, visited Hilldrop Crescent with DS Mitchell.

There they encountered a French maid and Ethel le Neve, who was wearing one of Mrs Crippen's brooches. Ethel said she was the housekeeper; she agreed to accompany the policemen to Albion House.

The three of them went by omnibus, and when they reached the building Ethel ran up the stairs to the third-floor office to let the doctor know who had come to see him. Having heard the reason for Dew's visit, Crippen said: 'I suppose I had better tell the truth.' 'Yes, that would be better,' Dew remarked. Crippen continued: 'The stories I have told about her death are untrue. As far as I know, she is still alive.' In between teeth-pulling and making up prescriptions, assisted by Miss le Neve, the doctor dictated a lengthy statement. It took five hours, with a break for lunch with Dew in an Italian restaurant. The doctor said that Mrs Crippen had left him for another man and that she had disappeared by the time he came back from work on 1 February. He said: 'I sat down to think it over as to how to cover up her absence without any scandal.'

At the conclusion of the statement and of the afternoon, Crippen and his assistant/housekeeper accompanied the two police officers back to

Hilldrop Crescent, and obligingly allowed the house to be searched. Both Crippen and Ethel watched from a doorway as Dew cast his eye over the coal-cellar. The only thing that seemed odd to him was the fact that Mrs Crippen had left a large quantity of her gorgeous gowns behind. He left the house, however, fairly satisfied that nothing was amiss, although he wondered why Crippen had gone to such lengths to hide the alleged reason for his wife's disappearance, especially as he seemed to be making the most of her absence with Miss le Neve.

Over the weekend the inspector pondered, remained unperturbed, and returned to Albion House on Monday, 11 July, for a few more routine enquiries.

He was astonished to hear from Crippen's partner, Dr Rylance, that on the previous Saturday Rylance had received a letter from Crippen instructing him to wind up his business affairs and household accounts. Wrote Crippen: 'In order to escape trouble I shall be obliged to absent myself for a time.' Dew learned that Crippen had also sent the office boy out to buy some clothing suitable for a boy.

Dew returned to Hilldrop Crescent. It was occupied by the French maid, whom the police later sent back to France. Of Crippen and Ethel there was no sign. At that moment they were in fact in Belgium, staying at the Hotel des Ardennes in Brussels, where they remained for eight days. Travel between countries was easier then – no passports were required.

In London, Crippen's house and garden were searched again and again, on 12 and 13 July, and at last Dew's persistence produced a result beyond anything he expected. Prodding the coal-cellar floor with a poker, he discovered that some of the bricks were loose. He and DS Mitchell prised them out. Underneath was a stinking heap of human flesh: viscera, skin, and hair, but no bones. Dew and Mitchell revived themselves with Crippen's brandy. They had found all that remained of Belle Elmore.

The medical experts who examined the remains were Dr Pepper and Dr Bernard Spilsbury, then aged thirty-three. His consequent appearance in court was the first occasion he gave evidence for the prosecution in a major murder trial. He and Pepper concluded that the remains had been part of a stout female, who bleached her hair and had had an abdominal operation, apparently when her ovaries were removed; there was a scar. Traces of hyoscine, enough to kill her, were found in various organs. Taken orally in sweet tea or coffee, the hyoscine would have caused delirium, then drowsiness, leading to unconsciousness within an hour, and ending within twelve hours in paralysis and death.

On 16 July a warrant was issued for the arrest of Crippen and Ethel le Neve, wanted for 'murder and mutilation'. The police bill, written by Dew, described Ethel as being 5 ft 5 ins, pale-faced, with light brown hair, large grey-blue eyes – 'Nice-looking, pleasant lady-like appearance. Quiet, subdued manner, talks quietly, looks intently when in conversation.'

On Wednesday, 20 July, the SS *Montrose* sailed from Antwerp bound for Quebec. Two hours later the ship's commander, Captain Kendall, became suspicious about two of his passengers, Mr John Philo Robinson and his sixteen-year-old son John, who both came on board in brown suits, soft grey hats, and white canvas shoes – Crippen had shaved off his moustache. The couple were unusually affectionate.

Two days later, Captain Kendall sent a lengthy wireless message to the ship's owners in Liverpool, outlining his certainty that the Robinsons were the wanted couple. He detailed his observations:

> She seems thoroughly under his thumb, and he will not leave her for a moment. Her suit is anything but a good fit. Her trousers, very tight about the hips, are split a bit down the back and secured with large safety pins . . . He continually shaves his upper lip and his beard is growing nicely . . . The mark on his nose caused through wearing spectacles has not worn off . . . He sits about on deck reading (*Pickwick Papers, Metropolis, A Name to Conjure With,* and *The Four Just Men*) . . . When my suspicions were aroused I quietly collected all the English papers that mentioned the murder . . . All the 'boy's' manners at table were most lady-like . . . Crippen kept cracking nuts for her and giving her half his salad . . . On two or three occasions when walking on the deck I called after him by his assumed name, and he took no notice. I repeated it, and it was only owing to the presence of mind of Miss le Neve that he turned round . . . He would often sit on deck and look up aloft at the wireless aerial and listen to the crackling electric spark messages being sent by the Marconi operator. He said: 'What a wonderful invention it is!'

The voyage lasted eleven days, during which 'The Chase of Crippen' featured every morning in the *Daily Mail.* The Robinsons, in blissful but anxious ignorance, strolled arm-in-arm along the decks.

As the ship steamed slowly up the St Lawrence River towards Quebec on Sunday, 31 July, a pilot boat came alongside about 9 am. On board was Dew, dressed as a pilot. He had sailed from Liverpool on 23 July on a faster ship, the SS *Laurentic.* Mr Robinson was on deck, relishing the sight of land; in a few hours he would be safe. Master Robinson was in Cabin No. 5 reading a novel. 'Who are all these people?' Crippen asked the ship's surgeon. 'It's the pilot boat,' was the reply. 'There seem to be a good many pilots,' murmured Crippen. Once on board, Dew went to the bridge and met Captain Kendall. Looking down on the deck below he saw a man he thought he knew. He descended the companion-way, his heart pounding. He approached the little man, who looked oddly naked without his moustache. 'Good morning, Dr Crippen,' he said. 'I am Chief Inspector Dew.' It was the finest moment of his life. Crippen's arms went up, as if to parry a blow. 'Good morning, Mr Dew,' he replied.

He was formally arrested and charged. Inspector Dew then saw Miss le Neve in her cabin. She was dressed in an ill-fitting boy's suit. 'Miss le Neve?' he enquired. 'I am Chief Inspector Dew.' She looked at him, screamed and fainted.

Later Crippen said: 'I am not sorry – the anxiety has been too much . . .

It is only fair to say that she knows nothing about it. I never told her anything.' Dew sent a triumphant message back to Scotland Yard – *Handcuffs, London. Crippen and le Neve arrested. Dew.*

Detained in Quebec for nearly three weeks, Crippen and le Neve were brought back to England on the SS *Megantic*, boarding the ship from a tug as she sailed towards Quebec from Montreal en route for Liverpool. On board the *Megantic* Crippen travelled as Mr Nield and Dew as Mr Doyle. Crippen read a lot (love stories), and had many agreeable conversations with his captor. Kept separate from Ethel le Neve, who was guarded by wardresses, he was never allowed to see her.

One evening Dr Crippen was taking his exercise on the boat-deck, walking up and down handcuffed to Dew. He suddenly said: 'I don't know how things may go. They may go right or they may go all wrong with me . . . I want to ask you if you will let me see her. I won't speak to her. She's been my only comfort for the past three years.'

Dew complied with his request.

Crippen was brought to the door of his cabin that night and Ethel to the door of hers. Some distance apart they gazed at each other. Not a word was spoken. Dew felt embarrassed and averted his eyes. The couple next saw each other in court.

Huge crowds booed and jeered the arrival of Crippen and his mistress in England. They were besieged at Liverpool and at Euston station. Both were committed for trial.

A month or so later, Mrs Crippen's remains were interred at Finchley Cemetery on 10 October. Some bits of skin were retained to be put in evidence, and at the trial were passed around the court in a soup-plate.

The trial of Dr Crippen began at the new Old Bailey – recently rebuilt and reopened by Edward VII in 1907 – on Tuesday, 18 October 1910, before the Lord Chief Justice, Lord Alverstone. Mr Richard Muir appeared for the Crown and Mr Aspinall Tobin for the defence. Miss le Neve was to be tried separately, and only with being an accessory after the fact. Crippen's moustache once more adorned his face.

His defence was that there was no proof that the remains in the cellar were those of a woman, let alone of Belle Elmore. They had been buried, it was suggested, without the accused's knowledge, even before he came to the house. The prosecution's medical evidence to the contrary was reinforced by the fact that three suits of pyjamas – a piece of one had been found with the remains – had been sent to 39 Hilldrop Crescent by Jones Brothers of Holloway in January 1909, and not in 1905 as Crippen had claimed. The trial ended on its fifth day when Crippen, having been found guilty – the jury were out for twenty-seven minutes – was sentenced to death.

'I still protest my innocence,' he said.

The trial of Ethel le Neve began on 25 October before the same judge and with the same prosecutor. She was defended by Mr F. E. Smith, KC, afterwards Lord Birkenhead. The trial lasted one day. She did not give any evidence. She was acquitted and freed.

Crippen's appeal was heard and dismissed on 5 November. He was hanged in Pentonville prison on 23 November 1910.

Three days before this he made a public statement, saying that Ethel le Neve was entirely innocent. He extolled their love:

> This love was not of a debased or degraded character. It was ... a good love ... Her mind was beautiful to me ... Whatever sin there was – and we broke the law – it was my sin, not hers ... As I face eternity, I say that Ethel le Neve has loved me as few women love men, and that her innocence of any crime ... is absolute ... Surely such love as hers for me will be rewarded.

Shortly before his execution he wrote to her:

> There are less than two days left to us. Only one more letter after this can I write to you, and only two more visits ... Your letter, written early Saturday, came to me last Saturday evening and soon after the Governor brought me the dreadful news about ten o'clock. When he had gone I kissed your face in the photo ... It was some consolation, although in spite of all my greatest efforts it was impossible to keep down a great sob and my heart's agonized cry.

His last request was that her photograph and letters should be buried with him. They were.

It is said that Ethel le Neve emigrated to Australia, where she died in 1950. Another account of Ethel's end is that for forty years, using an assumed name, she ran a Tea Room at Jumper's Corner, Iford Bridge, near Bournemouth.

CHAPTER 13

Steinie Morrison
The murder of Leon Beron, 1911

Leon Beron was a Russian Jew and a forty-eight-year-old widower. His English was poor: he spoke mainly Yiddish and French. He had in fact come to England in 1894 from Paris with his aged father, two brothers and a sister. To all appearances, with his waxed moustache, imperial beard, natty clothes and cosmopolitan affectations, Leon Beron was a man of some substance and even importance. He was indeed a man of property, although the only merit of the nine mean little houses he owned in the East End of London in Russell Court, Stepney, was that they provided him with most of his income. The rents totalled about ten shillings a week. Two shillings of this went towards the payment of his accommodation, a room above a fruit-shop in 133 Jubilee Street, Stepney, and one and sixpence a day was spent at the Warsaw restaurant at 32 Osborn Street, Whitechapel, a kosher eating-place. There, for an all-inclusive price, he could buy lunch, dinner and countless glasses of tea, and spend the whole day gossiping and arguing with other Jews, mainly emigrés with no leaning towards or perhaps any need for work.

As a landlord, Beron was more affluent than most and exhibited this status in his dress. He wore a large gold watch and chain, from which also hung a five-guinea piece. In a purse attached to his waistcoat by a safety pin were, it was said, about twenty golden sovereigns.

In December 1910, Steinie Morrison began to be seen in the Warsaw restaurant at Leon Beron's side. Morrison, aged about thirty, was also a Russian Jew, although he claimed to have been born in Australia. His real name may have been Alexander Petropavloff, although at other times he called himself Moses Tagger and Morris Stein. He came to England about 1898. A fine figure of a man (6 ft 3 ins tall) and darkly handsome, he was a charmer. His mien and good manners belied the fact that he was a professional burglar who had served five prison sentences, amounting to twelve years, and had in fact been released from jail about six weeks before he and Beron met.

At 8.10 am on Sunday, 1 January 1911, Beron's body was discovered by PC Mumford at Clapham.

Concealed in some furze bushes near a footpath on Clapham Common, it lay on its back with its legs neatly crossed. It had apparently been dragged a short distance, as there was mud on its front, on the backs of the hand and the toes of the boots. Beron, who was wearing a melton overcoat, muffler and patent leather boots, had been struck on the head by a blunt instrument and stabbed three times in the chest as he lay dead on the ground. He had been robbed – no coins or money were found in his possession. There were seven superficial cuts or scratches on his face. Two, one on each cheek, were thought by a police surgeon to be S-shaped and not made accidentally. He later described them in court 'as being rather like the "f" holes of the violin, on each side of the strings'.

The police discovered that Morrison had worked from late September 1910 for seven weeks for a baker in Lavender Hill and accordingly knew the Clapham Common area. They also discovered that on the morning of 1 January, Morrison, calling himself Banman, had deposited a paper-wrapped package in the cloakroom at St Mary's station, Whitechapel. It contained a revolver and forty-four cartridges.

The relevant cloakroom ticket was found in the lining of a billycock hat discovered in the rooms of a prostitute, Florrie Dellow, who resided south of the river at 116 York Road, Lambeth. Morrison had moved in with her on 1 January, after telling his East End landlady at 91 Newark Street, Mrs Zimmerman, that he was off to Paris. He met Florrie at midday – she lived in the house of a watchmaker acquaintance of his – and allegedly asked her if he could live with her. 'Yes,' she replied. 'If you will look after me.' He stayed with Florrie for a week, having, he later said, deposited the revolver in the cloakroom so as not to frighten her. In fact he did this *before* he met her.

Morrison was apprehended at about 9.30 am on Sunday, 8 January, at Cohen's restaurant, Fieldgate Street, just as he finished breakfast. He was taken to Leman Street police station, ostensibly because, as a convict on parole ('a ticket-of-leave man'), he had neglected to tell the police about his move to Lambeth. Two days later he was charged with the murder of Leon Beron.

The nine-day trial of Steinie Morrison began at the Old Bailey on 6 March 1911. Mr Justice Darling was the judge. Mr Richard Muir led for the Crown and Mr Edward Abinger for the defence. The trial was characterized by several colourful East-Enders, mainly aliens, who gave evidence. They tended to be disputative and unawed by the majesty of the court. On the eighth day, during Abinger's final speech for the defence, Solomon Beron, the dead man's bachelor brother, who lodged for seven pence a night in Rowton House, was so provoked by the suggestion that *he* might have killed his brother that he attacked Abinger and had to be removed, raving, from the court and immured in a lunatic asylum.

Throughout the trial the accused stood – he refused to sit – observing the court with disdain and with one hand on his hip.

According to Morrison, he had spent New Year's Eve, 1910, selling imitation jewellery. He had supped at the Warsaw restaurant, he said, at about 8 pm. Then he visited the Shoreditch Empire of Varieties, whose artistes that night included Gertie Gitana, Harry Champion and Harry Lauder. He was there from about 8.45 to 11.10 pm. After the show he returned to the restaurant to pick up a flute, wrapped in a paper, which he had left with one of the waiters, Joe Mintz. Morrison had in truth bought a flute for four shillings in the Aldgate that morning. He observed that Beron was in the Warsaw, but did not sit with him, and, having downed a cup of tea, he proceeded about 11.45 pm to his lodging in Newark Street, where he went straight to bed, sleeping on a sofa in the Zimmermans' downstairs front room. On his way to Newark Street, he said, he saw Beron and a very tall man on the corner of Sidney Street, scene of the famous siege. 'Bon soir, monsieur!' Beron had called.

In support of Morrison's account of his movements, Janie Brodski, aged sixteen, and her sister Esther, later told the court that he had indeed been at the Shoreditch Empire on New Year's Eve – somewhat inconsequential evidence as Beron was murdered at about 2.45 am – although Janie had neglected to tell the police so when they originally interviewed her. She and her sister, she said, had obtained seats in the orchestra stalls for one shilling each – Morrison was in the same row. Janie's evidence – 'I swear that I saw Morrison there on the night of 31 December. Nobody can deny my own eyes!' – was largely discredited when the acting manager of the Shoreditch Empire said that no seats for the stalls could have been bought at the door (they were all sold), and anyway the price had been raised that night to 1s 6d.

It seems that Janie was much enamoured of Morrison. She had only met him in the last week of December, and within days he had talked of marriage.

The Zimmermans, Maurice and Annie, assured the court that Morrison could not have left their house without rousing them, as the front door had such a noisy bolt that it regularly woke the household. The prosecution pointed out that he could have left by a window.

According to the prosecution Morrison spent most of the evening of 31 December with Beron in the Warsaw – from about 8.30 to 11.45 pm, as alleged by the proprietor, Alexander Snelwar, as well as the waiter, Joe Mintz – and had somehow inveigled Beron to go with him to Clapham Common. There, so the prosecution said, in the early hours of the New Year, Morrison murdered the other man by striking him with an iron bar or a jemmy (the skull was fractured) and by stabbing him three times.

The evidence was largely circumstantial, confused, and the prosecution witnesses easily impugned. Beron's belligerent brother Solomon swore he had seen Leon in Fieldgate Street at 10.45 pm on New Year's Eve. A gasfitter's wife, Mrs Deitch, who also ran a brothel, said she had seen Morrison and Beron in Commercial Road, Stepney, about 2.15 am on 1 January. Joe Mintz was not so sure that the package Morrison had left with him about 6 pm on 31 December was indeed a flute – it seemed too long (about 2 ft) and heavy.

Two hansom-cab drivers, Hayman and Stephens, and a taxi-cab driver, Castlin, said respectively (a) that Morrison and Beron had been picked up at about 2 am on 1 January at the corner of Sidney Street and Mile End Road, and had been driven a distance of six miles to Lavender Gardens,

Clapham, where Morrison had paid the five shillings fare; (b) that Morrison, on his own, had been driven from Clapham Cross to the Hanover Arms near Kennington Church about 3.10 am; and (c) that Morrison and another man had been picked up at 3.30 am at Kennington and taken to Finsbury Gate in North London. Stephens described his 'Morrison' as being about 5 ft 10 ins in height and looking like an actor or professional man.

It is odd how the cabmen's accounts detailing Morrison's journeys give him just enough time to dispose of Beron about 2.45 am and then walk across the Common. Moreover, that night there was no moon, and it was so dark that identification cannot have been easy.

Two of the cabmen, Hayman and Stephens, came forward some days *after* 6 January, when the police issued a notice asking cabmen for information about any man or men they had taken to and from Clapham Common between 2 am and 6 am on 1 January. A reward was offered. By the 6th Morrison's picture had appeared several times in the newspapers.

In his summing-up, the judge asked the jury about the evidence of the cabmen: 'With what certainty can you, do you think, swear to a man whom you saw on a night like that, by the kind of light there was at these places? Can you feel certain that a man would not be mistaken?'

Mr Abinger sought to imply that Beron was a police spy who had betrayed the anarchists responsible for the Houndsditch Murders (on 10 December 1910) as well as those who died in the Siege of Sidney Street (on 3 January 1911). Accordingly, he had to be killed. The alleged 'S' cuts on the cheeks of Leon Beron signified, he suggested, the Russian or Polish words for 'spy' – 'spic' or 'spiccan'. But DI Wensley, in charge of the case, refuted this last idea, denying that Beron had ever been an informer or was involved with Peter the Painter or any other anarchist. No one put forward the idea that 'S' might signify the *English* word 'spy' – even 'sodomite'. The prosecution suggested that the supposed double 'S' had been cut by Morrison to confuse the police.

The judge remarked that anyone who could see the letter 'S' in the scratches must have better eyes or a more vivid imagination than he himself possessed. Indeed, police photographs of Beron's corpse show little more than some scratches on his face. Dr Freyberger, who carried out the post-mortem, accounted for this by saying: 'They do not come out well in photographs.' They had also, he said, been distorted by rigor mortis.

It is conceivable, although the point was never raised, that the slight cuts were caused by the furze bushes into which Beron's body was flung. The so-called 'S' cuts, magnified by Morrison's defending counsel and by the press, have since become part of the myths and legends that accumulate around famous trials.

The jury were out for thirty-five minutes. They found Steinie Morrison guilty. As the judge passed sentence of death on him, saying, 'May the Lord have mercy on your soul,' Morrison shouted – 'I decline such mercy! I do not believe there is a God in heaven either!'

Although the verdict was upheld by the Court of Criminal Appeal, the

Home Secretary, Mr Winston Churchill, intervened. Morrison was reprieved on 12 April and his sentence commuted to penal servitude for life. He was sent to Dartmoor, and on his way there created a disturbance at Waterloo station.

He found prison conditions and his existence in jail intolerable, and continually protested his innocence. It is said that he petitioned four times for the death sentence to be carried out. In despair, he staged a series of hunger-strikes, and ultimately became so feeble that he died in Parkhurst prison on 24 January 1921.

Several authorities have thought that Morrison was wrongly convicted, and that although he may have known more about the circumstances of Beron's death than he admitted he was not the murderer. Some have suggested that a third man, looking not unlike Morrison, was involved – that this man drove with Beron to Clapham, and having murdered him joined up with Morrison at Kennington. It certainly seems odd that Morrison should take Beron six miles to Clapham Common to rob him and let himself be seen by three cabmen on the way there and back. Moreover, although Morrison moved to Lambeth, he kept in touch with his friends and did not run away. However, it may be worth noting that the cabman, Alfred Stephens, who said he had driven Morrison from Clapham to Kennington about 3.10 am, was assaulted by four men on 20 January – allegedly because he had kissed the wife of one of his assailants. Stephens said at the time that five days earlier he had been threatened because he was assisting police enquiries.

There seems little doubt that at the Morrison trial more witnesses than usual lied in court about events and people, and that Steinie Morrison, although loved by some, was more loathed than liked and was a great liar himself. Although the police working on the case were convinced before and after the trial that Steinie Morrison was the guilty man, it is possible that Morrison only acted as a decoy, taking Beron to Clapham Common on some pretext (perhaps to do with some sexual entertainment or the introduction of Beron to a receiver of stolen goods or 'fence'). Morrison may then have left – Beron then being murdered by some representative of the Houndsditch gang, who used a hammer or chisel. For indeed the dent on Beron's head does not look like a blow from a jemmy – or even from a flute.

CHAPTER 14

Mr and Mrs Seddon

The murder of Eliza Barrow, 1911

Money is the mainspring of not a few murders – sheer greed, the acquisition without too much trouble or work of what others have acquired or earned. Some murderers are also very mean about money themselves, never eager to spend, ever eager to get a bargain or something for nothing.

Frederick Henry Seddon was an insurance agent, the district superintendent for Islington of the London and Manchester Industrial Assurance Company, for whom he had worked for over twenty years. In 1911 he was forty, a short, bald-headed, narrow-eyed, wax-moustached, Lancashire businessman, conceited, unfeeling, exact and exacting, who was so obsessed with thrift, money-making and the possession of property that these things had become his religion, with gold as god. He was for ever counting his gold sovereigns and notes, totting up sums, zealously plotting and calculating how to save a bit here, make a bit there; and he was never loath to deal in anything that might show a profit, however small. He was not a pleasant man. He exacted 6s a week from his two teenage sons as payment for living at home. He studied the details of wills published in the papers and would say, seeing someone who had died intestate: 'All that money thrown into the gutter. It's criminal!' At a music-hall, he once created a scene when he was given change for a florin (2s) instead of half-a-crown (2s 6d). A freemason and formerly a chapel-goer and preacher, his pleasures appeared to be smoking, drinking, music-halls and married women.

His wife was three years his junior. A sharp-nosed, weak but capable woman, Margaret Ann Seddon was ruled by her tyrannical husband, whose servants (maid and charwoman) and children (there were five), seemed nervous of him, if not frightened. On the other hand she ruled their home. As she said: 'I did not tell my husband everything I done, and he never told me everything.' She also said: 'He never used to take any notice when I said anything to him – he always had other things to think of.' Despite 'a little difference on family matters' (as he put it) at the end of 1909, when there was a brief separation, the marriage seemed quite equable.

The story begins in January 1910 when they moved into 63 Tollington

Park, N4. Seddon, having persuaded the owners to reduce the asking price to £320, bought the house on a mortgage of £220 with a down-payment of £100. He intended to turn it into flats, but instead decided to use it himself, sub-letting the top floor. The other two floors and the basement were occupied by the Seddon household, consisting of husband and wife, his old father, William (aged seventy-three), his four children – a fifth child was conceived soon after the separation – and an eccentric servant, Mary Chater, whose brother and cousin were in lunatic asylums. She herself was a former mental nurse and was something of a case herself, shouting and breaking crockery and telling all manner of lying tales.

'This house I live in,' said Seddon in 1912, 'fourteen rooms, is my own, and I have seventeen other properties.' Four of these rooms formed the top-floor flat. Of the other ten, one was his bow-windowed front basement office, another a conservatory and only three were bedrooms. Mr and Mrs Seddon had a double room on the first floor above the ground-floor drawing-room. The first-floor rear room was divided by a partition: the two Seddon daughters and Mary Chater slept on one side, Grandfather William and the two Seddon sons on the other. Apart from the six shillings each of his sons paid for their weekly board, Seddon got five shillings a week from the insurance company as rent for the room used as his office, and twelve shillings and sixpence from the tenant of the four unfurnished top-floor rooms. They were occupied for six months, then vacated in June.

In July 1910, Miss Eliza Mary Barrow took over the top-floor tenancy.

At the time of her death Mary Barrow was forty-nine: a plump, unprepossessing female, about 5 ft 4 ins tall, who dressed poorly, was parsimonious, squalid, ignorant, asthmatic, self-indulgent, deaf and drank gin. Her failings were more acceptable to Seddon because she had money, apparently inherited from her mother.

According to an engine-driver, Robert Hook, she had £420 4s 3d, nearly all in gold coin, kept in fifteen bags in a cash-box, in which were also some bank-notes. Mr Hook said he helped her count it out in 1906, when Miss Barrow was living in her sister's house. It was later established that the cash-box could hold as much as £1,500 in gold.

She had known Hook since 1896, when she lodged with his mother in Edmonton. When old Mrs Hook died in 1902 Miss Barrow moved in with Robert's sister, Mrs Grant. The Grants were heavy drinkers, it seems, and always feuding, throwing bottles and fire-irons about. Mr Grant died in 1906. When Mrs Grant died in 1908, Eliza Barrow took charge of the youngest Grant, six-year-old Ernie, leaving his sister Hilda in an orphanage.

When Robert Hook married in 1909, aged thirty-seven – although he was nine years younger than Miss Barrow he said they had once been sweethearts – Miss Barrow went to live with a cousin, Frank Vonderahe and his wife, taking Ernie with her. She paid 35s a week for board and lodging for them both. The Vonderahes thought she was excitable, irritable and had peculiar ways; she once spat at Mrs Vonderahe. After a year there was some quarrel and Miss Barrow – 'dissatisfied' according to Frank

Vonderahe – moved out, soliciting the help of Robert Hook, who had continued to visit her and now sold her some of his sister's (Mrs Grant's) furniture for her new lodging in Tollington Park. Further, Hook and his wife also moved in with Ernie. They lodged with Miss Barrow rent free, in return for Mrs Hook's domestic services.

So, by 1 August 1910, twelve people were crammed into 63 Tollington Park. Before long Miss Barrow, according to Seddon, found fault with the Hooks; she said she was frightened of them, could not trust them, and enquired whether she could leave her cash-box, in which she said there was about £35, in Mr Seddon's safe. There was a row, fired by drink, on a Saturday night in the top flat, and on Sunday morning the Hooks took Ernie with them to Barnet, leaving Miss Barrow in sickness and tears and unattended all day. All this displeased Mr Seddon – 'They were creating a disturbance in the house which I was not used to; they proved undesirable tenants.' So he gave all four notice to quit.

But Miss Barrow was loath to leave. Hook, she said, was the cause of the trouble, and having no friends or advisors at hand she sought the help and advice of the Seddons. He suggested that she give Hook written notice to quit. She did, beginning her note: 'As you and your wife have treated me badly . . .' Hook replied by scrawling on the back of the notice, which had been delivered by Maggie Seddon, then aged fifteen – 'As you are so impudent to send the letter to hand, I wish to inform you that I shall require the return of my late mother's and sister's furniture, and the expense of my moving here and away – Yours R. D. Hook.'

This brought a summons from Seddon. Said Hook: 'I went down to see him. He said to me: "So I see you don't mean to take any notice of Miss Barrow's notice ordering you to leave?" and I said: "No, not this time of night." He then gave me the order to clear out within twenty-four hours, and I said I would if I could, and if I could not, I would take forty-eight hours. He said: "I do not know whether you know it or not – Miss Barrow has put all her affairs in my hands." And I said: "Has she?" I asked him if she had put her money in his hands and he said: "No." I said: "I will defy you and a regiment like you to get her money in your hands."'

Seddon took him at his word and pinned his own typewritten notice to quit on the Hooks' bedroom door. On Tuesday, 11 August, the Hooks moved out, taking all the furniture in their room – Miss Barrow paid for the removal. As she was now on her own, apart from little Ernie, Seddon suggested that his daughter Maggie might cook and clean for her for 1s a day. Comparative calm returned.

But then the top-floor lodger began to worry and fret about her properties and income. She consulted Mr Seddon. He said: 'She came down one Sunday in the month of September into the dining-room, and had a chat with me about her property . . . She said she had a public-house at Camden Town called the Buck's Head, and it was the principal source of her income. She had had a lot of trouble with the ground landlord, and she said that Lloyd George's budget had upset licensed premises by increased taxation; that her tenants, Truman, Hanbury, Buxton and Co. had a lot of licensed houses, and she was afraid they might have to close some of them. She also owned the adjacent barber's and had invested £1,600 in India stock, which had gone down in value – it had cost her £1,780. What with the gold and notes hoarded in her cash-box – she mistrusted banks – and the money in her savings bank, she was worth about £4,000, a small fortune then.

Seddon must have been most interested in the extraordinary wealth of this dowdy, dumpy lodger. Further discussions took place, he said later, in which she expressed an interest in purchasing an annuity, as a friend of hers had done. He advised her to consult a solicitor or the post office, but she mistrusted them as well. She chose to put her trust in him.

A year later her fortune had disappeared and Miss Barrow was dead.

On 14 October 1910, Miss Barrow transferred the £1,600 India 3½ per cent stock to Seddon in return for an annuity of £103 4s a year. About this time Mrs Seddon began to change £5 notes for gold at various stores, endorsing them with a false name and address. Twenty-seven £5 notes were eventually traced to Mrs Seddon and six went into her husband's bank account, five on 13 January 1911. The leasehold of the Buck's Head and the barber shop were likewise made over to him on 9 January 1911, for a further annuity of £52 a year. Although the transfers were legally made, there was no written agreement concerning an annuity – at least none could be found later. But Mr Seddon began paying Miss Barrow £10 a month in advance (for which she gave him a receipt), and allowed her to live in Tollington Park rent-free.

Mrs Seddon's explanation of the £5 notes (the proceeds of cheques paid to Miss Barrow by Truman, Hanbury, Buxton and Co.) was that Miss Barrow had asked her to cash them for her. She said: 'I think she had been out herself to get one cashed, and someone would not cash it for her, so she asked me if I would get it cashed. I took it to the post office, and they asked me for my name and address. I thought it was rather funny, as I never cashed a note in my life before, so I gave the first name that came into my head ... M. Scott, 18 Evershot Road ... and I gave the cash to Miss Barrow when I came back, five sovereigns. After that day Miss Barrow from time to time asked me to change notes for her ... At the shops I went to where I was known I gave my right name and address, because they already knew it ... I always gave the money to Miss Barrow.'

Mrs Seddon gave birth to a baby girl, Lily, on 3 January 1911, and when the annuity transactions were completed, she said, the happy lodger gave Mr Seddon a diamond ring. She herself, she said, was given a gold watch and chain on her birthday and her daughter Maggie was given a gold necklet and locket.

Seddon's explanation of the ring was that it was given to him to defray part of the legal costs in arranging the property transfers – 'She said she had no money to spare ... I wore that diamond ring on my little finger until Miss Barrow's death, and then I had it made to fit this other finger. I have a diamond ring of my own, which is four times the value of that ring.' The prosecution's explanation of these 'gifts' was that they were acquired *after* the lodger's demise.

On 25 January 1911 Seddon instructed Arthur Astle, a stockbroker, to sell the £1,600 India stock. It realized £1,519 16s and was paid by cheque to F. H. Seddon, who put it in a deposit account. Of this £119 16s was withdrawn on 1 February and put into another bank, his own, where it was split roughly between his current and deposit accounts. Then on 6 March the remaining £1,400, plus interest, was withdrawn and the account closed. With this money he bought the leasehold on fourteen houses in Coutts Road, Stepney, and added another £30 to his own deposit account to bring it up to £100.

That month Miss Barrow went to a funeral. Said Seddon: 'She came in talking about funerals and death and one thing and another and she said, how would it be if anything happened to her now regarding the furniture and jewellery she had got which had belonged to Ernest and Hilda Grant's parents? I told her that she ought to make a will.' Apparently she was afraid of the Hooks and Vonderahes getting possession of all she had left. He advised her to see a solicitor. But that night he received a letter from Miss Barrow through his wife, in which Miss Barrow named three first cousins, all called Vonderahe, as her nearest relatives and said: 'It is not my will or wish that they, or any other relation of mine, should receive anything belonging to me at my death . . . They have not been kind to me, or considered me.' 'I took it that she meant the letter to be a kind of will,' said Seddon, 'and I put it away in my secretaire.'

His salary had just been increased and he was now earning £5 15s 10d a week. About this time the Charing Cross and Birkbeck banks crashed, making Miss Barrow afraid for money she had in a savings bank in Clerkenwell. After closing an investment account she had at the bank in April (£10 7s 9d), she and Mrs Seddon went to the bank on 19 June and drew out £216 9s 7d; it was put into two £100 bags of gold coin, with the rest in loose gold and silver. The account had been opened in 1887 – the last payment was made in 1908 and the last withdrawal in 1907. When the women returned to Tollington Park, Seddon apparently rebuked Miss Barrow for keeping all that gold in a trunk in her room – 'I do not like the idea' – and she said she knew what to do with it. Neither of the Seddons saw the money again, they said.

On 1 August Miss Barrow went to see Dr John Paul in Isledon Road, accompanied by Mrs Seddon. Miss Barrow was suffering from 'congestion of the liver', and constipation. She paid further visits on the 3rd, 17th and 22nd; on the last visit she complained of asthma.

Meanwhile, all the Seddons, Miss Barrow and little Ernie went to Southend-on-Sea for the weekend of 5/8 August. Ernie, now aged ten, delicate and adenoidal, slept with his ageing foster-mother. He called her Chickie. Mr Seddon disapproved – 'I advised her to buy a small bed and to let him occupy the room.' But Ernie continued to keep Miss Barrow company in bed.

The last week in August and the first week in September were very hot: London sweltered in a heat wave.

On the morning of Friday, 1 September, Miss Barrow felt ill; she sat in the kitchen and complained of feeling sick and bilious. Mrs Seddon took her upstairs, where she lay down on her bed; a cup of tea made her sick. 'I had seen her like this before,' said Mrs Seddon, 'off and on, with these sick bilious attacks every month.' The next day she was still sick and had diarrhoea. Dr Paul was sent for but was too busy to attend. The Seddons' family doctor, Henry Sworn, arrived instead about ten o'clock that night. He prescribed bismuth and morphia, the latter for her stomach-pains. He thought she was very ill, and that her mental state was as poor as her health.

Returning on Sunday and Monday, Dr Sworn noticed no improvement. Mrs Seddon told him his patient would not take the thick, chalky bismuth. Instead, he prescribed an effervescing mixture of citrate of potash and bicarbonate of soda and gave her nothing for her diarrhoea, which was not too severe. But he suggested, raising his voice to counteract her deafness, that she should go to hospital. Miss Barrow refused. She also refused to have a nurse. She said Mrs Seddon 'could attend to her very well indeed and she was very attentive'. Indeed, Mrs Seddon, who prepared the patient's food – no solids, just soda water and milk, gruel, milk puddings and Valentine's meat juice – must have been up and down stairs all day, seeing to her various needs. Already the top-floor bedroom stank with the smell of faeces. Because of the heat the windows were open: flies swarmed in. Mrs Seddon and her daughter fanned the patient to keep the flies away.

On Monday, 4 September, Miss Barrow (said Mrs Seddon) instructed her to get some fly-papers, not the sticky ones, but 'those that you wet . . . I got these fly-papers at Meacher's, the chemist's, in Stroud Green Road, just around the corner from our house. An old gentleman served me. I think I ordered at the same time a 9s 6d bottle of the baby's food, Horlicks malted milk . . . I also bought a pennyworth of white precipitate powder, with which Miss Barrow used to wash her head. I have also seen her cleaning her teeth with it.'

Mrs Seddon bought four fly-papers for threepence, and back in the top-floor bedroom put each one in a saucer of water, wetting them thoroughly. Two saucers were put on the mantelpiece and two on a chest of drawers.

On Tuesday Miss Barrow was slightly better. She summoned little Ernie to sleep with her, as she did every night. For the next three days Dr Sworn continued to prescribe the effervescing medicine. But on the 9th he added 'a blue pill which contained mercury' as 'her motion was so very offensive' – so much so, that the stench pervaded the house and carbolic sheets were hung in the rooms. Ernie seemed not to notice the aroma around Miss Barrow, possibly because of his adenoids.

Dr Sworn took a day off on Sunday the 10th, returning on the Monday before midday. His patient was weaker. He advised Mrs Seddon to give her some brandy. It was still very warm and close, and what with the heat and Miss Barrow's weakness he was prepared for a sudden relapse and heart failure. He thought she was in some danger but not a critical condition. Her pulse was rapid and feeble, but her temperature had only once reached 101°F.

That afternoon Mr Seddon went upstairs to see his ailing lodger, who was worrying again about her possessions. She told Seddon: 'I don't feel well, and I would like to see if anything happened to me, that Ernest and Hilda get what belonged to their father and mother.' He advised her, he said, to call in a solicitor, but she asked him to draft a will for her. He agreed.

Mr Seddon's married sister, Mrs Emily Longley, and her daughter, had just arrived on a visit from Wolverhampton, and it was not until about half-past six, after dinner, that he returned to the sick room with his father and his wife as witnesses to Miss Barrow's will.

Mrs Seddon later said: 'We propped her up in bed with pillows in a sitting position to get her to sign it . . . My husband read the will to Miss Barrow, and then she asked for her glasses to read it herself, which she did, and then she signed it . . . I signed it on a little table, and my father-in-law signed it.' The will, revoking all others, made Frederick Henry Seddon sole executor – 'to hold all my personal belongings, furniture, clothing and jewellery in trust' until Hilda and Ernest Grant came of age, when Seddon was to hand them over (or the cash he made from selling them – 'But no article of jewellery must be sold') to the young Grants. 'Thank you. Thank God, that will do,' said Miss Barrow, according to Seddon. He said later that he fully intended to take the will to a solicitor and get it properly made out. The fact that no mention was made in the will of all the hoarded gold in Miss Barrow's cash-box seemed to have escaped his money-conscious attention. He said later. 'I never gave it a thought.'

That evening, as Miss Barrow lay ill in bed with Ernie, Frederick Seddon took his wife, his father and his sister for a night out to the Finsbury Park Empire, leaving his daughter Maggie to look after the lodger.

They returned about midnight, to revised sleeping arrangements: the Seddons moved out of their bed, which was now occupied by Mrs Longley and her daughter; they took over the bed where the two boys had slept with their grandfather, who in turn were moved into a large extra bed set up in a top-floor room, once occupied by the Hooks and next door to Miss Barrow's bedroom.

Nothing untoward happened on Tuesday the 12th – except that Mrs Seddon knocked one of the fly-paper saucers off the mantelpiece. She then put all four papers into a soup plate on a table between the windows.

Dr Sworn made no visit. But when he called before noon on Wednesday the 13th, he thought his patient was rather worse: she seemed weaker. Her diarrhoea was bad again, but she did not seem to be in much pain. He prescribed a bismuth and chalk mixture to be taken after every motion. Mr Seddon himself was not very well that morning. While the rest of the family, apart from his wife and Maggie, went to the White City, he stayed in bed. But about half-past seven in the evening he went to the Marlborough Theatre, where occurred the row about the wrong change for his half-crown.

About midnight, Mrs Seddon and Mrs Longley were chatting at the gate, waiting for Fred's return, when they heard a cry from the open top-floor window – 'I'm dying!'

Mrs Seddon rushed upstairs; her sister-in-law followed. Miss Barrow complained of severe pains in her stomach and that her feet were cold. A flannel petticoat was wrapped around them and hot flannels were laid on her stomach. Seddon, returning about twelve-thirty, was told by his wife about the lodger's 'dying' cry. He looked at his wife and said: 'Is she?' Mrs Seddon said: 'No,' and smiled. Mrs Seddon later explained to the court: 'I have a usual way of smiling at almost every thing, I think. I cannot help it. It is my way. No matter how serious anything was I think I would smile.'

Seddon was still complaining about being done out of sixpence at the theatre when Ernie called down the stairs – 'Mrs Seddon, Chickie wants you!' Mrs Seddon was resting on a couch. 'Never mind,' said her husband. 'I'll go and see what she wants.'

But both the Seddons went upstairs with Mrs Longley, who was so overcome by the smell and by Ernie's presence in the patient's room and on her bed that she soon retreated. Mr Seddon also found the smell nauseating – 'I have a delicate stomach' – and after rebuking the patient for making so many demands on his wife he gave her a drop of brandy.

The Seddons went to bed about two-thirty, and within minutes Ernie called Mrs Seddon again, and again half an hour later. 'She had the diarrhoea bad,' said Mrs Seddon later, adding: 'She did not seem sick – she was only once or twice sick during the night; she seemed to be retching, not proper vomiting, but a nasty froth came up.'

A third time Ernie called, crying: 'Chickie is out of bed!' It was now nearly four o'clock. Seddon told his wife to stay in bed – he would go. 'It's no good *you* going up,' she said, as on all the other occasions Miss Barrow had to be assisted on and off the commode and given hot flannels. But this time Seddon went with her.

Miss Barrow was sitting on the floor, moaning and in pain; Ernie was holding her up. 'Whatever are you doing out of bed?' asked Seddon. He waited outside while the commode was used and when he was able to enter the room he remonstrated with the exhausted patient. 'You must remember Mrs Seddon has got a young baby and she wants a rest. If Mrs Seddon sits up with you all night she'll be knocked up . . . Really we shall have to get a nurse, or you shall have to go to hospital.' Miss Barrow said she couldn't help it. She asked for Ernie, who had been ordered back to his own bed (not for the first time) and was very weary himself. Mrs Seddon thought she had better stay in the bedroom. She said: 'What's the good of going to bed, getting undressed and being called and having to get up again?' Her husband agreed. 'I'll put a pipe on and keep you company,' he said, and while Mrs Seddon sat in a basket-chair near the end of the bed, he stood at the door smoking his pipe and reading a newspaper. Sometimes he went downstairs to see how the baby was.

Miss Barrow seemed to sleep; Mrs Seddon dozed in the chair. For over an hour Miss Barrow snored as dawn began to light the top-floor room.

Suddenly the snoring softened and stopped. Seddon came forward. 'She's stopped breathing!' he said, rousing his wife. He felt Miss Barrow's pulse, lifted an eyelid and exclaimed: 'Good God, she's dead!'

It was just after a quarter past six, on Thursday, 14 September 1911.

About seven o'clock Seddon went to Dr Sworn's house and told him his patient had died. The doctor then and there made out a death certificate, giving the cause of death as 'epidemic diarrhoea'. 'I did not expect it then,' said Seddon.

He returned to 63 Tollington Park, where all the blinds were down. His wife and the charwoman, Mrs Rutt, were laying out the body. In the presence of both women he unlocked Miss Barrow's trunk with her keys. Inside was the cash-box. He put it on the bed beside the corpse. But no fortune lay within it. In the cash-box was only £4 10s. Three sovereigns were later found in a drawer, according to the Seddons, and £2 10s in a hand-bag. The trunk was ransacked, and apart from clothes, two watches, some brooches and a bracelet were unearthed.

About half-past nine the youngest children, including Ernie, who knew nothing of his foster-mother's death, were packed off to Southend.

Later in the morning Seddon visited Mr Nodes, an undertaker, and a cheap and instant funeral was arranged as a favour for £4, which was further reduced to £3 17s 6d when Seddon complained that all the cash he had for the funeral costs and the doctor's fees was the £4 10s found in the cash-box. The saving of 2s 6d was regarded by Seddon and Nodes as the former's commission. The cost of the funeral included 'a coffin, polished and ornamented with handles and inside lining, a composite carriage (for the mourners and the coffin), the necessary bearers, and the fees at Islington cemetery.' Miss Barrow was to be buried in a public grave, despite the fact that there was room for her – later denied by Seddon – in a family vault.

Nodes came and measured the body, removing it that night to a mortuary after Seddon had decided the funeral should be the following afternoon – 'It being a slack business day for me.'

He later claimed he had typed a letter on black-edged paper to Frank Vonderahe, informing him succinctly of his cousin's death, of the funeral times and of the terms of the will. The letter was addressed to 31 Evershot Road and, he said, posted before 5 pm. As it happened, the Vonderahes had moved two months before this to an address in Corbyn Street. Nonetheless, although other letters addressed to Evershot Road eventually reached them at Corbyn Street, they never received Seddon's letter – probably because it was never sent. Nor were any mourning cards, although he had some printed. They were inscribed: 'In ever loving memory of Eliza Mary Barrow' and contained this verse:

> A dear one is missing and with us no more;
> > That voice so much loved we hear not again;
> Yet we think of you now the same as of yore,
> > And know you are free of trouble and pain.

Most of Thursday afternoon was spent by Seddon in his basement office with his two assistant managers, Taylor and Smith, apart from an hour or so when he went to bed complaining of feeling very tired. Meanwhile the insurance collectors called with their weekly takings, which amounted that day to £63 14s 3d. Smith and Taylor worked from noon to midnight on the accounts. About 9 pm they observed a large amount of loose gold on Seddon's desk; he was counting it and putting it in four cloth bags, which the assistants later surmised must have held about £400 worth of gold.

In a very good humour Seddon picked up one of the bags and plonked it on Smith's desk. 'Here's your wages he joked. 'I wish you meant it, Mr Seddon,' replied Smith. Seddon then locked all four bags away in a safe. He later denied all this and said he was merely 'counting the gold and silver brought in by the collectors.

On Friday, 15 September, he was very busy. He made two payments into his bank account that amounted to £96 0s 8d, paid mainly in gold. £30 was also put into his post office savings bank, again mainly in gold coin. Mrs Seddon went with him to a jeweller in Holloway Road, where they left a diamond ring and a gold watch for alterations – the ring's band was to be widened, 'E. J. Barrow 1860' was to be erased from the back of the watch, and the enamel dial was to be replaced with a gold one.

When Mrs Seddon returned home she was vexed to find that the blinds had been raised by Mrs Longley. 'Let us show a little respect!' exclaimed Mrs Seddon and lowered the blinds.

She had already been out with her sister-in-law and father-in-law and had ordered a cross of flowers for the deceased. After lunch, about two o'clock, the same trio took the cross to the undertaker's mortuary in Stroud Green Road, where it was placed on the coffin – but not before the lid had been removed and Mrs Seddon had kissed the corpse.

Later that day, Mrs Longley and her daughter returned to Wolverhampton, and the Seddons to their own beds. The top floor was empty once more.

On Saturday afternoon Miss Barrow was buried, the two Seddons and Grandfather William travelling with the coffin in the composite carriage from the undertaker's to Islington cemetery. Less than a year before this, the few remains of Mrs Crippen had also been buried there.

Sunday was a day of rest for all concerned. But on Monday 18 September, Seddon was active again, buying three shares totalling £90 3s in a building society; he paid in gold coin. The following day he wrote to the society asking about the exact amount required to pay off the mortgage on 63 Tollington Park.

Meanwhile, the Vonderahes happened to hear that their cousin, whom they had not seen in the district for six weeks or so, was ill. Mr Vonderahe called at No. 63 on Wednesday, 20 September, and was amazed to be told by the eccentric servant, Mary Chater: 'Don't you know she's dead and buried?' He said: 'No. When did she die?' 'Last Saturday,' replied the maid. 'But if you call about nine o'clock you will be able to see Mr Seddon and he'll tell you all about it.' When Vonderahe returned with his wife that night, he was told by Maggie that both her parents were out.

The following morning Mrs Frank Vonderahe called with her sister-in-law, Mrs Albert Vonderahe about 10 am and were shown by Maggie into the sitting-room. After a long wait, both the Seddons appeared. 'Why didn't you answer my letter and come to the funeral?' demanded Mr Seddon. Mrs Frank Vonderahe said: 'We never got no letter.' Whereupon he produced a carbon copy of the letter allegedly sent on the day Miss Barrow died. He also gave Mrs Frank Vonderahe a statement about the terms of the will and the annuity which died with her, as well as a copy of the will and three mourning cards. Mrs Seddon remarked that they had had a very, nice funeral – 'Everything was done very nicely,' she said. Seddon told Mrs Frank Vonderahe that their cousin had been buried in a public grave. 'Fancy!' said Mrs Frank. 'And she had a family vault.' 'It's full up,' said Seddon. 'No, it isn't,' she retorted. He said: 'Oh well, it will be an easy matter for the relatives to remove the body.' Mrs Frank Vonderahe said a public grave was good enough for Eliza Barrow who had been a bad, wicked woman all her life. She spoke about scenes and quarrels that had occurred. 'Really,' said Mrs Vonderahe, 'it's a good job for the boy that she passed away . . . She even spat at us before we left.' 'She was a woman that wanted humouring,' Seddon opined. 'You ought to take into consideration her infirmities: she was to be pitied.' The Vonderahes then asked about Ernie. Seddon said he was quite prepared to look after the boy, unless any of his relatives could give him a better home. They enquired about the Buck's Head and the India stock; Seddon told them Miss Barrow had been anxious to buy an annuity and had parted with all her investments to this end. 'Well,' said Mrs Albert Vonderahe, 'Whoever persuaded Miss Barrow to do that was a very clever person.'

Neither wife was surprised that nothing had been left to their husbands, the actual cousins of the deceased. They asked if Seddon would see their husbands that evening, but he said it was out of the question – enough time had been wasted and he was going away the next day and he could not possibly see them until his return.

All the Seddons went to Southend on 22 September, where Ernie was informed about his benefactress's death. They returned on 2 October, and several days later Ernie was sent to Frank Vonderahe with the message that Seddon was back.

On 9 October Mr Vonderahe called with a friend, Mr Walker; his brother, he said, was not well. 'What did you want to bring a stranger for?' demanded Seddon. 'This only concerns the next-of-kin.' He said all the information Mr Vonderahe need have or know had already been given to his wife. 'Can I see the will, the original will?' asked Mr Vonderahe. 'No,' said Seddon. 'You already have a copy . . . I don't know why I should give you any information. You're not the eldest of the family. You have another brother, Percy.' This brother had in fact disappeared some time ago. 'He might be dead for aught I know,' retorted Mr Vonderahe. 'I don't think so,' Seddon returned. 'You've been making enquiries and talked about consulting a solicitor.' He had been told this by Nodes, the undertaker. Vonderahe persisted: 'Who is the owner of the Buck's Head now?' 'I am, likewise the shop next door . . . I am always open to buy property at a price.' 'How did you come by it?' 'I've already told you that.' 'Who bought the India stock?' Seddon answered: 'You'll have to write to the Governor of the Bank of England and ask him. Everything has been done in a perfectly legal manner.'

According to Seddon, the interview ended amicably, with enquiries about the well-being of Ernie and Hilda Grant. But the Vonderahes were very dissatisfied and deeply suspicious about the circumstances of their cousin's death and the total disappearance of her fortune. They communicated their anxieties to the police.

On 15 November Miss Barrow's body was exhumed and examined by Dr Spilsbury and Dr Willcox. The body was remarkably well preserved, a fact attributed to some preserving agent – such as arsenic – and sufficient traces of arsenic (2.01 grains) were found in the body to suggest that the cause of death was not epidemic diarrhoea and heart failure caused by gastro-enteritis, but 'acute arsenical poisoning' although the symptoms were the same. It was thought that a large dose of arsenic had been administered about three days before death, most of it having been purged by the body. It was calculated that one fly-paper, if boiled, could produce as much as 5 grains of arsenic (2 grains were said to be fatal) and one fly-paper soaked in cold water would produce nearly 1 grain.

While the body was being dissected in St Mary's Hospital, Paddington, Seddon was being shown around the hospital in connection with a business deal.

An inquest began on 23 November and was adjourned until the 29th.

At 7 pm on 4 December Seddon was arrested outside his home. On hearing the charge he said: 'Absurd. What a terrible charge – wilful murder! It is the first of our family that has ever been accused of such a crime ... Poisoning by arsenic? What a charge! ... Murder ... Murder.'

Mrs Seddon was arrested on 15 January 1912. On 2 February both the Seddons were committed for trial.

The arrests had attracted little attention, but the trial was avidly followed and the court was crowded every day. The trial began on Monday, 4 March 1912, at the Old Bailey and occupied ten days. The Attorney-General, Sir Rufus Isaacs, KC, was the prosecutor, assisted by Mr Richard Muir and Mr Travers Humphreys. Mr Edward Marshall Hall, KC, led Seddon's defence and Gervais Rentoul his wife's. The judge was Mr Justice Bucknill. Both the Seddons gave evidence, Frederick Seddon over a record three days.

He was fully in command of himself and his defence, and was never at a loss for an answer. His self-confidence was overweening; his responses were meticulous, his manner sometimes jaunty, but more often cold and arrogant. His whole demeanour, too clever by half, seemed to confirm every prejudice already felt against him and antagonized everyone in the court, even the Attorney-General who, as if from deep personal dislike, concentrated almost entirely on the case against the male accused – as did the judge in his summing-up. If Seddon had not given evidence, revealing himself as a man who certainly seemed capable of the crime as charged, the

Crown would have had a harder task and the all-male jury might have given him the benefit of the doubt. For the evidence was entirely circumstantial, concerned mainly with motive and opportunity. There was no evidence that Seddon had ever bought or used any arsenic or knew anything about it. There were also serious doubts about the way the police had conducted the investigation; and the Marsh test, which was applied to the arsenic in the body, was improperly applied to the *quantity* of arsenic therein, not just to the quality. As Seddon himself wrote after the trial: 'There was no motive for me to commit such a crime; I would have to be a greedy inhuman monster, or be suffering from a degenerate or deranged mind, as I was in good financial circumstances. 21 years in one employ, a good position, a good home with every comfort, a wife, five children and aged Father (73) depending on me, my income just on £15 per week.'

Despite the fact that the evidence offered against Seddon was the same as that offered against his wife – and, if anything, there was more to incriminate *her* – it was he alone who was found guilty by the jury after an absence of exactly an hour. Mrs Seddon was acquitted.

When she was pronounced 'Not guilty' Seddon leaned across and gave her a resounding kiss. She became hysterical and was taken below in tears. When asked if he had anything to say for himself before sentence of death was passed, he stepped forward in the dock, and made a very long, lucid speech, quoting facts and figures from his notes, explaining this, justifying that, leading to a powerful protestation of his innocence.

The judge, like Seddon, was a freemason. The condemned man concluded his speech by raising a hand as if taking a freemason's oath. He said: 'The prosecution has not traced anything to me in the shape of money, which is the great motive suggested by the prosecution in this case for my committing the diabolical crime, of which I declare before the Great Architect of the Universe I am not guilty, my lord. Anything more I might have to say I do not suppose will be of any account. But still, if it is the last words that I speak, I am not guilty of the crime for which I stand committed!'

The judge's secretary arranged the black cap on his wig; a chaplain appeared; the usher, crying 'Oyez, oyez, oyez!' called on all to be silent as sentence of death was passed. The doors of the court were locked.

The judge replied in a low, faltering voice to the points raised in Seddon's final speech. Seddon nodded twice in grave agreement when the judge said he believed the jury's verdict on Mrs Seddon was the right one and that the trial had been a fair one. Seddon spoke three times, quietly interrupting the judge's words, saying: 'I have a clear conscience . . . I am at peace . . . She done nothing wrong, sir.' Towards the end the judge said: 'You and I know we belong to one brotherhood . . . But our brotherhood does not encourage crime – on the contrary, it condemns it. I pray you again to make your peace with the Great Architect of the Universe. Mercy – pray for it, ask for it.' He was in tears as he said: 'The sentence of the court is that you be taken from hence to a lawful prison, and from thence to a place of execution, and that you be there hanged by the neck until you are dead . . . And may the Lord have mercy on your soul.'

An appeal was heard on 1 April and dismissed the following day. Meetings were held and a petition organized. It was signed by more than 250,000 people, but to no avail. Seddon was hanged at Pentonville prison on 18 April 1912, not long after hearing the news that his house had been sold for next to nothing. 'That's finished it!' he exclaimed.

A very large crowd, seven thousand people, gathered outside the prison as the hour of his execution approached.'

He made no confession. But Mrs Seddon did. A few months after the execution she remarried and moved to Liverpool, eventually emigrating to America. On 17 November the *Weekly Dispatch* published a signed confession in which she said that she had seen her former husband give poison to Miss Barrow on the night she died and that he had compelled her to say nothing by threatening her with a gun. But a fortnight later *John Bull* published another statement. Mrs Seddon swore on oath that the confession was a lie, that she had made it to stop people saying she was a murderess – and to gain the large sum of money she was offered by the *Dispatch*.

CHAPTER 15

George Smith

The murder of Bessie Mundy, 1912

Men who murder women generally do so under the stress of extreme provocation. What varies in each case is the cause of this stress. Some men have found their wives' lack of respect unbearable, others have been incensed by submissiveness. An excess of compliance often encourages a man already vain, unfeeling and bent on gain to believe that he can get away with murder.

Like other lady-killers in this book George Joseph Smith was a charmer, but the most cold-blooded and callous of them all. He was utterly vile. Like other murderers, he was a petty criminal before he began to kill.

A cockney, born at 92 Roman Road, Bethnal Green in the East End of London on 11 January 1872, he was only nine years old when he was sentenced to eight years in a Gravesend reformatory: an upbringing and a background that must have developed his criminal tendencies and total contempt for the law. When he came out he stayed with his mother. According to his first wife: 'He said he had a stepfather whose name was Smith. He said he had a good mother, but he had broken her heart.'

More thieving and brief spells in jail were followed by three years with the Northampton Regiment. Next, after persuading a woman to steal for him, he was jailed for a year in 1896 for larceny and receiving stolen goods. Released in 1897, he went to Leicester, where he opened a baker's shop at 28 Russell Square, using £115 (the equivalent of two years' wages) from a cash-box which the same woman had stolen for him from her employers.

In Leicester, on 17 January 1898, calling himself George Love, he married Caroline Beatrice Thornhill, aged eighteen, despite her bootmaker father's disapproval. Smith was twenty-six. She said of him: 'During the time I knew him I never knew him do any work.' She described him thus: 'Complexion fair, hair brown, ginger moustache, peak chin, on left arm a very large scar, military walk, stands 5 ft 9 ins.'

What this falls to indicate is his evident sexual attraction. He had a masterful way with women – some women. There was something hypnotic in the small dark eyes set in a bony face. His first bigamous wife, whom he married in London in 1899, said of him: 'He had an extraordinary power ... This power lay in his eyes ... When he looked at you – you had the feeling that you were being magnetized. They were little eyes that seemed to rob you of your will.'

He and Mrs Love moved to London soon after their marriage in 1898. Posing as her employer and providing references, he began his peregrinations, finding jobs for her in London, Brighton, Hove and Hastings. Educated by Smith she stole from the families who employed her as a maid. But in the autumn of 1899, at Hastings, she was arrested in a pawnbroker's shop where she was trying to sell some silver spoons. Sent to prison for twelve months she was able on her release to find, identify and incriminate Smith, who was, on 9 January 1901, jailed at Hastings for two years for receiving stolen goods. A local reporter wrote: 'For his spooning at Hastings, Love has gone to prison.'

Released in 1903, Smith went in pursuit of Mrs Love. To escape him she emigrated to Canada. Though separated from him she remained, despite the pseudonym, his only legal wife.

He returned to the middle-aged boarding-house keeper whom he had bigamously married in London *before* his incarceration. Having milked her of what money he could, he left, and having found what an easy way this was of acquiring bed, board and money – without doing a stroke of work – he travelled about the south of England wooing, wedding, and walking out on an unknown assortment of lonely or lovelorn women, whose humiliation led them to say little or nothing of the disappearance of their spouse.

Next to nothing is known about his activities for three years. But in June 1908 he met a widow from Worthing, Mrs Florence Wilson. After a three-week courtship they were married in London, where, after pocketing the £30 she withdrew from a post office savings account, he took her to the Franco-British Exhibition at the White City, went to get a paper and walked out of her life – but not before removing and selling all her belongings left in their Camden digs.

That was on 3 July. On 30 July he married Miss Edith Mabel Pegler in Bristol, using his real name. A dark-haired, round-faced twenty-eight-year-old, she had replied to his advertisement in a local paper for a housekeeper – he now had a shop in Gloucester Road, Bristol.

From then on, using their various homes as a base for his operations, which necessitated frequent and lengthy absences in pursuit of his trade as an antique-dealer, they moved to Bedford, Luton, Croydon, London and Southend. It was not a regular life, but Edith Pegler accepted it without question. Her husband would disappear for weeks and months at a time, sometimes saying he was off on business or off to help 'a young fellow' with some business deals. During his absences he sent her occasional letters and postcards as well as the odd pound note. When she ran out of money she returned to her mother in Bristol, where he would pick her up or send her a note telling her to come to him. His added wealth after his absences he attributed to the selling of rare antiques, pictures or jewellery. Sometimes he said he had been abroad, to Canada or Spain.

In October 1909, he married a spinster clerk from Southampton, Miss

Sarah Freeman. He called himself George Rose, claiming to be a man of means with a mythical moneyed aunt. He always dressed up for his wooings in a frock-coat and top-hat. They took lodgings in London and he had to wait a few days before she could withdraw all her post office savings; he had told her he was short of the wherewithal to set up an antique business. She also sold some government stock. He pocketed the lot and took her on 5 November to the National Gallery. She sat and waited while he went to the lavatory. He never returned. While she waited for him he journeyed to Clapham, where he removed and sold her belongings, leaving her totally destitute.

In all he made about £400 out of Miss Freeman, the equivalent of the average wages of a working man over four years.

With the money, Miss Pegler and a second-hand furniture shop were for a time established at 22 Glenmore Street, Southend, bought for £270 with £30 remaining on mortgage. Then the Smiths returned to Bristol, where he bought 86 Ashley Down Road, largely on loan.

Although he at one time owned eight properties and was worth a fortune, he made a loss on the sale of all of them. He was too mean to be a good businessman, ever suspicious, arrogant and demanding in his many ill-spelt, ill-composed letters to solicitors, insurers, banks and building societies. He was also mean with his brides, travelling third class, lodging them cheaply and taking them by bicycle or on foot to places of free public entertainment.

In August 1910, a tall and winsome girl, Miss Beatrice (Bessie) Constance Annie Mundy, aged thirty-one, was living in a boarding-house in Clifton. Her father, who had died in 1904, had been a bank manager at Warminster in Wiltshire and had left her well provided for with over £2,500 in gilt-edged securities, managed for her by a family trust headed by her uncle, who thought her a fool where money was concerned and from whom she received £8 a month.

One day she happened to meet a picture restorer, Henry Williams (George Smith) when out for a walk, and in a matter of days they were on their way to Weymouth, she with no luggage but a hat-box. They lodged at 14 Rodwell Avenue and were wed at the registry office on 26 August, 'Dear Uncle' she wrote, 'I got married today, my husband is writing tonight. Yours truly, B. Williams.' Smith wrote: 'Bessie hopes you will forward as much money as possible at your earliest by registered letter. Am pleased to say Bessie is in perfect health, and we are both looking forward to a bright and happy future. Believe me, yours faithfully, Henry Williams.'

But Smith had to wait until 13 December before he could lay his hands on £135, which was the interest that had accrued on her securities. He then absconded, leaving a lengthy letter of instruction for Bessie, repeating everything as if she were a child and cruelly explaining his departure.

Dearest, I fear you have blighted all my bright hopes of a happy future. I have caught from you a disease which is called the bad disorder. For you to be in such a state proves you could not have kept yourself morally clean ... For the sake of my health and honour, and yours too, I must go to London ... to get properly cured of this disease. It will cost me a great deal of money, because it might take years ... Tell the landlady and everyone else that I have gone to France. But tell your uncle the truth ... If he happens to ask you about money, tell him that you kept all the money which was sent to you in a leather bag, and two days after I had gone you happened to go on the beach and fall asleep and when you woke the bag of money was gone ... Whatever you do, stick to everything you say. Never alter it or else you will get mixed up and make a fool of yourself ... Mark what I say. Now tear this letter up at once and throw the pieces in the road.

Smith went straight from Weymouth to Bristol, back to Edith Pegler. They moved once more to Southend, where he bought another house. From there they went to London and then back to another address in Bristol, which may have been financed by another 'marriage', for nothing is known about Smith's activities in 1911.

Then in March 1912 there was a fatal meeting in Weston-super-Mare.

Bessie Mundy, who had been lodging with a Mrs Sarah Tuckett since February, went out at 11 am to buy some daffodils. By some extraordinary chance she met her vanished husband, Mr Williams. She returned at one o'clock. Mrs Tuckett said: 'She was very excited. She said as soon as she went out she found her husband looking over the sea.' At 3 pm he arrived at the house. Some women, like Mrs Tuckett, took an instinctive dislike to Smith. 'I asked him,' she said later, 'how it was he had left her eighteen months before at Weymouth. He replied that he had been looking for his wife for more than twelve months ... He knew her relatives and knew where they lived ... Miss Mundy said she wished to go back to her husband. She had forgiven the past. They had been to a solicitor, and she had promised to return to him. I told [Mr Williams] it was my duty to wire to her aunt to come at once ... She left with him without taking away any of her belongings. She promised to come back that same night, but I never saw her again ...'

Smith took Bessie from town to town while he made official enquiries about how he might legally get possession of her fortune. In May they were in Herne Bay, renting a small house at 80 High Street, which had neither bathroom or bath. On 2 July Smith heard from his lawyer that if he and Bessie both made wills and she died, he would inherit everything. The information signed her death-warrant. This time he had to kill his bride in order to get hold of her money and he had to act quickly, in case her relatives altered the terms of the settlement on her. Wills were drawn up and attested on 8 July.

The next day Smith bought a zinc bath (without taps) from an ironmonger, beating down the asking price of £2 to £1 17s 6d. In fact he never paid for it, returning the bath six days later, its purpose served.

On Wednesday, 10 July, he took his wife to a young and newly qualified doctor called French, alleging she had had a fit. All Bessie Mundy complained of was a headache. At 1.30 am on the Friday, Dr French was summoned to 80 High Street – Bessie had apparently had another fit. She was in bed. He found nothing amiss: she looked as if she had just woken up, was flushed and heavy-headed – it was a very warm night. The doctor prescribed a sedative. That afternoon he chanced to see the Williamses out of doors; she seemed in perfect health. That night, evidently on Smith's instructions, she penned a letter to her uncle:

> Last Tuesday night I had a bad fit, and one again on Thursday night . . . My husband has been extremely kind and done all he could for me. He has provided me with the attention of the best medical men here, who are . . . visiting me day and night . . . My husband has strictly advised me to let all my relatives know of my breakdown. I have made out my will and left all to my husband. That is only natural, as I love my husband . . .

Poor Bessie. The following morning, about 7.30, she prepared to have a bath in a spare room, making about twenty journeys up and down the stairs with a bucket to and from the kitchen, while Smith went out to buy some fish. She got in the bath, her hair in curling-pins. Smith returned.

About 8 am a note reached Dr French as he was dressing – 'Can you come at once? I am afraid my wife is dead.' Delaying to snatch a quick breakfast, he then hurried to the house. Mrs Williams was lying submerged in the bath on her back, naked and dead. A bar of Castile soap was clutched in her right hand.

When French left the house he informed the police of the fatality, and about ten o'clock PC Kitchingham arrived to take a statement from the bereaved husband. Bessie Mundy's body now lay, uncovered, on the floor by the bath, and it was still there when at 4 pm a woman came to lay the body out.

Smith wired Miss Mundy's uncle – 'Bessie died in fit this morning. Letter following.' The letter began: 'Dear Sir, words cannot describe the great shock I suffered in the loss of my wife. The doctor said she had a fit in the bath . . .'

There was no post-mortem. The inquest on Monday, 15 July – Smith wept throughout – found that she had died from 'misadventure'. She was buried in a common grave at 2.30 pm on the Tuesday, before any of her relatives could get to Herne Bay. They tried to contest the will, but within six months over £2,500 was paid to Bessie's sole executor and legatee, Henry Williams. He opened several bank accounts, bought seven houses in Bristol and an annuity for himself.

Edith Pegler was instructed in August to join Smith in Margate. She said later: 'I told him I had tried to find him at Woolwich and Ramsgate, and he was very angry about it . . . He said I should not . . . interfere with his business, because he did not believe in women knowing his business . . . He remarked that if I interfered . . . I should never have another happy day.'

It seems she was not unhappy, although he used to beat her from time to time. From Margate, they moved to Tunbridge Wells, Bristol, Weston-super-Mare and back to Bristol. In the summer of 1913 Smith disappeared again.

In October he was in Southsea, where he met and married short and plump twenty-five-year-old Alice Burnham, private nurse to an elderly invalid man and daughter of a Buckinghamshire fruit-grower.

Her father, Mr Charles Burnham, met George Smith before the marriage took place and was thoroughly repelled by him. However, there was nothing he could do to stop the marriage, which took place in Portsmouth registry office on 4 November, Smith using his real name and describing himself as 'bachelor, independent means'. But afterwards, when Smith wrote to Mr Burnham demanding the £104 which Mr Burnham was keeping for his daughter, he got a solicitor to enquire about his son-in-law's antecedents.

Mr Burnham soon received the following postcard from Smith: 'Sir – In answer to your application concerning my parentage, etc. My mother was a bus-horse, my father a cab-driver, my sister a rough-rider over the arctic regions – my brothers were all gallant sailors on a steam-roller.'

The day before the marriage, Alice's life was insured, for £500. Smith then set to work, and having got the £27 9s 5d that was in her savings bank, having extracted the £104 which her father owed her, and having paid the premium on Alice's insurance, he persuaded her to make a will. They then set off on an out-of-season seaside holiday.

This time Smith chose the main northerly English resort, Blackpool, where they arrived on Wednesday, 10 December 1913, a bleak and breezy day.

The first lodging-house they visited on spec, in Adelaide Street, had no bath. From here they were directed to 16 Regent Road, which had a bath; the rent was 10s a week. Again, a doctor was consulted (Dr Billing) about the buxom bride's health; she had a headache, not surprisingly after the long and tiring train journey across England from Portsmouth. Mrs Smith was then persuaded to write to her parents – 'My husband does all he can for me, in fact I have the best husband in the world' – and on Friday evening, 12 December, the couple went out for a walk after asking the daughter of their landlady, Mrs Crossley, to prepare a bath. They returned just after eight o'clock.

The bathroom was partly over the kitchen in which, at about 8.15 pm, the Crossleys were having tea. They heard nothing untoward, but suddenly observed stains spreading over the ceiling and down a wall – the bath had overflowed. Just about then Smith appeared in the kitchen door, seeming out of breath and looking rumpled. He had two eggs in his hand. He said: 'I've brought these for our breakfast.'

He then went upstairs, and a few minutes later shouted from the landing: 'Fetch the doctor! My wife cannot speak to me!'

The shocked Crossleys waited below as Dr Billing examined the unfortunate Mrs Smith, her body still in the bath. 'Oh, she is drowned – she is dead,' Dr Billing told Mrs Crossley. She could not believe what she must have suspected, but the death in her house and Smith's callous indifference to it were too much for her. She could not bear to have him stay there that night. She told him so and he slept next door.

But in the morning, Saturday the 13th, he was back, seeing to the burial and matters to do with his wife's death. In the afternoon he played Mrs Crossley's piano in the front room and drank a bottle of whisky. As a result he was able to be emotional (he wept copiously) at the inquest on Mrs Alice Smith, née Burnham, which was held at 6.30 pm. The verdict was accidental death.

Alice Burnham was buried in a common grave on Monday, 15 December, at noon. Smith refused to have a deal coffin, saying: 'When they are dead, they are done with.'

Immediately after the funeral he took the train back to Southsea. Before he left he gave Mrs Crossley an address card. She wrote on the back – 'Wife died in bath. We shall see him again.' She thought him 'a very hard-hearted man ... I did not like his manner.' As he left the house, she shouted: 'Crippen!'

After selling all Alice Burnham's belongings that had been left in her Southsea digs, Smith rejoined Edith Pegler in Bristol and was soon £500 richer. He increased his annuity. Once more he and Miss Pegler set off on their travels, going to London, Cheltenham and Torquay. By August they were in Bournemouth, and were staying in Ashley Road when the First World War began.

'While there,' said Edith later, 'my husband was out in the evenings. About the middle of September 1914, my husband said he was going to London for a few days.'

He had wooed and won another bride, a maidservant, Alice Reavil. Dressed in white flannels, white boots and a boater he encountered her as she sat listening to a band in the sea-front gardens. They were married in Woolwich by special licence on 17 September, he calling himself Charles Oliver James, and they lodged in Battersea Rise. She was lucky – she wasn't worth killing – and having made £90 out of her by stealing her savings and selling her belongings he left her in some public gardens after a tram-ride. Some of her clothes he generously gave to Edith, saying he had 'been to a sale in London and had bought some ladies' clothing'. The Smiths returned to Bristol, and he returned to his next victim, whom he had first met in June in Bath.

Miss Margaret Lofty was thirty-eight, the daughter of a clergyman long deceased. Occasionally a lady's companion, her last employment ending in July, she lived with her sister and aged mother. Disappointed in love earlier that year – her fiancé had turned out to be already married – she went out for tea on 15 December and never returned.

Two days later, on 17 December, without telling any of her family, she married 'John Lloyd, estate agent' in Bath. That same day the Lloyds went to London and took rooms at 14 Bismarck Road (now Waterlow Road), Highgate. The house had a bath. That night he took her to see a Dr Bates, and the following morning she went to a solicitor and made her will – her life had already been insured for £700. She wrote to her mother about her marriage, describing her husband as 'a thorough Christian man . . . I have every proof of his love for me . . . He has been *honourable* and kept his *word* to me in everything. He is such a nice man . . .'

About 8 pm on that Friday night, 18 December, she had a bath. The landlady, Miss Louisa Blatch, was ironing in the kitchen below the bathroom. She said: 'I heard a sound from the bathroom. It was a sound of splashing. Then there was a noise as of someone putting wet hands or arms on the side of the bath, and then a sigh . . . a sort of sound like a child might make . . .'

Next she heard the harmonium being played in the front room – 'Nearer my God to Thee'. About ten minutes later the doorbell rang. It was Mr Lloyd. 'I forgot I had a key,' he said. 'I have been for some tomatoes for Mrs Lloyd's supper. Is she down yet?'

At Smith's trial the medical experts, Dr Spilsbury and Dr Willcox, agreed that Smith probably drowned his brides by raising their legs, his left forearm under their knees, as he thrust their heads under the water with his right hand and held them down.

Margaret Lofty was buried on 21 December, and Smith was back with Edith in Bristol in time for Christmas. One day she said she was going to have a bath. He said: 'I would advise you to be careful of those things, as it is known that women have often lost their lives through weak hearts and fainting in the bath.'

The inquest on Margaret Lofty was held on 1 January 1915, and the resulting story in the *News of the World* – 'Bride's Tragic Fate on Day after Wedding' – was read by Alice Burnham's father and by Mrs Crossley. Both were powerfully struck by the similarities between the deaths of Mrs Lloyd and Mrs Alice Smith, and communicated their anxieties to the local police and to Scotland Yard.

On 4 January Smith called on a solicitor, Mr Davies, at 60 Uxbridge Road, and instructed him to have Mrs Lloyd's will proved and the insurance policy made good.

As Smith waited for the money to come in, the police were pursuing exhaustive enquiries that took them to towns all over England during the next four weeks. At last they had enough information to make a holding charge. When Smith returned to his solicitor on 1 February he was detained as he left the building by Detective Inspector Neil and two police sergeants. He admitted he was George Smith, who had married Alice Burnham, and was then charged with bigamy.

That same day, Margaret Lofty's body was exhumed and examined by Dr Spilsbury, who later travelled to Blackpool and then to Herne Bay to supervise the exhumations of Alice Burnham and Bessie Mundy and carry out the post-mortems. Spilsbury had by now become the Home Office's honorary pathologist.

After further police investigations, Smith was charged on 23 March with the wilful murder of Bessie Mundy, Alice Burnham and Margaret Lofty. Remanded at Bow Street several times he frequently shouted abuse at the witnesses and lawyers, denouncing and reviling them.

On 7 May the liner *Lusitania*, on her way from New York to Liverpool, was torpedoed by a German submarine fifteen miles off the Old Head of Kinsale, with the loss of 1,198 lives.

The trial of George Smith, aged forty-three, began at the Old Bailey on Tuesday, 22 June 1915, when he was indicted with the murder of Bessie Mundy.

The Times, reporting on the trial the following day, was full of war news: the Roll of Honour in the paper that day contained the names of over 3,000 soldiers and 80 officers who had been killed; 3,772 servicemen were listed as being Mentioned in Despatches. It was very hot in London that month, with temperatures over 80°F. But the court was packed, mainly with women eager to see the accused, whose denunciatory outbursts from the dock – he gave no evidence – became more frequent as the trial proceeded. He called Mrs Crossley a lunatic and Inspector Neil a scoundrel. 'I don't care twopence what they say,' he told the judge. 'You cannot sentence me to death! I have done no murder. I have nothing to fear.' He vilified his lawyers and shouted at the judge during the summing-up – 'You'll have me hung the way you are going on!' – 'Sentence me and have done with it!' – 'It's a disgrace to a Christian country, this is! I'm not a murderer, though I may be a bit peculiar.' The prosecutor referred to him as 'a systematic bigamist'.

The trial was long, concluding on Thursday, 1 July. There were 264 exhibits and 112 witnesses. At one point the jury were taken into an ante-room, where Inspector Neil demonstrated with a nurse (in a bathing-costume) and one of the baths how the brides could have been drowned. Artificial respiration had to be used to revive the nurse.

Smith was defended by Mr Edward Marshall Hall, KC, assisted by Mr Montague Shearman. The prosecutor was the senior Treasury Counsel, Mr Archibald Bodkin, assisted by Mr Travers Humphreys. The judge was Mr Justice Scrutton, who said in his summing-up: 'Since last August all over Europe ... thousands of lives of combatants, sometimes of non-combatants, have been taken daily, with no warning, and in many cases with no justification ... And yet, while this wholesale destruction of human life is going on, for some days all the apparatus of justice in England has been considering whether the prosecution are right in saying that one man should die...'

The jury retired at 2.52 pm and took twenty-two minutes to find George Smith guilty. After he was sentenced – and he took this quite calmly – he leaned over the dock and said to Marshall Hall: 'I thank you, Mr Marshall Hall, for everything you have done. I still have great confidence in you. I shall bear up.'

The judge commended the police who had carried out the investigation, in particular Inspector Neil, for their care and assiduity. The jury said: 'Hear, hear!'

Outside the court, Edith Pegler wept.

Smith's appeal was dismissed. He was removed from Pentonville to Maidstone prison on 4 August. Unrepentant, though often in tears and prostrated, it is said, by fear, he was taken at 8 am across the sunny prison yard on Friday, 13 August, and hanged in a high shed. Ellis was the executioner.

Inspector Neil formally identified the body, and the former bridegroom, naked and exposed to strangers as his wretched brides had been, was buried in a pit of quicklime within the jail.

The following day in Leicester, Caroline Thornhill, formerly Mrs Love, Smith's first wife and now a widow, married a Canadian soldier serving with the RE, Sapper Tom Davies, by special licence.

In 1916 the chief executioner, Henry Albert Pierrepoint, retired after ten years in office. The highest number of executions he carried out was in 1909, when he hanged nineteen people. His own account of the hanging of Abel Atherton in December 1909 can be found in Appendix B. In all, Harry Pierrepoint executed ninety-nine people, six of his executions being double hangings. Soon after his retirement his memoirs appeared in Thomson's Weekly News. *A Yorkshireman from Clayton near Bradford, he was succeeded by his older brother, Thomas William Pierrepoint, whom he had trained himself, and by John Ellis, who became the 'Number One'. Tom Pierrepoint was a carrier, as his brother had been. Ellis was a barber. Their wages, unchanged since Berry's time, were still ten guineas for the head hangman and two for his assistant.*

CHAPTER 16

Alfred Bowes

The attempted assassination of Sir Edward Henry,

1912

There is a kind of premeditated murder in which the victim, a person of political, social or religious significance, happens to emitomize all the deep-seated grievances that the assailant has grown to feel and can only exorcize by destroying the imagined symbol or cause of his suffering. Murders where a political motive appears to be paramount are called assassinations. But most of the public figures who are shot at are also the victims of misguided, malignant obsession as well as of a perverted and morbid desire for fame.

Edward Henry was appointed Chief Commissioner of the Metropolitan Police in 1903. Until Sir Joseph Simpson was appointed in 1958, no Commissioner had ever been a policeman himself; they were elderly gentlemen, reputable civil servants, colonial administrators or senior army officers, appointed by the government after years of public service to supervise the Metropolitan Police.

Born in 1850 – his father was a London doctor – Edward Henry was educated at a Roman Catholic school, St Edmund's College in Hertfordshire, and began work at the age of sixteen in the offices of the insurance company, Lloyd's. Dissatisfied with his position as a lowly clerk, Edward Henry studied for and successfully sat the Indian Civil Service exams and was sent to work for the Bengal taxation service in Calcutta when he was twenty-four. He learned Bengali, played polo and hunted jackals in his spare time, and an unexceptional civil service career might have followed had not his curiosity been aroused one day on a visit to a Calcutta cashier's office, where he first came across the system of identifying illiterate Indian workers which Sir William Herschel, a senior ICS official, had initiated. Each Indian workman made a thumb-print by sticking his left thumb in an ink-well, wiping off the excess with a rag and then pressing his thumb on a wages sheet.

Edward Henry realized, as others had done, that the resulting prints – no two of which were the same – might be used to identify and track down criminals. But how? Using duplicates of the thumb-print payment sheets of Bengali workmen, he began to study the differences and similarities in the prints and tried to work out some system of classification.

In 1888, the year of the 'Jack the Ripper' murders in London, Edward

Henry became a Magistrate-Collector, presiding over civil courts in which tax claims and disputes were settled. Two years later, aged forty, he married the young daughter of an Irish vicar when on leave in Britain. She was called Louisa Moore, and sailed with him back to Calcutta, where he had now lived and worked for sixteen years. The following year the ICS appointed him Inspector-General of Police in Bengal.

He was now able to study the fingerprints of thousands of Indian malefactors, and gradually evolved a numerical system that classified the prints of each finger on a man's hand according to its loops, whorls, arches, composites and lines.

Dr Francis Galton, a cousin of Charles Darwin, published a book called *Fingerprints* in 1892. His conclusions, however, were not favourable towards using them as a positive means of identification: there was still no proof that the line-patterns on people's fingers did not alter between the cradle and the grave; their variety seemed to be endless, and there seemed no simple way of classifying them. In the meantime Scotland Yard detectives, using a French system, continued to measure and photograph criminals for their records – although some fingerprints were taken in case they might prove useful in identifying villains, many of whom used aliases in those days.

Then, in 1894, Edward Henry at last felt sufficiently confident about his findings and his system to write an official report, describing and advocating his system of identification by fingerprints. He sent it to the Government of India. The system was adopted throughout the country, and Henry published a text-book, *Classification and Use of Fingerprints*, which eventually became the accepted textbook on the subject all over the world. Nonetheless, magistrates in India continued to be reluctant to convict anyone on fingerprint evidence alone.

In 1899, at Galton's suggestion, Henry was invited to address a meeting of the British Association in London about his fingerprint researches and conclusions, as well as a government body, the Belper Committee, which had been set up to consider the various methods of identifying criminals and determine which might be best.

And so, after twenty-five years in India, Edward Henry resigned from the ICS and returned with his family to England, hoping to find some senior police post which would enable him to put his theories into practice. Nothing transpired, and he went to South Africa to take up a police job there, which involved the reorganization of the Transvaal police force. In so doing he instituted new labour passes for coloured workers which bore the fingerprints of the holders. But the Boer War put an end to any further experiments and improvements. Then in 1901 he heard that Sir Robert Anderson, Assistant Commissioner and head of the CID at Scotland Yard, was about to resign. Edward Henry applied for the post and got it. He took up his duties at the Yard on 31 May 1901.

Two months later, the Central Fingerprint Branch of the Metropolitan Police was established at the Yard under Detective Sergeant Stockley Collins.

It operated under many difficulties, much doubt and some opposition. Indicative of the scornful mistrust of many was this letter from 'A Disgusted Magistrate' to a national paper: 'Scotland Yard, once known as the world's finest police organisation, will be the laughing-stock of Europe if it insists on trying to trace criminals by odd ridges on their skins. I, for one, am firmly convinced that no British jury will ever convict a man on "evidence" produced by the half-baked theories some official happened to pick up in India.'

Another correspondent, writing in 1902, denounced Henry's system as 'hopelessly inaccurate, dangerous, and completely un-British'. But on Derby Day that year, the fingerprints of fifty-four people who had been arrested on Epsom Downs were taken and checked by Henry, Collins and a constable against the 2,000 or so that had by that time been filed away by the Fingerprints Branch. Twenty-nine of the fifty-four were found to have had previous convictions, and the next day, as a result, received heavier sentences from the magistrates who heard the charges against them.

The first trial at the Old Bailey in which fingerprint evidence formed the main part of the prosecution's case involved a burglar called Jackson, newly out of prison, who had left a neat impression of his prints on some new paint in a house he had robbed in Denmark Hill. He was found guilty, chiefly on account of the adept evidence of DS Collins, who had given the young barrister prosecuting Jackson (Richard Muir) a crash course on fingerprint deduction before the trial.

However, these successes met with little public attention, and even in the Yard Henry's oddball enthusiasm for fingerprints was dismissively regarded by most of his colleagues. But when, in 1903 , his book on fingerprints was published for the first time in Britain, police forces in other cities – and other nations – slowly began to put the Henry system into practice, the town of Bradford in Yorkshire being the first English town to start its own fingerprint collection.

Then, on the retirement of the Commissioner, Edward Bradford, after thirteen years of service, Edward Henry was asked to be the next Chief Commissioner of the Metropolitan Police. He was fifty-three.

The fingerprint section at the Yard now flourished under Assistant Commissioner Melville Macnaghten. But it was the murder of the Farrows in Deptford in March 1905 that firmly established the value of fingerprinting as evidence of identification. At the ensuing trial of the Stratton brothers at the Old Bailey Richard Muir was again the prosecutor, and the most damning evidence, despite the reservations of the judge, was Alfred Stratton's thumb-print on the cash-box.

A further advance in the science of fingerprinting was made when it was discovered that prints not immediately visible could be made so by dusting them with a very fine yellow powder called licopodium. Yet it took a candle and a burglary in Huddersfield in 1909 to fix fingerprinting as evidence that was legally beyond all doubt.

The burglar, Herbert Castleton, had been convicted of breaking and entering – no defence was put forward and he subsequently appealed. A candle he had gripped and used to light his search for valuables had served to convict him – it bore a fine set of fingerprints. He claimed that various thieving acquaintances had also handled the candle. In the appeal court Justice Darling asked the prisoner's counsel if he could produce anyone else whose fingerprints exactly matched those on the candle. This he could not do and the appeal was dismissed. Thenceforth 'The Castleton Judgement' became a point of law.

Three years later the Commissioner himself appeared in the Old Bailey as a witness for the prosecution in the case of his own attempted murder.

Edward Henry's responsibilities as Commissioner included the protection of foreign potentates and politicians and of the royal family, and as a result he had become acquainted with King Edward VII and Queen Alexandra. When the King died in 1910, Henry supervised the full-scale security operation surrounding the coronation of George V in June 1911. After this he was knighted. But his biggest security headache was the state visit of the new King and Queen to India later that year. With them travelled the former Lloyd's clerk and junior ICS official, overseeing security arrangements throughout the royal tour, which culminated in the imperial splendours of the grand Durbar at Delhi.

By 1912 Sir Edward had stopped riding a horse to work, as had been his wont, and generally walked the five or six miles between his Kensington home and Scotland Yard. Sometimes, however, he made use of the car and chauffeur officially placed at his disposal, as he did on 27 November that year.

About 7 pm that evening the car taking him home, driven by Albert English, drew up outside Campden House Court. Sir Edward's wife and his two young daughters were awaiting his arrival – he also had a four-year-old son who was then in bed. His second daughter, Hermione, aged eleven, watched from the window of her bedroom above the front door porch as her father got out of the car. Sir Edward told English that he would not be needed again that night and turned towards the house.

As he did so a young man approached him and said there was something he wanted to talk about. 'Can't speak to you now,' said Sir Edward. 'I'm busy. Call my office.' Whereupon the man pulled out a pistol and fired three times. Two shots missed their target. Wounded by the third, Sir Edward staggered to the front door of his house, opened it, and was helped to a chair by his eldest daughter, Helen, who happened to be in the hall. The assailant had in the meantime been seized by the chauffeur, who was assisted in the resulting struggle by a porter and a decorator working in a house across the road. 'Let me go!' cried the young man. 'This man has done me a great wrong! Let me go!'

Sir Edward's injury was found not to be serious, but he suffered severely from shock. His assailant was taken to Kensington police station and identified as Alfred George Bowes, from Acton in West London. Having failed to pass his driving test and having been refused a licence as a taxi-driver, Bowes had developed distorted feelings of injustice and humiliation which focused for some reason on the Commissioner. Bowes imagined that the Commissioner was personally responsible for his failure to get a licence.

He was tried at the Old Bailey. No fingerprint evidence or any other was required as the accused pleaded guilty. Sir Edward, supporting himself on a stick and still unwell, was the chief witness. He asked the judge to be merciful towards Bowes. 'He was ambitious to become a taxi-driver,' explained Sir Edward. 'All ambition is a good thing, and I would not wish him to suffer unduly because of that ambition.'

The judge sentenced Bowes to fifteen years' penal servitude.

This distressed Sir Edward, who as Commissioner was in a position to know much more about his assailant's background and character than the usual victim of such an attack. He knew that Bowes, an only son, had been anxious to better himself and earn a good and regular income as a taxi-driver so that he could improve his widowed mother's lot. She kept herself from abject poverty by washing and sewing for others.

After Bowes was imprisoned, Sir Edward periodically drove to Acton, where he dismissed his chauffeur-driven car before calling on Mrs Bowes. He gave her enough money to satisfy her needs and keep herself comfortable and warm. After each visit – and they continued for several years – he returned to Kensington by public transport. For a long time no one, not even his wife, knew about these visits.

When Alfred Bowes was released from prison in 1922 Sir Edward paid for his passage to Canada, giving him enough money for him to make a new start in life.

Sir Edward, meanwhile, remained as Commissioner throughout the First World War, although he could have retired in 1915 when he was sixty-five. When in 1918, after years of governmental procrastination, the police went on strike at midnight on 29 August, demanding various improvements in pay, pensions and conditions, Sir Edward, who had supported their cause and had been sadly disillusioned by the whole experience, resigned soon after the government capitulated. The strike lasted two days.

Laden with honours and distinctions bestowed on him for his invention, classification and promulgation of a fingerprint system which was now in successful world-wide use, Sir Edward lived out the rest of his life in a house called 'Cissbury' at Ascot. He became a magistrate. He was chairman of the Athenaeum Club in London and on the central committee of the NSPCC. Then in 1930 his only son, John, who had just completed his three-year course at Trinity College, Cambridge, suddenly became ill and died, aged twenty-two.

Six months later Sir Edward died at the age of eighty, on 19 February 1931.

Meanwhile, further improvements had been made at Scotland Yard. In August 1914, when the First World War began, a PC was earning thirty shillings a week; in 1918 the basic pay was put up to forty-three shillings; and by 1931 it had risen to seventy shillings. By the First World War the first detective training school had been started and the Criminal Record Office set up. By then the Metropolitan Police were equipped with a few official bicycles and cars, and twenty years after the first telephone was installed at the Yard (in 1901) the first police telephone box was erected, in 1921.

CHAPTER 17

David Greenwood

The murder of Nellie Trew, 1918

Seldom have more trivial items helped to trap a murderer than the button and badge that were lost from an overcoat and left behind at the scene of this crime. Seldom has a murderer been so hopeless or pathetic, or he and his victim so young.

Nellie Grace Trew was sixteen. A junior clerk, she worked in the offices of Woolwich Arsenal and lived with her parents at Juno Terrace, Eltham Well Hall. She was known as Peg. On the evening of Saturday, 9 February 1918, she left her home to go to Plumstead Library to change a library book. When she failed to return home by midnight her father went to the police.

Her body was found the following morning on Eltham Common, near the Eltham–Woolwich Road, and about a quarter of a mile from her home. She lay on her back, and although still wearing her knickers, she had been raped. Covered in mud, she had been struck on the head, dragged about thirty yards and strangled manually. Beside her lay her handbag and a library book called *The Adventures of Herr Baby*.

Nearby, trodden into the grass and mud, was a replica of the badge of the Leicestershire Regiment (the Tigers), and an overcoat button. The button had been threaded through two holes – not with cotton or wool but with a piece of wire, one end of which was sharp, the other end being broken. The police acted promptly, and by Monday morning photographs of the badge and button appeared in every popular newspaper.

Ted Farrell, who worked for the Hewson Manufacturing Company in Newman Street, between Oxford Street and Tottenham Court Road – the firm made aeroplane parts – drew the attention of the pictured badge to a twenty-one-year-old workmate, a turner called David Greenwood. Farrell thought the badge was just like one that Greenwood wore in the lapel of his overcoat – and he had been wearing it, Farrell felt sure, the previous Saturday. Now it was missing. He pointed at the newspaper and remarked: 'That looks uncommonly like the badge you were wearing.' Greenwood agreed, and when asked what had happened to *his* badge, replied that he had sold it on Saturday afternoon for two shillings to a man he had met on a tram between Well Hall and Eltham. His colleagues suggested that for his own good he should 'clear the matter up' with the police.

Accordingly, at lunchtime, Greenwood went to Tottenham Court Road police station and told his story about the badge and the man in the tram – 'His accent appeared to me as though he came from Belfast . . . I should say he was a man that had had an outdoor life.'

The police discovered that Greenwood had been a neighbour of Nellie Trew and lived at Jupiter Terrace, Well Hall. They visited the Hewson works the following day, showed Greenwood the badge, and asked him if it was in fact his. He said it was. He was then asked to accompany Inspector Carlin back to Scotland Yard.

En route, the inspector casually enquired: 'What buttons have you on your coat?' adding as he saw for himself – 'Why I see they are all off.' Indeed they were – and Greenwood said they had been 'off for a long time'. The inspector, taking a close look at the coat worn by the young man beside him, now noticed that there was a little tear where one button had been. 'That is where it was pulled out, I suppose,' Greenwood explained.

The button found by Nellie Trew's body was later proved to have come from his overcoat and the wire attachment to have been part of a spring of a type used at Hewson's. Greenwood was arrested and charged.

His trial began at the Old Bailey on 24 April 1918 before Mr Justice Atkin. Sir Travers Humphreys was the prosecutor and Mr Slesser defended.

Greenwood, who pleaded not guilty, said he had never liked his overcoat, which had been issued to him on his discharge from the RAMC in 1917. The buttons were poorly sewn on and had come off easily. He was not, he claimed, wearing the coat on the day of the murder.

Mr Slesser revealed the record of Greenwood's valiant war service and tried to get Spilsbury to admit that Greenwood would not have been able to overpower a healthy young girl. He had enlisted at the beginning of the war when he was seventeen and had fought at Ypres, where he had been buried alive by the earth thrown up by an exploding shell. He was now suffering from neurasthenia, shell-shock and a weak heart. Spilsbury refused to commit himself either way.

The jury took three hours to find Greenwood guilty, adding a recommendation for mercy because of his youth, his services to his country and his good character. Curiously, when asked if he had anything to say before sentence was passed, Greenwood repeated that he was innocent but urged that the recommendation be disregarded. It was – he was sentenced to death.

He appealed, and was reprieved on the eve of his execution, set for 31 May, being sentenced instead to penal servitude for life. For some years people continued to agitate for his release – petitions were organized and signed by thousands. But he spent fifteen years in jail, being released in 1933 at the age of thirty-six.

CHAPTER 18

Major Armstrong

The murder of Mrs Armstrong, 1921

Very few murderers seem to have been of any great height or, for that matter, of any great weight, and they have had a correspondingly exaggerated idea of their own importance and an excess of personal vanity. Vanity is a trait to be found in most murderers, who lavish much care on their dress and appearance, especially when appearing in court. One such was Major Armstrong, the only solicitor ever to be hanged. He was about five feet three inches tall, and always wore a fresh flower in his buttonhole.

Herbert Rowse Armstrong, a neat little man with ice-blue eyes, was fifty-one at the time of his wife's death. He wore spectacles, spats, button-hole flowers and a walrus moustache, spikily waxed at each end. Apart from being small he was also extraordinarily slight, weighing only about seven stone. He lived with his wife and three young children in the charming Welsh border town of Hay-on-Wye, in Brecknockshire, where he was clerk to the local JPs, Worshipful Master of the Hay Lodge of freemasons, and had a reputable solicitor's practice in Broad Street.

He was born in Devon, in Plymouth, on 13 May 1869; his father was a merchant. The family moved to Liverpool and young Armstrong, after studying at St Catherine's College, Cambridge, and then in Liverpool for a law degree, became an articled clerk in that city in 1895. He was commissioned during the Boer War in 1900, serving with the First Lancashire Royal Fusiliers. In 1901, pursuing his profession as a solicitor, he went to Newton Abbot in Devon, lived there for six years, and eventually, after a three-year engagement, married a printer's daughter, Miss Katherine Mary Friend, in Teignmouth in 1907, when she was thirty-four.

They moved to Hay-on-Wye, where, at 9 Broad Street, Armstrong became the junior partner of Mr Cheese in a solicitor's firm that was then renamed Cheese and Armstrong. The couple settled in a valley south-east of Hay called Cusop Dingle, where they acquired a large house, Mayfield, as well as three children in as many years, two girls and a boy. The house, situated on the English side of the border (which was marked by a wooded stream running down the valley), had a large garden, a tennis-court, and a plethora of plantains and dandelions that required large quantities of weed-killer to keep them under control.

On 26 April 1914 Mr Cheese died (of cancer) and his wife collapsed and died the following day (of a heart attack). Whereupon the solicitor's practice became Armstrong's alone, with only his name on the brass plate at the door. It read: *Mr H. Rowse Armstrong, Solicitor and Notary Public, Clerk to the Justices.* But he had little chance to enjoy his professional elevation – which some people would later see in a very sinister light – for in August war was declared.

In November 1914, Armstrong enlisted in the RE and served throughout the Great War (although never abroad), becoming a major in 1916, a rank he also held as a part-time soldier after the war in the Territorial Army. In 1917 Mrs Armstrong, nervous about her children's future, made a will leaving them everything she had, aside from bequests to friends, and just £50 a year to her husband.

Major Armstrong was demobbed in May 1920. Two months later he was entertaining a middle-aged widow in London: they had dinner together and went to a theatre. This was Mrs Marion Gale, who lived with her mother in Ford Cottage, Christchurch. She had first met Armstrong in August 1915 when he was stationed in the Bournemouth area.

It is worth noting here that in April 1920 the body of Mrs Mabel Greenwood was exhumed at Kidwelly in South Wales and found to contain about half a grain of arsenic. Her husband, Harold Greenwood, was a forty-five-year-old solicitor practising in Llanelly; and four months after his wife's sudden death, in June 1919, he had taken a younger woman, Gladys Jones, as his second wife. In June 1920 the jury at the inquest on Mrs Greenwood concluded that she had been poisoned by Mr Greenwood. He was sent for trial. Weed-killer containing arsenic was alleged to have been given to her in a bottle of burgundy at lunch. The case excited much interest, not only in Britain but also in America. It must have caused much comment in that other town in South Wales, Hay-on-Wye.

A month before the major met Mrs Gale in London and just about the time that Greenwood was sent for trial, Mrs Armstrong made a *new* will, leaving everything to her husband and making no special provisions for her three children. The will was in *his* hand-writing and counter-signed by the housekeeper and a maid – although not at the same time, and in the case of the maid not in Mrs Armstrong's presence. Her signature and the will were almost certainly forged.

About this time her mental state began to deteriorate. She had never been in the best of health, suffering from chronic indigestion, rheumatism and neuritis, and was something of a hypochondriac: she believed in homoeopathic medicines, of which over fifty bottles were found in her bedroom after her death. A tall and gawky, intelligent, cultured woman, who wore spectacles and played the piano with skill, she was also a cranky, teetotal autocrat who allowed no wine, spirits or smoking in the house and who ruled her home, husband and children with some severity. The Armstrongs were nonetheless thought locally to be an affectionate couple – they were impolitely known as Mutt and Jeff – and her public rebukes were born by the major with mild and good-humoured forbearance.

According to him he first noticed signs of a mental breakdown on 9 August 1920 when (five days after he had bought three tins of powdered weed-killer) he returned home from his office and learned that Mrs Armstrong had told the children they would never see their father again. She believed he had been arrested for something she had done.

Her melancholia and delusions arose, it seems, from a deep sense of failure. Acutely introspective, she felt she was unworthy, that she was not looking after the children properly, was defrauding tradesmen and underpaying the servants. She heard voices and footsteps, and was anxious about imaginary intruders. 'She imagined things were happening in the house,' said the elderly housekeeper, Miss Pearce.

These delusions rapidly worsened, and then Mrs Armstrong became really ill.

Doctors and family friends were consulted and on 22 August after Sunday lunch, which was attended by Major and Mrs Armstrong, by her sister, her niece and by the Major's lifelong friend, a solicitor named Mr Arthur Chevalier, the necessary forms were signed and Mrs Armstrong was driven to Gloucester, to Barnwood House Hospital for Mental Disorders, a private asylum. She was there for five months.

Free of her strictures, the major indulged in his little vices, like drinking and smoking and going up to London at the weekend, when he pursued the pleasures of a middle-aged philanderer. Before long he was paying for these pleasures – in November he contracted syphilis, and was not fully cured until the following spring. In November he must also, like everyone else, have read with extraordinary interest that the jury at the Harold Greenwood trial in Carmarthen had brought in a verdict of 'Not guilty'. Indeed, it was not long after this that he began to agitate for Mrs Armstrong's return home, writing letters on the subject to the asylum's superintendent.

Then, on 11 January 1921, he bought a quarter of a pound of arsenic from Mr John Davies, the principal chemist in Hay – in very early anticipation of using it as a weed-killer in his garden.

Three days later he again wrote to the superintendent of Barnwood about his wife's illness, saying: 'The original delusions have absolutely ceased, and I feel sure that a return to her home and light household duties will be beneficial.' Although her general health had improved, the superintendent, Dr Townsend, knew that her delusions had persisted – she believed she was being poisoned by the asylum. But as she herself was eager to go home, to redeem herself as a dutiful wife and mother, and as her husband's request could not reasonably be denied, Mrs Armstrong returned to Mayfield on 22 January.

She was still quite feeble, and a nurse, Muriel Kinsey, was hired from the 23rd to assist Mrs Armstrong in washing and dressing. But Nurse Kinsey felt unable to cope with her charge's mental condition after Mrs Armstrong 'asked if it would be sufficient to kill anyone if they threw themselves through the attic window.' A full-time nurse, Eva Allen, took over on the 27th.

Meanwhile, the Armstrongs' family doctor, Dr Tom Hincks, a large man with a dark moustache and a fondness for hunting and riding, was puzzled by his patient's reference in an examination to the fact that she felt she was walking on springs. Although an invalid she left her sick-bed every day, anxiously venturing downstairs to check on the running of house and home. On 8 February she was forty-eight.

Then on Sunday, 13 February, Mrs Armstrong was stricken with vomiting, pains and muscular spasms. It was thought she had caught a chill from sitting out on the porch, although she had been wrapped in an eiderdown and had had hot-water bottles at her feet and in her lap.

She recovered, but after lunch on the 16th (boiled leg of mutton, junket and preserved gooseberries), she was dreadfully sick again. Dr Hincks noted that her sallow skin had darkened, becoming almost coppery; there were sores about her mouth. That evening she retired to her bed and never left it, being fed on soft foods like tapioca, sago and Benger's foods, intermittently vomiting and suffering from diarrhoea, with a pulse rate of 120 and terrible pains in her stomach.

Dr Hincks now attended her daily, and raised no objection when the major asked if his wife could take some of her homoeopathic brews – which the major prepared for her himself.

Two days later Mrs Armstrong's arms and legs became paralysed, and, on Monday, 21 February, Dr Hincks told the major that his wife would not recover.

Very early next morning Nurse Allen heard Mrs Armstrong say: 'Nurse, I'm not going to die, am I? Because I have everything to live for – my children and my husband.' At 8 am Nurse Allen summoned the major from the bedroom he had used since his wife's return: she was all but unconscious. Dr Hincks arrived, and having done what he could for the dying woman he drove the major into town and dropped him off at his office in Broad Street about nine o'clock. Some fifteen minutes later, Nurse Allen telephoned the major to say that Mrs Armstrong was dead.

Her demise was succinctly noted in Major Armstrong's pocket diary (Full Moon 9.32 am) – 'K died.'

Two nights later he asked one of the maids, Inez Rosser, to bring a candle to the main bedroom, where Mrs Armstrong's body now reposed in a coffin, her hair twined into long plaits. The maid watched as, by candlelight, the major soaped his dead wife's fingers and removed her rings.

Dr Hincks continued to be perplexed by the conflicting symptoms of Mrs Armstrong's last illness. He wrote on her death certificate that she had died of heart disease, arising from nephritis and gastritis.

She was buried on 25 February. The major's diary entry read – 'K's funeral 3 pm Cusop.'

Within three weeks Major Armstrong rewarded himself with a month-long holiday in Italy and Malta, where he picked up a skin infection that produced a rash over most of his body. On his return to England he visited Bournemouth and asked Mrs Gale to marry him. She demurred. But the marriage of a solicitor did take place in Hay that summer, on 21 June – that of Mr Oswald Martin and Miss Constance Davies.

Mr Martin, aged thirty-two, was the senior partner in the firm of Griffiths and Martin, and had become so when old Mr Griffiths died in November 1920. Mr Martin had come to Hay the year before. Wounded in the last months of the Great War, in which he had served throughout as a private, he had sustained an injury that half-paralysed one side of his face. This made him seem to wear a permanent half-smile, which some people found rather disconcerting. Something other than this, however, must have irritated the major during the three months that followed his professional rival's wedding, for on 20 September, a 1 lb box of Fuller's chocolates was posted to Mr Martin by an anonymous well-wisher.

Fortunately neither he nor his wife were partial to chocolates, although they sampled one or two. These had no ill-effects and the rest were put aside, to be brought out and placed in a silver sweet-dish on 8 October, when the Martins gave a dinner-party for his two brothers and their wives, who were in Hay on a visit. Of the six Martins only Gilbert Martin's wife, Dorothy, ate any of the chocolates. Later that night she was violently ill – much to the embarrassment of her hosts and the vexation, no doubt, of Major Armstrong.

Oddly enough, a local inspector of taxes was also taken ill at about this time after dining at Mayfield, and an estate agent from Hereford, Mr Willi Davies, at odds with the major over some deal, actually died on 4 October. Local gossip was later to put a poisonous cast on both of these other mishaps.

A month after the chocolate-box incident the major had definite cause for aggravation apropos Mr Martin. They were both involved in the sale of the Velinnewydd estate: Armstrong was acting for the vendor, Martin for the purchaser. Completion was more than a year overdue. On 20 October 1921 Mr Martin gave written notice of his client's desire to rescind the contract, at the same time demanding repayment of deposits totalling £500, with costs and expenses. This apparently much agitated the major, who wished to defer the matter as his client had, without his previous knowledge, taken out two mortgages on the estate.

However, in an apparent attempt at conciliation, he asked Mr Martin to tea at Mayfield on Wednesday, 26 October. Mr Martin went there by car.

He said later: 'When I arrived at Major Armstrong's house [about 5.10 pm], I met him in the drive. We went round the garden, and went into the house . . . into the drawing-room on the left as you go into the hall. There was a small table by the window laid for tea, and by it there was a three-tier cake-stand . . . The teapot and hot water were brought in by the maid. I sat with my back to the window facing him. It was getting dusk at the time. Major Armstrong poured out a cup of tea and handed it to me, and then he handed me a scone in his fingers.' It was a buttered scone and the gesture was uncharacteristically uncouth. 'Excuse my fingers,' said the major in mitigation. Mr Martin also ate some currant bread.

Within a few hours Mr Martin began to feel ill. After dinner with his wife (jugged hare and coffee custard), he dashed upstairs and was horribly sick. He continued to retch and vomit throughout the night; he was ill for five days.

Dr Hincks, who attended him, was more than puzzled by this patient's symptoms and rendered most uneasy when Mr Martin's father-in-law, Mr Davies (the town's chief chemist), informed the doctor that the major regularly purchased large quantities of arsenic from his shop. It was Mr Davies who then remembered the sudden sickness of Mrs Dorothy Martin. The two men agreed it might be advisable to have a sample of the invalid's urine analysed – as well as the remaining chocolates, which were still in the Martins' house – and on 31 October a parcel containing the urine sample and the chocolates was sent to the Clinical Research Association in London. At the same time Dr Hincks wrote to the Home Office, outlining his suspicions.

The Association's laboratory found that two of the chocolates had been tampered with and that one was stuffed with 2.12 grains of white arsenic. The urine sample contained 1/33 of a grain of arsenic. The Association informed the DPP about this. But Dr Hincks, Mr Davies and the Martins were kept in suspense until 9 December, when a representative of the DPP met Dr Hincks in Hereford. Dr Hincks made a statement and a secret police investigation was instituted straight away.

It lasted for a month, during which the persistently friendly major assailed Mr Martin with further invitations to tea – as he had done throughout November. 'I think I had about twenty invitations to tea,' said Mr Martin, desperately trying to postpone the event with a series of increasingly lame excuses.

To avoid having to pass Mayfield on his way home he began to take tea in his office. The major began to do likewise, and as the two offices were on opposite sides of Broad Street it was most difficult for the intended victim to find plausible reasons for not accepting an invitation whenever the major telephoned and suggested that Mr Martin nip across the road for a genial business chat over a cup of tea – especially after the police instructed him to give the major no cause for alarm.

Matters came to a head when, just before Christmas, Major Armstrong issued a formal invitation to both Mr and Mrs Martin. It was for 28 December. Martin had run out of excuses, but found some weak reason for his wife's and his own absence from this festive treat. Then at last, on 31 December, Inspector Crutchett of Scotland Yard came to the rescue.

Accompanied by Sergeant Sharp and Superintendent Weaver (the Deputy Chief Constable of Herefordshire), the inspector called on Major Armstrong in his antiquated office in a converted shop at ten o'clock that morning. They entered his office without knocking. They stayed until four.

The major, who was wearing a snappy Norfolk jacket, riding-breeches and trench boots, was asked if he had anything to say about the suspicious circumstances of Mr Martin's recent illness. 'This is a very serious matter,' he replied. 'I will help you all I can.' He then made a detailed statement, after which he was arrested on a charge of attempting to murder Mr

Martin, and his clothes and the office were searched. A small packet of arsenic was discovered in one of his pockets. It was the twentieth part, he said, of one ounce of arsenic purchased to eradicate twenty dandelion roots in his garden. Another two ounces of arsenic were found in his office desk.

Major Armstrong was taken to the local police station where he was temporarily lodged, to the stunned disbelief of the local worthies, before being remanded in custody in Worcester jail.

On 2 January 1922, Mrs Armstrong's body was exhumed from the snowy graveyard of Cusop church and examined the following day by Dr Bernard Spilsbury. Her remains, when analysed, were found to contain 3½ grains of arsenic, a remnant of the massive dose that had killed her. As the grave-diggers worked in the churchyard on the 2nd, Major Armstrong made his first sensational appearance at Hay in the magistrate's court in which he had often assisted in the processes of justice. Throughout the hearing he was transported by car between Worcester and Hay.

He was charged on 19 January with the murder of his wife.

Unseasonal snow was falling when the trial of Major Armstrong began at Hereford Assizes on Monday, 3 April 1922, the day after Cambridge won the Boat Race – a good omen, as it seemed to him. The trial lasted ten days.

The presiding judge was Mr Justice Darling, aged seventy-three. The Attorney-General, Sir Ernest Pollock, led for the Crown. Sir Henry Curtis Bennett, for the defence, suggested that Mrs Armstrong had committed suicide when of unsound mind and had taken the arsenic herself. It was also pointed out that hardly any of the money left to the major by his wife (£2,278) had been touched.

The major, himself a lawyer, was a confident witness and an acquittal was expected. But Mr Justice Darling's questions – he asked over a hundred – were incisive, and Major Armstrong, five hours in the witness-box, could give no satisfactory explanation for the presence of arsenic in his office and in his pocket.

'If you were simply dosing dandelions,' inquired the judge, 'why did you make up that one ounce of arsenic into twenty little packets such as that found in your pocket wrapped up in paper?'

'Because of the convenience of putting it in the ground,' replied the major.

The judge: 'Why go to the trouble of making up twenty little packets, one for each dandelion, instead of taking out the ounce you had got and making a hole and giving the dandelions something from the one ounce?'

'I do not really know.'

'Why make up twenty little packets, each a fatal dose for a human being, and put them in your pocket?'

'At the time it seemed to me the most convenient way of doing it.'

Major Armstrong was found guilty of the murder of his wife on Thursday, 13 April. An appeal was dismissed and, having put his affairs in order and given small gifts to his lawyers and his warders, he was taken from his cell in Gloucester prison on 31 May 1922 and hanged.

The Armstrong children were taken care of by an aunt; Mayfield was sold and its name was changed; Hay-on-Wye returned more or less to normal, and Mr Martin became the leading solicitor in the town. But the attempts on his life, the notoriety and the trial had deeply affected his health. He suffered from depression and became afraid of the dark. In 1924 he and his wife moved to East Anglia, where he died within a few years. Dr Hincks died in 1932 from a heart attack that struck him one day as he rode on the hillside above Mayfield. The judge, the Attorney-General and Sir Henry Curtis Bennett all died in 1936. The twice unhappy widow, Mrs Gale, known at the trial as Madame X and thereafter in reports of the case as Mrs G, outlived them all. She died in a Bournemouth nursing-home in 1960 at the age of ninety-one.

Armstrong's office in Broad Street, Hay-on-Wye, is still occupied by a firm of solicitors, Williams, Beales and Co., and across the street, where Mr Martin once held sway, is a sign that now says: 'R. Trevor Griffiths and Co., Solicitors'. Nothing much, apart from the plethora of bookshops, has really changed in charming Hay-on-Wye.

CHAPTER 19

Ronald True

The murder of Gertrude Yates, 1922

More prostitutes have been murdered than persons of any other profession, including policemen, and several men have murdered women for resisting their sexual advances. Sexual problems are indeed at the root of many murders that are not committed for gain – but Gertrude Yates was murdered mainly because Ronald True was mad. An extreme example of the totally amoral murderer who fantasizes and lies, Ronald True had, like so many other convicted murderers, learnt to kill during a war. In fact, a wave of serious crime followed the First World War, and the Flying Squad was formed to deal with it. The Squad inherited their first vehicles from the Royal Flying Corps; some were equipped with wireless sets that transmitted in morse code.

True was born in Manchester on 17 June 1891, the son of an unmarried sixteen-year-old girl. She married a wealthy man when Ronald was eleven, and he was sent to Bedford Grammar School. Even as a boy he habitually lied, played truant and was cruel to his pony and rabbits. When he left school at seventeen he did no work and his stepfather followed the usual line with family incompetents and misfits by sending him abroad again and again to learn some job, like farming. For brief periods True lived and worked in New Zealand, Argentina, Canada and Mexico, leaving each country after being dismissed from his job or merely walking out. He kept coming home, as dissolute and as feckless as ever. He started taking morphia.

In 1915 he joined the Royal Flying Corps and crashed in February 1916 on his first solo flight at Farnborough, suffering severe concussion. The head injuries he sustained may have affected his mind: his behaviour became odder and he developed an aversion to wearing hats. A month later he crashed again, and then had a nervous breakdown. Pilot Officer Guy Dent said of him: 'He had a feverish air about him; he was always given to rushing about and laughing with a loud voice, and he seemed deficient in common sense . . . He was unstable, boastful . . . He was a very bad pilot . . . He gave me the impression of a man always on a strain – tense.'

Invalided out of the RFC in October, True acquired and soon lost a job as a test pilot at Yeovil. He went to New York, where he regaled ladies at parties with stirring tales of air-battles with German planes. As an indirect result he obtained a brief job as a flying instructor and married an impressionable young actress, Frances Roberts. He was an attractive man, tall (6 ft 1 in), dark and handsome, with large eyes and a moustache.

He wandered with his wife from America to Mexico, to Cuba, and then back to England, whence he was despatched to a Gold Coast mining company in February 1919. His lies and odd conduct again caused his dismissal within six months. A colleague, John Thompson, an engineer, said that True was not only bombastic, irresponsible and erratic but was 'in the habit of laughing and joking and generally playing about with the native black men, which was considered very infra dig . . . which no white man does or would do . . . One must not hob-nob with the blacks.'

On True's return to Bedford his stepfather washed his hands of the young man, giving him an allowance but no further help.

His fantasies by this time had increased, as had his morphia-addiction. For eighteen months he was treated for both, in and out of nursing-homes. While hospitalized in Southsea he was wheeled about in a bath-chair, which was decked with flags and toys – a monkey, a cat, a hooter and a dog that barked. He giggled a lot; he shouted and swore; at other times he just sat and stared, at a tree, at the sea or the sky.

In September 1921 he was convicted and fined in Portsmouth for obtaining morphia from a chemist using forged prescriptions.

Two months later, back home once more, he began displaying hostility towards his wife – she had taken up her acting career again. Anything disagreeable that happened to him was now blamed on another Ronald True, who became his bogeyman and the symbol of his split personality. He believed this man was impersonating him and forging his cheques (the ones that bounced).

Sometimes he was violent, sometimes morose and brooding. His wife did what she could to humour and care for him. But when he became hostile towards their two-year-old son, whom he had once adored, she gave up, accepting his mother's decision that he should be certified as insane. He used to wet and comb the child's hair several times a day.

He told his aunt, who rebuked him for staying out late: 'I may as well enjoy life when I can; I am going to be killed through a woman soon.' He said that three palmists, in Buenos Aires, Shanghai and San Francisco, had told him so.

Early in January 1922 he disappeared in London, where he haunted West End bars and clubs. Now aged thirty, he lived richly, signing dud cheques, walking out of hotels without paying his bill, stealing from coats, purses and people's homes. He was out having a good time every night, dining, drinking, dancing, picking up women and telling fantastic tales about his own achievements, wealth and plans. He formed instant friendships and liaisons, but was always on guard against his enemies, including the imaginary Ronald True.

One friend he acquired in the first week of February was an out-of-work motor tradesman, James Armstrong. They were introduced in the Corner House, Leicester Square. For some reason they took to each other and for the next few weeks were together nearly every day, travelling about, amusing themselves, with True the eccentric but congenial host. Interestingly, it was the *women* he met who thought him insane. True bought a pistol off Armstrong for £2, to protect himself against the other Ronald True. There was, in fact, a Ronald *Trew*, a singer of whom True may have heard in some club.

His wife, much concerned about his state of mind, traced his whereabouts in London and managed to see him twice over a period of two months. She was so alarmed by his conversation and appearance that on 3 March she sought the help of Scotland Yard – True had vanished again – and employed an enquiry agent to seek him out.

Some weeks before this, on Saturday, 18 February, True had met Olive Young – 'a member of the unfortunate class', according to the prosecution. Aged twenty-five, her real name was Mrs Gertrude Yates. She had given up working in a shop to become a call-girl and was doing rather well, with money in the bank and some rather expensive jewellery. True stayed the night in her basement flat at 13a Finborough Road, Fulham, and on leaving removed a £5 note from her handbag. She resolved not to see him again, and succeeded for a while, although True kept on calling at the flat at night and pestering her with telephone calls.

On 2 March, posing as Major True (he was staying at the Grand Hotel, Northumberland Avenue without paying any bills) he acquired a chauffeur-driven car from a hire firm – the driver was Luigi Mazzola – and in unpaid-for luxury drove about with Armstrong to Richmond, Reading, to tea-rooms, dance-halls, hotels and clubs, after which True was penniless. At one tea-dance he pointed out a man to an acquaintance, Robert Scales. Mr Scales later told the court: 'He said this man was not treating a girlfriend of his right . . . He said the man had been at Bedford Grammar School when he first met him. He said the girl lived at Bedford, and that her name was Olive . . .'

Every night before midnight on the 2nd, 3rd and 4th of March, Mazzola drove True to Finborough Road and then drove him away. Each time Miss Young was out.

But just before midnight on Sunday, 5 March, she was at home, and let him in – Mazzola was dismissed.

True spent the night with her.

The following morning a newspaper boy delivered the *Daily Mirror* at about 7.10 am. The milkman arrived about 7.30 am. Some time after this Ronald True made tea for himself and Miss Young. He took her cup into the bedroom. As she sat up to drink it he struck her five times on the head with a rolling-pin. It appears that he then drank his own cup of tea and ate some biscuits.

About 9.15 am, Miss Young's daily, Miss Emily Steel, arrived, letting herself into the flat with her own key. She went to the kitchen, observing in passing that a man's coat and scarf were in the sitting-room and that the glass panel of the bedroom door was newly cracked. She began cooking some sausages for her own breakfast and did some tidying in the sitting-room. She was there when True, whom she had seen before, breezily entered the room.

'Good morning, Major True,' she said. He told her: 'Don't wake Miss Young; we were late last night . . . She's in a deep sleep. I'll send the car round for her at twelve o'clock.' Miss Steel helped him on with his coat and he gave her half-a-crown before leaving to get a taxi.

It was about 9.50 am when she knocked on the bedroom door and went in. Blood was everywhere. There seemed to be a body in the bed, but on pulling back the bedclothes she discovered only two blood-stained pillows. A rolling-pin lay under the eiderdown; the dressing-table had been ransacked; some jewellery had disappeared. She found Miss Young's naked body in the bathroom: a towel had been rammed down her throat and a dressing-gown cord tied around her neck. She had died of asphyxia.

Miss Steel ran out of the flat to get some help, and an inspector from Chelsea police station arrived on his bicycle at the flat not long after 10.15 am.

Meanwhile, True had taken a taxi to a post office, where he phoned Mazzola and then drove on to a menswear shop, Horne's in Coventry Street, where he bought a bowler hat (18s 6d) and a ready-made brown suit (5 guineas) which he put on, after showing the salesman some blood on his trousers – 'He said he had had a smash that morning in an aeroplane and hurt himself in the groin. He said he had come over from France and in landing he had had a smash.' He was very jocular. He then took the same taxi, which had waited, on to 21 Wardour Street. There he had a shave at a barber's and then a few doors along (No. 27) he pawned two rings for £25 and redeemed a silver cigarette case and a watch, which he had pledged the previous Saturday. He then met Armstrong at the Strand Corner House about eleven o'clock, and with Mazzola at the wheel they drove to Hounslow (to look at engines), to Feltham, to Croydon for tea – True bought the *Star* which featured Olive Young's murder on the front page – then on to Richmond, where he bought a shirt which he put on. They eventually reached the Hammersmith Palace of Varieties about 8.40 pm, and Mazzola was then dismissed.

He returned to his garage, where the police were waiting. Having heard Mazzola's story, four senior police officers returned with him to the Palace of Varieties, arriving about 9.45 pm.

Detective Inspector Burton later told the court: 'I saw the accused and the witness Armstrong in a box in the theatre . . . I entered the box and got hold of the accused by both hands and said to him: "I am a police officer. Come out with me." I took him outside the box, still holding his hands, and Superintendent Hawkins took from his hip pocket a revolver . . . It was loaded.'

True made a brief statement in which he said that a tall man, aged thirty-one, was in Mrs Yates's flat the previous night when he arrived there; he left when a stormy scene ensued.

On 7 March, he was charged with the wilful murder of Gertrude Yates. Held for observation in Brixton prison's hospital, he attacked a prisoner whom he thought was stealing his food, and was jolly with Henry Jacoby, an eighteen-year-old pantry boy who had murdered an elderly hotel guest, Lady White.

'Another one to join our Murder Club!' cried True. 'We are only accepting members who kill them right out!'

His trial began at the Old Bailey on Monday, 1 May 1922. The judge was Mr Justice McCardie, who had just sentenced Henry Jacoby to death after a two-day trial.

True's defence was that of insanity, two psychiatrists agreeing with the prison doctor that True was suffering from a congenital mental disorder, aggravated by his drug-addiction. There was a lengthy legal debate about the meaning of homicidal insanity and the McNaughton case was much discussed. The prosecutor, Sir Richard Muir, called no experts, relying on his cross-examination of witnesses to prove the defendant was not altogether mad.

Victor Trew, twin brother of Ronald Trew, was produced at one point – his brother was in hospital with pneumonia – to show that his brother was quite unlike True in appearance, and to say that he never carried a gun and did not know Olive Young.

The jury concurred with the prosecution; the doctors might say True was mad, but they could not believe that he was truly a lunatic. On 5 May they found Ronald True guilty of the murder of Gertrude Yates. He was sentenced to death.

An appeal was dismissed by the Lord Chief Justice. But while True was in Pentonville prison he was re-examined by three other medical experts on the orders of the Home Secretary and declared to be insane. Whereupon he was reprieved and sent to Broadmoor Criminal Lunatic Asylum, later renamed Broadmoor Institution. This caused an outcry in the Commons and the press, especially as Henry Jacoby had just been hanged. It was felt that social position had damned the one and saved the other.

True spent the rest of his life in Broadmoor, a popular and cheerful chap. He died there in 1951, aged sixty.

CHAPTER 20

Bywaters and Mrs Thompson

The murder of Mr Thompson, 1922

Nothing seems to incite one man to kill another as strongly as the urge to be the sole possessor of the other man's woman of wife. Desire for a woman can become so obsessive that nothing but the most drastic action will resolve the situation. Rational thought is seldom employed. In this case, as in that of Mrs Casserley, the wife could have left her husband; she could have deserted him and gone to live with her lover. But she chose not to do so. Love seldom conquers all. Apart from the fact that women are more responsive to social expectations and the sanctity of the status quo, some primitive instinct seems to demand that the possessor be aggressively dispossessed and the woman carried away. Moreover, so complex are the interactive feelings of those involved, that two people who become part of an unhappy triangle can only be realigned as a happy pair when the triangular involvement is torn apart.

Frederick Edward Francis Bywaters was a good-looking, virile young man, self-willed and well travelled. Although susceptible to emotion, he was not a man of imagination or a thinker. He was more a creature of instinct and of action, and, although impressionable, not the innocent lad his counsel later described. Nor was Edith Jessie Thompson the dominating seductress portrayed at the trial. A sensual, attractive lady, she was a dreamer, in love with love and anything that lifted her out of the shallows of her pedestrian life with Percy Thompson in Ilford.

They had married on 15 January 1915, when she was twenty-two and he was twenty-six. There were no children. At the time he was a shipping clerk with a firm in the City and she was the book-keeper and ultimately the manageress of a wholesale milliner, Carlton & Prior, at 168 Aldersgate Street, EC1, a quarter of a mile north-east of the Old Bailey. Both the Thompsons continued with their jobs for seven years until the night of the murder, she earning as much as he, £6 a week.

In 1916 Percy enlisted in the London Scottish Regiment, but was soon discharged as unfit because he was suffering from heart trouble. About this time Freddy's father, a ship's clerk who had also enlisted in the army at the start of the Great War, was killed, and his mother moved from Manor Park to Norwood, south of the river. Two years later Freddy Bywaters, then aged sixteen, joined the Merchant Navy as a writer or clerk.

In July 1920 the Thompsons, who had both been born and brought up in Ilford, a north-eastern suburb of London, took up residence in 41 Kensington Gardens, Ilford. They bought the terraced house from a crabbed old lady, Mrs Lester, who with her ailing husband remained in the house as the Thompsons' lodgers. Every weekday morning the Thompsons set off about quarter past eight to work in the City, returning about quarter to seven at night. They dined with friends or went to shows, but seem to have had few interests – except that Edith Thompson was an avid reader of popular fiction and magazines.

On 4 June 1921 Freddy Bywaters, then aged eighteen, returned from a four-month voyage to Australia on the steamship *Orvieto*. He had been friendly with Edith's younger brothers and sister since his schooldays – her maiden name was Graydon – and at Percy's invitation he joined the Thompsons and Edith's sister, Avis Graydon, for a week's holiday at Shanklin on the Isle of Wight. Edith was able to escape with the younger people and have fun, to have swimming and tennis lessons, and to exchange her first kiss with Freddy. A year later, on 14 June 1922, she was to write: 'One year ago today we went for that memorable ride round the island in the charabanc do you remember? – that was the first time you kissed me.'

At the end of the holiday, 18 June, Freddy was invited by Percy, who liked the young man, to lodge with them, presumably so that Freddy could be nearer the Graydon boys and Avis. The Graydons lived a mile and a half south of the Thompsons in Shakespeare Crescent, Manor Park. But Freddy's romantic interest in Avis, if it ever existed, had already been diverted.

Although he and Edith both denied in court that they had made any declaration of love until that September, she wrote to him in a letter dated 20 June 1922: 'It's Friday now darlint . . . I am wondering if you remember what your answer was to me in reply to my question "What's the matter?" tonight of last year. I remember quite well – "You know what's the matter, I love you" . . . but you didn't then darlint, because you do now and it's different now isn't it?' On 20 June 1921 Freddy Bywaters had been lodging with the Thompsons for just two days.

Friday 27 June was his nineteenth birthday, a date and a day she looked back on several times in her letters as being of some significance.

They met for lunch in the Holborn Restaurant. Bywaters later told the court: 'Mrs Thompson told me she was unhappy, and I said: "Let me be a pal to you – let me help you if I can" . . . Mrs Thompson and I had been having an argument, and she suddenly burst into tears, and I advised her to wait, not to give up hope, and not commit suicide . . . I extracted a promise from her to wait five years, so that she should not commit suicide.' In the interim she was to try to obtain a divorce or separation, and if this was not possible they would go away together or both kill themselves in a suicide pact.

A month passed, with Freddy still lodging in Kensington Gardens. By now the Thompsons had been married for more than six years. She said later, 'I think I was never really happy with my husband,' and added that the question of a separation had been discussed between them long before Bywaters came to stay.

On Monday, 1 August, it was aired again. She told the court: 'I had some trouble with my husband that day. I think it originated over a pin.' She was sewing and Freddy went to fetch a pin for her. 'But eventually it was brought to a head by my sister not appearing at tea when she said she would. I wanted to wait for her, but my husband objected, and said a lot of things to me about my family that I resented. He then struck me several times, and eventually threw me across the room.' Her arm was badly bruised. 'Bywaters was in the garden ... He came into the room and stopped my husband. Later on that day there was a discussion about a separation ... I wanted a separation and Bywaters entreated my husband to separate from me. But he said what he usually said, that he would not. At first he said he would, and then I said to him. "You always tell me that ... and later, you refuse to grant it to me." '

Not surprisingly Freddy was asked by Percy Thompson to leave, and did so four days later.

'We were friends,' Freddy said later of his relationship with Mrs Thompson at that time – 'I was fond of her.' But it seems the affair had already been consummated. In one of the only two surviving letters he wrote to her, found at Carlton & Prior's and written two days before the murder, he wrote: 'I do remember you coming to me in the little room and I think I understand what it cost you – a lot more darlint than it could ever now. When I think about that I think how nearly we came to be parted for ever. If you had not forfeited your pride darlint I don't think there would ever have been yesterday or tomorrow.' The little room was most probably where Bywaters lodged in Kensington Gardens.

After 5 August he stayed in his widowed mother's small house in Westow Road, Upper Norwood, a long way from Ilford. But he continued to meet Edith – or Edie, as her family called her.

The first extant letter she wrote to him is dated 11 August 1921. It says: 'Darlingest – Will you please take these letters back now. I have nowhere to keep them, except a small cash box I have just bought and I want that for *my own letters only* and I feel scared to death in case anybody else should read them ...' Apparently she was referring in the first instance to 'personal' letters written to him by a girl-friend he had acquired in Australia.

Her next letter was a note dated 20 August – 'Come and see me Monday lunchtime, please darlint. He suspects. Peidi.' She explained in court: 'I meant that my husband suspected I had seen Bywaters. I think it was on the Friday previous to that date. I usually saw him on Fridays and I continued to see him until he sailed on the ninth of September.'

On Fridays the Thompsons invariably visited her family, the Graydons, in Manor Park. So did Bywaters, calling on Avis and her brothers; the parents also liked him and made him welcome.

It was before he sailed on the SS *Morea* to the Mediterranean, working as a mess-room steward, that he and 'Peidi' ('Child') affirmed their love for each other. Their letters, with hers breathing an 'insensate, silly affection' according to the judge, now began their lengthy travels across the world.

Forty-nine letters, notes and telegrams were produced as exhibits at the trial – thirty-four were not. This discrimination gave undue prominence to Mrs Thompson's apparently incriminating remarks about removing her husband which, if taken in their full context, would have seemed more fantastical and less calculating. The defence never insisted, however, on *all* the letters being put in evidence – for the very good reason that some referred damagingly to Mrs Thompson's abortions.

She wrote more than sixty letters to Bywaters over the period of a year, during which he was at sea five times: from 9 September to 29 October 1921; 11 November 1921 to 6 January 1922; 20 January to 16 March; 31 March to 25 May; and finally from 9 June to 23 September 1922. These five voyages were all in the SS *Morea*, where he was employed as a mess-room steward, a writer and then as a laundry steward.

She wrote to him nearly every day, often at her desk in Carlton & Prior's, with a brass monkey he had given her sitting on the desk before her. Some of the letters were very long, running on like a diary from day to day, full of gossip and chat about the weather, relatives, shows, books, her thoughts and feelings. Very often she included newspaper cuttings, advertisements, invitations or other items that she thought might interest him – in fact fifty enclosures were found with the letters. She also sent him books, chocolates and other gifts, probably using Carlton & Prior's postage; he addressed some of his replies to her office, although later she used a poste-restante address at the Aldersgate post office under the name of 'Miss P. Fisher'. He reciprocated as best he could with letters and gifts, and sometimes, it seems, he humoured her fantasies; though on his fifth and longest voyage his enthusiasm flagged.

His two surviving letters to her, written just before the murder, could have been composed by her. The style is very much the same: rambling, effusive, loosely constructed and punctuated, with the occasional French or coded phrase. He signs himself 'Freddy'. He calls her 'Peidi Mia – Ma Chere – Darlint little girl – The darlingest little sweetheart girl in the whole world . . . and big pal.'

Always signing herself 'Peidi', she invariably calls him 'Darlingest boy', and ubiquitously 'darlint'. She describes their relationship as 'the Palship of two halves'. 'We're not ordinary human beings,' she wrote, 'We're apart – different – we've never known pleasure . . . until we knew each other.'

No letters survive from his first voyage on the *Morea*.

She wrote of their reunion on 31 October 1921: 'I'll never forget it, I felt – oh, I don't know how, just that I didn't really know what I was doing, it seemed so grand to see you again, so grand to just feel you hold my shoulders, while you kissed me, so grand to hear you say just 3 ordinary commonplace words "How are you." Yes I did feel happy then.'

They saw each other nearly every day. Then he visited Kensington Gardens on the afternoon of 5 November, specifically to see Percy

Thompson – 'We shook hands when we met' – and asked the other man to agree to a separation from his wife. According to Bywaters, there was a reason for this confrontation. He said: 'I had taken Mrs Thompson out previously. Apparently he [Mr Thompson] had been waiting at the station for her and he had seen the two of us together. He made a statement to Mrs Thompson – "He is not a man or else he would ask my permission to take you out" – and she reported that statement to me the following day. In consequence of that I went and saw Mr Thompson . . . I said: "Why don't you come to an amicable agreement? Either have a separation or you can get a divorce." And he hummed and hawed about it. He . . . said: "Yes – No – I don't see it concerns you." I said: "You are making Edie's life a hell. You know she isn't happy with you." He replied: 'Well, I've got her, and I will keep her."'

On 11 November 1921 Freddy sailed for India on the *Morea*, bound for Bombay via Marseilles, Port Said and Aden. It was his second voyage.

From dreary Ilford, about a week after Freddy left her, Edith Thompson wrote:

At night in bed the subject – or the object the usual one came up and I resisted, because I didn't want him to touch me for a month from Nov. 3rd . . . He asked me why I wasn't happy now – what caused the unhappiness and I said I didn't feel unhappy – just indifferent, and he said I used to feel happy once. Well, I suppose I did . . . but that was before I knew what real happiness could be like, before I loved you darlint. Of course I did not tell him that but I did tell him I didnt love him and he seemed astounded. He wants me to forgive and forget anything he has said or done . . . I told him I didnt love him but that I would do my share to try and make him happy . . . I was feeling awful.

In her next letter, undated but written on the 21st or 28th, she wrote:

I gave way this week (to him I mean) its the first time since you have been gone. Why do I tell you this? . . . We had – was it a row – anyway a very heated argument again last night (Sunday). It started through the usual source, I resisted – and he wanted to know why since you went in August I was different – 'Had I transferred my affections from him to you.' Darlint its a great temptation to say 'Yes' but I did not. He said we were cunning, the pair of us . . . He said 'Has he written to you since he has been away,' and when I said 'No' he said 'That's another lie.'

There was more of the same on 6 December.

I am feeling very blue today darlint, you havn't talked to me for a fortnight . . . I fear that we, you & I, will never reap our reward, in fact, I just feel today darlint, that our love will be in vain. He talked to me again last night a lot, darlint . . . He said he began to think that both of us would be happier if we had a baby, I said 'No, a thousand times No' & he began . . . to plead with me, oh darlint, it's all so hard to bear . . . He hasn't worried me any more, except that once I told you about . . . You know I always sleep to the wall, darlint, well I still do but he puts his arm around me & oh its horrid.

What do you think he is going to learn dancing – to take me out to some nice ones, wont it be fun . . . About myself darlint, its still the same & I've not done anything yet – I don't think I shall until next month . . .

Her birthday was on Christmas Day: she was twenty-eight. On 3 January 1922 she wrote:

Darlint, I've surrendered to him unconditionally now – do you understand me? I think it the best way to disarm any suspicion, in fact he has several times asked me if I am happy now and I've said 'Yes, quite . . . ' Darlint, you are a bad bad correspondent really darlint I absolutely refuse to talk to you at all next trip, if you dont mend your ways. Darlint, are you frightened at this – just laugh at me.

The *Morea* returned to England on 6 January. She saw Freddy the following day. His shore-leave was short, for the *Morea* sailed again on 20 January, bound again for Bombay.

The prosecution was to imply later that the December letter contained an expression of intent to remove Percy Thompson by poison or some other means. But what it was she had to do becomes clear in a letter written on 24 January, just after he went to sea again.

About 10.30 or 11 am I felt awfully ill – I had terrible pains come all over me – the sort of pains that I usually have – but have not had just lately – do you understand.

She fainted in her office three times and at 3.30 pm was taken home in a car with a hot-water bottle in her lap. She went straight to bed.

About 7 something awful happened, darlint I don't know for certain what it was, but I can guess, can you, write & tell me.

This letter was not one of the exhibits read out in court, as the revelation that she had had a miscarriage or abortion would in those days have damaged her defence and damned her in the eyes of the jury. The prosecution and the defence probably made some deal about which letters were to be put in evidence. But the suppression of the foregoing piece of information, which helped the defence, also assisted the prosecution, allowing them to add a murderous intent (as in the letter of 3 January) to anything ambiguous Mrs Thompson wrote. They were undoubtedly also assisted by Mrs Thompson herself.

10 February 1922 – You must do something this time ... opportunities come and go by – they have to – because I'm helpless and I think and think and think ... It would be so easy darlint – if I had things – I do hope I shall ... Have enclosed cuttings of Dr Wallis's case. It might prove interesting.

The cuttings from the *Daily Sketch* of 9 February, referred to *Mystery of curate's death*. He had been poisoned by hyoscine – his wife seemed to be involved. The same letter contained a cutting: *Poisoned chocolates for university chief. Deadly powder posted to Oxford Chancellor. Ground glass in box.* Clearly she wished Freddy to provide her with some poison and tell her what to do.

On 22 February she wrote:

I do hate this life I lead – hate the lies hate everything and I tell so many that it hurts ... if only I could make an absolutely clean – fresh start ... Darlingest boy, this thing that I am going to do for both of us, will it ever make any difference between us, darlint, do you understand what I mean. Will you ever think any the less of me ... because of this thing that I shall do. Darlint – if I thought you would Id not do it ...

The letter dated 14 March 1922 continued this theme.

Will you do all the thinking and planning for me darlint – for this thing – be ready with every little detail when I see you – because you know more about this thing than I, and I am relying on you for all plans and instructions – only just the act I'm not. What about Wallis's case? You said it was interesting but you didn't discuss it with me.

In this letter, a very long one, she also said she had been looking for an unfurnished flat.

Freddy Bywaters returned to England on 16 March. In court he admitted to having given her some quinine – to humour her ideas of suicide, he said, knowing it wouldn't kill her. *His* interpretation of the letters in court (as well as hers) was that she was referring in the ambiguous sentences to suicide or her freedom, which was to be gained by divorce, separation, or by running away – not by murder.

She saw him just before he sailed away again on 31 March, when she gave him a watch as a present. The day before she had written:

After tonight I am going to die ... not really ... but put on the mask again until the 26th May ... This time really will be the last you will go away ... like things are, won't it? We said it before darlint I know and we failed ... But there will be no failure this next time darlint, there mustn't be ... if things are the same again then I'm going with you ...

In her next lengthy letter (1 April) she mentions hearing of an unfurnished three-room flat in Kensington for thirty-five shillings a week – 'Darlint it is just the thing we wanted.' She reverts to their farewell and then to more sinister matters:

Darlint you're not and never will be satisfied with half and I don't ever want to give you half ... You said to me 'Say no Peidi, say No' on Thursday didn't you – but *at that very moment* you didn't wish me to say 'No' did you? ... I knew this – felt this – and wouldn't say 'No' for that very reason.

Don't keep this piece. About the Marconigram – do you mean one saying Yes or No, because I shant send it darlint I'm not going to try any more until you come back ... He puts great stress on the fact of the tea tasting bitter, 'as if something had been put in it' he says. Now I think whatever else I try it in again will still taste bitter – he will recognise it and be more suspicious still ... I wish we had not got electric light – it would be easy. I'm going to try the glass again occasionally – when it is safe. I've got an electric light globe this time.

Three days later she wrote:

He knows or guesses something ... As I was getting into bed a car drew up outside & he came in looking, well you know how with that injured air of mystery on his face attempted to kiss me and then moved away with the expression 'Phew – drink.' ... If he has any sense he could easily put 2 & 2 together. Your last night last time & your last night this time – I went to a theatre on both occasions ... I'm afraid I let go & said several things in haste ... I was told I was the vilest tempered girl living.

After the Easter holiday, during which she amused herself by going to a tea-dance at the Waldorf and by attending a Sunday League Concert at the Ilford Hippodrome, she wrote on 24 April: 'I used the "light bulb" three times but the third time – he found a piece – so I've given up – until you come home ... I had a doctor's bill in yesterday ... You want me to pay it, don't you darlint – I shall do so.'

She was writing more often now, posting letters to Aden and Bombay which were packed with her thoughts on all manner of things. But the theme of most was *When?* and *How?*

On 1 May 1922 she wrote:

About those fainting fits darlint ... I'm beginning to think its the same as before ... What shall I do about it darlint, if it is the same this month ... I still have the herbs ...

We must learn to be patient ... Such a love was not meant to be in vain. We'll wait eh darlint, and you'll try and get some money and then we can go away ... You said it was enough for an elephant.

Perhaps it was. But you don't allow for the taste making only a small quantity to be taken ... Darlint I tried hard. [She was apparently referring to the quinine he had given her.]

The mail was in this morning and I read your letter darlint and I cried ... it sounded so sad ... I was buoyed up with the hope of the 'light bulb' and I used a lot – big pieces too – not powdered – and it has no effect – I quite expected to be able to send that cable ... Oh darlint, I do feel so down and unhappy. Wouldn't the stuff make small pills coated together with soap and dipped in liquorice powder ... You tell me not to leave finger marks on the box – do you know I did not think of the box but I did think of the glass or cup ... Do experiment with the pills while you are away – please darlint.

During the trial Bywaters was asked if he ever believed she had attempted to poison her husband. 'No,' he said. 'It never entered my mind at all. She had been reading books.'

Dr Bernard Spilsbury told the court that he had found no trace of any powdered glass in Percy Thompson's remains, nor any trace of any of these things having ever been administered. Spilsbury's post-mortem examination was carried out on 3 November, a month after the murder.

Earlier that year, Bywaters' fourth long voyage was coming to an end – he was due home on 25 May. Ten days before this Edith Thompson wrote to him about the money she had lost betting on horse-racing, about the weather – 'It has been a beautiful weekend' – and about her boss, Miss Prior, who had asked Edith to go to the West End and buy some mourning clothes for her newly divorced widowed sister.

There were widows hats with some veils at the back and nobody had the pluck to try them on – they all say it is unlucky – so because of it being unlucky to them I thought it might be lucky to me and tried them all on. I think they all think terrible things are going to happen to me now – but darlint I am laughing I wonder who will be right, they or I?

On 18 May she wrote lengthily about the weather, clothes, cooking, and family news and quoted a passage from a book about the deadly effects of digitalin if taken to excess – 'Is it any use?' She discussed at great length two other books, romantic novels, and then wrote: 'Old Mr Lester died last night. All their side of the house the blinds are drawn. I havent drawn mine and Im not going to. I think they think Im a heathen.'

Two days before his return she wrote (23 May) about an adventure she had had with an admirer – 'the usual type of man darlint ... that expects some return for a lunch.' He had bought her a pound box of marrons glacés. But she was depressed – 'Your news about – from Bombay – and waiting till next trip, made me feel very sad and downhearted ... You talk about the cage you are in ... that's how I feel ... Mine is a real live cage with a keeper as well ...'

He saw her constantly during the fortnight he was ashore, before sailing on 9 June on his longest voyage, to Australia via Colombo. As well as lengthy lunches, they indulged themselves by using her alleged theatre visits to spend a few hours together in hotels like the Regent Palace. They became increasingly careless, and people began to talk.

Four days after he sailed she wrote (13 June):

On Thursday – he was on the ottoman at the foot of the bed and said he was dying and wanted to – he had another heart attack – thro me. Darlint I had to laugh at this because *I knew* it couldn't be a heart attack. When he saw this had no effect on me – he got up and stormed – I said exactly what you told me to and he replied that he knew thats what I wanted and he wasnt going to give it to me – it would make things far too easy for both of you (meaning you and me) . . . We're both liars he says and you are making me worse and he's going to put a stop to all or any correspondence coming for me at 168.

Anticipating this, on 9 June (the day Freddy sailed) she had sent a telegram to the *Morea* at Tilbury Docks – 'Send everything Fisher care GPO.' Her letter continued:

On Saturday he told me . . . I have always had too much of my own way and he was a model husband . . . He also told me he was going to be master and I was to be his mistress and not half a dozen mens (his words) . . . Avis . . . said that *he* said at 231 'I thought he was keen on you [Avis] – but now I can see it was a blind to cover his infatuation for Edie.' Darlint its not an infatuation is it? Tell me it isnt.

It was now a year since the Shanklin holiday, since their first kiss, since Freddy lodged with the Thompsons in Kensington Gardens, since the row and his departure, and since the declaration and consummation of their love. She now remembered and referred to these highlights in her life with fondness and yearning, and looked forward to his birthday, when he would be twenty.

She wrote to him on 14 June 1922:

On our birthday [27 June] you will be left Aden on your way to Bombay – you'll be thinking of a girl whose best pal you are in England wont you . . . Time hangs so dreadfully . . . We are not busy this week and are leaving at five . . . Darlint, how can you get ptomaine poisoning from a tin of salmon? One of our boys Mother has died with it . . . Darlint this month and next are full of remembrances – arent they . . . ?

I was taken faint in the train this morning . . . On Saturday I'm going to see a Doctor.

Six days later she wrote:

When you are not near darlint I wish we had taken the easiest way . . .
The days pass – no they don't pass, they just drag on and on and the
end of all this misery and unhappiness is no nearer in sight . . . There
are 2 halves in this world who want nothing on earth but to be joined
together . . .
    I went to see a doctor on Saturday he asked me lots of questions –
could he examine me etc – I said no . . . Eventually he came to the
conclusion I have 'chronic anaemia.'

The doctor asked her if she had had an accident and lost a lot of blood. 'I
said "No" – because it wasn't really an accident and I didn't want to tell
him everything – he might have wanted to see my husband . . . I lost an
awful lot of blood.'
Despite what appears to have been a second abortion and a general
depression, she was soon (if briefly) enjoying herself.
Her next letter was dated 23 June:

Darlint, your own pal is getting quite a sport. On Saturday I was first
in the Egg & Spoon race & first in the 100 yards Flat race . . . Then I
was MC for the Lancers . . . We had a very good day indeed – until we
got to Lpool St coming home & then he started to make a fuss – says I
take too much notice of Dunsford and he does of me . . . He gets
jealous & sulks if I speak to any man now . . .
    It was rather fun on Thursday at the Garden Party – They had
swings and roundabouts & Flip Flaps cocoa-nut shies Aunt Sallies –
Hoop la & all that sort of things I went in for them all & on them all
& I shocked a lot of people I think. I didnt care tho . . . It was rather
fun.

On 4 July she wrote:

Last Wednesday I met your mother and she cut me . . . things get
worse and worse . . . Why arent you sending me something – I wanted
you to – you never do what I ask you darlint – you still have your own
way always – if I don't mind the risk why should you?

Absence and distance had by now not made Freddy's heart any fonder,
rather the reverse. It seems he had a good time on shore-leave in Australia:
in Fremantle, Melbourne and Sydney. He missed the boat at Sydney and
rejoined the ship at Melbourne.
    In England, the Thompsons went on holiday for a fortnight to
Bournemouth, an event much dreaded by Mrs Thompson – 'No swimming
lessons or tennis or anything that Id really enjoy. However I must make the
best of it & dance – Im so tired of it all tho – this dancing and pretending.'
She was also concerned about the paucity of his letters and an attempt to
distance himself.
    In her letter of 14 July she said:

You do say silly things to me – 'try a little bit every day not to think about me' . . . When you've got something that you've never had before and something that you're so happy to have found – you're always afraid of it flying away – thats how I feel about your love . . . I never want to lose it and live.

Bournemouth, she thought, was 'a very stiff and starchy place', not a bit like the fondly remembered Isle of Wight. On her return to Kensington Gardens, where Mrs Lester was 'horrid' to her, she found herself becoming an insomniac like her husband.

In her letter dated 15 August:

Ever since Ive been back in Ilford Ive had most awful nights rest . . . I dream – sometimes theyre not very nice dreams They are nearly always about you . . . One night I dreamed I had been to a theatre with a man I knew – I had told you about him & you came home from sea unexpectedly & when you found me you just threw me over a very deep precipice & I was killed . . .

That dream strangely foreshadows fatal events that were less than eight weeks away.

Yet any thoughts or plans about divorce or the disposing of Percy seem now to have been abandoned. She wrote on 28 August: 'I said I would wait 5 years – and I will darlint . . . its only 3 years and ten months now.'

Then her 'darlingest boy', now homeward bound, stopped writing. Later, he told the court: 'I said I would not see her when I came to England, as it would not be so hard for her to bear . . . I was doing that for her sake, as I wanted to help her.' This was something she was unable to accept or acknowledge.

On 12 September she complained:

I don't hear from you much you don't talk to me by letter and help me and I don't even know if I am going to see you . . . I feel so hopeless – just drifting . . . Things here are going smoothly with me – I am giving all – and accepting everything and I think I am looked upon as 'The Dutiful Wife' . . . Darlingest, only lover of mine – try to cheer me up.

And on 19 September she wrote:

Darlingest boy – I don't quite understand you about 'Pals'. You say 'Can we be Pals only, Peidi, it will make it easier.' Do you mean for always? Because if you do, No, no, a thousand times . . . Have you lost heart and given up hope? . . . Yes, darlint you are jealous of *him* – but I want you to be – he has the right by law to all that you have the right to by nature and love – yes darlint be jealous, so much that you will do something desperate.

In this letter she included a cutting from the *Daily Sketch* headed *Rat Poison Consumed by Fowl Kills Woman*.

The *Morea* docked at Tilbury on Saturday, 23 September. Freddy Bywaters never put to sea again.

He went straight home to Upper Norwood, avoiding any meeting with Mrs Thompson, and refrained from seeing her until the Monday. Even then it was only for an hour after work. They met at Fenchurch Street station – as they did on Tuesday, Wednesday and Thursday.

What was discussed? Bywaters later told the court that he had never thought of marrying Mrs Thompson, or even of taking her away, for 'financial reasons'. Yet she was earning £6 a week and he £200 a year. She herself valued her job with Carlton & Prior's very much, as much as Mr Carlton valued her – he said she was 'a very capable woman.' But if she were involved in some scandal she would forfeit that job. It seems likely that she deceived herself and Freddy about her real intentions, subconsciously loath to lose her home, her job, her respectable status, even her husband by letting her dreams become reality. Perhaps Freddy subconsciously realized all this, and fired once again by her presence, frustrated by snatched embraces and by her curious reluctance to seek a separation or divorce through proper channels – she never pursued this common-sense approach – was goaded into making fact of all the fantasy, talk and emotional uncertainty of the past year (on which she seemed to thrive) and ending all the deceit and lies, which, it seems, he genuinely disliked.

Certainly something happened that weekend, some passionate experience that lit the touch-paper of his emotions and shattered the unequal triangle.

In court he described the weekend as follows: 'On Friday the 29th I met Mrs Thompson about midday and took her to lunch, and then she went back to her business. I went to Fuller's tea-shop between three and four ... Later on Mrs Thompson came in. I left her in Ilford that evening about quarter to seven, and then I went home to my mother's. On the Saturday morning, about nine o'clock, I took her for a walk in Wanstead Park' – with a break for her to do some shopping. He left her there at one o'clock. She went home to cook her husband's dinner and Bywaters returned to Norwood, where he remained for the rest of that day and all of Sunday.

On the morning of Monday, 2 October, she telephoned him and they met for lunch and again later in Fuller's, after which he again saw her home, leaving her in Ilford at quarter to seven. He then went to the Graydons, for a couple of hours before making the long journey back to Norwood.

On the Saturday, the Sunday or the Monday – she said it was the Monday, although she saw him twice that day – she wrote her last, undated letter.

Darlingest lover of mine, thank you, thank you, oh thank you a thousand times for Friday – it was lovely – its always lovely to go out with you. And then Saturday – yes I did feel happy ... Darlint, we've said we'll always be Pals haven't we, shall we say we'll always be lovers . . . Or is it (this great big love) a thing we can't control . . . Your love to me is new, it is something different, it is my life . . . It seems like a great welling up of love – of feeling . . . just as if I am wax in your hands . . . its physical purely . . . Darlingest when you are rough, I go dead – try not to be please.

She went on to talk about a book she was reading and continued:

I tried so hard to find a way out tonight darlingest but he was suspicious and still is – I suppose we must make a study of this deceit for some time longer. I hate it . . . I'd love to be able to say 'I'm going to see my lover tonight.' If I did he would prevent me – there would be scenes and he would come to 168 [Aldersgate St] and interfere and I couldn't bear that . . . Darlint its funds that are our stumbling block – until we have those we can do nothing. Darlingest find me a job abroad. I'll go tomorrow . . .
    Darlint – do something tomorrow night will you? Something to make you forget. I'll be hurt I know, but I want you to hurt me – I do really – the bargain now seems so one sided – so unfair – but how can I alter it?

If she gave him the letter on the Monday, 'tomorrow night' refers to Tuesday night, when she had arranged to go to the theatre with her husband and her uncle and aunt, the Laxtons. She told the court that what Freddy was to do was to take Avis out, which would hurt her – as *he* would be hurt when she was out with Percy. Freddy did in fact see Avis at the Graydon's home on Monday and Tuesday night, although he never took her out.
    The letter ended: 'He's still well – he's going to gaze all day long at you in your temporary home – after Wednesday. Don't forget what we talked in the Tea Room, I'll still risk and try if you will – we have only 3¾ years left darlingest. Try & help. Peidi.'
    Her explanation in court of these ambiguities was that 'he' was the brass monkey which Freddy had given her and the 'temporary home' was a sketch of the *Morea* that she was having framed for her desk. What they talked about in Fuller's, she said, was him getting her a job abroad.
    The mention of '3¾ years' would hardly seem to indicate that she was plotting her husband's murder.
    Two letters from him that were found later that week at Carlton & Prior's portray his tempestuous feelings. Though undated, they were probably written on Friday night and on Sunday evening.

Darling Peidi Mia. Tonight was impulse – natural – I couldnt resist – I had to hold you . . . I thought you were going to refuse to kiss me – darlint little girl – I love you so much and the only way I can control myself is by not seeing you and I'm not going to do that. I must have you – I love you darlint – logic and what others call reason do not enter into our lives . . . Peidi you are my magnet . . . I shall never be able to see you and remain impassive.

Sunday (1 October):

Peidi Mia I love you more and more every day – it grows darlint and will keep on growing. Darlint in the park – our Park on Saturday, you were my 'little devil' – I was happy then Peidi – were you? . . . I mustn't ever think of losing you . . . My darlint little girl I love you more than I will ever be able to show you. Darlint you are the centre . . .

Did they plan murder that weekend? Did she urge him once too often to do something before he sailed again? Or quite without her knowledge was *he* planning to kill?

On Tuesday, 3 October, Mrs Thompson phoned Bywaters about 9 am and they met for lunch at the Queen Anne restaurant, Cheapside. After lunch she went back to Carlton & Prior's. In the afternoon he went once more to Fuller's, where she turned up at about ten-past five, meeting him at the door. They conversed for about fifteen minutes and he walked with her back to Aldersgate Street station, leaving her there about half-past five.

They both said later that arrangements for the following day were discussed: they would meet again for lunch. That was all in fact that was possible that day, for at 5 pm on the Wednesday both the Thompsons had arranged to go to Paddington station to meet an arrival from Cornwall, a maid, Ethel Vernon, hired by Percy to relieve his wife of some of her domestic duties. Naturally Mrs Thompson would have to stay at home that night, tutoring the maid, and any meeting between the lovers was out of the question.

Bywaters knew of the maid's coming. He also knew and had known for some days that the Thompsons and the Laxtons were going to the Criterion Theatre on Tuesday night to see Cyril Maude in *The Dipper*. When he left Peidi at Aldersgate Street station she was met by her husband. Perhaps Freddy watched them walk away together, on their way to the West End. It would have been the first time he had seen the despised possessor of Peidi for many months.

Freddy went east to Manor Park, to see the Graydons in Shakespeare Crescent; Avis was there, with her parents and a brother, Newenham. Freddy stayed with them for over four hours, until 11 pm.

In his overcoat pocket was a knife, which he said later he had bought the previous November. Such knives were on sale in Aldersgate Street. He said he always carried it in his overcoat pocket. It was a sheath-knife – but the leather sheath was never afterwards found.

Before leaving the Graydons he asked Avis to come to the pictures the following evening. Then he walked to East Ham station.

'I thought,' he said later, 'I don't want to go home; I feel too miserable – I want to see Mrs Thompson . . . I walked in the direction of Ilford. I knew

Mr and Mrs Thompson would be together, and I thought perhaps if I were to see them I might be able to make things a bit better ... I went to see Thompson to come to an amicable understanding for a separation or divorce ... It kind of came across me all of a sudden ...

He must have had to wait. For it was not until midnight that the Thompsons began to walk up Belgrave Road from Ilford station. They had left the theatre about 11 pm, said goodbye to the Laxtons at the Piccadilly Circus underground station, and had travelled on to Liverpool Street station, where they got the 11.30 pm to Ilford.

It was a long walk up dark and badly lit Belgrave Road, which was intersected by suburban avenues left and right. The Thompsons walked along the right-hand pavement. Mrs Thompson was, she said later, trying to persuade her husband to take her to a dance in a fortnight's time.

They were near the Kensington Gardens intersection when a man in an overcoat and hat overtook them in a rush. He pushed Mrs Thompson out of the way and she fell, banging her head on something. She was momentarily dazed.

Said Bywaters later: 'I pushed Mrs Thompson with my right hand, like that. With my left I held Thompson and caught him by the back of his coat and pushed him along the street, swinging him round ... I said to him: "Why don't you get a divorce or separation, you cad?" ... He said: "I know that's what you want. But I'm not going to give it to you. It would make it too pleasant for both of you." I said: "You take a delight in making Edie's life hell." Then he said "I've got her – I'll keep her – and I'll shoot you" ... going at the same time like that with his right hand – as if to draw a gun from his pocket. As he said that he pushed me in the chest with his left fist, and I said: "Oh, will you?" and drew a knife and put it in his arm ... I had the knife in my left hand.' Bywaters was right-handed. 'All the time struggling, I thought he was going to kill me ... and I tried to stop him.'

That was what he told the court. Two months earlier, on 5 October, he had told the police: 'I said to him: "You've got to separate from your wife." He said: "No." I said: "You'll have to." We struggled. I took my knife from my pocket and we fought and he got the worst of it ... I didn't intend to kill him. I only meant to injure him.'

Percy Thompson was slightly cut in four places on his left side below the ribs; there were also two superficial cuts on his chin, two deeper cuts on the right of his lower jaw, one on the inner right arm by the elbow, and two two-inch stab-wounds in the back of his neck, one of which severed the carotid artery. He died, drowning in his own blood, a few minutes later.

The damage done, Bywaters fled, running in and out of the pools of lamplight through Seymour Gardens, where he thrust the knife down a drain, and on through Wanstead and Leytonstone to Stratford. By taxi and on foot he passed south across London, getting home about 3 am. 'Is that you Mick?' said his mother, hearing him come in. 'Yes, Mum,' he said.

Mrs Thompson, meanwhile, struggled to her feet. 'When I came to my senses,' she said, 'I looked round for my husband and I saw him some distance down the road. He seemed to be scuffling with someone . . . I saw somebody running away, and I recognized the coat and hat.' She went to her husband. Blood was pouring from his mouth; but she had no idea, she said, that he had been stabbed. 'He fell up against me and said "O-er" . . . I helped him along by the side of the wall, and I think he slid down the wall onto the pavement . . . I went to get a doctor.'

He collapsed in one of the large dark spaces between the street-lights. She ran back down the road, meeting a couple, Dora Pittard and Percy Clevely, who were walking up Belgrave Road from the station. She was sobbing, hysterical and incoherent. She cried: 'Oh, my God! Will you help me? My husband is ill – he's bleeding!'

They took her to the house of a Dr Maudsley, who was eventually roused from his slumbers. Mrs Thompson ran back to her husband, where Mr John Webber, drawn there by a match being struck, found her kneeling by a man who was propped against a wall. Webber, on the point of going to bed, had heard 'a woman's voice saying "Oh, don't! Oh, don't!" in a most piteous manner'. He was certain the voice was that of Mrs Thompson. But it may have been her husband's. On the other hand, his house was by no means the nearest to the stabbing – he may have made the story up.

The doctor arrived, and was followed at about 1 am by Police Sergeant Mew. After the body was removed, the sergeant escorted Mrs Thompson the fifty yards or so around the corner to her home. 'Will he come back?' she asked 'Yes,' said the sergeant, assuming she meant her husband. 'They'll blame me for this,' she said.

Frederick Bywaters was arrested at the Graydons' house in Manor Park on the night of 4 October and taken to Ilford police station. Edith Thompson was detained later the same night.

He made a lying statement saying he went straight home after leaving the Graydons. She made a lying statement the following morning, after which she happened to see Bywaters in the room where he was being detained. She said: 'Oh, God! Oh, God! What can I do? Why did he do it? I didn't want him to do it! I must tell the truth.'

She then made a brief statement naming Bywaters as her husband's assailant. That evening he was told that he and Mrs Thompson would be charged with the wilful murder of Percy Thompson. 'Why her?' said Bywaters. 'Mrs Thompson was not aware of my movements.' He then made a second statement, outlining his actions on the night of 3 October. They were then both charged.

It was not until a week later that her letters were found in his sea-chest, or ditty-box, in his cabin on the *Morea*, anchored at Tilbury.

The trial began at the Old Bailey on Wednesday 6 December. There were five other indictments against Mrs Thompson besides that of murder – of conspiring to murder, of attempting to murder and of inciting Bywaters to murder Percy Thompson. But the couple were only tried on the first count. The judge was Mr Justice Shearman. The Solicitor-General, Sir Thomas Inskip, KC, led for the prosecution – Travers Humphreys was his second.

Cecil Whiteley, KC, defended Bywaters, and Sir Henry Curtis Bennett, KC, acted for Mrs Thompson.

Against the advice of her counsel she gave evidence, as did Bywaters. Curtis Bennett said later: 'She was a vain woman and an obstinate one. She had an idea she would carry the jury. Also she realized the enormous public interest, and decided to play up to it by entering the witness-box.'

She was rigorously cross-examined. The letters and her adultery seemed damning; there seemed to be no doubt in the letters she had incited Bywaters to kill her husband.

'I never considered them as such,' said Bywaters. Mrs Thompson's explanation of her talk of poison was: 'I wanted him to think I would do anything for him, to keep him to me.'

'She worked and preyed on the mind of this young man,' said the Solicitor-General, and the judge appeared to agree. His summing-up was prejudicial and remorseless. Spilsbury's evidence – about the total absence of any poison or glass in Mr Thompson's body – was ignored. It seemed as if the jury were being asked to view the case as a breach of the third commandment, not the second.

The judge said: 'This charge really is – I am not saying whether it is proved – a common or ordinary charge of a wife and an adulterer murdering the husband ... You are told this is a case of great love. Take one of the letters as a test – "He has the right by law to all that you have a right to by nature and by love." If that means anything, it means that the love of a husband for his wife is something improper ... and that the love of a woman for her lover, illicit and clandestine, is something great and noble. I am certain that you, like any other right-minded person, will be filled with disgust at such a notion.'

On Monday 11 December both the accused were found guilty. Bywaters said: 'I say the verdict of the jury is wrong. Edith Thompson is not guilty. I am no murderer – I am not an assassin.' After sentence was passed Mrs Thompson cried: 'I'm not guilty! Oh, God, I'm not guilty!'

Separately removed from the dock, they never saw each other again.

Despite many protests, the verdict against her was upheld in the Court of Criminal Appeal.

On 9 January 1923, Edith Thompson was dragged from her cell in Holloway prison in a drugged stupor and hanged by John Ellis, the executioner, and two assistants – at the same time as Frederick Bywaters was hanged by Thomas Pierrepoint in Pentonville half a mile away.

Ellis, a neurotic man who drank a lot, retired in 1923, several months after the execution of Mrs Thompson – some said, because of it. In August 1924 in Rochdale – eighteen months after she was hanged – Ellis tried to commit suicide by shooting himself. His aim was poor and he only succeeded in fracturing his jaw and lodging a bullet in his neck. 'Bloody hell,' said executioner Tom Pierrepoint to his nephew Albert. 'He should have done it bloody years ago. It was impossible to work with him.' When Ellis recovered he was sent for trial for the offence before a magistrate, who remarked: 'If your aim had been as true as the drops you have given it would have been a bad job for you.' On promising to stop drinking and to behave, Ellis was discharged. But seven years later, in 1931, he cut his throat and died.

CHAPTER 21

Patrick Mahon

The murder of Emily Kaye, 1924

The ghastliest murder case dealt with by Scotland Yard between the wars made police history of another kind. It led to the introduction of the Murder Bag, a case of forensic, medical and other items that were taken thereafter to the scene of every murder visited by detectives of the Metropolitan Police. This murder also illustrates yet again the terrible lengths to which a murderer will go to dispose of a corpse, and the unique terrors he faces. Mahon's method of disposal was so sensational, albeit unsuccessful, that it actually started a trend.

Miss Ethel Primrose Duncan was thirty-two and unmarried. A tall and dark-haired, well-built woman, she lived with her sister in Worple Avenue, Isleworth. On Thursday, 10 April 1924, about ten o'clock at night, she was on her way home in pouring rain. In the High Street near Richmond station she met an attractive man in his thirties with merry eyes and a ready smile. He offered to escort her part of the way towards Isleworth. This meant crossing the River Thames by way of Richmond Bridge. As they walked along with the rain dripping off his trilby hat, he told her that his name was Pat, that he was married, lived in Richmond and worked in Sunbury. His marriage, he said, was 'a tragedy'. Before he left her, he asked her if she would dine with him soon, and when she replied in the affirmative he said he would get in touch. She gave him her address, and he wrote it down in his diary.

'You'll probably hear from me on Wednesday,' he said, with murder in mind – though not that of Miss Duncan.

The following Tuesday she received a telegram in the late afternoon which read – 'Charing Cross seven tomorrow. Sure. Pat.'

As requested, on Wednesday, 16 April, she went to Charing Cross at 7 pm. But it was not until about 7.50 pm that Pat appeared. His wrist was bandaged, and he said he had sprained it saving a lady from falling off a bus. He also said he had travelled up from Eastbourne, where he had borrowed a bungalow from a friend, and he asked Miss Duncan over dinner at the Victoria station restaurant whether she would like to spend the Easter holiday with him in the bungalow. She agreed, and it was arranged that in two days' time (on Good Friday) he would meet her at Eastbourne. They left the restaurant at about half-past ten, by which time he had missed the last train back to Eastbourne. So after booking himself in for the night at the Grosvenor Hotel beside Victoria station, he courteously accompanied her to Waterloo station and saw her safely on to the 10.36 pm for Isleworth. There had been nothing at all in Pat's manner to suggest to Miss Duncan that he had just murdered another woman.

The next day, Thursday, Ethel Duncan received a telegraphic order for £4 and a telegram that said – 'Meet train as arranged. Waller.' Up to that point she had had no idea what Pat's surname was.

On Good Friday she travelled on the 11.15 am train from Victoria to Eastbourne, arriving at 1.57 pm. Pat met her at the station – he was wearing a fawn-coloured suit – and after leaving her luggage in the station cloakroom they had lunch at the Sussex Hotel. In the afternoon they went for a drive in a taxi-cab and dined that evening in the Royal Hotel, Eastbourne, leaving there about 10 pm. A taxi took them both (after they had collected her luggage) along the coast for about three miles towards Pevensey Bay, to a village called Langney and finally to a bungalow by a shingly beach and the sea.

Here Pat and Ethel spent three nights, sleeping in the bedroom that was first on the left in the hall. Ethel realized as soon as she entered the room that another woman had been there before her, for a tortoiseshell brush and some cosmetics lay on a chest of drawers. Then the following morning, in tidying up, she discovered a pair of ladies' buckled shoes.

Pat said they belonged to his wife: she had been down the previous week, he said, and would return there after Easter. He told Ethel she need not bother about cleaning the bungalow as his wife would do that. Ethel never saw the shoes again on her visit – Pat had hidden them away. But he could not conceal the bruising she had noticed on the back of his right arm.

On Saturday morning they drove into Eastbourne, where Pat left Ethel to do some shopping while he took the taxi on to Plumpton races, twenty miles to the west. Unknown to Ethel, Pat stopped off at Lewes and entered the general post office, from where he sent a telegram to 'Waller, Officer's House, Pevensey.' It read: 'Must see you Tuesday morning nine Cheapside. Lee.'

Pat reached the race-course about 1.30 pm and remained there until the last race had been run. He had retained the taxi-driver who had brought him there and returned in the same taxi to Eastbourne. There he met up again with Ethel at the railway station about 6.30 pm. They dined that night at the Sussex Hotel. On the way there he called in at the Sussex Stores and made some purchases.

On Easter Sunday Pat busied himself in trying to change the lock on the door of the bedroom next to theirs. There were four bedrooms in the bungalow, as well as a sitting-room, dining-room, bathroom, kitchen and scullery. There was also a telephone. Pat's explanation for his task was that a pal of his had some valuable books in the room and he was concerned about their safety.

The chisel he was using slipped and cut his left hand. Ethel bound it up for him, and through the partly open door glimpsed a bed and a large brown trunk. Pat said that if he had known the trouble the lock was going to be, he wouldn't have started. Later that afternoon he solved the problem another way. He told Ethel: 'I've screwed the door up. I don't know why I didn't think of that before.'

That night they dined at the Clifton Hotel in Eastbourne, travelling to and fro by taxi – Pat seemed to have a lot of money on him in cash.

Earlier that day, Pat had shown her a telegram which had apparently arrived the night before when they were out. He opened it, told her what was in it – it was from someone called Lee – and said: 'We'll have to go up to London tomorrow. I have to be in town at nine o'clock on Tuesday morning.'

So at 3.30 pm on Easter Monday the couple left the bungalow and returned by train to London, where they dined together before going to the Palladium Theatre. After the show Pat travelled with Ethel from Waterloo to Richmond station, where at midnight he left her, no doubt promising to see her again. Ethel's romantic weekend was over.

She did not see him again for more than five weeks. But a fortnight after their parting she was horrified to read in the newspapers that in a bungalow on Pevensey Bay the headless, mutilated remains of a woman had been found in a large brown trunk.

Pat's real name was Patrick Herbert Mahon. He was thirty-four. Thin-faced, nice-looking, tall (about 5 ft 10 ins) and with an athletic build, his most noticeable features were his deep-set eyes and thick brown wavy hair which was already streaked with grey. His father was a stock-keeper in a clothing warehouse. Born in 1889 and brought up in West Derby, Liverpool, by Irish parents, he was as a boy a regular church-goer, good at games, a good mixer, intelligent, smart and an avid pursuer of girls, his activities in this field being undiminished by his marriage on 6 April 1910 to Jessie, aged twenty-three, from Walton, Liverpool. He gave his occupation as 'literary publisher's book-keeper'. A year after his marriage Mahon spent a weekend on the Isle of Man with another girl, a visit paid for by some forged cheques. For this he was bound over, but he was soon sent to prison on another charge of embezzlement. He moved to Surrey, and his constant picking up of women got him into trouble with his employers and eventually with the police. In 1916, during a robbery, he struck a maidservant with a hammer, but was so overcome by his action that he remained on the scene until she recovered consciousness, reassuringly kissing her and apologizing for what he had done. He was sentenced to five years in jail for this attack.

When he was released he joined his wife and she got him a job as a £12 a week salesman in Sunbury with Consol Automatic Aerators (1914) Ltd, which marketed soda fountains. She worked as a secretary with the firm. The Mahons lived with their surviving child in Richmond – another child, a boy, had died while his father was in prison.

But in May 1922 the company went bankrupt and came under the receiver. A chartered accountant, Mr Hobbins, was appointed by a firm of

CAs, Robertson, Hill and Co., to sort out the company's affairs, and in effecting this he retained the services of Mr and Mrs Mahon and a chemist. In fact he appointed Patrick Mahon as sales manager on a salary and commission that averaged £42 a month. Mahon's duties took him into the City of London to the offices of Robertson, Hill and Co. in Copthall Avenue, Moorgate, where Mr Hobbins worked. His secretary and shorthand typist was Miss Emily Beilby Kaye.

Aged thirty-eight (born in November 1885), she was a tall, athletic woman, with fair bobbed hair and a round face – 'a cheery, lovable girl' according to a cousin. Her parents had died in Manchester when she was seventeen, since when she had supported herself locally as a clerk for over twenty years while living with her married sister, before eventually coming to London in October 1922.

It was in January 1923 that she was engaged as a typist by Robertson, Hill and Co. at £17 6s 8d a month, and in May she went to live in the Green Cross Club, Guilford Street, off Russell Square; where for a time she shared a room with Miss Edith Warren. Miss Kaye was described by Edith as placid and not easily roused. But she was also 'strong physically and unusually strong mentally'. Edith thought that Emily, whom she called 'Peter', was 'capable of very deep feeling'. Peter called Edith 'Phiz'.

Peter was also a prudent woman. Over the years she had accumulated some £600 which she had invested in stocks and shares. In the course of office business she soon met Patrick Mahon.

He said later: 'Miss Kaye was aware that I was married, knew my wife by sight, and had spoken to her on many occasions on the phone. Miss Kaye frequently rang me up, and towards the end of August or September ... suggested a day on the river, which suggestion, as I was anxious to gain some impartial knowledge of the legal proceedings in connection with the litigation in which the company was concerned, I accepted.' The events of that day, he said, showed him that Emily Kaye was 'a woman of the world'. After that she often wanted to see him, he said. He continued: 'She reproached me on several occasions as being cold, and told me plainly she wished my affection, and was determined to win it if possible.'

On 21 October she was dismissed from Robertson, Hill and Co. but was able to obtain employment elsewhere. Over the New Year she went to stay with her sister, Mrs Elizabeth Harrison in Cheshire, and when she returned to London she got a new job working as a shorthand typist and book-keeper for a financier, Lewis Schaverien, in Old Bond Street. She was only there a month.

In February 1924 she began to sell shares and to cash her savings, putting the proceeds into an account with the Midland Bank in Coleman Street. On 16 February she cashed a cheque for £404, receiving the money in four £100 notes and four £1 notes. In March she was ill with influenza and went down to Bournemouth for a week to recuperate. At the end of this visit she was joined by Patrick Mahon in Southampton, where he bought her a diamond and sapphire cluster ring at Cranbrook's, a jeweller's in the High Street. That night they shared a double room in the

South Western Hotel, signing the register as Mr and Mrs P. H. Mahon, Richmond.

On Emily Kaye's return to the Green Cross Club she showed the ring to Edith Warren and said she was engaged to Pat. Edith thought that Peter seemed to be 'very fond' of Pat but not 'passionately in love'. Later she asked Edith not to use his name in front of the other girls as they knew some of his business acquaintants. Edith was to refer to him as 'Derek Patterson'.

Emily also told the club secretary, Ada Smith, about her engagement – 'She came bounding into my room exclaiming: "It's fixed, my dear – the date!"' – and that she and her fiancé were going to emigrate to South Africa. She wrote in a similar vein to her sister on 5 April on the very day that Mahon, calling himself Waller, travelled to Langney to inspect a bungalow that had been advertised to let in *Dalton's News*. He agreed to rent it at three and a half guineas a week from 11 April to 6 June.

On Monday, 7 April, Emily Kaye packed her bags, said her goodbyes and moved out of the Green Cross Club. She went to Eastbourne and took a room in the Kenilworth Court Hotel, Wilmington Square, where she stayed until Saturday the 12th; Mahon had met Miss Duncan in Richmond on the 10th. About 2 pm on the 12th Emily Kaye received a telegram – 'Regret extremely cannot come three-fifteen. Coming four forty-nine. Meet train. Pat.' Before she left the hotel she asked the receptionist to forward any letters to 'Poste Restante, Paris.' The receptionist noticed that Miss Kaye was wearing a smart grey costume, grey suede shoes and a fur coat with a dark collar.

In London earlier that day, about lunchtime, Mahon had paid a visit to Staine's Kitchen Equipment Company in Victoria Street, and had bought a ten-inch cook's knife and a small meat-saw.

That evening he met Emily Kaye in Eastbourne, as arranged, and they drove out in a taxi to the bungalow by a stretch of coast known locally as The Crumbles.

It was called the Officer's House and was one of a row of white-washed houses once occupied by the coastguard on Pevensey Bay. Nearly three years earlier, and within a short distance of the bungalow, a seventeen-year-old London typist named Irene Munro had been battered to death and robbed of her holiday money by two men, Jack Field (nineteen) and Bill Gray (twenty-nine), who were subsequently hanged.

The bungalow had been let furnished to Mahon by Mr Muir of Ashley Gardens in London on behalf of a Mrs Hutchinson of Prince's Gate. It had been cleaned up and made ready by Mrs Hutchinson's cook-housekeeper on 11 April, the day that Mahon had travelled from London to meet Mr Muir at the bungalow and to receive the keys. He returned to London that afternoon without seeing Emily in Eastbourne.

Strangely, Muir happened to meet Mahon again the very next day (Saturday) in Victoria Street between 12 noon and 1 pm. Mahon was carrying a kitbag in which would soon repose the newly bought knife and saw. That night he collected Emily Kaye and took her to the Officer's House.

No one knows for certain when she died.

She survived their first night together in the bungalow, which was spent in the bedroom that was occupied by Miss Duncan the following weekend. She was seen through a window on the Sunday morning (13 April) by a butcher who called to deliver some meat. On the same day Emily called at a neighbouring bungalow to borrow some milk.

On Monday, 14 April, she apparently visited Eastbourne, for a letter she wrote to Edith Warren was marked 'Kenilworth Court Hotel, Eastbourne, Monday', although it need not have been written there. The letter was not in fact posted until 16 April, when it was dropped by Mahon into a letterbox in south-west London. It said:

Pat arrived intact, but with his arm in a sling, on Saturday, and we are having a very nice time of it; quiet, a nice change from town. He particularly wants to get to Paris for Easter, and would like you and Fred both to have dinner with us when we return to town. We shall have a few days, about a fortnight, before setting on our final journey ... All news when we meet. Lots of love to all the pals and yourself, old bean – Pete.

Miss Warren tore the letter up and threw the pieces into a bin.

This letter ties in, although somewhat loosely, with the fact that the last time Emily Kaye was seen alive was at the Kenilworth Court Hotel on either Monday or Tuesday (the 14th or 15th) when she called and enquired whether any letters or a parcel had arrived. The receptionist was uncertain about the exact date.

Despite Mahon's later insistence that Miss Kaye died on the *Tuesday* night after a day-trip to London – where he pretended to go to the passport office while she went to the club – it seems likely that she died on Monday the 14th.

In cross-examination at his trial he said that Miss Kaye was with him in Hastings on the 15th, when at 3.40 pm he sent the telegram to Miss Duncan asking her to meet him the following day at Charing Cross. If Miss Kaye was with him in Hastings they could have gone there from London. But no evidence was ever produced to show that either Mahon or Miss Kaye was in London on the 15th or that she was ever in Hastings.

What is fairly certain, however, is that she wrote a second letter to Edith Warren, dated 14 April – although Mahon later claimed that she actually wrote it on Tuesday the 15th. This letter said:

Dear old Phiz ... I am sorry that I shall not after all be able to see you before my departure. As you can imagine, there has been a lot to do ... We shall be travelling overland through France and Italy en route to the Cape. On arrival there I will write regarding prospects and other matters in general. I wish to thank you for all the kindness and friendship you have shown me in the past. One cannot put into words just what one feels, but I am sure you will understand and

appreciate just what is in my mind. Any letters addressed to me care
of Standard Bank, Cape Town, will find me. As I have said earlier, I
will write fully on my arrival – Believe me, yours, Emily Kaye.

There is something oddly formal about this letter. One wonders
whether it was in some way forged or written under duress. It is hardly
the kind of farewell letter that a woman writes to her best friend.

Mahon's accounts of the death of Emily Kaye vary in detail (and date).
This is the story he told the court at Lewes when he gave evidence in his
own defence.

He said that after they returned to the bungalow on Tuesday evening,
15 April, he lit a fire. In doing so he carried the coal-scuttle from the
dining-room into the sitting-room. There were some large lumps of coal in
the scuttle which he broke up with a small wooden-handled axe, laying it
afterwards on the sitting-room table at which Miss Kaye was seated,
writing letters. He said she wrote *two* letters that night, both to Edith
Warren. When she finished writing, he said, she looked up and stated:
'Pat, I'm determined to settle this matter one way or the other tonight.'
She tossed the two letters over to him and said; 'These letters and my
actions mean that I have burned my boats.' By this he understood that she
meant leaving the club. 'For me there is no turning back,' she continued.
'Can't you realize, Pat, how much I love you, and that you are everything
to me, and that I can never share you with another?' He said: 'Why can't
we be pals?' She replied: 'What is the use of palship to me, to one of my
nature?' 'That's all I can offer you,' he replied. Then, according to him,
she became very excited. He realized that a crisis was coming. She was, he
said, 'distracted and overwrought'.

At this point the judge intervened. 'This is a descriptive sort of
narrative,' he said. 'We want to know what happened.'

Mahon continued: 'I said to Miss Kaye: "I'm going to bed," and I
moved away from the table to go to the bedroom. Miss Kaye said
something, and as I turned by the bedroom door she threw the axe. I
barely had time to avoid it striking me on the right shoulder. It hit over
the door or framework of the door. I was astounded by the suddenness of
the attack. She leapt across the room clutching at my face – '

Here Mahon's voice broke; he staggered; his shoulders heaved and he
burst into tears. When he had composed himself, drying his eyes with a
silk handkerchief, he went on with his narration.

'I did my best to keep her off. We struggled backwards and forwards,
and I realized in a minute that I was dealing with a woman almost mad
with anger. I tried to keep her off, but I realized she was getting the better
of me . . . In an almost despairing throw I pushed Miss Kaye off and we
both fell over the easy chair on the left of the fireplace. Miss Kaye's head
hit the cauldron and I fell with her – she was underneath. She had gripped
me by the throat and I had gripped her by the throat. We were locked
together. I think I must have fainted with the fear and shock. When I did
become conscious of what had happened, Miss Kaye was lying by the

coal-scuttle and blood had flowed from her head. I tried to rouse her, pinched her, and called her by name, but she never moved or answered. I think I must have fainted again, or lay in a sort of stupor. I remember dashing water into her face. I must have gone half-mad. I went into the garden crazy with fear. I remember coming back to the bungalow later. Miss Kaye was still lying there, dead. That would be hours later, towards daybreak or at daybreak. It suddenly struck me what a fool I had been not to call for assistance, and it dawned on me what a horrible thing it was she was lying there, and dead. The fact that she was dead flooded my mind.'

The judge said: 'You are asked what you did – not all this imagination . . .'

Mahon then told the court how he had dragged Miss Kaye's body into the second bedroom and covered it with a fur coat. He went to Eastbourne about breakfast-time, he said, and then to London to keep his appointment at Charing Cross with Miss Duncan.

It was on this day that the first letter to Miss Warren was posted from somewhere in south-west London, and it was that night which he spent in the Grosvenor Hotel, returning to Eastbourne the following day, Thursday. Before he did so he sent a telegram at 9.55 am to his wife from Vauxhall Bridge Road near Victoria station – 'Expressed you urgent letter. Sorry impossible today. Mahon.'

It was not until the morning of Good Friday (18 April), according to Mahon, that he began to dismember Miss Kaye's corpse.

He cut off her legs and then her head in order to pack her body into a trunk in the second bedroom. Having done so, he said, he then went by taxi to Eastbourne to meet Miss Duncan at the station just before 2 pm. He later told the police: 'I should have gone stark raving mad if I had not had her with me. It was ghastly.'

He and Miss Duncan returned to London on Easter Monday, and very late that night Mahon went home to Pagoda Avenue. But on Tuesday he was away again. He returned to the bungalow where he burnt the corpse's head in the sitting-room grate, as well as the feet and legs. Apparently he did this during a thunder-storm, and later he told his counsel that when he put the head on the blazing fire the eyes opened – just as there was a clap of thunder overhead. Lightning flashed, and he fled from the room in terror.

Returning yet again to the bungalow on the Saturday he disposed of further portions of the now putrefying corpse.

He explained what he did in his first statement to the police. 'I had to cut up the trunk. I also cut off the arms. I burnt portions of them and then I had to think of some other method of disposing of the portions. I boiled some portions in a large pot in the bungalow. I cut the portions up small, packed them in a brown bag, and I threw them out of the train while I was travelling between Waterloo and Richmond . . . I had intended to go home Sunday night, and as I could not dispose of all the portions between Waterloo and Richmond I went on to Reading and stayed at the Station

Hotel in the name of Rees.' This was on the night of 27 April. He arrived about 7 pm, and as he had some luggage with him no deposit was required. 'Next morning I came to London and left the bag in the cloak-room at Waterloo – on the Monday morning.'

One wonders at Mahon's dreadful persistence, at the enormity of his terrible task and the mess he made of it. One wonders how the soda fountain salesman remained in his right mind, and what Mrs Jessie Mahon thought of his comings and goings and of the strain that must have shown itself in his eyes, face and behaviour. She must have been very concerned, and suspicious – but of what? Was she distressed by the thought that he was in the throes of another torrid affair? Or did she suspect something else?

On the last day of April she took her worries to a friend, a former railway policeman. She also gave him a cloakroom ticket which she had found in her husband's pockets, and asked the ex-detective to find out what it was that Pat had left at Waterloo.

This he did, presenting the ticket at the cloakroom of the south station at Waterloo. He was given a locked Gladstone bag. Easing the sides apart he was able to see what appeared to be blood-stained female underwear, and a knife. He returned the bag to the cloakroom and the ticket to Mrs Mahon, instructing her to put it back in her husband's suit.

On Thursday, 1 May, the ex-detective communicated what he had been told and seen for himself to the Chief Constable of the CID, Frederick Wensley. DCI Percy Savage was asked to investigate. He visited the South station cloak-room himself about 7.15 pm with DS Frew, and after undoing the straps of the bag he was able to peer into it from the side. From then on the bag was kept under direct observation by the police, who were ordered to detain and question whoever came to collect it. They did not have long to wait.

About 6.30 pm the following day (2 May), Patrick Mahon paid 5d to retrieve the Gladstone bag from the cloakroom, and as he walked towards the station's York Road exit he was brought to halt by DS Thompson. 'Is that your bag?' enquired Thompson. 'I believe so,' said Mahon. Thompson asked if he might have a look inside the bag. Mahon replied: 'I haven't got the key.' Thompson said. 'You'll have to come with me to Kennington police station.' 'Rubbish!' retorted Mahon. Thompson said it was not rubbish and that the other man would have to do as he was told.

At the police station Mahon was searched: a set of keys, 1,805 francs and a post office savings book were found on him. He was seen at about 8.30 pm by DCI Savage, who took both Mahon and the bag (still unopened) for examination to Scotland Yard, where they arrived about 9 pm. Mahon was offered a drink and some sandwiches but refused them. The interrogation began about forty-five minutes later in the chief inspector's room.

'Look at the bag carefully,' said Savage. 'Is it yours?' Mahon said: 'Yes.' Savage opened the bag and took from it a torn and bloodstained pair of bloomers, two pieces of bloody white silk, a bloody scarf, a cook's knife and a brown canvas racket bag initialled 'EBK'. Everything had been liberally sprinkled with a disinfectant, Sanitas. 'How do you account for the possession of these things?' asked Savage. 'I'm fond of dogs,' replied Mahon – 'I suppose I carried home meat for dogs in it.' 'That explanation won't do,' said Savage. 'I'll have to detain you while we make further enquiries.' Mahon said: 'You seem to know all about it.' To which Savage replied: 'I cannot tell you what I know. It is for you to tell me what *you* know, and how these things came into your possession.'

At this point Savage had absolutely no idea what crime, if any, had actually been committed. He waited. The two men sat in silence for fifteen minutes, Mahon with his head upon his hand.

Then Mahon said: 'I wonder if you can realize how terrible a thing it is for someone's body to be active and one's mind to fail to act.' Savage said nothing.

Mahon remained silent for another half an hour before speaking again. He remarked: 'I'm considering my position.'

Fifteen minutes later he said: 'I suppose you know everything. I'll tell you the truth.'

After being cautioned he made the first of several detailed and voluntary statements to the police. His story was taken down by DI Hall, and took well over two hours to tell. About 1.30 am Mahon collapsed and had to be revived with some whisky before he could complete the statement, which he did by 2 am. Then he read through what Hall had written. He made some corrections, initialled each page and signed the last.

In this first long statement he revealed how he had quarrelled with Emily Kaye on *16* April in the bungalow, and that during a struggle she had hit her head on the coal-scuttle and died. It was on the *17th*, he said, that he bought a knife and saw in Victoria Street, and on the 18th that he began to dismember the body. He said he returned to London on Easter Monday. He made no mention of Miss Duncan. It was about 3.30 am before Savage left the room.

Wensley was informed about Mahon's statement straightaway and in the early hours of Saturday, 3 May, he and Savage drove down to Sussex. After liaising with the East Sussex Constabulary they went to the Officer's House, still with no sure idea of what they might find.

The bungalow's porch was overhung with rambling roses. Inside, it stank. In a large locked trunk marked 'EBK' was the quartered limbless body of a woman. In a hatbox and biscuit tin were the heart and other organs. In a saucepan were portions that had been boiled. There were charred remains in the dining-room and sitting-room grates, and a quantity of bone fragments on an ash-dump outside. There were blood-stains on the sitting-room floor and on the door-frame. There was no mark, however, on or near the door to indicate that it had been struck with an axe. The axe-head itself was eventually discovered hidden under some coal in the coal-house; its broken shaft was found in the scullery. A saw was found by a fireplace and the coal-scuttle was in the dining-room.

Miss Kaye's personal possessions and clothes, some of which had been torn up and wrapped around pieces of her flesh, had been stored in the same bedroom as the trunk.

Savage returned to London where Mahon had in the meantime corrected and expanded on his first statement, now revealing details about Miss Duncan's involvement.

On Sunday morning Sir Bernard Spilsbury visited the bungalow, and out in the back garden began to piece together the remains of Emily Kaye on a table, protected from the eyes of the curious – hundreds of people had gathered at the scene – by a high wall. The police began digging up the garden, searching for the missing limbs and the head. These were never found, and it was thought that Mahon had, as he claimed, destroyed them in the sitting-room fire. Spilsbury was able to establish that Miss Kaye had been about two months pregnant.

On the afternoon of Monday, 5 May, Patrick Mahon, in a grey suit, was taken to Hailsham in Sussex and charged with the murder of Emily Kaye. He replied: 'I've already made a statement. It wasn't murder, as my statement clearly shows.'

Police investigations later that month revealed that Emily Kaye had given him the four £100 notes, presumably to pay in part for their trip abroad and the setting up of a home in South Africa. He had cashed two of the notes at the Bank of England before her death, and one after. The fourth note was thought by the police to have been changed at Plumpton races.

A motive for murder now appeared. Having misled Miss Kaye into thinking that he would marry her, he acquired and spent most of her savings. When she became anxious about the non-realization of his promises – and also became pregnant – he decided to kill her, for she had become a threat to his marriage, his financial solvency and his apparent innocence. He persuaded her to tell her friends that she was engaged to a man called Patterson and that they were going to South Africa to start a new life. She would then conveniently disappear. In his statements he said that *she* was the motivating force in their association, demanding that he leave his wife, that they get married and go abroad. He said that *she* bought the 'engagement' ring and that he never knew she was pregnant.

Probably, if it had not been for Mrs Mahon's discovery of the cloak-room ticket, Miss Kaye would in due course have vanished entirely from the bungalow on The Crumbles and nothing would have connected Mr Waller of Eastbourne with Mr Mahon.

The trial of Patrick Mahon began at the Sussex Assizes in Lewes on Tuesday, 15 July 1924. Mr Justice Avory presided. Sir Henry Curtis Bennett, KC, led for the Crown, and the prisoner was defended by Mr J. D. Cassels, KC, MP. Thousands of people mobbed the court-house and 200 were actually allowed inside.

The Times correspondent wrote: 'The accused appeared to be in much better health than when he appeared at the police court, although showing signs of weariness and fatigue.' In fact he was looking his best: his face bore an artificial tan created, it is said, by tobacco juice; his hair was immaculate, his hands manicured; and he wore a smart, blue, specially tailored seven-guinea suit. He carefully scrutinized the all-male jury as they were sworn in – three were challenged by Mr Cassels and asked to stand down.

The second day of the trial was interrupted by the separate illnesses of two jurors, who had to be replaced. Two new ones were sworn in and the proceedings were recapitulated for their benefit. A third juryman then fainted, and a fourth asked to be excused. So another two jurors were sworn in and the prosecution's case was outlined again before the trial continued.

On the third day, Thursday, Miss Ethel Duncan sobbed hysterically as she took the oath, and when she was asked by the judge to identify the prisoner as the man she had met at Richmond she cried: 'Oh, don't! Please!' and sobbed. When he stood up in the dock for her inspection she stared at him fixedly, then burst into tears. Giving evidence, her voice was almost inaudible.

Sir Bernard Spilsbury followed her. He supported the prosecution's view that Miss Kaye could not have received any fatal injuries from falling on to the coal-scuttle, as the scuttle (a cheap one with insubstantial hollow legs) was undamaged. He did not think that her throat had been cut. But the absence of her head prevented anyone from proving the theory that she had been hit on the head with the axe, and possibly strangled.

Later that afternoon, Mahon himself gave evidence on his own behalf. In telling of his renting of the bungalow he said: 'I promised Miss Kaye that we would go through with this experiment – this love experiment we called it. I thought if I took the bungalow for two months it would kill two birds with one stone. After Miss Kaye had finished – ' The judge interrupted: 'After Miss Kaye had *finished*?' Mahon explained: 'After we had finished our experiment and Miss Kaye had returned, my wife and I could use the bungalow.' Later on he was overcome with emotion when he related how she had attacked him; he wept. Outside the weather was close and sultry. During Mahon's narration of the dismemberment of the body, lightning flashed and there was a clap of thunder. Mahon shuddered and blanched, reminded perhaps of the thunder-storm that had accompanied his burning of the head and limbs.

He was cross-examined for nearly three hours on the Friday morning. When asked by Sir Henry about Miss Kaye's alleged assault on him, Mahon again broke down in tears. Towards the end of Sir Henry's interrogation, Mahon's face ran with sweat. He wiped his eyes repeatedly; he shuddered and seemed about to faint. When he was given a chair he sat on it with his left hand tucked under his right arm; his right hand shook.'

Mr Justice Avory's one-and-a-half hour summing-up was delivered on the morning of Saturday, 19 July. During it Mahon never raised his head; he was quite listless and seemed to be in despair. Found guilty by the jury, he suddenly became animated, making a passionate denouncement of 'the bitterness and unfairness' of the summing-up before he was sentenced to death.

Patrick Mahon was hanged at Wandsworth prison on 9 September 1924.

When Spilsbury arrived at the Officer's House on 4 May, he found DCI Savage using his bare hands to pick up pieces of decomposing flesh. 'Are there no rubber gloves?' he asked, concerned about the risk of infection. There were none. But the Yard, in consultation with Spilsbury and other forensic experts, then devised and assembled a Murder Bag that was henceforth taken to the scene of any such crime.

CHAPTER 22

Norman Thorne

The murder of Elsie Cameron, 1924

Sheer stupidity seems to be a characteristic of most murders – not surprisingly, as murder is seldom the act of a sensible person. But having committed the fatal deed some murderers behave so stupidly that even if not technically insane they would certainly seem to be abnormal. They are careless, they lie, they make a mess of disposing of the body and the evidence, and they cannot resist assisting the police. It sometimes seems they want to be caught, or else cannot believe they ever will be, as if they thought they had put themselves beyond the reach of society and the law.

Elsie Emily Cameron was far from being a typical pretty flapper. A London typist, aged twenty-six, she was small, plain, bespectacled, nervous (even neurotic), and very obstinate. None the less, she was engaged to John Norman Holmes Thorne, a chicken farmer two years younger than she, who lived in a hut on a run-down, muddy smallholding at Crowborough in Sussex.

They had met in 1920 at Kensal Rise Wesleyan church in North London, and although Norman may not have been the brightest boy around she decided he was quite good-looking and better than nothing, for besides being nice and amenable, he was also a Sunday school teacher, attended Band of Hope meetings and concerts, helped to run the local scout group and was involved in all kinds of chapel work. Perhaps more than anything else, he had a certain physical attraction. Elsie began walking out with him and eventually determined to marry him.

Norman was then an electrical engineer with Fiat motors at Wembley. He had been born in Portsmouth in 1902. His mother died when he was seven; his father, who remarried, was an engineer, an overseer and inspector for the Admiralty. In March 1918 Norman joined the Royal Naval Air Service as a mechanic. Stunned by a bomb-blast after he went to Belgium in October 1918 (three weeks before the end of the war), he was demobbed in November the following year and on returning to England became a civilian mechanic. But with thousands of others he was forced to go on the dole in the summer of 1921. Norman, however, was not prepared to put up with this – he was made of sterner stuff – and having bought a field with money from his father (£100), he established the Wesley Poultry Farm, Blackness, Crowborough, Sussex, on 22 August.

To begin with, he used to lodge locally while he built his chicken-runs and huts. At weekends he bicycled back to London. Then, to simplify matters, he turned one of his brooding-houses into a shack for himself, where he set up a sort of home. At this point Elsie began travelling down by train to see him at weekends, staying with local people at night and with Norman during the day.

They became engaged at Christmas 1922.

The following month Elsie was sacked from her job, after being with the same firm for nine years; she was said to be moody and forgetful. Four other jobs followed in fairly quick succession.

But in June 1923 she had something else to occupy her mind. It was about then, as Norman later told the police, that 'we became on intimate terms, that is feeling one another's person and from that it went that I put my person against hers, but in my opinion I did not put it into her. This practice continued on almost all the occasions when Miss Cameron came to the hut. We had previously made up our minds that she should not become pregnant.'

Having given herself to him in this way Elsie, both sexually aroused and frustrated, wrote a long letter to Norman on 28 June, full of passion and repeated endearments like 'Oh my pet – lovey – beloved – dearie – treasure – sweetheart – darling'. She wrote:

> Our courtship is like a fairy-tale and it will end with 'They lived happily ever after' ... Oh my treasure, how I adore you, you mean everything to me, and oh, if only we could get married, Oh pet, let's try and do so this year and manage as I said, Lovey. We can manage in a little hut like yours; your Elsie is quite well now and there is no fear of any children for three or four years ... Oh, my Darling, how I adore you, what you mean to me you cannot realise ... For ever and always. You own true little sweetheart Elsie. PS. Do not forget my weekend letter.

Elsie's brother and sister both married in 1923, but the anniversary of her engagement came and went (she spent Christmas with Norman's neighbours, Mr and Mrs Cosham) without Norman showing any inclination to name the day – understandably, as the chicken-farm was doing such poor business. It was not a success, and Norman was in debt. But Elsie was quite prepared for any sacrifice; love in a hut was after all still love.

Unfortunately, Norman's waning interest was diverted in the spring of 1924 by a simpler, more immediate attraction. For at a local dance that Whitsun he met a jolly young dressmaker, Miss Elizabeth Coldicott (Bessie). He began to walk out with her, and she ventured as far as his shack in September where she had tea with him. Norman found she was warm and understanding and much more fun than Elsie and, casting about for some way of damping his fiancée's ardour, he took her one day to the Wembley Exhibition where they visited the stand of the Alliance of

Honour. Norman, already a member, paid his subscription and persuaded Elsie to join the Women's Section for one shilling. The Alliance was of those who pledged to keep themselves pure in deed as well as words.

By this time Elsie had been out of work for months. Her mental and physical condition, which had never been stable, had begun to deteriorate. She became hysterical and abusive, or deeply depressed and lethargic, where before she had been moodily listless. A doctor diagnosed neurasthenia and prescribed sedative remedies.

At the end of October Elsie stayed in Crowborough for a week. She lodged with the Coshams, and according to Norman they had no sex. Nonetheless towards the end of November, becoming desperate, Elsie wrote to him informing him she was pregnant – he would have to marry her now.

To convince him, and herself, she met him at Groombridge (between Crowborough and Tunbridge Wells) and talked repeatedly of her pregnancy and their forthcoming marriage. She urged him to fix a date for their wedding and to get the banns called at Tunbridge Wells. Norman was somewhat sceptical of Elsie's pregnancy – in fact it was imaginary – and by now he was quite enamoured of Miss Coldicott, whom he was seeing every night between half-past eight and half-past ten, mainly at the shack.

He wrote to Elsie on Tuesday, 25 November, after the Groombridge visit: 'You seem to be taking everything for granted. I shall not be going to Tunbridge Wells this week . . . There are one or two things I haven't told you . . . It concerns someone else . . . I am afraid I am between two fires.'

Elsie replied on 26 November:

My own darling Norman . . . Certainly I take everything for granted, and especially after what you said on Friday, and I shall expect you to go and arrange our marriage as soon as possible. I really do think you might comfort me in your letters . . . This worry is very bad for the baby . . . I feel sick every day and things will soon be noticeable to everybody, and I want to be married before Christmas . . . I really do think an explanation is due to me over all this.

He wrote back the next day:

What I haven't told you is that on certain occasions a girl has been here late at night . . . When you gave in to your nerves again and refused to take interest in life I gave up hope in you and let myself go . . . She thinks I am going to marry her, of course, and I have a strong feeling for her or I shouldn't have done what I have . . .

His clumsy letter destroyed her. She wrote on 28 November:

You have absolutely broken my heart. I never thought you were capable of such deception. You have deceived me, and I gave you myself and all my love . . . You are engaged to me and I have first claim on you . . . Oh Norman, I wouldn't have believed it of you. It's a poor thing for a man to let himself go because his girl has her nerves bad . . . You don't seem to care how I feel. You don't write a single word of love to me, and I have stood by you through all your out of work and farm trouble . . . Well, Norman, I expect you to marry me, and finish with the other girl, and as soon as possible. My baby must have a name, and another thing, I love you in spite of all . . . I have been told in times gone by that 'You can't trust no man,' but oh Norman, I thought you were different . . . For ever and always, your own loving Elsie.

On Sunday, 30 November, Elsie arrived unexpectedly at the chicken-farm before eleven in the morning. She was aggressive and demanding. Who was the other girl? Was she in trouble? Why hadn't he gone to Tunbridge Wells? When were they going to be married? To pacify her, Norman assured her they would get married soon and managed to defer the matter of the date by saying he had to sort that out with his father.

Mollified but still suspicious, Elsie left the farm at 7.50 pm, getting the 8.18 train from Crowborough back to London. Having seen her off, Norman hurried back to the farm, where Bessie Coldicott duly arrived after half-past eight. He told her about his plight; she consoled him and was sympathetic.

Three days later, on Wednesday, 3 December, Norman's father called at the hut in response to a letter from his son. They discussed his financial problems and his fiancée. Mr Thorne suggested that Norman, if he had doubts about the pregnancy, should wait until after Christmas before committing himself to any marriage.

Norman wrote a note to Elsie saying his father had been to the farm. On receiving it Elsie made up her mind: she decided to force the issue. As far as she was concerned she was practically married to Norman already, so she might as well burn all her boats and go and live with him.

On Friday, 5 December, she had her hair done in a new style. She was cheerful, according to a female lodger living in her parents' home, and when she left the house, 86 Clifford Gardens, Kensal Rise, about 2 pm, she was wearing a green knitted dress, a new jumper and new shoes. She set off for Victoria station carrying an attaché case containing no underwear and nothing but two pairs of shoes, toiletries, and a baby's frock.

All she had when she walked from Crowborough station towards the farm was a penny-halfpenny in her purse, and an iron resolve.

Five days later her father, a commercial traveller and a Scot, sent a telegram to the chicken-farm early on 10 December – 'Elsie left Friday have heard no news has she arrived reply.' Norman's answer came by return – 'Not here open letters cannot understand'.

Mr Donald Cameron waited a day then informed the police about his daughter's disappearance.

On 12 December PC Beck visited the farm and was given a photo of Elsie by her helpful fiancé. The following day Norman called at Crowborough police station, eager and anxious to help. He gave them the following account of his movements around the time that Elsie disappeared.

He said that on the actual day of her disappearance he cycled to Tunbridge Wells about 1.30 pm, bought some shoes and a chess-set. Returning home about 3.45 pm he fed his fowls and got milk from the Coshams. He then had his tea. He was in the shack, he said, from about 5 pm to 9.45, when he went to Crowborough station to meet Miss Coldicott and her mother; they had been to Brighton for the day and he had arranged to meet them on their return and escort them home from the station. He did so and was back in his shack about 11.30 pm. On Saturday, 6 December, he went to Groombridge station, he said, expecting to meet Elsie – she had written to him, he said, asking him to meet her there. On finding no sign of Elsie at the station he got the next train to Tunbridge Wells, where he did some shopping and then came home. As usual about tea-time he collected some milk from the Coshams, and learning from them that a party at their house that night had been cancelled, he went instead to the cinema with Miss Coldicott. The next day he wrote to Miss Cameron – 'My own darling Elsie . . . Well, where did you get to yesterday? . . .'

The police were able to confirm much of this. But they also discovered that Elsie, carrying her attaché case, had been seen by two homeward-plodding flower-growers, Bert and George: she had been walking purposefully along a road that passed the chicken-farm at about 5.15 pm on the 5th.

Meanwhile, Norman – 'I want to help all I can' – was showing policemen and reporters around the farm, inviting them into the shack (11 ft 8 ins by 7 ft 5 ins) and guiding them about the chicken-runs. He talked freely with the reporters, posing for photographs with his dog and among his chickens. 'What about here?' he asked. 'Feeding the chickens?' – and was snapped in the very chicken-run under which Elsie was buried.

Questioned again by the police, Norman, though as helpful as ever, was definite – Elsie Cameron had never arrived at the farm – the horticulturists were mistaken.

On New Year's Eve he wrote to Bessie:

My darling Bessie. Looking back over the last few months I perceive many changes in my life . . . I have been in love twice . . . the second was with Elsie . . . [She] had a strange disposition and strange parents . . . They tried to force her on me . . . Honour bright darling, I never felt for any girl as I do for you . . . No one knows the struggle that has raged within, but dearest of pals, you have pulled me through. Love, Honour, Bessie – my watchwords for 25 . . .

A month had passed since Elsie disappeared, but the local police were still doggedly pursuing their enquiries.

At the beginning of January they made a routine call on one of Norman's neighbours, Mrs Annie Price, who, when asked, said she had actually seen Elsie walk through the chicken-farm gate on 5 December about 5.15 pm.

Scotland Yard were called in by the Sussex police, and before long Chief Inspector Gillan of the Yard decided he had no option but to arrest Norman Thorne on suspicion of having had something to do with Elsie's disappearance or death.

At 3.30 pm, on 14 January 1925, he was picked up at the farm by CI Gillan and detained at Crowborough police station. When the police arrived at the shack Norman was sitting at a table with a letter to Bessie in front of him, which suggested that they should not see each other for a while. While he was in the police station the farm buildings were searched, and an Oxo-cube tin, discovered in a tool-shed, was found to contain Elsie's wrist-watch (damaged), some jewellery and a bracelet. Meanwhile the police, armed with spades and shovels, had begun to dig.

They struck lucky the very next day. At 8.25 am on a cold, wet morning, Elsie's sodden attaché case was unearthed by PC Philpott. Among its contents were her broken glasses.

At 9.30 am, at Crowborough police station, CI Gillan told Norman he might be charged with murder, if and when they found her body. The police assumed he had buried it somewhere on the one-acre farm.

All day Norman sat in a cell thinking, while the police continued to dig. At 8 pm he said: 'I wish to tell you the truth of what happened . . . ' He then made a statement. He said he didn't kill her, but he knew where her body was buried.

He was, he said, having tea when Elsie arrived, much to his surprise. She was belligerent, he said, but when she calmed down she joined him in a cup of tea and had some bread and butter. He said: 'I asked her why she had come down without having written and where she intended to sleep. She replied that she intended sleeping in the hut; furthermore, she also stated she intended stopping until she was married.' At about 7.30 pm he went to the Coshams, to see whether they would put her up for the night. But they were out. On his return to the hut there was an argument about his association with Miss Coldicott and about his unfaithfulness. They had some supper. About 9.30 pm, he said, he told her he had to go to the station to meet the Coldicotts. 'She protested . . . and she suggested that we should go to bed. I again refused . . . and told her to go to bed.' He departed at quarter to ten. 'She remained in the hut with the dog . . . When I returned about half-past eleven, the dog came down to meet me. When I opened the hut door I saw Miss Cameron hanging from a beam by a piece of cord as used for the washing-line. I cut the cord and laid her on the bed. She was dead. I then put out the lights. She had her frock off and her hair was down. I laid across the table for about an hour. I was about to go to Doctor Turle and knock up someone to go for the police and I realized the position I was in . . . I got my hacksaw and sawed off her legs, and the head, by the glow of the fire.'

The head with its new hair-do he crammed into a biscuit tin, and the other pieces were wrapped in newspapers, all being buried in the chicken-run in which he kept his Leghorns – 'the first pen from the gate'.

It was there, at 10.46 pm, after Norman had completed his statement, that the police discovered the remains of Elsie Cameron.

Two days later Sir Bernard Spilsbury, who had been knighted the year before, examined the decomposing body, and on 26 January it was reburied in Willesden.

But a month later the remains were exhumed on Norman's insistence: he was sure the mark of the rope, which Spilsbury had failed to find, must be visible on Elsie's neck. He had *seen* such a mark, he said.

When her body was finally reburied, he sent a wreath saying: 'Till we meet again.'

Norman Thorne was charged with the murder of Elsie Cameron and sent for trial at Lewes Assizes on 4 March 1925. The judge was Mr Justice Finlay. Thorne was defended by Mr J. D. Cassels, KC; Sir Henry Curtis Bennet led for the Crown.

The medical experts disagreed about the cause of Elsie's death. She seemed to have died from shock. Spilsbury, for the prosecution, said there were several bruises and injuries on her head and body, all caused shortly before her death, and no evidence of hanging. He also said that a 'crushing blow' on her forehead could conceivably have been caused by one of the Indian clubs found outside the hut. The experts agreed, however, that she had died one and a half to two hours after eating a light meal and was dismembered six to seven hours after her death.

The defence's chief medical expert, of the three who were called, was an extrovert Irishman, Dr Robert Brontë. He had examined the corpse a month *after* Spilsbury, and now said that creases on the neck might have been made by a rope. Spilsbury said the marks were naturally found on most female necks. The police said there were no traces of any rope-markings on the only wooden beams in the hut, across its centre – 'The upper beam was very dusty ... The lower beam was entirely free from dust.' There were hats on the lower beam, and Norman told the court, while giving evidence and speaking of the cord that Elsie had used to hang herself – 'I believe it was tied around some of the paper I used to keep the dust off my hats.'

He also said about her unexpected arrival – 'She seemed to be highly strung' – and of her death – 'I realized the awful end that neurasthenia had brought to her.'

Her glasses were on the table, he added, along with her brooch, bracelet and hairpins. He was unable to say how her watch and glasses were damaged and why he had burnt her dress and jumper. Mr Justice Finlay enquired: 'You never thought of getting a doctor, and you did not get one?' To which the answer was 'No.'

The accused also said, explaining his actions, that he was 'trying to build up evidence that I knew nothing about Miss Cameron's death ... I had gone so far and I could not stop. One lie meant another ...'

On the night of Elsie's death, however it happened, he may have been fatally influenced by his apparent interest in and knowledge of the grisly murder that had occurred earlier that same year less than twenty miles away. In April another determined and possessive shorthand typist, Emily Kaye, had been murdered by her lover, Patrick Mahon. He had also been tried at Lewes Assizes, and was convicted largely through the forensic evidence of Sir Bernard Spilsbury. Mahon had been hanged on 9 September 1924, almost three months to the day before Elsie Cameron's death.

Newspaper cuttings about the Mahon case were discovered in Thorne's hut. The idea of dismembering Elsie's body probably came from them, teaching him how to profit (as he thought) from Mahon's mistakes.

Norman Thorne was found guilty of Elsie Cameron's murder and sentenced to death.

The next day, 17 March, he wrote to 'Dad and Mother' about the 'extraordinary verdict . . . They say a man has to be *proved* guilty; in what way was it proved against me? . . . What happened while I was out I do not know.'

An appeal was rejected, although he expected it to succeed. He was taken from the Appeal Court crying: 'It isn't fair! I didn't do it.'

He was hanged in Wandsworth prison on 22 April 1925, on what would have been Elsie's twenty-seventh birthday.

The day before this he wrote a last letter to his parents: 'The world seems bright and beautiful, but how much better must be the Kingdom of Heaven . . . A flash and all is finished, *no*, not finished, but just starting; and I shall wait for you, just as others are waiting for me. By Christ I am free from all sin; all forgiven, I go to Him. All's well. With all my love, your loving son, Norman.'

Perhaps he told the truth – that Elsie stage-managed her death, timing it to coincide with his return so that he might save her. This could account for the lack of marks of hanging – if she stepped off a chair or the bed as he opened the door. Perhaps she bungled it somehow and was shocked to death by the experience. Her injuries may have been caused by his clumsy manoeuvres when he cut her down – they certainly happened near the time of her death. Or they may have been caused by his fist during some violent row, in which he struck her several times and threw her out of the hut. Perhaps, thus rejected and despised, she died of shock, heart-broken.

In any event, Thorne would probably never have been hanged if he had been wholly honest from the start about the manner of Elsie's death, however it happened, if he had not dismembered her body, if he had not concealed it in the ground, and if he had not continuously lied, so persistently and for so long.

CHAPTER 23

John Robinson

The murder of Minnie Bonati, 1927

Dismemberment of a murdered person never inclines a judge of jury towards a tolerant view of the murderer. Not only is this a clear attempt to thwart justice by hiding the body and thus the evidence, but it also shows disrespect and is, as it were, double murder. Within three and a half years of the Mahon and Thorne dissections of their lady-loves, John Robinson was at it himself, believing no doubt that it was the only way to remove a body from his premises, which happened to be opposite a police station. Surely there have not been many times that murder has been committed so close to the eyes of the law.

On Friday, 6 May 1927, a man with a soldierly bearing deposited a large black trunk in the left luggage office at Charing Cross railway station. It had a rounded top and was made of wicker-work, the whole encased in black American cloth and bound with a wide strap. He urged that the trunk be carefully handled and departed in the taxi in which he and the trunk had arrived. The left luggage attendant on duty the following Monday noticed an offensive smell coming from the trunk. A policeman was sent for and the trunk was opened.

Inside it, roughly parcelled in brown paper and tied with string, were five portions of a woman – her limbs had been severed at each shoulder and hip-joint and the sections wrapped in items of female clothing, towels and a duster, the latter being wound around her head. A police surgeon was actually called to certify that the woman was dead before the bits of her body were removed to a mortuary.

The Home Office pathologist, Sir Bernard Spilsbury, pieced the body together and concluded that several bruises on the woman's forehead, stomach, back and limbs had been caused before she died. The cause of her death, he decided, was asphyxia, resulting from pressure on her mouth and nostrils while she was unconscious. She had been dead, he deduced, for about a week, and when alive had been short and stout and about thirty-five years old.

A pair of black shoes and a handbag were also found in the trunk. Some of the clothing was marked; two items bore laundry marks (581 and 447) and a pair of knickers carried a tab marked 'P. HOLT'.

Initials were painted on the trunk itself – FA – and a label read 'F

AUSTIN to ST LENARDS.' The initials and the name were later found to be blameless and to have no connection with the case. But the police were now checking the other clues.

Within twenty-four hours the knickers and the laundry-marks were traced to a Mrs Holt, who lived in Chelsea and was very much alive. The woman who was likely to have purloined her clothing must have been in Mrs Holt's employment, and the police now set about checking the whereabouts of ten female servants employed by Mrs Holt in the past two years. All but one were accounted for, and to clinch the matter the genteel employer was asked to identify the severed head. She did. The dead woman was a Mrs Rolls.

A *Mr* Rolls was soon found, but it transpired he was not her husband – she had merely lived with him for a time. Her real but estranged husband turned out to be an Italian waiter called Bonati, who was soon cleared of suspicion. The victim's real married name was Mrs Minnie Alice Bonati; her maiden name was Budd. She was thirty-six, on the game, it was said, and had last been seen alive in Sydney Street, Chelsea between 3.45 and 4 pm on Wednesday, 4 May.

In the meantime, photographs of the trunk had appeared in the newspapers under lurid headlines and with satisfying results. A Brixton Road dealer in second-hand luggage told the police he had sold the trunk for 12s 6d on or soon after 4 May to a dark man with a small moustache: a man of average height, well-dressed, well-spoken, a military sort of man, who looked as if he might have served in India.

A shoeblack produced the left-luggage receipt, which he had happened to pick up in the station forecourt after seeing it thrown out of a taxi window as the taxi left the station. The ticket was numbered, and by tracing the owner of the ticket issued immediately *before* it the police established that the black trunk had been deposited in the left luggage office soon after 1.50 pm on Friday, 6 May.

Then the taxi-driver concerned came forward with information about his passenger and the trunk. He said that some time after 1 pm on the Friday he had taken two young men from the Royal Automobile Club in Pall Mall to the police station in Rochester Row, SW1, at the back of the Roman Catholic Westminster Cathedral. The charge-sheet at the station revealed that the two men had been summonsed for motoring offences and arrived in the station at 1.35 pm. After dropping his passengers, the taxi-driver was hailed by a gentleman standing in the doorway of an office block across the street, and assisted him in carrying a heavy trunk from the building, across the pavement and into the cab. When he commented on the trunk's weight, the cabbie was told that it was full of books. His destination was Charing Cross station (although Victoria station was much nearer) and there the trunk, which the taxi-driver identified, was left after being taken to the left luggage office by a station porter.

The office block in Rochester Row was identified as No. 86, which was now viewed with considerable interest by the police in their premises diagonally opposite.

Most of 86 Rochester Row was occupied by a firm of solicitors. But one of the occupants of a seedy two-roomed, second-floor office overlooking the street was missing. He turned out to be a struggling estate agent, who had written on 9 May to his landlord saying he was moving out because, frankly, he was broke. His name was John Robinson. His office was named: *Edwards and Co., Business Transfer Agents.*

Born at Leigh in Lancashire, young Robinson had been taken from school at the age of twelve and sent to work. Over the years he had worked variously as an errand-boy for the Co-op, as a clerk, a tram-conductor, a bartender – and a butcher's assistant. He married in 1911 and his first wife bore him four children. His second wife was a girl from Tasmania.

Nothing incriminating was found in his office in Rochester Row and not a speck of blood. However, a window-pane was cracked and the fireplace fender was found to be broken and an iron bar to be detachable.

Mr Robinson's clerk, Miss Moore, was traced. She said that on 4 May Mr Robinson had returned about 3 pm to the office, obviously drunk, with a man in military uniform. Alarmed by this, no doubt by something that was said or done, she left the office early at 3.30 pm and never returned.

The police visited John Robinson's lodgings in Kennington. But he had gone from there without leaving a forwarding address. However – and this was another stroke of luck for the police – a telegram addressed to 'Robinson, Greyhound Hotel, Hammersmith' had been returned to his lodgings, addressee unknown, and this led them to the Greyhound Hotel where they found, not Robinson, but *Mrs* Robinson, who worked there. The telegram had been returned to the sender by a new maid ignorant of Mrs Robinson's presence in the hotel. She in turn was ignorant of the sorry fact that she was not Mr Robinson's wife, for he had another, his first.

She agreed to co-operate with the police, and when she went to meet Robinson at his request on Thursday, 19 May, at a pub, the Elephant and Castle in Walworth, Chief Inspector George Cornish went with the aggrieved woman.

John Robinson, aged thirty-six, was quite amenable to being interviewed at the Yard that evening and to taking part in an identity parade. Here he was very lucky. For neither the taxi-driver, the station porter nor the trunk-dealer recognized him. As he naturally denied any knowledge of his crime, of buying the trunk, or of Mrs Bonati, he was released.

There was a conference at Scotland Yard on 21 May, in which all the evidence was reviewed. Chief Inspector Cornish decided that the blood-stained and grimy duster should be washed. His hunch proved correct, for a thin tab on the hem was revealed bearing the word 'GREYHOUND'.

In the meantime, a fresh scouring of Robinson's office in Rochester Row produced a blood-stained match: it had been caught in the wicker-work of a waste-paper basket.

Robinson was picked up at his lodging on 23 May and brought back to the Yard. Now his luck deserted him. For fearing perhaps that the police knew more than they did – or possiby overwhelmed by a feeling of guilt – he elected to make a statement. He said: 'I realize this is serious . . . I met her at Victoria and took her to my office. I want to tell you all about it. I done it and cut her up.'

His story was that on 4 May, about 4.15 pm in the afternoon, he was accosted by Mrs Bonati at Victoria Station. Back in his second-floor office she asked him for money but he refused to give her any, saying he had none. She became abusive and made as if to strike him. He shoved her away and she fell, hitting her head on a coal-scuttle. Having thus silenced her – and perhaps it was the presence of the police station across the road that made him fearful of the noise she made – he left the office. He said he thought she was only dazed and would go away when she recovered. But when he returned the following morning, he said, she still lay on the carpet, face down. How was he to get rid of her?

Perhaps he remembered Mahon and Thorne. It seems more than coincidence that led him to the very shop in Victoria Street where Mahon had bought a carving-knife and a saw. Here Robinson merely purchased a knife. Then, in that shabby office of his, under the eyes of the law, he set about dismembering Minnie Bonati.

Having parcelled up her remains in brown paper after wrapping them in her own clothes, in the duster and a towel, he went away, no doubt exhausted. Doggedly he returned to the office on the following morning. He brought a trunk with him and travelled by omnibus, and the bus conductor helped him carry the trunk up the stairs to the top deck. Having got off the bus in Vauxhall Bridge Road about 10 am, he dragged the trunk along Rochester Row and up the stairs to his office. Here he loaded the trunk with the parcelled portions of Mrs Bonati, throwing her shoes and her handbag into the trunk as well, and then dragged it out on to the landing. Perhaps he also did some scrubbing and cleaning of the premises to ensure that no sign of Mrs Bonati's visit remained.

About noon his labours came to an end, and in need of a drink he went out to a local pub, where he fell into conversation with a Mr Judd. They chatted about property. Robinson told Mr Judd about a flat which he had to let and the two men returned to the office, where Judd was furnished with the flat's particulars. He was then asked if he would mind giving Robinson a hand with the trunk and helped him take it downstairs to the hall. Judd obliged. The trunk was very heavy. 'Are you travelling in lead?' he puffed. 'No, I'm taking some books to the country,' Robinson replied.

A few minutes later Robinson hailed the taxi that had just stopped under the blue lamp of the police station. It seems incredible that he could behave so matter-of-factly and yet be so stupid. For after having acted with such deliberation and care that morning and the day before, he now publicly associated himself with the trunk and left it where it was bound to be discovered before long. The knife, as he later showed the police, was buried under a hawthorn tree on Clapham Common.

The trial of John Robinson began at the Old Bailey on Monday, 11 July. The judge was Mr Justice Swift. Mr Percival Clarke led for the Crown, assisted by Mr Christmas Humphreys. Robinson was defended by Mr Lawrence Vine.

Robinson himself gave evidence, in which he admitted more or less everything, except an intention to kill. When asked why he did not go to the police, he said: 'Because I was in a blue funk and did not know what to do.'

Dr Brontë was called by the defence to combat Sir Bernard Spilsbury's evidence. Spilsbury had said, and was supported by the police surgeon who did the post-mortem, that the bruises on Mrs Bonati had been caused by direct blows and pressure, probably from a knee; congestion in the lungs showed that she had lain on her back for some time; no coal-gas poisoning, heart disease or epilepsy was involved; she had been asphyxiated after a violent assault; and a cushion found in the office seemed the most likely object to have been used to silence her cries. Brontë, supporting Robinson's contention that on returning to the office he had found Mrs Bonati face-down on the floor, suggested that she could have suffocated with her face in the folds of the carpet (which was threadbare), or in the crook of her elbow. He disputed Spilsbury's timing of the bruises, saying they could have been caused several hours before death, before she and Robinson met.

Another witness for the defence was the dead woman's former husband, Mr Frederick Rolls, who said Minnie Bonati was much addicted to drink and was sometimes very violent – she had attacked him many times.

The jury were not convinced by Dr Brontë's vigorous assumptions, nor was the judge impressed. As in Thorne's case, the judge asked the accused why he did not summon help and inform the police when he found the woman dead in his room. Robinson replied: 'I did not look at in that light.'

After being out for an hour the jury returned a verdict of 'Guilty'. John Robinson was sentenced to death on Wednesday, 13 July and hanged at Pentonville prison on 12 August 1927.

CHAPTER 24

Browne and Kennedy

The murder of PC Gutteridge, 1927

Apart from soldiers in wartime, the men on public duty most likely to be killed are policemen. Unarmed, unless in special circumstances, they have little defence against the law-breakers they attempt to apprehend in the execution of their duties.

At dawn on Tuesday, 27 September 1927, a post office worker called Bill Ward was driving north across Essex from Romford to Abridge, delivering mail. He stopped at Havering and Stapleford Abbotts. His next port of call was Stapleford Tawney. Just before six o'clock, as he approached Howe Green, he came to a right-hand bend in the road on a slight incline and on rounding the bend he saw a man propped up against the opposite bank with his legs sticking out into the road.

Mr Ward stopped his car and investigated. A thick trail of blood led across the road to where the body lay; it was that of a uniformed and caped policeman. His helmet lay near him, as did a pocket-book. A pencil was still clutched in his right hand. Despite the fact that the policeman's head was a bloody mask, Mr Ward recognized the dead man as PC George Gutteridge.

Ward ran up the road to Rose Cottage. His knocking awakened Alfred Perritt, an insurance agent, who dressed and went back to the body with Ward. Mr Perritt, picking up the feet, swung the body round so that it lay parallel to the hedge and was not in danger of being run over. Next on the scene was the driver of a country bus. Ward drove on to Stapleford Tawney, from where he telephoned Romford police station.

By about quarter to eight Detective Inspector Crockford arrived and saw that PC Gutteridge had been shot in the face. The dead man seemed to have been taken completely by surprise as he was about to make a note in his pocket-book: his truncheon was in its place at his side, his torch was in a pocket. His whistle hung loose, however, outside his tunic.

Dr Robert Woodhouse was called out from Romford by nine o'clock and surmised that the murdered policeman had been dead for four or five hours. The body was removed to a cart-shed at the Royal Oak public-house and taken the following morning to Romford mortuary, where Dr Woodhouse made a post-mortem examination. He found that PC Gutteridge had been shot four times at close range, twice through the left cheek, near the ear – and once in each eye.

PC Gutteridge had lived with his wife, Rose, at Stapleford Abbotts. He had been out on night patrols on the 26th and 27th, covering his beat on foot. It had been his custom and duty to meet up with another policeman, PC Taylor, for a conference about 3 am outside Grove House at Howe Green. Taylor was a little late in the early hours of the 27th and when he turned up at the rendezvous the two men stood chatting in the quiet night until 3.25 am. 'It was not an exceptionally dark night,' said PC Taylor. 'But it was fairly dark. There was a fog, or what I would describe as a summer mist, in certain of the lower places . . . But not on the high hill.' Taylor was home and in bed by half-past four. Gutteridge set off homewards along the Ongar–Romford road, passing Rose Cottage and Howe Green and walking downhill as the road turned left. As he approached this bend a car came speeding towards him.

Less than an hour before this, ten miles to the east, a blue four-seater Morris-Cowley car, TW 6120, had been stolen from the garage of Dr Edward Lovell's house in London Road, Billericay. He had put it away about 7.30 pm on Monday the 26th and had locked the garage door, leaving two cases of surgical instruments and dressings and a small case with some drugs inside the car. The following morning, after breakfast, he found the garage door had been forced and the car had gone. Later, two neighbours remembered a car being started up about half-past two and passing with headlights ablaze down the Mountnessing Road. Dr Lovell reported the theft of his car to the police and was able to tell them that the mileometer must have read about 6640.9 when the car was stolen.

The Morris had already been spotted forty-two miles away in South London, in a narrow passage behind 21 Faxley Road, Brixton.

Albert McDougall, a crippled clerk, left that address by the back door at about half-past seven on his way to work. 'It was a very cold morning,' he said, 'with a mist.' He edged around the car, and happening to touch it 'on account of my disability,' noticed that the radiator was 'very warm'. When he returned home about 5.50 pm the car was still there. He noticed that he nearside mudguard had been torn off, and after some thought reported his find to a policeman he chanced to find in Brixton Road. PC Alfred Edmonds casually inspected the car – it was empty of any cases – and telephoned Brixton police station.

About 6.45 pm Sergeant Hearn arrived, and as it was now dark he drove the car to the police station yard, where he and DC Hawkyard examined it by the light of a torch. They now knew, having checked the registration number, that it was Dr Lovell's stolen car and had come from Essex. They discovered an empty cartridge case under the front nearside seat, marked on the cap RLIV, indicating it was a Mark IV made at the Royal Laboratory in Woolwich Arsenal – a type of flat-nosed bullet that had been issued to the British Expeditionary Force in 1914. It was later seen to have been scarred by a fault in the breech-block of the gun that had fired it. The two policemen also discovered bloodstains on the running-board by the driver's door. The mileometer read 6684.3.

The distance frm Dr Lovell's house to Brixton police station, Faxley Road, was later found to be about forty-two miles.

There were no further developments for four months, although hundreds of policemen were employed in a determined hunt to find the killer of PC Gutteridge.

The murder weapon had been a Webley revolver, according to the expert gunsmith Robert Churchill, and two Webleys were found in the mud of the Thames. But it was proved that neither had fired the cartridge found in the car, for neither left the same small mark on the cartridge cases of test bullets fired by Mr Churchill. Meanwhile, a watchful eye was kept on known car thieves and associated criminals in South London.

One of these suspects was Frederick Guy Browne. His real name was probably Leo Brown. Aged forty-six, he was described as a 'tall (5 ft 7 ins), well-built, dark-complexioned man with a heavy moustache' and grey eyes. A strong, powerful man, born in Catford in 1881, he was a very capable mechanic, was easily provoked to anger and as easily assuaged. He suffered from complex feelings of resentment against society and the law – not surprisingly, as he had been in and out of jail (four sentences of hard labour and four years' penal servitude) since the age of twenty-nine, when he had been living with his widowed mother in Eynsham, repairing bicycles by day and stealing them at night.

His first conviction was in 1910 for carrying firearms. In 1915 he married a cook-housekeeper called Caroline; they had a daughter and settled in Clapham. 'With all his faults,' said Mrs Browne, 'my husband has been decent to me.' Indeed he was not a typical ruffian, being a teetotaller, a non-smoker, and faithful to his wife. In March 1917 he joined the Royal Engineers, serving in the Railway Operating Department; he never went overseas. 'I was never a soldier,' he said. 'I was a worker in khaki.' Convicted for stealing a motor-cycle in Petersfield, he was discharged from the army on 5 November 1918 – 'character, indifferent' – after which he worked in garages in Clapham and Essex, stealing and altering cars and fraudulently claiming the insurance on them. For this he was arrested with others on Christmas Eve 1923 and sentenced at the Old Bailey on 20 February 1924 to four years' penal servitude.

He became too violent for Parkhurst prison and was eventually moved to Dartmoor. There he met and made friends with Fred Counter, who was serving three years for burglary. He was released in March 1927.

In June, Browne rented what had been a milk-yard next to the Globe cinema in Lavender Hill and turned it into a garage/repair-yard/paint-shop, also called the Globe, at 7a Northcote Road. 'I profess to be a motor-engineer,' said Brown in court. 'And my instruments, I say, are far different to the average garage man; that is to say, I do better-class work, finer things.' There were spaces for seven cars, a fitter's shop, and a primitive office at the back in which there was also a bed. Here slept a man employed to keep the books and do odd jobs, of whom Browne said: 'I got him from the Salvation Army to give him a start.' This was forty-two-year-old Pat Kennedy.

They had probably already met, in Dartmoor jail. Kennedy, whose Christian names were either Patrick Michael or William Henry, was born in Ayrshire in 1895. His parents were Irish and he retained an Irish accent all his life. Trained as a compositor, he worked mainly in Liverpool, where in 1911 his first conviction (for indecent exposure) earned him two months' hard labour. Before that, he was a teenage soldier in South Africa from 1902 to 1903, and for the next eight years served with the Loyal North Lancashire Regiment as William Herbert, ending as a Lance-Corporal ('character, indifferent'). Other fines and convictions soon followed the first one: for theft, for being drunk and disorderly, for loitering, again for indecent exposure, for house breaking and larceny. For the last offence he was sentenced to three years' penal servitude. On his release in April 1916 he enlisted in the Hussars, deserted, enlisted in the King's Liverpool Regiment, deserted, rejoined the King's under a different name and was discharged with ignominy. His petty criminal career continued from 1920 to 1927. He was hardly ever out of prison, doing time as before for theft, indecent exposure and burglary.

In 1927, the Discharged Prisoners' Association got him a job on a farm in Cheshire. He was there when he received a letter from Fred Browne.

Said Kennedy later: 'He invited me to come down and act as manager. He said he would probably have a number of boys under him later, and that he would want me to look after them whilst he was away on repair jobs. He said he could not offer me much money at first, but it would cost me nothing for board and lodgings, as I could live at the garage. He sent me my fare, exact amount, and I borrowed ten shillings ... My duties consisted of attending to correspondence, keeping the books, making and dealing with accounts. The man Fred Browne was also sleeping on the premises at the time.'

Mrs Browne was still in service then. A handyman, John Dyson, came to work at the garage in August for 25s a week, and Curly Billy, aged twelve, helped here and there.

Business prospered, and on Saturday, 24 September, Browne and his wife rented two rooms in 33a Sisters Avenue, Lavender Hill. Mrs Brown later told the court: 'Occasionally, if anyone was coming into the garage late, so as to not disturb me he slept in the garage.' But, she said, on the night of 26 September 'he returned from work between nine and ten that night ... He was at home all night.'

Kennedy told the police a different story, in a very carefully considered and lengthy statement which he made after his arrest.

'I well remember the day of 26th September,' he said, 'Browne suggested that I should accompany him to Billericay, to assist him in stealing a Riley car at the end of the High Street, away from the station.' They went there by train from Liverpool Street station, arriving about 8 pm. They hung about waiting until people went to bed. But Browne was unnerved and deflected from his purpose of taking the Riley from its garage by the barking of a dog. He told Kennedy: 'We'll try somewhere else.' They walked off down the road – both were wearing overcoats and trilby hats – and at the other end of the village they came to Dr Lovell's house, which had a garage. They waited in a field until well after midnight. Then Browne forced the doors of the garage. Inside was a Morris-Cowley with plenty of petrol in the tank. They pushed it down the gravelled drive on to the road and then for another hundred yards along the road before getting in, Browne in the driver's seat, Kennedy beside him. The car started noisily and they raced away, avoiding the main roads, having to check sign-posts as they drove westwards through country lanes, heading back to London. They were on a road leading to Ongar when a man by a bank ahead of them flashed a light as a signal for them to stop.

'We drove on,' said Kennedy, 'and then I heard a police whistle and told Browne to stop. He did so quite willingly, and when the person came up we saw it was a policeman ... He came up close to the car and stood near Browne and asked him where he was going and where he came from. Browne told him we came from Lea Bridge Road garage, and had ben out to do some repairs. The policeman then asked him if he had a card. Browne said "No." The policeman then again asked him where he came from and Browne stammered in his answer, and the policeman said: "Is the car yours?" I then said: "No – the car is mine." The policeman flashed his light in both our faces, and was at this time standing close to the running-board on the offside.' PC Gutteridge could also see the occupants by the dim light from the dash-board; being six feet tall he had to stoop to talk to them. 'He then asked me if I knew the number of the car and Browne said: "You'll see it on the front of the car." The policeman said: "I know the number, but do you?" I said: "Yes, I can give you the number," and said: "TW6120". He said: "Very well, I'll take particulars," put his torch back in his pocket, pulled out his notebook, and was in the act of writing when I heard a report, quickly followed by another one. I saw the policeman stagger back and fall over by the bank at the hedge. I said to Browne: "What have you done?" and then saw he had a large Webley revolver in his hand. He said: "Get out quick." I immediately got out and went round to the policeman, who was lying on his back, and Brown came over and said: "I'll finish the bugger," and I said: "For God's sake don't shoot any more – the man's dying," as he was groaning. The policeman's eyes were open, and Browne, addressing him, said: "What are you looking at me like that for?" and, stooping down, shot him at close range through both eyes.'

They returned to the car, driving on into London. Browne told Kennedy to reload the revolver, and in his excitement Kennedy dropped a spent cartridge. The other three he threw out of his window. Hitting a patch of fog, Browne smashed the car into a tree, sheering off the nearside mudguard. The car was abandoned about 5.30 am in Brixton, and laden with the doctor's cases, the pair returned by tram to the Globe garage, where 'business carried on as usual'.

Kennedy had moments of panic, wanting to flee when he read accounts of the murder in the papers. Browne told him: 'You'll stop here and face it out with me.' Kennedy said later that Brown also threatened him with a gun.

But after two months had passed Browne must have thought they were safe, and Kennedy, whose drinking habits had begun to distress the older man, was allowed to go. Said Browne: 'He is a persistent drunkard. I tried all I could – I kept him short of money. I watched him from half-past nine to ten at night, and I could not stop him from drink, and I gave him the sack.' On 17 December Browne drove Kennedy to Euston station, where Kennedy got on a train for Liverpool.

He remained in West Kirby until 13 January 1928 when he returned to London with a woman whom he married five days later.

In the meantime Browne had gone on a binge of burglary, theft and stealing cars, making eight such criminal forays that winter with other villains, starting in October. Robbing railway station offices became a speciality.

One of the cars he stole, a Vauxhall that was taken in Tooting in November, was sold a few days later by Browne to a butcher in Sheffield, Benjamin Stow, who gave him £100 and a grey Angus-Sanderson car, CW 3291, in part exchange. Browne used the car to drive down to Devon in the New Year. 'I do a lot of driving,' said Browne. 'I do thousands of miles. I do more miles than the average man, because the average man will stop at night to put up and garage and I do not. I keep straight on.'

In Devon he picked up Fred Counter, who had been released from Dartmoor on Friday, 20 January. Browne, who intended to employ Counter in the garage, had dressed himself up as a chauffeur in a blue coat and a peaked cap. He drove Counter the two hundred miles back to London, dropping him off near New Scotland Yard, where Counter had to report to the Convict Registration Office. This done, Browne returned to his garage near Clapham Junction about 7.50 pm. The police, having traced the stolen Vauxhall car by now, were waiting for him in force.

The police version of what happened next, as related in court with the use of notebooks, was generally stilted and stiff. Browne was presented as a dangerous thug and the police as stern and silent. Browne's version, substantially the same, is far more lively and more likely.

'I went into the garage,' he said, 'and saw a light in there, and found Mrs Browne there. She said: "I thought you would be back soon," and I said: "I've brought the man's luggage." And I went out to get the luggage – that was a big case and a small case – and I put it in the office. I started talking to my wife, and – well, in rushed a man who was – I will tell you it was a detective. And behind him rushed a lot more.' DS Miller reported: 'I entered the inner office belonging to the garage with Inspector Barker, and I was present when Inspector Barker arrested Browne and searched him.' *Inspector Barker*: 'He seemed to be boiling inwardly, holding himself in . . . He went pale and gripped his hands tightly together, as though he was trying to master his feelings.' *Browne*: 'I really do not know what happened, because I had my back to him, but anyhow he caught hold of me and said: "I am going to charge you with stealing a Vauxhall car." I said: "I know nothing about a Vauxhall car," and that is all I troubled.' *Inspector Barker*: 'He said: "What do I know about stealing a car?"' *Browne*: 'Then he went on to explain that I got a Vauxhall car and sold it, and then I knew the car he was referring to was a car I sold to a butcher at

Sheffield. I then said to him: "Yes, I sold the car. But why say I *stole* it? I got the car and paid the price for it" – words very similar to that – "and I sold it."' *Inspector Barker*: 'He said: "Well, you can't prove I stole it."' *Browne*: 'There was some argument about it and I said: "Well, anyhow, I was going to make myself some cocoa, because I have had a long run and I have had nothing." He said: "Well, wait a minute, I'm going to search you." I had these cartridges in my pocket, and I did not want him to see them. I made an excuse I wanted to go to the lavatory, and I did not want to – I wanted to get rid of the cartridges. He got the cartridges, and I said: "That's done it now."' *Inspector Barker*: 'He said: "That's done it. Now you've found them, it's all up with me."' *Browne*: 'The atmosphere was changed ... Presently this revolver was brought in.' *Inspector Barker*: 'Browne looked at it and said: "Ah, you've found that, have you? I am done for now."' *Browne*: 'I said: "It's all up now," because I knew they would have me for having firearms and ammunition and no licence.' He was escorted to the lavatory by four policemen. *DS Miller*: 'He said: "Why all this precaution? I have never seen so many officers in my life!"'

He was then taken in a car – by two men, according to the police; by five, according to Browne – to Tooting police station. Nothing had yet been said about the murder of PC Gutteridge.

'They were quite decent,' said Browne. 'They put me in a big room with a big table, and they were laughing about something about "You won't go for a 200 mile run ..." There was a lot of chatter. In the midst of it in comes another detective with a little revolver. He put it down on this table and he passed some remark ... Anyway they were laughing about it and I said: "Oh yes, you can laugh about it. You think it's a toy. But it wouldn't only tickle you ..." I knew there was something in it.'

DS Miller: 'Browne said; "Oh, you've found that, have you? That's no good. It would only tickle you unless it hit you in a vital part."' *Browne*: 'They explained they wanted to get me while I was in the car, and one said: "No. Wait until he's in the garage!" I didn't hear this – this was explained to me. And one said to me: "What would you have done, Browne, if we had stopped you in the car?" And I said: "I do not know." He said: "Perhaps you would have stopped us." And I said: "I have not been put to the test." ... Then it came to my knowledge that there were ten men who had come to arrest me – ten! And all those ten men were armed. And they said had I tried it or something ... they would have blown me to pieces, if I had shown any resistance. That is what it amounted to. But they were good-tempered ... laughing about it.' *DS Miller*: 'No laughing at all.' *Browne*: 'It was to this effect – "There would have been little left of you, Browne, if you had used it ..." I said: "Good heavens! Ten! Why – it would take a man with a machine-gun to cope with you." Those were the words.' *DS Miller*: 'What he did say was: "I shall have to have a machine-gun for you bastards next time."'

The police searches discovered twelve .45 cartridges in the back hip-pocket of Browne's trousers; a stockinette mask in his jacket pocket; a forceps and a Webley revolver, fully loaded with six cartridges, in a pocket inside the driver's door of the Angus-Sanderson; sixteen .45 cartridges wrapped in some paper in the inner office, as well as another forceps, several rolls of bandages, some gauze, lint and an ethylchloride spray. In the Brownes' rooms off Lavender Hill were found a roll of plaster, a convex lens, an ear speculum, twenty-three .22 cartridges, a small nickel-plated revolver, loaded, and a fully loaded Smith and Wesson. A further search of the Angus-Sanderson revealed another fully loaded Webley revolver in a secret recess behind the driver's seat. This was the revolver that was later proved to have fired one at least of the fatal shots: its breech block had the peculiar fault that imprinted itself on every cartridge case fired by the gun.

Kennedy, ignorant of Browne's arrest, arrived at the garage at 2 pm on Saturday, 21 January.

Since his return to London he had been there twice before. Said Browne: 'I was surprised to see him again, because I told him not to come near the place again on account of the drink . . . On the first occasion he insinuated would he come back to the garage? And I would not have anything to do with him. On the second occasion he wanted to know if he could come to Devon . . . And again I said: "I cannot have you for drink." And he finished.'

On the day that Browne had driven to Devon – Wednesday, 18 January – Kennedy had married.

On the 21st, finding the garage doors looked and two men who he thought were detectives inside, Kennedy hurried back to his wife in 2 Huguenot Place and urged her to pack. They returned to Liverpool on the midnight train from Euston. The Kennedys had three more nights of married bliss before the police closed in.

It was on Wednesday the 25th that Kennedy was arrested. That night, about 11.40 pm, he was hurrying away from his home along St Andrew's Street, hiding his face, when DS Bill Mattinson, who knew Kennedy of old, approached him from behind and said: 'Come on, Bill. Now then, come on, Bill.'

Kennedy's response was to swing around and pull a pistol out of his pocket. He recognized the policeman, said: 'Stand back, Bill – or I'll shoot you!' and fired. There was a click. Mattinson seized Kennedy's gun-hand with his left hand, hit him with the other, and wrenched the pistol, a Savage, from the other man's grasp. Shouting to his distant colleagues, Mattinson propelled Kennedy back up St Andrew's Street into Copperas Hill, where three other policemen came to his assistance. It's all right!' cried Mattinson raising the pistol. 'I've got it!' Realizing now how close he had been to being shot, he collapsed and was sick. In fact, the safety catch was found to be in the safety position.

Kennedy was taken into custody. He had clearly left his digs in a hurry, for under his coat he wore no shirt, just a vest; his trousers were undone and his boots unlaced. Having heard some policemen arrive in a taxi in the street below – they gave the cabbie a clear instruction to drive around the corner – he had taken flight. 'I had a premonition something was going to happen to me today,' he said.

He met Mattinson again at Warren Street police station, where he was charged with being concerned with Browne in stealing a Vauxhall motor car. He said to Mattinson: 'I'm sorry. I've no grudge against the police. But you should be in heaven now. And there was one for me.' Mattinson looked at him and said: 'I did not expect that from you.'

The following evening, Chief Inspector Berrett visited Kennedy, now in custody in New Scotland Yard, and asked him if he had any information to give about the murder of PC Gutteridge. Kennedy asked to be allowed to think, and did so for several minutes, head in hand, elbows on a table. 'Can I see my wife?' he eventually asked. Mrs Kennedy, who had travelled with him from Liverpool, was fetched. She kissed him. Berrett noted their conversation.

Kennedy said: 'Well, my dear ... These officers are making enquires about that policeman murdered in Essex.' She exclaimed: 'Why – you didn't murder him, did you?' 'No,' he replied. 'I didn't. But I was there, and know who did. If I'm charged with murder and found guilty, I shall be hanged, and you will be a widow ... If I'm charged and found guilty of being an accessory I shall receive a long sentence ... and be a long time away from you. Will you wait for me:' She said: 'Yes, love. I'll wait for you anytime.' Kennedy asked: 'Well, what shall I do then?' 'Tell these gentlemen the truth of what took place,' she said. He replied: 'All right, I will.'

It took him over three hours to dictate his statement, which Browne derided later in court as 'one pack of wilful or imaginative lies, either wilfully told or misled by some kink of the brain ... It is a horribly concocted statement that has taken hours to consider. That is my opinion.' However, what Kennedy said is probably largely true, although he naturally tried to minimize his involvement in the death of PC Gutteridge. It is quite possible that Browne and Kennedy were *both* armed – even that Kennedy fired the first or second pair of shots.

Browne could make no counter-allegations, as his defence was that he was never in Essex that night. He claimed he was in bed with his wife.

On 6 February, Browne and Kennedy were both charged by Berrett with the murder of PC Gutteridge. 'It's absurd,' said Browne. 'I know nothing about it.' Kennedy said nothing.

Their trial began at the Old Bailey on Monday, 23 April 1928, before Mr Justice Avory. The Solicitor-General, Sir Boyd Merriman, led for the Crown; Mr Lever defended Browne and Mr Powell appeared for Kennedy. Browne's appearance in the witness-box unleashed a torrent of verbosity: generally impatient with the proceedings and indignant, one minute he muttered, the next he ranted. The barristers, including his own, intervened with difficulty. He even argued about taking the oath. 'How can I tell the whole truth,' he cried, 'of something I do not know?'

Kennedy elected to make a statement from the dock. He said that he had loaded the Webley after Gutteridge had been shot because he was terrified and did not know what he was doing. Browne also gave him the Savage, he said – and he only intended to frighten Sergeant Mattinson. He concluded:

'I can only now express my deep regret to Mrs Gutteridge that I should have been in the car on the night of the crime.'

The ballistics evidence, concerning the bullets, the cartridges, and the gun-prints made by the breech-shield of the Webley, was damning – the first time such evidence had been used to such effect in a murder trial. Four firearms experts were called, including Robert Churchill, the Crown's chief expert in this and other trials involving guns.

Both Browne and Kennedy were found guilty. Both made a speech, Browne repeating that he had had nothing to do with the murder, but was 'quite content to leave it' as penal servitude was worse than death. Kennedy said the verdict was pre-ordained – it was fate – and they all were accessories of that fate. He said he wasn't afraid to die, and asked if he could see his wife.

The appeals were heard on 22 May and dismissed. On 31 May 1928, Browne was hanged at Pentonville and Kennedy at Wandsworth.

The night before his execution Kennedy, who had been converted to Roman Catholicism while awaiting execution, wrote a long, eloquently passionate letter to his wife, urging her to join him soon in heaven – 'Our word is au revoir.'

He added two postscripts, written a few hours before he died. 'Perhaps the worst is to know the exact hour, and yet perhaps the best . . . Darling, my last word. I again assert that I had no previous knowledge of what was going to happen that night. I go to my death knowing that, and that my statement is true, and that my own darling believes me. B x x x x.'

In 1930 executions reached another low, only five people being hanged – the same number as those executed in 1921 – and in the years before the Second World War some overdue reforms were made in the laws governing capital punishment. The Infanticide Act of 1922, which had abolished the execution of mothers who killed their newborn babies, was tardily followed in 1931 by the Sentence of Death (Expectant Mothers) Act, which decreed that pregnant women should not be hanged.

Then in 1933 the Children and Young Persons Act raised the age of convicted persons who might be hanged: no one who was under the age of eighteen when murder was committed could from henceforth be sentenced to death. They were to be detained during His Majesty's pleasure.

CHAPTER 25

Samuel Furnace

The murder of Walter Spatchett, 1933

There seems little doubt that various forms of mayhem, from mugging to murder, attract some imitators when sensationally and lengthily described by the press. For instance, a mentally unbalanced youth called Ernest Rhodes was so obsessed with the murderers Patrick Mahon and Norman Thorne that, when the latter was awaiting execution, Rhodes went out on 9 April 1925 and cut the throat of a girl he thought he loved. He was found guilty but insane. The much publicized murder committed by Alfred Rouse in November 1930 may have had a similar effect. He faked his own death by strangling a complete stranger and burning the body in his car so that he might assume a new identity. Two years after Rouse was sentenced to death, a man called Furnace tried the same fiery trick.

On the evening of Tuesday, 3 January 1933, Mr Wynne, of 30 Hawley Crescent, a road north of Camden Town underground station and now containing the new studios of TVam, was startled to see that a shed in his backyard was on fire. It had been rented from him by a builder and decorator, Sam Furnace. After firemen had extinguished the blaze they discovered the charred body of a man sitting on a high stool before what had been an office desk.

Furnace's home was in Crogsland Road, Chalk Farm, about five hundred yards to the north-west. A native of St Neot's, he was married with children, the eldest being a ten-year-old boy. Earlier in life he had been a ship's steward, and had served in the Rifle Brigade and with the Black and Tans. A tenant of his, Mr Abbot, was able to identify the body as that of his late landlord. A note was found that said: 'Goodbye all. No work. No money. Sam J. Furnace.'

At the inquest, which began on 6 January in St Pancras coroner's court before Mr Bentley Purchase, a life insurance claim was declared to be void as the person insured had committed suicide. The sympathetic insurance company agreed, however, to provide the widow with a generous grant.

The coroner, Mr Purchase, more suspicious than sympathetic, took it upon himself to examine the charred remains personally. He concluded that he was dealing with neither *felo de se* nor Furnace. For there was what appeared to be a bullet wound in the corpse's back, and its teeth were those of a man younger than forty-two-year-old Sam.

A full post-mortem revealed that the burnt man had in fact been shot *twice*, and had probably been dead before he was set on fire. He was identified by a sodden post office savings book found in an overcoat in the shed. Both coat and book belonged to Walter Spatchett, aged twenty-five, a rent collector for Messrs T. B. Westacott and Son of Camden Road, who lived with his parents in Dartmouth Park Road, Highgate. He was last seen on the evening of the Monday before the fire, when he had about £40 of rent on him. He and Furnace were known to have been acquainted.

A nation-wide hunt for Furnace was instituted by the police. On 9 January, BBC Radio brashly announced that the missing man was wanted for murder.

Furnace, said to have been sighted all over the country, was finally traced to Southend. There he made the not uncommon mistake of criminals on the run: he wrote a letter – in his case to his wife's brother, Charles Tuckfield, who received it on Saturday, 15 January.

It said:

I am at Southend, quite near the station, making out I have been ill with the flue ... I am far from well through want of sleep. I don't think I have slept one hour since the accident happened. Now what I want you to do is not for me but for May and the kiddies. My days are numbered. I want you to come down on Sunday, on your own, please. Catch the 10.35 from Harringay Park, that gets you down in Southend at 12.8. Come out of the station, walk straight across the road and down the opposite road. Walk down on the left side. I will see you. I am not giving my address in case you are followed. Just walk slowly down. If you come, will you bring me 15½ shirt and two collars, any colour will do. Also one pair of socks, dark ones, and one comb. I think that is all now. Best of luck. Mine is gone.

Tuckfield gave the letter to the police. Shadowed by them, he went as instructed to Southend and walked down Whitegate Road. A curtain twitched in No. 11, and Furnace looked out and beckoned. Tuckfield entered the house and conversed as easily as he could with his brother-in-law until the police, led by Superintendent Cornish, entered the house through a rear door. Furnace, who was thought to be armed, was rushed and overpowered. He was taken back to London.

In a statement made at Kentish Town police station that night he claimed that the shooting of Spatchett was accidental. Furnace said that on the Monday evening they had both been in the shed, which also served as an office. He said: 'I showed him the revolver. He cocked it. I told him it was loaded ... I was showing him through the door, with the gun in my left hand, and as he was going through the door the gun went off and shot him. He fell to the ground groaning. I realized my position and lost my head. I went out. When I got back there I found that he was dead ... I took the gun away and did not tell anyone I had shot him ... Next morning about 7.15 I dragged him into the office ... The idea struck me to destroy the body by a fire at my shop, making out that the body was mine. The idea at first seemed too terrible, but no other way seemed possible.' The same afternoon he returned to the shed. He sat the body on a chair and poured spirits and oil over it. 'I screwed up a lot of paper on the floor and set a candle, which I lit, in the middle of it . . . I came outside and pulled the outer door to, locking it.'

One wonders whether his story, if it had been used as a defence, would have been believed in court. But there was no trial.

Having made the statement, Furnace was locked overnight in a cell in Kentish Town police station. During the night he could be heard pacing restlessly about. As it was very cold, he asked for his overcoat to be returned; it was the one article of clothing that had not been searched. Towards dawn on Monday there was silence. A PC peered through the spy-hole at 7 am, and saw Furnace raise something to his mouth. The PC hastily opened the cell door, to find the prisoner now writhing on the floor. He had swallowed some hydrochloric acid, the contents of a small bottle that had been sewn into the lining of his overcoat.

He died twenty-four hours later, on Tuesday, 18 January, in St Pancras hospital, in whose mortuary Spatchett's body already lay. A coroner's jury concluded that the death of Spatchett was not accidental and they found Furnace guilty of murder.

CHAPTER 26

Parker and Probert
The murder of Joseph Bedford, 1933

Murders committed in the course of a robbery are almost as common as sexual or domestic murders, and the murderers are commonly a pair of thugs, usually young, whereas their victims are usually middle-aged or old. The following case history was brutally commonplace. It is unusual in that the executions which settled the law's and the victim's account were the last, it is believed, to have been witnessed by a reporter – in this case the chief crime reporter of the Press Association, W. G. Finch.

Joseph Bedford, an eighty-year-old bachelor, maintained a dilapidated general store in Clarence Street, Portslade, a run-down suburb between Worthing and Hove. On a slate in one of the shop's windows was written – 'Bankrupt Stock'. Somewhat doddery and deaf, he was also something of a miserly recluse, keeping his money in two chocolate boxes. But one or two women in the neighbourhood kept an eye on him and cared for him in a small way.

Bedford's shop usually remained open until 8 pm, and it was about fifteen minutes before this on Monday, 13 November 1933, that Miss Kathleen Russell called on the old man to prepare a simple evening meal for him, as was her wont. When she left the shop about eight o'clock she saw two young men, both strangers, outside – 'hanging about' as she put it. One of them said something to her, but she was later not allowed by the courts to reveal what that was.

The suspicions of another neighbour were aroused about two hours later when at 9.50 pm or so he observed that the light in Bedford's shop was still on. This neighbour, Edward Myers, the son of the publican whose hostelry was on a street corner opposite the shop, was puzzled by the irregularity. Not only that, some of the old man's stock was still outside on the pavement. Myers summoned a police constable.

PC Peters was also aware of Mr Bedford's habits and investigated. He tried the shop door – it was locked. Hearing sounds 'as if someone was stumbling against something', he flashed his torch into the dimly lit interior through the glass panel of the door, across which a ladder had been placed. He said: 'The light fell full across the face of Mr Bedford, and I could see that it was covered with blood. The next moment I saw him stagger backwards. He fell against some gardening shovels resting against a showcase. I then forced the door, and found Mr Bedford lying in a heap on the floor.'

Mr Bedford was taken to hospital, where the following morning he died of shock occasioned by multiple injuries to his head.

On the same day, Tuesday, Scotland Yard were called in, and DCI Askew, after examining the premises, came across a bowler hat with a dent in the crown and an overcoat button which seemed to have been torn off. Both were on the shop floor among several copper coins that were scattered about: halfpennies, pennies and farthings. The old man had kept his coppers in a chocolate box and his silver coins – sixpences, shillings, florins and half-crowns – in another.

Mr Bedford was buried in Portslade Cemetery a week after the attack on him. His two assailants had already been picked up in Worthing, on or about Thursday, 16 November, and charged with loitering with intent to commit a felony.

The circumstances of their arrest are now known, but a week later, on the morning of Thursday, 23 November, they appeared before the Worthing magistrates, who gave them a nominal sentence of one day's imprisonment. After being taken back to their cells the two men were re-arrested by Superintendent Fairs at 10.40 am on a charge of murder. Handcuffed, they were driven to Portslade police station, where they were officially charged. Fifteen minutes later they appeared before a special sitting of the Hove County Bench and were remanded until 1 December. Both men were granted legal aid. The chairman of the Bench and the younger of the accused men had the same name, Frederick Parker.

Frederick William Parker was a twenty-one-year-old labourer; his partner in crime was a fitter, Albert Probert, aged twenty-six.

While in custody in Worthing, Fred Parker had been asked by Inspector Lewis about the attack on Joseph Bedford. Parker, who had not been told that Bedford was dead, said: 'Why don't you ask my mate? I don't see why I should give someone else away.'

Later he confessed. 'I don't see that I shouldn't tell you,' he said. 'We knocked an old man out in a shop at Portslade on Monday night. It was a shop where they sold bankrupt stock, and we took the money from the till.' Lewis then asked Parker if he realized the seriousness of what he was saying. 'Yes,' replied Parker. 'I want to get it off my mind. We decided to hold up a chap in a shop in Portslade. It was an old dirty shop of bankrupt stock. We both walked to the shop window to see that all was clear. After investigating we walked into the shop and spoke to the old shopkeeper. I then turned and locked the door. No one was passing at the time, and I brought my revolver into play. The gun was not loaded, but I had no other choice of making the old shopkeeper put up his hands. I held him up and the other chap with me – I don't want to mention his name – went around the counter and just knocked him out. I went to the boxes, and we both took money out and put it in our pockets. Those farthings you found on me are some I took from the till. It was somewhere about £6 that we both got from the till . . .'

Later that night Fred Parker asked Inspector Lewis how Bedford was. Lewis was presumably non-committal, for the young man went on to say, still ignorant of Bedford's death: 'I wish it had been a bigger job. It was not worth doing for £6. He was an old miser; I thought we should have found buckets of money . . .'

Parker first knew that Bedford was dead when told so by DCI Askew. 'You don't mean to say the old chap is dead?' asked Parker, who then made a statement elaborating what he had told Lewis and naming Probert as his partner in the raid on Bedford's store.

He said he first met Probert 'by accident' in the Church Army Hostel at Brighton. The police later established that on 7 November the two were in lodgings in Portslade from which they disappeared on the 10th. The next day, Saturday, Parker was temporarily employed selling tickets for a sweepstake draw. Sometime during this period Parker gave Probert his blue overcoat, as the other man wanted one to match his blue suit. To replace it, Parker stole another coat.

On Monday the 13th, said Parker, 'Probert asked if I would "do" a jeweller's. I said that the shop was bound to have alarms all over, but Probert said he was desperate. I tried to get him to talk sense. We walked round Portslade and we came to the shop. I explained to Probert that it was a big risk and I would not take any part except holding the gun.' They entered the shop.

The gun, according to Parker, had been given to Probert by a man he knew. His statement continued: 'While Probert was talking to the old man I turned the key, already in the door, and coming back I told Probert that the old man was deaf and could not hear what we were saying, but if he did hear to hit him gently. I took the revolver from my pocket and asked the old man to put up his hands. He resisted at first and Probert struck him. Probert was leading him backwards and as he struck the old chap went down. Probert did not take any notice of what I said and kept on asking if I had got the money. I told him to put a scarf under the old man's head. He was knocking his head on the floor and I could hear that distinctly. I told Probert: "I have found the money," and he left the old chap and we left the shop together.'

The police discovered that later that night, between 9.30 and 10 pm, the pair had had a meal in a tea-room in Worthing. The following morning they went to an outfitters' and bought new suits and shirts. While they were there Probert had a new button sewn on to his overcoat to replace the one that was missing.

After their arrest and after Probert had been told about Parker's allegations, he denied any involvement in Bedford's death and having ever been in his shop. But he could not or would not say where he was on the night in question. When arrested, Parker was found to have twenty-seven farthings on him; Probert had twenty-nine.

During their various appearances before the magistrates at Hove in the first week of January 1934, Parker fainted seven times in the dock and had to be revived.

On 4 January DCI Askew also collapsed. He was being cross-examined when he suddenly fell backwards down the steps of the witness-box. After being given first-aid Askew re-entered the box and almost immediately fell forward in a faint. He was taken into an adjoining room where he was revived by the doctor who had been standing by to resuscitate Parker.

Fred Parker made a statement denying that he had struck the fatal blow. He said: 'I held up the old man with a gun and told him we had come for money. He put his hands up eventually. I stepped back for Probert to tie him up. . . We had tied my scarf and Probert's together for that purpose. I thought we were going to carry out the whole thing by merely tying him up. I told him to stop hitting him. . . Finally, I hit Probert over the knuckles to separate him from the old man. I told him the old man had had enough . . . He told me to keep my mouth closed, and said that if I did not, he would do the same to me as he had done to Mr Bedford.'

Parker and Probert appeared at Sussex Assizes in Lewes on Wednesday, 14 March 1934. Both gave evidence. Mr Justice Roche was the judge and Sir Henry Curtis Bennett, KC, was the Crown's chief prosecutor. Mr John Flowers defended Probert.

Mr J. D. Cassels, KC, defending Parker, claimed that the charge against his defendant should be at the most one of manslaughter, as Parker alleged it was Probert who used the excessive violence that resulted in the old man's death. The judge remarked: 'I am afraid I shall have to tell the jury that the proposition is not correct in law.' Mr Cassels then suggested – as did Mr Flowers for Probert – that Bedford, in falling backwards, possibly frightened by PC Peters's flashlight, had struck his head on something sharp, had fractured his skull, and so died by misadventure.

The Crown's view, supported by the judge, was that if two persons set out to commit a robbery and if one used violence, the other standing by was as guilty as the person striking the blow. Mr Justice Roche in his summing-up told the jury that if they accepted Parker's evidence that he contemplated robbery and the use of some degree of violence, it was not manslaughter but murder. If they thought Mr Bedford fell because of the injuries he had previously received and died from the effects of that fall, then the original injuries were the cause of death.

After retiring for thirty-five minutes, the jury found both men guilty of murder. They were sentenced to death. An appeal was dismissed on 18 April by the Lord Chief Justice, Mr Justice Avory and Mr Justice Humphreys, and Parker and Probert were hanged in Wandsworth prison on Friday, 4 May 1934.

CHAPTER 27

Charlotte Bryant

The murder of Frederick Bryant, 1935

Poisoners, especially female poisoners, who, with very evident malice aforethought, deliberately plan the deaths of their victims, have invariably been treated with a corresponding lack of pity by the law.

Charlotte McHugh was an illiterate Irish girl and something of a slut, whom Frederick Bryant, a corporal in the military police, met when he was serving in Ireland. This was during 'The Troubles', the guerrilla warfare and savage reprisals of 1920–21 that followed the First World War, resulting in the official division of Ireland into Eire and Ulster in 1921–22. Corporal Bryant was at that time serving in Londonderry. He brought young Charlotte back with him to England and they were married in Somerset in March 1922. She was just nineteen and he was twenty-five or six.

But life with the upright amiable Fred soon deteriorated. Jobs were hard to find – the country no longer needed or wanted its soldiery, and the best employment Fred Bryant could find was as a farm labourer. In 1925 they moved into a tied cottage on a Dorset farm on the Somerset border, at Over Compton, east of Yeovil. Here Mrs Bryant soon acquired a reputation for harlotry and excess. She was known locally, mainly in the public bars of inns, as 'Compton Liz', 'Black Bess' and 'Killarney Kate'. It seems she had an insatiable desire for amorous adventure and sex.

Although her hair was lousy and she was virtually toothless, she had many affairs, which presumably consoled her mind and body and distracted her from the humdrum poverty of a labourer's life. Along the way she produced five children, whose paternity must have been in doubt, and let the cottage slide along with her local fame into squalor and disorder. However, her extramarital activities supplemented the family income, and this was apparently of some importance to Fred. He was earning less than £2 a week. As he said to a neighbour: 'Four pounds a week is better than thirty bob. I don't care a damn what she does.'

Accordingly, he was not displeased when at Christmas 1933 a pedlar and horse-dealer of gipsy origin, Leonard Parsons, began lodging at the cottage as a paying guest, sleeping on a couch in the kitchen and sharing Fred's razor – and his wife.

Fred was forced out of his complacency when early in 1934 he was sacked by the farmer, largely on account of the scandal caused in the neighbourhood by Mrs Bryant's amours. All the Bryant's did, however, was to move east to another cottage on another farm not far away, at Coombe, a mile north of Sherborne, and carry on much as before.

Parsons was not a regular lodger, since his roving nature and occupation took him periodically elsewhere, sometimes in the direction of his 'natural wife', Priscilla Loveridge, a gipsy woman who bore him four children and later described him as 'a woman's fancy man, the kind of man who would break up any man's home'. But his reappearances at the Bryants' cottage, unshaven and unkempt, apparently excited Mrs Bryant so much that like a drug, she wished to have more – could not have enough of him in fact – and began to consider how she might rid herself entirely of her marital obligations, loose as they were.

She was fairly besotted with Parsons, and more than once went with him on his travels, staying with him as his wife in Dorchester and Weymouth. During these absences as well as during his visits, her duties as mother and housewife were further neglected and the cottage would lapse even further into squalor and filth.

Parsons was lodging with the Bryants in May 1935, when on 14 May Fred Bryant became suddenly ill, vomiting and suffering from acute pains in his stomach. The local medic, Dr MacCarthy, diagnosed gastroenteritis, and his patient's strong constitution soon assisted Fred towards a full recovery. Another such attack on 6 August was similarly diagnosed and Fred Bryant was soon on his feet again and back at work.

By October, Parson's feelings for Charlotte Bryant seem to have cooled, for towards the end of the month, deterred perhaps by her demands, he went away and never returned. In fact he told her he was not coming back. She became more distraught as time passed, and on 11 December a third poisonous attack on her husband's innards laid him very low.

A week later, when he was still incapacitated, although believed to be recovering, she travelled north to a gipsy camp near Weston-super-Mare, seeking Parsons. She encountered instead Priscilla Loveridge and her pipe-smoking crone of a mother, Mrs Penfold. Mrs Bryant was heartily abused by both and sent away.

The next day, Friday, 20 December, Fred Bryant's condition suddenly worsened. On Saturday he was in agony, saying there was something inside him like a red-hot poker that was driving him mad. A neighbour, Mrs Stone, saw him that day, and when his employer's wife, Mrs Priddle, called, he was so ill he could not speak. On Sunday he was removed from the cottage in an ambulance to the Yeatman Hospital, Sherborne, and that afternoon he died. He was thirty-nine.

This time Dr MacCarthy was suspicious and refused to sign a death certificate. He communicated his concern to the police. There was an inquest.

'What is an inquest?' asked Mrs Bryant, and waxed indignant when she understood – not surprisingly as on 28 December 4.09 grains of arsenic were discovered by the Home Office analyst, Dr Roche Lynch, in the corpse of poor Fred. But even before this, Scotland Yard's assistance had been sought by the Dorset police.

Meanwhile, Mrs Bryant and her five children were lodged in the Poor Law institution at Sturminster Newton, a former workhouse, while the Bryants' cottage was minutely examined by the police in the shape of DCI Bell and DS Tapsell of Scotland Yard. It was virtually taken apart, but not before Tapsell, equipped with three paintbrushes, had gone about carefully sweeping shelves and cupboards and acquiring in all about 146 samples of dust, dirt and refuse, of which thirty-two later revealed traces of arsenic.

Parsons was questioned and was luckily able to convince the police that he had had nothing to do with Mr Bryant's demise. He said he met Mrs Bryant towards the end of 1933 when he was lodging at Babylon Hill and going under the name Bill Moss. Soon afterwards they became intimate and remained so for two years. In the summer of 1935, he said, she remarked more than once that she 'would soon be a widow', after which they might marry. To this he had unkindly replied: 'I wouldn't marry any woman.'

An elderly widow, Mrs Lucy Ostler, who had lately lodged with the Bryants, told how Mrs Bryant had once said: 'I hate Fred.' When Mrs Ostler asked her why she didn't leave him, Mrs Bryant replied that she did not want to leave the children. The older woman revealed that on the night of 21 December (Bryant died the following day) his wife had coaxed him to take some liquid Oxo, a meat extract. On another occasion Mrs Bryant, said Mrs Ostler, had disposed of a tin of weed-killer saying: 'I must get rid of this.' And on being told what an inquest implied, the young widow had said: 'If they can't find anything, they can't put a rope around your neck.'

The police discovered that an insurance agent, Mr Tuck, had been approached by Mrs Bryant in December 1934, when she said: 'I would like to insure my old man.'

This was not followed up, but a year later, on 20 December 1935, Mr Tuck happened to call at the Bryants' cottage. Mr Bryant, he thought, looked a very sick man – gastritis, said his wife – and Mr Tuck concluded that the husband was not a fair risk. However, he effected some insurance for the children. On 22 December Bryant died. But Mr Tuck, unaware of this, returned to the cottage on Monday the 23rd. Finding only the children at home he drove off, but on the way met Mrs Bryant and Mrs Ostler, returning to the cottage on foot. He gave them a lift. Mrs Bryant had a bundle with her and she told him that she had been to the hospital to pick up her dead husband's clothes. 'Well, he's gone,' she said. 'I've been a good wife to him – nobody can say I haven't. And nobody can say *I* poisoned him.' Mr Tuck, mystified by this remark, said: 'No. Why should they?' She replied: 'Well, you never know what will come of these things.' She did not seem to the insurance agent like a woman who had just been widowed.

The police also made an exhaustive search of the area about the cottage, and an empty, battered tin was found in some rubbish, and in it traces of arsenic. The tin was identified by a firm who manufactured weed-killer.

On Monday, 10 February 1936, Superintendent Cherett of the Sherborne police visited Mrs Bryant in the Sturminster Newton institution. After being cautioned and formally charged with the murder of her husband, she said: 'I have never got any poison from anywhere, and that people do know. I don't see how they can say I poisoned my husband.' She was taken by car to Exeter prison. Her five children, aged twelve, ten, six, four and fifteen months, remained in the institution despite an offer from the NSPCC to find them a home.

On Wednesday, 27 May 1936, the trial of Charlotte Bryant began in Dorchester at the Dorset Assizes. The judge was Mr Justice Mackinnon; the Solicitor-General, Sir Terence O'Connor, KC, led for the Crown; and the accused was defended by Mr J. D. Casswell.

Neither the defendant nor the principal witnesses for the prosecution, Parsons and Loveridge, seemed to comprehend the gravity of the situation – Mrs Bryant munched caramels in the dock. In giving evidence she said she knew nothing about poison and had never bought any weed-killer, and she denied nearly all the prosecution's allegations, including what Parsons and Mrs Ostler had told the court. She was, she said, on very good terms with her husband – 'Never a breath wrong with my husband in my life until Leonard Parsons came along.'

On Saturday, 30 May 1936, she was found guilty of murder and duly sentenced to death.

An appeal was heard on 29 June and dismissed. Ten days later the Labour MP for Nelson and Colne, Mr Silverman, asked the Home Secretary, Sir John Simon, whether he was aware that the appeal judges had refused to admit certain additional evidence on the ground that it could have been produced at the original trial, where, said Mr Silverman, the defence had been conducted by junior counsel only – whereas 'such a heavy battery of leading counsel' appeared for the Crown that 'the minds of a rustic jury' might have been considerably affected.

The Home Secretary replied that counsel for the Crown were not a battery directed against the accused, and that in his view the defence was most adequately conducted.

Meanwhile, in Exeter prison, Mrs Bryant's hair turned white at the roots. She refused to see her children so as not to upset them any further. The day before her execution she sent a telegraph appealing for mercy to the new, uncrowned king, Edward VIII – to no effect.

Charlotte Bryant was hanged in Exeter prison on Wednesday, 15 July 1936. She was thirty-three.

It is said that she went to her death bravely. Said a priest: 'Her last moments were truly edifying.' Mrs van der Elst, a leading campaigner for the abolition of capital punishment, staged a small demonstration outside the prison and was fined £5 for obstructing an officer. She also handed in £5 for the police sports fund and said she was going to pay for the maintenance and education of Mrs Bryant's five children.

At the inquest on the body of Mrs Bryant the jurors asked the coroner if they might give their fees to her children. The coroner replied that it was a small amount and provision had already been made for the children. The jury then handed their fees to the prison governor to give to the Discharged Prisoners' Aid Society.

Three months before the execution of Charlotte Bryant, another woman was hanged for murder, Dorothy Waddingham. She was thirty-six, and also had five children. Nurse Waddingham, who ran a small nursing home in Nottingham, had been charged with the murder by poison (morphia) of two elderly women in her charge: Louisa Baguley, aged eighty-nine, and Ada Baguley, fifty, who weighed sixteen stone and suffered from disseminated sclerosis. Found guilty of the murder of Ada Baguley, Nurse Waddingham was executed at Winson Green prison, Birmingham, on 16 April 1936.

It was the last time that two women (both poisoners) were hanged in the same year – in which six other women who had been sentenced to death were reprieved. No woman would be executed in Britain for over twelve years, the next being a forty-two-year-old lesbian, Margaret Allen, hanged on 12 January 1949 for the murder with a hammer of an elderly eccentric, Mrs Chadwick.

CHAPTER 28

George McMahon

The attempted assassination of Edward VIII, 1936

Edward Albert Christian George Andrew Patrick David, aged forty-two, formerly Prince of Wales and now King Edward VIII after the death of his father George V on 20 January 1936, was riding in state along Constitution Hill on 16 July 1936 on his way back to Buckingham Palace after presenting new Colours to the Brigade of Guards in Hyde Park, when a man in the crowd, George Andrew McMahon, pulled out a gun.

If he had fired it, if he had shot and killed the king, the abdication crisis over Mrs Simpson would never have happened and King Edward would have become the first king regnant to be assassinated since William II. But McMahon was not a marksman – nor a madman, as was later claimed. He was a publicity-seeking fantasist. The revolver, which was brand new, had probably never been fired. It was loaded and found to be cocked, but was later proved to be inaccurate beyond ten yards; and the king, on horseback, was more than twice that distance away.

McMahon told the police that he had been hired by a foreign power to kill the king for £150; agents of the foreign power had given him the revolver. He was disbelieved, as few people believed that any foreign power would employ so inadequate an assassin, who had never, on his own admission, fired a gun before. Besides, the man seemed mad.

Nonetheless, for whatever reason, he had stood in the crowds lining Constitution Hill with the loaded revolver concealed in a newspaper. As the king rode by, McMahon drew out the weapon and raised his arm. A special constable, especially alert, happened to be near him, and seeing the movement and the revolver knocked it out of McMahon's hand. It skidded across the road, startling the horses. But no shot was fired.

McMahon was charged under Section 2 of the Treason Act 1842 and found guilty at the Old Bailey of 'producing a revolver near the person of the King with intent to alarm His Majesty'.

He was sentenced to twelve months' hard labour – during which time Edward VIII abdicated (on 10 December), became the Duke of Windsor and married Mrs Simpson (in June 1937), a month after his younger brother was crowned King George VI.

CHAPTER 29

Leslie Stone

The murder of Ruby Keen, 1937

Only one policeman has ever been tried for murder at the Old Bailey. This was PC William Teasdale, who strangled his wife in bed in their Clapham home during a row about his association with another woman. Teasdale was tried at the Old Bailey in April 1938, found guilty and sentenced to death. He was reprieved in May. The year before this, two policemen were among the main suspects in a murder case outside London to which the Metropolitan Police's CID were called.

Ruby Anne Keen was an attractive young woman, aged twenty-three, who lived with her widowed mother, elder sister and her lorry-driver brother in Leighton Buzzard, Bedfordshire. She worked in a factory in the nearby town of Dunstable, and when she was free liked to go out and have a good time, which several young men in the district were glad to provide. She enjoyed the attention, the affirmation and exercise of her attractions, and if invited out by one of her admirers was not loath to accept.

One of her regular boy-friends was a builder's labourer, Leslie George Stone, aged twenty-four, who lived in the hamlet of Heath and Reach, a mile north of Leighton Buzzard. He and Ruby had been friends for some time, since 1931, and it was thought by their families that one day they would get married. But Stone was a soldier, serving with the Royal Artillery, and in 1932 he was posted to Hong Kong. After a year of so, Ruby's letters became less frequent and then stopped altogether. Out of sight meant out of mind. Besides, her other admirers were not slow to occupy her time and affections – in particular, two young policemen. Before long one of them was favoured above all other suitors, and in 1936 she became engaged to a PC with the Bedfordshire Constabulary. Not long after this, in December 1936, Stone was discharged from the RA on medical grounds and returned to Leighton Buzzard.

It was more than two months before he saw Ruby again: she was in the company of another man. Stone said later: 'I did not speak to her as I did not want to look a fool.'

However, he spoke to her the following Sunday, 4 April. He bought her a drink in a pub, the Golden Bell, and she said they must have a night out together for old time's sake. She would not commit herself to an actual date.

But a week later, after going to evening service in a local church with a girl-friend, she dropped in again at the Golden Bell about seven o'clock, where Stone was waiting. In expectation and in honour of the occasion he had put on a new blue serge suit, one he had never worn before. He had three pints of mild and she had a glass of port. They moved on to the Cross Keys and ended up in the Stag Hotel. They say in a corner of the saloon bar, their conversation being overheard in part by some of the locals drinking at the bar – Leslie Stone was trying to persuade Ruby Keen to give up her fiancé and marry him. After he had drunk two more pints and she two ports, they left just before closing time at ten o'clock.

Two of the more inquisitive locals followed the couple, who walked past Ruby's home in Plantation Road and entered a lover's lane, the Firs, on the outskirts of the town, about 300 yards from her home. The locals gleefully hurried back to the Stag with this bit of gossip, leaving the couple alone.

Stone later told the police that he left Ruby about 10.15 pm outside the Stag, when they went their separate ways, he reaching home about 10.45 pm.

Ruby's presence in the Firs was accidentally confirmed in a curious way by a married couple who chose to take a short cut home along the lane about 10.30 pm. In the shadows they saw Ruby in the arms, they said, of a *policeman* – an assumption easily made, for the man was dressed in what they swore was a dark blue uniform with silver buttons. And who but a policeman would be embracing Ruby?

Early next morning, about 7 am, her almost naked body, wet with dew, was found in the lane by a railwayman, Mr Cox, on his way to work. No attempt had been made to hide her. She had been strangled with her own black silk scarf. Although most of her clothing had been torn off she was still wearing her gloves, and there was no sign of sexual assault. But there was every evidence in the sandy ground of the desperate struggle she had made, presumably to avoid being raped. She had been struck on the chin before being strangled, and her assailant had knelt as he killed her. The assault must have been swift and silent, for dogs in a nearby cottage had not been disturbed sufficiently to bark.

On the afternoon of 12 April Stone called at the house of PC McCarthy, who was out. Mrs McCarthy thought that Stone looked very worried and agitated. He said he had heard about Ruby's death and asked her to telephone Leighton Buzzard police station, as he had been with Ruby the previous night and wanted to make a statement to clear his name. He did so. But the police were more concerned about the evidence of the couple in the lane and the involvement of two local policemen with the murdered girl.

The assistance of Scotland Yard, in the person of Chief Inspector Barker, was speedily sought. He had been closely involved in 1927 in the arrest of Frederick Browne. It fell to Barker to question the two young policemen who had been the friend and fiancé of Ruby Keen, as well as the young workman who had been drinking with her on the night she died. The fiancé said he had last seen Ruby on the Sunday afternoon, before he went on duty at the village of Hockliffe, three miles east of Leighton Buzzard. It was an unbreakable alibi. But he and the other PC owed their ultimate elimination from the inquiry to Leslie Stone's new suit.

All the footprints beside the body had been trampled and defaced in the frantic struggle between Ruby and her assailant. But his knee-marks, shallow, rounded depressions in the ground, remained. Plaster of Paris casts were made of them, and when they were examined by Sir Bernard Spilsbury a clear imprint of the trouser crease and the material was revealed.

The dark blue trousers of the main suspects were inspected. Despite the fact that the trousers of Stone's new suit, as well as the jacket, had been cleaned or brushed – so hard at the knees that the nap had worn away – Spilsbury's microscope picked out granules of sandy soil in the fibres of the suit, and similar specks in the turn-ups. They were identical with the trampled earth by the dead girl's body. The fact that the suit had been worn by Stone on 11 April for the first time meant he could not claim to have got earth on his suit on any other night.

As incriminating was a single silk fibre found embedded in the lining of Stone's jacket. It matched the cream underslip Ruby had been wearing the night she died.

Stone was charged with her murder on Wednesday, 24 April 1937.

His trial began at the Old Bailey on Monday, 28 June, before the Lord Chief Justice, Lord Hewart. The chief prosecutor was Mr Richard O'Sullivan, KC, assisted by Mr Christmas Humphreys, son of Mr Justice Travers Humphreys. Christmas Humphreys had become a Treasury Counsel in 1934, when he was thirty-three. Mr Maurice Healy, KC, defended the accused.

The evidence was scant and circumstantial. But on the second day of the trial, Stone changed his story in the witness-box, saying in his defence that he and Ruby had quarrelled – she had struck him and he had choked her. He explained, saying that in the old days Ruby had had a trick of poking her little fingers in his ears and tickling them. This annoyed him. He had once struck her when thus provoked, but had missed and hit a brick wall. On the night of the murder she referred to this, and asked him if he had any trouble with his hand. He told the court: 'I told her she was lucky that I hit the wall instead of hitting her. She called me a dirty devil and hit me above the left ear. It was a full-arm swing. I was surprised and went up to her, and she struck again at me with the other hand. It made me jump at her. I caught hold of her scarf I think and pulled it. I think I knotted it again after that. . . She started to fall down and I caught hold of the front of her clothes. I was in a kind of rage. Her clothes were torn off as she was falling.' Then, he said, he knelt. He decided that she was not dead, only stunned. He said he did not try to interfere with her and walked away, thinking she would revive. When he got home he brushed his clothes.

The jury were out for twenty-five minutes. They found him guilty and he was sentenced to death.

When he appealed against the verdict on the grounds that the jury had been misdirected, it was on the basis that the judge had replied: 'Yes, undoubtedly,' to the jury's question – sent to him as they considered their verdict – 'If as a result of an intention to commit rape a girl is killed – although there was no intention of killing her – is a man guilty of murder?' Stone's appeal was dismissed.

He was hanged at Pentonville prison on Friday, 13 August 1937.

CHAPTER 30

Edward Chaplin

The manslaughter of Percy Casserley, 1938

Mr and Mrs Casserley married in 1927 when he was forty-seven and she was twenty years younger. Nothing is known of their lives till then, except that in his youth he had been a long-distance runner of some distinction and had represented his country in France; his club was South London Harriers. In 1937 they were living in suburban comfort in Wimbledon, at 35 Lindisfarne Road.

Percy Arthur Casserley was managing director of John Watney and Co., Ltd, a London brewers, earning £1,500 a year. Tall, spare and still with an athletic build, he was due to retire in February 1938, but certain circumstances caused him to stop work the previous September. He was an alcoholic. His wife later told the police that he drank a bottle and a half of whisky every day, that he began drinking after returning home from work and continued, hardly bothering to eat dinner with her, until well after midnight. Irascible rather than violent, he was abusive, unsociable and moody, and as a result the Casserleys had few friends locally and seldom went out together. They had no children. This was said to be Mr Casserley's wish and not his wife's.

There may have been other reasons, for in 1936 he had an unspecified operation which led to the total cessation of sexual relations between them. His consumption of whisky increased in 1937, and Mrs Casserley's frustrations, seeking some release, focused on Ted Chaplin.

Lindisfarne Road was a cul-de-sac south of Wimbledon Common. In the spring of 1937 work began on the building of a house next to the Casserleys' home. The builders' foreman, there every day, was a strapping, handsome man aged thirty-five, Edward Royal Chaplin. Married in 1928, he had been divorced in 1934.

One day Mrs Georgina May Casserley (Ena) asked him if he would like a cup of tea. The association deepened into an affair.

By September, Mr Casserley stopped going to work, and his state of health was such that he started having treatment for his alcoholism. He was in a home for inebriates between 16 January and 17 February 1938. In his absence, Chaplin more than once stayed overnight in 35 Lindisfarne Road. Mrs Casserley also visited him in his flat two miles away in Abbotsbury Road, Morden. On her husband's return she had news for him – she was pregnant.

This was another painful humiliation for Mr Casserley: his pride was hurt as well as his manhood. On 23 February he told his brother-in-law, Mr James Barry: 'One way out would be for me to shoot myself.' He presumed that his wife's lover must be 'a tea-planter home on six months' leave from Ceylon'.

Before long he was back in the nursing home (described in court as a 'home for nervous disorders'), said to be suffering from a nervous breakdown.

While he was away, from 8 to 22 March, Ted and Ena indulged themselves, albeit unhappily, careless now of what people might think or say. The live-in maid, Lydia Scott, had already been cast as Mrs Casserley's confidante and messenger. But something had to be done about making the baby legitimate; there was no question of an abortion. Ena Casserley, at the age of thirty-eight, wanted the baby very badly and she also wanted its father to be her husband. Chaplin wanted both woman and baby to be his in name as well as in fact. So while Percy Casserley was still in the nursing home Ena wrote to him asking for a divorce. He replied: 'Do you think I am such a fool as to give you up for someone else?'

Mr Casserley came home on 22 March, and the next night he was dead.

On the morning of Wednesday, 23 March, Lydia Scott, who had the evening off, asked Mrs Casserley if she would like to go to the pictures that night. Mrs Casserley agreed, but later on said that her husband did not want her to go – he had threatened, she said, to shoot her, and had put her into a state of fear and great distress. As Lydia Scott left the house at 6.45 pm, Mrs Casserley said to her: 'If you happen to see Ted, tell him I shall only be able to see him for a minute or two. I won't be able to get out. If he comes to the back door I'll be able to see him . . . Do try and see him.'

Chaplin had in fact arranged to meet Mrs Casserley at 7.30 pm at Coombe Lane. Lydia Scott turned up instead. She said: 'Madam can't get out tonight. Will you go up to the house to see her if only for a few minutes?'

He walked up the road to the Casserleys' home and arrived, according to him, as Mrs Casserley came out of the front door, wearing hat and coat and in tears. They walked to Copse Hill, where at 7.45 pm she bought a bottle of whisky at an off-licence – presumably to account for her absence to her husband if required to do so. She told him of her husband's threat and that she was afraid to go home.

They returned to the house in Lindisfarne Road and conferred in the scullery. Chaplin, wearing a raincoat over his sports jacket and trousers, and still wearing his hat, said: 'You had better leave this to me.' He sent her upstairs to her bedroom, from where she heard men's voices raised in anger, the sounds of a scuffle, two gunshots, and then someone coming up the stairs. The door opened – it was Chaplin.

That was the story she told to the police. Chaplin's story was told in court, as follows.

Percy Casserley was in an armchair beside the fireplace when Chaplin entered the lounge intending to have a man-to-man talk. 'Good evening,'

Left: Charles Peace
Above: Sketch of the body of
Catherine Eddowes by
Dr F. Gordon Brown

Left: James Maybrick
Above: Florence Maybrick

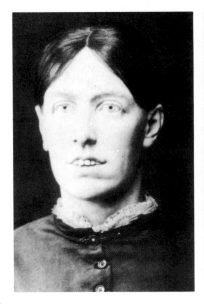

Waxwork of Mrs Pearcey from
Madame Tussaud's

The rope Berry used to hang
Mrs Pearcey

Dr Cream

Frederick Deeming

The murder
weapon used by
Richard Prince

Left: William
Terriss

Samuel Dougal with Georgina
Cranwell

The remains of Miss Holland in
the greenhouse at Moat House
Farm

Masks and coshes used in the raid by the Stratton brothers

Dr Crippen

Belle Elmore

Frederick Henry Seddon

Eliza Barrow

George Smith

The bath used in court to
show how a victim could
be drowned

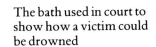

Right: Herbert Rowse
Armstrong, at the
time of his marriage
Below: Ronald True
Bottom: Freddie
Bywaters, Edith
Thompson and Percy
Thompson

Left: Patrick Mahon and his daughter
Above: Emily Kaye

Elsie Cameron and Norman Thorne

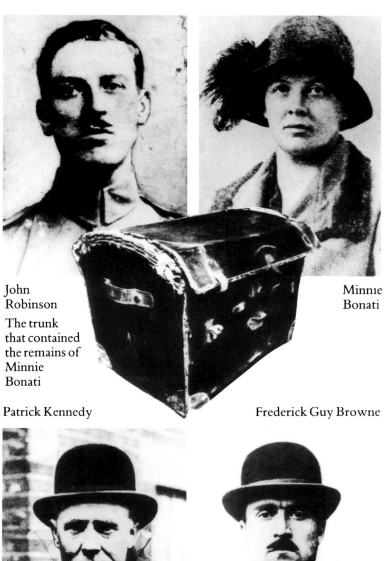

John
Robinson

The trunk
that contained
the remains of
Minnie
Bonati

Minnie
Bonati

Patrick Kennedy

Frederick Guy Browne

Above: Charlotte
Bryant
Right: The
Bryants' cottage at
Coombe Farm

Below: The arrest
of George
McMahon

Far left: Ruby Keen

Above: The scarf
with which Ruby
Keen was strangled

The body of Percy Casserley as it was discovered by the police

Below: Gordon Cummins
Right: Evelyn Oatley

Elizabeth Jones — 'Georgina'   Karl Gustav Hulten — 'Ricky'

Left: John George Haigh

Below: Daniel Raven with his bride

Above: Christopher Craig

Left: Derek Bentley

John Christie   Timothy Evans

From left to right (top row): Ruth Fuerst, Muriel Eady, Ethel Christie
(bottom row): Kathleen Maloney, Rita Nelson,
Hectorina MacLennan

Left: Ronald Chesney, alias John Merrett

Below: Veronica Murray

Below left: Michael Dowdall as a drummer-boy

Below right: Harry Roberts

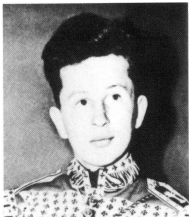

Above: Guenther Podola on 28 July on his way from Brixton prison to the West London Magistrates' Court

Reginald and Ronald Kray

Arthur and Nizamodeen Hosein   Muriel McKay

said Chaplin, and removed his gloves to shake hands as Casserley got to his feet; his spectacles had fallen on the carpet. Chaplin made a speech: 'I've called to see what the trouble is between you and Mrs Casserley. I've just left her and she's terribly upset. You known about her condition. I'm responsible for it. I want to suggest to you that either she comes away with me tonight or I'll phone and get her police protection, as I understand you've threatened Mrs Casserley.' Percy Casserley stared at the other man as if shocked or dazed – or drunk. He said: 'Oh, so it's you, you swine.'

Chaplin waited, pulling on his gloves again, as Casserley went and sat at a writing-bureau with his head in his hands. Then he opened a drawer and took out a pistol. Chaplin dived forward and seized the other man's right forearm with both his hands, twisting the arm so that Casserley was forced to drop the pistol. Chaplin then released his grip as the older man 'looked ill'; he was half supporting him. Casserley then leaned over and picked up the pistol with his *left* hand, which was grasped at once by Chaplin's right hand. With his left he seized the other man's right wrist and there was a stand-up, face-to-face struggle, during which Chaplin endeavoured to keep the pistol pointing in the air and away from him. It went off.

The bullet penetrated the back of Casserley's neck, exiting at once – a superficial wound. Whereupon Chaplin released his grip on Casserley's right wrist and put his left arm around the other man's waist, intending to throw him to the floor and disarm him. As he did so Casserley's right hand (the left one still held the gun) gripped Chaplin's testicles – referred to in court as 'a portion of his body'. Enraged by this and in some pain, Chaplin reached out for a torch lying on the bureau and, left-handed, struck Casserley on the head three times. Casserley's head – he was stooping – was by then on a level with Chaplin's stomach and his left arm and the pistol were held high in Chaplin's right-handed grasp. After the second blow on Casserley's skull, the head of the torch came off. The third blow was struck with the base of the torch.

Casserley let go of the younger man's genitals as Chaplin made another determined effort to throw him to the ground. Casserley stumbled and fell backwards, pulling Chaplin down on top of him; their faces touched, and in their fall Chaplin banged his head on a bookcase. All the time fifty-eight-year-old Casserley struggled violently, trying to point the pistol at Chaplin and using both his hands now; there were a couple of clicks from the gun. 'He was like a maddened bull,' said Chaplin. With both of his hands he seized the other man's left wrist and pulled his left arm down and across his neck. Casserley, overpowered and unable to move under Chaplin's weight, said: 'All right. I give in.'

Chaplin relaxed his hold and began to get up. As he did so he heard another click and saw that both of Casserley's hands were on the pistol. He pounced and forced the other man's hands back to the side of his head. The gun went off. Casserley went limp – shot in the head, just in front of his left ear.

Chaplin removed the pistol from Casserley's left hand and stood up, wrapped the gun in a handkerchief and put it in his raincoat pocket. He closed the open drawer in the bureau after taking out a box of cartridges he saw there and putting that too into a coat pocket. Noticing his gloves were stained with blood he wiped them on his raincoat. He then went into the hall and upstairs to Mrs Casserley. 'My God!' he said.

They both came down and went to the kitchen. Chaplin then returned to the lounge where Casserley lay on his back, stretched out diagonally opposite the door and in front of the small bookcase, on top of which was a large framed photograph and a bowl of yellow tulips. His head was near the skirting-board resting in a pool of blood. He was still alive, groaning but unconscious. Chaplin knelt and touched the wounded man's head. He panicked; he thought of getting medical help, then thought of staging a burglary 'to save the publicity and to keep Mrs Casserley's name out of it as far as possible'.

When the police arrived about 9.30 pm they found the house in some disorder. They had been summoned after Mrs Casserley rushed to a neighbour's house at 9.10 pm, sobbing and crying out that something terrible had happened – an intruder had broken into her house and her husband had been injured. The neighbour, Mr Burchell, went next door with his son, turned on the lights in the sitting-room and saw Mr Casserley lying on the floor with every sign of an interrupted burglary. He sent for the police.

Mrs Casserley told the police she had gone out for a walk earlier that evening, being absent for about forty minutes. On her return, she said, she found her husband dying in the lounge and the house much disordered. Indeed, in the hall a coat-stand had been knocked over; the kitchen window was open; silverware stood and lay on the dining-room floor and other pieces were scattered on the floor of the lounge. A broken and blood-stained torch also lay on the lounge carpet and a grey button by the door. On the settee reposed one of the dying man's slippers; an empty cartridge case lay against the skirting-board by his head, and about a foot above it there was a bullet-hole in the wall, which was spattered here and there with blood, as was the furniture and the floor. It was like a scene from a play.

Casserley died soon after the police arrived.

Meanwhile Chaplin went to Raynes Park and thence to his flat in Morden. There he put the pistol, handkerchief and box of cartridges in the drawer of a bedside cabinet. Also in the drawer was a life-preserver (a cosh), which Chaplin said later he had bought for his ailing father in October the previous year. He washed the front of his raincoat, burned the handkerchief and later the box, and then washed the life-preserver, as some blood from the pistol or handkerchief had got on to it. The following morning he went very early to Epsom and hid the gun and the cartridges in the cavity wall of a half-completed villa. Then he went to work.

Soon after the police investigation started they began to suspect that burglary was not the background to Percy Casserley's death.

The autopsy, carried out by Sir Bernard Spilsbury, was on the 25th. On 29 March the police visited Ted Chaplin, builders' foreman, on his current site in Northey Road, Epsom. 'Are you Mr Chaplin, known as Ted?'

enquired Detective Inspector Henry. 'Yes, that's right,' responded Chaplin. DI Henry continued: 'I wish to speak to you concerning the death of Percy Arthur Casserley.' 'Yes,' said Chaplin. 'It's terrible. I read about it in the papers.' He was asked to accompany DI Henry to a police station to be interviewed. Chaplin fetched his raincoat from a shed and put it on. It was still damp and was missing a button.

At the police station, after making a statement denying that he had been to Lindisfarne Road the night before, he suddenly decided to confess, and have done so, took the police to the villa where the pistol was hidden. 'I'll show you where the gun is,' said Chaplin. 'You'll never find it on your own.'

He was charged at Wimbledon police station with the murder of Percy Casserley on the same day that the murdered man was buried at Gapp Road Cemetery, Wimbledon; his wife sent a wreath of red roses from 'Sorrowing Ena'.

Three days later she was arrested in a nursing home and charged with being an accessory after the fact. She was remanded in custody in the hospital in Holloway prison, where she was forbidden to have a bath and made to scrub floors. Her lawyer protested about this when he asked for bail, saying his client was a lady, whose social position, refinement and pregnancy did not justify such harsh and humiliating treatment. Bail was granted.

The trial of Edward Royal Chaplin began at the Old Bailey in Court No. 1 on Tuesday, 24 May 1938, before Mr Justice Humphreys. Mr Norman Birkett, KC, defended Chaplin, and Mr St John Hutchinson appeared for Mrs Casserley, whose trial for being an accessory was to follow Chaplin's. Mr G. B. McClure, KC, led for the Crown, assisted by Mr Christmas Humphreys, the judge's son.

Sir Bernard Spilsbury, appearing for the prosecution, said the blows on the dead man's head could have been caused by the life-preserver, as could three marks or injuries on his back. Casserley's body was in fact bruised or injured in more than seventeen places. Not a single mark had been found on Chaplin when he was examined by a doctor soon after his arrest.

The judge told the jury in his summing-up: 'What you have to decide is – did Chaplin unlawfully cause the death of Mr Casserley, and if he did, did he do it with the intention of causing his death or causing him grievous injury?'

The prosecution's case was that Chaplin went to the house, and knowing Casserley had a pistol took the life-preserver with him, which he then used to batter the older man before shooting him twice. Having lodged in the house in Mr Casserley's absence, Chaplin might well have known where the gun was kept – it was also possible that Mrs Casserley could have told him. He might have intended that Mr Casserley's death should look like suicide. Perhaps the struggle in the lounge was not caused by Casserley's efforts to kill Chaplin, but by his efforts not to be killed himself. Spilsbury suggested that the blows to Casserley's head had been struck from *behind*, and that the bullet which sliced through the back of his neck must have been fired from a distance of *more* than twelve inches, as there were no powder-marks on the neck. Neither man was left-handed. But Chaplin said he struck the other man with the torch in his *left* hand, and that the pistol was in Casserley's *left* hand each time it was fired.

Another problem was that Casserley, who was fifty-eight and ill, was unlikely to have put up much of a fight against a thirty-six-year-old with large strong hands (Chaplin was asked to hold them up in court), even if he was fighting for his life. The prosecution also pointed out that Chaplin was unmarked in the struggle and that he had made no attempt to get help for the injured man – there was a telephone in the house. When Mr McClure asked Chaplin: 'Why didn't you hit him in the face with that large hand of yours?' – Chaplin answered: 'I had no intention of harming Mr Casserley.'

Mr McClure, in his closing speech, again drew attention to the blood that had been washed off the life-preserver – how did it get there? There were other questions. Why was a diamond ring worn by Casserley found hidden in a basket in Chaplin's flat? How could he have been in a panic if he troubled to remove the ring? Why did the accused never mention that Mr Casserley cocked the gun before the first shot was fired? Did this mean the gun in the bureau drawer had already been cocked? Why did Chaplin, with his superior strength, need a weapon with which to strike the older man? Would not Casserley, having been struck three times, be dazed at least and even less capable of resistance? Why, after disarming Casserley once when the gun was in his right hand, was it so difficult to disarm him when he held the gun in his left hand? Were the jury to believe that a man like Chaplin would take his eyes off the gun for a moment, and allow Casserley to get both hands on it? 'Chaplin was holding the hand that was holding the pistol,' said Mr McClure. 'Whose was the force that was pressing that pistol against the skin? The man was flat on his back. . .' His suggestion was that Chaplin's story was made up later to fit the facts.

A point in the accused's favour was that the little pistol, a .25 Webley and Scott automatic, had a defective mechanism. The firearms expert, Robert Churchill, concluded that the weapon would be more effective in the hands of the man accustomed to handling it, its owner. Casserley, therefore, when the gun misfired, would be more knowledgeable and quicker at clearing the jammed cartridge. On the other hand the pistol had not been oiled, which seemed to indicate that Casserley knew or cared little about guns.

The judge reminded the jury that if they decided that Mr Casserley had been shot 'in the heat of passion in the course of a quarrel so serious that the accused lost complete control of himself' they might convict the accused not of murder, but of manslaughter.

This they did, and on Friday, 27 May, Chaplin was found guilty of manslaughter and sentenced to twelve years' penal servitude.

Mrs Casserley, waiting outside the courtroom, fainted when she heard this. Twenty minutes later, supported by policewomen and six months pregnant, she was brought into the court to be dealt with as an accessory after the fact. She wept without pause.

Her counsel, Mr Hutchinson, began his plea by saying that for years she had been an excellent wife. The judge, Mr Justice Humphreys, interposed – 'You are not putting her forward as an excellent wife *now*?' Later, Mr Hutchinson said: 'Also, I would ask you to take into account her condition at the moment.' 'We know she is pregnant,' snapped the judge, 'as hundreds of other women are pregnant. But there's nothing the matter with her, no disease or anything like that?' 'No,' replied Mr Hutchinson. 'But the nervous strain . . .' 'She can pull herself together if she wants to,' said the judge.

As with Mrs Thompson and Mrs Rattenbury, the judge's censure of the dead man's wife was severe. He said: 'The less said about you and your part in this case the better. I am not going to treat you with lenience because I think there is nothing particular in your condition that calls for it. Your case has aroused the most ridiculous nonsense. A great many people have treated you as though you were a sort of heroine. You were a participator in a vulgar and sordid intrigue.' He ended – 'Now please go!'

Mrs Casserley was given a nominal sentence of eleven days in prison and immediately released.

Ted Chaplin served eight years of his sentence. When he was freed from prison on the Isle of Wight after the war, Ena Casserley was waiting at the gates. He put on a new suit and they went to a register office. On 17 May 1946, they became man and wife.

CHAPTER 31

William Butler

The murder of Ernest Key, 1938

The body of Ernest Percival Key, a sixty-four-year-old jeweller, was found in his lock-up shop at 74 Victoria Road, Surbiton, just before noon on Saturday, 24 December 1938, by his son, Jack Key, and his daughter, Mrs Arthur Bell. Covered in blood and unconscious, the old man was still alive, despite one of the most savage knife attacks on record. He had been stabbed about thirty-one times in his head, face and neck, and there were well over a dozen cuts on his arms, made as he tried to defend himself. He died on the way to hospital.

Mr Key, a Yorkshireman from Hull, was well known locally, having been in business as a jeweller in Surbiton for over twenty years. He had been murdered during the course of a robbery – some jewellery was missing from the shop. A bowler hat, however, had been left behind by the assailant, and Dr Eric Gardner, the County Pathologist for Surrey, was able to use the size of the hat and hairs found within it to give the police investigating the murder some hints about its owner before Sir Bernard Spilsbury arrived on the scene.

The owner turned out to be an unemployed driver called William Thomas Butler, aged about twenty-nine. He was married with two children and lived in Laurel Road, Hampton Hill, Teddington, about three miles north-east of the jeweller's shop, beyond Hampton Court Palace and the park. He had previous convictions for housebreaking.

Less than an hour after the knife attack on Mr Key, Butler took a taxi from Kingston railway station to the Kingston county hospital. Blood was issuing from his gloves. He was seen by Dr Day, who also examined Mr Key. Butler said he was Charles Jackson, of Norbiton, and had been accidentally injured by a wood-cutting machine. He later told the police that his hands had been cut when he was knocked down by a motor-cycle combination and that he gave a false name and address at the hospital because he could not afford the fees. The cuts had in fact been caused by a dagger or knife without a guard, which he had used to stab Mr Key.

Butler was charged with the murder of Mr Key on 17 January 1939, and was put on trial at the Old Bailey a month later, on Wednesday, 15 February. The judge was Mr Justice Singleton, and the prosecutor Mr G. B. McClure. Butler was defended by Mr David Maxwell Fyfe, KC, MP, later to become Solicitor-General, and in 1951 Home Secretary. He claimed that

Butler had acted in self-defence, and that the charge should be reduced to manslaughter.

The trial ended on its second day. Butler was found guilty and sentenced to death. An appeal was lodged on 23 February and dismissed. He was hanged at Wandsworth prison on 29 March 1939.

CHAPTER 32

Vincent Lawlor

The attempted assassination of Marina,
Duchess of Kent, 1939

Ledgwidge Vincent Lawlor was a forty-four-year-old Australian with inordinate attachments to a .22 German rifle and to the British royal family. Arriving in England in 1938, he found employment on the construction of the new Waterloo Bridge and at weekends he travelled about visiting Windsor Castle, Buckingham Palace and other royal homes – to see 'the dukes and kings' as he put it – with the gun stuffed down a trouser leg. For the sake of comfort, and no doubt concealment, the rifle barrel had been sawn off right back to the wood and the stock had also been shortened. Thus equipped, Lawlor stumped around the royal residences, secure in the knowledge that he possessed a firearms certificate issued by the Metropolitan Police. This, as he later told the police, entitled him to fire the rifle as and when he liked. He also told them he never intended to kill – certainly no member of King George's family, all of whom he much admired.

Be that as it may, on the night of 4 June 1939 he was in Green Street, Mayfair, and fired a shot at No. 32, the London home of the Earl of Harewood. The bullet penetrated a window, but caused no other damage and no injury. The occupants were mystified. People in the street heard the shot, but presumed it was some car back-firing.

The following afternoon Lawlor went to Belgrave Square, and occupied the porch of a house opposite No. 3, which happened to be the home of the king's youngest brother, the handsome Duke of Kent, who had married the fashionably beautiful daughter of Prince Nicholas of Greece, Princess Marina, in 1934. They now had two very young children: Prince Edward and Princess Alexandra. That evening the Duchess of Kent left the house about 7 pm and got into a chauffeur-driven car which was to take her to a social engagement. As the car pulled away from the kerb, Lawlor fired. His shot struck a wall.

This time he was seen and apprehended. Although the rife, with its foresight and most of its barrel removed, was not an accurate weapon, it was still dangerous. The Duchess was fortunate – as was Lawlor. For at his trial he was bound over for a month, on condition that he returned to Australia, where no royal person or residence would prove a tempting target.

CHAPTER 33

Udham Singh

The murder of Sir Michael O'Dwyer, 1940

On Wednesday, 13 March 1940 – a comparatively quiet day in the Second World War, which had begun (as far as Britain was concerned) on 3 September the previous year – there was a joint meeting at Caxton Hall of the East India Association and the Royal Central Asian Society. Held in the Tudor Room, it was attended by about 160 people who had assembled to hear a lecture – 'Afghanistan: the Present Position' – given by Brigadier-General Sir Percy Sykes. The Secretary of State for India, Lord Zetland, was in the chair and several distinguished elderly gentlemen sat beside him on the platform, including Sir Michael Francis O'Dwyer, who had been Lieutenant-Governor of the Punjab in 1919 at the time that the Amritsar riots were brutally suppressed by General Dyer. Sir Michael, now seventy-five, had succeeded Sir Louis Dane, who was now nearly eighty-four. Also seated on the platform were Lord Lamington, aged seventy-nine, former Governor of Bombay and President of the East India Association and Sir Frank Brown, the Association's honorary secretary.

After the lecture, which lasted for about forty-five minutes and concluded at about four o'clock, Sir Michael O'Dwyer made, according to *The Times*, 'a witty speech, which was warmly received. The substantial unanimity of the Moslem world in support of the Allied cause in the war was emphasized. After Mrs Malan (formerly Miss Audrey Harris) and Sir Louis Dane had spoken, a vote of thanks was moved by Lord Lamington.' It was now about half-past four.

When the applause had died away the officials on the platform stood up and moved to congratulate each other on the success of the meeting. As they did so, a burly Sikh walked down a gangway to the front of the hall and at very close range fired all six rounds of a .45 Smith and Wesson revolver into the group on the platform.

Sir Michael O'Dwyer, who had sat at the end of the front row, was shot twice in the back, one bullet passing through his heart and right lung, the other through a kidney. A bullet broke Sir Louis Dane's arm. Lord Lamington's right wrist was injured. Lord Zetland had a miraculous escape. He was hit by two bullets in the chest, but their impact was minimized by his clothes and by the Sikh's use of .40 ammunition, which was thirty years old and whose cartridges were a loose fit and failed to engage with the rifling grooves. 'I felt a sharp pain in my ribs,' he said later.

'It rather knocked me out, and while I was lying down I heard some other shooting going on, but did not see what happened.'

The Sikh was overpowered by two members of the audience (one in RAF uniform) as he ran for the exit, shouting 'Make way!' and waving the revolver. Found also to be carrying a knife, he was charged at Bow Street police station on 14 March with the murder of Sir Michael O'Dwyer, whose death was described by Mr Attlee in the House of Commons as an 'abominable outrage'. In India it was also officially deplored and condemned and Mr Gandhi said it was 'an act of insanity'.

The assassin was Singh Azad, a thirty-seven-year-old engineer who lodged in Mornington Crescent. He was also known as Udham Singh. A note of Sir Michael's name was found twice in Singh's diaries for 1939 and 1940, once spelt 'O'Dyer'. It seems Singh confused O'Dwyer with General Dyer.

In custody Singh, who was excitable and spoke English badly, made several disjointed statements: 'I did it because I had a grudge against him. He deserved it. I don't belong to any society or anything else. I don't care. I don't mind dying. What is the use of waiting until you get old? That is no good . . . Is Zetland dead? He ought to be. I put two into him. I bought the revolver from a soldier in a public-house. My parents died when I was three or four . . . Only one dead, eh? I thought I could get more.'

In prison, awaiting trial, Singh went on a forty-two day hunger strike.

His trial began at the Old Bailey on 4 June 1940 – a most desperate time for Britain in the war: the British Expeditionary Force had just been evacuated from Dunkirk; the Germans were pouring into France and the Russians into Lithuania, Latvia and Estonia. Paris fell on 14 June and France capitulated eleven days later.

The judge at the trial was Mr Justice Atkinson. Mr G. B. McClure led for the Crown and Mr St John Hutchinson for the defence. Singh said in his defence that the shooting was an accident. He had intended, he said, to fire at the ceiling in protest at the difficulty of getting a passport and at the treatment of Indians by the British government in India.

Sir Bernard Spilsbury gave evidence. Looking far from well (having had a slight stroke a few weeks earlier), he spoke from the well of the court and was not cross-examined.

On 5 June the jury retired for ninety-five minutes before deciding Singh was guilty. He made a speech which the judge directed should not be reported in the press.

An appeal heard on 15 July was dismissed, and on 31 July Udham Singh was hanged in Pentonville prison.

In the first twelve months of the Second World War, Albert Pierrepoint, born in 1905 at Clayton in Yorkshire and brought up in Huddersfield and Manchester, was given his first job as the 'Number One' executioner, and as such carried out his first execution at Pentonville prison in 1940 (see Appendix C for his account of this). Albert, following in the footsteps of his father, Harry, and his Uncle Tom, had become an assistant executioner in 1931, the year of Ellis's death. Uncle and nephew ('Our Albert') worked together on many executions, and although Uncle Tom worked as a hangman for forty-two years, retiring when he was seventy-five, it was 'Our Albert' who was able to say on his retirement: 'I have carried out the execution of more judicial sentences of death (outside the field of politics) than any executioner in any British record or archive.' To this end he executed many war criminals in Germany on behalf of the allies, twice hanging seventeen men and women in one day. Altogether, Albert Pierrepoint hanged over 400 men and women in his twenty-five years of office.

CHAPTER 34

Harold Trevor

The murder of Mrs Greenhill, 1941

Few murderers have exhibited quite as many of the characteristics of an archetype as H. D. Trevor, whose self-interest, self-pity, self-deception, self-dramatization, stupidity, conceit, mendacity, charm and indolence were unbounded and apparently unending. Nonetheless, of minor criminals he seemed the least likely to end up as a hanging man. In doing so he provided the police with one of their swiftest solutions of a crime, made at the scene itself.

Mrs Theodora Jessie Greenhill was the sixty-five-year-old widow of Major Greenhill and lived in a block of flats in Elsham Road, West Kensington. In the autumn of 1941, anxious to move out of bombed and blacked-out London, she decided to let her flat, furnished, and advertised this fact through a local estate agent.

On Tuesday, 14 October, she was visited by a tall, slim elderly gentleman, wearing a monocle and with thinning grey hair, who expressed a keen interest in renting the flat. Indeed, he was so pleased by it that he agreed to take it then and there. The few pounds she had requested as a down-payment were forthwith produced – an advance or first instalment of the rent. No doubt much gratified by this speedy and satisfactory development, Mrs Greenhill seated herself at her bureau in the drawing-room and began writing out a receipt for the money in her large bold hand – 'Received from Dr H. D. Trevor the sum of s . . .'

The pen jerked in her hand, making a jagged line down the notepaper, as the monocled gentleman struck her on the head with a beer bottle, using such force that it shattered: pieces fell on the floor and into a wastepaper basket. Mrs Greenhill collapsed unconscious on to the carpet, where the phoney doctor got down on his knees and strangled her with a ligature.

This done he ransacked the flat, rifling through the drawers of the bureau and emptying a cash-box that he found in the bedroom. He prized it open with a nail-file. Having retrieved the rent advance he left the flat. But before doing so he laid a decorous handkerchief over the dead woman's face.

Thus she was discovered by a daughter of her first marriage, Miss Tattersall, who, on receiving no reply from her ringing of the door-bell, let herself into her mother's flat.

DCS Fred Cherrill, called to the scene from Scotland Yard to assist the investigation begun by DCI Salisbury, examined the various fingerprints that had been found – four on fragments of the beer-bottle, two on a small table near the body, and one on the cash-box.

Something seemed familiar to Cherrill about the name on the incomplete receipt: 'Trevor'. Yet surely no one would be so stupid as to leave his *actual* name on the murdered woman's desk – in her own hand? The name must be fictitious. Nonetheless, Cherrill contacted the Criminal Record Office at the Yard and asked for all the files bearing that name to be brought to him. When they arrived he began, with the aid of a magnifying glass, to compare the records of fingerprints in the files with the suspect prints in the flat. Before long he was able to tell the astonished Salisbury that the murderer was Harold Dorian Trevor.

A warrant was issued for Trevor's arrest and he was traced to Birmingham, where he had pawned and sold a cabin trunk and other articles which he had removed from Mrs Greenhill's flat by taxi to King's Cross station. There he had pawned two of her rings.

He was picked up on Saturday, 18 October, as he stepped out of a telephone box in Rhyl, North Wales.

After being cautioned by DCI Salisbury, Trevor said: 'It wasn't murder. There was never any intent to murder. I have never used violence to anyone in my life before. What came over me I do not know. After I hit her my mind went completely blank and is still like that now. Something seemed to crack in my head.'

It was not surprising that the name 'Trevor' was familiar to DCS Cherrill – the sixty-two-year-old Yorkshireman had spent nearly all of his last forty years in jail. In that time he had in fact known only eleven months of freedom, and had just been released from prison when he called on Mrs Greenhill with robbery, it seems, in mind. He had never before, however, been involved in any kind of violence, the crimes for which he was so often incarcerated being those of petty theft and fraud. Posing as Commander Crichton, Sir Charles Warren or Lord Herbert, he would ease money from any susceptible source, preferably female. His apparent aim was to avoid work and to live in the style and comfort he affected in his impostures. His subconscious intention seems to have been to dramatize and magnify a vacuous existence by making himself the centre of attention in police investigations and in a court of law. He must also have unconsciously sought the organized security of life in prisons, where he was known and cared for.

The murder of Mrs Greenhill is so uncharacteristic and unnecessary, and his stupidity in virtually leaving his calling-card (his name and finger-prints) so extraordinary, that he appears to have almost consciously sought the final satisfaction in his old age of being tried on a capital charge and making a perfectly legal exit. Certainly he never lost the chance in all his court appearances to address the judge and jury, speaking the utmost humbug with dignity and courtesy, and with his honour unsoiled.

Trevor was tried at the Old Bailey on 28 and 29 January 1942. Mr Justice Asquith was the judge. Mr L. W. Byrne appeared for the Crown and

Mr John Flowers, KC, and Mr Derek Curtis Bennett for the defence, which tried to prove that the accused was insane.

Harold Trevor's greatest moment came when he was asked if he had anything to say before sentence of death was passed.

'I would like once and for all,' he declared, 'finally to say this, that I, as a man who stands, so to speak, at death's door, would like to confirm all I have already said regarding this lady's death, that I have no knowledge of it. Even as I am speaking the moving finger is writing on the wall, and the words once written, can never be recalled. I sincerely hope that each of you, gentlemen of the jury, and the judge too, in passing sentence will remember these words – that when each of you, as you surely must some day, yourself stand before a higher tribunal, you will receive a greater measure of mercy than has been meted out to me in this world . . . If I am called upon to take my stand in the cold grey dawn of the early morning, I pray that God in his mercy will gently turn my mother's face away as I pass into the shadows. No fear touches my heart. My heart is dead. It died when my mother left me.'

There was much more; and if this were not enough, in the death-cell he penned a long farewell in which he said: 'I have lived my life not as I would have liked to live it – but as it was forced upon me by fate. I was educated at a first-class school in Birmingham, and was the friend and playmate of men who are Bishops today. Some of them are sitting in the Episcopal Chairs, while I am waiting the short walk from the condemned cell to the scaffold.'

He was hanged on 11 March 1942 in Wandsworth prison.

CHAPTER 35

Gordon Cummins

The murder of Evelyn Oatley, 1942

The fantasies of many murderers are seldom as fantastic as the stories about them perpetrated by some newspapers in the guise of news and truth. Facts are misrepresented, elaborated and dressed up in a feverish style that is supposed to attract the public and sell papers, or in the case of television to fill the spaces (as it sometimes seems) between the advertisements. Nothing unlocks the crime-writer's cupboard of clichés more than the sexual murder of a woman or child, when the murderer is presented as a monster or beast and the victim as pretty, if not attractive, and as innocence personified. In many cases the victims have been far from pretty and have often been much more sophisticated than the reports suggest. No man is a monster, however monstrous his acts, and it is an unfortunate fact that many sex-murderers have been good-looking, good company and good fun.

Such a one was Gordon Frederick Cummins, aged twenty-eight, who went on a sudden, barbarous murder binge in wartime London in 1942. He killed four women in six days, horribly mutilating three of them. He picked up his victims in West End pubs and clubs, older women who were on the look-out for pleasant young servicemen to give them a good time.

Nice-looking, agreeable Gordon Cummins was a most unlikely Ripper. But so was the recent Yorkshire Ripper, lorry-driver Peter Sutcliffe, who at the age of thirty-four was sentenced to life imprisonment on 22 May 1981 for the murder of thirteen women over a period of six years. Another pleasant and plausible lady-killer was Neville Heath, a twenty-nine-year-old ex-air force officer, who was active four years after Cummins. The two are in fact quite similar; and there are curious similarities between Cummins, Sutcliffe and the *original* Ripper. But because Cummins's atrocities were committed in wartime, they never received the press attention that made the other two men notorious. However, the attacks on Cummins's four known victims are unparalleled in their perverted savagery. They are also the most inexplicable. Little has been written about him – the few known facts are these.

Gordon Cummins was a well-educated boy, of good family and of average height (5 ft 7 ins), but unreliable, dishonest, and unable to hold down a steady job. His father was the superintendent of an approved school. A Yorkshireman, Cummins was born in New Earswick, to the north of York. He was educated at Llandoveris County School, and when his family moved to Northampton he attended the technical school there before going to work in London in a laboratory. He married a theatre producer's secretary in 1936; they had no children. Called up in 1941, two years after the outbreak of war, he joined the RAF, became an Air Cadet, trained for the air-crew, and was billeted in the new year in North London. His air force colleagues remarked on his phoney Oxford accent and pretentions and called him 'The Duke'.

On Saturday, 8 February 1942, he left an RAF establishment in a requisitioned block of flats in St John's Wood, visited his wife, borrowed some money and then went into the West End for a night on the town.

Early on Sunday the body of Miss Evelyn Margaret Hamilton, a chemist's assistant aged forty, was discovered by an electrician in a brick-built air-raid shelter in Montagu Place, W1, just north of Marble Arch. She had been in London on her way from Hornchurch in Essex, where she worked, to her home in Newcastle-upon-Tyne. Her clothes were disarranged and her scarf had been wound around her head. But Cummins's motive for murder, apart from an unexplained lust to kill, seems to have been theft: her handbag had vanished and with it £80. Although she had been strangled there was no sign of sexual assault.

This was only a prelude.

That night, a thirty-five-year-old former actress and Windmill show-girl, now a prostitute, Mrs. Evelyn Oatley (also known as Nita Ward), encountered Cummins and took him home to her Wardour Street flat. Here she was strangled. Her nearly naked and crudely mutilated body was found on her bed on Monday, 10 February. After she was strangled, her throat had been cut, and the lower part of her body cut open with a tin-opener or a knife. Nearby was a pair of curling tongs.

A few days later, on Thursday, 13 February, another prostitute, Mrs Margaret Florence Lowe, aged forty-three and known as Pearl, was murdered in her tiny flat in Gosfield Street, W1, parallel to Great Portland Street. She was strangled on her divan bed with a silk stocking and then cut and disfigured. By the body were the knife and razor used on her. There was also a candle. In the kitchen was a half-empty bottle of stout.

While DCI Greeno, Sir Bernard Spilsbury and DI Higgins were still at the scene of the Lowe murder they received news of yet a fourth.

This time the victim was Mrs Doris Jouannet, aged thirty-two. The wife of an elderly hotel manager, she was also known as Doris Robson. Strangled with a scarf, and with her naked body obscenely mutilated, she lay in the two-roomed ground-floor flat she shared with her husband in Sussex Gardens, north-west of Marble Arch. A fountain pen and a comb had been taken from the flat. As with Miss Hamilton, her home town was Newcastle-upon-Tyne.

DCI Greeno, who with DCS Cherrill was investigating the murders, realized after the discovery of the bodies of Mrs Lowe and Mrs Jouannet that a new Ripper was at large. Even the case-hardened Bernard Spilsbury was moved to say on viewing Mrs Lowe's injuries that they were 'quite dreadful' and that their perpetrator was a savage sexual maniac.

On Friday, 14 February, Cummins, now insatiable but careless, chatted up Mrs Greta Heywood in Piccadilly. They went for a drink and a sandwich in the Trocadero and then walked down Haymarket. She said later that he became unpleasantly forward, so she said goodbye and tried to leave him. 'You must let me kiss you goodnight,' he said, trying to do so. Having no wish to be his Valentine she hurried away in the blackout. He chased after her, she claimed, catching up with her in St Alban's Street. In a dark doorway he seized her by the throat and began to choke her. She struggled in vain and passed out.

But her life was saved by a delivery-boy who happened to be taking some drink to a bottle-party in the nearby Captain's Cabin. He heard some scuffling and saw a flash of silk stocking as Mrs Heywood's legs gave way. He went to investigate. Cummins ran off, leaving behind an RAF gas-mask which bore his name, rank and number (525987).

A few hours later, still bent on a fifth kill, he acquired another companion, a young prostitute called Mrs Mulcahy, in Regent Street and returned with her in a taxi to her Paddington flat in Southwick Street. On the way there he gave her five £1 notes. It had been snowing and was very cold. Mrs Mulcahy lit the gas-fire, and as her room was icy she kept her boots on while she removed her clothes. Cummins had hardly removed his great coat and belt when a 'strange expression', as she later said, came over his face. He gripped her neck and squeezed. Mrs Mulcahy kicked him hard on the shins, making him cry out. As if recovering his senses he shook his head, put on his coat, and left – but not before giving her another £5 in notes. Perhaps he panicked, fearful of the noise he himself had made and of being caught in the act again. This time he left behind his belt.

This and the gas-mask and the £1 notes enabled DCI Greeno to trace Cummins to his St John's billet, where Greeno at once came up against an apparently perfect alibi – Cummins's name in the billet pass-book showed that he had reported back to the billet and been signed in before midnight all that week, and must accordingly have been in bed when Evelyn Oatley, Mrs Lowe and Mrs Jouannet had been murdered. He, of course, when interviewed, denied having anything to do with the killings.

It was not until Greeno ascertained that the airmen in the billet often vouched for each other's return and that on the nights in question Cummins, leaving the building by way of a fire-escape, had gone out with another airman *after* being checked in, that the alibi was proved false.

There was enough other evidence to clinch the case against Cummins. A white metal cigarette case belonging to Mrs Lowe was found in a pocket of his tunic. Items belonging to Mrs Hamilton were found in a dustbin outside the billet. The fountain pen belonging to Miss Jouannet (and marked 'DJ') was found in his number one uniform, and a cigarette case belonging to Mrs Oatley was discovered in a refrigerator in the billet.

In her flat a print from a left thumb on a mirror and a print of a left little finger on the tin-opener were identified as his. In Mrs Lowe's flat, fingerprints from a left hand were detected on the bottle of stout and a candlestick. Cummins was left-handed.

He was arrested on Sunday, 16 February, the day after Singapore surrendered to the Japanese.

Two other murders, then unsolved, were later attributed to him: that of nineteen-year-old Miss Maple Church, whose body had been found the previous October in a bombed house in Hampstead Road, near Euston station, and that of a Mrs Humphries, whose body was discovered in Gloucester Crescent, north-east of Regent's Park.

Gordon Cummins was charged on 17 February 1942 with the murders of Mrs Oatley, Mrs Lowe, and Mrs Jouannet, and on 20 February with assaulting Mrs Heywood and Mrs Mulcahy. Finally, on 27 March, the murder of Miss Hamilton was added to the list.

While on remand in Brixton prison, Cummins was escorted to and from prison by DI Robert Higgins, who, with a detective sergeant from Tottenham Court Road police station, had discovered the body of Mrs Lowe after forcing open the door of her flat with a jemmy. Higgins was also with Cummins in court, and in his memoirs had this to say of his charge:

He chatted to me on everyday subjects as though he had not a care in the world. He seemed to be completely unaware of the seriousness of the charges against him . . . [He] had an irritating habit of wanting to shake hands each time we met . . . Observed at close quarters, he was not an obviously unpleasant person . . . He was inclined to be slow and steady in his speech. From the physical point of view he appeared quite normal, being well built and proportioned, and would not have attracted special notice if put among a group of ordinary people. I did, however, take particular note of his unusually large, strong hands, which had been well kept. He was deceptively gentle in manner and quite good-looking – a man not unattractive to women . . .

The trial of Gordon Cummins began at the Old Bailey on Monday, 27 April 1942, before Mr Justice Asquith, and he was indicted, as was usual, on just one count – the murder of Evelyn Oatley. The prosecutor was Mr G. B. McClure, KC. Cummins was defended by Mr John Flowers, KC. The evidence was conclusive and the trial was brief, ending the following day on 28 April. The jury took thirty-five minutes to find him guilty.

Cummins was hanged in Wandsworth prison on 25 June during an air-raid.

His wife, who had stood by him throughout, visited him until the day of his execution, believing, it seems, that he was totally innocent – as he himself continued to claim. The post-mortem on his body, as with many other executed murderers, was carried out by the pathologist who had examined the victims, in this case Sir Bernard Spilsbury.

CHAPTER 36

Jones and Hulten

The murder of George Heath, 1944

No full-length study has been made of the relationship between murder and wartime, when official military murder is rife. Some connections undoubtedly exist, as is shown by the increase and the casual nature of wartime murders, when life seems cheap; living is difficult, passions are raised and people are on the move. Many post-war murders also have their roots in wartime: the imagination of boys, fired by dreams of death and glory, by the guns their fathers wore and used, later seeks some equivalent peacetime realization. Then there are also the demobilized servicemen, their reason and feelings marred and bent by slaughter. In fact, while the majority of all murderers have previous criminal records, another large proportion related to the first, are servicemen or ex-servicemen.

In the autumn of 1944, the allies were following up the D-day invasion on all fronts, in Europe and in the Pacific. The liberation of Paris on 23 August had preceded the recapture of Antwerp and Brussels, as well as the allied advance through Belgium, Holland and France to the borders of Germany, forestalled for a time by the Arnhem disaster and the German counter-offensive in the Ardennes. British forces then invaded Greece on 5 October. Meanwhile, V2 rockets had begun falling on the south-east of England and on London, as well as doodlebugs – the flying-bombs.

In the late afternoon of Tuesday, 3 October 1944, an American GI met a striptease artiste in wartime London.

He was Private Karl Gustav Hulten, aged twenty-two, dark-haired, Swedish in origin, and absent without leave for six weeks from his paratroop regiment. He was now passing himself off as a lieutenant and called himself Ricky (Richard Allen). She was Elizabeth Maud Jones, aged eighteen, fair-haired and blue-eyed. Her stage-name had been Georgina Grayson, and it was as 'Georgina' that Betty Jones was introduced to 'Ricky' in a little café in Queen Caroline Street, Hammersmith Broadway, by Len Bexley, a coach trimmer who happened to know them both.

Said Hulten: 'I saw Len Bexley sitting there with a young lady. I took another seat, but he asked me to come over and join them, which I did.' She said: 'I thought he was a gentleman.' 'We were there a while in the cafeteria,' said Hulten, 'and afterwards we all got up together and left together. Mrs Jones and I walked down towards the Broadway. I asked her if she would care to come out later on . . . She agreed and then she left us. I told Bexley: "I don't believe she will turn up."'

Hulten went off to see a girl-friend, Joyce Cook, whom he had known only for three days. They had met the previous Sunday by chance at the local Gaumont cinema. Betty Jones returned to her rented room in 311 King Street, Hammersmith.

Born in South Wales on 5 July 1926, she had married at the age of sixteen. Her husband was a Welsh soldier and ten years older. On their wedding-day he struck her and she left him there and then. Two months later, in January 1943, she came to London, obtaining employment as a barmaid, usherette, waitress and ultimately as a striptease dancer at the Panama and Blue Lagoon clubs. But from the spring of 1944 she was out of work, living on the separation allowance of £1 15s 6d a week provided by her husband. He was serving abroad; he went missing in September, and the letter confirming that fact was delivered to her on 13 October, the day she was formally charged with murder.

On the night of Tuesday, 3 October, she turned up at the Broadway cinema at 11.30 pm as arranged, but Hulten failed to make an appearance. She was walking back to her room in King Street when a two and a half ton ten-wheeled US army truck pulled up in front of her, driven by Hulten, now in a leather jerkin and khaki slacks. He hailed her and she climbed into the huge truck beside him. 'I told her I was a paratrooper,' he said, 'and she said that was a dangerous profession to be in. I told her it was . . . She said she would like to do something exciting, like becoming a "gun moll", like they do back in the States. At first I thought she was kidding . . . I then explained to her that we had a stolen truck. We drove on towards Reading.' He also told her that he had broken into a pub and had run around with a mob in Chicago. He showed her a stolen pistol.

About 1 am, just outside Reading, they passed a girl on a bicycle. Hulten turned the truck around, drove past the girl again and stopped the truck. He got out, and as the girl cycled by he shoved her over. She scrambled away, and he seized her purse which was hanging from the bicycle's handle-bars. After throwing the purse up to Betty Jones he got into the cab (it had a left-hand drive) and they drove back to London. Their haul was a few shillings and some clothing coupons, which he later sold for £1. 'During the night,' she said, 'he taught me to drive.'

About 5 am he dropped her off in King Street, parked the truck in a car-park and slept there.

He saw her again on the Wednesday night, but they made no foray in the truck. Hulten discovered she had a rash on her stomach. 'That put me cavy,' he said, and accordingly, although they slept together, they went only as far as 'the next thing to sexual intercourse'.

On Thursday, 5 October, he called on her about 5 pm. They went out for a meal and then to the Gaumont cinema in Hammersmith. On leaving the cinema at about 8.45 pm they entered a café. 'Just as we got to the door,' she said, 'the sirens sounded.'

After the air-raid they went to the car-park, got in the truck and drove towards Reading again, to a pub near Sonning which he intended to rob. But either his nerve failed or something disturbed him, for he drove the truck back to London, to Marble Arch.

'When we got there she suggested that we rob a cab. She pointed one out to me and I followed it . . . out to Cricklewood.'

Although Hulten, having forced the taxi to stop, pulled a gun on the driver and said: 'Let me have all your money,' the presence of a passenger in the back alarmed him and he fled. He and Betty Jones drove slowly back through deserted, blacked-out London to Marble Arch. In Edgware Road, at Jones's suggestion he offered a young girl pedestrian a lift to Paddington, where she hoped to catch a train to Bristol. Hulken offered to take her as far as Reading. He put her suitcase (which was tied with rope) into the back, and she sat in the cab between Jones and Hulten, thankful for the lift.

Said Hulten: 'When we were almost through Runnymede Park going towards Windsor I stopped the truck off the road. I told the girls we had a flat tyre. We all got out . . . I told Georgina to get the girl's back to me. She said: "All right." Georgina gave the girl a cigarette and lit one for herself . . . I hit the girl over the head with an iron bar.' As she did not fall he put an arm-lock around her neck, forced her to the ground and knelt on her back as Jones went through the helpless girl's pockets. She found about five shillings. 'By this time the girl had ceased struggling. I picked up her shoulders and Georgina picked up her feet. We carried her over and dumped her about three feet from the edge of a stream.' She survived.

The robbers returned to Georgina's bed in King Street and stayed there till 3 pm on Friday afternoon. When Hulten left King Street an hour or so later he went to see his other girl-friend, Joyce. They went out to the pictures, and then returned to her house in Fulham Palace Road. He left about 11 pm.

Betty Jones had been expecting her American friend since six o'clock. She now had a very bad cold. Despite this and his broken promise she went out with him, apparently without complaint or reservation, when he whistled for her down in the windy street. They decided to rob a taxi.

They were sheltering from the wind in a doorway opposite Cadby Hall in Hammersmith Road when a grey Ford V8 saloon slowly approached them as if seeking their custom. Betty Jones called out – 'Taxi!' – and the car stopped.

It was a private hire car, driven by thirty-four-year-old George Heath. Earlier that night he had twice called for work at a Godfrey Davis garage in Eccleston Street, the last time at about 11.05 pm. But no work was forthcoming and he set off on his own to find some passing trade. His charge for taking his two young customers to the Chiswick roundabout that marked the end of the Great West Road was an exorbitant ten shillings. Between them Jones and Hulten then had less than £2; she had 10s 3d. They expected to have more money soon.

The Ford set off with its two passengers sitting in the back, Hulten behind the driver. It was now about 2 am.

Once past the Chiswick roundabout, Hulten, the loaded gun in his lap, told Heath: 'We'll get out here.' The car stopped at the kerb and Heath leaned to his left over the back of the front seat to open the near-side door for the female passenger. Hulten fired – accidentally, he said later, claiming his jacket sleeve caught on something on the door and jerked his arm as he started to get up. Later, Betty Jones said: 'As Heath was leaning over I saw a flash and heard a bang. I was surprised there was not a loud bang because Ricky had told me it would make a big noise when it went off . . . Heath moaned slightly and turned a little towards his front. Ricky said to him: "Move over or I'll give you another dose of the same." I saw that he still had the automatic in his hand. Heath seemed to understand what Ricky had said, because he moved further over to the left-hand side of the front seat . . . I heard him breathing very heavily and his head slumped on his chest.'

Heath had been shot through the middle of his body. Hulten now occupied the driver's seat and drove speedily towards Staines.

Said Jones: 'Ricky then told me to go through Heath's pockets. I leaned over and I heard his breath coming in short gasps. Ricky told me to look for his wallet in the breast pocket of his jacket. I felt in that pocket but did not find the wallet. I found it instead in the left-hand outside pocket of his overcoat.' She emptied the dying man's pockets, including his trouser pockets. She removed his wrist-watch; the pound notes, pennies, fountain-pen, silver pencil, and cigarette case were given to Hulten. Everything else was thrown out of a window: his cheque-book, identity card, licence, petrol coupons, photos and letters. Paralysed by a bullet deflecting off his spine, Heath died of haemorrhage within fifteen minutes, drowning in his own blood.

His body was dumped in a ditch on the edge of Knowle Green near Staines. Jones found the bullet that had killed Heath – it had ricochetted off the front near-side door, striking the dash-board and dropping to the floor. It too was thrown from a window.

The couple drove back to London, parking the Ford in the old Gaumont car-park behind Hammersmith Broadway at about 4 am; they wiped it clean of fingerprints. They ate in the Black and White café and asked some cab-drivers there to take them home. None of them would, so they walked. In Jones's room they examined all their trophies before going to bed about 5 am on Saturday, 7 October.

Three hours later, about eight o'clock, an electrician's apprentice, John Jones, was walking along the Great Southwest Road that leads to Staines when he came across the wallet, identity card, driving licence and cheque-book that had belonged to George Heath. The body was discovered soon after 9 am by an auxiliary fireman attached to the National Fire Service, Robert Balding. He had just finished a night duty at the Ship garage, London Road, and was taking a short cut across Knowle Green on his way home.

Tyre-marks on the grass verge helped to identify the car. Police enquiries about the murdered man traced his movements the previous night and a description of his car, RD 8955, was circulated to all police stations.

Meanwhile, Jones and Hulten got up at ten to eleven. He went out to a barber's shop at 16 Queen Caroline Street and sold Heath's wrist-watch to a hairdresser, Morris Levene, for £5. The fountain-pen and silver pencil were sold to Len Bexley for eight shillings. 'He said he was broke and wanted some money,' said Bexley, who then went to a pub with Hulten before returning with him to 311 King Street. On the way there Hulten bought a small bunch of flowers for Georgina.

The three then took a taxi to the White City Stadium where they bet on the greyhound races. Jones looked very tired, according to Bexley; but the couple, he said, seemed very fond of each other.

She won some money, and when she and Hulten returned to King Street she asked her landlady, Mrs Evans, to mind some money for her, £7 in all. 'I said to her,' said Mrs Evans, 'if she had any money at any time – as the buzz-bombs are about, I put anything of mine in the oven, and let me put it in the oven for her ... and she did.' Later, Mrs Evans (like Bexley and Levene) said Hulten was 'a very decent chap'.

The couple went out for a meal and then saw a film, *Christmas Holiday*, starring Deanna Durbin.

On Sunday, 8 October, Hulten spent the afternoon with Joyce and most of the night with Georgina, during which they drove about in the Ford V8, using it as a hire-car, having further unknown adventures and returning to King Street (the car was parked behind an air-raid shelter) about 7.30 am. They slept until about 1.45 pm.

When Hulten left King Street he picked up the car, saw Joyce at the bakery where she worked, drove to his camp near Newbury in Berkshire, and called on Joyce about 6 pm when he had promised to visit Georgina. He parked the car in Lurgan Avenue.

About ten-past eight on the night of Monday, 9 October, PC William Walters observed the Ford and its number, RD 8955, when he was out on his beat. After telephoning Hammersmith police station from a police-box he was soon joined by Inspector Read and a sergeant, who arrived at the scene in a police car. All three waited, with PC Walters at the rear of the Ford.

About nine o'clock Hulten emerged from Joyce's house and entered the stolen Ford.

Walters dashed up, seized his hand, and said: 'Is this your car, sir?' Hulten was silent. Walters shouted – the police car put its lights on and the other policemen ran up. Hulten was dragged out and searched. In his left-hand hip pocket there was a Remington automatic, the safety catch cocked; ammunition was found in a trouser pocket. He was taken to Hammersmith police station where he said he was 2nd Lt Richard Allen, 501 Parachute Infantry Regiment, US army.

The police communicated with the American authorities, as an act passed that year had laid down that no American serviceman could be tried in a British court.

At 3 am on Tuesday, 10 September, Lt Robert Earl de Mott, aged twenty-seven, an American CID officer who had once been a lawyer in Denver,

Colorado, interviewed the suspect and established his real name and that he was a deserter. Hulten said he had found the car abandoned near Newbury. He was removed to the American CID HQ in Piccadilly and questioned further. This time he said he had spent the night with Georgina Grayson.

On Wednesday morning he offered to show de Mott where Georgina lived. He did so, and two British inspectors entered the house at noon, found Jones in bed and took her to Hammersmith police station, where she made a statement and was allowed to go home, not as yet being thought to have been involved in the shooting of Heath.

That afternoon at about half-past four she happened to go into a cleaners' in Hammersmith where she met a War Reserve constable, Henry Kimberley, whom she had not seen for two years, not since she had been a very young waitress. He had gone to the cleaners' to pick up a suit. She said: 'Hello.' Struck by her haggard appearance, he remarked how tired she looked. 'I should think so,' she said. 'I've been over at the police station for hours about this murder.' She pointed to a newspaper she held which reported the murder of George Heath. The papers called it the 'Cleft Chin Murder' and the 'Inky Fingers Murder', both descriptions applying to Heath. Kimberley asked her why that should worry her if she had nothing to do with the murder. She said she knew the man they had got inside – he couldn't have done it as he was with her all Friday night. Before she left he commented once again on her worn-out appearance. She said: 'If you had seen someone do what I have seen done, you wouldn't be able to sleep at night.'

A few hours later, Inspector Tansill and Kimberley called at 311 King Street. Betty Jones arrived at the same time. Alone for a moment with Kimberley she asked him why he had brought the inspector. 'I think you should tell him the truth,' said Kimberley. 'All right, I will,' she said.

She made a full confession, implying that Hulten had led her astray and that she was only obeying his orders. She denied helping him carry the body out of the car.

A fortnight later she elaborated this idea, writing to the police and saying she had acted throughout in fear of Hulten's threats and violence. This was to be the mainspring of her defence.

Hearing of her confession Hulten made a statement, blaming her for egging him on 'to do something exciting' and participating far more than she had admitted. 'If it hadn't been for her, I wouldn't have shot Heath,' he told the police.

The American government waived its rights on the Visiting Forces Act and allowed Hulten to be tried in a British court.

As the Russians completed the capture of Warsaw, and while the British and American forces pushed on towards Cologne and Berlin and the Americans occupied the Philippines, Hulten and Betty Jones appeared before Mr Justice Charles at the Old Bailey, on Tuesday, 16 January 1945. Mr L. A. Byrne led for the prosecution, Mr John Maud and Mr J. D. Casswell for Hulten and Jones respectively. Mrs Lloyd Lane also appeared for Jones, the first woman barrister to defend a prisoner accused of murder. And for the first time a female accused in a murder trial was allowed to appear hatless and with no covering on her head.

After a six-day trial both the accused were found guilty and were sentenced to death. Eighteen-year-old Betty Jones was taken shrieking and sobbing down to the cells. Appeals pleading manslaughter were heard and dismissed in February.

Dresden was bombed by the British on 13 and 14 February – 25,000 people died – and on 19 February the Americans landed in Iwo Jima. As the recapture of Burma proceeded apace, Elizabeth Jones was reprieved, just two days before the date set for her execution.

There was no reprieve for Karl Hulten. He was hanged at Pentonville prison five days after his twenty-third birthday, on 8 March 1945. The war in Europe ended two months later.

Betty Jones was released from jail on licence in January 1954. She was twenty-seven.

CHAPTER 37

Jack Tratsart

The murders of John and Claire Tratsart, 1945

Lyons Corner Houses, tea-rooms and restaurants of some distinction, were celebrated features of the London scene for more than fifty years. In their heyday before the Second World War there were 250 of them, employing hordes of swift-footed aproned waitresses known as 'nippies'. The first Corner House was opened in Piccadilly in 1894, and the last bearing that name closed in 1969. They were phased out in the 1960s, being converted into self-service restaurants called Jolyon. The Corner Houses were large, bright, cheerful establishments, providing cheap but agreeable teas and meals. They were popular places of rendezvous and formed the familiar setting of many tête-à-têtes and scenes of domestic affection, argument, parting and celebration. The Oxford Street Corner House, near Tottenham Court Road, was once the setting for a murder.

At about 5 pm on 20 April 1945, the ground-floor restaurant was crowded, buzzing with conversation and busy nippies. The end of the war was in sight – the surrender of Germany was only a fortnight away. Few people glanced at the family of six gathered around one of the tables, although one or two of those sitting nearby noticed that a young man wearing glasses was fooling, so it seemed, with a pistol – a water-pistol or an air-pistol, they thought, naturally enough as the other members of the family continued to laugh and joke as if nothing at all was amiss.

Then six shots cut across the teatime chatter.

Customers screamed and some ducked below tables, as three members of the family fell from their chairs, their heads and bodies spurting blood. The young man wearing glasses stood over them, a smoking gun in his right hand.

Two soldiers, quicker to react than most, seized him, and the police and a doctor were sent for. The initial panic soon subsided: after five years of war and bombing, Londoners were accustomed to violent sights and sounds. The Corner House staff soon calmed their customers and persuaded them to stay put, coolly screening off the scene of the crime. No more teas were served that day.

Meanwhile, the first police constable to arrive on the scene – he had hurried in from Oxford Street – informed the local police station in Tottenham Court Road.

By the time DI Robert Higgins arrived the bodies were being removed. One man was dead; a woman was dying; and a young man was seriously injured, shot through the jaw. The bespectacled gunman, still guarded by the two soldiers, sat calmly on a chair. Higgins asked where the gun was. No one could tell – no one knew. He approached the gunman, assuming that he had concealed the murder weapon somewhere on his person, and after introducing himself Higgins asked the young man for the gun. Speaking clearly and firmly the assassin informed the police officer that as *he* was a detective it was up to him to find out.

A search of the gunman and of the floor-space round him produced no gun, although nineteen bullets were found in a pocket. Higgins was becoming anxious when something odd in one of the light fittings on a pillar caught his eye. Through the bowl-like glass of the lights he saw the silhouette of a gun. It had been thrown there after the shooting, but to Higgins's amazement no one in the restaurant had noticed the gunman doing this. No one, it also appeared, had actually seen the shooting – presumably because, on hearing the bangs, everyone automatically dived for cover under the nearest table or chair.

The short-sighted young man was removed to Tottenham Court Road police station for questioning. To this he was not at all averse and spoke freely, his words being carefully written down in longhand as he sipped at a cup of tea.

His name was Jack Tratsart. He was twenty-seven, unmarried, and a toolmaker by trade. His father, John Tratsart, was a Belgian who had come to Britain before the First World War and had settled in Norbury, South London; he designed shoes for a living. He and his wife had six children. When she died in 1937 he married his housekeeper. After the start of the Second World War the Tratsarts were evacuated to Northampton, except for the eldest son, Jack, who remained 'for business reasons' in Norbury.

As the war came to an end, the family in Northampton began to think about returning to Norbury. A meeting to discuss the move was arranged by Jack, who had plans of his own. It was decided that Mr Tratsart (aged fifty-seven), his son Hugh and two of his daughters (Claire, twenty-eight, and Anne, thirteen) should meet Jack and Mr Tratsart's first wife's middle-aged sister, Miss Coemans, at the Lyons Corner House in Oxford Street.

Claire had been an epileptic for seven years; young Hugh suffered from a kind of palsy. Jack himself was an insomniac and a manic-depressive. He had been to see a specialist about his depressions, but having no faith in doctors he soon terminated his visits. The casualties and suffering caused by the war used to excite his concern. He was particularly outraged, according to his aunt, by the Italians' treatment of the Abyssinians. As it was, life seemed to him to be full of almost intolerable pain, delusions and difficulty; and when disabilities were added, as in the case of his sister Claire and brother Hugh, the sufferers might as well be dead. So might his father, whom he hated and despised.

Privately he resolved to kill the three of them and then commit suicide himself, and he decided that the family gathering in the Lyons Corner

House would provide the best occasion for the deed. He already had a revolver, bought two years previously 'from a sailor' for £5. 'They say that opportunity only comes once,' remarked Jack Tratsart.

In the long statement he made to the police he said: 'I have considered killing my brother Hugh and my sister Claire for some time, four or five years really, ever since I came back from Belgium when I was nineteen. My sister Claire is an epileptic and my brother Hugh has never been able to use his hands – a sort of semi-paralysis. They've never stood a chance and my father didn't help them in their deficiencies. He is miserably, terribly bigoted, and the worst person to have as a father. You know what an epileptic is? She can't get married, and her life isn't worth living whatsoever. My sister Claire is a staunch Roman Catholic, and all she thinks about is going to heaven. She's got every possible disadvantage and couldn't keep here job. I have been contemplating killing myself for a number of years. I tried once, but failed. That was in Belgium. I was the only one of the family who could help Claire and Hugh. My father only thought of making money. I had decided to commit suicide, so I thought I would do a good job while I was about it.'

So on the afternoon of 20 April, ten days before Hitler's suicide in the Berlin bunker, Jack Tratsart travelled up to London with his aunt to meet the other members of his family at the Corner House. In a pocket was his pistol and twenty-five cartridges, six of which had been loaded in the magazine. The family took their seats and gave their orders to the waitress. The three women, Anne, Claire and the aunt, sat opposite the three men, Mr Tratsart, Hugh and Jack.

'I sat in the right position,' said Jack, 'so that nobody could interfere with me shooting them and myself. We all sat talking normal gossip. I got the gun out and the funniest thing happened. I tried three times to fire it and couldn't. I didn't know you have to pull the top back. I decided to shoot Claire first then my father, then Hugh, then myself. I pointed the gun across the table at Claire and pulled the trigger. But nothing happened and only Hugh saw me and grinned. Ten minutes later I repeated the performance and pulled hard at the trigger, with the gun only about two feet from Claire. But again nothing happened. They did not seem to realize that I was going to kill, and when my aunt asked jokingly, what I had there, I said: "Only a water pistol." They joked about it and I put it under the table. Then I carried my plan through. I fired two bullets at Claire, but did not see what happened. I then fired two at my father and two at Hugh, coming round in a line. I was then standing up and pointed the gun at my head and pulled the trigger once or twice. But nothing happened.'

Mr Tratsart died almost at once. His daughter died on the way to hospital. Hugh, shot through the chin, survived.

Jack Tratsart was charged with double murder and attempted murder. After a preliminary hearing at Marlborough Street court he was sent for trial at the Old Bailey. But he never appeared there. Doctors and psychologists who examined him in prison decided he was unfit to plead.

He was declared insane and sent to Broadmoor, where two years later he died.

Before he died he learnt how to play tennis and to play the piano. He became quite good at both. He also began writing a book which opened – 'This is a world of youth, all men over forty scram.

CHAPTER 38

Neville Heath

The murder of Margery Gardner, 1946

Some people seem to invite their own murder by provocative or needling words or acts. Such a one was Mrs Margery Aimée Brownell Gardner, a thirty-two-year-old film extra, who had recently separated from her husband and led what was then known as a 'bohemian' life. She had rather masochistic tendencies, her bent being flagellation and bondage.

In May 1946 she went with a good-looking, well-built younger man to the Pembridge Court Hotel in Notting Hill Gate, where she was saved from a fate worse than flogging by the intrusion of a hotel detective.

Some weeks before this another woman, likewise naked and bound, was saved in a hotel in the Strand by a similar intervention that had been prompted by her screams. This woman later refused to prefer charges against her assailant, presumably to avoid appearing in court and to escape the ensuing publicity.

Yet Yvonne Symonds, who had no predilection for bondage or anything of the sort, was saved a few weeks later when she spent a night in a hotel room with the same man, saved by what one can only presume was her own innocence and trust.

Miss Symonds was nineteen. She was staying at the Overseas Club, and on Saturday, 15 June 1946, she went to a WRNS dance in Chelsea. There she chanced to meet a charming army officer in civvies who called himself Lt Col Neville Heath. He was ten years older than she, quite young to be a colonel, but it was possible for him to have achieved such a rank in the war. He took her to the Panama Club in South Kensington and then back to the Overseas Club. Much enamoured of him, she spend most of Sunday in his company and agreed, after he made a proposal of marriage, to spend Sunday night with him at the Pembridge Court Hotel, 34 Pembridge Gardens, Notting Hill Gate. He booked them in as 'Lt Col and Mrs NGC Heath'. Nothing untoward happened to her in Room 4, despite her partner's recent and frustrating experiences with the lady in the Strand hotel and with Mrs Gardner.

None the worse the next day, she returned to her parents' home in Worthing, leaving Heath alone in the hotel and free to pursue his own devices.

He telephoned Yvonne in Worthing several times and amused himself in unknown ways on Monday, Tuesday and Wednesday. He also telephoned his recent acquaintance, Margery Gardner, and as fate would have it she agreed to see him on Thursday, 20 June.

That night they visited the Panama Club in Cromwell Place and left just after midnight, getting a taxi back to Pembridge Gardens. Both were the worse for drink. Heath took a minute or so to count out the fare – 1s 9d, to which he added 5d – and then walked off towards the hotel with his arm round his companion's waist. The taxi-driver, Harold Harter, later recalled that Heath wore a grey, pin-striped suit and that Mrs Gardner 'had a tight-fitting hat and a three-quarter tweed coat'. To the man on the door at the Panama Club she had seemed 'rather dowdy'.

Heath, who had stayed twice before at the hotel under the name of Lt Col Armstrong, let himself into the nineteen-bedroom hotel with a front door key – there was no night porter – and took Mrs Gardner up to Room 4 on the first floor. It had two single beds.

The occupants of three other adjacent bedrooms slept on, undisturbed by any sound.

The following afternoon, a chambermaid, receiving no answer to her knocking, went into the unlocked room. The curtains were drawn; both beds were disordered; and a body under the bedclothes of one so alarmed her that the assistant manageress was fetched. Mrs Alice Wyatt entered the room and drew back the curtains.

When she recovered from her shock and horror at seeing the state of the body in the bed nearest the door, the police were called. Sergeant Fred Averill walked over from Notting Hill police station, arriving at the hotel at about 2.35 pm.

The naked body of Margery Gardner lay on her back under the bedclothes, her right arm underneath her. Her ankles were tied tightly together with a handkerchief, and her hands had also been tied behind her back. This was later deduced from marks on her wrists, although any ligature was missing – as was the material with which she seemed to have been gagged and which would have stifled her screams. Her face and chin were bruised, as if she had been hit by a fist, and as if a hand had gripped her jaw to prevent her opening her mouth or moving her head. She had been scourged seventeen times by something that had left a cross-cross diamond-like pattern on her face (twice) and on her front and back. Her breasts had been bitten and the nipples nearly bitten off. In addition some rough instrument had been thrust up her vagina and fiercely rotated, causing much bleeding. All these injuries had been inflicted before her death, which had been caused by suffocation – either by the gag, a pillow or the bed-clothes, or by having her head, face-down, pressed into a pillow.

There were many bloodstains in the bedroom, especially on the sheets of the other disordered bed by the window. This suggested that the main injuries had been inflicted there, and that the woman's body had been moved.

Her face had been washed, but there was still some dried blood caught in her nostrils and in the lashes of her left eye. There was no evidence that any intercourse had taken place.

The handkerchief that bound her ankles was embroidered with a 'K' and marked 'L Kearns'. But this clue was later found to be misleading and the handkerchief's owner to have had nothing to do with Mrs Gardner's death.

That morning – Friday, 21 June – Heath telephoned his unofficial fiancée in Worthing and travelled down by train to see her. They had lunch together and he booked himself a room at the Ocean Hotel. Miss Symonds met him again the following morning, when he mentioned a murder in London that was featured in the morning papers. He said he would tell her something about it later. She introduced him to her parents and they all went to the local golf club. That night he took Miss Symonds out for dinner at the Blue Peter Club in Angmering. During the meal she said: 'Look here, you told me you were going to tell me more about the murder.' He obliged.

'He told me,' she said later, 'that it happened in the room he booked at the Pembridge Court Hotel.' The amazed Miss Symonds heard that he had actually seen the body – 'a very gruesome sight,' he said – and that he had met the victim earlier in the evening and lent her his keys; she had had a man with her and they had nowhere else to go. He had slept elsewhere. He told her Inspector Barratt had telephoned him at this other place, had picked him up and taken him to the hotel where he was shown the body. She continued: 'He said Mr Barratt had said he thought she had been suffocated . . . that a poker had been used on her . . . had been stuck up her . . . had probably killed her.' Heath seemed concerned about the victim. He said that the sort of person who could do a thing like that must be 'a sexual maniac'. After dinner he took her home.

The Sunday morning papers were full of the murder, and Miss Symonds's parents were most distressed to read that Scotland Yard wished to interview a six-foot man named 'Neville George Clevely Heath', aged twenty-nine. Their daughter anxiously telephoned her fiancé at the Ocean Hotel. She told him her parents were rather worried by what they had read. 'Yes, I thought they would be,' he said. He reassured her, saying he was going back to London to talk to the police and would telephone her that evening. He never did.

Fortunately for Miss Symonds she never heard from him or saw him again until she gave evidence at West London magistrate's court and then at the Old Bailey.

Heath left Worthing that Sunday afternoon and went to Bournemouth. Before he left he posted a letter which he had begun, or written, the day before. It was addressed to Chief Inspector Barratt of New Scotland Yard (who had never met Heath) and arrived at the Yard on Monday, 24 June. The letter, signed 'NGC Heath', embellished what he had told Miss Symonds, excluding any reference to Barratt himself.

Heath said that he had lent his hotel key to Mrs Gardner, who had met an acquaintance 'with whom she was obliged to sleep' for financial reasons. Mrs Gardner, he said, intimated to him that if he returned after 2 am he 'might spend the remainder of the night with her'. He did so, he said, and on his return 'found her in the condition of which you are aware. I realized that I was in an invidious position, and rather than notify the police, I packed my belongings and left.' He then described Mrs Gardner's acquaintance, called Jack, and ended: 'I have the instrument with which Mrs Gardner was beaten and am forwarding this to you today.'

This he neglected to do, and the police neglected to provide the newspapers with any photo of him – with the result that he was able to stay at the Tollard Royal Hotel in Bournemouth for thirteen days without attracting much attention, other than that he was over-familiar with the head porter and seemed to have nothing other than a light brown sports jacket, flannel trousers and some shirts to wear.

He arrived at the hotel on the evening of Sunday, 23 June, calling himself Group Captain Rupert Brooke. The hotel was on the West Cliff, overlooking the sea. He was given Room 71, and was moved on 27 June to Room 81 on the second floor as he wanted a room with a gas fire. He complained of being cold. Room 4 at the Pembridge Court Hotel had also had a gas fire but, according to the manageress there, a poker had not been part of the furnishings. Otherwise, according to the Tollard Royal's head porter, Heath was just like any other male guest, reading, drinking beer and going out at night to shows and dances. There was also dancing at the hotel twice a week.

Ten days passed without apparent incident, except that Heath met a girl called Peggy at a dance at the Pavilion.

On the morning of Wednesday, 3 July, he was sitting on the promenade under the West Cliff when he saw her again, walking along the front with another girl. He joined them, and when Peggy left in about half an hour he asked the other girl, Miss Doreen Marshall, who was staying at the Norfolk Hotel, to have tea with him that afternoon. She was twenty-one.

Heath later told the police something of what happened that afternoon and night.

'I met her along the promenade,' he said, 'about 2.45 pm in the afternoon, and after a short stroll we went to the Tollard Royal for tea at about 3.45. The conversation was fairly general and covered the fact that she had served in the WRNS. She mentioned the fact that she had been ill [with influenza] and was down in Bournemouth to recuperate. She left the hotel at about 5.45 after accepting my invitation to dinner in the evening. At approximately 7.15 I was standing outside the hotel when I saw Miss Marshall approaching the hotel on foot down West Hill Road.' She had in fact left the Norfolk Hotel in a taxi. 'I entered the hotel, went to my room to get some tobacco and came downstairs again just as she was entering the lounge. We dined at about 8.15 pm and sat talking in the lounge after dinner, moving into the writing-room at about 10 pm.'

His timings were vague as he had no wrist-watch. 'The conversation was again general but she told me she was considering cutting short her holiday in Bournemouth and returning home [to Pinner] on Friday instead of Monday. She mentioned an American staying in the hotel (her hotel) and told me that he had taken her for car rides into the country and to Poole. She also mentioned an invitation to go with him to Exeter, but I gathered, although she did not actually say so, that she did not intend to go. Another American was mentioned – I believe his name was Pat – to whom I believe she was unofficially engaged some while ago . . . Conversation continued general until approximately 11.30 pm. At 11 pm (approx) Miss Marshall suggested going away, but I persuaded her to stay a little longer. At about 11.30 pm the weather was clear and we left the hotel and sat on a seat near the hotel overlooking the sea . . .'

The night porter, who had served them with drinks, thought that Miss Marshall seemed tired and pale and a little distressed. It seems she asked another hotel guest to order a taxi for her and that Heath countermanded this, saying he would walk her home. When they left just after midnight, he told the porter he would be back in half an hour. 'No – in quarter of an hour,' said Miss Marshall. Hatless, she was wearing a black frock and a yellow camel-hair coat and carried a handbag. Around her neck was a single string of twenty-eight pearls. She was 5 ft 3 ins.

According to Heath, they walked down towards the Pavilion and he left her at the pier, from where she headed back to the Norfolk Hotel in Richmond Hill through the public gardens. He said he returned to his hotel on foot via Durley Chine, west of the hotel – a very circuitous route. 'It rained heavily before I reached the hotel,' he said. He continued: 'I guessed that he [the night porter] would be waiting for me to come in, and as a ladder had that day been placed up against my window, I decided to practise a small deception on him, and entered my hotel bedroom via the ladder . . .'

So he did, and there he was, asleep in bed, when the night porter, wondering whether the playful group captain was in or not, peeped into Room 81 at 4.30 am. He noticed that Mr Brooke's shoes outside the door were caked with sand.

The following morning Heath joked about his little deception with the staff. He continued to stay at the hotel, his manner and appearance unchanged apart from the fact that he had a couple of scratch marks on his neck, took to wearing a scarf, and for once paid for his drinks in cash.

On Friday, 5 July, the manager of the Norfolk Hotel notified the police that Miss Marshall had been missing for two days. He also telephoned the Tollard Royal manager, Mr Relf, as he believed she had dined there the previous Wednesday.

On Saturday morning, about 10.15 am, Mr Relf asked Group Captain Brooke whether his dinner guest on Wednesday had been a Miss Marshall from Pinner. Heath laughed this off, saying: 'Oh, no. I've known that lady for a long while, and she certainly doesn't come from Pinner!' The manager suggested nonetheless that Mr Brooke should get in touch with the police. He did so, telephoning Bournemouth police station within half an hour. The officer in charge of the case was out, so Heath said he would phone again.

He did so at half-past three and spoke to DC Souter, who asked him if he would come and look at a photograph of the missing Miss Marshall. Heath agreed and arranged to visit the police station at 5.30 pm.

There he happened to meet Doreen's father and sister, who had travelled to Bournemouth from London. He consoled them, looked at Miss Marshall's photo, and was able to say that the girl with whom he had dined was indeed the missing girl.

As he gave an account of his dealings with her, DC Souter was struck by the group captain's resemblance to the photo of a man, wanted for murder, which had been circulated by Scotland Yard.

He told his superiors about his suspicions and suggested to Mr Brooke that his real name was Heath. Although the group captain denied this, he was detained in the police station by delaying tactics until DI George Gates saw him at about 6.30 pm. Heath was searched. £4. 10s was found on him in notes and cash. It was later established that he had pawned Doreen Marshall's ring for £5 on Friday and her watch for £3 on Saturday morning.

When Heath was told he was being officially detained for further questions, he complained of feeling chilly and asked if he could get his jacket from the Tollard Royal – he was wearing a buttoned-up, tieless flannel shirt and flannel trousers. He said he would come back. Gates fetched the jacket himself.

It was searched at the police station in front of Heath. In a pocket was found a cloakroom ticket issued at Bournemouth West railway station on 23 June, as well as a single artificial pearl and the return half of a first-class railway ticket from Bournemouth to London which had belonged to Doreen Marshall. Heath said he found it on a seat in the lounge of the Tollard Royal.

Gates then went to the railway station to claim the luggage Heath had left there. It turned out to be a suitcase.

Inside was some clothing, a mackintosh, a hat, and other articles marked with the name 'Heath'. There was also a blue neckerchief and a dark blue woollen scarf, both blood-stained, the latter with several hairs stuck to it that had come from Margery Gardner's head. Finally, there was a leather-bound riding switch, with a striking criss-cross weave. Where the end had worn away, a bunch of wire filaments was exposed. The switch had been washed or wiped but some blood still remained on it. This was the instrument used on and in Mrs Gardner

About 9.45 pm, Gates told Heath he knew who he was and that he would be further detained until officers of the Metropolitan Police arrived to interview him in connection with the murder of Mrs Gardner.

'Oh, all right,' said Heath.

He began writing out a carefully worded statement about half-past eleven, finishing it at 2.45 am on 7 July.

That day Detective Inspector Reg Spooner arrived in Bournemouth and checked and followed up the investigations already made by the Bournemouth police. He eventually saw Heath in the early hours of Monday, 8 July, at about 5.20 am. Heath said: 'I will make a statement after I've had some sleep.' He was taken by car to London a few hours later. That evening he was charged with the murder of Margery Gardner. He said: 'I have nothing to say at the moment.'

About the time he was charged, the body of Doreen Marshall was found.

Earlier the same day a young woman, Miss Evans, out exercising her black spaniel dog in Branksome Chine after returning home from work, noticed a swarm of flies in some rhododendron bushes. Later, after reading a newspaper account of the missing girl, she discussed her suspicions with her father over their evening meal. Mr Evans was intrigued. About eight o'clock he and his daughter visited the chine and found the body. By half-past eight the find had been reported to the police.

Branksome Dene Chine is a deep wooded valley running inland from the sea, about a mile west of what used to be the Tollard Royal Hotel, in the opposite direction from the pier and the Norfolk Hotel. It can be reached by a long walk past three other chines, along the sea-front under the cliffs. The body was found some distance away from the beach, to the right of a path in a subsidiary chine, dumped in some thick rhododendron bushes and covered first with the victim's clothes, the black dress and the yellow coat, and then with a fir-tree bough. The body, naked except for a left shoe, had apparently been moved a short distance: bloodstains and a broken string of pearls were found some twenty feet away, and nearby was a torn stocking. Another stocking was found high up in some bushes, and a blue powder compact seventy yards south of where Doreen Marshall's body lay.

She had been struck several times on the back of her head. There were also abrasions on her back, a bruise on her right shoulder and an area of redness around the left collar-bone, as if someone had knelt on her. The left side of her chest was bruised and a rib had fractured, piercing the left lung. Her left arm was bruised, as were both wrists, which appeared to have been tightly tied; they also bore finger-nail imprints of her assailant. The fingers of both her hands were badly cut on the inside, as if she had seized a knife in self-defence. All these injuries had been inflicted before she died, her death itself having been caused by a haemorrhage resulting from two deep knife-cuts across her throat.

After death a nipple had been bitten off and her body had been mutilated. A jagged series of slashes reached from her vagina vertically up to her chest, where they were joined by a deep diagonal cut from each nipple to the centre of her body, forming a Y. A rough instrument, possibly a branch, had also perforated and torn her vagina and anus.

No knife was ever found, nor was any blood on any of Heath's clothing. It is thought he stripped naked before the attack; and afterwards washed himself in the sea, into which he also threw the knife.

Heath's trial at the Old Bailey began on Tuesday, 24 September, concluding on the Thursday of that week at 5.45 pm. He pleaded not guilty. The judge was Mr Justice Morris; Mr E. A. Hawke led for the Crown and Mr J. D. Casswell for the accused.

The question was not whether Heath was guilty but whether he was insane. He gave no evidence in his own defence; as his counsel felt that his calm detachment and agreeable manner would never support the defence's contention that he was mad. Mr Casswell, in his cross-examination of DI Spooner, tried to establish Heath's instability and criminal nature by a detailed account of his career.

Neville George Clevely Heath was born on 6 June 1917 at Ilford, Essex. His father was a barber, and his mother is said to have been a large dominant woman. He was educated to begin with at a local Catholic school, where he seems to have been a bully and a tormentor of animals. He was good at athletics and rugby, but failed his exams. An office-boy at £1 a week for a time, he joined the Artists' Rifles when he was seventeen, and finding a service life to his liking he enlisted in the RAF on a short-service commission in February 1936. Court-martialled the following year for being absent without leave, for escaping while under arrest and for stealing a car, he was dismissed from the RAF in September 1937. In November he was charged with fraud and false pretences, eight other offences being taken into consideration, including two of posing as Lord Dudley. He was put on probation. In July 1938, after working for a fortnight as a sales assistant in an Oxford Street store, he was sent to a borstal in Suffolk for three years for robbing a friend's house of jewellery worth £51. Ten other offences were taken into consideration. Released on the outbreak of war – years later he revisited the borstal at Hollesley Bay, giving the inmates a talk on how he had made good – he joined the RASC as a private, being commissioned in March 1940 when he was sent to the Middle East. This time he got into trouble with a brigadier, mainly over dishonoured cheques. He went absent without leave, was again court-martialled and then cashiered in August 1941. Sent back to Britain on the troopship *Mooltan*, he absconded at Durban and went to Johannesburg, where he masqueraded as Captain Selway MC for a time, until he enlisted in the South African Air Force, calling himself Armstrong. His past record came to light eventually, but because of his good work he was allowed to remain – although he was never put on operational duties. Obtaining the rank of captain, he was seconded to the RAF in May 1944, to 180 (Bomber) Squadron, and flew a few sorties over Holland. In October his Mitchell bomber – he was the pilot – was hit by anti-aircraft fire and he and his crew bailed out.

Early in 1945 he returned to South Africa and in October his wife (he had married in February 1942) divorced him for desertion, taking custody of their son. She was a wealthy woman and he tried to blackmail her family over the divorce. In December he was court-martialled for the third time, being convicted of undisciplined conduct and of wearing unauthorized decorations. Dismissed from the service he returned to England, to Wimbledon, where his parents lived in Merton Hall Road. Before long he was fined £10 at Wimbledon magistrate's court in April for wearing medals and a uniform to which he was not entitled. He studied for a 'B' commercial flying licence but failed to turn up for the necessary exams.

The assault on the woman in the Strand hotel occurred in March, and the first assault on Mrs Gardner in May. He killed her in the early hours of 21 June 1946.

Mr Casswell's defence was that Heath's mind was 'not behind his hand', that he was not responsible for his actions and was 'morally defective' or 'morally insane'. Was there any anticipation or premeditation? Were his actions in London, Worthing and Bournemouth the actions of a sane man – not hiding, discussing the murder with Miss Symonds, writing to the police, reporting to the police, behaving in an apparently normal manner after the most savage of crimes? He may have known what he was doing, said Mr Casswell, but he did not know that what he was doing was wrong. Besides, the man must have been mad to have done what he did. Therefore his deeds came within the scope of the McNaghten Rules on insanity and Heath must be found guilty but insane.

Dr W. H. de Bargue Hubert, produced by the defence as an expert psychiatrist who could vouch for this line of reasoning, was carved up in cross-examination. Within a year Dr Hubert, a drug-addict, committed suicide. Two prison doctors, testifying for the crown, announced that Heath was a most abnormal person, a sadist, a sexual pervert and a psychopath, but that although he had behaved in an extraordinary way he was not insane.

Heath seemed indifferent to what was being said. Wearing a light grey suit with a wide chalk stripe, he presented a clean, almost heroic appearance with his fresh complexion, blue eyes, and fair wavy hair, carefully brushed and pomaded.

The question of why his petty criminality took such a sadistic, murderous bent in 1946 was hardly raised and never answered. Nothing was said of his early sexual experiences – Heath himself was reluctant to talk about them to the doctors who examined him – but as a schoolboy he had assaulted a girl, and then a woman much later in South Africa. No wife, relative, or friend or parent was called to say anything on his behalf.

The jury, who included one woman, were out for an hour. They found him guilty of murder. Asked if he had anything to say, Heath replied: 'Nothing.' There was no appeal.

He never showed any remorse or made a confession. He wrote to his parents: 'My only regret at leaving the world is that I have been damned unworthy of you both.'

Just before he was hanged at Pentonville prison by Albert Pierrepoint on 26 October 1946, he is said to have asked for a whisky, and then added: 'I think I'll make it a double.'

CHAPTER 39

Jenkins, Geraghty and Rolt

The murder of Alec de Antiquis, 1947

Chance plays as large a part in murder as in life, and it was pure chance that motor mechanic Alec de Antiquis happened to be riding on a motorcycle along Charlotte Street one sunny April afternoon just after two o'clock. Aged thirty-four and married with six children, he had a garage and repair business at Collier's Wood in South London, and was on his way back there after picking up some spare parts for his workshop. It was not chance that he acted the way he did, but it was chance that the man whose path he blocked had a gun and had no hesitation in using it. The inadvisability of having a go was seldom better demonstrated than in this case, which is also notable for the emergence of one of Scotland Yard's celebrated investigators, Superintendent Robert Fabian, and for the last appearances of Sir Bernard Spilsbury and Robert Churchill at an Old Bailey murder trial.

Just before 2 pm on Monday, 28 April 1947, three masked gunmen burst into Jay's, a jeweller's shop at 73/75 Charlotte Street, W1, on the corner of Tottenham Street and not far from the Scala Theatre. A new building, an out-patients' department of the Middlesex Hospital (a VD clinic), now stands on the site. Two of the gunmen went in by the front door, the third by a side entrance – this man ordered the two assistants in the back to keep quiet. The two bandits in the front of the shop grabbed at the jewellery on the shelves.

What happened next has been confusedly reported. It seems that during the raid a gun was thrown at the firm's director, Ernest Stock, as he slammed shut the door of a safe. One of the raiders clubbed him to the ground with another gun. The assistant manager, Bertram Keates, aged seventy, managed to set off a burglar alarm, and when he was asked for the safe's keys he threw a stool at the gunmen, whereupon a shot was fired. It missed him, passed through a glass door leading to the inner room and struck the panelled wall beyond. No doubt alarmed by the noise, resistance, and their own violence, the gunmen fled outside, empty-handed apart from the guns that two of them held. They piled into a getaway car, found their exit was blocked by a lorry and scrambled out. They then ran, it seems, across Charlotte Street towards the section of Tottenham Street that leads into Tottenham Court Road. Women screamed; pedestrians scattered; some dropped to the ground. But Mr de Antiquis drove his motorcycle across their path in an attempt to obstruct their escape.

One of the raiders shot him in the head. He fell dying into the gutter while the three robbers vanished among the crowds and traffic. He is alleged to have said before he died: 'I'm all right . . . Stop them . . . I did my best.'

Another passer-by, a surveyor from Kenton in Middlesex named Charles Grimshaw, also had a go. He described how he saw the three gunmen come out of Jay's and then run towards him. 'At that moment a motorcyclist drew up in front of me. He more or less stood up from his machine on one leg, as though to dismount, and I heard a shot and saw him fall. I saw two men come round the front of the machine, which had fallen over, still running towards me across Charlotte Street. They were side by side and the taller of the two was removing a white scarf from his face. There seemed to be a third person on the other side of the fallen motorcyclist. I stepped off the kerb behind a stationary car and as they drew near to me, trip-kicked the shorter man. He fell full length on the pavement and dropped the gun he was carrying. I jumped on top of him, but his companion, who had run on a few paces, turned back and kicked me on the head. That made me release the man, as I was dazed, and he pushed me over the stood up. He picked up the gun, pointed it at me and said: "Keep off." I stayed where I was.'

Albert Pierrepoint, the executioner, who happened to walk down the street soon after the shooting, saw a lot of people gathered round a body in the road. But he walked on, late for an appointment with some friends in a pub.

One of Pierrepoint's police friends, acting Superintendent Robert Fabian, was put in charge of the case, assisted by DCI Higgins and DI Hodge. The many eyewitnesses accounts of the robbers varied considerably, and it was wrongly thought they escaped in a car.

But two days after the shooting a taxi-driver walked into Tottenham Court Road police station and said he had seen two men in a hurry enter Brook House, an office block at 191 Tottenham Court Road. They had had knotted handkerchiefs around their necks. When the building was searched, a raincoat was found in an empty top-floor office, where one of the gunmen at least had sought temporary shelter. Stuffed into the coat's pockets were a cap, a pair of gloves and a piece of white cloth, triangularly folded and knotted. The maker's name had been torn from the coat and cap, but a dissection of the coat revealed (in the lining) a manufacturer's stock label bearing trade numbers of marks. The expert help of a man in the clothing business enabled the police to trace the raincoat to a multiple tailors' in Leeds. They in turn informed the police that the coat was part of a consignment delivered to three of their branches in London. The coat found in Brook House was traced to a tailor's shop in Deptford High Street.

At that time, to prevent the acceptance of forged clothing coupons, a customer's name and address were noted as a precaution, and as a result, a record of the coat's sale on 30 December 1946 led the police to a man in Berdmonsey who said, after some prevarication, that his wife had lent the coat a few weeks before the shooting to her brother, Harry Jenkins.

Charles Henry Jenkins, aged twenty-three, was soon picked up. A handsome braggart and ex-borstal boy, he was a minor criminal with a record for assault, including two convictions for assaulting policemen – he broke the jaw of one of them.

But twenty-seven witnesses failed to pick him out at an hour-long identity parade.

In the meantime, an eight-year-old schoolboy discovered a gun lying just above the low-tide mark of the River Thames at Wapping. It was a .32 loaded with five rounds (three of which had misfired) and an empty case, which proved to have been that of the bullet that killed Alec de Antiquis. Then another gun was recovered from the foreshore of the Thames, a rusty old .455 Bulldog revolver loaded with six rounds, one of which had been fired. This bullet was extracted from the woodwork in the jewellers' shop. The rounds in the Bulldog were over fifty years old. Both guns were found a quarter of a mile from the block of flats in Bermondsey where Jenkins' wife's parents lived.

Two years before this, Harry Jenkins's older brother Thomas had been convicted of manslaughter for a very similar crime. In another raid on a jewellers', this time in the City (on 8 December 1944) a retired naval captain, Ralph Binney, a passer-by, tried to stop two thieves from getting away by stepping into the road and stretching out his arms before the getaway car. The driver, Ronald Hedley, knocked him down with the car and ran over him twice. The captain's clothing caught on the bodywork of the car and he was dragged for over a mile, across London Bridge, before his broken and battered body was flung clear. He died soon afterwards. Hedley was sentenced to death, but was later reprieved and given life; he was released in 1954. Thomas Jenkins, who was with him in the car, was sentenced to eight years' penal servitude. Both he and Hedley belonged to a South London gang called the Elephant Boys.

Harry Jenkins was not so fortunate as his brother. Two of his friends were also picked up by the police and interrogated – Christopher James Geraghty, aged twenty, and Terence John Peter Rolt, who was seventeen. Geraghty had been with Jenkins in borstal and had twice escaped. Both he and Rolt eventually made incriminating statements and all three were charged on 19 May with the murder of Alec de Antiquis.

Rolt's story was that two days before the shooting, the three of them had broken into a gunsmith's shop, F. Dyke and Co., in Union Street, between Waterloo and London Bridge stations, on Saturday, 26 April. Here they spent the night, playing with the guns on display and eventually choosing the three that were used in the Charlotte Street raid. On the morning of Monday the 28th they met up again at Whitechapel underground station and travelled by tube to Goodge Street. Walking here and there, all armed, they tried to evaluate the possible pickings in jewellers' shops in the vicinity of Tottenham Court Road. This took some time as they edgily nerved themselves for the robbery. Jay's at last was chosen, but by this time it was the lunch hour and the streets were thronged. The raiders retreated to a café for lunch.

They now encouraged each other by sneaking across the street to make further assessments of what was in the window of Jay's – first Rolt, then Geraghty, who derided Rolt's timorous estimates, saying the contents of the window were worth £5,000. Procrastinating yet further, they decided to acquire a getaway car. But after a black Vauxhall 14 saloon had been stolen from Whitfield Street by Jenkins and Rolt there was nothing now to stop them staging the raid.

Rolt drove the car up Charlotte Street with Geraghty beside him. Jenkins walked ahead. The plan was that all three, having parked the car near the shop, would first assemble on the pavement and then, when the coast was clear, would enter the shop. Rolt parked the car and Geraghty joined Jenkins. Then Rolt, in a high state of tension and nervous excitement, mistook a signal from Jenkins and scrambled out of the car. He burst into the shop, brandishing a gun. Jenkins and Geraghty, hastily pulling up their scarves as masks, followed him in.

In the confusion the two elderly salesmen were assaulted and a shot was fired from the Bulldog. The gun that was thrown at Mr Stock had faulty ammunition, which rendered it incapable of being fired. When the robbers fled outside they found that a lorry had pulled up in front of their getaway car and obstructed its departure. In a panic they ran down the street. It was Geraghty who shot the motorcyclist who got in his way.

All three were found guilty at the Old Bailey of the murder of Alec de Antiquis. Their trial began on Monday, 21 July, before Mr Justice Hallett and ended a week later. The chief prosecutor was Mr Anthony Hawke. Jenkins was defended by Mr Vick, KC; Rolt by Mr O'Sullivan, KC, and Geraghty by Mr Wrightson.

The jury were out for fifty minutes. Rolt, because of his youth – he was not yet eighteen – was ordered to be detained at His Majesty's pleasure for at least five years. Although Jenkins killed no one, he was deemed to have been an accessory engaged in a joint enterprise of armed robbery. He was sentenced to death with Geraghty. Despite pleas for a reprieve on account of their youth, he and Geraghty were hanged at Pentonville prison by Albert Pierrepoint on 19 September 1947.

Their executions caused an outcry, reinforcing the demands for the abolition of the death penalty. But very little was said or done about Mrs de Antiquis and her six children – except that the police gave her a medal commemorating her husband's bravery.

Terence Rolt was released from prison on licence in June 1956.

Sir Bernard Spilsbury committed suicide two months after Jenkins and Geraghty were hanged; he was seventy. He had never fully recovered from the wartime deaths of his wife and two of his sons. His mental and physical health had deteriorated – he had become absent-minded and unobservant, and had suffered from several strokes and arthritis in his hands. On 17

December, after leaving the Hampstead hotel where he lived, he performed a post-mortem, gave his staff Christmas boxes, destroyed notebooks and papers in his laboratory in University College, Gower Street, and wrote out his last post-mortem report. After an early dinner at his club he returned to the laboratory and turned on the gas. A post-mortem said he died of coronary thrombosis and carbon monoxide poisoning. He was cremated at Golders Green.

CHAPTER 40

Donald Thomas

The murder of PC Edgar, 1948

Another petty criminal shot a policeman to avoid arrest in 1948. This case was different in that the gunman had a North London and middle-class background and, because of a temporary suspension of capital punishment, he was never hanged.

Soon after 8 pm on 13 February 1948, a woman was walking along a suburban road, Broadfields Avenue in North London, with her brother. They heard three shots coming from the direction of another road, Wades Hill, and then a man ran past them, in and out of the street-lights. The couple found a badly wounded man, who turned out to be a policeman, lying in the drive of 112 Wades Hill, They summoned help.

The policeman, PC Nathaniel Edgar, aged thirty-three, married with two children, had been patrolling in plain clothes an area called Winchmore Hill on the look-out for any break-ins – there had been a spate of burglaries in the Southgate district. Seeing a young man acting suspiciously, he had stopped to question him, going as far as writing the man's name and address in his notebook, when the suspect suddenly pulled out a pistol, fired three times and fled.

PC Edgar, shot in the back, in the base of the spine, buttock and right thigh, was able to tell his colleagues what happened – 'I got his identity card and name . . . The pocketbook's in my inside pocket' – before he died an hour later in hospital. The notebook referred to 'Thomas Donald 247 Cambridge Road, Enfield. BEAH 257/2'.

Donald George Thomas turned out to have a record. He was twenty-three and had been born and brought up in Edmonton, a suburb adjacent to both Enfield and Southgate. A member of the Boys' Brigade, he had been educated at a good school where he had become the cricket captain and had done well academically. However, he had been put on probation more than once, and once, when he was sixteen, was sent to an approved school. Called up for military service in January 1945, the last year of the Second World War (when he was nineteen), he had soon deserted. After nearly two years on the run he gave himself up and was sentenced to 160 days in detention. On being returned to his unit he absconded again.

This was in October 1947, since when the army had been on the look-out for him.

The police now joined the hunt, but failed to find Thomas at his Enfield address. They appealed for help on the radio as well as in the papers, saying that the police wished to interview Donald George Thomas as he 'might be able to help them in their enquiries'. It was apparently the first time that this familiar formula was used in a press release.

A Mr Winkless, living in Camberwell, South London, got in touch with them. He had known Thomas for about three months, and within that time Mrs Winkless had fallen passionately in love with the debonair younger man and had absconded with him, leaving her home, husband and three children.

Her photograph, supplied by Mr Winkless, was published in the papers on 17 February. It was seen that morning by a Mrs Smeed, the landlady of a house converted into bed-sits in Clapham. She immediately telephoned the police, saying that the woman in the picture was, she thought, in the top flat with a young man.

Four policemen arrived a few minutes later and it was agreed that Mrs Smeed should, as usual, take a breakfast tray up to her lodgers. This she did, closely attended by the police. She put the tray down outside the door of the top-floor room, knocked and said that breakfast was outside. There was a pause before a key turned in the lock. The door opened an inch or so.

Simultaneously the police and Thomas, in his underpants, glimpsed each other. The police rushed forward, preventing him from shutting the door. He sprang for the bed, in which was the hapless Mrs Winkless and a Luger pistol under the pillow, but was overpowered and disarmed before he could use it. He said: 'You were lucky. I must just as well be hanged for a sheep as a lamb.'

Bullets from the Luger matched those extracted from PC Edgar. Mrs Winkless made a statement saying that Thomas had told her about his involvement in the shooting. Seventeen rounds of ammunition were found in the bedroom as well as a jemmy and a rubber cosh.

Donald Thomas was tried at the Old Bailey in April 1948, before Mr Justice Hilbery, and was found guilty and sentenced to death.

But the Home Secretary had announced that no executions would be carried out while the House of Commons debated an experimental five-year suspension of the death penalty. So Donald Thomas did not hang.

Nor did James Camb, a ship's steward who was sentenced to death in March (also by Mr Justice Hilbery) for the murder of twenty-six-year-old Miss Eileen Gibson, known as 'Gay', a first-class passenger on the *Durban Castle* en route from Cape Town to Southampton. She was believed to have been strangled and her body, which was never found, pushed through the porthole of Cabin 126.

The sentences on Donald Thomas and Camb were commuted to life imprisonment. Soon afterwards the 'no hanging' clause, passed in the Commons by twenty-three votes, was deleted from the Criminal Justice Bill in June in the House of Lords by 181 votes to 28. Lord Goddard, making his maiden speech, spoke against the amendment. The death penalty was restored.

Nonetheless, a Royal Commission was set up in May 1949 to consider whether capital punishment should be modified or limited (see Appendix D).

James Camb was released from prison in 1959. Donald Thomas was released on licence in April 1962.

Between 1909 and 1949 life imprisonment lasted for eleven years on average. No one was detained for more than twenty years during this period and only a few served as many as fifteen years. Most so-called lifers now serve ten years or less.

CHAPTER 41

Harry Lewis

The murder of Harry Michaelson, 1948

In the early hours of Sunday, 26 December 1948, Boxing Day, the night porter at Furzecroft, a large block of flats in George Street, Marylebone, was startled out of his night-time reverie by a cry for help. It came from the basement. The porter trotted down the interior stairs and saw, standing outside the entrance door of No. 75, one of the basement flats, Mr Harry Saul Michaelson, a well-known commercial artist and cartoonist. Mr Michaelson was dazedly using a towel to dab the blood that spilled from a deep wound on his forehead. Although seriously injured and in pain, he was quite coherent. But he had absolutely no idea how the injury had been sustained. His wife, who lived with him in the basement flat, happened to be away on holiday.

Mr Michaelson was taken to St Mary's Hospital, Paddington, where his condition swiftly worsened: his ribs had been fractured as well as his skull. An operation on his brain was performed, but he died on the 27th without regaining consciousness. The head-wound had not been self-inflicted or caused by accident. But who had struck him, with what, and why?

The police soon answered the first two questions. The assailant had left bloody finger and palm-prints on a tubular metal chair, which had clearly been the unwieldy and unusual weapon used to batter Mr Michaelson. The prints matched a set in the Criminal Record Office at Scotland Yard. They belonged to a known thief, Harry Lewis, aged twenty-one.

He was arrested on 18 January 1949 and charged with murder.

His story was of a chance break-in. Penniless at the time, he happened to be on the prowl in George Street when the sight of an open basement window invited his inspection. He clambered over the railings edging the basement area and cautiously climbed through the window. He found himself in a bedroom: a man lay asleep in a bed. In the darkness Lewis fumbled his way about the room, finding a pile of clothes, some loose change and a wallet, which he pocketed. Exploring further, he opened the bedroom door and crept into the hallway of the flat. As he did so a fuddled voice behind him called out from the bedroom – 'Who's there?'

Lewis panicked. He told the court: 'I went back into the bedroom. The chap was getting out of bed. I picked up the metal chair. It was the first thing I could put my hand on . . . I admit I gave him two bashes.'

Having temporarily incapacitated the occupant of the flat, Lewis fled via the basement window. Out in the street he hailed a passing taxi and left the scene of the crime.

He was tried at the Old Bailey on 7 March 1949. The judge was the Lord Chief Justice, Lord Goddard; the prosecutor was Mr Anthony Hawke. Lewis's counsel tried to attribute Mr Michaelson's death to the hospital operation – it was not Lewis who killed the cartoonist but the surgeon. Pathologist Dr Donald Teare, appearing for the Crown, said the patient would have died in any case whether or not he had been operated on.

The defence hoped for a verdict of manslaughter. But Lord Goddard told the jury that the accused man should be found guilty if they thought that the deceased had been killed by a burglar seeking to evade apprehension. Persuaded by this and by the facts of the case, the jury found Lewis guilty of murder, although they added a recommendation for mercy.

The recommendation was ignored. Harry Lewis was duly sentenced to death.

An appeal was likewise ignored by the Home Secretary, and at the age of twenty-one, on 21 April 1949, Lewis was hanged at Pentonville prison.

CHAPTER 42

John Haigh

The murder of Mrs Durand-Deacon, 1949

Gross insensitivity and vanity characterize most murders, as does a very limited imagination. In some cases the daring, almost divine aspect of depriving a human being of life seems to infect the murderer with a belief in his own invulnerability. Or perhaps some death-wish is at work. For whatever reason, many murderers, like Haigh and Norman Thorne, feel compelled to assist the police with their inquiries, convinced, it seems, that they can get away with murder. Or is that they feel they should not be allowed to get away with murder and wish subconsciously to be caught?

Mrs Olive Henrietta Helen Olivia Robarts Durand-Deacon, aged sixty-nine, was a stout, intelligent widow whose husband had left her well provided for. For over six years she had lived in South Kensington at the Onslow Court Hotel, Queen's Gate.

She was in the habit of exchanging pleasantries with another long-term resident, a neat, smiling little man with twinkling eyes and nice manners, who sat in the dining-room on his own at a table next to hers and had done so for over four years. He was somewhat younger than the other residents, being only thirty-nine, and when he first appeared in the hotel about six months before the end of the war she was probably curious about his single status and the source of his income, but was too well-bred to ask personal questions. However, a nodding acquaintance developed in time to a certain friendship, and whatever he told her about his antecedents and irregular absences – she was a lady of regular habits herself – must have sounded very plausible. Although he was clearly not a gentleman born and bred – he had a slight accent and was rather flash – she learned he was a Yorkshireman, an engineer, a company director and patented inventions. She often chatted to him as they sat at their separate tables.

She had no idea and would never have believed that nice Mr Haigh had already cold-bloodedly murdered five people for gain.

On St Valentine's Day, 1949, Mrs Gwendoline Birin, assistant secretary of the Francis Bacon Society, lunched (as she usually did on a Monday) with Mrs Durand-Deacon, and during the meal her hostess, after excusing herself, produced a box of plastic finger-nails which she showed to Mr Haigh and discussed briefly with him. She told him about an idea she had had for a new type of artificial finger-nail. Later she showed him some she had made of paper and glued to her own nails. Could he make something of her idea, she wanted to know. Would it be possible to manufacture and market such finger-nails? He said he would think about it – it seemed like a good idea. But the idea she had actually given him was quite a different one.

John George Haigh was in debt; his gambling losses, on horses and dogs, had of late been rather heavy, and he had no regular income. His bank account was overdrawn by £83; his cheques were beginning to bounce, and he had not paid his hotel bill (£5 15s 6d a week, plus 10 per cent for services) since the beginning of January. He now owed the Onslow Court Hotel nearly £50, as the manageress discreetly but firmly continued to remind him. To avoid further embarrassment he had to acquire some instant cash.

He looked at Mrs Durand-Deacon and saw money in what she wore.

The next day, Tuesday, he set about depriving her of her jewellery and of her life. He drove south to Sussex, to Crawley (then little more than a large village), motoring to Leopold Road, where he had acquired the use of a small workshop in Giles Yard. The ramshackle, weedy yard also contained some lock-ups for cars; the workshop itself belonged to Hurstlea Products Ltd, for whom Haigh had once worked, and when they discarded it he borrowed it off them.

He called on a business acquaintance, a welding engineer called Mr Davies, and asked him to collect some acid from London. Mr Davies had performed a similar task for Haigh a year before. He also called on the manager of Hurstlea, Mr Jones, and asked him for a £50 cash loan. This he was given on condition the money was repaid that week.

On the Wednesday he paid his hotel bill in full, using the money he had borrowed, and was left with 4s 11d in change.

In Crawley, Mr Davies went to Haigh's workshop in Giles Yard and emptied one of three carboys of sulphuric acid that were there by filling up the other two. He took the empty one away, and on Thursday exchanged it for a full one at White's, Dallington Street, EC1 – one carboy contained about ten gallons of acid. Haigh had previously telephoned White's and ordered the carboy in his own name. Davies brought the carboy back to Haigh's workshop and dumped it there.

That afternoon Haigh himself went to Barking, and at Victor Blagden's wharf obtained a forty-five gallon black drum, which he then exchanged for a green drum, specially prepared to resist corrosive acids. He had in the meantime told Mrs Durand-Deacon that he thought he could do something with her idea for false finger-nails and suggested that she should come down to his factory at Crawley. He asked whether Friday would be convenient for her.

In the hotel dining-room at breakfast on Friday, 18 February, he told Mrs Durand-Deacon that everything was arranged and that he would confirm the appointment at lunch-time. He drove down to Crawley, helped Mr Jones to move some steel sheeting from Giles Yard to the Hurstlea premises in West Street, and was back at the hotel in time for lunch.

Mrs Durand-Deacon had already eaten, and he met her in the Tudor Lounge and asked her if she was free to come with him to Crawley. He drove her there in his Alvis. They left about half-past two.

On the back seat was a square leather hat-box, in which was a .38 Enfield revolver and eight rounds of ammunition.

The last time Mrs Durand-Deacon was seen by anyone else was when she and Haigh called in at an ancient coaching inn, the George Hotel in Crawley, and visited the cloakrooms. It was about 4.15 pm.

What happened next was later described by Haigh himself in his third statement to the police.

'She was inveigled into going to Crawley by me in view of her interest in artificial finger-nails. Having taken her into the storeroom at Leopold Road, I shot her in the back of the head while she was examining some paper for use as finger-nails. Then I went out to the car and fetched in a drinking-glass and made an incision. I think with a penknife, in the side of the throat. I collected a glass of blood, which I then drank. Following that, I removed the coat she was wearing, a Persian lamb, and the jewellery, rings, necklace, earrings and cruciform, and put her in a forty-five gallon tank. Before I put the handbag in the tank I took from it the cash – about thirty shillings – and her fountain-pen and kept these, and tipped the rest into the tank with the bag. I then filled the tank up with sulphuric acid, by means of a stirrup-pump, from a carboy. I then left it to react. I should have said that in between having her in the tank and pumping in the acid I went round to the Ancient Prior's for a cup of tea.

He also had a poached egg on toast with his tea and chatted cheerily to the proprietor. At one time the owner of the restaurants and bars which now occupy the historic timbered building was the former middleweight boxing champion, Alan Minter.

Haigh's account of his activities in Giles Yard omits the fact that soon after shooting Mrs Durand-Deacon, at about 4.45 pm, he called on Mr Jones in West Street. Haigh told Mr Jones that the person he had intended bringing down to Crawley to discuss artificial finger-nails had not turned up. Mr Jones was in a state (he had just sacked some of his employees) and Haigh left a few minutes later.

He was next seen about ten-past six by a van-driver who left his van in Giles Yard, where there were also several lock-up garages. By the light of the headlights the van-driver saw a man in a fawn overcoat going to and fro between a car and the workshop, the bottom half of whose windows were blacked out.

It was not until about 6.45 pm that Haigh went to Ye Old Ancient Prior's restaurant in The Square for some refreshment. Having consumed his poached egg and drunk his tea, he left the restaurant just after seven o'clock, returning to the workshop to fill the drum with acid. Soon after 9 pm, with his tasks completed, he was back in the George Hotel, where he treated himself to a full-blown three-course dinner. He then drove back to London and was safely ensconced in the Onslow Court Hotel before 11 pm.

The following morning at breakfast, the waitress, Mary, asked Haigh if anything was wrong with Mrs Durand-Deacon as she had not been down to dinner the previous night. Mrs Constance Lane, who had lived at the hotel for nine years and was 'a great friend' of Mrs Durand-Deacon, was then approached by Mr Haigh, 'a nodding acquaintance only'. After an exchange of polite 'good mornings' he asked her: 'Do you know anything about Mrs Durand-Deacon? Is she ill? Do you know where she is?' 'No,' said Mrs Lane, who had noticed that her friend's table had been unoccupied the night before. She added: 'I haven't seen her . . . Don't know where she is? I understood from her you wanted to take her to your factory in Horsham?' 'Yes,' said Haigh. 'But I wasn't ready. I had not had lunch, and she said she wanted to go to the Army and Navy Stores and she asked me to pick her up there.' He said he had waited an hour for her there but she never arrived. Mrs Lane was worried. 'Well,' she said, 'I must do something about it.'

She went upstairs to Room 115, Mrs Durand-Deacon's room, and spoke to a chamber-maid. But the room had clearly not been used overnight, and Mrs Lane, becoming increasingly anxious, sought some explanations from the staff and other guests for her friend's disappearance.

Meanwhile, Haigh was elsewhere employed that Saturday, as he later told the police.

'I eventually went back to Crawley, via Putney, where I sold her watch, en route, at a jewellers' shop in the High Street for £10.' It was a ruby and diamond wrist-watch and he signed the receipt with a false name and address. 'At Crawley I called in to see how the reaction in the tank had gone on. It was not satisfactorily completed, so I went on to Horsham, having picked up the coat and put it in the back of the car. I called at Bull's the jeweler;s for a valuation of the jewellery, but Mr Bull was not in. I returned to town, and on the way dropped in the coat at the "Cottage Cleaners" at Reigate.' The second-hand value of the black Persian lamb coat was about £50.

On Sunday morning Haigh again approached Mrs Lane's table in the dining-room and solicitously asked her if she had any news. 'No,' said Mrs Lane. 'I haven't had any news.' She added that she intended going to Chelsea police station after lunch to ask them to take the matter up. Haigh went away, but before long came back to Mrs Lane in the Tudor Lounge where she was reading a morning paper. Haigh said: 'I think we had better go together to Chelsea police station.' 'I think so too,' said Mrs Lane.

He drove her there about 2.15 pm. Unhappily for Haigh, he and Mrs Lane were interviewed by a policewoman, Sergeant Lambourne, whose instincts based on experience led her to mistrust the male informant. She visited the hotel and what she learned about Mr Haigh from the manageress gave colour to her suspicions.

On Monday, a call was put through to the Record Office at Scotland Yard and very soon Chelsea police station was supplied with the information that Mr Haigh had thrice been imprisoned for crimes connected with the fraudulent obtaining of money,

Meanwhile, on Monday morning, Haigh drove south again. 'I returned to Crawley to find the reaction almost complete, but a piece of fat and bone was still floating on the sludge. I emptied off the sludge with a bucket and tipped it on the ground opposite the shed, and pumped a further quantity of acid into the tank to decompose the remaining fat and bone. I then left that to work until the following day. From there I went to Horsham again and had the jewellery valued, ostensibly for probate. It was valued at just over £130. I called back at the West Street factory and eventually returned to town.

At the hotel two police officers were waiting to see him, Detective Inspector Symes and DI Webb. The former said to Haigh: 'I am a police officer and I am making enquiries with respect to a lady named Mrs Olive Durand-Deacon who is missing from the hotel.' Haigh replied: 'Yes, I thought you would see me as I went with her friend, Mrs Lane, to the police station to report her missing. I will tell you all I know about it.'

He made a statement, written down by DI Webb, about his appointment with Mrs Durand-Deacon at the Army and Navy Stores, her failure to arrive, his trip to Crawley (without her) and his subsequent conversations with Mrs Lane.

Apparently undisturbed by the police visit and with money uppermost in his mind, he returned to Horsham on Tuesday, 22 February, and sold the jewellery to Bull's the jeweller's for £100, of which he was given £60 – the remaining £40 was handed over the following day. He gave the jeweller's a false name and address. Money in hand he drove to Crawley and gave Mr Jones £36 of the £50 debt.

At the workshop Haigh decided the acid had done its work and emptied the drum of its sludgy contents in the yard. Mrs Durand-Deacon's plastic handbag had not been much affected by the acid's action, although its handle and base had come apart, and Haigh stuffed the handbag behind some bricks beside a fence. But decomposition was not as complete as he thought: the minor contents of the handbag and bits of Mrs Durand-Deacon remained, hidden in the sludge.

On Wednesday Haigh was back in Horsham, collecting the £40 that was owed him by the jeweller's. He put £5 into his bank account in Crawley. He then called on Mr Jones just before lunch to settle his debts. But Mr Jones had other matters on his mind, for the police had interviewed him the night before. He said he hoped Haigh was not in any trouble. Haigh shrugged, said 'No,' and laughed. 'If there is any trouble,' said Jones, 'I prefer you not to come to the works – I prefer you to stay away.' Haigh left and Jones never received the £14 Haigh owed him.

The next afternoon the police returned to the Onslow Court Hotel and interviewed Haigh again.

He helpfully provided them with a second statement very similar to the first, but with more details. He must have realized that Jones would lead the police to the workshop, but nothing daunted he stayed on at the hotel, full of foolish confidence that nothing would be found. Nothing happened on Friday, except that the police continued to pursue their inquiries and had a conference.

It was on Saturday, 26 February, that Mr Jones took DS Pat Heslin of the West Sussex Police to Giles Yard.

The workshop door was padlocked and had to be forced as Haigh had the keys. Inside, Heslin noted the presence of three carboys, a stirrup-pump, a rubber apron, rubber gloves, a mackintosh, a gas-mask, an attaché-case and a locked leather hat box. A key from the attaché-case opened the hat-box, in which were found a revolver, ammunition and a receipt from a Reigate cleaners' for a black Persian lamb coat.

On Sunday and Monday DI Shelley Symes visited Crawley, Horsham and Reigate and picked up various items. At 4.15 pm on Monday, 28 February, DI Albert Webb was waiting at the hotel when Haigh drove up in his Alvis. 'I want you to come to the Chelsea police station at once,' said DI Webb, 'and see Superintendent Barratt and Detective Inspector Symes.' 'Certainly,' said Haigh, 'I'll do anything to help you, as you know.'

But at the police station Barratt and Symes were still occupied, and it was not until about 7.30 pm that Symes appeared and said: 'I have continued my inquiries into the disappearance of Mrs Durand-Deacon and I want you to answer some more questions.' Haigh nodded. 'I'm quite willing to answer anything I can,' he said. 'And to help you all I can.' Symes then questioned him about the Persian lamb coat and Haigh's visits to Horsham. How many times had Haigh been there? 'I used to go to Horsham a lot,' said Haigh. 'But lately I've only been there once in the evening, to the pictures.' 'You've been there in the morning recently on no less than four occasions,' said Symes. 'Ah,' said Haigh. 'I can see you know what you're talking about. I admit the coat belonged to Mrs Durand-Deacon and that I sold her jewellery, as you know, to Bull's in Horsham.' Symes then produced the cleaners' ticket. Haigh said: 'Yes, I wondered if you'd got it when you started.' 'How did you come by this property?' demanded Symes. 'And where is Mrs Durand-Deacon?' He then cautioned Haigh about anything he might say.

There was a pause before Haigh replied. 'It's a long story,' he said. 'It's one of blackmail and I shall have to implicate many others. How do I stand about that?' Symes retorted: 'What you have to say is entirely a matter for you.'

At this point some other business summoned Symes and Barratt from the room for about ten minutes. Haigh was left alone with DI Webb.

Haigh looked at him and said: 'Tell me frankly, what are the chances of anyone being released from Broadmoor?' Said Webb: 'I can't discuss that sort of thing with you.' 'Well,' said Haigh. 'If I told the truth, you wouldn't believe me. It sounds too fantastic for belief.' Webb cautioned him. Haigh interrupted: 'I understand all that – I'll tell you all about it. Mrs Durand-Deacon no longer exists. She's disappeared completely – and no trace of her can ever be found again.' Webb was non-committal. 'What's happened to her?' he asked. 'I've destroyed her with acid,' replied Haigh. 'You'll find the sludge that remains at Leopold Road. Every trace has gone. How can you prove murder if there's no body?'

Webb fetched Symes and Barratt. In Haigh's presence, Webb remarked:

'He's just told me that Mrs Durand-Deacon doesn't exist, and that he's destroyed her by acid.' 'It's perfectly true,' said Haigh. 'But it's a very long story and it'll take hours to tell.' 'I'm prepared to listen,' said Symes.

What the police officers thought as Haigh told his story about the death of Mrs Durand-Deacon is not on record. If they were not amazed and astounded at the end of it they certainly were when Haigh mentioned McSwann and Henderson – 'the subject of another story'. Invited to narrate it, Haigh briefly said he had disposed of Mr W. D. McSwann and his mother and father, as well as Dr and Mrs Henderson, 'in a similar manner to the above'.

Pressed for details, he said that in the summer of 1944 he chanced to meet William Donald McSwann, a man in his thirties whom Haigh had first met in 1936. The acquaintance was renewed. Haigh was also popular with McSwann's parents, often visiting them. One night (9 September 1944) the two men had a drink at The Goat in Kensington High Street, and then went to 79 Gloucester Road, where Haigh had a basement workshop in which he was repairing a pin-table for McSwann. He hit McSwann on the head with a cosh, drank his blood (he said), removed any valuables and put his body in a purloined water-butt which he had filled with acid, later disposing of the sludge down a manhole in the basement. He visited Mr and Mrs McSwann and told them their son had gone underground to avoid being called up. The deception was maintained by Haigh, who forged letters from young McSwann to his parents, posting them from Glasgow and Edinburgh.

In July the following year, Haigh dealt separately with Mr and Mrs McSwann in the Gloucester Road basement, disposing of them as he had their son.

Posing as the son he then obtained legal control of all his victims' assets, including the freehold in four properties, their furniture and belongings (which he sold) and the gilt-edged securities they owned. He made over £4,000 out of the extermination of the entire McSwann family.

Haigh then told the astonished police how he had then cultivated and disposed of another couple, Dr and Mrs Henderson, whom he met in 1947 over a property deal.

In February 1948 he took them one by one from the Metropole Hotel, Brighton, where all three were staying, to his new workshop in Crawley. Here both Hendersons were shot and dumped in two drums of acid, but not before he had drunk their blood and removed any money and valuables they had on them. Their hotel bill in Brighton was paid by Haigh and he took charge of their red setter dog until it contracted night blindness, when he sent it to the kennels. Again he kept the relatives quiet by forging occasional letters to Mrs Henderson's brother who lived in Manchester.

Six victims were more than enough for the Chelsea police officers. After his confession Haigh was detained in custody. The next day, Tuesday, 1 March, Symes searched Haigh's room at the Onslow Court Hotel (Room 404) and removed certain items and papers. He, DCI Mahon and the Home Office pathologist, Dr Keith Simpson, drove down to Crawley to examine the scene of Mrs Durand-Deacon's alleged disappearance.

Specks of blood were found on the whitewashed wall above the workshop bench, a hat-pin was found in the bottom of the green drum, and a gall stone was spotted by the observant Dr Simpson in the sludge outside the yard. The sludge itself was ladled into five wooden boxes and carted to the police laboratory in New Scotland Yard. Carefully sifted and analysed, it produced 28 lb of animal fat, two more gall stones, part of a foot, eighteen corroded bone fragments, a lipstick container, the handle of a handbag, and a full set of dentures, which were later identified by Mrs Durand-Deacon's lady dentist.

Left in acid or even in the sludge these exhibits would all have dissolved within a month (apart from the gall stones), thus preventing the identification of the remains and proving Haigh's claim that Mrs Durand-Deacon had indeed vanished without trace.

He was charged with her murder at Horsham police station on 2 March, and taken to Lewes prison in Sussex.

Two days later he asked to see DI Webb and made another statement in which he said he had murdered three other people, strangers whom he met accidentally, coshed and disposed of in acid. One was a woman in her thirties whom he met in Hammersmith and killed in February 1945; the second was a man in his thirties called Max whom he encountered in The Goat in Kensington and coshed about September 1945; and the third was a Welsh girl called Mary whom he met in Eastbourne in the summer of 1948. The first two, he said, were disposed of in the Gloucester Road basement, the third in Crawley. Haigh said he robbed all three of what they had, which was very little, and drank their blood.

No evidence was ever unearthed by the police to substantiate these claims. Most probably Haigh fabricated these murders to enforce the idea of insanity, which was to be his defence. He may have thought, like Christie, that the more the merrier, and decided to invent victims who were slaughtered just for their blood and not for their money, as the other six obviously were.

There is no evidence to prove whether or not he drank anybody's blood, except that a penknife with faint traces of blood on it *was* found in his Alvis. Blood if drunk would, however, tend to act as an emetic. The blood-supping and his alleged dreams of blood and crucifixion were elaborated by the defence at the trial, as was Haigh's claim that he had habitually drunk his own urine since he was a boy. At the trial he was reported to have done just that in the presence of a prison doctor.

His life had in fact been rather unusual. He was born on 24 July 1909 at Stamford in Lincolnshire, and brought up in a Yorkshire village, Outwood, situated between Wakefield and Leeds. The only child of a colliery foreman, his solitariness was enforced by the fact that his parents belonged to a religious sect, the Plymouth Brethren, who frowned on sport, light entertainment, social amusements of any frivolous or unedifying sort, and daily prayed together and read the Bible, isolating themselves from the sins, pleasures and evils of the world and refusing to have even a wireless or a newspaper in the house. But Haigh was not unhappy and was fond of his mother and father. He was always neat and smart. Educated at Wakefield Grammar School until he was seventeen, he was a good mixer, eager to please, and mischievous; and although no scholar or athlete, he wrote well and won a Divinity prize with an essay on St Peter. At the same time, to avoid trouble or offence, he became an accomplished liar. He was also an accomplished pianist, music being his greatest indulgence and passion. Between the ages of ten and sixteen he sang with the Wakefield Cathedral Choir, and occasionally played the organ at minor services.

Much was also made at his trial of the presumed disturbing dichotomy between the lavish High Church cathedral rituals and the austere religion of his parents, but it is doubtful whether his sensitivity or intellect were sufficiently deep to be disturbed.

Apprenticed for a time to a motor engineer, he began at the age of twenty-one to experiment with various speculative business ventures concerned with insurance and brokerage. Then on 6 July 1934 he married, left home and stopped attending meetings of the Brethren. Looking around for some means of making money he devised a method of swindling a hire-purchase company dealing in cars by forging documents for non-existent cars hired by non-existent owners. Within a few months he was found out and was sentenced at Leeds Assizes in November 1934 to fifteen months for conspiring to defraud.

He wrote later: 'When I first discovered there were easier ways to make a living than to work long hours in an office, I did not ask myself whether I was doing right or wrong. That seemed to me to be irrelevant.'

While he was in prison his wife left him and he was rejected by the Brethren. His next venture, a successful dry-cleaning business, collapsed when his partner was killed in a car crash; the firm went into liquidation. Haigh came to London in 1936.

He was employed as a chauffeur and secretary of the manager of an amusement arcade called McSwann, whom he later murdered. He became quite friendly with the McSwanns, but soon he embarked on another swindle. Posing as a small-town solicitor who was winding up a client's estate and wished to dispose of some non-existent shares at a good price, he offered them for sale to anyone who paid a 25 per cent deposit. For a time he was successful, collecting the cheques and moving on from town to town. In all he made over £3,000. But eventually the law latched on to him and in November 1937 he was charged at Surrey Assizes in Kingston with obtaining money by false pretences. He pleaded guilty and was sentenced to four years' penal servitude.

He was released in August 1940, and during the blitz was then employed as a firewatcher in Pimlico. Within a year he was back in prison, sentenced to twenty-one months for stealing household goods.

This third experience of prison, together with his experiences as a firewatcher, seems to have hardened and darkened his mind. He wrote later: 'The ghastly sights after two land-mines had wiped out a block of buildings are fixed indelibly in my memory.' He began to doubt the existence of God. In prison he is thought to have studied the effects of acid on mice, seeing how long their bodies took to dissolve if immersed in a mug of sulphuric acid. He resolved not to get caught again and to abandon the petty crimes of the cheap crook.

On his release he became a salesman for an engineering business at Crawley, where he lived for about two years, often being seen in the lounge of the George Hotel having tea.

In March 1944 he was involved in a motor accident in which his head was cut. Some months later, now living in London, he chanced to meet young McSwann.

The brief trial of John George Haigh began at Lewes Assizes court in Sussex on Monday, 18 July 1949. It finished the following afternoon. The judge was Mr Justice Humphreys. The Attorney-General, Sir Hartley Shawcross, KC, MP, led for the Crown, and Sir David Maxwell Fyfe, KC, MP, for the defence.

The prosecution produced the evidence of thirty-three witnesses, of whom only four were cross-examined (and then briefly) by the defence. Haigh gave no evidence and only one witness was called for the defence, Dr Henry Yellowlees, a leading psychiatrist, with little or no court experience. Dr Yellowlees was an early exponent of forensic psychiatry and appeared for the defence in other trials, successfully supporting verdicts of guilty but insane. Of nine doctors who had examined Haigh in prison he was he only one prepared to speak up on the prisoner's behalf, after talking with him on three occasions for a total of twenty-four hours and ten minutes.

Dr Yellowlees maintained that Haigh had a paranoid constitution which could produce paranoid insanity. Early influences in his life had contributed, the doctor said, to this condition. But when cross-examined, Dr Yellowlees was forced to admit that Haigh knew he had done something which was 'punishable by law', and therefore 'wrong by the law of the country'. In his book *To Define True Madness*, published in 1953, Yellowlees wrote about the 'sadly overrated Haigh case', and said that the only point of real interest was that Haigh was 'medically mad' but not 'McNaghten mad'. Yellowlees said that he had been prepared in court to admit that 'Haigh did not satisfy the McNaghten criteria'. But so 'unfriendly and hostile' was the atmosphere in the court that his evidence was attacked *in toto* and, he felt, 'improperly treated'.

No medical evidence was called by the Crown, the Attorney-General submitting there was nothing to rebut. The judge, commenting in his summing-up on Dr Yellowlees' statement that there was no sex element in the case, said that this was 'really rather a comfort in a way; one gets rather tired in these courts of sex complexes.'

The jury were out for seventeen minutes, returning at 4.40 pm. They found Haigh guilty of murdering Mrs Durand-Deacon. Asked if he had anything to say, Haigh replied: 'Nothing at all.'

Before his execution he wrote a remarkable account of his life, which appeared in the *News of the World*.

He was hanged by Pierrepoint at Wandsworth prison on 10 August 1949, seventeen days after his fortieth birthday. The cause of death as given on his death certificate was: 'Injuries to central nervous system consequent upon judicial hanging'. Pierrepoint used a special strap of pale calf leather to bind Haigh's wrists – as he had done with Heath. He used this special strap on only about a dozen occasions; and on these occasions he made a red ink entry in his diary on the day of the execution – to indicate, as he said, 'more than a formal interest in this particular execution'.

CHAPTER 43

Daniel Raven

The murder of Mr Goodman, 1949

Among the murderers who kill without apparent motive are a number of sons who for some reason or other cannot exist without extinguishing members of their families, frequently a mother or father or both. Such inimical offspring tend to plead guilty or to be found insane, and so no explanation or motive is ever officially put forward for their fatal deeds.

In this case the deadly relative was a son-in-law. No motive for his extraordinary actions was ever aired before or during his trial. But on Monday, 10 October 1949, after visiting his young wife, Marie, in a maternity home in Muswell Hill (where on 6 October she had given birth to their first child), a dapper Jewish advertising agent called Daniel Raven, aged twenty-three, drove to the home of his parents-in-law and battered them both to death.

The fact that Mr Leopold Goodman, aged forty-nine, and Mrs Esther Goodman, aged forty-seven, were Russian Jews and possessively proud of their daughter, Mrs Raven, and of their new grandson, is probably not as relevant as the fact that they were also at the maternity home that evening, sitting beside their daughter and watched by their son-in-law. Something surely must have been said, some opinion, prejudice or attitude expressed by the middle-aged couple that provoked the nervy Mr Raven to eliminate them.

They left the nursing home at 9.05 pm, followed soon after by their son-in-law. He drove to the Goodman home in Ashcombe Gardens, Edgware, where at about 9.30 pm he went berserk, battering Mrs Goodman seven times on the head and Mr Goodman at least fourteen times. In both cases the weapon was the base of a television aerial.

The presence of a television set in the house gives some indication of the Goodmans' affluence, for television was then in its infancy and sets showing the few black and white programmes the BBC broadcast on one channel were expensive. (The BBC's transmissions from Alexandra Palace, begun in November 1936, had been discontinued during the war, only being resumed on 7 June 1946.) Danny Raven, earning about £20 a week, was not rich enough to own a TV set.

After the attack Danny drove around the corner to Edgwarebury Lane, where he lived with his wife in a house bought for them by Mr Goodman. Here he tried to remove the bloodstains on his dark blue suit, and having failed to do so satisfactorily he stuffed the shirt into a coke-boiler in the kitchen, hastening the burning process by leaving a lit gas poker in the boiler.

About 10.30 pm he received an unexpected telephone call from the police – possibly while he was still trying to clean his suit. The police requested him to come round to his in-laws' house straight away – they had some bad news for him. If the telephone call interrupted him in his efforts to clean the suit he must have set about burning it in some haste, before dressing himself in a new shirt and tie and suit.

Unfortunately for Danny, what had happened about twenty minutes after he left Ashcombe Gardens was that Mrs Goodman's brother-in-law, Mr Frederick Fraiman, called at the house with his wife and eldest daughter. At about 9.55 pm they had driven over from Marlborough Avenue to enquire about Marie Raven and the baby. Mr Fraiman was a business partner of the Goodmans in L. Goodman Radio Ltd. When the three Fraimans received no response to their knocking and ringing at the front, side and back doors, Mr Fraiman climbed into the house through an open window and came across the savaged bodies of the Goodmans in their blood-soaked dining-room. He dialled 999 at 10.02 pm. The police and a doctor were soon at the scene, the police investigations being led by DI Diller. The aluminium aerial was found in a sink in the scullery.

Robbery as an associated motive for the murders was discounted when bundles of notes were found untouched in the house, including one cache of notes under a mattress. There was over £2,500 in a safe.

When Danny Raven arrived he was overcome with emotion and sat sobbing on the stairs, crying: 'Why did they tell me to go? Why didn't they let me stop?' He had wanted to stay, he said, as his in-laws were apprehensive about being burgled. But they had insisted, he said, that he left. 'I don't get on with Mr Goodman too badly,' he confessed. 'Although we do quarrel at times. But Mrs Goodman and me didn't get on at all well.'

DI Diller was doubtful about Raven's explanations and sorrow, and had cause to be so when one of his policemen, who had questioned other relatives of the Goodmans, passed on the information that the young man had been wearing a dark blue suit earlier that evening – not the light grey suit he now wore. Diller also noted that Raven's shirt seemed very crisp and fresh.

The lamenting son-in-law was asked to accompany the police to Edgware police station for further questioning. But before this happened Diller asked Raven for the keys to his house. Danny handed them over reluctantly, adding: 'But you won't find anything there – I only had a bath.'

It was not until 11.45 pm that Diller entered the Ravens' nest. As soon as he did so he noticed a smell of burning. It came from the kitchen. He saw the gas poker projecting from the blazing boiler. He removed it, closed the vent and flue, and was able to retrieve part of a suit. Later it was found to be stained with blood (from the Goodmans' rare blood group AB) as were a pair of shoes which had been washed and hidden in the garage. The driver's seat in Raven's car had also been scrubbed.

When asked to account for the burning, bloody suit in the boiler – he admitted the suit was his – Danny replied: 'How the blood got on it I don't know.' He had left it, he said, in the bathroom – where the police found no evidence of a bath having been recently taken.

Daniel Raven was charged by DCI Albert Tansill at Edgware police station on the night of Tuesday, 11 October, with the murder of Mr Leopold Goodman. In proclaiming his innocence, Raven said that his father-in-law had made several enemies as a result of crooked business deals.

This was elaborated in court by counsel for the defence, who suggested that Mr Goodman had been a police informer, assisting the police with information about persons suspected of currency offences, and that the elderly couple had been murdered in revenge by a person or persons unknown. Raven's story by now had also been elaborated. When he gave evidence he said that after leaving the Goodmans alive and well he had called on his cousins nearby (who were out) and then decided to return to Ashcombe Gardens, as he knew the Fraimans would probably call that night. Receiving no reply, he said, to his knocking at the door, he entered the house through a window and found Mrs Goodman in the dining-room, her skull cracked open. He felt sick at the sight, he said – and in the witness box he swayed and appeared on the point of collapse. He continued by saying that blood got on his clothes and shoes when he knelt by her body. Overwhelmed by fear, he said, he fled from the house and drove to his own home where he burned his suit and washed his shoes.

No defence involving the accused's mental instability or even insanity was broached.

He was tried at the Old Bailey on Tuesday, 22 November 1949, before Mr Justice Cassels, with Mr Anthony Hawke appearing for the Crown and Mr John Maude, KC, for the defence. Found guilty on 24 November, Daniel Raven was sentenced to death.

In support of an appeal, a solicitor, Mr Rutter, then produced evidence that Raven was insane, that on account of his 'severe anxiety neurosis' he had been discharged from the RAF (which he had joined when he was sixteen) after a plane-crash that he alone survived. A doctor who had treated Raven in the past stated that he used to suffer from 'blackouts and brainstorms'. Another said he had a kind of epilepsy. The appeal was heard on 20 December and dismissed.

All other appeals for clemency as well as a petition failed. Raven was hanged in Pentonville prison on Friday, 6 January 1950.

CHAPTER 44

Craig and Bentley

The murder of PC Miles, 1952

Few murder trials exemplify the instinctive 'Them and Us' attitudes of those who uphold the law as starkly as Regina v. Bentley and Craig in 1952. Seldom has an execution raised so many agonizing problems. Questions were later asked in the House of Commons. Mr R. T. Paget said: 'A three-quarter witted boy is to be hung for a murder he did not commit, which was committed fifteen minutes after he was arrested. Can we be made to keep silent when a thing as horrible and as shocking as this is to happen?' But the law was determined to make an example of Craig and Bentley in order to deter young criminals in post-war Britain. In doing so it succeeded in making a disturbing example of itself. Bentley was hanged; he was nineteen. But crimes of violence committed by boys and youths continued to increase.

Christopher Craig was born on 19 May 1936, three years after Derek William Bentley. Both lived in South London, in Norbury, and both went to Norbury Secondary Modern School and left when they were fifteen. Craig suffered from word blindness – dyslexia – a disability that was hardly recognized then and rarely treated. As a result he was scarcely able to read or write, only comics being within his comprehension. Other boys, he said, 'used to take the mickey out of me'. To improve his status he cultivated athletic skills – he was a good swimmer – and carried weapons, revolvers and knives; the guns he took to school, displaying them and swapping some with other boys. Between the ages of eleven and sixteen he possessed in all about forty pistols and revolvers; his ambition was to be a gunsmith. This interest arose from the fact that his father, a chief cashier in a bank, had been an army captain with the London Scottish during the First World War and was himself the possessor of two wartime revolvers. He also took his sons target-shooting, using air-guns; Christopher, the youngest of nine children, was included. He proved, however, not to be a good shot, unlike his oldest brother, Niven.

Christopher's fantasies involving firearms were fed by the films he saw – he went to the pictures three or four times a week – and gangster films were his favourites.

Niven, who was ten years older, had turned those fantasies into fact. Convicted of shop-breaking when he was fourteen, he was found guilty as a juvenile of two other offences and sent to an approved school. He was convicted twelve times in the army, being eventually court-martialled for armed robbery and given a five-year sentence. In March 1952 Niven was involved with four other men, one of whom died later in prison, in an armed robbery at Waltham Abbey. The haul was a cigarette lighter and £4. Niven Craig, aged twenty-six, a motor mechanic, denied any involvement in the robbery – he said he was elsewhere at the time. Nonetheless he was convicted of the offence and of possessing a pistol at the time of his arrest. He denied making a grab at it when the police burst into his bedroom. On Thursday, 30 October 1952, he was sentenced at the Old Bailey to twelve years in prison.

Some of his family were in court, including his youngest brother, Christopher. They heard the judge, Mr Justice Hilbery, say to the prisoner: 'You are not only cold-blooded, but . . . I believe that you would shoot down, if you had the opportunity to do so, any police officer who was attempting to arrest you . . .'

Three days later, on Sunday, 2 November, Christopher Craig, aged sixteen, went to the pictures with a girl-friend. They saw a film in which the hero was hanged after a gun-fight during which a policeman was shot. The film was called *My Death is a Mockery*.

Between 8 and 9 pm, after going home for a meal, Craig called at the home of Derek Bentley.

Bentley, born on 30 June 1933, was then nineteen; his father owned an electrical business. Bombed out twice during the blitz, he had suffered head injuries, which possibly resulted in the fact that he was of below average intelligence and illiterate. He was later adjudged by a prison doctor to be 'feeble-minded'. Perhaps to compensate for his intellectual failings, he took up body-building; he was proud of his physique, and was a tall, nice-looking boy. On leaving school he worked occasionally as a dustman or removal-man. Convicted of shop-breaking, he was sent to an approved school. About the time of Niven Craig's arrest in 1952 he began an infrequent association with young Christopher Craig whom he rather admired, an association that his parents did their best to stop after some trouble in May that year. Worth a mention here is the fact that Bentley once refused to go on a raid with Craig when he found out that Craig carried a loaded firearm.

On 2 November, when Craig called at the Bentley home about 8.30 pm, Mrs Bentley said Derek was out. Derek was in fact watching television. He said later: 'A little later Norman Parsley and Frank Fazey called . . . My mother told me that they had called and I then ran out after them. I walked up the road with them to the papershop where I saw Craig standing. We all talked together and then the other two left. Chris Craig and I then caught a bus to Croydon, a 109 bus.'

'What for?' demanded the judge at the trial. Said Bentley: 'Just for a ride, sir. An ordinary ride.'

He and Craig had already met that morning. According to Craig, who gave Bentley a knuckle-duster on the short bus-ride into Croydon, Bentley had dared him to break into a butcher's shop. This Bentley later denied. But both were now armed. Craig had a revolver with a sawn-off barrel, some ammunition, and a sheath-knife which he wore on his belt. Bentley had a smaller knife and the knuckle-duster, which Craig said he had made. He also said in court: 'I did not know what Bentley had got, sir, and he did not know what I had got.' According to him their common intent that night was burglary.

They got off the bus at West Croydon station and went down Tamworth Road. Said Bentley: 'We walked down to Reeves' Corner and crossed over, and then we came back up ... We looked into the window of the sweet-stuff shop ... I was still looking in it and Craig had got over this iron fence.' It was in fact a six-foot-high iron gate.

A woman chanced to be putting her little girl to be in a house opposite the wholesale confectioner's, which was called Barlow and Parker. It was about 9.15 pm. The child drew Mrs Ware's attention to the two men near the side entrance of the confectioner's. 'They were just standing there,' said Mrs Ware, 'talking for a few minutes, and pulling their hats over their eyes.' 'I was always messing around with my hat, sir,' said Bentley later. Mrs Ware: 'All of a sudden the shorter one jumped right over the fence at the side on the left.' The taller man, she said, 'waited for a few more minutes, and then a motor came round the corner and he waited for that to go by, and when there was no one in sight he jumped over.' Her husband telephoned the police.

Bentley said: 'Chris then climbed up the drain-pipe to the roof and I followed. Up to then Chris had not said anything. We both got out on to the flat roof at the top ... Someone shone a light in the garden, and so we got behind a stack or lift-shaft ... Someone called out down in the garden. Chris said: "It's a copper. Hide behind here ... " We were there waiting for about ten minutes.'

It was a dry night, but dark – 'there was not much moon', according to a police witness.

At about 9.25 pm a police van arrived outside the confectioner's, moments before a police car. In the van were DC Frederick Fairfax in plain clothes, PC Norman Harrison, PC Budgen and PC Pain. In the car were PC Sidney Miles and PC James McDonald. All six were from Z Division.

What happened in the next thirty minutes or so was to be variously interpreted by the accused and the police.

Fairfax's story, and that of his colleagues, was as follows. He said his attention was caught by a foot-print on a window-sill of the warehouse and that he then climbed up a drainpipe on to the flat roof. Somehow aware of the presence of the burglars behind the lift-shaft at one end of the roof, he approached them, walking carefully between a set of four roof-lights. 'I'm a police officer!' he shouted. 'Come out from behind that stack!' Craig retorted: 'If you want us, fucking well come and get us!' 'All right,' said Fairfax, and showing great courage and determination he rushed towards the lift-house and grabbed the nearest figure he saw, who happened to be Bentley. Fairfax dragged him out into the open. Still holding Bentley he tried to close in on Craig. But Bentley broke free shouting: 'Let him have it, Chris!'

Craig fired, six feet away from Fairfax, whose right shoulder was grazed by a bullet. He fell, got up and chased after the nearest fleeing shadow. This again turned out to be Bentley. Fairfax floored him with his fist and Craig fired again.

With Bentley as a shield, Fairfax ducked down behind a roof-light and frisked his captive, finding a knuckleduster and a knife. 'That's all I've got, guvnor,' said Bentley. 'I haven't got a gun.' Firmly holding on to Bentley, Fairfax edged around the roof-lights, finally finding shelter behind the staircase head to one side of the roof. Craig retreated back to the area of the lift-shaft and was now about forty feet away from them.

PC McDonald, whose weight had made climbing the drainpipe difficult, was assisted on to the roof by Fairfax, who let go of Bentley in the process.

Then Fairfax called to Craig: 'Drop your gun.' 'Come and get it!' was the answer, accompanied by another shot. According to McDonald, Fairfax said to him: 'He got me in the shoulder,' and Bentley said: 'I told the silly bugger not to use it.'

Meanwhile, PC Harrison had climbed on to an adjacent roof to the right of the lift-shaft (from the policemen's point of view) and to the left of Craig, who fired two shots in Harrison's direction when the policeman edged out on to a connecting roof of asbestos and glass tiles. Harrison retreated behind a chimney-stack, which he said was struck by a bullet – although no corroborative evidence of this was ever produced.

McDonald then asked Fairfax: 'What sort of a gun has he got, Fairy?' Bentley intervened saying: 'He's got a .45 Colt and plenty of bloody ammunition too.'

Several minutes later police reinforcements arrived below. Some were armed. At least six guns are believed to have been issued to the police, who surrounded the warehouse.

PC Miles, who had arrived at the scene with PC McDonald, had gone in search of the confectioner's manager. From him Miles obtained the keys to the warehouse. On his return Miles was one of the policemen who entered the building and came up the interior staircase to the roof. PC Harrison was with him. Miles kicked the roof door open and stepped out. As he did so, a shot was fired and he fell down dead, a bullet having entered his head above the left eyebrow – it made a horizontal exit wound at the back.

A second shot was fired as Fairfax and McDonald dragged Miles's body behind the stair-head, leaving Bentley again unattended.

Moments later PC Robert Jaggs climbed on to the roof from the drain-pipe and joined his colleagues. Whenever he poked his head around the stair-housing he heard shots. Craig shouted: 'Come on, you brave coppers! Think of your wives!' Bentley said to Jaggs: 'You want to look out. He'll blow your head off.' PC Harrison, after hurling his truncheon, a milk-bottle and a piece of wood in Craig's direction – during which Craig cried: 'I'm Craig! You've just given my brother twelve years! Come on, you coppers! I'm only sixteen!' – dashed out of the stairhead door and joined his three colleagues.

Meanwhile, PC Lowe Stewart, who had arrived about 9.45 pm, had climbed a drainpipe to the roof, seen that Miles was dead, climbed down again and positioned himself in a small yard west of the building and below Craig's vantage-point. There was a dilapidated greenhouse in the yard. He heard Craig say: 'It's a Colt .45 – Are you hiding behind a shield? Is it bullet-proof? Are we going to have a shooting-match: It's just what I like . . . Have they hurt you, Derek?'

Fairfax, McDonald and Jaggs now pushed and pulled Bentley around the open stair-head door and inside the entrance. Bentley shouted: 'Look out, Chris! They're taking me down!' The three policemen and Harrison went down the stairs with Bentley.

Before long Fairfax returned, armed with a .32 automatic. 'Drop your gun – I also have a gun!' he shouted. Craig replied: 'Come on, copper – let's have it out!'

Fairfax darted out of the stair-head. A shot was fired, and he fired two shots in return as he rushed around the roof-lights, dodging behind them and moving towards Craig, whose own gun, misfiring, clicked more than once – four times, according to PC Stewart, who then heard a shot and Craig say: 'See – it's empty.' Craig said later there were just two clicks. He swung his body over the railings that edged the roof, stood for a moment and said: 'Well, here we go. Give my love to Pam! He jumped.

The drop was twenty-five feet. But on the way down, according to Stewart, Craig hit the edge of the greenhouse, which was 15 ft 6 ins away from the warehouse wall. Stewart ran over to Craig.

Later, Stewart said: 'I jumped on him and he said: "I wish I was fucking dead! I hope I've killed the fucking lot."' Craig's spine was fractured, as was his breastbone and his forearm. However, it seems highly unlikely that his leap took him as far as the greenhouse fifteen feet away. His injuries may have been caused when he hit a shed in falling: it was immediately below him on his right. Some may have been caused by Stewart.

It was now about 10.45 pm. Craig was put in the same ambulance as DC Fairfax and taken to Croydon General Hospital, where he and Fairfax lay overnight in adjacent cubicles.

Although Craig was in considerable pain, he was only given two codeine tablets (at 2 am on Monday the 3rd) in the twelve hours that passed between his admission and the operation to set his wrist – at 11 am on the Monday morning. At 9.45 pm on the Monday night he was given a pain-killing injection of pethedine, another dose of the same at 4 pm on Tuesday, and more codeine at 10 pm on Wednesday. On Wednesday morning he had another operation on his wrist.

Craig said later in court that he dived head-first off the roof, intending to kill himself. He said he landed on his head and knocked himself out. He remembered nothing thereafter until the early morning of the 3rd. He said: 'I was in hospital and I woke up when someone hit me in the mouth and called me a murdering bastard, sir.' He claimed later – and this must refer to the operation on his wrist on Monday morning: 'They were pushing me down a corridor on a trolley and they were running me into the walls and all over the bumps so they could hurt me.' He added, explaining his difficulty in remembering what the police claimed he had said: 'I was injected every twelve hours, sir . . . I was hardly conscious half the time, sir.' 'Hardly conscious!' exclaimed the Lord Chief Justice. 'Don't talk such nonsense!' Said Craig: 'I was only half conscious. I was crying for my mother.'

Six policemen from Z Division gave evidence at the trial about Craig's callous and boastful remarks as he lay in a hospital bed under police surveillance – 'Is the copper dead? How about the others? We ought to have shot them all – Did I really kill a policeman? – I shot him in the head and he went down like a ton of bricks – All you bastards should be dead – Is the policeman I shot in the shoulder still in hospital? I know that the one I shot in the head is dead – That night I was out to kill because I had so much hate inside me for what they did to my brother.' Much of this was later denied by Craig.

DS Shepherd said in court that he went to Croydon General Hospital at 11 pm on 2 November and saw Craig, who later denied seeing Shepherd until 11 November.

DCI John Smith, who had already visited the scene of the crime, seen the dead policeman's body and spoken with DC Fairfax, who was in the next cubicle, said he charged the young gunman at about 11.30 pm with the murder of PC Miles.

This is contradicted by Fairfax himself, who some years later told author David Yallop: 'Craig did not talk to anyone either voluntarily or any other way until the following day. He was *out* and stayed that way.'

At 1.15 am Smith and Shepherd went to Craig's home, where they found a .45 bullet in his bed and 137 rounds rounds of ammunition in a tin box in the attic.

At 4 am they saw Bentley in Croydon police station. Bentley said to Smith: 'Are you in charge of this, guvnor? . . . I didn't kill him, guv. Chris did it.' He was then cautioned and made a statement, written down by DS Shepherd. It was read back to the illiterate Bentley, who scrawled a signature on each page. He was then charged. He said: 'Craig shot him. I hadn't got a gun. He was with me on the roof and shot him then between the eyes.' In his statement he said: 'I did not have a gun and I did not know Chris had one until he shot.'

This contradicts a remark Bentley is said to have made in the police car taking him from Tamworth Road to the police station. After being taken down the stairs Bentley had been handed over by Inspector Bodley to PS Edward Roberts, who cautioned him. Bentley said to him: 'I didn't have a gun. Chris shot him.' Sitting between PC Roberts and PC Alderson in the rear of a police car driven by PC Stephens, Stephens and Roberts heard Bentley say: 'I knew he had a gun, but I didn't think he'd use it. He's done one of your blokes in.' According to Roberts, nothing else was said by anyone in the car. Stephens, however, added that Roberts also said: 'I shouldn't make any other statement now. You'll be given a chance to make a statement at the station.'

Apart from the fact that both Craig and Bentley later denied most of what police witnesses alleged they had said – on the roof, in the police car, and in hospital – including the phrase 'Let him have it, Chris!' which was said to have been heard by Fairfax, McDonald and Harrison, these officers and others sometimes disagreed about other shouts and remarks made by Bentley and Craig, who both also denied that Fairfax apprehended Bentley in the manner he described.

Their version was that Fairfax, having seized Bentley, took him back across the roof – McDonald was then struggling up the drainpipe. It was then, said Craig, that he fired 'to frighten him away' – when Fairfax was about thirty feet from him. He said he fired at the ground, six feet in front of himself, and his defence suggested that the bullet flew up and grazed Fairfax's shoulder. Said Bentley: 'Fairfax leaned on me and fell over like *that*. He did not touch the floor though . . . He got up, well, leaned up, and put me behind that staircase . . . I gave him the knuckleduster; I took it out of my pocket myself.'

Oddly, the alternative interpretation of the phrase 'Let him have it, Chris' – i.e. 'Hand him the gun' – was never mentioned in court, not even by the defence.

Craig's defence was that although guilty of manslaughter, he was innocent of murder – he never intended to injure or kill. He fired at the policeman, he said, obliquely, not directly, and what he shouted was – 'Bluff, sir, so that they would not come at me.'

His version of PC Miles's death was this. 'The door flew open and I thought someone was rushing at me, sir, saw someone was coming out, and I fired another one to frighten them away . . . over the roof' – to his right. The fatal bullet, he said, 'might have ricochetted off'. Of Fairfax's final armed charge at him, he said: 'Someone fired two shots at me from somewhere I could not see.'

Bentley's defence was that the 'joint enterprise' had ended fifteen minutes *before* Miles died, that at the time of Miles's death he was already under arrest, had made no move to rejoin Craig or to escape when he might have done, did not know Craig had a gun, and did not urge him to use it.

The prosecution had to prove that Bentley and Craig had a common purpose. The law is that an accomplice, although he does nothing, is as guilty as the person who strikes or shoots. It had to be proved that Bentley knew Craig had a gun before the shooting began and that he was prepared to use it – as Bentley urged him to do, according to the prosecution.

Bentley himself had two weapons in his possession, a knife and a knuckleduster. But it was the latter that excited Lord Goddard's interest and disapprobation. Slipping it on his hand, he asked the jury: 'Have you ever seen a more horrible sort of weapon? . . . Did you ever see a more shocking thing than that?'

As regards Craig, the judge told the jury that in the special law concerning policemen, if a person 'does a wilful act which causes the death of the officer, he is guilty of murder, whether or not he intended to kill or to do grievous bodily harm.' The defence, said the judge, had to show the *act* was accidental in order to reduce the charge to manslaughter.

The trail of Bentley and Craig (who was still on crutches) began at the Old Bailey, on Thursday, 9 December 1952 – less than six weeks after the shooting. It ended on the morning of Saturday, 11 December. The judge was the Lord Chief Justice, Lord Goddard. The chief prosecutor was Mr Christmas Humphreys, son of Mr Justice Humphreys. Craig's counsel was a barrister from Leeds, Mr John Parris, and Bentley's was Mr F. H. Cassels, son of Mr Justice Cassels.

Mr Parris, busily employed in a trial in Leeds, was given the brief concerning Craig three days before the Old Bailey trial was due to start – originally on Monday 6 December. When he complained, the start of the trial was postponed for three days.

Twenty-four witnesses were called by the prosecution – sixteen were police officers of Z Division – and only, two by the defence, the accused themselves.

The police witnesses failed to agree on how many shots were fired and some of their evidence was inconsistent. But, as the judge told the jury, speaking of Fairfax, McDonald and Harrison: 'Those three officers in particular showed the highest gallantry and resolution; they were conspicuously brave. Are you going to say they are conspicuous *liars*? Because if their evidence is untrue – that Bentley called out "Let him have it, Chris" – those officers are doing their best to swear away the life of that boy. If it is true, it is, of course, the most deadly piece of evidence against him.'

Craig himself said he reloaded his gun once and fired it eleven times, two shots being misfires.

The prosecution produced Mr Lewis Nicholls, MSc, Director of the Metropolitan Police Laboratory, as their ballistics expert. He revealed that the gun was not strictly speaking a Colt .45 but a First World War standard issue .455 Eley service revolver with a sawn-off barrel. He said: 'This weapon . . . was quite an inaccurate weapon,' and agreed that it would be inaccurate to a degree of six feet at a range of thirty-nine feet, although 'if one aimed at the centre of a human being, one would more or less guarantee to hit him at six feet.'

This seemed to suggest that Craig was far more likely to have hit Miles (some thirty-nine feet away) if he had *not* been aiming at him – a point that the defence failed to follow up.

Nicholls said that of the twelve bullets and cartridge cases given to him on 15 November – nearly a fortnight after the shooting – one was a .32 and three were undersized and would make a shot completely inaccurate. These three had been fired, one being found later caught up in Fairfax's braces. The rest were .45 tommy-gun rounds, two of which were duds. The police found only two spent bullets on the roof, and apparently none (apart from that in Fairfax's clothing) elsewhere. One .45 bullet (Exhibit 8) was inside the doorway of the staircase head, and the other was in a far corner of the roof. Mr Nicholls agreed that Exhibit 8 was 'badly distorted' and had been fired by a revolver similar to Exhibit 6, Craig's gun. However, he said: 'I could find no evidence of blood on it whatsoever. Therefore, in all probability, it is not the fatal bullet.'

Mr Haler, who carried out the post-mortem on Miles, told David Yallop some years later that the bullet that killed Miles was a large-calibre bullet of a size ranging between .32 and .38.

What happened to the bullet that killed PC Miles? It was never produced as such in court. Nor was any forensic expert or indeed any other ballistics expert asked by the defence to examine and comment on the bullets, the ammunition and the gun.

It has been alleged that one of the policemen involved in the later stages of the confrontation at the warehouse, and situated on an adjacent roof, could have shot PC Miles by accident or mistake – although Craig himself always seemed to believe that *he* had shot Miles. However, Yallop quotes him as saying years later: 'What I've never been able to understand is how I shot him between the eyes when he was facing away from me and was going the wrong way.'

During the brief trial Lord Goddard made over 250 interjections, most of them harmful by implication to the accused. As the jury retired, the foreman asked the judge if they could examine Fairfax's jacket and waistcoat. Lord Goddard retorted: 'You will remember you are not considering the wounding of Sergeant Fairfax. You are considering the murder of a policeman!' He was still wearing the knuckleduster, which he put on his hand toward the end of his summing up. He now smote the bench with it.

The all-male jury were out for seventy-five minutes, between 11.15 and 12.130 am. While they were our Lord Goddard dealt with another case in which Craig and a sixteen-year-old grammar school boy, Norman Parsley, both masked, had robbed an elderly Croydon couple at gunpoint. Parsley was sentenced to four years in jail.

Craig and Bentley were both found guilty of the murder of PC Miles, but in Bentley's case the jury added a recommendation for mercy. Neither prisoner said anything when invited to speak before sentence was passed. Lord Goddard donned his black cap and formally sentenced Derek Bentley to death.

Christopher Craig was too young to hang. He was, said the judge: 'One of the most dangerous young criminals who has ever stood in that dock.' He was sentenced to be detained at Her Majesty's pleasure. 'You are the more guilty of the two,' said Lord Goddard. 'Your heart was filled with hate, and you murdered a policeman without thought of his wife, his family or himself, and never once have you expressed a word of sorrow for what you have done . . .'

The Lord Chief Justice then asked Fairfax (now a detective sergeant), PCs McDonald and Harrison, and the Chief Inspector of Z Division to step forward. He told them that their conduct was worthy of the highest commendation and that the thanks of all law-abiding citizens was their due.

Three weeks later, on 6 January 1953, *before* Bentley's appeal was heard, it was announced that DS Fairfax had been awarded the George Cross, PC Harrison and PC McDonald George Medals, and PC Jaggs a BEM.

Bentley's appeal was heard on 13 January and dismissed. Although the press were largely in favour of his execution – four policemen had been killed by villains in 1951 – there were widespread protests, petitions and expressions of outrage by MPs and many others. But the Home Secretary, Sir David Maxwell-Fyfe, remained inflexible and did nothing.

Derek Bentley, aged nineteen, was hanged in Wandsworth jail at 9 am on Wednesday, 28 January 1953, just over three months after the shooting of PC Miles.

Some 5,000 people demonstrated outside the prison, crying 'Murder!' and singing, 'Abide with me' when the hour struck. The notice of Bentley's execution, hung on the prison gates, was torn down and smashed. His death certificate recorded his cause of death as 'Fractured neck and crushing of cord. Judicial hanging'.

It was rumoured that Bentley wept as he was taken to be hanged. His executioner, Pierrepoint, has categorically denied this, saying in his book: 'I did not shake hands with the prisoner on the afternoon before his death. I did not make any notes about him. The Governor of Wandsworth did not have to urge me to get on with my job. Bentley did not cry on the way to the scaffold.'

At the Bentley home in Norbury the clocks in the house had all been silenced. Mrs Bentley lay upstairs in bed, heavily sedated. In the living-room sat Mr Bentley, his daughter Iris, and his youngest surviving son, Dennis aged nine. Mr Bentley wore a wrist-watch and he could not help glancing at it from time to time as the hour of his eldest son's execution approached. At nine o'clock he suddenly rose from his chair and grabbed Dennis. 'No one's ever going to take my son away from me,' he said and wept.

Christopher Craig spent ten and a half years in prison and was released on licence in May 1963. He settled in Buckinghamshire, became an engineer and married in 1965 when he was twenty-eight. Lord Goddard died in May 1971, at the age of ninety-three.

Bentley's family tried for years to get the verdict on their son repealed, but to no avail. Mr Bentley died in July 1974 and his wife two years later. Iris struggled on alone. Dennis, who grew up to be a bitter, sullen young man, himself fell foul of the law more than once. In 1980, when he was thirty-eight, he was sentenced to a term of imprisonment for various driving offences.

Before Derek Bentley died he told his parents: 'I didn't kill anyone. So why are they killing me.'

In his last letter to them someone wrote at his dictation: 'I tell you what Mum, the truth of this thing has got to come out one day.

CHAPTER 45

John Reginald Christie
The murder of Mrs Christie, 1953

More has probably been written about the murders at 10 Rillington Place than about any other case investigated by the Metropolitan Police. At least six women were murdered there. But what has caused the greatest argument is whether or not two murderers were at work at the same time in the same house. The extraordinary fact is that a man who had already strangled two women was the chief witness for the prosecution at the trial of another man who lived in the same house and was alleged to have strangled his wife and child.

John Reginald Halliday Christie was a thin, bald, weak, neurotic, unlikeable person, a hypochondriac, a liar and one-time thief. One of seven children, five of whom were girls, he was born on 8 April 1898 in Yorkshire and brought up in Chester Street, Boothtown, on the edge of Halifax. His father was a carpet designer. As a child Christie was often ill, often beaten by his father and known as a cissy at Halifax Secondary School, where he proved to be quite bright and sang in the school choir. He was also a boy scout and liked gardening.

After leaving school when he was fifteen he got a job with the Halifax police. He was sacked for petty pilfering, and then sacked for petty theft by the carpet factory that gave him his next job. He became a cinema operator at the Gem and then at the Victoria Hall cinema in Halifax, from where he was called up in April 1917 just after his nineteenth birthday. He served as a signalman with the Duke of Wellington's Regiment and with the Notts and Derby Regiment in Flanders and France. Injured by an exploding mustard-gas shell, he was gassed twice, blinded for some months, and lost his voice (as he claimed) for over three years. Thereafter he always spoke in low, uncertain tones. He was also short-sighted and wore glasses. His sex drive was apparently as feeble as his constitution – he had pneumonia when he was seventeen – and a girl who led him down a lover's lane in Halifax dubbed him 'Reggie-no-dick' and 'Can't-do-it-Christie'.

He married Ethel Simpson Waddington in May 1920; they had no children. He moved from job to job, working as a cinema operator, a clerk and a postman, and in April 1921 he was sentenced to three months' imprisonment for stealing postal orders. Two years later he was bound over for obtaining money by false pretences and put on twelve months' probation for violence.

Presumably disgruntled with the attentions of the lawmen and the imperfections of his all but sexless marriage, he came to London in 1923, leaving his wife in Sheffield, where she worked as a shorthand typist. The pattern of shiftlessness continued. He moved from place to place from job to job. In September 1924 he was given nine months' hard labour at Uxbridge for theft.

Two months after this Timothy John Evans was born in South Wales.

Christie then held down a clerical job for five years until, in May 1929, he was sentenced to six months' hard labour for striking a woman with whom he was living with her son's cricket-bat. His last sentence, in 1933, was three months for stealing a car.

His wife visited him in prison and on his release came to live with him in London, ten years after their separation. Her presence gave him some stability, for it was twenty years before he was again charged with an offence – her murder. Their sex-life, although it apparently revived for a time, was sporadic and eventually ceased.

In 1938 they rented three small rooms, the ground floor flat in 10 Rillington Place. It was then a seedy cul-de-sac near Ladbroke Grove underground station. Since demolished and rebuilt as a terrace of modern houses, the street, off St Mark's Road, is now known as Ruston Mews.

Christie lived in Rillington Place for fifteen years, during which seven women were murdered in the house.

The first was Ruth Fuerst, a tall Austrian girl, aged twenty-one at the time of her death, who came to England in 1939 as a student nurse and was then employed in a wartime munitions factory in Davies Street, Mayfair. In 1939 Christie had begun to wear the dark blue uniform and peaked cap of a special constable in the War Reserve Police. Based at Harrow Road police station, he patrolled the streets making sure black-out regulations were observed and law and order maintained. This he apparently did with a thoroughness that verged on the officious. Off duty one day, but making enquiries about a man wanted for theft, he met Ruth Fuerst in a snackbar. As his wife was away in Sheffield, where she fled when the bombing became unbearable, he asked Miss Fuerst back to Rillington Place on two or three occasions.

It was August 1943 and Christie was forty-five.

'She was very tall,' he said later. 'Almost as tall as me, and I was 5 ft 9 ins . . . One day . . . she undressed and wanted me to have intercourse with her. I got a telegram while she was there, saying that my wife was on her way home. The girl wanted us to team up together and go right away somewhere together. I would not do that. I got on to the bed and had intercourse with her. While I was having intercourse with her, I strangled her with a piece of rope. I remember urine and excreta coming away from her. She was completely naked . . . She had a leopard-skin coat and I wrapped this around her. I took her from the bedroom into the front room and put her under the floorboards. I had to do that because of my wife coming back. I put the remainder of her clothing under the floorboards too. My wife came home in the evening; my brother-in-law, Mr Waddington, came with her. Mr Waddington went back home the next day and during the afternoon my wife went out. I think she was working at Osram's. While she was out I picked the body up from under the floorboards and took it into the outhouse [the wash-house]. Later in the day I dug a hole in the garden, and in the evening, when it was dark, about ten o'clock I should say, I put the body down the hole and covered it up quickly with earth. It was the right-hand side of the garden, about halfway towards the rockery. My wife never knew. I told her I was going to the lavatory. The only lavatory is in the yard [beyond the wash-house].'

That statement was made nearly ten years after the event it describes, and like most of what Christie so cautiously said has to be viewed with equal caution. The fact is that Ruth Fuerst was last seen on 24 August 1943 in her Notting Hill digs and that her skeleton was recovered in the area indicated by Christie in March 1953. There was no evidence to show how in fact she met her death.

Four months after the Austrian girl's disappearance, Christie ceased to be a War Reserve constable because of his association with a married woman employed at Harrow Road police station. Her soldier husband, returning home on leave, assaulted Christie and cited him as co-respondent in the ensuing divorce case.

Meanwhile, Christie, whom everyone knew as Reg, got a clerical job with Ultra Radio in Acton. There he met a small, stout woman, Miss Muriel Eady, aged thirty-two, who worked in the canteen. She had a boyfriend, and the two of them used to visit the Christies in Rillington Place.

'On one occasion,' said Christie, 'she came alone. I believe she complained of catarrh, and I said I thought I could help her. She came by appointment when my wife was out. I believe my wife was on holiday. I think I mixed some stuff up, some inhalants, Friar's Balsam was one. She was in the kitchen, and at the time she was inhaling with a square scarf over her head. I remember now, it was in the bedroom. The liquid was in a square glass jar with a metal screw-top lid. I had made two holes in the lid and through one of the holes I put a rubber tube from the gas into the liquid. Through the other hole I put another rubber tube, about two feet long. This tube didn't touch the liquid . . . She inhaled the stuff from the tube. I did it to make her dopey. She became sort of unconscious and I have a vague recollection of getting a stocking and tying it round her neck. I am not too clear about this . . . It may have been the Austrian girl that I used the gas on. I don't think it was both. I believe I had intercourse with her at the time I strangled her. I think I put her in the wash-house. That night I buried her in the garden on the right-hand side nearest the yard.'

Last seen alive on 7 October 1944 at her Putney home, Muriel Eady's skeleton was unearthed in the garden in March 1953. The cause of her death could not be established, but that same month the police discovered a square glass jar (but no lid) in the kitchen of Christie's flat. They also found that a gas-pipe on the kitchen wall by the window had been stopped up with putty and that one of the burners on the gas-stove, minus its top, was merely a nozzle.

Christie probably devised a method of gassing women visitors so that he could indulge his sexual whims with their immobile unconscious bodies. This may have involved some form of masturbation rather than intercourse. For as the women were apparently willing – with the possible exception of Miss Eady – there was no need to gas them before a normal act of intercourse. None of his later victims died of carbon monoxide poisoning: the gas was used to incapacitate them.

Miss Fuerst and Miss Eady may not have been the only women so treated, but in their case strangling may have resulted when they panicked and resisted, or when they suddenly revived. Strangulation in the case of his last three victims may by then have become part of some masturbatory rite in which necrophilia was also involved. Christie's statements probably 'improved' on what he did, making it more manly.

Few men with unusual sexual tastes – and Christie was otherwise quite a prim and proper person who neither smoked nor drank – are willing to admit in detail the special tricks and techniques by which they obtain ejaculation.

What is especially odd, among so much that is queer about this case, is that after killing two women (in 1943 and 1944) he killed no more – if one excepts Beryl Evans – for nine years. And then he killed four women in four months.

Why did he stop after Muriel Eady? Possibly because his wife was more or less permanently in the house. Or perhaps he found some partner who suited his peculiar sexual requirements. Perhaps his health, which was always poor, became his main preoccupation. He had been visiting Dr Odess since 1934 with a string of minor complaints, fibrositis being the most consistent and severe.

Dr Odess said at Christie's trial that he was a 'nervous type . . . He had fits of crying, sobbing; he complained of insomnia, and headaches, and giddiness.' He also suffered from diarrhoea, flatulence and amnesia.

After the war Reg Christie became a clerk in a post office savings bank, a job that lasted four years – until his previous convictions came to light. His next and final job was a clerical one with British Road Services.

Meanwhile, on 20 September 1947, Timothy evans (who was now twenty-three) married Beryl Thorley, a pretty but dull eighteen-year-old telephonist working at Grosvenor House in Mayfair.

Evans was a van-driver, a thin and wiry Welshman (5 ft 5½ ins) with an uncertain temper, whose constitutional, tubercular weakness kept him in sanatoria when he was a boy and kept him out of national service, from which he was rejected on medical grounds. Poorly educated and hardly able to read or write, he was none the less not illiterate. For he read comics, signed his own name, and must have had some understanding of the writing on the packages, receipts, etc., which he handled in his job. He was not, as has been claimed, a pathetic 'near mental defective'.

Beryl Thorley, who came from a respectable family and worked in upper-class surroundings, is unlikely to have married an idiot. The Tim Evans whom she met on a blind date must have been an attractive, sparky young Welshman, not too bright perhaps, but not a dim-witted lout either. He was also a bit of a braggart, a heavy drinker and a fantastic liar. A senior police officer thought him 'quite worldly'.

For a while the young couple lived with Evans's mother, Mrs Probert (she had remarried), in St Mark's Road, and when Beryl learned she was pregnant the couple decided to move into a place of their own. This they did in March 1948, renting the two rooms on the top floor of 10 Rillington Place – the middle flat was occupied by a solitary, elderly man called Kitchener. The Christies lived on the ground floor.

Geraldine Evans was born on 10 October 1948.

A year passed without apparent incident, except that Mr and Mrs Evans often had rows, mainly about money but also about a blonde girl, Lucy, who came to stay for a few weeks in August. She was seventeen and a friend of Beryl. It is said that the two girls shared the marital bed while Evans slept on the kitchen floor. Before long Mrs Probert and a probation officer were involved: once Evans threatened to throw his wife out of a window. Eventually he walked out with Lucy, staying away for two nights before he returned to Beryl.

Then, in October 1949, Beryl told him she was expecting another baby.

It seems she decided to have an abortion, apparently reluctant to lose her figure and possibly her husband, as well as the extra money she earned through part-time work. Both the Christies knew of her intentions and advised her against the abortion. Evans himself was also opposed to the idea, as he explained in his first statement to the police.

'She told me she was about three months gone. I said: "If you're having a baby, well, you've had one – another won't make any difference." She then told me she was going to try to get rid of it. I turned round and told her not to be silly, that she'd make herself ill. Then she bought herself a syringe and started syringing herself. Then she said that didn't work, and I said: "I'm glad it won't work." Then she said she was going to buy some tablets. I don't know what tablets she bought because she was always hiding them from me. She started to look very ill, and I told her to go and see a doctor, and she said she'd go when I was in work. But when I'd come home and ask her if she'd been, she'd always say she hadn't. On the Sunday morning, that would be the sixth of November, she told me that if she couldn't get rid of the baby she'd kill herself and our other baby, Geraldine. I told her she was talking silly. She never said no more about it then, but when I got up Monday morning to go to work she said she was going to see some woman to see if she could help her . . .'

In his *second* statement Evans told a different story.

'About a week before my wife died, Reg Christie . . . approached me and said: "I'd like to have a chat with you about your wife taking these tablets . . . If you and your wife had come to me in the first place I could have done it for you without any risk." I turned round and said: "Well, I didn't think you knew anything about medical stuff." So he told me that he was training for a doctor before the war. Then he started showing me books and things on medical . . . He told me the stuff he used one out of every ten would die with it. I told him I wasn't interested – so I said goodnight to him and I went upstairs. When I got in, my wife started talking to me about it. She said that she had been speaking to Mr Christie and asked me if he had spoken to me . . . I told her she wasn't to have anything to do with it. She turned round and told me to mind my own business and that she intended to get rid of it and she trusted Mr Christie . . . On the Monday evening [7 November] . . . My wife said that Mr Christie had made arrangements for the first thing Tuesday morning. I didn't argue with her. I just washed and changed and went to the KPH [a pub] until ten o'clock. I came home and had supper and went to bed. She wanted to start an argument, but I just took no notice. Just after six I got up the following morning to go to work . . . I had a cup of tea and a smoke and she told me: "On your down tell Mr Christie that everything is all right. If you don't tell him, I'll go down and tell him myself." So as I went down the stairs he came out to meet me and I said: "Everything is all right." Then I went to work.'

In his first statement, Evans had said that on the Monday he met a man at a transport café who gave him some 'stuff' in a bottle that would fix the matter of his wife's pregnancy.

He said that on Tuesday when he returned from work at about 6.30 pm the lights were out and he found his wife, who had apparently taken the liquid 'stuff', dead on the bed. That night, he said, be put her body down a manhole or drain outside the house and got someone to look after the baby the next day. This statement was made on the afternoon of Wednesday, 30 November, to the Merthyr police. When they told him later that night that there was no body in the drain and that three men had been needed to lift the manhole cover, Evans then said: 'I said that to protect a man named Christie. It's not true about the man in the café either.'

He then made the second statement, the longest of the four he made, accusing Christie of causing his wife's death in an attempt to carry out an abortion.

Evans said: 'When I came home in the evening [Tuesday] he was waiting for me at the bottom of the staircase. He said: "It's bad news. It didn't work."' Christie refused to tell him what happened except that Beryl had died about three o'clock and that her stomach was 'septic poisoned'. Evans found his wife lying on the bed – 'I could see that she was dead and that she had been bleeding from the mouth and nose and that she had been bleeding from the bottom part. She had a black skirt on and a check blouse and a kid of light blue jacket on.'

This story was repeated by Evans at his trial.

He also said that about seven o'clock he helped Christie, who was 'puffing and blowing', to carry Beryl's body down the stairs and into Mr Kitchener's kitchen, as the old man was away in hospital. According to Evans, Christie said he would dispose of the body 'down one of the drains' and would see about getting someone to look after the baby. This was done in Evans's absence at work on the Thursday, when a 'young couple from East Acton' – so Christie informed him – took the baby away.

What actually happened on the Thursday (and from now on Christie's and Evans's versions of events roughly tally) was that Evans was sacked from his job, although he told everyone he had left of his own accord. 'He seemed extremely angry,' said Christie at Evans's trial, 'really wild.' That evening Evans told his mother that Beryl and the baby had gone to her father in Brighton.

On Friday the 11th Evans visited a second-hand furniture dealer in Portobello Road, and went out drinking and to the pictures over the weekend – the Christies fed him on Sunday – and on Monday afternoon the furniture dealer bought and took away most of the Evans's hire-purchase possessions, including the lino on the floor.

Evans received £40.

He then left Rillington Place, going again to the pictures and to various pubs before he caught the 12.55 am milk-train from Paddington station to Wales.

Early on Tuesday, 15 November, he arrived at the home of his aunt, Mrs Lynch, in Merthyr Vale. He told her and her husband that Beryl and Geraldine had gone to Brighton and would spend Christmas there. Apparently no further questions were asked and Evans idled about Merthyr for almost a week until, on Monday, 21 November – the day after his twenty-fifth birthday – he returned to London.

His whereabouts on Monday and Tuesday are unknown, but he appeared at the door of 10 Rillington Place on Wednesday the 23rd and had a discussion on the doorstep with Christie, allegedly about the baby's well-being. That night Evans was back in Merthyr.

By now his mother and her married daughters in St Mark's Road were becoming anxious: they had heard neither from Beryl nor from Evans for over a fortnight. The Christies, when asked for information, said they knew nothing of Beryl, except that she had gone away with the baby.

A telegram was sent on 29 November to Beryl's father in Brighton and resulted in the disclosure that she was not there either. On that same day Mrs Probert wrote to Mrs Lynch in reply to a recent letter from her sister-in-law saying that Tim had been in Merthyr for two weeks on his own and was jobless. Mrs Probert wrote:

> I don't know what lies Tim have told you down there I know nothing abut him and I have not seen him for 3 weeks ... there is some mystery about him you can tell him from me he don't want to come to me I never want to see him again ... he have put years on my life since last August [When Lucy lodged with the Evanses] ... he is like his father no good to himself or anybody else ... his name stinks up here everywhere I go people asking for him for money he owes them. I am ashamed to say he is my son ...

At breakfast on the 30th Mrs Lynch read this letter to Tim Evans, who was dismissive and made little comment. but that afternoon at 3.10 pm he walked into Merthyr Vale police station and told an astonished DC Evans: 'I want to give myself up. I have disposed of my wife.'

'What do you mean?' enquired DC Evans. 'I put her down the drain,' said his namesake. 'You realize what you're saying?' responded DC Evans. 'Yes,' the other man replied. 'I know what I'm saying. I can't sleep and want to get it off my chest.'

Evans then made his first statement – about his wife's abortion attempts and the man in the café – in which neither himself nor Christie were implicated in Beryl's death.

The Welsh police telephoned London, and the manhole cover outside 10 Rillington Place was raised with great difficulty by three policemen and no body was found 'down the drain'. When informed of this, Evans made a second statement, naming Christie as the abortionist and killer.

At Evans's trial, Christie denied knowing about or assisting in any abortions, and no evidence was ever produced to refute this.

He said that on Tuesday, 8 November: 'I was in bed a lot of the time with the illness I had, which is enteritis and fibrositis in my back. I was in a great deal of pain and I rested as much as possible under doctor's orders with a fire in the room day and night, and on Tuesday evening at about twenty-past five I went up to the doctor.' Doctor Odess lived in nearby Colville Square. On the way back Christie collected his wife at the local public library, where she had gone while he was seeing the doctor. The Christies went home and he went to bed 'feeling pretty bad' and his wife prepared some milk food for him. 'As a matter of fact she slipped and fell and the milk food went over the bed, and I didn't have it.' About midnight, he said, they were both in bed when they were startled awake by a very loud thud. 'We listened for a few seconds and didn't hear anything, and I gradually knelt up in bed and looked through the window which overlooks the yard. It was very dark and I couldn't see anything there, and so I went back and we laid down, and shortly after that I heard some movement which appeared to be upstairs . . . as though something heavy was being moved.'

Mrs Christie said in court it was 'as if furniture was being moved about'.

There was no sign of Beryl or the baby on Wednesday, according to both the Christies, and when Evans returned that night at about half-past ten he told Mrs Christie, in answer to her question: 'Where's Beryl and the baby?' – 'Oh, she's gone away to Bristol.' 'Gone away to Bristol?' queried Mrs Christie. 'She never told me she was going.' 'She said she would write,' Evans replied, adding: 'She didn't tell my mother either.'

None of this was ever contradicted or refuted by either of the Christies, by Dr Odess, or by any other witness at Evans's trial – apart from Evans himself.

At Christie's trial, Dr Odess said that his patient had had a severe attack of fibrositis that had lasted from 1 November to 27 December 1949, and he doubted whether Christie could lift a human being down two flights of stairs. He said: 'At the time I was seeing him, he could hardly get off the chair sometimes; I had to help him up.'

He said later that Christie visited him on Tuesday the 8th complaining of enteritis, or diarrhoea, and again on the 12th when his fibrositis was so bad his back had to be strapped.

On 1 December 1949, the day after Evans made his first two statements, the police in Merthyr Tydfil and London pursued their enquiries by interviewing Mrs Lynch, Mrs Probert and Mr and Mrs Christie, who were questioned at some length and independently. The two rooms of Evans's former flat were found to be empty, apart from a stolen briefcase and some newspaper cuttings about the 'Torso Murder' of Stanley Setty. The yard and garden, which were also examined, showed no signs of digging or disturbance.

In Merthyr, Evans added some details to his second statement saying he helped Christie to carry his wife's body down the stairs and that he visited Christie on Tuesday the 15th.

Investigations in Brighton and Bristol concerning the whereabouts of Beryl and the baby likewise drew a blank. She might have gone elsewhere, but Evans's statements seemed to indicate that her body – if there was a body – was somewhere in or around the house at the end of the cul-de-sac.

On the morning of Friday, 2 December, a thorough search was made of 10 Rillington Place by Chief Inspector Jennings, accompanied by DCS Barratt. The door of the wash-house was found to be locked. Mrs Christie said the wash-house was not used as such, adding that the tap inside was used to swill out the slop-pail. The lock, she said, was faulty, and the door locked itself; it could be opened with a piece of metal which pushed back the catch. She proceeded to do so.

Christie was also present, with his hands pressing into the base of his back, suffering from an attack of fibrositis.

Under the sink, hidden by bits of wood, was a bundle wrapped in a green tablecloth and tied up with sashcord. Mrs Christie was invited by the police officers to explain its presence, even to touch the bundle. She did so and was mystified. The bundle was dragged out into the yard, the cord was untied and a pair of feet flopped out.

Baby Geraldine, with a striped tie knotted tightly around her neck, was found concealed by some kindling behind the door.

Dr Donald Teare, the Home Office pathologist who carried out the autopsies, established that both mother and daughter had been strangled, Geraldine by the tie and Beryl by what appeared from the abrasions on her neck to have been a rope. Clothed but without any knickers, she was more than three months pregnant, and the only evidence of interference was a slight bruise in her vagina and an old scar.

She had evidently been struck in the face about twenty minutes before she died – her right eye and upper lip were marked and swollen – and there were two bruises on the inner, upper part of her left leg.

Timothy Evans, ignorant of these discoveries, was brought to London that night and taken to Notting Hill police station. He was show two piles of clothes, Beryl's and Geraldine's as well as the tablecloth, a blanket in which Beryl had been wrapped, and the striped tie. He was told by CI

Jennings that the bodies of both mother and daughter had been discovered in the wash-house that morning 'and this clothing was found on them'. Both had been strangled, said Jennings.

It was disputed at Evans's trial whether Jennings also revealed the exact positions of the bodies and that they had been obscured by pieces of wood.

As Jennings talked, Evans picked up some of the garments. He picked up the tie. Tears came to his eyes.

If his first two statements were true, this was when he discovered that his baby was dead and how she had died and where her body had been put. Said Jennings: 'I have reason to believe you were responsible for their deaths.'

'Yes,' said Timothy Evans.

He made a brief statement, his third. 'She was incurring one debt after another,' he said. 'I couldn't stand it any longer, so I strangled her with a piece of rope and took her down to the flat below the same night ... I waited till the Christies had gone to bed, then I took her to the wash-house after midnight. This was on Tuesday, 8 November. On Thursday evening after I came home from work I strangled my baby in our bedroom with my tie, and later that night I took her down into the wash-house after the Christies had gone to bed.'

According to Jennings he then said: 'It's a great relief to get it off my chest. I feel better already. I can tell you the cause that led up to it.' He then went on to make a long statement, his fourth. As in the third there was no attempt to incriminate Christie and no mention of any abortion attempt.

Beryl, he said, was always moaning about the long hours he worked and about how little he was paid. She was in debt, and he worked overtime to pay off her debts; he also borrowed money himself. Then he discovered she was behind with their HP payments and with the rent. There was a row. 'I told her if she didn't pull herself together I would leave her, so she said: "You can leave anytime you like."' There was another row on the on the morning of Sunday, 6 November; then he went out to the pictures and she nagged him on his return and until he went to bed. The following morning, he said, 'she gets up and starts and argument straight away. I took no notice of her ... My wife told me that she was going to pack up and go down to her father in Brighton ... She was going to take the baby with her ... So I said it would be a good job and a load of worry off my mind.' When he returned from work that night he put the kettle on, sat down, and his wife walked in. 'I thought you was going to Brighton,' he remarked. She replied: 'What, for you to have a good time?' He went downstairs to fetch the push-chair. 'I came upstairs and she started an argument again. I told her if she didn't pack it up I'd slap her face. With that she picked up a milk bottle to throw at me. I grabbed the bottle out of her hand. I pushed her, she fell in a chair in the kitchen, so I washed and changed and went out.' When he got home later, they argued again.

On Tuesday morning he went to work as usual. 'I came home at night about 6.30 pm, my wife started to argue again, so I hit her across the face with my flat hand. She then hit me back with her hand. In a fit of temper I grabbed a piece of rope from a chair, which I had brought home off my van, and strangled her with it. I then took her into the bedroom and laid her on the bed with the rope still tied round her neck. Before 10 pm that night I carried my wife's body downstairs to the kitchen of Mr Kitchener's flat . . . ' He fed and sat up with the baby and then put her to bed. Later, 'when everything was quiet', he wrapped his wife's body in a blanket and a green tablecloth from the kitchen table and tied the bundle up 'with a piece of cord from out of the kitchen cupboard.' He took the bundle – Mrs Evans was quite small – down to the wash-house, put it under the sink and 'blocked the front of the sink up with pieces of wood so that the body wouldn't be seen.'

For two days, on Wednesday and Thursday, he fed, washed and changed the baby and went to work, sitting by the fire in the evenings. After he was sacked on Thursday he came home, he said, 'picked up my baby from her cot in the bedroom, picked up my tie and strangled her with it.' That night he hid the baby's body in the wash-house 'behind some wood'.

Why would Evans kill the baby? One explanation was put forward, but never used in the court, by PS Trevallian, who guarded Evans in his cell at Notting Hill Gate. Trevallian said later that as they conversed he remarked that he was unable to understand how or why anyone would kill a baby. Evans replied, according to Trevallian, that it was the continual crying of the baby that got on his nerves and that he strangled it to silence its noise.

There are other questions. Why did he remove the rope from his wife's neck and not the tie from Geraldine's? The tie, if it was his – and this was never clearly established – would obviously incriminate him. How was it that the baby was silent for two days, though left unattended for twelve hours at a stretch two days running? If alive, she must have cried and must have been heard by the Christies. It was on *Wednesday* evening that Mrs Christie asked Evans: 'Where's Beryl and the baby?' To which he replied that they had gone away to Bristol.

Why did he say he strangled the baby on the *Thursday* night? Was there some reason for this in his story in the second statement about the baby being given by Christie on Thursday to a couple from East Acton? Was he again trying to protect Christie? Or indeed someone else, some woman to whom he had given the baby on the *Tuesday* night?

It seems unlikely that Evans should wish to protect Christie. There is no reason to suppose that either man had any respect or liking for the other, or that Evans was dominated by the older man. Evans, a heavy-drinking excitable, brawling, coarse Welshman, must have been despised by his tall, quiet, nervous, teetotal neighbour. The Christies tended to keep themselves to themselves. The wives might have become familiar, but next to nothing is known about this.

Although Mrs Christie's role in the events of that week is far from clear, the police apparently never doubted her innocence or her mystified reaction to the bundle under the wash-house sink. She was believed when she said in court that the last time she saw Beryl and the baby was on the Monday of that week – she had looked after the baby when Beryl was out.

There is also no reason to suppose that the police terrorized Evans into making a false confession – no complaint or allegation about this was ever made by Evans, by his lawyers, or by his relatives.

On 3 December Timothy Evans was charged with the murder of his wife. He replied: 'Yes, that's right.' When charged with the murder of Geraldine he made no reply.

On his way to the magistrate's court in a police car he told Inspector Black: 'After I killed my wife I took her ring off her finger and sold it for six shillings in Merthyr.' The ring was in fact found in a Merthyr jeweller's shop. But when his mother, Mrs Probert, saw him after the magistrate's hearing he told her: 'I never done it, Mum – Christie done it. Tell Christie I want to see him. He's the only one who can help me now.' She tried to talk to Christie, but he refused to see here and sent for the police.

When Evans was examined by the prison doctor in Brixton, he voluntarily repeated his account of Beryl's death as contained in his fourth statement, and made no accusations against Christie. He was cheerful in prison, playing dominoes and cards, and never professed to be innocent – until he saw his solicitor on 15 December, when once again Evans accused Christie.

Timothy Evans was tried at the Old Bailey on Wednesday, 11 January 1950, before Mr Justice Lewis, a sick man who died a few weeks later. Mr Christmas Humphreys, now Britain's leading Buddhist, led for the Crown: it was his first case as Senior Treasury Counsel. As a Buddhist, he believed in reincarnation. Five years later he would successfully prosecute Ruth Ellis, and in all he was prosecuting counsel at 250 murder trials. He became a judge in 1968, retiring eight years later, and died in April 1983 at the age of 82.

Evans was defended by Mr Malcolm Morris. He was charged with the murder of Geraldine, as it was assumed by the prosecution that there would or could be no excuse or provocation – which might have been put forward as a defence in the case of Mrs Evans.

Christie was a good but cautious prosecution witness and Evans himself was the only witness – a poor and muddled one – for the defence. He was patently a liar.

His counsel's assault on Christie, revealing his previous convictions, was viewed with disfavour by the court, as were counsel's allegations that Christie was an abortionist, a murderer and a liar. All this was firmly denied by Christie. Evans's explanation of his last two statements, a 'load of lies', was that they were made because he was 'upset' after hearing about Geraldine's death, because he thought the police would 'knock him about' if he said otherwise, and because he wanted to protect Christie.

When asked by Mr Humphreys to suggest why Christie had strangled Mrs Evans, the accused replied: 'Well, he was home all day.' 'Can you suggest why he should have strangled your wife?' demanded Mr Humphreys. 'No, I can't,' said Evans. 'No,' he said again when the question was applied to his daughter.

Mr Humphreys's closing speech was probably the shortest ever made in a murder trial – it lasted less than half an hour. The defence's allegations and attack on Christie were dismissed as 'Bosh!'

On Friday, 13 January, the jury took forty minutes to find Evans guilty of the murder of Geraldine Evans. Christie, who was in court, burst into tears. Evans said nothing. He was sentenced to death.

Taken to Pentonville prison, he was as cheerful as he had been in Brixton. He showed no sorrow for his dead family, nor displayed any outrage at his sentence or when his appeal was dismissed, although he still maintained that 'Christie done it.' He was well behaved, good-tempered and calm.

Before he was hanged on 9 March 1950, Evans, a Roman Catholic, received the sacrament and made his last confession to a priest.

There were no petitions, demonstrations or outcry before or after the execution of Timothy Evans.

In August 1950, 10 Rillington Place was bought by a Jamaican, Charles Brown, a hotel commissionaire. The upstairs rooms – Kitchener had left – were occupied by several Jamaicans and others, much to the annoyance and distress of both the Christies. They complained several times to the Poor Man's Lawyer Centre about noise, intrusion and assault, which they said were affecting their health. Fibrositis, enteritis, insomnia and amnesia were still Christie's ailments. His wife suffered from nerves and depression – she was regularly taking sleeping-pills and phenobarbitone as a sedative.

In the spring of 1952 Christie was advised to go to Springfield Mental Hospital for treatment for an anxiety neurosis, but he was reluctant to leave his wife. Mentally and physically declining, he stopped seeing Dr Odess in September and gave up his £8 a week job with British Road Services on 6 December. He was fifty-four. Three years had passed since the death of Beryl Evans.

On 10 December 1952, Mrs Christie wrote a letter to her sister. Christie kept it and altered the date to the 15th, when he posted it. By then Ethel Christie was dead. She was last seen at a laundry on Friday, 12 December.

Christie later told the police: 'She was becoming very frightened from these blacks ... and she got very depressed. On 14 December [Sunday] I was awaked at about 8.15 am. I think it was by my wife moving about in bed. I sat up and saw that she appeared to be convulsive, her face was blue and she was choking ... I couldn't bear to see her, so I got a stocking and tied it round her neck to put her to sleep ... I left her in bed for two or three days and didn't know what to do.'

He alleged she had taken an overdose of phenobarbitone, but no traces of it were found later in her body. He eventually buried her under the floorboards of the front room after wrapping her body (which was naked apart from unsecured stockings) in two dresses and a blanket, with a pillow-case around her head and a vest between her legs.

Why did he kill his wife, with whom he had lived closely and amicably for nineteen years? Despite the alteration of the date on the letter – which could have been lying about, accidentally not posted, and then put to use as an afterthought – there is little to suggest premeditation. Nor is there any reason, beyond being wise after the event, to suggest that he wanted to rid himself of her so that suddenly, after a nine-year gap, he could revert to his murderous wartime habits. There is also no reason to suppose that three years after the murder of Beryl Evans Mrs Christie had to be killed because what she knew had made her so fearful and guilt-ridden that Christie had to silence her in case she talked. Fictional murderers may be infinitely cunning, but Christie was sunk in apathetic despair.

The murders that followed were made more possible after she died and because of his isolation. They probably happened because of her death, and not the other way around.

What is interesting is the coincidence of events between his and Timothy Evans's actions after the deaths of their wives: Mrs Christie's body was wrapped up and hidden under wood: her wedding ring was sold on the 17th for £1 17s; the neighbours were told she had gone away; Christie sold nearly all his furniture (for £13) to the same dealer Evans had chosen; and eventually he also left the house.

The furniture was sold on 6 January 1953, but Christie kept a mattress, some blankets, a table, two chairs, some crockery and cutlery. For ten freezing weeks he squatted in the back room with his mongrel bitch, Judy, and a cat. One of the chairs was a deckchair, with knotted webs of string in place of canvas. Once a week he received £2 14s from the unemployment exchange. Daily he disinfected the hallway, the drains, the front and back of the house with Jeyes Fluid, as he had begun to do towards the end of December.

During this period he murdered three prostitutes and put their bodies in a coal-cupboard in the kitchen.

On Friday, 13 March, a week after the last murder, he sublet his three rooms to a Mr and Mrs Reilly for £7 13s – three months' rent in advance. After taking his dog to a vet to be destroyed he walked out of 10 Rillington Place on 20 March with all he owned in a battered suitcase. That night he turned up at a Rowton House hostel for down-and-outs in King's Cross.

The Reillys, despite an unpleasant smell in the kitchen, moved into Christie's rooms and unknowingly spent one night with the corpses of four women before they were visited by the landlord, Charles Brown, and thrown out.

Three days later Mr Beresford Brown, a Jamaican who lodged upstairs, was clearing up the mess in the downstairs flat before it was re-occupied, and was inspecting the fabric as he did so. He knocked on a kitchen wall and heard a hollow sound. He tore off a loose piece of patchy wallpaper, covering what had been the coal-cupboard door, and through a gap in the boards and by the light of a torch he saw a naked back.

It was not until DCI Griffin, senior police officers and the Home Office pathologist, Dr Camps, had gathered at the house at about 7.30 pm that the cupboard was opened up. Inside were three bodies. They were photographed, and removed in the reverse order of their concealment.

First out was Hectorina MacLennan, aged twenty-six, from the Hebrides. She was naked apart from her brassiere, and was squatting, head bowed, on a heap of rubble and ash. Next was Kathleen Maloney, also twenty-six. She as partly clothed and wrapped in a blanket, as was Rita Nelson, aged twenty-five, from Belfast; the latter was six months pregnant. The last two had probably been killed towards the end of January, and Ena MacLennan about 6 March.

All three prostitutes had had VD and had been strangled with some ligature, not manually. All three had also been gassed – there was carbon monoxide in their blood – but not fatally. All three had a vest or some material between their legs, like a diaper, and intercourse had taken place about the time of their deaths.

Later that night the decomposing body of Mrs Christie was discovered under the floorboards on the front room. Although she also wore a kind of diaper there were no signs of intercourse. She had been strangled by some ligature and had not been gassed, injured or bruised.

The morning papers, reporting the findings of the three bodies in the cupboard, must have been read by Christie. He left Rowton House on 25 March, leaving his few belongings in a locker. He wandered about London for six days, sleeping rough, while 10 Rillington Place was stripped and searched and the garden dug up – a disruption that so crazed Christie's cat that it had to be destroyed.

In the garden a mass of bones was unearthed, which when pieced together formed two skeletons, those of Ruth Fuerst and Muriel Eady. In the yard a tobacco tin was found which contained four sets of pubic hairs.

Despite the photographs in every newspaper and an intensive police hunt, the thin, bald, middle-aged man with glasses went unobserved until Tuesday, 31 March.

About ten-past nine on a cold grey morning, PC Tom Ledger was walking along the embankment south of the river by Putney Bridge. He saw a shabby, unshaven, hungry-looking down-and-out leaning on the embankment wall, looking at the river.

PC Ledger went up the man and said: 'What are you doing? Looking for work? The man replied: 'Yes, but my employment cards haven't come through.' Ledger asked the man for his name and address and was told it was 'John Waddington, 35 Westbourne Grove.' Said Ledger: 'Have you anything on you to prove your identity?' 'Nothing at all,' the man replied. Some instinct or suspicion prompted the PC to ask the man to remove his hat. He did so, revealing a bald dome, and PC Ledger recognized John Christie.

The wanted man was taken to Putney police station. Coins amounting to 2s 3½d were found on him, as well as a wallet containing identity cards, ration books (his own and his wife's), his marriage certificate, a union card, a St John's Ambulance badge, three pawn tickets, a rent-book and a newspaper cutting outlining the evidence Christie had given at the trial of Timothy Evans.

When told by DCI Griffin that his wife's body had been found under the floorboards of his flat, Christie began to cry. He said: 'She woke me up. She was choking. I couldn't stand it any longer. I couldn't bear to see her suffer.'

He then made a long statement describing the murders of his wife and the three prostitutes. He was diffuse and vague, often saying he 'thought' or 'believed' or 'must have done' something and failing to remember details. Not once did he actually admit to strangling any of them, or gassing the last three, or having sex with them. All four unaccountably seemed to die after some sort of struggle.

He was charged at Notting Hill police station with the murder of his wife and taken to Brixton prison after a preliminary hearing at the West London magistrate's court, to which he was accompanied by a very young PC called Bill Waddell – who also sat with him in a cell. That PC is now the Curator of the Black Museum.

On 15 April Christie was also charged with the murders of the three women in the cupboard, by which time his lawyers had told him his defence had to be one of insanity. To this end he was interviewed more than ten times by Dr Hobson, a psychologist.

At the first interview Christie indignantly denied killing Mrs Evans. But after 22 April, when he first heard that the skeletons in the garden had been dug up and identified, he told Dr Hobson he had also murdered these women – by gas or strangulations or both.

It was five days later that he said he had killed Beryl Evans – but not the baby, Geraldine. 'The more the merrier,' as he remarked to the prison chaplain.

On 18 May Mrs Evans and the baby were exhumed and their bodies examined.

It was not until 5 June, however, that Christie made a statement to the police in the presence of his solicitors, saying he was responsible for the deaths of Miss Fuerst and Miss Eady. For the first time he mentioned strangling and gassing, though confusedly, and admitted for the first time that he had had intercourse with his victims. In his last statement, made on 8 June, he described how he had killed Mrs Evans.

He said that in November 1949 he disturbed her in a suicide attempt – she was lying on a quilt on the kitchen floor with the gas on. The next day he happened to go upstairs at lunch-time, he said, and she asked him to help her commit suicide. 'She begged of me to help her to go through with it . . . She said she would do anything if I would help her. I think she was referring to letting me be intimate with her . . . She lay on the quilt . . . I got on my knees but found I was not physically able of having intercourse with her owing to the fact that I had fibrositis in my back and enteritis. We were both fully dressed. I turned the gas tap on . . . held it close to her face. When she became unconscious I turned the tap off. I was going to try again to have intercourse with her but it was impossible . . . I think that's when I strangled her. I think it was with a stocking . . . ' When Evans returned that evening, Christie told him his wife had gassed herself. Evans carried her body into the other room and put it on the bed. 'I told Evans that no doubt he would be suspected of having done it because of the rows and fights he had had with his wife. He seemed to think the same. He said he would bring the van down . . . and take her away and leave her somewhere . . . He did not know his wife had been strangled . . . I never mentioned it to him. I never had intercourse with Mrs Evans at any time. We were just friendly acquaintances, nothing more. I went up that first afternoon to have a cup of tea . . . I had some shoring timber and old floorboards from my front room which had been left behind by the work people and I asked Evans to take it to the yard for me, as I could not carry it owing to my fibrositis . . . I suggested he put it in the wash-house out of the way. I saw it in the wash-house afterwards and some of it was stacked in front of the sink . . . I feel certain I strangled Mrs Evans and I think it was with a stocking. I did it because she appealed to me to help her commit suicide . . . I don't know anything about what happened to the Evans's baby.

He then went on to say that he had gassed the three prostitutes as they sat in the deck-chair by the kitchen window. He attached a piece of rubber piping to the plugged gas-pipe at the window – 'I put a kink in the tube with a bulldog clip to stop the gas escaping' – and, letting it dangle behind the chair, he then removed the clip.

Some substantiation of this was provided by the fact that a bulldog clip and a piece of half-inch rubber tubing were discovered in the flat – although how did he avoid being gassed himself?

However, his version of Beryl Evans's death, about the assisted suicide and the invitation to intercourse, seems most unlikely. Few activities, let alone these, are likely to be contemplated or carried out by a sick man suffering from backache and diarrhoea. The autopsies on her showed that she had not been gassed, that she had been punched more than once, and strangled not with a stocking but with a rope. Nonetheless, he may well have tried, when unexpectedly provided with an inert female body, to have intercourse with her – after her death.

Whatever the truth, it seems that Christie's self-love was such that he could admit to nothing nasty or perverted about himself. Reluctantly and cautiously he confessed, not to 'murder', but to having killed; and he tried to dignify and obscure his motives and his actions as much as he could. In no circumstances would he ever admit, to himself above all, to such vile and vicious behaviour as baby-killing, sadism, onanism, abortion and necrophilia.

Was there, nonetheless, some truth in Evans's story about the fatal abortion attempt?

One fact contradicts this, and poses many more questions – a fact that was mentioned but never attested to at both trials. In the week that Beryl Evans died there were workmen in the house as well as in the yard.

They were actually at work on the wash-house, repairing the roof, pointing and plastering. It was not a big job but they worked slowly, storing their tools and equipment in the wash-house overnight. They finished working on the roof on Tuesday, 8 November – the day Mrs Evans is said to have died – but did not finish their plastering until the Friday, when they removed their tools and left the wash-house bright and *empty*.

In addition to these two workmen, there was a carpenter at work inside the house, repairing the floorboards in the front room and in the hall. He worked from Thursday the 10th until noon on Monday the 14th, when at Christie's request he gave him the broken bits of floorboard for firewood.

The presence of workmen in and about one's house is disruptive at the best of times: they make requests and require cups of tea. It is most unlikely in these circumstances, with workmen *and* Mrs Christie in the house, that Christie planned an abortion – which could have waited until the following week – or carried out a murder. After all, it was only when he was alone in the house that he felt safe enough to set about killing the first two and the last three of his victims.

It is, however, conceivable that at night, in the heat of a row, Evans might well have struck and strangled his wife. But if so, how could he or Christie or both of them have put her body in the unfinished wash-house?

There can be little error about the workmen's dates: their employer kept time-sheets, and they all made statements in 1949 to the police. These statements were never, it seems, supplied to Evans's counsel and never used by the prosecution – probably because they made nonsense of Timothy Evans's confession of murder (on which the prosecution based their case) in respect of his alleged date of the disposal of the bodies.

Were the bodies hidden in Kitchener's flat until after all the workmen had gone and Evans had sold his furniture? And if Beryl's body was put in the wash-house on *Monday* night, was that why Evans caught such a late train, at 12.55 am, to South Wales?

Perhaps Christie, investigating the bumps and movement of Tuesday night, came across Beryl's body in Kitchener's unoccupied flat the following day. What would he do? He would hardly welcome the attentions of the police. But her body might have invited the attempt at intercourse which he later described. Later that night, avowedly anxious to help Evans, might he not have advised Evans to leave everything to him to sell up and go? And might not the concealment of the bodies in the wash-house on the Monday have been a *temporary* measure – as it had been with Fuerst and Eady? Might not Christie have intended *burying* the bodies, but have been prevented from doing so because of his fibrositis?

All might have been well, as far as he was concerned, if Evans had kept quiet. This he failed to do. But what, unless a feeling of guilt, led Evans to make that first odd confession to the Merthyr police?

The trial of John Reginald Halliday Christie for the murder of his wife began in the No. 1 Court at the Old Bailey before Mr Justice Finnemore on Monday, 22 June 1953. The Attorney-General, Sir Lionel Heald, was the prosecutor and Mr Curtis-Bennett, QC, appeared for the defence, which aimed to show that Christie was guilty but insane.

It was Curtis-Bennett who brought the attention of the court to the murders of all seven women, including that of Mrs Evans, which the accused said he had also committed. His memory of events, however, was poor and vague. Christie spoke slowly, with long pauses, and in such a low voice that a microphone was set up so that he could be heard.

The only other witness for the defence was Dr Hobson, who said the accused suffered from gross hysteria which affected his reason, and that it was highly probable that at the time of the crime he did not know that what he was doing was wrong. Hobson also said: 'He has this abnormal memory. I am prepared to believe that the abnormality of his memory is in some way purposeful, but that he himself is not aware of the fact that it is motivated . . . He often makes statements one after the other which to the listener seem self-contradictory, but Christie is unable to see the contradiction. I found . . . that those things about which he has been most certain, and most sure, and most indignant when the opposite was suggested, were things we ultimately found him most mistaken about or deceiving himself about.'

He was most indignant, said Hobson, when it was suggested that his wife had died in other ways and for other reasons than those described by Christie, and that he had picked up Kathleen Maloney in a pub. Dr Hobson said: 'I have never . . . felt able to place any reliance on any of his statements without confirming the facts externally . . . I think he has tried to be as co-operative as possible. I believe that these tricks of memory, or avoidance of getting down to disturbing topics, is to preserve his own self-respect . . . rather than to avoid incriminating himself.'

Dr Matheson, prison doctor at Brixton, appearing for the prosecution in rebuttal, described Christie thus: 'He is a man of weak character; he is immature – certainly in his sex life he is immature; he is a man who in difficult times and in face of problems tends to exaggerate in an hysterical fashion . . . I would call him not a man suffering from hysteria, but a man with an hysterical personality . . . He spoke quite freely, but when it came to what might be incriminating facts . . he became vague, and started saying: "Well, it must have been so' – "I think it must be that" – "I can't be certain" – "I can't remember."'

Dr Curran, a psychiatrist, who also interviewed Christie on behalf of the prosecution, said he was 'an inadequate personality with hysterical features, and a very extraordinary and abnormal man.'

Summarizing the ward reports, Dr Curran said: 'Christie was somewhat emotional; tremulous and fearful on admission but soon settled down. He has been meticulously clean and tidy in his person and habits; he has always kept himself well occupied; he has mixed freely with the other patients. He has been noticeably egocentric and conceited. He keeps a photograph of himself in his cell. He has been a great talker and has seemed to enjoy discussing his case, bringing the conversation round to it. He has been cheerful and boastful; he has compared himself to Haigh; he has admitted in conversation that he "did some of them in". He appeared to be above average intelligence; he has always been polite and well behaved . . . He has slept well, his appetite has been good and he gained 11 pounds in weight.'

Dr Curran added: 'I do not believe Christie's alleged loss of memory is genuine. It is in my opinion too inconsistent, variable, patchy and selective to be genuine . . . His lies seem to be purposive if not convincing . . . [He has] like many other criminals and murderers, a remarkable capacity for dismissing the unpleasant from his mind . . . He is a man with a remarkable capacity for self-deception.'

The trial ended on 25 June. The jury were out for eight-five minutes, and found Christie guilty of the murder of his wife. He was sentenced to death.

Much unease was felt before and after the trial about the case of Timothy Evans – had an innocent man been hanged? – and a private enquiry initiated by the Home Secretary, Mr David Maxwell-Fyfe, QC, MP, was carried out by a senior QC, Mr John Scott Henderson. After reading all the relevant depositions, documents, transcripts and briefs – including the statements of the workmen – and interviewing the police and lawyers concerned as well as Christie himself (who was more guarded and ambiguous than ever), Scott Henderson concluded that Evans *had* killed both his wife and child. His report was published on 13 July and presented to parliament.

On 15 July Christie was hanged in Pentonville prison by Pierrepoint, who had also hanged Evans.

Some Labour MPs believed that Scott Henderson's report was a piece of official whitewashing aimed at protecting the police, and so the matter was strongly debated in the House of Commons on 29 July. The Home Secretary refused to order a public enquiry. It was again debated in November, and the Evans case continued to be discussed whenever the issue of the abolition of the death penalty was raised.

On 10 February 1955, the Rt Hon. James Chuter Ede, Home Secretary at the time of Evans's trial and execution, told the Commons: 'I think Evans's case shows . . . that a mistake was possible, and that, in the form in which the verdict was actually given . . . a mistake was made.'

Later the death penalty was abolished for most crimes in a free vote in the Commons. But the pressure to re-investigate the murder of Beryl Evans and her daughter continued.

In the winter of 1965/6 the case was reheard in public by Mr Justice Brabin. The main hearings of the enquiry covered thirty-two days. In a definitive report, published by HMSO in 1966, the judge concluded that it was 'more probable than not' that Evans *had killed* his wife and that he *did not kill* his daughter.

As Evans had been convicted and hanged for the murder of Geraldine, and not of his wife, he was given a free and posthumous pardon. His remains were exhumed and reburied outside Pentonville prison.

Among all the uncertainties of his statements, Christie said 'I feel certain' twice – that he strangled Mrs Evans and that the pubic hairs in the two-ounce tobacco tin found in the yard came from the three women in the cupboard and from his wife.

It is highly likely that his very certainty indicated a lie. He later amended this secondary certainty, telling his solicitor that one of the sets of hair in the tin might have come from Beryl Evans. Forensic experts established that the type of one of the four teased-out tufts was the same as Beryl's, but was also common to millions of women and could not in fact have been cut from her at the time of her death. One of the souvenirs was of a type that could have come from Mrs Christie. But none could have come from the three prostitutes, although two of the trophies might have come from Muriel Eady and Ruth Fuerst. It was impossible to be sure.

On the other hand, *all four* could have come from four completely unknown women.

It was Christie who claimed ownership of the tobacco tin. But was it his? It could have belonged to Timothy Evans – he was a heavy smoker and Christie never smoked at all. Or did the tin have nothing to do with either, having been thrown into the yard by Mr Kitchener or some other occupant of 10 Rillington Place?

On 13 July 1955 the last woman to be hanged in Britain, Ruth Ellis, was executed in Holloway prison for the murder of her lover. The executioner was Albert Pierrepoint. He resigned the following year on 23 February 1956 and was succeeded by two men who between them carried out thirty-four executions in the next eight and a half years. Pierrepoint retired to the pub he and his wife Anne had run since 1946. Situated at Hollinwood, Manchester, it was called 'Help the Poor Struggler'.

The real reason for Pierrepoint's resignation was never revealed. What happened was that in November 1955 he was employed to carry out an execution in Manchester. The night before the execution, after Pierrepoint had got everything ready, the condemned man was reprieved. The weather was so bad, according to Pierrepoint, who had gone out to a local club, that – 'I couldn't drive home in that weather. It was atrocious. So I had to stay in a hotel overnight. I phoned up the wife and told her.' *He drove the fifty-two miles back home the following morning.*

In due course, he received a letter from the Dundee sheriff, who was then in overall charge of executions. It contained no fee; just £1 for expenses. The hangman was highly offended. 'So what I did,' *he said,* 'was I returned it. I sent it back with my compliments.' *The sum of £4 then arrived in the post.* 'I sent it back. I wrote to the Prison Commissioners. They couldn't do anything about it.' *Eventually he was sent another £5, which brought the sum to £10 – the executioner's fee. But his hotel expenses were not forthcoming, and so Pierrepoint resigned.*

Mr Sidney Silverman's Death Penalty (Abolition) Bill, given a second reading in 1956 in the Commons by 286 votes to 262, was rejected by the House of Lords. However, in March 1957 the Homicide Act was passed. The death penalty was now only to be exacted for five kinds of murder (a) committed in the course of furtherance of theft, (b) caused by shooting or by an explosion, (c) in the course or for the purpose of resisting or avoiding or preventing a lawful arrest, (d) of a police officer acting in the execution of his duty or a person so assisting him, (e) of a prison officer or murder done by a prisoner. A previously convicted murderer who killed again could also be sentenced to death.

CHAPTER 46

John Donald Merrett

The murders of Vera Chesney and Lady Menzies,

1954

Unlike lightning, murder sometimes strikes twice. In recent years more than one convicted murderer has within a year or two of his release from jail or Broadmoor killed again. In fact about one per cent of the dangerous criminals released from Broadmoor commit crimes similar to those for which they were incarcerated. Donald Merrett's two murders are doubly unusual in that they occurred twenty-seven years apart.

Vera Chesney, aged forty-two, was surprised to see her forty-five-year-old husband on the night of 10 February 1954. Not only had she seen little of him in recent years, but the last time he called on her in the old people's home she ran with her mother in Montpelier Road, north of Ealing Broadway, he had looked quite different. He had then been his usual self, hugely extrovert (if unusually amiable), and with his bulk, his beard, his big nose and one gold earring, he had looked as piratical as ever. They had had a fine night out, going to the cinema and downing quantities of gin, Vera's favourite tipple. Now, exactly a week later, he was back again and quite altered – without a beard or the earring, with his hair brushed back and wearing horn-rimmed glasses.

He had flown over from Germany, as he had done the last time, specially to see her. She did not know he was travelling with a false passport, falsely using the name of Lesley Chown, a real photographer whom he resembled in this disguise. She probably never realized the purpose of this second visit, as she was fortunately in a drunken stupor when he towed her into the bathroom and held her face down in the bath in six inches or so of water.

It was all part of a plan to provide Ronald Chesney with some money – money that he must have felt was rightly his. For after he and Vera had married in 1928 (by eloping to Scotland when he was twenty and she was seventeen) he had at the age of twenty-one inherited a fortune of £50,000 from a grandfather, of which he settled £8,400 on his teenage bride. The interest on this sum was to be hers as long as she lived. When she died, the capital would revert to her husband.

For a time this did not mean much to him, as he spent the rest of the inheritance in the ten years before the Second World War, acquiring in the process a taste for adding to his diminishing income by criminal means –

theft, smuggling, blackmail and fraud. Any thoughts of acquiring his wife's nest-egg were further diverted by the war and by various illegal wartime involvements. During the war he served in the RNVR and was captured by the Italians at Benghazi. After the war his criminal career branched out into black-market activities, mainly in the ruins of post-war Germany. But by 1954 he was short of funds and devised a new scheme to enrich himself. He was not sentimental. After twenty-five years of marriage, much interlarded with mistresses, he decided to reclaim the £8,400 that had been part of his inheritance by killing his wife.

It was not the first time he had killed a woman. The first had been his mother.

Chesney's real name was John Donald Merrett – Donnie to his friends. Born in New Zealand on 17 August 1908 at Levin in the North Island, he was the only son of an electrical engineer who deserted his wife, Bertha, in 1924. Whereupon she returned to England with sixteen-year-old Donnie, who was sent to school at Malvern College. He was an intelligent, enthusiastic boy, good at languages. He was also very tall for his age and well developed, and his enthusiasm for the pursuit and conquest of girls soon resulted in his being removed from the school and in Mrs Merrett's move in January 1926 to Edinburgh, where Donnie was sent to the university to study art.

On 10 March mother and son moved into a first-floor flat at 31 Buckingham Terrace. In the meantime, Donnie had been enjoying himself, spending much of his time in the Palais de Danse studying the art of the foxtrot and the female form, his studies being financed by his unsuspecting mother. For by now he had discovered another talent, that of forging her signature on cheques. By this means he withdrew £458 from her two accounts by means of twenty-nine cheques, and was prevented from making it an even thirty by a worried letter that reached Mrs Merrett from a bank manager querying the size of her overdraft.

This filled her with a certain unease, which was nonetheless nothing compared to the uneasiness felt by Donnie, who in order to avoid any future financial embarrassment – and to avail himself of her annual income of £700 – decided to kill her.

Her death was carefully planned, but the plan misfired. It was supposed to look like suicide.

On Wednesday, 17 March 1926, at 9.40 am, the Merretts' maid, Mrs Sutherland, was disturbed in the kitchen by the large seventeen-year-old youth who rushed in crying – 'Rita, my mother has shot herself!'

And indeed, Mrs Merrett lay on the sitting-room floor by her bureau with a gun-shot wound in her right ear and a gun in her hand. However she was still alive, though unconscious.

She was removed to the Royal Infirmary – the grieving Donnie being driven there by the police – and as an attempted suicide (a criminal act) she was isolated, and when she recovered consciousness she was asked no questions. However, she was able eventually to tell Dr Roy Holcombe: 'I was sitting down writing letters and my son Donald was standing beside me. I said: "Go away, Donald, and don't annoy me," and the next thing I heard was a kind of explosion, and I don't remember anything more.'

She died on 1 April. Her death might have been classed as suicide had not the Edinburgh police discovered one of her cheque-books in Donnie's bedroom.

Further enquiries revealed that the signatures on some of Mrs Merrett's cheques were forgeries, and almost reluctantly, it seems, so unbelievable was the charge, Donald Merrett was arrested on 29 November 1926 for the murder of his mother. He was at that time staying with family friends at Hughenden Vicarage in Buckinghamshire – 'preparing for an academic career'.

His trial began at the High Court of Justiciary, Parliament Square, Edinburgh, on 1 February 1927 and lasted until 8 February. The Lord Justice-Clerk, the Rt Hon. Lord Alness, was the judge and the Lord Advocate, the Rt Hon. William Watson, KC, led for the prosecution.

Mr Craigie M. Aitchison, KC, defended the tall, pleasant-looking teenager, now eighteen – the defence being that Mrs Merrett had shot herself and had not been shot by her son. The suicide theory was disputed by the absence of any powder marks on or near Mrs Merrett's ear – no blackening or 'tattooing'. Sir Bernard Spilsbury, appearing for once for the defence, said that this fact could also be consistent with suicide or accident.

The jury were bemused by the whole matter and returned a verdict possible in Scottish courts – 'Not Proven'.

Donald Merrett was, however, found guilty of 'uttering as genuine' twenty-nine forged cheques. For this he was sent to jail for a year, and after serving eight months of his sentence he was released. While in jail he was visited by a friend of his mother, Mrs Mary Bonnar, and on his release he went to stay with her in Hastings. A few months later he eloped with and married her daughter Isobel, who was known as Vera.

Mrs Bonnar apparently never believed that Donnie *did* shoot his mother. But Vera, in later years, when her husband insisted they call themselves Chesney, sometimes borrowed a book from the local lending library – a book in the Notable British Trials series – and read about the trial in 1927 of young John Donald Merrett. What did *she* believe?

Whatever it was, she could never have believed that twenty-seven-years after shooting his mother, Donnie/Ronnie would drown his wife.

But in 1954 Vera Chesney died, drowned in her own bath by her matricidal husband.

Unfortunately for Chesney/Merrett, the perfect murder plan once again went wrong. Mrs Bonnar, now calling herself Lady Menzies, saw him in the house. She had to be silenced. Small and elderly though she was, she fought for her life until she was eventually overpowered, and battered and strangled by her hulking son-in-law.

He escaped from the house and flew back to Germany. But someone had noticed a heavily built stranger in the neighbourhood that night, of the same build as Mr Chesney – and the police knew from their files that Mr Chesney had once been Mr Merrett. Was it possible after all this time that he had now killed not only his wife but also his mother-in-law?

The police in France and Germany were alerted and asked to find Chesney/Merrett. But less than a week after the murders of Vera and her mother, on 16 February 1954, his body was found in a wood near Cologne. He had shot himself.

Pink fibres from Lady Menzies's scarf were found on his clothes, as were hairs from her dog and traces of blood. Dark hairs similar to his were found on her cardigan, and under her fingernails were slivers of skin. They came from his arms, scratched and bruised by the frail old woman as she struggled for her life, arms that were later displayed at a coroner's inquest in England and are now the most strikingly grisly exhibit in the Black Museum – two arms, severed above the elbows and crossed, erect, in a tank of formaldehyde.

CHAPTER 47

Ginter Wiora

The manslaughter of Shirley Allen, 1957

Ginter Wiora was a Polish art student aged thirty-four, who lived with his twenty-four-year-old girl-friend, Shirley Marguerite Allen, in a basement flat in 21 Leinster Square, Bayswater. They moved into the flat in November 1956, she posing as his wife and calling herself Wiora. He was known as 'Peter'. A jealous man, he suspected her of having posed for pornographic pictures and was angered by her carefree attitude to and association with other men.

On Saturday, 4 May 1957 – it was Cup Final Day (Aston Villa beat Manchester United 2–1) – the landlady, Mrs Doreen Dally, aged fifty-five, was awakened at 8 am by a loud banging noise – she slept in a basement flat opposite that occupied by Wiora and Shirley Allen. Mrs Dally then heard a woman cry out: 'No, Peter! No! Oh, Peter, please.' This was followed by a terrible scream of agony and fear.

The landlady agitatedly went to the door of her flat, opened it and looked out into the passage. She saw Shirley Allen, wearing a red dressing-gown, begin to emerge from the door of Wiora's flat, with blood streaming down her neck from a head-wound. But something or someone seemed to be holding her back and Miss Allen, seeing Mrs Dally, said softly: 'Oh, Mrs Dally – help me, please. Peter's gone mad.' Mrs Dally seized the other woman's right arm and was able to pull her away. The door was only slightly ajar and she saw nothing of Wiora.

She pushed Shirley Allen into her own flat and told her to lock the door. She then hastened towards the basement stairs, intending to reach a telephone on the floor above, but had only mounted two or three steps when she heard a sound behind her. She turned and in that instant saw Wiora standing in the passage, gazing at the door of her flat. His hands, crossed high on his chest, held a curved, long-bladed Burmese *dha*, or sword. He turned and looked at her. Suddenly grasping the sword by its hilt, he lunged at her – the sword's point piercing her left breast and entering her chest. He then returned the sword to its previous position.

Mrs Dally ran up the stairs, blood staining her nightdress. She roused the occupant of another flat and telephoned for the police. Meanwhile, screams could be heard coming from her flat below.

When the police arrived they found Mrs Dally sitting in an armchair in a ground-floor flat, waiting to be taken to hospital. She told them what had happened. PC Tennyson went down into the basement.

The door of Mrs Dally's flat was open, and Shirley Allen lay dead on her back behind the door, her head against the wall. A Burmese sword with a bent blade lay on the floor by her right leg. Nearby was a broken standard lamp with which she had been battered on the head. She had died of a haemorrhage caused by a deep stab-wound in her chest.

With PC Tennyson was DC Patrick Drown. He discovered that the door to Wiora's flat had been locked. He listened, and could hear the sound of a radio and some moaning. There was also a smell of gas. The door was kicked open and the police burst in, hastening to turn off an unlit and hissing gas fire and kitchen stove. On a bed in a corner lay Wiora, writhing and moaning. He had tried to commit suicide by stabbing himself with another sword and by cutting his wrists with a bread-knife. He and Mrs Dally were taken to St Mary's Hospital, Paddington.

Wiora was tried at the Old Bailey on 25 July 1957. His defence was that of diminished responsibility. The jury found him guilty of manslaughter and he was sentenced to twelve years in prison.

He was moved to Broadmoor on 31 October 1958, where he remains to this day.

CHAPTER 48

Michaeal Dowdall

The manslaughter of Veronica Murray, 1958

The body of Veronica Murray, a thirty-one-year-old prostitute, was found in her room in a boarding-house at 58 Charteris Road, Kilburn, on Christmas Eve 1958. She had been dead for five or six days. She was naked except for a pullover drawn up over her head, which had been battered six times by a blunt instrument – apparently by a blood-stained 6 lb dumb-bell; it was found on the floor by the bed. The fatal injuries she sustained, which had fractured her skull and caused her death, were on her forehead above the left eye. There were slight lacerations and abrasions on her body, including a series of small circular marks which had been inflicted after death.

Fingerprints of her possible assailant were found on a cup, but police investigations into the murder produced no results for nearly a year.

Then, on 10 October 1959, a Mrs Hill, celebrating her birthday in the West End, met a youth whom she invited back to her flat in Ismailia Road, Fulham. When she refused to have sex with him he hit her, tore her clothes off and strangled her with a silk stocking until she became unconscious. She survived, and from her evidence and the young man's fingerprints the police were able to connect the attack with another assault on a sixty-five-year-old woman who had been battered with a poker as she slept in her home near Sloane Square. She had been robbed, as had Mrs Hill – of money and a bottle of whisky. The assailant's fingerprints also connected him with a series of break-ins and burglaries over the past year, including three in Chelsea, one in a Fulham pub and another in the Westbury Hotel, Mayfair.

Apart from possessing the burglar's fingerprints, the police now knew he was young, drank heavily, chain-smoked and was called Mick.

DI Peter Vibart of Chelsea police station, investigating the Fulham attack, was struck by a curious feature of the assault on Mrs Hill – on her body were odd circular marks, indicative of some sexual perversion. Vibart recalled that such marks had been found on another woman's body sometime ago. He checked the files, studied the unsolved murder of Veronica Murray, and saw that the fingerprints in the Murray file matched those of the youth called Mick who had attacked and robbed Mrs Hill.

The police were now convinced that they were dealing with not just a dangerous criminal but a psychopathic, perverted killer who might murder again.

Previous burglaries and assaults on women in the London area were double-checked and a further detail emerged – Mick had a cigarette-lighter bearing the unusual name 'Texas Gulf Sulphur Co.' A picture of a similar lighter was published in the newspapers one month after the attack on Mrs Hill. It produced a response – from a young guardsman stationed at Pirbright in Surrey, the depot of the 1st Battalion Welsh Guards. He informed his CO that another guardsman, called Mick, had just such a lighter. His full name was Michael Douglas Dowdall.

The police were informed. Dowdall's army record was checked against the police file on Veronica Murray, the attacks on Mrs Hill and other women, and the weekend burglaries.

At the time of Miss Murray's murder Guardsman Dowdall, then barely eighteen, had been absent without leave. He frequently spent his weekends off duty in London and he drank and smoked a great deal. He had in fact been AWOL four times, and once, when in military detention, had tried to hang himself. His CO, Lt Col. Mansell Miller, later described Dowdall as 'a bit odd' – the boy had delusions of grandeur arising from the fact that he was in reality 'small, weak and insignificant'.

Dowdall had joined the Welsh Guards as a drummer boy. He was born on 12 December 1940 and his father, an army captain, was killed in 1943. Described as 'quite uncontrollable' at school, he had been a problem child from the start, being referred to a child-care officer with the LCC when he was six and a half. He was also said to be 'destructive'. He would become hysterical, and once, according to his brother, he tried to set fire to the Dowdall home. His mother died in 1948, after which he was brought up by an aunt in Wales. He was an unruly child and a violent, vicious youth. After joining the Welsh Guards he would brag about his prowess with women and burst into tears when he was disbelieved. To prove himself he drank heavily, stealing money to buy both drink and women

On his eighteenth birthday he went with Sgt Clotworthy, Cpl Hopkins and other guardsmen, all older than he, to a hotel in Guildford, where he drank four or five half pints of gin. At Dowdall's trial the judge asked Sgt Clotworthy: 'You did not feel it incumbent upon you to stop him? Did you have no responsibility for him?' Replied Clotworthy: 'Not while he was out of barracks.' Cpl Hopkins, who said that the rest of the group drank beer, told the judge that after two hours – and two pints of gin – Dowdall had to be carried out of the hotel and taken back to camp in a taxi. He was unable to go on parade the following morning and was taken for a walk by Hopkins.

On 24 November 1959 Dowdall was interviewed by the police at Pirbright. His fingerprints were taken and they matched those in the Murray file. He was brought to London, to Chelsea police station, where he was questioned by DCI Acott. Dowdall said: 'Everybody had been against me. It's when I get drink in I do these things. I'm all right when I'm sober. It's been worrying me for a long time, and I wanted to go to a doctor. I'm glad it's over. I'll tell you all I can remember.'

He said: 'Just before Christmas 1958, I had been drinking in the West

End and I got very drunk. I picked up with a prostitute in Trafalgar Square. She called a taxi and I remember she gave an address somewhere in Kilburn. We got to her house and climbed the stairs to her room. I had sex with her and went to sleep. When she woke up we had a row over something and she called me a filthy little Welsh bastard. I threw a vase at her. I believe it smashed. She came at me and hit me with something on the back of the neck and head and scratched my nose and eyes. I rushed at her, and I knocked her down and hit her head or face. I think she was half getting up. I pulled her on to the bed and I remember chucking some clothes over her. I took a bottle of whisky and then I left the place. I went back to the Union Jack Club and went to sleep. When I woke up, I found blood on my hands, and my shirt and suit were covered in blood. I chucked the shirt away in the dustbin at the camp. I tried to wash it, but I could not get rid of the blood. I sent the suit to the cleaners. A day or two afterwards, I read in the newspapers that a prostitute had been found murdered at Kilburn, and I knew then I had killed the woman.'

He went on to confess to a series of house-breakings and burglaries and to the assault on Mrs Hill.

'There are a lot of other jobs I've done in the last year,' he said. 'But I can't remember where all of them were exactly.' Trying to explain his criminal activities, he said: 'My army mates think I'm queer; I've tried to show them they're wrong . . . My mates make me feel a nobody. So I have a drink, and then I feel better and more important. Once I started the heavy drinking-bouts, I liked it and kept it up. When I was drunk, very drunk, I would try anything. I wasn't fussy about what I did or what woman I went with. I'm glad I've been caught. I feel much better now already.'

He was charged with the murder of Veronica Murray on 3 December 1959, nine days before his nineteenth birthday.

Dowdall's two-day trial began at the Old Bailey on 20 January 1960. The judge was Mr Justice Donovan; the prosecutor was Mr Alastair Morton, and Mr Desmond Trenner defended the accused, who pleaded not guilty to murder. His defence was that of diminished responsibility, which if accepted would reduce the charge to one of manslaughter.

The pathologist Dr Donald Teare gave evidence for the Crown. The defence produced a child-care officer, as well as Dowdall's brother, various guardsmen and officers, and the principal MO at Brixton prison, Dr Brisby, who described the accused as 'a psychopath', a 'social misfit' and 'an untruthful type', who believed people mocked and maligned him.

Dr Leigh, a psychiatrist at Bethlehem Hospital, said Dowdall was a psychopath and sexual pervert. The characteristics of a psychopath, he said, were aggressiveness, impulsiveness, lying, sexual perversion and often alcoholism, with no remorse or sense of guilt. The judge, in his summing-up, told the jury that if they accepted that the accused was suffering from an abnormality of mind which substantially impaired his responsibility for the killing, they should find him guilty of manslaughter.

The jury were out for three hours before returning to seek advice on the degree of impaired responsibility necessary to mean 'substantially impaired mental responsibility'. After another eight-minute retirement the jury found Dowdall guilty of manslaughter on the grounds of diminished responsibility. On 21 January 1960, the judge sentenced him to life imprisonment, to be detained until, as he said, the authorities 'are satisfied that you can safely mingle with your fellow creatures once again'.

An appeal was dismissed.

Mick Dowdall was released on licence from prison in July 1975, suffering from a serious illness from which he died in November 1976. He was thirty-six.

CHAPTER 49

Guenther Podola

The murder of DS Purdy, 1959

Between 1900 and 1975, thirty-three men serving with the Metropolitan Police were murdered on duty, mainly by criminals evading arrest. The trial of one such murderer made legal history on the opening day. The accused was said to be unfit to plead, because he had lost his memory.

Guenther Fritz Erwin Podola, the only child of a banker, was born on 8 February 1929 in Berlin. He was a studious, piano-playing boy, the tenor and direction of whose life was altered irrevocably by the Second World War. His early teens were spent in the lawless atmosphere of the bombed and ruined city; he became a member of the Hitler Youth. He was fourteen when his father was killed at Stalingrad and sixteen when the Russians invaded the city and Hitler died in his bunker. The men in the block of flats where Podola lived were machine-gunned by the Russians, and the women, including his mother, were raped.

He survived the deprivations and hardships of post-war Germany and in 1952, when West Germany became an independent nation, he escaped from East Berlin to the West, leaving behind him a woman, Ruth Quant, with whom he had lived and who had borne him a son, Micky. Podola emigrated to Canada and stayed there for six years. But in July 1958 he was deported after being jailed for a year for theft and burglary. For a time he worked in Dusseldorf. Then in May 1959, when he was thirty, he came to London, affecting a gangster pose in Soho night-clubs and calling himself Mike Colato. During the day he was involved in various legitimate though shady activities. At night he added to his wages by housebreaking and burglary.

One of the flats he burgled, on 3 July 1959, was occupied by Mrs Verne Schiffman, a thirty-year-old English-born American model, on holiday in London. The flat was in Roland Gardes, South Kensington, and she lost some furs and jewellery. A few days later she received a letter from a man called Levine, who claimed to be an American private detective and said he possessed some compromising photos and tapes. These would be returned to her, he wrote, on the payment of $500.

Five days later on Sunday, 12 July, Mrs Schiffman was telephoned by Podola, posing as a Mr Fisher. He said he was acting on behalf of Mr Levine and wanted to know her response to the letter. Unimpressed by the letter and the threat of blackmail, she had already complained to the police investigating the burglary. On their advice her telephone was tapped, and when the blackmailer rang again at about half-past three on Monday, 13 July, she kept him talking for fifteen minutes while the call was traced to a telephone box in South Kensington underground station – KNI 2355.

At 3.50 pm she heard the man say: 'Hey – what do you want?' There was a sound of a scuffle and she heard another man say: 'Okay, lad, we're police officers.' The same man then spoke to her: 'Mrs Schiffman,' he said. 'This is Detective Sergeant Purdy. Remember my name.'

DS Raymond William Purdy, aged forty, was a married man with three children. He had driven over from Chelsea police station with DS John Sandford to apprehend the caller. They hauled Podola out of the call-box. But as they went up the stairs that led to the street, he broke loose and ran down Sydney Place into a block of flats in 105 Onslow Square, about a hundred yards from the tube. He hid behind a pillar in the hall but was soon spotted and seized by the two detectives, both of whom were in plain clothes and unarmed.

DS Purdy took charge of Podola, ordering him into a corner of the hall to the right of the entrance, where there was a window.

Here Podola was briefly questioned, but not searched. Purdy removed the blue sun-glasses Podola was wearing – the summer of 1959 was the hottest and driest for fifty years – and stuffed them in the suspect's breast pocket. He told Podola to behave himself and sit on the window-sill. Podola did so, hoisting himself on to the marble ledge, as DS John Sandford crossed the hall to ring a bell summoning the caretaker, his intention being to enlist some assistance before he himself returned to the police car and communicated with the police station.

There was no response to his ringing of the bell and Sandford so informed Purdy, calling out to him across the hall. Purdy, momentarily distracted, turned his head towards the other detective.

Podola pulled out a gun, a 9 mm FB Radom V15, shot Purdy through the heart, and fled out of the door and into the sunny street.

Sandford rushed over to his fallen colleague. When he ran outside there was no sign of the gunman.

DS Purdy was not Sandford's usual partner, who that afternoon had been elsewhere engaged. Although Purdy had been about to go off duty when Sandford was detailed to go to the call-box, he volunteered to partner the other sergeant. Before he did so he telephoned his wife to say he would be late coming home that evening.

Sandford later described Podola as: 'A man about thirty, height about 5 ft 10 ins, slim build, brown hair, speaking with an American accent, last seen wearing dark glasses, a light sports coat, light grey trousers and suede shoes.'

Podola was identified by fingerprints left on the marble ledge in the hall of 105 Onslow Square. Two days after the shooting, Purdy's widow said that the address-book which had been returned to her with his personal possessions was not his. It belonged to Podola. Purdy, seeing it in the call-box when Podola was picked up, probably put it in his pocket.

Although Podola's name was not in the address-book, the names, addresses and telephone numbers of many other people were. They were all contacted, and variously confirmed Sandford's description of the gunman. Some thought he was German, others Canadian.

Then a hotel manager told the police that one of his guests, Paul Camay, was acting 'very strangely' – he seemed to be in hiding in the hotel.

On the same day the Royal Canadian Mounted Police sent particulars and a photograph of an immigrant German, Podola, who had been deported in 1958. The hotel manager thought that Camay and Podola were one and the same.

The police went to the Claremont House Hotel, 95 Queen's Gate, Kensington, where Mr Camay had hidden himself in Room 15.

Here he had cowered for two days since the shooting, in great fear of the law, it seems, and of being caught – not eating, nervously smoking and listening to the news on the radio about the police hunt for him. He had hidden his gun and its ammunition in the attic of the hotel, wrapping the weapon in a copy of *The Times* dated 13 July. It was later found there by the police.

At 3.45 pm on the afternoon of Thursday, 16 July, there was a banging on the bedroom door.

'Police! Open the door!' said a voice.

After a brief hesitation Poldola, wearing a vest and trousers, went to the door. Perhaps he removed the key to peer through the keyhole, for the police outside said later that they thought they heard a click like the cocking of a gun.

DS Albert Chambers, who weighed sixteen stone, charged the door. It burst open, the handle striking Podola in the face as Chambers crashed down on him. Podola was overpowered and put on the bed by DCI Acott and DI Vibart. He then apparently became unconscious and fainted.

When he had somewhat recovered he was taken from the hotel at about 4.14 pm, minus the shirt and shoes and with his jacket thrown over his head.

Some newspapers later exaggerated the doubtful aspects of Podola's arrest, including the actions of a police dog, which was also present with its handler. It was rumoured that Podola had been beaten up by the police and bitten by the dog.

But Podola himself never made any complaints, nor did his lawyers. What was seldom mentioned was that the police officers concerned had showed some courage in tackling an armed (as far as they knew) gunman, and that DS Chambers had received a George Medal four years earlier in October 1955, awarded for his courageous actions in overpowering and arresting an armed gunman in Mayfair.

A police surgeon, Dr John Shanahan, was summoned to examine Podola within half an hour of Podola's arrival in Chelsea police station, and found him to be 'dazed, frightened and exhausted' and suffering from muscular tremors, as if he were shivering, with a 'withdrawal reaction to his arrest'. Minor injuries included a cut over the left eye, some bruises and some scratches on his face. The worst bruise was under his left eye – it still showed at his trial two months later. Dr Shanahan examined Podola again at midnight and found no change.

Podola was taken to St Stephen's Hospital on the following day, 17 July, where he was handcuffed by one wrist to a bed in a public ward and guarded by two policemen. Here he was seen by Dr Harvey, the consultant physician. Podola seemed to be in a stupor and only partially aware of his surroundings. But tests revealed no fractures or internal bleeding. He seemed severely shocked.

Over the next few days he began to recover, although he remembered hardly anything of his life before 17 July. Interestingly, although he wanted to know where he was and why, he apparently never asked why he was chained to the bed.

On 20 July Dr Harvey allowed him to be seen by the police and a solicitor. That afternoon Podola was removed from the hospital and taken to West London magistrate's court, where in a state bordering on collapse he was charged with the murder of DS Purdy. He was then driven to Brixton prison, where a posse of doctors examined him over the ensuing weeks to determine whether or not his loss of memory was real.

His trial began at the Old Bailey on 10 September before Mr Justice Edmund Davies; Mr Maxwell Turner led for the Crown. Podola was represented by Mr Frederick Lawton, QC.

Although the Homicide Act of 1957 had limited the death sentence to seven kinds of murder – with a gun, with explosives, in the furtherance of robbery, of a police officer, of a prison warder, while resisting arrest or escaping, and committing two separate murders – Podola's crime was such that he could, if found guilty, be hanged. But first, certain legal issues had to be resolved about his alleged amnesia. Were the prosecution or the defence to open the debate? On which of them was the burden of proof, and what was the nature of that proof.

The judge ruled that it was up to the defence in the first place to prove that the loss of memory was genuine. If they succeeded they would have to submit that Podola could not therefore be tried as charged. This legal discussion took nine days.

Mr Lawton said at the start of his opening address to the jury: 'I stand here today, my learned friend by my side, Podola's solicitor in front of me, and the three of us have no idea what his defence is at all.'

He said that Podola's loss of memory meant that he was unable to defend himself, and suggested that it had been caused by concussion and severe fright occasioned by the circumstances of his arrest at the Claremont House Hotel. Podola's injuries, acquired then, were not severe, said Mr Lawton – 'A good deal of blood was shed, however. Two pillowcases were deeply stained with blood; a coverlet was stained . . . There was blood spattered on his trousers.' All this was unlikely to have come from a cut above Podola's eye. It was more likely to have come from a nose-bleed. Not that there was so far any complaint against the arresting policemen. Said Mr Lawton: 'Podola does not know whether he has any complaint at all. It may have been an accident. It may have been that he struggled violently . . . It may be, of course, that more force was used than was necessary.'

Mr Lawton detailed the findings of Dr Shanahan and Dr Harvey and then those of Drs Edwards, Ashby and Larkin, who concluded that Podola's amnesia was geniune.

All these doctors had given evidence at the medical trial before the murder trial.

The last four, who had studied Podola, agreed that although it was possible for him to be feigning amnesia, it was most unlikely. He could not have the psychiatric knowledge or superior intelligence, they said, to sustain such as deception. And the fact that he had not lost certain acquired skills – he remembered how to play chess, pontoon, and could speak English, German and French – was quite consistent with his claim. Nonetheless, two doctors found it surprising that his virtually total loss of memory had persisted until September.

Podola himself gave evidence. He said he remembered two names, Micky and Ruth, whom he thought were his son and a girl-friend. He also remembered a time when he was lying under a train, and another time when a policeman whispered: 'I am your friend – say it was an accident.' He remembered nothing else of his life before 17 July, although he said he knew how to speak English and German, to play cards and chess, and certain bits of general knowledge, like the names of national rulers.

The prosecution produced a letter he had written from Brixton prison to a man called Ron Starkey, who was also produced and said he had met the accused three times and that the accused once stayed with him. Podola said he had no memory of this man and had only replied to the man's postcard in order to acquire a visitor and some cigarettes.

Starkey's postcard read: 'Dear Mike. Is there anything I can get you in the way of tobacco and eats? If so, drop me a visiting card and I will come and see you. Best of luck, Ron.' Podola replied:

Dear Ron. Thank you for your card. I was very pleasantly surprised to hear from you. How are you keeping yourself these days, old boy? I reckon you have heard all about the mess I am in . . . I think it is very nice of you to write and now you want to come all the way to London to see me. You don't need a special visting-card, you can see me any day Monday through Saturday from 10 to 11.30 and 1.30 to 3.30. Naturally I would appreciate anything in the line of smokes and eats but it really isn't necessary . . . However, Ron, if you should be able to pick up a bunch of old magazines or reading matter I will be sure glad and grateful . . . There is not much doing around here. The food isn't bad but lacks variety . . . It was sure nice to hear from you, Ron. Cordially yours, Mike.

Two doctors were called by the prosecution – Dr Brisby, the prison doctor at Brixton, and Dr Leigh, who saw Podola on ten occasions.

They concluded that Podola was malingering, faking his amnesia. They said there had never been a case of hysterical amnesia involving such total memory loss that did not have some clinical or medical symptoms. In rebuttal the defence summoned another psychiatrist, Dr Strafford-Clark, who said that he had dealt with twenty cases of complete hysterical amnesia and that such persons might lose all personal knowledge but retain certain skills and general knowledge.

These medical discussions covered four days.

On 23 September, the ninth day of the trial, the judge asked the jury to go away and consider whether the defendant was or was not suffering from a genuine loss of memory 'covering at least all the events with which he was concerned between 1 July 1959 and the time of his arrest on 16 July 1959', and whether he was fit to stand trial. The jury returned after three and a half hours: Podola, they thought, was not suffering from a genuine loss of memory. This had not, they felt, been established.

Podola's actual trial for murder, with a new jury but the same judge and lawyers, began on 24 September. It lasted two days.

The main prosecution witness was DS John Sandford, who told how Podola had shot DS Purdy. In his defence Podola made a statement from the dock: 'I understand the various accusations that have been made, and now the time has come for me to defend myself against these accusations. I cannot put forward any defence ... I cannot remember the crime. I do not remember the circumstances leading up to the events or to this shooting. I do not know if I did it or whether it was an accident or an act of self-defence ... For these reasons I am unable to admit or deny the charge against me ... Thank you, my lord.'

The jury took half an hour to find Podola guilty and the judge sentenced him to death for a 'foul and terrible deed'.

Guenther Podola, the last man to be hanged for killing a policeman, was executed at Wandsworth prison on 5 November 1959 after an appeal to the House of Lords was turned down by the Attorney-General. The appeal judge said: 'Even if the loss of memory had been a genuine loss of memory, that did not of itself render the appellant insane.'

DS Purdy's widow received a pension of £546 a year.

The last two men in Britain to be sentenced to death for murder and hanged were executed on the same day at the same time – at 8 am on 13 August 1964. They were Peter Anthony Allen, aged twenty-one, and Gwynne Owen Evans, aged twenty-four, who had been convicted of the murder in the furtherance of theft of John Alan West, aged fifty-two, in Seaton, Cumberland. A laundry-van driver, West was brutally beaten to death with a cosh in his home and stabbed. This happened on 6 April 1964. Allen and Evans were tried in June and their appeal was dismissed on 21 July by the Lord Chief Justice, Lord Parker, by Mr Justice Widgery and Mr Justice Winn. Allen and Evans were hanged three weeks later, the former at Walton prison, Liverpool, and the latter at Strangeways, Manchester.

Four months after the executions, Mr Sidney Silverman's Murder (Abolition of Death Penalty) Bill, which suspended capital punishment for murder for an experimental period of five years, was given a second reading by the House of Commons by a majority of 185 votes. However, the bill did not become law until 9 November 1965.

CHAPTER 50

Harry Roberts, Witney and Duddy

The murders of DS Head, DC Wombwell and PC

Fox, 1966

The murders of policemen always result in letters to the newspapers demanding the restoration of capital punishment – something the police themselves would generally support. After the triple murder of DS Head, DC Wombwell and PC Fox there was such a public outcry, such widespread demonstrations of outrage, that it seemed the death penalty might be restored for some sorts of murder.

The last time three policemen had been shot dead in one incident was at midnight on 16 December 1910 in Houndsditch, when seven anarchists were surprised digging their way through the rear wall of a jeweller's shop. These deaths resulted in the fiasco of the Siege of Sidney Street, when two of the gang were trapped in a three-storey tenement at 100 Sidney Street, Whitechapel, on 3 January 1911. In the ensuing gun-battle, in which thirty-six guardsmen and many policemen were involved, the building burnt down, two anarchists were killed, and a fireman died when part of the building collapsed. Four other firemen were badly injured, and five policemen, four civilians and a soldier were wounded. Of the nine persons arrested by the police in connection with the shooting of the three policemen, not one was convicted, because of lack of evidence. The deaths of the policemen were later dignified by a memorial service in St Paul's Cathedral.

Between 1910 and 1966, twenty-four policemen had been murdered on duty, eleven after 1956. Since then, there had also been a general rise in crimes of violence, of gang warfare and robbery in London, and many people believed that because hanging had been abolished, the growing number of criminals armed with guns would not fear to use them.

It was warm and sunny on Friday, 12 August 1966 when the three-man crew of Q car Foxtrot Eleven took over their car, a Triumph 2000, at Shepherd's Bush police station in Uxbridge Road. The three men, who were on duty from 9 am to 5 pm that day, had been working together for just a few weeks. The area they patrolled, F Division, centred on Hammersmith and took in Shepherd's Bush and Fulham.

A major murder enquiry in F Division, concerning the strangling of six prostitutes whose naked bodies had been dumped around the division, mainly by the river, had recently been closed after the suicide of the chief suspect, a security guard.

The driver of Foxtrot Eleven was forty-one-year-old PC Geoffrey Roger Fox. Married with three children, he lived in a council flat north of Northolt and had been a PC at 'the Bush' for the sixteen years he had been in the police force. His wife, Marjorie, said later: 'I always knew my Geoff would get killed some day.' PC Fox was the regular driver of the Q car and, like the other two, he was in civilian clothes.

DS Christopher Tippett Head, aged thirty and unmarried, was in charge of the team. Born in Dartmouth on 24 December 1935, one of four children, he was five when his mother was widowed; she brought the children up on her own and Christopher went to the local grammar school. He became police cadet when he was seventeen and did his national service with the RAF police in Scotland. When he was demobbed he worked in an aircraft factory in Newton Abbot until June 1958 when he was accepted by the Metropolitan Police in London and posted to Fulham after his training. He joined the CID in 1964 and was promoted to sergeant just before his move to Shepherd's Bush.

DC David Stanley Bertram Wombwell, aged twenty-seven, was also a newcomer to 'the Bush' and had only just become a temporary detective constable, three years after joining the force. The only child of divorced parents, he had been brought up by his father and grandmother. After studying motor engineering at a polytechnic he became a car salesman. When he was twenty-three he married a seventeen-year-old hairdresser, Gillian Hague, in St Albans in 1962. They had two children and lived in East Acton.

On the morning of Friday the 12th, the crew of Foxtrot Eleven took DI Coote to Marylebone magistrate's court, where he gave evidence against five men who had escaped from Wormwood Scrubs prison in June. Coote had with him several court exhibits, such as the ropes which had been used in the escape.

Foxtrot Eleven went back on patrol, and the three policemen had lunch in the Beaumont Arms in Uxbridge Road before setting off again, driving up Wood Lane, past the BBC TV Centre and the White City stadium, where they turned left into Western Avenue.

About 3 pm Foxtrot Eleven was in the East Acton area. So was a battered blue Standard Vanguard estate car, containing three other men.

All three were petty criminals with previous convictions and they were on the lookout for a car to replace the one they were in. The stolen car would then be fitted with a pair of false number-plates which lay in the back of the Vanguard, and would be used in the robbery of a rent collector which the three planned to carry out the following week. The Vanguard was untaxed and uninsured; it had failed an MOT test, and the insurance covering the car had expired at noon that day.

Its owner was John Edward Witney, aged thirty-six and unemployed, who lived in a basement flat with his wife, Lilian, in Fernhead Road, Paddington. Previously a lorry-driver, he had ten convictions for petty theft

– his longest prison sentence had been eighteen months. Earlier that year he had met another lorry-driver and petty criminal, Harry Roberts, and the two teamed up, stealing metal and lead until they were joined by a third man, John Duddy, aged thirty-seven, when they began raiding betting shops and robbing rent-collectors. Duddy later said that Witney was 'the brains of this outfit'.

Duddy himself was a Scot, born in Glasgow's Gorbals district on 27 December 1929. He was 5 ft 5 ins, slightly corpulent, brown-haired, fresh-complexioned, and his right forearm was tattoed with a skull, a heart and the motto 'True to death'. Four of his convictions were for theft; the offences had all been committed before he was twenty and none had involved violence. He was sent to borstal once and imprisoned twice for three months. But after 1948 no further convictions had been added to his record. He married and came to London, working from there as a long-distance lorry-driver, and for seventeen years kept out of trouble. Then in 1966 he began drinking heavily and frequenting dubious West London clubs, in one of which he met Roberts and Witney.

Apart from the fact that they all had previous convictions, had all been lorry-drivers, wanted easy money and lived within a mile of each other in London W9, they had little in common – except that Duddy's father had been a policeman and that Roberts as a boy had wanted to be one. Oddly, in 1966, Roberts was living with an ex-policeman's wife.

Harry Maurice Roberts was three weeks past his thirtieth birthday at the time of the shooting, having been born on 21 July 1936 at Wanstead in Essex, where his parents managed a pub, the George. An only child, he was cared for by a nanny who called him Robin. On the outbreak of war his father, who had a savage temper and sometimes assaulted his wife, joined the RAF. 'I thought he was mental,' she said much later. 'He was always taking money off me and putting it on the dogs or drinking it.' When her son was seven or eight she sent him to a Roman Catholic boarding-school in Norwood, for which she had to pay, being determined that he would have a good education – she was convent-educated herself. Hard times followed. Mr Roberts walked out, and Mrs Roberts was left to bring up young Harry in post-war London. She slaved to pay for his education, sometimes working twenty-two hours a day, and lived on a council estate near Euston. She became manageress of a local restaurant. When Harry was thirteen he became, at his own insistence, a day boy at St Joseph's, and as his mother was out working nearly all the time he began to play truant. He started taking money from her handbag and pilfered the restaurant till.

'Every time my boy got into trouble,' she said, 'and I tried to thrash things out of him, I got nowhere. I just couldn't seem to get through to him somehow . . . I know now where the turning-point was. It was when he was sixteen or seventeen, and I hauled him out of a fellow's flat. He hadn't been working; but he would go out all dressed up, obviously up to something . . . The man was no good. A criminal type. I went up one afternoon and banged on the door till they let me in. In front of my son, and this man's wife, I told him I knew he was no fit company for a young lad, and he was never to see my son again. I made Robin come home with me. He said nothing until he got into my flat, then he turned on me like a savage and punched me in the face, splitting my lip open. I couldn't believe he would do such a thing to his mother . . . I didn't go to the police; I couldn't bring myself to turn my own boy in . . . All his life he has liked the company of rotten people.'

Her care and devotion, and his education, were wasted. Already, by the time he was fifteen, he had been put on probation for receiving stolen goods, and when he left school (early) he was variously a porter, electrician's mate, street-trader and lorry-driver, filling in time until national service claimed him.

He then joined the Rifle Brigade, became a marksman and a lance corporal and served in Malaya during the emergency; jungle training and guerrilla warfare taught him much and hardened him.

After he was demobbed, according to his wife Margaret (who called him Robbie): 'He seemed bitter, and talked about killing and the fear of battle and the danger . . . He seemed to have become slightly ruthless and much more tough.' He had met his future wife – a small, attractive barmaid and former vaudeville dancer, Margaret Rose – at a party while he was on leave. He was very clean and tidy and made no demands on her sexually. They were married on 3 March 1958 when he was employed as a motor mechanic/driver earning £7 14s 1d a week, less than his wife who worked for £8 a week as a barmaid.

For a time the couple lived with his mother; there were rows. Then in January 1959 he was convicted at Chelmsford in Essex for attempted store-breaking and larceny and sentenced to a total of twenty-one months in prison. While he was inside, the knowledge that he had robbed and beaten up a seventy-eight-year-old man the previous November worried his wife, for before her marriage she had lodged with the old man. He was now dangerously ill in hospital, and it was said a ring had been cut off his finger. Roberts had admitted the assault when she questioned him. But – 'I didn't know what to do,' she said. 'I was his wife after all.'

When he was released he seemed different to her. 'All his quiet manners had gone,' she said. 'Only his tidy habits and neat dressing remained. He did not seem to care how he got money from somewhere.' They had a serious row when he suggested she could make some money for them both if she picked up men.

A few nights later they were both in a Soho night-club, drunk, when he repeated the suggestion. She was furiously indignant. He knocked her off the bar-stool, punched and kicked her. She staggered out to a call-box, phoned the police, and told them about the assault on the old man.

Harry Roberts, aged twenty-two, was sentenced in March 1959 to seven years for robbery with violence. 'You are a brutal man,' said the judge.

The maximum sentence was life, and Roberts could have been hanged if the old man had died. Instead he was in jail for four years and eight months. When he was sentenced he swore he would be revenged on his wife. She was seven months pregnant. She collapsed in court and soon afterwards miscarried. She later became a stripper, calling herself Mitzi, and was billed as the Pocket Venus. She never saw Harry Roberts again.

In prison, despite an erratic, explosive temper that erupted over card games, Roberts was quite popular, although he had no interest in betting and football. He took courses in bricklaying and plumbing and did well in both.

In January 1963 he was transferred from Wormwood Scrubs to Horfield prison in Bristol. A 'trusty', he was allowed to live in a prison hostel and do a normal job, bricklaying, provided he returned to the hostel by 10.45 pm. At weekends he went drinking with other inmates, some of whom, tempted by so much freedom, absconded.

It was in a pub that Roberts met Mrs Lilian Margaret Perry. She was auburn-haired, about thirteen years older than he, and was in the process of getting a divorce from her ex-policeman husband. She and Roberts became friendly.

When he was released in November 1963, he lodged with her in Horfield, continuing to work as a bricklayer for Wimpey's in Weston-super-Mare. He worked hard, earned good money, and bought a second-hand Daimler for £650, his only personal extravagance.

But by March 1966 he had had enough. Leaving a large overdraft and several sizeable debts behind him he returned to London. Mrs Perry went with him. They stayed in Maida Vale with a married couple, the Howards, who had witnessed his wedding to Margaret. He was now twenty-nine.

A police description of him issued later that year said: 'Height 5 ft 10 ins, slimmish build, slightly sunken cheeks, quiff of hair in centre of forehead that falls down frequently, George Robey eyebrows, left side of mouth twists up slightly, a big eater, drinks little and then brown or light ale or Coca Cola, has a passion for suede shoes, occasionally takes purple hearts, smokes tipped cigarettes fairly heavily, spends freely ... has long fingers and bites his nails ... needs to shave only occasionally.'

Mrs Perry said later: 'We never had a cross word the whole time we were together ... He said he had often rowed with his mother and would walk out of the room to avoid one. He was a very quiet man who kept himself to himself. He hated pubs and clubs and just liked to sit at home and watch television or read ... I think he had never had a real home life before. He loved getting home at night, seeing a big fire and finding a steak grilling for him. He used to say that was the life, and we'd sit there so peaceful and happy. Wrestling was his favourite programme and he read all the James Bond books. He was a deeply lonely man and wanted me to go everywhere with him ... If the Labour Government hadn't put the squeeze on and killed the building trade, Robbie wouldn't be inside now. It was only when the building trade flopped that he took to doing jobs ... Robbie had to have money. He always had money as a boy. His mother gave him plenty because she was working and could not spend much time with him ... He reckoned it salved her conscience ... He could always buy friends with money but he could never rid himself of this horrible loneliness. That's why he was happy with me ... There was no sex between us. I'm sexless, and Robbie didn't like it either ...'

He vowed, she said, that he would do anything to avoid going inside again – that he would shoot it out rather than go back to prison.

Mrs Perry and their landlady, Mrs Howard, knew of Roberts' association with Witney and Duddy – he was very fond of Witney – and Mrs Howard often warned him about the loaded guns they had. 'You'll get fifteen years if you're caught with them!' she would say. 'If only they hadn't had the guns,' said Mrs Perry. 'Robbie always swore they were for frighteners.' Said Mrs Howard 'if they were only for frighteners, they wouldn't have been loaded, would they?'

At 3.10 pm on Friday, 12 August, Witney's ramshackle, noisy blue Vanguard left East Acton underground station car park with Witney at the wheel, Roberts beside him, and Duddy in the back with the false number-plates, a stocking mask and some overalls. A small canvas bag containing three guns occupied the space between the two front seats.

Apart from a break for lunch in Eastcote they had spent the day driving around the Harrow and Wembley areas looking, mainly in station car parks, for a car to steal. No suitable car, or opportunity, had presented itself, and on leaving East Acton the three decided to abandon their search, take a break, and discuss their next move. Witney was also reluctant to go home as his wife thought he was at work. They headed for nearby Wormwood Scrubs common, intending to lie in the sun on the grass not far from the prison walls.

At 3.10 pm Foxtrot Eleven received a radio message from DI Coote in Marylebone magistrate's court: the five men who had escaped from the prison had just been committed for trial, and Coote asked the Q car to pick him up with his exhibits. DS Head told Coote they would be at the court in twenty minutes – they were then in Acton.

Exactly where they were and how they chanced to spot and follow the blue Vanguard is unknown. But something about its appearance or movements must have attracted the policemen's attention. DS Head probably decided to check the other car before they headed east to Marylebone Road.

All six men, three in one car, three in the other, were totally unprepared for what happened in the next five minutes.

The Vanguard entered Braybrook Street, whose southern end runs along the thirty-foot-high perimeter wall of the prison; the rest of the street is bordered on the north by the wide stretch of the common. The residents of the council houses lining the opposite side of the road were used to drivers parking in the quiet street for a nap or a snack. That sunny afternoon women idled about their household duties and children on holiday played on the pavement and out on the common.

The police car overtook the Vanguard and DS Head flagged it down. Both cars came to a halt, the police car some yards in front of the other, which was much closer to the kerb. Head and Wombswell got out of the Q car and approached the Vanguard, both coming to the driver's window. Fox remained in the Q car, the engine running.

Head asked Witney if he was the owner of the car. Witney said: 'Yes.'

Then he was asked for his road fund licence. He replied that he didn't have one. Head enquired why. Witney said he couldn't get the car taxed until it had been given an MOT certificate. Head asked to see his driving licence. Having examined it, he asked for the car's insurance certificate. After studying it he remarked: 'It's three hours out of date.'

Wombwell produced a notebook to write down the car's and the driver's particulars. So far Roberts and Duddy had said nothing. Head moved away to inspect the rear of the car. 'Can't you give me a break?' cried Witney. 'I've just been nicked for this a fortnight ago.'

As DC Wombwell inclined his head to talk to Witney through the open window, Roberts shot him in the left eye.

Wombwell staggered back and fell.

Roberts told Duddy to grab a gun and leapt out of the car, closely followed by Duddy, as Head ran for his life towards Foxtrot Eleven. 'Get the driver!' Roberts shouted at Duddy.

Roberts fired at Head and missed. 'No, no, no!' cried Head, trying to hide behind the bonnet of Foxtrot Eleven. Roberts shot him in the back, and Head fell dying in front of the car.

Shocked senseless, Fox was slow to respond. But in any case, with Head in front of the police car he could not advance, and if he reversed he would approach the gunmen. Duddy fired at him three times, once through the rear near-side window, shattering the glass. This and another shot missed Fox. The third shot, which Duddy fired through the open passenger window, entered Fox's left temple and exited the other side.

As it did so his foot stamped on the accelerator. The car lurched forward over DS Head, who was still alive. He was caught underneath the car. Smoke poured from the engine as the rear wheels, lodged against his body, repeatedly banged against him, unable to advance. Fox lay dead at the wheel.

Witney had stepped out of the car to see what was happening. Roberts and Duddy ran back towards him and piled into the Vanguard.

'Drive!' cried Roberts. 'You must be fucking potty!' yelled Witney. 'Drive, you cunt!' Roberts retorted. 'Unless you want some of the same!'

Unable to stomach passing the fallen policemen, Witney reversed, and the blue Vanguard careered backwards with its loose exhaust, tied with string, sparking on the road. The brakes screeched as the car stopped, was swung left and sped down Erconwald Street and away from what would come to be known by the press as the Massacre of Braybrook Street.

A young couple, Bryan and Patricia Deacon, driving up Braybrook Street on their way to see his parents, were alarmed by the Vanguard reversing towards them. Mr Deacon, a thirty-year-old security officer who had been on duty the previous night, swore at the men in the blue car, and thinking that they might be mixed up in some prison-break shouted at his wife, who was seven months pregnant – 'Get the number!' He drove on, cursing, intending to telephone the police about the incident.

'Then I came across the first body,' he said later. 'I now know it was David Wombwell. He was lying with his feet towards the common. There was blood everywhere. Pat said: "He's dead!" There was a green police car in the middle of the road, with smoke pouring from it. A lorry-driver ran down the street, shouting: "Get the police! Get the police!"'

It was the lorry-driver who reached across PC Fox and switched off the ignition – the engine died and there was silence in the street.

About this time a blackbird flew in the kitchen window of Mrs Roberts's flat in Euston. She was unable to get rid of it for sometime and felt it was an omen.

Bryan Deacon drove on past the police car and found a telephone in a nearby butcher's shop. He dialled 999. Although his wife was sobbing and hysterical he returned to Braybrook Street on foot and gave the Vanguard's number, which he had written down on the butcher's wrapping-paper, to the driver of one of the many police vehicles that were soon on the scene. The number was PGT 726.

There were other witnesses, women and children. But there were discrepancies in their statements, and their descriptions of the three men involved in the shooting proved to be very inaccurate.

It took some time to trace the owner of PGT 726 (this would never happen now) as the records of car owners were kept in county offices and at 5 pm they had closed for the day.

DCS Richard Chitty was put in charge of the murder enquiry, and by 9 pm DI Steventon and a sergeant were knocking at the door of Witney's basement flat in Paddington.

'We are making enquiries concerning the owner of a blue Vanguard shooting-brake, PGT 726, which we understand is yours.' 'Oh, no – not that,' said Witney, and explained: 'We've just seen on the telly about the coppers being shot.' He told Steventon that he had sold the car that day to a stranger for £15. 'You told me you'd been to work,' said Mrs Witney. 'You didn't tell me you'd sold the car. What's going on?' 'I haven't been to work for five weeks,' Witney replied. 'I had to get some money for you.'

He was trembling and sweating; he mopped his face with a towel. Steventon, after further questions, asked Witney to come to the police station. Mrs Witney, much upset by now, said: 'Please, darling, tell them the truth.'

Witney was questioned at Shepherd's Bush police station. He made a statement, elaborating what he had told DI Steventon, and was detained. A search of his flat revealed no weapons or anything incriminating.

Meanwhile, the car's number and descriptions of the wanted men had been issued to the press and broadcast on radio and television. Masses of information, most of it useless began to pour in, and at a press conference on Saturday evening the police appealed for other witnesses and information. Witney's detention was not mentioned.

The previous evening Harry Roberts had returned to Wymering Mansions at seven o'clock. 'I knew at once something was wrong,' said Mrs Perry. 'He looked as if he had been running; he was all breathless and very flushed. I told him I had some nice rock salmon and chips for his tea. He looked disgusted. "I can't eat anything," he said, complaining of a headache.' Soon after this Mrs Howard left the flat and Lilian Perry mentioned the shootings – she had heard about them on the radio. 'Did you hear about the three policemen?' she said. 'Shut up!' said Roberts, and added – 'It was us.' He told her what had happened. Repeatedly he said: 'If only that fool hadn't asked to look inside the car. I knew if the coppers turned the car over they'd find the guns and put us all away. I thought it was better to shoot it out than go down for fifteen years.' If the police had found the guns, he said, they would have done time for nothing.

He neither ate nor drank and sat staring at the television set all evening, seeming to Mrs Perry to be very far away. She didn't know what to say or do.

On Saturday morning they went shopping. On their return John Duddy was in the flat; he had the guns. Roberts hid them under a bed.

In the afternoon Roberts, Duddy and Mrs Perry went for a walk in Paddington Recreation Ground, taking a pram and two of Mrs Howard's children with them, Barry, aged four, and Samantha, two, whom Roberts carried in his arms to hide his face. They returned to the flat in time for the wrestling on ITV.

Roberts wanted Duddy to go with him and get rid of the Vanguard, which Witney had left in a lock-up garage in Tinworth Street, Vauxhall, near the river. But Duddy refused to go anywhere near the car. Eventually, at about 8 pm, Mrs Perry agreed to accompany Roberts to Vauxhall, leaving Duddy behind in the flat to baby-sit, as the Howards had gone out. Duddy poured himself a drink.

The lock-up garage was under the arches of the main railway line to Waterloo. Mrs Perry and Roberts peered through the slats of the garage door at the car within – it was locked and they did not have the garage key or car key. Roberts said he wished Duddy would help him do something to get rid of the car, burn it or something. But he did nothing himself. Returning to the flat with Mrs Perry, he kept on at Duddy to do something, to help him – but the other man said: 'No.'

Later that night a man telephoned the police to say that he had seen a blue Vanguard being driven into the Tinworth Street garage on Friday. Within minutes the police visited the scene, and some time after midnight the police discovered that the lock-up was rented by Witney. Three .38 cartridges were found in the car from the .38 Colt that Duddy had fired.

The next day, Sunday, the Commissioner, Sir Joseph Simpson, and the Home Secretary, Roy Jenkins, called at Shepherd's Bush police station, outside which a crowd was shouting: 'Bring back the rope!'

That evening John Witney was charged by DCS Chitty with the murders of all three policemen 'with others' and taken back to his cell. Soon afterwards he decided to make another statement. 'I'm not scared for myself,' he said. 'I know I'm going away for a long time, but I'm frightened for my family. As God is my judge I had absolutely nothing to do with the shooting of the three policemen.' He told the police his version of what had happened in Braybrook Street, naming Roberts and Duddy as the gunmen. Unable to remember their exact addresses, he was taken in a police taxi late at night to point out where Roberts and Duddy lived. Both buildings were discreetly surrounded by armed policemen.

They were raided at 5 am on Monday, 15 August, to the shock and alarm of the occupants. Duddy's two teenage daughters were on their own; they had not seen their father since Saturday, and their mother had walked out weeks ago. The Howards and their children were alone in their flat – Mrs Perry and Roberts were absent. Mrs Roberts's flat in Euston was also visited by the police and searched; it was kept under observation from then on. Harry Roberts's wife was put under police protection. But of Roberts himself there was no sign.

On Sunday morning Roberts and Duddy had gone to Hampstead Heath to bury the guns. On their return Duddy opted to go to Scotland and Roberts decided to go to ground. He told Mrs Perry to pack a suitcase for him, and that afternoon they went to the Russell Hotel. He booked them in as Mr and Mrs Crosby. After a meal in a local restaurant – he couldn't eat as food still made him feel sick – they went up to their twin-bedded room. They lay on top of the single beds, talking; Roberts smoked. It was a very warm night, for London was having a heatwave. He said: 'What a mess I've made of things. What a bloody mess. If only that fool hadn't wanted to inspect the car . . . I've got to get away, pet. If I can keep hidden, lie low for a while, the whole thing may blow over.'

It seems he intended to go to Scotland, for on Monday morning they walked from the hotel to Euston Station, where Roberts changed his mind and the direction of his flight. He put his case in a left-luggage office, and then tore up the ticket he had bought.

They then went to a second-hand army surplus store near King's Cross where he bought some camping equipment, including some clothes, a haversack, a primus stove and a sleeping-bag. He also bought some tins of food from a grocer. From King's Cross they journeyed by bus to Camden Town, where they got on a Green Line bus for Epping. He hardly spoke. They left the bus beyond the Wake Arms and walked back to the cross-roads opposite the pub.

He looked at her and said: 'This is as far as you go, love . . . I'm on my own now. I'll have to make my own way from here.' She asked him where he was going. 'I don't know,' he said, 'I haven't really made up my mind.' He began to cry. So did she. 'You better go,' he said, 'before I get any worse.' Taking £6 out of a pocket he gave her 6s 6d, and told her how to get back to Maida Vale from there. 'That should be enough for your fare,' he said. 'I reckon I'm going to need the rest more than you.' Although she wanted to stay with him, he told her to go and saw her on to a coach.

On her return to Wymering Mansions she was interviewed by the police. She told them what she knew about Roberts and his whereabouts.

On Tuesday, 16 August, another hot sunny day, a photograph of Harry Roberts was issued with a description of the khaki combat jacket, khaki trousers, shirt, socks and boots he might be wearing. The public were warned he might be armed.

That same morning the police, acting on a tip-off, arrested John Duddy in Glasgow, catching him in bed in a Calton tenement. He did not resist arrest.

That night he was brought back to London on a scheduled flight from Glasgow airport. Handcuffed, he sat between two Yard detectives, DCI John 'Ginger' Hensley and DI Slipper. The latter took a statement from him on the plane, which Duddy later denied having made. It said: 'I must tell you what happened ... It was Roberts who started the shooting. He shot two who got out of the car and shouted to me to shoot. I just grabbed a gun and ran to the police car and shot the driver through the window. I must have been mad.' At Shepherd's Bush police station Duddy made another statement; it ended: 'I didn't mean to kill him. I wanted quick money the easy way. I'm a fool.'

At dawn on Thursday over 500 policemen, many of them armed, began searching the 6,000 acres of Epping Forest, backed up by police dogs and tear-gas guns, with a helicopter overhead observing and directing. On Saturday the search was called off – Harry Roberts had gone to ground elsewhere.

The man-hunt intensified, spreading all over Britain and into the Continent, where Interpol were alerted. Roberts was seen everywhere: sightings were as many as the theories about where and how he was living – was he disguised? – and every piece of information had to be followed up. There were further raids, chases and searches. A £1,000 reward was offered and advertised on 16,000 posters. It was the biggest police operation since the Great Train Robbery in August 1963.

In London the police had two rest days, on 31 August and on 6 September. On the first day the three murdered policemen were buried after a funeral service in the church opposite Shepherd's Bush police station. Over 600 policemen lined the route of the funeral procession. At Scotland Yard, in the wind and rain, a lone piper played a lament in the courtyard. On 6 September a memorial service was held in Westminster Abbey, attended by 2,000 policemen from all over Britain, as well as by the Prime Minister, Mr Wilson, by Mr Heath, by the Home Secretary and other leading politicians. In Whitehall, signatures were collected for a petition demanding the restoration of the death penalty.

More sightings than ever before were reported – over 6,000 in all. Roberts was seen in Ireland, Wales, the Isle of Man, on planes, trains and boats. A hundred and sixty reported sightings came from Liverpool, 106 from Bournemouth. And over 50,000 people sent money and gifts to the Bush for the dead men's families.

September ended. Press and public interest waned and was diverted by another sensation – the escape, on 22 October, of the spy George Blake from Wormwood Scrubs prison, where Roberts had met him. Blake had been sentenced in 1961 to forty-two years in prison, the longest sentence ever passed by a British court.

October ended. The trial of Witney and Duddy was set for Monday, 14 November. By then the real Harry Roberts had been seen by several people who thought they recognized him but did nothing about it.

It must have been in October that three teenage boys, hunting rabbits in Thorley Wood near Bishop's Stortford in Hertfordshire – three miles up the A11 from Epping Forest – found a camouflaged tent, hidden in undergrowth and surrounded by a low stockade of twigs and branches. A man was inside and a radio was on. Without disturbing him they went away. One of the boys told his mother about the man in the woods. He said: 'I wonder if it's Harry Roberts.' 'That's not possible,' she said with a laugh.

Since the beginning of October a dishevelled man in a combat jacket had regularly visited a grocery shop two miles away from the wood; he went there once a week and bought bread, eggs and tins of food, for which he paid in silver and other coins. 'My gosh, that chap looks like Harry Roberts,' said the manageress to her assistant, who laughed. They continued to see him. Said the manageress later: 'I meant to telephone the police. But I was afraid of feeling a little foolish. Now I feel an even bigger fool.'

Then in November, four days before the trial of Witney and Duddy began, a gipsy farm labourer, twenty-one-year-old John Cunningham, was prowling at night in Thorley Wood armed with a catapult and looking for small game. His eye was caught by a light from a tent buried in the undergrowth and fallen autumn leaves. A tin can rattled; the occupant was having a meal. Cunningham returned to the family caravan and mentioned his discovery to his father, who was incurious and dismissive. But on Saturday a policeman making inquiries about thefts in the area chanced to visit the caravan and heard about the stranger in the wood. He determined to investigate. With another policeman he set out for the wood that afternoon.

After some difficulty they found the hideaway. There was no one inside. But it was admirably situated and constructed, its carefully built framework of boughs and branches being covered with tarpaulin and plastic sheeting painted green and brown. Branches screened it all around; a hand-made chimney poked out of the roof, connected within to an iron stove; kindling cut to size was stacked in a box; a camp-bed, sleeping bags, blankets, a primus stove, a cache of food tins, two transistor radios, a fishing-rod, and all the necessary equipment for cooking and washing completed the homely scene; two suits and some shirts were neatly folded away.

The policemen watched and waited all day and night, but the tent's occupant failed to appear.

Fingerprints in the hideaway were taken by the Hertfordshire police and identified the occupant as Harry Roberts. Scotland Yard were informed.

DCS Chitty received the news in the Old Bailey on the first day of the Witney/Duddy trial. That night Thorley Wood was silently surrounded by well over 100 policemen. At dawn on Tuesday they moved in.

Harry Roberts was found just before noon on the edge of neighbouring Nathan's Wood.

PS Smith and PS Thorne were poking around bales of straw piled up in a disused hangar. Smith noticed a jar of methylated spirits. Pulling apart the bales behind the jar, he unearthed a primus stove and a torch. Heaving aside another bale he saw a sleeping-bag. He prodded it with a rifle. At one end Roberts's bearded face emerged – he had been asleep. He said: 'Don't shoot. You won't get any trouble from me – I've had enough. I'm glad you caught me.' A loaded Luger lay inside the sleeping-bag – the one used to kill Head and Wombwell. But this time he let it lie.

News of his capture reached DCS Chitty, the police and the press in the Old Bailey as they listened to Mrs Perry's evidence. Some left the court at once. But nothing was said officially before the court adjourned for lunch and for the day.

Chitty saw Roberts that afternoon in Bishop's Stortford police station. He denied killing PC Fox but made a statement admitting everything else. A large crowd had gathered outside Shepherd's Bush police station when he was taken there that night. His mother saw him for ten minutes. At first she failed to recognize him, with his ginger beard and long hair. He looked thin and tired, she thought. She wept, and he hugged her. She asked him if the police had harmed him, and he said: 'No, they've been the essence of kindness.'

On Wednesday, 16 November, Roberts made brief appearances at West London magistrate's court and at the Old Bailey, where it was decided that he should be tried with Witney and Duddy. A new date was set for the new trial.

It began at the Old Bailey on Tuesday, 6 December 1966. Witney and Duddy, represented respectively by Mr W. M. Hudson and Mr James Comyn, QC, pleaded not guilty to all the indictments against them. Roberts, defended by Mr James Burge, QC, pleaded guilty to the murders of DS Head and DC Wombwell and not guilty to the murder of PC Fox. He admitted the other charges: of being an accessory to the murder of PC Fox, and to possessing firearms. The Crown was led by the Solicitor-General, Sir Dingle Foot, QC. The judge was Mr Justice Glyn-Jones.

All three accused were found guilty of murder and of possessing firearms. The judge said: 'You have been justly convicted of what is perhaps the most heinous crime to have been committed in this country for a generation or more ... Lest any Home Secretary in the future should be minded to consider your release on licence I have to make a recommendation. My recommendation is that you should not be released on licence, any of the three of you, for a period of thirty years, to begin from today's date.'

Roberts and Witney appealed, but their applications were dismissed.

John Cunningham, the gipsy, was given £300, part of the £1,000 reward offered for information leading to Roberts's capture. Mrs Wombwell, Mrs Fox and the mother of DS Head each received £26,250, three-eighths of the £210,000 that was raised for and given to the dead policemen's families. The rest of the money was put into a trust fund for the children.

Mrs Dorothy Roberts, Harry Roberts's mother, went to work in a hotel. She said: 'When I come home from work I shut myself away and keep

myself to myself. Everybody round here knows who I am. It's not pleasant
... I've got to go on living for my son's sake. When everybody else has
forgotten him, I'll be visiting him. But there doesn't seem much point in
living now, and most nights I cry myself to sleep.'

David Wombwell was, like Harry Roberts, an only child. His mother
said: 'I saw Roberts at the trial. I had to go ... He was so cocky, so
arrogant. I couldn't understand why he should be there, alive and
swaggering, when my boy who was so good was dead. Yet I couldn't hate
him, because it all seemed so unreal ... It was all so pointless, so wicked
... Everybody wants something for nothing these days it seems. That's the
attitude that breeds the Harry Roberts of this world, and then it's the
honest, hard-working boys like my son who have to die ... What was it all
for? What's it all about? Why did it have to happen to him? ... Sometimes
I feel I shall break, or go out of my mind.'

John Duddy died in the hospital of Parkhurst prison on the Isle of Wight
in February 1981, having served half of the recommended thirty years of his
life sentence, to which the automatic one-third remission did not apply. He
was fifty-two.

No one this century has ever served a full thirty-year prison sentence. But
it may not be until 1986, twenty years after the massacre in Braybrook
Street – if then – that Witney and Harry Roberts will be released from jail.

CHAPTER 51

The Kray Twins

The murders of George Cornell and Jack McVitie, 1966/7

The trial of the Kray brothers and eight other men at the Old Bailey in 1969 was at that time the longest and most expensive criminal trial in British history. It was also unique in that the main defendants, both charged with murder, were thirty-five-year-old identical twins, although by then their varying life-styles and their divergent mental and emotional problems had subtly altered their appearances. If ever two men were fated to follow a violent life of crime it was these two, doomed by their nature and their circumstances, and bound by the very fact of being identical twins to imitate and protect each other and finally to share in each other's ruin.

They were born on 17 October 1933 at Hoxton in the East End of London. Their father was Charles Kray, aged twenty-six, an itinerant dealer in old clothes, silver and gold. Their mother, Violet, aged twenty-one, called the first child Reginald and the second, who arrived an hour later, Ronald. The Krays already had another son, Charles, a placid, pleasant child. The twins were different. Said their mother: 'They were so lovely when they were born, so small and dark, just like two little black-haired dolls.'

Their Romany ancestry showed more than the Jewish and Irish blood in them. Ronnie nearly died when they both got measles and diphtheria. After that he was moody and slower than Reggie who was more of an easy-going charmer.

In 1939 the family moved to Vallance Road in Bethnal Green, then an East End ghetto and a hot-bed of boxers, gamblers, hard drinkers and assorted villains. Half of it was destroyed in the war, but the Kray twins survived, constantly fighting each other and other boys; they were little demons and were known as the Terrible Twins. They were nonetheless polite and considerate to their elders, and although inseparable never stopped competing, vying with each other all the time. 'Even as a kid,' said Reggie, 'if I was challenged to a fight and I backed down, Ronnie would know. He'd be a sort of conscience, and I'd find it hard to face him afterwards.' Other boys thought them weird. They had no interest in girls and fought with a cold fury, piling into enemy gangs with coshes, bicycle-chains and broken bottles; and Ronnie used a sheath-knife. 'You're a born devil, Ronnie,' said Aunt Rose, adding that his eyebrows, meeting in the middle, meant he was born to hang. This of course also applied to Reggie.

In 1950, a sixteen-year-old Hackney boy called Harvey was found badly beaten up by fists, boots and bicycle-chains. There were witnesses, but when the twins were put on trial at the Old Bailey – their first appearance there – the case was dismissed for lack of evidence.

They bought their first revolver when they were sixteen. In 1951, aged seventeen, they became professional boxers, lightweights. Reggie was the better boxer, Ronnie the slogger. They always won. On 11 December 1951, Reggie, Ronnie and Charlie all appeared in a boxing contest at the Albert Hall. Charlie lost; Ronnie was disqualified; Reggie won.

Sometimes they hit their father, especially when he had drunk too much; he began to avoid them. They loved their mother and she them. 'I used to worry about the twins . . . I wasn't their mother for nothing. But if they was involved in any trouble I didn't want to know. It only upset me . . . Both of them was good boys at heart . . .'

Called up for national service they reported to the Waterloo Building in the Tower of London on 2 March 1952, decided they didn't care for the Royal Fusiliers or the army and walked right out, after dotting a corporal on the jaw. 'We're off home to see our Mum,' remarked Ronnie. The next day they were picked up by the police.

For the next two years they were either on the run, in jail, in guard-room cells or military prisons. On the run and in jail they learned many lessons from minor criminals. From the army they learned about weapons, discipline and power – the power of propaganda and of fear. United they could get away with nearly anything, behave as badly as they liked and make nonsense of society's conventions. Once they assaulted a policeman sent to arrest them – it was Christmas and they were reluctant to spend it in a barracks. 'Kray Brothers Beat Up PC' said a local paper, and showed a photo of them. They spent a month in Wormwood Scrubs. All this added to their status and their self-esteem.

Awaiting court-martial in a Canterbury guard-room, they went crazy, screaming abuse, refusing to eat, setting fire to their bedding and their uniforms, wrecking what they could and escaping again. The army could have thrown the book at them, but at their trial on 11 June 1953 they were charged with striking an NCO, going AWOL, and with conduct prejudicial to good order and discipline. They pleaded guilty and were sentenced to nine months in custody.

These were spent in Shepton Mallet military prison, making contact with incipient and actual criminals and preparing for a life of crime to achieve their vision of the good life: wealth, property, cars, fame and power. Ronnie's heroes were T. E. Lawrence, Wingate and Al Capone. He wanted to be as feared and as famous.

They acquired a billiard hall in Mile End which became their HQ and centre for the advising and aid of petty criminals. They started a protection business and waged war on other gangs. Within six months of being dismissed from the army Ronnie was known as the Colonel; the twins' organization became known as the Firm, and their mother's home Fort Vallance.

By 1956 their control over thieves, clubs, pubs and businesses had spread over Hackney, Stepney, Bow and Shoreditch. They ruled through fear and thrived on danger. But they still lived with Violet in Vallance Road, which now contained an armoury of assorted guns and knives. Ronnie dressed like a gangster, and had his own barber; but at night he slept with the light on and a gun under his pillow.

Then Ronnie shot a young docker in the leg. The docker was a member of a rival gang and had threatened a car-site owner favoured by the Krays. Money changed hands, threats or promises were made; and the docker, in hospital, found he couldn't quite remember how or where the accident happened, and although he picked out Ronnie in an identity parade the police had no option but to let him go when he said: 'I'm not *Ronnie* Kray. I'm *Reggie* Kray. I wasn't nowhere near where this bloke was shot.'

Reggie was however furious with Ronnie. 'You must be raving mad!' he shouted. 'You shoot a man and leave me to clear it up!' 'All you're fit for is clearing up,' retorted Ronnie. 'You couldn't shoot a man if you tried.'

In the summer of 1956 two business friends of the Krays, club-owners, were beaten up by the Watney Street gang. A punitive raid was made by the Firm on a pub where the gang was thought to be. As the Firm's large cars arrived at the entrance the gang escaped out the back. But a boy who happened to remain behind was seized, slashed and stabbed with a bayonet – he was also kicked unconscious.

This time the victim couldn't be fixed, and at the Old Bailey, on 5 November, Ronnie Kray was sentenced to three years for causing grievous bodily harm to Terence Martin of Stepney. But nothing was proved against Reggie.

With his dangerous brother in Wandsworth jail, Reggie now took the lead and much improved the Firm's business operations. He opened a club in Bow Road, the Double R. A club owned by Terence Martin's family in Poplar was destroyed by fire. The Double R prospered, being a success with both villains and celebrities. The twins' older and married brother, Charlie, became involved. They bought a car site, another club in Stratford, and set up an illegal gambling club beside Bow police station.

Meanwhile, in Wandsworth, Ronnie made friends with a gentle psychopathic giant called Frank Mitchell. He also read books and behaved well. Then he was moved to Camp Hill prison on the Isle of Wight. Isolated from his contacts and his family he lost touch with reality, becoming obsessed with Reggie's successes and his own apparent failure. He became silent and refused to eat, certain that everyone was his enemy and out to get him. For a time the only thing that reassured him was his reflection in a mirror. Then one night he went berserk.

He was moved to Winchester jail. The MO said he had prison psychosis. Heavily sedated, he appeared to recover. Then Reggie wrote saying that Aunt Rose had died. The following day Ronald Kray was certified insane. He was twenty-four.

On 20 February 1958 he was transferred to an asylum in Surrey, Long Grove Hospital, suffering from paranoid schizophrenia. He soon responded to the drugs he was given and was about to be sent back to prison – the doctors concluded he was now 'quiet, co-operative, and mentally sub-normal' – when Reggie arranged his escape by swapping places with his twin during Sunday visiting-hours.

Ronnie was hidden away in a four-berth caravan in Suffolk to begin with, making secret and sensational appearances at old haunts in London. But his dementia remained, and despite all the family's attempts to cure him (psychiatrists were hired), Ronnie's condition worsened. One night he tried to kill himself. His family were forced to accept the unimaginable – they informed Scotland Yard of his whereabouts.

He was picked up and taken back to Long Grove, then returned to Wandsworth. Still prone to violence and delusions, he was released in the spring of 1958, a changed man indeed. No longer the image of Reggie, his face and figure thickened; he looked brutish – the picture, it was said, of a homicidal psychopath.

The twins still lived in Vallance Road with their mother. They had fearful rows. Reggie guiltily modified his pursuits and ambitions to fall more in line with Ronnie's, whose aggression now began to imperil the Firm's business. 'He's ruining us,' said Reggie. 'I know we ought to drop him. But how can I? He's my brother and he's mad.'

East End violence grew; gang-fights became bigger and more bloody. Then in February 1960, Reggie was accidentally caught backing up a demand for protection money and sentenced to eighteen months in Wandsworth jail.

Now Ronnie was on his own. The Double R began to lose money. Then Ronnie met Peter Rachman. Rachman's whole empire was threatened by the frequent beating up of his rent-collectors, and so he arranged to pay off the Krays by giving them a fashionable nightclub in Knightsbridge, Esmeralda's Barn, which later became a discothèque. Freed from East End opinion, Ronnie now openly paraded his homosexuality with a fast turn-over of teenage boys. His contacts in this direction proliferated: politicians, businessmen, actors, academics, DJs and clerics. 'I'm not a poof,' he said. 'I'm homosexual.' He despised pansies as much as he despised women.

Reggie came out of prison when he was twenty-seven, and fell in love with a sixteen-year-old schoolgirl, Frances Shea, sister and look-alike of Frankie, a Hoxton boy whom Ronnie had once admired. Reggie put Frances on a pedestal. Ronnie vilified them both. There was a terrible row and Ronnie walked out of the Barn and the West End, back to the East End to a flat in Cedra Court, Walthamstow, where parties at which he and his boys were the centre of attraction were very well attended.

Meanwhile he planned to set up an English branch of Murder Incorporated, a private army of East End villains. He read *Mein Kampf*; he believed he was Attila the Hun reincarnated.

Reggie expanded the protection business and rackets involving fraudulent companies. Between them the Krays dominated London's criminal world.

In March 1962 after the gala première of *Sparrers Can't Sing* in Bow

Road, the cast and their friends celebrated at the twins' new club, the Kentucky. Their fame and power spread. They moved in on other clubs in Birmingham and Leicester. In 1962 three attempts to kill them were thwarted by their excellent network of informers. They were making about £500,000 a year. They bought their mother a race horse and themselves a restaurant in Kingston, the Cambridge, where Ronnie, insulted one night by an old friend, a boxer called Joe, knifed him in the washroom; Joe's face needed seventy stitches. Another old friend, Jonathan, also offended Ronnie, and his face was branded. Ronnie's depressions, drinking, paranoia and sadism increased along with his wealth, notoriety and power.

A sensational revelation in the *Sunday Mirror* on 12 July 1964 of the alleged homosexual relationship between a peer and a well-known gangster resulted in a detailed denial of the allegations by Lord Boothby in *The Times*, an apology by the *Sunday Mirror*, the payment of £40,000 in compensation, and the total embarrassment of the press and the police.

This was compounded when in 1965 the twins, together with Teddy Smith, were arrested and charged with demanding money with menaces from Hew McCowan, owner of the Hideaway club in Soho. Bail was refused. The Firm got to work. The jury failed to agree about their verdict. In the re-trial, McCowan was successfully discredited as a witness and the trial was stopped. The Krays were freed and celebrated by buying the Hideaway, renaming it El Morocco. They celebrated there with the biggest party they had ever given, to which the police and press were also invited.

Partly because of the McCowan case, the law was changed so that verdicts in future could be accepted from a majority of the jury.

The West End party of the year was followed by the East End wedding of the year. On 20 April 1965 Reggie married Frances Shea. They went to live below Ronnie in Cedra Court. Two months later Frances left her husband, going back to her parents. Six months after her marriage she was visiting the same Harley Street psychiatrist who was seeing Ronnie.

He was now dreaming of being an international racketeer, dealing in drugs, guns, forgery and crooked deals. The twins became involved with the Mafia, disposing of securities stolen in Canada. They acquired a stuttering Jewish banker called Alan Cooper to handle their affairs. He needed their protection, having been threatened by the Richardson gang. The Krays needed him. The middle-class Richardsons had made Ronnie feel threatened – they were getting too big, encroaching on the West End where the Krays hoped to enter into business in the gambling world with the American Mafia, then attempting to invade London.

At Christmas 1965 there was a confrontation between the Richardsons and the Krays at the Astor club. A Richardson henchman, George Cornell, referred to Ronnie as a 'fat poof'. An all-out gang war was declared. Two attempts were made on the lives of the twins.

Then early on 8 March 1966 there was a shoot-out at Mr Smith's club in Catford between the Richardsons and a local gang. The Krays were not involved, but one of their allies, Richard Hart, was killed. One of the Firm said: 'One of ours had gone, so it was up to Ronnie to do one of theirs.' But of the leading members of the Richardson gang only George Cornell, who had been absent from the Catford shoot-out, was not behind bars. This suited Ronnie, who had a personal insult to avenge.

He asked Jack Dickson, a Scot, to drive him to the Blind Beggar in Whitechapel Road. With him was another Scot, Ian Barrie. Both had guns, Ronnie a Mauser pistol. There were few people in the pub apart from the barmaid. Cornell, sitting on a bar-stool, was drinking a light ale with two friends when Ronnie and Barrie entered. The juke-box was playing 'The Sun Ain't Gonna Shine Anymore'. Barrie fired two shots into the ceiling. Everyone froze. Then Ronnie drew his pistol from a shoulder holster and shot Cornell between the eyes.

No one talked. Ronnie Kray was included at a police identity parade at Commercial Street but the barmaid failed to recognize the killer in the line of men. She had a poor memory for faces, she explained.

However, the Firm's business suffered as a result. The twins were now very bad news. They themselves became nervous. They fled abroad for a time to Morocco, from where they were soon ejected. Reggie now drank more than ever; his wife attempted suicide.

In an effort to improve their status the twins helped Frank Mitchell, the mad Axeman, to escape from Dartmoor on 12 December. Just before this Ronnie went into hiding in a Finchley flat to avoid giving evidence in a police corruption trial.

Mitchell, cooped up in a flat in Barking Road, became impatient and dangerous and threatened to shoot policemen or the Krays, although he was provided with a blonde night-club hostess called Lisa with whom he fell in love and who later declared: 'His virility was greater than that of any man I have ever known.'

On Christmas Eve Mitchell disappeared. One of his keepers later said that Mitchell was shot in a Thames van occupied by three men and that his body was dismembered and disposed of. The murder has never been solved and Mitchell is still officially on the run from Dartmoor.

There were other disappearances: one was Ronnie's driver, Frost; another was Teddy Smith.

There was also a death in the family. Frances Kray, aged twenty-three, took an overdose on 7 June 1967, the day after Reggie bought them both tickets for a second honeymoon on Ibiza. Her funeral at Chingford was a lavish one. She was buried in her wedding-dress.

Reggie went to pieces, drank more than ever, and was full of hate. He began to seek revenge on those who had betrayed him. Drunk on gin he shot at a man whom he thought had maligned his wife. All the shots missed, except for one that struck the victim's leg.

'Drunken slag!' said Ronnie later. 'Risking our necks like that – you risk everything shooting one of our friends, you drunken pig . . . You couldn't kill a man if you tried. You're too soft. When I did my one, I made a job of it.'

Reggie shot another man who owed the Firm money, again through the leg. He knifed a third in the face.

The Firm's business expanded into fruit-machines, drugs and pornography. Assassination plots occupied Ronnie's mind – of President Kaunda and Colin Jordan. He also had a death-list of the Firm's enemies. He got the idea that murder would unite the Firm's members, test their loyalties and make them a brotherhood.

He decided to try out his idea on a drunken, loud-mouthed suspect associate called Jack 'The Hat' McVitie – he wore a hat to hide his baldness. Ronnie gave him a gun and £100 to rub out a former associate, Leslie Payne, for which McVitie would then get £400. Payne was on his guard and remained alive. Ronnie failed to get his money back, so Reggie went to collect it. But McVitie told him a sob-story and Reggie gave him £50 instead. Ronnie went wild, abusing Reggie and demanding payment. McVitie, feeling aggrieved and frightened by the twins' blowing hot and cold, got drunk, and armed with a sawn-off shot-gun went looking for them in the Regency club, saying he was going to get them.

Such defiance was unendurable. A few nights later in November 1967, Reggie, drunk himself, entered the Regency looking for McVitie, intending at last to emulate Ronnie's murder of Cornell. McVitie wasn't there.

Meanwhile, Ronnie was making other arrangements. He took over a basement flat in Cazenove Road, Stoke Newington, belonging to a woman called Carol, and, when Reggie returned there, he sent their cousin (a former merchant seaman called Ronnie Hart) and two half-Greek brothers called Lambrianou, who had yet to be blooded, to find McVitie and ask him to a party at Carol's place. Two boys were with Ronnie; they danced together as Ronnie and Reggie waited with a man called Bender.

Just before midnight the drunkenly bold McVitie barged in, looking for a party. 'Where's all the birds and booze?' he cried, and Reggie, behind the door, pointed a gun at McVitie's head and fired. The gun jammed.

There was a furious struggle. Ronnie's boys fled. McVitie got half out of a window – his hat fell off. He was hauled back by the legs. Ronnie seized him from behind, pinioning his arms. Reggie now had a carving-knife.

'Kill him, Reg!' screamed Ronnie. 'Do him! Don't stop now!' 'Why are you doing this, Reg?' cried McVitie.

He was stabbed in the face, the stomach and chest, and finally impaled through the throat on to the floor – by Reggie, according to Ronnie Hart, who was later counter-accused by Reggie. But the twins' honour had been satisfied.

McVitie's body was never found. Rumour said it had been buried in concrete, consumed by pigs, cremated in a furnace, or concealed in a coffin by a fearful undertaker and then cremated. The twins took a week's holiday at an expensive hotel in Suffolk.

A month earlier Scotland Yard had set up a special team led by Detective Superintendent Leonard (Nipper) Read to investigate the Krays and find some charge against them that would stick. Leslie Payne, McVitie's intended victim, was routinely questioned about his former business associates and decided to talk.

He was secretly interrogated for three weeks; his final statement ran to over 200 pages. Other statements were acquired, but many people would not speak until the Krays were safely inside. There was no corroborative proof against them. Meanwhile the twins were planning their retirement. They knew about Read's investigation, and considered killing him. Ronnie's mind was still on murder.

To test Alan Cooper, Ronnie suggested he should kill a minor villain whose death would score off one gang while putting another in his debt. Cooper agreed, even though it meant killing the man when he appeared as a witness at the Old Bailey, and he produced an unusual murder weapon – an attaché case that would jab a cyanide-filled hypodermic needle into the man's leg. Cooper also arranged for a tall, bespectacled young man called Paul Elvey to do the job. He failed – the victim never appeared, said Elvey.

Another weapon was provided by Cooper, a crossbow. Again Elvey's mission failed.

Ronnie went to New York with Cooper but mysteriously failed to meet the Mafia. On his return, to impress them as the boss of criminal London, he took on a contract to eliminate a Las Vegas gambler staying at the London Hilton, who proved to be very wary and elusive. An easier target then presented itself, a Maltese nightclub owner, George Caruana, whom Ronnie thought of blowing up in his car, a red Mini. He asked for Cooper's assistance and Cooper again brought in Paul Elvey, sending him by plane to Glasgow to fetch four sticks of dynamite. As he boarded the plane on his way back he was arrested.

The attaché case and crossbow were found in his house. Elvey confessed, implicating Cooper.

Cooper's story was almost incredible. He told Nipper Read that he was an undercover agent, working largely on his own and for himself, and had been working for the Yard and the American Treasury Department for two years, trying to compromise the Krays. The weapons he supplied, he said, were faulty (e.g. the gun that jammed when used against McVitie), and Elvey could be relied on to bungle everything.

It had been a most dangerous game – and was hard to believe. But now Nipper Read had three attempted murders, arranged by Cooper, to pin on the Krays, as well as Payne's statement.

At dawn on 9 May 1968 the police raided Violet Kray's new council flat in Braithwaite House, Shoreditch. Reggie was in bed with a girl from Walthamstow, Ronnie with a fair-haired boy. They had spent the night until 4 am at the Old Horn pub in Bethnal Green and at the Astor Club, Berkeley Square.

With the Krays behind bars, people were now persuaded by the police to talk – like the barmaid from the Blind Beggar. Twenty-eight criminals were promised freedom from prosecution if they talked. Ronnie Hart and Jack Dickson were among those who turned Queen's evidence.

The Krays were charged with the Cornell and McVitie murders. Others of the Firm, like Charlie Kray and Bender and the Lambrianou brothers, were charged with being accessories.

The trial, before Mr Justice Melford Stevenson, lasted thirty-nine days, beginning in January 1969 and ending on 8 March. Ronnie Kray gave evidence, arrogantly denying everything, claiming it was all a police plot. He shouted at the prosecutor: 'You're a fat slob!' He told the judge: 'You're biased too!'

Reggie Kray's defence could have been that he was dominated by his brother Ronnie. But the twins, pleading not guilty, were tried and sentenced together to life imprisonment, the judge recommending that this should not be less than thirty years. They were thirty-five years old.

They were later found not guilty of the murder of Frank Mitchell. Other charges are still on the files.

For a time the twins were reunited, in 1972, in Parkhurst jail. But in 1979 Ronnie Kray was again declared to be insane and moved to Broadmoor. In 1981 Reggie Kray was temporarily transferred to Long Lartin prison in Leicestershire before being returned to Parkhurst.

'For humanitarian reasons' he has been allowed more than once to visit his twin in Broadmoor: they lunch together, exchange news and views and talk about old times. Their mother, Violet, died in August 1982 and their father, aged seventy-five, some six months later. The twins were allowed to attend both funerals, but declined in the case of their father as there had been a press and TV beanfeast at their mother's funeral. Ronnie Kray may never leave Broadmoor, and it is unlikely that Reggie Kray will be released from prison before his fifty-third birthday in 1986.

In November 1969 the five-year experimental period during which the death penalty for murder was suspended came to an end, and on 16 December 1969 the House of Commons confirmed the abolition of capital punishment by a majority of 158 votes. The decision was reaffirmed by the House of Lords two days later – by a majority of 46.

A motion supporting the return of capital punishment for certain murders was debated by the Commons in July 1983. The motion was defeated by 361 votes to 245 – a majority of 116.

However, the scaffold at Wandsworth prison has never been dismantled, as the death penalty still could (and can) be exacted for treason and for piracy with violence – and still remains in force on the Isle of Man, where it is within the jurisdiction of the Manx courts. In December 1982 a nineteen-year-old ex-labourer, Stephen Moore, convicted of the murder of his girlfriend's baby son in Douglas, Isle of Man, was sentenced to death by the Island's senior judge, Deemster Jack Corrin. In an outmoded ritual, now outlawed on the mainland, he formally donned a black cap and said: 'You will be taken from this place to the Isle of Man prison and thence to a place of lawful execution where you will be hanged by the neck until you are dead.' To date, the sentence has not been carried out.

CHAPTER 52

Stanley Wrenn

The murder of Colin Saunders, 1969

Violent offences against homosexuals have increased since the passing of the Sexual Offences Act of 27 July 1967, which legislated that 'a homosexual act committed in private shall not be an offence, provided that the partners consent thereto and have attained the age of twenty-one years.' This increase in violence is probably due to the fact that so-called gays have tended, since the Act was passed, to pursue their sexual activities more openly and so make themselves more obvious targets for those opposed to them or antagonised by them. Murders of homosexuals are not often solved, because of the random nature of the pick-up that is frequently involved. The following case is unusual in the deliberate but casual way the murderer chose and killed his victim, in the choice of weapons, in the absence of any attempt to conceal the crime or to evade capture, and in the ackowledgement of guilt.

Stanley Wrenn was born in Liverpool on 20 January 1950. When he was sixteen he joined the army as a junior private in the RAMC but was discharged later the same year. After that he drifted, finding employment as a car-sprayer, shop-assistant, labourer and barman. In October 1969 he was in London, and one night during the first half of the month he was in the concourse of Piccadilly Circus underground station when an older man came up to him and said: 'How are you getting on? Haven't I met you before?'

Wrenn was nineteen. The other man was thirty-five-year-old Colin George Saunders, who was born in Bedford on 12 June 1934 and was now a chauffeur with Warley Car Hire Services in Bromley, Kent. Saunders, who had previous convictions for importuning and gross indecency, continued: 'Where are you living?' 'Nowhere,' replied Wrenn. Saunders took him for something to eat in a café and asked him if he would like to come back to his place. 'Yeah,' said Wrenn.

They went to 13 College Road in Bromley, a Victorian type of terraced house which was divided into various flats and single rooms. Saunders occupied a ground-floor room at the front. That night they slept in a double bed, but Saunders soon acquired two single beds. According to Wrenn, the older man had sex with him – 'I did nothing' – every night.

This went on for five or six weeks – during which there were demonstrations in America against the war in Vietnam, Apollo 14 was launched to orbit the moon, and colour television programmes began on BBC 1 and ITV.

Then in the third week of November Wrenn discovered that Saunders had infected him with gonorrhoea. The relationship became very strained, and on Monday, 24 November, 'out of spite', Wrenn made up his mind to kill Saunders.

He went shopping for a knife, and having passed over one that cost 12s 6d – it was too dear – he bought a fisherman's knife for 4s 6d. He also dismantled and removed a gas-ring from another room in 13 College Road and concealed both it and the knife in a cubby-hole by the television set in their shared bed-sitting-room.

The following night Wrenn hid both weapons under his bed, going to bed himself at 10.45 pm.

He later told the police that he stayed awake until 5 am on the morning of Wednesday, 26 November, listening to Saunders snore. Then he got out of bed – he was wearing a T-shirt – took the gas-ring and knife from their place of concealment, and with the gas-ring struck Saunders, who was asleep on his side, on the head.

'The second time I hit him,' said Wrenn later, 'he looked up – he was facing the wall. I then stuck the knife in his throat.' Wrenn went berserk, stabbing Saunders many times about the head.

After drying his hands on his T-shirt, Wrenn pulled a sheet up over Saunders's bloody head and covered it with a dressing-gown. He then washed and shaved.

He remained in the room for some time, going through the dead man's possessions. Eventually Wrenn took what he wanted – money, clothes, car-keys and some other articles – packed the larger items into a suitcase, and went out.

Saunders's employer's car, a Humber, was outside and Wrenn got in. He was not, however, familiar with cars or with automatic gears; the Humber reversed at speed and struck a Ford Consul being driven along Hammelton Road. The driver remonstrated with Wrenn, saying: 'That's a nice thing to do.'

There was an argument that concluded with the driver of the Ford suggesting that they should telephone the police. Wrenn volunteered to do so and returned to 13 College Road, where he made no phone call but put Saunders's chauffeur's cap on the dead man's bed. He returned to the impatient driver of the Ford and pretended he had telephoned for the police. Once more he returned to the house, this time leaving the car-keys on Saunders's bed before walking to Bromley North railway station, where he got on a train to London.

Wrenn spent that night in the West End.

In the morning he bought a newspaper and saw that he had been named in connection with the death of Colin Saunders – police investigating the car accident had gone the previous day to Saunders's address and discovered his body. Wrenn, seeing his name in the papers, decided to give himself up.

He approached a police constable in Piccadilly Circus and said who he was. The PC took him to West Central police station, where he was charged on Thursday, 27 November.

Put on trial at the Old Bailey on 24 March 1970 before Justice Sir Ralph Cuack, Stanley Wrenn pleaded guilty and was sentenced to life imprisonment.

He served ten years of his sentence, being released from prison in June 1980 when he was thirty.

CHAPTER 53

Arthur and Nizamodeen Hosein
The murder of Mrs McKay, 1969/70

Kidnap victims must be among the most pathetic and wretched victims of crime, living in acute discomfort, isolation and terror until, as sometimes happens, they are done to death. Kidnappers must be among the most cowardly and callous of killers. One of the many extraordinary features of the McKay case was that it was the first kidnap-and-ransom crime ever perpetrated in Britain. It was also one of the worst examples of co-operation between the police, the press and the victim's family, and the ensuing investigation suffered as a result. It was also only the third case in fifty years in which a murder conviction was obtained without the body ever being found. The questions still remain. Whatever happened to Mrs McKay? When, and where, and how did she die? The prime irony is that she was kidnapped by mistake.

Muriel Freda McKay, née Searcy, aged fifty-five, was the epitome of a wealthy middle-class woman, with a large comfortable house in Wimbledon, many social and charitable interests, three fond married children, and a successful, loving husband, Alexander Benson McKay (Alick). They were both Australians.

Born in Adelaide on 4 February 1914, Muriel Searcy met and fell in love with Alick McKay at a Sunday school when she was thirteen and he was eighteen. They married in June 1935. It was through her brother that Alick became involved in the newspaper business, in the management of Sir Keith Murdoch's News Ltd. Eventually, in 1957, he came to London as the advertisement director of Daily Mirror Newspapers. The family settled in a red-brick, mock-Georgian mansion, St Mary House, 20 Arthur Road, Wimbledon.

Alick McKay continued to prosper, becoming advertisement director of the newly formed IPC in 1963 and acquiring many powerful friends in politics and the newspaper world. Two years later he was awarded the CBE. He was all set to retire in August 1969 after two heart attacks – he was now sixty – when Rupert Murdoch, son of Alick's first newspaper employer, offered him a job.

Murdoch's company, News Ltd, had gained control in January 1969 of the world's best-selling Sunday paper, the *News of the World* (circulation: six million). Its success was based on the public's appetite for sensational stories about sex, crime, scandal and murder. In June, Murdoch became the paper's chairman, and then bought an ailing daily paper, *The Sun*, from IPC, relaunching it in November. The previous month Alick McKay had retired from the IPC with a golden handshake said to amount to £40,000. Instead of returning to Australia as his wife had hoped and his colleagues expected, he accepted Murdoch's offer of a job as deputy chairman of the *News of the World*, becoming temporary chairman when Murdoch decided to return to Australia with his attractive young wife for a six-week holiday.

Alick McKay was left in charge on 19 December and given the use of the company car, a dark blue Rolls Royce.

The car had already caught the eyes of two Muslim brothers from Trinidad who wanted to know where Rupert Murdoch lived. They had looked in the London telephone directory, tried directory enquiries, consulted a library copy of Kelly's Street Directory – all without success. They then drove to the *News of the World* offices in Bouverie Street where some chance sighting or snippet of information led them to identify the blue Rolls Royce as the chairman's car. Who else but he would have such a car at his disposal?

They noted its number, and on Friday, 19 December – the very day that Rupert Murdoch flew with his wife to Australia – the younger Trinidadian brother, Nizamodeen Hosein, called at the offices of the GLC at County Hall and, using a false name, said he was anxious to trace the owner of ULO 18F with which, he said, he had been involved in a slight accident. A girl in the vehicle registration department could only tell him that the Rolls was owned by the *News of the World*. This merely confirmed what the brothers knew.

They now surmised that the simplest way of finding out where the chairman lived was to follow the car from Fleet Street to its destination. This they did just before Christmas, oblivious of the fact that the identity of its passenger had changed a few days before. They followed the Rolls across London. It led them to 20 Arthur Road, Wimbledon, to the kind of up-market house a wealthy executive was likely to inhabit. They went home to plan the kidnapping (as they thought) of Mrs Anna Murdoch, for whom they intended to ask a ransom of one million pounds.

Home for the Hosein brothers of Railway Road, Dow Village, Trinidad, was now a run-down seventeenth-century farmhouse set in eleven acres of Hertfordshire, forty miles north of London. Rooks Farm, by the hamlet of Stocking Pelham, had been bought by the older brother, Arthur Hosein, on a mortgage in 1967.

Arthur Hosein was a vain and natty little man – 'like an advert for Babycham', said a publican – about 5 ft 4 ins, moustached, ever-talking, volatile, jokey, ambitious, boastful, and determined to make good in England, to make money – lots of it – to make and be worth a million. He had immigrated to England in September 1955, hoping to become a student. He became a ledger-clerk instead, earning £7 a week. He was then called up for national service. Army life had little appeal for him and he often absconded, finally being court-martialled for desertion in 1960. 'Immeasurably the worst soldier it has been my misfortune to have under me,' said one officer, and Private Hosein of the Royal Pioneer Corps was sentenced to six months in Aldershot military prison and discharged. However, as a British soldier stationed at Colchester, he had met Else Fischer, a married woman ten years his senior. They married after she got a divorce from her soldier husband. She had a ladies hairdresser's in Mare Street, Hackney, and it was there that Arthur began a tailoring business that won him a solid reputation as a very good trouser-maker and craftsman. He was also a keen gambler and owned two greyhounds which he raced at various tracks around London. The East Enders called him 'Nutty Arthur', and he might have stayed among them and prospered – he was now earning up to £150 a week of which £65 a month was sent to his parents in Trinidad – but for his ambition to become a country gentleman and realize some of his fantasies.

This led him to abandon his 'business in town' and acquire an 'estate in the country', Rooks Farm. He moved there in May 1968 and relied mainly on hire-purchase to furnish the house in style: there was a gilt cocktail bar in the lounge. One of the outhouses became a tailor's workshop where he cut his famous trousers, taking them into the East End to be finished. He had two cars, a dark blue Volvo saloon and a Morris Minor. At night he liked cutting a dash in local pubs, buying lavish rounds of drink for village worthies – whisky was his favourite tipple – and talking grandly of the money he had made and planned to make, of influential friends and contacts. He also liked making up calypsos mocking the Labour government; Arthur was a Liberal. He saw himself as an English squire – some villagers called him 'King Hosein' – and when an altercation with Captain Barclay, Master of the Puckeridge Hounds (they had cut across Arthur's land), involved the police and legal correspondence and the actual social acquaintance of a real country gentleman, Arthur must have felt he had made his mark. He applied to Barclay to become a member of the Puckeridge Hunt.

None of this appealed to Nizam, who was an awkward youth, introverted and emotional. He came to England, lured by Arthur's fantasies, in May 1969, a year after he had wounded his father in a fight. He was twenty-one. He worked as a labourer on the farm in return for pocket-money and his keep. But little pleased him and he was disparaging about Arthur's illusions and exaggerations. Where was the wealth, the affluent and socially successful life that Arthur had bragged about in Trinidad, and which he had promised his parents should they come to visit England?

The discrepancy between Arthur's heady aspirations and cold reality had to be faced. The solution was obvious – get rich quick. But how? How could Arthur realize the ultimate fantasy of making a million, which would in turn make fact of all his dreams?

The answer was provided by a television show. On 30 October the brothers were watching David Frost interviewing Rupert Murdoch about the ethics of reprinting Christine Keeler's memoirs. But what was of greater interest to the brothers was the huge amount of money mentioned in connection with the takeover of the *News of the World*. Clearly Mr Murdoch was a millionaire many times over. They heard he also had a young, attractive wife. Obviously he would part with one of his millions to ransom her if she were kidnapped.

The brothers probably made some preliminary enquiries in November, but did not go into action until after 13 December when Arthur's German wife, their two children and his thirteen-year-old sister left England on a Christmas visit to Else's parents in Germany. They would return on 3 January, soon after which Nizam's visitor's permit was due to expire. The brothers had three weeks in which to make a million.

It took them a week to find out where, as they thought, Mrs Murdoch lived. Then there was the Christmas break, a long one as Christmas Day fell on a Thursday. Nobody would be back at work until Monday, 29 December.

The McKays spent a pleasant family Christmas at Lingfield in Sussex with their daughter, Diane, who was married to David Dyer, a business executive with the Wilkinson razor-blade company. The Hoseins were on their own in Rooks Farm, although they were joined on Boxing Day by a Trinidadian nurse called Liley, who was Nizam's girl-friend. She was twenty-nine and had left her husband and three children. Her presence excited Arthur, who thought all women found him irresistible, and there was a punch-up between the brothers in which Nizam was worsted and was so distraught that he reported Arthur to the police. But when Liley departed on the following day fraternal harmony was restored.

On the morning of Sunday, 28 December, two policemen visited Rooks Farm, making enquiries about an assault on an old farmer the previous Sunday. Both Hoseins denied being involved in this case of grievous bodily harm and the detectives withdrew. That night, about 9.30 pm, the brothers appeared in a pub, the Plough at Great Munden. Arthur was full of beans. He said he had been invited to a dinner party at Mr Rupert Murdoch's house, but had had to refuse. The following morning, about 11 am, PC Felton called at the farm in connection with Nizam's complaint against his brother. Nizam said he didn't wish to prefer any charges. Of Arthur and the Volvo there was no sign.

Later that day, at 8 pm and again at 10.30 pm, Liley telephoned the farm to talk to Nizam. No one answered the first call. The second was answered by Arthur, who said Nizam was out.

That morning Alick McKay set off for work at half-past nine in the dark blue Rolls Royce, driven by his chauffeur, Bill. Mrs McKay waved goodbye at the door of St Mary House. It was very cold: the ground was still white with frost.

Not long afterwards Mrs McKay got into her own Ford Capri and drove to Haydon's Road to collect the household help, Mrs Nightingale. Back at the house, after dealing with various tasks including the preparation of two steaks for the evening meal, Mrs McKay went shopping on foot, visiting a cobbler's, a bank, and a smart dress-shop where she bought a silk dress and matching coat for £60. She lunched in the kitchen with Mrs Nightingale and then visited her dentist in Wimpole Street for a routine check-up, returning home about 5 pm, when she drove Mrs Nightingale home, stopping to buy the evening papers. She must have been back in St Mary House about 5.40 pm, when she made herself a cup of tea and settled down to read the papers in the snug at the rear of the lounge, with a log fire blazing in the grate and her dachshund, Carl, at her feet.

She turned on the television to watch the news but, as was her wont, kept the volume down until news-time arrived. The front door was locked, with a chain across it – Mrs McKay had become wary of strangers ever since the house had been burgled three months before: silver, jewellery, a television set and a record-player being taken from the house.

At about ten to six the doorbell rang.

At six o'clock a neighbour, Mrs Lydiatt, walked by the house and noticed a dark car parked in the drive. She also saw that the light above the front door was on.

Alick McKay returned from work at 7.45 pm. After dismissing the chauffeur-driven Rolls he rang the doorbell in a pre-arranged code (three shorts and a long) to let his wife know who it was. There was no response. He tried the door – it was neither locked nor chained. He went into the house.

The scene in the hall, as DS Birch described it later, was 'as if it had been set up for an amateur production of an Agatha Christie thriller'. The telephone lay on the floor, its lead ripped from the wall, as well as Mrs McKay's reading-glasses. The contents of her handbag were scattered on the stairs; and littering various pieces of furniture were a tin of Elastoplast, a ball of string and a wooden-handled billhook. Everything else was in order, and Carl the dachshund lay dozing in front of the fire in the snug.

At 8 pm Alick McKay telephoned the police from a neighbour's house. Within five hours the house was besieged by the press and garrisoned by CID and uniformed policemen. Mrs McKay's two married daughters moved in with their husbands, and several influential newspaper friends arrived, including the editor of *The Sun* and the chairman of IPC.

The disappearance of Mrs McKay was potentially just the kind of story that would be blasted across the front page of *The Sun* and the *News of the World* – as in fact it was – and the police, headed by DCS Bill Smith and DI John Minors from Wimbledon, were at first suspicious about everyone's motives and about everything to do with the case.

They thought that Mrs McKay's disappearance might be part of some publicity stunt (the *News of the World* had a regular item dealing with missing persons, as it happened); that Mr McKay, who seemed strangely calm, might be in some way involved; that Mrs McKay had run off on her own accord, possibly with another man; that there had been a family row; or that she had had some kind of breakdown. In any event they felt that 'the whole thing smelt' and that her disappearance had been stage-managed. They rather doubted she had been abducted, as it seemed. There was after all no ransom note, and middle-aged women who went missing were a regular occurrence in London, numbering about fifty a week. Earlier that year another Wimbledon housewife, Mrs Dawn Jones, aged thirty-seven, had vanished in similar circumstances, her body being eventually found in a hut in Morayshire, Scotland.

What irritated the police most was the involvement of the press. A *Sun* reporter and photographer were the first journalists at the scene, and a statement was sent by *The Sun*'s editor to the Press Association in time to catch the morning papers.

That night, at 1 am, Mrs McKay's disappearance was announced in very vague terms by BBC radio. Fifteen minutes later the McKays' telephone, which had been busy all night after being reconnected, rang.

David Dyer, the McKays' more aggressive son-in-law, answered it. The operator said he was putting a call through from a call-box at Bell Common, Epping. A voice said: 'Tell Mr McKay it is M3, the Mafia.' The house fell silent as the family and the policemen who were there looked at Mr McKay. He took the receiver from Dyer. DS White picked up an extension in the kitchen. The voice, evidently disguised and later described by the operator as 'an American or coloured voice' continued: 'We are from America – Mafia. M3. We have your wife . . . You will need a million pounds by Wednesday . . .' 'This is ridiculous!' cried Mr McKay. 'I haven't got a million!' 'You had better get it,' said the voice. 'You have friends. Get it from them. We tried to get Rupert Murdoch's wife. We couldn't get her – so we took yours instead . . . You have a million by Wednesday night. Or we will kill her.' 'What do I have to do?' demanded Mr McKay. 'All you have to do is wait for the contact . . . Have the money or you won't have a wife.'

The family were both relieved and horrified: Mrs McKay was apparently alive but in the hands of a lunatic gangster. The police found it hard to believe that any kidnapper would make a ransom demand from a public call-box, and 'Mafia M3'! It was most unlikely and must be a hoax.

The Sun's front-page headline on the morning of Tuesday, 30 December was 'MYSTERY OF PRESS CHIEF'S MISSING WIFE'. Mr McKay felt that the maximum publicity could only help in his wife's return. But the police were far from sure about this, as were some members of his own family.

From the police point of view Mr McKay was still the most obvious suspect. The house, the attic and the garden of 20 Arthur Road were carefully searched. Frictions developed between the family and the police, who they thought should be pursuing their enquiries elsewhere. This was in fact being done, and a press conference revealing details of the one million pound ransom demand was held that morning.

At the same time a description of Mrs McKay – '5 ft 9 ins, medium build, dark complexion, dark brown hair, straight nose, green eyes, oval face' – was circulated, and a crime index was set up at Wimbledon police station. The index comprised a filing system, heavily cross-referenced, dealing with all the sightings, statements and other information that began to come in as the police made enquiries about cars and people seen in the area. They questioned friends and neighbours of the McKays and investigated the activities of local cranks and crooks. A tape-recorder was provided by a detective working on the case – it would have taken over two months to obtain one through official channels – and was fixed to the telephone in the snug, which had been taken over by the police. The McKays' number was soon jammed by hoaxers and reporters, but there was not a word from M3. This tended to confirm police suspicions that the Mafia call was a hoax.

But at 4.56 pm M3 finally got through. He was ringing again from a call-box. David Dyer, who took the call, heard the pips. The voice said: 'Your wife has just posted a letter to you. Do co-operate . . . for heaven's sake. For her sake, don't call the police . . . You have been followed. Did you get the message? . . . Did you get the money?'

That was all – again no instructions were given as to where or how the money was to be delivered. The family's fears increased, and that night Diane Dyer appeared on the 8.50 BBC TV News – much to the vexation of the police and with a corresponding increase in nuisance calls.

But on Wednesday morning a letter, postmarked '6.45 pm. Tottenham. N17', arrived. On lined blue paper was a feeble unaligned scrawl from Mrs McKay: 'Please do something to get me home. I am blindfolded and cold. Only blankets. Please co-operate for I cannot keep going . . . I think of you constantly . . . What have I done to deserve this treatment? . . . Love Muriel.'

The police decided to keep the letter's contents secret and it was not mentioned at the midday press conference. None the less it was leaked to *The Sun* and the Press Association, and most morning papers carried the text in full. The police in charge of the case were furious, and DCS Smith felt he now had no option but to enlist the family's full co-operation and explain his every move – against all police principles.

That night (New Year's Eve) both Mrs McKay's daughters and David Dyer, who had become the McKay's spokesman, appeared at the evening press conference, and Diane Dyer made another emotional appeal on television, this time on ITN's news.

Early that same morning the Hoseins had had a visitor. He was a business friend and a master tailor and arrived by appointment at Rooks Farm about 7.30 am to collect some trousers. This he did, seeing nothing of Arthur nor anything suspicious. Later that morning both brothers picked up Liley in London by car and brought her back to the farm, where she stayed until 2 January, during which time she noticed nothing odd. She said Arthur spent most of the time watching television.

The telephone in 20 Arthur Road continued to ring. One call came from a nurse who recommended that a medium be consulted. Then the McKay family, determined to explore any avenue to obtain Mrs McKay's release, contacted a spiritualist, who said she was too busy to see them just then but had already received a message from the spirit world about the abduction. Three people were involved, she said, as was Seven Sisters Road – which ended just south of Tottenham, N17. The motive was spite or malice, she said, and Mrs McKay was being held in a 'very scruffy place'. This impressed the family and they resolved to go further, without telling the police.

They next consulted a famous clairvoyant, Gerard Croiset, who lived in Utrecht in Belgium. A family friend took a photo of Mrs McKay to Croiset, who said: 'The impression I get is of a white farm . . . Around it are trees and a green barn.' It was approached by a road going north-north-east out of London. In the vicinity, said M Croiset, were another farm, a disused airfield, a concrete building, and a pond in which was an old motor-cycle. He added: 'If she is not found without fourteen days, she will be dead.'

Somewhat reluctantly the police followed up the information, finally identifying a deserted building on the Essex – Hertfordshire border. Rooks Farm was only a few miles away.

When the newspapers published their accounts of the McKays' dealings with M Croiset the police were doubly aggrieved, firstly by the implication that the supernatural might be more reliable than police detection and secondly by the influx of related information that now swamped them.

'Because of Croiset's intervention,' said Commander Guiver of the CID, 'we wasted thousands of man hours. Not through following up his ideas, but because of all the imitators.' In addition the McKays' telephone was again jammed by useless, cranky calls.

But on the evening of Thursday, 1 January, at 7.40 pm, M3 got through again.

Diane Dyer answered the untraceable STD phone call. M3 was unwilling to talk to her. 'I'll contact you later,' he said. 'Why don't we talk now?' asked Diane. 'You've gone too far,' said M3. 'It has gone too far now.' 'What's gone too far?' persisted Diane. But M3 rang off. A few minutes later he was back. He said: 'You tell them they've gone too far . . . They've gone to the police . . . They've got to get a million, a million pounds. I'll contact them tomorrow, and they've got to get it in fivers and tenners.' 'Where do you get a million pounds from?' demanded Diane. 'That's not my business,' said M3 and rang off. Nothing more would be heard from the kidnappers for nine days.

On 3 January Mrs Hosein and the children returned to Rooks Farm. Nine day later, when she found that Liley had stayed at the farm in her absence, there was a row – Arthur hit Else and she walked out with the children, going to live with a friend for a few days.

By now the police, the press and the family all tended to believe that Mrs McKay had indeed been kidnapped – but by whom? The ransom demand was so excessive as to appear absurd, and it was felt that the kidnapping could be an act of malicious revenge directed against the *News of the World* by someone who had been exposed in its pages or who disapproved of the paper's lurid and explicit stories. In the meantime Ian McKay (the McKays' son) and his wife Lesley had arrived in England from Australia. Displeased with the way things were going, he would none the less soon be instrumental in getting his family to treat the police approach with more respect.

The telephone in 20 Arthur Road rang constantly. There were always two policemen in the house as well as two or more outside, where the press and television crews still stuck to their posts, their numbers swelled by sightseers.

On Friday, 2 January a man telephoned offering to return Mrs McKay for £500 – the hand-over was to be effected on Platform 5 at Wimbledon railway station. DI Minors, in Mr McKay's hat and coat and carrying a suitcase containing £150 and some paper money, kept the appointment – as a result of which a nineteen-year-old waiter was arrested and later fined £100 for attempting to obtain money by deception.

On Saturday evening at the press conference the police were harassed by questions they were unable to answer. By then, although most senior officers were inclined (like the McKays and the press) to believe that Mrs McKay *had* been kidnapped, some were still suspicious of Alick McKay. So the house, the garden and the garage were searched again.

He was now allowed to read a statement and was photographed in his dressing-gown and pyjamas: this was arranged to give the impression that he was ill. The statement implied that Mrs McKay was also ill and needed certain drugs to maintain her health. It said: 'I ask whoever is holding Muriel to get in touch with me immediately and let me know exactly what they want. If it is money, then I must know how and where it can be exchanged for my wife. In order to be certain I am dealing with the person who is holding Muriel I must have positive proof that she is safe.' Six days later he appeared on television appealing for proof his wife was still alive.

During that week the police effort was largely dissipated in the necessary but useless investigation of phone calls and sightings all over Britain. There were more hoax ransom demands.

In following up one of them, DS Chalky Whyte, disguised as Diane Dyer in a wig and mini-skirt and carrying £5,000 in a suitcase, travelled on a 47 bus across London to a hand-over point at Stamford Hill, as instructed by an anonymous caller. Two other detectives, dressed as workmen and sitting separately, accompanied Whyte all the way, and the bus was shadowed by two Q cars – so closely that the bus-driver reported their suspect presence to the Stamford Hill police. In another hoax, the telephone caller was caught outside a public toilet in an East London underground station and jailed for three years.

Increasingly, the police were accused of doing too much – because of the status and connections of the McKays – and also of not doing enough. One lead they followed led them to Hertfordshire, to Bishop's Stortford, eight miles from Stocking Pelham. The billhook found in the hall was said by a Sheffield manufacturer to have been one of many sold and used in Hertfordshire. But the trail was apparently followed no further.

When twelve days had passed since Mrs McKay's disappearance, and nine days since the last communication from M3, the accumulated fears and frustrations of all those most closely concerned with the case were relieved for a while during the morning after Mr McKay's television appearance. A letter received by the editor of the *News of the World* on

Saturday, 10 January, complained that the writer had telephoned Arthur Road several times but the line had always been engaged; the million-pound ransom was now to be delivered in halves, at two collection points. Instructions would follow.

But again there was silence, this time for four days. Then on Wednesday, 14 January, M3 rang both the *News of the World* and Arthur Road, the latter call being taken by Alick McKay.

Both calls were brief, and neither contained any new information. 'You co-operate,' M3 told Mr McKay, 'and you'll get your madam back.' The tape-recording of this conversation, as of the others, was sent to an acoustics laboratory – the first time this had happened in a murder case. Voice-printing, then as now, was an uncertain but improving method of identification. M3's voice was deduced to be West Indian with American overtones.

The next and longest call to date, lasting thirty-five minutes, was answered on the afternoon of Monday, 19 January, again by Alick McKay, who was in an emotional state after the police had openly admitted their fears that Mrs McKay was dead, a fear already expressed by some of the family.

M3 asked for a first payment of half a million pounds and said, as before, that instructions would follow. Mr McKay demanded that some proof be sent that his wife was still alive. 'Bring a gun here and shoot me,' he cried, 'rather than make impossible demands! ... Nobody's got a million pounds ... and it's ridiculous to talk about it ... I can't give you what I haven't got!' 'If you don't co-operate,' said M3, 'you will be responsible for not seeing your wife again.' 'What have I done to deserve this?' 'I don't know,' said M3. 'But I'm very sorry we had to do this because your wife is such a nice person.' When Mr McKay offered to pay £20,000, M3 said: 'That's not enough ... It must be half a million, first delivery.' 'Take me instead!' said Mr McKay. M3 rang off.

By this time the press interest in the story had waned, as had the interfering telephone calls. After Mr McKay's outburst the police persuaded the family that Ian McKay should reply to all calls and try to establish some rapport with the kidnappers. He answered the next call, which came two days later on Wednesday, the gist of which was that the family should have no dealings with the police and that two letters from Mrs McKay were on the way.

These, and a ransom demand with detailed instructions, arrived on Thursday the 22nd inside an envelope postmarked Wood Green, a northern suburb parallel to Tottenham. The letters referred to Diane's television appeals (on 31 December and 2 January), one of which Mrs McKay had apparently *heard*. Her faltering hand wrote: 'I am deteriorating in health and spirit ... Excuse hand-writing, I'm blindfolded and cold ... Please keep the Police out of this and co-operate with the Gang ... The earlier you get the money the quicker I may come home ... Please keep Police out of it if you want to see me alive ... The gang is too large to fool ...'

The ransom demand told Mr McKay to put half a million pounds, in five and ten pound notes, into a black suitcase and to bring it, using his wife's Capri, to a telephone box on the corner of Church Street and Cambridge Road (the A10) in Edmonton at 10 pm on 1 February; there he would receive further instructions.

The following day, Friday, Ian McKay answered three calls from M3, who was anxious to confirm that the letters and the demand had been received and to repeat his threats. Ian's belligerent attitude and counter-demands for proof of his mother's well-being produced an excited volubility from the caller and two more letters from Mrs McKay, plus another ransom demand and three bits of material cut from the clothes she had worn on 29 December. They arrived in one envelope on Monday, 26 January.

The letters were hard to decipher: they were despairing, and, it seems, the last that she ever wrote – probably weeks earlier. 'If I could only be home . . . I can't believe this thing happened to me . . . It seems hopeless . . . You betrayed me by going to the Police and not co-operating with the M3 Gang . . . Love Muriel.'

The ransom note ended: 'Looking forward in settling our business on the 1st February at 10 pm as stated on last letter in a very discreet and honest way, and you and your children will be very happy to join Muriel McKay, and our organisation also will be happy to continue our job elsewhere in Australia . . . You see we don't like to make our customer happy, we like to keep them in suspense, in that way it is a gamble . . . We give the order and you *must* obey. M3.'

The police made their plans. The ransom was made up of £300 in real five-pound notes, provided by Mr McKay, and convincing forgeries in bundles with real notes at either end. An electronic homing device was attached to the suitcase.

It was decided that DI Minors would dress as a chauffeur while DS Roger Street posed as Ian McKay, with his arm in a sling in which a two-way radio would be concealed. 'I'll have to come in the Rolls,' the real Ian told M3 on 30 January, after several other conversations between the two. 'I don't know the north of London very well, and I've also injured my hand a bit and I want to bring the chauffeur.' 'Oh, I see,' said M3 doubtfully. But he raised no objections.

On Sunday, 1 February, the Hoseins left Rook Farm at about 6.30 pm in the Volvo, after entertaining some friends to lunch. At 9 pm the Rolls set off from 20 Arthur Road. Lying in wait about the A10 were over 150 policemen and over fifty unmarked police cars.

Roger Street entered the Church Street call-box soon after 10 am. The phone rang. 'Who's that?' said a voice. Street replied: 'Ian McKay. Who's that?' 'This is M3. These are your instructions . . . ' Street was directed to another call-box further up the A10, on the corner of Southbury Road. The Rolls set off again. In the second call-box M3 told Street that further instructions were written in a cigarette pack on the floor – a pack of Piccadilly cigarettes which was empty apart from directions to High Cross where the suitcase was to be left. M3 said that if Street then returned to the first call-box at Church Street, he would receive a call saying where Mrs McKay could be found.

The Rolls drove on north, past a petrol station in High Cross, until it came to a left turning leading to Dane End. Here, two paper flowers stuck in a bank marked the spot where the suitcase was to be abandoned. This was done – it was midnight. The Rolls headed back to London.

But the trap failed. So many policemen, variously disguised – some as Hell's Angels – drove up and down the road and lurked in ditches and hedges that the fantasy of catching the kidnappers turned into a farce. In the two and a half hours that followed the drop, almost five times as many police vehicles as civilian cars were noted by the CID men concealed across the road. Only ten of the latter were logged in that time.

One was a Volvo 144. In it, unknown to the police, were the Hoseins, who drove slowly past the suitcase to a transport café where they parked and debated their next move. Two policemen in plain clothes happened to pull in after them, giving themselves and the game away by their loud comments on the operation. The Hoseins fled back to Stocking Pelham, eight miles to the east. At the farm Else gave them a meal and they went to bed.

Early that morning Ian McKay was primed at 20 Arthur Road by DI Minors and DS Street on where they had gone and what they had done, in case M3 rang again. It seemed a hopeless prospect. Everyone in St Mary House was badly depressed.

But a day later, on 3 February, an indignant M3 telephoned, accusing Ian McKay of setting a trap – police cars, he said, had been seen around the pick-up spot. Ian tried to convince M3 that he knew nothing of this. The conversation was, as usual, a lengthy one. M3 said he would only talk in future to Alick McKay; he was now off, he said, to a meeting of the gang to discuss Mrs McKay's fate. 'I am going to plead for your mum,' said M3. 'I'm fond of her – your mum – you know . . . She reminds me of my mum.'

The day before this, and not until then, the Hertfordshire police became officially involved in the enquiry. At the same time some Flying Squad detectives, making routine investigations around the scene of the drop, asked a sergeant in the local police station if any West Indians lived in the neighbourhood. The sergeant replied in the negative, but added that he believed two Pakistanis were living in Stocking Pelham. The detectives went there and made further enquiries, establishing that the 'Pakistanis' were called Hosein and were not too popular. The sergeant, questioned again, said he knew about the Hoseins because of some motoring offences; they had two cars, a Morris Minor and a Volvo. On the detectives' return to London the information was filed away in the crime index.

The Hoseins, undeterred by the evident odds against them and blindly confident about the outcome of the game they were playing – and probably excited by the sight of the suitcase – telephoned Arthur Road twice on Thursday, 5 February, the day after Mrs McKay's birthday.

This time M3 spoke at length to Mr McKay. The £500,000, he said, was to be put in two suitcases and taken by Mr McKay and his daughter Diane in the Rolls to the Church Street call-box at 4 pm the following day.

Preparations were swiftly made, and more wisely after the overkill of the previous Sunday. In Wimbledon DI Minors shaved off his moustache in order to impersonate Mr McKay and donned a fur hat and a camel-haired coat; DC Joyce Armitage dressed herself in Diane's clothes. This time the Rolls had an unseen passenger. DS John Bland was hidden in the unlocked boot with an oxygen mask and two cylinders.

They set off at 3 pm on Friday, 6 February, half an hour after M3 made his final call. It came from the East End where Arthur Hosein was delivering trousers. Ian McKay answered the call.

'They're on their way,' he said. 'This is the last and final chance,' said M3. It was, for all concerned.

Minors was kept waiting at the Church Street call-box for forty-five minutes. When M3 rang, he was told to go to the East End of London to a call-box in Bethnal Green Road, six miles away.

Commander Guiver, supervising police manoeuvres from an ops room in Scotland Yard, moved some of his forces south. The Hoseins, who were in the area already, parked not far from the second call-box and at about 6 pm observed the Rolls arrive. They then moved on to make the call that Minors had awaited. He and Joyce Armitage were now told to leave the Rolls at Bethnal Green underground station and to take the Central Line tube to Epping, where they would receive another call on a booking-hall telephone. Unwilling to risk any trouble on a train crammed with commuters, the police took another risk.

After consulting the ops room, Minors drove the Rolls to Theydon Bois – the stop before Epping – and boarded a train there. He drove slowly so that the police forces could again be repositioned. When he and Joyce Armitage reached Theydon Bois underground station, DS Bland, who had been in the boot for over four hours, got out. With Minors carrying the suitcases, all three boarded a train bound for Epping, as did assorted policemen in various civilian disguises. Nothing happened on the short journey. All the policemen left the train and disappeared, except for Minors and Armitage who waited beside the suitcases in the hall.

Meanwhile, at about 7.15 pm, Arthur Hosein turned up on his own in a pub, the Raven, in Berden, Essex, a few miles from Rooks Farm.

It was 7.34 pm when the next and final telephone call was answered by the police waiting at Epping station. The call is believed to have been made by Nizam from a pay-phone in a house converted into flats in Bishop's Stortford.

Minors and Armitage were told to go by taxi to Bishop's Stortford, thirteen miles to the north on the A11 and eight miles east of Stocking Pelham. They were to leave the two suitcases beside a mini-van, UMH 587F, parked in the forecourt of Gates Garage. 'We deal with high-powered telescopic rifles,' said M3. 'Anyone trying to interfere with the cases, we will let them have it.'

A mini-cab driver, Robert Kelly, was sent by his office to pick up a 'Mr

McKay' at Epping station after that gentleman had telephoned for a cab. Kelly found that 'Mr McKay' was accompanied by a young woman and that they had two white suitcases with them. He put the cases in the boot. They set off, and had hardly gone two hundred yards when 'Mr McKay' told him to stop the car – whereupon a man (DS Bland) dashed out of the darkness, plunged into the back of the car and curled up on the floor at the female passenger's feet. Kelly, enquiring about this strange behaviour, was told: 'We're playing a joke on a friend.' He was also advised to ask no more questions and drive on. At Bishop's Stortford, he was told to drive past Gates Garage, do a U-turn and stop beside a hedge. Here the woman got out and the man in the back crawled out and disappeared into the hedge. The suitcases were then removed from the boot and deposited by a beige mini-van outside the garage. Minors and Armitage then returned in a mini-cab to Epping station, where they waited for a call that never came. Kelly also waited, as curious as he was apprehensive, and eventually drove the couple back to Theydon Bois to the Rolls. He was paid £5 for his five-hour mystery tour. He said later: 'There were times when I thought of leaving the car and running for it ... I didn't sleep properly for about three days puzzling over it, and I don't mind admitting I was frightened.'

Meanwhile DS Bland concealed by the hedge across the road from the garage, observed the slow approach of a dirty dark blue Volvo, XGO 994G. Its driver seemed to take an interest in the cases. Other cars passed. Then thirty minutes later the Volvo returned, went past the garage, did a U-turn, passed the cases again, and then – the driver having apparently been alarmed by people pouring out of a bingo-hall – drove on back into Bishop's Stortford.

Arthur, meanwhile, had been enjoying himself in the Raven, remaining there until 10 pm, chatting with an actor, Griffith Davies (who lived locally), and two girls. He boasted about the fact that he would soon be a millionaire. He was joined at the Raven by Nizam and after an earnest private conversation they both left.

The Volvo reappeared again outside the garage at 10.47 pm. This time there were two men inside. Again it slowed noticeably as it passed the cases. Bland and other policemen hidden about the garage cocked their guns. They were waiting for the kidnappers to pick up the cases and take them back to their hide-out, where Mrs McKay might be or might have been. But the Volvo moved away.

Then at 11 pm the trap was sprung – by the wrong mice.

A public-spirited couple, the Abbotts, seeing the cases lying unattended in the garage forecourt, became concerned. Mrs Abbott kept watch on the cases while her husband reported their find to the local police, who in due course visited the garage and removed the cases, taking them to the local police station where the duty officer was astounded to see what was in them – half a million pounds.

The operation was abandoned at 11.40 pm.

Back in Wimbledon, Minors and Armitage, sitting with the McKays in case M3 telephoned, were as depressed as the family – they had failed again. But about 3 am DCS Smith came to the house; he was smiling. Bland's sightings of the Volvo had tallied with other entries in the crime index. 'We think we may be on to them,' said Smith.

At 8 am on Saturday morning the police visited Rooks Farm in force; they saw that a Volvo was parked outside.

Mrs Else Hosein answered the door. DCS Smith said he was investigating the disappearance of some jewellery (Mrs McKay's). Arthur Hosein appeared and cheerfully invited the police inside, despite the flooded kitchen and living-room – the washing-machine had just burst. With Arthur's consent the house was searched. 'You can look where you like,' he said. 'I know nothing. I earn over £150 a week. I do not deal in stolen property.'

The police found some paper flowers made by Liley for the Hoseins' children. They found an exercise book whose pages had been used for Mrs McKay's letters, a billhook, a sawn-off shotgun, a tin of Elastoplast, a packet of Piccadilly cigarettes, and a paper flower on the floor of the Volvo. DS Bland identified Nizam as the man who had driven the Volvo the previous night.

The brothers were taken to London for further questioning by the police.

Arthur Hosein's fingerprints were the same as those that had been found on the ransom demands, the envelopes and the cigarette packet.

He and Nizam were charged on Tuesday, 10 February. Handwriting experts agreed that Arthur had probably written two ransom notes, and voice experts concluded that Nizam had made most of the phone calls. But neither brother said anything incriminating. Arthur seemed to exult in all the attention and hardly ever stopped talking. Nizam, on the other hand, tried to kill himself twice, and seemed constantly afraid and on the point of tears; he hardly spoke at all. There was little doubt that he was, and always had been dominated by his older brother. 'Arthur always gets me into trouble!' wailed Nizam.

They were remanded in custody – appearing seventeen times in Wimbledon magistrate's court – over a period of seven months.

For weeks, hundreds of policemen scoured Rooks Farm and the neighbourhood. But no pathologist was brought there, and not a trace of Mrs McKay was found.

The trial of Arthur and Nizamodeen Hosein, charged with murder, kidnapping and blackmail, among other indictments, began at the Old Bailey on Monday, 14 September 1970. The judge was Mr Justice Sebag Shaw; the Attorney-General, Sir Peter Rawlinson, led for the Crown; Arthur was defended by Barry Hudson, QC, and Nizam by Douglas Draycott, QC. The trial ended on 6 October.

On the last day all the McKays were present, as was Else Hosein and the brothers' father from Trinidad. Arthur wore a dark blue suit, made specially for the occasion. Both Hoseins were found guilty, the jury adding a recommendation for leniency in Nizam's case. Asked if he had anything to say, Arthur shouted: 'Injustice has not only been done, it has also been seen and heard by the gallery to have been done! They have seen the provocation of your lordship and they have seen your immense partiality!'

Both brothers were sentenced to life imprisonment on the murder charge. Arthur was also given twenty-five years on the other charges and Nizam fifteen years. Their appeals were dismissed.

St Mary House and Rooks Farm were both sold, the house for £30,000 and the farm for £18,500. Mrs Hosein obtained a divorce. *The Sun*'s circulation rapidly increased, passing the two million mark in February 1971. A special tie was made for those policemen who had worked on the case: dark blue, its crest was a black, red-eyed rook and two crossed billhooks.

Alick McKay remarried in 1973, his second wife being Beverley Hylton, the widow of the impresario, Jack Hylton. In 1976 he became Managing Director of News International, the company owning *The Sun*, the *News of the World*, *The Times* and *The Sunday Times*. He was knighted in 1977 and died of a heart attack, aged seventy-three, in January 1983.

What happened to Mrs McKay? The police believe she was murdered and disposed of at Rook's Farm. Some believe her dismembered body was fed to the pigs at the farm, seven Wessex Saddlebacks. When the police eventually raided the farm the boar and four of the sows had been sold and slaughtered – although this did not happen until 19 January. Two sows and their litters remained. But none of these, sold by Mrs Hosein on 26 February, was killed or examined for any traces of the drug cortisone, which Mrs McKay had been taking.

It would have been difficult to conceal her at the farm after Else Hosein, the children and Miss Hosein returned to Rooks Farm from Germany on 3 January. The police theory is that Mrs McKay was drugged, then shot before being dismembered.

There are two other possibilities: that Mrs McKay died of natural causes, of shock perhaps or hypothermia; and that she was never at Rooks Farm, being held captive and killed somewhere else.

A few of the police officers who worked on the case are of the opinion that a third man was involved, someone who was the brains behind the kidnap and then dropped out when Mrs McKay died.

None the less, the obvious suppositions remain the most likely explanation of what happened. There were reports of a gun being fired at the farm on or about New Year's Day and of a burning smell coming from the farm after 6 January, and of unidentified men and cars being seen near the farm. But only the Hoseins, who will remain in prison until 1984, at least, know what happened to Mrs McKay.

More Murders of the Black Museum
1835–1985

Gordon Honeycombe

Contents

The years given above refer to the year in which the named victim was killed, not to the year of the ensuing trial.

In cases of multiple murder, the victim named is the one for whose death the accused was charged and tried.

CHAPTER 1

James Greenacre and Sarah Gale
The Murder of Hannah Brown, 1836

The New Police, in their top hats and blue-belted coats, were but seven years old when they were faced with the kind of murderer whom their successors would often encounter over the next 150 years: a plausible and persuasive man, charming, amoral, avaricious, egocentric, self-deceiving, stupid and vain, with an urge to talk and write, to make his cleverness known, but not to acknowledge his evil and guilt – and to give himself away. For having killed and dismembered his victim, who but such a murderer would scatter the separate parts around London for anyone to find? The police involved efficiently pieced together the body, and the case. But, as would be the case in years to come, it was solved for them by the killer's crazy carelessness, by helpful witnesses and citizens, and also by sheer chance.

The Whigs, led by Lord Melbourne, were in power in 1836. William IV, aged 71, the third son of George III, was king. An old sea-captain and now Lord High Admiral, he was married to the much younger Queen Adelaide. Their children had all died in infancy, and the teenage Princess Victoria, only daughter of William's brother, the late Duke of Kent, was now heiress presumptive. William's seven-year reign was approaching its end. It had begun in 1830, when the Duke of Wellington attended the opening of the Manchester and Liverpool railway – an event of as much significance as his victory at the Battle of Waterloo, 15 years before. Times were changing: machines driven by steam were being dreamt of and made; trade unions were being formed; the Tolpuddle Martyrs, sentenced to transportation in 1834, had been pardoned; and in 1835 the word 'socialism' was coined. Winters were worse in those days: it was colder, and there was more snow.

It had been snowing in London since Christmas. On the afternoon of Wednesday, 28 December 1836, a labourer, Robert Bond, was trudging down the western side of Edgware Road near a toll-gate called Pineapple Gate, when he noticed a large bundle stowed behind an up-ended flagstone propped against a wall. The road was being widened thereabouts and new buildings built, so the snowy footpath was obstructed with piles of bricks and builders' supplies. No doubt on the look-out for something to filch, Bond examined the bundle, whose bulky contents were wrapped in a sack partly covered in snow and tightly parcelled with cord.

'I pulled the stone aside,' he said later. 'At first I thought it was meat, but on feeling it and pulling it about, I felt a hand.'

Alarmed, he summoned another labourer, James White, who was employed in the construction of Canterbury Villas near by. He cut the cords around the bundle and the twine at its neck. After removing various bloody bits of cloth and rag that enveloped what was hidden within, the two men exposed a headless torso with its folded arms tied across its breast.

Bond ran off to find a policeman and hailed PC Sam Pegler, who was on the other side of the road. On inspecting the workmen's grisly discovery, he sent Bond to fetch a wheelbarrow from the Paddington poorhouse, whither the remains, the rags and cords were conveyed about half-past two. It was not until then, when the torso was removed from the coarse, dirty sack and the arms untied, that the naked trunk, without legs, was seen to be that of a mature woman. The ragged bandages proved to be torn parts of a child's frock, a towel, and a shawl, some of which had been secured by small safety-pins, of a sort used on children's clothes.

PC Pegler, carefully examining these items, noticed that the sack smelled of mahogany dust, and that some mahogany shavings were lodged within – 'similar', he said later, 'to what a cabinet-maker would scrape off a mahogany table with a steel instrument'. He had also astutely observed, while in Edgware Road, that there had been no snow under the sack. It had evidently been dumped behind the flagstone on or before Christmas Day.

A post-mortem examination was carried out later that afternoon in the 'deadhouse', or mortuary, attached to the poorhouse, by a local surgeon, Gilbert Girdwood. He reported: 'The hand is a full woman's size, and dirty; there is no mark of needlework on the left forefinger; the mark of a ring exists on the left ring-finger . . . There are no marks of violence on the body . . . The thigh-bone on both sides . . . is sawn through . . . and then broken off.' The organs and the body were healthy, he said, and entirely drained of blood, which led him to suppose that the woman had been dismembered after death – after her throat was cut. She had eaten a meal and drunk some spirit shortly before her death, which must have been sudden. She was aged about 40, had been about 5' 6", and had never produced a baby. This latter fact was substantiated by what Girdwood called a 'remarkable peculiarity' – the dead woman had no uterus.

An inquest was held in a large room in the White Lion tavern in Edgware Road on the Saturday morning before a 'venerable' coroner, Mr Stirling, who was attended by his barrister son. Evidence was heard, and the proceedings observed by Inspector George Feltham, who had been put in charge of the case. He made copious notes. After retiring to the far end of the room for a discussion, the 12-man jury returned a verdict of 'wilful murder against some person or persons unknown'. *The Times* reporter noted 'a most singular coincidence'. Behind the coroner's chair was a full-length painting of an execution at Valencia in Spain, in which the executioner held up the decapitated head before the assembled multitude, who exhibited 'the greatest horror at the sight'.

A week after the inquest, the woman's head was found.

Matthias Rolfe, a lock-keeper on the Regent's Canal, was shutting the gates of the Ben Jonson lock at Stepney at 8.30 am after the passage of a coal barge, when the falls, or sluices, failed to close. Investigating the cause, he was horror-struck to see a human head, to which he assumed a body was attached. Summoning assistance and climbing down a ladder into the lock, his groping hand in the water informed him no body was attached. The head was a hideous sight, bloated and disfigured, with long dark slimy hair. It also lacked one eye.

Taken to the bonehouse in Stepney churchyard, it was examined by a surgeon, who deduced it was that of a woman aged between 40 and 45, and had been in the water for about five days. In fact, it had been in the freezing water of the lock for about two weeks. The jaw had been crushed and twisted by the gates. The right eye had evidently not been dislodged by them, but by a heavy blow that had caused severe bruising and swelling to the brow and cheek.

The canal superintendent, thinking that the head had been severed from the body of someone who had fallen into the water, had the locks emptied and the canal dragged – without result. Meanwhile, Inspector Feltham, hearing of the discovery while at the station-house in Hermitage St, Paddington, sought official permission to obtain the head from Stepney. Although he went to fetch it himself, accompanied by PC Pegler, it was not handed over until 10.00 pm on Sunday night. It seems the local police and parish authorities were reluctant to let it leave Stepney town hall, where the head now reposed and where a large crowd clamoured outside, wanting to view the find. It was wrapped up and taken to Paddington in a basket, as the torso, which had been buried on Thursday, was being exhumed.

On Monday morning Mr Girdwood, surrounded by medical men and parish officials in a poorhouse room, successfully joined the torso to the head. Both were closely examined for over two hours and Girdwood issued another report. He said:

> The head is that of a female, and of middle size; the skin is fair, and the hair is of a dirty brown colour, with a trace of grey here and there in it. The longest tresses are two feet long. The eyebrows are well marked, and, with the eyelashes, which are not very long, are of a dark brown colour. The eye is gray, with a shade of hazel in it. The frontal sinuses are strongly marked . . . The mouth is middle-sized, the lips large, more especially the upper, and prominent. The front teeth are good . . . Both ears are pierced for the ring. The left ear for that purpose has been pierced a second time, the original hole having apparently given way . . . The profile struck all of us as being very much that of the lower order of Irish.

A couple called Spencer, from the village of Willesden, were brought by PC Pegler to view the head. They thought it might be that of Sarah Ricketts, who had left the village to collect a legacy and never returned. But having seen the head they declared its features were not those of Mrs Ricketts and they went away.

Reports of missing women had proliferated since the finding of the trunk and arms. Now the one-eyed head excited even more interest and morbid curiosity. It was preserved in a jar of spirits in the Paddington poorhouse and shown to those whom the churchwardens deemed to have reasonable grounds for supposing it might belong to their mother, sister, daughter or wife. The trunk was reinterred, but not before the severed thigh-bones had been removed from their pelvic sockets, in case a match was required for the missing pair of legs. In the meantime, the Regent's Canal, which skirted northern London from the lower to the upper Thames, was dragged where it passed under Edgware Road. For it was surmised that the head and missing legs might have been dumped in the canal, not far from the trunk, and that the head's hair, becoming entangled in a barge's steering gear, might have been dragged all the way to Stepney lock. But although reports and rumours abounded over the rest of January, nothing relevant occurred until 2 February 1837.

A labourer, working in a bed of osiers (willows) in a marshy meadow beside Coldharbour Lane (between Brixton and Camberwell), discovered and opened a large sack. It contained a pair of bloodless legs, severed below the thighs. Each was bent backwards and tightly tied, like the trunk and arms, to make a compact bundle.

They and the sack were removed to a police station and examined the following day by the Paddington surgeon, Mr Girdwood, and by Inspector Feltham. The broken thigh-bones made a perfect fit, and Girdwood was now able to say that the dead woman had been 5' 6", that her legs, though large, had been well proportioned, with very small ankles, and that her feet, which were 'large and broad', had the appearance 'of having belonged to a person accustomed to walk barefoot'.

The piece of torn sack containing the legs was marked with capital letters: LEY and ERWELL. It was soon identified as being the property of a coal and corn merchant from Camberwell, Mr Moseley. He had many such sacks, but had no idea who might have so misused one, or when or how. However, the cords employed were the same as those used to tie up the Edgware sack, though that one was quite different from Mr Moseley's. All the evidence was taken to Paddington, and the legs interred in the churchyard with the trunk. The head remained on show.

Seven weeks passed without any further developments. It seemed as if the murdered woman's identity would never be known, nor the murderer found. Then, nearly three months after the torso was discovered in Edgware Road – on Monday, 20 March – an anxious man called William Gay expressed a wish to see the head. Reluctantly, the churchwarden concerned complied. Mr Gay stared at the terrible object with emotions that can scarcely now be imagined. But he said he was certain the head was that of his sister, Mrs Hannah Brown, aged 46, who had disappeared on Christmas Eve.

It was not, however, until the Thursday that Inspector Feltham heard Mr Gay's story and that of his sister's few friends. Within a few days he was able to make an arrest.

Hannah Gay was born in Norfolk in 1790, on a farm two miles from Norwich. Her father was a yeoman farmer. Apart from her brother William, she had two sisters, Mary and Rebecca; there were probably more. Aged 16 (and about a year after the Battle of Trafalgar), she went into service at Crimley Hall, the home of Lord Wodehouse. She was there for four years, after which she came to London and married a shoemaker, Thomas Brown. It was not a happy marriage. But after two years her husband sailed for the West Indies, in the expectation of claiming some property there as an inheritance. However, during the voyage he fell overboard, and was drowned. This would have been in about 1812, three years before Waterloo.

Over the next 20 years Mrs Brown worked for various respectable families as a cook, ending with a hatter, Mr Perring, in the Strand. During these years of hard kitchen work, being of frugal and temperate habits, she saved a good deal of money, some of which she then used to set herself up in business, buying a mangle and renting a kitchen basement at 45 Union Street (now Riding House Street), where she took in washing. The house, behind the Middlesex Hospital, belonged to a shoemaker, Mr Corney, and his wife who, like most shop-owners in London, took in lodgers paying a weekly rent. Here Mrs Brown lived quite comfortably, with a caged bird for company. Her savings consisted of a bag of sovereigns. But she also possessed some valuable pieces of jewellery: brooches, ear-rings and rings.

In appearance she was a tall, big woman – 5' 6" was tall for a woman in those days. She was 'very high chested', with strong large hands, long fingers, a high forehead and 'short, thickish teeth'. Her long brown hair was streaked with grey. She was very reserved, even secretive, and sometimes never spoke to anyone for several days.

About two years before her death her brother, William Gay, came to London, and Mrs Brown was instrumental in getting him a job as an assistant to a broker (a dealer in second-hand furniture etc), called Mrs Blanchard, whose business was at 10 Goodge Street, off Tottenham Court Road, a few hundred yards from his sister's lodging. He and his wife also lodged there. Brother and sister were very friendly at first, but after some disagreement Mrs Brown cold-shouldered her brother, even ignoring him when she visited Mrs Blanchard's shop.

The last time he saw her was on Thursday, 22 December, when she called on Mrs Blanchard to tell her that she was going to marry a Mr James Greenacre in Camberwell on Christmas Day. The banns had already been read at St Giles's Church. Greenacre waited for Mrs Brown outside the shop, and when she rejoined him, her brother William watched them walk away.

Her women friends would later say that she could not have known Greenacre for more than three months. Mrs Corney knew of the proposed marriage, and also that Mrs Brown had sold or disposed of her mangle and furniture prior to the marriage, saying that Mr Greenacre had told her to keep what she got for them as pocket money. The rest of her belongings she packed into some boxes before her departure.

None of her friends, or family, had met Greenacre before 22 December, apart from Evan Davis and his wife. They had known Hannah Brown for five years. He was a cabinet-maker, and they lived in Bartholomew Close, near Smithfield Market. About nine days before Christmas, Mrs Brown brought Greenacre to their house and introduced him as her beau. The two men went out to a pub, the Hand and Shears, for a drink, and Davis learned that Greenacre had an estate of about 1,000 acres at Hudson's Bay in Canada, from where he had returned about five weeks ago and whither he would return with his bride. The Davises then entertained the couple to supper in their home. Mr Davis would later say of Hannah Brown that she was 'remarkably sober, and a more social, agreeable woman did not exist'.

On 22 December, about 6.30 pm (after seeing Mrs Blanchard), Mrs Brown and her beau again visited the Davises' home. According to Mrs Davis, they 'appeared to be cordial, and like people who were about to be married'. She approved of the match, but advised Mrs Brown, when they were on their own, to be cautious about going abroad. The two men again went out to the pub for a drink, where Greenacre once more talked about Canada and America. After supper, while he and Mrs Brown sat on the sofa, he said:

> Well, we may as well tell you our intentions, as we aren't children. We intend to get married on Christmas Day, Sunday morning, at ten o'clock, at St Giles's Church. And as you've kindly offered us a dinner on that occasion, we accept of it. You, Mr Davis, will act as the father and give her away, and your daughter shall be bridesmaid. Meet us at Ramsay's public house near the church, and then we'll all go in together.

Mrs Brown also invited the Davises to visit her temporary new house in Camberwell, and Greenacre said they would have to excuse its appearance, as on account of their impending departure, it was in something of a mess.

Not long after this the happy couple left Bartholomew Close, with Mr Davis accompanying them a short distance down the road. Neither he, nor his wife and daughter, who were both called Hannah, ever saw Hannah Brown, alive, again.

She was seen by a friend, a plasterer's wife, Mrs Glass, at noon on Saturday, 24 December, when Mrs Brown called at the Glasses' house in Windmill Street to confirm that she would stay there that night, the night before her marriage. That afternoon, in Union Street, assisted by Greenacre, Mrs Brown put her trunk and boxes into a hackney-coach and told Mrs Corney she would return on the Monday, to pay the final instalment of her rent and remove the rest of her things. Mrs Corney said later: 'I received the key of Mrs Brown's room from one of my lodgers on the Tuesday . . . A week's rent was due on the Tuesday, and on the following day my husband and I went into the room and found nothing there but a bird cage.'

That night, about 11.00 pm, Mrs Davis was very surprised to be visited by Greenacre, without his future wife. She was even more taken aback when he asked her if Mrs Brown was there. Mrs Davis said later: 'I said No, and that I did not expect her. He then told me that he had broken off the match, having found out that Mrs Brown had no property, and it would not do to plunge themselves into poverty. I asked him to walk in, but he declined, and seemed agitated.'

Three days later, about 7.00 pm on Tuesday, 27 December, it was Mrs Blanchard's turn to receive a visit from Greenacre.

Unknown to him, William Gay, who was in the broker's shop at the time, listened to their conversation. He said later:

> I heard him tell my mistress that the wedding was broken off, and that he did not approve of [my sister's] character. He had heard that she had no property, and said he should take a shop in London instead of going to America . . . He said he went to the people, where they were to have dined on the Sunday, at 11 o'clock on the Saturday night to decline the invitation, because [Mrs Brown] and he had had a few words that night, and she had refused to go herself.

He could not, Greenacre said, in all justice, allow the Davises to be put to unnecessary trouble and expense. He said Mrs Brown had run him into debt in the Strand, and if she did that before the marriage she could do it after. He told Mrs Blanchard that the representations made by Mrs Brown and her friends concerning her property were incorrect, and that he had been deceived by her and them. Asked by Mrs Blanchard where Mrs Brown was now, he replied that she had, he believed, taken some lodgings in Camberwell, as it was too far to bring her boxes back to Union Street.

Mrs Blanchard, noticing that Gay was near by, then pointed at him and said: 'This is Mrs Brown's brother. You had better walk in.' Greenacre's expression altered. 'No, thank you. I'm in a hurry,' he said. 'I have an appointment to keep at ten o'clock.' He muttered something, bowed to Gay, and a few minutes later he left the shop.

When William Gay got home, he told his wife, Sarah, about this strange turn of events. Mrs Blanchard, in the meantime, expected that Mrs Brown would soon return to Union Street, to give her own account of what had happened. But when she failed to appear after a fortnight, Mrs Blanchard called on Mrs Corney, who had also seen or heard nothing of Mrs Brown since Christmas Eve. The room key had, however, been returned – given to a lodger by a boy, who had been given it by a man.

The two women concluded that the disagreement between Mrs Brown and her beau had been resolved, that they had married privately, and gone to America. Neither expected to see Mrs Brown again.

William Gay, however, was a worried man. The lurid newspaper reports of the finding of the torso, head and legs of a female in various suburbs had filled him with unease, especially the detailed description of the head. When he read that the legs had been found in Camberwell, where his sister's intended husband was believed to have dwelt, he decided, without telling his wife, to make casual enquiries as to her whereabouts.

To this end he visited her few known acquaintances and friends. It was a slow process as, like every shopman, he worked 12 hours every day: he was only free on Sundays. He walked, rather than travel by horse-drawn omnibus or hackney-cab. It transpired, however, that no one had had any news of his sister for more than two months, since Christmas. When the Davises provided him with Greenacre's alleged address in Camberwell, he decided to pursue his enquiries there.

He did so on Sunday, 12 March. There were people residing in 6 Carpenter's Place, but Greenacre was not among them; nor did they know where he lived. He made various enquiries locally, and hearing about a certain Mrs Gale and her child and other matters prejudicial to James Greenacre, Gay concluded at last that his sister had been murdered.

But before going to the police he was, it seems, determined to discover where Greenacre lived. For on Sunday, 19 March he returned to Camberwell, to talk further with the occupants of 6 Carpenter's Place (now Mission Place, off Peckham High Street).

Mrs Susan Dillon, who rented the house, told Gay that Greenacre had called there the previous Monday to collect his rent – he owned the house. He would not call tomorrow (the 20th), she said, but would send a representative. Gay suggested to Mrs Dillon that she should refuse to pay the rent to anyone other than Greenacre, thereby hoping that he would be forced to call and that his whereabouts, as well as himself, would be revealed. As it happened, Mrs Gale appeared on the Monday, and when no rent was forthcoming she agreed that Greenacre would call the following week.

But Gay had done enough. When he went home to Goodge Street, on the night of Sunday the 19th, he decided not only to tell his wife about his mysterious outings, but to go and look at the dead woman's head. 'Oh, heavens!' he said to Mrs Gay. 'I'm sure my poor sister has been murdered, and if the Lord spares my life until tomorrow I'll go and see her features!'

Why did he not do so sooner? Possibly it was a truth he was reluctant to face. But on the morning of Monday, 20 March he made his way to the Paddington poorhouse, and having explained his reasons for wanting to see the head to its guardian, a churchwarden, Mr Thornton, he was allowed a viewing. Battered and one-eyed, its long tresses floating in spirit, it must have presented a horrid sight. But William Gay was able at last to aver that the profile was that of his sister, whose left ear had been pierced a second time, after a fellow-servant had torn off an ear-ring.

Corroboration was needed, however, before the churchwarden was convinced – many people had wanted to see the head over the past two months – and Gay returned on the Wednesday night with two others (possibly the Davises) to confirm his conviction that the head was that of Hannah Brown. Even then the churchwarden had to be persuaded to pass on the outcome of all Mr Gay's patient enquiries to the police.

On Easter Sunday, 26 March, Inspector Feltham, accompanied by PC Pegler, went to Lambeth to arrest James Greenacre and Mrs Gale, arriving at 1 St Alban's Place about 10.45 pm. It is not known how he discovered the whereabouts of Greenacre's new abode, but *The Times* believed the information came from 'a gentleman connected with the family of one of his former wives'. Feltham later told the court:

The landlord told me that [Greenacre] was in bed in the front parlour. I knocked at the door, when a voice from within said: 'What do you want?' I said: 'Open the door,' and the prisoner said: 'Wait until I strike a light.' I heard him in the room, and having raised the latch I entered and saw him standing beside the bed. I told him I had a warrant against him for the wilful murder of Hannah Brown. I then asked him if he knew such a person, and he answered that he did not. I then said to him: 'Were you not both asked in church?' He replied: 'Yes, we were.' He was then putting on his stockings, and I again asked him if he knew where Hannah Brown was. He answered: 'No, I do not, and you have no right to ask me such questions.' I then said: 'I do not intend to question you any more, but mind, whatever else you may say I shall be bound to repeat elsewhere.' I was then in the act of searching the trousers of Greenacre when I saw the woman Gale in bed for the first time. I said: 'Hallo! What woman is that?' Greenacre said: 'She is a woman that sleeps with me.' Hearing something rattle in the bed, and observing the woman endeavouring to hide something, I said: 'What have you got there?' Gale handed me the watch now produced. I then said I must take her into custody also, and as she was dressing herself I searched her pockets, and took from them several pawnbrokers' duplicates, a pair of cornelian ear-rings and other articles . . . After Greenacre had put on his clothes, he observed that it was a cold night, and requested that he might be allowed to put on a greatcoat, which was in a box, corded up. I objected at first, but subsequently opened the box, and gave him the coat. As soon as Gale had dressed herself I desired a constable, who was with me, to go for a hackney coach, when Gale said: 'My little boy is sleeping in the next room, and he must go too' . . . Greenacre said it was lucky I had come so soon, as he should have sailed for America on the following day.

A later search of the room produced a quantity of female attire which was identified as having belonged to Mrs Brown. Other articles had been pawned near Walworth Road by Mrs Gale on 17 January. These included a pair of shoes, two veils and a handkerchief, all of which were wrapped in an old silk handkerchief stained with blood. Mrs Gale would later insist the cornelian ear-rings were hers.

She and Greenacre were taken to Hermitage Street police station, Paddington, and at 11.30 am were locked in separate cells. It seems that her little boy, George, aged 4, accompanied his mother. Soon after this, at 12.25, the police sergeant on duty happened to visit Greenacre and found him unconscious, 'black in the face' and lying on his back. He had tried to strangle himself, using a handkerchief as a noose. When he was revived he said: 'I don't thank you for this. You might as well have let me die. I wished to die . . . Damn the man that's afraid to die! I am not!' As a result of this suicide attempt he was put in a strait-jacket and closely guarded day and night.

Later on that day, Easter Monday, Feltham and Pegler were searching Greenacre's rooms in St Alban's Place when a man knocked at the door. He enquired whether Mr Greenacre was at home and was greatly surprised to learn that he was in custody, charged with murder. The man turned out to be Captain Henry Tanner, with whom Greenacre had planned to sail to America on the Tuesday. Tanner was taking his wife, but Mrs Gale was apparently not included. Greenacre said later: 'Three of us were to have gone to America together, Captain Tanner and his wife, who were entered in the ship's books as Mr and Mrs Henry Thomas, and I. I signed my name as James Thomas, and we paid £24 for our passage. This Tanner took out a cargo some time ago, and sold it, and came back after selling it.'

The Tanners had in fact paid £18 for the voyage and Greenacre £6 – which meant he would have travelled as a single man in the steerage, and not in a cabin. The departure for Quebec of the sailing-ship, the *Mediator*, was delayed, and four large chests were found in the hold in Greenacre's assumed name. Three were full of 'very valuable tools and implements of various descriptions'. The fourth belonged to Mrs Brown and contained household items and other belongings which she had packed away before her 'marriage'.

The *Mediator* sailed on 3 April, two days after Greenacre and Mrs Gale appeared in Marylebone magistrates' court. From there they were separately taken for their own safety to the New Prison and the House of Correction in Clerkenwell – so violent were the demonstrations against them in Marylebone High Street.

It was at the magistrates' court on 1 April, in a police court cell, that Greenacre began to confess, while talking to the constable, PC Brown, who was with him. Brown commented on all the people who had come to look at Greenacre. He agreed that the affair had caused much excitement, more than any that had occurred in London for some time. Many people, he added, seemed to think that 'it' had been carried to Edgware Road in a cart. 'What do you mean?' enquired PC Brown. 'The body?' 'Yes,' said Greenacre. 'It wasn't moved in a cart, but in a cab.' After cautioning him, Brown asked: 'Was it on the same night that it happened?' 'No,' the prisoner replied, and continued: 'I believe it was between 2 and 3 o'clock . . . There has been a great deal of mystery about the head, and people appear to run away with the idea it was thrown into the tunnel at Maida Hill . . . There is, in fact, no proof to the contrary.' PC Brown warned the prisoner again. He retorted: 'Oh, never mind that! All I've said to you would go for nothing.'

From then on Greenacre became loquacious, and when not talking was writing. His hands, it seems, were not confined by the strait-jacket all the time.

After hearing the evidence against him for the first time in the magistrates' court, he made a long and voluntary statement, which he signed. He said:

On the Saturday night before Christmas Day, Mrs Brown came down to my house, rather fresh from drinking, having in the course of the morning treated the coachman, and insisted upon having some more rum, a quantity of which she had had with her tea. I then thought it a favourable opportunity to press upon her for the state of her circumstances. She was very reluctant to give me any answer, and I told her she had often dropped insinuations [that] she could command at any time £300 or £400. I told her I had made some inquiry about her character, and had ascertained that she had been to Smith's tally-shop in Long Acre, and tried to procure silk gowns in my name. She put on a feigned laugh, and retaliated by saying she thought I had been deceiving her with respect to my property ... During this conversation she was reeling backwards and forwards in her chair ... I put my foot to the chair, and she fell back with great violence against a chump of wood that I had been using. This alarmed me very much, and I went round the table and took her by the hand ... But she appeared entirely to be gone. It is impossible to give a description of my feelings at the time; and in the state of excitement I was in I unfortunately determined on putting her away ... I thought it might be more safe that way than I gave an alarm of what had occurred.

He insisted that Mrs Gale, who was not in the house, had no knowledge of the accident or what he did thereafter. He had sent her to another lodging before Mrs Brown's arrival and did not see her, he said, for several days. When Mrs Gale returned to Carpenter's Place, he told her that as Mrs Brown had left all her boxes and other things behind, they would pledge all they could. 'The whole of the articles pawned,' he said, 'fetched only £3.' He added that Mrs Brown had eleven sovereigns on her and a few shillings in silver.

Mrs Gale stated that she was not at Camberwell at the time of Mrs Brown's demise. It was later proved in court that she had lodged, without giving her name, with a Mr and Mrs Wignell in Portland Street, off Walworth Road, on 22 December. She brought her little boy with her. Greenacre visited her on the morning of the 23rd, as he did on the 24th, and that night she went out between 9.00 and 10.00. She and Greenacre dined on 'a scrag of mutton and turnips' on Christmas Day, when he was with her between 2.00 and 9.00 pm. The following night she was away all night, leaving her child locked up in her room. He was heard calling 'Mother! Mother!' On Thursday, 29 December, the day after the torso was discovered in Edgware Road, Mrs Gale paid her rent and went away, taking the child. She returned the following day. On Sunday, 1 January, while she and Greenacre were in her room, Mr Wignell read aloud to his wife a newspaper account about the finding of the torso. On the Monday morning, Greenacre, who had spent the night with Mrs Gale, left the house with her, helping her with her things.

Neighbours noticed that the windows of 6 Carpenter's Place were shuttered on Christmas Day and remained so for three days. They saw Mrs Gale (whom they knew as Mrs Greenacre) leave the house at 7.00 pm on Boxing Day (Monday) with 'her bonnet carelessly on'. Her child was crying, and she picked him up, saying: 'You naughty cross thing!' Earlier that evening, Frances Andrews, who lived at No. 11, called on Mrs Gale to give little George a piece of plum pudding. She called again on the evening of the 28th, when Greenacre offered her a glass of whisky. Before Christmas, Mrs Gale had told Mrs Andrews that a lady, a friend of Greenacre, was coming to stay for a few days. No one seems to have seen Mrs Brown, and her boxes, arrive. And none was aware that Mrs Gale had temporarily moved out of the shuttered house.

A week or so after Christmas, an out-of-work shoemaker called Chisholm was walking along a lane in Camberwell when he was tapped on the shoulder by Greenacre and asked if he wanted a job – which was to assist in moving some goods. A boy was co-opted as well. All three went to Carpenter's Place. Chisholm said later: 'A number of boxes were placed all ready, tied up. Greenacre placed the boxes on a truck, together with some articles of furniture, and having secured them all together with ropes, he appeared very much agitated, and said: "Now all's right, I'm going to leave the country." A woman with a plaid cloak on [Mrs Gale] was standing by, and said to Greenacre: "Now you have done for yourself."'

Chisholm and the boy, who were paid 6d and 3d, pulled the truck to the Elephant and Castle, to a pawnbroker's shop. Greenacre and Gale accompanied them. Soon after this, the house at 6 Carpenter's Place was advertised as being *To Let*. Callers noticed that it had been fumigated with brimstone and that the fireplace had been boarded up. Mrs Dillon moved in.

It seems evident from all this that Mrs Gale was not as innocent as she claimed. She may not have been in the house when Hannah Brown was killed and dismembered. But she clearly helped Greenacre dispose of Mrs Brown's possessions and probably cleaned the house before it was let.

In ascertaining these matters the police, and *The Times*, also pieced together, partly from Greenacre himself, an account of his life, previous marriages, and career. He also wrote his own high-flown account, which was published by a paper on 9 April.

James Greenacre, at the time of his trial, was 51. He was born in 1785 – in Norfolk, like Hannah Brown; and his father, like hers, was a farmer. His birthplace was a hamlet called West Winch, two miles south of King's Lynn, and he was one of seven children. When his father died, about 1807, his mother remarried a local farmer called Old Towler, who had two young children of his own. It was about then, when Greenacre was 23, that he was sent on spec to a grocer in King's Lynn. But after four months he felt he had learned all he could and asked his parents to send him to London, where he expected to learn more, and more quickly, and be a success. They gave him 20 guineas, part of which was for the purchase of an apprenticeship. By somehow contriving to see the manuscript of *Times*' job vacancies before they were printed, he obtained work with a grocer at Tower Hill. There he remained for three years, during which he saved £45, and thence moved to a shop in Oxford Street. When Greenacre was 19, Old Towler helped to set his stepson up in business by buying a grocer's shop and putting him in charge. He also sent his daughter Betsy Towler, aged 16, to London to act as Greenacre's housekeeper. This was a mistake, as Greenacre tried by various means to seduce her and then to rape her. Betsy succeeded in fighting him off and fled back home. Her father turfed Greenacre out of the shop, although the young man tried to prevent this by barricading himself inside.

Soon after this Greenacre married the 18-year-old daughter of a publican,

Charles Ware, in Woolwich, where he opened his own grocer's shop. She had two children, and then died 'of a putrid, sore throat'. His second wife was an Essex farmer's daughter, and she also died, 'of brain fever', after bearing two children. Despite these domestic tragedies, his business thrived. For in 1814, aged 29, he took over a more prestigious establishment in the Borough (Southwark) and married Jane Simmonds of Bermondsey. She bore him seven children, of whom two survived – as did three from his first two marriages. For nearly 20 years he lived and prospered in the Borough, becoming a very well-known local tradesman. He wrote of himself: 'I have always abhorred a public-house and the babble of drunken men: the society of my books, my wife and children, have always been to me the greatest source of delight that my mind could possibly enjoy ... My apprentices and servants have always manifested much pleasure in their situations ... As a friend I can give the most incontrovertible testimony.' So what went wrong?

In 1833, after committing some offence against the excise laws, he absconded to America, taking his eldest son, James, aged 14, with him, and leaving his third wife and other children in London to await his summons to join him. Three weeks after his departure, however, she died of cholera. He stayed in New York for two years. Later he complained that in this period he was swindled and cheated out of nearly all the property he took with him by pretended friends. He also said he was imprisoned in New York for libel. On his release, he went with his son to Boston and married for a fourth time. But before long he was arrested again for a similar offence and jailed once again in New York. Clearly, he was incautious about expressing his grievances in letters to individuals, to officials and to the press. According to him, this arrest was so sudden – it occurred in the street – that he saw neither his wife nor his son again before he returned to London. This may have been of his own choosing. Or he may have been deported.

Back in London (in 1835), he waged an epistolary war against his creditors, who had declared him bankrupt, and against his third wife's relatives, who had disposed of the property left to him when she died. He succeeded in obtaining possession of 6 Carpenter's Place, and the house next door, and embarked on the manufacture of what he called 'amalgamated candy', made of cinnamon, peppermint, lemon and cloves. The secret ingredient was a herb which he had discovered while in America. Medicinal, the candy was advertised as a cure for coughs, colds, sore throats, hoarseness, asthma, and shortness of breath. He also invented and patented a washing-machine. At some point he met Sarah Gale, and she and her child moved in with him in October 1835. Her maiden name was Sarah Farr.

It seems she had 'married' more than once, and was living with a man called Thomas Gale, near the Elephant and Castle, when on 30 January 1833 she gave birth to a boy, who was named George. While living with Greenacre she bore another baby boy, at about 5.00 am on 17 February 1836. But the doctor who attended her never saw the infant after that day. Three days after the birth she was up and well – but the baby had disappeared. A day later, a male baby was found buried under a clod of grass by a ditch near Bermondsey. It was said by a doctor to have been dead for about 24 hours and to have been three days old when it died. Accused by a neighbour of murdering the child, Mrs Gale retorted that it was alive and well and being cared for by a friend in the Old Kent Road. Greenacre, when questioned, told one person that the baby was with a friend in Edgware Road. He told another the infant was dead.

It is not known how or when he met Mrs Brown. But the introduction, perhaps in September 1836, was made by a carpenter called Ward, who lived in Chenies Mews, off Tottenham Court Road. Ward is also described in *The Times* as a cabinet-maker and mangle-maker. By the time the police began their investigation, he had disappeared. Perhaps Mrs Brown was having her mangle repaired or buying a new one when Greenacre met her at the carpenter's shop, where he, perhaps, was having a discussion about his washing-machine with Ward – who may have constructed it. Somehow he learned that she had money, as well as jewellery, and determined, by offering her marriage, to rob her of all her possessions, and her life.

Why? He probably needed extra finance for his business ventures, and to restore a life-style he had lost. He would also have required money for the voyage to America and to set himself up in business once again, selling candy and washing-machines. Mrs Brown's death was clearly calculated, and not an accident, as he claimed.

He and Sarah Gale appeared for the third time before the magistrates on Wednesday, 5 April 1837, in the unusual setting of a large room in the Governor's residence in the New Prison, Clerkenwell. Gale was brought there by coach. Very pale, she trembled from head to foot when she alighted, followed by her child, who held her hand and smiled as he tripped along.

She and Greenacre sat on a bench before the magistrates, with a sturdy policeman between them. Evidence given by witnesses at the previous hearings was read, as were the statements of the accused. Greenacre proposed a minor correction and cheerfully rose to sign his statement. Gale was fearful of signing hers. 'Sign! Sign!' Greenacre urged her. 'Don't frighten yourself at what people say about your going to be hanged, and all that sort of stuff!'

The question of whether the trial should be postponed until the next session was debated. But Mr Price, Greenacre's counsel, urged on the prisoner's behalf that it should take place without delay. After being committed for trial the following week, both the accused were removed in a prison van to Newgate Prison, which was situated at the western end of Newgate Street, not far from St Paul's and near the street known as Old Bailey. In existence since the reign of Henry I (1100–35), the prison was rebuilt several times, having been destroyed in the Great Fire of London in 1666 and again in the No Popery riots of 1780. The Central Criminal Court, established in 1834, was next door.

Here the trial of James Greenacre and Sarah Gale began on Monday, 10 April 1837 at 10.00 am. The streets outside, like the court, were packed. Greenacre, dressed in a blue coat, fancy waistcoat and black stock, was remarkably self-possessed throughout the proceedings; Gale sat with lowered head and eyes. Lord Chief Justice Tindal headed the trio of judges, the other two being Mr Justice Coleridge and Mr Justice Coltman. The Recorder of

London sat with them. Mr Adolphus appeared for the prosecution, assisted by Mr Clarkson and Mr William Henry Bodkin. The prisoners, who were allowed to sit, were defended by Mr Price and Mr Payne.

The indictment against Greenacre contained three lengthy counts, in which he was accused of killing Mrs Brown by various means and dismembering her. This was called 'mutilation' by the court. Mrs Gale was charged with feloniously 'aiding, assisting and counselling' him in the murder. They both pleaded 'Not guilty'.

After outlining the prosecution's case, Mr Adolphus remarked: 'Happily but few instances have occurred in this country of similar atrocity [involving dismemberment].' These few he then listed – the case 'of Catherine Hayes about 100 years ago' who murdered her husband; of a Frenchman named Bardell, who murdered his landlady 70 years ago; of the murder of Mr Paas, of Holborn, by a man named Cook. The Bardell case was remarkably similar, said Mr Adolphus, in that the Frenchman had also made a statement saying that after a row, he had pushed his landlady's chair and caused her to fall backwards and fracture her skull. Mr Adolphus commented that Greenacre and Gale 'would have one advantage which persons in their situation were, until lately, deprived of – the advantage of having a speech from counsel in their favour'. This would, however, he felt sure, be largely unsupported by evidence. Twenty-seven witnesses were called by the prosecution and proceedings ended at 8.00 pm. The jury were lodged overnight in a nearby coffee-house.

On the second day of the trial the statements made by Greenacre and Gale before the magistrates were read in full. They were both found guilty. But such was the riotous behaviour of the mob outside the court that sentence was not passed, as was then the custom, on the last day of the sessions, but in secret on the following afternoon by the red-robed Recorder. It was prefaced by a legal dispute about the wording of the indictment, engineered by Mr Payne, and by Greenacre's attempt to make a speech in his defence. In it he complained about press prejudice and false evidence – 'such as might be collected in any pothouse or ginshop' – and said: 'It is contrary to reason and common sense to suppose that I should have meditated the death of the woman . . . because of the property she had. If that had been my object, I could have had it all on the next morning, when our marriage was to have taken place, and then it would have been mine. Where, then, was my motive for the murdering of her? It is –'

The Recorder interrupted, saying that this should have been urged by Greenacre's counsel during the trial and should be directed now to the Secretary of State. Greenacre then reaffirmed Mrs Gale's innocence, concluding: 'I deem it a religious duty to exculpate her from having any concern in this unfortunate affair. I have no more to say.'

He stood as sentence of death was passed, and while Mrs Gale sat on a chair at the rear of the dock. He stood for some time, as the Recorder had much to say and was much moved by his own strongly worded sentiments and observations. He said: 'The appalling details of your dreadful case . . . will long live in the memory and . . . in the execration of mankind, and generations yet to come will shudder at your guilt. You have, indeed, required for yourself a revolting celebrity, an odious notoriety in the annals of cruelty and crime.' The Recorder went on to refer to 'the amputated limbs and the dis-severed body', to 'the mutilated trunk and mangled remains'. He said: 'The still warm corpse was barbarously mutilated and mangled by you, in the hope that the eye of man would not detect your guilt. But the eye of God was upon you!' He conceded that he was addressing 'an individual not devoid of education, of reasoning faculties, and strength of mind', and attempted to re-vive 'the last remaining sparks of virtue and religion' in Greenacre's heart by reading a long passage about repentance from 'an excellent work' – *The Analogy of Religion, Natural and Revealed*.

Greenacre listened without moving, and unmoved, even when the death sentence was eventually passed. He was led to the back of the dock as Mrs Gale was brought forward to be sentenced, in fewer words. 'Perhaps you considered that what had been done could not be undone,' said the Re-corder, concluding: 'This Court do adjudge that you be transported beyond the sea to such place as His Majesty, with the advice of the Privy Council, shall direct and appoint, for the term of your natural life.'

That night Greenacre, back in the prison ward at Newgate, and confined in a 'strait-waistcoat' every night when he went to bed in case he tried again to kill himself, saw, at his request, an alderman he had known when he lived in social affluence in Southwark. He now gave a different version of the man-ner of Mrs Brown's death, in order, it seems, to remove any aspect of premeditation and hopefully have his sentence reduced to transportation for life. He told the alderman that while Mrs Brown was washing up the tea-things she admitted she had deceived him about the property she possessed, and laughed. Whereupon he had lost his temper, and struck her with a piece of wood used as a rolling-pin, which was originally a roller for silk – 'a sort of swinging side blow on the right eye'. She fell insensible to the floor and he fled from the house for an hour. On his return he deemed her to be dead, and decided then and there to dismember her and dispose of the parts. He attri-buted the fact that the neighbours had heard no sounds of altercation to their absence at market, it being Christmas Eve, and accounted for the absence of blood-stains on the floor when he cut up the body by saying that he had soaked up the blood with a flannel and thrown it in the privy.

Advised to make a detailed statement to this effect, for forwarding to the Home Secretary, Lord John Russell, Greenacre spent the whole of Thursday in writing, and in reading what he had written to the two turnkeys (warders) who closely observed him day and night. Frequently dissatisfied with his composition, he would tear it up and thrust it into a fire in the room, exclaiming: 'No, that won't do!' In so doing he used up a quire of foolscap.

Cheerful and loquacious, he continued to say that Mrs Gale knew nothing of Mrs Brown's death and dismemberment – and so did she. When she re-turned to his house, she said, and asked about all the boxes, he told her that Mrs Brown had left them there and wondered when she would retrieve them.

Greenacre completed his statement on Thursday morning and handed it to his counsel, Mr Price. He was also visited by the Sheriff and Under-Sheriff, but (said *The Times*) he refused to see 'a well-meaning and pious gentleman, who has been for some years in the habit of visiting capital convicts in the prison for the purpose of affording them religious consolation'. Greenacre said he had always despised 'religious cant'. However, he did not object to the prison chaplain's visits, although he remarked: 'The reverend gentleman might spare himself the trouble of advice and admonition, as I want no priest to tell me how to die.' *The Times* commented: 'How long this feeling will sustain him remains to be seen; but it would appear from his occasional abstracted and meditating moods, and the seeming attention which he bestows upon the Bible with which he is provided . . . that the light of religion may yet break in upon his mind.'

In his latest statement, Greenacre now claimed that after striking Mrs Brown with the roller on Christmas Eve he did not leave the house but paced up and down the room, 'not knowing how to act'. On realising she was dead, he considered how to dispose of the body and decided eventually to cut her up. This he did, he now said, with a dinner knife. He did not, however, as stated in a morning paper, hold the severed neck over a pail 'until the blood had ceased to flow'. He wrapped the head in a silk handkerchief and then put it in a canvas bag. Uncertain about what to do with it at first, he resolved at last 'to hide it in some distant place'. So he left the house, locked the door, and walked to the Elephant and Castle, with the head under his arm. From there he travelled by omnibus to Mile End, with the head in his lap, and then walked down to the Ben Jonson lock where, unwrapping the head, he 'shot it into the Stepney lock'. On his way back to Camberwell, he called on the Davises in Bartholomew Close. He spent the night in his own home – with the headless corpse. On the morning of Christmas Day, a Sunday, he cut off the legs, and carried them on his back to Coldharbour Lane, where he dumped them in the osier bed. After returning to Carpenter's Place, he put the torso and arms in a sack and tied it up, and on leaving the house with the sack on his back he hitched a lift with a carter as far as the Elephant and Castle, from where he and his bulky parcel were taken by cab to Edgware Road. Unobserved, he shoved the sack behind the flagstone near the Pineapple Gate.

He said later he chose to get rid of the dismembered body by day because he was less likely to be noticed by the police: carrying a large sack at night would look much more suspicious. Why he ventured as far as Stepney and Edgware Road – both were about seven miles from Camberwell – and why he chose these particular locations, remains as much a mystery as his carelessness about concealment. He could have buried his parcels, or, like the head, thrown them, weighted, into a pond or in the river. Asked what he had done with the roller and the silk handkerchief, he said he had burnt them with those of his clothes that were stained with blood; and that after washing out any stains on the floor, he went out to dine that afternoon with Mrs Gale in Walworth.

Further evidence of Greenacre's iniquity was published by *The Times* on 17 April, when it was revealed that a month after the death and dismemberment of Hannah Brown, Greenacre had advertised on 23 January on the front page of *The Times* as follows: 'Wanted, a partner, who can command £300, to join the advertiser in a patent to bring forward a new-invented machine, of great public benefit, that is certain of realizing an ample reward. Applications, by letter only, post-paid, for JG, at Mr Bishop's, No. 1 Tudor Place, Tottenham Court Rd.'

Perhaps it was through some similar device that he met Mrs Brown. For among the replies he received to this ad was one, *The Times* said, from 'a female of great respectability', who 'indiscreetly wrote to him on the subject, and afterwards had two or three interviews with him'.

He responded to this woman's initial letter with an unabashed offer of marriage. Writing on 4 February (the day of the inquest on the reunited pieces of Hannah Brown), he said:

> It is my wish to meet with a female companion, with a small capital, one with whom a mutual and a tender attachment might be formed, who would share with me in those advantageous pecuniary prospects which are now before me . . . No man can have a greater aversion than myself to advertising for a wife; nevertheless, this advertisement was intended to give an opportunity, by which I might make propositions of an honourable nature to one whom I might prefer as a companion for life . . . I am a widower 38 years of age, without any encumbrance, and am in the possession of a small income arising from the rent of some houses . . . Excuse the dissimulation by which I have obtained an introduction to you, and believe that my present proposal is dictated by every honourable and affectionate feeling towards you. I am, dear Madam, yours most sincerely, James Greenacre.

Perhaps the temporary success of this or other ventures caused him to defer his departure for America to the end of March. But *The Times* was censorious, exclaiming that 'at the very moment he wrote that letter, not only was he cohabiting with his fellow-convict, Sarah Gale, but was then, and is now, a married man, having left his fourth wife, a young woman of considerable personal attractions, behind him in America'. The newspaper had also learned that she, and his son by his first wife, were 'in a state of distress' in New York, where Greenacre had abandoned them.

The Times also reported two conversations which Greenacre had had in Newgate Prison with Alderman Humphrey, in which he denied having a wife in America. He said: 'A wife! No such thing! I never was married there. It is true I knew a woman called Martin there, and was as intimate with her as if I was her husband, and I intended to marry her, but I never did . . . There were two sisters of the house, and I was to have married one of them. But nobody knew anything about it.' Asked whether, as was rumoured, he was one of the Cato Street conspirators, who in 1820 had plotted to murder most of the Government at a banquet and then set fire to London, Greenacre replied: 'I never had anything to do with it. But I must be great food for the newspapers. Their business is to find out everything against me, and then to invent. I hope that report will be contradicted. It is quite absurd.'

He denied that Mrs Gale's baby had been murdered, and said that the silk roller, with which he struck Mrs Brown, belonged to her: 'It was in her trunk. It did not belong to me.' He also denied that she was killed upstairs, where some suspicious stains had been found. He said: 'It is true she went upstairs to make the bed in the back room, while I was lighting the fire, but she soon came down again.' Asked how no blood splashed over the walls and floor, he replied: 'I took care to let all the blood out of the throat before I cut off the head.' 'Into what did you let it flow?' Humphrey enquired. Greenacre answered: 'Into a brown pan, and I wiped up what was spilled with two flannel cloths, which I threw, blood and all, into the privy . . . There are two cesspools, and it is impossible they could be found.' He added: 'If I'm going to be hanged, I wish they'd hang me at once. I wish they'd hang me tomorrow.'

Hoping somehow, perhaps, to realise his wish and forestall the hangman, he wrote to Lord John Russell, ten days after he was sentenced to death, saying:

> Could I, my Lord, be relieved from the torture of the strait-jacket, and be permitted to recline upon my mattress occasionally, by day, instead of being compelled to sit in close company with two talkative keepers, I could derive that consolation of self-communion and secret prayer which the Bible so often enjoins us to strive for, by pouring out our sorrows before God in prayer, and by watering our pillows and our couches with our tears . . . I have, my Lord, another complaint to make of cruel, hard, and unfair usage . . . I mean, my Lord, the cruel falsehoods, the fabricated reports, and the perverted statements of newspaper advertisements. It is these falsehoods that make my death terrible indeed . . . PS. Should you feel disposed to permit me more liberty to pursue my devotions, there is, indeed, my Lord, no danger in me abusing that liberty.

Nothing, it seems, was done about Greenacre's request. The sheriffs reported to the Home Office that 'the strait-waistcoat which is placed upon Greenacre does not confine him to any uneasy position, it being so loose as to enable him partially to move his hands and arms'.

The order for his execution was communicated by the prison chaplain, Dr Cotton, and the Governor, Mr Cope, on 26 April. Greenacre was writing at a table in his room. On seeing the chaplain with a paper in his hand, to which a black seal was attached, he rose to his feet – strait-jacketed still, it would seem. As reported in *The Times*, the chaplain formally announced: 'The Recorder has made his report to the King, and I am sorry to inform you that it is unfavourable to you.' 'It cannot be helped,' Greenacre said. 'I am sacrificed through prejudice and falsehood.' Dr Cotton expressed the hope that the condemned man would occupy the time that was left to him 'in earnest and hearty prayer'. Greenacre replied: 'I have a confidence in the mercy of God, and will trust to that. I care not a pin for death. But I abhor the thought of going out of the world branded as a wilful murderer. I committed no murder.' On being handed a book of prayer, he said: 'I can't attend to those long prayers. I must look to inward prayer for relief. All prayers from the heart are short.' Said Dr Cotton: 'The blood of the unfortunate woman is upon your hands. For it was by your means she came by her death.' 'Yes,' said Greenacre. 'But it might as well be said that I murdered her, if a cart-wheel passed over her and I afterwards committed the mutilation. I have fallen a sacrifice to prejudice and the press.'

Dr Cotton aroused Greenacre's displeasure after the service in the prison chapel on Sunday, 30 April. Greenacre was now lodged in the condemned cell. He said: 'Sir – I do not know whether it was your duty to make the allusions you did in your sermon today. But whether your duty or not, you treated me as though I was a murderer.' Dr Cotton replied: 'My dear sir, you stand a convicted murderer by the verdict of a jury of your country, and as such I must speak of you.' 'But you said a good deal of the necessity of a confession,' Greenacre protested. 'Why need you have done that? You know I have already confessed. What can I say more?' To which the chaplain said: 'I am aware you have made statements more than once. All that is required is that there should be no mental reservation.' 'But sir,' retorted Greenacre, 'you spoke of me as a murderer! I have never acknowledged myself as such. Why should I – when I know to the contrary? . . . I consider that you made observations which might have been spared.' He was also upset when the authorities refused to allow him to see Mrs Gale before he died.

James Greenacre was hanged outside Newgate Prison at 8.00 am on Tuesday, 2 May, by which time some 20,000 persons had crammed the Old Bailey and every adjacent street, from Ludgate Hill to Smithfield Market.

They began gathering outside the prison well before midnight, where a sort of fair was held: piemen sold penny sandwiches and Greenacre tarts; ballad-mongers touted their wares; some hawkers sold pictures and life stories about Greenacre and Sarah Gale, as well as fake confessions. Others distributed religious tracts; and pickpockets plied their trade. Coffee-shops and pubs were open; first-floor rooms opposite the scaffold could be hired for as much as £12; windows were thronged. Every new activity or event was greeted with excited cheers and whistles, hisses and boos, even when women fainted or boys were trampled underfoot. Despite barriers and policemen, the crush and riotous incidents increased. At 4.00 am workmen emerged from the Debtors' Gate of the prison to erect the scaffold, a process that was hailed at every step by a cacophonous crescendo of sound, culminating in the executioner's appearance to fix the noose to the overhead beam. At 7.45 the bell of St Sepulchre's Church began to toll. Said *The Times*: 'From the moment that signal of the approaching execution was heard, the screams and groans occasioned by the pressure from the two extremities of the crowd upon the centre was perfectly appalling.' A few minutes before Greenacre appeared there was a general cry of 'Hats off!' and every man uncovered his head.

Within Newgate the condemned man had slept little, getting up and dressing himself at 3.45 am, after which he wrote several letters and conversed with the turnkeys. The previous night he had refused to take the sacrament with Dr Cotton, and when the chaplain entered his cell and offered consoling words and advice, Greenacre said he had no doubt Christ was a very good man, but he did not believe him to be the Son of God. About 7.00, while he drank a cup of tea and ate some bread and butter, he wept. It was the first time he had shed tears since being jailed. He remarked that he was very differently situated now to what h' was some years ago: he had been highly respected then, and had been re_..ned as one of the overseers of St George's parish with one of the largest majorities ever known. As 8 o'clock approached he became very agitated, but said nothing. The sheriffs and other officials assembled at 7.45 and Greenacre's arms were pinioned by Calcraft, the chief executioner, who had performed this office since 1828. The procession formed up, and set off through the prison to the Debtors' Gate. Greenacre's last request, after giving a small parcel to a sheriff for Mrs Gale (said to be his spectacles), was that he would not be exposed to the multitude for too long and his execution be swiftly done. *The Times* said:

> No sooner did those officers, who usually precede the criminal to the place of execution, become visible, than [the concourse] burst forth in a loud, deep and sullen shout of execration against Greenacre . . . As soon as he had mounted the scaffold, which he did with a firm and steady step, the populace again exhibited their detestation . . . by setting up a wild hurrah in approval of the retaliation which he was about to endure under the hands of justice . . . It appeared as if he was either perfectly unmoved by it, or regarded it as no additional bitterness to the agony of the hour . . . The bolt was withdrawn, Greenacre fell, and the vengeance of the law was accomplished. In two minutes from his first appearance on the platform he ceased to be a living man. He died, we think, instantly. One convulsive grasp of the hands was observed – nothing more.

He hung there for an hour. Then his body was cut down to 'a yell of triumph' from the crowd. A plaster cast was taken of his shaven head, and he was buried within the jail at 9 o'clock that night, near the graves of five of the Cato Street conspirators.

Before his death he had penned long and moralising letters of farewell to his family; to Mr Price; to Mr Hobler, his solicitor (to whom he left his silver hunting-watch, with its gold chain, and a key); and to his five surviving children, most of whom, it seems, were boys. He proclaimed his innocence to all. He also left a manuscript, written in Newgate and entitled *An Essay on the Human Mind*. This was seized by the sheriffs, denounced as 'a crude and wild farrago of visionary speculations founded upon the excellence of a moral religion', and destroyed.

To his sons he said:

> No precaution can be of any avail, for that which has happened to me may prove the Fate of any man . . . To avoid such a Fate I might admonish you never to throw at any person, nor to yield to passion . . . I would have you blend in your Hearts' Study your Worldly as well as your Spiritual welfare. For be you assured that upon your Temporal circumstances depends your Happiness or your Wretchedness in this life . . .

There is no enemy to man equal to that of poverty. It is poverty fills the country with sin and crime.

To his brothers and sisters he said:

Most sorry am I that the name of our family should be disgraced by any act of mine . . . that name which has not been stained by any crime cognizable to the laws of our country for centuries past . . . I feel this the more since I know that none amongst you, nor any person in London, has been more careful to maintain a good character than myself . . . Sobriety, industry, integrity, humanity and a quiet demeanour have always been the careful study of my life . . . My untimely end is an awful proof of the vicissitudes of life, and that no care or prudence can protect us from the decrees of fate.

He was an extraordinary murderer, and a more than ordinary man.

Three weeks after James Greenacre was hanged, Princess Victoria celebrated her 18th birthday on 24 May. Four weeks later, in the early hours of 20 June, her uncle, King William IV, died at Windsor Castle. The Archbishop of Canterbury and the Lord Chamberlain were driven from there to London, to Kensington Palace, and at 6.00 am Victoria, aroused from bed by her mother, the Duchess of Kent, put on a dressing-gown and went to meet the two gentlemen, alone, in an outer room. They told the short, slim, fair-haired girl that she was Queen.

CHAPTER 2

Daniel Good

The Murder of Jane Jones, 1842

Times were increasingly hard in 1842 for the teeming urban and industrial-ised mass of the population. Children aged six were working in mills and mines for 12–14 hours a day; the boys earned at most 3s 6d a week, the girls much less. An Act of 1840 had prohibited the employment of anyone under the age of 21 in sweeping chimneys by climbing them, but the Act was ignored for many years. Chartism, a nationwide movement for social, in-dustrial and political reform, particulary where it affected the artisan and labouring classes, was rampant, resulting in torchlit meetings, processions, petitions and strikes. Transportation, although it had ceased to New South Wales in Australia, still continued. But gas-lighting, level wooden-blocked streets, umbrellas and waterproofing had provided some general benefits, as had the railways. Ninety-three Railway Acts had been passed since 1825, and 1,500 miles of track had been laid: London was now linked to Birming-ham, to Southampton, Dover and York. The middle classes prospered, as did those values of family morality epitomised by the young Queen, now 23, and her young German husband, Prince Albert. Married in February 1840, they had already produced two children, the future Princess Royal and the Prince of Wales, and would have nine in all.

The Tory Prime Minister was Sir Robert Peel. The New Police that he had fathered were still getting a bad press. Punch, launched the previous year and with W. M. Thackeray now on its staff, treated policemen with derision, even contempt. The police themselves still suffered from problems of cred-ibility and poor communications, and were over-eager to be open about their activities with the press. As Charles Dickens said, they were forever 'jobbing and trading in mystery and making the most of themselves'. Their mishandling of the Jane Jones murder – a case of much bad luck for all con-cerned, including Good – caused considerable public criticism and internal ructions. But it led to the creation of a detective branch, which later became the CID.

It was unfortunate for Daniel Good, and for PC William Gardiner, that both of them happened to be in Wandsworth High Street at about 8.45 pm on Wednesday, 6 April 1842, and that the casual theft of a pair of trousers would lead to the revelation of what *The Times* would describe as 'a murder of a most frightful and appalling nature'.

PC Gardiner was on patrol in the High Street when a shopboy ran up to him to report a theft. Led by the boy, he proceeded to a pawnbroker's owned by a Mr Collingbourne, who complained that an Irish coachman had filched a pair of black trousers, after haggling over, and buying, a pair of black knee-breeches. The shopboy, Sam Dagnell, had noticed the swarthy coachman conceal the trousers under his greatcoat, before stuffing them under the cushions of a four-wheeled pony chaise. He told Mr Collingbourne, who darted outside and asked the coachman if he had made some mistake. The coachman was at first dismissive, and then became abusive when accused of theft and drove the chaise away.

All this had been observed by a youth called Robert Speed standing outside an adjacent grocer's shop, where he lived and worked as Mr Cooper's assistant. He had recognised the Irish coachman – as did Mr Collingbourne, who also knew for whom the coachman worked, and where in Putney Park Lane. Armed with this information and determined to bring the felon to justice, PC Gardiner set off at once, with Speed and the shopboy, Sam, both of whom he evidently enlisted to identify the thief. Perhaps they also went along for a bit of excitement. If so, they would not be disappointed. It would be a night they would remember all their lives.

Putney Park Lane, a long avenue lined by trees running north and south between Upper Richmond Road and Putney Heath, was nearly two miles away, with the little village of Roehampton near its foot. No doubt, being early April, the night was cold as well as dark. But Gardiner had a lantern to guide him and the boys along the rough and unlit roads.

The district was then a pleasant one of parks and fields dotted with large country-houses, in one of which, called Granard Lodge, lived an aged, retired East India merchant, Mr Queeley Shiell. According to the 1841 census, he and his wife were in their early eighties. With them lived their son John, a barrister in his fifties, his much younger wife and four children, all girls, the youngest of whom was two. They employed about a dozen servants, most of whom were female.

On entering the gates of Granard Lodge, Gardiner and the boys approached the front door, where he rang the bell. The door was opened by a footman, who, when asked where the coachman might be, directed the PC to a farming complex of stables and kitchen gardens a few hundred yards up the road. There were two blocks of stables, with different sections for horses, conveyances, feed and equipment. Above one block were four rooms, which were used as sleeping quarters by some of the staff, including the Irish coachman and the son of Mr Shiell's chief gardener and bailiff, Thomas Houghton. That night the son, John Houghton, the estate's second gardener, was in his father's dwelling beside this stable block.

The stable-yard had a bell by a gate, which was rung, on PC Gardiner's instruction, by Speed, and a thin, dark man in his forties appeared, attended by a smaller boy.

'Has the coachman come home?' Speed enquired. 'I am the coachman,' replied the other man. 'Daniel Good.' Whereupon Gardiner stepped forward and, as he attested later, said: 'I have come to take you into custody on a charge of stealing a pair of black trousers from the shop of Mr Colling-bourne, the pawnbroker, of Wandsworth.' Good replied: 'Why, yes. I bought a pair of breeches from Mr Collingbourne. But I haven't paid for them yet.' He took a purse out of a pocket and added: 'I'll give you what we agreed on, and you can take the money to him.'

Gardiner reported later: 'I told him I could not take the money as it had nothing to do with the charge I came upon. He then said: "Very well, I'll go with you to Wandsworth, and settle with Mr Collingbourne." I asked him if he would allow me to look into the chaise, and over the stables, to which he said: "Yes." And I went in, accompanied by the lads.'

First Gardiner searched the chaise-house and the stable on the north side of the yard. Then he moved towards the stable on the south side. Suddenly Good put his back to the door and refused to let the others enter. There was an altercation, heard by Houghton, the chief gardener, aged about 57. He emerged from his dwelling, and when he understood what the matter was about, told Good to stand aside and let the search proceed. All six entered: Gardiner, holding his lantern, Houghton, Good, Speed, Sam, and the small boy who had been with Good.

PC Gardiner told Speed and Sam to keep an eye on Good while he inspected the first two stalls, which were empty, and the hay-racks. Good seemed very uneasy, and shifted about, like the two ponies in the third stall. As Gardiner inspected the interior of a corn-bin, Good exclaimed that he would willingly go back to Wandsworth to pay what he owed. Gardiner refused to listen and said: 'No. I'll not go until I've searched the stable and made a diligent search.' He said later:

I then desired the lad Speed, in the presence of Good, to stand by him while I finished the search; and Good having walked to the bottom stall while I was searching the bin, I followed him. I saw him move the hay from one side of the stall to the other – which I forbid – and told him to go and stand outside [the stall] with the lad. I then moved two trusses of hay . . . and on disturbing some loose hay I discovered something under it. I said: 'What is this here? A goose?'

Suddenly, Daniel Good ran for the door. Surprised, the others were too late to prevent him closing the door behind him and locking them in. 'Now we are done!' cried Gardiner, and added, according to Speed: 'Oh, my God! We have lost the prisoner!' For some seconds Gardiner, aided by Speed, attacked the door with a pitchfork, before resigning himself to official displeasure, even dismissal, over the departed thief, and he went back to examine his peculiar find, the plucked goose. On closer inspection it proved to be too large for a goose. Was it the carcass of a sheep, or, as the little boy thought, a pig? None of the five had seen anything like it before. 'Oh, my God!' cried Sam, who was now holding the lantern. 'It's a human being!' Speed turned the body over and they saw it had breasts. They now realised, aghast, they had found a naked female torso, without head, legs or arms, and with the lower stomach ripped open and the entrails removed.

PC Gardiner must now have felt even more sick: he had let a murderer, not a thief, escape. But it was 15 minutes before he was able to break open the stable-door and send Sam to raise the alarm.

After 20 minutes or so, PC Hayter and then PC Tye arrived. The latter galloped off on one of Mr Shiell's ponies to Wandsworth station-house, while Hayter made a brief search of the neighbourhood. He found a broken paling in a fence and footprints heading for Putney in the soft earth of a field.

When Sergeant Palmer arrived at about 11.00 pm he took charge. A further search was made of the stables. A dried-up pool of blood was found near the torso, and in another stall, hidden under hay, a mattress stained with blood and urine was found, rolled up with two blankets and tied. In the separate but adjacent harness room, whose locked door had to be forced, 'a very fulsome smell' was noticed by PC Tye. 'It resembled the odour of the rind of pork when burnt,' he said later. 'It nearly threw me on my back,' said Palmer. They investigated – Houghton senior was with them. He later told the court: 'The grate is what is called Cobbett's register-grate, much larger than an ordinary one, and the fire was laid when I entered with the officer. It was composed of wood and coals, of an unusual quantity. I should think about two wheelbarrows full . . . The day before the search was made I observed a quantity of smoke issuing from the harness room, from which I found a smell similar to that from the singeing of horse-hair.'

So he must also have told Sgt Palmer. Houghton's son, John, aged about 22, would later add to this, saying:

> On Tuesday morning, about half-past six o'clock, I came down from my room and perceived a very uncommon smell. [Good] was in the stable and I asked him if he been singeing the horses. He replied that he had been in liquor overnight, and had been roasting some cheese to refresh him. I did not see the fire in the harness room at the time, but I heard the cracking of wood . . . Good said he was drying the harness.

In the ashes of the grate the policeman discovered some calcined bones, including two pieces of a skull. A further search revealed two strips of flannel petticoat on the saddle-rack, some torn female linen, a bloody knife in a table drawer, a saw, and by the fireplace a blood-stained axe. An assistant surgeon, Alfred Allen, a local man, inspected the torso and pronounced that the dismemberment had been done after death about three days earlier. Apart from a portion of the bladder, the abdominal and pelvic viscera had been entirely removed.

It seems that some of the Shiell family were not at home at this time. Granard Lodge had been sold and the Shiells were about to move to a grand house in Clarges Street, off Piccadilly. None of the Shiells gave evidence later on, and of their servants, only the two male Houghtons, as well as the footman and cook, appeared in court. The Shiells may have been making the most of Easter – the previous Monday had been Easter Monday (4 April) – and they may have been staying with relations or friends. This might explain why Good had had so much free time, and was able to borrow the chaise on Wednesday, 6 April for about eight hours.

The Houghtons, and in particular the son, John, whose room in the stables was next to Good's, had much to tell the police. John said of the coachman: 'He never had a good character. No one would trust him much . . . He was a kind of swindler.' None the less the young gardener, who, having seen the remains – 'What a wretch he must be!' – and having sworn never to sleep in the stables again, had to admit that he had heard nothing unusual on the Sunday, Monday and Tuesday nights. This was not because he was inebriated – he went to bed sober – but because he was a heavy sleeper, he said.

Both Houghtons, father and son, added further details to their accounts of the stench and smoke emanating early on Tuesday morning from the harness room and its chimney.

Good, who had been with the Shiells for two and a half years, had been visited at the stables by two women, with whom he had had tea in the harness room. One of them, the younger one, who had worked at the Rose and Crown in Wimbledon, had been to the stables four or five times over the past year. On her last visit, a fortnight ago, she had stayed the night – thus the mattress in the stall. The other woman, Good had said, was his sister. She had been seen at the stables three times, the last time at the end of March. The police also learned that this sister had looked after the coachman's 10-year-old son, also named Daniel Good.

Where was the boy? He was in Thomas Houghton's cottage, whither he had fled in tears at 9.30 that night, after escaping from the stables. He had been locked in with the others, and seen the torso. He had also been out most of that day with his father in the chaise. Now he sobbed because his father had run away – and where was his aunt?

What little Daniel told the police, and when, we do not know. But this is what he told the magistrates' court.

He had lived with his aunt, whom he called 'Mother' to please her, in the front kitchen of 18 South Street, Marylebone for just over two years. His father used to come and visit them there. He last saw his mother in South Street on Easter Sunday, when he went to a C. of E. Chapel in Baker Street. On his return, she had gone. But this was not unexpected, as she had arranged for him in her absence to spend the night with a widow, Mrs Young, at 99 East Street, which he did, going to school as usual on Monday morning in Dorset Street. Later that day his father fetched him from the school and told him that his mother had gone into service and that he would not see her again for six months. On leaving South Street they went to Blandford Street and then to George Street. A man put him on an omnibus, which took him to Roehampton. A publican there, Mr Ricks, then escorted him to Mr Shiell's house, where he arrived about 9.00 pm. He slept there that night (presumably with his father in a room above the stables) and at 5.00 pm the following day, Tuesday, was taken by his father to sleep at Mrs Hester's house in Pear Place, Roehampton. She was out, but returned at half-past eight. On Wednesday, 6 April, he returned to the stables, and that afternoon he and his father set off in the chaise for Woolwich, for 13 Charlotte Place, arriving there about 1.00 pm. His father had a small band-box with him, in which was a blue bonnet that had been worn by his mother for about a year. At Woolwich his father took him to see Susan Butcher, saying that she was a cousin, and gave her some apples and pears and other items in the kitchen, where they had tea with Susan's little sister. Her father was a shipwright. Afterwards, Susan came with them in the chaise as far as New Cross Station, where she and his father went into a public house. On the way he was allowed to drive, after he had agreed to call Susan Butcher 'Mother'. Later, on their way back to Putney Park Lane, his father had pulled the chaise up in Wandsworth High Street to buy a pair of black trousers, which he put under the cushions on which little Daniel sat. Back at the stables, a policeman arrived looking for his father, who before long locked them all in the stables and ran away.

No one knows what little Daniel thought, and suffered, that night. But the police now knew that Susan Butcher could not have been the woman murdered in the stables. The victim must have been the little boy's 'mother' and his father's 'sister', last seen on Easter Monday. She called herself Jane Good. Before that she had been Jane Jones.

The police had much to do and a murderer to find. There was never any doubt in their minds, and in the papers, that Good *was* the murderer. But having caught him by chance, they had let him escape. Thereafter, because of their parochialism, poor communications, inter-divisional rivalries, and a shortage of men, he would evade arrest for more than a week. Even then he was caught by sheer chance. Daniel Good had some very bad luck.

The police would later claim, in an official document headed 'Outline of Steps taken by the Police', that 'about half-past nine o'clock on Wednesday night, the 6th of April . . . information of the charge and the escape, with a description of Good, was circulated immediately to all the Divisions of the Police . . . and known at every Police Station of the Metropolitan Police District [being a circumference of about sixty miles] before four o'clock'. This may have been the intention, but it could never have happened, for Gardiner and the others did not break out of the stables until half-past nine, when the coachman's little boy went crying to the gardener's home. The next policemen to appear, PCs Hayter and Tye, arrived some 20 minutes later. Gardiner himself declared: 'I sent the younger lad to give information of the circumstances to all the police he could meet with, while I remained with the body. In about half an hour Constable Hayter, who said he knew the prisoner well, arrived, and he, accompanied with another constable, went to give information to Superintendent Bicknell, who on his arrival proceeded with me and others to make a further search.'

The information could not have been given to Bicknell before about half-past ten, and it is unlikely that he passed it on straightaway. But even if the murder report had reached the police stations in central London by 4.00 am, the policemen on the beat would probably not have known about it until they paraded at 6.00 am – by which time Good had entered and slept in Jane

Jones's room, before absconding by cab with a large box, a large bundle and a bed. This he did at 5.15 am.

An internal inquiry would later be held into the police failures that night and various officers were censured for a less than urgent and efficient application to their duties. Some were suspended. PC Gardiner was discharged.

The next policeman to displease his superiors was Police Sergeant Stephen Perdrian, who had happened to observe Good order a cab in South Street at about 5.00 am and had noted its number, 726. He said later: 'While I was talking to the cabman, [Good] came out and called the cabman. I then crossed to the other side, and saw Good pass a large trunk to the cabman.'

But it was not until 4.30 on the afternoon of Thursday, 7 April that Sgt Perdrian was sent for by an inspector and told to find out where the cab had gone. No doubt Perdrian was already being blamed for not having had the foresight to question Good when he left South Street so conspicuously that morning, or to arrest him on suspicion.

By this time the police had decided that Jane Jones, missing from South Street since Easter Sunday, was most probably the murdered woman. Said to have been about 40, she had lodged at No. 18, where John and Jane Brown had a greengrocer's shop, for three years, and for most of this time had lived in the front kitchen, where she took in washing. A painted sign outside the house said: *Mangling done here by J Good*. She had begun calling herself Mrs Good about the time she moved into the kitchen, which was rented and paid for by Daniel Good. His small son, Daniel, had been living with her for about two years. He called her 'Mother'. Good told Mrs Brown that the boy's real mother had died a year and a half previously. Mrs Brown said later:

He used to come daily to see Jane Jones, but not so frequently after he went to live at Putney. He never stayed long . . . She was a neat-looking woman, not stout, about five feet two inches high, and a person of close habits. I had no means of knowing whether she was in the family way or not . . . I last saw her alive on Sunday, 3 April. She had on a blue bonnet, a black shawl with flowers on it and a cotton dress. She went out between two and three o'clock in the afternoon.

Before she departed, Jane Jones told Mrs Brown she was going to visit her husband's place of work and that if she took the little boy, who called her 'Mother', he would 'massacre' her. Jane hoped it would pour with rain to prevent her having to go, as she was worried about what her husband wanted. She didn't know why he had sent for her or what he was up to.

Earlier, she chatted to Elizabeth Christie, who occupied the first floor of No. 18. She said she had been sent for by Good, and was distressed about where the boy would sleep that night, having been instructed not to bring him with her. Christie later said:

She came to my door at twelve o'clock and said 'Do you think it will rain? I hope it will pour with rain all the afternoon.' I have known her to go to Putney, but never to stay out all night. Good used to visit her as early as five o'clock. I often heard him say on going away: 'Goodbye, my dear. Take care of yourself' . . . She told me, about three months back, that she thought she was pregnant, but subsequently that she was not.

South Street (now an extension of Blandford Street) was a few hundred yards north of Manchester Square, and it must have been the starting-point of Sgt Perdrian's investigation, which he pursued with great single-mindedness, evidently hoping to find Good and arrest him on his own. Promotion and praise were on his mind, not the public censure that ensued. It took him nearly 12 hours to trace the cab and its driver, John Littlebody, during which time he must have visited nearly every cabstand in central London. But at 3.45 am on Friday, 8 April, he was back at Marylebone police station, reporting that Good and his luggage had been dropped at Mr Shepherd's livery stables in Dorset Place, Pall Mall East at 5.45 am the previous day. It seems he was told, or decided himself, to make further enquiries, and succeeded in finding out that a second cab had taken Good on to the Spotted Dog in the Strand, where the luggage was booked in under the name of Stanley. At the Spotted Dog, Sgt Perdrian must have learned – as was later declared in court by a barmaid – that Good and a woman had collected the luggage at 11.30 am and driven away. A waiter also revealed that when the couple were in the tap-room, Good said he was very tired, as he had been 'travelling all night by the railway'. When asked which railway, he said he didn't know. Good was very restless, frequently going out into the street. As the waiter cooked Good some steak, he overheard him tell the woman: 'That bugger won't trouble you no more.'

All this must have much encouraged Sgt Perdrian. Fired with new enthusiasm, he now set out to find the *third* cab and its driver, assisted by a crossing-sweeper, who had seen Good and the woman leave the Spotted Dog, and knew the cabman who drove them away. He was found in Drury Lane. He said he had taken the couple, the bed and other articles to an address in Spitalfields. To save time, Perdrian hired the cab to take him on to Flower and Dean Street, to No. 4, where all the items had been unloaded and taken upstairs, to a room occupied by a Mrs Molly or Mary Good, aged 59, a fruit-seller in Bishopsgate.

What happened next that Friday morning was described by Perdrian himself, calling himself PS 16, in a report he later submitted to the Joint Commissioners of the Metropolitan Police.

On PS 16 entering the House he ascertained the woman who lived upstairs was named Good but that she was out. PS 16 also found that Good had been there on Thursday morning and taken Mrs Good, his wife, out with him and returned in the middle of the day, bringing with them a bed and a Trunk which they took away with them again in the afternoon when they went out together. While PS 16 was hearing this from the lodgers downstairs, Mrs Good came in and went upstairs. PS 16 then went upstairs to her and said to her good morning, I think I saw you at the Spoted Dog in the Strand yesterday. She said she went there with her Husband who she had not seen for the last 7 year until Thursday morning when he came home and said he was in trouble and had left his place. She then called him a vilain and said he had left her to live with another woman. I said to Her whose things were those he had with him. She said she did not know, she also stated that Good took her out in the afternoon with the intention to go and see some relation he had living in the Strand, but subsequently left her in a coffee shop at 5 pm on Thursday, since which she as not seen anything of him. PS 16 considered that the only motive Good had for going to see his wife was to get her to assist him in disposing of the things which PS 16 found to have been pledged by Good and his Wife at F Somes No 200 Spitalfields – and identified the things as being those removed from 18 South St . . . PS 16 thought it better to be explicit with her being convinced that she would soon hear of it, then told her of the Murder. She said I hope he may be taken, for he as been a raskal to me. PS 16 remained with Mrs Good up to 6 pm on Friday and finding there was no chance of gaining any further clue in tracing Good left to give the above information to the H Division. PS 16 also has to state that he found a bundle and two small work boxes at Mrs Good which she said Good had brought there.

Mr Soames's pawnbroking assistant must have told Perdrian (as he later told the court) that Good first offered to pawn a bed. But as he was a stranger, Soames refused to take it in. Good went away and returned with Mary Good. She said he was her husband, who had just come ashore from a voyage, and that it was all right. Good added that he had come to London by train and that the articles he wanted to pawn had belonged to a person who had died on the voyage home from China. Later, he brought in some female apparel to pawn.

Alas for Perdrian. When at length he reported all his discoveries, his enterprise and initiative were met with disapproval and blame. The 'Outline', previously quoted, declared: 'The Sergeant of Police belonging to the Marylebone Division, who had traced Good to this place, not being acquainted with the neighbourhood, from perhaps an excess of zeal more than discreet, made inquiries in the neighbourhood without communicating – as he ought to have done – with the Superintendent of Police of the Division, and any certain trace of Good has been lost since that time.' Inspector Nicholas Pearce, who had been put in charge of the investigation, also complained about Perdrian's 'incautious conduct'.

Pearce was also vexed by the carping clamour of the press, typified by a paragraph in *The Times* on Saturday, 9 April: 'The conduct of the Metropolitan Police . . . is marked with a degree of looseness and want of decision which proves that unless a decided change is made in the present system, it is idle to expect that it can be an efficient detective police, and that the most desperate offender may escape with impunity.'

But the police were doing all they could. Instructions were sent to all Divisions to check on 'all persons going away by any Coach, Railroad, or by the River, or any of the roads out of Town'. A description of Good was also sent 'to all the sea ports and principal Towns' and posters, proclaiming MURDER! and printed on 7 April, were distributed far and wide. These contained the following description of Daniel Good: 'He is an Irishman, aged about 46 years, 5 ft 6 ins high, very dark complexion, black hair, long features, and bald at the top of the head; walks upright; was dressed in a dark Great Coat, Drab Breeches and Gaiters, and Black Hat.'

As a result, swarthy sinister Irishmen were sighted all over the place, although most sightings were reported hours, even days, after the event. The police themselves kept a watch on Mary Good, whom the papers invariably described as 'Old Molly'. Of this surveillance the 'Outline' said:

> It has been ascertained, that an Irishman who comes from the same place as Good has been in frequent communication with Mrs Good – apparently the Bearer of some messages to and from her. When he goes to her room the utmost caution is used to prevent observation, and a Cloth is hung up within the door to prevent anyone looking through the Keyhole or any opening. Upon his leaving her he has been followed to a Court near Tooley Street in the Boro', where great numbers of the low Irish people lodge, and from thence has been traced again to Mrs Good's ... Observation is still kept upon the girl Lydia Susannah Butcher, with whom Good is known to have been intimate latterly, and at her father's house at Woolwich.

The watch on Molly Good produced another suspect, and another unhappy result, which was described in some detail by the *Morning Advertiser*. Soon after midnight on Saturday the 9th, a young man 'of rather diminutive stature, with a large bundle of papers under his arm' knocked loudly on the street door of 4 Flower and Dean Street. Old Molly descended but refused to open the door. Whereupon the youth wrote something on a slip of paper and passed it to her. Apprehended by a constable, he was taken to the police station at Spital Square, where he 'strutted about with great apparent indifference'. He told the duty sergeant that he had called on Mrs Good to offer the professional assistance of his master, a solicitor. Sgt Coleman rebuked the youth before releasing him, saying his action at such a late hour might show some industry and perseverance, but not much professional respectability. The young man responded that the Sergeant was mistaken. More than once, he said, he had obtained a client by this means. Besides, the trial would be notorious, and benefit his master if he were involved. And there were 'many very nice and critical points of law' concerning the identification of the remains.

This particular matter was in part resolved by a mole on the right side of the torso's neck – Jane Jones had had such a mole, so two of her female neighbours said. The torso itself was buried on 15 April in Putney church-yard by the parish constable, watched by over 200 people. He had retrieved it after what was left of Jane Jones was put on display in a pub the previous Sunday. 'It is even asserted', said the *Advertiser*, 'that money was received, on that sacred day, for admission to the heartrending and sickening spectacle.'

The horror and emotion aroused by the murder was compounded by the popular conviction that Jane Jones had been about four months' pregnant. So a Putney doctor, who examined the remains, would later aver in court. But Mr Allen, the only other doctor to comment on this, would not commit himself, as the evidence had been removed. A broadsheet published at that time reflected the general revulsion. It began:

Great God of all, who rules on high, Our secret thoughts to Thee are known. The darkest deeds before Thine eye Are all exposed before thy throne . . . Worse than Greenacre we allow, Like him all feeling thou didst spurn; He cut his victim up, but thou The body afterwards did burn . . . A double murder thou hast done, Unequalled yet by savage wild. For when the mother's blood did run, Thou didst destroy her un-born child . . .

It was later deduced from the stinking state of the travelling-box on the chaise – 'I nearly fell back in a faint,' said PC Tye – that Jane Jones's entrails had been transported to the Lower Richmond Road near Putney Bridge and cast into the Thames. A piece of flesh was found on the tow-path.

Good neglected, however, to destroy her clothes, and behaving with the unbelievable thoughtlessness that characterises most murderers (those that are known) pawned Jane Jones's belongings, including her bed, and gave items of her clothing to Susan Butcher and Molly Good. He also stole three shawls and a fur tippet from a shop in Welbeck Street on 5 April, the day before he stole the fatal trousers from the pawnbroker's in Wandsworth. All of which was done with a characteristic indifference – or subconscious invitation – to being found out.

By this time the inquest, first held in the Angel Inn, Roehampton on 8 April and adjourned until Tuesday the 12th, had been adjourned again, and a re-ward of £50 was offered by the parochial authorities of Putney.

On the Monday, *The Times* had published an account of Molly Good's early life and her version of what had happened the previous Thursday. She claimed to have married Daniel Good when she was 26 or 27 and while she was a housemaid in a gentleman's house in Kinsale, near Cork. Good, she said, was then a footman in another such house, that of a captain. They married and came to London where, after three years, he deserted her. She saw him eight years later, when he said he now had a son. Then he vanished again, to reappear on Thursday, 7 April.

If this was true, he must have been about 13 when they met. More likely, she was about 31 and he 18 or so. Interestingly, *The Times* had revealed the previous week that Good had been an officer's servant throughout most of the Peninsular War (1808–14), since when he had received a pension of five shillings a week. His master (the Captain?) had been killed near the end of the war, after which Good may have returned to Kinsale, when, in 1814, he would have been about 18. Perhaps he married Molly then. His real name is said elsewhere to have been Sullivan, or Dinovan, not Good.

According to Molly Good, when Daniel turned up in Flower and Dean Street on the Thursday at breakfast-time, he told her he had been away at sea. She upbraided him, and he replied: 'What ails you, my heart? I know I've been a very bad man. But God Almighty has at last turned me to you, and we'll be happy and comfortable yet.' Whereupon he embraced her and burst into tears. He then gave her sixpence to buy some rum, which they downed with their breakfast. He also gave her some women's clothing, and left the oilskin cover for his hat in her room. At the pawnbroker's shop managed by Mr Soames (whom they must have visited about noon, after leaving the Spotted Dog in the Strand), Good, saying he was William Stanley, pawned a bed, a rug, a counterpane, four pillows, four blankets and five sheets, as well as two waistcoats, two pairs of boy's trousers and a tablecloth, several scarves and shawls, a tea-caddy, several cups and saucers and other pieces of china, plus two dozen knives and forks. He sold all he could of Jane Jones's possessions – he told Susan Butcher to take her mangle.

After this, according to Molly Good, they walked westwards to Cheapside, where they paused to have a coffee. Hungry, she asked him to get her an egg. He walked out, and never returned.

That's what she said. The following morning Sgt Perdrian called. From then on a watch was kept on the house in which she lived, and on Tuesday, 12 April Inspector Pearce replaced previous police observers with an experienced and soldierly sergeant, Stephen Thornton, who noted the almost daily visits paid to Molly Good by an Irishman, Richard Gamble, and endeavoured to trail him wherever he went. But there was still no sign of Good, although agitated Irishmen looking like him were spotted in Essex, in Greenwich, in assorted pubs and streets and eating-houses and barber's shops – apparitions who paled and fled when anyone mentioned murder. More interesting was a Mr Dixon's piece of information. He said that an Irishman called Daniel Good had been in his father's service about nine years previously as a coachman. This man committed a felony in Brixton and was sentenced to seven years' transportation, a sentence then commuted to one or two years which were spent in the Millbank Penitentiary.

The *Morning Advertiser* reported on Friday, 15 April: 'Yesterday the office of the Commissioner of Police in Scotland Yard was besieged with anxious inquiries as to whether the murderer Good had been taken into custody, and the police on duty were compelled to return the mortifying answer that he had not.' During the day, continued the *Advertiser*, several people had purported to have important information. But 'their intelligence was in most instances vague and shallow, and in some instances truly absurd'. A middle-aged gentleman had gravely informed the police that he had seen Good, dressed in female attire, selling apples in Finch Lane, Cornhill.

The police themselves were better informed about Good's appearance on 16 April, when a very detailed and useful description of him was circulated within the divisions. It originated in a report from an Inspector Macgill in Sidcup. He had visited Elmstead Farm, where Good had once worked as a coachman for a Mr Fitzgerald. His enquiries led him to a Mrs Head, who had 'lived as fellow servant' with Good in Mr Fitzgerald's service. She told Macgill:

He speaks very fast, is quick in all his movements, eats fast, and his cheeks are thin and hollow from the loss of his back teeth; his eyes are small and very dark, his brow much wrinkled, and knits his brow and shakes his head when speaking; has a scowl upon his face and looks very morose, and when he smiles he seems altogether as well pleased; his nose is rather conspicuous, for near the point, it seems as if a small piece had been chopped off; this however is natural.

Macgill added: 'While in the service of Mr Fitzgerald Good was assaulted by his master, and Mrs Head bathed the wound whilst he lay on a dresser in the kitchen; this wound was on the left side of the upper lip near to the nose. Mrs Head states that Good speaks 4 languages, French, Italian, Irish and English.'

But he was unable to read or write. If he had been able to do so, he may, like Greenacre, have deluged others with his prose. As it is, he managed to send two letters to Mr Shiell, one of which was dictated to an Irish paviour, John McEvoy, taken by Good from his employment in the Poultry (a road in the City) to the Three Tuns in Coleman Street, where he was provided with some paper and a quart of gin to assist his literary output. This was at about 6.15 am on Thursday, 7 April. The letter that resulted was so badly written and spelt that McEvoy himself took an hour to read it aloud in court. It expressed the hope that Mr Shiell would take care of Good's 'destitute boy' and that £7 10s allegedly owed to Good would be used to look after his son. Among disjointed sentences it said: 'I am a single man since I buried my dear wife five years the 14th of January last . . . You will find two blankets and a mattress in the stable which Susan Butcher and me slept on. I was a RC until I became acquainted with Susan Butcher, and she was the cause of all my trouble and misfortune . . .'

Another poorly written epistle, but much shorter, was also sent to Mr Shiell. Now in the Public Record Office archives in Kew, it was also probably penned by an Irishman – or woman – and is hard to decipher. It says: 'Sur – i wright thys to inform u to pa the 7 pounds 10 due to mee to mi desolate boy. I shall thro miself into the thames just bi waterloo brydge tonight where mi body wil be found. Good by god bless yu all – tak kare of mi poor boy and I shall dy in piece. Dan Good.'

Although a man's body found in the Thames at Richmond was thought for a while to be that of Good, this proved wrong. On 15 April the *Advertiser* complained: 'The retreat of the murderer has not yet been discovered, and that unhealthy excitement which pervades all minds suffers no abatement, but on the contrary, it increases as the chances lessen of the police being able to capture a man of such atrocious and fiendish character.' He had been missing now for nearly ten days. Where *was* he?

On 16 April, through another piece of bad luck, Daniel Good was found. It seems that he did not leave London until Sunday, 10 April. For on that day he entered a barber's shop in Bromley in Kent to have himself shaved. Dressed as a bricklayer – in a fustian jacket and trousers, dirty blue-striped shirt, black waistcoat, black neckerchief, low shoes and a dark cloth cap without a peak – he carried a large bundle and a new bricklayer's hod. The barber, Anthony Foyle, became suspicious when his customer insisted on moving his chair to a dark part of the shop. Foyle deliberately began to discuss the murder with another customer, a young market gardener, Bill Addis. 'What a dreadful thing that murder was at Putney,' Foyle remarked, razor in hand. 'I should like to have the punishing of the villain.' This upset his customer so much that the shaving was abandoned. But he paid his penny for the shave and was not averse to exchanging some words before he left. He said he'd been knocking about for several days and was on his way to the country to get a job. 'On a Sunday?' queried Foyle. 'I would venture to swear you haven't been a bricklayer's labourer for the past three months.' 'To tell the truth,' the stranger replied, 'I've not been so long. For I was in a capacity where I was obliged to shave every day, and I don't feel comfortable without it.'

He left, and proceeded on his way – on foot, although he may have got a lift in a cart – to Sevenoaks. From there he journeyed to Tonbridge where, it is said, he arrived at about 11.00 pm and lodged overnight at the Bull. At about 5.30 am on Monday, 11 April he entered the Angel public house (which was then on the southern edge of Tonbridge) and asked the landlord, Mr Adams, if there was any work to be had. Mr Adams said there was a good deal of building going on in the neighbourhood and that a job should be easy to get. After consuming a penny loaf and supping a half-pint of beer, Good succeeded in obtaining a job with a builder and began work on some cottages near the new South-Eastern railway station. He appeared to know his business, but spoke to no one. That night, he acquired a lodging at Mrs Hargreave's house, telling her he used to be a hawker and dealer in hare and rabbit skins. She said later he was very restless and could be heard sighing and moaning at night. Whenever anyone came to the door he became anxious, and wanted to know who it was.

For five days and nights he lived and worked in Tonbridge undisturbed. But on the morning of Saturday, 16 April, he was approached by another bricklayer, Thomas Rose, who was labouring on the new station near by, and thought there was something familiar about the other man. Rose happened to be not only a former police constable, but also one whose beat in Wandsworth less than two years ago had included Putney Park Lane.

'Why – you are the man Good!' he said. 'Your name is Daniel Good.' 'No, it's not!' retorted the Irishman. 'My name is James Connor.' Rose persisted: 'Why, you are he I've seen in Putney Park Lane. You was coachman to a gentleman there.' The Irishman insisted that Rose was mistaken – he had never been a coachman. Rose exclaimed: 'Oh, I've seen you frequently at the stables opposite to Mr Hulton's. And you know young Houghton.'

He went away to find a policeman, asking someone in his absence to keep an eye on Good. Rose told PC Humphrey, who duly had a careful look at the suspect, acquired two other constables, Ludlow and Peckham, as reinforcements and invited Good to join him in the Angel for a glass of ale. There Good was handcuffed and guarded while Humphrey hastened to Good's lodging to search his room. In a bundle were garments usually worn by a coachman, which had in fact been worn by Good on the night he fled from Putney Park Lane. Back at the Angel, a search of the suspect produced a silver watch, a purse containing £3 17s 6d, and an apron made from a black muslin petticoat and stained with blood.

News of the capture soon spread, and 'an immense crowd' attended Good's removal at 1.00 pm to the magistrates' office, where he was formally charged and remanded. Good, who gave his name as Richard Hall, said: 'I'm an innocent man, and evidence can be produced before the twelve judges to prove it.' He was then conveyed in a cart, accompanied by Ludlow and Peckham, to Maidstone Jail. Three times, as they passed through the villages of Hadlow, Mereworth and Teston, Good asked for permission to get himself shaved. The constables refused, in case he would attempt to cut his throat or escape. However, they stopped at the King's Head in Mereworth, so that the prisoner could partake of some bread and cheese and beer.

They reached Maidstone at 7.00 pm. The prison governor, after studying the descriptions of Good and narrowly viewing the suspect, pronounced him to be the murderer. This conclusion was happily reinforced when Good took a comb from a pocket and rearranged his hair to cover a bald patch.

On Sunday he was brought to London. The hackney-coach in which he was conveyed as far as Greenwich was assailed by so many people along the way, by booing, hisses, shouts and missiles – the windows were broken – that he was transferred to a prison van. Escorted thence by policemen on horseback, he reached Bow Street police station about 8.00 pm. Good now began talking freely, admitting his real identity and that Jane Jones had been with him on Sunday, 3 April. But how she died, he did not know. He conceded that appearances were 'rather black' against him, but joked about his escape and the locking-up of PC Gardiner and the others in the stables. He chatted with two constables detailed to sit with him, and after enjoying a pint of coffee and some bread and butter, fell asleep at 3.00 am.

The previous night (Saturday), Inspector Pearce and his observer, Sgt Thornton, had pounced on Molly Good and her visitor, Richard Gamble. Both were arrested and charged with receiving stolen goods, namely three old dresses.

The *Morning Advertiser* took the opportunity once again to disparage the police. It said:

The old woman made no secret whatever of having these things; on the contrary, she exhibited them to various members of the police, and even asked many of them to take them away . . . For some reason best known to the police themselves, they were allowed to remain there for a whole week . . . The numerous respectable persons who have known the old woman for upwards of 20 years, believe her to be wholly incapable of the slightest participation in the frightful crime . . . and her apprehension, under the circumstances, is considered by them . . . as somewhat extraordinary. The secret of the matter appeared to be, that the police, feeling annoyed at the slovenly manner in which the case had been managed, as well as their own almost culpable negligence in permitting the murderer to escape, were determined to apprehend some person as a sort of *flash in the pan*.

Mrs Good herself objected strongly to being arrested, saying it was for 'Nothing at all, at all.' On being told of Good's arrest she said: 'Then bad luck to him! Serve him right – if he has done the deed!'

She became fractious again on the Monday, when she and Gamble were taken to Bow Street court, where the charge against them was changed to murder. Before being removed from Spital Square police station she was brought some breakfast by friends, who had also provided her with food and refreshment the day before. Constable Evans took the breakfast to her cell. But she insisted that her friends be allowed to bring it in person. On being told this could not be allowed, she became violent and abusive, claiming that the police had brought her there to murder her and were poisoning her food. She refused to leave the cell when a hackney-cabriolet arrived to take her to Bow Street and, still raving, was forcibly plucked from her cell by Sgt Coleman and dumped in the cab.

On that same Monday (18 April), at 10.30 am, Daniel Good appeared in Bow Street court, before Molly Good and Gamble were charged. *The Times* reporter remarked: 'His countenance was rather unpleasant, his eyes sunken, and his hair, nearly black, rather long and combed from the right side of the head to the left.' Dressed once again in his coachman's gear, he stood for most of the time with his chin on his left hand and his left elbow resting on the edge of the dock. Nine witnesses were called, including PC Gardiner, and Robert Speed. Lydia Susannah Butcher also gave evidence and wept throughout. Good was also moved to tears.

In reporting the proceedings in detail the following day, the *Advertiser* now thought it fit to commend the police, and declared:

It is said to be rare that a man so accomplished in the art of crime has for so short a period evaded justice. From this it will be seen that the police, to whom so much blame has been attached, are, after all, anything but culpable, and that in the present instance the attribution of the want of energy and ability are, at least, unjust and unwarranted . . . The officers employed, instead of exhibiting any negligence, seem to have been most vigilant and active.

When Good reappeared in Bow Street court on Thursday, 21 April, he was attired in blue prison clothes and attended by a jailer, Tyrrell, from Coldbath Fields Prison. The court was packed; tickets of admission, and seats, were the privilege of a favoured few, who included several noblemen, distinguished persons and MPs. This time the witnesses, 33 altogether, were questioned by a Treasury solicitor, Mr Maule, as well as by the magistrate, Mr Hall. The accused was also allowed to question the witnesses, although he seldom did so.

During PC Gardiner's evidence, Good fainted and was revived by the jailer. He also became emotional when Susan Butcher appeared, as did she; and when his ten-year-old son, Daniel, was brought in to the court to give evidence, which he did in a most clear and sensible manner, Good burst into tears and collapsed on a seat in the dock. At the conclusion of the boy's examination, during which Good sporadically wept, he said: 'Your worship – will you allow me to shake hands with the boy before he goes away?' Mr Hall acquiesced to this, and at the end of the hearing Good, again in tears, was allowed to embrace his son in front of the court before being removed to Newgate Prison.

The trial of Daniel Good, which lasted 11 hours, took place at the Central Criminal Court on Friday, 13 May. It began at 10.00 am, and was attended, among other notable persons, by the Queen's 69-year-old uncle, the Duke of Sussex. The prosecution was headed by the Attorney-General, Mr Waddington; the defence, by Mr Doane. The judges were Lord Chief Justice Denman, Baron Alderson and Mr Justice Coltman. On this occasion Daniel Good and Molly Good were arraigned side by side, he being indicted on 32 counts, which covered every possible way and means by which he might have killed Jane Jones. He pleaded 'Not guilty'. Mary Good was now charged with unlawfully harbouring, concealing and comforting him, knowing he had committed felony and murder. Mr Doane then applied for the prisoners to be tried separately. This was granted and Mary Good was removed from the court. The charges against her and Gamble were later dropped.

During the examination of Alfred Allen, the young surgeon, he stated that the torso of Jane Jones was 'in a most healthy state' and was empty of blood. He said: 'I should be inclined to think the deceased was pregnant, but I cannot speak decidedly . . . She was a plump, fine woman . . . The bosom was plump and full, and I do not think from their appearance that she had ever suckled a child.' The other doctor, Mr Ridge, who thought Jane Jones had been pregnant, said she died 'while in perfect health'.

Her movements on the Easter Sunday were pieced together in the evidence of five witnesses, who had seen her that day with Good. A confectioner, Lavender Layton, saw the couple at 3.45 pm walking arm in arm on the Barnes road, between the Red Lion and the Hammersmith suspension bridge. Good introduced Jones as his sister. 'We met by accident,' emphasised Mr Layton. 'I avoided conversing with them. My son, seven years old, was with me.' At 4.05, the landlord of the Coach and Horses in Barnes said the couple had some gin and water in his parlour. The woman was again introduced as Good's sister and said by him to be Welsh. He also said she had been good enough to bring him a present of some cream, sugar and tea. At 4.30 they called on Mrs Fanny Hester, the wife of an ornamental painter, whose husband was away in North America. The blue-bonnetted woman was introduced this time as Good's sister-in-law. Mrs Hester offered them tea and they stayed for an hour. At one point Mrs Hester confided that the old gardener, Houghton, had been saying 'something disrespectful about Susan Butcher sleeping in the harness room'. This much upset Jane Jones, who told Mrs Hester that she knew nothing of this Susan Butcher, and demanded to know of Good who she was. He replied she was a friend of his and that it was time they left. Jones said she could plainly see that he wished to drop the subject. She clearly didn't, for at 6.15 they were seen by a policeman in the Upper Richmond Road, not far from Putney Park Lane, conversing 'in a loud angry tone'. The woman appeared, he said, to be 'finding fault with the man, and not him with her'.

At 7.00 pm they were in the King's Head in Roehampton, having bypassed Granard Lodge. They were again drinking gin and water. The landlord noticed that Good seemed to be urging the woman to drink, and that she did so with reluctance, pushing away the glass he offered her several times.

Good and Jane Jones finally reached the stables of Granard Lodge at about 7.30 pm. It was about then that Shiell's footman saw Good and told him his master wanted him to take some letters to the post office. Good collected them from the Lodge and told the footman he was going to the Green Man, a pub on Putney Heath, to see a person about taking his son to Ireland. Did Jane Jones go with him? Did he urge her to drink more gin? Did he kill her, as seems likely, later that night?

A motive for the murder seems to have been the fact that Susan Butcher, after spending a night at the stables a fortnight earlier, had agreed to marry Daniel Good. At his trial, between tears, she said he used to visit her when she was in service in Wimbledon. She was now out of work. He had been very kind to her, she said, and used to give her presents. He became her suitor, and told her his wife had been dead for five years. Although he asked her to marry him several times, she refused him at first, saying she wouldn't like to marry a Catholic. 'Nor I neither,' he said. On the night she slept in the stables, she slept alone, she said, on a mattress in the harness room. Good locked her in. The following morning she returned to Woolwich and to her father's home via the steam-boat from Putney. The last time she saw him was on 6 April, when he gave her several items which he said had belonged to his wife, including a blue bonnet, a shawl, a fur tippet and a pair of boots. He asked her to wear the bonnet, but she refused. With him on this occasion was his little boy, whom she had never met before. Good told the child, as they drove to New Cross, to call her 'Mother'.

Mr Doane, speaking on behalf of the prisoner, told the jury that there was nothing to show that Jane Jones met her death at the hands of another person, and that, on suddenly learning that the accused had been unfaithful to her, she took her own life. He begged the jury to bear in mind that 'the disgusting and horrible circumstances of the mutilation of the body' formed no part of any charge against the prisoner. And even if he did such a thing, to conceal her death, this did not mean that he had caused it. Why would he wish to kill her? She had no claims on him, and he could have ended the association when he pleased.

The Attorney-General, so sure was he of the prosecution's case, waived his right to reply.

In his summing-up, Lord Denman remarked that although the jury could not tell what motive might operate on the prisoner's mind, it was quite clear that no adequate motive could be assigned for the revolting and brutal act of dismembering the body after death and consuming the limbs by fire. If she destroyed herself, could a man with whom she had been living on friendly and intimate terms for a considerable time, be so lost of all proper feeling as to proceed to dismember her body without giving the least alarm or endeavouring to obtain any assistance?

The jury retired at 7.30 pm and returned at 8.05. The foreman declared the prisoner to be guilty. In sentencing Daniel Good to death, the Lord Chief Justice delivered a powerful speech condemning the 'most foul and wicked murder'. He said:

> There is no doubt that it is owing to the indulgence of your inclinations for one woman after another, that being tired of the unhappy deceased, and feeling that you could not enjoy to its full extent, in your view, the fresh attachment you had formed, that you resolved upon destroying the unhappy woman who was the former object of your affection . . . You coldly calculated, long before the act was committed, upon depriving the unfortunate woman of her little property . . . There is no doubt that on that Sunday night you lured the unhappy deceased to your stable intending to take her life, and to hide her afterwards from the eyes of men. That place was entirely under your control . . . But although you were watched by no human eye, your proceedings were brought to light in such a manner as to afford a powerful warning to all other criminals . . . It is absolutely necessary that your life should be forfeited to the laws of God and man.

In reply Good made a passionate attack on Susan Butcher, who was 'always getting intoxicated' and was the cause of Jane Jones's death. This he now explained in a spirited defence that took the court, and his counsel, by surprise. He said:

> When we left Mrs Hester's, Jane declared that she would destroy herself . . . I told her I could not let her sleep in the harness room, for that the old gardener told everything that occurred to my master. She was very

angry with me about Butcher, and declared she would drown herself. I told her she should not fly in the face of God by doing such a thing, and I prevented her going out of the stable. I shook down some hay in the stall where the trunk was found, and told her to stay there till I came back, and when I returned I found her lying dead in the same stall with her throat cut, and a razor and sharp penknife, with which she had done it, lying by her side. She was lying dead before me when I went into the stable, and I did not know what to do ... I threw the knife over Hammersmith Bridge. I went out of the stable and locked the door, and did not know what to do. But I afterwards went back and covered her over with hay. On the Monday morning a man, of whom I had occasionally bought matches, rang at the bell, and I told him what had happened, and showed him the body, and asked him what I had better do, and he said: 'I'll tell you – we'll conceal the body.' I offered him a sovereign if he would conceal it for me, and he consented. And he came on the Tuesday morning and I gave him the axe and the knife, and left him in the harness room, and locked him in and told him not to make a noise ... And he made a fire, and burnt the head and the limbs. I declare to God I had nothing to with it ... He was to have come the next day and fetched the trunk and have thrown it into the river. But he did not come. I took her ear-rings out of her ears, and the ring from her finger. It was my wife's wedding-ring. *She* was not my wife ... The next day I went to Susan Butcher and gave her the ring and the bonnet, and the shawl, and told her what had happened. And she said she was glad of it – that *she* was out of the way. She kept the cap, the shawl, and the ring, and did not give them up to the police ... Ladies and gentlemen, I wish you all a very good night. I have a great deal more to say, but I am so bad I cannot say it.

By 'bad' he meant 'upset' or 'fatigued'. But more than bad did Good seem now. His blatant lies, the last-minute invention of the match-seller, the cruel incrimination of the servant-girl he had meant to marry, and the removal of Jane Jones's ear-rings and ring in addition to the disposal of her property and clothes, all made him seem like evil incarnate. He was removed from the dock as the great crowd that had gathered outside heard of his fate. 'They uttered a tremendous volley of cheers,' said the *Advertiser*. 'And the unhappy wretch was taken to his cell with the cheers of the multitude ringing in his ears.'

It seems likely that Jane Jones was killed – hit on the head with the axe – as she lay in the furthest stall on the mattress, wearing little except her petticoat. For the mattress was found to be stained with blood and urine; and no marks of blood were apparently found on her outer garments, which Good later gave away.

Daniel Good was hanged outside Newgate Prison on Monday, 23 May 1842. The crowd that assembled to witness his execution was said by prison warders to have been the largest they had ever seen. People began gathering outside the prison 12 hours before the execution. At 3.00 am, prison carpenters began erecting the scaffold, completing their task before 6.00 am.

Inside the prison Good, who had slept for less than three hours, got up at 5.00 am, remarking cheerfully to one of the warders that it was 'a very fine morning'. When the Governor, Mr Cope, appeared, Good assured him: 'Mind, I am no murderer – I am no murderer.' Meanwhile, the prison chaplain, the Revd Carver, had been exhorting the condemned man to confess – to no avail, as Good continued to deny any guilt. At 7.00 am he hungrily consumed the breakfast that was was brought to him.

But by 7.45, when the sheriffs, under-sheriffs, reporters and others arrived to witness his final minutes, Good broke down. Sitting on a bench beside the Revd Carver, he wept, clasping his hands and rocking from side to side. 'The Lord be with you all!' he cried. 'The Lord have mercy upon me!' He clung on to anyone who came near him, repeatedly shaking any hands that he could reach, thanking all and sundry for their kindnesses and attentions between saying again and again: 'I never took the life of that woman! I never took a life! I never took a life from anything!' To the Revd Carver he said: 'Oh, sir! You have done everything that a man could do. I love the very ground you walk upon.' Carver responded: 'Think now of what you are saying, and remember that you now have but a few minutes to live. And think of that text which I have so often endeavoured to impress upon you – "If we confess our sins, God is faithful and just to forgive our sins, and to cleanse us from all unrighteousness. But there is no forgiveness of sin without sincere repentance, and a forsaking of sin in the heart."' Good, placing his hand on his heart, replied: 'Oh, sir! I know it! I know it! I would confess everything to you. But I never took a life – I never took a life!' He said this so many times that one of the sheriffs rebuked him, saying: 'You had better remain quiet, as you are only making your case worse!' But Good would not be silent, and continued to declare his innocence and lament his fate.

Minutes before the procession to the scaffold formed up, the Governor gave Good a tumbler of port wine to drink, which he did. The executioner then tied his wrists together, pinioned his arms and removed the coachman's white cravat from his neck. He was wearing a long dark frock-coat, black trousers and a waistcoat, and looked thinner and less healthy than at his first appearance in court. By 7.55, when the grim procession set off through the jail and out to the scaffold, Good was temporarily more composed, though he still tried to shake people's hands.

The *Morning Advertiser*'s reporter wrote: 'The tolling of the chapel bell, the reading of selected portions of the funeral service, and the indistinctly heard shoutings of the mob without, altogether combined to produce a most solemn and impressive effect.'

Outside, Good was overcome with dread. He seemed terrified by the sight and sound of the crowd, and of the scaffold itself. He ascended it slowly, and looking 'more dead than alive' his lower jaw dropped as the rope was adjusted and the cap drawn over his face. It is said he cried: 'Stop! Stop!' and tried to address the crowd. But Calcraft, the executioner, told him not to waste his breath, and to pray. Seconds later, the lever was pulled, and the floor fell from under his feet. The *Advertiser* reported: 'He struggled very little, and appeared to die almost immediately. The only motion observed was about the hands, which, the instant he fell, he raised up in the attitude of prayer, as far as the pinioning rope would allow them to go.'

Before he died, Good dictated three letters, the longest being a general letter of thanks to several people, including the Lord Mayor and his wife (who had paid him a visit), the sheriffs, the Governor, the clergymen, and three of his former masters, Mr Dando, Mr Nottidge and Mr Shiell. In this letter he said: 'I put my trust in James Spencer and his wife, Mrs Spencer, that they will have an eye after my boy.' He also said:

> I do acknowledge, as I am parting this world, that Susan Butcher was the cause of that poor woman, Jane Jones, through jealousy, making away with herself; and Jane Jones told me that she would make away with herself through hearing about Susan Butcher ... I wish to say I never cut her up. The matchman said he could not make away with the body without taking the limbs off. I locked him up in the stables, and I was cleaning my harness. He promised to come on the 6th of April and take the remaining part away, but he never came. He told me he lived in the neighbourhood of Brentford. I knew this man as coming with matches about fourteen or fifteen months.

A short letter was addressed to the Spencers, and a third to Molly Good. In this he said: 'My dear Molly – I write these few lines to bid you farewell, and I'm glad you got acquitted. I hope the things I put in pledge you will be able to redeem, and keep them for yourself. My best respects to you, with tears, and also your friends; and the Lord be with you all, and may the Lord have mercy upon my poor soul. From your unfortunate – Daniel Good.'

The one redeeming feature of Daniel Good's last months is his evident concern for his son, although he pawned the little boy's spare trousers. One wonders what happened thereafter to the boy and whether his father's last wishes were carried out. Was young Daniel rescued from the Lambeth Workhouse, where he had been dumped, and given a home by the Spencers – or by the Shiells? Or did he end up with Molly Good? Did he ever recover from the horrors of that April and May, from the dreadful deaths of his 'mother' and father? Unfortunately, murder trials and tales have little to say about those other victims, the family's survivors – and less if anything at all about the children of the hanged.

In June 1842 – as the result of the Jane Jones murder and that of a policeman on duty – the Joint Commissioners of the Metropolitan Police, Colonel Rowan and Richard Mayne, sent a memorandum to the Home Secretary, Sir James Graham, advocating the setting-up of a plain-clothes 'Detective Force' to co-ordinate and carry out investigations into certain crimes. This force, created that month, consisted of two inspectors and six sergeants.

Two more sergeants were soon added to the team, and from 1846 two constables from each Division were regularly trained in detective work to assist in operations. But there would be no increase in the basic complement until 1864. Even four years later the detectives numbered a mere 15, out of a police force of nearly 8,000 men.

Of the original eight who formed the Detective Force, forerunner of the CID, one was Sgt Stephen Thornton. Another, the senior detective inspector in charge of the force, was Inspector Nicholas Pearce.

CHAPTER 3

William Palmer
The Murder of John Cook, 1855

If speculation and other writers are to be believed, the murder of John Cook was the last in a series of murders that Palmer committed over a period of ten years, during which as many as 15 men, women and children were poisoned by him. His trial, the first for poisoning by strychnine – although none was found in the body of the deceased – was one of the longest and most sensational of the century. It was remarkable also for the length of the defence and prosecution speeches, the overt partiality of the judge, and the profusion and confusion of the medical experts. In its way, the trial was as much a damning contemporary comment on the medical profession, its ignorance and ineffectuality, as the recent deaths of thousands of soldiers in the Crimean War mainly through disease and despite Florence Nightingale's endeavours. The war came to an end in 1855 with the Russian surrender of Sebastopol – two months before the death in a Staffordshire inn of a young racehorse-owner, John Parsons Cook.

He was a slight and pale young man, aged 29, who played village cricket and regularly rode with a hunt. But he had a weak constitution and was liable to headaches and bilious attacks. He also had bad teeth, spots and ulcerations, some of the latter being minor syphilitic symptoms. Some two weeks before his death, he visited his doctor, Henry Savage, who noted that one of Cook's tonsils was red and enlarged and that there were some superficial ulcers on his lips. He assured Cook that he did not have syphilis and that his general health was good. Dr Savage said later: 'He was a weak man, and apt to take the advice of any person he might be in company with . . . I recommended him to go abroad for two years, as I wished to get him away from his turf associations.' One of them was William Palmer.

Cook had been a solicitor. But when he inherited some £12,000 he abandoned that profession, became a racehorse-owner and frequenter of race-tracks. He met Palmer about a year before his death. They soon became friends, and for a while they were joint owners of a mare, Pyrrhine, until, in settlement of a debt or loan, she became Palmer's property. Although both men owned several horses, they were virtually broke when on Monday, 12 November 1855 they went to the Shrewsbury Races, taking two bedrooms and a sitting-room at the Raven Hotel. Cook had some cash, which he had won at Worcester Races the previous week. But Palmer was deep in debt, owing one money-lender £11,500, and another, £2,000. Both, however, had horses running in the races, and it would literally be a matter of life and death, as to which horse, if either, won. In the event, Cook's won and Palmer's lost and Cook was doomed.

William Palmer was 31, boyish, blue-eyed, short and chubby, with thinning hair. Baptised at Rugeley in Staffordshire on 21 October 1824, he was the second son in a family of five boys and two girls, whose father, Joseph, a sawyer, had so improved his lot that when he died in 1836 he owned a sawmill and left his family £70,000 – of which William received about £9,000 when he was 21. Apprenticed to a firm of wholesale druggists in Liverpool, he stole from them and was redeemed by his mother, Mrs Sarah Palmer, who continued to rescue him from financial troubles (not always knowingly) for the rest of his life. She herself was already a source of local scandal – as were a drunken uncle and brother of William (both of whom he later killed) – because of various unseemly love affairs that followed her husband's death.

Apprenticed next to a surgeon near Rugeley, from whom he also stole and in due course absconded, William then moved to Stafford Infirmary to continue his medical studies. There he remained for four years, finally obtaining his diplomas as a surgeon at St Bartholomew's Hospital in London in August 1846. He then returned to Rugeley, setting up an alternative doctor's practice in the High Street to that of 74-year-old Dr Bamford. Palmer was 22.

The chief pleasures of his youth were women, horses, money and drink. Quite without scruples of any kind, he cheated, lied and stole to achieve his ends, while maintaining a good appearance of social respectability and concern: he was a regular church-goer and generous to his horsy friends. He also possessed an abundance of energy and boyish charm. It is said that, before he married, he fathered 14 illegitimate children of as many girls.

His first victim is said to have been a man called Abley. Palmer was having an affair with Mrs Abley, and her husband died after a drinking session with Palmer, who supposedly put strychnine in his brandy – partly to see how it worked. Then one of his illegitimate children, born to a local girl, Jane Mumford, died after visiting him. But it was not until the young Rugeley doctor married, in 1847, that poison became his panacea for any inconvenient problem.

His wife, Annie, was the illegitimate daughter of a Colonel Brookes, who had served in India and settled in Stafford; the housekeeper, Mary Thornton, was Annie's mother. When the Colonel died, his estate, amounting to about £20,000, was divided between the two women, although Annie's share was tied up in Chancery. No doubt it was her inheritance that made Annie so precious to Palmer – he wooed her for over a year, until she was 21 and free to choose whom she married. But she was obviously not unattractive. She produced five children in the seven years before she died. Four of those children also died in infancy, the first in January 1851; the eldest, Willie, was the only one to survive.

A letter that William Palmer wrote to his wife has also survived. Undated, it gives some indication of the literary style and measure of the man.

My ever adored Annie. I feel certain you will forgive me for not writing to you last night when I tell you that since I last saw you I have not had two hours sleep. I do assure you I never felt so tired in my life. I am almost sick of my Profession. Sorry I am to say my Mother has had another attack & one of my Sister's children I think will be dead before morning . . . My dearest Annie, I purpose all being well being with you tomorrow about three & depend upon it nothing but ill health will ever keep me away from you. Forgive me my duck for not sending you the papers last night. I really could not help it – I will explain fully tomorrow . . . My sweetest and loveliest Annie, I never was more pleased with you in my life than I was on Friday afternoon last. It was a combination of things. God bless you. I hope we may live together & love each other for 100 years to come. Excuse now for I must go. Till tomorrow accept my everlasting love.

Annie's mother, Mrs Thornton, was the next to die. Said to have been an intemperate, domineering woman, she was not fond of her son-in-law, and suspicious. Invited in January 1849 to stay in Rugeley, she grimly remarked to a neighbour that she did not expect to survive more than a fortnight. She was wrong: she died sooner than that, screaming: 'Take that awful devil away!' when her attentive son-in-law appeared by her bed. According to the local physician, Dr Bamford, who, it seems, was not just aged but unqualified and accepted all his confident younger colleague's diagnoses and assertions, Mrs Thornton died of apoplexy. Her possessions and property were duly inherited by her daughter and absorbed by Palmer, and converted to cash, and spent.

The following year, after a visit to a race-meeting at Chester, Palmer found himself owing £600 to a companion and brewer called Bladon, a debt he was unable or reluctant to pay. Invited to stay with the Palmers at Rugeley, Bladon expired within a week. Mrs Bladon arrived just before her husband's very sudden demise, and although friends encouraged her to seek a post-mortem or involve the police, she neglected to do so, succumbing instead to the seductive charms of her host.

A similar calamity visited another racing companion, called Bly, whom Palmer owed £800. As with Bladon, Dr Bamford signed a blameless death certificate, and Bly's widow was told that it was her husband who owed Palmer £800, not the other way around, and that she should honour this debt.

But this was small beer, resulting in the cancellation of Palmer's debts without augmenting his income, and in 1852, when he abandoned his moribund and unprofitable medical practice to pursue a full-time career as a racehorse-owner and gentleman of the turf, he looked to his own family to finance his investments, which involved a string of horses and his own stud and stables at Hednesford.

Expecting to inherit a modest legacy at least from an uncle, Joseph Bentley, Palmer invited his debauched and drunken relation to take part in a brandy-drinking contest, which the uncle won, dying not unexpectedly a few days later, mourned by his less indigent nephew. A wealthy aunt was the next object of Palmer's familial attention. Taken ill while on a visit to the Palmers' house in Rugeley, she was given some special pills by her solicitous nephew, which he advised her to take before she slept. Feeling better, she dispensed with his remedy by disposing of the pills by throwing them out of a window. The following morning several occupants of an adjacent chicken-run were discovered to have died. Whereupon the blessed and not suddenly sainted aunt discovered she was well enough to travel and had urgent business elsewhere.

In 1852, in addition to Uncle Joseph, two of Palmer's infant children also died, in January and December that year. It is said that he let them suck at a finger while they were cradled in his arms, having dipped the finger in a fatal sauce of honey and some poison. 'What will people say?' wondered sad Annie, speaking to a sister-in-law. 'My mother died here, then Mr Bladon, and now all these children!'

Local gossip was presumably saying in whispers quite a lot. But infant mortality was far from unknown, and hard-drinking, over-eating and un-hygienic adults might succumb suddenly and mysteriously to one of many virulent mid-Victorian diseases. And who among the racing fraternity and tradesmen of Rugeley really thought that carousing, church-going, cheerful William Palmer could be a killer in their midst? Nor could Annie Palmer ever believe that the loving man who had fathered her five children and called her his duck, was now plotting to kill her – but not before he had insured her life for £13,000.

In 1853, Palmer's financial situation, despite the benefits accruing from the deaths of family and friends, was worse than ever. With reckless abandon, he had placed bets amounting to £10,000 on his mare, Nettle, winning the Oaks. She lost, and he lost the lot. Other bets and gambles failed; he defaulted on some and was blacklisted by Tattersall's. To pay his debts he borrowed from money-lenders at high interest rates, and as security drew up documents in his mother's name and faked her signature. Eventually his debts, with interest and other charges added, amounted to some £20,000.

With the help of a round-faced Rugeley solicitor, Jeremiah (Jerry) Smith, who had been one of his mother's lovers, Palmer sought to insure his wife's life for £25,000. This failed, but he succeeded in January 1854 (soon after his fourth infant died) in effecting a policy for £13,000 at an annual premium, which was paid, of £760. It was not until September, however, that Annie Palmer fell ill and died, poisoned over a period of nine days by stiff doses of antimony. Palmer wrote in his diary for September 29, Friday: 'My poor, dear Annie expired at 10 past 1.' And Dr Bamford, now an octogenarian, wrote 'English cholera' in the section of her death certificate describing the cause of death. After some delay and with some reluctance, the insurance company paid.

Nine days after Annie's death, the sorrowing widower took his only surviving offspring, Willie, to church to receive the condolences of the community. Nine months later, his housemaid, Eliza Tharm, gave birth to their illegitimate child. It is said that he was in bed with her the night that Annie died.

Such was the success of this venture, although the money was soon swallowed up by Palmer's creditors, that he tried to duplicate it by insuring the life of his drunken younger brother, Walter, for £82,000. Three companies were approached, with Jerry Smith acting on Palmer's behalf. Eventually, as with his wife, he managed to take out a policy with the Prince of Wales Company for £13,000. This policy was lodged with a London money-lender, Thomas Pratt, as security to cover a number of debts, which then began to be slowly repaid. Palmer also forged his mother's name as a guarantor on various loans. To forestall the £13,000 going to brother Walter's widow after his death, William agreed to lend Walter £400 in return for all the policy's rights and to pay the premium. Again, the deed was witnessed by Jerry Smith for a £5 fee.

Two other brothers of William in Rugeley were respectable men, being an honest solicitor and a vicar. But Walter Palmer was a dissolute sot, allegedly downing three bottles of gin every day. It was not difficult to add some prussic acid to his intake, and on 16 August 1855, Walter Palmer died.

But this time the insurance company concerned were more than suspicious and sent agents to check on the circumstances of Walter's death. His doctor had warned the company that William had 'insured his late wife's life for many thousands, and after first payment, she died. Be cautious'. And the postboy at the Talbot Arms, where Walter died, James Myatt, attested that he had seen William put something in Walter's glass. Soon after this, Myatt was persuaded to have a drink with Palmer and was laid low with agonising pains in his stomach. He recovered after a couple of days. In the meantime, Walter's widow laid claim to the policy on her husband's death, on the grounds that the £400 loan had never been paid.

Palmer was now becoming desperate. Pratt was pressing him for part payment of some of his debts, as was another money-lender, Padwick. So, having suffered a setback with Walter, he looked elsewhere for another life to insure, and fastened on the overseer of his stud and stables, George Bates, a former farmer who was paid, though not regularly, a sovereign a week for his labours. Said Bates: 'I looked after his stud and saw that the boys who had the care of the horses did their duty. I had no fixed salary.' Bates, a single man, had lodgings in Rugeley, for which he paid 6s 6d a week. It was in September, after a dinner in Palmer's home (when the other guest was John Parsons Cook) that the subject of insuring Bates's life was broached.

In October the necessary application was formulated by Palmer and Jerry Smith (it seems that Bates was virtually illiterate, though he could sign his name) and his life was insured for £10,000. Smith, acting as the company's local agent, for which he received a percentage of the premium, described Bates as 'a Gentleman of good Property and possessing a Capital Cellar of Wine'. No doubt he was also paid well by Palmer. Unfortunately, the insurance company reneged on the policy after making some checks, and the agents investigating Walter Palmer's death threatened to call in the police. So Palmer had to consider other means and other persons to solve his ever-present pecuniary problems. He now owed the money-lender, Thomas Pratt, £11,500.

On 6 November, Pratt issued two writs for £4,000 against Palmer and his mother. The following Saturday (10 November), Palmer visited Pratt in London and paid him £300. He prevaricated about paying off two large loans made on the expected payment on Walter's policy, and Pratt apparently threatened him with the writs, which had not been served. If and when the writs *were* served, Palmer would be revealed as a forger of his mother's name, and possibly others – he had forged Cook's signature endorsing a cheque for £375. On 13 November, when Palmer and Cook were both at Shrewsbury, Pratt wrote that steps must be taken to enforce the policy on Walter Palmer's life. 'I count most positively on seeing you on Saturday,' said Pratt. At the same time Palmer was being blackmailed by Jane Burgess, a Stafford girl, whom he had paid to have an abortion. Letters concerning this and other matters were in her possession, and she asked him for £50 for their return. On 13 November he wrote to her: 'I cannot do what you ask. I should not mind giving £30 for the whole of them, though I am hard up at present.'

It was at Shrewsbury on Tuesday, 13 November 1855, that a temporary solution to Palmer's many money problems presented itself. Cook's horse, Polestar, unexpectedly won the Shrewsbury Handicap at 7–1. His winnings amounted, with the stakes, to £2,050. He was as good as dead.

According to another doctor friend of Cook, William Jones, who spent the day with him and whose home at Lutterworth in Leicestershire was where Cook lived when not chasing to race-meetings around England:

> After the race was run he was so excited that for two or three minutes he could not speak to me. He was elated and happy the rest of the day, but he was not at all intoxicated. He was a very temperate man ... We dined together in the evening at the Raven Hotel. He accompanied me when I left the hotel at 10 o'clock for the station. On our way there we called at the house of Mr Fraill, the clerk of the course. I was present during a conversation they had along with Whitehouse, the jockey. Cook produced his betting book and calculated his winnings.

Palmer, it seems, was elsewhere that night, apparently in Rugeley, whither he had dashed to procure some antimony, or tartar emetic, with which to commence his poisoning of Polestar's owner.

On Wednesday, 14 November, Cook collected some of his winnings and, with what he had won at Worcester, now had some £750 on him in banknotes. He attended the races that afternoon with Palmer, and the two of them were seen in the Unicorn Hotel at about 9.00 pm before they returned to their rooms in the Raven, where several racing companions assembled about 11.00 pm to drink some grog (brandy and water). Among them were Cook's agent, a wine merchant, Ishmael Fisher; another wine merchant, George Reid; a law stationer, Thomas Jones; and a Rugeley saddler, George Myatt, who had arrived, at Palmer's invitation, in Shrewsbury that night. He later slept in Palmer's bedroom. They sat around a table, drinking from a decanter of brandy, and smoking. Myatt would say later that Cook 'seemed the worse of liquor', though Fisher said he 'certainly was not drunk'.

Earlier that evening, Mrs Anne Brooks of Manchester, an occasional attendant at races without her husband's knowledge, had met Palmer in the street at about 8.00 pm. They conversed about racing prospects and odds for the following day, when Palmer's horse, Chicken, would run. He asked her to procure some information about Lord Derby's horse, and at 10.30 pm she went to the Raven, leaving her friends to wait for her below. She went upstairs and found Palmer standing by a small table in a corridor, with a glass in his hand. 'I'll be with you presently,' he said, holding the glass up to a gas-light and shaking a small quantity of colourless liquid within the glass. He made some casual remark about the weather, to which Mrs Brooks replied, then entered an empty adjacent sitting-room (not his own), whose door was partially open. In a minute or so he reappeared, still carrying the glass, and went into his own room, shutting the door behind him. Before long he emerged from his sitting-room bearing a glass of brandy and water for Mrs Brooks. As she sipped it, they discussed the next day's racing.

She suffered no ill effects from her drink. But curiously, and probably coincidentally, several racing persons were taken ill that day. Mrs Brooks said later: 'There was a wonder as to what had caused their illness, and something was said about the water being poisoned. They were affected by sickness and purging.' We do not know *when* on Wednesday people were smitten; and as Palmer was apparently in Rugeley on Tuesday night and on Wednesday morning, he was probably not to blame. But what happened to John Cook on Wednesday night was certainly of Palmer's doing.

Some time before midnight the party in the Cook/Palmer sitting-room was coming to a jovial end. Thomas Jones had left, and George Reid had just arrived, when Cook complained about the taste of his glass of grog, and asked Palmer to get him another. Palmer said he would do so if Cook emptied his glass – which he did, protesting: 'It burns my throat dreadfully.' He also said: 'There was something in it.' 'There's nothing in it,' retorted Palmer, seeming to take a sip of what was left, after which he handed the glass to Reid, who said: 'What's the use of giving me an empty glass?' Myatt said nothing, while Fisher sniffed the glass and commented that it smelled of brandy, and strongly so. A few minutes later the party broke up. Reid departed, while Palmer and Myatt retired to their shared bedroom (the bedrooms seem to have been on an upper floor), remaining there undisturbed and probably in a drunken torpor until dawn.

Cook was left with Fisher, and in ten minutes or so Cook rushed out of the room to be sick. Returning, he took Fisher outside and into Fisher's sitting-room, where he said he thought Palmer had been playing a trick on him and had put something disagreeable in his drink. Some similar jest had happened to him before. He gave Fisher his £750 for safe-keeping and then was violently sick again. After a third such seizure, this time up in Cook's bedroom, Fisher sent for a doctor, Mr Gibson, who arrived about 12.30. Cook complained of pains in his stomach and a burning throat, and said he thought he had been poisoned. Gibson advised him to take an emetic, which he did and was sick yet again. After this Gibson dosed the young man with rhubarb pills containing calomel and a draught of mistura sennacum. Fisher sat up with Cook until 2.00 am, when he exhaustedly fell asleep.

The following morning, Thursday, Palmer sent Myatt to check on Cook, who was still unwell and in bed. He told Myatt about his sickness and the doctor's visit and demanded to know what had been put in his grog. Myatt expressed total ignorance and fetched Palmer, who proclaimed his amazed innocence and hurt. 'I never play such tricks with people!' he told Fisher later. 'But I can tell you what he was – he was very drunk.' It seems that Cook believed Palmer. At any rate, he recovered sufficiently to have some breakfast later in the sitting-room and, though looking pale and ill, accompanied the others that afternoon to the racecourse. The weather was poor: it was cold and damp. Palmer's horse, Chicken, ran, and lost, and in losing deprived its owner of £5,000 of potential winnings, not to mention some £500 in bets. If it had won, Cook might have lived.

But Palmer had more to make of Cook, and his signature, which he intended to forge on money transactions, as he had done before. That evening, after an early meal in the Raven, Palmer and Myatt returned to Rugeley, about 6.00 pm, taking John Cook with them. They travelled by train from Shrewsbury to Stafford (Palmer paid) and then drove for nine miles in a fly (a one-horse hackney-cab) to Rugeley, during which journey *Palmer* was sick, and vomited out of the window. On arriving, Cook found accommodation in the Talbot Arms in the High Street, which was opposite Palmer's house. Still feeling poorly, he went to bed about 10.00 pm.

On Friday morning he was visited at 10.00 am by Palmer's solicitor, Jerry Smith, a small-eyed, fat-bodied man, who later told the court:

> He was having breakfast in bed – a cup of tea with a wineglassful of brandy in it. I dined with him and Mr Palmer about two o'clock. We had a beef steak and some champagne. After dinner we had three bottles of port wine, of which Cook drank his share. We rose from the table between five and six, and Cook and I went to my house, and then to the Albion Hotel, which is next door, and had a brandy and water each.

Smith asked Cook for £50, which he was owed. Cook gave him £5, saying he would pay the balance when he returned from claiming the rest of his winnings at Tattersall's in London on Monday. He said he had already loaned Palmer some money to settle a debt. And indeed that day he had written to Ishmael Fisher in London, and told him to pay £200 to Mr Pratt of Queen Street, Mayfair, in part settlement of a £500 debt. 'It is of great importance to both Mr Palmer and myself,' wrote Cook, adding, 'I will settle it on Monday at Tattersall's. I am much better.' This was engineered by Palmer as a sop to forestall any action being taken on Saturday, as threatened by Pratt, who received a letter from Palmer, saying: 'A friend of mine will call and leave you £200 tomorrow.' This Fisher did.

On Friday night Cook again went early to bed. On Saturday morning the process of poisoning him began again and continued on Sunday. Antimony was apparently the poison used.

First, Cook was sick after drinking some coffee while Palmer was in his bedroom. Then Palmer's charwoman was sent to fetch some broth from the Albion, and after he had warmed it up (and doctored it) in his kitchen, she took it over to the Talbot Arms, having been instructed to say it came from Jerry Smith. Cook refused to sample it, but on Palmer's insistence, did so later and was sick again. Some barley water and arrowroot was next taken up to his room by the chambermaid, apparently without ill effects. They were probably ordered by aged Dr Bamford, whom Palmer, after lunching with Smith and another crony, the postmaster, Samuel Cheshire, prevailed upon to visit Cook about 3.00 pm. He also arranged, at the suggestion of the housekeeper at the Talbot Arms, for Jerry Smith to sleep in Cook's room that night (it had two beds) when Cook was sick after eating some toast and water. Cook was also constrained to use what Smith referred to as 'the night-chair'. Evidently he was also suffering from diarrhoea. The inn was noisy that night, but Smith seems to have slept like a log.

He was woken by the arrival in the morning of Palmer and Bamford. Cook said: 'I'm rather better this morning. I slept from about two or three o'clock, after the confounded concert was gone.' 'I'll send you some more medicine,' Bamford said. Later, Palmer sent the patient another large cup of broth, this time via his gardener. The chambermaid, Elizabeth Mills, took it upstairs, but not before sampling it in the kitchen. Half an hour later she was very sick. So was Cook. She retired to her bed about 1.00 pm, but recovered by 5.00. Cook also recovered, and when Mills saw him again about 10.00 pm he was in good spirits. So much so that Palmer, who was in constant attendance on his friend, assured the housekeeper, Miss Sarah Bond, that no one need sleep in the room that night, not even Daniel, the boots. Palmer knew that Cook would have an undisturbed night, and day, as he (Palmer) had to go to London. It would never do if Cook expired in his absence and when he was not in charge, and he had probably decided to use another, and more deadly poison.

He had also already written to Cook's friend in Lutterworth, William Jones, saying: 'Mr Cook was taken ill at Shrewsbury . . . Since then he has been confined to his bed here with a severe bilious attack, combined with diarrhoea, and I think it is advisable for you to come and see him.' Jones was ill on Monday and could not comply at once. Palmer probably needed him as an innocent witness to Cook's demise.

So, when Palmer saw Cook about 7.15 on Monday morning, the coffee Cook drank had no effect on him, and by one o'clock he was well enough to wash, shave and get dressed. Elizabeth Mills brought him some arrowroot, and he was visited later by, amongst others, his trainer, Mr Saunders, and Dr Bamford, and drank some brandy and water. About 4.30 pm, Cook had another cup of coffee, and at 8.00 Mills took a pillbox, sent by Dr Bamford, to Cook's room and placed it on the dressing-table. By this time Palmer was well on his way back from London, having caught the 5.00 pm express for Stafford at Euston Station. A slow, smoky and noisy train, it arrived three minutes late, at 8.45. Palmer was back in Rugeley by half-past nine.

In London he had seen an agent, George Herring, with the assumed purpose of settling Cook's debts on his behalf, using his Polestar winnings, which added up to £984. Herring was instructed to pay Padwick £550 out of the winnings and Pratt £450. After collecting all but £110 of the money at Tattersall's (a Mr Morris had only paid £90 of the £200 he owed), Herring sent a cheque for £450 to Pratt and wrote to Cook, care of 'Palmer, Rugeley', saying what he had done. This letter was intercepted by the postmaster, Cheshire, and given to Palmer. The two of them had been at school together and Cheshire had already been persuaded, with gifts and/or money, to intercept any official-looking letters addressed to Mrs Palmer.

After deluding Herring, Palmer then went to see Pratt, to whom he gave £50 and told him that £450 was on its way. This meant that with £200 already sent by Cook, the £2,000 once owed to Pratt had been reduced to £1,300. No doubt well pleased with himself, Palmer returned to Rugeley for the final kill.

On arriving he called at Dr Salt's pharmacy and persuaded the young assistant there, Charles Newton, to give him three grains of strychnine. Newton did so without charging Palmer or making any note in a poison register. He later told the court: 'Mr Salt was not on speaking terms with Mr Palmer, and I thought Mr Salt would be angry at my letting him have it.' Palmer then called on John Cook in his room at the Talbot Arms.

Some minutes before midnight, the inn's waitress, Lavinia Barnes, was in the kitchen when the bell for Cook's room rang madly on the wall. 'I went up to his room,' she said, 'and found he was very ill. He was screaming "Murder!" and was in violent pain. He said he was suffocating. He asked me to send for Mr Palmer. His eyes looked very wild, and were standing a great way out of his head. He was beating the bed with his hands. I sent the boots for Palmer, and went and called Elizabeth Mills.' Her bedroom was on the floor above Cook's room. Mills said:

I heard a noise of violent screaming whilst I was dressing . . . I heard the screams twice. As soon as I entered the room I found him sitting up in bed. He desired me to fetch Mr Palmer directly. I walked to his bedside, and I found the pillow upon the floor. There was one mould candle burning. I picked up the pillow and asked him if he would lay down his head. At that time he was sitting up and was beating the bedclothes with both his arms and hands stretched out. He said: 'I can't lie down – I shall suffocate if I do! Oh, fetch Mr Palmer!' His body, his hands and neck were moving then. A sort of jumping or jerking . . . Sometimes he would throw back his head upon the pillow, and then he would raise himself up again. This jumping and jerking was all over his body . . . Both the eyes were much projected. It was difficult for him to speak, he was so short of breath. He screamed three or four times while I was in the room. He called aloud: 'Murder!' twice. He asked me to rub one hand. I found the left hand stiff. The fingers were something like paralysed.

Cook was conscious throughout. When Palmer appeared, he gasped: 'Oh,

Palmer, I shall die!' 'Oh no, you won't, my lad,' said Palmer. He went away, returning a few minutes later with some pills. Cook said he could not swallow them, so Mills gave him, at Palmer's instruction, a teaspoonful of toast and water. Cook's body was still contorted with spasms. She said later:

> He snapped at the spoon like *that* – with his head and neck, and the spoon was fast between his teeth. It was difficult to get it away . . . Mr Palmer then handed him a draught from a wineglass – three parts full, with a liquid of a dark, heavy-looking nature. Cook drank it. He snapped at the glass just the same as he did at the spoon. He swallowed the liquid, which was vomited up immediately. I supported his forehead . . . The stuff he vomited smelt, I should think, like opium. Palmer said he hoped the pills were not returned, and he searched for the pills with a quill. He said: 'I can't find the pills.' After this Cook seemed to be more easy.

Cook told Palmer he thought he was dying and he must not leave him. He asked Palmer to feel his heart. Palmer said it was all right, still going – perhaps with an edge of ironic surprise.

The waitress, Lavinia Barnes, was also present during most of this, but left the room before 1.00 am. Mills stayed until about three. When she left, Cook was dozing, and Palmer was asleep in a chair. She returned about 6.00 am, to find Cook alone – Palmer had left at quarter to five. When asked how he felt, Cook replied that he was no worse. He asked the chambermaid if she had ever seen anyone suffer such agony. She said: 'No, I never have,' and continued: 'What do you think was the cause of all that, Mr Cook?' And he said it was the pills that Palmer gave him at half-past ten. But this was apparently said without suspicion or any blame.

That Tuesday morning, 20 November, Palmer was still busy trying to make the most of Cook's Polestar winnings and concocting a conclusively fatal dose. The postmaster, Cheshire, was summoned to Palmer's house to write out a cheque, in Palmer's favour and at his dictation, for £350, which was what Cook allegedly owed him, but was in fact the total amount of the Shrewsbury Handicap stakes. Cook, said Palmer, was too ill to write the cheque himself. All Palmer had to do then was to forge Cook's signature and send the cheque to the Secretary of the Jockey Club.

Later that morning Palmer called at Mr Hawkins's chemist's shop, where he was served by an apprentice, Charles Roberts. He asked for some prussic acid, some opium and six grains of strychnine. Roberts was making up the order when Newton, Dr Salt's assistant, came in. Palmer, not wishing Newton to know what he was buying, turned him about and took him outside, where he indulged in idle chat. When another man happened to arrive and begin conversing with Newton, Palmer went back into the shop to pick up his purchases and then walked off towards his house. Newton, once he was free of the other man, re-entered the shop, and enquired what Palmer wanted – it was two years since he had bought anything there. Roberts is said to have replied that Palmer had bought enough poison to finish off the whole parish.

That afternoon, Cook's friend from Lutterworth, Dr William Jones, arrived in Rugeley by train and reached the Talbot Arms by half-past three. He examined Cook in Palmer's presence and found that the patient's pulse was normal and that his tongue was clean. 'You should have seen it before,' said Palmer. Jones also saw no symptoms of the bilious attack described in Palmer's letter.

Both men were in and out of the bedroom all afternoon, attending to Cook, who seemed to improve, although he vomited some coffee and toast and water, brought upstairs by Elizabeth Mills and handed to Palmer. Dr Bamford appeared at 7.00 pm, and the two doctors and Palmer had a consultation on the landing about the case, concluding that Bamford should make up some morphine pills and send them over later. Cook was now strong enough to get up and sit in a chair. 'He was very jocose,' Jones said later, 'speaking of what he should do during the winter, and of his future plans and prospects.' 'He was in very good spirits,' said Elizabeth Mills, 'and talked about getting up the next morning.' She brought him some arrowroot at about half-past ten. Palmer asked Cook if she could do anything more for him, and he said he would want nothing more. So she said goodnight and went downstairs to the kitchen, where she and Lavinia Barnes remained for some time, in case they were needed again. 'I was anxious,' said Elizabeth Mills.

At about 11.00 pm, Palmer entered Cook's room with a box of pills, which he said had been sent by Dr Bamford. He had in fact collected such a box from Bamford an hour earlier. Drawing Jones's attention to the directions on the box, Palmer remarked: 'What an excellent hand for a man upwards of 80 to write.' Jones agreed. Cook was reluctant to take two of the pills, protesting that they had made him ill the previous night. Reassured, however, by the other two men, he swallowed them with toast and water, and once again was sick. Palmer suggested that the utensil in which Cook had vomited be searched for the pills. But they had been retained. Satisfied, Palmer left the room and the inn, returning to his house.

With Cook seeming comfortable, Jones went downstairs for some supper, returning to Cook's room in half an hour, when he undressed while talking idly to Cook, who was sleepy and seemed quite well. Jones climbed into the other bed, leaving a single candle burning darkly in the room.

He was still awake when, ten minutes later, Cook sat up in his bed, crying: 'Doctor, get up! I'm going to be ill! Ring the bell for Mr Palmer!' Below, in the kitchen, the bell for Cook's room rang violently just before twelve. With what apprehension and alarm did the two servant-girls gaze at each other before running upstairs? Lavinia Barnes remained outside Cook's room, while Elizabeth Mills went in, to be told by the agonised man being supported by Jones, who was rubbing the back of his neck: 'Fetch Mr Palmer!' She ran out of the inn and across the street to Palmer's house. She said later: 'I rang the surgery bell at the surgery door. I expected him to come to the window, and as soon as I stepped into the road he was at the bedroom window. He did not put up the sash . . . I asked him to come over to Mr Cook directly, as he was much the same as he was the night before. I then went back to the hotel.'

She was in Cook's bedroom helping William Jones when Palmer entered a few minutes later, remarking: 'I was never so quickly dressed in my life.' He told her to wait outside, and produced what he said were two ammonia pills for Cook to swallow. Cook did so and began to scream, throwing himself back on the bed. He cried to Jones: 'Raise me up – or I shall be suffocated!' Then his whole body was seized by violent convulsions, so extreme that his head and heels bent back as if they would meet. Jones, with Palmer's assistance, tried to lift or control the contorting body but failed, because of the spasms and the rigidity of Cook's limbs. The convulsions lasted for about ten minutes, after which Cook's agony diminished and his heartbeat faded. He was dying. Jones sent Palmer out to fetch some spirits of ammonia, and on the landing he answered Mills's enquiry about the patient by saying he was not so bad as last night – 'not by a fiftieth part'. On Palmer's return, Jones turned Cook, at his request, on to his right side and listened to his heart, holding Cook's clenched left hand in his. He was not able to take the ammonia,' said Jones. 'His heart was gradually sinking, and life was almost extinct. He died so very quietly that I could hardly tell when he did die.'

Palmer sent Mills to fetch Dr Bamford. She did so, and when Bamford left the bedroom later he said: 'He's dead. He was dead when I arrived.' She sat on the stairs for a while until she was summoned into the room by Jones. 'Palmer wants you,' he said. She said to him: 'It's not possible that Mr Cook is dead?' 'Oh, yes. He's dead,' Palmer replied. They discussed who should lay out the body, and when Jones went downstairs to see Miss Bond, both Mills and Barnes, engaged in tidying the room, noticed Palmer rummaging through the pockets of Cook's clothes as well as under the pillow and bolster. They both left as Jones returned to find Palmer with Cook's coat in his hands. With smooth self-possession Palmer remarked that Jones, being Cook's closest friend, should take charge of his effects; and he handed over Cook's watch and purse, containing five sovereigns and five shillings. His betting-book, papers and the balance of his Polestar winnings had already been purloined by Palmer. As he left the inn, Palmer confided in Jones that Cook owed him about £4,000 and expressed the hope that his friends would honour these debts. 'If they don't assist me,' he said, 'all my horses will be seized.'

Palmer's blinkered and obsessive goal of gaining all he could and more from Cook's demise led him to further ill-considered and astounding acts of indifference to the opinions, suspicions and feelings of others. Having killed so often without being caught, he seems to have become convinced of his own immunity from discovery and retribution, presuming that people were more stupid than he, and that he who dares, wins.

On Wednesday, 21 November, Palmer noted in his diary: 'Cook died at 1 o'clock this morning.' Although busy later, making arrangements for Cook to be buried and lunching with Cook's trainer, he found time to write to Thomas Pratt in London:

Ever since I saw you I have been fully engaged with Cook and not able to leave home. I am sorry to say, after all, he died this day. So you had better write to Saunders [Cook's trainer]. But mind you, I must have Polestar, if it can be so arranged, and should anyone call upon you to know what money or moneys Cook ever had from you, don't answer the question till I have seen you . . . I sat up two full nights with Cook, and am very much tired out . . .

To which Pratt replied: 'I have your note, and am greatly disappointed at the non-receipt of the money as promised, and at the vague assurances as to any money . . . If anything unpleasant occurs you must thank yourself.'

The following day Palmer made a more thorough search of Cook's room, ostensibly for a paper-knife. He also summoned Cheshire and produced a document, apparently signed by Cook, which acknowledged, in effect, that Cook owed Palmer £4,000. 'I want you to witness it,' Palmer said. To which Cheshire replied: 'Good God – the man is dead!' He refused to append his signature, as he was not present when the document was drawn up and signed (by Cook). Palmer seemed unconcerned: he would get someone else to witness the deed.

Meanwhile, William Jones had gone to London to inform Cook's step-father, William Stevens, of his stepson's death. Mr Stevens, a retired merchant, who had married Cook's mother 18 years previously, had last seen his stepson at Euston Station on 5 November, when he said: 'My boy, you look very well. You don't look anything like an invalid now.' Where-upon John Cook had manfully struck his chest and said he was quite well. Shocked by Jones's revelations about the manner of Cook's sudden and dreadful death, he travelled with Jones to Lutterworth to collect some personal effects, documents and Cook's will. The two men arrived in Ruge-ley on Friday, 23 November, and proceeded to the Talbot Arms. Stevens and Palmer had only met once before. Stevens said later:

Mr Jones introduced us in the inn, and we then went up and viewed the body. I was greatly struck by . . . the tightness of the muscles across the face. We all then went down to one of the sitting-rooms, and I said to [Palmer] that I understood from Mr Jones that he knew something of my stepson's affairs. He replied: 'Yes. There are £4,000 worth of bills out of his, and I'm sorry to say my name is to them. But I've got a paper drawn up by a lawyer and signed by Mr Cook to show I've never had any benefit from them.' I told him I feared there would be no money to pay them, and asked if he [Cook] had no horses or property. He replied that he had horses, but they were mortgaged . . . I then said that whether Cook had left anything or not, he must be buried. Palmer immediately said: 'Oh, I'll bury him myself, if that's all.' I replied I could not hear of it . . . I said it was my business, as executor, to bury him, and that I in-tended to bury him in London in his mother's grave . . . Some short time afterwards I asked Palmer for the name of some respectable undertaker in Rugeley, so that I might order a coffin at once. He replied: 'I've been and done that. I've ordered a shell and a strong oak coffin.' I expressed my surprise, and said he had no authority to do so.

The three men had lunch together and Stevens left Rugeley by train at 4.15 pm. Before his departure he asked Jones to collect any correspondence, as well as the betting-book from Cook's room. Palmer went along with Jones, who returned empty-handed before long. 'No betting-book, Mr Jones?' exclaimed Stevens, then demanding of Palmer: 'How is this?' 'Oh, it's no manner of use if you find it,' said Palmer. 'No use, sir!' Stevens retorted. 'I'm the best judge of that.' 'It's no manner of use,' Palmer repeated. 'I'm told it *is* of use,' said Stevens. 'I understand my son won a great deal of money at Shrewsbury. And I ought to know something about it.' Palmer said: 'It's no use, I assure you. When a man dies, his bets are done with.' To which Stevens responded: 'Very well, the book ought to be found, and must be found.' 'Oh, it will be found,' said Palmer. 'No doubt of that.'

The next day, Saturday, Palmer entrained for London, where he gave Pratt £100 in part payment of his debts. Returning to Rugeley on the 2.00 pm from Euston he encountered Mr Stevens, who had been taking legal advice and now intended to employ a local solicitor to investigate his stepson's affairs and to arrange a post-mortem. This he told Palmer, who offered to introduce him to a solicitor (Smith). Over the weekend he kept checking on Stevens's intentions and offering advice, to no effect. By now Stevens had learned that enquiries were being made into Walter Palmer's death.

On Sunday, maintaining appearances and social conventions, William Palmer went to church. At some point he called on Dr Bamford about Cook's death certificate, and Bamford, at Palmer's suggestion (for he had been in regular attendance) attributed Cook's death to 'apoplexy'. Meanwhile a post-mortem was organised for the following day. That night Palmer summoned Mr Salt's young assistant, Newton, to his house. Said Newton later: 'There was no one else there. He asked me what dose of strychnine would kill a dog, and whether it would be found in the stomach. I told him a grain, and that there would be no inflammation, and I did not think it would be found. I think he said: "That's all right then", as if speaking to himself, and snapped his fingers.'

The post-mortem, held in a room in the Talbot Arms at about 11.00 am on Monday, 26 November, was one of the most imperfect and farcical ever held. Supervised by a physician from Stafford, Dr Harland, it was carried out by a medical student, Charles Devonshire, assisted by Newton, and attended by Drs Bamford and Jones, by local chemists, surgeons and tradesmen, by Smith and Cheshire, by the publican, Masters, and by William Palmer, who was now under suspicion of causing Cook's death six days previously. The corpse lay naked and pale on a table, the hands still clenched, before the curious and morbid eyes of up to 20 men.

Earlier, Palmer had met Dr Harland when he arrived in Rugeley. They had met several times before. 'I'm glad you've come to do the post-mortem,' said Palmer. 'Someone might have been sent whom I didn't know. I know you.' 'What is this case?' asked Harland. 'I hear there's a suspicion of poisoning.' 'Oh, no!' said Palmer. 'Not at all! He had an epileptic fit on Monday and Tuesday night, and you'll find an old disease in the heart and in the head.' Soon after this he told the nervous Newton, whom he invited to his house for a pre-post-mortem brandy: 'You'll find this fellow's been suffering from a diseased throat. He's had syphilis.'

The stomach and intestines were the first items to be removed and examined. As Devonshire was opening the stomach with a pair of scissors, Palmer gave Newton a shove, which made him bump into Devonshire – with the result that some of the stomach's contents were spilled. 'Don't do that!' said Dr Harland, thinking the persons concerned were just fooling about. What was left in the stomach, about three ounces of brownish liquid, was then inspected by the experts. Nothing unusual was noted there and so announced by Harland. Whereupon Palmer remarked to Bamford: 'They won't hang us yet!' The stomach was then placed in a jar, as was a portion of the intestines. The jar was then wrapped in a double layer of bladders, or parchment, tied up and sealed and placed on a table. It seems not to have had a lid.

The dissection continued: the liver, lungs and heart were examined, and the brain and throat removed. Harland suddenly noticed that Palmer, who had been restlessly moving about, was missing, as was the jar. 'Where's the jar?' demanded Harland. 'It's here,' replied Palmer, from the other end of the room. 'I thought it more convenient for you to take it away.' Harland reclaimed the jar, and discovered that a small cut or slit had been made in the parchment covering the jar. 'Who did this?' he demanded. But Palmer, Newton and Devonshire denied any responsibility. Harland rearranged and retied the wrapping, and the post-mortem eventually established that Cook had been moderately healthy, and had suffered from no disease or defects that might have caused his death. There were papillae or follicles at the back of his tongue which would have caused some discomfort in eating and swallowing. But there were no indications of syphilis, apart from a venereal scar.

It is not clear what Palmer was doing or hoped to do with the jar. Discovered at the end of a long room, near a door which was not the main entrance but a door that led to another room and then a passage, he may have been about to walk away with the jar. More likely, unobserved by the others, he hoped either to empty the stomach's contents through the slit or to inject some chemical that would neutralise the poison within.

It seems he may have succeeded. For when the contents of the jar were later examined by Professor Taylor, an expert in poisons at Guy's Hospital, there was nothing left in the cut-open stomach – which had been squashed by the intestines and much shaken about on the journey south. He tested the jar's contents for several poisons, for strychnine, prussic acid, oxalic acid, arsenic, mercury, antimony, hemlock and hellebore, among others. He also sent for Cook's kidneys, liver and spleen. All Taylor discovered were some traces of antimony – which might have caused Cook's death, although less than a quarter of a grain was found.

The jar had been taken to London by the wary Mr Stevens and a solicitor's clerk, two days after the post-mortem. Before the jar left Rugeley, Palmer made another crazily blatant attempt to destroy the evidence therein. He offered the postboy at the Talbot Arms (who was also a cab-driver) £10 to overturn the fly in which Stevens and the jar were about to be conveyed to Stafford. The postboy refused to comply.

But that was not the end of Palmer's machinations. On 1 December, when in London, he told the porter at a boarding-house to make up a hamper containing a brace of pheasants, a codfish, a turkey and a barrel of oysters, and send it anonymously to W. W. Ward, Esq, of Stoke-on-Trent. Mr Ward was the coroner who conducted the inquest on the death of John Cook. The inquest, held at the Talbot Arms and twice adjourned was much mismanaged by Ward. The jury asked more questions than he. It came to an end on Saturday, 15 December.

The previous day Palmer had written to Ward, most foolishly quoting from a letter written by Professor Taylor on 14 December to Mr Stevens's solicitor in Rugeley – which Cheshire intercepted and opened at Palmer's behest and whose contents were shown to him. On 14 December Taylor's conclusion appeared in Palmer's letter to Ward, in which a £10 note was also enclosed. Palmer wrote:

My dear Sir – I am sorry to tell you that I am still confined to my bed. I do not think it was mentioned at the inquest yesterday that Cook was taken ill on Sunday and Monday night in the same way as he was on the Tuesday night when he died . . . I also believe that a man by the name of Fisher is coming down to prove he received some money at Shrewsbury . . . Had you better not call Smith to prove this? And again, whatever Professor Taylor may say tomorrow, he wrote from London last Tuesday night to Gardner to say 'We have this day finished our analysis, and find no traces of either strychnine, prussic acid, or opium.' What can beat this from a man like Taylor? . . . I know, and saw it in black and white, what Taylor said to Gardner. This is strictly private and confidential, but it is true. As regards his betting-book, I know nothing of it, and it is of no good to anyone. I hope the verdict tomorrow will be that he died of natural causes, and thus end it – Ever yours.

But that was not the verdict, nor was it the end; and William Palmer, apprehended earlier on a writ served by the money-lender, Mr Padwick, was arrested on a charge of wilful murder and taken to Stafford Jail.

Although the bodies of Annie and Walter Palmer were exhumed the following week and their murders ratified by a Grand Jury in Stafford in March 1856, Cook's murder was the only one with which William Palmer was indicted at the opening, on 14 May, of his trial at London's Central Criminal Court. Normally he would have been tried by an assize court in Staffordshire. But local feeling was so biased against him that it was felt he would not have a fair trial. An Act was accordingly passed in Parliament to allow for such a situation and for the trial to take place in London. It is still known as Palmer's Act.

The trial lasted two weeks, and was considered for many years to be one of the greatest trials in the history of English law. Most unusually, three judges presided, led by the Lord Chief Justice, Baron Campbell, then aged 77 and soon to become Lord Chancellor. The other judges were Mr Justice Cresswell and Mr Baron Alderson, aged, respectively, 62 and 68. The prosecution was led by the Attorney-General, Sir Alexander Cockburn, regarded as 'the most accomplished orator of his generation'. A QC since 1841, and a bachelor, he, like Campbell, came from an ancient Scottish family. Assisting him were Mr Edward James, QC, aged 44, who five years later would have debts amounting to £100,000, would be disbarred and become an actor in the USA; Mr W. H. Bodkin, aged 65, who was later knighted and became a judge; Mr William Welsby, aged 61, who had written numerous books about the law; and Mr John Huddleston, aged 41, a brilliant conversationalist and a devotee of both the theatre and the turf, who became a QC after the trial and then an MP, marrying when he was 57. The defence was led by Mr Serjeant Shee, a grey-haired Irishman, aged 51, who had never before defended in a murder trial and replaced another serjeant (ranked higher than a QC) who had been taken ill. Appointed a judge in 1863, Shee became the first Roman Catholic judge since the Reformation. He was assisted by Mr William Grove, QC, aged 45; Mr Edward Kenealey, another Irishman, aged 37; and a Scot, John Gray.

The court was packed. Many noble lords, aldermen and MPs attended the trial, including the Earl of Derby, and admission was by ticket. The *Illustrated London News* said: 'It was generally remarked that [Palmer] looked little like a man who had committed murder, and that he had grown exceedingly stout since his committal to prison. He is a good-humoured, ordinary-looking man and appears much older than he really is.'

Evidence for the prosecution, in which 40 witnesses were called, lasted six full days. Serjeant Shee's eight-hour speech for the defence took up the whole of the seventh day, and he called 21 witnesses, of whom 15 were medical experts. They dilated at length on the effects of strychnine on humans and assorted animals, drawing various conclusions as to the cause of Cook's death, and attributing it to traumatic or idiopathic tetanus, unknown causes, convulsions, arachnitis and even angina pectoris. This was the nub of the defence – that Cook's symptoms indicated he died from some *disease*, not strychnine, of which none was found in his corpse. Most of these experts were extensively cross-examined by the prosecution and the trial was largely a forensic contest full of hypothesis and disagreement. Ten medical witnesses had also been called by the prosecution, whose chief witness, Elizabeth Mills, spent several hours in the witness box.

Serjeant Shee's one-day speech endeavoured to make a detailed and innocent interpretation of some of Palmer's actions and words. Early on, Shee stated: 'I commence his defence – I say it in all sincerity – with an entire conviction of his innocence. I believe there never was a truer word pronounced than the words he pronounced when he said "Not guilty" to this charge.' This earned him the reproof of the Attorney-General and the Lord Chief Justice. Shee also erred when he spoke of Palmer's love for his wife, saying: 'He loved her as ardently as he now loves her first-born, his only surviving child, a boy of seven years old, who waits with trembling anxiety the verdict that will restore him to the arms of his father, or drive that father to an ignominious death upon the scaffold.' At this point the accused covered his face with his hands and wept. Shee went on to read a love-letter from Palmer (which ended: 'with best, best love, believe me, dearest Annie – your own William'); to speak of Palmer's 'dear sister' and 'a gallant and devoted brother', and his aged, grieving and agonised mother; and to urge the jury 'to stem the torrent of prejudice'. Shee was criticised for all these sentiments by a leading legal journal, which said:

> The defence of Mr Serjeant Shee was clever, ingenious and eloquent, but wanting in judgment and taste ... The allusion to the family of the prisoner, and to his supposed affection for his wife, grated sorely, and almost ludicrously, on the sense of propriety in the face of the undisguised fact, known to all his audience, that he was accused of murdering his wife, that he slept with his maid-servant on the very night she died, and that he had confessed himself guilty of forgery upon his mother. Equally injudicious was the philippic against the insurances offices. In worse taste still was his solemn assertion to the jury that he was convinced by the evidence of the prisoner's innocence.

The Attorney-General's address to the jury, said to have been delivered without any notes, was a masterful exposition of the facts and an incisive refutation of the defence's claims. It was given on Saturday, 24 May.

The Lord Chief Justice, having spent 14 hours on the Sunday preparing his summing-up, began his charge to the jury at 10.00 am on the Monday. He spoke for ten hours, during which he dealt with the proofs for the prosecution. The case for the defence was less carefully treated on the Tuesday, much of it merely consisting of the reading of what witnesses had said.

A powerful and wealthy coterie of racing men later organised a concerted and abusive attack on the judge, by letter and in print, likening him to Judge Jeffreys and accusing him of bias and infamous conduct. They hoped to obtain a pardon or reprieve on the grounds that Palmer had not had a fair trial. They said:

> You weakened, by all the means within your power, the effect of the evidence when it told for the prisoner ... Did you not step out of the way to comment (like an advocate) on the evidence? To get up this witness and to knock down that one, to praise those who supported Dr Taylor's theory, and to censure those who were independent of such nonsense? Did not your lordship convey, as clearly to the jury, by meaning looks, by thumping the desk with peculiar energy, by laying emphasis on certain parts of the evidence and then pausing and gazing intently upon the jurymen; by shaking your head, as if your thoughts of [Palmer's] guilt were too dreadful for utterance; by repeating over and over again those parts which told heaviest against him; by running on the evidence for the prisoner so that it was impossible for the jury to understand it?

Mr Baron Alderson was also lambasted as 'that learned functionary, who inaugurated the first day's proceedings by falling asleep and nearly tumbling over his desk during the Attorney-General's opening speech'. He was said to have amused himself during the progress of the trial by suggesting questions to Mr James, the counsel for the prosecution, by lifting up his hands in apparent astonishment when anything favourable to the prisoner was elicited, by looking at the jury with every mark of incredulity and contempt when Serjeant Shee suggested any matter beneficial to the prisoner, and by joining your lordship in overruling every legal objection which was raised by the counsel for the defence.

The jury retired for an hour and 18 minutes, returning with a verdict of 'Guilty'. Palmer was silent when asked if he had anything to say before being sentenced to death. It is said that after the Attorney-General's speech, he passed a note to his defence which said: 'It was the riding that did it.'

While in prison he was buoyant and cheerful, cracking grim little jokes.

He was hanged outside Stafford Jail at 8.00 am on Saturday, 14 June 1856, reiterating: 'I am innocent of poisoning Cook by strychnia.' And indeed this may have been, strictly speaking, correct, some other allied poison having been used in addition to antimony. The hangman was George Smith of Dudley, who wore a top hat and a long white coat.

Before a crowd of 30,000, some of whom were seated in grandstands, having paid a guinea for a place, Palmer composedly climbed the ladder to the scaffold and positioned himself directly below the noose. His body was buried in the precincts of Stafford Jail.

Some residents of Rugeley, embarrassed by the town's image as a sink of immorality, drunkenness, corruption and vice, and as a centre of mass murder, sought to change its name. They failed, and Rugeley is still on the map. The Talbot Arms, after its name was changed to the Shrewsbury Arms, is now called the Shrew Kafé-Bar. Palmer's house is now occupied by a video shop and a shop selling women's wear, and although the tombstone over the Palmers' family vault in the graveyard has been broken and battered by vandals, it still records the deaths of William's father in 1836, of his mother, Sarah, in 1861, and of his brother George and his wife in 1866 and 1870. William's brother, Walter, his wife Annie, and their four infants, are also buried there – but their deaths are not recorded. At a distance stands the unravaged gravestone of John Cook, singing his praises and saying: 'Whose life was taken away at Rugeley on the night of 22 November 1855 in the 29th year of his age.'

Robert Graves wrote a book, published in 1962, asserting Palmer's innocence and entitled *They Hanged My Saintly Billy.* In it a footnote records that Palmer's surviving son, Willie, committed suicide, aged 72, in 1925.

What a contemporary and a judge, Sir James Stephen, who had made a study of murderers, said of Palmer is worth quoting here, as it could apply to most murderers – few if any of whom are the 'monsters' created by the popular press.

His career supplied one of the proofs of the fact . . . that such a thing as atrocious wickedness is consistent with good education, perfect sanity, and everything, in a word, which deprives men of all excuse for crime. Palmer was respectably brought up; apart from his extravagance and vice, he might have lived comfortably enough. He was a model of physical health and strength, and was courageous, determined, and energetic. No one ever suggested that there was ever a disposition towards madness in him. Yet he was as cruel, as treacherous, as greedy of money and pleasure, as brutally hard-hearted and as sensual a wretch as it is possible ever to imagine. If he had been the lowest and most ignorant ruffian that ever sprang from a long line of criminal ancestors, he could not have been worse than he was.

CHAPTER 4

James Mullins

The Murder of Mary Emsley, 1860

Murder is mostly committed out of a compulsion to possess, or to dispossess – to get, or to get rid of, someone or something. When not motivated by rage, self-loathing, lust or frustration, most murderers kill in the course of a robbery, in taking what is not theirs. They could take without killing. But some basic denial of the owner, and his or her rights, seems to be an associated necessity. In order for the taker to feel fully secure and to take full possession, the owner, especially if weak or elderly, must lose not just property, but life as well.

On 17 August 1860, Inspector Hayes of K Division, which covered Stepney, sent a Murder Report to the Detective Department of the Metropolitan Police. He wrote:

> I beg to report that at 12 noon this day, Mr Rose, Solicitor, of No. 19 Change Alley, Cornhill, informed Sergeant Dillon, K19, that he had called at the house of Mrs Hemsley, Widow, No. 9 Grove Road, Mile End Road, Stepney, for the purpose of seeing her, but could not make anyone hear, & that he thought something was wrong. The Sgt went through the next house & over the garden wall, when he found the back door & window shutters of No. 9 unfastened; he proceeded upstairs & in the front room (2nd floor) he found Mrs Hemsley, dead, lying on her left side with her head against the doorpost. Dr Gill, of Bow, who was passing at the time examined deceased & stated that death had been caused by the fracture of the back part of the skull . . . There is a great quantity of congealed blood on the floor & it is supposed that deceased had been lying where found for – at least – 2 or 3 days. The deceased was last seen alive on Monday afternoon last. She was a very eccentric person, of independent means, & lived alone. I respectfully beg that one of the Detective Force may assist in the inquiry.

Inspector Stephen Thornton was put in charge of the case, and on 18 August he dispatched Sgt Dick Tanner, aged 28, and Sgt Bill Thomas, an ex-grocer from Bagshot, to investigate the circumstances surrounding the elderly woman's death.

Three days later Inspector Thornton penned his own report to the Assistant Commissioner. He wrote:

The deceased was about 70 years of age, resided quite alone in her house and was possessed of considerable house property situated in very low neighbourhoods of Bethnal Green, Ratcliff, Stratford, Barking, Dagenham, etc, and she was in the habit of personally collecting the greater portion of her rents on a Monday, and in consequence of her frequent litigation with the tenants, her very plain way of dressing and living, she became well known at the East End of London. On the 2nd August last the deceased purchased a large quantity of paper hangings at an auction (part of a bankrupt stock), the major portion of which was put into the room where the deceased's body was found, and I am of opinion that some person or persons called on the deceased on Monday evening last (13 August) under pretence of buying some of the said paper hangings, and she went upstairs to the top room to show it when she was murdered and robbed of 3 or 4 rings from her fingers and whatever rents she collected on that day estimated at present at about £40, which is all the property that at present can be ascertained to be stolen. I directed a thorough search of the Coal Cellar, privy, etc of the house in order if possible to find the weapon with which the deceased was murdered but it cannot be found, but a tin box containing £32 in gold, and £16-2-0 in silver has been found among the Coal in the cellar, and now is in the hands of the police. There is no doubt the deceased was murdered on Monday evening as she was not seen alive after that time and it was not discovered until about 12 noon the following Friday [17 August]. At present there is no clue to the perpetrator of the crime . . . There is nothing stolen which can be traced beyond a Ten pound cheque which has been stopped, but I am of opinion the murderer will not make use of that . . . The deceased employed a number of persons to assist to collect her rents, and many others to do her jobbing work at her houses; her custom of living alone, collecting and taking home rents on a Monday was also well known among her tenants numbering some hundreds, some of whom are of the most depraved and lowest class, and who have frequently threatened her. Her solicitor, Mr Rose, a very highly respectable man, informs me that he has frequently told the deceased that he thought she would be murdered, going about as she did alone among such bad and dangerous characters. The deceased has also a number of very poor relations who have also a great interest in her death, and she had made up her mind to make a will to build Almshouses with the whole of the money and not leave anything to her relatives which fact the deceased had talked publicly about and all the relatives knew it . . . Myself and Sergeants Tanner and Thomas are still pursuing the inquiry.

Among the many suspects was a soldier based in Portsmouth, Edward Jackson, said to be a nephew of Mrs Emsley and 'a very bad character'. Thornton, in another report, seeking instructions and also dated 21 August, wrote: '[Jackson] has often inquired by letter to his sister to know if his Aunt was dead, and has appeared anxious for her death, as he believes he will have considerable property at her death.' Thornton asked whether he should send

Tanner to Portsmouth to make enquiries, or telegraph the local police. The Assistant Commissioner replied, writing at the foot of Thornton's report: 'Telegraph inquiry to the Police – and if the soldier has been absent PS Tanner may be sent at once.' Promptly Thornton sent a message and on the same day received the following reply from the Portsmouth Superintendent: 'Edward Jackson was not absent but obtained leave today to go to London about the murder of a Relative.'

We do not know whether the soldier or any of those who claimed to be related to Mrs Emsley eventually inherited part of her fortune. It was a considerable one: she is said to have owned literally hundreds of houses and to have had an annual income of £5,000. Most people then earned £50 a year, or less. Her husband, another eccentric, and a building contractor and brickmaker, had died about four years earlier. They had been married for 17 years. Both, it seems, had had previous partners. So Mrs Emsley had been a very wealthy widow indeed. She was also very miserly and mean: she only bought the cheapest food at markets – stale vegetables and meat – and her house, without the attentions of a single live-in servant, exhibited every sign of dust, dirt and general neglect. Anything of value, like jewellery and silver plate, had been safely stored elsewhere or was hidden, like the tin box in the cellar containing coins of gold and silver. But every Monday, when she went out to collect her rents, she had the equivalent of a poor man's annual wage on her person. This money she brought home, no doubt to count and tabulate, before taking it that same evening to be locked away in a safe in the New Globe Tavern in Mile End Road.

On Monday, 13 August – as Thornton and his team soon established – Mrs Emsley was visited by a niece, Mrs Gotz, who apparently 'dined' with her. That afternoon she was out rent-collecting in Barnsley Street near Bethnal Green Station, one of her more insalubrious possessions. That evening she was seen by a neighbour sitting at a first-floor window of her house, between 7.00 and 8.00 pm. She was probably killed soon after this, before it got dark, as no shutters were closed and no candles were found to have been lit or taken to the second-floor lumber room where she died. The police thought she must have known and trusted her killer, as she was wary of letting anyone in, and there was no sign of a forced entry. Thornton's theory was that someone had called on her to collect or buy some of the paper hangings stored in the lumber room. Why else was she killed up there?

On the Tuesday, a youth called Edwin Emm went to the house to pick up two brass taps for his father, Walter Emm, a shoemaker, who did odd jobs for Mrs Emsley and sometimes acted as her rent-collector. No one answered his knocking at the front door. Nor was there any reply or reaction to the follow-up visits made on Wednesday, Thursday and Friday by Walter Emm. He reported the matter to Mrs Emsley's solicitor, Mr Rose, who went to see for himself; and when he also failed to gain entry, he sent for the police and notified a Mr Faith and a Mr Whitaker, who had each married a stepdaughter of Mrs Emsley. The two sons-in-law, with Emm and Rose, waited in the street while Sgt Dillon entered the house at noon, via the garden wall and the unlocked back door. He let the others in and Mrs Emsley's body was found on the second floor, her head so badly battered by a blunt instrument that pieces of bone had been driven into the brain.

A search revealed that Monday's rental payments had been stolen, as well as some rings, a £10 cheque (received on the Monday), and a few knick-knacks, like spoons and a silver pencil-case. The lower rooms were in a state of considerable confusion: they had evidently been ransacked, and were littered with hundreds of documents, agreements and deeds. One of them, a receipt, had been signed in the house on the day of the murder by a paperer and plasterer, who like Emm did odd jobs for Mrs Emsley. His name was James Mullins.

A middle-aged man with a slight Irish accent, he had once been a police sergeant in K Division, until some misdemeanour caused him to be dismissed. About ten years ago he had been sentenced to six years' penal servitude for larceny, part of which was spent in the county jail at Leicester. An official said later: 'His conduct here was very bad and required constant watching by the officers.' He was removed as 'incurable' to Dartmoor Prison in November 1854, but despite that label and an attack on a police officer he was eventually released.

According to a charlady, it was Mullins who had carried Mrs Emsley's bargain buy of hundreds of paper-rolls up to the second-floor room on Saturday, 4 August – for which she paid him six shillings. It was because of his association with the scene of the murder, and his criminal record, and the receipt, that Inspector Thornton had Mullins briefly tailed and watched. Walter Emm was also under suspicion, as being another odd-job man who was known to enter the house. However, both men had alibis for the evening of 13 August, and much of the initial police inquiry was taken up in investigating a host of other suspects: German Jews, disaffected tenants and penurious relations headed the list. It was not in fact until 28 August that Mullins was interviewed by Sgt Tanner.

By this time there had been another, accidental death at 9 Grove Road. PC Watson, acting as a security guard, had been living in the house since Mrs Emsley's body was found. His family were with him. On the morning of Friday, 24 August, his four-year-old son fell out of a window at the back and was killed.

By this time also, a large reward amounting to £300 (£200 of which was contributed by Mrs Emsley's sons-in-law) had been offered for any information that might lead to an arrest. But no arrest was made, or seemed likely to be made, and *The Times*, on 8 September, three weeks after the body was found, reported that the police were 'ready to abandon the investigation as hopeless'. Then, on that very day, the killer, in trying to incriminate someone else and claim the reward, gave himself away.

The ex-policeman, James Mullins, visited Sgt Tanner at his home in Stepney, professing to have some information about the murderer, whom he suggested was Walter Emm. Mullins had earlier called on Inspector Thornton, but (it was a Saturday) he was out. Mullins said that ever since 28 August, when he had been interviewed by Tanner, he had been giving the case a good deal of thought, capitalising on what he had learned as a policeman, and had concluded that the most likely suspect was Emm. That morning, he said, he had secretly observed Emm's home at about 5.00 am, while pretending to be picking herbs, and had seen him leave his cottage and make his way to a ruined outhouse in a brickyard, 40 yards away, known as Emsley's Fields. He came out of the outhouse carrying a parcel, which he took into his cottage. Ten minutes later he reappeared bearing a much smaller parcel, which he concealed in an adjacent shed. Mullins felt certain that whatever was in the parcel had something to do with the case.

Tanner was properly cautious, and perhaps already suspicious of Mullins's manner as well as his words. He said he could not take any action before he had consulted Thornton, but agreed to meet Mullins the following day. As Mullins left he made a stupid and self-incriminating remark: 'If this goes off all right, I'll take care of you' – meaning that he would give Tanner part of the £300 reward.

On the Sunday morning, Sgt Thomas called at 11 Oakham Street, Chelsea, where Mullins was now lodging with his wife. They discussed the case. 'You know I am clever in these matters,' said Mullins. 'I've been working day and night to discover the murderer of Mrs Emsley, and I have found him out.' They teamed up with Thornton and Tanner, and all four travelled in a hackney-cab to the brickyard, where, telling Mullins to stay out of sight, they made (it seems intentionally) an inconclusive search of Emm's cottage, the shed and the ruined outhouse. No parcel, or anything untoward, was found. On being told this, Mullins was prompted to exclaim: 'You haven't half searched the place! Come – I'll show you!' Entering the shed, he said: 'Look there now! Pull down that bloody slab.' Sgt Thomas did, and discovered a small parcel, tied with tape and containing one large spoon, three small spoons marked WP, and a £10 cheque. Mullins seemed very pleased with himself.

Walter Thomas Emm was arrested and taken to Arbour Square police station and charged. Mullins went with the police, ostensibly as the happy recipient of the £300 reward. Then he was charged as well – on suspicion of also being involved in the murder. He exclaimed: 'Is this the way I'm to be served after giving you the information?'

Later, at the magistrates' court, Emm was discharged, for his alibi was unshakeable, and James Mullins was committed for trial.

Thornton and his sergeants now set about finding witnesses and other evidence to convince a jury of Mullins's guilt. His alibi for the night of the murder now seemed suspect – it had been provided by two of his sons. Emm's alibi was that on the Monday night, at about 9.00 pm, he had travelled to Bromley-by-Bow and Stratford in a pony-cart with his wife and two friends, returning at about 11.30 that night. And he had a toll-ticket to prove it. He was even able to prove, when he was supposedly concealing the parcel in the ruin on the morning of the 8th, that he was somewhere else and not even at home.

Sgt Thomas, in searching Mullins's lodgings at 33 Barnsley Street (where Mrs Emsley had been collecting rents on the afternoon before her murder), found some tape similar to that used to tie the parcel. He also found a plasterer's hammer which might well have been the murder weapon. At the lodgings in Orford Street, Chelsea where Mullins had lived at the time of the murder with his wife, Thomas noticed that Mrs Mullins had a spoon marked WP – later identified, by Mrs Gotz, as having belonged to Mrs Emsley. He also found a boot in a dust-hole (rubbish dump) which the landlady claimed to have seen being thrown out of the Mullinses' window. The marking on the boot's sole corresponded with a bloody boot-mark on the wooden stairs of 9 Grove Road. Thornton later produced the relevant piece of the stair in court, so that the jury could compare the boot with the mark. A silver pencil-case was also produced in court. It was said to have been sold by Mrs Mullins to a potboy in a pub.

The trial of James Mullins at the Central Criminal Court began on Thursday, 25 October 1869, and lasted two days. It was held before the Lord Chief Baron Sir Frederick Pollock, aged 77, and his son-in-law, Mr Baron Martin, aged 59. Sir Frederick Pollock, the son of a saddler of Scottish origins patronised by George III, had been the Lord Chief Baron for 16 years. He had previously held the post of Attorney-General and was also the Tory MP for Huntingdon. He married twice: his first wife had eleven children, and his second seven. He retired in 1866 and died four years later. His eldest daughter Fanny married Samuel Martin in 1838. He became a Baron of the Exchequer in 1850, was knighted, and died in 1883.

Serjeant Parry led for the prosecution, and Mr J. Best and Mr J. E. Palmer appeared for the defence. John Humffreys Parry was 44 and had been a Serjeant-at-law for four years. Born in London, the son of a Welsh antiquary and, like Pollock, twice married, he was noted for his 'admirable appearance and voice' and for the clarity of his thinking and of what he said.

The prisoner, according to *The Times*, looked 'hardly so old' as his alleged age, 58 – 'though he wears spectacles' – and had an 'intelligent and rather prepossessing appearance'. Witnesses were produced to say they had seen Mullins near Grove Road (now Globe Road) before and after the murder. One, a tailor, said that while waiting to enter a urinal at the end of Grove Road at 7.50 pm on Monday, 13 August, Mullins, in the working clothes of a plasterer, had emerged and walked off towards No. 9.

Thomas Mullins, aged 16, and his older brother, John, an unemployed dock-labourer, were called by Mr Best to substantiate their father's alibi, which was that the three of them were in 33 Barnsley Street from about 6.45 pm on 13 August until the following morning. After supper they had gone to bed about 9.00, although they then lay awake, talking, for another three hours. Mullins had slept on a trestle and some sacking, and his two sons on some rushes on the floor. They claimed that a Mrs Musick, who used to sleep in the back kitchen of the house, saw Mullins on the Tuesday morning; but she had since disappeared.

Serjeant Parry produced a laundress, Caroline Brinson, who swore that Mrs Musick, who had looked after her aunt at 33 Barnsley Street, was not there on the Tuesday morning (and by implication had left the previous night); for the laundress went there on Tuesday at 10.00 am to take Mrs Musick's place. She said she only saw Thomas Mullins there, and not his older brother or father. She added that the ceiling of a corridor in the house had not been waterwashed on the Tuesday by Mr Mullins, as his sons alleged, but on the Thursday.

In cross-examination, both the Mullins brothers gave confused and un-convincing replies about where they were and what they were doing on the days and nights before and after the murder. They were only certain about the events of the Monday night. 'I don't know why we didn't go to sleep at once,' said Thomas. 'Because we couldn't, I suppose.' 'You go along too fast for me,' John complained to Serjeant Parry – and there was laughter in court.

The Lord Chief Baron, in his summing-up, which lasted over three hours, was dubious about aspects of the prosecution's case. He was uncertain about the reliability of the identifications of Mullins around the night of the murder; and the two pieces of tape, of a very commonplace sort, did not cor-respond *exactly* – nor did the print on the stair with the sole of the boot. The hammer, he thought, had not been positively proved to be the murder weapon, or to belong to the accused. Moreover, a smear of blood on the pencil-case was not necessarily Mrs Emsley's. Nor were three hairs found on the hammer indisputably hers: plasterers used human hair in their mortar. The case against Mullins depended on whether or not the jury thought Mul-lins, and his sons, were lying about his whereabouts on the night of the murder, and whether he had deliberately lied about Walter Emm.

The judge's caution was probably caused by his injudicious acceptance of medical evidence in the trial of Dr Smethurst in August 1859 and his con-sequent summing-up against the accused. This evidence was reconsidered by the Home Office, found to be flawed, and Smethurst was released.

The jury at Mullins's trial had fewer doubts than the Lord Chief Baron. They retired at 6.15 pm on the Friday, and after an hour returned with a ver-dict of 'Guilty'.

Before sentence of death was passed, Mullins stated: 'I am not guilty. I know that I have not many days to live, and I am now speaking the truth. I am most happy to have had such a trial – an attentive jury and also such able counsel.' He said the hammer was not his, nor was the boot. In conclusion, he said, striking his breast: 'My heart is light at being able to tell all my friends about me that what I say to you now is the real truth. I am extremely obliged to the jury, and I am happy to have had such a patient jury. I am obliged to your lordship also, and to the gentlemen, both against and for me.' He also thanked Mr Best and his solicitor, Mr Ward, ' who has taken more trouble than I would expect a gentleman in his class to take. He has done all he could to find witnesses for me, and as yet I am sorry to say that I have not paid him'.

In passing sentence, the Lord Chief Baron managed yet again to indicate his dissatisfaction with the prosecution's case and with the evidence pro-vided by the police. He said: 'I am still of the opinion that some of the circumstances urged against you [Mullins], instead of increasing the weight of evidence for the prosecution, only tended to embarrass the jury in coming to a conclusion. But with that conclusion I am bound to state I am perfectly satisfied.'

On 27 October, Inspector Thornton was able to report to his superiors, with some satisfaction, that 'James Mullins was yesterday found guilty at the Central Criminal Court of the Wilful Murder of Mrs Emsley on the 13th August last, and he was sentenced by the Lord Chief Baron Pollock to be executed'.

Before the execution, at Newgate Prison, Mullins was visited three times a day by his wife and children, and continued to proclaim his innocence. An appeal was denied by Sir George Lewis, the Home Secretary, on 16 November, and Mullins was hanged by Calcraft outside Newgate before a crowd of some 20,000 persons on Monday, 19 November. As he was a Roman Catholic, no words from the Anglican funeral service were read.

Minutes before his execution, he handed a lengthy written statement to the prison officials, in which he repeated he was innocent and reiterated the details of his alibi. 'My children proved the truth,' he said. 'But the truth was not believed.' He also asked for donations for his 'poor family' who were 'in the greatest destitution'.

Buried in this statement was a single sentence that seemed to acknowledge he had lied over one matter. He wrote: 'I believe Emm to be innocent of the murder of Mrs Emsley.' He had at least, and at the last, exculpated Walter Emm.

The hangman, William Calcraft, then aged 60, is said by the Dictionary of National Biography *to have been 'very fond of his children and grandchildren' and to have taken 'a great interest in his pigeons and other pet animals'. A kindly, mild-mannered, grey-whiskered man, he hanged about 1,000 people in his 45-year career. Born at Baddow, near Chelmsford, in 1800, he was a shoemaker, watchman, gentlemen's butler and hawker, before officially becoming the chief executioner in April 1829. He succeeded John Foxton, who died that year and had himself been executioner for 40 years. A chance meeting with Foxton had led to Calcraft being employed to flog boys at Newgate for ten shillings a week. Standing in for Foxton, he performed his first execution, a double hanging in Lincoln, in 1828. As the chief hangman, Calcraft was paid a guinea a week, and a guinea for every execution. He also received half a crown for every man he flogged, and was given an allowance to provide 'cats' and birch rods. For an execution out of town he might receive as much as £10. His last hanging was of James Godwin on 25 May 1874. He retired on a good pension of 25 shillings a week and died at Hoxton in London five years later, on 13 December 1879.*

CHAPTER 5

Franz Müller

The Murder of Thomas Briggs, 1864

Committed on a train, it was the first railway murder, and caused an outcry in the press. Although horse-drawn wagons conveying goods or coal had trundled along on rails in certain districts since 1800, the first conveyances carrying passengers and drawn by a George Stephenson locomotive would not rattle along the Stockton and Darlington line until 1825. Five years later, at the grand opening of the Liverpool–Manchester railway, the first passenger fatality occurred: Mr Huskisson, a VIP, was killed by a passing locomotive as he stood on the track. By 1848, some 5,000 miles of track had been laid in Britain and hundreds of bridges, cuttings and embankments had been built. The amalgamation of small regional companies had also led to the rise of the big national companies, like the LNER, LMS and GWR, and in 1863 people could travel from London King's Cross to Edinburgh without changing trains. They could also travel from Paddington to Hammersmith on the new Metropolitan Railway, the first underground railway in the world.

There were three classes of railway carriage, first, second and third, with separate compartments in each, and the top speed was 40–45 mph. Trains were symbols of progress in more ways than one. Noisy, bumpy, smoky and dark though they were, their standards of regularity, comfort, punctuality – and safety – were very high.

Mr Thomas Briggs was 69, and chief clerk in a City of London banking-house in Lombard Street, called Robarts, Lubbock & Co. After leaving his place of work at about 4.30 pm on Saturday, 9 July 1864, he journeyed south across the Thames to have an early dinner with his married niece and her husband, David Buchan, a woollen warehouseman, at 23 Nelson Square, Peckham. Formally dressed for work, he wore a high silk hat, and a heavy gold chain across his waistcoat attached to a heavy gold watch. In one hand he carried a black leather bag, whose contents he gave to the Buchans, and in the other a sturdy walking-stick with a solid handle. He was 5' 9" tall and the picture of Victorian respectability, portly, affable and silver-haired, with a full white beard.

Conversation at the dinner-table, apart from a mix of family and business matters, no doubt touched on recent battles and events in the American Civil War, on President Lincoln and Generals Grant and Sherman, on the aims and activities of the governing Liberal Party led by Viscount Palmerston, and on the unhappy situation of 45-year-old Queen Victoria, widowed since December 1861. Perhaps the merits of Dickens's latest novel, *Our Mutual Friend*, currently being published in monthly parts, was discussed.

Soon after the clocks in the house chimed the half-hour after eight, Mr Briggs departed, collecting his hat, stick and now empty bag and kissing his niece at the door. David Buchan walked with Mr Briggs to the Old Kent Road – the latter twice checked the time on his watch – and saw the elderly gentleman safely on to a horse-drawn omnibus. 'He was perfectly sober,' said Buchan later. 'Indeed, he was a man of very temperate habits.' The omnibus conveyed Mr Briggs back across the Thames to King William Street, where he descended, not far from his Lombard Street bank, and walking past the Monument, proceeded along Fenchurch Street to the railway station there. After showing his return ticket, he entered a first-class carriage and settled in a corner of a two-door compartment, his back to the engine. The train left the terminus at 9.50 pm, five minutes late, and proceeded via the North London railway line on its round of smoky northern London suburbs, via Shadwell, Stepney and Bow, to Hackney, Islington and Chalk Farm. Mr Briggs's destination was Hackney Central; his home was in nearby Clapton Square.

A dim ceiling-light glowed overhead. The night was warm. Perhaps Mr Briggs, having dined well and worked all day, gently dozed.

At Bow station, a property-owner and gentleman called Thomas Lee, who was waiting on the platform for the train (he was also going to Hackney Central), exchanged a few words with Mr Briggs through the open door or window before moving up the train to a second-class carriage. The two men were casually acquainted. 'Goodnight, Tom,' said Mr Briggs. Lee answered: 'Goodnight, Tom.' He was surprised to see the older man out so late and noticed there were two other men in the compartment: one was a thin, dark man, and the other, opposite Mr Briggs, was 'a stoutish thick-set man with light whiskers'.

At 10.01 the train left Bow. It was due at Hackney Wick four minutes later, at 10.05.

In a first-class compartment next to that in which Mr Briggs was seated sat a draper and a lady, unnamed. The draper, yet another Tom (Thomas Withall), would later say: 'When the train was near Hackney Wick I heard a horrid howling. I believe it was a dog. A lady, a stranger to me, who was riding in the same carriage as myself, remarked on it being a dog.' Another lady in an adjacent compartment would say that her dress was spattered with drops of blood flying in through an open window. She, however, said she heard nothing untoward, no sounds of violence or cries for help.

When the train pulled into Hackney Wick, two young clerks, Henry Verney and Sydney Jones, who both coincidentally worked at Mr Briggs's bank and were going to Highbury, stepped into the gloomy and now empty compartment where Mr Briggs had sat. After seating themselves Jones found there was blood on one of his hands. They then noticed there was blood on the seat cushions, on a window, on a black leather bag and a walking-stick.

Under a seat lay a black beaver hat, crushed, as if someone had stood on it. Much alarmed, they reported their discoveries to the guard, Benjamin Ames. He searched the compartment in the light of his hand-lamp, locked it, and as the train steamed on to Hackney Central, Ames telegraphed to the station-master at Chalk Farm, where the carriage was disconnected and shunted on to a siding to await the arrival of the police.

At about 10.20 the guard on a southbound train of empty carriages happened to see a dark object lying on the six-foot way between the railway lines. The train, which had just crossed a bridge over Sir George Duckett's Canal and was about 800 yards out of Hackney Wick station, was brought to a halt. The guard, William Timms, investigated, as did the engine-driver and the fireman. They found the body of Mr Briggs, lying on his back with his feet towards the City. Though badly injured and bloody about the head, he was still alive, albeit unconscious. With difficulty they carried him down the track to Wick Lane, where he was deposited on a table in the Mitford Castle tavern. A policeman, who chanced to be in Wick Lane, came to their assistance and a doctor was summoned. He arrived at about 11.00 pm. An examination revealed that wounds on the left side of Mr Briggs's head had probably been caused when he fell from his train. Two severe blows had also fractured his skull.

Mr Briggs's home was notified, and he was formally identified by one of his servants before his second son, Thomas James Briggs, a waterproofer, arrived with the family doctor at 6.00 am on the Sunday morning to take the injured and still-insensible man to his house in Clapton Square. He died there late on Sunday night.

'MURDER ON THE IRON WAY' proclaimed one newspaper. Another protested: 'It is monstrous that a thousand persons should be encased in a series of boxes and hurled along a line at the rate of forty miles an hour, and that they should be debarred from means of communicating with the only person who has control of the rushing mass.' 'Who is safe?' cried the *Daily Telegraph* on 13 July. 'It would be impossible to imagine circumstances of greater apparent security than those which seemed to surround Mr Briggs. Well known – expected at home – travelling First Class for a mere step of a journey, on a line where stations occur every mile or so, and fringed with houses – if we can be murdered thus we may be slain in our pew at church, or assassinated at our dinner table.' Train carriages were suddenly precincts of fear: women became very apprehensive about travelling at night, and alone; respectable men eyed rough-looking strangers with silent suspicion, concealing their watches and clutching their sticks or a hidden, protective life-preserver (a cosh).

Inspector Dick Tanner, assisted by Sgt George Clarke, was put in charge of the investigation, which soon established that the motive for the attack was robbery – although a diamond ring on the victim's little finger, a silver snuffbox, four sovereigns and some silver had not been taken. Missing were Mr Briggs's gold watch, valued at about £12, and its chain – as well as his high silk hat. The crushed black beaver hat was evidently the assailant's. Had he picked up the wrong hat in his flight, or deliberately purloined the more expensive item? It transpired that Mr Briggs's hat, which had a bell crown, had been specially made for him by a well-established hatter's managed by Daniel Digance and situated in Cornhill, near Lombard Street. It bore Briggs's name on an inner band. The beaver hat bore the name of its maker: Mr Thomas Walker of 42 Crawford Street, Marylebone. It had an unusual broad-striped lining and a merino rim.

Descriptions of the missing hat, as well as of the watch and chain, were published in the papers. They soon elicited a response from a Mr Death.

Robert Death, who apparently pronounced his name Deeth, was an assistant to his brother in a jeweller's shop at 55 Cheapside, a quarter of a mile west of Mr Briggs's place of work in Lombard Street. He told the police that on the morning of Monday, 11 July, a young man with a foreign accent had visited the jeweller's and offered to exchange a gold watch-chain in his possession for another of equal value. Death's brother, John, assessed the chain to be worth £3 10s, and in exchange the customer was given another gold chain (worth £3 5s) and a ring (5s) which were wrapped up in a small cardboard box.

There was no major development in the police investigation for a long frustrating week. It seemed the murderer would never be found.

Then, on Monday, 18 July, a 35-year-old cabman, Jonathan Matthews, began reading a poster outside the Great Western Hotel at Paddington Station, while his horse slaked its thirst at a trough. He had been prompted to do so after hearing the murder discussed on the cab rank. The poster – and hundreds had by then been splashed across London – announced that a reward totalling £300 (offered by the Government, Mr Briggs's bank and by the North London Railway) would be given for information leading to the capture of the murderer. Reading slowly through the details and noting the beaver hat, Matthews's eye was transfixed by the sight of 'Death'. Such a name, he recalled, had been inside a small cardboard box given to his daughter the previous Monday by a German acquaintance, a young tailor who wore a beaver hat – Franz Müller.

Matthews drove off at once to his home off Lisson Grove, found the box in a drawer and took it that evening to the Hermitage Street police station. He provided the police with a description of Müller, as well as his address and a photograph, and said that he had recently bought *two* beaver hats, one for Müller (for 8s 6d) and one for himself. He also revealed that the young German was no longer in London. He had emigrated to America four days ago, and was on his way to New York.

With commendable speed and enterprise, Inspector Tanner and his team soon discovered that Müller had pawned Mr Death's chain and some other items to raise the necessary cash to pay for his transatlantic voyage, as a steerage passenger, on the sailing-ship *Victoria*. The ship had left London a day late, at dawn on the previous Friday. On the Saturday, while the ship was still within view of the coast, Müller had written a farewell letter to the Blyths, in whose house he had recently lodged. The letter was posted at Worthing. It said: 'On the sea, 16 July, in the morning. Dear Friends, I am glad to confess that I cannot have a better time as I have, for the sun shines and the wind blows fair, as it is at present moment everything will go well.'

The Blyths, Ellen and George (he was a messenger), lived at 16 Park Terrace, Old Ford, Bow, not far from Wick Lane. Mrs Blyth told Inspector Tanner that Müller had lodged with them for about seven weeks, and that on the night of Saturday, 9 July, she had waited up for him until 11.00 pm.

As he had not returned by then, she and her husband went to bed. Müller had a latch-key. She said later: 'I saw him the next morning, Sunday, when he came down to breakfast with us, as usual. I did not notice anything unusual in his manner. He appeared to be a little lame from a sprain of the ankle, which he had spoken of on the Friday. He said he had got his foot between a bus and a kerbstone in crossing the road near London Bridge.' On Saturday he had, in fact, been wearing a slipper on the injured foot. On the Sunday, she said, Müller was in the best of spirits, laughing, chatting and enjoying his meals. He remained at home all Sunday, and went out with the Blyths in the evening. On Monday evening he showed the Blyths a gold chain which, he said, he had bought from a man at the docks. Müller, said Mrs Blyth, was 'a quiet, well-behaved, inoffensive young man, of a humane and affectionate disposition'.

Tanner followed up other leads provided by Mrs Blyth and the cabman, Jonathan Matthews, who had bought the beaver hat for Müller the previous December, in exchange for a waistcoat Müller made for him. Matthews identified the crushed beaver hat found on the train as Müller's. So did Mrs Matthews, who remarked that Müller, not liking a flat brim, had 'turned up the sides in the fashion worn by foreigners'. They had known him for nearly a year, having become acquainted through mutual friends, a couple called Repsch.

Godfrey Repsch was a tailor, living at 12½ Jewry Street, Aldgate. He and his wife had known Franz Müller for about two years, since he arrived in London from Germany, via Cologne. It was Mr Repsch who had helped Müller find a job with a tailor's, Mr Hodgkinson's, in Threadneedle Street (not far from Lombard Street), where he was paid 25 shillings a week. Müller left the business on 2 July, saying he was going to emigrate to America.

The last time I saw him [said Mrs Repsch] was on the morning of Thursday, 14 July, the day he sailed. He told us he was going in the ship *Victoria* from the London Docks to New York. On the previous Saturday, the 9th, I had seen him at my house, where I left him at about half-past seven o'clock at night, talking to his friend, John Hoffa. He had not told me he was going anywhere. When I came back at about half-past eight, Hoffa was still there, at work, but Müller was gone. I did not see Müller at all on the Sunday. But he called on Monday between ten and eleven o'clock, and seated himself on the shop-board beside my husband. He then took out of his pocket the gold Albert [chain] and said he had paid £3 15s for it, and he showed us a ring upon his finger with a white stone and a peculiarly shaped head upon it, and he told us he had bought it for 7s 6d . . . He told us that he bought the chain and the ring of a man at the docks, whom he met when he was going down to take his passage ticket, and he thought it was a good bargain. I joked him about it and said it was not worth the money, upon which he took up the shears and scraped the chain, to show me the way of testing it. He said: 'You see it is pure gold.' I observed that the hat he was wearing was quite new, and I said to him: 'How extravagant you are with your hats!' He said he had smashed his old one and thrown it into the dust-hole. I had particularly noticed his old hat, because it had a striped lining . . . He used to put his letters in the lining.

When Müller said he had paid 14s 6d for his new hat, Mr Repsch remarked that it looked more like a guinea hat.

On Thursday morning, the day on which the *Victoria* was scheduled to sail, Mr Repsch had accompanied the young tailor to London Docks and saw him on to the ship. He was probably wearing his smart new hat. Why did he keep it? Perhaps, being a tailor, he appreciated its worth and appearance more than most, and had not the heart to throw it away.

John Hoffa was another young tailor and a friend of Franz Müller, having met him at Hodgkinson's, where he also worked. On the Saturday night referred to by Mrs Repsch, Müller told Hoffa when he left the house that he 'was going to see his girl – his sweetheart'. Her name was Mary Ann Eldred. But although he called at her lodgings, he never saw her that night. He robbed and killed Mr Briggs instead.

It seems that Hoffa had arranged to take over Müller's little first-floor room at the back of the Blyths' house. For he moved there from the Repschs' home on the Monday before Müller sailed. It seems they shared a bed. It was by no means unusual for male members of a family or friends to sleep together then. Travellers staying overnight at an inn were also accustomed to share a bed with total strangers. Hoffa moved in with Müller three nights before he vacated the room. He said later: 'Müller slept with me on the Monday, Tuesday and Wednesday nights.'

On the Tuesday Müller pawned the Albert chain obtained from Mr Death at 21 Minories – he had pawned his own watch and chain a month previously. He received £1 10s for the Albert chain, and then sold the ticket to Hoffa for 12 shillings, which Hoffa borrowed from someone else. Müller said he needed the money as he did not have enough for his passage to America. This he bought, in his own name, for £4 on the Wednesday morning at London Docks. What else he did and how he celebrated his last two days and nights in London is not known. Hoffa said: 'He left me in bed at six o'clock on Thursday morning and said "Goodbye", as he was going to the ship.' Hoffa presumably never expected to see his friend again.

Tanner and Sgt Clarke accumulated most of all this information in the 24 hours after Matthews went to the police (on Monday, 18 July). The known facts and the strong suspicion that Müller was Mr Briggs's murderer were presented to the Chief Commissioner of Police, Sir Richard Mayne, late on Tuesday afternoon, and such was the popular and political concern and interest in the case that he authorised Tanner and Clarke to proceed to New

York on a faster ship and arrest Müller when the *Victoria* docked. No expense was spared and no legal chances taken. To identify the wanted man both Robert Death and Matthews were invited to accompany the two detectives, who were armed with all the warrants, letters and other documents necessary for extradition. Matthews's wife (she had four children) was given 30 shillings a week from the Police Fund to compensate for his absence and loss of earnings.

On Tuesday evening, at a private hearing in Bow Street magistrates' court, Müller was charged with murder in his absence and a warrant was issued for his arrest. That night, Tanner, Clarke, Matthews and Death entrained at Euston for Liverpool, from where on Wednesday, 20 July, they embarked on a steamship, the *City of Manchester*, for New York.

While they were at sea, Inspectors Williamson and Kerressey supervised further police investigations in London and unearthed some more facts, via the German authorities, about the unsuspecting suspect on the *Victoria*.

They learned that Franz Müller was born on 31 October 1840 at Langendernbach in the Grand Duchy of Saxe-Weimar. Weimar, a small town in central Germany, was celebrated for its literary associations with Goethe, Wieland and Schiller. Müller had been apprenticed as a gunsmith before getting into some money troubles in Cologne and fleeing from there to London in March 1862. He was 5' 3", with light-brown reddish hair and no whiskers, moustache or beard. A New York reporter described him later as having 'small, grey, inexpressible eyes'.

The *City of Manchester* reached New York on 5 August, three weeks ahead of the *Victoria*, which docked on 26 August. All the steerage passengers were summoned on deck and Müller's arm was seized by Sgt Clarke. 'What's the matter?' asked Müller. An American police officer said: 'You are charged with the murder of Mr Briggs . . .' When he failed to remember the details of the charge, Clarke intervened. 'Yes,' said Clarke. 'On the North London Railway, between Hackney Wick and Bow, on the ninth of July.' Müller replied: 'I was never on that line that night.'

He was taken to the saloon and searched, as were his belongings. Among them were Mr Briggs's gold watch and his remade silk hat, reduced by an inch or so when Müller had carefully cut out the inner band, marked with the owner's name. He had then sewn the two parts together. In conversation with the ship's officers, Tanner and Clarke learned that Müller's manner during the voyage had been 'overbearing' and that he had suffered a black eye after calling a fellow-passenger a liar and a robber. Trying to make some money, he had wagered that he would eat five pounds of German sausages. He failed, and paid up with two of his shirts.

On shore Müller was picked out in an identification parade by Death. Presumably Matthews was also involved. But the records never mention him. Perhaps he was taken ill on the voyage.

Extradition proceedings began later that day before Commissioner Newton, who sat in the United States district courtroom in New York in the capacity of a committing magistrate. Müller's extradition was strongly opposed by several German organisations and individuals in the city, who took up his cause and paid lawyers to defend his rights. Other opposition came from Yankees aggrieved by England's support of the Southern States in the Civil War. The prosecuting counsel was provided by the British Consul; Müller's counsel was Mr Chauncey Schaffer, who spoke passionately if not always pertinently and evoked a good measure of partisan applause from the spectators in the court.

He said at the start that there was nothing in the evidence to justify the commitment of the accused on the charge preferred against him. He stated that any man who came to America was presumed to be innocent of any crime. He continued:

> I do not regard the treaty under which it is sought to extradite this man as anything else than a violation of the constitution of the United States, and utterly inoperative . . . The extradition of this man is claimed by virtue of a treaty between this country and England . . . I will show that it is at present suspended after the act . . . A state of war between two nations suspends the operation of all treaties. But it may be said that there is no war between this country and England . . . There does exist what the eminent Groteus terms 'a mixed or unclean state of war' between the two nations . . . and this, as in any war, leads to the suspension of treaties . . . England cannot say she is neutral in this matter when she furnishes our rebellious subjects with vessels of war, mans them, opens her ports to them, furnishes them with arms and ammunition, and sends them forth on their errand of destruction, burning merchant ships and destroying the commerce on the seas of a friendly power. The *Alabama*, built and armed in England, and manned by Englishmen, sank and burned 120 of our ships . . . But when a man is found murdered in London, they pursue the supposed murderer to our shores and cry: 'Treaty, treaty, treaty!' They tore that treaty to pieces three years ago!

Loud applause interrupted this oration. Schaffer went on to assert that the extradition treaty was a dead letter, that 'England, to claim this man, must come into court with clean hands!' He said: 'She must not come here and ask of us to honour her justice when she dishonours her own justice, breaks her treaties, and cries peace and neutrality while at the same time she lets slip the dogs of war!' He concluded by saying: 'The pride and honour and courage of America is at stake!' Again, there was much applause.

Mr Marbury, speaking for the British Government, disposed of this argument as 'immaterial' and 'irrelevant' and suggested that the defence had spoken thus because the case afforded no entertainment – 'which the counsel is always expected to produce whenever he appears in court'. Commissioner Newton's simple conclusion was that there was sufficient testimony to commit Müller for trial. 'It is not necessary for me', he said, 'to determine absolutely that he is guilty of the crime . . . But . . . so clear and distinct is the question of probable cause that I cannot for one moment have a doubt as to the proper course to pursue. Under these circumstances I am constrained to

The Chapel and Visiting-Yard at Newgate. On the right stands the Execution Shed (1898)
(Illustrated London News Picture Library)

Condemned cell, Newgate (1862) *(Hulton Deutsch)*

Full Particulars of the Examinations of *James Greenacre & Sarah Gale*
CHARGED WITH THE

MURDER **and** MUTILATION

Of Mrs. Hannah Brown;
WITH THE AWFUL CONFESSION OF JAMES GREENACRE,
And every Circumstance connected with this most monstrous Tragedy.

James Greenacre *(Westminster City Archives)*

Sarah Gale, also implicated in Mrs Brown's murder *(Westminster City Archives)*

* Head of the Woman,
As preserved in Spirits in the Workhouse at Paddington.

Edgware

Death's head of Greenacre *(Black Museum)*
Left: Pineapple Gate, Edgware Road where the trunk of the body was discovered *(Westminster City Archives)*

METROPOLITAN POLICE OFFICE, 7 April, 1842.

MURDER!

A WARRANT HAS BEEN GRANTED FOR THE APPREHENSION OF

DANIEL GOOD,

COACHMAN, who has absconded from his Master's Residence, PARK LANE, PUTNEY, charged with ROBBERY and Suspicion of MURDER: The Trunk of a Female, without the Limbs and Head, has been found by the Police in one of the Stalls of the Stable, some of the Bones of which were in the Harness Room, nearly consumed by Fire, and are now in possession of the Police.

Description of Daniel Good.

He is an Irishman, aged about 46 years, 5 ft. 6 ins. high, very dark complexion, black hair, long features, and bald at the top of the head; walks upright; was dressed in a dark Great Coat, Drab Breeches and Gaiters, and Black Hat.

Information to be given to any of the POLICE STATIONS in the METROPOLITAN POLICE DISTRICT.

ROEHAMPTON MURDER

EXAMINATION OF GOOD

BOW STREET.—Yesterday morning the great vicinity of this Court, it b s evening, that Daniel Tunbridge-wells for the veyed to town for the before the Magistrat f the journey in a lu ich, where he was pl on van, and conduc ing. Previous to ed to be allowed l reasons was refus house of the F d emain with him mself very quietly reation. had been disp should dispose to enable the accommodated brought in t he bench we upon the bar. He was attired in

Lennox, Mr. R. C. Dawson, of the Rev. T. B. Whitehurst, a Magistrat ford; the Rev. Dr. Pinkney, of M.P.; Sir Charles Aldis, Lord M barrister; Lord Faversham, Dr. B Cottingham, Magistrate of Union- Precisely at half-past ten o'clo at the bar. He was attired in and blue handkerchief and bla

Death's head of Good *(Black Museum)*

GOOD THE MURDERER.

HIS APPREHENSION AT TUNBRIDGE, AND ARRIVAL AT BOW-STREET.

Information having reached town on Saturday evening, that the murderer Good had been apprehended on that morning at Tunbridge, we made inquiries on the subject, and having reason to believe that such report had some foundation in fact, we at once dispatched our reporter to that place; and from the information which he was enabled to collect on the spot, and which follows, he has no doubt that the miscreant murderer is at this moment in the hands of justice, and locked up in Maidstone gaol. Should he turn out to be Good, the murderer and mutilator of the unfortunate woman, whose body had been found on the premises of Mr. Shiell— and of this, we repeat, there can be but little doubt—his apprehension, it will be seen, is not less singular than that of the discovery of the murder itself.

It appears that about half-past five o'clock on Monday morning last, a man with a furtian jacket and trousers, with a dark waistcoat, entered the Angel public-house, at the southern extremity of Tonbridge, with a hod, in which was found a small bundle, and addressing Mr. Adams, the landlord, asked him if he could assist him to a job as a bricklayer's labourer. Mr. Adams told him that there was a good deal of building going on in the neighbourhood, and it was very likely he would get something to do. The man upon this observed that if he procured work he would come to lodge at his house, and he then called for a penny loaf and half a pint of beer, which he had.

The appearance of the man was such as to raise considerable suspicion in the mind of Mr. Adams that he was not what he represented himself to be, and the suspicion was considerably heightened by the fact of his having a perfectly new hod, a circumstance of not very frequent occurrence in this fraternity, particularly in such his attention was at

The High Street, Rugeley, showing William Palmer's house and the Talbot Arms where Cook died *(from* The Life and Career of Dr William Palmer of Rugeley *by George Fletcher)*

Below left: The trial of William Palmer at the Central Criminal Court, May 1856 *(Mansell Collection)*

Below: William Palmer (drawing by Joseph Simpson) *(from* The Trial of William Palmer *by George Knott)*

Foot: Letter from Palmer on black-edged paper *(Black Museum)*

Metropolitan Police
Detective Department
27th October 1860

Report

I beg to Report in reference
to the Murder of Mrs Emsley, alluded
to in annexed papers that the
Prisoner "James Mullins" was Yesterday
found Guilty at the Central Criminal
Court of the Wilful Murder of
Mrs Emsley on the 13th August last,
and he was sentenced by the Lord
Chief Baron Pollock, to be
executed.

Seen.
W. C. H.

J Thornton
Inspector

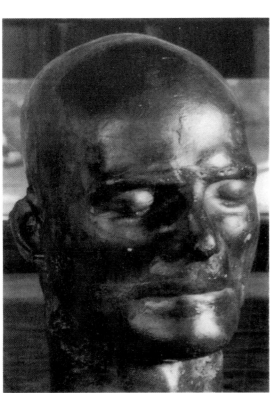

Above: Police Report on the sentencing
of James Mullins *(Public Record Office)*

Death's head of Mullins
(Black Museum)

Franz Müller *(Hulton Deutsch)*

Below: Death's head of Franz Müller
(Black Museum)

Middle picture: The SS *Victoria*
(Hulton Deutsch)

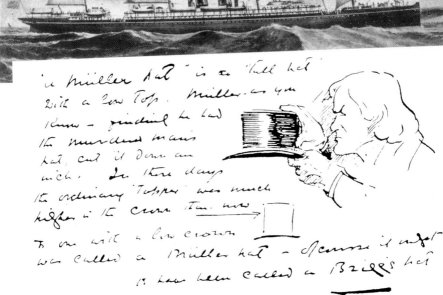

Cartoonist's comment on Müller's hat
(Black Museum)

2 St John's Park, Blackheath, the house burgled by Peace on 10th October 1878 and where PC Robinson was shot *(Black Museum)*

Below: Charles Peace the day before his execution in Armley Jail, Leeds *(Syndication International)*

Foot: Phillips' memoir on Charles Peace with a map drawn by Peace showing the scene of PC Cock's murder *(Black Museum)*

Below left: Charles Peace 's violin *(Black Museum)*

Left: John Lee sketched in court in 1884 *(Torquay Central Library)*

Below: Sketches of Miss Kate Farmer, Miss Keyse, Elizabeth Harris, Eliza Neck, Jane Neck *(British Newspaper Library)*

Above: Babbacombe, showing the Cary Arms and the Glen, where Miss Keyse was murdered *(Torquay Central Library)*

Below: Postcard from Lee to a Miss A. Gibbs (1910) *(Black Museum)*

Lee after his release in 1907, aged 43 *(Torquay Central Library)*

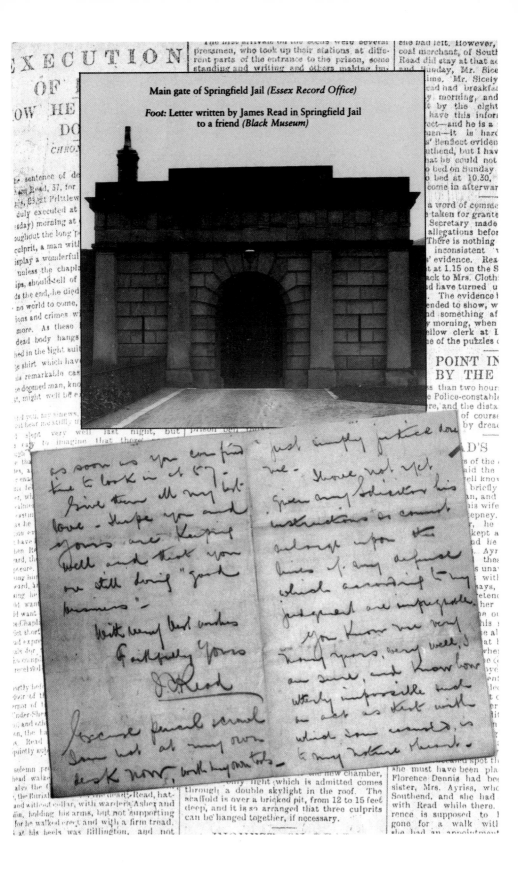

Main gate of Springfield Jail *(Essex Record Office)*

Foot: Letter written by James Read in Springfield Jail to a friend *(Black Museum)*

(c/o Mary Evans
Picture Library)

Below: PC Tyler
*(Topham Picture
Source)*

Tottenham Tragedy
P.C. Tyler was Shot Dead

Car, with driver and messenger boy that brought
the wages to Schnurmann's factory, Tottenham
(New Scotland Yard)

"Oak Cottage" Hale End

Above: Oak Cottage, where Lepidus died
(Mary Evans Picture Library)

Left: Paul Hefeldt and the bridge where he
was shot *(Metropolitan Police)*

Below: Walker's 14-point agenda on black-lined notepaper *(Black Museum)*

Foot: The new Central Criminal Court which now covers the site of Newgate Jail in *The Sphere*, March 1907 *(Illustrated London News Picture Library)*

MESSENGER BOY MURDER.

ACCUSED "INSANE AT THE TIME."

JUDGE AND THE LEGAL DEFINITIONS.

Before Mr. Justice Roche, at t... Criminal Court yesterday, Ernes... Walker, 17, footman, was found ... the murder of Raymond Charle... District Messenger boy, in Low... The jury also found that he was i... time and not responsible for his ... Mr. Justice Roche directed ... detained during his Majesty's pl...

MESSENGER BOY'S DEATH.

ALLEGED CONFESSION BY YOUNG FOOTMAN.

At Westminster Police Court yesterday, before Mr. Chapman, Ernest Albert Walker, 17, footman, in the employ of Colonel C. W. Trotter at 30, Lowndes-square, S.W., was charged with the wilful murder, at that address, of Raymond Charles Davis, 14, a District messenger. The prisoner, a tall youth of slight build, was defended by Mr. Ivan Snell.

Detective-inspector Burton said that on Sunday he went with Detective-inspector Hedley to Tonbridge police station, where he saw the prisoner, who had surrendered to the local police. The witness told the prisoner he would be arrested on the charge of murdering a District messenger boy on Saturday night by striking him on the head with a piece of iron, and cautioned him. The prisoner replied, "Yes, sir; I don't know what made me do it. I don't think I knew what I was doing at the time." On the way to London he spoke again, and the witness said he had better not say anything until he reached the police station.

At Gerald-road police station, added the witness, the prisoner, after being cautioned as before, said, "I quite understand what that means, but I wish to say that when I hit the boy with the piece of iron I did not ... what I was doing. I want ... to the laun...

...NGER BOY'S MURDER.

...-examined by Mr. St. John ... appeared for Walker), the ... told him about his mother ... very depressed for about a ... suggestion is that he ... gun out for the purpose ... self?—Yes, sir. ... hat would be about the same ... her's death?—Yes, sir. ... He was in a state of depressio... He was quite a decent young ... Morally?—Exceptionally so, ...

The next witness was Clar... ...smaid at 30, Lowndes-squ... ...last to be in the house w... Saturday afternoon. She had t... servants' hall, and he then ... all right and was not annoyed ... alone. She said she would be ... and he remarked that he w... thing to read. She lent him a b... Oppenheim.

The Alleged Conf...

Police-constable Sheepwash ... stated that at 8.30 p.m. on S... Walker came up to him and said, ... go to the police-station as I have done a ... After being cautioned, ...

...on, in reply to Mr. St. John ... said that on the prisoner's ... a relative was ...

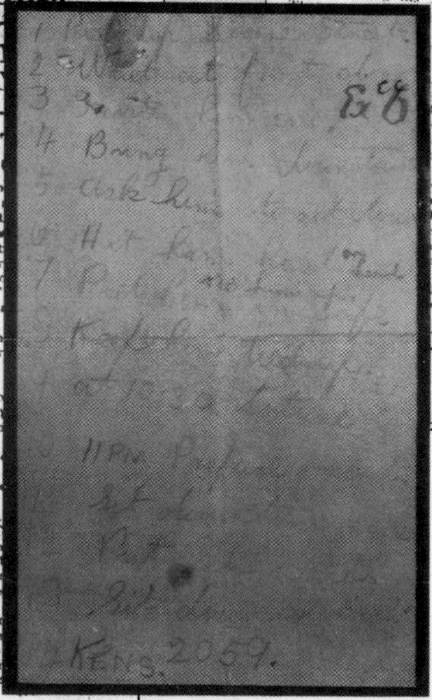

Chief Inspector Peter Beveridge introduces himself to Florence Ransom then arrests her for the Matfield triple murder *(British Newspaper Library)*

Left: Gun used by Florence Ransom *(Black Museum)*

Right: Ruth Ellis in April 1955 *(Topham Picture Source)*

Below: David Blakely *(Syndication International)*

Below left: Gun used by Ruth Ellis *(Black Museum)*

Foot: The Magdala Tavern, Hampstead *(Popperfoto)*

Inset: Ruth Ellis celebrating with friends, Desmond Cussen third from left *(Syndication International)*

G 49 **5 JUL 1955**

In replying to this letter, please write on the envelope:—

Number....9656.... Name........ELLIS. R.........

HOLLOWAY,..Prison

Dear Frank,

Thank you, for your letter, & lovely flowers, Yes, I was allowed, to see them, they are now, in the chapel, I shall see them again, on Sunday.

Sorry to hear of your accident, hope you get well soon.

I am overwhelmed, with the thought of so many people, waiting to help me. And am, deeply grateful, to one, and all.

No doubt, you have heard, I do, not want to live. You may, find this, very hard to believe, but that, is what I want.

I am, quite well & happy, under, the circumstances, And very well looked after, I have plenty to amuse me.

Well Frank that must be all for now.

Thanks Once Again.

Yours Ruth Ellis

No. 243   (21442—3-11-42)

Letter from Ruth Ellis in Holloway prison *(Popperfoto)*

Main picture: Crowds outside Holloway prison the morning Ruth Ellis was hanged *(Syndication International)*

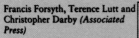

Francis Forsyth, Terence Lutt and Christopher Darby *(Associated Press)*

Below: Forsyth's shoes which killed Allan Jee *(Black Museum)*

Norman Harris *(Associated Press)*

Below: (c/o Hounslow Leisure Services Department)

THE COUNTY OF

Middlesex ✚ Chronicle

with which is
BRENTFORD

incorporated the
CHRONICLE

TWICKENHAM & WHITTON CHRONICLE
STAINES, ASHFORD & SUNBURY CHRONICLE
SOUTHALL & EALING CHRONICLE

HOUNSLOW & DISTRICT CHRONICLE
FELTHAM, BEDFONT & HANWORTH CHRONICLE
PUBLISHED AT 136, HIGH STREET, HOUNSLOW, MIDDLESEX
(Phone: HOUnslow 0016-7-8)

REGISTERED FOR TRANSMISSION BY POST (Postal Rates ... per annum)

THREEPENCE

102nd YEAR   No. 5292

FRIDAY, JULY 1st, 1960

BRUTAL MURDER: WHAT WAS MOTIVE?

Young Man Struck Down In Footpath

ENGAGED TO WED THE DAY BEFORE

A S a full-scale murder hunt was launched by police in
... week for the killer or killers who
... -old engineer,

Sunday  Dispatch

June 4, 196.

TWO POLICEMEN DIE: THEN THE BIGGEST MANHUNT

A call from WANstead 4199, a shot, a scream—and it is all over

LONDON GUNMAN
SHOT IN PHONE BOX

Above: Telephone box in Wanstead *(Topham Picture Source)*

ALDWORTH ROAD

INSPECTOR SHOT AT END OF ROAD

GUNMAN RAN OFF THIS WAY

POLICE SERGEANT AND CONSTABLE SHOT HERE

TENNYSON ROAD

Above: Inspector Pawsey, DS Hutchins and PC Cox *(Associated Press)*

Top: John Hall *(Associated Press)*

Right: Tennyson Road, where John Hall shot Inspector Pawsey and DC Hutchins *(John Frost Historical Newspaper Service)*

Left: The house in Sutton Lane, Chiswick, where Mrs Essens was murdered *(Black Museum)*

Main picture: Ashstead Wood by the A243, where Mrs Essens's dismembered corpse was buried *(Black Museum)*

Reynolds's sketch, compared with a drawing of Mrs Essens *(Press Association)*

Left: Donald Neilson, *Daily Mirror,* 22 July 1976 *(Syndication International)*

Below: Lesley Whittle's home in Highley *(Syndication International)*

Inset: Ronald Whittle, Lesley's brother *(Hulton Deutsch)*

Main picture: Aerial view of Bathpool Park after the discovery of Lesley's body, March 1975 *(Syndication International)*

Below left: Lesley Whittle at her brother's wedding in 1972 *(Syndication International)*

PATH TO BATHPOOL PARK

2nd ENTRANCE TO SHAFT

RAILWAY LINE TO STOKE

TO KIDSGROVE

TENT OVER SHAFT WHERE LESLEY'S BODY WAS FOUND

POLICE VAN

assassin's tiny killer

PINHEAD PELLET ▶ OF DEATH

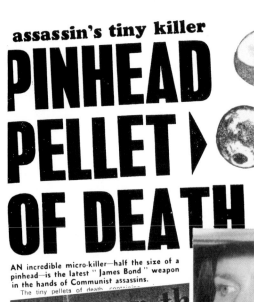

AN incredible micro-killer—half the size of a pinhead—is the latest "James Bond" weapon in the hands of Communist assassins.

The tiny pellets of death containing...

'stronger th cobra veno

By GUY

A METAL pellet cont deadly as cobr Georgi Markov, 49, who "hated the regi inquest decided yeste

The poison was ricin, castor oil plant. The p fractionally larger than a pinhead.

Mr Gavin Thurston, the Inner West London Coroner decided that Mr Markov, who regularly broadcast to Bul garia on the BBC's Worl Service, was "killed unlaw fully."

Mr Markov died four da after telling how he was jabb in his right thigh with an u brella while waiting for a b on Waterloo Bridge.

Among the witnesses yes day. was Commander Ja Nevill, head of Scotland Ya Anti-Terrorist Squad, who that during investigati police officers had travelle France, Italy and Germany quiries had also been ma America.

"But we still have n dication who was respon or how the pellet was a stered."

Test on pig

During the two-hour i at Battersea, a patholog the Government research at Porton Down, Wilts, pig, injected with a amount of ricin, died 25 later.

The first witness Markov's widow, Annabel, dark-haired and attractive, told

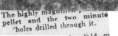

The highly magnified pellet and the two minute holes drilled through it.

Left: (c/o John Frost Historical Newspaper Service)

Inset: Annabel Markov leaving Battersea Coroner's Court, 2 January 1979 *(Press Association)*

Below: Markov, 13 September 1978 *(Topham Picture Source)*

Above: Simon Tipper and his bride *(with thanks to Lt.-Col. Parker Bowles)*

Main picture: Lt.-Col. Parker Bowles (top right) at the scene of the car-bomb explosion *(Topham Picture Source)*

Far right, above: Lt. Daly *(with thanks to Lt.-Col. Parker Bowles)* and *below:* Nichola Daly and her sister at Hyde Park *(Syndication International)*

Right: SQMC Roy Bright *(with thanks to Lt.-Col. Parker Bowles)*

Left: Dennis Nilsen *(Express Newspapers)*

Below, from top to bottom: Martyn Hunter-Craig *(Syndication International)*
Douglas Stewart *(Syndication International)*
Trevor Simpson *(Press Association)*
Carl Stottor *(Rex Features)*

The house in Melrose Avenue, Kilburn *(Topham Picture Source)*

Left: Dennis Nilsen's flatmate, David Gallichan *(London News Service)*

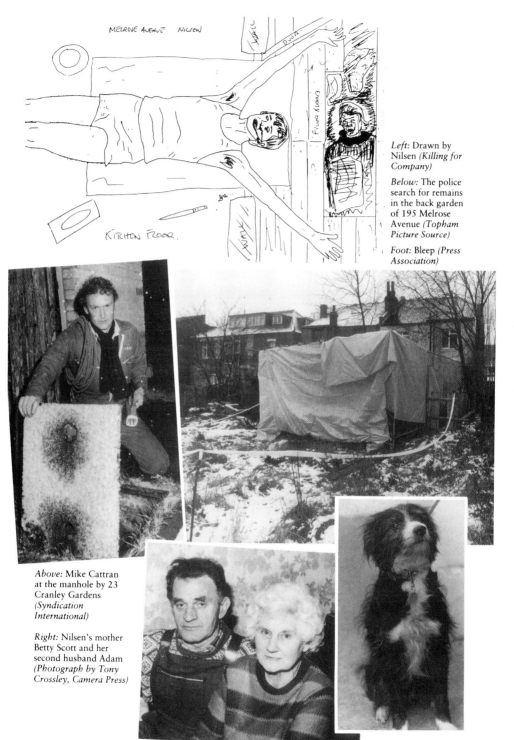

Left: Drawn by Nilsen *(Killing for Company)*

Below: The police search for remains in the back garden of 195 Melrose Avenue *(Topham Picture Source)*

Foot: Bleep *(Press Association)*

Above: Mike Cattran at the manhole by 23 Cranley Gardens *(Syndication International)*

Right: Nilsen's mother Betty Scott and her second husband Adam *(Photograph by Tony Crossley, Camera Press)*

Left: (c/o Hulton Deutsch)
Below: William Calcraft *(Hulton Deutsch)*

William
Marwood
*(Hulton
Deutsch)*

Left: James Berry *(Hulton Deutsch)*
Below: Pierrepoint *(Hulton Deutsch)*

grant the certificate [of extradition], and the prisoner therefore stands committed.'

Inspector Tanner's comments on this are contained in a letter he wrote on 28 August to Sir Richard Mayne. He said:

It will be seen by the Newspapers which I send, also by the mail, that strong language was used by the prisoner's counsel in references to England ... When the papers are ready, I go on to Washington to obtain the warrant from the President [Abraham Lincoln] to take the prisoner home. I do not know how long it will take but I shall endeavour to leave there by the steamship *Etna* on the 3rd September for Liverpool ... Extraordinary as it may seem, strong sympathy is felt here for the prisoner and it is rumoured that an attempt to rescue him from my custody will be made ... But I shall take such steps as I hope will prevent that.

Marbury also wrote to Mayne saying that Tanner's duties had been discharged 'with such discretion, energy and propriety as to commend my unqualified approbation'.

Nothing evidently happened to interfere with Müller's return to England, and on 3 September Tanner and Clarke embarked on the *Etna* with Müller, Matthews and Death. The prisoner is said to have enjoyed the voyage: the food was superior to that given to steerage passengers on the *Victoria*, and he found time to read and enjoy *Pickwick Papers*, as well as *David Copperfield*.

The *Etna* reached Liverpool on the night of Friday, 16 September. Tanner telegraphed Inspector Williamson in London: 'Cannot come tonight. Will come by nine o'clock train tomorrow morning.' The five men stayed in Liverpool overnight, Müller in a police station. On the Saturday morning Müller set off on his last journey by train.

On his arrival at Euston Station and in London's streets he was reviled and booed by the crowd. After appearing at Bow Street magistrates' court he was removed to Holloway Prison (built in 1850). At Bow Street on 26 September he was committed for trial, a few hours after the jury at the coroner's inquest in Hackney Town Hall returned a verdict of wilful murder. The foreman portentously added: 'The jury ... will take this opportunity of expressing their dissatisfaction with the present state of railway accommodation, as affording facilities for the perpetration of various crimes.'

Before the trial began, German nationals in London and elsewhere were busy on Müller's behalf, disseminating favourable opinions to influence the press and finding evidence and an alibi for his defence, which a well-respected solicitor, Mr Beard, was well paid to prepare. The notable advocate, Serjeant Parry, was employed to defend Müller at the trial, which began in the Central Criminal Court at 10.00 am on Thursday, 27 October 1864 before two judges, the Lord Chief Baron (Sir Frederick Pollock) and his son-in-law, Baron Martin. Sir Robert Porrett Collier (the Solicitor-General) led for the Crown.

Müller, who pleaded not guilty, agreed to be tried by 12 Englishmen; and after the defence had challenged the choice of 16 of the jurors (the prosecution challenged one) the trial began. At that time the jury's names and occupations were published; and this jury included three accountants, a baker, a grocer, and a tobacconist (the foreman, Isaac Moore). *The Times* reporter noted that the accused was 'a short and slightly made young man almost boyish in appearance, and with light brown hair – neatly dressed in a plain, brown morning coat buttoned on the chest – quiet, self-possessed and respectful'. It was difficult to believe that the little tailor could have made such a savage and murderous attack on an elderly man.

In his opening speech, the Solicitor-General said: 'Undoubtedly, the evidence in this case is what is called circumstantial evidence chiefly. But I may remind you that it is by circumstantial evidence that great crimes are most frequently detected. Murders are not committed in the presence of witnesses, and to reject circumstantial evidence would be to proclaim immunity to crime.'

Serjeant Parry did his best to case doubt on that evidence by providing Müller with an alibi and implying that Matthews or some revengeful bank employee killed Mr Briggs. Matthews's alibi, as well as his manner, was somewhat vague. Having been unable at the Bow Street hearing to account for his movements on the night of 9 July, he now said he had made enquiries and established that he was at the cab-stand at Paddington Station between 7.00 and 11.00 pm. The fact that he claimed to have known nothing of the murder until 18 July (when he read the poster) also seemed suspect, especially as his wife said she knew of the murder on 11 July. Matthews's past was also aired in court: in 1850, aged 19, he had spent three weeks in prison for theft (he had stolen a boot and a spur). Parry suggested that Matthews's aim had been to incriminate Müller and at the same time claim the £300 reward. 'Do you expect a portion of the £300?' Parry enquired. Said Matthews, unctuously: 'I leave that entirely to my country – if it thinks I have done my duty.' 'Then you do expect a portion of the reward?' insisted Parry, persisting with the question as Matthews variously replied: 'If they think proper to give it' – 'If they are only satisfied with my conduct' – 'If it had been a shilling, I should have done my duty the same.' To this Parry retorted: 'I do not ask you to compliment yourself.'

Parry also pointed out that no blood-stained clothes had been found on Müller or in his room (although a rag he used to clean his shoes had some blood on it). He claimed that the little tailor could never have assailed and thrown Mr Briggs off the train in three minutes: Briggs was six inches taller and about four stone heavier. He also claimed that Mr Briggs's stick was not the weapon used, and that *two* men had committed the crime – the men seen by Mr Lee in Briggs's compartment at Bow, minutes before the attack.

Lee was, however, unable to identify Müller as one of the two, and Sir Robert Collier was able to impugn his reliability by demanding why he had not spoken to the police for more than a week. Mr Lee said lamely he had thought it 'unimportant' and a 'bother'. He said: 'I only went to Bow for a stroll.' The real reason for his tardiness and confusion was that he had had an assignation with a girl that night and did not wish his actual whereabouts to become known to his wife.

Parry's main effort was expended on an alibi. He produced an omnibus conductor who said that at about 9.50 pm on 9 July a passenger had got on his bus in Camberwell wearing a carpet slipper on one foot. And he called Mrs Jones of Stanley Cottage, James Street, off Vassall Road in Camberwell, to say that Müller was in her house at 9.30 pm: he had gone there (after leaving Hoffa at the Repschs' home) to see Mary Ann Eldred. If this was true, Müller could not have been on the same train as Mr Briggs – it left Fenchurch Street Station at 9.50. 'I had a clock in the kitchen,' said Mrs Jones. 'I looked at the clock, and called out when it was nine o'clock, and then Miss Eldred went out.' Müller arrived after that, she said, and stopped for five or ten minutes to chat.

Unfortunately, the omnibus conductor was unable to identify Müller as the man with the slippered foot. And Mrs Jones, who was 36 and lived with a Mr Kent, admitted that her two female lodgers were 'young women who receive the visits of men'. Mary Ann Eldred was a prostitute. According to the prosecution, Müller, whom Mrs Jones called 'the little Frenchman', would have known that she always went out on Saturday nights. And even if he went to Camberwell, he could easily have got there by 9.00 pm, after leaving Hoffa at 8.00 – with time enough in hand to travel back to Fenchurch Street to catch the delayed 9.45 train.

Mary Ann Eldred, who was also called by the defence, was not a convincing witness, although she supported Mrs Jones's assertion that she left the house at 9.00, before Müller arrived. She had known Müller for a year, she said, and had last met him a week before 9 July, in Cheapside. She revealed that Müller had asked her to go with him to America; he had said he had a sister there.

In his summing-up, the Lord Chief Baron remarked:

> The evidence of Mary Ann Eldred – whom it is impossible to see here without some compassion for the situation of life which she is in – counts certainly very much more in saying what she *cannot* recollect, rather than what she can . . . Then there is the evidence of Mrs Jones. And respecting her husband, I think a man who is living on the profits of such a calling as that pursued by his wife, is about the most infamous of mankind. How far the wife is some shades better than her husband is for you to judge.

Serjeant Parry might have made something of Müller's amazing carelessness in concealing the crime: he assaulted a man to steal a watch and chain but neglected to empty the victim's pockets; he left his hat at the scene of the crime and wore that of the man he had killed; both the hat and the chain he unconcernedly showed to friends; he gave the jeweller's box to the cabman's daughter instead of throwing it away; he booked the voyage to New York in his own name; and he told people the name of the ship. Serjeant Parry could have claimed that such actions were those of an innocent man, not a murderer, who would have sought to avoid, not invite, detection.

It certainly seems that Müller never expected that he would be caught, and that once at sea and then in America he would be safe. It also seems that he never intended to *kill*, but only to incapacitate Mr Briggs, in order to seize the gold watch and chain to pay for his passage to New York. In his own mind he was innocent of any intent to kill.

Parry's speech for the defence, which began on the Friday at 2.30 pm, *before* his witnesses were called, lasted two-and-a-half hours. In it he complained, as others had done, about not having the opportunity to sum up, like the prosecution, *after* all the evidence had been heard. The following year the law was altered, by 'Denman's Act', and the defence was provided with a closing speech, which was made after that of the prosecution and before the judge's summing-up.

This took place on Saturday, 29 October – two days before Müller's 24th birthday. The jury was absent for 15 minutes, returning with a verdict of 'Guilty'. Mr Baron Martin, in passing sentence of death on Müller, said: 'We are perfectly satisfied with the verdict. If I had been one of the jury, I should have concurred with it.' When asked if he had anything to say, Müller responded, speaking softly: 'I am perfectly satisfied with my judges and with the jury. But I have been convicted on false evidence, and not on a true statement. If the sentence is carried out, I shall die innocent.'

The German community now strove even harder to save their countryman from the rope. Petitions were signed, protests made about a miscarriage of justice, and a telegram signed by the King of Prussia and some German princes was sent to Queen Victoria. The Home Secretary, Sir George Grey, was likewise beset. But pleas and petitions all failed. On Friday, 11 November, at 3.00 pm, Müller's solicitor, Mr Beard, visited the condemned cell in Newgate Prison and told Müller he would not be reprieved.

A week earlier a Lutheran minister, the Revd Walbaum, described in *The Times* one of his daily visits to the doomed little tailor:

> He is reserved and uncommunicative, without, however, being in the least morose. He eats and sleeps well. Last evening he had gone to bed about 7 o'clock, and in less than an hour afterwards he was sound asleep. He usually sleeps right through the night and rises about half-past six. He attends the morning service in the chapel daily, and is permitted to take exercise in a yard adjoining his cell, attended by a warder . . . He spends much of his time reading – the Bible principally.

But it was not to the Revd Walbaum that Franz Müller turned in his final days of life. Dr Louis Cappel, pastor of the German Lutheran Church in Goodman's Fields, had also been a regular visitor. An hour and a half before the execution Cappel, while conversing with Müller, in German, urged him to declare finally whether he was innocent (as Müller had always maintained) or guilty. Dr Cappel wrote later: 'With an earnest and passive look he remained one or two minutes silent, standing before. He then suddenly cried out, with tears in his eyes, and throwing his arms round my neck: "Do not leave me! Remain with me to the last!" I judged by this that he had determined to make a confession.'

The execution was set for 8.00 am on Monday, 14 November. Calcraft was the executioner. He had had a busy year: eight people were hanged at Newgate in 1864, out of a national total of 19. This had whetted, not satiated, the appetite of the mob, whose behaviour at the execution was best described in *The Times* by two reports: one outside the prison and the other within. They wrote:

The barriers to check the crowd were begun across all the main streets which lead to Newgate as early as on Friday last, and all through Friday night and on Saturday and Sunday, a dismal crowd of dirty vagrants kept hovering around them ... It was, however, different on Sunday night. During the early part of the evening there was a crowd as much of loungers as of drunken men, which stood the miserable drizzle with tolerable patience, while the public-houses were open and flared brightly through the mist. But at eleven o'clock the greater part of the rough mass moved off, leaving the regular execution crowd to take their early places ... A thick, dark noisy fringe of men and women settled like bees round the nearest barriers, and gradually obliterated their close white lines from view. Many had jars of beer; at least half were smoking, and the lighting of fuses was constant, though not more constant than the cries and laughter ... Occasionally, as the rain, which fell heavily at intervals, came down very fast, there was a thinning of the fringe about the beams, but, on the whole, they stood it out very steadily, and formed a thick dark ridge round the enclosure kept before the Debtors' door, where Müller was to die ... Newgate was black enough in its blind massiveness, except at one little point high over the walls, where one window in the new wing showed a little gleam of light ... Not more than some four thousand, or at the most five thousand, were assembled. Every now and then came a peculiar sound, sometimes followed by the noise of struggling, almost always by shouts of laughter, and now and then a cry of 'Hedge.' ... Till three o'clock it was one long revelry of songs and laughter, shouting, and often quarrelling. But about three the workmen came to finish the last barriers, and from that time the throng rapidly increased in numbers. Someone attempted to preach ... Then, again, another man, stronger in voice, began the old familiar hymn of 'The Promised Land' ... Another and apparently more popular voice gave out some couplet in which at once, and as if by magic, the crowd joined with the chorus of – 'Of, my, think, I've got to die' – till this again was substituted by – 'Müller, Müller, he's the man!' All these vocal efforts, however, were cut short by the dull rumbling sound which, amid cheers, shouts, whooping, clapping of hands, hisses and cries ... heralded the arrival of the dirty, old gallows ... The shouts and obscene remarks which were uttered as the two upright posts were lifted into their places were bad enough, but they were trifles as compared with the comments which followed the slow efforts of the two labourers to get the cross beam into its place ... And then, amid such yells as only such sightseers could give vent to, a strong force of police filed in and took their places, doubly lining the enclosure round the drop . . . Then, as every minute the day broke more and more clear, the crowd could be seen in all the horrible reality in which it had been heard throughout the long, wet night . . . Among the throng were very few women; and even these were generally of the lowest and poorest classes. The rest of the crowd was, as a rule, made up of young men . . . sharpers, thieves, gamblers, betting men, the outsiders of the boxing ring, bricklayers, labourers, dock workmen, German artisans, and sugar bakers, with the rakings of the cheap singing-halls and billiard rooms, the fast young 'gents' of London . . . Then, as the sun rose clearer, did the mysterious, dull sound explain itself . . . It was nothing more than the sound caused by knocking the hats over the eyes of those well-dressed persons who had ventured among the crowd, and, while so 'bonneted', stripping them and robbing them of everything . . . There were regular gangs, not so much in the crowd itself within the barriers, as along the avenues which led to them . . . Sometimes their victims made a desperate resistance . . . In no instance, however, could we ascertain that 'Police!' was ever called. Latterly, nearly fifty thousand people were crammed between the walls of this wide thoroughfare. Wherever the eye could rest it found the same dim monotony of pale but dirty faces, which seemed to waver as the steam of the hot crowd rose high. At last, when it was near towards eight o'clock, there came shouts of 'Hats off!' and the whole mass commenced, amid cries and struggles, to wriggle to and fro as the bell of Newgate began to toll . . .

Inside the prison the convict had retired to rest at half-past ten, and slept soundly for about four hours, but was anxious and uneasy during the remainder of the night. He rose at six o'clock and dressed. Shortly afterwards, Dr Louis Cappel joined the convict in his cell . . . As the hour fixed for the execution drew near, Dr Cappel administered the sacrament to him . . . The convict frequently clung to him and embraced him, observing, with tears in his eyes, that he was the only friend he had then in the world . . . About half-past seven o'clock the Sheriff of London, Mr Alderman Dakin and Mr Alderman Besley, with the Under-Sheriffs, Mr Septimus Davidson and Mr De Jersey, went from the London Coffee-house, in Ludgate Hill, where they had passed the night, to the Courthouse of the Old Bailey, where they remained until a quarter to eight. There they were met by Mr Jonas, the governor of Newgate, and by Mr Gibson, the prison surgeon, and, forming themselves into a procession, the authorities passed from the sessions-house to the gaol. The way lay through a series of gloomy passages . . . and over the graves of malefactors who had been buried there during the last thirty years. Emerging at length into an open courtyard they paused, until a door was unexpectedly opened and Müller presented himself, attended by a single warder . . . He was pale, but quite calm and collected. A comely-looking young man, he walked with his hands clasped in front of him, looking upward with a touching expression. He was dressed with scrupulous care in the clothes which he wore on his trial

. . . From the courtyard he passed into the press room, followed by the authorities. There he submitted himself to the executioner, and underwent the process of pinioning with unfaltering courage. While all about him were visibly touched, not a muscle in his face moved . . . At this trying moment, Dr Cappel approached and endeavoured to sustain him again and again. Repeating in a docile and affectionate manner words which the reverend gentleman put into his mouth, the convict more than once said: 'Christ, the Lamb of God, have mercy on me' . . . As the executioner was removing his neckerchief and shirt collar, on the arrangement of which some care had evidently been bestowed, the convict moved his head about to allow of that being done . . . Mr Jonas, the governor, approached the convict and asked him to take a seat, but he declined the offer, and remained standing until the prison bell summoned him to his doom . . . One could not help being struck with the appearance of physical strength which his figure denoted, and still more with his indomitable fortitude. Though short in stature, he was compactly and symmetrically made, and there were manifest indications of strength about his chest, arms, hands, and the back of his neck in particular. A signal having been given by the governor, the prisoner was escorted to the foot of the scaffold, the Rev Mr Davis leading the way, and reading as he went some of the opening verses of the burial service.

At the little porch leading to the gallows the Sheriffs and officers stopped. Dr Cappel alone ascended it with Mr Davis and the guilty man. The clergymen at once took their places on the line of sawdust, which had been laid to mark the outline of the drop . . . Close after them came Müller. His arms were pinioned close behind him; his face was very pale . . . He took with a steady step his place beneath the beam, then, looking up, and seeing that he was not exactly beneath the proper spot whence the short, black link of chain depended, he shifted a few inches, and then stood quite still. Following him close came the common hangman, who at once pulled a white cap over the condemned man's face, fastened his feet with a strap, and shambled off the scaffold amid low hisses. While this was being done Dr Cappel, addressing the dying man in German, said: 'Müller – in a few moments you will stand before your God. I ask you again, and for the last time, are you guilty or innocent?' He replied: 'I am innocent.' Dr Cappel said: 'You are innocent?' Müller answered: 'God knows what I have done.' 'Does he also know if you have committed this crime?' Müller replied: 'Yes. I did it' – 'Ja. Ich habe es gethan.' And these were his last words. Almost as soon as these words had left his lips, his kind spiritual guides quitted the platform, and the drop fell . . . So greatly relieved was Dr Cappel by the confession that he rushed from the scaffold, exclaiming: 'Thank God! Thank God!' and sank down in a chair . . . Those who stood close to the apparatus could just detect a movement twice, an almost imperceptible muscular flicker that passed through the frame. This was all, and before the peculiar humming noise of the crowd was over Müller had ceased to live, though as he hung his features seemed to swell and sharpen so under the white cap that the dead man's face at last stood out like a cast in plaster. For five or ten minutes the crowd, who knew nothing of his confession, were awed and stilled by this quiet, rapid passage from life to death . . . But before the slight, slow vibrations of the body had well ended, robbery and violence, loud laughing, oaths, fighting, obscene conduct, and still more filthy language, reigned around the gallows far and near.

The body was cut down and stripped, and after a plaster cast was taken of the shaven head, the naked corpse was placed in a rough deal box filled with shavings and quicklime. Franz Müller was buried near Greenacre and Good under the flagstones of a narrow passage within the jail, roofed by a cross-barred grating. An 'M' was carved in the stone wall above his head.

Thomas Briggs junior sent a cheque for £55 to Inspector Tanner via Sir Richard Mayne – 'as a small token of our appreciation of the courteousness and delicacy with which he conducted the case'.

The reward of £300 was eventually (in May 1865) paid to Jonathan Matthews. But most of it went to his many creditors, who had succeeded, a month after Müller's death, in having the cabman imprisoned for debt. Released from Horsemonger Lane Gaol on 17 December, Matthews called on Tanner to complain about the treatment he had received from the Government, who, he claimed, had let his wife and family starve. 'His manner appeared mysterious,' Tanner wrote in a report. 'There does not appear any truth in him.'

Some good was done as a result of this, the first railway murder: corridors were slowly introduced in most carriages and communication cords in all trains. The process was accelerated by the next railway murder, in June 1881, of a 64-year-old gentleman, Mr Gold, who was shot and stabbed on a London to Brighton train by a journalist, Percy Mapleton, and thrown out of a first-class compartment.

Müller's murder also made minor history of another sort – in men's fashion. For a while, the cut-down topper that the little German tailor had made and worn was copied by smart young men in London. It was known as a 'Müller' hat.

In 1866, a Royal Commission, set up to consider the whole question of capital punishment, presented its report. It recommended that capital punishment should only be meted out to those who had committed high treason or murder; that the laws on child murder by women should be changed; that different degrees of murder should be recognised by the law; and that public executions should cease. This recommendation was the only one to be put into effect. And the last public hanging in England – the last in Scotland had happened two years earlier, in Perth – was staged outside New-gate Prison on 26 May 1868, the year in which Sir Richard Mayne, co-founder of the Met, died.

The last man to be hanged in public was Michael Barrett, executed for his part in a Fenian plot to free two prisoners, Captain Burke and his aide,

Casey, *from the Clerkenwell House of Detention. The plan was that on 12 December 1867, while Burke and Casey were taking some exercise in the prison yard, an explosion should demolish the prison wall, allowing the two men to escape. It was arranged that Burke should throw a white ball over the wall to signify his presence and readiness. The explosive device, a 36-gallon beer cask packed with about 500 lbs (it is said) of gunpowder, was parked on a dray alongside the wall. When a white ball flew over into the street, the Fenians outside had trouble with the fuse – it failed to ignite. They tried again the following day, Friday, 13 December. In the meantime, the Prison Governor had been warned that an escape attempt was planned, and had kept Burke and Casey locked up in their cells. He also put a temporary end to any prisoners exercising in the yard. At 3.50 pm, although no white ball had flown over the wall, the edgy Fenians successfully lit the fuse and retired. The resultant explosion, which was heard for many miles around, not only demolished the prison wall but wrecked some tenement buildings opposite. Six people were killed, including two children, and many were injured. Michael Barrett, arrested in Glasgow, was the only Fenian to be charged with the crime and was hanged at Newgate in May 1868, still protesting that he neither planted the gunpowder bomb nor lit the fuse.*

The Fenian Society was an Irish-American organisation formed in 1848 to promote and accomplish the overthrow of British rule in Ireland and establish the island as a republic. In 1867 an attempt at a popular rising in Ireland against British authority failed and resulted in several attacks and outrages in England. Order was restored, but Fenianism continued to smoulder for many years, and some of the movement's aims and ideals were adopted by Arthur Griffiths, who founded the radical nationalist party, Sinn Fein, in 1902.

CHAPTER 6

Charles Peace

The Murder of Arthur Dyson, 1876

Murder is often compounded with theft or sex – which is to say that it fre-
quently results from a compulsive desire to deprive, or a compulsion not to
be deprived of one's desire. Another aspect of the equation is that thieving
seems to be related to a low or inadequate sexual appetite or capability and
acts as a compensatory surrogate for sex, providing similar thrills. The act of
burglary, known as breaking and entering, is a sort of rape, a secretive un-
lawful penetration of private property made without the owner's consent.
The metaphor is enforced by those who take weapons with them, guns or
knives. When disturbed, the thief or burglar invariably suffers from instant
withdrawal and runs away. But an armed, aggressive and over-sexed thief is
more of a danger and has greater problems. He is so highly charged that
faced with capture he is likely to explode. Such a one was Charles Frederick
Peace.

His story was told in The Murders of the Black Museum, *published in*
1982, since when a memoir, written by the Inspector who investigated the
case, came to light, containing much original material and information. This
first-person account added so much to the life and crimes of Peace that his
story was worth revising, retelling and including here.

He was born in Sheffield on 14 May 1832, the son of a respected shoemaker;
he was not a good scholar, but was very dexterous, making artistic shapes
and objects out of bits of twisted paper. Apprenticed at a rolling-mill, he was
badly injured when a piece of red-hot steel rammed his leg, leaving him with
a limp. Later on, his jaw was fractured, and this enabled him to alter his
lower features more or less at will. He took part in amateur theatricals, and
learned to play the violin with some flair and skill, billing himself at local
concerts as 'The Modern Paganini'.

When he was about 18, in search of other excitements and reluctant to
earn a living, he began to thieve. He was not too successful at first, and between 1851 and 1866 was jailed for burglary four times, with sentences of
one month, four, six and seven years. When he was not in jail he wandered
from town to town. In 1859 he met and married Mrs Hannah Ward, a
widow with a son called Willie. He returned to Sheffield in 1872. About three
years later, he set up shop in Darnall, then a village a few miles east of Sheffield, trading as a picture-framer and gilder. He was also a collector and
seller of musical instruments and bric-à-brac.

In 1875 Peace was 43. He was, according to a Sheffield police description issued after the murder of Arthur Dyson – 'Very slightly built, height 5 feet 4 inches, hair grey; lacking one or more fingers of his left hand; cut marks on the back of both hands; cut marks on forehead; walks with his legs wide apart; speaks somewhat peculiarly, as though his tongue was too large for his mouth, and is a great boaster.' He looked about ten years older than his actual age, and apart from being plain ugly, he was as agile as a monkey and very strong. He was also utterly selfish, salacious, mendacious and shrewd.

Towards the end of 1875 or early in 1876 he became involved with his neighbours, next door but one, in Britannia Road, Darnall. Their name was Dyson.

Arthur Dyson, very tall (6 ft 5 ins) and genteel, was a civil engineer, employed by a railway company. He had met his future wife, a young Irish girl called Katherine, when he was in America. She was tall, buxom and blooming, and fond of a drink. They married in Cleveland, Ohio about 1866. Returning to England some seven years later, they lived for a time with Dyson's mother in Tinsley before coming to Darnall. It seems they often had rows.

Peace, commissioned by the Dysons to frame four pictures, including a portrait of Dyson's mother, became familiar with them and was soon enamoured of Mrs Dyson. 'If I make up my mind to a thing,' he once said, 'I am bound to have it.' She unwisely responded to his attentions. It seemed they visited pubs, music-halls and fairs together and that their place of assignation was a garret in an empty house between their two homes. Peace took to calling on the Dysons at any time, including meal-times, until Mr Dyson put his foot down. But Mrs Dyson continued to associate with Peace, sending him notes informing him when her husband was not at home.

In June 1876, Peace was forbidden by Arthur Dyson to call on his neighbours any more. Dyson wrote on a visiting-card: 'Charles Peace is requested not to interfere with my family.' He threw the card into Peace's yard.

Peace was much affronted. He began to harass and threaten the Dysons. 'We couldn't get rid of him,' said Kate Dyson, talking later to the *Sheffield Independent*'s reporter. 'I can hardly describe all that he did to annoy us after he was informed that he was not wanted at our house. He would come and stand outside the window at night and look in, leering all the while . . . He had a way of creeping and crawling about, and of coming upon you suddenly unawares . . . He wanted me to leave my husband!'

On Saturday, 1 July 1876, Peace tripped up Mr Dyson in the street. That same evening he chanced to encounter Mrs Dyson outside her home in Britannia Road as she was complaining to three female neighbours about the assault. He demanded to know if they were talking about him; he was told they were. Asked by him to repeat what she had been saying, Kate Dyson did so. Whereupon Peace pulled out a revolver and said: 'I will blow your bloody brains out and your husband's too!'

The following morning a magistrate's warrant was obtained for his arrest and he fled with his family to Hull, where Mrs Peace found employment as the supervisor of an eating-house.

For a time, the Dysons were, it seems, undisturbed by their former neighbour. But on 26 October, still apprehensive about Peace's reappearance – or perhaps Arthur Dyson was still suspicious about his wife's association with Peace – the Dysons moved to the other side of Sheffield, to Banner Cross Terrace off Eccleshall Road. Their furniture went ahead of them in a wagon, and when they arrived at their new home that evening to take possession of it, Peace walked out of the front door and confronted them. After he and Dyson had exchanged some remarks Peace said: 'You see, I am here to annoy you wherever you go.' Dyson reminded him that there was a warrant out for his arrest. Peace retorted that he cared nothing for the warrant, nor for the police. He then entered a grocer's called Gregory's, next door to the Dysons' house, to buy some tobacco.

A month later, on Wednesday, 29 November 1876, Peace was seen hanging about Banner Cross Terrace between 7.00 and 8.00 pm. He visited Gregory's, asking for Mr Gregory, who was out. He requested a woman in the street to take a message to Mrs Dyson, asking her to come and see him. The woman told him to deliver the message himself. He continued to loiter, and just before 8.00 pm accosted a labourer, Charles Brassington, outside the Banner Cross Hotel and began to malign the Dysons. Brassington moved away. Peace's behaviour may have been connected with the fact, as was later suggested in court, that he had had a rendezvous in the Stag Hotel the night before with Mrs Dyson. The outcome of a murder trial in Manchester was also on his mind. But more of that later.

At about 8.00 pm that evening, Mrs Dyson put her little boy, aged five, to bed. She came downstairs to the back parlour, where her husband was seated in an armchair reading, and about ten-past eight she put on her pattens, or clogs, took a lantern and, leaving the rear door open, went to the outside closet, which stood in a passage at the end of the terrace. It was a moonlit night. Peace later claimed that she left the house when he whistled for her.

Her closet visit concluded, Kate Dyson opened the door. Peace stood before her, gun in hand. 'Speak, or I'll fire,' he said. She shrieked, slammed the door and locked it. Mr Dyson, alarmed, rushed out of the rear door of his house and around the corner of the building. As he did so his wife emerged from the closet. He pushed past her, pursuing Peace down the passage, across a forecourt, down some steps and on to the pavement. According to Mrs Dyson, the two men never came to grips. According to Peace, there was a struggle. He fired one shot, he said, to frighten Dyson. It missed. 'My blood was up,' said Peace. 'I knew if I was captured, it would mean transportation for life. That made me determined to get off.' He fired a second shot, that struck the much taller man in the forehead. The shots were fired in quick succession.

Mr Dyson fell on to his back, and his wife screamed: 'Murder! You villain! You have shot my husband!'

Peace ran across the road, hopped over a garden wall and ran across a field. In so doing he dropped a small packet, containing more than 20 notes and letters and Dyson's card requesting Peace not to interfere. The notes, obviously written by a woman, said such things as: 'You can give me something as a keepsake if you like' – 'Will see you as soon as I possibly can' – 'You must not venture for he is watching' – 'Not today, anyhow he is not very well' – 'I will give you the wink when the coast is clear . . . Will sure tell you' – 'He is gone out, come now for I must have a drink' – 'Send me a drink, I am nearly dead' – 'Meet me in the Wicker, hope nothing will turn up to prevent it' – 'He is out now so be quick.'

Arthur Dyson was carried into the Gregorys' house and then into his own home, where a surgeon, Mr Harrison, found him propped up in a chair, a bullet-hole in his left temple, the bullet being lodged in Dyson's brain. He died at about half-past ten.

From then on Charlie Peace was on the run and wanted for murder, with a reward on his head of £100. He disguised the missing two fingers on his left hand by fitting a tube over that arm, to which he appended an iron hook, so that he appeared to be minus a hand and arm. He acquired the nickname 'One-armed Jemmy'. Burgling as he went, he travelled from town to town, from Sheffield to Bristol, to Oxford, to Derby, to Nottingham and Hull. During an attempted burglary in Hull, in February 1877, he was surprised by the householder, a Mr Johnson, and fired two shots at him, both of which missed.

From Hull, Peace went back to Nottingham, and there he met Susan Thompson, a widow aged about 30, who was also known as Susan Bailey, or Grey. They lived together as man and wife, and Peace supported them by committing several burglaries locally, until one day the police called at his house. He escaped via a back window and fled south, to London, where he found lodgings in Lambeth. Here Susan joined him – and so, before long, did Hannah Ward and her son, whose presence, as the police later believed, 'protected his mother from sudden death'. For Hannah 'possessed the great secret of the Banner Cross murder' – which one day she divulged to Susan Thompson 'in a bad temper'. The two women, sworn on a bible to secrecy by Peace, managed to suppress their mutual animosity and 'act the part of friendship between themselves and the man'.

The Peace household now moved to Greenwich, before settling at 5 East Terrace, Evelina Road, Nunhead, near Peckham. Hannah Ward was installed in the basement with her son. Charlie occupied the other rooms with Susan Thompson – 'a dreadful woman for drink and snuff', according to him – and they passed themselves off as Mr and Mrs Thompson. Before long she bore him a son.

The house was richly furnished, adorned with a quick turnover of other people's possessions and alive with dogs, cats, rabbits, canaries, parrots and cockatoos. As the women were always quarrelling it must have been quite a clamorous household. In the evenings Peace sometimes entertained friends and neighbours with musical soirées, at which he played a fiddle he had made himself, recited monologues and sang.

Meanwhile, he continued his trade, driving around South London by day in his pony and trap, looking for likely 'cribs' to crack, and returning to them at night with his tools concealed in a violin case. He dressed well on these outings – 'The police never think of suspecting anyone who wears good clothes', he said – and looked quite different from his Sheffield self, having shaved off his beard, dyed his hair black and stained his face with walnut juice; he also wore spectacles. He became more successful, more daring than ever, and although his exploits attracted much attention in the papers, no one knew who he was. Every Sunday he and Mrs Thompson went to church.

It seems in the end that someone grassed on him, perhaps one or other of his women. Certainly the police were out in unusually large numbers in the early hours of Thursday, 10 October 1878 in the suburbs south-east of Greenwich Park.

About 2.00 am, PC Edward Robinson noticed a flickering light in the rear rooms of 2 St John's Park. He acquired the assistance of PC William Girling and Sgt Charles Brown, and the latter went round to the front of the house and rang the door-bell, while the other two policemen perched on or by the garden wall at the rear. They saw the roving light within the house go out and a figure make a swift exit from the dining-room window on to the lawn. PC Robinson gave chase, running across the moonlit garden, and was six yards away when Peace turned and shouted: 'Keep back, keep off, or by God, I'll shoot you!' PC Robinson said: 'You had better not!'

Peace fired three times, according to Robinson, narrowly missing the constable's head. He rushed at Peace, who fired a fourth shot that missed, and as they struggled – 'You bugger, I'll settle you this time!' exclaimed the burglar – a fifth shot entered Robinson's right arm above the elbow. Undaunted and no doubt now enraged, Robinson flung Peace on the ground, seized the revolver and hit Peace with it several times. 'You bugger!' said Peace, 'I'll give you something else!' And he allegedly reached for some weapon in a pocket. But by then PC Girling, followed by Sgt Brown, had come to Robinson's assistance and Peace was overpowered.

While he was being searched, Peace made another attempt to escape and was incapacitated by a blow from Girling's truncheon. A spirit flask, a chequebook and a letter case, stolen from the house, were found in his possession, as well as a small crowbar, an auger, a jemmy, a gimlet, two chisels, a centre-bit and a hand-vice.

As Robinson was now feeling faint through loss of blood, the two other policemen took charge of the captive burglar. He was escorted to Park Row police station near the Royal Naval College at Greenwich and not far from the River Thames. There he was charged with burglary and with the wounding of PC Robinson with intent to murder. He gave his name as 'John Ward', and when asked where he lived replied: 'Find out!' Inspector John Bonney, of Blackheath Road police station, was put in charge of the case, and later that morning Peace was brought before Detective Inspector Henry Phillips, local head of the newly formed Criminal Investigation Department of Scotland Yard, the CID.

DI Phillips later wrote a vivid and as yet unpublished memoir of the case. Writing in 1899, he said that Peace's 'repulsive' appearance could be verified by the wax image of him in Madame Tussaud's – where it is to this day.

On the morning of 10 October 1878, DI Phillips and Inspector Bonney tried to elicit information from the bloody-minded burglar, who exclaimed:

'If you want to know where I live, find out! It's your business!' When he became insolent, Bonney threatened to thrash him. 'All to no purpose,' wrote Phillips.

So the two inspectors tried to trap him, using a trick not sanctioned by the police authorities.

After the prisoner was remanded he was put in one of the Police Cells alone [wrote Phillips]. I then made up a man under my charge, and the Gaoler put him into the Cell with the prisoner. He was pushed in head foremost and very nearly fell on the top of Mr Ward. The newcomer commenced by using abusive and threatening language towards the Police Gaoler. Mr Ward then offered a little sound advice for the benefit of his fellow prisoner. He said: 'Young man, don't never kick up a row with the Police. It's a bad plan and you will always find they get the best of you.'

Unfortunately for Phillips, Peace revealed nothing about his own circumstances, other than that he had been brutally treated by the arresting policemen and charged with burglary.

Peace was then incarcerated in Newgate Prison, where he was visited by Phillips more than once. Phillips wrote later: 'He was very talkative and boasted of his misdeeds as if they were something to be proud of.' He concluded that although Peace could seem 'religious-minded' and a 'nice quiet old man', he was really 'a canting hypocrite'.

The following month, Peace was tried under the name 'John Ward' at the Central Criminal Court in the Old Bailey on 19 November 1878, charged with the attempted murder of PC Edward Robinson. The judge was Mr Justice Hawkins. Mr Pollard was the prosecutor and Mr Montague Williams spoke on the prisoner's behalf.

After a four-minute consultation, the jury found Peace guilty. Asked by Mr Reed, the Clerk of the Court, if he had anything to say before judgement was pronounced, the prisoner made a lengthy, whining speech that apparently impressed most of his listeners, except the judge. Peace said:

My Lord, I have not been fairly dealt with, and I swear before God I never had the intention to kill the policeman. All I meant was to frighten him in order that I might get away. If I had the intention to kill him I could easily have done it. But I never had the intention to kill him. I declare I did not fire five shots. I only fired four shots . . . If your Lordship will look at the pistol you will see that it goes off very easily, and the sixth barrel went off of its own accord after I was taken into custody at the station. At the time the fifth shot was fired the constable had hold of my arm and the pistol went off quite by accident. I really did not know the pistol was loaded, and I hope, my Lord, you will have mercy upon me. I feel that I have disgraced myself and am not fit to live or die. I am not prepared to meet my God, but I fear that my career has been made to appear much worse than it really is. Oh, my Lord, do have mercy upon me, and I assure you that you shall never repent it. Give me one more chance of repenting and preparing myself to meet my God. As you hope for mercy yourself at the hands of the great God, do have mercy upon me, a most wretched miserable man – a man that am not fit to die. I am not fit to live, but with the help of my God, I will try to become a good man [etc].

Peace was sentenced to penal servitude for life.

The judge then called PC Robinson forward, commended his courageous conduct and recommended him for promotion and for a reward of £25. Robinson was duly promoted to sergeant, and for a time a waxwork of him stood in Madame Tussaud's beside that of Peace.

The prisoner was then moved to Pentonville Prison, which in 1878, according to Phillips, was 'a preparatory prison for all convicts sentenced to Penal Servitude. It was here they performed the first nine months of their sentence, under what was known as the solitary system'.

By this time Peace's real identity had been established, as well as the fact that he was wanted for the murder of Arthur Dyson in Sheffield. What happened was that some two weeks before the Old Bailey trial, while Peace was in Newgate Jail, he wrote a letter requesting a certain gentleman, a Mr Brion, to visit him. This Mr Brion did, and was tailed when he left the jail and returned to his home in Philip Road, Peckham Rye. Phillips and Bonney decided to call on him that night (on Saturday, 3 November), although they were 'in some sort of doubt as to who the man was'. He might have been an accomplice of Peace.

'However,' continued Phillips in his memoir, 'we took a straightforward course after inspecting the house in which Mr Brion resided, which appeared to be of a highly respectable appearance and not at all like the haunt of Burglars. We were fortunate in finding Mr Brion at home, and we were still more fortunate in finding we had met with a very respectable man, very willing to assist us in this interesting enquiry.' Mr Brion, a map-maker, had apparently believed 'Mr Thompson' to be equally respectable and had been as surprised as Mrs Brion to hear that their acquaintance was in Newgate. They had believed Peace's story that he was inventing 'an unsinkable boat', and had taken out a patent. He had explained his night-time excursions by saying that he was testing his boat on the Thames at night so that no one could observe him.

The Brions were able to tell the two inspectors where Mr Thompson lived and with whom: Susan Thompson and Hannah Ward. But their house, said Mr Brion, had 'broken up', Mrs Ward having gone to the north of England and Mrs Thompson to Nottingham. The latter, however, who had been staying with the Brions, was expected back very soon. The policemen asked to be informed, by telegram, the moment she returned.

On Monday, 5 November, a telegram came from Mr Brion, and the inspectors returned to Peckham. At the Brions' house they were introduced in the front parlour to Susan Thompson. 'She was a tall, angular-featured woman,' according to Phillips, 'with a certain amount of determination and reserve in her disposition'. She was 'the Key to the whole situation', he wrote. 'But the Key was rusty at first and required some lubrication. First persuasion was used, and then threats.'

After two hours [wrote Phillips], we were well nigh tired of our work, which seemed so fruitless. We begged of her to tell us who the man was. She refused pointblank. I had been successful in finding a small silver watch in a bedroom she occupied, and this was brought into use when terror was brought to the front. We told her we should arrest her for receiving the stolen watch. Mrs Brion implored her to tell all she knew. She said: 'I cannot tell you. I have taken an oath not to tell you anything.' The torment she was going through began to tell upon her. I pointed out the disgrace she would bring upon Mr Brion if she was arrested at his house. She looked at me with tears in her eyes and said: 'I dare not tell you.' I said: 'You need not tell me one word with your lips – write it.' I pulled out my pocket book and handed her a pencil, and this is what she wrote: *I know that is name is not Ward is Charles Pease of Sheffield.*

Phillips continued: 'The Key had opened the door and now her conscience was relieved as to the Oath. Information as to John Ward's antecedents began to flow freely. She said: "He is the greatest criminal that ever lived and so you will find out. He used to live at Darnall near Sheffield and is wanted for murder and there is a reward for his arrest."'

Susan Thompson eventually received that reward – £100.

Inspector Bonney thought Peace was a most inappropriate name for a burglar and alleged murderer and doubted Mrs Thompson's story. But he and Phillips went off to report to the recently appointed Director of the CID, Mr Howard Vincent, who immediately, to their surprise, sent them north along with Mr Brion, 'at the Public Expense'. Phillips wrote: 'The Director knew nothing of red tape and waited on no occasion for Office rules to be complied with.'

It seems that Phillips had never been north of Finchley, and his experiences over the next few weeks, as well as Peace's character and crimes, left a lasting impression. Over 20 years later, he wrote: 'We went by the Midland Railway, all the way in the dark. The Country looked very dismal, but was lighted up by various bonfires, it being the 5th November. At Trent we separated. Bonney with Brion went on to the town of Nottingham, while I kept on with the Express and soon found myself in Sheffield.' He continued:

It is a strange feeling of loneliness to be suddenly landed in a great City, having no knowledge of any person within its boundaries. After some enquiry I found myself at the Central Police Office. It was 9.45 pm and an Inspector was then parading the night duty men, very much after the system of the Metropolitan Police. I thought them a very fine body of men. I now introduced myself to the Inspector, and having told him I had come to Sheffield to make enquiries, something like the following conversation took place. 'Is there a place near Sheffield known as Darnall?' 'Yes, there is a village named Darnall near Attercliffe.' 'Have you ever heard of the name of Peace as a family living near Sheffield?' 'Oh, yes. We have been looking for a man named Charles Peace for some time – he is wanted for a Murder at Banner Cross near here. But our Chief has received some information that he died in a Coal Pit in Derbyshire.' I said: 'What is your man like? Has he lost some fingers?' 'Yes,' said he. Then I said: ' My friend, you may depend upon it that Charles Peace did not die in a Coal Pit, but is at the present time in Newgate Prison awaiting trial for attempted murder.' He said: 'You had best see Chief Constable Jackson in the morning.'

I asked for a recommendation to some good hotel and I was taken to the Hen and Chickens, kept by one Tingle. Now Tingle was a man anybody could take to because he was homely, and after 5 minutes interview and a Chat, I felt I had known the man for a much longer time. Here I stayed then till after breakfast on the 6th Nov, and upon going to the Central Police Station I had an interview with Chief Constable Jackson, who died in 1898, 20 years after my first introduction to him. A finer stamp of a Police Officer I have never met. No formalities with him. Common sense was his motto before all technicalities. He at first doubted if the man Ward in Newgate was Peace. He put several Photographs of Criminals before me and I was soon able to point out the one most resembling John Ward, and then he told me that that was the portrait of Peace.

However, in order to make matters perfectly clear on this point, he sent off a Police Officer to London, telegraphing to Mr Vincent, and by the time the Officer arrived at Scotland Yard, Home Office Authority had been obtained for the inspection of John Ward, who of course was identified as Charles Peace – much to the discomfort of that person. A telegram soon arrived at Sheffield notifying the result of the interview.

DI Phillips then set out to find Hannah Ward, assisted by an Inspector from Attercliffe. 'A true type of Yorkshireman', wrote Phillips. 'I have never got in contact with such men before. They seemed to have the Knack of making you feel you had known them for years.' They journeyed to Darnall – 'a wild barren-looking country, the more so in November' – and found where Hannah Ward, now aged 50, was staying, in a cottage with her daughter (by Peace) and son-in-law. Phillips wrote:

As luck would have it she came to the door in answer to my Knock. I told her I wanted to know if she would give up the possession of the house at Nunhead, trying to make her believe that I was Agent for her Landlord. I got inside the house under this pretence and at once noticed a Clock on a Chest of drawers which answered the description of one stolen at Blackheath. The Inspector came up with the Village Constable and then Mrs Peace began to look rather discomfited. I at once arrested her upon the charge of receiving the Clock with a guilty knowledge, and

I searched the house and found property consisting of valuable wearing apparel, such as a sealskin jacket, silver plate and various articles which looked quite out of place in a four-roomed Cottage, whose real occupant was a Collier. Having packed up this property, we set out for Sheffield with our Prisoner and a very heavy bundle of goods which were never expected to find the way back to their owners, but they did.

On 9 November, having heard of Hannah's arrest, Peace wrote from Newgate to 'a gentleman of Sheffield', beseeching him to save Hannah – 'She is inesent, she knows nothing of my doings . . . It is me and not her.'

Hannah Ward appeared before the Sheffield magistrates, was remanded for a week, and some time before Christmas was taken by Phillips back to London on an overnight train and charged by him 'at Bow Street one Saturday morning about 4.00 am'. On 14 January 1879 she appeared at the Old Bailey before Mr Commissioner Kerr, charged with receiving stolen goods. She was discharged, however, on the grounds that she was Peace's *wife* – although this was never proved or established by a search of civil records (as could easily have been done) – and had acted under *his* authority.

Eight days after this, and early on the morning of Wednesday, 22 January, Peace was taken from Pentonville Prison and, handcuffed and attended by two warders, was put on the 5.15 am express from London to Sheffield for the magistrate's hearing. It was very cold: up north there was snow on the ground. Peace was very troublesome, but all went well until the train neared Sheffield.

Peace was well acquainted with the locality [Phillips wrote]. He expressed a wish to pass water, and for that purpose the window was lowered and he faced it. He was wearing handcuffs with a chain 6 inches long, so that he had some use with his hands – and he immediately sprang through the window. One of the warders caught him by the left foot. There he held him suspended, of course with the head downwards. He kicked the Warder with the right foot and struggled with all his might to get free. The Chief Warder was unable to render his colleague any assistance because the Warder's body occupied the whole of the space of the open window. He hastened to the opposite side of the Carriage and pulled the Cord to alarm the Guard, but the Cord would not act. But some gentleman in the next compartment, seeing the state of affairs, assisted the efforts of the warder to stop the train. All this time the struggle was going on between the Warder and the Convict, and eventually Peace succeeded in kicking off his shoe and he fell, his head striking the footboard of the Carriage, and he fell on the line.

The train eventually came to a halt before it reached Kiveton Park, and the two warders ran for over a mile back along the railway line and found their prisoner prostrate in the snow and apparently dead. To their relief he soon recovered consciousness, professing to be in great pain from the bloody wound on his head and dying from cold. A slow train heading for Sheffield chanced to appear and was stopped by the warders. Peace was lifted up and placed in the guard's van. The train proceeded on its way, arriving in Sheffield at 9.20 am.

An immense crowd had assembled to get sight of this great Criminal [continued Phillips] and the excitement became intense when the 8.54 Express arrived without him. The Guard reported that Peace had escaped. The crowd were unbelieving and they suggested that the statement was a ruse to get the crowd away. But when they saw a sword and a rug and a bag belonging to the Warders brought from an empty carriage and handed to Inspector Bird, it was then generally believed that the statement was true and that Peace had escaped from Custody and that the Warders were on his track.

At the Sheffield Police Court great preparations had been made for the reception of Charles Peace and the Court was crowded. All the persons required to be in attendance were present, except one, and that was the Prisoner. The Magistrate, Mr Welby, was there. Mr Pollard of the Treasury was ready with all his documents to carry out the Prosecution on behalf of the Crown, while Mr Clegg, a solicitor, was there to defend. Mr Jackson, Chief Constable of Sheffield, entered the Court in a state of some excitement and made the startling statement to the Bench that Peace had escaped from the Warders. The ordinary business of the Court proceeded, when it suddenly became known that Peace had been captured and was actually in Sheffield – although it was doubtful if he would be able to attend the Court that day in consequence of his injuries.

On reaching the Police Station Peace was carried to a Cell, where he was seen by Dr Stewart, the Police Surgeon, and a Mr Hallam, a Surgeon of Sheffield. They found him suffering from a severe scalp wound and concussion of the brain. He appeared to be in an exhausted state and vomited freely, and it was with some difficulty that stimulants were administered to him. His wounds were carefully dressed and he was laid in a bed in a Cell and covered with rugs. There the little old man lay, with his head peeping out of the rugs, guarded by two Officers. During the first hour he was frequently roused and he partook of some brandy. At first, force had to be used to get him to take it, but subsequently he drank without any trouble: at the same time he said he should prefer whiskey if he was compelled to take spirit. When he was handled by his Police attendants, for the purpose of giving these stimulants, he ground his teeth, clenched his hands and appeared to be in a fit. But when extra force was used he obeyed the Officers. On one of these occasions a Police Officer who knew him well said: 'Now, Charlie, it's no use. Let's have none of your hanky-panky games here. You will have to take it.' And he did take it (A Coward you see when subdued). He next complained of being cold and extra clothing was provided for him, the object of the Authorities being of course to bring him round as soon as possible so as to get him before the Magistrate. In a few days the Surgeon certified him as being fit to attend the Court.

In fact, the court went to Peace, and the magistrate's hearing was held on Friday, 24 January by candlelight in the corridor outside his cell.

Swathed in rugs and bandages, he cursed, groaned, complained and endlessly interrupted. 'What are we here for? What is this?' he protested. The stipendiary replied: 'This is the preliminary enquiry which is being proceeded with after being adjourned.' Said Peace: 'I wish to God there was something across my shoulders – I'm very cold! It isn't justice. Oh dear. If I'd killed myself it'd be no matter. I ought to have a remand! I feel I want it, and I must have one!'

The hearing was attended by Mrs Dyson, who had been brought back to England from America, whither she had gone after her husband's death. As the prosecution's principal witness she seemed to enjoy the drama of her situation and was evidently not put out by Peace's presence, appearance and his aspersions. When she took the oath without lifting her veil, he exclaimed: 'Will you be kind enough to take your veil off? You haven't kissed the book!' At one point he put his feet on the table. At the end of the hearing, he was carried back into his cell blaspheming.

Committed for trial at Leeds Assizes, he was taken by train to Wakefield Prison. A large crowd again assembled at Sheffield railway station to witness his departure. Professing to be helpless, he was carried from the police van by prison warders. He looked pale and haggard, despite his brown complexion, and had a white bandage around his head. 'He wore his Convict suit,' wrote Phillips, 'and very comical he looked in the cap surmounting the bandage and appeared as feeble as a Child.'

When Peace arrived at Wakefield, less sympathetic, or more astute, officials compelled him to walk unaided to his cell. There he spent the next few days dictating penitential and moralistic letters. One, on 26 January, was to Mrs Thompson.

My dear Sue. This is a fearful affair which has befallen me, but I hope you will not forsake me, as you have been my bosom friend, and you have oftimes said you loved me, and would die for me. What I hope and trust you will do is to sell the goods I left you to raise money to engage a Barrister to save me from the perjury of that villainous woman Kate Dyson. It will have to be done at once . . . as the Assizes commence on January 28th. I hope you will not forget the love we have had for each other. Do your best for me. I should like you to write or come and see me if you can. I am very ill from the effects of the jump from the train. I tried to kill myself to save all further trouble and distress, and to be buried at Darnall. I remain your ever true lover till death.

Sue Thompson replied:

Dear Jack, I received your letter and am truly sorry to receive one from you from a Prison, and in regard to what you ask me I have parted with all the things in my possession. I sold some of the goods before Hannah and I went away and I shared with her the money that was in the house, and what I had, had to be sold for my subsistence as you well know. I had nothing to depend upon, and have not a friend of my own, but what have turned their backs upon me, my life is indeed most miserable. I have 2 friends who have not turned upon me for which I am most grateful. I am sorry you made such a rash attempt upon your life, for your sufferings are greater than they would have been . . . You are doing me a great injury by saying I have been out to work with you. Do not die with such a base falsehood upon your conscience, for you know I am young and have my home and character to redeem. I pity you and myself to think we should have met. In conclusion, I hope and trust you will be very penitent and that we shall meet in Heaven. Yours, etc – Sue.

On Tuesday, 4 February 1879, Charles Peace was put on trial at Leeds Assizes before Mr Justice Lopes. The prosecutor was Mr Campbell Foster, QC, and the accused was defended by Mr Frank Lockwood. The Mayor, the Sheriff, MPs and a peer were present, and the court was packed, many of the women being armed with opera glasses. Peace, wizened, but wiry and unshaven, his scarred head and hollow features bristling with thin grey hairs, sat in an armchair within a semi-circular spiked enclosure.

Mr Campbell Foster contended in his opening remarks that the shooting of Arthur Dyson was premeditated and committed 'with malice aforethought'.

The prosecution's chief witness, Mrs Dyson, although evidently embarrassed by the implications of some of the defence's questions in cross-examination, behaved with a degree of flippancy, even levity. When asked by Mr Lockwood how wide the passage was outside the closet, she replied: 'I don't know – I am not an architect.' Lockwood, bent on getting her to admit that Dyson and Peace had come to grips before the shots were fired, quoted what she had said before the magistrate – 'I cannot say whether he, that is my husband, attempted to get hold of him or not'. She now declared: 'He never touched him. He did not get close enough.' She was obdurate, although badgered by Lockwood on this point for some time. She was shown her signed deposition and he read from it: 'I cannot say my husband did not get hold of him.' 'He did not try to get hold of him,' the witness responded. 'Do you remember saying what I have read?' demanded Mr Lockwood. Mrs Dyson: 'I said he did not try to get hold of him.' Lockwood: 'Do you remember saying the words I have repeated to you?' Mrs Dyson: 'Yes. I do remember saying it, but the word "try" is left out.' 'Do you remember?' 'I can't say I do.' 'Will you swear that you did not?' 'I won't swear I did *not*, because it is written down.' 'Will you swear your husband did not get hold of him?' 'I say he did not, because he was not near enough to him.' 'Did you give that as the reason when you were before the magistrate?' 'Yes. They did not press me so hard – not as hard as you!' There was laughter in court.

Mr Lockwood pressed on regardless until the judge intervened: 'Whatever you said before the magistrate is correct?' 'Yes,' Mrs Dyson replied. But Mr Lockwood would not let go. To his question 'Did this man touch him with his fist?' she replied: 'No, the *bullet* touched him.'

He was more successful in implying that Mrs Dyson had had an association with Peace, that he gave her a ring, that she continued to meet him after her husband had expressed his dislike of Peace and had been photographed with him at the Sheffield Summer Fair in 1876. She denied that letters and notes referring to assignations were in her handwriting. She was forced to admit, when confronted by witnesses, that she had gone with Peace to a pub called the Marquis of Waterford in Russell Street, Sheffield, to the Norfolk dining-rooms in Exchange Street, and to the Star music-hall. But she denied that she bought drink at the Halfway House in Peace's name, that she gave a man called Kirkham notes for Peace, that she was ever evicted from a pub for being drunk, and that she was with Peace in the Stag Hotel the night before her husband was killed.

Throughout Mrs Dyson's cross-examination, Peace leaned forward looking at her, occasionally summoning his solicitor and whispering.

Mr Lockwood, in his speech for the defence, proposed that the shooting was accidental, that Peace's threats were meaningless and that the prosecution's principal witness was unreliable and her evidence tainted and uncorroborated. The prosecution, he said, had not established their charge. In conclusion, he urged the jury not to lay themselves open to the reproach that they had 'wrongfully taken away the life of a fellow man'.

The judge told the jury that the plea of provocation failed altogether 'where pre-conceived ill-will against the deceased was proved'.

The jury took 15 minutes to reach a verdict of guilty of wilful murder and Peace was sentenced to death. On being asked if he had anything to say before sentence was passed, he muttered: 'Will it be any use for me to say anything?'

Peace was removed to Armley Jail in Leeds where, playing the penitent, he made a full confession of all his crimes to the Revd Littlewood, vicar of Darnall. He revealed that four months *before* the killing of Arthur Dyson he had also shot and killed a police constable, in Manchester.

At the time, in 1876, two young Irish brothers, called Habron, had been accused of the constable's murder and one had been sentenced to death. Their story was also told by Inspector Phillips in his 180-page memoir on Peace.

About 1870, four young labourers named Habron left their village home in County Mayo and in a suburb of the City of Manchester they settled down. Thomas Habron went into the service of Mr Grealey, a Farmer. The others, William, John and Frank were engaged by Mr Francis Deakin, Farmer, and there the brothers remained without further notice until the summer of 1875. They bore excellent characters on the whole and regularly remitted a portion of their earnings to the old folks at home. All that stood to their disadvantage took the form of

3 summonses for drunkenness. Two were issued in July 1876 at the instance of a young Constable, Nicholas Cock, who however seems to have made a mistake and the summons were dismissed on the 1st August 1876. John and William went to a Beer house known as the Royal Oak where they were regular customers. John drank to his safe return, while William was heard to say: 'Here's Damn the Bobbies,' adding if the Bobby did him, he would do the Bobby. John, contending that the Constable had no right to summon him, said: 'If he does, by God we will shunt him!' The landlady said: 'Why, Jack, what do you mean?' And the reply was: 'We will shift him. We will get our Gaffer, Mr Deakin, to shift him.'

The night was a dark one, and the well-to-do neighbourhood of Whalley Range with the great houses and large gardens seemed more than ordinarily deserted, and while the 3 brothers slept as was their wont in the outhouse in Mr Deakin's premises, the object of their spleen, Police Constable Cock, commenced his beat from Charlton Village along Chorley Lane to West Point, where he was due at midnight. In Charlton Lane he was met by a pedestrian, a Mr Simpson, and at West Point they were met by PC Beanland. Immediately after, the figure of a man was seen moving along in the shadows towards the garden of a house that had been in the occupation of a Mr Gratrix, and when Mr Simpson had said: 'Goodnight, Beanland,' he went into the garden where the mysterious figure had apparently disappeared and examined the door of the house. He had barely turned away again when 2 shots fired in rapid succession were heard. Hurriedly retracing their steps, Beanland and Simpson were horrified to find Constable Cock lying in the roadway, shot through the right breast. The sound of wheels was heard and a night-cart coming along, on this rude vehicle the body of the insensible Policeman was conveyed to the nearest surgery. The wounded Constable did not live long.

The local Superintendent immediately suspected the Habrons, and within an hour, in company with some Constables, had taken possession of the outhouse where the brothers slept. Promptly bidding the brothers to get out of bed, he instituted a rigorous search, ordering each man to put on the clothes he was wearing yesterday ... By 3 am the 3 Habrons were in the cells at Northumberland St Station.

The charges against Frank Habron were dropped through lack of evidence. But John and William (the youngest brother) were sent for trial at Manchester Assizes on 27 November 1876.

The prosecution implied that Cock had been shot by one or other of the Habrons out of spite and in revenge. Various witnesses recalled various threats the brothers had made, that William had inspected a revolver in the ironmonger's, and that John had said 'shoot him' not 'shift him'. *Two* men were alleged to have been seen lurking near the scene of the crime, one of whom allegedly wore a coat and hat similar to those worn by William Habron. Although Mr Simpson described the mysterious figure he had seen as 'elderly and with a stooping gait', PC Beanland was positive that the man had walked erect and definitely resembled William Habron. Footprints found near the scene allegedly matched those made by the boots of the accused, and some percussion caps were found in a waistcoat pocket worn by William. Mr Deakin, convinced his employees were innocent, explained that he had given the waistcoat to the accused and had probably left the caps in the pocket himself.

On 28 November, the jury, having consulted for two and a half hours, found John not guilty and William guilty, adding a recommendation for mercy 'on the grounds of his youth'. William was 19. Mr Justice Lindley, who had summed up in the prisoners' favour, observed in passing sentence that he did so in the execution of his duty.

Peace had watched the whole trial from the public gallery. He kept silent. 'What man would have done otherwise in my position?' he later demanded.

The following night, in Sheffield, on 29 November, he shot and killed Arthur Dyson.

For three weeks William Habron was confined in the condemned cell. But on 19 December, the Home Secretary, Mr Cross, granted a reprieve and the sentence was commuted to one of penal servitude for life. William Habron was sent to Portland Prison as Convict 1547, where he remained for over two years – until Peace, now under sentence of death himself, chose to confess. He told the Revd Littlewood that he thought it right 'in the sight of God and man to clear the young man'.

Peace's written confession, dated 17 February 1879, and reprinted in Phillips's memoir, said that all the witnesses who appeared for the prosecution perjured themselves, except one (presumably Mr Simpson). A detailed map, drawn by Peace, was included in the confession, indicating with dotted lines the movements of the main protagonists. Peace said that about midnight, as he entered Seymour Grove, he saw two policemen and two civilians standing near a duck-pond. He crossed the road, hurried away from them and slipped into the garden of a house by the gate. When Beanland followed him in and tried the front door, turning on his bull's-eye lantern, Peace returned to the road via the garden wall, crossing the road to the other side. Cock must have seen him, for he came down the road towards the burglar, shouting at him to stand where he was.

This policeman was as determined a man as myself [Peace admitted later], and after I had fired wide at him, I observed him seize his staff, which was in his pocket, and he was rushing at me and about to strike me. I then fired the second time. 'Ah, you bugger,' he said, and fell. I could not take as careful an aim as I would have done, and the ball, missing the arm, struck him in the breast. I got away, which is what I wanted.

At the confession's end Peace wrote: 'As a prouff of his [Habron's] inescence you will find that the ball that was taken from Cox's breast was one of Haley's No. 9 Pinfire cartridges, and was fired out of my revolver now at the

Leeds Town Hall.' He ended: 'What I have said is nothing but the truth and that is my dying words. I have don my duty and leave the rest to you.'

On 19 March 1879, William Habron was moved from Portland to Mill-bank and then set free with a full pardon. Mr Deakin was there to meet him, with the news that William's father had died six months earlier 'of a broken heart'. He was given £1,000 in compensation 'to ease his pain and anguish'.

Years later Phillips wrote: 'No part of the case gave Bonney and myself so much satisfaction as the release of the Convict William Habron, an innocent man.'

Charles Peace was hanged at Armley Jail in Leeds at 8.00 am on 25 February 1879.

His last days were spent in interminable letter-writing and prayer and the Christian exhortation of others. But his real reprobate self prevailed. Of his last breakfast, he said: 'This is bloody rotten bacon!' And when a warder began banging on the door as Peace lingered overlong in the lavatory on the morning of his execution, he shouted: 'You're in a hell of a hurry! Are you going to be hanged or am I?' On the scaffold he refused to wear the white hood – 'Don't! I want to look' – and insisted on making a speech of forgiveness, repentance and trust in the Lord.

Four journalists who were present wrote down his last words, spoken as his resolution left him: 'I should like a drink. Have you a drink to give me?' As he spoke, William Marwood, the executioner, released the trap-door. Peace fell: the vertebrae at the base of his head fractured and dislocated, and his spinal cord was severed. A doctor wrote on his death certificate: 'Hanging by virtue of a sentence of law.'

Peace wrote his own epitaph for the memorial card which he himself printed in jail: 'In memory of Charles Peace who was executed in Armley Prison, Tuesday, February 25th 1879. For that I done but never intended.'

In due course DI Henry Phillips donated the tube that Peace had used to cover his arm, a crucible and a collapsible ladder to the Black Museum at Scotland Yard. A hundred years later, Phillips's very informative, hand-written memoir was in turn donated to the Museum by lorry-driver Peter Coyle on behalf of Phillips's great-niece, Mrs Bell.

The Criminal Investigation Department at Scotland Yard was created in 1878. Its first Director was Howard Vincent. Under his successor, James Monro, the CID was put under the nominal control of the Commissioner and Monro became the Assistant Commissioner. To cope with the Fenian outrages in 1883–5, Monro set up the Special Irish Branch.

CHAPTER 7

John Lee

The Murder of Emma Keyse, 1884

Hanging was hardly ever an instantaneous method of execution until William Marwood, public executioner from 1874 to 1883, developed a system of execution involving a sudden drop or fall, calculated to break the victim's neck. The fall could vary in depth from 5 to 15 feet, depending on the weight, age, sex, height and physical condition of the condemned person. Previously, he or she was hoisted off the ground or platform with a noose around the neck, or left dangling when whatever supported the feet was removed. As a result the condemned were slowly strangled or suffocated, hanging by the neck until they were dead. Sometimes executioners, or even relatives or friends, hung on to the hanging man's legs to hasten the process. Some were difficult to hang; and some were cut down too soon and found to be unconscious but alive. Whereupon they were hanged again. Sometimes relatives paid large sums of money to the hangman for a quick cutting-down and permission to acquire the body straightaway. Whereupon it was secretly restored to life. Some were thus saved; others, at the last hour, were reprieved. But one man entered local and criminological legend as the Man They Could Not Hang. He was saved from death by a structural fault. Or, as he believed, by God.

Babbacombe was a small fishing village in Devon, about two miles north-east of Torquay. The largest buildings, situated between a hillside and the beach, were an inn, the Cary Arms, and the Glen, a spacious two-storey house (in those days termed a villa) with a high thatched roof, shuttered windows and a long, low colonnade or verandah facing the sea. Lawns, bowers and gardens surrounded the house, which was full of old paintings and furniture and was valued in 1884 at £13,000. But, according to the *Torquay Times* of November that year, 'the spot is a weird and lonely one in the winter, and especially unsuitable for the living-place of an aged and solitary female. The approach to it is such that no vehicles can be got near it, and the occupant has to mount a very rough and steep hill in order to reach the high-road'.

The owner was a 68-year-old spinster, Miss Emma Anne Whitehead Keyse. Her father had died when she was very young and her mother had remarried a Mr Whitehead, by whom she also had some children. There seems to have been a Scottish connection, as Miss Keyse's sister, who lived a few miles inland at Compton, was called Mrs Maclean, and a step-brother, Mr

George Whitehead, lived in Edinburgh. It seems that Miss Keyse, who had once been one of Queen Victoria's Maids of Honour (or lady-in-waiting), was a very proper, religious woman, severe, though well regarded socially, and strict with her staff. Nonetheless, she had sufficient vanity to have her grey hair dyed a reddish hue.

Two of her servants, Jane and Eliza Neck, who were both in their late sixties, had served the family for well over 40 years, Jane, the parlour-maid, since 1836. The cook was a young woman called Elizabeth Harris, who at the time of the murder was pregnant though unmarried and none too well. Her half-brother, a sturdy, not unattractive young man, was the only other servant. Said to have been a footman, he was more of a gardener and general dog's-body. He was 20 and his name was John Henry George Lee.

Baptised on 4 September 1864, the son of a yeoman farmer, John Lee had lived in a lowly cottage in Abbotskerswell, two miles south of Newton Abbot and not far from Babbacombe, until he was 15. At that age he was first employed as a servant by Miss Keyse and went to work and live in the Glen. But in due course a nearer acquaintance with the sea, with fishermen and sea-men – Torquay's development was partly influenced by the use of Torbay as a naval anchorage during the Napoleonic wars and the building of accom-modation for officers' families on the shore – persuaded the teenage Lee to join the Royal Navy. However, after a year and a half, he was invalided out, apparently because he had a weak chest. Bad company or example on board ship or ashore, or a criminal bent, prompted him to steal from his next employer, a Colonel Brownlow, whom he served as a footman, and he was sentenced to six months' hard labour. Hearing of this, Miss Keyse wrote a well-meaning but fatal letter to the Governor of Exeter Prison, proposing that her house would be a better environment than the jail for the youth's im-provement and correction.

So it was that Lee re-entered her service in January 1884 and returned to the Glen, where he was paid 2s 6d a week.

The house's regimes revolved around religious observances and the exer-cise of thrift, especially in heat and light and probably food. No oil-lamps were lit where a candle would do, and no fires blazed in any grate except in the kitchen. At night the house was dark and cold. Twice a day there were prayers for all in the dining-room, and apart from attending church every Sunday, Miss Keyse also went there on Fridays; and every night, when she filled in her diary, she invariably included some religious observation or text.

There was nothing odd that we know about Friday, 14 November, except that the cook's pregnancy was making her ill and upsetting routines; that most of the household were late to bed; and that, possibly after some slating or reprimand from Miss Keyse, her young male servant was contemplating her death. Elizabeth Harris, the cook, said later:

I saw Miss Keyse for the last time in the morning at 10.30. This was at prayers in the dining-room. Eliza and Jane Neck and me were there . . . I heard Miss Keyse's voice during the day. She was in and out. She went to church as she always does on Fridays . . . I went to bed about five o'clock as I was ill . . . I have not been ill long. I asked Jane not to say anything to Miss Keyse about my illness as she might think more of it than was necessary . . . I fell asleep until nearly 11 o'clock. At that time one of the other servants, Eliza, came to me before she went to bed to see if I wanted anything. I stayed awake a little while longer and then went to sleep.

Jane Neck was on her feet until late that night. She filled the oil-lamps before dusk and later went around the house closing and fastening all the internal shutters and bolting the windows and doors. It was a windy night, with a strong easterly wind blowing off the sea against the front of the house. When Miss Keyse was ready – she had no supper that night – Jane summoned her sister and John Lee for prayers at about half-past ten. He had gone out, as was usual, about 6.30 or 7.00 to post some letters, and stayed out, as usual, until 10.30 or so. He said later he returned at eleven. After prayers Miss Keyse had some tea and toast, made by Jane, and at about 11.00 pm she noticed that John was in his bed and apparently asleep. He said later that he went to bed at midnight.

Lee slept in a pull-down bed in the pantry, a narrow room in a passage near the foot of the hall stairs and within sight of the dining-room door. It was separated from the passage by a partition which had a 1' 10" gap at the top, through which any sound, or smoke, would easily penetrate. It seems that Jane Neck entered the pantry to collect or deposit something, or to give John a message. But as Eliza also saw him in bed they may have glimpsed him through the pantry door, which was always open.

A note from Miss Keyse was later found on a table in the pantry. But it is not known who left it there or gave it to Lee. It said: 'John – You had better do some raking of the paths first and go to Compton afterwards.' This referred to a package that Miss Keyse had put together that night for Lee to take to Mrs Maclean the following morning.

Jane still had some other little domestic jobs to do, like putting a hot-water bottle in Miss Keyse's bed; she also put the house-keys on a bedroom seat. It seems that she and Eliza sat with Miss Keyse for a while, possible sewing. At about 12.30 Jane went to make Miss Keyse some cocoa, which as usual she left on the kitchen stove. It was 12.40 when she returned to the dining-room to wish Miss Keyse goodnight, and left her writing in her diary in the light of a single lamp. Just before Jane went upstairs she heard Lee coughing in the pantry.

Jane Neck and her sister slept in a bedroom on the first floor, adjacent to Elizabeth Harris's room. They were both in bed before 1.00 am, and soon asleep. 'I was not long awake when I got into bed,' said Jane.

Not long after this Miss Keyse, it seems, left the dining-room and went upstairs. Having changed into a flannel nightdress, she donned a woollen jacket and, as was her wont, came downstairs to the kitchen carrying a candle (she would have passed the pantry), and after warming the cocoa took a cup of it and a plate of biscuits up to her bedroom. She had drunk but half of the cocoa when for some reason she ventured downstairs again.

Was it then that she left the note for John Lee on the pantry table? Or was there some minor domestic matter that sprang to mind and required her attention? She was in the hall at the foot of the stairs when a hatchet struck the back of her head.

Some two hours later, at about 3.30 am, Elizabeth Harris awoke. It was fortunate that she had been in bed since 5.00 pm the previous day and was not as tired, or as old, as the Necks. Otherwise, she and they might have perished with Miss Keyse, and the murder, as was intended, never discovered. She said later: 'I was awakened by the smell of smoke. I was not woke up by a noise. There was no sound of anything but the wind. So far as I can say there was no smoke in my own room. I thought at first I would not take any notice of it. But afterwards I smelt it stronger, and struck a light. I called to Jane and Eliza three or four times before I could make them hear.'

She was slow getting dressed and out of her room. The Neck sisters were more quickly alarmed and on their feet. Pausing only to light a candle, and calling 'Miss Keyse! Miss Keyse!' they hastened in their nightdresses to her bedroom – to find a sofa, the curtains, the bed canopy and a corner of the bed ablaze. Jane Neck, thinking Miss Keyse was in the bed, tore back the bed-clothes, exposing the hot-water bottle but no sign of Miss Keyse.

What happened next is confused, as is the evidence of the sisters, especially Jane's. At some point, dense smoke snuffed out the candle held by Jane. Eliza was the first to feel her way downstairs: part of the bottom steps and the ban-ister were smouldering and on fire. But the worst blaze was in the dining-room, whose door was open, although the flames were largely obscured by the smoke. 'What's the matter?' she heard Lee say from the direction of the pantry. It seems she fetched some water from the kitchen and threw it on the dining-room flames. In doing so she stumbled on Miss Keyse's body, scorched and nearly naked, lying on its back near a couch with the fingers clenched. 'Here is Miss Keyse!' she cried. Although most of the nightdress, stockings and jacket had burnt away, the face and hair, though bloody, were untouched. Charred heaps of paper lay about and there was a smell of paraffin oil.

Meanwhile, Jane had abandoned any attempts she might have made to ex-tinguish the bedroom fire and had retreated to the landing, doubtless coughing and choking. She saw John Lee, who was wearing (although un-noticed by her then) a blue collarless shirt, socks, and trousers with the braces hanging down. He supported her to the balustrade. 'He seemed frightened at the fire,' she said. Later, she would find that the upper part of her nightdress was smeared with blood.

Elsewhere, Elizabeth Harris, who had remained on the first floor, was throwing water on the flaming walls of a guest bedroom called the Honey-suckle room above the dining-room. She saw John Lee but said nothing to him. This room, where the bed was also badly burned, was set alight by the fire below. The police later deduced that there were five separate seats of fire: the dining-room, the two first-floor bedrooms, the hall carpet and the stairs. At the magistrates' court the prosecution would say:

In the dining-room heaps of charred paper were found under the sofa and on an arm-chair. But it was apparent that the fire could not be got to burn, and as a last resource paraffin was obtained and used, being poured over the carpets, over the table, and various parts of the room and then ignited. More paraffin was poured over the carpet in the hall . . . and over the first two stairs, which places were also set on fire.

The police superintendent would say that the dining-room was set on fire an hour before Miss Keyse's bedroom – where some paraffin oil was also scattered about. It seems clear that because the windows were all closed and shuttered and the air in the rooms so still, the flames were slow to spread and most burning items smouldered. If doors and some windows had been opened, and the wind let loose in the house, the fires would have become a conflagration and burned the Glen to the ground.

Apparently the female servants and Lee tried haphazardly to dowse the flames for as much as 20 minutes (according to Jane), before Eliza unbolted the kitchen door and sent John Lee into the windy night to fetch some help. Thinly dressed as he was he ran to the nearby Cary Arms and to Beach Cottage, calling out: 'Miss Keyse's house is on fire!'

The landlord of the Cary Arms, William Gasking, and his niece, were the first to respond. Gasking dressed himself, and equipped with a lantern, made for the Glen, from which billowed volumes of smoke. 'Well, John – what's the matter?' asked Gasking. Lee replied: 'Oh, Mr Gasking, Miss Keyse is burnt to death!' 'Where to?' enquired Gasking, and Lee led him to the dining-room. Gasking took charge. He said later:

> I went to the left-hand side of the body and said: 'Help me to get her out of this.' He began to talk about some other matter and I said: 'Hold your tongue, John! I don't want to hear anything about that.' I also told him to 'Come on!' And then he helped me to move her. John put his left hand to her arm and his right hand under her right thigh. The legs dropped down because they were limp. We took her as far as the kitchen door and then I sent John to get a carpet. I saw the wounds on the body. Her right foot was the portion most burnt. The features of the deceased were not disfigured, but all about the cut in the throat was burned.

Lee managed to drop her body in the hall, where Gasking noticed a pool of blood near the stairs. While he waited for Lee to return, a fisherman, Richard Harris, arrived at the kitchen door, followed by his wife, sister and son. He said: 'I got there about five minutes to four . . . I asked whose the body was, and Gasking said it was Miss Keyse. I did not notice at first that the lady's throat was cut. I thought it was a burn . . . I made use of the words "What a wonderful burn in her throat," Lee being present at the time.'

He and Gasking placed the body on the piece of carpet, folded over the sides and carried it to an outhouse. 'When I left John,' said Gasking, 'I told him to look sharp and get some water.'

It was probably about now that Jane Neck opened the shutters and the french window in the dining-room and went out on to the lawn. The evidence she gave in court is confused, as she went outside more than once, but she stood there or ran about shouting 'Fire!' until Lee led her back inside. It was about then that he cut his arms deliberately by smashing some panes in the window.

Jane said later: 'The first place I saw John was on the landing. I had no conversation with him until I had been out on the lawn. He did not tell me he had cut his arm until after I had been on the lawn. He also told me he had broken the window to let out the smoke . . . I noticed that his arm was bleeding when he called my attention to it.' Lee's intention was to account for the blood-stains on Jane's nightdress, caused when he took her arm earlier on the smoke-logged landing. He must have noticed the stains and was afraid that others, apart from she, would wonder how they got there. It was of course Miss Keyse's blood, that had soaked his shirt and trousers when he cut her throat, which he tried to conceal by setting paper alight on her throat to obscure the wound. On the lawn he took Jane's arm once again, now smearing *his* blood on her nightdress. The blood-stains on his blue shirt and plaid trousers were probably not evident in the smoke and darkness to Gasking and Harris. But Lee's bare arms, with the sleeves rolled up, were more in view.

When and *how* the nightdress became blood-stained, as well as *when* the dining-room window was broken, were matters much questioned at the various hearings. Gasking later told the inquest: 'When Lee helped me out with the body I saw no stain of blood on his arms. I have examined the clothes I was wearing and can't find a trace of blood on them. If blood came off Miss Keyse's body it would have stained me as well as him. The body was as dry as a horn.' 'I did not notice any blood about her,' said Harris. Nor did he notice any blood flowing from John Lee's arms. Both men also swore that the dining-room shutters were closed when each arrived. Said Gasking later: 'I went around afterwards to the dining-room window, and saw that one of the panes of glass was broken. The outer shutters were opened and fastened back . . . Had the inside shutters been open the wind would have blown in violently . . . I asked Lee when he broke the glass and he told me it was before he called me up. I also asked him how he did it, and he said: "With my fists."'

In fact he must have cut his arms *after* Gasking's arrival. And several panes of glass were broken, not one. Lee probably closed the *inner* shutters, allowing some smoke to escape, when he took Jane back to the dining-room.

By this time, further helpers had arrived, including four coastguards and some fishermen. Firemen from the local volunteers were prevented from bringing their equipment to the scene because of poor access and the steep hill behind the house. Water was collected from a well, from taps and the water-butt; and a pole was used to bring down smouldering sections of ceiling. This, and a handspike, were fetched from a woodshed by Lee. He also produced a hatchet on request. Witnesses would later aver that the hatchet appeared very quickly – the implication being that it was already in the house.

By 5.00 am the various fires had been extinguished and about this time the police began to arrive, some summoned by Lee. The ensuing investigation was conducted by Police Sergeant Nott, assisted by three PCs.

Their arrival may have prompted Lee's departure from the Glen at 5.15 am, although he had already been told to go to Compton House by Jane Neck, to tell Mrs Maclean about her sister's death. Whether he took Miss Keyse's package with him is unknown. He put on an overcoat, which was marked by his bleeding arms, and, carrying a lantern, set off up the hill.

On the way he encountered an elderly chimney-sweep, George Russell, who thought at first, as he told the inquest, that Lee was a policeman. Russell was heading for Sir Frederick Ryden's house and later recalled the ensuing conversation.

'Holloa!' called Lee, holding up his lantern. He told the sweep he was going to Captain Maclean's house to tell them Miss Keyse had died. 'Is she really dead?' asked Russell. 'We should all have been burnt to death,' said Lee, 'if it hadn't been for my sister.' 'How did she know about it?' 'She smelt smoke, came downstairs and saw the sofa afire in the dining-room.' 'Is that all?' queried Russell. 'Was there any lamp capsized?' 'No,' replied Lee. 'There was no lamp or candle . . . I'm very sorry for it. But as she's dead we shall never know how it occurred.' The two then continued on their separate ways.

Some time after half-past five, Mrs Maclean's maid, Mary Blatchford, heard someone knocking at a door. 'Oh, Miss Blatchford!' called Lee. 'Come down! Miss Keyse's house is burning!' She told the inquest later:

> I then opened the housemaid's door and went into her room and spoke to Lee through the window. I asked him if it was much, and he said the dining-room was burning. I asked him if the engine was there and he said it was sent for. I said: 'Where is Miss Keyse?' and he did not answer me for a moment. But then he said: 'Miss Keyse is hurt.' I said: 'Where is she?' And at last he said: 'Her's dead.' I said: 'No! It isn't possible!' And he said: 'Yes, her is, and you must tell Mrs Maclean.' I said: 'I can't tell her!' And he said: 'You must. Jane told me to come and tell you, and you must tell Mrs Maclean.'

The cook, Ann Bolder, also talked to Lee, who told her: 'Miss Keyse's house is on fire and she's burnt to death.' The cook saw that his arm was bleeding and he told her he had cut himself breaking glass to let the smoke out.

The next person whom Lee spoke to was PC Boughton, who had arrived at the Glen at about 5.30 am and been told to guard the outhouse in which Miss Keyse's body lay. He was there when Dr Herbert Chilcote of St Mary-church carried out an initial examination of the body, concluding that Miss Keyse had been hit on the head before her throat was cut and her body partly burnt after death.

Boughton said later:

> At 6.15 I saw John Lee coming down the hill towards the house. I asked him where he had been and he said: 'I've been to Compton. Isn't this a bad job?' I said: 'Yes, it is.' Lee said: 'Isn't my arm bad?' I said: 'What's the matter?' And he replied: 'I cut it in breaking the dining-room win-dow to let out the smoke.' I told him it was a foolish thing to do, and he

said: 'I was obliged to do it. The smoke was so thick, I couldn't find my way back to the door.' At nine o'clock I saw him again. He was shaking very much and I said: 'Hallo, old man – you're feeling the cold.' He replied: 'So would you if you'd been running about all morning with only your shirt and trousers on.' He added: 'Good God! That ever such a thing should happen! I've lost my best friend.' I said there was no doubt about that, and asked him if he had heard anything during the night. He said: 'No. I was dead asleep, and the servants had great trouble to wake me . . .'

This was not what Jane and Eliza Neck would tell the inquest. But it was probably what Lee told the police superintendent, Captain Douglas Barbour, who began his investigation of the premises and of the circumstances surrounding Miss Keyse's death, when he reached the Glen at 7.00 am on the Saturday morning.

At 8.00 am Dr Chilcote, back in his St Marychurch surgery, was visited by the injured John Lee, whose cut arms had by then been washed and bandaged at the Glen by his half-sister, Elizabeth Harris. Chilcote noted that Lee's right arm was punctured, and that there were two circular wounds 'about the size of a florin' on his left forearm. He opined later that 'they might have bled a good deal'.

Captain Barbour also inspected John Lee's injuries, as well as his bloodstained clothing. An attempt had been made to wash out blood-stains on Lee's trousers. Apart from the pool of blood in the hall, there was blood on the handles of two hall doors, on the glass of the broken windows, and blood smeared or spattered elsewhere, in and out of the house. There were marks of blood on the hall carpet near the stairs, as if a knife had twice been wiped on it. There was blood on an empty oil-can found in a pantry cupboard, to which access was limited when the bed was pulled down. The can's cork lay on the pantry floor. And there was blood on a knife in a pantry drawer. The knife had been used by Miss Keyse when gardening and had been kept in the hall by a small whetstone. It transpired that she must have sharpened the blade that would be used to cut her throat.

In her bedroom Sergeant Nott found a match on the carpet, similar to those in a box of matches found on Lee, along with some letters, when he was searched. Most damning of all was the smell of paraffin which the police noticed, as others had done before, emanating from various items, like the hall carpet and some dining-room furniture; from the burnt shreds of Miss Keyse's nightdress; and from the trousers and socks of John Lee.

Apart from all this, it was evident that none of the windows or shutters or doors had been forced open by an intruder. The arson and murder had been committed by someone within the house.

That morning, when the police investigation ended, Captain Barbour and Sgt Nott cautioned Lee in the pantry where he had been detained, guarded by a policeman. Lee was informed that he would be taken into custody on suspicion of murder. 'Oh, on suspicion?' he said. 'Aye. That's all right.'

The arrest and the crime created an immediate sensation in Babbacombe, in Torquay, in Exeter and beyond.

The inquest, before a jury, opened on Monday, 17 November in the music room of the Glen at 11.00 am. The room, said the *Torquay Times*, was 'a pleasant apartment, overlooking the sea and furnished with rare pictures and old china'. The county coroner, Sidney Hacker, addressed the jury, who were then shown over the house by Sgt Nott and were also allowed to view the body of Miss Keyse laid out in a bedroom. Everyone then moved to the town hall in St Marychurch and the inquest resumed at about half-past twelve. The room was crowded; few spectators had seats, these being re-served for the coroner, certain gentlemen, clergymen, local dignitaries, and the witnesses. Lee was brought from Torquay police station in a cab. 'He was trembling violently, and looked pale and distressed', said the *Torquay Times*.

The evidence of the first witness, Elizabeth Harris, was interrupted by the arrival of George Whitehead, Miss Keyse's step-brother, from Edinburgh. Throughout the inquest, John Lee was allowed to question witnesses, which he did with some vigour, concentrating on Elizabeth Harris and William Gasking, and disputing minor facts. Jane and Eliza Neck answered the coroner's many and confusing questions as best they could; Jane said Miss Keyse had encouraged Lee to emigrate and had lent him some money. The sisters were followed by Dr Chilcote. He reported on the post-mortem exam-ination of the body that had been carried out that morning by him and Dr Steele. Chilcote said the skull was fractured in two places, that the body was scorched mainly on the feet, chest and hands, and that the throat had been cut with great force, so much so that the knife had notched the vertebrae. He thought a hammer or knob-stick might have caused the blows on the head. At half-past seven the inquest was adjourned.

It resumed on Tuesday at 11.00 am. The *Torquay Times* reporter noted that the prisoner 'smiled ostentatiously and tripped up the steps with a jaunty air. Sgt Bastin had him in charge. The prisoner's sweetheart, Kate Farmer, was sitting near the jury'.

This time, Gasking and the other fire-fighters gave evidence, as did the chimney-sweep, Mrs Maclean's maid and cook, and Dr Steele, who deemed that Miss Keyse died from loss of blood and was 'not quite dead' from the blows on her head when her throat was cut. If this had happened first, he said, her blood would have spurted, instead of flowing out 'quietly'. He found *three* wounds on the head, two of which had fractured the skull. The third, he said, was 'a large square wound', which was probably effected by the base of a hatchet he had previously seen. It was shown to him again. The blade had, he thought, caused the other two wounds. This contradicted some of Dr Chilcote's evidence. But Steele was believed, and the hatchet, along with the clothes that Lee had worn, were sent to London to be examined by experts.

A surprise witness was a postman, William Richards, who had known Lee for six years. He revealed that two months earlier he had spoken to Lee in the grounds of one of Miss Keyse's other properties. Lee had a rake in his hands.

'Hard at work?' asked Richards. Lee said he was tired of his job. He said: 'If the Missis doesn't get me a good job soon, she'll bloody soon wish she had.' He added: 'I will put an end to one in the house before I leave.' 'You had better be careful, Jack,' said the postman. 'If anyone gets hold of your words, you'll be locked up.' 'I don't care,' said Lee. On another occasion, when the two of them met at the Glen's back door, Lee was carrying a stick with a black knob at one end. 'You might as well give me that,' said Richards. 'No,' replied Lee. 'It's the one I carry. It would give anyone a hit on the head, wouldn't it?' 'I shouldn't like to have one from it,' the postman replied.

John Lee stood up to question Richards about these remarks, demanding: 'Are you certain these words were spoken?' To which Richards said: 'Yes.' Lee put other questions about the stick, concluding: 'Well, I threw a stick into Mr Horne's garden when I was walking out with a young woman, and if they find the stick, you'll be able to know whether it was the one or not . . . Are you certain of the words?' 'Yes.' 'Very good. They weren't spoken by me.'

He sat down, and the inquest was adjourned until the Friday of the following week.

On Wednesday, 19 November, the magistrates' hearing at Torquay Police Court began and was adjourned for six days. A solicitor, Mr R. G. Templer, appeared on Lee's behalf. Much of the hearing was taken up by the two doctors' evidence, concerning wounds, weapons, clothing and paraffin oil. That afternoon Sgt Nott visited Lee's girlfriend, Kate Farmer, at Ellacombe. She had been seen wearing a diamond ring; and a valuable diamond ring had vanished from one of Miss Keyse's fingers since the fire. But it was soon proved that the ring being worn by Kate Farmer had belonged to her mother, who had recently died. Kate was still in mourning and wearing black.

So were those who attended the funeral of Miss Keyse on Thursday afternoon. Mr Gasking was the undertaker. The remains were enclosed in three coffins: what was called a shell, then a leaden coffin, and a coffin of polished oak, bright with brass fittings. The *Torquay Times* reported:

> A strong body of bearers conveyed the coffin up the ascent, and placed it in the hearse . . . Numerous crosses and wreaths had been sent to the house, and these were laid upon the coffin . . . They were mainly composed of white chrysanthemums and dahlias and arum lilies . . . At the head of the procession were a number of Babbacombe and St Marychurch tradesmen, and next in order were 16 bearers – fishermen and others, four coastguards . . . Some 30 carriages composed the main body of the cortege, at the sides of which hundreds of the general public walked. The blinds of all the houses were drawn.

Mr Whitehead, Jane and Eliza Neck led the mourners at the church, and after 'a solemn choral service', Emma Keyse was laid to rest in the family vault.

The inquest resumed on Friday, 28 November. The magistrates had intimated that the coroner was turning his inquiry into an unnecessarily lengthy judicial investigation – a point that also aggrieved Lee's solicitor, Mr Templer, who suggested that the object of the inquest was only to ascertain the cause of death. Mr Hacker was unmoved, and responded by saying that as the Government analyst, Dr Stevenson, could not come to St Marychurch until Monday, he would continue with the inquest then. In the meantime he questioned Sgt Nott, Captain Barbour and PC Boughton in some detail. Lee was not present, to the disappointment of the large crowd outside the town hall. His behaviour had been so indifferent and disrespectful ten days earlier that he stayed in jail – partly for his own safety, as he had also antagonised the crowd by making faces at them through an ante-room window, and even looping a window-cord around his neck.

Mr Hacker also had an ace up his sleeve, and was determined not to be deprived of the pleasure of playing it. He recalled Elizabeth Harris. Questioned by him, she said:

Some months ago I had a conversation with John Lee. We were talking and reading in the kitchen. I said: 'Suppose Miss Keyse won't give you a character.' He said if she wouldn't, he would level the place in ashes to the ground. I said: 'Don't burn me with it,' and he said he would let me know ... On 28 October I had another conversation with Lee in the kitchen. He came in and sat down crying. I asked him what he was crying for and he made no answer. He afterwards said that Miss Keyse was only going to pay him two shillings a week. I said I thought the agreement was for 2s 6d and he said there was no agreement. He grew very angry and said he wouldn't stay there another night ... He said he would have his revenge, and that on another occasion, when Miss Keyse had been grumbling at him, if she had been near a cliff, he would have pushed her over.

This caused a sensation. When the coroner asked the pregnant young cook why she had not said this before, she replied: 'I tried to screen him. Now I've told the whole truth.' She revealed, with apparent reluctance, that Lee had said something about setting the house on fire and going up on the hill to watch it burn.

On the fourth and final day of the inquest, on Monday, 1 December, the medical expert from Guy's Hospital in London, Dr Stevenson, gave a detailed description of his findings, with regard to the articles sent to him for analysis; the hatchet, the gardening knife, the oil-can, Jane Neck's bloody nightdress, Lee's blood-stained shirt, trousers and socks, a lock of the victim's hair. He had found blood on all the items, and mineral oil on Lee's clothes. Grey hairs with a reddish tint found on his socks matched the piece of Miss Keyse's hair.

Sgt Nott and Jane Neck were briefly recalled and the coroner then indulged himself with an extensive summing-up, lasting over an hour. The jury retired at 2.20 pm. Half an hour later they returned and the foreman declared: 'We find unanimously that the deceased ... was murdered ... by the prisoner, John Lee, by striking her on the head with some blunt instrument and afterwards cutting her throat with the knife found in the pantry drawer, which is stained with human blood.'

Twenty minutes later, Dr Stevenson, who had to return to London, repeated his evidence before the magistrates in Torquay. This hearing was resumed on the Tuesday, with an opening by Mr Isidore Carter for the prosecution, followed by frequent cross-examining of witnesses by Mr Templer, who also objected to an artist sketching the accused. Lee glared at Elizabeth Harris when she repeated her evidence; and when she sat down after signing a transcript of what she had said, Lee stared at her 'with so stern an expression on his face that she burst into tears and had to leave the court'.

On the third day of the hearing, John Lee was committed for trial at the next Devon Assizes on two charges, of arson and murder. As he was removed from the court, he laughed.

Many years later, PC Boughton would recall the journey he made with Lee and another policeman from Torquay to Exeter Prison, setting off at 6.00 am. He told a reporter:

> The police feared that there might be a disturbance if he was seen by the public, and consequently we did not go by the railway to Exeter. Instead, we drove the whole distance in a carriage drawn by a pair of fine horses. I remember well it was a beautiful morning: the air was fresh and invigorating, the sky a lovely blue, and all around was a splendid picture, even though we had reached the winter . . . We had a drive which in any other circumstances would have been the most delightful conceivable, right away over Haldon, through Chudleigh, into the city. We stopped at Chudleigh for refreshment, but no one knew that Lee was one of our number . . . On reaching Exeter we had to pass along High Street. There we saw the newspaper placards, and the accused man, looking out of the window, read them aloud – 'Babbacombe Murder: Prisoner before the Magistrates' – without the slightest comment upon them. That was the only reference he made to the crime . . . He was a powerful young fellow . . . He gave us no trouble at all.

The trial of John Lee was held in Exeter Castle before Mr Justice Manisty, with Mr Collins, QC, and Mr Stonehouse Vigor prosecuting, and Mr Molesworth St Aubyn leading for the defence. The trial began on Monday, 2 February 1885.

The *Torquay Directory* said that the prisoner 'wore his usual air of indifference. His appearance was somewhat improved; his hair was brushed and trimmed, and he wore a coat of a dark grey mixture'. Elizabeth Harris, looking 'much careworn', was offered a chair but did not take it. As with other witnesses, her evidence was a repeat of what had been said before. The jury were lodged in the White Hart Hotel overnight, and when the trial resumed on Tuesday, Lee resumed his place in the dock with 'almost serene indifference', although on the Monday he had occasionally appeared uneasy at some things that were alleged and had sourly smiled when some witnesses contradicted themselves. Sgt Nott was the first to give evidence, for nearly three hours, and it was he who read aloud the contents of two letters, written by the accused and his girlfriend, Kate Farmer, who was not at the trial, although she attended the inquest. The letters are remarkable for their literacy and the honesty of the sentiments expressed.

Lee wrote from the Glen on Friday, 10 October:

My dearest Katie – I write to tell you I am very unsettled in what I am going to do in my future life. I am tired of service, and I am going to look out for something else to do, which might not be to your liking. And, my dear, don't let me keep you from going anywhere that will be for your good. My dear, you may get a better chance going away, and we may not be always the same as we are now, in love. I implore you, if you think we shall not come together, let us break off our engagement before it is too late. I am beginning to love you so much that it will break my heart if we should leave in time to come. So let us break it off at once. My dearest, let what we have going by die out of our thoughts, but our love never can. My dear, you have been the kindest I ever met with in my love and all things . . . If I had kept your company when first I seen you, I would have married you and made you happy. But I am unsettled now, and don't know what my fate may be. Goodbye, my sweetest love, from one who will ever love you the same. John Lee.

She replied on Tuesday:

My dearest love – Your letter to hand, which has caused me the greatest pain and grief. What can you possibly mean by telling me one time you will leave me, and then writing to know if I wish to break off the engagement? I cannot make it out, as you are undecided as to what you intend to do for the future. Are you also undecided about me? I tell you now . . . that our engagement shall not be broken off with my consent. As to what you intend to do in the future, if it was your lot to crack stones in the street, and would ask me to be your wife, I would not say no. Have a little pity for me, and think how dearly I love you. Perhaps if I had loved you less you might have valued me a little more . . . Do you think I wish you to marry me before you see your way clear? No, my darling, I am quite prepared to battle my way in the world till you think fit to make me your wife. I will never be the one to grumble at waiting for you . . . Jack, I think if we part you would be the cause of grieving me to death and breaking my heart. After what you said on Sunday I never dreamt of your writing me now in the same strain as your last letter was written in. But never mind, I freely forgive you. At the same time I will not give you up. My mother will naturally come into your mind. Would to God it had been my funeral you went to instead of hers. Then I should never have got your letter, and you would never have written it. She was my only friend, but I have always depended upon you to be something more than a friend. You have been my chief support in all my troubles

... Grant my last request by coming down tomorrow evening. Accept my fondest and truest love, and believe me ever your true love, Katie Farmer. Please excuse this scrawl, as I am very unwell today.

The trial ended on Wednesday, 4 February. Mr St Aubyn, for the defence, suggested that the cook's lover might have been the murderer and that she would have had the greatest inducement to protect him and blame someone else. John Lee was found guilty and sentenced to death. The judge remarked on his calmness. Lee replied: 'Please, my lord, allow me to say that I am so calm because I trust in my Lord, and He knows I am innocent.'

In the condemned cell in Exeter Prison, Lee continued to confuse people by his apparent indifference. The *Western Morning News* reported:

His health was not visibly affected either by his confinement or the anti-cipation of his fate. He partook of his meals with heartiness and regularity and, in short, evinced little of the depression which would be naturally looked for in the case of one so situated. When visited by his mother and other relatives his demeanour was by no means indicative of a man who realised, much less dreaded, the approach of death by hanging. While persistently asserting his innocence he assumed a cheer-fulness, and even a jauntiness of manner, which to his Friends was not less painful than surprising. In bidding his last farewell he betrayed not the slightest emotion – not even when his grief-stricken mother finally embraced him and reluctantly withdrew from his cell.

The execution was fixed for Monday, 23 February. On the Friday before this, the new public executioner, James Berry, travelled from his home in Bradford to Bristol, where he lodged overnight, and on Saturday morning entrained from Bristol to Exeter. Arriving at the prison at noon, he signed the Register Book, saw the Governor and had lunch in the town before being shown his bedroom, a room in the prison hospital. Accompanied by two warders, he then made his inspection of the place of execution. It was a coach-house, in which the prison van was usually kept. From a high beam and a bolt hung an iron rod with a hole at the end, to which the rope would be attached. Below, a double trap-door in the stone-flagged floor opened on to a pit about six feet wide and eleven feet deep. A lever, when pulled, drew back the bolts that held the trap-doors in place, releasing them to fall down against the walls of the pit. Berry tested the apparatus twice and was satisfied that it worked, although he complained to the Governor that the trap-doors were only an inch thick instead of four, that the ironwork was frail, and that springs should be fixed in the pit to prevent the fallen doors from re-bounding. The Governor agreed to put these matters right.

We do not know where Berry went or what he did in the way of pleasure on Saturday night. Sunday he spent within the prison, mainly in his room, going to bed at about 9.45 pm. That night it rained, as it had on Saturday night.

On the Monday morning, Berry rose at 6.30 and an hour later entered the coach-house, where he tied a suitable length of rope to the overhead rod and made other preparations, like positioning the white cap and straps to pinion the condemned man's legs. He did not try the trap-doors again, as they had functioned adequately in his Saturday afternoon tests.

Berry has left us two accounts of the execution, in a letter to the Under-Sheriff of Devon, Henry James, dated 4 March, and in his autobiography. But his descriptions are somewhat partial and compressed. The fullest and most objective account of what happened is probably that of the *Western Morning News* reporter, who witnessed the extraordinary and harrowing events of the attempted execution of 20-year-old John Lee.

At five minutes to eight the reporters, ten in number, were stationed within the main corridor of the building at a point to be passed by the culprit . . . A few seconds later the procession, headed by the Chief Warder [Mr Rainford] entered the corridor. The Chaplain [Revd J. Pitkin] and the Schoolmaster [Mr Libby] came next and were immediately followed by Lee, who walked with pinioned hands between a couple of warders. The Prison Surgeon [Mr Caird] and the Governor [Mr Cowtan] also accompanied the procession, while other warders, and beside them Berry, the executioner, brought up the rear. The slow and deliberate tread of Lee and his companions, the tolling of the prison bell, added to the impressive tones of the chaplain as he repeated portions of the burial service, combined to make the occasion one of deep solemnity. The look of the doomed man . . . bore no signs of anything like fear. He walked with firmness and with head erect . . .

The scaffold, which was the same as that employed in the execution of Anne Tooke about five years ago, had been removed to another part of the building. It was sunk into the ground and formed, in fact, the flooring of a small brick shed . . . The gloomy and repulsive character of the gallows was, if possible, intensified by its enclosure within brick walls. As Lee walked into the building and . . . placed himself on the fatal planks, there was no faltering or sign of fear. He cast a glance at the rope above him, as if to assure himself that its fastenings were perfectly secured, and then inaudibly muttered something to Berry as the latter functionary adjusted the noose around the culprit's neck. There was even a dash of bravado in the unhappy man's demeanour as he glanced at the ghastly paraphernalia of death. A white cap was, in the usual manner, placed over the head and face of the convict, and as the closing words of the burial service died away on the lips of the chaplain, Berry, at a given signal, drew the lever. The only response was a grating sound and a slight movement of the trap . . .

A second and third attempt were made to draw the bolt, but with no more success than attended the first effort. Something was evidently wrong, and Berry, assisted by some of the warders, made an examination of the apparatus, having in the meantime withdrawn the rope and cap from the culprit's neck and face and moved him a little forward. In this terrible position Lee never flinched, but stood erect as before . . .

Not so with the officials, whose hurried movements and pale faces betrayed signs of deep anxiety and even terror. The apparatus having again been prepared, Lee's legs were once more pinioned and the rope and cap adjusted. Again the fatal signal was given, and the loud click of the lever once more startled the witnesses to this terrible scene.

The bolt having once more defied the repeated efforts of the hangman, Lee was freed from the fatal noose and removed, this time to the back of the building . . . By this time the convict had become an object of the supreme sympathy of every man present. Still seemingly unmoved . . . the condemned man surveyed the preparations which were going on before him. After a suspense of several seconds he was once more placed, and Berry ran hurriedly to the back of the shed to drop him. As the bolt again and again refused to yield, Berry made a desperate effort to force the trap down by stamping it with his feet . . .

As the convict had once more to be set aside, a feeling of inexpressible horror . . . seemed to seize everyone present. After a hurried conference of the officials he was conducted to the interior of the prison. In the meantime the services of a carpenter were procured, and by the process of planing, it was sought to remedy the cause of previous failures. This occupied something like five minutes, when for the fourth time the condemned man was placed in readiness for execution . . . The apparatus seemed, if possible, more rigid than ever . . . and Lee was accordingly returned to the cell from which he had been taken . . . The great strain upon him . . . was followed by a certain amount of physical prostration. The Governor assisted him to his cell and offered him stimulants, but he pointedly refused.

So began the legend of The Man They Couldn't Hang. A white dove was said to have perched on the scaffold before the execution began. Lee is said to have cried: 'Oh, God – help me!' He himself claimed to have dreamed the previous night that he would not be hanged and that what happened was a miracle. His incredible survival was also seen as a sign of his innocence.

What was extraordinary – as revealed in Berry's account – was that when Lee was removed from the trap-doors they functioned well enough. Berry wrote: 'I worked the lever after Lee had been taken off, drew it, and the doors fell easily. With the assistance of the warders the doors were pulled up, and the lever drawn a second time, when again the doors fell easily.' He also said: 'It was suggested to me that the woodwork fitted too tightly in the centre of the doors, and one of the warders fetched an axe and another a plane.' A crowbar was also brought. Berry said the Governor and Mr James were 'almost frantic'. The chaplain fled, it seems, after the third attempt. He said later: 'A great noise was heard, which sounded like the falling of the drop. But to my horror, when I turned my eyes to the scaffold, I saw the poor convict standing upon the drop as I had seen him twice before. I refused to stay any longer.'

Legend and most writers say that three attempts were made to hang John

Lee. Berry implies there were two attempts. But the reporter's account indicates *four*. Legend, however, likes the number three.

The distraught officials decided to defer the execution while the Home Secretary's instructions were sought, and the reporters left the prison to tell their astonishing tale to the crowds of people still outside, who had wondered why no black flag was raised half an hour ago. That night a reprieve was granted on humanitarian grounds, and as 'it would shock the feelings of everyone if a man had four times to bear the pangs of imminent death'. Lee's sentence was commuted to penal servitude for life.

What happened that morning, other than a miracle? Berry blamed the mishap on defective ironwork and on the doors, which should have been heavier, he said. He discounted the supposition in the prison that the woodwork had become swollen in the damp produced by two nights of rain, and that the doors jammed when stood upon. None the less, this seems the most reasonable explanation. Although the coach-house had a roof, it may well have leaked and the stone floor may have been flooded by the rain. What was probably crucial was Lee's weight – enough to compress and wedge the doors, but not enough to pitch him eight feet into the pit.

After spending nearly 23 years in jail, John Lee was released from Portland Prison, where he was something of a hero, in December 1907, by which time the Glen had long been razed to the ground. Lee was now 43. Travelling from Weymouth to Newton Abbot by train, he took a cab from there to his mother's cottage at Abbotskerswell. They were besieged by reporters, but both had nothing to say.

One reporter traced Kate Farmer, who now lived in Plymouth. Lee had been in prison for less than a year when she married a man called Parrish and left Torquay. Four years later she left her husband, taking her daughter with her, who was now 21. When interviewed, Mrs Parrish said:

> He has suffered. I hope his future life will be happy. His way will not be my way, for I am now settled in life after my vicissitudes. I hope he may be able to prove his innocence . . . I was then a silly sentimental girl, and did not know my own mind. I am wiser now . . . I remember most vividly the last time I saw him. It was at the inquest. I recall he walked with his head in the air, although he was in such deadly peril. He recognised me and smiled, and said: 'Goodbye, my dear.' Those were the last words I heard him utter. He never sent a letter from prison to me, and never asked me to visit him in Portland . . . My friends told me that Lee would be kept in prison as long as he lived, and a life's devotion would be thrown away. So I put him out of my heart.

A life of John Lee was published and his story was much later made into a film. He is said to have become a publican in London, and in the Black Museum there is a postcard, dated September 1910 and showing the Rustic Bridges of Torquay, that is addressed to a Miss Gibbs at 45 High Road, Borough, London SE. This seems to suggest that he was living in London then. Other than that, little is now known about his life after 'life'. But he is said to have been in America in 1932. Did he ever meet up with his Kate again? Did he marry? And when in the end did he die?

Lee's unsuccessful executioner, James Berry, was a thick-set, muscular man with sandy hair; 5' 8½" in height and weighing 13 stone, he was born on 8 February 1852 at Heckmondwike in Yorkshire. In 1874, the year that he married (he had six children), he became a policeman in Bradford, and during the course of carrying out his duties met the public executioner, William Marwood, the originator of the long drop. When Marwood died in 1883, Berry, by now an impoverished boot-salesman, applied for the job, among 1,400 others. The post was given to Bartholomew Binns. But Berry was recommended by the English authorities to carry out a double execution, of Robert Vickers and William Innes, in Edinburgh on 31 March 1884. Binns was found to be unsuitable after four or five months, and Berry was appointed in his place.

His first task was to execute David Roberts for the murder of David Thomas at Llanblethian in Glamorgan. Berry miscalculated the length of the drop and Roberts's neck failed to break – he was left struggling at the end of the rope. Those present were asked to withdraw as Berry went down into the pit and, grabbing the struggler's legs, added his 13 stone to that of the condemned man. His failure to execute John Lee followed in February 1885. Later that year, in November, at Norwich Castle, Berry failed again. This victim was Robert Goodale, who had murdered his wife; he weighed 15 stone. Berry reduced the recommended drop for some reason from 7' 8" to 5' 9", with the horrid result that the sudden jerk severed the head from the body and both parts fell to the floor of the pit. The attendant Governor, already overwrought and highly strung, burst into tears.

Another condemned man, John Conway, was nearly decapitated by Berry in August 1891, after which, at the age of 40, he retired – 'on account of Dr Barr interfering with my responsible duty at Kirkdale Gaol, Liverpool, on the last execution there'. There had been a dispute about the mechanics of the drop. Thereafter, James Berry went on a series of lecture tours, recommending the abolition of capital punishment, and appeared in music-halls. He also wrote a book.

CHAPTER 8

James Canham Read

The Murder of Florence Dennis, 1894

Energy characterises the late Victorians more than their prudery. Those who survived the depredations of disease, pollution and poverty became epitomes of industry, activity and zeal. They worked long hours in badly lit and aired conditions, slept little, ate, smoked and drank a great deal and produced large families. They had stamina, and for the most part, strong constitutions. Their social and charitable concerns were as great as their appetite for the comforts of religion, and sex. They were great believers, and great deceivers. Public morality might rule the middle class, but it was countervailed by rich seams of private vice. Prostitution was rampant, as were many kinds of crime and social abuse. These matters fascinated many, as they did Conan Doyle's Sherlock Holmes, who first appeared in 1887. Apart from Thomas Hardy, the most famous writer of the 1890s was Oscar Wilde, whose cultivation of the aesthetic was satirised by W. S. Gilbert in Patience *as early as 1881. In 1894, Queen Victoria was 75: she had reigned for 57 years. Gladstone resigned, after a fourth term as Prime Minister, and in 1895 the Liberals were replaced by ten triumphant years of Tory rule and imperialism, when the British Empire ruled half the world.*

Although the jury's verdict of 'Guilty' was undoubtedly a proper one in the case of James Read, there was room for doubt – not for the first time, alas, or the last – about the propriety of police methods in obtaining evidence and a conviction. After the trial, the conduct of identification parades, which were being mishandled and abused, was cleaned up and improved. And the centuries-old unjust anomaly of an accused person not being allowed to give evidence, if he or she so wished, was abolished in 1898.

Soon after six o'clock on the evening of Monday, 25 June 1894, the body of a young woman, fully clothed, was found in a ditch by a footpath in fields near the village of Prittlewell in Essex. She had been shot once in the head. Prittlewell, an ancient settlement mentioned in the Domesday Book, was a mile or so north of Southend-on-Sea, which came into being in the reign of Henry VIII and was originally the South End of Prittlewell. It was now a fashionable health resort, known for its dry climate, safe sea-bathing, amusements, and a very long pier, that stretched out into the Thames estuary for nearly one-and-a-half miles.

The dead girl, who had been murdered on the Sunday night, was Florence

Dennis. Aged 23, she was not married, but was heavily pregnant. She had been staying in Southend with a married sister, Mrs Ayris, who had much to tell the police about the likely father of her younger sister's unborn child, and of one of her own.

He was James Canham Read, aged 37, and known as Jim. A third-class clerk, with a first-class character at work, he was employed at the Royal Albert Dock at North Woolwich, on the north shore of the Thames. He had worked there for nearly 20 years and was well paid and trusted, his salary amounting to £1⁄ ⁄r year. His home was in Stepney, where lived his wife and their eight children. But he was not at home when the police called, nor was he at his place of work, which he had left on the Monday afternoon, two hours before the body of Miss Dennis was discovered. He took with him £160 of his employers' cash and disappeared.

Within two weeks, however, the police succeeded in tracking him to a small cottage at Mitcham in Surrey, where he was living with a young woman called Mrs Benson, who had a six-month-old baby. Read was posing as Mr Benson. A search of the premises produced £83 in cash. Read was arrested and taken to Southend. On 30 July he was incarcerated in Springfield Jail in Chelmsford, the Essex county jail, and after being remanded in custody six times, he was committed on 7 September for trial at the next Essex Assizes in Chelmsford, some 18 miles north-east of Southend.

The trial began in the Shire Hall on Monday, 12 November 1894 before Mr Baron Pollock. The newly appointed Solicitor-General, Mr Frank Lockwood, QC, MP, led for the prosecution, assisted by Mr C. F. Gill and Mr Stephenson. Mr Cock, QC, led for the defence, assisted by Mr Warburton.

The Pollock family had flourished in the legal profession for over a hundred years; the Pollock features, long, pale and strongly marked, had presided over many trials. Mr Baron Pollock, who was a very pious, just and learned man, was the last judge to bear the title of Baron of the Court of Exchequer, as distinct from those of the Queen's Bench and of the Common Pleas, which merged in 1880. Mr Cock was also the last of the type of QC characterised as having 'lungs of leather and a voice of brass'. Besides being loud, he was a bit of a bully in court, aggressive and blunt. It was said he was better at demolishing the opposition's case than building his own. Mr Lockwood, on the other hand, had a fine voice and presence; he was handsome, charming and frank, with a sense of humour and a penchant for making comical drawings while at work. A Yorkshireman, he was said to look older than his 50 years. In 1879 he had defended Charles Peace.

Baron Pollock arrived in Chelmsford by train from Norwich on Thursday, 8 November, and was accommodated at a house called Maynetrees in New Street. He presided over the trials of 22 persons, mainly charged with stealing, on the Friday and Saturday and attended church on Sunday. On the Monday, after robing himself at Maynetrees, he was taken in the Sheriff's carriage at half-past ten to the Shire Hall. It was pouring with rain. Read was taken there from the prison in a fly at 6.00 am, accompanied by two warders, to avoid the crowds.

Over 300 applications for tickets to the court had been received, and the

Essex County Chronicle reporters noted (there were two): 'Greater interest and excitement were caused by the trial than by any that has taken place at Chelmsford within living memory.' Two things, they wrote, accounted for this: 'One being the great element of mystery surrounding the murder, and the other the strange and unhappy life of sensuality which is alleged to have been led by the prisoner.'

All eyes were on him when he appeared in the dock. He was wearing the light grey suit in which he had been arrested, and a black tie. He looked spick and span: his hair and moustache had been carefully trimmed, as had his beard, which prison regulations had obliged him to grow. He stood erect and seemed confident, saying 'Not guilty' in a firm, clear voice.

Before the murder trial began, he pleaded 'Guilty' to another charge, that while in the service of the London and East India Docks Joint Committee he stole £159 12s 6d from his employers. He then sat between his two warders with folded arms. Outside, the falling rain and grey skies added a certain gloom to the scene within the court.

The Solicitor-General rose to present the prosecution's case, and, after his opening remarks, related the story of James Canham Read's recent life and crimes.

So far back as August, 1889, the prisoner made the acquaintance [on the pier at Southend] of Mrs Ayris, the wife of John Ayris [a dairy man] and the eldest sister of Florence Dennis. That acquaintance ripened into an intimacy, and there is no doubt that immoral relations existed between the prisoner and Mrs Ayris ... In December 1889, Mrs Ayris removed [from Clapham Junction] to 189 St John's Hill Road, Wandsworth. The prisoner was then corresponding with her, but not under her own name or at the address where she was living with her husband – this for obvious reasons. He was writing under an assumed name ... He addressed her as Mrs Neville, and his letters were sent to 137 St John's Hill Road, a stationer's shop ... We find the prisoner and Mrs Ayris spending a day at Leigh in the spring of 1891 ... We subsequently find they were staying at Buckingham together. The immoral relations between Mrs Ayris and this man ceased about March, 1892. There was another meeting in March 1894, at Victoria Station, when she told him it was her intention to take a lodging-house at Southend, and asked him to recommend lodgers ...

In September 1890, on one occasion when Mrs Ayris and the prisoner were out walking [on Clapham Common], they met Florence Dennis, I suggest by chance. Mrs Ayris introduced Florence Dennis [and another sister, Mrs Deed, who was with her], and they passed on ... Florence [who was not yet 19] was then living part of her time with her mother, but throughout the case you find she has resided alternately with her mother [at Sheerness in Kent] and Mrs Ayris. In May 1892, a child was born – I think it was Mrs Ayris's second child. Florence Dennis went to her sister's. There was a nurse there, a Mrs Schmidt, and she will tell you that during that time ... she posted two letters for Florence Dennis, at her request, and both the letters were addressed to Mr Read, at the Albert Docks. One night Florence was absent from her sister's house, and she remained out until late . . .

In 1893 we find Mrs Ayris living at Hanwell, and Florence Dennis at Sheerness, and we find Florence Dennis corresponding with Read, addressing letters from and receiving them at 63 High Street, Sheerness, where a woman of the name of Hughes was manager. Evelina Dennis, a younger sister of the murdered woman, fetched the letters for Florence, and these letters were addressed to 'Talbott' . . . Some of the documents we have are in disguised writing by the prisoner . . . One of the visits paid by Florence Dennis to Mrs Ayris at Hanwell was in October 1893, and when the body of this unfortunate woman was examined, it was found to contain a child that must have been begotten about that time. After Christmas 1893, letters were addressed to the name of Talbott to the Post Office, Sheerness . . . The correspondence ceased in May 1894, and Florence Dennis was murdered in June 1894 . . .

I take you now, gentlemen, to another scene, and introduce you to another name. In 1892 the prisoner made the acquaintance of a young woman named Kempton, who was living in Gloucester Road, at a [confectioner's] shop. The prisoner met her at a railway station [Gloucester Road], and introduced himself as a Mr Edgar Benson, of 16 North Street, Poplar. He described himself as a traveller on behalf of Messrs Peck, tea merchants, of Cheapside. Correspondence took place, and meetings took place, and according to the sad story Miss Kempton will tell you, she was seduced by the prisoner in the spring of 1893. Miss Kempton had a home at Cambridge, but she left there to go to Hallingbury, where she lived under the care of the prisoner. The prisoner explained his absence from her there by stating that his business kept him away. But he was able to spend from Saturday to Monday with her. On 6 January, 1894, a child was born to Miss Kempton by the prisoner. In February, Miss Kempton moved into lodgings provided for her by the prisoner at Rose Cottage, Mitcham . . .

The prisoner has a brother, named Harry Read. The name by which he was introduced to Miss Kempton was 'Mr Edwards,' a friend. 'Benson' told Miss Kempton that he himself had a sister at Canterbury, married to a man named [Walter] Parker . . . Harry Read – 'Edwards' as he was known to Miss Kempton – lived at 16 North Street, Poplar. But he was dismissed from there . . .

In April 1894, Miss Kempton notices that the prisoner is exhibiting considerable anxiety, and he tells her it is his pecuniary position that troubles him. But, gentlemen, what was it really? Florence Dennis conceived her child in October 1893, and by this time, April 1894, no doubt her condition must have been made known to herself, and to the prisoner . . .

I told you the prisoner spent from Saturday to Monday, as a rule, with Miss Kempton. From Christmas 1893 to the day of the murder, June 1894, he never spent one Sunday at his own house, where his own wife and family lived, at Jamaica Street, Stepney. With three exceptions he spent a portion of the Saturdays, and a portion of the Sundays, during 1894 with Miss Kempton at Rose Cottage, Mitcham. Gentlemen, these three dates are 20 May, 10 June, and 24 June . . . He wrote to Miss Kempton to excuse himself for his absence on the first date, and stated that he had gone to Canterbury, on most important business on behalf of Walter [Parker] whose child was ill with bronchitis. Gentlemen, there was no such child ill, and what he said was false. Florence Dennis at this time was living in Sheerness [in Kent]. On Saturday, 19 May, she went out at night and did not return home until about 10.30 . . . I now come to the next date, 10 June. On 8 June he writes to Miss Kempton: 'I am making arrangements to go to Canterbury tomorrow, Saturday, on important business, so let me beg of you to do your best to keep up your spirits until I come back. I do not expect I shall be back before Monday' . . . On 22 June, this is the excuse the prisoner gives for not going down to Miss Kempton: 'I am sure you fully share with me my regret that I shall not be with you this weekend. I have to go to Canterbury on most important business of Walter's. He has asked me to do this, and I cannot refuse . . . If I can utilise this opportunity to lift myself out of my present critical condition I will do so. But if I do not succeed in this, God knows what I shall do. I'm dead broke.' Absolutely untrue! There was no business at Canterbury – he did not go to Canterbury – he had no relations at Canterbury . . . I shall be able, I think, to show you . . . that he was at Southend – that he was at Prittlewell . . .

I will now resume the story of Florence Dennis. In June 1894 she was eight months advanced in pregnancy. A communication was made to her mother, with whom she was living at Sheerness, and on 19 June she was removed to Mrs Ayris's house at Southend. On Friday, 22 June, the prisoner wrote to Miss Kempton to say that he was going on Saturday to Canterbury on most important business. That Friday he was loitering away his time with his brother and a friend named Kendall [they met at 10.05 pm] . . . and another telegram is dispatched to Florence Dennis. I am prepared to show that the telegram is in the handwriting of the man who was in company with the prisoner at the time – I mean Harry Read. Harry Read it was who sent that telegram from a Post Office near Charing Cross [at 9.25 pm] . . . That telegram was received by Florence Dennis on 23 June [Saturday]. You will hear that Florence Dennis went out . . .

All these telegrams were dispatched in a curious way. Instead of being handed over the counter, they were put into the post, so as to give no opportunity of the sender being identified. The prisoner carried about with him, it seems, telegraph forms and stamps . . .

I come now to the Sunday, 24 June, the day on which the murder was committed . . . Florence remained about [her sister's] house until the evening of that day, and an arrangement had been made by her, with her sister's knowledge, that owing to the crowded state of her sister's house, she should pass the night in a room taken for her at an adjoining house.

On that evening she went out to meet somebody – and by any of her relations she was never seen alive again . . .

That Sunday afternoon, a lady named Mrs Kirby met the prisoner in a
wheatfield, coming from Prittlewell. The prisoner asked her the way to
Leigh. She said she didn't know, and he said: 'Oh, I may as well go back
to Rayleigh again.' And he turned back . . . He was not seen again by
anyone we are in a position to call until a little after ten, when a man
named Robert Dowthwaite, coming from Prittlewell, meets a man and
a woman, whom he identifies as the prisoner and – having seen the dead
body – the murdered woman, walking arm in arm along an avenue
towards the field in which the murder was committed. Another witness,
Richard Golding, who with his family had been in a public-house at
Prittlewell, came along this same road, and he saw a man coming down
the avenue alone – a man whom he afterwards identified as the prisoner.
The man who went up the avenue was with a woman – the man who returned was alone . . . But the prisoner is seen again, by a policeman
named Daniel, at Benfleet, early the next morning [at 1.15 am]. The
prisoner said he wanted the road to London . . .

Later we find him calling at the house of a fellow clerk at Leytonstone, who was ill [at about 9.20 am]. When he called at the house his
appearance was not as usual – he had not that smart, dapper appearance which he usually presented. He had no gloves in his hand, and
presented a dishevelled appearance. At about ten o'clock [on the Mon-
day] he arrived at his office at the docks, a little later than usual. But that
was explained by his call at the fellow clerk's. At 12.30 he went out and
got shaved . . . Later, a clerk named Burgess went into the prisoner's
room at the office, and found him burning a fire. He asked what it was
for, and the prisoner made some remark about foul air. At 3.00 pm, a
telegram is received [at the office] by him from Mrs Ayris . . . The telegram was one inquiring: 'Where is Florrie?' The answer was a letter
saying that he had not seen Florence Dennis for 18 months.

On Monday, 25 June Mrs Ayris goes round to the house where her
sister had been staying the previous day. She is startled to find that
Florence Dennis is not there. She waits . . . After waiting some time she
gives information to the police, and then telegraphs to the prisoner, asking where Florence was . . . The body at that time had not been
discovered. Mrs Ayris did not know that her sister was murdered . . .
When [the prisoner] got that telegram from Mrs Ayris he knew perfectly
well that the hue and cry had commenced. He knew that Mrs Ayris
knew his address in Jamaica Street, and that there he would probably
meet an officer to arrest him. He knew that to stay at the Royal Albert
Docks was to court apprehension . . . But there was one place Mrs Ayris
did not know, a place known only to his brother Harry – viz, Rose Cottage, Mitcham. Therefore you are not surprised to hear he leaves his
work earlier than usual, without signing off [and] takes with him a bag,
which probably contained the money, to stealing which he has pleaded
guilty . . . Why was he fleeing? Because, I say, he was the only man who

knew of that murder . . . He goes to the address known practically only to himself and his brother, in whom he has confidence . . . And at 4.30 he dispatches the following letter-card to his brother: 'My dear Harry – Secure my desk contents and report everything to me at M——. In strict secrecy. Will explain when I see you. Allay all fears. JCR' . . .

Well then – between eight and nine o'clock on the Monday night the prisoner arrives at Rose Cottage, Mitcham. He is dressed in a black coat and vest, grey trousers, a light brown hat, and a light coloured tie. He has money with him, and he accounts for that by saying he has borrowed it from Mr Parker. There is some alteration in his whiskers – he has them cut more closely to his face – and this is the commencement of a disguise which he afterwards developed. Miss Kempton remarks on his appearing tired and weary. He accounts for it by saying that he has been to Canterbury. That is untrue . . .

On 26 June the prisoner went to Croydon, where he bought a ready-made suit [light grey], the clothes, I think, in which he now sits in the dock. From that time he no longer wears the clothes he was wearing on 25 June. He leaves off shaving, and when Miss Kempton asks him why, his first reason was that he had no razor with him . . . When Miss Kempton suggested that he should go out to be shaved, he said it was too much trouble . . . He stays indoors much more than usual . . . On 27 or 28 June he is absent from Rose Cottage, and Miss Kempton receives a telegram from him, asking if all is right. On 30 June she receives another telegram asking her to wire if all is well. What was the cause of his anxiety? His anxiety was to ascertain if any person was on his track – if so, he would not return . . .

In July, Inspector Baker and Sgt Marden go to Rose Cottage to apprehend the prisoner . . .

Now how was this young woman, Florence Dennis, killed? Beyond all doubt it was by a bullet wound. Gentlemen, the revolver is not forthcoming but the bullet is . . . Above the left ear there is a circular wound, about a quarter of an inch in diameter. The edges of the wound are blackened and singed, showing that the revolver must have been held very near to the head of that woman, and the conical bullet was found embedded in her brain. What was the weapon used? You may remember in the opening part of my speech, I alluded to an address: 16 North Road, Poplar. That was the place from which Harry Read was discharged at Christmas 1892, for some misconduct. Some time before that Harry Read purchased a revolver. He, at this time, got very low in spirits, and on one occasion threatened to take his own life. The prisoner, who was present at the time, expostulated with him, calling him a fool, and took the revolver away. Mrs Kelly, a sister, took the cartridges away.

In January 1894 this revolver was seen in the house of the prisoner at Jamaica Street, and was afterwards seen also by Miss Kempton, while they were at Hallingbury. In April 1894 the prisoner's daughter [Emma Read] will tell you she saw at the house in Jamaica Street a revolver case in the sitting-room – and the prisoner had a pocket made to carry it . . . I can show the bullet was a 7-Eley, was in a pin cartridge, and was of conical shape. This woman's death was caused by a bullet which would fit exactly the cartridges which were used in this revolver, which is traced to the prisoner's possession, and is seen in the prisoner's possession until April 1894, and which has not been seen since.

After conceding that Mrs Ayris had lied to the coroner and magistrates – she said she had *seen* James Read in Southend on the night of the murder – Mr Lockwood brought his opening speech to a well-modulated close by 1.40 pm, when the court adjourned for half an hour for lunch.

All that the Solicitor-General alleged was confirmed and elaborated by the many witnesses he called. Frederick Rush, a local youth, deposed that he had discovered the body (with her hat on her breast) at 6.00 pm on the Monday night. PC Alfred Marden, to whom Rush told his tale, deposed that the body had clearly been pushed through a hedge in the ditch. He also described the prisoner's eventual arrest. He and Inspector Baker observed Read return to Rose Cottage, in a light suit and cap, on 7 July. Baker went to the door and knocked. Miss Kempton appeared, and then the prisoner (who said he was Edgar Benson). Told he was being arrested as James Canham Read for the murder of Florence Dennis, he said: 'You're on the wrong scent.' He added: 'There's a lady living here with me – she doesn't know who I am.' Seized and taken inside, he was searched, as was the cottage. Money was found. During the search, Read remarked: 'Mrs Ayris can tell you where the revolver is.' When he was escorted from the cottage, Harry Read appeared at the gate. He followed the others. Jim Read said: 'Mrs Ayris knows more about this than I do.' Later he said: 'It's all rot about Southend. I was considering whether or not I should offer myself at the coroner's inquiry to be examined.' He said to Harry: 'What do you think of the little milkmaid [Mrs Ayris] now? Isn't she a –?' and he failed to finish the sentence.

Although it was never mentioned in court, Marden and Baker traced Read to Mitcham by closely monitoring Harry Read's movements and possibly intercepting his mail.

Other witnesses were called. Mrs Emma Deed, an older sister of Florence, who was with her when she first met Jim Read on Clapham Common in the autumn of 1890, deposed that her husband put a stop to Florrie receiving letters addressed to 'Talbott' at their Sheerness home. Mrs Sophie Schmidt, a midwife, remembered posting two letters at Wandsworth (where Mrs Ayris had a baby, in 1892), written by Florrie to 'Mr Read, Royal Albert Docks'. Mr Cock, cross-examining, implied that the letters may have been dictated to Florrie by the prostrate Mrs Ayris, and Mr Lockwood enquired: 'Were those letters written on behalf of Mrs Ayris?' Mrs Schmidt answered: 'They couldn't have been, because I had to promise Florence that I wouldn't tell Mrs Ayris about them.'

Julia Price, a stationer in Wandsworth, agreed that letters addressed to 'Miss Latimer' came to her shop. She did not know who collected them. But when Mr Lockwood asked Mrs Ayris to come forward, and said: 'Is that the woman?' the witness flatly announced: 'No. She was a young and nice-looking person.'

The sudden and brief appearance in court of Mrs Ayris was one of several 'sensations' in court. The *Chronicle*'s reporters noted that though she had 'a very sober air' and looked discomfited, she was 'of prepossessing appearance' and was fashionably attired in a dark dress with a high-shouldered and full-sleeved brown jacket, and a stylish hat – 'black straw trimmed with crape'.

The first day's proceedings concluded at 4.30 pm with the evidence of three post office officials and that of Florence Dennis's brother Fred, a seaman, and of her 14-year-old sister, Evelina. Both recalled Florence posting letters in 1893 and 1894 addressed to 'Mr Read'.

Overnight, the all-male jury were lodged in a large room in the Saracen's Head Hotel, attended by two court officials. One part of the room was furnished with 14 beds, the other part was used as a refectory, where the jury shared four bottles of wine during dinner and afterwards were allowed a cigar each and a glass of 'grog'.

The morning of Tuesday, 13 November was fine and bright. The *Chronicle*'s reporters, who occupied seats 100 and 101 in the crowded press gallery, nearest the judge, were pleased to note, after being forced to write on their knees on Monday, that: 'Today there is a desk constructed at seats 100 and 101, where the occupants may write in comfort and ease.'

After further post office evidence, Mrs Emma Dennis, Florence's mother, appeared. Dressed in deep mourning, she shed tears as she disclosed that on 19 June 1894, at her home in Sheerness, she learned that her daughter was pregnant, as well as who the father was, and 'where intimacy took place'. She took Florrie to stay with Mrs Ayris in Southend later that day. Mrs Dennis wept when she identified her daughter's handwriting on some letters, and told Mr Cock: 'Florrie never did anything by way of earning a living.'

The next and principal prosecution witness was Mrs Louisa Bertha Ayris. Attired as on the Monday, and obviously abashed by her exposure as an adulteress, she replied with brevity, mainly 'Yes' and 'No'. She admitted that while on holiday at Southend in September 1889 (two years after her marriage) she had met Read on the pier and had cohabited with him periodically until March 1892, two months before his child was born. He used to write to her, though not to her home, addressing her as Mrs Neville, Miss Harris or Miss Dennis – never as Miss Latimer or Talbott. She was not aware that Florence was writing to Read until September 1892, or that she was pregnant, until 19 June when, advised by Mrs Ayris, Florence wrote a letter to Read, saying: 'Dear Sir – I have left Sheerness and am staying at Southend. Please write me what arrangements you have made. Write to the General Post Office, Southend, in the name of Miss Dennis.' On Saturday, 23 June, Florence received a telegram – 'Meet me tonight. Great Eastern Station, Southend, 9.30.' She left the Ayris home at 24 Wesley Road at about 9.00 pm and it was 'very, very late' before she returned.

On the Sunday night Florence moved temporarily into the nearby house of Mrs Eggers, and was last seen by Mrs Ayris at half-past nine. The following morning, at 7.00, Mrs Ayris, visiting her neighbour, found that Florrie had been out all night and had not returned. She waited for two deliveries of mail to be made before going to the police, whom she provided with descriptions of her sister and of 'someone else'. That afternoon her husband sent a telegram to Read at the Royal Albert Docks – 'Where is Florrie? Telegraph at once'. That night the police told Mrs Ayris that Florrie had been found dead and she formally identified the body. The next morning she received a letter-card from 'J C Read'. It said: 'Dear Mrs Ayris – What is the meaning of your extraordinary wire? Please write fully. I have not seen the young person for quite 18 months, when you were at St John's Hill.'

She admitted that she never saw Read on the Saturday or the Sunday night, and that when she told the magistrates she had, and described his clothes, what she had said then was quite untrue.

This was seized on at once by Mr Cock in his cross-examination, his aim being to present her as a liar and a deceiver. He suggested that *she* was really Miss Talbott and Miss Latimer and that Read was only writing to *her*. He implied she was badgering Read for money or blackmailing him. For she had called at his Stepney home with their baby, and in March 1894, when she asked to meet him at Victoria Station, she told him (alleged Mr Cock) that she was poor and that her sister had 'got into trouble' with a soldier from Hounslow Barracks, near Hanwell. This Mrs Ayris denied. She had no idea, she said, that Florence was pregnant until June, and only sought Read's advice in March about legal and other matters. She knew from the start he was married, she said; Florence thought he was divorced.

Mr Ayris and Mrs Eggers then spoke of events on the 24th and 25th of June, and four witnesses were called to prove that Jim Read was in Southend on Sunday, 25 June. Two were possibly not telling the truth.

An elderly woman, Mrs Kirby, agreed that at about three o'clock on the Sunday afternoon, crossing wheatfields near the scene of the murder, she met a man who asked her the way to Leigh. She said she couldn't tell him, and he said: 'I may as well go back to Rayleigh.' Both villages were to the west of Southend. The man had 'piercing eyes', she said, and a quick walk; he was wearing a hard hat and a light tie. Questioned by Mr Cock, she admitted that she told the police about the encounter *two months* after the murder, by which time Read's appearance and dress had been well publicised. She did not speak to the police sooner, she said, because 'I was not well. I had a bad cold.'

An umbrella-maker, Robert Dowthwaite, said he saw a man and a woman walking arm in arm through the midsummer fields. He saw her face, but not that of the man, who was wearing, he said, a light coat and dark trousers. In the dock, Read chuckled and smiled: Dowthwaite was clearly confused. For Read, according to the prosecution, had been wearing a *dark* coat and *light* trousers that day. The witness added that the man had 'a very smart, genteel walk' and looked 'superior to his companion'. The next witness, a labourer, Richard Golding, deposed that the man *he* saw, about 10.00 pm, wore light trousers, a dark jacket and a hard felt hat. Golding, out for a walk with his wife and children, noticed that the man, appearing behind them, seemed reluctant to pass and eventually turned off the road and walked on quickly towards Leigh.

Presumably, although the midsummer sun had set an hour or so before, the sky was still light and not overcast – for both Dowthwaite and Golding could see the man in some detail, well enough to recognise him later. But this potentially awkward point was never mentioned in court.

The fourth of these witnesses allegedly came across Read much later, at 1.15 am. This was PC Daniel, who was patrolling his beat in South Benfleet (west of Leigh), and no doubt carrying a lantern, when a man approached him from the direction of Southend. 'Hallo, guv'nor!' Daniel called. 'You're up and dressed early this morning.' 'Yes,' said the other man, who was dressed in a dark *suit*, wore a round hat, and carried a *walking-stick*. He asked the policeman: 'Can you direct me to Benfleet?' Daniel retorted: 'You're in Benfleet now. Whom might you want?' 'I want no one here,' said the stranger. 'I want the road to London.' 'Where have you come from?' 'Southend.' Said Daniel: 'You've come a mile or two out of your way.' He put the other man right and they wished each other 'Good morning'.

PC Daniel, at an identification parade in Southend police station on 9 July, had picked out Read, who was wearing the light grey suit in which he had been arrested. Dowthwaite and Golding also correctly identified him, as did Kirby. It wasn't difficult: his description was well known. And Read was the only man in each line-up to be correctly dressed. The others were labouring men.

But, having accepted Daniel's identification and story (and that of the other two men) the police were lumbered with the unlikely hypothesis that, after the murder (the last train from Southend to London having left at 9.19 pm), Read *walked* the 30 miles from Prittlewell to Leytonstone, via Leigh and Benfleet – in the dark night along country lanes. For he was definitely seen at Leytonstone at 9.20 on the Monday morning, when he paid a duty call on Theresa Scannell's sick husband, a former colleague of his. Mr Scannell told the court that Read was dishevelled, carried no gloves (or a walking-stick) and hadn't shaved.

It was then proved in court that at 10.15 am he was back in his office, where he lit a fire (to burn letters?) and left early without signing off. He was carrying a black bag. Between 4.45 and 6.00 pm he posted his letter-card to Mrs Ayris in the EC district, replying to the telegram 'Where is Florrie?' He then took a train to Mitcham.

The evidence of former sweetshop assistant, Miss Beatrice Diva Kempton, occupied most of the afternoon. Dressed entirely in black and, like Mrs Ayris, wearing a black straw hat trimmed with crape, she spoke softly, never once looking at the man in the dock, whom she had known as Edgar Benson. No one doubted the detailed account of her seduction and life with Read. It was obvious he had told her many lies about himself, his absences, his friends and relatives, and his work. Large sections of his loving letters to her – 'My darling Beatie' – were read out in court by Mr Lockwood. Miss Kempton agreed that she had seen a revolver in January 1894 and that she knew Read's brother, Harry, as 'Harry Edwards', and had met him once. Read had produced a fake marriage certificate to silence her parents, and assured her he would marry her after her baby was born.

Miss Kempton's sad story was deeply damaging to Read. All Mr Cock could do was ask whether the accused man had been kind and affectionate. 'Very kind and affectionate,' she replied, with tears in her eyes. 'He seemed fond of me, and was kind to the child.'

On the third day of the trial there was another change in the weather, and high winds blew 'mournfully round the grey Shire Hall'. So wrote the *Chronicle*'s reporters, their fingers stiff and inky with scribbling. They noted that Read 'was paler, and wore a very anxious look. He seemed occasionally to wander into dreamland'. But he must have listened carefully when his brother, Harry, gave evidence. He was preceded by Thomas Gurrin, a handwriting expert, who opined that various telegrams and letters *were* written by the prisoner, although some of the writing was disguised or printed. After him came William Kendall, an artists' colourman, who said he had met the Read brothers at Marble Arch at 10.05 pm on Friday, 22 June. They drank in a public house until 11.30, conversing chiefly about family matters. There was no mention of Jim Read going to Canterbury on important business the following day or anywhere else. Kendall said he had known the prisoner since he was seven years old. They parted at Baker Street Station, Harry going home with Kendall, with whom he stayed until the Monday.

So that was Harry's alibi – if anyone had imagined that *he* shot Florence Dennis on his brother's behalf.

The *Chronicle*'s reporters described Harry Victor Read, when he appeared, as being 'in gentlemanly attire, in a heliotrope tie, and with a white chrysanthemum in his button-hole. He is a good-looking fellow, with a moustache inclined to be sandy'. It seems he may have been a bit of an aesthete and an admirer of Oscar Wilde, then reaching the peak and ruin of his career.

Harry was evasive about letters addressed to him as 'Edwards' and about his brother being 'Edgar Benson'. But he admitted he had no married sister in Canterbury called Parker. He professed not to know what his brother did at weekends, although they were, he said, on very intimate terms. He denied any knowledge of a telegram being sent to Florence Dennis by him or his brother on the night of Friday, 22 June from Charing Cross, although he admitted they got off a bus there before walking to Marble Arch to meet Kendall at 10.05 – and although a violet pencil, such as Harry had, was used to write the telegram. 'Where was your brother on that Sunday?' asked Mr Lockwood. Said Harry: 'I do not know.'

The last prosecution witness was Inspector Baker. A statement made by the prisoner was then read, asserting his innocence, and no witnesses were called by the defence. Mr Cock then applied for his closing speech to *follow* that of the prosecution, saying: 'I am entitled to reply . . . on the rule that was laid down at the meeting of the judges . . . who decided that it was only the Attorney-General, when he appeared in person, who could have the last word.' The point was debated; and lost by Mr Cock. The judge said: 'My ruling must be that the Solicitor-General, appearing here as the representative of the Crown, has the same right as the Attorney-General.'

After the court had adjourned for half an hour for lunch, Mr Cock rose to speak at 1.45. He complained 'of the enormous difficulty of conducting a criminal investigation without the person against whom the charge is made having an opportunity of giving explanations'. He also complained about the biased reporting, the theories and suggestions of the press, and concentrated on Mrs Ayris as the villain of the case, supposing that all the letters that Florrie received were really for Mrs Ayris, and that *she* was not only bent on 'injuring' her former lover, but intent on sending him to the scaffold. To this end Mr Cock interpreted much of the evidence to support his thesis, and implied that Read, wearying of Miss Kempton, was in the arms of a new paramour on 23/34 June, and that either Mrs Ayris or the soldier from Hounslow Barracks had something to do with Florrie's death. He offered no excuses about Read's affair with Miss Kempton or the theft of his employers' money. But these matters were not part of the charge, he said. And he claimed that the police had failed to prove the prisoner was in Southend on the Saturday night. Or on the Sunday. For the witnesses who said they had seen him were unreliable and not to be trusted. Moreover, there was no blood on the prisoner's clothes – no one had heard a shot – and the medical experts had said Florrie died much later (about 1.00 am) than the prosecution averred. 'No fact proved before you,' declared Mr Cock, 'is sufficient to bring home any guilt to this man.' The court adjourned at half-past four.

The fourth and last day of the trial was 'wet and gloomy'. The Solicitor-General dealt smoothly with Mr Cock's 'theories' and criticised him for 'a most bitter attack' on Mrs Ayris. Where was this *third* woman who might have cleared up the mystery of Read's whereabouts on 23/24 June? Where was the evidence that he was tired of Miss Kempton? Who was this soldier who wrote or printed telegrams with such an educated hand? And where *was* the prisoner on the night of the murder? Said Mr Lockwood: 'It is not one hour which is unaccounted for. It is not six hours. It is 36 hours of this man's life which are absolutely unaccounted for except by the prosecution! ... Why, gentlemen, one poor moment of that time ... would relieve him from this most terrible charge!'

Dealing with the sound of the shot, Mr Lockwood said the noise of the revolver shot would have carried no more than 200 yards and be no louder 'than the crack of a whip'. He concluded his speech at 11.25.

Five minutes later, during which Read cheerfully chatted with his warders, Mr Baron Pollock began his summing-up.

After urging the jury to omit from their consideration what they had heard 'of immoral and licentious conduct', he provided them with an explanation of Mrs Ayris's only known lie (that she had *seen* Read in Southend) – 'What she probably meant to say was that she had a strong, intense feeling that he was at Southend that day.' Of the four witnesses who said they saw Read in Southend, the judge remarked: 'It may be said that their evidence is not precise enough. But what evidence of this nature would be precise? The fair rule is to take it as a whole, and if you find substantial agreement in what is important to prove – with circumstantial variety as to the colour of the dress, and so forth – that is in one sense the best evidence you can have.' And where was the revolver, known to have been in the prisoner's possession? If he had disposed of it, why was the person to whom he had given or sold it not called? And why was no one called to prove where he was, if not at Southend?

The judge spoke for 80 minutes, concluding at 12.50 pm, when the jury retired. They returned at 1.30.

Their foreman, Mr G. Thorpe Bartram, of Braintree, was very pale and appeared to be suffering from palpitations when he announced the verdict – 'Guilty'. Jim Read, who also paled at the word, soon recovered his composure and spoke clearly and coolly when asked by the Clerk of the Court: 'Have you anything to say why sentence of death should not be passed upon you?'

Read declared:

> I would wish to repeat that I am perfectly innocent of this charge; that it is now two years since I have ever seen Florence Dennis; that I have never written to her; that I have only received one letter from her – one of the two sworn to by Mrs Schmidt. I have received from her one telegram . . . I have never fired a revolver in my life . . . I have never been to Hanwell in my life. It was in March *last* – which Mrs Ayris swore was in the March preceding – that I received from her a letter making an appointment there [at Victoria Station]. I met her . . . She wanted to borrow a sum of £50. I had not 50 pence, and if I had 50 pence I wanted them for my own family . . . In her evidence she told us that the meeting lasted ten minutes. It lasted three hours. The last thing I have to say is that at the time the murder was committed according to the evidence, I was as nearly as possible 50 miles from the spot.

He sat down and watched, with his arms folded, as the judge donned the black cap. Told to stand for the sentence, he thrust his left hand in his trouser pocket, and pulled his moustache with his right.

Mr Baron Pollock, in pronouncing sentence of death, was brisk and brief. 'Amen!' said the chaplain and others. Many of the spectators, especially the women, wept.

But Read was all smiles when he left the courthouse in a prison van. Wearing a white straw hat with a black band, he waved cheerfully at the crowd, who shouted 'Murderer!' and 'You wretch!'

Mrs Ayris now wrote to the *Chronicle*, saying that after Read's arrest, she received a threatening letter, apparently from Read or his brother. It said: 'If he is committed, you are a ruined woman. So beware!' She also revealed – having seen part of Read's petition against his sentence of death – that in it he now claimed he was out with *Mrs Ayris* on the Sunday night (24 June), walking about Southend. She wrote: 'Was anything ever more absurd?'

If this was his plea, which she of course denied, it meant he now conceded that he *was* in Southend, and not '50 miles from the spot'.

While awaiting the Home Secretary's response to his petition, Read wrote several letters from his quarters in Springfield Jail. In one he wrote: 'You may all satisfy yourselves that my murder, which is fixed for a fortnight today, and which I do not fear at all, is the sacrifice of a perfectly innocent life, which I do not now value at twopence since I have learned the value of earthly so-called friendships, and that so-called "divine justice" which permits such an outrage as this.'

A story was published about him serving as a choirboy at St Mary's Chapel-of-Ease in Shadwell, and his agnosticism was attributed to a schoolmaster, a sceptic, who lent the boy books casting doubt on the Bible and urged him to keep an open mind.

On the morning of Friday, 30 November, Jim Read was visited by his wife for the last time. She was accompanied by his brother, Harry, and an unmarried sister, Miss Read. Still cheerful, he maintained his innocence and said he was hopeful of a reprieve. But there were tears in his eyes as he bade his wife and sister goodbye, though all expressed the hope it would not be a final farewell. Mrs Read and Miss Read called on a Catholic priest before returning to London by train.

Harry Read was back in Chelmsford on Saturday afternoon. Jim was full of jokes, and kept repeating: 'I'm sure I shan't be hanged – you see!' Both regarded the long-delayed response to his petition as a good omen. At one point Harry left the prison to buy a new collar for his brother – he wanted a clean one to wear on Sunday – and when eight o'clock had come and gone with still no news from London, the brothers were even more optimistic. They parted, not expecting to hear anything so late at night. 'Goodnight, old chap,' said Harry. 'See you tomorrow.' 'Goodnight, old fellow,' said Jim.

A thick fog hung around the prison. Harry spent an hour in the George Hotel before catching the 9.25 back to London.

The train bearing the Home Secretary's decision, sent by express mail instead of by special messenger, must have passed Harry's train in the fog. Because of the fog, it was late arriving at Chelmsford, and the missive, stamped 'Official' and 'Immediate', reached the Under-Sheriff just before half-past ten. A copy went to the Prison Governor. Dated Whitehall, 1 December, it said: 'Sir – I am directed by the Secretary of State to acquaint you that . . . he regrets that he has failed to discover any sufficient ground to justify him in advising Her Majesty to interfere with the due course of the law . . .' Jim Read was told that night, unofficially, that there would be no reprieve. He would hang on Tuesday.

His brother learned of the decision in the Sunday papers. He returned to Chelmsford on the afternoon of Monday, 3 December. Stopping off at the George Hotel, Harry opened a telegram which had arrived for him minutes before. He showed it to a local reporter. It was in reply to a telegram he had sent to the Queen appealing for clemency, 'as a case does not appear to have been proved against my brother beyond reasonable possibility of doubt'. The telegram said: 'OHMS. Windsor. Your application should come through the Home Secretary. Signed: Private Secretary.'

Harry Read was not discouraged. He said: 'A member of my family and a lawyer are having a private audience at Windsor today.' 'Keep your pecker up!' said a bystander. Harry walked to the jail, smoking a pipe and knocking the ashes out before he entered the visitors' gate.

Jim was dejected. He said he was 'disgusted' at the Home Secretary's decision. But his sister, Mrs Kelly, who arrived soon afterwards, was able to tell him that her letter to the Queen had received a more positive reply: 'Your letter has been sent to the Home Secretary.' But no change of sentence, no news, had reached the prison by the time brother and sister had to leave. Mrs Kelly left first and returned to London. Harry stayed as long as he could, and when he departed, the two men, trying to control their feelings, bid each other an emotional farewell.

At 10.00 pm Harry returned to the prison to see the Governor. But there was no word from Windsor. He spent the night at the George Hotel, and remained in his bedroom, in bed, while his brother was hanged within Springfield Jail.

Outside the jail, a small crowd began gathering in the early morning fog at about 7.00 am. Among them were several reporters, some policemen, a preacher, an eccentric gentleman called 'The Major', who was prepared to act as hangman if Billington failed to appear, and a milkman, who arrived in his milk cart to make his daily deliveries to the jail. Various officials entered the jail, and at 7.45 the funeral bell began to toll.

Within, Read asked for a little brandy and the reassurance that his death would be instantaneous. He looked haggard but remained composed. Asked by the chaplain if he had anything to say, he said: 'Nothing at all – except to thank you and the others.' He had dressed himself with great care, brushing his hair, combing his beard and twisting his moustache. When the officials and hangman arrived he faced them bravely, and having been pinioned, was led in procession from his cell, across a hall, through a passage and across an open yard to the small execution shed. A cross-beam stretched from wall to wall, from which dangled a chain, and the noose. The pit below, some 15 feet deep, was lined with brick. Overhead, a double skylight afforded some illumination. The condemned man weighed 125 lbs, and the hangman had allowed a drop of 7' 8". The only sound was the tolling bell and the chaplain's mournful recitation – 'Man that is born of woman hath but a short time to live . . . In the midst of life, we are in death.'

At 7.55 the fog began to clear from the prison, and the black flag was unfurled at 8.03. Voices in the crowd murmured: 'There he goes!' A few seconds later 12 warders emerged from the prison on their way to breakfast. All looked gloomy and sad; some had tears in their eyes.

At 10.30 the inquest on the body was held in the Governor's office. The jury went to view the body, as it lay in a coffin in a storeroom. The face bore 'a peaceful expression', but there was slight abrasion on the neck. Jim Read still wore the light suit in which he had been arrested, tried and hanged. His red socks showed above his tan-coloured shoes, and his body, it is said, was still warm. He was buried within the jail.

Before he died, on the Sunday, Read wrote to his brother, Harry, saying he had written to the Home Secretary asking that his whereabouts in Southend (and his alibi) be checked anew. He said: 'I had beforehand referred him to the medical evidence, which showed the girl was murdered between 12 midnight 24/6 and 5.00 am 25/6.' He added that '4 witnesses at Mrs Clothier's, No. 1 Granville Villas, Southchurch Road, Southend, could answer for my being in bed the whole of that time'.

If this was so, why were these four witnesses never produced in court?

This statement, elaborating his petition's admission that he *was* in Southend, again negated his claim in court that on the night of the murder he was 50 miles away.

One of the *Chronicle*'s reporters investigated, on the very morning that James Read died. He found that Gresham (not Granville) Villas was near the railway station and that the landlady, Mrs Clothier, was not at home. But a coal merchant, Mr Sicely, who was lodging there, stated 'most positively' that Read had breakfasted there at about 7.00 am on the Monday morning and was thought to have left Southend by the eight o'clock train. Mr Sicely had gone to bed at half-past ten the previous night, and heard another lodger, possibly Read, return somewhat later. The reporter checked with the police, who confirmed that after studying Read's petition they had seen Mrs Clothier and established that Read returned to his lodging at 11.15 on the Sunday night.

So it was now confirmed that he *had* been in Southend on the night of the murder. In which case PC Daniel had been mistaken – or was telling a lie. For although it was possible for Read to have walked the eight miles to Benfleet between 11.15 and 1.15 am (when PC Daniel claimed to have met him) and then returned to Southend in time for a few hours' sleep before having breakfast at 7.00 am, it seems most unlikely that he did.

The implication at the trial that Read had *walked* the 30 miles from Southend to Leytonstone now seems even more absurd. He could easily have travelled on the Monday morning to Leytonstone by train, leaving Southend at 8.00 am and arriving at the Scannells' home at about 9.15. But if he was in Southend at Mrs Clothier's on the Sunday night (and on Saturday), why didn't the police find out? Or having done so, not present this damning fact in court?

It seems that the police, having accepted PC Daniel's evidence and being stuck with the consequent conclusion that Read walked back to London via Leigh, failed to enquire whether he might have lodged in Southend – not just on Sunday – but also on Saturday night. But even more odd is the apparent silence of Mr Sicely and Mrs Clothier. How did they fail to report that a stranger, a man answering Read's description, had lodged at Gresham Villas over the very weekend that Florence Dennis died?

There was another death a few days after the execution of James Read. His loyal and loving brother, Harry, shattered by the events of the last six months and without a job, threw himself into the River Thames, and drowned.

Two events occurred in 1895 that would have a far-reaching impact on the world, and on the study of criminals and the detection of crime. A young Italian with an Irish mother, Guglielmo Marconi, who had left his birthplace to pursue his experiments in wireless telegraphy in London, sent his first message over a mile. And in Vienna, Sigmund Freud published his first work on psycho-analysis.

A more immediately important legal event, and long overdue, occurred in 1898, when the Criminal Evidence Act decreed that any person being tried on a criminal charge could give evidence on his own, or her own, behalf. The Act also allowed a husband or wife of the accused to give evidence in court.

The scaffold, described by Billington's successor, Harry Pierrepoint, as 'the finest scaffold in the whole country, being fitted to hang three persons side by side', was moved to Pentonville Prison in 1902, when Newgate Prison was demolished. The first hanging at Pentonville took place on this scaffold on 30 September 1902 – an event that was also marked by the discontinuance of the practice of flying a black flag in London when an execution occurred. Instead, a bell was tolled.

In 1903, the number of people executed for murder in Britain rose to its highest level for over 70 years – 27 people being hanged. This, however, was well below the average for the years between 1811 and 1832, when about 80 people were hanged per year. This in turn was far less than the average rate of executions in the brief reign of Edward VI (1547–53), when about 560 people were executed each year at Tyburn (at Marble Arch).

Once Newgate Prison was demolished, building on the site began in 1903, concluding three years later. Topped by a large bronze figure of Justice, the new and imposing Central Criminal Court rose in its place, to become more familiarly known by the name of the street over which it towered – the Old Bailey.

CHAPTER 9

George Chapman

The Murder of Maud Marsh, 1902

Poison is rightly regarded as a woman's weapon when it comes to murder. Of the 68 women hanged for murder between 1843 and 1955, 37 were poisoners. But certain men of some education and social standing, especially doctors, are also apt to use poison to effect their murderous ends and seem to relish the power it gives them over their victims' lives and the suffering slow poisoning can cause. Such murders, premeditated and clinically performed, are particularly vile, and those who commit them the most callous and cruel of murderers. For they kill without passion, without a blow being struck, with the victim dying before their coldly curious eyes.

His real name was Severin Klosowski. The son of a carpenter, he was born on 14 December 1865 at Nagornak, a village near Kolo, west of Warsaw. Leaving school in 1880, when he was 14, he was apprenticed for four-and-a-half years to a surgeon in the village of Zvolen. At that time, Poland did not exist, having been swallowed up by Russia, Prussia and Austria. Warsaw was in the Russian sector, and it was to Warsaw that young Klosowski went in October 1885. There he was employed as an assistant surgeon until November 1886, during which time he studied practical surgery at the hospital in Praga, a suburb of Warsaw. The following month he received the degree of a junior surgeon. Wherever he went he collected certificates of employment and various commendations, which praised his diligence, zeal and good behaviour. A travel pass issued three weeks before his 21st birthday describes him as 'height, medium; hair, dark; eyes, blue; nose and mouth, medium; chin and face, longish; birthmarks, none'.

The last of these certificates, which were found much later in Chapman's possession and seem to be genuine, places him in Warsaw in March 1887. After that, there is no record of him until he appears in London in 1888. He is said to have joined the Russian army and to have served for 18 months. If so, he would surely have kept his service record (unless it was defamatory and bad). A witness at his trial, Wolff Levisohn, who had served with the Russian army for seven years, said: 'The accused could not have been a soldier, because he was too young when he came over here.' Chapman was 23 in December 1888.

It was Levisohn, a traveller or sales rep in hairdressing supplies, who established the year of Chapman's arrival in London. He told the Police

Court that he first met Chapman in a hairdresser's shop under the White Hart public house, 89 High Street, Whitechapel, in 1888. Chapman gave his name as Ludwig Zagowski. They discussed the efficacy of certain medicines, Chapman speaking a mixture of Polish and Yiddish. He said he came from Warsaw. According to Levisohn, the other man worked as an assistant to the hairdresser in this shop until 1889, when he became the proprietor. He was there until 1890. During this time, Chapman was joined by his wife and two children. But, said Levisohn, 'he did not support them, and now and again I and another man gave the woman some coppers'.

If Mrs Klosowski appeared on the scene in 1889 – with *two* children – she must therefore have married the junior surgeon in 1887, if not before. There seems no reason to doubt the fact that she was his real wife, and a Catholic, and would therefore have never countenanced any divorce. This would explain why Chapman never married his four subsequent 'wives', although he pretended to do so. Mrs Klosowski, like his later 'wives', seems to have been or become an inconvenience and an embarrassment. She disappears from the scene, almost as soon as she appears. Perhaps Chapman poisoned her, and the children. More probably, he disappeared himself, leaving his family to fend for themselves. It is recorded that Klosowski, using his real name, worked as an assistant for five months at a hairdresser's in West India Dock Road in Poplar. But this was, it seems, in 1888.

It is not known why Chapman never worked as an assistant surgeon in England. Historically, barber-surgeons were a joint occupation in England until 1745, serving as primitive doctors and dentists as well as barbers – the red ribbon on a barber's pole signifying the ribbon bound around a patient's arm before blood-letting. The practice may have survived much longer in rural Russian Poland.

The next sighting of Severin Klosowski, as he still called himself, was in the Polish Club in Clerkenwell in 1889. Here he met a Polish tailor, Stanislaus Baderski, who was living with a married sister, Mrs Polacryk. She and another sister, Lucy, used to visit the club on Sunday nights, and about a month after Chapman met Lucy Baderski they 'married', celebrating with a party on August Bank Holiday, 1889. At the time, Chapman had a barber's shop in Cable Street, Whitechapel. Here the couple lived for a few months before moving to Greenfield Street, also in Whitechapel. Another of Lucy's sisters, Mrs Rauch, who came to London from German Poland in August 1889, visited the Klosowskis in Greenfield Street, and when their first baby, a boy, was born, she recalled that the father washed the infant 'just like a nurse'.

In May 1890 the Klosowskis went to America, where it seems the baby boy died. Lucy returned to London, alone, in February 1891, and gave birth to a second child, a daughter, on 12 May. About two weeks later, according to Mrs Rauch, the father appeared and for a time the couple lived together, moving from lodging to lodging. But in 1893, or earlier, Lucy left her 'husband', apparently because of his ardent interest in other women.

He is next heard of in Tottenham, where in 1893 he worked for a hairdresser, Mr Haddin, at 5 West Green Road. Here he was known by another assistant as 'Schloski', and here the ubiquitous salesman, Wolff Levisohn, re-encountered Chapman in 1894, describing him later as 'a la-di-da then, with black coat, patent boots, and a high hat'. Another woman was with him then, and in 1895, when Chapman, using his real name, sublet a hairdresser's shop in High Road, Tottenham for a few months, he 'got a girl in trouble'. He later moved to another High Road shop opposite Bruce Grove railway station.

This woman and girl was Annie Chapman. She met the man who was to assume her surname towards the end of 1893, when he was working for Mr Haddin in West Green Road. She said later: 'I went there one day and made his acquaintance. After that I went out with him for a little while. I think he said he was either single or a widower. He was living at Haddin's, and he proposed I should go as his housekeeper, and after a time I did so. I lived with him as his wife. We passed as Mr and Mrs Klosowski.'

They were together for a year. Annie Chapman moved out in December 1894 when Lucy Klosowski moved back in – 'He brought her to the shop where I was living with him. He said she was his wife . . . That was the reason I left.' But on discovering a month or so later that she was pregnant, she returned to the shop opposite Bruce Grove railway station – 'I went there . . . and asked him to help me in my trouble. I was going to have a baby. I also asked him to give me a reference to get a situation . . . He did not take much notice.' She saw him once again, in February 1895, when he bicycled over to her Tottenham lodging – perhaps to dissuade her from seeing him again, or to exact his 'marital' rights.

It was in 1895, seeking to obscure his Polish origins, to confuse debtors and demanding 'wives', that Klosowski began calling himself George Chapman. Even after his arrest, he refused to acknowledge that he was Severin Klosowski, saying: 'I don't know anything about that fellow.'

As George Chapman he replied to an advertisement for a hairdresser's assistant in 1895, and was employed for about seven months by William Wenzel, whose shop was at 7 Church Lane in Leytonstone. There a customer, John Ward, offered to rent him a furnished room at his home in Forest Road. Mr Ward happened to have another lodger, Mrs Spink, who had been abandoned by her husband. She became Chapman's first victim, dying of poisoning two-and-a-half years after they met.

Her family came from Otley in Yorkshire and her maiden name was Mary Isabella Renton. While living with a cousin, a corn chandler, Joseph Renton, and his grandmother, in Leyton (her parents died when she was in her teens), she married a railway porter at Leytonstone Station, Shadrach Spink. He, according to Mr Renton, 'was not a sober man', and she 'was also intemperate'. They had a son, also called Shadrach, and a few years later, Spink deserted his wife, taking young Shadrach with him. A few months later, Mrs Spink gave birth to a boy, possibly not Spink's. Called Willie, he was five when his mother took a room in Mr Ward's house in Forest Road. By this time George Chapman was 29 and Mrs Spink about 39. Despite her age, her intemperate habits, and her son, she had a certain appeal – her grandfather had left her nearly £600 in trust when he died.

Before long, Mrs Ward complained to her husband about the 'carrying on' between Mr Chapman and Mrs Spink. Mr Ward spoke to Chapman, saying: 'My wife has seen you kissing Mrs Spink on the stairs. We cannot allow that sort of thing to go on in the house.' 'It's all right, Mr Ward,' said Chapman. 'We're going to get married about Sunday week.' And early on a Sunday morning in October, 1895, they went out together, allegedly to a Catholic church in Whitechapel, and returned that night. On seeing the Wards, Chapman announced: 'Allow me to introduce you to my wife!'

The Chapmans and little Willie left Leytonstone in March 1896, moving for some reason to Hastings. They settled in 10 Hill Street, where a family called Helsdown also lived. For a few months Chapman ran a hairdressing business in a poor part of the town. Then in June, the first Mrs Chapman withdrew £195 of her money so that her husband could open a barber's shop in Albion Mansions, George Street, where she acted as his assistant, lathering the customers' faces and occasionally trying to shave them. A small plump woman (5' tall), with short dark hair cut like a man's, she must have been something of a character and a bit of a laugh. She also played an upright piano in the shop. Chapman had hired it to attract more custom, and business improved: a female hairdresser was unheard of then and 'musical shaves' were a novelty. That summer he also bought a small sailing-boat and, attired in nautical gear, took his spouse for brief cruises along the coast. Once the boat capsized, and both were saved from drowning by some fishermen – saved in both cases for a more dreadful demise.

Meanwhile, little Willie was leading a miserable and neglected life, sometimes sleeping in a cellar or in the shop; and his mother's addiction to drink now led to rows and blows. She told Mrs Helsdown that her husband had smacked her face and once grabbed her by the throat. She also complained of pains in her stomach and sickness, although no doctor was ever called.

In February 1897, the Chapmans moved to new lodgings in 1 Coburg Place. Another lodger, Mrs Greenaway, who only knew the Chapmans for a month, would later remember that Mrs Chapman, who drank, but seemed in good health though 'dazed', said that her first husband had been killed on the railway and that her second husband had a revolver. She also borrowed four volumes of Cassell's *Family Physician* from Mrs Greenaway which were never returned.

A frequent customer at the Albion Mansions barber's shop was a chemist, William Davidson, who had lived in Hastings for 18 years. He and Chapman used to chat about medical matters, and the barber sometimes called at his High Street shop. On 3 April, Chapman bought an ounce of tartar-emetic, a white powder, for which he paid two pence. Davidson entered the purchase in his poison register book – Chapman signed the entry – and on a red label printed *Poison*, which he attached to the bottle, he wrote: '*Dose, ⅙th grain to ¼ grain: to be used with caution*'. He also sold the barber two old medical books.

Tartar-emetic was sometimes used to treat sick horses. It was used before long to make Mrs Chapman ill. In May, the housekeeper at Albion Mansions noticed that the barber's wife was 'vomiting a good deal' and afterwards 'appeared very poorly'.

About this time, a maidservant, Alice Penfold, was accosted one Sunday evening by a man called Smith, alias Chapman, who said he was single and managed a piano shop. She went out with him three times, and on one occasion accompanied him to St Leonards, to view a public house which he said he was thinking of buying. Then she received a letter from him in London, asking her to come and see him. She did not go.

This letter was written at an East End pub, the Prince of Wales, Bartholomew Square, off Old Street. Having sold the barber's shop and all therein, Chapman had turned himself into a publican. But to do so, to buy a lease on a pub – and before he killed off his wife – he required some, if not all, of her money. At her request, the balance of her Yorkshire trust, nearly £300, was sent south and banked in her name in Hastings on 31 August. Two days later, £50 of this was withdrawn in gold and a cheque for £200 was cashed the following week. On 28 September, George Chapman opened a bank account in London with £230, to which he soon added £55. The first Mrs Chapman died three months later, on Christmas Day.

Four women attended her dying, two neighbours, a part-time nurse and the pub potman's wife, Susan Pagett, who helped behind the public bar when Mrs Chapman was confined to her bed. To begin with, Mrs Chapman complained of feeling 'very bad' with 'pains in her head and all over'. Chapman would tell her, when she appeared behind the bar: 'Get out of it! You can't get drunk down here!' He told Mrs Pagett his wife was suffering from *delirium tremens*, and when she queried what sort of medicine he was giving his wife, he said: 'I told you before that she's delirious. You must take no notice of it.' Mrs Pagett replied: 'Delirious or not – I quickly moved in and I can quickly move out.' She did so, as did her husband, who told Chapman: 'If you've no respect for your wife and want to kill her, I have respect for mine. And you won't kill *her*.' Before they left, Mrs Pagett threatened to send for the parish doctor, and Chapman sent a note via her husband to a local doctor, Dr Rogers, who had also been recommended by Martha Doubleday.

Mrs Doubleday was a neighbour, a pub regular, it seems, who became friendly with Mrs Chapman, whom she described as 'a nice, little-built person, with a fresh colour'. After a month or so, Mrs Doubleday noticed the other woman was white-faced and very thin. Two weeks before Christmas Chapman asked her to sit up with his wife, who was now very ill. She agreed. Three days later Dr Rogers's services were sought. Mrs Doubleday said later:

I stayed with Mrs Chapman every night. She was in bed in the front room on the second floor, all the time I was there. The accused used to sleep on the couch. She was suffering very much – she vomited frequently and had diarrhoea very badly. I had to get her out of the bed. I never gave her any food. After the doctor came, the accused gave her brandy and medicine. He brought the brandy up with him at night. After she had the brandy she vomited. When the accused came into the room he used to lean over her. Once or twice he told me to go outside, and then I would hear her say: 'Pray God – go away from me . . .' When

Dr Rogers came, he and the accused talked together in the bar about Mrs Chapman. I asked the accused what was the matter with her. He replied that the doctor said she was wasting away . . . I was only there at night. I saw Mrs Mumford there during the day . . . Towards Christmas she got much worse. Dr Rogers asked me to go and get Mrs Waymark to nurse her, as I could not do it any longer.

When Mrs Mumford, another neighbour, asked Chapman about his wife's illness, he replied: 'She drinks a good deal of brandy.' She saw him reading medical books in the bar: he said he was giving his wife something to cure her of *delirium tremens*. 'She seems very bad,' said Mrs Mumford. 'Oh, she'll get better when she gets on,' he said. He told her he had been a doctor on board a ship. The nurse, Mrs Waymark, later told the court:

> He used to go up to the bedside and feel her pulse. I sometimes said: 'She's very bad', and he would reply: 'Yes, I know what to do.' She used to say: 'Do kiss me.' She put out her arms for him to bend over and kiss her, but he did not do so. He would take her hand . . . She complained of diarrhoea and vomiting, and violent pains in her stomach. I very often saw her vomit . . . She always complained of thirst. She did not take much food, only a little beef tea, brandy, milk and soda, and water. The accused gave them to her. After she had had the drink, she was sick, and then used to go off in a stupor . . . She got worse and worse.

Mrs Doubleday was present when Mrs Chapman died.

> On Christmas morning she got much worse and became unconscious. She had been vomiting very much. A severe flooding came on. I called out for the accused, but he did not come up for some time afterwards. When he did, he only leant over the bed. He shook his head, and then went downstairs without making any remark. Before she died I called him again – 'Chapman! Come up quickly! Your wife is dying!' But he was too late . . . He went to the bedside and said: 'Polly – Polly – speak.' He went into the next room and cried. She died at one o'clock. Then he went downstairs and opened the public-house. I said: 'You're never going to open the house today?' He said: 'Yes, I am.'

The women were shocked when they laid out the body: it was like a skeleton, and the flesh was discoloured and yellow. That night Chapman summoned an undertaker, and Mary Isabella Chapman, aged 41, was buried in a common grave in Leytonstone on 30 December. Dr Rogers, who would die before Chapman was arrested, attributed her death to a consumptive, wasting disease, phthisis.

Throughout this period, Willie Spink had slept in an adjacent room, but not much longer. Chapman tried to put the boy into one of Dr Barnardo's homes, saying he had no relations. The enquiry officer was suspicious, and Willie was not accepted. But in March 1898 he was admitted to Shoreditch workhouse. Chapman told the officials there (truthfully) that Willie's mother, Isabella Spink, was dead and that her husband had deserted her. As references, he gave the names of Miss E. Painter and Bessie Taylor. Both lived at addresses near the Prince of Wales pub, and Willie's address was given as No. 8 Haberdasher Street, the same as that of Bessie Taylor, who was described as Chapman's housekeeper.

Apparently Chapman advertised for a barmaid or housekeeper soon after Mrs Spink died. Bessie Taylor was chosen. Born Elizabeth Taylor, the daughter of a Cheshire farmer, she was a maidservant in London before becoming the housekeeper/manageress of a restaurant in Peckham. In view of the fact that Chapman was evidently acquainted with both Elizabeth Painter and Bessie Taylor in March, it is possible, as the women were friends and were lodging near the Prince of Wales, that *both* assisted in helping Chapman run the pub, and that Painter was the first to be employed. At Chapman's trial she admitted, without saying *when*, that she sometimes assisted behind the bar, and that he kissed her 'once or twice', although 'he never made any overtures to me, nor said I could be Mrs Chapman'. But by Easter it was Bessie Taylor, aged 33, who moved into the Prince of Wales and before long 'married' the owner – perhaps in July 1898, when a £50 cheque, sent to Bessie by her father, was credited to Chapman's account. On 23 August, he closed the account, withdrawing £370 in notes and cash. In that month the Chapmans moved north, to Bishop's Stortford in Hertfordshire, where they leased another pub, The Grapes. Perhaps local gossip about the death of the first Mrs Chapman and the speedy appearance of a second 'wife' in the Prince of Wales prompted the move.

Not much of special interest happened at The Grapes, except that Elizabeth Painter stayed there for a fortnight before Christmas, apparently standing in for Bessie when she entered a hospital for treatment to her teeth: she had 'lumps on her face from her gums'. According to Mrs Painter, Chapman was 'very unkind' to Bessie on her return – 'He carried on at her all the afternoon, and in the evening he frightened her with a revolver.' None the less, Painter later told the court that the Chapmans were on 'very good terms'. She said: 'Most people are changeable, and he was no exception to the rule.'

In May 1899, the ever-mobile publican moved back to London, leasing The Monument in Union Street, in Southwark, where the second Mrs Chapman would die within two years, during which the Boer War was fought in South Africa, and Ladysmith, Kimberley and Mafeking besieged and then relieved.

Bessie Taylor was a charitable, genial woman, well regarded by the customers and by the sisters at the local mission. Like her predecessor she played the piano and she took up bicycling to please her husband. Her parents and her brother, William, who stayed more than once at The Monument, were favourably impressed by Chapman. Bessie's mother, Mrs Taylor, said she 'had never seen a better husband'. So why did Chapman decide to kill her?

It was not for her money. Bessie, alive, a favourite daughter, could expect to inherit a large sum of money when her parents died. So why? Did Chapman tire of her – as he seemed to tire of all his women after a couple of years? Did a younger woman catch his eye and excite his lust? Did he relish the power over life and death that lay in his hands as he dispensed his poisonous doses? Did he seek to relive some of the hospital dramas of his youth? He was clearly a poseur and liked play-acting, pretending to be other, and more, than he was. Did he also like playing the doctor, the husband, the lover, as well as the man of the world?

As the Christmas of 1900 approached, Bessie, who had been out of sorts for several weeks, became seriously ill. She had complained to a neighbour, Martha Stevens, who was a nurse, of being 'fatigued, languid, and having pains in her stomach'. Mrs Stevens recommended a visit to Dr James Stoker, who thought the sick woman had constipation and prescribed a dose of salts. She visited him more than once, and he first called on her at The Monument on 1 January 1901, when he found her to be suffering from pains in the stomach, vomiting and diarrhoea. Mrs Stevens, who had been acting as a day nurse for about two weeks, was now employed on a 24-hour basis, assisted on some evenings by Elizabeth Painter and then by Bessie's mother, Mrs Taylor. Dr Stoker now called on the patient nearly every day.

He said later: 'She used to get better and then go back again.'

Mrs Stevens said:

She complained a little about her throat burning, and it was very red. On about two occasions I noticed perspiration. When she vomited it was severe, green, thick and slimy. She did not complain much of being thirsty. When she did complain I saw milk, water, brandy and water, and champagne given to her . . . I sometimes prepared the nourishment she had, sometimes her mother, and sometimes the accused. [He] was there during the night until Bessie's mother came, and then he went and slept in the parlour. I went back to my home in the daytime for an hour sometimes. Mrs Taylor did not go out very often.

Elizabeth Painter said:

She always felt sick, and it always came on after she had had anything to eat or drink . . . When the accused came into her room he felt her pulse with his watch in his hand. After a time I saw medicine bottles in the room. The accused would shake them and then look up to the light through them. I asked him what was the matter with her, and he said it was a complication of diseases. When I went into the bar, I would ask him how Bessie was, and sometimes he would say: 'Your friend is dead.'

But she did not take him seriously. 'It was just his way of putting it,' she said.

On 22 January 1901, Queen Victoria died, and The Monument, like London and the Empire, was garbed in mourning, in purple and black. Bessie's brother, William Taylor, who came to see his sister more than once, said that in February: 'She appeared to be very ill and shrunken . . . thin, like a little old woman.'

Three other doctors were consulted at Mrs Taylor's suggestion. Each examined the patient and came to three different conclusions: that she was suffering from some womb trouble; that she had a cancerous disease of the stomach or intestines; that she was afflicted with a severe form of hysteria, i.e. imagining things and malingering.

One Sunday, Bessie was suddenly better. Mrs Stevens told the court:

She got up and went about the house, and then sat down and played the piano in the club-room adjoining her bedroom. As she was playing, Dr Stoker came in and put his finger up so that I should not interrupt her. And he then said: 'Capital!' She looked round and discovered him there. I went home to sleep that night. I was sent for again on Monday or Tuesday. Bessie seemed quite prostrated ... I was with Bessie on 13 February, and at about 1.30 am I thought she was dying. So I called the accused. He looked at her, and I think he said: 'Oh, she has gone!' And he commenced to cry.

Dr Stoker gave as the cause of death 'intestinal obstruction, vomiting, and exhaustion'. He still believed that the primary cause of her illness was constipation. There was no post-mortem. Two days later, Bessie Taylor's body was transported to St Pancras Station. Chapman went with the hearse. At the station the coffin was received by William Taylor, who took it by train to Warrington. He paid all the funeral expenses, as Chapman claimed to be short of money.

Bessie Taylor was buried, aged 36, in the family plot in Lymm churchyard in Cheshire, where a gravestone, presumably raised by William, records that she was a daughter of Thomas and Betsy Taylor, who were to die within two months of each other in 1902. There is no mention of Chapman or how she died. The death of another daughter, Mary, is also given; she died in 1893 aged 28 – presumably she was Bessie's twin.

On a memorial card, a verse was inscribed, possibly composed by Chapman himself:

> Farewell, my friends, fond and dear,
> Weep not for me one single tear;
> For all that was and could be done,
> You plainly see my time is come.

Mrs Stevens remained at The Monument for a week or so until, as she said, 'a woman appeared in response to an advertisement'. We do not know this woman's name, only that Mrs Stevens called her 'Madam'. Whoever she was, she evidently left without agreeing to be the third Mrs Chapman. That fatal role would be assumed by an 18-year-old girl, Maud Marsh.

Some writers have characterised George Chapman as baboon-like, repulsive, illiterate, ugly, of meagre physique and coarse. He was most probably none of these things. He was not illiterate, although his spelling was poor, and he was clearly something of a dandy, making the most of his dress and appearance with his colourful ties and breast-pocket handkerchiefs, his rings, his gold watch and chain, his carefully brushed hair and luxuriant droopy moustache. Although thin of face, even gaunt, and possibly scrawny, he must, after years on his feet as a medic, barber and publican, have been fairly sinewy and fit. He was a keen cyclist: he would bicycle the ten miles from Southwark to Croydon and back, to see Maud's parents, and when licensee of the Prince of Wales he belonged to a police cycling club. He was also a keen photographer, taking photos of himself and his wives and developing the results. Interested in matters criminal, as well as medical, he cultivated the custom and good opinions of the local police – he even possessed a copy of James Berry's autobiography. The pubs he ran were adorned with guns, swords and pistols, flags, photos and souvenirs of his travels. Apparently he used to regale his customers with exaggerated tales of his adventures at sea and in America, and of hunting game. Sometimes he used an American revolver to kill rats lurking in his cellars. He is said to have affected a republican stance and to have pretended to be an American. During the Boer War, whose late peace was concluded in May 1902, he made himself unpopular by siding with the Boers and drinking to their success.

In the spring and summer of 1901, Chapman must have employed one or more replacements for Bessie Taylor as barmaid/housekeeper at The Monument. Whoever these women were, they walked out, or were sacked, the last in August, and thereby possibly saved their lives. Still seeking to employ another 'wife', Chapman replied to an advertisement in the *Morning Advertiser* placed by Maud Eliza Marsh in August 1901.

Maud's father was a labourer, and the family, which included at least four daughters and a son, lived at 14 Longfellow Road, West Croydon. Maud had been working locally as a barmaid since she was 15 and seems to have hankered after a London job. Her mother accompanied Maud to The Monument when a reply to her ad was received, and learned that the publican, Chapman, was a widower and an American, and that a family occupied the pub's top floor – which was untrue. Despite Mrs Marsh's doubts, Maud was employed there and then, and moved in within a few days.

Within a month, in mid-September, when Maud and George Chapman visited Mrs Marsh in Croydon (her husband was ill in a local hospital), she was doubtless surprised to hear from Chapman that he had taken a great fancy to Maud and wished to marry her. Mrs Marsh said she would consult her husband, whom the couple also visited at a later date. It seems that neither parent was keen on the match, although Chapman promised to make a will, leaving £400 and all his furniture, etc, to his 'wife' in the event of his death.

About this time, possibly before the visit, Maud wrote to her mother to say that Mr Chapman had given her a gold watch and chain. Then this letter arrived in Croydon:

Dear Mother – Just a line to say on the QT Mr has gone out, so I now write this to you to say that George says if I do not let him have what he wants he will give me £35 and send me home. What shall I do? It does worry me so; but still I am engaged, so it will not matter much, and if he does not marry me I can have a breach of promise, can't I?

Mrs Marsh wrote and told her daughter to come home at once, with or without the £35. Maud refused, and wrote again, more or less refuting the gist of her previous letter. Her father then visited The Monument, and urged his daughter to behave herself – to no avail. When Mrs Marsh paid a visit to the pub on Sunday, 13 October, she saw some confetti lying about and was told by her 14-year-old daughter, Nellie, who was there on a working visit that lasted two months: 'Maud was married this morning.'

This was soon confirmed by the happy couple – Maud was wearing a wedding ring – and Chapman asked Mrs Marsh to stay for dinner and join in the celebrations. The story was that they had married in a Roman Catholic church in Bishopsgate. Although Mrs Marsh asked to see the certificate – and was told by Maud: 'George has got it, and has put it with his other papers' – she was not disposed to believe that her daughter would lie. Chapman himself was welcoming, and, as she said later, treated her nicely. Her husband, who visited the Chapmans just before Christmas, was likewise placated, later telling the court that he and Chapman, whom he found pleasant and agreeable, were on 'the best of terms'. He said: 'I minded his house for him on two occasions ... He always answered my inquiries about my daughter perfectly frankly ... and, as far as I could see, she was very happy with him. I thought he treated her very well.'

That pre-Christmas visit was paid to The Crown, Chapman's latest acquisition, at 213 Borough High Street, Southwark. The move was necessitated, in part, by a fire at The Monument, not long before Chapman's lease on that pub was about to expire. Oddly, the Chapmans were not at home at the time, the tills had been emptied, doors were open, and some of the furniture had been removed. Although the Fire Brigade's headquarters were a few minutes away, the pub was badly damaged. Chapman made an insurance claim and sued a newspaper, which voiced suspicions about the fire's cause, for libel. However, he failed to pursue both claims, and no insurance was paid. Even more oddly, as he very probably set fire to the pub himself, no action was taken against him by the police, and he soon acquired the lease of The Crown, some 500 yards away.

He was a litigious man, and the following summer succeeded in a claim of financial deception, although *he* was in the wrong. Interestingly, Arthur Hutton, a tall man who wore a monocle and prosecuted at Southwark on Chapman's behalf, would appear for the defence nine months later at Chapman's trial.

When Chapman and his third 'wife' moved to The Crown, Mrs Marsh received no communications from her daughter, nor saw her, for seven months. However, her son and other daughters were regular visitors at The Crown, and Mrs Marsh heard from them that Maud was happy and well. But a married daughter, Mrs Louisa Morris, neglected to report that Maud had had an abortion in about April or May.

This was induced by Chapman himself, using certain appliances and con-coctions. Maud was much upset by not being allowed to have a baby. She wanted a family of her own, and when her sister, Louisa, brought *her* baby to The Crown, Maud would become 'very distressed and cry a good deal'. She complained that George didn't want any children, not until his business and income had improved. She also complained that George was reluctant to let her leave the pub, restricting her to the bar or the rooms upstairs. On one occasion, when the sisters went out for a walk, Maud began to cry. 'You don't know what he is!' she sobbed, and when questioned revealed that George had beaten her more than once, grabbing her hair and banging her head. In retaliation, she said, she had kicked him.

Clearly, Chapman wanted his women to be useful but passive and decorous doormats, submitting fully to his every professional and personal need. Fear and hatred of women were probably deeply embedded within his psyche. But he needed them for domestic and sexual purposes, and to con-stantly reassert his own, and others', high opinion of himself.

Maud's intractable youth and tears may have shortened her life. Or Chap-man, now 36, may have sought more frequent conquests and thrills. But the appearance of Florence Rayner in The Crown in June seems to have been the spur that hastened the third Mrs Chapman's demise. Louisa Morris would later remember a tea-time conversation when Maud remarked, in her hus-band's presence: 'What do you think? George says I won't live to be 28.' To which Chapman responded: 'No more you won't!'

Florence Rayner, who came from Peckham, was employed locally and be-came accustomed to dropping into The Crown about mid-day. Happening to mention that she had some previous experience behind the bar, she was asked one day by Chapman to lend a hand, after which he offered her a job as a barmaid at 5 shillings a week, plus board and lodging. She agreed. This was in the middle of June. She used to eat with Chapman upstairs while Maud managed the bar below. Before long he was being very attentive, kissing the barmaid and asking her if she would come to America with him. 'You've got a wife downstairs,' said Florence. 'You don't want me!' He retorted: 'I could give her *that* – and she'd be no more Mrs Chapman.' He said he would send Florence to America, then sell the business and join her there. 'Be my sweet-heart, will you?' he asked, and she said: 'No!' One afternoon he entered Florence's bedroom. But we do not know whether Florence said: 'Yes!' However, three weeks after her arival, Maud became sick, suffering from vomiting and diarrhoea.

It seems that Florence then blotted her copybook by becoming drunk on duty one Saturday night, and Chapman threw her out, refusing to give her a reference. Her version was that she departed to avoid his advances. Several weeks later he visited Florence at her next place of employment, The Fores-ter's in Twickenham. He told her that his wife was in Guy's Hospital suffering from constipation, and said: 'If you hadn't been such a fool, you would have been at The Crown now.'

It was not his idea that Maud should be hospitalised. What happened was that her sister, Alice, called at The Crown towards the end of July (after

Florence had gone and after a servant, Louisa Cole, had been employed in her place) and found that Maud was unwell. 'Where's Maud?' she enquired on arrival. Said Chapman: 'In bed. Dying fast.' Going upstairs, Alice found her sister sitting up in bed, sipping some senna tea; she complained of being constipated and in great pain. Alice took charge. She told Chapman: 'I think Maud ought to have a doctor, or go to the hospital.' He said he didn't want her to be messed about. None the less, Alice persuaded her sister to get up and get dressed – she was so weak that this took an hour – and they went out together, to a local doctor. He was out, so they walked on to Guy's Hospital, where Maud collapsed and was admitted, on 28 July. Chapman was far from pleased.

Suffering at first from a high fever (up to 103°), a rapid pulse and such pains in her abdomen that she could not bear to be touched, Maud slowly recovered. The assistant obstetric surgeon at Guy's surmised she had peritonitis. But her husband was opposed to any internal examinations and insisted he could care for her at home. Had he not been a junior surgeon? So when her temperature returned to normal and her health improved, the doctor had to let her depart, on 20 August, prescribing light food, occasional aperients and some opiates for any pain. Chapman fetched her himself, taking her away in a cab. Two months later she was dead.

Although her parents and sisters had visited her in the hospital, it was Maud's older sister, Mrs Louisa Morris, who, apart from the servant, Louisa Cole, and Chapman himself, saw the most of the dying young wife (she was now 19 and a half) from the day Maud returned to The Crown.

Mrs Morris said later: 'She was sitting on a chair in the bar. She appeared very ill, and I told her she had no business there. I made her go upstairs and lie down . . . I had to help her. I visited her subsequently: sometimes I found her well and sometimes unwell. She was generally up. On one or two occasions I found her lying down.'

At some point Chapman remarked: 'She should have done as I told her.' Mrs Morris asked: 'What was that?' He answered: 'She should have took the medicine I give her.' 'She never would take medicine,' said Mrs Morris, adding: 'It's funny the doctor couldn't find out what was the matter with her.' To which Chapman replied, snapping his fingers: 'I could give her a bit like *that*, and 50 doctors wouldn't find out.' 'What do you mean?' demanded Mrs Morris. 'Never mind!' he said and walked away.

None the less, on Friday, 10 October, Chapman decided he needed a doctor to witness Maud's illness and imminent death. He himself called on Dr Stoker, who had been so effectively ineffectual in knowing what was wrong with Bessie Taylor, and would prove so once again.

That night Stoker called on Maud Marsh – Chapman had revealed to him that she was not really his wife – and prescribed a mixture of catechu, bismuth, opium and chalk, and a diet of soda water and milk, boiled milk, brandy, beef tea, and ice. Two days later he changed the medicine to bismuth, morphia and ipecacuanha. The next day Maud was worse. She now suffered from spasms, and the pain in her stomach was severe. He thought she might have gastro-enteritis and stopped any oral intake of food, or medicine apart from bismuth, and told Chapman that the patient must be fed by rectal injections of a mixture of beef tea, milk and egg. A nurse, he suggested, should be employed.

On 16 October, Chapman asked the charwoman, Jessie Toon, if she could do any nursing. She replied: 'It all depends what it is. Is it a miscarriage, or is it premature?' He said: 'No. Nothing of the kind. She's been sick, and the doctor has ordered her to have food injected.' Mrs Toon said: 'I don't understand anything of that kind.' Nevertheless, she was employed, after seeing the patient, who lay in her second-floor bedroom and cried. Maud said if no one could be found to look after her, she would have to go to the hospital, which she did not want. 'I don't understand it, Mrs Chapman,' the charwoman said. 'But would you like me to look after you?' 'Yes, please, Jessie,' sobbed Maud. 'If you will.' She had just been sick. Unknown to Dr Stoker, it was Chapman who would give Maud the injections, using a syringe with a rubber attachment.

Mrs Toon said later:

> The injections didn't stay with the deceased. They came back again quickly, and she was in terrible pain. No one brought anything into the room for her use except the accused. I didn't see where he got what he brought, or how it was mixed. Dr Stoker sent some medicine to be kept by the bed, but she never took any of it. The accused took it into the kitchen with him and brought it back when he came in with the injection . . . When the attacks of diarrhoea came on, I had to help her out of bed. It was as much as I could manage to hold her, there was such dreadful pain. Her limbs would go stiff, and she complained frequently of thirst . . . She said her throat was burning, and that it seemed to be always burning . . . Everything she drank she vomited within a few minutes. The vomit was green.

On Saturday, 18 October, Maud's father, worried by what his daughter, Mrs Morris, had told him, visited The Crown. He sat with Maud for three hours, during which Chapman was 'up and down stairs every few minutes'. The two men said very little to each other, but when Mr Marsh left at about 10.00 pm, he was deeply disturbed and suspicious, although he took no action for two days. When he did, Chapman gave Maud a final, fatal dose.

In the meantime, on Monday, 20 October, both Mrs Marsh and Mrs Morris went to The Crown. They did what they could; Maud was very ill, in a stupor most of the time, and still having rectal injections. She was in pain and vomiting a good deal; Chapman gave her some brandy and water. Mrs Marsh said to him: 'Don't you think you had better have another doctor?' He replied: 'No. It's no good.' That night Mrs Morris and Mrs Toon went home, leaving Mrs Marsh to tend her daughter. On the Tuesday, Dr Stoker called at noon. Mrs Marsh said: 'Is there anything you can give her to stop the sickness?' 'No,' he replied. 'I'm at my wit's end to know what to do.' 'If she dies,' said Mrs Marsh, 'don't you think you ought to have a post-mortem? If you do, I'll pay the expense out of my pocket.' Chapman, when asked, blamed Maud's condition on a rabbit stew that he claimed had also made him sick.

The unexpected arrival of Dr Grapel at about 3.00 pm surprised all those on their feet in The Crown. That morning Mr Marsh had called on him, expressing deep concern about his daughter, and asked him – he was the Marsh's family doctor – to visit Maud. When Dr Grapel arrived, Chapman tried to pretend that Grapel was not only misinformed but at the wrong address. Muttering that a doctor was already in attendance, Chapman sent for Dr Stoker and the two doctors examined the patient. Dr Grapel said later: 'Her skin was sallow, jaundiced and muddy in appearance, tongue coated, her pulse fairly quick, and her breathing shallow. She was in a semi-comatose condition. I examined her stomach and found it was extremely tender to the touch. When I touched it, she groaned and retched.'

After a consultation with Dr Stoker and a private word with Mrs Marsh, Dr Grapel left, convinced that the patient was 'suffering from some acute irritant poison, probably ptomaine'. Arsenic was also in his mind as a cause, and he decided on his way home that an analysis of the patient's excreta might resolve the matter. At The Crown, Mrs Marsh confronted Chapman. 'Dr Grapel thinks Maud has been poisoned,' she said. To which he replied that he couldn't think how, unless it was the rabbit. She said: 'Dr Grapel says you don't find arsenic in rabbits.' He retorted: 'I can't think what it was then.'

That night Mrs Marsh sat in an armchair in her daughter's bedroom after Mrs Toon had left; Chapman lay on a couch. He brought some brandy in a glass tumbler upstairs and placed it on a safe by the bed. For a while, all three slept. About 4.00 am Maud awoke and asked for some liquid. Her mother gave her a tablespoonful of the brandy mixed with soda. Maud was sick. An hour or so later, Mrs Marsh, who had eaten nothing since her arrival and drunk only tea and stout, swallowed some of the brandy to revive herself. She said later: 'After I had taken it I had severe diarrhoea and sickness and pain in the lower part of my stomach, which continued till about 7.00 am. I had about six attacks of diarrhoea and vomiting during that time. Maud's bedroom was on the second floor; the WC was on the first floor. When I had to go there the accused was left with my daughter. He opened the house to the public about 8.00 am.'

It was Wednesday, 22 October. Mrs Marsh sent the servant, Louisa Cole, to fetch Mrs Toon, who arrived about 8.30 am. She asked Chapman: 'What's the matter? Is she worse?' 'No,' he said. 'Her mother is bad now.' 'What's the matter with her?' 'Sickness and diarrhoea,' he replied. She said: 'What! Two of them now!' 'You had better go upstairs, Jessie,' he said. 'And tell her to get to bed out of the way, the old cat.' He also said: 'Be careful, Jessie, what you say to her, and take particular notice of what she says to you . . . The old cat wants to have her cut about and show me up.'

Upstairs, Mrs Toon watched as Chapman brought another tumbler of brandy into the sick room. He poured some water into the glass and gave it to Maud to drink. Mrs Marsh then came in and spoke of her sickness. She said Chapman should send for a proper nurse. He said she was over-tired and he left the room. Maud asked for another drink. Mrs Toon offered her the brandy. But Maud raised her hand, saying: 'No, no, no.' She drank some water instead. Mrs Toon then tasted some of the brandy to test its strength. It burned her throat, and she went downstairs to wash out her mouth and eat some bread.

Maud was dying. At about 9.00 am she had a spasm or fit. Green fluid seeped from her mouth. Her face and hands were discoloured and dark; her lips were black. At about noon Mrs Marsh summoned George Chapman. He stood beside the bed, looking down at Maud. She whispered: 'I'm going, George.' He said 'Where?' She murmured: 'Goodbye, George.' And within a little while she died.

Chapman wept. He was wiping his eyes when Dr Stoker arrived, too late to do anything, but now resolved to do something. They conversed on the landing. Dr Stoker said he would like a post-mortem, as he could not account for the cause of Mrs Chapman's death. 'What use is that?' asked Chapman, adding that she had died of exhaustion. 'What caused the exhaustion?' demanded Dr Stoker. Chapman replied: 'Diarrhoea and vomiting.' Dr Stoker persisted: 'What caused the diarrhoea and vomiting?' To which Chapman made no reply.

The following day, Thursday, Dr Stoker carried out a private post-mortem. Before he began, he received a telegram from Dr Grapel, suggesting that he look for arsenic. Grapel had decided on this course of action after hearing from Mrs Marsh that Maud had died. But Dr Stoker was not a specialist and found nothing that might have caused her death. However, he bottled her stomach and other organs and sent them on Friday to Dr Bodmer, a chemist and the public analyst for Bermondsey. Reinsch's test was made and revealed some evidence of antimony, as well as arsenic. He so informed Dr Stoker, who communicated with the police very late that night and wrote to the coroner's office.

At noon on Saturday, 25 October, Detective Inspector George Godley and Detective Sergeant Kemp went to The Crown, and Chapman was detained, pending further enquiries. Although two full days had elapsed since Maud's death, he had destroyed none of the evidence that would help to convict him: bottles containing brandy and water, medicine bottles, medical books, a diary, memorial cards and undertakers' accounts for Bessie Taylor and Mrs Spink, photographs, a will, certificates and other documents, some in Polish, and even the red label that Mr Davidson had stuck on the bottle of tartar-emetic in Hastings. All these things were seized by Godley, including gold and silver coins and notes amounting to £268.

George Chapman was charged with the wilful murder of Maud Marsh at 10.15 that night. He said: 'I am innocent. Can I have bail?' Godley said: 'No.' Earlier, Chapman had said: 'I don't know how she got the poison.' He told Sgt Kemp: 'I wouldn't hurt her for the world. I've had a lot of trouble with my barmaids. But I took a great fancy to this one. There was some jealousy lately. She said to me: "I've not had a baby yet. If I don't soon have one, you won't have me with you long."'

It was not until 30 October that Dr Stevenson, a Home Office analyst and expert in poisons, made a thorough examination of the body and established that Maud Marsh had been poisoned by antimony.

He later told the court: 'I found traces of arsenic in a small quantity, and I formed the opinion that death had not resulted from it. Arsenic is sometimes found in antimony when it is impure. I came to the conclusion that death was caused by poisoning with antimony in a soluble form – tartar-emetic, or metallic antimony.' 7.24 grains of antimony, representing 20.12 grains of tartar-emetic, were found in Maud Marsh. A dose of 15 grains would have been enough, he thought, to kill her. But a very large amount of what she had been given would have been quickly ejected or purged. He said:

> Vomiting and purging make people waste away. It produces gastro-enteritis, and they also appear to die from failure of the heart. Antimony depresses the circulation and quickens the pulse . . . The effect of the poison itself generally takes a considerable time before it causes death . . . The symptoms are great depression, profuse perspiration, followed by nausea and vomiting. Purging is set up with pain in the abdomen, and usually after a time there is a burning or metallic sensation in the throat and stomach; there is a great thirst. Spasms are quite common, and patients fall sometimes into a comatose state. They are generally very pallid, and sometimes get quite jaundiced and dark under the eyes, and thin and worn.

Dr Stevenson also carried out post-mortems on the bodies of Bessie Taylor and Mrs Spink, who were exhumed, respectively, on 22 November at Lymm, and at Leytonstone on 9 December. Both bodies were remarkably well preserved – a side effect of the antimony that had destroyed them. 3.83 grains were found in Mrs Spink (much would have disappeared after five years underground) and 29.12 grains in Bessie Taylor. Stevenson concluded that she had been given a large dose of antimony not long before her death.

On Monday, 27 October 1902, George Chapman appeared before the magistrates at Southwark Police Court; the coroner's inquest was opened the following day. On 31 December he was charged in the name of Severin Klosowski with the wilful murders of Mrs Spink and Bessie Taylor. 'By what means?' he asked. 'Stabbing, shooting, or what? Who is this other fellow? I don't know the other fellow.' He never acknowledged that he and Klosowski were one and the same.

There were four sittings of the coroner's inquest, the last on 18 December. Police Court proceedings progressed simultaneously, taking place on 14 separate days until 11 February, and so setting a record for the number of appearances by a prisoner before being committed for trial.

This began in Court No. 11 at the Central Criminal Court, soon to be demolished, on Monday, 16 March 1903. The trial lasted four days. The judge was Mr Justice Grantham, an imperious figure, with a resonant voice, whose preconceived ideas about a prisoner's guilt tended not to be concealed. The chief prosecutor was the Solicitor-General, Sir Edward Carson, KC, MP, who had prosecuted Oscar Wilde. He was assisted by Charles Mathews and Archibald Bodkin, both later knighted and successive Directors of Public Prosecution. Mr Bodkin had led for the prosecution when

Chapman appeared at the Police Court. The defence was led by Mr George Elliott, assisted by Arthur Hutton. Mr Elliott tried to prevent the prosecution citing and examining the murders of Bessie Taylor and Mrs Spink – they were separate indictments. He was overruled by the judge. Chapman, who seemed overawed and nervous, pleaded 'Not guilty, sir', thrice. The all-male jury were then instructed to try him for the murder of Maud Marsh. Forty-three witnesses were called by the prosecution; the defence called none.

Both closing speeches lasted less than 15 minutes, the defence arguing, while Chapman wept, that as he was 'a hated alien', the jury might be prejudiced against him.

Summing up, as if in continuation of Sir Edward Carson's closing words, the judge remarked that the case was unique from medical, chemical, legal and criminal points of view. 'It is the first time,' he said, 'in which the antecedents of the prisoner have been investigated in the way in which they have been on the present occasion, and on which it has been found possible, as well as legal, to bring forward evidence of two other cases in which persons have died at the hands of someone . . . and, as it is suggested, by the prisoner at the bar.' He went on to speak scornfully of the apparent stupidity and incompetence of most of the doctors involved. 'It is a very sad thing,' he said, 'that a person who has up to now occupied only the position of a hairdresser, has been able to defy the doctors . . . to baffle the surgeons for five or six long years.'

The jury were out for a mere ten minutes, returning an inevitable verdict of 'Guilty'. Chapman seemed numb with terror, as Mr Justice Grantham, having donned the black cap, pronounced sentence, saying at the start: 'Severin Klosowski – for I decline to call you by the English name you have assumed – the only satisfactory feature in the case we have just completed is that I am able to address you as a foreigner, and not as an Englishman.'

An appeal addressed to the Home Secretary was rejected (there was then no Court of Criminal Appeal).

In prison Chapman was morose and restless. He refused to see anyone except a Catholic priest – not even his first and real Polish wife – and still maintained he was an American, George Chapman. In one of several letters that he wrote he said: 'One thing whod I wish is this to be Remembered as I am an American orphend of good family and I left my foster father, against his wish, and I took to erning my own living at age of ten.' He also wrote:

> Believe me, be careful in your life of dangers of other enimis whom are unnow to you. As you see . . . I was unjustly criticised and falsly Represented. Also you can see I am not Believed. Therefore you see where there is Justice. They can take my life, but they cannot kil my soul . . . As to crime I am innocent . . . Believe me I am werry grievously sorry but it could not be help now . . . Shall be now starting preparing for my Deth.

He was hanged at Wandsworth Prison on 7 April 1903. In his will he left items worth £140 to the surviving family of Bessie Taylor, and a ring and some clothes to the parents of Maud Marsh.

Some writers have suggested that George Chapman may have been Jack the Ripper – a supposition based on vague coincidences, misconceptions and a suppression of logic and facts. The Ripper's five murders were committed between August and November 1888 in the Whitechapel area, where Chapman lived and worked after arriving in London, although it is not known exactly when. It is most unlikely, however, that an insecure young foreigner in a strange city, speaking little or no English and ignorant of social customs and local geography, would have suddenly set about a series of horrific murders involving mutilation – and then stopped, and married (Lucy Baderski) the following year. In May 1889, the couple went to America, settling in Jersey City, where a series of alleged Ripper-like murders is said to have happened at about this time. The actual dates and nature of these killings would need to be known before they could begin to be ascribed to Chapman. It is said that they ceased at the beginning of 1892. If so, Chapman had already been back in London for a year. The evidence of Lucy's sister, Mrs Rauch, is very clear. She said at the trial: 'She came back alone in February 1891. Another child was born on 12 May. When the child was about a fortnight old the accused came back from America, and I then left my sister, as they were going to live together.'

Mrs Spink died several years later, in December 1897. Apart from a generic similarity to two of Sir Melville Macnaughten's main suspects (one was a Polish Jew, Kosminski, and the other a Russian doctor), there is nothing, no fact, to make a reasonable connection between Jack the Ripper and Chapman the poisoner, except that Chapman was probably in London in the latter half of 1888. So were thousands of other male foreigners – with a moustache and of medium height, as the Ripper was described in the only likely, though very doubtful, sighting of him. This man was also said to be 34 or 35, to be well dressed and look respectable. Chapman was then a poor hairdresser's assistant, aged 22.

What is most inconceivable is that one man could switch from a quick series of frenzied, sexual slaughters of prostitutes done with a knife and mainly outdoors, to the slow, secretive, indoor poisoning of 'wives' over several months and separated by more than a year. The only characteristic the Ripper and Chapman shared, as with other lady-killers, was their loathing of the opposite sex.

CHAPTER 10

Paul Hefeldt and Jacob Lepidus
The Murder of PC Tyler, 1909

It takes two to make a murder – that is to say, no one would be a murderer if no appropriate victim was present, nor would someone become a victim if someone else was not in a murderous frame of mind. It also sometimes takes two, or three, to murder someone else – usually during a robbery, when a conjunction of character flaws and personality failures erupts in an explosive display of murderous violence, that destroys not only others but also the despairing, doomed relationship that bound the two, or three, together. There must have been something very amiss with the association of Hefeldt and Lepidus, aside from their social alienation. For they destroyed not only the lives of two others, but also themselves one fatal day. They could have surrendered: they did not need to die. But they did.

Poles, Russian and German Jews had had a bad name in London for many years, mainly because they were aliens. All aliens were generally regarded as 'undesirable', whether they were refugees, immigrants or genuine thugs. Their foreign languages, accents, customs and practices were enough to make them seem suspect to the average Londoner, especially if they were of the lower orders, impoverished and young. Deprived usually signified depraved, dangerous and bad.

Russians were a comparative rarity, and Russia a dark enigma, where amidst thick snow, wolves and bears, a debauched, corrupt and cruel aristocracy, headed by the Czar, was believed to control and crush legions of starving serfs. In between were a few mad revolutionaries, soldiers and students, seeking to overthrow the status quo with bullets and bombs.

Clearly those Russians who came to London, to the East End or to any of the city's sprawling Edwardian suburbs, would not be of the Czarist or peasant class. They were more likely to be of the dangerous, revolutionary kind – anarchists! And so the London papers, who in five years' time would be hailing Russian soldiers engaged in the First World War as 'our gallant allies', were as hyperbolic about Hefeldt and Lepidus, branding them as anarchists and revolutionaries and what they did as 'The Tottenham Outrage – an amazing series of outrages, singularly rare if not entirely without parallel in a civilised country'.

What happened *was* amazing, particularly the amount of bullets that were fired, not only by the villains, but also by the public and the police, who also exhibited an amazing amount of mad bravery, matching that of the villains they chased. Amazing also was the variety of vehicles used.

Not much is known about Paul Hefeldt and Jacob Lepidus, except that they were in their mid-twenties, Russian, and out of work. *The Times* would say later that both came from Riga in Latvia and that they were engaged in conveying revolutionary literature, which was printed in England, to Russia by sea. They belonged to something called the Lettish League. Lepidus had a brother, according to *The Times*, who was a member of one of the 'Terrorist' societies in Paris and had died when a bomb he was carrying exploded. The police said that Jacob Lepidus had worked for a while at a furniture factory in Tottenham, owned by Messrs Lebus & Co. Hefeldt, they said, had been employed at Mr Schnurmann's rubber factory, also in Tottenham, but only for a few days. Perhaps there was a row. Perhaps he was dismissed. But on the morning of Saturday, 23 January 1909 he and Lepidus went to the office of Schnurmann's factory in Chestnut Road to take a kind of revenge.

The day before, there had been a private memorial service at the Frogmore Mausoleum, Windsor, commemorating the eighth anniversary of the death of Queen Victoria and the accession of Edward VII. It was attended by the 67-year-old King and his family. At Horse Guards Parade in London a 41-gun salute was fired. Asquith was the Liberal Prime Minister, and although most theatres were still presenting pantomimes like *Dick Whittington* and *Red Riding Hood*, *The Gondoliers* was on at the Savoy, *The Merry Widow* at Daly's, *Our Miss Gibbs* at the Gaiety, and at Covent Garden audiences were enjoying Wagner's *The Ring*.

It was dull and overcast that Saturday morning, and there was a cold north-easterly wind. Hefeldt had a mask, probably just a scarf, in case he was recognised by any of Mr Schnurmann's workers. He and Lepidus tried to look unobtrusive as they loitered outside the factory office, waiting for the return of the motor-car that had been sent, as usual, to the London and South Western Bank in South Hackney to collect the employees' weekly wages. It had no guard – only the 17-year-old youth who made the collection and the driver of the car. No one apparently expected that the object of the bank expedition, a canvas bag containing £80 worth of gold, silver and bronze coins in brown paper bags, would become the objective of a daring daylight robbery. For the rubber factory was just off Tottenham High Road, which was busy with Saturday shoppers – Bruce Grove Station was a few hundred yards away. More importantly, Tottenham police station was immediately opposite the factory. Who would dare to carry out a robbery at such a time and in such a place?

The two who dared did so because they had guns – a Browning and a Hauser, with enough bullets, about 100 each, to start a war. Because of this the two Russians must have thought they would have little difficulty in making their escape. The police, after all, carried no firearms, only their 'little sticks', their truncheons. All the robbers had to do was threaten, or shoot, anyone who got in their way. None the less, they seem not to have worked out any plan of escape. There was no getaway vehicle, or car – neither could drive, and cars were still a novelty. It seems they expected to melt away in the crowd. They were simply not prepared, nor was anyone else in the vicinity, for what happened so suddenly, and so thrillingly, next.

It began at 10.30 am, according to the police, and an hour earlier, according to Mr Schnurmann, who was on the look-out for the arrival of his workers' wages – he may have been at the factory door. He was probably rather anxious about the two men 'who had been hanging about all the morning'. Mr Paul, a partner, was not far away.

At last the car, driven by Joseph Wilson, aged 29, arrived, and Albert Keyworth, aged 17, got out, carrying the canvas bag full of cash, and stepped across the pavement to the office door.

What followed is best told in a report headed *Murders, Attempted Murders, Shooting and Arrest of the Murderers* and written two weeks later, which was submitted to the Commissioner, Sir Edward Henry, by Superintendent Jenkins of N Division, Stoke Newington. His report, edited, amended and put together with other eyewitness accounts and statements, now tells the story of the next three extraordinary hours.

Supt Jenkins: Two men of foreign type stood at the entrance of the premises, one at each side. Lepidus seized the boy and the bag and shot at him, but inflicted no injury. There was a momentary struggle. They both fell, but the man got up with the money.
Mr Schnurmann: He was taking a bag of money from the car to the office when two men who had been hanging about all morning made a dash for the messenger. One of the men was wearing a mask, which made it difficult to identify him. They wrenched the bag from the boy, when another man came to the boy's rescue.
Supt Jenkins: The chauffeur, Wilson, went promptly to the boy's assistance. He grasped Lepidus by the throat. Both fell and struggled desperately. Hefeldt shot at the chauffeur repeatedly – his overcoat was riddled with bullets and a slanting shot passed through every garment, including his under vest, in the region of the stomach. Lepidus released himself and discharged his revolver at the chauffeur. In a miraculous and unaccountable way he escaped injury. The chauffeur cried loudly for help, and a man named George Smith, a gas stoker, went and tripped Lepidus and threw him – the bag of money falling upon the pavement. Whilst struggling with Lepidus, Smith was shot in the chest by Hefeldt. Lepidus released himself and took the money, at the same moment discharging his revolver at Smith, whose escape from death was equally remarkable. The assailants then ran off towards Tottenham marshes, proceeding by way of Chestnut Road, Scales Road, and Mitchley Road.

The revolver shots were heard by the police at the Tottenham Police Station situated immediately opposite the rubber factory. PCs Tyler and Newman, who were on reserve duty, ran out. The chauffeur rapidly explained the position of things, and with the latter PC [Newman] got into the car and followed. PC Tyler pursued on foot.

PCs Bond and Fraser, hearing the alarm, jumped through the open boot-room window of the station into Chestnut Rd, followed by other officers, who were aroused from sleep and who hastily put on some clothing and ran out by the front entrance and took up the chase.

Mr Schnurmann: I jumped into the car and several policemen got in with me. We made off after the men. After chasing them for about 200 yards we gained on them rapidly. But one of the robbers turned and fired at the front of the car. The first shot passed through the glass windscreen, hit the body of the car, and grazed the neck of the motor driver. Another shot entered the radiator and disabled the car. The police then took up the chase on foot, and at this point I gave up the pursuit.

Supt Jenkins: PC Newman received a graze on the cheek and a small wound on the lobe of his right ear. A crowd of persons joined in the chase. Among them was Ralph Joscelyn, aged 10, a schoolboy. He was mortally wounded by a bullet wound in the right breast. He was conveyed to Tottenham Hospital, where he was found to be dead. He was subsequently identified by his mother.

After these incidents, the murderers proceeded rapidly in a northeasterly direction to the Dust Destructor, situated on the marshes. Constables Tyler and Newman [who had left the car] crossed in a northerly direction, with a view of heading them off. When opposite the Dust Destructor, PC Tyler was approaching them from the marshland and called upon them to surrender. But the man Hefeldt stood and took deliberate aim and shot him in the head. Constable Newman remained with his fallen comrade. When Sub-Divisional Inspector Large arrived, Tyler was carried into a house nearby. An ambulance was sent for, and he was conveyed with all speed to Tottenham Hospital, and five minutes after admission he died.

The chase, which had now become most desperate, was continued with splendid determination. The murderers proceeded over the footbridge spanning the Great Eastern Railway, then continued in a north-easterly direction to the west bank of the River Lea. They then went north beside the river to Chalk Bridge, which spans the river just beyond the Rifle Butts, and thence onto the Millstream Bridge, where they held the crowd at bay for a considerable time.

Mr Paul: We followed them all the way to the banks of the Lea. After having gone some distance we saw several men on the other side of the river with guns. We shouted to them to try and shoot the robbers, and they fired. But the shots did not carry far enough to take effect. All the way along, people were trying to stop the desperados. But the two men were firing indiscriminately at all who ventured to arrest their progress. We followed till we got to Chingford Rd, where the tramways run.

Supt Jenkins: It was at the Millstream Bridge that PC Nicod went a short distance ahead of the crowd, and knelt down upon the bank with a view of shooting the murderers. But the revolver which he had, a private one, was found to be defective. Before he could beat a retreat, both miscreants fired upon him, and both shots took effect. He was wounded in the calf of his left leg and thigh. Just previously, a lad named

Cyril Burgess was wounded by a bullet fired by one of the men, in the inner side of the right ankle.

The murderers then passed on along a footway on the south side of Banbury Reservoir, and thence northwards through a narrow pathway towards Higham Hill. Sidney Slater, aged 30, a horsekeeper, out of work, rather recklessly followed the men into this pathway and they fired six or seven shots at him. He was hit in the left thigh and disabled. First aid was rendered by the police.

Frederick Easter, aged 27, a single man [and bricklayer], of 1 Billet Rd, had also joined in the chase. In Folly Lane, the murderers turned again and fired upon their pursuers, and Easter was shot. He was also hit in the left thigh, the bullet passing through the fleshy part of his leg.

They now crossed by the base of Higham Hill through some allotments and entered a field where there was a gipsy encampment. In the same reckless way the miscreants fired among the gipsies, fortunately without causing any hurt. They now entered the premises of Salisbury Hall Farm and took temporary shelter behind a haystack. From either side of it they continuously fired upon the pursuers, who were fully exposed to the deadly fire, many saving themselves by lying down flat on the ground. It was during this severe encounter that William Roker, aged 32, a labourer, married, was very seriously injured, being shot in both legs. He was promptly attended to and conveyed to the Walthamstow Cottage Hospital, where he now lies in a critical condition.

The murderers now passed through the farmyard to the Chingford Rd. Without a moment's hesitation they commandeered an electric tram car [Car No. 9] en route southwards to the Bakers Arms publichouse, Lea Bridge Rd. The driver [Joseph Slow] and the conductor [Charles Wyatt] were held up at the point of a gun.

Joseph Slow: We were journeying in the direction of Lea Bridge Rd when I saw a crowd of excited people rushing across Salisbury Farm. I did not know what the matter was, but when we reached a spot near the Crooked Billet I heard cries of 'Stop!' – 'Murder!' I immediately pulled up, and looking round saw a man at the back of the car covering the conductor and myself with a revolver. There was a crowd behind and many of them had guns and were firing in the direction of the car. Several bullets whistled past my head, and it seemed to me that death was inevitable. Had I remained at my post I felt that I should be a dead man in a few seconds. I therefore scrambled up the steps onto the top of the car. I crouched down and was not aware of what was going on below.

Charles Wyatt: Suddenly a man who had jumped over a hedge or ditch rushed onto the platform. In his hand he held a revolver, and he was calling to another man who was about 50 yards up the road. The second man also carried a revolver, and as he ran he turned and fired at the crowd who were in pursuit. The first man was apparently a foreigner, about 5 feet 9 inches in height, and was dressed in a dark suit and wore a cap. He was about 27. As he jumped on the car he shouted 'Stop!' and pointed the revolver at my head. I then saw the driver hurriedly leave his place and rush to the top of the car. Then the bullets commenced flying all around us. Some of the pursuing crowd took cover behind the hedges and fired repeatedly with their guns. The man who had cried at me to stop, motioned to me to drive on.

There were three passengers on board, an elderly gentleman [Edward Loveday, a glass merchant, aged 64] and a woman with her child. The elderly man said excitedly that he would get out. But the desperado, placing the revolver close to my temple, said in a determined voice: 'I ask you to drive on!' I said at first I could not. But he looked so determined and held the pistol so near to my face, that I moved along to the front of the car. By this time the second man had come up and jumped onto the back of the car. He still continued to fire his revolver at the crowd.

I started the car and commenced to drive slowly. All this time bullets were striking and whizzing past the car. The woman passenger and the child crouched down, and it is a marvel how they escaped, as several of the bullets crashed through the windows and splintered the interior of the car with glass. I felt that every instant I should be struck. The man who had first boarded the car held the revolver so close to my cheek that I could feel the warm glow of the barrel. At times he would turn the revolver to the side and fire at some passing object which he thought was a pursuer . . . I was apprehensive whether the driver above would do anything that would involve danger to myself. He could, if so minded, have placed his weight upon the trolley bar, cut the circuit, and by so doing brought the car to a standstill. I was sure that had that been done, the ruffian would have come to the conclusion that I had intentionally stopped the car and would have shot me dead. I had, however, to slow down at a loop [at the Victory public-house, St John's Road] to let another car pass. The woman and child scrambled out and apparently escaped unhurt.

Near here, an advertising cart came towards us from behind. It contained, in addition to the driver, a man, who I believe was a policeman, armed with a gun, and another man. These were in pursuit. But before they could come up with us, the man on the back platform of the car brought the pony to earth with a shot from his revolver, and all three occupants of the cart were hurled into the road.

Supt Jenkins: PC Hawkings was following the murderers in an advertisement cart. He was armed with a gun but did not use it. One of the murderers shot the pony, causing it to fall, and Hawkings and the men with him were thrown out. Bullets had passed through the leg and seat of his trousers. He was grazed over the left eye and leg.

Charles Wyatt: There was no lack of ammunition. I thought that surely the time would come when the men would have exhausted their store. But no sooner were the chambers of the revolvers emptied than they dipped their hands into their pockets and brought forward a fresh supply . . . All this time the crowd was in hot pursuit, and scores of bullets flew by me. It staggers me to think how I escaped being hit.

I now thought it best to continue the journey [to Kite's Corner] as quickly as I could, in the hope that on reaching a busy thoroughfare the men might be overpowered. Then another thought struck me. As we approached a turn in the road, I said to the man who still held his revolver to my head: 'You had better get off here, as there's a police station just around the bend.' The man answered gruffly: 'There is not!' I then said: 'All right – we'll go on.' On reaching Kite's Corner, or just before that, the elderly man in the car, who was very excited, came towards me as if to make a plucky attempt to seize my assailant. The latter, however, was too quick for him. In an instant he fired his revolver, and the old man was struck, I believe, in the neck . . .

At Kite's Corner I saw a milk-cart standing at the kerb and the man who drove it coming towards a gate. He was about to climb the gate when the man at the back of the car shot at him. The two assailants then dashed off the tramcar together and, making for the cart, jumped into it, and lashing at the horse disappeared down Kenilworth Avenue, in the direction of Forest Rd.

Supt Jenkins: George Conyard [the milkman], aged 19, who was inside a shop, seeing the horse being driven off, rushed out to stop it. But he was immediately shot down, the bullet passing through his right arm and chest.

Charles Wyatt: My driver then came down from the top of the car, and we drove as fast as we could to the Bell, thinking we might intercept the desperados. But they were too quick for us. When we examined the tramcar we found that it was riddled with bullets. Never have I had such an exciting time in my life before.

Supt Jenkins: They drove down Kenilworth Avenue to Forest Rd. Here they were overtaken by a horse and van driven by Thomas White, greengrocer. [Another version is that the milk-cart the robbers were driving overturned and they then seized White's van.] One of the men pointed a revolver at White's head and he jumped off his seat. The men took possession of the van and drove rapidly [along Forest Road, eastwards] to Wood St. Meanwhile, PC Adams had commandeered a motor car and followed, blowing his whistle.

Fred Williams: I was driving a car, LN 1662, belonging to my employers Ferdinand and Edward Reiss, along Forest Rd at 11.30 am, and when near the Bell public-house I heard police whistles blow and I looked round and saw a crowd and policemen following. Two policemen [one of whom was PC William Shakespeare] got into the car, and told me to follow two men in a van. I did so. When the policemen got in the car, some of the crowd climbed up behind and bent both wings of the hind wheels.

Supt Jenkins: PC Adams attracted the attention of PS Jowitt and PC Francis, on duty at Hagger Bridge. These officers made an attempt to stop the van, and one of the murderers fired at them. The bullet passed between them and broke the glass panel of the side door of a greengrocer's at 849 Forest Rd. But the action of the officers diverted the miscreants' course, and they turned into Kingsley Rd, before driving across wasteland [northwards] to Fulbourne Rd.

Thomas Brown: I heard my son Thomas calling out: 'Dad! Come quick!' I saw him running up Kingsley Rd, and then a PC named Adams [whose vehicle must have been disabled or abandoned] running up Forest Rd. He said: 'Don't go too near! They've got shooters!' I still kept running down Kingsley Rd, and then I saw two men in a van, the one driving whilst the other was at the tailboard with a revolver in each hand, and suddenly he fired at me, the bullet whizzing past my right temple. [He] again fired at me, and this time the bullet passed through the cloth of the right leg of my trousers. I still continued in the chase, following the murderers up Fulbourne Rd. They were still firing at random at their pursuers.

Fred Williams: When we caught them up in Fulbourne Rd they fired upon us with revolvers. I eased up to keep out of range and they went on. I kept about 30 yards behind.

Thomas Brown: They then turned to the left up Brookscroft Rd, still firing, until they reached Beresford Rd. After this they turned into Wadham Rd. Then I went around into Chingford Rd. Here I met a PC who was doing point duty. I said: 'Come with me quick! The murderers are up there!' He and another PC came running along with me, and then we saw a motorcar [driven by Mr North] that was in pursuit. Into this we all got, also a gentleman who happened to arrive with a breech-loading gun. We proceeded along Wadham Rd as quickly as possible, and whilst on our way were firing at our assailants. Soon the gentleman in possession of the breech-loading gun left the car and let me have the use of the gun and some cartridges. I fired at our assailants in Wadham Rd, and the tallest of the two murderers, who held a revolver in each hand, was keeping up a furious fire on us all the time. Soon they were in Winchester Rd, Highams Park. Here Mr North and myself fired on the two men in the van.

Supt Jenkins: Through this part of their route, Lepidus was driving. Hefeldt possessed both revolvers and kept up a continuous fire upon the pursuers. In Winchester Rd they abandoned the van and ran to the River Ching.

Fred Williams: They jumped out of the van near a level-crossing.

Thomas Brown: I noticed the tallest of the two hand his mate one of the two weapons he had been using, and then they made off for a fence that was close by.

Supt Jenkins: They clambered down the narrow bank of the river. Lepidus succeeded in climbing the fence that bounds it. Hefeldt attempted to do so and failed.

Thomas Brown: Here it was that Mr North and myself fired at the tallest of the two. He fell this side of the fence.

Supt Jenkins: He turned round and saw that his position was hopeless. He cried out to Lepidus: 'Go on! Save yourself! I've only got two left!'

He sank upon the ground, and shot himself through the head. He was seized by the police, disarmed, and taken as soon as possible to Tottenham Hospital in a van requisitioned on the spot.

Thomas Brown: One of the PCs picked up the revolver, which had been used by the assassin. I asked the PC, 747, for the revolver. We then continued to chase the murderer who was now alone. He made his way across to a place called Beech Hall Estate. Here they were erecting some houses, and more shots were fired by the assailant, and a plasterer, by name F. Mortimer, was shot in the right breast.

Supt Jenkins: Lepidus was hotly pursued by PC Zeithing, and was within a few yards of him when he turned and fired three shots at him, one of which passed over his left shoulder, and entered the chest of Frederick Mortimer [a master plasterer], aged 38, and came out at the back of him. This man had just thrown a brick at Lepidus. The PC had a very narrow escape, as one or more of the bullets passed through the lapels of his greatcoat.

Thomas Brown: Then he ran across Oak Hill, through the hedge, around the back of the Oak public-house towards some cottages. I then reloaded the gun I had with me. Then I saw our assailant creeping behind a hedge with his revolver in his left hand, and he saw me taking aim at him. Then he made for one of the cottages nearby and admitted himself by the back door.

Supt Jenkins: Lepidus had run across Hale End Rd into a field at the rear of Oak Cottage, Hale End, occupied by Charles Rolstone, a coal porter. He sought shelter in this small house, consisting of four rooms and a lean-to. He first ran to the front room where, judging from the amount of soot which was found lying in the room, he had made an attempt to climb into the chimney. I may say that before entering the kitchen he had peered through a small window in the door of the lean-to. His face was covered with blood, no doubt caused by the small shot from the fowling-pieces of men who had shot at him when he was crossing the fields in the earlier part of the chase. Mrs Rolstone saw him, screamed, and ran out of the place [by the back door], crying: 'Oh, my children!'

Lepidus then shut and bolted that door, also the front door. Charles Schaffer, a baker, who had chased these men throughout, went to the door of the lean-to, and with the assistance of PC Dewhurst burst it open. Both passed into the kitchen and brought the children [a baby and a little boy] out safely.

After failing in his attempt to hide in the parlour chimney, Lepidus went upstairs into the front bedroom. He gave a stealthy look through the window, which was seen by his pursuers. They had now arrived in large numbers and some of them were armed. They at once poured a volley in his direction, shattering most of the contents of the room.

Thomas Brown: I saw him at one of the bedroom windows. Then I fired at him, the shots piercing some of the windows. Then Detective Dixon came through the house and said: 'Don't fire any more, for God's sake! There are three or four of us inside now!'

Supt Jenkins: At this juncture PC Dixon of the CID, PC Eagles and PC Cater rendered good service. [PC Dixon had cycled over from Edmonton.] PC Eagles obtained a ladder from an adjoining premises and placed it against the back bedroom window. He obtained a loaded gun from a bystander, climbed the ladder, opened the window and looked in. PC Dixon had sent a dog up into this room, which Eagles encouraged to go under the bed. He turned and saw Lepidus with the door of the front bedroom ajar, pointing a revolver at him. Finding that his gun was unworkable, through a safety catch which he did not understand, he rapidly descended the ladder. He changed the weapon for a police revolver which PC Dixon had. The three officers then climbed this very narrow staircase, Eagles being in front, Dixon in the centre, and Cater behind. It was perfectly clear that if the miscreant secured the first shot, these men would have been seriously hurt or killed. Eagles fired twice and later once through the panel of the bedroom door.

Thomas Brown: I entered the house and heard Dixon shout up the stairs to the assailant to surrender. But no answer came. PC Eagles fired up the stairs at the door, and soon all was quiet for some seconds. Suddenly a loud report rang out, I then followed Dixon and PC Eagles [up the stairs]. I then saw a man lying on a bed, bleeding from a wound in the right temple, and a revolver lying on the bed by his side.

Supt Jenkins: Eagles asserts that Lepidus opened the door slightly and presented his revolver at him. But in the fearful excitement of the moment, the PC could have been mistaken. Evidence has since proved that a police shot did not despatch this man. He shot himself. Upon police entering the room, Lepidus was found upon a small bed in the corner in the throes of death. Immediately afterwards he expired. The body was carried down into the yard ... It was then conveyed in a police ambulance to the Walthamstow Mortuary, Queens Rd ...

I drove to the scene with my groom and a PC in plain clothes armed with a revolver and ammunition, taking a direct course to Woodford, that being the last place where I heard the murderers were making for. When I reached the Napier Arms public-house, Woodford, I was informed by police scouts of the death of Lepidus at the cottage nearby and the arrest of Hefeldt. I proceeded there and took general charge.

Upon Lepidus there were found two paper bank bags, one of which contained £5 in silver, the other being empty ...

This extraordinary manhunt was carried out over a course extending about six miles. It would be impossible for me to speak too highly of the splendid conduct of the police of N and J Divisions. In response to my call to duty they were most prompt, and in action cool, tactful, and fearless. The conduct of the public engaged was equally praiseworthy and brave.

Paul Hefeldt died in hospital nearly three weeks later. He and Lepidus, apart from killing PC Tyler and 10-year-old Ralph Joscelyn, shot and wounded 18 other people. In addition to the eleven civilians and policemen mentioned above, six others were injured. They were: William Devine, aged 13, shot in the right leg; George Harwood, 26, wounded in the right hand at the railway bridge; George Rawson, aged 40, wounded in the right wrist at the Mill-stream Bridge; Joseph Ayley, aged 30, wounded in the left knee while tending PC Tyler; George Cousins, aged 29, shot in the left shoulder; and William Edwards, aged 28, shot in the left elbow 'near where PC Tyler fell'. Only four, however, remained in hospital more than a week: George Conyard, the milkman; Edward Loveday, one of the passengers on the tram; Frederick Easter, bricklayer; and Frederick Mortimer, master plasterer. All recovered in due course.

Four policemen were injured through other causes: PC Forde sprained his left thigh; PC Wadden cut his right thumb; PC Brown cut his left hand; and PC Bond 'contracted a chill through taking up the chase partly clothed'.

Another kind of reckoning also resulted. Thirty-two civilians put in various claims for compensation arising out of injuries, damages and distress caused during the chase.

Fred Williams asked for £23 2s 9d for damage to his employers' car. A Mr Rowntree wanted 3/9 for repairs to his bicycle borrowed by PC Hawkings. Thomas Brown asked for 12/6 for damage to his trousers caused by a bullet. G. White, greengrocer, wanted £2 10s 'for loss sustained through having to rest his pony for four days in consequence of the treatment which he alleges it received on the 23rd'. His assistant, Thomas White, was driving the cart when it was seized by Hefeldt and Lepidus. William Roker, a plasterer's labourer and local pugilist, who was shot in both legs and had a wife and three young children to support, put in an unspecified claim. As did someone on behalf of George Dawkins, aged 41, a cart-driver, who 'was terrified by the shooting . . . and has not been right in the head since'.

The most niggardly claim came from Mr F. Thorogood, of Oak Villa, Thackeray Avenue, Tottenham, into whose house PC Tyler was carried after being shot. Thorogood asked for £1 10s – for the damage done to three pieces of carpet, a table cover and an overcoat 'by the blood which came from the officer's wound'.

Six civilians and several policemen received financial rewards for their bravery. The civilians, all married men, were: George Cousins, a labourer; George Smith, who struggled with Lepidus outside Mr Schnurmann's factory; the chauffeur, Joseph Wilson; William Roker; Charles Schaffer, who helped to rescue the children from Oak Cottage; and Mr North, a greengrocer, whose car took Thomas Brown and others as far as the River Ching.

Brown himself received no reward nor, it seems, did the wages-carrier, Albert Keyworth, or the driver and conductor of Car No. 9. Perhaps their temporary local and national fame was reward enough. The police were given amounts ranging from £5, for senior officers, and £2, for PCs. In addition, several were given medallions recording their bravery, and the salaries of PCs Newman and Zeithing were bumped up at once to the highest rate a PC could receive. Five were promoted to sergeant: PCs Nicod, Dewhurst (who helped rescue the children), Cater, Dixon and Eagles.

On 27 January, the 71-year-old Baron (formerly Sir Francis) Knollys, who had been Edward VII's Private Secretary for 39 years, wrote to the Commissioner, Sir Edward Henry:

> My dear Sir Edward – I have shown your letter both to the King and the Prince of Wales, and His Majesty desires me to thank you for sending him such an interesting and graphic account of the tragedy at Tottenham. It is almost inconceivable that such a thing could have occurred in these days on the very outskirts of London. The King thinks the Police behaved with great gallantry . . . He would likewise ask you to express to the Widow and Family of the unfortunate Constable who was killed, his sincere sympathy with them in their great sorrow.

It is not known what official sympathy or compensation was given to the parents of Ralph Joscelyn for the loss of their 10-year-old son. But PC William Tyler's widow received a substantial sum of money from a special fund – £11 was donated by the Wiltshire police alone.

PC Tyler, aged 30, who had been a policeman for seven years (before that he was in the Royal Artillery), was buried after a grand and very well-attended funeral, with honours, at Abney Park Cemetery. A memorial service followed on 18 July at All Saints' Church, Child's Hill, and in October a stone monument, costing £134, was erected in Abney Park Cemetery, with a memorial brass in the village church.

Mrs Tyler later married PC Williams, who died in 1925.

It is not known where Paul Hefeldt and Jacob Lepidus were buried. Their only memorial is the commemoration in the annals of crime of the fact that they shot and killed a policeman and a boy in Tottenham in 1909 – and that their dramatic pursuit across north-east London is remembered, by some, to this day.

There were other more far-reaching events in England that year; old-age pensions began, and Blériot's flimsy monoplane flew across the English Channel. Elsewhere, the Union of South Africa was formed, and Henry Ford began mass-producing cheap motors – the Model T. In 1910, on 6 May, Edward VII died at Buckingham Palace. His eldest surviving son, George V, aged 45, became King.

In the five years before the First World War, eight policemen were murdered in London, two in 1909. The murder of PC Tyler broke a ten-year period (1898–1908) in which no policemen on duty had been killed. The worst year for the murder of policemen was 1876, when six policemen died.

CHAPTER 11

Ernest Walker

The Murder of Raymond Davis, 1922

1922 was a famous year for murder and murderers. On 5 April, Jack Hewett was arrested for the murder of Mrs Blake. On 13 April, Major Armstrong was sentenced to death at Hereford for the murder of his wife. Raymond Davis was murdered on 22 April. And on 28 April, a pantry boy, Henry Jacoby, was sentenced to death for the murder of Lady White. On 5 May, Ronald True was found guilty of the murder of Gertrude Yates, but insane. On 7 May, Thomas Allaway was charged with the Bournemouth murder of Irene Wilkins. And on 5 October, Freddie Bywaters murdered Mrs Thompson's husband, Percy. He and she were both sentenced to death on 11 December 1922.

Bywaters was 19, Jacoby 18, and Hewett 15 when each of them killed. Walker was 17; his victim was even younger.

After Hewett was sentenced at Oxford in June to be detained during His Majesty's pleasure – he had confessed to the killing of Mrs Blake, licensee of the Crown and Anchor, Gallows Tree Common, near Henley and then retracted his confession – the judge said that it was somewhat appalling to consider the number of crimes committed by young people. There were a great many of them, he said, at the present day – crimes of 'motiveless ferocity'. Like that of Ernest Walker.

Soon after 6.00 pm on Saturday, 22 April, a telephone call was received at the District Messenger office in Sloane Street. The caller requested that a messenger boy should be sent at once to 30 Lowndes Square, Knightsbridge.

This was the handsome London home of Colonel Charles Trotter, CB, and the Hon. Mrs Trotter, daughter of Lord Hamilton of Dalzell. Their country home was at Barton in Buckinghamshire. That weekend they were not at their London residence, possibly because it was the end of the Easter week and they were holidaying or staying elsewhere.

Lowndes Square was very near Sloane Street, and the uniformed messenger boy who was sent there happened that evening to be 14-year-old Raymond Davis, a small bright lad, whose home was far removed in appearance from that of the Trotters, being situated near the clangour of trains, the smoke and whistles, of Clapham Junction Station. Raymond had been with the District Messenger service for about two months, and must have been pleased with his smart new uniform, if nothing else: he wore a pillbox hat and a cape and carried a letter pouch. Thus attired, at about 6.15 on a fine but chilly night, he rang the front door-bell of 30 Lowndes Square.

Some two hours later and 30 miles away, at Tonbridge in Kent, PC Sheepwash was proceeding down a street near the railway station when a tall, slim youth approached him and said: 'I want to go to the police station, as I've done a murder in London.' Although the youth looked very pale and ill, he spoke calmly when questioned by Sheepwash, who was sufficiently impressed by the seriousness of the replies to take the confessed murderer to Tonbridge police station. Besides, he had dried blood on his hands.

There the youth was cautioned, and after giving his name and occupation – Ernest Walker, footman – and his address, he made and signed a statement. He said: 'I do not know what made me do it. I did it between 6.00 and 6.30. I hit him with a piece of iron bar. I have felt bad since last Wednesday, and I lost my mother last January, when the flu was about. I came to Tonbridge as it would give me plenty of time to think and tell the police there. I caught the 7.35 from Charing Cross.'

Although Victoria Station was much nearer Lowndes Square than Charing Cross, Walker's home was at Stanford, near Folkestone in Kent, and trains from Charing Cross to Folkestone stopped at Tonbridge. Perhaps Walker thought of going home, then changed his mind.

At about 9.30 pm the Tonbridge police telephoned Gerald Road police station in Belgravia, and in due course DI Hedley and DS Steel visited the scene of the alleged crime. After knocking and ringing to no avail – No. 30 seemed unoccupied – the policemen forced open the area door.

In the basement pantry they saw blood on the floor by a chair. Streaks of blood then led them to a closed door. There was, however, a key in the lock, and on opening the door they were met with a rush of gas. Taking whatever precautions they could to protect themselves and to avoid a gas explosion, they entered the room, and discovered the body of a messenger boy under a table. He was lying face down; he was fully dressed, and his hat and head had been dealt a heavy blow. Near him was a gas radiator; and on the blood-stained floor was an iron bar enclosed in an umbrella-case cover, and a length of rope with a noose. Around the boy's neck was a bloody teacloth, knotted at the back. He was still alive.

He was soon identified and was taken to nearby St George's Hospital. There, briefly regaining consciousness, he managed to say that a tall man had invited him to come inside and wait for a letter. He then remembered waking up in a gas-filled room with a gag in his mouth. He succeeded in removing the gag before passing out again.

The room in which the boy was found was the butler's bedroom. In Walker's bedroom, DI Hedley found several bits of paper covered with a pencilled scrawl, as well as some books, which the coroner would later describe as 'sensational detective trash'.

While Hedley was thus engaged perhaps, at about 10.15 pm, the head housemaid, Clara Miles, returned to Lowndes Square from her Saturday night out.

That afternoon she and the young footman, Ernest Walker, had had tea together in the servants' hall. All the other servants were out or away. He had seemed 'quite all right' to her, and he was not annoyed, he said, at being left alone when she went out. She told him she would be back just after ten. When he remarked that he would like something to read, she had lent him a book by Edward Phillips Oppenheim, one of the most prolific crime and mystery writers of the day.

There was much for Clara Miles to see in London's theatreland that night. George Robey was at the Hippodrome; Harry Lauder at the Princes; and Tom Wallis and Leslie Henson were in a farce called *Tons of Money*. Several plays by Galsworthy and J. M. Barrie were being presented, as was Jerome Kern's *Sally* with George Grossmith and Dorothy Dickson. Other stars to be seen on stage included Matheson Lang, Seymour Hicks, Godfrey Tearle, Owen Nares, Fay Compton and Phyllis Nielson-Terry; while in the few and new picture houses, Charlie Chaplin could be seen in *The Kid* and the Gish sisters in *Orphans of the Storm*.

Just before 6.00 am on Sunday morning, in St George's Hospital, Raymond Davis died. His father, Steve Davis, a railway-carriage cleaner employed by the London, Brighton and South Coast Railway Company, identified the boy's body. Later that day DI Hedley and DI Burton travelled down to Tonbridge, where they told Walker that he was being arrested on a charge of murder. After being cautioned, Walker said: 'Yes, sir. I don't know what made me do it. I don't think I knew what I was doing at the time.'

On the way back to London he began to talk, but was told to say nothing until Gerald Road police station was reached. There, after being cautioned again, he said in a statement: 'I quite understand what that means. But I wish to say that when I hit the boy with the piece of iron, I didn't know what I was doing. I wanted to send a letter to the laundry, and I telephoned for a messenger boy. I had never seen the boy before, and when he came to the house something came over me and I hit him with the iron. I've had a bad headache since last Wednesday. That's all I wish to say.'

On Monday, 24 April, Ernest Albert Walker, aged 17, appeared at Westminster Police Court charged with the wilful murder of Raymond Charles Davis, 14, and was remanded in custody.

At the coroner's inquest, which took place two days later before Mr Ingleby Oddie, the Trotters' butler, James Pallant, was among those who gave evidence. Most of the scrawled notes that Walker had written were addressed to Pallant, and he identified them as being in Walker's handwriting. When questioned by the coroner, Pallant said that the young footman, who had been with the Trotters for 18 months, had spoken about his mother's death in January, and had been very depressed for about a week. So much so, in fact, that Walker, unknown to Pallant, took one of Colonel Trotter's guns and considered shooting himself. 'He was quite a decent young man?' asked the coroner. Pallant said: 'Yes.' 'Morally?' enquired the coroner. 'Exceptionally so, I should say, sir,' Pallant replied.

DI Hedley read out what Walker had written: One note was scrawled on the back of a printed hand-out advertising menswear. It said: 'Mr Pallant. I prepared this in the afternoon. I covered the boy with my [unreadable] then prepared some more effects. Give my best love to Mrs P and R. I have felt queer this week or so, so goodbye all. I am, Ernest. Please let my dad know.' On the small black-edged envelope of a memorial card was written: 'You can have my shirt and bows also collars. My dad is to have the rest. Ernest. I hope Rachael is well.'

Hedley then produced a letter, written in pencil on black-edged note-paper. One wonders whether someone in the Trotters' family had recently died? Or was it paper saved after the funeral of Walker's mother? This letter was headed '30 Lowndes Square, London, SW1' and dated 'The Fatal Day in the afternoon'. It is one of the few accounts of a murder hand-written by the murderer himself.

It said: 'Dear Mr Pallant, I expect you will be surprised to see what I have done. Well, since my mother died I have made up my mind to die also. You know at Barton you said the guncase had been moved you were right it had I had a gun out loaded it made a sling for my foot to pull the trigger then my nerve went and I put it away. The boy here I had for a companion to –'

The coroner here interrupted Hedley's reading of the letter and asked to see it. 'This is curious,' he remarked. 'He's put a dash after the word "to".'

What the dash signified still remains a mystery. Perhaps Davis was to have been a companion in death, and the missing word is 'die'.

Walker then wrote, after the dash:

I rang up the Sloane St office and said Please send a messenger to 30 Lowndes Square and he came to the front door. I asked him to come in and wait, brought him to the pantry and hit him on the head with the coal hammer *so simple* then I tied him up and killed him. *I* killed him *not* the gas, then I sat down and turned the gas *full* on and passed over the border. I am sane as ever I was and only I can not live without my dear mother. I didn't half give it to the damn boy I made him squeak. Give my love to dad and all my friends, I remain yours truly, Ernest.

He then added, most oddly: 'Minnie Shorts clapper drives me nearly mad also the cold water.'

On another piece of black-rimmed notepaper Walker had drawn up a chilling 14-point agenda concerning the murder and his own suicide, which contradicted his original statements to the police ('I didn't know what I was doing' – 'Something came over me').

1 Ring up Sloane Street
2 Wait at front door
3 Invite him in
4 Bring him downstairs

  5 Ask him to sit down
  6 Hit him hard on head tie him up
  8 Keep him tied up
  9 At 10.30 torture
 10 11 pm Prepare for end
 11 Sit down turn it on
 12 Put letter out
 13 Sit down shut windows
 14 Kens 2059

The telephone number was that of the District Messenger service.

It is clear from the agenda that the killing of the messenger boy was planned and not a matter of mad impulse. Whatever was in Walker's fevered mind at the time, he evidently intended to gas himself, and the boy, after keeping his victim tied up and out of sight in the butler's bedroom or in 'the safe' which is where meat, fish and vegetables would have been stored. Mr Pallant, it seems, was away; and Walker had possibly expected to be alone in the house that night. Perhaps his agenda was spoiled by Clara Miles saying she would return just after ten. Perhaps she was lucky not to have been killed herself. At any rate, it seems as if Walker hit the boy too hard and was then put off by all the blood. Perhaps he thought Davis was dead. Untying him from the chair, to which Davis had been bound after being hit by the coal hammer – or by an iron bar used to break up coal – Walker then dragged the boy to the butler's bedroom, where he turned the gas on, but could not persevere with his own destruction. So he wrote his notes to Pallant, put on his cap and left the house.

How sane was Walker? At his trial, which began and ended at the Central Criminal Court before Mr Justice Roche on Wednesday, 21 June, Walker's counsel for the defence, Mr St John Hutchinson, said that there was no motive for the murder, that the letters were those of a madman, and that at the time of the murder the accused was under the influence of an epileptic seizure.

To this end he called a teacher at Walker's old school, who said that the prisoner had shown peculiar traits: he was absent-minded and weak; he wrote poetry and had an aversion to taking part in games. Walker's father also gave evidence, saying that his son had been prone to have fits since he was five, and that his mother had been a nervous and excitable woman, who thought she would have to go to an asylum. It was also proved that a relative had died in an asylum in 1893; that another relative died in another asylum in 1898; that two others were admitted to asylums and a fifth died of brain disease.

None of this proved, however, that Walker was mad, dangerous or liable to kill. Nor did the defence's contention that Walker was epileptic, although a Harley Street physician, Dr Macnamara, was produced to aver that after studying the prisoner's family history and symptoms, he had concluded that Walker was suffering from 'the condition of epileptic automatism or its psychic equivalent' when Davis was killed. This meant that Walker, who in prison had professed to have an imperfect recollection of what had happened – and denied writing the agenda or the letters – was only partially conscious and not fully aware of what he was doing. Nor would he be able to control his actions at that time.

For the prosecution, which was led by Mr Percival Clarke, Dr East, the medical officer at Brixton Prison, declared that he had observed *no* symptoms of epilepsy, although they might not have been manifest when the prisoner was being observed. He also said he had seen no evidence that the accused might, on the day of the murder, have been suffering from mental disease.

Asked by St John Hutchinson, for the defence: 'It is a very mad murder?' East replied: 'It is a very unusual murder.'

The judge urged the jury not to be influenced by recent discussions in the press about the nature of criminal insanity, which had arisen out of the trials, in April and May, of Henry Jacoby and Ronald True. But doubtless influenced by the fact that Jacoby, aged 18, had been hanged on 8 June, they brought in a verdict, after five minutes of chat, of 'Not guilty' – but insane at the time.

Mr Justice Roche directed that Walker be detained during His Majesty's pleasure, and he was removed – as with True and Jack Hewett – to Broadmoor Criminal Lunatic Asylum, later renamed Broadmoor Institution.

It is not known when, if ever, he was released.

On the afternoon of Saturday, 22 April, a few hours before Walker thought of suicide and Davis was killed, another young man committed suicide most publicly, stepping in front of a car in Piccadilly Circus and then shooting himself. His inquest was held on 25 April before Mr Ingleby Oddie. The young man's name was Martin Bateson. He was 22, and had become a drama student after leaving Cambridge with a first-class degree in Natural Science. His father, Professor William Bateson, had been a Cambridge don, and in May would be elected as a trustee of the British Museum.

Martin died through his unrequited love for a girl, who was already engaged to someone else. He visited her home on the morning of his death. She sent him away and wrote him a letter, in which she said: 'Dear Martin – After your extraordinary visit to me this morning, I have decided to write this to you. You must never come here again, as I shall always be "Not at home" and I shall return any letters unopened. I am engaged, and your persistence annoys me so much that I consider it dishonourable. I am sorry.'

The letter must have been delivered by messenger boy, as Martin shot himself that afternoon. He wrote several farewell letters, leaving all his money to the girl, about £1,000 after some debts were paid. In one letter he wrote:

> *She is the loveliest child*
> *And her heart is made of gold*
> *Gold that is undefiled*
> *As it was in the days of old*

He added: '*I hope she will be lucky, she will be happy. She will be blessed, if my dying wish is of any avail.*'

In 1922, T.S. Eliot's poem, The Waste Land, *was published. It begins:* '*April is the cruellest month . . .*'

CHAPTER 12

Florence Ransom

The Murder of Dorothy Fisher, 1940

In 1940 Britain was at war. But it was not until April, when Norway and Denmark were invaded by Germany, that the 'Phoney War' came to an end. On 10 May the Germans overran Holland and Belgium. Chamberlain resigned that day, giving place as Prime Minister to Churchill, who on 13 May was speaking to the Commons of 'blood, toil, tears and sweat' and 'victory at all costs'. On 27 May the evacuation of the British forces from Dunkirk began. By the end of June, Paris and France had fallen, and Britons stood alone, facing 'their finest hour'. Invasion seemed imminent, and a German invasion was indeed planned. The Channel Islands were occupied on 1 July and nine days later the Battle of Britain began, although it was not until August that the full-scale bombing of English airfields in Kent ensued, followed by mass air-raids on London in September. It was during the dark uncertainties of that glorious summer that Mrs Ransom went mad.

Mrs Gibbs was 80, and every Tuesday afternoon she expected her married daughter, Mrs Dorothy Fisher, to come and visit her – whether there was a war on or not. Both women lived in the village of Matfield, about five miles south-east of Tonbridge in Kent. Mrs Fisher and her younger daughter, Freda, resided in a two-bedroom cottage called Crittenden, which the family had used as a weekend retreat before the war; since September it had become their permanent home.

Freda Fisher, aged 20, was, according to the local paper, 'a familiar figure in the village of Matfield, being an exotic type of beauty, of striking appearance in her somewhat Bohemian attire'. Her mother, Mrs Dorothy Fisher, was also somewhat unconventional. With the approval and assistance of her complacent husband, she had recently applied for a permit allowing a male friend, a Dane called Westergart, to live near her in Matfield. Such a permit was needed as the district had been declared a protected area, out of bounds to aliens and others who were not service personnel or indigenous. The application had been turned down.

Mrs Fisher, who was 48, had in fact been amicably living apart from her husband, though in the same house in west London, for several years. He had had a mistress and she her Danish lover, until Fisher moved with his mistress to Oxfordshire and she and her younger daughter, Freda, to Kent. The other daughter, Joan, a repertory actress aged 26, had sailed to India two years previously to marry a doctor there. So Mrs Fisher and Freda were left to face the prospect of invasion in their cottage, attended only by a house-keeper, Miss Saunders, who was 46 and had served the Fishers for eight years.

At 5.00 pm on Tuesday, 9 July, old Mrs Gibbs became impatient. Where was her daughter? She began telephoning Mrs Fisher's house, continuing to do so at frequent intervals until half-past six, when, before the wartime black-out became an inconvenient necessity, she sent John Leury, a carter-cowman and her part-time gardener, to Crittenden cottage, to find out what, if anything, was wrong.

He arrived at the cottage at about 6.45 pm and saw a woman's body, that of Charlotte Saunders, lying on the drive in front of the house. Leury hurried off to inform the local policeman, in the person of a part-time Special and a full-time teacher, Harry Crickmay. He inspected the body and the cottage, which was in a state of some disorder, as if there had been a burglary. All the doors were open, and of the other occupants there was no sign. He sent for further police assistance, waiting at the cottage until several other officers arrived. He later found a yellow woman's bicycle lying by a gate with its handlebars bent, about 50 yards away from the cottage on the road to Ton-bridge.

Assistance in the form of DI Frank Smeed, DS Smith and PC Donald arrived at about 9.15, by which time it was dark, and because of the black-out the officers had to examine the premises and the corpse by flashlight. It seemed at the time as if Charlotte Saunders had died from severe head injuries. She had in fact been shot in the back of the head.

If robbery had been the mainspring of the murderous assault, as indicated by the mess in the lounge and bedrooms, nothing seemed to have been stolen. Although drawers had been pulled open and papers and clothing scattered about, jewellery and money had not been taken, nor apparently any item of value. Two oddities struck both Smeed and Smith: some letters found in a writing bureau in the lounge bore none of the surnames and christian names of the three women known to have lived there, although Freda was men-tioned more than once. And in the kitchen some broken crockery and a tray that lay on the floor, indicated that a *fourth* person had been expected for tea. For among the items, which Smeed pieced together, were *four* cups, saucers and plates.

DI Smeed and the others also searched the three-and-a-half acres of land around the cottage and the outhouses at the rear. There they found a path that led through some undergrowth to an old orchard. In the gateway to the orchard lay the lifeless body of Freda Fisher. A further search revealed that at the other end of the orchard, where the ground rose steeply, lay the corpse of Dorothy Fisher. Both women had been shot in the back. It was PC Donald who found what would be a vital clue: about halfway between the mother and daughter lay a left-hand lady's glove.

At midnight, a medical examination of the three bodies was carried out by the superintendent from the county hospital at nearby Pembury, Dr Grasby. He worked in the light of torches held by policemen and shaded from enemy aircraft by their capes. It was a mild night; the day had been cloudy and warm.

By this time the Kent County Police, based at Maidstone, had summoned the assistance of Scotland Yard.

DCI Peter Beveridge, who that very day had moved from the Flying Squad to the Murder Squad, was having a drink at 11.00 pm with a close friend, Inspector Greeno, when a message about the Matfield murders reached him. Beveridge was a tall, fair-haired, well-dressed man, a disciplinarian and a Scot. In recent years he had supervised raids on illegal gambling dens, on nightclubs and bottle parties. After talking on the telephone to DI Smeed he sent for his favourite sidekick, DS Bert Tansill, a stout and extrovert man, and they drove through blacked-out London to the West London flat of Mr Westergart. There was no point in visiting the scene of the crime until day. Besides, the Dane, Mrs Fisher's lover, was a possible suspect. His shocked reaction to the news of her death was real enough, however, to remove him from the inquiry, especially as his whereabouts that day excluded him from having had the time for a trip to Kent.

Early on the following day, Wednesday, Beveridge and Tansill drove north to the home of another natural suspect – to Carramore Farm at Piddington, an Oxfordshire village between Aylesbury and Bicester. This was where Mrs Fisher's husband lived, although he worked in London. It was his custom to leave the farm at about 8.00 am and drive to Aylesbury, where he caught the 8.43 to Marylebone Station, going from there to his office. He edited a technical magazine, the *Automobile Engineer*. But on this particular morning he was stopped by the police on his way to Aylesbury and invited to return to the farm.

There Beveridge informed Mr Fisher of the death of his wife and daughter. He broke down at the news, and while he recovered, attended by Tansill, Beveridge took the opportunity to examine the house. In the main bedroom he found a woman in one of a pair of beds. On going outside he encountered the foreman, from whom he learned that the woman was 'Mrs Fisher'. She was difficult and dictatorial, according to the foreman. He said that over the past few weeks, the cowman, Fred, had been showing her how to ride a bicycle, as well as how to aim and fire a gun. Beveridge also learned that Fred's surname was Guilford, that his wife, Jessie, was the dairymaid, and that his mother, Mrs Mary Guilford, did the housework at the farm. All three lived in a separate cottage and had been employed by 'Mrs Fisher'.

On returning to Mr Fisher, Beveridge was introduced to his alleged wife. She was a small, slim, over-made-up woman, aged 34, with bright auburn hair, red-painted fingernails and lips, and was dressed in a bright jersey and blue trousers. She turned out to be a friend of Mr Fisher, and was called Mrs Florence Ransom.

Nothing was said to her about the murders at Matfield, and after some comments about the weather and the war, Beveridge and Tansill made their excuses, shook hands with her and left, taking Mr Fisher with them. This was so that he could formally identify the bodies at Matfield and make a statement. But it was a 90-mile drive, traversing wartime London, and Mr

Fisher, who had reason to be deeply uneasy about the murderer's identity, was inclined and willing to talk – about his marriage and his life.

Walter Lawrence Fisher was a dapper, blue-suited businessman, aged 54. Born in London in 1886, he was educated at the Merchant Taylors' School and then at the Guilds' Technical Institute. After being employed by the Standard Motor Company and the Dunlop Rubber Company, he became editor of the *Automobile Engineer* in 1914, a year after his marriage, aged 27, to Dorothy Saunders Pound. She was then 21. The marriage was not a happy one. After the birth of Freda, the Fishers ceased to cohabit, although they continued to live together in a house at Richmond in Surrey. Before long Mrs Fisher met Mr Westergart and he became a frequent visitor to the house. In 1932 the Fishers and their two daughters moved to Rosslyn Road in Twickenham – a year after the cottage at Matfield was bought as a country retreat, where Mr and Mrs Fisher could conduct their separate affairs. There never seems to have been any question of a divorce. Perhaps one or other, or both, were Catholics. At any rate, and with his wife's tacit consent, Mr Fisher was free to indulge in his own lusts and loves, and about 1934 he met a young and exciting widow, Mrs Florence Iris Ouida Ransom.

Her husband, Douglas Ransom, had died in 1930 after five years of marriage. She also became a frequent visitor to the Fishers' family home, and the *ménage à quatre* continued on its loose, liberated way until 1938, when Mr Fisher bought the farm at Piddington. It was a dairy farm, and was managed for a while by a foreman, until, in March 1940, Fisher went to live there with Mrs Ransom (now posing as Mrs Fisher). His real wife and their daughter Freda had already moved into the cottage at Matfield to escape the expected aerial bombardment of London.

At Piddington, Mrs Ransom, acting as secretary/manager, ran the farm, while Mr Fisher commuted every weekday from Aylesbury to London, returning each evening to the farm at about 6.45 pm. About once a fortnight he travelled down to Matfield to see his daughter and his wife, to whom he paid a monthly allowance, and had visited them at the beginning of July, accompanied by Mrs Ransom. The purpose of this visit was to try to assist Mrs Fisher in obtaining a permit for Mr Westergart to come and live at Matfield. All three – the Fishers and Mrs Ransom – drove to Maidstone to see the police. But the application for a permit was refused.

Mr Fisher told Beveridge that although his wife had never visited him at Piddington, his daughter, Freda, had stayed there for a while in June, when Mrs Ransom had given Freda some clothes from her wardrobe. Beveridge also learned that another oddity of the Fisher *ménage* was their liking for nicknames. Mrs Fisher was 'Lizzie' or 'Mrs Kelly'; Mr Fisher was 'Peter'; and Florence Ransom was 'Julie'.

When the police car reached Tonbridge, the widower was left at the police station while Beveridge and Tansill motored out to Matfield. 'Bert,' said Beveridge. 'What do you make of Mrs Ransom?' 'A good-looker but tough,' was Tansill's reply. 'Her eyes are a bit queer. Sort of vacant.'

Newspaper reporters were already at the cottage. First to arrive had been the representative of the *Tonbridge Free Press*, who was also the first to inform many of the villagers about the murders. Even people living in cottages near Crittenden were unaware that something was amiss and none, it seemed, had even heard any shots. The *Free Press* reporter discovered a local butcher who had called at the house, as he did daily, at 9.15 on the morning of the murders when he saw both Mrs Fisher and Miss Saunders. The part-time gardener, John Leury, was also found and questioned by the reporter, who was soon overwhelmed by the arrival of 22 'newshawks' from the national papers. He was proud to reveal later in a *Free Press* exclusive:

> Among the well-known crime reporters who covered the story were Percy Hoskins (author of a number of books on crime), Edwin Tetlow (*Daily Mail*) and Norman Rae (*News of the World*). Just back from the European war-front was O'Dowd Gallagher (*Daily Express* ace war correspondent), who trekked down to cover the murder story at Mat-field after having covered the Abyssinian, Spanish and Chinese wars. Ewart Brooks (*Daily Mirror*) only a few weeks ago obtained a tempor-ary commission to take his own motor-boat out to Dunkirk to assist in the evacuation of the BEF.

Thrilled though he may have been by all these 'aces' and by such an assign-ment, the local reporter was still diligent enough to report on the 'civilian sensation-hunters who flocked to Crittenden on Wednesday'; on the re-sulting police road-blocks; on the police search for the weapon – they dragged nearby ponds; and their checking up on the movement of vagrants in the district, of gypsies and tramps. And he was sufficiently well informed to write in the *Free Press* on Friday: 'The possibility of burglary is not ruled out, though it is not yet definitely established whether anything was stolen from the house . . . Another theory which is being considered by the police is that the murderer may have attempted to stage a fake burglary in order to cover up the real motive for the crimes. It is thought that the disorder in the house may have been caused deliberately.'

Such had been DCI Beveridge's conclusion after viewing the bodies of the three women and the cottage interior. He noted the broken tea things pre-pared for four people. He was told about the lady's bicycle found not far away – it was Mrs Fisher's (Freda had another) – and he took possession of the lady's left-hand glove found in the orchard. A light-brown hogskin glove, almost white, it must, he thought, have been dropped by the killer as she re-loaded her gun – although no cartridges had been found in the orchard or elsewhere.

It seemed to Beveridge that Freda Fisher had been the first to be shot in the back after she and her mother, both wearing gumboots, had been inveigled outside. Or had they gone for a walk? Mrs Fisher was carrying a handbag. Perhaps the gun had been hidden by the orchard gate. Mrs Fisher, fleeing to the other end of the orchard, had evidently been pursued by the killer, who reloaded the gun and fired again. Miss Saunders, hearing the shots, may have gone outside via the kitchen door and, on seeing the killer approaching with a gun, have tried to escape by darting around the cottage to the drive, where she too had been shot. The tea tray in the kitchen may have been deliberately upset by the killer. On the other hand, Charlotte Saunders may have dropped it in her fright, before fleeing from the house.

The letters that DS Smith had found in a desk indicated that there had been some row or disagreement in June and that relations between the female Fishers and Mrs Ransom had become quite strained. In one, dated 7 June, Julie (Mrs Ransom) had written to 'Dear Mrs Kelly' (Mrs Fisher) to say she was sorry that Freda had felt she must return home. She had been a little upset, she wrote, although Freda had told her she had 'enjoyed herself immensely'. Freda, said Julie, was 'very sensitive, sentimental, and touchy'. Four days later Lizzie (Mrs Fisher) wrote to Peter (Mr Fisher) as follows: 'I have received the enclosed peculiar and I think unnecessary letter from Julie, and I am now sending it to you, as I really do not know how to deal with it. It is obvious to me it was written while under some mental strain caused no doubt by business worries and responsibilities to which she refers. Otherwise why all this fuss?'

Three days later Julie (Mrs Ransom) wrote again to Mrs Kelly:

I am sorry that you took the trouble to send my letter to Peter, as he already had a copy . . . I am certainly a little worried, but I could not run this place if I were labouring under any mental strain, as you suggest . . . I very seldom write letters, but when I do they are penned after much thought. I also make copies of them which are filed. I think it much safer to do this as people are so careless with words and facts. I may be extremely dense, but there seems to be some mystery about the whole situation which I am unable to solve, mystery not being a strong point with me unless in a cheap detective story. So I fear I must withdraw and leave her to you, as her father seems as mortified as I.

In a letter to Freda, whom elsewhere Julie called 'Freda, my duck', Julie wrote: 'You will remember your little outburst on the Saturday morning before you departed. Owing to that your Daddy and I had a good talk about you in the evening and it was then we made our decision . . . I can assure you we were fully agreed that you should not come again.'

Whatever Beveridge thought of all this he must have believed that Mr Fisher knew much more than he said. And later that Wednesday some leading questions may well have been asked on the two-hour drive back to Piddington. Earlier, Beveridge had sent for the Yard's fingerprint chief, Superintendent Fred Cherrill, and a top police photographer. He also called in the Home Office pathologist, Sir Bernard Spilsbury. The bodies of the three women had by now been removed to the mortuary in the county hospital at Pembury, where Mr Fisher had been taken to identify them before accompanying Beveridge and Tansill back to Oxfordshire.

However, he did not stay at Carramore Farm that night. And it is possible that he never returned to Piddington, but was dropped off instead in London – which would imply he was too upset to face Mrs Ransom. In fact he did not see her again until 12 July.

What did he say to Beveridge in the car? We do not know. But on returning to Carramore Farm on the night of Monday, 8 July (as he later told the court), he had noticed a tobacco tin with cartridges in it beside Julie's bed. The cartridges were those of a single-barrelled 4.10 shotgun, known as a poacher's gun, which he had bought in Bicester some months ago, at the request of Fred Guilford, and given to him. And in the adjacent bedroom was a canvas bag from which protruded the cleaning rod of a gun.

On the day of the murder, Tuesday, he had returned as usual to the farm at about 6.45: Julie was not in the house. This was very unusual and had never happened before. He ate his dinner, served by the older Mrs Guilford, alone. Julie came in, distressed, at about 8.50 pm with Fred's wife, Jessie, and explained that she had seen a lost cat and chased it and had fallen down and bumped her head. She had then gone, she said, to the Guilfords' cottage to lie down and recover; she lay on Jessie's bed. 'She was crazy and bewildered,' Mrs Guilford would later tell the court, and Mr Fisher would say how restless she was, going to bed that night and getting up and spending half the night awake in the bed beside his.

Was any of this disclosed to Beveridge then, or revealed later? Did Fisher tell the other man, as he later told the court, that Julie had had a miscarriage a few years ago and had been very ill – that she had suffered once from a brainstorm and loss of memory? Did he try to protect her, as the Guilfords did when questioned by Beveridge? With every reason, for Mrs Guilford and her son, Fred, were Mrs Ransom's mother and brother, and Jessie was her sister-in-law.

This was something Fisher could never have told Beveridge, because he was totally unaware of this fact – that Julie's maiden name was really Florence *Guilford*, and that her nearest relations were the trio who had worked at the farm for several months.

Beveridge, on his return to Carramore Farm, eventually became aware who the Guilfords were. But first he talked to Mrs Ransom, asking her what she did and where she was on Tuesday. Her manner and answers were imprecise, although she was definite that she had never left the farm all day. Mrs Guilford, she said, would confirm this. She had recently been to Matfield, but not on Tuesday. We do not know what else Beveridge asked her, and what impression she made on him. But at some point he produced the glove that had been found in the orchard and asked Mrs Ransom to put it on. 'Certainly,' she said. 'But I think it's too small.' Without showing a flicker of concern she donned the glove and waved her hand about, before casually removing the glove and, without a word, returning it to Beveridge. He later told the court: 'It fitted perfectly.'

When he interviewed Mrs Mary Guilford she seemed anxious and uneasy, but agreed that she had seen Mrs Ransom on the farm on Tuesday, although the details were vague. The cowman, Fred Guilford, said that Mrs Ransom had been in the farmhouse scullery at about 8.15 am on the Tuesday, when she gave him a note to give to his mother; she said she was not feeling well and was going back to bed. He admitted he had a 4.10 shotgun, which fired single shots and had to be reloaded every time, but not that it had been missing on the Tuesday. He agreed he had been teaching Mrs Ransom to shoot –

to shoot rabbits, he said. Jessie Guilford had not seen Mrs Ransom on the Tuesday until about 8.45 pm, when she appeared at the Guilfords' cottage complaining of having fallen after chasing a cat. She had then been wearing a red jumper and navy-blue bell-bottomed trousers.

It is not clear how or from whom Beveridge elicited the fact that Mrs Ransom was Mrs Guilford's daughter and the sister of Fred. Perhaps a slip of the tongue, or some family resemblance, led to the disclosure. Most probably the information came from the embittered foreman. It is clear, however, that all the Guilfords had conspired to keep Mr Fisher in ignorance of the true relationship.

Beveridge and Tansill returned to Tonbridge that Wednesday night, to meet up with Sir Bernard Spilsbury, who had dined in a local hotel after conducting the post-mortems in Pembury. He was of the opinion that all three women had been shot at close range, that *six* shots had been fired, one at Charlotte Saunders, two at Mrs Fisher and three at Freda Fisher. His interpretation of this was that the two Fisher women had each been shot once, and as they lay dying the killer had gone back to each woman and fired – twice in Freda's case.

Meanwhile, in Kent, DI Smeed, whose promotion to detective superintendent would come into effect the following week, had with local assistance been making further enquiries, which continued on Thursday and were extended to Oxfordshire and Paddington Station.

Witnesses would later say in court that Mrs Ransom had caught the Wolverhampton to Paddington train at Bicester at 8.56 am on Tuesday, 9 July. At 12.45 Miss Fisher and Miss Saunders were seen on the road near Crittenden and heading towards it: Freda was on a bicycle and Miss Saunders was walking beside her. Mrs Ransom was next spotted by a 14-year-old charcoal-burner, William Smith, who was cycling from Matfield to Tonbridge, at about 3.20 pm. He saw a lady's bicycle lying on the ground with one of its handlebars caught in a gate, and further on he passed a woman walking towards Tonbridge carrying a brown paper parcel about a yard long and four inches wide. She was wearing blue trousers, a fawn overcoat, brown shoes with crêpe soles, and a blue handkerchief around her auburn hair. He saw her again later, at Alders Hill. This time she was running towards Tonbridge. At Alders village a labourer saw her, and then at about 3.45 she asked a baker who was loading his van at the family shop for a lift. She wanted, she said, to get to Tonbridge quickly. As the baker and his father, called Playfoot, were going in that direction, they took the woman with them. On the way she told them that she was meeting some friends in Tonbridge, that her husband was in the Air Force, that her children had been evacuated to Cornwall, and that her mother was very ill. She was carrying a long brown paper parcel, which she held on to all the time. The Playfoots dropped her off in St Mary's Road at about 4.10, near the police station, and at about 4.15 a ticket collector at the railway station was questioned by this same woman about the time of the next train to London. Misunderstanding what he said, she rushed out of the station and told a taxi-driver to take her to Sevenoaks to catch a train. Wondering what was in her long thin parcel, he asked her what train she meant, and as she seemed confused, he sought the advice of the ticket collector, returning to tell her that the next train to London left Tonbridge at 4.25. 'You must have misunderstood me,' said the ticket collector when she went back to him. 'I told you the next best train was the 4.25.'

All these witnesses roughly remembered what Mrs Ransom wore and described her appearance, her manner and her parcel. She was evidently so obsessed about returning home *before* Mr Fisher that she made no attempt at concealment or disguise. Her actions clearly show she was deranged and of unsound mind at that time. But this point was never made by her defence.

Armed with most if not all of this information, DCI Beveridge set off from Tonbridge early on the morning of Friday, 12 July to arrest Mrs Ransom, accompanied by DS Tansill, DI Smeed and Mrs Smeed. The latter's presence was co-opted as no policewoman was available.

On arriving at Carramore Farm they discovered that Mrs Ransom was not there. She had caught a train from Aylesbury to London, where, it was thought, she intended to visit Mr Fisher. The police at New Scotland Yard were warned about this, and on communicating with Fisher at his office they learned that Mrs Ransom had telephoned from London about noon to say that she was very worried: the police had been ransacking the farm. She wanted to meet him at the York Road exit of the Underground station at Waterloo at half-past four.

Jessie Guilford, Fred's wife, would later tell the court that early that morning Mrs Ransom asked her if she would come to Oxford with her to do some shopping. But she changed her mind and they went in a van, driven by he foreman, to Aylesbury after Mrs Ransom said: 'We'll go to London. I want to see my doctor.' On arriving in London the two women went by the Underground to Waterloo, where Mrs Ransom telephoned Mr Fisher and her doctor. They then took a train to Wimbledon, where Mrs Ransom left Jessie Guilford for a few hours. The two women were together again when a call was made to Piddington. Fred answered and spoke to Mrs Ransom, who said agitatedly to Jessie: 'Someone's been to the cottage and taken the gun. I must see a solicitor.'

At about 4.00 pm, Mrs Ransom rang Fisher, telling him to meet her at 5.30 pm at a solicitor's in Warwick Court, off High Holborn and near Gray's Inn.

She and Jessie Guilford got there first, and when the solicitor, Mr Manooch, prevaricated, saying that he could do nothing until he had spoken to Mr Fisher, both women left the building. Fisher then arrived. Jessie Guilford returned *without* Mrs Ransom, who had gone shopping, she said. Then Beveridge and the others appeared. Where was Mrs Ransom? Jessie Guilford said they were supposed to have met at a certain shop in High Holborn. Beveridge went below, fearing that Mrs Ransom might have fled. But there she stood outside a shop.

It was 6.00 pm. As she seemed not to know him, he told her who he was and that he was making enquiries into the deaths of three women at Crittenden. 'Oh, yes,' she said. 'But I must first see my husband. He's in an office around the corner.' A meeting was held between Beveridge, Mrs Ransom, Fisher and Manooch, and she was then taken to New Scotland Yard. There, after being cautioned, she made a statement and was detained.

In this statement she denied being anywhere near Crittenden on 9 July. She said: 'If there is any doubt about me or any suspicion that I was concerned with the death of Freda or the others, I am willing to do whatever is asked of me. I can assure you, however, that I am not concerned, and I do not believe that Mr Fisher is either.'

She also denied that the Guilfords were related to her.

In her shopping-bag was a letter (dated 16 June) from Freda Fisher to Julie, in which Freda thanked her for sending a coat and for her 'nice, long letter'. She wondered why Julie and her father did not want her to stay at the farm any more. She wrote: 'I feel I must have offended you. This I have not meant to do, and I am sorry. You say you are mystified. I am, too, and cannot understand why there has been all this trouble. Mummy thanks you for her letter. With love, Freda.'

On Saturday, 13 July, Mrs Ransom was brought from London to Tonbridge police station, and on Sunday the police scoured the town, looking for eight red-haired or fair-haired women, similar to Mrs Ransom, to take part in an identification parade. They were required to wear dark blue trousers and colourful blouses or jerseys. The parade took place on Monday morning, and several witnesses identified Mrs Ransom as the woman they had seen near Matfield on 9 July.

At 3.00 pm that day, in the presence of DCI Beveridge, Florence Ransom was charged at Tonbridge police station by DI Smeed with the murders of Mrs Fisher, Miss Fisher and Miss Saunders. 'I didn't do it! I didn't do it!' she said. 'How could I? No, no!'

When she was examined later by Dr Grasby, bruises were found on both her legs, consistent with a fall from a bicycle. Dr Grasby and Mr Fisher both gave evidence at the inquest, which was held at 4.00 pm that afternoon in the billiard room at the county hospital. Packed with police officers and the press, it was adjourned after the bodies had been formally identified and the cause of death announced.

Mrs Ransom appeared at Tonbridge Police Court at 10.10 am on Tuesday, 16 July, and was remanded in custody for two weeks. The local reporter from the *Free Press* was there. He wrote:

Assisted into Court, the accused – a red-haired woman of smart appearance, wearing a grey two-piece suit – entered the dock. She was obviously very distressed and in a half-dazed condition. In the dock, accused sat huddled up, with her head against the shoulder of Mrs Millicent Wiffen, wife of the lock-up keeper at Tonbridge Police Station. Mrs Wiffen had one arm around the accused, and once or twice whispered to her.

Afterwards, Mrs Ransom was taken to Holloway Prison in a large black car with its curtains drawn.

The funeral of Mrs Fisher and her daughter was held at Paddock Wood the following morning. There were four mourners: Mr Fisher, Mr Westergart, Mr Rainer, a cousin of Mrs Fisher, and Mrs Johnson, a lifelong friend. The floral tributes were few. A cross of red roses placed on the double grave bore a message from Mrs Gibbs: 'To my darling daughter, who was all the world to me. That love will never fade until we meet again – Mother'. Charlotte Saunders was buried in London. It is possible that she was a poor relation of Mrs Fisher, whose maiden name was Dorothy Saunders Pound.

After another remand, on 30 July, there was a two-day hearing at Tonbridge Police Court before the magistrates on Tuesday, 13 August. Mr G. K. Paling, appearing for the Director of Public Prosecutions, attributed the motive for the murders to Mrs Ransom's jealousy – although this is not particularly evident from the letters. He produced the glove, the letters, the bicycle, and Fred Guilford's gun as exhibits. Of the gun he said: 'If this was the gun used, six cartridges were fired, and at least five times did the assailant have to remove the cartridges and put a fresh one in.'

The police never found any of the spent cartridges, nor the right-hand glove. Mrs Ransom must have disposed of both.

At the hearing, the three Guilfords revealed what lies Mrs Ransom had told them about her whereabouts on the day of the murder and what she had persuaded them to tell the police. Mrs Mary Guilford was overcome by emotion when giving evidence: she broke down and wept and had to be given a glass of water. A statement from a gun expert, Robert Churchill, was read. He testified that the wads and pellets removed from the bodies of the three women could have been fired by a 4.10 shotgun, like that produced in court.

Although Mrs Ransom appeared for trial before Mr Justice Hallett at the Old Bailey on 23 September (by which time the Battle of Britain had been won and Hitler's invasion plans abandoned), the trial was then postponed so that the defence, led by Mr Stuart Horner, could have the accused examined by a neurologist and her medical history ascertained. Mr Horner also explained that he had been briefed only a week before.

Mrs Ransom, he said, had been in several hospitals and had suffered from mental troubles for many years. 'Hysteria and a desire for publicity, or what?' demanded the judge. 'No,' said Mr Horner. 'Lapses of memory which may be due to a basic source.' The judge remarked: 'I do not understand lapses of memory. A person is either sane or insane. I am not aware of any third stage.' Mr Horner said this might well be a case of delusional insanity. 'I don't see what lapse of memory has to do with it,' retorted the judge. 'Insanity is not always continuous insanity,' Mr Horner replied, adding: 'One may be insane tomorrow, but perfectly sane yesterday and today. This woman would be prejudiced in her defence if the trial comes on before the defence has had an opportunity to investigate this question of insanity.'

After further argument, Mr Justice Hallett grudgingly acceded – 'So that no one can be given the least possible chance to say he had not been given every chance.'

The four-day trial began at the Old Bailey on Thursday, 7 November

1940, before Mr Justice Tucker. Mr Horner defended, and the prosecution was led by Mr St John Hutchinson, KC, who had been a leading *defence* counsel until very recently – he defended Ernest Walker in 1922. Mrs Ransom was only charged with the murder of Mrs Dorothy Fisher.

The trial made minor legal history as, on account of German air-raids at night, and for the first time in a murder trial, the jury were allowed to go home each night instead of being locked up in a hotel room. During the day 'spotters' on the top of the building kept an eye out for imminent danger during an alert. The court had a glass roof.

Despite the postponement of the trial, no medical expert or prison doctor was produced by Mr Horner, who could only imply that the defendant was unstable, had lapses of memory and might have been epileptic. He also proposed that if the defendant had planned the killings with so much care, as the prosecution claimed, why did she not prepare a better alibi? And there was not one shred of a motive, he said.

The only witness for the defence was Florence Ransom herself. She seemed fairly calm and positive. Guided by Mr Horner, she said that since the age of 16 or 17 she had suffered from a bad memory and had been in hospital many times. Sometimes she had fainted in the street. Later, she suffered from giddiness and had frequently been a victim of such attacks that summer. She sometimes had two or three of these attacks in a fortnight at the farm, and on one occasion had been found, she said, wandering in a lane. Questioned about 9 July, she said:

> I meant to go to London that day. I was worried about my health and wanted an opinion whether I should see a specialist. I remember standing in a field when I saw the 8.27 train – the train I would have caught . . . I must have stayed there a little time because I then saw the 8.56 pass by. I do not remember what happened afterwards until I went back to bed. The next thing I clearly remember is falling in a field and striking my head.

She said that she and Mrs Fisher and her daughter 'were on very good terms indeed'. Asked to examine the off-white hogskin glove, she denied ever owning such a pair. 'I have had only one pair of hogskin gloves in my life,' she said. 'I still have them.' 'Where?' the judged enquired, and Mrs Ransom held up a hand to show the pair she was carrying. They were passed to him and after comparing them with the single glove, he ordered them to be passed to the jury.

Asked by Mr Hutchinson to put on the single glove, she did so and he remarked: 'It fits all right, doesn't it?' She replied: 'Well, it's not a comfortable fit. It's not big enough.'

When handed the shotgun, Mrs Ransom said: 'I asked my brother for lessons ever since he had the gun. I had tried with Mr Fisher's rifle to shoot some years ago. I wasn't even able to hold the gun properly.' She said she returned the gun to her brother after it had remained overnight in the farmhouse. Mr Hutchinson later pointed out that Mrs Ransom received the gun on 8 July, that the women were shot on 9 July, and that she returned the gun on 10 July.

In reply to a prosecution question she said: 'I have never believed that Mrs Guilford is my mother.'

Mr Justice Tucker asked: 'You say you feel quite confident you did not go to Kent on the ninth?' To which Mrs Ransom replied: 'I feel certain I did not. I cannot possibly imagine I could have gone.'

On Tuesday, 12 November, the jury retired for 47 minutes: the verdict was 'Guilty'. Mrs Ransom drooped and shuddered. 'I am innocent,' she said quietly, when asked.

When the judge pronounced the death sentence she collapsed, moaning, and had to be assisted from the dock.

There was an appeal against the judge's directions to the jury about Mrs Ransom's state of mind. It was heard at the Central Criminal Court on 9 December before the Lord Chief Justice, Lord Caldecote, Mr Justice Humphreys and Mr Justice Hallett. Mrs Ransom was wearing the grey costume, blue blouse and grey hat she had worn during the trial – though the hat, as the *Free Press*'s faithful reporter observed, was 'carelessly worn'. He added: 'Two wardresses sat on either side of her, holding her hands and trying to calm her as she rocked in the seat in the dock. Her cheeks were blanched, her lips were pale.' When her insanity was discussed she waved her hands and swayed from side to side. And when the appeal was dismissed, she was heard to mutter: 'I want to go home. I want to go home.'

On 21 December the death sentence was cancelled and Mrs Ransom was reprieved, following a medical inquiry carried out at the request of the Home Secretary, Herbert Morrison. By this time the worst of the London blitz was over, although on 29 December much of the City was set on fire by incendiary bombs: seven Wren churches and the Guildhall were destroyed.

Mrs Ransom was sent to Broadmoor, where later she took part in some of that institution's in-house plays, acting, it was said of one show, 'with an aplomb that would have startled many experienced actors and actresses'.

She was transferred to Whitchurch Hospital in March 1966 and was discharged from there in January 1967, at the age of 60, having been locked away for over 26 years.

It was in 1940 that Albert Pierrepoint, born on 30 March 1905 at Clayton in Yorkshire, became the chief executioner and carried out his first hanging as such, in Pentonville Prison. Following in the footsteps of his father, Harry, and his Uncle Tom, he had been an assistant executioner since 1931, the year James Ellis died.

Two convicted murderers, James Camb and Donald Thomas, escaped being hanged in the spring of 1948. Camb, a ship's steward, had been sentenced to death in March for the murder of Eileen (Gay) Gibson, a first-class passenger on the liner Durban Castle, *en route from Cape Town to Southampton. Her body, which was never found, was believed to have been pushed through the porthole of Cabin 126. Thomas, a young petty criminal, was sentenced in April for the murder of PC Edgar in North London. The Home Secretary had recently ruled that while the House of Commons debated an experimental five-year suspension of the death penalty, no executions would be carried out. So the sentences on Camb and Thomas were commuted to life imprisonment. But in June that year the 'No Hanging' clause, passed by the Commons by 23 votes, was deleted from the Criminal Justice Bill by the House of Lords – by 181 votes to 28. Camb and Thomas were lucky they killed when they did.*

Camb was released from prison in 1959, Thomas in 1962.

The hanging of convicted murderers continued until 1964.

CHAPTER 13

Ruth Ellis

The Murder of David Blakely, 1955

No women were hanged in Britain for over 12 years between the execution of Charlotte Bryant in Exeter Prison in July 1936 for the murder, by poison, of her husband, Fred, and the execution of a 42-year-old lesbian in January 1949 for the murder, with a hammer, of an elderly eccentric, Mrs Chadwick. The last woman to be hanged in Britain was Ruth Ellis, executed for the murder of her lover in July 1955.

Ruth Ellis was born on 9 October 1926 at Rhyl in North Wales. Her real surname was Hornby. But her father changed his name to Neilson for professional reasons, and it was as Ruth Neilson that his fourth child was baptised.

Her grandfather was a Manchester-based musician, who gave piano lessons and played the organ in the cathedral. Ruth's father, Arthur Neilson, was a cellist. He prospered until the dance bands, the palm court players and cinema musicians became less popular and obsolete. He then had to travel further and further afield to get work. His wife, Bertha, was Belgian and a Catholic. She had had a turbulent childhood. Her mother had died when Bertha was two years old and she had been raised by nuns. At the start of the First World War, she was brought to England as a blanket-clad refugee. She had then gone into service, the only available occupation then for an untrained foreign woman.

She and Arthur had six children, spaced over 20 years: Julian, the eldest, was born about 1919; Muriel, born in 1921, would become 'mother' to the younger siblings; the third child, Granville, contracted a disease diagnosed by the family doctor as sleeping sickness and sea air was recommended. As Arthur occasionally worked on liners sailing out of Liverpool, the family moved to the seaside resort of Rhyl in 1926, when Bertha was pregnant with her fourth child, Ruth. Jackie, the fifth child, was born in Rhyl but died 18 months later. The Neilsons' last child, Elizabeth, was born at the outbreak of the Second World War.

The family lived at 74 West Parade, Rhyl, and when Ruth was five she went to the local infants' school. It seems that Bertha was not a good mother and found it difficult to cope with the family and domestic duties; she would often join Arthur on his travels, leaving the responsibility for the younger children and the household to Muriel, who of necessity learned to care for fair-haired little Ruth and the two older boys, making sure that Ruth was properly washed and dressed and that the glasses she wore for her short-sightedness were clean. It was Muriel who protected Ruth from any bullying at school and from their short-tempered father when he was at home.

In 1933 Arthur Neilson obtained work with a cinema band at Basingstoke in Hampshire and the family moved south. Despite a regular pay-packet, he resented the demeaning nature of this employment and vented his frustrations on his family. This worsened when the cinema sacked the band. But he managed to get a job as a hall porter and telephonist at a local mental hospital. It was the end of his career as a musician and he became even more irascible and morose.

Muriel and Ruth went to Fairfields Girls' School, where Ruth learned very little. Her spelling was never good later in life, and when she spoke she dropped her aitches. A short, skinny girl, with straight fair hair and glasses, she was 'as plain as hell' – as she later described herself. She was also headstrong and impudent, and determined to do as she liked. She took to wandering off on her own, appearing later with no explanations and causing further rows at home. Muriel usually took the brunt of her father's anger and, sometimes, his blows.

Bertha Neilson later said: 'Ruth hated us to be poor. She hated boys too at that time . . . But she always liked clothes, and she would borrow mine and dress up in them. She wasn't like my other children. She was so very ambitious for herself. She used to say: "Mum, I'm going to make something of my life."'

Arthur's uncertain temper cost him his post at the hospital in 1939, as the Second World War began. He then obtained a caretaking job in Reading and the family moved again.

Ruth left school in 1941 – she was 15 in October that year. She had already begun to earn some money by working as a waitress in a café. But what she earned she spent on clothes and make-up. Her body had filled out and she was beginning to be aware of the effect she had on the opposite sex. She stopped wearing her glasses and started collecting boyfriends. She was probably still a virgin, as Bertha's religious upbringing meant she was unable to tell her three daughters even the most basic facts of life.

In the middle of 1941, Arthur Neilson obtained a position as a chauffeur in wartime London, in Southwark. He was provided with a flat, and despite the bombing, Ruth and a girl friend of hers called Mac moved in with him, eager to sample the pleasures and thrills of wartime London, and the men. Arthur did some sampling of his own, and Bertha, paying an unexpected visit to Southwark, found him and Mac together in bed. After that Bertha decided to stay with her husband in Southwark. Muriel joined them. Julian and Granville had joined the Army, and were serving overseas.

Ruth was now bleaching her hair and making the most of her appearance: she was 5′ 2″ and had a 34″ bust. She and Muriel, now 20, worked for a while in a munitions factory. At night they went out to local dance-halls, cafés and clubs. Ruth was determined to have a good time, and Muriel had difficulty remembering all her sister's boyfriends. She herself had fallen in love with a young engineer, a Lithuanian, and was waiting patiently to marry him. She could not understand her teenage sister's feckless ways. Once when she remonstrated with her, Ruth said: 'You may be my older sister – but I'm ten bloody years older than you in experience.' She was afraid of nothing and no one. When the Neilsons' home was wrecked by a bomb-blast, Ruth calmly helped to dig her injured father out of the rubble. Arthur was a sick man after that and he never worked full-time again.

The family were temporarily housed in various lodgings until they were reunited in Camberwell, at 19 Farmers Road. They were there when they heard that Julian had been severely injured. The second son, Granville, was also wounded, and captured by the Germans; he became a prisoner of war. Bertha's last child, Elizabeth, had been born at the beginning of the war, and nights spent in air-raid shelters or in the Underground exacerbated the baby's asthma.

Meanwhile, Ruth had left the munitions factory and went to work as a machine-minder in the OXO factory at Southwark. But every night she was out enjoying herself, making the most of being a vivacious, teenage peroxide blonde. London was teeming with servicemen looking for a good time with girls like her, and she was fêted and desired at various dance-halls, restaurants and clubs. For a few months in the spring of 1942 she was stricken with acute rheumatic fever. But she was soon back on her feet, dancing the night away. She was 'dance mad', according to her mother. She was 16 in October.

Ruth was sometimes asked if she was a professional dancer, model, or actress, and she decided to do something about this by leaving the OXO factory (where the other girls thought she was 'stuck up') and then taking some singing, drama and elocution lessons at Richmond, after which her aitches were pronounced – though they tended to disappear when she was excited or drunk. She survived financially during this period by singing with a band in a club, and when that ended she took up various spare-time jobs, one of which was as a photographer's assistant in the Locarno dance-hall in Streatham.

It was there that she met and fell in love with a French-Canadian soldier called Clare (his surname is unknown). Her parents, and Muriel, liked him, and as he was a Catholic, her mother was pleased. In his late twenties, good-looking and mature, he seemed to have plenty of money, was generous with it, with flowers and gifts, and seemed to dote on Ruth. He proposed to her, and her happiness was hardly shaken when she discovered, soon after Christmas 1943, that she was pregnant. Clare said he would ask his commanding officer for permission to wed straightaway.

But permission was unexpectedly slow in being granted. So Bertha wrote to the CO, on Ruth's behalf, explaining the need for haste. He replied that Clare was already married and had three children back in Canada. Clare assured Ruth that he truly loved her and would get a divorce, so that they could marry. But she was unconvinced. She cried a lot and renounced her dancing days, obtaining a humdrum job as a cashier in a café. Although Clare continued to visit the Neilsons, and Ruth, and made regular payments to her out of his wages, the money stopped after he returned to Canada with his regiment in 1945. A society for unmarried mothers arranged for Ruth to have her baby at a nursing-home in Gilsland, not far from the Scottish border and near Hadrian's Wall. Andrea Clare Neilson was born on 15 September 1944, a few weeks before his mother's 18th birthday.

Ruth told everyone thereafter that the baby's father was an American pilot who had been killed in the war. Although she took Clare's betrayal calmly, with assumed indifference, she felt used and abused. She told the *Woman's Sunday Mirror* later: 'I did not feel that anything could hurt me any more, and I had become emotionally rather cold and spent. Outwardly I was the same.'

When she returned to London, she and the baby stayed for a while with Muriel, who had married her Lithuanian and now had three children of her own. She then moved in with her parents. She needed to earn some money to keep Andy, as the little boy was called, and she was loth to work full-time. So like hundreds of girls in her position, she decided to capitalise on her charms. She answered an advertisement for a camera club requiring a model for 'Nude but artistic poses . . . Evening work only'. She got the job.

The pay was very good (£1 an hour) and she eventually found posing easy and agreeable. Ruth said later: 'At first I felt frightfully embarrassed, but I soon got used to it . . . The men treated me very decently. Often, after work, one or other of them would take me to one of the clubs for a drink.'

At one of these clubs, the Court Club, at 58 Duke Street, she met Morris (Morrie) Conley, who owned four nightclubs in central London. He invited her for a drink at one of them in Mayfair.

This was in 1946, and Morrie Conley was on his way to becoming 'Britain's biggest vice boss' – so-called by the *People* nine years later. He was 44, fat and ugly, but affable, shrewd and rich. He was also a convicted fraudster and well known to the police. His clubs were staffed by young hostesses who were encouraged to make men feel welcome and prostitute themselves. As a result they enjoyed a high standard of living in postwar London, where the black market and ration books still survived, thanks partly to the 'overtime' payments from club members who sought and bought their favours. Such a life, of financial security and good times in glamorous Mayfair, was much desired by Ruth, who was eager to escape from Padfield Road, where her parents now lived. And when Conley offered her a job at £5 a week, plus a commission on all drinks she persuaded customers to buy, she agreed.

Soon after starting work at the Court Club, Ruth was earning more than £20 a week – enough to pay her parents' rent, enough to pay Muriel to look after Andy, enough to buy better clothes and make-up and have her hair more expensively done. At the same time she was mixing with 'society', with the occasional titled person and film star, with broadcasters and sportsmen, and above all with men with money to spend. When the Court Club closed at 11.00 pm (it opened at 3.00 pm) she moved on to another of Morrie's clubs that stayed open until 2.00 am. Afterwards, she could choose with whom and how she spent the night – unless Conley decreed she would spend it with him. She aimed to please and was not averse to group sex, or to sex, if required, with other women. 'Specials' earned more, and Morrie's approbation. Sometimes she and another girl, Vicki Martin (who became the girlfriend of the Maharajah of Cooch Behar and was killed in a car crash early in 1955), would go off with some men for a weekend at a country hotel. But she was still a good Catholic, or not very practical, and soon became pregnant again. This time she went to a private nursing-home for an abortion. She would have two or three more.

Then in the spring of 1950, when she was 23, she met George Ellis, a dental surgeon and an alcoholic, at the Court Club. He was 41 and had been divorced the previous year by his wife, Vera, who was given custody of their two sons. He became obsessed with Ruth and badgered her to go out with him. Finally she agreed.

She said later:

> I thought he was rather pathetic: he told such wild tales. I think he really believed them. He used to spend a lot of money and was always good for champagne . . . One particular night [in June], Vicki, Pat and I were in company with some members and George Ellis walked in. He wanted me to join him, but I didn't want to – he used to frighten me with his wild ravings. Vicki and I had planned to go out that night to a party. George Ellis kept pestering me. So to get rid of him, I said: 'You go to the Hollywood and I'll meet you there later.' I had no intention of going there.

But Ellis did, and his face was slashed with a razor when he left the Hollywood with another man's girl. Ruth felt responsible for Ellis's injury and tried to make amends. They went out for dinner at his golf club at Purley Downs, taken there in a chauffeur-driven car – George hired cars and drivers whenever he went out for a drink.

Ruth said later:

> I spent a lot of time in his company. He took me out shopping, bought me lots of expensive things. We ate at the best places – in fact he showered me with everything . . . It was summer holiday time, so we went off to Cornwall. I didn't tell Morrie I was going, so he was rather annoyed. I think we went in July and we came back in September. I don't think Newquay will have forgotten us in a hurry.

Back in London, Ruth moved into Ellis's house at Sanderstead in Surrey, telling people, including George's mother, that they had just returned from their honeymoon. Despite rows centred on Ellis's heavy drinking and spendthrift ways, they were married at Tonbridge Register Office on 8 November 1950.

The following day Ellis entered Warlingham Park Hospital for treatment for his drink problem. This was one of Ruth's conditions, to which he agreed, before she would marry him. Another was that he would sell his practice and house, so that the two of them could start afresh in another town. The proper education of Ruth's son, Andy, who was now six, must also have featured in the arrangement. She did not love Ellis, although she told her sister, Muriel, that this was 'the real thing'. But she was prepared for sacrifices, and toned down her make-up, appearance and dress. For marriage to a well-off, well-educated professional man would give her, apart from some security, a respectable status and, at last, a home of her own. She also expected him to inherit a fortune when his mother died.

Ellis obtained a job, by lying about his recent past and the scar on his cheek, in one of several practices owned by a dentist in Southampton, Ronald Morgan, and occupied the house that went with the job, at Warsash, near Southampton Water. He began work in the New Year – he had already begun drinking again – and within five months he was sacked.

A job in Newquay followed, as did two other drying-out stays at Warlingham Park Hospital. Ruth periodically walked out on her husband, returning to London to lodge with her mother, and the rows, threats and accusations on both sides continued, to which blows were sometimes added. She would throw drink over him and he would hit her. She abused him as 'a drunken old has-been' and he called her 'a bloody bitch from Brixton' – which was where her mother now lived. His dissipation, concerning money and drink, obsessed her less, however, than his imagined infidelity. Once married, and without company when he was at work, she began to suspect him, unreasonably, of having affairs. She knew, from her experience with Clare and the club customers, that married men could not be trusted and easily lied. She began checking up on him, phoning him at work, following him about and visiting him during the day, expecting to catch him in the arms of 'some old bag'. This began at Warsash, and she accused him of having sex with patients and staff – not only there but also at Newquay and Warlingham, where she created a scene, shouting four-letter abuse ('fucking adulterer') at him. She had to be physically restrained and was sedated.

Throughout most of this time she was pregnant. But this failed to impress Ellis or soften his attitude, and a year after their marriage, in November 1951, he tried to obtain a petition for divorce on the grounds of cruelty. The application was refused (they had not been married for three years) and a reconciliation was urged. Ruth would have acceded to this, as in October 1951 she had given birth, with difficulty, to a baby girl, who was called Georgina. Ellis was indifferent. He paid for a layette and undertook to give the mother £4 a week. But he refused to pay for a pram and suggested the baby should be adopted. She returned to Morrie Conley and the only easy way of earning a living she knew. Men, as lovers and husbands, were 'shits', and were only useful as money-machines, to be played for all they could give.

The two children were parked with her parents in South London – they had moved from Brixton to Tooting Bec – and Ruth, now 25, became a hostess once more at Carroll's, which was the new name of the Court Club. It was now open until 3.00 am, and provided a cabaret, dancing and a restaurant. Vicki was still there and now a platinum blonde, as Ruth became from then on. She mocked men and marriage and towns like Warsash – 'In that bloody hick dump you can't even buy a pair of nylons.' But life was pleasant in 1952. Once more she was admired and desired, in control of her men and their money, and of herself. Conley still exacted his pound of flesh, but in return found her a flat in Gilbert Court, Oxford Street (with a Mayfair telephone number), which was owned by his wife. His more superior hostesses were housed therein, paying the rent out of their call-girl activities. Ruth's activities broadened: she dished out cards containing off-key verses and pornographic poses to favoured customers, and advised others on where to purchase specialist rubber, and other, gear.

Early in 1953, she had an ectopic pregnancy (a foetus began growing outside the womb), and was off work for several months. In April, a party was held at Carroll's to celebrate her return. In June the nation celebrated the coronation of Elizabeth II, who was six months older than Ruth Ellis. It was a good summer for Ruth. A regular customer took her on holiday and was so satisfied he gave her a gift of £400. And then the motor-racing gang from the Steering Wheel Club in Brick Street, Mayfair, led by the tall, blond 23-year-old motor-racing champion, Mike Hawthorn (who died in a car crash six years later), chose to spend some of their drinking time at Carroll's. Among them were the two men who would destroy her life two years later – Desmond Cussen and David Blakely.

Desmond Cussen was 33. A director of the family firm, Cussen & Co, who owned several tobacconists in London and South Wales, he had been an RAF bomber pilot during the War, flying Lancasters; after being demobbed, he became an accountant. Unmarried, he lived in a flat in Devonshire Street, London W1, at 20 Goodwood Court. Unprepossessing, short, with a thin moustache, he was unambitious, ordinary and rather shy. He had known David Blakely for about a year, and they shared a common interest in drink, loose women and fast cars – Cussen had a black Ford Zodiac. They were also both strongly influenced (as was George Ellis) by their mothers.

Cussen used to tag along with the motor-racing gang, and it was Blakely who brought him to Carroll's in September 1953. Ruth met him before she met Blakely: she was 26, and Blakely, who had recently celebrated his birthday, in June, was 24.

Ruth said later:

I was at Carroll's Club, as a guest this time, with the motor-racing boys, including Desmond Cussen, whom I had only just met, when in strolled David wearing an old coat and flannel trousers. I did not like his manner from the start. I thought he was too hoity-toity by far. He greeted the other lads in a condescending manner and was offhand in his acceptance of the proffered drink. He lounged at the bar with his back to the other girls and started making derogatory remarks, referring to the club as 'a den of vice' and jerking his head towards the hostesses' and saying 'I suppose these are the so-called hostesses' and so on . . . I turned to the other boys and in a plainly audible voice, so that he could hear, I said: 'Who is that pompous little ass?' He turned to me and said: 'I suppose you're another of them?' I said: 'No. As a matter of fact I'm an old has-been.' He finished his drink and said: 'Come on, boys. Let's get out of this sink of iniquity', and lounged out of the bar.

She told another hostess: 'I hope I won't see that little shit again.' She did, the following month.

After her 27th birthday on 9 October, when she threw a lavish party at Carroll's Club (*Cocktails and buffet, at 7 pm*), Morrie Conley asked her to become the manageress of the Little Club, a first-floor drinking-club at 27 Brompton Road, Knightsbridge. She was paid £15 a week and given a weekly £10 allowance for entertainment. A two-room flat above the club went with the job, rent-free. Two rooms above this were occupied by a couple of call-girls unconnected with the Little Club. David Blakely was already a member of the club, and on Ruth's first day in charge, he was the first person she served.

David Moffett Drummond Blakely was a Yorkshireman. He was born in a posh Sheffield nursing-home on 17 June 1929, the youngest son of a well-to-do GP, who already had two sons, Derek and Brian, and a daughter, Maureen. His mother was an Irish woman (her father had been a horse-dealer) with blue eyes and considerable charm. David was largely brought up by a nanny, whom he adored, and was particularly close to his sister.

In February 1934, when David was four, his father was accused of murder and acquitted by a magistrates' court. The case was reported in the *Daily Telegraph*:

> After hearing a speech for the defence, the Sheffield magistrates last night dismissed the charges brought against Dr John Blakely, 49, of the murder of an unemployed waitress, Phyllis Staton, 25, and of supplying a certain drug to the girl, knowing it to be intended for unlawful use. The presiding magistrate said the evidence was so weak that no jury would convict. For the prosecution it was alleged that Dr Blakely had procured a miscarriage in such a way that a post-mortem would not implicate him and that a drug had been used.

It was also alleged that the waitress, who died of acute septicaemia, had been the doctor's mistress for at least 18 months.

Although his patients forgave this lapse, Mrs Blakely never did. Appearances were maintained, but there was constant friction and unspoken animosity until she filed for divorce. It was made absolute on 2 December 1940, when David was eleven years old. Mrs Blakely was granted custody of the four children.

Two months later, on 4 February 1941, she married Humphrey Cook, at Caxton Hall in London. Both were 47. He was a wealthy man, the son of a draper, with a passion for racing-cars. They moved to 4 Culross Street, between Park Lane and Grosvenor Square. It was wartime and the two older boys were serving overseas. Maureen was at school and David went to board at Shrewsbury, a public school in Shropshire. He made little academic or athletic impression, but was a member of the Army Training Corps. He got on well with Humphrey Cook and usually spent his holidays with his mother and stepfather. When he was 18 he was called up for National Service and, being ex-public school and a former member of the ATC, he was commissioned as a second-lieutenant in the Highland Light Infantry. Charming, selfish and weak, he was prone to playing silly pranks, getting drunk, and to boasting about his driving and mechanical skills and his successes with women, those who were attracted by his boyish high spirits and eager brown eyes, his long eyelashes and lithe, lean frame – he was 5' 9". He also had an uncertain temper and a tendency to sulk; he was cowardly when trouble loomed, hiding or creeping away.

After leaving the Army, his stepfather secured a job for him as a management trainee at the Hyde Park Hotel in Knightsbridge, and a mews flat was found for David, his brother Brian and their nanny at 28 Culross Street. David was too lazy and undisciplined to enjoy hotel work, but he liked pandering to and being flattered by older female guests, while maintaining an association with a theatre usherette, a small platinum blonde who tolerated his erratic and unreliable ways. Women wanted to mother him; he is said to have been an indifferent performer in bed.

The hotel soon realised that David was not cut out for his job, but the management was persuaded by his stepfather to keep him on for a while. As his wages were meagre, his mother made him an allowance of £5 a week, and Mr Cook indulged him by paying some of his debts and giving him loans, which were rarely repaid. For his 21st birthday (in June 1950), Cook bought David a sports car, which soon became David's ruling passion. A good mechanic, he enjoyed tinkering with cars and driving at speed, and accompanied by his stepfather, he attended various racing events in England, entering a few junior races, which he never won. Along the way he chummed up with other racing enthusiasts and he used to meet up with them at the Steering Wheel Club, which was not far from the Hyde Park Hotel. It was frequented by racing-drivers like Mike Hawthorn, Pete Collins, Stirling Moss and Cliff Davis. Even nearer the hotel, virtually across the road, was the Little Club, whither David would vanish during working hours and at nights, for a quick drink and some fun.

David's playboy lifestyle blossomed when his father died, aged 67, in February 1952 and left each of his children £7,000. His hotel work by now ran a very poor third to his racing and social life, and the management fired him in October after a row. Mr Cook may have felt partly responsible for David's failure. At any rate he sent his wife and stepson off on a world cruise. He also bought a small mansion, the Old Park, at Penn in Buckinghamshire, and a separate flat was provided there for his stepson and the nanny. Near Penn was a small engineering company, Silicon Pistons, and David went to work there on returning to England, although he spent most of his time in London. In Penn he started having an affair with a married woman. In London, in 1953, he had an affair with an American model older than him. At the same time he was courting the young, buxom daughter of a Huddersfield businessman, with a wealthy marriage in view.

Ruth Ellis became the manageress of the Little Club in October 1953, and it was in that month that she met David for the second time. Despite her professed poor opinion of him and despite his forthcoming engagement to the

Huddersfield manufacturer's daughter (it was announced in _The Times_ on 11 November), she and David began sleeping together two weeks after that second meeting. Later she said that he was playing 'hard to get' and that this was part of his attraction. He began staying overnight in her flat above the Little Club, returning at weekends to Penn. He was overwhelmed by her sexual energy and invention. He told a friend she was 'one of the finest fucks in town'.

In February 1954, she had an abortion, for which she paid. Although David, on being told that he was the father, said that he would marry her, she was still married to George Ellis, and David was still engaged to the Yorkshire girl. Ruth said later, in court: 'He offered to marry me, and he said it seemed unnecessary for me to get rid of the child. But I did not want to take advantage of him . . . I was not really in love with him at the time, and it was quite unnecessary [for him] to marry me.' She called him 'Loverboy'.

Cliff Davis (who was older than David), later said of him and those days:

Racing-drivers weren't like they are today. You lived at a very fast rate – booze, women, everything . . . I used to see a lot of David. If we'd go to Silverstone we'd have piss-ups in the local pub either before or after a meeting. He liked his booze – he was really a drinker . . . He wasn't averse to poncing, and he certainly ponced on Ruth. His parents kept him and he had a flat just off Park Lane paid for by them. He was looked after by a housekeeper, and his stepfather paid her wages too. I went round there several times, though he didn't encourage too many visitors there. I don't know if he even took the odd bird there . . . [Ruth] was a typical club-girl . . . very attractive [but] too clued-up, too sharp. She'd been around . . . On the other hand, as a woman – not to marry but to fuck – she was wonderful. What an artist! She started at your toes and she went all the way up with her tongue. She gave you the full treatment. Terrific. I only had the experience once . . . But apart from sex, I rated her very highly as a person. As far as I know she didn't take money for sex and she always bought her round. She never ponced on anyone, not once. She had a bloody sight more principles than Blakely – David was a good-looking, well-educated, supercilious shit. But you couldn't help but like him. She was nuts about him . . . I knew he used to knock her around, because she used to have black eyes and bruises. Theirs was the absolute in love–hate relationships. They should never have been allowed to meet . . . They wanted each other, and the feeling was so diabolically strong that it excluded everybody else. If she was talking to somebody else or flirting with someone, it immediately sparked off an explosion. And of course she felt the same over his behaviour. They were usually very good. For after all David was basically a gentleman, although he could be a bastard on occasion . . . The real villain of the piece was Desmond Cusson. He was a snaky bastard. I knew him well. He was well dressed and suave. Not so young as most of us. Thick-set chap. He always used to sit in the corner of the Steering Wheel and drink on his own. That is, until he could get somebody to talk to him . . . Cussen was madly in love with Ruth and hated Blakely's guts.

Both Ruth and David liked to display each other to selected friends: he took her to race-meetings; she took him to the theatre and to other clubs. She began, as he did, to neglect her work, although she still performed as a call-girl during the day while Andy, who was nine, was at school. He and two-year-old Georgina were living with their mother in the flat above the Little Club. The bruises Ruth exhibited may have come from clients as well as David. She said in court: 'He was violent on occasions. It was always because of jealousy in the bar. He only used to hit me with his fists and his hands. But I bruise very easily, and I was full of bruises on many occasions.'

She was also jealous – in particular of Carole Findlater, whom David had met in 1951. Carole was then 27, and her husband, Anthony Seaton Findlater (ex-public school, a mechanic and car-engine designer, known as Ant), was 29. They had met during the war, when Carole Sonin (who was Jewish) was in the WAAF and Ant was an RAF sergeant. An interest in cars brought David and Ant together, as well as David's interest in Carole, who was dark, dynamic and wore flashy glasses. She was also a journalist, a sub-editor on *Woman* magazine. David tried to persuade her to leave Ant and live with him. He failed, but the three of them remained friends. And in April 1954, when Carole was eight months' pregnant, David employed Ant, at £10 a week, to assist him on the design and development of a new HRG sports car, which they called the Emperor.

It was in that month, at Ant's birthday party, that Carole and Ruth first met.

The party was held in the Findlaters' second-floor flat at 29 Tanza Road in Hampstead, on the southern edge of Parliament Hill. Carole later said of Ruth: 'She was wearing a black dress with a plunging neckline. She had a small bust, small wrists and ankles – the effect was shrimp-like. She said "Hallo" to me in a tiny voice . . . and then ignored me for the rest of the evening. She spent all her time talking to every man at the party.' Ruth said: 'Carole behaved like the Mother Superior herself, but I took no notice.'

About this time George Ellis reappeared, visiting the Little Club when he was in London – he was now a schools' dentist in Lancashire. Sometimes, drunk, he slept overnight on a divan in Ruth's flat. He took the infant Georgina north with him to be adopted and lodged a petition for divorce in May, soon after Carole Findlater's baby, Francesca, was born.

By now, David's heavy drinking (double gins) and tantrums were becoming a problem for Ruth. She said later:

I began to think that it was time that the affair ended, because we seemed to be getting too deeply involved. The business at the club was beginning to suffer because of my now frequent absences and the fact that I was being monopolized. Furthermore [Conley] had started charging me a rental for the flat, because he knew that David was living there . . . He had already warned me – he considered it was bad for me and the business.

By now, Ruth was borrowing money from Desmond Cussen, and was puzzled when he apparently expected nothing in return. Spinning tales about her imagined and actual woes, past and present, was a ploy she used to financial and emotional effect. A man-friend said: 'She told me all her troubles . . . I thought I was the only one . . . She used to tell the most awful lies to get money from you.' Deceiving others, and deceiving herself, had become a way of life.

In June 1954, David Blakely took part as a co-driver in the Le Mans 24-hour race and neglected to return to England, although he sent postcards to Ruth, for about three weeks. In his absence she turned to Desmond Cussen, her 'alternative lover' as he was later called in court. She invited him to sleep with her in her flat. Cussen said later: 'I was terribly fond of her at the time.' Ruth told the court: 'I thought that Desmond would tell David we had been intimate, and I thought that would finish it' – the affair with David. Instead, it was renewed with vigour.

The main reason for this was that David's engagement was annulled in the Hyde Park Hotel, on the night of a belated birthday party Ruth gave for him in the Little Club. His fiancée probably broke it off, having heard about Ruth or some other affair. David told Ruth: 'I've got news for you. You're not going to lose me after all.' He asked her to marry him, going down on his knees and in tears. She said later: 'From then on he paid even more attention to me. He literally adored me . . . Now he was free, I'm afraid I allowed myself to become very attached to him . . . I put him on the highest of pedestals. He could do nothing wrong.'

She decided not to prolong her divorce proceedings by claiming maintenance or by defending herself in any way. She was going to marry David, with or without the Cooks' approval, and thus resolved, she became more possessive, and as obsessed as she had been with George Ellis about money, marital security, and other woman, although she humoured and indulged David at first.

In August 1954 he went to a motor-racing event in Holland to drive an MG for a friend. The car broke down. This failure, and the expense of the outing, added to David's financial problems: the money his father had left him was much depleted; the development of the Emperor, which was moved from an Islington garage to one in Culross Street, was time-consuming and costly; and Humphrey Cook, when asked for a loan, had refused to comply. David was still being paid by Silicon Pistons, paying no rent for his accommodation, and receiving his mother's allowance. But his heavy drinking and socialising – he spent his lunch-breaks in a pub at Penn and his nights in the Little Club – drained his income away. He neglected to pay Ant Findlater – who obtained a job selling second-hand cars – and began to rely on Ruth supplying him with free drinks and free meals at the club. She also provided him with cigarettes and clothes. If they went out to eat in a restaurant, she gave him the money to pay the bill. She insisted on accompanying him to other clubs, to keep an eye on him, and again she paid for their drinks. In effect, she was keeping him and in so doing was imperilling her job. There were rows, and sometimes blows: each was jealous of the other's interests and friends. She later told the court: 'He was violent on occasions. It was always because of jealousy in the bar. At the end of the evening when we got upstairs, it was always about the things he had been seeing me do, and so on and so forth.'

All these payments caused Ruth, who was also a heavy drinker (gin or Pernod) and smoker, additional money problems. These were alleviated in part when Desmond Cussen was persuaded to pay the fees for a boarding-school, to which Andy went in September 1954 when he was 10. Spoilt by his mother and undisciplined, he was frequently left on his own and used to roam around London. Now he was out of her way.

In October, Ruth Ellis was 28, and she gave a party at the club. On David's flowery birthday card, sent from Penn, was scrawled: 'Sorry I couldn't find a better card, but in this part of the world they are unheard of. Happy birthday Darling, BE GOOD. Love, David.' He promised to take her to Paris for a weekend, but lied his way out of it. Neither of them trusted the other. Ruth had found out about his affair with Carole Findlater and made him promise never to go to Tanza Road. If he did, he would be banned from the club.

Meanwhile, takings at the Little Club fell, and David's constant drunken, boorish and aggressive presence at the club was making both him and Ruth unpopular. Morrie Conley's business sense overcame his lustful need of her and in December he gave her the sack. Desmond Cussen had already asked her to live with him at Goodwood Court, and now she did, acquiring rent-free accommodation in a prestigious address and an agreeable home for Andy during his Christmas holiday.

David was incensed. But as he had often urged her to leave the Little Club and stop being a hostess, so that she would be more socially acceptable to his family, he could not be angry for long – especially as, she assured him, she would not be sleeping with Desmond and would sleep with him at some hotel as often as he wished. She added that if he really loved her, he would provide her with a home of her own. But of course he had insufficient funds.

None the less, he generally paid the £3 for their nights out at the Rodney Hotel in Kensington, where they stayed on 15 nights between 17 December 1954 and 5 February 1955, posing as Mr and Mrs Blakely. They would arrive about midnight and have breakfast in their room before coming downstairs mid-morning for a drink at the bar. David began taking amyl nitrate capsules to delay his ejaculations, the better to satisfy Ruth. She was becoming very demanding, as well as possessive. A serious crisis loomed.

David told Cliff Davis: 'I'd give anything to get away from her. But as soon as we meet it all starts again.' Ruth told Davis: 'I've given him some money, and he's out somewhere, probably poking the arse off some tart.'

Desmond Cussen had to be satisfied with Ruth's explanations for her absences that she was staying overnight with friends, or visiting them or her little girl, Georgina, up north.

That Christmas, Ruth gave identical silver cigarette-cases to Desmond and David, and as David was in Penn on the 25th, she invited a few friends to Goodwood Court for a party, one being the barmaid at the Little Club, Jackie Dyer. Cussen was at an official function and was unable to be there before 9.00 pm. Ruth put Andy to bed and, leaving a note on the door saying where she was, went off with her friends to a club for a pre-party drink.

Meanwhile, David was becoming bored at Penn; he had been drinking most of the afternoon, and as he also had a present to give to Andy, a toy revolver, decided to call on Ruth. David drove south to London and was vexed when he read the note on the door. He telephoned the club, asked to speak to Ruth and then upbraided her for leaving Andy alone in the flat. Ruth returned with her friends to Goodwood Court and everyone entered Cussen's flat, where a row at once ensued between David and Ruth. He railed at her for being a tart and sleeping with Cussen because he paid Andy's school fees. Ruth swore at him and said that Cussen didn't ponce on her as David did. She accused him of 'poking' Carole Findlater and David retaliated by telling her to go to the Findlaters' home in Hampstead and ask Carole herself. Still furious, they both went out and got into David's car, oblivious of Cussen, who had just arrived and saw them drive away. Cussen also saw how drunk David was and he followed them in his car to Tanza Road. The Findlaters were away in Bournemouth. But David had a key to the flat and went inside with Ruth. Cussen hung about and then drove back to Goodwood Court to play the party host.

At Tanza Road, Ruth and David continued arguing and accusing each other until, exhausted, they went to bed. When she returned to Goodwood Court the following morning, she told Cussen that David had threatened to kill himself if she left him on his own. So she had stayed. Cussen chose to accept her story and others that she later told.

Another night she persuaded Cussen to driver her to Penn to see whether David, as he claimed, would leave his local, The Crown, and go straight home. She watched as David drove to the house of his married woman-friend, whose husband was often away, not leaving until 9.00 am. She then accused David of being unfaithful and tried to stage a confrontation with the other woman. This David succeeded in avoiding, by lying and by taking Ruth to Penn, to The Crown, when he knew the other woman, with whom he used to play darts, would not be there. On another occasion, David happened to see his mother going into The Crown, and insisted on Ruth remaining in the car while he went inside. He brought their drinks out to the car.

On Boxing Day, the day after the Christmas-party row, David, worn out with argument, drink and sex, drove the Emperor in its first race, at Brands Hatch. He came second.

In January 1955, Ruth took some lessons in French, so that she could seem more cultured when she went with David to Le Mans later that year. Her tutor, Mrs Harris (a male tutor was banned by David), remarked on the fact that Ruth was tense, chain-smoked and could not concentrate. Drinks were constantly offered, and Mrs Harris was told that Ruth and her fiancé were continually attending or giving parties or dinners. She had in fact attended the surgery of Dr Rees, who had tried to cure George Ellis's alcoholism. Rees prescribed tranquillisers, which Ruth took from then on to calm her fevered imaginings. She would threaten to visit David's mother in Penn, as well as the married woman, and tell them all about her affair with David. She threatened to call in some of her underworld friends. She told the court: 'The tables had been turned. I was jealous of him, whereas he, before, had been jealous of me. I had now given up my business – what he had wanted me to do – left all my friends behind, connected with clubs, and things.'

Then, on 14 January, a decree nisi was granted to George Ellis, which meant that marriage to David was possible in three months' time. But the irrational pattern of violent quarrels and passionate reconciliations continued, and several hurtful and emotional scenes were enacted requiring the intervention and support of friends. Cussen was co-opted to chauffeur Ruth in pursuit of David, bent on checking where he was and with whom. Cussen himself was checking on *them*. He spotted them drinking together at certain clubs and knew about their assignations at the Rodney Hotel. However, he said and did nothing about Ruth's lies and her pretence that *he*, not David, was the main man in her life.

The worst fight between Ruth and David, involving black eyes, cuts and bruises, occurred in Desmond's flat on the evening of Sunday, 6 February, after a sustained spree of drink and sex. Each accused the other of infidelity. Desmond was out at the time. Ant Findlater and a friend, Clive Gunnell (in whose garage the Emperor now reposed), were summoned by phone to rescue David, who told them Ruth had tried to knife him. Frightened, he wanted to flee, but was prevented by Ruth, who took his car keys – he never thought to leave by taxi or on foot. He told Ant: 'She won't let me go!' And outside, in Devonshire Street, there were more histrionics as Ruth sat in David's car to prevent him leaving and then lay in the road in front of Ant's car. She later complained to Cussen that David had beaten her up, without saying what she had done to him or why.

That same night she ordered Cussen to drive her around looking for David, and early on Monday morning, she was banging on the door of David's flat at the Old Park in Penn. A confrontation between the three took place later that day outside a pub in Gerrards Cross, when Cussen told David ('You gutless little bastard!') to apologise to Ruth. He did so, and fled after she threatened to tell his mother, and the police. Later, a bouquet of red carnations arrived for her, with a note saying: 'Sorry Darling, I love you, David.' A reconciliation followed and Ruth moved out of Cussen's flat.

She moved from Goodwood Court to a furnished serviced room at 44 Egerton Gardens in South Kensington on 9 February. Ruth paid the rent with money she borrowed from Cussen, having told him she was moving out to save him from further embarrassing scenes. A week later she paid 20 guineas to join a modelling course in March. The money was again borrowed from Cussen but soon repaid, evidently from what she earned from clients.

David, absolved from paying for the Rodney Hotel, now lodged at Egerton Gardens overnight during the week, travelling to and from Penn to work and escaping thither at weekends. There he sought the consoling company of his nanny and the married woman, to whom he confided: 'Ruth is madly in love with me, but I hate her guts.' He was also becoming scared of her. There was another violent row about his (and her) unfaithfulness on 23 February. Bruises on her shoulders had to be disguised by Cussen with make-up a few days later before he could take her to a racing-drivers' dance, with David's permission, at the Hyde Park Hotel. That night she said to Cussen: 'I don't know whether I love him or I'm going mad.'

David was also at this dance, with his mother and Humphrey Cook. Ruth danced with both David and Desmond and told them that her divorce had been made absolute that day – which was a lie. She suggested a toast to her freedom. David refused to drink to this and Ruth became alarmed, thinking that he never meant to marry her.

A week's estrangement followed, during which she began attending the modelling course and demanded that David return his set of keys to Egerton Gardens. This was achieved by Cussen knocking him down outside the Steering Wheel Club and Ruth seizing the keys. But several days after this he was waiting outside 44 Egerton Gardens one night when she returned. She wrote later:

I said: 'What are you doing here?' He said: 'You said if I stopped the affair at Penn, everything would be all right.' I said: 'Have you?' He said: 'Yes.' I believed him. He seemed so genuine and sincere. Later on, he said: 'I've been wanting to come home to you all week. It's been hell. I've missed you so much. I've slept with you so long, I can't sleep without you.' I said: 'That's no excuse for sleeping with somebody else.'

The next day Ruth got Cussen to drive her to Penn at lunchtime. David and the married woman were together in The Crown. Embarrassed, he came over to Ruth, bought her a drink and then left. He said to her later: 'I can't help it if *she* goes into The Crown.'

Ruth now found she was pregnant yet again. This did not endear her to David, who could not be certain the child was his. Nor did it ensure their marriage. When she complained, yet again, about his conduct, he lost his temper. According to her, he hit her face with his fist, grabbed her by the throat and punched her in the stomach. 'Oh God, don't let me do it!' he said (according to her). She choked: 'You're mad – you're stark, raving mad!' He said: 'One of these days I'll kill you!' She said: 'You've done that already.'

She later told the court that a miscarriage followed this scene. She told *Woman's Sunday Mirror*: 'On 28 March, I had an abortion, and I wasn't at all well. David took no interest in my welfare and didn't even bother to inquire if I was all right. I was very hurt indeed about this, and I began to feel a growing contempt for him. The results of my abortion in fact continued until Tuesday 5 April.'

None the less, she would later quote David as saying on Wednesday, 30 March (two days after the abortion): 'I wish we had enough money. We could have kept our little David. I didn't want you to get rid of it . . . No one is ever going to part us. I do love you so much.' And before they left London to race the Emperor at Oulton Park near Chester, Ruth telephoned friends to say matters had improved and that the marriage would soon take place.

Another version of the situation that week is that David was so exasperated by Ruth telephoning him at the garage and pestering him that, in order to get some peace to work on the car with Ant and Clive Gunnell, he agreed to marry her after the race-meeting at Oulton Park.

This took place on Saturday, 2 April. On the Friday, in a practice run in the rain, the car broke down and was withdrawn from competition. Carole Findlater, now woman's editor of the *Daily Mail* (she was writing an article on women's fashion at the meeting), arrived in Chester that night and found that Ant, David, Ruth and Clive were all 'down in the dumps'. David contrived to blame the car's failure on Ruth's nagging and intrusion into his work. 'It's all your fault – you jinxed me!' he said, complaining that he could not afford to get the car repaired. Ruth felt bitter about David borrowing £5 from her to help pay their hotel bill and then paying by cheque. She said later: 'I used to be good company and fun to be with. He had turned me into a surly, miserable woman. I was growing to loathe him . . . He was so much in love with himself.'

She and the others returned to London with the Emperor on the Sunday – a week before David Blakely died.

He and Ruth continued to bicker and battle, publicly and privately, over the next few days. Andy's presence was a strain: it was the Easter holiday and he was sleeping on a camp bed in the same room as David and Ruth, who had a heavy cold. But on Wednesday, 6 April, David was cheerful and optimistic. He talked about getting married and gave Ruth a photograph of himself as a future member of the Bristol team at Le Mans. It was signed: 'To Ruth, with all my love, David'. He also talked about selling the Emperor. When she protested, he said: 'If you can find me £400, I won't need to sell it.'

On Thursday, driven by Cussen, Ruth visited the photographer who had taken the photos for Le Mans to find out whether David had given any to other women. Cussen also checked to see whether David was in The Crown at Penn with the married woman, but he was there on his own. That night, in a cinema, Ruth became annoyed when David talked to her – 'He was telling me he loved me and all kinds of things' – during the film.

At about 10.00 am on Good Friday, 8 April (according to Ruth), David, having spent the night at Egerton Gardens, left in a fairly good mood – 'on the best of terms', she said. He told her he was going to team up with Ant to do some work on the car and that he would be back in the evening at eight and take her out. The Findlaters later said that David arrived at their local, The Magdala in South Hill Park, opposite Hampstead Heath Underground station, complaining about Ruth, saying that she was unstable and violent and he couldn't stand her any longer. 'I want to get away from her,' he said. Ant sympathised and suggested that David spend the Easter weekend with him and Carole at their flat in Tanza Road. He assured David that if Ruth arrived and made a scene, he and Carole would deal with her.

That same Friday morning, Desmond Cussen had collected Ruth and Andy from Egerton Gardens (all week he had driven her to her modelling course) and took them to Goodwood Court for lunch. Afterwards, they went out to a cinema. Then Ruth took Andy home, put him to bed, and prepared herself for David's return. She waited until about 9.30 pm and then telephoned Tanza Road.

The Findlaters' 19-year-old nanny answered and told Ruth that everyone was out and she didn't know where David Blakely was. An hour later, Ruth rang again. Ant answered. Ruth told him she had been waiting for David since half-past seven. Ant admitted that David had been at the flat earlier on, but was not there now. Ruth was not convinced. She said later that she was sure that David *was* at Tanza Road, that the Findlaters would not let him speak to her and were laughing at her behind her back. She kept ringing up. Sometimes Ant would answer and try to placate her; at other times the phone was replaced. Ruth became increasingly frustrated and furious. She tried telephoning Desmond Cussen, but he was out.

Meanwhile, in the Findlaters' flat, David was reacting nervously to the continuing telephone calls. Carole tried to reassure him: she gave him a kiss and told him that if Ruth came after him, she and Ant would protect him and not let her in. Then she took a sleeping pill and went to bed. David was to sleep in the sitting-room on a divan.

Just after midnight Cussen returned to his flat in Goodwood Court. The phone rang – it was Ruth. She asked him to pick her up and drive her to Tanza Road. Cussen did so. David was obviously with the Findlaters as his grey-green Vanguard van was parked outside No. 29. Ruth ran up the steps at the front of the house and rang the street door-bell. She thought she heard a woman giggle. When no one answered, she kept her finger on the bell – 'I just wanted to see David and ask for the keys.'

Inside the house, Ant came down from the second-floor flat to the hall. He listened and was relieved when the ringing stopped and he heard Ruth going down the steps. But she had not abandoned her mission. She went to the nearest telephone box and began ringing the Findlaters' flat from there. Within the flat the receiver was lifted and then replaced. Ruth walked back to the house and rang the door-bell again. There was no response. Now in a fury of rejection and spite – 'rather a nasty mood', she said – she borrowed a rubber torch from Cussen's car and attacked the windows of David's car. She later told the court: 'I knew the Vanguard windows were only stuck in with rubber. So I pushed at one of them, and it came clean out from the rubber. It didn't break, just made a noise. And I did the same with two other windows. I didn't break any – I just pushed them in.'

Ant had seen what she was doing and telephoned the police. He now emerged from the house in pyjamas and dressing-gown and confronted Ruth on the steps. It was about 2.00 am. She demanded to see David, and Ant denied that David was there. He continued to argue with her until a police car arrived. The police officer in charge heard accusation and counter-accusation, vociferously put from Ruth, less so by Ant. Ruth said she had partly paid for the Vanguard, so what she did to the car was nothing to do with the police. Ant insisted that David had no wish to see Ruth or speak to her again. She said: 'I shall stay here all night until he has the guts to show his face.' The policeman viewed the incident as a domestic rumpus. Placatory, he advised Ruth to go home: if she continued to create a disturbance, he would have to charge her with a breach of the peace. He then drove away. But Ruth would not be pacified: she began to shout.

Ant once more rang the police. But Ruth had left the scene by the time the police returned. She walked to the top of Tanza Road, where Cussen had parked, and he drove her back to Egerton Gardens at about 2.45. For over two hours he had sat in his car, making no move to interfere or appease.

Apparently Ruth stayed awake for most of that night, her mind seething with injustice and slighted love. She told herself how much she loved David and how much she had done for him. And how had he repaid her? He had sponged off her and treated her badly, even brutally. Because of him she had lost her job at the Little Club and her security at Goodwood Court. He had promised to marry her, but had failed to do so. He had lied to her, and she was sure he continued to sleep with younger and richer women. She couldn't trust him, and she felt that the Findlaters had pressured him into giving her up.

At about 8.30 on the Saturday morning she rang the Findlaters' flat. The receiver was picked up and replaced. She then got a taxi to Tanza Road and hid in a doorway two houses away from No. 29. She was there for more than an hour. At about ten o'clock Ant Findlater appeared and looked cautiously around. Then he motioned behind him and David emerged. The two men inspected the damaged Vanguard, then got into the car and drove away. Ruth guessed that they would take the car to Clive Gunnell's garage in Rex Place, Mayfair, for the necessary repairs.

She walked to a telephone box and, having waited until she thought they would have reached the garage, she rang its number. Giving a false name she asked for Ant Findlater. When he answered, she thanked him sarcastically for calling the police the previous night. He rang off. She then took a taxi to Goodwood Court and got Cussen to ring the garage on her behalf. Ant recognised his voice and put down the phone. Ruth concluded that by the time Cussen drove her to the garage, Ant and David would probably have left. She heard Cussen telling her that 10-year-old Andy was on his own and would be hungry. She agreed to be driven back to Egerton Gardens, where she gave Andy some lunch. Then they took him to Regent's Park Zoo and left him there, Cussen having given him enough money to enjoy himself and to pay his bus fare home.

At about 2.30 pm, Ruth prevailed on Cussen to drive her north to Hampstead. They saw David's car outside The Magdala pub, but decided to drive on to Tanza Road, intending to confront David there on his return. Some decorators were working on the ground floor of a house opposite No. 29. Ruth went over, and on learning that the flat was up for sale, pretended to be a prospective buyer. From her chair in a front room she could see No. 29, and in due course David and Ant returned from the pub. The nanny was not with them. Ruth made her excuses, left her observation post and moved back to the doorway where she had concealed herself that morning.

Before long she saw David, Ant, Carole, and the fair-haired nanny, who was carrying the baby, leave the house, get into the Vanguard and drive away. Ruth could have spoken to David there, or earlier at the garage, but it seems she was now averse to staging a confrontation and was bent on adding fuel to her feelings of bitter rejection and cold-eyed hate.

She waited for Cussen— he had been driving around looking for her since she had disappeared into the house opposite No. 29. They drove together to The Magdala, but there was no sign of the Vanguard or the others. Cussen persuaded her to return to Egerton Gardens, where Andy, back from the Zoo, was fed and bathed and put to bed.

Ruth had had little sleep for 36 hours, but later that Saturday night she asked Desmond to drive her yet again to Tanza Road. David's car was parked outside No. 29 and a party was now in progress in the second-floor flat. Ruth watched from the road. Someone opened a window and she heard voices and laughter. She said later that she heard David's voice and that when he stopped talking, a woman laughed. She had convinced herself that David was having an affair with the nanny, encouraged by the Findlaters, and her fervid imagination supplied the evidence. When David and Ant emerged from the house at about 9.30 pm with a young, dark-haired woman, she assumed it was the nanny, even though the nanny was fair-haired. At her trial Ruth claimed she heard David say: 'Let me put my arm around you for support'.

She did not see the three again, as she apparently then left Tanza Road to find a toilet. But on her return she again heard giggling and David's voice (the windows were open). Later, at about 12.30, she noticed that the blinds of a front room below the Findlaters' sitting-room were pulled down. She thought this was the nanny's bedroom. Although the party continued above, she could no longer hear David's voice, and imagined that he and the nanny had gone to bed. She told the court: 'I thought David was up to his tricks.' In fact, the nanny's room was at the back of the house.

After about another half an hour of watching and waiting, she let Cussen drive her home, where she spent another sleepless night tormented with jealousy, anguish and hate. When asked in court: 'What state of mind were you in?' she replied: 'I was very, very upset.'

By the morning of Easter Sunday, 10 April, Ruth was emotionally and physically very distressed. She had been on her feet for two days and had probably been drinking heavily and taking drugs. She had also had an abortion less than two weeks before.

At about 9.00 am she dialled the Findlaters' flat. The phone rang for a long time and then Ant answered. Ruth said: 'I hope you are having an enjoyable holiday, because you've ruined mine.' Ant hung up the moment he heard her voice.

In court Ruth was asked how she spent Easter Sunday. She said: 'I have completely forgotten what I did. My son was with us and we amused him in some way . . . About 7.30 I put my son to bed . . . I was very upset, and I had a peculiar idea I wanted to kill him [David].' At some point she took down all her photographs of David and replaced them with some of herself.

Desmond Cussen told the court that he collected Ruth and Andy at about noon and brought them to Goodwood Court, where they all had lunch. He then drove them home at 7.30 pm, and that, he said, was the last he saw of them.

But statements made the day before Ruth Ellis was hanged, corroborated by what she told her friend Jackie Dyer, and others, tell a different story. Ruth's sister, Muriel, who was looking after 10-year-old Andy immediately after Ruth's arrest, claimed she asked him what he had done on Easter Sunday afternoon. According to Muriel, he told her he had seen Uncle Desmond give his mother a revolver, and having oiled it, show her how to use it. And Ruth told a solicitor that after lunch on Sunday, Cussen drove her and Andy first to Hampstead and then to Penn to try to find David. Cussen allegedly stopped the car at Epping Forest (or Gerrards Cross) so that Ruth could walk into some woods and practise firing at a tree. Some of this (not the shooting practice at Gerrards Cross) was confirmed by Andy, who was quoted in the *People* after his mother's death as saying that, on their way back to Egerton Gardens, Ruth Ellis said: 'If I had a gun, I would shoot him.' To which Cussen allegedly replied: 'I've got one – but it's old and rusty and needs oiling.'

Andy was put to bed at about eight o'clock in Egerton Gardens and Ruth then left the flat. According to her, she left with Cussen, who drove her back to Goodwood Court.

The day before her execution she was persuaded by a solicitor, Victor Mishcon, to make a statement, in which she said:

I had been drinking Pernod (I think that is how it is spelt) in Desmond Cussen's flat and Desmond had been drinking too. This was about 8.30 pm. We had been drinking for some time. I had been telling Desmond about Blakely's treatment of me. I was in a terribly depressed state. All I remember is that Desmond gave me a loaded gun. Desmond was jealous of Blakely, as in fact Blakely was of Desmond. I would say they hated each other. I was in such a dazed state that I cannot remember what was said. I rushed out as soon as he gave me the gun . . . I rushed back after a second or two and said: 'Will you drive me to Hampstead?' He did so, and left me at the top of Tanza Road. I had never seen the gun before. The only gun I had ever seen there was a small air pistol used as a game . . .

In 1977 Cussen told a TV reporter:

I did not give Ruth the gun. Nor, on that occasion did I drive her up to Hampstead . . . The statement that Ruth gave isn't true in any way. There was no question of us drinking Pernod together. To the best of my recollection, it was a gin and tonic I poured her and she said: 'I don't feel like drinking. I'd rather have a cup of tea.' And she went off and made one. Besides, the police would have smelled Pernod on her breath if she'd been drinking heavily.

He claimed they spent the day listening to the radio, playing records and entertaining Andy, before taking him and his mother back to Egerton Gardens. Cussen added: 'She was a dreadful liar, you know.'

Ruth told the police after the murder:

> I waited all day [Sunday] for David to phone, but he did not do so. About eight o'clock I put my son, Andrea, to bed. I then took a gun which was given to me three years ago in the Club by a man whose name I do not remember. It was security for money, but I accepted it as a curiosity. I did not know it was loaded when it was given to me. But I knew next morning when I looked at it. When I put the gun in my bag I intended to find David and shoot him. I took a taxi to Tanza Road, and as I arrived, David's car drove away from the Findlaters' address. I dismissed the taxi and walked back down the road to the nearest pub [The Magdala], where I saw David's car outside. I waited . . .

David had gone back to The Magdala with Clive Gunnell. They had already been there, at lunchtime, accompanied by the Findlaters and a female friend of Clive. David had cashed a £5 cheque. That afternoon he and the Findlaters had visited the Easter Fair on Hampstead Heath. There was safety in numbers as far as David was concerned, and he walked about with the Findlaters' little girl on his shoulders. Later on, David drove to Clive's home to collect him and his gramophone and some records. Carole went too, and the three of them stopped at The Magdala for a drink before returning to Ant at Tanza Road. They sat around, smoking and drinking and playing records, until about 9.00 pm, when Carole ran out of cigarettes; the party was also short of beer. She asked David to buy some cigarettes for her at The Magdala and get some more beer. Clive went along to give him a hand. They drove the short distance down the hill in David's Vanguard, and parked outside the pub.

It was dead unlucky for David Blakely that he left No. 29 when he did. And if Carole had not run out of cigarettes he might not have gone out at all. Also, if Ruth had ambushed him outside the house, she might well have missed when she fired at him from further away, and he might more speedily have fled.

In the pub, Clive and David bought some beer, in quart flagons and bottles, and Carole's cigarettes. They stayed for a drink. Outside, Ruth watched and waited. She was carrying a .38 Smith and Wesson revolver, and was wearing a pair of black-rimmed glasses. A customer saw her peer through a stained-glass window of the pub.

It was close on half-past nine when Clive and David drained their glasses, picked up their purchases and came out of the pub. Clive walked around to the front passenger door of the car. As David, carrying a flagon, felt for his car keys, Ruth called out 'David!' He ignored her. She took her gun out of her bag and cried 'David!' again. He swung round, saw the gun and as he ran round the back of the car, she fired twice. He screamed 'Clive!' Ruth chased after him. She shrieked at Clive 'Get out of the way!' and fired again. David dodged past Clive, around the front of the car and moved up the hill towards

Tanza Road. Again she fired and he fell, face down. A total of four bullets tore through David: one was fired less than three inches away from his back; another lodged near his tongue.

Of the two other bullets fired from the revolver, one ricocheted and hit a passer-by, Mrs Gladys Yule, aged 53, in the thumb. Another apparently missed. There were clicks as Ruth fired again at David's back. It was later claimed by onlookers that she put the empty gun to her head but then lowered her arm.

She stood on the pavement by David's body as Gunnell ran into the pub. 'She's got him!' he cried. A policeman in plain clothes, PC Alan Thompson, who had been having a drink in The Magdala, went up to Ruth. She said: 'Will you call the police?' He replied: 'I am the police,' and removed the gun. She was taken to Hampstead Police Station on Rosslyn Hill.

At about 11.00 pm three CID officers, DCS Leonard Crawford, DCI Leslie Davies and DI Peter Gill, interviewed Ruth Ellis. She told them: 'I am guilty. I am rather confused.' She then agreed to make a statement, which began with the words: 'It all started about two years ago – when I met David . . .' She gave the police a calm and succinct resumé of the past three days and of the shooting of David Blakely. She blamed no one. Nor did she mention Desmond Cussen. She said that the gun was given to her three years ago 'by a man whose name I do not remember'. As she spoke, she drank some coffee and smoked a cigarette.

A post-mortem was carried out on the body of David Blakely at 9.30 am on Easter Monday. The cause of death was attributed to 'shock and haemorrhage due to gunshot wounds'. Ruth was charged with his murder at 12.30 pm, and after a brief appearance at Hampstead magistrates' court she was removed to Holloway Prison, where she became Prisoner 9656.

She asked for a bible and a photo of David. She told visitors, including Cussen, she was prepared to die. 'An eye for a eye,' she said. 'A life for a life.' Her friend, Jackie Dyer, was asked to check on David's funeral arrangements. Said Ruth: 'Go and see him, and tell me what he looks like.' When David was buried at Penn on Friday, 14 April, she sent a wreath of red carnations, her favourite flower – she had often received them from Clare.

She had already written to David's mother, Mrs Cook:

No dought these last few days have been a shock to you. Please try to believe me, when I say, how deeply sorry I am to have caused you this unpleasantness. No dought you will hear all kinds of stories, regarding David and I. Please do forgive him for decieving you, has regarding myself . . . The two people I blame for David's death, and my own, are the Finlayters. No dought you will not understand this but *perhaps* before I hang you will know what I mean. Please excuse my writing but the pen is shocking. I implore you to try to forgive David for living with me, but we were very much in love . . . Unfortunately David was not satisfied with one woman in his life . . . I shall die loving your son. And you should feel content that his death has been repaid. Goodbye. Ruth Ellis.

At the time of the murder an industrial dispute had prevented the printing of the national newspapers. It lasted 26 days, ending on 20 April, on the day that Ruth Ellis made her second appearance in the magistrates' court. The following day the murder was front-page news, along with the election of Sir Anthony Eden as the new leader of the Conservative Party for the forthcoming General Election (on 26 May) – 'BLONDE MODEL ACCUSED OF KILLING ACE RACING CAR DRIVER' (*Daily Mirror*) – 'MODEL ON MURDER CHARGE' (*Daily Mail*). She was described as wearing in court an off-white, or grey tweed two-piece suit, edged with black piping, and black high-heeled shoes. Her platinum hair was said to be 'dyed silver-blue' by the *Daily Express*; to be 'ash blonde' by the *Daily Mirror*; and 'dyed silver-grey' by the *Daily Mail*. She was remanded in custody for another week.

At the third hearing, George Ellis appeared in the court's foyer, drunk. He declared: 'Stop this trial! Stop the trial! I want to see my wife's lawyers!' He was taken away.

Witnesses were called at this hearing, among them Ant, Clive Gunnell and Desmond Cussen, who revealed details of Ruth's private life and loves that she had hoped to conceal. The housekeeper at Egerton Gardens, Mrs Winstanley, would later recall Cussen's nervousness in the waiting-room. 'He just couldn't sit still,' she said. 'He was sweating like a pig. I asked him if he was well, but he just ignored me . . . He kept pacing up and down the floor. You could sense that he knew much more than he was ever going to say.'

Cussen showered Ruth with gifts of flowers, make-up, scent and books while she was awaiting trial. He wrote letters and visited her several times. When sentence was passed, all the gifts, letters and visits ceased. It is alleged by some writers that Ruth Ellis made a deal with Cussen – she would say nothing about his actions on the day of the murder, if he promised to provide for Andy after the trial.

In Holloway, she was interviewed by psychiatrists for the prosecution and for the defence. The former concluded that the accused woman was not suffering from any mental illness and knew what she was doing. The latter, Dr Duncan Whittaker, wrote in his report:

> She indignantly denies that her behaviour at the weekend was hysterical, and said that on the whole she is a calm person. Nevertheless, her whole history is that of an emotionally immature person, and her present equanimity is '*la belle indifference de l'hystérique*', whose intolerable problem has been solved at an immature level of behaviour and who is prepared to pay the price for this solution. Jealousy, of course, played a very large part. But it was her incapacity to get out of an intolerable situation which finally precipitated her action . . . An emotionally mature woman would have been prevented from this action by thoughts of her children . . . She told me that she never once thought of them.

Before the trial Ruth Ellis wrote a long account of her life and the events leading up to the shooting for the *Woman's Daily Mirror*. It was heavily edited and rewritten for publication after the trial – partly because her lawyers dared not prejudice a possible reprieve, and also because she wished nothing unsavoury about her past to be known. But her own account of the shooting of David Blakely is worth giving here:

I felt somehow outside of myself – although I seemed to be registering impressions quite clearly. It did not seem to be me ... When I got to Tanza Road I saw David's car drive away, and I followed on foot down Tanza Road towards the Magdala, where I saw the car outside. It must have been between 9.00 and 9.30 pm ... I certainly do not remember looking in the window of the Magdala, and I do not think I did, although I walked down past the Magdala and up again. Anyway, after what seemed to me to be only a few minutes, I saw Clive Gunnell, followed by David, come out of the door of the Magdala. I thought they were both carrying bottles. Clive went round to the nearside door – the car was facing downhill on the same side of the road as the Magdala and immediately outside the [saloon bar] door. David walked up to the door on the driving side. I have a vague impression that he saw me, but went to the door of the car without taking any notice of me. I know I was in a frightful temper, and I think I started forward and took the pistol out of my handbag as I was walking towards him. I believe I stopped a few paces away from him and fired. But what he was doing or whether he was facing me or had his back to me, I cannot say ... I did not hear him call out. But he started running round the back of the Vanguard. I had no experience in firing a gun before, and I did not think he had been hit, because he was running. I think I followed, and when I was beside Clive I said: 'Stand still, Clive!' or something like that. He was petrified. And then when I got to the front of the bonnet of the car I think I fired again. David was still running and I must have followed, because when I got back to the other side of the Vanguard on the pavement near the rear, he was running along the pavement up the hill towards Tanza Road. He looked round as I shot again, and he fell forward flat on his face. During the whole of this time I felt that I was in a kind of cold frenzy ... At one time I seem to remember someone saying: 'Stop it, Ruth!' It may have been David – it may have been Clive ... I do not remember firing any more shots, although the pistol must have been empty. I vaguely remember it clicking. I am sure there were no more shots because I meant to shoot myself. I remember standing there, watching him in a completely detached sort of way. I did not feel anything, except I seemed to be fascinated by the blood. I have never seen so much blood [which flowed down the gutter, mixing with the beer from the burst flagon]. He seemed to gasp two or three times, heaved, and then relaxed. I think that must have been when he died. I saw his outstretched arm, his watch and signet ring. I was rooted to the spot ... Someone felt David's pulse and said: 'He's gone.' Clive was hysterical and screaming: 'Why did you kill him? Why didn't you kill me? What good is he to you dead? You'll both die now.' Someone said [to Clive]: 'Pull yourself together. You're a man, aren't you?' ... I stood beside David, watching him, until the ambulance arrived.

The trial of Ruth Ellis began at the Central Criminal Court on Monday, 20 June 1955 – three days after what would have been David Blakely's 26th birthday. It lasted two days. She pleaded not guilty and spoke in her defence. The judge was Mr Justice Havers, aged 65. The prosecution was led by Mr Christmas Humphreys, a leading Buddhist, aged 54, the son of a judge. He was assisted by Mr Mervyn Griffith-Jones and Miss Jean Southworth. The defence was led by Mr Melford Stevenson, QC, aged 52, with Mr Sebag Shaw and Mr Peter Rawlinson, aged 35.

Ruth Ellis wore a black two-piece suit with an astrakhan fur collar and cuffs and a white blouse. Her hair had been specially redyed. She looked pale, but seemed totally unmoved throughout the trial, except when she was asked in the witness box to identify David's photograph. It was the one on which he had written: 'To Ruth, with all my love, David'. As it was given to her she began sobbing and turned her head away.

Mr Humphreys commenced, on behalf of the Crown: 'Mrs Ellis is a woman of 28, divorced, and in a word, the story which you are going to hear outlined is this – that in 1954 and 1955 she was having simultaneous love affairs with two men, one of whom was the deceased . . .' He ended: 'Whatever may have been in her mind up to the time when she took that gun – if you have no doubt that she took that gun with the sole purpose of finding and shooting David Blakely and that she then shot him dead – in my submission to you, subject to his Lordship's ruling in law, the only verdict is wilful murder.'

None of the first three witnesses for the prosecution, including Mrs Winstanley, was cross-examined by Melford Stevenson, who seemed almost as indifferent to Ruth Ellis's situation as she was herself. Desmond Cussen, who was next, was given an easy time: there were no testing, embarrassing or awkward questions about the relationships between him and Ruth and David; or about her drinking or her taking of drugs; or about her children; or about Cussen's whereabouts on the day of the shooting; or about the gun. The police had found an air-gun and a starting-pistol in a drawer in Cussen's flat, but this was never mentioned in court. All that Melford Stevenson established was that Ruth Ellis had lived at Goodwood Court and had been bruised by David more than once. It seems as if any hint of a conspiracy to murder was deliberately avoided by all the lawyers concerned.

Anthony Seaton Findlater, who followed Cussen into the witness box, was similarly treated, although he was deliberately unhelpful when asked about Ruth's constant phone-calls on the Easter Sunday. He refused to admit she was desperate or disturbed. He said: 'She rang me up, as she had done hundreds of times, and asked if I knew where David was. It was just a telephone conversation.'

Ruth's solicitor, John Bickford, said much later:

Not to cross-examine the witnesses for the prosecution in a derogatory manner was the counsel's decision . . . If they had been cross-examined, that would have caused Ruth Ellis to give her evidence in a very, very different way indeed, and created, I think, an exceptionally good impression. But in point of fact, she was so upset that the witnesses for the prosecution had not been cross-examined that she virtually threw her life away. And as a result her counsel, Mr Melford Stevenson, was deprived of his right to address the jury after the evidence for the defence.

Just one other prosecution witness, Clive Gunnell, was questioned by Melford Stevenson, whose slow and methodical opening address for the defence, conceded that although 'this woman shot the man', she was guilty of manslaughter, not of murder; that Ruth Ellis was 'driven to a frenzy which for the time being unseated her understanding'; that 'the effect of jealousy upon the feminine mind can so work as to unseat the reason'; and that this jealousy constituted 'this defence of provocation'.

His main witness was Ruth Ellis, who spoke in such a toneless and offhand way that she seemed without feelings, morals or remorse. Her apparent coldness made a poor impression on the jury and it baffled the defence. Melford Stevenson's lack of comprehension of the accused's character and background led him to a fatal close. He asked: 'When you say you had a peculiar idea that you wanted to kill him – were you able to control it?' 'No,' said Ruth. Mr Stevenson continued: 'And you went up, and you in fact shot him? Is that right?' 'Yes,' said Ruth.

Christmas Humphreys had only one question to ask after that. 'Mrs Ellis,' he said. 'When you fired that revolver at close range into the body of David Blakely, what did you intend to do?' Ruth matter-of-factly told the court: 'It is obvious that when I shot him I intended to kill him.'

The defence's other witness, Dr Whittaker, was demolished by Mr Humphreys's question: 'In your view, was she at the time, within the meaning of the English law, sane or insane?' 'Sane,' said Dr Whittaker.

Neither George Ellis nor Andy Neilson, who had much useful information to reveal, was called by the defence.

The jury were then dismissed while Melford Stevenson tried to have the charge reduced to one of manslaughter, claiming that jealousy had worked on Ellis's mind to such an extent as to cause provocation. It was a novel defence and it failed. The jealous fury of a woman scorned was no excuse for murder. Nothing in English law allows a defence of *crime passionnel*, and when the court reassembled on Tuesday, 21 June, the judge told the jury, 'the evidence in this case does not support a verdict of manslaughter on the grounds of provocation.' It was murder, or nothing. Melford Stevenson then waived his right to a closing speech, as did Mr Humphreys. The judge summed up and the jury, of ten men and two women, retired at 11.52 am.

One of the jury, a man, said later:

The others were going backwards and forwards to the toilet. I reckon that of the 23 minutes we were out, only about 13 were spent actually discussing the case . . . I said she should be found guilty of murder, and this other chap thought we ought to be a bit lenient on her, because of all that she had gone through. The fact was the judge didn't direct us towards leniency. Either she meant to kill this lover of hers or she didn't . . . There was really nothing to argue about. I mean, it was Mrs Ellis herself who admitted she meant to to kill him.

Their verdict was 'Guilty'. Ruth was seen to smile. Mr Justice Havers donned the black cap and told the condemned woman: 'The jury have convicted you of murder. In my view it was the only verdict possible.' He sentenced her to death. A woman at the back of the courtroom sobbed. Her father quietly wept. Ruth Ellis's expression never changed. But as she left the dock she smiled at her parents and friends.

It seemed obvious to those who had access to her in Holloway in the three weeks before her execution that she was shielding someone, but she would say nothing. There were several attempts to get a reprieve. Her MP, George Rogers, co-opted by Jackie Dyer, talked to Ruth about her son's future and persuaded her to let him ask for clemency on her behalf. His first visit affected him deeply. He said later: 'Everything was grey. Everything, even the wardresses . . . Here she was, facing death, and this had stripped her of all feminine vanity and behaviour in the sort of way she must have had it when she was pursuing her normal life in the Club. She was rather thin and very pale. A rather fragile sort of person, with brassy yellow hair. Her eyes were rather shallow, not much depth to them.' He recalled that she had a powder compact that, when opened, played 'La vie en rose'.

Fifty thousand signatures on a petition for mercy were sent to the Home Office. MPs of a liberal disposition raised questions in the House of Commons and, with leading churchmen, wrote to the press. John Bickford sent a letter to the Home Secretary, Major Gwilym Lloyd George, setting out extenuating circumstances. But the most powerful appeal was made in the *Daily Mirror* on 30 June by the columnist William Connor, writing under his pen-name, Cassandra.

He attacked capital punishment as 'this ghastly business, this obscene ritual', and concluded:

You who read this paper – and millions like you – are the key supporters of this sickening system whereby with panoply and brutality mixed with the very dubious sauce of religion and consolation we bury our worst malefactors in the quick-lime grave . . . The prospect of judicial execution never stopped any murderer. By all the records that have ever been examined, the scaffold does not prevent the use of the gun, the knife, the fatal blow, the strangler's hands or the phial of poison. Ruth Ellis does not matter any more than her two most recent female predecessors to the hangman's noose – Mrs Merrifield and Mrs Christophi. But what we do to her – you and I – matters very much. And if we do it, and if we continue to do it to her sad successors, then we all bear the guilt of savagery untinged with mercy.

The condemned woman, however, continued to tell visitors that she was resigned to her fate and wanted to die. On 5 July she wrote to a friend, Frank
Neale: 'I am overwhelmed with the thought of so many people, wanting to
help me. And am deeply grateful to one and all. No dought you have heard I
do not want to live. You may find this very hard to believe, but this is what I
want. I am quite well & happy under the circumstances and very well looked
after. I have plenty to amuse me.'

But when on the afternoon of 11 July the Home Office notified the
Governor of Holloway Prison, Dr Charity Taylor, that there would be no reprieve, Ruth Ellis reacted far from calmly to the news. She became hysterical
and lay on her bed screaming – 'I don't want to die! I don't want to die!'

Yet she said nothing to her mother and Jackie Dyer, who visited her soon
after Ruth heard she would *not* be reprieved. Mrs Bertha Neilson,
questioned by a reporter on the top of a 629 trolley-bus, said: 'Ruth seemed
just the same. Calm as usual.' Mrs Dyer said: 'She was just the same. She said
nothing about a reprieve being refused.' But when her solicitor, John Bickford, visited Ruth Ellis she was very abusive, blaming him for the failure of
the appeals. She said: 'I know what you've been doing. You've been taking a
bribe, in order that I should be hanged and Cussen go free!' She dismissed
Bickford and demanded to see her former divorce lawyer, Victor Mishcon. It
was Mishcon, on the morning of 12 July (the day before the execution), who
persuaded Ruth Ellis to say from whom she received the gun. He argued:
'Don't you owe it to your son to leave behind you a record of the truth?' She
said: 'I'll tell you what happened, if you promise not to use it to try to save
me.'

She then made a statement. She said: 'It is only with the greatest reluctance
that I have decided to tell how it was that I got the gun . . .' She named Desmond Cussen. The statement was signed at 12.30 pm.

Victor Mishcon moved fast. He phoned the Home Office for an interview.
Sir Frank Newsam, the Permanent Under-Secretary, was summoned from
the Ascot Races. Senior police officers were called in and at 4.30 pm DI Gill
and DC Claiden set out to try to find Desmond Cussen. Ruth's brother,
Granville, also tried to track him down. But where Desmond was that night
has never been revealed. He disappeared. Granville later claimed that he and
a reporter tracked Cussen to a flat and found him in bed with a woman. Cussen told them to 'Get lost!' A *Woman's Sunday Mirror* reporter, Duggie
Howell, later claimed that Cussen spent that evening with him at his home,
drinking.

Meanwhile, shirt-sleeved men and women in cotton dresses were gathering outside Holloway Prison, some with portable radios. There were chants
of 'Evans! Bentley! Ellis!' Inside the prison, Ruth Ellis wrote farewell letters,
to Jackie Dyer, Frank Neale and George Rogers, who was authorised to take
Andy away for a holiday. Andy had been told his mother was on a modelling
assignment abroad. Ruth refused to see her brother, Granville, although she
saw her parents that afternoon, about the time that the executioner, Albert
Pierrepoint, arrived.

At 6.30 am on Wednesday, 13 July 1955, Ruth Ellis was visited by a

Roman Catholic chaplain. She had reverted to that faith and a crucifix had been fixed to a wall of her cell. She knelt before it as the priest administered the last rites. At 7.00 am she wrote a final letter to Leon Simmons, Mr Mishcon's clerk. She said: 'This is just for you to console my family with the thought I did not change my way of thinking at the last moment. Or break my promise to David's mother. Well, Mr Simmons, I have told you the truth and that's all I can do. Thanks once again. Goodbye. Ruth Ellis.'

She was hanged by Albert Pierrepoint at 9.00 am. She had been given a glass of brandy beforehand at her request, and she walked to her death courageously, and without a word.

Outside the prison, about a thousand people, among them Julian Neilson, awaited the posting of the execution notice. At 9.00 am some had wept, some had knelt in prayer, and a musician had played Bach's *Be Thou With Me* on his violin. In Hemel Hempstead, Mrs Neilson prayed in her bedroom as her husband played a solemn lament on his cello below. Ruth's sister, Muriel, ran from room to room in her house, weeping and crying 'No! No! No!'

Granville Neilson identified his sister's body: a scarf had been tied around her neck to hide the marks of the rope. He said later: 'She was laid with a cross at the top of her head and two candles on either side . . . She was made up, with lipstick and powder. I turned around and said to the Governor: "Doesn't she look beautiful?"'

Ruth Ellis's body was interred in the prison grounds until 1970, when Holloway underwent a rebuilding programme. Andy Neilson, her illegitimate son and next of kin, was granted permission to remove the body, which was reburied under her real maiden name of Ruth Hornby in the graveyard at St Mary's Church in the parish of Amersham in Buckinghamshire – a few miles from where David Blakely lies at Penn.

Three months after Ruth's execution, in October, her younger sister, Elizabeth, died from cardiac arrest following an asthma attack. Julian Neilson died in the mid-1960s from wounds sustained in the Second World War. Bertha Neilson's mental state deteriorated rapidly after the execution and she was admitted to a psychiatric hospital, mentally deranged. She died several years after her husband, Arthur.

It is said that Andy Neilson, who was ten years old when his mother was hanged, had not found a satisfactory niche in life by 1977, when he was 33. And his half-sister, Georgina, also found living with her mother's notoriety difficult. At one time she wrote an article on Ruth Ellis for a tabloid newspaper, although she can have remembered little if anything of her mother and nothing of the trial. When a film about Ruth Ellis, *Dance with a Stranger*, was mooted, Georgina applied to play the part of her mother, although she had had no acting experience. Ruth's ex-husband, George Ellis, committed suicide at a hotel in Jersey in the Channel Islands, five years after Ruth's execution. He hanged himself.

Desmond Cussen was last heard of in 1977 living in Perth, in Western Australia, and running a florist shop, *Chez Fleur*. He continued to deny that he ever gave Ruth Ellis a revolver or drove her to Tanza Road on the night of the murder. He told a TV reporter: 'I never thought she would hang, you know. I always thought she would get a reprieve, right up to the end . . . She used to complain when I visited her in Holloway that they'd cut all the reports of her case out of the newspapers she was given to read. She wanted to know the headlines she was making. She loved the headlines. She always wanted to be a star. She achieved that, didn't she?'

The bar-staff at The Magdala public house in South Hill Park, Hampstead, still get the occasional query about the Ruth Ellis murder. Few visitors remember the victim's name.

In 1956, Sidney Silverman's Death Penalty (Abolition) Bill, after being given a second reading in the House of Commons by 286 votes to 262, was rejected in the House of Lords. However, in March 1957 the Homicide Act was passed. The death penalty was now confined to five kinds of murder: (1) committed in the course or furtherance of theft; (2)caused by shooting or by an explosion; (3)committed in the course of or for the purpose of resisting or avoiding or preventing a lawful arrest; (4) of a police officer acting in the execution of his duty or of a person so assisting him; and (5) of a prison officer, or murder done by a prisoner. A previously convicted murderer who killed again on release could also be sentenced to death.

Albert Pierrepoint resigned in February 1956, seven months after the death of Ruth Ellis. The two men who succeeded him carried out 34 executions in the next eight-and-a-half years. Pierrepoint retired to the pub he and his wife Anne had run since 1946. Situated at Hollinwood, south of Oldham, it was called Help the Poor Struggler.

He resigned over a money matter, not through conscience or remorse. What happened was that after making all the preparations to hang a man in Liverpool in November 1955, the condemned man was reprieved. The weather was so bad, according to Pierrepoint, that he was unable to drive the 52 miles back home and stayed in a hotel overnight. In due course he was sent £1 for his pains and nothing for the hotel bill. Highly offended, he sent the money back. The sum of £4 was then sent to him. He sent it back. Eventually the full sum of £15 was sent – the executioner's fee. But as his hotel expenses were not forthcoming, Pierrepoint resigned in disgust at this slight.

In his 25 years in office, as assistant and chief executioner, Albert Pierrepoint hanged over 400 women and men.

He died in July 1992 at the age of 87. His obituary appeared in the national papers on the 37th anniversary of the day on which he hanged Ruth Ellis – on 13 July.

CHAPTER 14

Francis Forsyth, Norman Harris, Chris Darby and Terence Lutt

The Murder of Allan Jee, 1960

Nearly eight years after Derek Bentley, aged 19, was hanged by Pierrepoint in January 1953 for his involvement with Chris Craig in the shooting of PC Miles, four young men were all found guilty of the murder of Allan Jee – although only one of them was responsible for his death. Two escaped hanging, one because he was under 18. But Francis Forsyth, who was 18, was hanged for a murder he did not intend to commit. Norman Harris was hanged for his involvement in the attempted robbery that occasioned the death of Jee, although he struck no blow. Like Bentley, he was hanged because he was there, and because an example, to discourage other young thugs, had again to be made.

It was Saturday night in Hounslow, a sprawling suburb in western London below the Great West Road. The A315 and A314 meet in Hounslow, which is constantly overflown by planes making their roaring descent to Heathrow Airport. It was 25 June 1960. Allan Jee, aged 23, was walking home. He had said goodnight to his 18-year-old fiancée, Jacqueline Herbert, a hairdresser, who lived in Stamford Brook, and at about 10.55 pm had caught a 657 trolley-bus back to Hounslow. She had walked with him to the bus-stop. That midsummer's afternoon they had been to Richmond and wandered along the riverside before having tea and seeing a film. After that they had returned to Jacqueline's home to watch TV. The day before this they had become engaged, planning to marry in two years' time.

Allan was a pleasant, athletic young man, a good ice-skater, and a trainee engineer. He had lived in Hounslow for most of his life, and had been educated at the Bulstrode Secondary Modern school. For five years he was a choirboy at the Holy Trinity Church. In February 1960 he had been demobbed from the RAF, having spent most of the two years of his National Service in Cyprus during the EOKA troubles. Once he had a narrow escape from death or injury when a booby-trap bomb exploded in a washroom. His mother said later: 'It seems terrible to think that he came through all that trouble safely, only to be killed like this near his home.'

It was about 11.10 pm when Allan stepped off the trolley-bus at the bus station and, taking the usual short-cut to his parents' home at 31 Hall Road, made his way via James Street to a poorly lit footpath that led to a footbridge over a railway line. The footpath was fenced; there was a small park on his right; allotments lay to his left. Ahead of him, where the path turned left, to run parallel with the railway before reaching the bridge, he saw four dark figures: the street-lamp there that lit the corner was out. Perhaps he felt a spasm of doubt or fear. But he was happy and going home, and he strode on hopefully towards the darkness at the bend in the path.

Earlier that night, four local youths, after visiting several pubs, had sat in Joachim's coffee bar. They were Norman Harris, an unemployed driver; Christopher Darby, a coalman; Terence Lutt, a labourer known as Lobe, and unemployed; and Francis Forsyth, known as Floss, a road worker and 18 years old.

Forsyth's fair hair was arranged in a Be-Bop style, rolling on to his forehead; he wore pointed Italian-style shoes. After passing his eleven-plus exam, he had gone for a while to Isleworth Grammar School, where, according to a schoolmate, he was 'touchy and hated to be laughed at'. Sent to an approved school when he was 15, he had two other previous convictions, the first, for larceny, when he was eleven. Norman Harris also had previous convictions and lived around the corner from Forsyth. At 23 the oldest of the four, pale-faced and dark, and darkly suited, he left school at the age of 14 and did his National Service in the Army, serving in Cyprus, like Allan Jee. Like Jee he had been to Bulstrode Secondary Modern, as had Darby and Lutt. Darby was 20, bearded, liked traditional jazz, and as a child had suffered from asthma. Excused from military service, he still carried a spray to relieve any asthmatic attacks. The youngest, Lutt, aged 17, was also the tallest and biggest, with thick, dark greasy hair.

All four lived near each other in West Hounslow, and that night had decided to do some thieving. Harris later told the police: 'I was skint and out of work. I meant to go screwing a shop or house.' Forsyth said a visit to a scrap-metal yard was mentioned. Then one of them said: 'Let's jump somebody.' This was probably Lutt. Forsyth said later: 'Lutt suggested rolling someone. He likes a fight. Come to that we all do when we've had a few shants [drinks].' Harris said: 'We followed some fellow through the path by the park and were going to do him. But some people were coming over the bridge, so we let him go.'

They waited, on edge. Then another man appeared. This was Francis Power, a big, well-built man, who was on his way home, as others were that Saturday night, taking the short-cut across the railway line to Chatsworth Crescent. Power saw four men standing in the dark at the bend in the path, two on each side. He heard their voices, and what sounded like a warning as he approached. They were silent as he passed between them. They refrained from attacking him because of his size, and Power returned safely home. It was now about 11.15 pm. The next person to approach them up the path was Allan Jee.

Lutt punched the young man hard in the face. Jee staggered against the fence, his hands to his face, and Harris caught him as he fell. 'What do you want me for?' cried Jee as Lutt and Harris held him down. Darby later claimed he took no part in the attack. Harris said: 'I put my hand in his inside pocket to get his wallet, but there was nothing in there at all . . . Forsyth was standing above us . . . I saw some blood on my hand . . . I realised Floss had put the boot in.' Forsyth said later: 'Lutt only hit him once. He packs a punch . . . As the fellow came up Lutt struck him . . . He was struggling, so I kicked him in the head to shut him up.'

Forsyth kicked Jee more than once with his Italian-style shoes, until Jee lay bleeding and semi-conscious on the ground. Then Forsyth followed as the others fled.

Although Harris had rifled Jee's other pockets, he had failed to find the small change amounting to 15 shillings, which was all Jee had.

It was over in seconds. The four ran down the path past Anthony Cowell, who was on his way to the main road. He then saw them standing on the corner of James Street. John Summerscale was probably the next to walk up the path; he was taking his mother home. He heard 'muttering and groaning' and saw a man lying full-length on his back. 'I thought the man was drunk,' he said later. Passing on and over the bridge he deposited his mother at her house, and on retracing his steps some minutes later, found an ambulance at the scene.

Meanwhile, a young typewriter mechanic, Douglas Reeve, who lived in the same road as Harris and had just taken his girlfriend home, had paused to peer at the body by the bend in the path and saw it was lying in a pool of blood. He went for help, banging on the door of a house at the end of James Street. It was 11.25 pm. But the occupant, Dennis Kemp, had to see the body for himself before he dialled 999. PC Derek Mizen arrived on the scene at 11.40. He reported later that the injured man was very restless and had to be comforted until an ambulance appeared. He said: 'We had to hold him onto the stretcher, because he started struggling.' Jee was bleeding from the nose and ears.

He was taken to West Middlesex Hospital on the Twickenham Road in Isleworth. A doctor saw him at 12.30 am. Apart from the bleeding, there was an abrasion at the base of his nose and some bruising, as there was around his left eye and ear. X-rays showed he also had a fractured skull.

His mother, Mrs Doris Jee, aged 51, visited the hospital on Sunday; she had last seen her son on Saturday afternoon. She told a reporter: 'He had a terrible black eye, and he lay there, unconscious, having a blood transfusion. I stroked his poor forehead and said: "What have they done to you, son?" I thought while he was sleeping he had a chance. But the hospital said he was critically ill.'

Allan Jee died in the hospital of cerebral contusion at 1.10 am on Monday, 27 June. Mrs Jee said: 'In the middle of the night they came to tell us he was dead . . . I'm sure he must have been attacked without warning. For he was a very fit boy, and would have given a good account of himself, if he'd had a chance . . . We keep asking: "Why, why, why?" And any minute I think that perhaps it hasn't happened and he'll walk up the path . . .'

A full-scale murder hunt was launched, led by Detective Superintendent Fred Hixson. Detectives were called in from other areas; all police leave was cancelled; and appeals were made to the public for any information. Meanwhile, the area around the footpath was minutely searched for a weapon or some clue to the identity of the assailant or assailants. No one imagined the weapon was a shoe. The murder was seemingly without a motive, for no money had been taken off Jee. For a while the police thought he had been attacked at 11.07, for his watch had stopped at that time. Jacqueline Herbert told them, however, that his watch was ten minutes slow.

Scores of people were interviewed – 3,000 in all – including known hooligans and those on police files. And such was the public response that on Thursday, 30 June, the police were able to issue detailed descriptions of three of the four young men seen in the vicinity of the crime on Saturday night. The day before this, Hixson himself interviewed Norman Harris, a known offender, and asked him about his movements on the night of the murder. Harris replied: 'I don't know anything about it, and I can tell you where I was and who I was with. I was indoors before then.' He then made a lying statement about his whereabouts, presumably backed up by Forsyth, and possibly by Darby and Lutt. Hixson told the *Middlesex Chronicle* reporter that there was no immediate prospect of a 'dramatic development'. Extensive enquiries, he said, might take weeks before the killer of Jee was found.

Nearly a fortnight after the murder, on 7 July, Superintendent Hixson was still appealing for people who were in the neighbourhood at the time to come forward. 'It is their public duty to do so,' he said. He added it was vital that the three persons whose descriptions were issued the previous week should be traced and interviewed. Perhaps he already had his suspicions, or was waiting for a lucky break. It came on Sunday, 17 July.

A teenager, Kevin Cullinan, had been feeling uneasy ever since Forsyth told him something of what had happened on the night of 25 June, when he (Cullinan) had seen Forsyth, Harris, Darby and Lutt, all of whom he knew, in Joachim's coffee bar. Forsyth had even revealed that Lutt had grabbed Jee and that he (Forsyth) had kicked him. Then on 17 July, Cullinan went to a pub with Lutt and on the way Lutt asked him who he thought had murdered Jee. Cullinan replied, somewhat boldly, that Lutt, Forsyth and the other two were probably responsible. Lutt was carrying a copy of the *People*, which was offering a reward of £500 for information leading to an arrest. He pointed at this item and said to Cullinan: 'I'll have to watch you now.'

Whether Cullinan then found he had a conscience or lost his nerve is not now known. But on Tuesday, 19 July, Lutt and the other three were taken to Hounslow Police Station for questioning. They were there all day, separately detained and interviewed by a team of dogged policemen. Before long all four began to talk, and by 7.00 pm they had all been charged with the murder of Allan Jee.

It seems that Norman Harris was the first to crack. He asked DI Humphreys: 'What killed him then?' Humphreys replied: 'He was knocked down and kicked on the head while he was on the ground and died from the injuries he received.' According to Humphreys, Harris then said: 'I'll have a fight, but I wouldn't kick a fellow lying on the ground. I didn't know the chap – but I feel sorry for him dying like that.' 'You may have known him,' said Humphreys. 'He went to Bulstrode School at the same time as you. He was about the same age.' 'I can't remember him,' retorted Harris. 'I got thrown out when I was 14 anyway.' Then he added: 'How did his people take it?' Humphreys answered: 'They thought a lot of their son, and they were very upset. In fact the shock's made his mother ill.' Harris was silent for a time, then said: 'I'm the oldest – so it's bound to be down to me.'

Elsewhere, the bearded Chris Darby asked PS Atkins: 'How long do you think we'll get for this?' Atkins replied: 'I'm not in a position to say.' Darby then said: 'It wasn't my idea to roll the bloke.' Ten minutes later he said: 'I didn't kick the chap. It was Floss who put the boot in.'

Harris was now with DS Saxby. According to Saxby, Harris said: 'I've been thinking this over – and if it all comes out, I think I'll dangle.' 'Did you do it?' Saxby asked. Replied Harris: 'If I give out on my mates we'll all dangle together.'

Forsyth was with DC Cowling, whom he asked: 'What am I likely to get for this? I reckon about a fiver . . . Suppose I get five years – what's the remission? I'd do about three years eight months, wouldn't I?' According to Cowling, Forsyth indicated his shoes, and said: 'These are the shoes I had on that night. Look – they're only soft ones. I only kicked him twice to keep him quiet . . .'

DC Barnes was present when Forsyth is alleged to have said: 'I reckon I'll get five years for this. I hope I don't go to the Scrubs . . . Lobe only hit him once . . . Really, it's sort of fading now. It's over three weeks ago. I know I only kicked him twice.'

Harris made a statement, which was shown to Forsyth. Forsyth said: 'That's about right. It was me that did the kicking. I didn't think I'd hurt him that much.' Forsyth then made a statement. Meanwhile, Darby was shown Harris's statement. He said: 'All right – I'll tell you my side of it.' He did so, denying that he had touched Jee. 'I didn't mean any harm to come to this fellow,' he said. Lutt was shown copies of the statements made by both Harris and Forsyth. He said: 'All right. What they say is true.'

Forsyth, Harris, Darby and Lutt appeared at Brentford magistrates' court on Wednesday, 20 July, and were remanded in custody for a week. A crowd of about 100 people, mostly housewives with children, gathered outside. Within, the parents of the four accused were allowed to see their sons in the cells. In the presence of a policeman Forsyth told his mother: 'I'm sorry, Mum. I did it.'

Their next appearance was on Wednesday, 4 August when, after a two-day hearing, they were committed for trial to the Old Bailey, charged with the capital murder of Allan Edward John Jee in the course or furtherance of theft. Another charge was brought against them, of assaulting Jee with intent to rob him. All four pleaded not guilty and reserved their defences. Mr Philip Radcliffe, prosecuting, said: 'They were all agreed to commit some sort of crime by way of larceny. Harris was short of money and his friends agreed to help him. Harris wanted to break into some premises but one of the others, Lutt, was more interested in what actually took place – which was highway robbery.'

Among those who gave evidence were Jee's father, Jee's fiancée, Jacqueline, Francis Power, John Summerscale, Douglas Reeve, and Kevin Cullinan.

Two hospital doctors also spoke, as did several Hounslow policemen, led by Superintendent Hixson.

The trial of Francis Robert George Forsyth, aged 18, and of Harris, Darby and Lutt, began in the No. 1 Court at the Old Bailey on Tuesday, 20 September 1960. The judge was the Hon. Mr Justice Winn, and the chief prosecutor was Mervyn Griffith-Jones. The four accused were represented by Edward Gardiner, QC (Forsyth); Peter Rawlinson, QC (Harris); David Weitzman, QC (Darby); and Victor Durand, QC (Lutt).

In his opening statement, Mr Griffith-Jones said: 'At the very best, it is robbery with violence. Planned and deliberate. The prosecution submit to you that it goes further than that, and on the law as it now stands, is murder.' Of Allan Jee, he said: 'He was set upon. He was knocked to the ground. He was held there, while his pockets were gone through. He was kicked into un-consciousness, and left lying, bleeding, moaning and semi-conscious on the ground, while these four young men made good their escape.' At one point Mr Griffith-Jones held up a black, pointed shoe and said to the jury of nine men and three women: 'The toe, you may think, is almost a lethal weapon.' Later, the pathologist who carried out the post-mortem on Allan Jee, Dr Teare, said he thought the main injuries to the head had been caused by *five* kicks, delivered with 'considerable force'.

At the end of the prosecution's opening speech the charge against Darby was reduced from capital murder to 'simple' murder, as he denied using any violence against Jee. This was accepted by the prosecution – a very fine dis-tinction, as Harris had also committed no actual violence on Jee, and Darby knew that violence was planned 'in the course or furtherance of theft'.

The first witness for the prosecution was Jacqueline Herbert. Another was the director of the Metropolitan Police Laboratory, Lewis Nicholls, who told the court he had found blood-stains on the right sleeve of a jacket belonging to Lutt and on a sleeve of Forsyth's jacket. There were also spots of blood near the turn-up on the right leg of Forsyth's jeans, as well as traces of blood in the welt and on the instep of his right shoe.

Harris and Forsyth both gave evidence. But although an attempt was made by their QCs to minimise the defendants' actions on 25 June and to re-fute what they were alleged to have said in Hounslow Police Station, their demeanour and replies were unconvincing. Harris said that Jee 'seemed to buckle at the knees and fell towards me . . . I just caught him. I bent down and lowered him to the ground. If not he would have fallen. I went to put my hand in his right-hand pocket. I felt something wet and sticky on my hand. I realised what a senseless thing I was doing and said "Let's have it away" and ran up the alley.' Harris added that he only put half his hand in Jee's inside pocket and touched no other pockets. There was no kicking of Jee when he was there, he said – 'I didn't think he had been seriously injured when I got home.' He was 'very much afraid and upset' when he heard that Jee had died. After giving evidence, Harris appeared to be on the verge of collapse and had to be given some water.

Forsyth, when asked by his QC whether he had intended to rob Jee or anyone else, replied: 'No.' He said that he and the others were chatting in the alley when Jee came along. He heard a whack and realised that Lutt had hit Jee. Forsyth said: 'I moved in to see what was going on and he fell down at my feet . . . He was shouting, and I thought someone might come along, so I kicked him a couple of times to keep him quiet.' Asked whether he intended to cause any serious injury, Forsyth replied: 'No, sir.'

In his summing-up on Monday, 26 September, Mr Justice Winn conceded: 'It is not suggested here that any of these men intended to kill Allan Jee or desired his death.' None the less, the question was whether each of the accused intended to cause serious injury or committed acts which were likely to cause such injury in the course or furtherance of theft – although no money was taken. It was enough that they *intended* to steal. 'One of the vital questions is whether there was a common purpose or design,' said the judge. 'And if so, which of these defendants was party to it, and was ready to give assistance in furtherance of that common purpose.'

After deliberating for 40 minutes, the jury returned at 4.25 pm to deliver verdicts of guilty of murder on all four men. Harris and Forsyth were sentenced to death.

Harris seemed half-dead already: his face was ashen; his eyes were closed; he swayed in the dock. Forsyth stood with his mouth open, swallowing and staring ahead of him; his face was white. Darby, found guilty of simple or non-capital murder, was sentenced to life imprisonment. Lutt, not yet 18, was sentenced to be detained during Her Majesty's pleasure.

Afterwards, Jacqueline Herbert said: 'I have no feeling for them at all. What happened to Allan was so terrible, I have no sympathy for them. They have got what they deserve for the dreadful thing they did.'

Two days later, Norman Harris's father, aged 53, who was seriously ill and knew nothing of his son's sentence, died. The news of his father's death was given to Harris in the condemned cell at Pentonville Prison by the Prison Governor.

Appeals were lodged and dismissed on 24 October by the Lord Chief Justice, Lord Parker, attended by Mr Justice Elwes and Mr Justice Ashworth. It was argued that Forsyth had kicked Jee *after* the failed theft, and *after* the others had fled. Therefore the deed was not committed in the course or furtherance of theft – nor was it part of a common purpose – and should not have been adjudged as capital murder. Nor did the four set out with a weapon, a gun or knife. The jury had been influenced by what they read in the papers and misdirected by the judge.

The Lord Chief Justice concluded his verdict on the appeals by saying:

This court has spent some considerable time on this case. We have heard the arguments by counsel on behalf of the appellants, and one thing clearly emerges for our consideration, and that is that the learned judge summed up the legal issues not only accurately and perfectly, but with great clarity. The only criticism that can be made is that in one respect [Darby] he was too favourable. There was no miscarriage of justice and no grounds on which this court can interfere.

Petitions against the death sentences were organised, one by Harris's girl-friend, 16-year-old Norma Mackie. She said: 'More people have got pity for Norman than for Floss. And a lot of people were against hanging as a whole. In fact, some people said they had no pity for the boys – but they were against hanging. So they signed.'

The chairman of the National Campaign for the Abolition of Capital Punishment, Gerald Gardiner, QC, wrote to the Home Secretary, R. A. Butler, begging him 'to remember that the existence of capital punishment did not prevent the murder, that the Christian purpose is redemptive, and that a large number of good citizens would be deeply shocked if our society were today deliberately to kill in cold blood a youth of 18, whatever he has done'.

The question of a reprieve for Harris and Forsyth was still under consideration in the first week of November, when a letter deploring the executions, particularly of Forsyth, appeared in *The Times*, signed by 31 distinguished persons, including Kingsley Amis, A. J. Ayer, Hugh Casson, John Freeman, Victor Gollancz, Gilbert Harding, Jacquetta Hawkes, Christmas Humphreys, Julian Huxley, Augustus John, J. B. Priestley, Michael Redgrave, Donald Soper, Stephen Spender, Sybil Thorndike, Leonard Woolf and the Lords Harewood, Harmsworth and Russell.

A letter-writer in the *Middlesex Chronicle* took another view, condemning the 'wicked and wanton crime'. He said:

With regard to the petition which is circulating in this district to save two young murderers from their very just punishment, a learned QC is quoted as saying that a very large number of people would be 'deeply shocked' if one – or I presume both of them – were hanged. A very larger number of people will be even more 'deeply shocked' if they are not. On what grounds should these killers be pardoned? That they are young? So was their victim. That capital punishment fails to deter? Of course it fails to deter, if culprits know very well beforehand that sentimentalists will rush to their rescue. Their whole attitude, both before and after their trial, indicates, to my mind, only selfish concern for their own skins, a totally unrepentant attitude, and anxiety only to escape the consequences of their actions. The only way to deal with such a petition is to tear it up.

On Monday, 7 November, Harris's mother and Lutt's father took a petition to the Home Office bearing over 1,000 signatures. Forsyth's mother sent a telegram to the Queen. On Tuesday it was announced that there would be no reprieves.

On Wednesday Mrs Ada Forsyth and her 74-year-old husband, Frank, who had been a soldier for 18 years, visited their youngest son in Wandsworth Prison. Afterwards, Mr Forsyth said: 'He was laughing and joking the whole time. He never once mentioned that the reprieve had been turned down. He's a very brave boy. He knows he's got to go, but he's taking it like a soldier, just like his old man.'

At 9.00 am on Tuesday, 10 November, Francis Forsyth, aged 18, was hanged at Wandsworth Prison, and Norman Harris, aged 23, at Pentonville.

Ten years later, in 1970, Christopher Darby and Terence Lutt were released on licence – Lutt in November and Darby in May.

CHAPTER 15

John Hall

The Murders of Inspector Pawsey

and DS Hutchins, 1961

Some correlation seems to exist between suicide and murder. Those who kill themselves are said to do so 'when the balance of their mind is disturbed'. This might also be said of those who kill other people. Neither murder nor suicide is, after all, the act of a wholly sane or rational person, but that of someone suffering from much mental and emotional stress; from an excess, or lack, of feeling; from total self-disgust, and/or a total lack of self-respect. Between 1900 and 1949, 29 per cent of those suspected of murder committed suicide; and 21.4 per cent of those found guilty of murder were adjudged to be insane or unfit to plead.

It is also the case that those who murder, sometimes kill themselves soon after, and in many cases, the act of murder can be viewed as an act of displaced self-destruction. The disturbed person, unable to kill himself, or herself, kills someone else instead, someone close. Thus a deeply disturbed woman, wanting but unable to kill herself, or a husband, or lover, will redirect her desire for death, and slaughter someone more vulnerable, like a child, as a substitute. Others, like John Hall, cannot destroy themselves without first killing someone else in an act of sacrificial revenge – a life for a life, a death for a death – so that they do not die alone.

1960 was a time of much social and international unease. The birth of new republics and independent states in Africa, like the Congo, Chad, Togo, Ghana, Nigeria, had been heralded by Macmillan's 'wind of change' speech in South Africa (soon to become a republic itself), and was underlined there by the Sharpeville Massacre. There was trouble in Algeria, the Congo, South Korea, and Laos, and the Cuban crisis loomed. In Britain, the Americans set up a missile early-warning system in Yorkshire, and the Navy's first nuclear submarine was launched by the Queen, a few weeks before John Kennedy became President of the USA. The first Polaris submarine arrived at Holy Loch in March 1961, and the first space-flights were made: that of a Russian dog in March, of Yuri Gagarin in April, and of an American, Alan Shepherd, in May. There were other changes that year: steam locomotives, trolley-buses and trams were being phased out fast; new £1 notes were issued, and the farthing ceased to be legal tender; betting shops were made legal; but homosexuality, despite the Wolfenden Report, was not. The Archbishop of Canterbury visited the Pope and a modern version of the New Testament (the first part of The New English Bible) appeared. In May 1961, the Queen and the Duke of Edinburgh visited the Pope; and in Vienna, on Saturday, 3 June, Kennedy and Khrushchev met.

The previous night, there had been what the police called 'a family dispute' in a house in Tavistock Road, off Romford Road in Stratford. A 30-year-old salesman, John Hall, also known as Helmwig, had attacked his wife, mother-in-law and sister-in-law with a chair. The local police were informed and left a message with the family that Hall, who had temporarily disappeared, should call on them to sort the matter out.

The police learned that Hall had recently remarried – his second wife, Sylvia Roberts, aged 21, having been a friend of his first wife, Joyce, whom he had left two years previously and divorced. The second marriage had taken place at the Forest Gate Methodist church nine weeks before, on Easter Saturday (1 April). There had been 100 guests. After a honeymoon in Spain, the couple had moved into rented rooms in Balfour Road, Ilford.

During his first marriage Hall, who was born in Woodford Green, had run a pet shop for about a year in Cranbrook Road, Gants Hill. For a time he kept two pet ocelots in his garden at Donald Drive, Chadwell Heath, but gave them away to a zoo when he and Joyce moved to Ilford. Neighbours described him later as a quiet, unassuming man, and very fond of animals. He was friendly, they said, but his wife kept herself to herself. However, they were both members of a flying club – Hall had a pilot's licence and had flown 100 hours – and he also belonged to a rifle club and was licensed to carry a gun. In fact he owned several guns.

The 'dispute' in the home of Sylvia's parents in Tavistock Road was apparently caused by her refusal to give him £5 to pay off a loan – he owed the money to the car firm who employed him. Sylvia's mother, Mrs Roberts, told a reporter: 'For some reason he went crazy and began hitting out with a chair. He hit Sylvia and he hit me. I put up my hand to defend myself and a blow broke my wrist. I had 10 stitches in my head and 12 in my arm. Sylvia had 22 stitches in a head wound, and Eileen [Sylvia's sister] was hurt too.'

After the assault Hall visited his parents' home in Empress Avenue, Woodford Green, before staying overnight with a friend.

At 12.05 on the afternoon of Saturday, 3 June, DI George Jones took a telephone call at West Ham police station in West Ham Lane, a few hundred yards south of Stratford Broadway. It was John Hall. He said: 'I understand you want to see me about the affair last night. Can I come and see you? Can I speak to the officer who is dealing with it?' DI Jones indicated that he would be pleased to see Hall and suggested he call at the police station. Hall did so, and arrived there, armed, at 1.05 pm, having driven to West Ham Lane in a red Austin Healey Sprite. He was wearing blue denim trousers and a royal-blue windcheater. John Hall was a tall, thick-set man, 6' 1", with fair hair going blond.

After he had reported to the front desk, DI Jones came to meet him and said: 'It's in your favour that you've come here of your own accord. But, as you know, your mother-in-law, wife and her younger sister were badly hurt at Tavistock Road last night.' Hall, interrupting, said: 'I know – and I'm sorry. I went on my knees to them and asked forgiveness. But they started pushing me about. I lost my temper and hit them with a chair. Are they badly hurt?'

Jones took Hall into the CID office, where DS Lewis was sitting at a desk. Also present was DC Walton. Hall was told that he would have to be detained while further enquiries were made. Presumably he was also charged with assault. But, although he may have been prepared to answer questions and to give his address, he was not willing to be detained.

On being told by DI Jones to empty his pockets and put the contents on the desk, Hall produced six bullets from his left-hand trouser pocket and put them on the desk. Then he pulled out a gun.

It was an automatic pistol [DI Jones said later]. Hall was about a yard from us. As he backed towards the door he had us all at gunpoint. He backed to the door covering us. I told him not to be silly, and he said: 'You're not keeping me here!' By that time he was by the door. He rushed out and down the stairs. An immediate hue and cry was raised, and several other officers joined in the pursuit. Sgt Hutchins and PC Cox were in the chase.

DS George Hutchins was 49. He had joined the police force in 1933 and had been at West Ham for six years. He and his wife, Betty, aged 47, had a 22-year-old son and a daughter, aged 14, and they lived in Elmcroft Avenue, Snaresbrook. PC Charles Cox, who was also married, had two young daughters. Aged 38, he was from Leicestershire and had been with the police since 1947 and at West Ham all that time.

Hall, ignoring his car, ran across the road and into a small park or recreation ground, in which children were playing on slides and swings before going home to lunch. It was a fine, warm, Saturday afternoon and there were quite a few people in the streets. Hall veered to his left, heading for some houses that backed on to Whalebone Lane beside the park. Crossing the lane, he charged through the back garden and back door of 54 Farringdon Road, and exited by the front door. He then made for No. 35, diagonally across the road.

A wood-machinist, Leonard Hilliard, aged 36, was on a ladder painting the front of his parents' house, observed by his father. He said later:

The bloke rushed into the house, and my father, who is nearly 70, went after him. The man barged into the kitchen and saw my mother was reading to my nine-year-old girl, Vivian. He said: 'I'm wanted by the police!' He tried to rush out of the back door to get into the garden. But my Welsh collie dog growled at him and he turned back. My father caught hold of this bloke, turned him round and said: 'Get out of here!' He did. He was puffing and panting, but he went out without making any fuss.

Hall turned left into Tennyson Road, passing a corner greengrocer's shop with Hutchins and Cox now close on his heels. They were within four feet of him when he turned and fired.

Hutchins fell on the pavement, shot through the stomach. Cox also collapsed, shot in a leg and an arm.

Several people saw it all. Mrs Winifred Norcott, who lived at 71 Tennyson Road, had just shouted to her son, Roy, to come in and have his lunch. Roy Norcott, aged 13, was outside sitting on a wall with his friend, Keith Pearman. He said later:

> I heard my mother shouting to me. I turned round and saw a man running towards me with a gun in his hand. He turned around and shot a man in plain clothes coming after him. This man fell to the ground . . . He fired at a policeman who was also chasing him and hit him too. When he saw us he turned back, but a policeman on a motorbike was coming after him, so he came towards us again. I was scared. I pushed my pal Keith and his mother into the house and we ran into the back garden. Afterwards I heard another shot in the distance.

Mrs Norcott said: 'It was like a television gangster serial. I couldn't believe it was real!'

In the greengrocer's, Mrs Doris Bethell, aged 37, was serving some customers when – 'I heard a schemozzle outside and I went to the door.' She said:

> As I got to the door the man opened his coat and pulled out a long pistol and shot the man. [He] doubled up, clasping his stomach, and fell to the ground. I was terrified. I thought [the gunman] might fire at me. My husband Harry called me back into the shop. I ran back inside to phone the police and then I heard a second shot. My husband came out and saw the two policemen lying on the ground . . . A uniformed policeman was not far from the other man. Blood was pouring from them . . . We got some blankets and put cushions under the two wounded men's heads.

Hall staggered on up the road, pursued now by a helmeted police motorcyclist, PC Leslie England, to whom Hutchins had called: 'Get him, Les! He's got us!' England drove his lightweight machine on to the pavement and cautiously followed. According to what he later told the coroner's court, he was within a few feet of Hall, when Hall turned and fired again – but missed.

According to the civilian eyewitnesses Hall, who said nothing throughout the chase, fired three shots – but none at England. Mrs George Mansfield, who was outside her home in Tennyson Road, said later: 'I screamed, "He's got a gun!" and began to run into the house. The gunman stopped and pointed the gun at another policeman on a motorbike. But he did not pull the trigger that time.' Mrs Florence Carter, aged 52, said: 'I saw him walk up the street with the motorcyclist behind him. Once or twice he turned round. Then at the corner he broke into a run. A moment later I heard another shot.'

This, the third, was probably fired, not at England, but at Inspector Pawsey, who was in a police patrol car. He had driven into Tennyson Road from the Romford Road, in an attempt to prevent Hall's escape.

Pawsey was 40, married, but with no children. He had been at West Ham for five years.

Said PC England later:

He saw Hall and drove the car across the road and stopped beside him. Inspector Pawsey opened the door of the car, as if to get out, and Hall turned and pointed the gun at him. He did not fire at that second, and Inspector Pawsey shut the door without getting out. He opened the door again, which gave me the impression he intended to get out and tackle Hall. Hall then shot him. He was very close, about three or four feet away, at pointblank range. Hall ran off, and the Inspector said to me: 'Get after him!' The Inspector was sitting and reaching across for the radio microphone. At that time I did not think he was seriously injured. But I knew he was hurt because he did not resume the pursuit. I went after Hall.

David Goddard, aged 11, who was standing in the porch of a house near the junction of Tennyson and Romford Roads, saw Hall approaching him up the road. 'He was lurching as he ran and breathing heavily,' said David later. 'In his right hand, which was pointing in front of him and held straight out, was a black pistol. A helmeted policeman on a scooter was following him along the pavement.' As the gunman passed the porch, Pawsey drove into Tennyson Road and screeched to a halt on the wrong side of the road. Said David: 'The policeman opened the door of the car and was going to get out when the man raised the gun opposite his shoulder and fired at him. The policeman fell forward over the steering-wheel and the horn started to blow.'

Hall now seems to have eluded the police by dodging through another house and more back gardens before crossing Romford Road (the A118) and slipping into a parallel street called Deanery Road. Walking along, he reloaded his gun.

John Wright, aged 13, standing outside his home, called out: 'Is that a real gun, mister?' Further on, another 13-year-old, Janet Bilverstone, was hovering at her front gate. She told a *Daily Telegraph* reporter: 'I saw a tall man – I should think he was about 5ft 11 – wearing a dark jacket, and a white shirt with a dark tie. He was loading a gun. He went past me and then turned on to a bomb-site, jumped over a wall and went into the open back door of a house at the basement. He ran out the other side through the front door and into Romford Road.'

Here he was seen at a distance by DI Jones. Hall got a lift in a red saloon car (perhaps it was someone he knew) and was taken a mile or so east towards Ilford, before asking to be dropped off. He got out of the car and disappeared.

Back in Tennyson Road, Inspector Pawsey, shot in the chest, lay dying in the driver's seat of his car, while a woman vainly tried to send an SOS over the car radio, which was crackling with messages about the shootings and Hall's escape. A man succeeded in operating the radio and told Control: 'A policeman has been shot! Send an ambulance and another police car straight away!'

It was too late. Pawsey died where he was. Hutchins died a few hours later in Queen Mary's Hospital, where PC Cox was also taken, seriously injured, but likely to survive.

Meanwhile, police forces for miles around were mobilised to find and apprehend the gunman. His description was widely circulated and road-blocks set up on major roads to Essex and the south. An all-car alarm went out, and the Commissioner, Sir Joseph Simpson, left Motspur Park in Surrey where he had been attending a police athletics meeting. It was the worst shooting affray involving the deaths of police officers for 50 years – since a jewel robbery in Houndsditch in December 1910, when three policemen were killed and four wounded by a gang of anarchists, two of whom were later trapped and died in the Siege of Sidney Street, in January 1911.

Nothing was seen or heard of John Hall, however, until that night, when he telephoned the *Sunday Express*.

The call was taken at the newsdesk by Nelson Sullivan, who was standing in for an absent colleague on the five-to-midnight shift. Sullivan happened to be a crime reporter, working mainly for the *Evening Standard* in liaison with Scotland Yard. The caller said: 'I'm the killer. I'm the man who killed the policemen.' The caller's voice sounded very agitated and at times incoherent. Sullivan asked for the man's name, and was told it was 'John Hall'. They talked for 14 minutes, while another journalist listened on another line and made notes.

Sullivan later told the coroner's court:

> I tried to quieten him down and told him I would arrange for someone to go to the telephone box and take good care of him. He said: 'I am very sorry, for everybody's sake. I've got a gun pointing at me at this moment.' I asked him to give me the telephone number from which he was ringing. I tried to get the location from him and told him that immediately in front of him there was a panel which gave him the location. He said: 'It's all scribbled. I can't read it.' He then gave a number – Wanstead 4199. Colleagues got through to the police, giving them the telephone number to enable them to trace the call. Hall said he had had some trouble the previous night with his wife and some relatives, and that after the trouble he had to go to the police station. He said he was sad and miserable about what had happened the night before and wanted to shoot himself all night long. Hall broke into uncontrollable sobs and kept saying: 'Tell everybody I am sorry – I didn't mean to do it.'

Hall said he still had the gun at his chest and had 20 rounds left, and Sullivan told the court he expected to hear a shot at any moment. He told Hall not to worry, and that if the police approached the box they would look after him. Hall said: 'If any policeman comes near me, I'll shoot him. I think I can see some police cars coming now. Yes – there are some opposite now. There are police all around. But I'll shoot the first person who comes forward. I expect they'll try to rush the door.' Sullivan said he tried to reason with Hall, who began sobbing again. Hall said: 'There's no one else around. Just police.' He continued: 'I'm terribly sorry. You must understand that. Is there anything else before I go? You'd better hurry up – because I'm going to die. Please don't make me out to be a bad boy. I didn't really mean to give trouble.'

A little later Hall started shouting, 'I am – !' He said no more. Sullivan heard what sounded like scuffling, and voices, and then 'something like a thud'.

The telephone box had speedily been identified as being in Lake House Road, which crossed Wanstead Flats to Aldersbrook and was less than two miles from where the policemen were shot. Empress Avenue and Balfour Road were about as far to the east. Within minutes the box was surrounded and the area cleared. The police closed in, some armed, some with dogs. The women's captain of the Aldersbrook Tennis Club near by said: 'The police formed a cordon across the road and advanced.' Within the box, Hall must have realised that this time there was no escape – from a trap he had made himself. It was a pleasant summer evening and lengthening shadows were being cast by the setting sun.

Colin Harding, aged 30, who lived in Lake House Road, was watching television. He said later:

> I heard the police bells gonging, and I dashed out of the house. There were about 60 police constables charging about; some were hiding behind trees, as if they were seeking cover; and there was one constable behind the phone box near my home . . . I walked towards the phone box and saw a man on the telephone. I tried to move nearer, but I was told to go back by the policeman. I wasn't sure what was going on . . . One policeman was standing just at the back of the box, and two others went up to the door. I heard a shot, and the man fell out of the kiosk just before the police got right up to the door. Suddenly the man fell back, his arms outstretched . . . When this happened, the policemen piled on top of him. I remember the police dogs were snarling on their leashes, but their handlers held them back.

Mr E. F. Lloyd was watching from a window in his house. He said: 'I saw two policemen walking carefully across the grass on the blind side of the kiosk, and as they got near I saw the man suddenly collapse. The door opened with his weight and he slid half out on the ground. As the man fell out of the box he groaned . . . One police officer in a flat cap seized the gun . . . They put him on a stretcher and took him away.'

Hall was still alive: he had failed to kill himself, although the bullet had exploded through his chest below his heart. The gun he had used was a Walther 9 mm automatic of Belgian make. Also retrieved from the telephone box was a copy of the *Evening Standard*, on which Hall had written in large capital letters: I AM SO SORRY.

DI Jones, who was at the scene, took charge, and accompanied the injured man in an ambulance to Whipps Cross Hospital. Hall kept mumbling: 'I'm sorry, I'm sorry . . . Why can't I die?' In the casualty department he appeared to recognise Jones and grasped his hand. 'Say you forgive me!' he pleaded. 'I'm sorry. I want to die.' He was operated on that night, but remained seriously ill.

His young second wife, Sylvia, her head bandaged, was not allowed to see her husband. She left, sobbing, with her father, Mr Roberts, who took her by taxi to Tavistock Road.

The following night, Sunday, President Kennedy and his wife arrived in London and John Hall was taken off the emergency list. He was said to be 'as well as can be expected'. In a private room, D33, propped up on pillows, he was attended at all times by two detectives.

Earlier that day, Mrs Muriel Pawsey was interviewed by reporters at her home in Oaks Lane, Ilford, about a mile from Hall's former pet shop in Cranbrook Road. She was 38, and had been married for 14 years. Her eyes were shadowed with weeping and lack of sleep. She said: 'I had Philip's lunch ready for him yesterday at one o'clock. He was a bit late arriving, but I didn't worry because I thought another job had cropped up.' She continued: 'Phil and I did everything together and had no outside interests. Of course he loved his work and was very thrilled when he got promotion. Then last summer we moved into this police house . . . I never thought anything could happen to us like this. Now I'll have to leave and find a new home.'

The other police widow, Betty Hutchins, spoke to reporters as her teenage daughter sobbed beside her. She said: 'My husband was going to retire in about three years. I looked forward to this so much, because we were going to have some time together.' In Queen Mary's Hospital, Mrs Cox said, after visiting her injured husband: 'He's more comfortable now, but will be in hospital for some time.'

Both widows received a letter on Monday from Mrs Irene Purdy, whose husband, DS Raymond Purdy, had been shot and killed by another gunman evading arrest, Guenther Podola, in South Kensington in July 1959.

On Thursday, 8 June, the Duke of Kent married Katherine Worsley in York Minster, and on the Friday, the funerals of Inspector Pawsey and DS Hutchins took place.

The nine-car cortège made a two-mile detour to pass West Ham police station and Queen Mary's Hospital, where PC Cox was taken in a wheelchair to watch the procession from a window. Two thousand five hundred policemen, including representatives from every force in Britain, lined the route and the road to the grey stone chapel in the City of London cemetery at Forest Gate. Among the dignitaries were the Home Secretary, R. A. Butler, Sir Joseph Simpson, and the Mayor of West Ham. Over 200 floral tributes and wreaths had been sent. That of Hutchins's children, Mark and Sharon, was a policeman's helmet fashioned from blue daisies; their card said: 'To the best Dad in the world. We shall miss you.' Mrs Pawsey's wreath was of red roses, which her husband had grown himself.

On Saturday, 10 June, Sylvia Hall was telephoned at 6.00 am – her husband had taken a turn for the worse. She went to Whipps Cross Hospital with her father. Hall was put in an oxygen tent. But, said Sylvia later, 'he was talking and appeared quite rational.' Her father wept, when Hall said: 'Will you forgive me, Dad?' They left the hospital at 3.00 pm. Sylvia said: 'John was asleep. And that's how I left him. I loved him. And he loved me.'

In Tavistock Road, the telephone rang again at 4.00 pm. Sylvia answered it. Her parents heard her scream: 'He's gone! He's gone!'

So there would now be no trial, and the report on the murders, already compiled at West Ham police station, would never be submitted to the Director of Public Prosecutions. The file was closed.

Sylvia's mother, Mrs Roberts, told a reporter: 'There are no hard feelings. As far as I'm concerned, he was a fine son-in-law, always civil and polite. But he was a sick boy. In a way I'm glad he died. Because it would have been awful if they had got him fit, only to use the hangman's noose on him. Or worse, if they had sent him to Broadmoor.'

The more sensational Sunday papers, cheated of a major trial, set out their findings on 11 June about 'POLICE KILLER JOHN HALL – GUN-CRAZY JOHN HALL'. The *News of the World* revealed: 'He once attacked a motorist, who he thought, had not shown him enough consideration . . . What made him go berserk? Hall's closest friends believe it was his fear of being sentenced for the attack on his family and locked in a cell. He suffered from claustrophobia. Even when he walked into a strange house he would open as many doors and windows as he could. Whenever possible he drove a convertible car with the hood down. When he had to drive a saloon car he opened all the windows.'

The *Sunday Dispatch* said: 'Hall married 21-year-old Sylvia Roberts after a nine-week whirlwind courtship. Each day the 6 ft salesman arrived at her house in a different expensive car. They were all from his car business, which he had been running for a year. Hall was a mental misfit when he was young, and had been in trouble for minor (non-indictable) offences. Juvenile courts had ordered him to approved schools.'

The *Sunday Telegraph*'s crime reporter said that Hall always dressed immaculately and had wealthy friends.

Flying, fast cars, speedboats, surf-riding and photography were among his hobbies, and he was extremely fond of animals . . . He described himself as a self-employed salesman, but he was a jack of all trades. Among the main jobs he had were lorry-driver, mechanic, traveller, and book-keeper in a furniture store . . . His father, Mr William Hall, 70, is a shoe-shop manager. At the Herts and Essex Aero Club, Stapleford, Essex, which he joined with his first wife, Joyce, in 1955 and where he learned to fly, members described him as 'the best of company, and the last man one would expect violence from' . . . Almost a year after joining the club he crash-landed an aircraft on a golf course on the edge of Epping Forest. He and his passenger escaped with slight injuries . . . He continued flying after the accident, but had not been seen at the club recently . . . Hall had received treatment in a mental hospital. He often insisted that no one could understand his mind – doctors were sceptical, and he was examined by a number of psychiatrists. He insisted he was in need of mental treatment.

Another paper referred to a medical report, which was said to have stated that Hall had been invalided out of the RAF because of 'mental instability'. If true, and if there had been a trial, it seems unlikely that John Hall would have been hanged, and would, as Mrs Roberts feared, have been incarcerated in Broadmoor.

At the inquest held in West Ham on 22 June 1961, Hall's widow, Sylvia Hall, dressed in a black costume and hat, was invited by the coroner to question, if she wished, any of the witnesses. She asked DI Jones: 'When John took the gun from his pocket [in the police station], did a certain change come over him? Did his eyes go blurry or something?' Jones replied: 'He seemed to develop a temper suddenly. His attitude certainly changed.' Mrs Hall said she asked the question because Hall's eyes 'had gone blurry' when he attacked her and her mother with the chair. She later declined to give evidence against her husband.

The eight-man coroner's jury brought in a verdict of double murder and suicide, and the coroner commended the bravery of all the policemen who had chased after Hall. He said: 'They were all taking their lives in their hands, in accordance with their duty. Each of them did that duty without hesitation.'

In due course, the widows of Inspector Pawsey and DS Hutchins received the Queen's Police Medal, awarded posthumously, on their behalf. It is not known how much they received in financial compensation. Mrs Irene Purdy, whose husband was shot by Guenther Podola in 1959, had received a total weekly income of £10 10s – from his police pension, family allowances and insurance benefits.

Mrs Miles, whose husband PC Sidney Miles was shot by Chris Craig in 1952, only received a police pension of £2 12s 4d a week.

Guenther Podola, who had shot DS Purdy on 13 July 1959, was the last man to be hanged for the murder of a policeman. He was executed at Wandsworth Prison on 5 November 1959.

The last two men to be sentenced to death for murder in Britain and then hanged were both executed on 13 August 1964. They were Peter Anthony Allen, aged 21, and Gwynne Owen Evans (real name John Welby), aged 24, and known as Ginger.

In the early hours of 7 April 1964, neighbours in King's Avenue, Seaton, a village near Workington on the Cumberland coast, heard thuds and a scream. They investigated and called the police. At the foot of the stairs of No. 28, lay the body of John West, a laundry-van driver, aged 53, clad only in a shirt and vest. He had been brutally battered with a cosh and stabbed. West, unmarried, had lived alone in the house since the death of his aged mother the previous year. A raincoat found in the house and not belonging to West led the police to Ginger Evans. He was arrested and implicated Peter

Allen, in whose possession was found a gold watch given to West by the Lakeland Laundry for 25 years' good service. Evans had once worked with West and had gone to his house that night with Allen to borrow some money. They had driven there in a car that also contained Allen's wife and children.

Evans and Allen were tried in Manchester Crown Court, found guilty of murder and sentenced to death. An appeal was dismissed on 21 July by the Lord Chief Justice, Lord Parker, by Mr Justice Widgery and by Mr Justice Winn. And a telegram sent by the mothers of Allen and Evans to the Queen at Balmoral had no effect. The two young men were hanged three weeks later, Evans at Strangeways Jail in Manchester and Allen at Walton Prison, Liverpool – both at 8.00 am. There were no demonstrations, no petitions, no clamour in the press; there were a few ill-attended vigils. Evans and Allen were hanged nine years after the death of Ruth Ellis and the storm of protest that her hanging had caused.

But four months after the execution of Ginger Evans and Peter Allen, Sidney Silverman's Murder (Abolition of Death Penalty) Bill, which suspended capital punishment for murder for an experimental period of five years, was given a second reading by the House of Commons by a majority of 185 votes. The bill did not, however, become law until 9 November 1965.

In August 1992, Harry Allen, the man who had succeeded Albert Pierrepoint as executioner and had hanged nearly 100 people – including Ginger Evans at Strangeways – died aged 80 at Fleetwood, Lancashire, a month after Pierrepoint's death.

CHAPTER 16

Alexander Vanags

The Murder of Eleonora Essens, 1968

Thousands of people disappear every year from their homes, their jobs, and other people's lives. They are mostly reported as missing and quite a few are never seen again. Some without doubt have been murdered, and their bodies have been concealed in cupboards, in attics or under floorboards, or are buried in back gardens, woods and fields, or sunk weighted in rivers and lakes. More murders are probably committed than we would like to think, and will ever know. If the killer is sensible, no one need ever know of his dreadful deed. But a sensible killer is a contradiction in terms.

The murderer's biggest problem, if he wishes to hide the evidence of his crime, is how to dispose of the body. If the murder happens indoors, in someone's home, the killer can either hide the body in the house or bury it in the garden. If it is to be hidden or buried elsewhere, some transport is necessary, and the place of disposal must be at a distance and deep. Dismemberment may seem another necessity, to render a bulky body less obtrusive and more transportable. But even if a murderer manages to hide or bury a body without being seen and with no suspicions being aroused, some mischance, some unconsidered event or act, may expose both corpse and crime. Although Al Vanags did not have a car, he disposed of his body most carefully. But he failed to bury his body deep enough, and forgot about the hungry foxes.

1968 was marked in Mexico by the Olympic Games, in Czechoslovakia by the invasion of Russian troops and tanks, and in America by the assassination of Robert Kennedy and Martin Luther King. In London, Eleanora Essens was murdered.

Three years later, on a fine Wednesday evening in September 1971, Dennis O'Flynn, a dentist from Fetcham in Surrey, near Leatherhead, was playing a leisurely round of golf with a friend, Mike Fisher, on Leatherhead golf course, two miles north of the town and beside the A243, which ran northwards up to Chessington and then to Kingston-upon-Thames. O'Flynn was a 24-handicap golfer, and at about 7.15 pm on the tenth hole he sliced a shot, sending a ball into thick rough by the fairway, not far from the main road. He never found the ball, nor finished the game. For as he poked about, he found something very horrid – a severed female forearm.

He told reporters later: 'I didn't realise what it was at first – it had become quite decomposed. It gave me quite a turn. It was obviously a woman's arm, quite slim, with a silver filigree ring and a blue stone on the wedding finger. The nails were quite long, and it seemed a well-manicured hand.'

O'Flynn and his partner went to a nearby house to telephone the local police, who were able to make a brief search of the area before it got too dark. They discovered part of a leg, much eaten, and a seven-inch bone.

A further search with tracker dogs was carried out the following day, Thursday, 2 September, with policemen waiting quietly as women golfers competing in Ladies' Day played their shots. But no other body parts were found on the golf course, and the police, led by DCI Paddy Doyle from Leatherhead, remained uncertain whether they were dealing with a murder, suicide or grisly prank. It seemed, from the state of the left forearm and hand, that its owner had died within the last two weeks and that she might have been about 25. There were teethmarks on the arm and on the remains of the leg, and it was evident that the leg had been gnawed, as had the bone. Golf-club groundsmen told the police that the limbs had been found on a foxes' trail. But where was the rest of the body? Where did it lie? Or had a fox dug it up? The arm and leg could have been carried by a fox for a mile or more.

The trail was followed up in both directions, one of which took the police away from the golf course and across the Leatherhead–Kingston road. There, in Ashstead Wood and not far from a bus-stop, they found a shallow grave, disturbed by foxes, from which the arm and right leg had been re-moved and dragged on to the golf course. But the left leg was still in the grave, wrapped in polythene in a hold-all. A dark blue corduroy slipper was still on the foot. It seemed as if a woman's dismembered arms and legs had been buried there together.

This looked like murder, and the Murder Squad at Scotland Yard were called in, led by DCS Peter Shemming. Other searches of the areas were carried out, but by Sunday morning nothing more had been found. It was then decided to seek the assistance of a local recluse. Ted Churcher, aged 71, who had lived in a tent in Rowhurst Woods off the Oxshott Road, for 30 years, was asked to employ his extensive knowledge of the area and look for anything untoward. Called 'Catweazle' after a wizard in a children's TV series of that name, he set to work on Monday, 6 September.

He said later:

I have been living in these woods in a tent for years and years and I know every square inch of them. I joined the hunt early this morning and went to the first grave. After examining it, I just walked round and round through the thick undergrowth until I noticed this mound of earth, which I know wasn't there the last time I walked through this place. I stuck my hook into the ground and felt something. So I started digging and a few inches down came across this parcel wrapped in polythene. Inside was the torso of a woman. It wasn't a very pleasant sight.

The torso was wrapped in a navy-blue slip and had been buried deeper in the wood than the limbs. Some concentrated digging of the area soon uncovered a third grave a few yards away. PC Duck first of all unearthed the bones of a hand wrapped in polythene, and then below this the victim's decomposed head was found in the remnants of a cardboard box.

DCI Doyle said: 'This is a tremendous break and we owe a lot to Mr Churcher.' DCS Shemming told reporters, before a post-mortem had been made: 'We think the victim was a girl in her late teens or early twenties and about 5ft 4ins tall.'

He was wrong about the victim's age and unaware, like others who had seen the sawn-up remains, that they had been marvellously preserved by the polythene bags in which they had been wrapped, and in which some articles of clothing used to staunch any bleeding were also found. Even after the post-mortem, in which it was revealed that the woman had had a hysterectomy, and had been savagely battered about the head, her age was wrongly given as being from 35 to 45. She would turn out to be 48 – although some newspapers gave her age as 51. She was evidently very well preserved in more ways than one.

But who was she? The police needed to identify the victim before they could begin the hunt for her killer. Dental records checked against her teeth would confirm who she was once a name was produced. The only immediate means of identification were the rings on the wedding-finger of her left hand, which her murderer had failed to remove. It was through these rings that he was eventually caught.

There were two rings – not one, as Mr O'Flynn had thought – and the stone on one was amber in colour not blue. It was surrounded by little *diamanté* stones. The other ring was a plain silver band, unmarked inside but for the number 835. Pictures of the rings were released and published in the newspapers. They produced a good response, and the information was added to the many reports of missing women, over 1,000, that the police were already checking. One of these women was a Mrs Essens from Mansfield. A woman in Mansfield, Mrs Kuicel, told the police that the rings could belong to her 'old friend Nora'. Mrs Kuicel came from Latvia, and so did Mrs Essens, whose first name was Eleonora.

In the meantime, forensic and other experts had concluded that the dead woman had been killed in December 1968 or in January 1969. Tree-roots were adjudged to have been damaged by the grave-digger before the spring of 1969; and part of a newspaper, the *Evening Standard*, which had been used to wrap the remains, was dated 5 December. A drawing of the woman was also made from her skull by a descendant of the 18th-century portrait-painter, Sir Joshua Reynolds.

Roy Reynolds had called at Leatherhead police station in response to a call for information. He said he had seen a man leaving woods near the golf course with a spade – a matter which was later found to have no bearing on the case. But in conversation with the police he mentioned that while working as an artist in Birmingham some time ago, he had drawn several portraits of wanted persons from descriptions provided by victims. He was now asked if he could recreate a human face from the bony proportions of a skull. He said he could, and after five hours of studying and measuring the skull, he went home and produced several sketches, which he showed to the police the following day. The woman's features, he felt sure, had included a long straight nose, a long chin, and eyes slightly recessed.

He told a reporter:

I used the basic methods of the Old Masters like Leonardo da Vinci and Michelangelo. They sketched the bone structure of human forms, then filled in the flesh around the skeleton. From my measurements and using my training in anatomy, I knew the face muscles could pull the face flesh only in definite directions. That gave me the all-important clues to the shape of the face. It proved to be accurate. It may have come as a surprise to the police, but I was certain from the outset.

For a while DCS Shemming was dubious about releasing the reconstruction – it might have been very misleading. But he took a chance. The picture was publicised, and featured in October, along with more factual clues, on ITV's *Police 5*.

The programme was seen by Mrs Essens's killer and his current girlfriend in his Chiswick flat. 'It looks like your old friend Nora,' she remarked. He shrugged, said nothing and went into the kitchen to do the washing-up.

Among the viewers who responded to the programme was the woman from Mansfield, Mrs Kuicel, who had thought she recognised the rings. She now provided the police with a photograph of Mrs Essens, with her eyes closed (as in Reynolds's sketch), and when it was compared with the sketch the resemblance was seen to be very close. DCS Shemming also had the photo blown up so that, when superimposed on a photo of the skull, there was seen to be an almost perfect match.

This was a significant advance in solving the case, but the police still needed irrefutable proof that the remains buried near the golf course were those of Eleonora Essens.

A dentist had found the severed forearm, and now another dentist discovered among his records a dental chart that matched the teeth of the skull. Clifford Allen had chanced to keep dental records going back for six years – usually they were destroyed after two. Mrs Essens had been a patient of his in Nottingham.

Her husband, Alexander Essens, was traced, and identified the two rings, one of which, the silver band, was a pair with one he wore. They had been made by a jeweller from a silver necklace and were used as wedding rings by Mr Essens and his bride.

The police learned that Eleonora Essens was born in the town of Riga in Latvia on 24 December 1920. She married there and had two children. But her husband and the children were killed in the Second World War when the Germans overran Latvia and the other Baltic states in 1941. The previous year the Russians had occupied the country, incorporating it within the USSR. They succeeded in driving the Germans out of Latvia towards the end of 1944, and it was about this time that the widowed Eleonora met Alexander Essens, who was also from Latvia, in a displaced-persons camp at Lübeck in northern Germany. After the war they both came to England and settled in Nottinghamshire, where Alexander Essens obtained employment as a coal-miner. They married in 1947 and made a home for themselves in a council house in Mansfield. Here they got to know another Latvian refugee, Alexander Leonard Vanags, who also worked as a miner in a Nottinghamshire pit. He first met Mrs Essens, who was seven years older than him, at a party in 1956 – she seduced him, he later claimed.

Like Mrs Essens, Vanags was born in Riga, on 5 August 1927. Like her, he had ended up in England after the war, and had married there in 1948. Like her, his marriage, to a German girl, broke down and he had been living apart from his wife, Ingrid, and their two children, since 1954. Mrs Essens and her husband had, however, compromised: they continued to live together but lead separate lives. In 1956 or soon thereafter, Alexander Vanags moved into the Essens' home. He remained there for several years, still working as a miner, until 1963, when a violent row between Mr Essens and his wife resulted in Mrs Essens and Vanags leaving the council house and setting up house together in Nottingham.

Alexander Essens said later: 'Occasional rows between my wife and I culminated with a fight at Christmas 1963, after which she took me to court for assault. After that I told her to get out, and she left ... She used to play around and sometimes got drunk. In fights she used her fingernails. Every woman does – it's their only defence.' Essens said that the last time he saw his wife was in 1964 on New Year's Eve, when they met at Mansfield magistrates' court in connection with legal proceedings about maintenance payments.

It was in 1964 that Alexander Vanags lost an eye and injured a shoulder in an accident on a motor-scooter. Thus incapacitated, he was prevented from pursuing his job as a miner. Instead, he found employment at a printer's. In 1967 he and Mrs Essens left Nottingham and went south to London, Vanags having obtained a job as an editor of aircraft books with a publishing company, Macdonalds. The couple moved into rented accommodation in Cheam, on the south-western edge of London, not far from Ewell and Epsom. Cheam was also about six miles from where Mrs Essens's dismembered body would be buried at the end of 1968.

Discontented with her suburban existence, she persuaded Vanags to move closer to central London, and he rented a flat in Chiswick, where she was later killed.

On Thursday, 18 November 1971, the police formally identified Eleonora Essens as the woman whose remains had been discovered near Leatherhead golf course in September.

The following day Alexander Vanags, now aged 44, went to West End Central police station to tell the police that Mrs Essens had disappeared from the flat in Chiswick on Sunday, 28 December 1968, after a row. She never returned to him, he said, although she had telephoned him at his office in January 1969. He told the police that she had walked out on him before, and was in the habit of consorting with Greek and Greek-Cypriot acquaintances in Soho. She was, he said, a terrible flirt, and often stayed out all night. She had several lovers, he claimed, and had left him four times in all. He called her Minky.

While the police checked various Soho nightclubs and restaurants which Mrs Essens was said to have frequented, Vanags was taken to Leatherhead for further questioning. He was detained for 24 hours while his home and his background were checked.

The police found that he had been living since June 1969 with a Guyanese girl, Denise Abbott, now aged 22, in a flat in a large Victorian house called Kendal in Sutton Lane, Chiswick, and that, as he said, he was the technical editor of aviation books published by Macdonalds of Poland Street in Soho. He earned £2,400 a year. He had met Miss Abbott in the Hammersmith Palais, where he often used to go to pick up young girls and bring them home. Some of them, including Denise, featured on a hand-written chart, in which his lovers' attributes were listed and awarded marks from 4 to 10. Mrs Essens (Nora) also appeared on the chart. She had been given the highest marks: her face, legs and figure rated an average of 6, but her bust was given 9–10, and her hair, make-up, conversation, kissing and love-life all scored 10.

Vanags was released on Saturday night. About this time he wrote to Alexander Essens in Mansfield, claiming that Mrs Essens had walked out on him and complaining about the way she had treated him. He wrote: 'It was a dog's life. The devil only knows what for her would have been the ideal man – maybe a lapdog . . . She would never admit that she was wrong. If I had been a strong man I would have shown her the door. But you know I could not do that.'

On Tuesday, 23 November, Vanags told a *Daily Mail* reporter: 'I'm going to hide. I'm going away from London for a while. I can't stand the strain of this inquiry any longer.' Miss Abbott (his fiancée, according to the *Daily Mail*) said: 'This business has turned me into a nervous wreck. The police have been watching Alex's flat, and people have been saying terrible things about him.'

What happened next between Vanags and his girlfriend is not a matter of record; nor is where he went. He was interviewed again by the police on 28 December (the third anniversary of Mrs Essens's disappearance and death).

But it was not until Monday, 10 January 1972 that Vanags was arrested in Chiswick High Road as he returned from work, and then charged on the eleventh with the murder of Eleonora Essens. At first he said: 'I didn't do it.' Then he told DCS Shemming: 'I did kill her. She was horrible to me.'

He made a statement. He said that on the Sunday after Christmas Mrs Essens began tearing up his books; he lost control when she taunted him and he hit her with a pistol-butt. He hit her more than once. When she collapsed, he listened to her heart and felt her pulse: both were very faint. He wrapped a cardigan around her head and sat beside her for a long time, wondering what to do. Then she died. After dragging her body between the two single beds in the room, he covered it up and tidied the flat. He went to work and told people Mrs Essens had gone away. But her body remained on the floor between the beds for three or four days before Vanags resolved to dispose of it by cutting it up. He told the police that Mrs Essens had twice attacked him physically and twice threatened to blind him in his one good eye.

He appeared before Epsom magistrates on 12 January and was remanded in custody. He was committed for trial on 2 March.

The trial began in the Central Criminal Court on 3 July 1972 before Mr Justice Swanwick. The prosecution was led by Mr Richard Lowry, QC, and the defence by Mr Basil Wigoder, QC. Vanags pleaded not guilty to murder, but guilty to manslaughter; his defence was provocation. He wore a smart grey suit, cream shirt, and a wine-coloured tie. He looked straight ahead, with his eyes on the judge. Occasionally he made notes.

Mr Lowry read out the statement made by Vanags to the police, in which he said that on 28 December 1968, just after Christmas and after Nora's birthday on Christmas Eve (when she was 48), she was in bed in the flat in Sutton Lane and he was doing the household chores. At that time he was 41. She began mocking him for his inefficiency, and when he suggested that they go out for a drink she laughed at him and said: 'I'm going out when I'm good and ready.' She also shouted at him: 'I'll see you ruined!'

Vanags's statement continued:

You couldn't stop her. She would never forgive or forget. She said I was good for nothing and I was no good in bed at all. Later, Nora was shouting and tearing up my books. I couldn't contain myself any longer. I grabbed a pistol and hit her. She screamed at me: 'You're nothing but a bastard!' and 'Your mother was a whore!' I hit her and hit her. I must have gone mad. I sat down and cried. I didn't know what to do. What could I do? I dragged the body, after checking she was dead, and put it between two single beds. I went to work next day without sleeping a wink. I ditched the pistol in a rubbish bin near Chiswick railway station. After three or four days I decided the only thing to do was to dismember her. So I went out and bought a bottle of vodka.

This was either on New Year's Eve or New Year's Day, a Thursday. He drank half of the bottle before cutting Nora up with a hacksaw. First he cut off her head, shutting his eyes as he began. Having done so, he was sick. He wrapped the head up and put it in a cardboard box, which he tied up with string. Having decided, after looking at a map, to dispose of the body in the Epsom Forest area, he took the box to Victoria Station, travelling by tube with the box on his knee. He put the box in a left-luggage locker near the air terminal office. He was glad to get rid of it as he thought of the head as being full of evil. Then he went to Woolworths to buy some large plastic bags. Returning to Sutton Lane he cut off the legs and wrapped them up separately. He did the same with the arms. The torso was too big, he felt, to dismember. After packing the severed legs and arms into a blue hand-grip, he took a taxi to Victoria, where he left the grip in another left-luggage locker and returned to the flat to deal with the torso. This he did the following day. He wrapped up the torso and squeezed it into a hold-all. Thus burdened he struggled with the hold-all up Sutton Lane to Chiswick High Road, where he hailed a taxi and proceeded for the third time to Victoria Station. The hold-all containing the torso was jammed into yet another locker. Mrs Essens was together again in one place, though not in one piece.

Vanags was now shocked to find, on opening his first locker, that it was empty – the head had disappeared. But having gone so far he did not panic and decided to do the obvious thing of enquiring about the missing box at the lost property office. He was told that the box had been removed from the locker, because the time allowed had expired. The box was returned to him and he took it by train to Mitcham. But the ground was frost-hard and he was unable to scrape a hole (he was apparently using a knife). So he returned with the box to London and put it back in another locker.

He needed a spade. He was also needed back at work. He bought a spade in Brewer Street, near his place of work in Soho. Retrieving the hold-all containing the torso from its locker in Victoria Station, he carried it (and the spade) to a Green Line bus-stop on Eccleston Bridge where he got on a bus for Leatherhead. This was probably on the Saturday. Getting off the bus across the road from the golf course, he lugged the hold-all into adjacent woodland, dumped it, and covered it up with branches. Then he returned to Victoria to collect the hold-all containing the legs and arms. He also bought some red roses, which he put inside the two hold-alls before burying them and their contents in separate shallow graves in the wood. Each was marked by a mound. He hid the spade and returned to Sutton Lane.

The next day (probably Sunday) Vanags collected the head from its locker, bought another bunch of red roses and went by train to Ewell, from where he walked for about three miles to his burial ground in the wood, carrying the box and the roses. He dug a hole and buried the box, and stuck the roses in the ground. Near by he carved the letter N, for Nora, on a tree. Then he went home. As if to restore his self-esteem he then embarked on a sexual spree.

All these winter journeys, on foot and by taxi, Tube, Green Line bus and train, were necessitated because Vanags did not drive: he had no car. He had to rely on public transport. But although he showed some resourcefulness as well as grim and dogged determination in disposing of Mrs Essens's remains, he neglected to remove the rings from her left hand or make the three graves deep enough. He also wrapped the remains in plastic bags (which served to preserve them), and in items of clothing (none of which, however, bore laundry-marks). A newspaper, which could be dated, was also used to staunch the blood. Then he marked the burial-place of the head with a small N carved on a young tree. It is not known if and when the police noticed the N and what they made of it when they did. But despite all the errors he had committed in concealing the remains, they would probably never have been found, had it not been for a hungry fox.

For nearly three years Vanags tried to put Nora out of his mind, and perhaps he succeeded – until a fox dug up one of his graves and Dennis O'Flynn drove a golfball into the rough.

The prosecutor, Mr Lowry, chose to take a line that was far from condemnatory and took him into the territory of the defence. He conceded that although Vanags had acted wrongly in killing Mrs Essens and in trying to conceal the circumstances of her death, there *had* been a measure of provocation. Vanags, he said, had been 'led an awful dance' by Mrs Essens: 'She made trouble at Vanags' workplace by ringing up a girl employee and suggesting he was carrying on with her. She came to his office and spied on him and made many nuisance telephone calls.' Mr Lowry went on to tell the court that in September 1967 Mrs Essens attacked Vanags with hot water from a kettle, causing him to have medical treatment; that she accused him of various misdemeanours concerning money and other women; and that in 1968 she rented a room in a house owned by the Latvian Welfare Society and had an affair with a Latvian seaman. According to Mr Lowry, manslaughter was a possible verdict for the jury to think about.

When Denise Abbott entered the witness box to give evidence at the start of the second day of the trial, she became hysterical and ran shrieking out of the court. It was agreed that a statement that she had made to the police could be read aloud instead.

Alexander Vanags also went into the witness box to tell the court about his life with Mrs Essens and how she met her death.

He said that on the day she died he was doing the housework while she stayed in bed, passing all kinds of remarks. She demanded a 12-egg omelette. He made it and brought it to her, but all she said then was – 'You are a fool!' Vanags carried on dealing with some household chores, and after a while he noticed that Mrs Essens had gone to a bookshelf. She began to pull out various books and tear them up. Some of the books were rare editions. She said: 'I'll see all this destroyed – all these damned papers destroyed. That's all you want – papers!' He tried to reason with her. He said: 'Please, please, leave my books alone.' Then he grabbed hold of her hand. She screamed at him and suddenly attacked him, hitting him with her hands. She screamed: 'I'll blind you for good!' He said she scratched him near his right eye and on his cheeks and hand. He seized her wrists but could not subdue her. He was standing by the bookshelf on which lay the broken pistol. He told the court: 'I grabbed it. I just wanted to knock her out. I could not control her.' He hit her once with the butt of the pistol as she faced him, but not very hard. He said: 'She spat in my face and screamed: "You're nothing but a bastard! Your mother was a common whore!" Then I just lost control. I have never ever hit her or lifted my hand against her before. I hit her a number of times. I held her by the dressing-gown and then I just let her drop . . . I had no intention of killing her. All I had in my mind was to knock her out.'

Vanags's virtues and Mrs Essens's awfulness were emphasised by the managing director of Macdonalds, James MacGibbon, who said: 'He was a meticulous worker, even to a fault. He was extremely conscientious, very unassuming and always very helpful. I thought he had a certain lack of confidence outside his professional work . . . Once he arrived at the office with a black eye. His mental distress was often noticeable.' A colleague, Dennis Green, proclaimed: 'He was one of the most gentle men I have ever met – at times almost irrationally calm in accepting what he obviously suffered at [Mrs Essens's] hands.'

Continuing the apparent consensus in court that there should be a sympathetic verdict, Mr Wigoder, in his closing speech for the defence, outlined the sufferings, bravery and honest endeavour of Vanags's early life.

When Latvia was occupied by the Russians in 1940, Alexander Vanags's father, a Latvian air force officer, was arrested by the Russians and executed.

After the Germans overran the country in 1941, the teenage boy and his mother searched for his father's body among the hundreds of corpses disinterred from three mass graves. After three years of privation, hiding and hardship, Vanags, aged 16, volunteered for the German air force in 1944. In March 1945 he was serving on the Eastern front when he was captured by the Russians. In May, the war in Europe came to an end with the surrender of the Germans. Vanags ended up in a displaced-persons camp in Lübeck (at the very same time Mrs Essens was there). But in 1946 he absconded, and made his way to the British zone in West Berlin. He met his future wife, Ingrid, there and came with her to England in 1948.

Mr Wigoder asked the all-male jury to consider the effect of Mrs Essens's abuse and taunts of sexual inadequacy on such a man, described by one witness as 'the gentlest man I know'. He said: 'Imagine yourself in his place, as a child of 14 walking with your mother along a row of recently disinterred graves, inspecting hundreds of dead bodies in order to try to see if you could recognise the body of your own executed father. If someone called you, in those circumstances, a bastard and the son of a common whore, is not that provocation that might make anybody, any reasonable person, see red?'

It was an illogical question, to which the reasonable answer should have been 'No'. But Mr Wigoder continued to paint a very sympathetic picture of the defendant, saying that it was entirely through his own efforts that he had raised himself to a responsible position as a publisher's editor. He had spent many years on research, said Mr Wigoder, and his files represented a lifetime's work. 'Put yourself again in his position,' said Mr Wigoder. 'You suddenly see somebody, for no reason, flaying them, ripping and tearing them up. Provocation? Enough, perhaps, to make a reasonable person see red.' And the prosecution had admitted that there *had* been provocation.

In his summing-up, the judge told the jury that there was no dispute that Vanags had killed Mrs Essens by aiming several blows at her head with a pistol. They would have to ask themselves, he said, two questions: 'Are you satisfied beyond reasonable doubt that when the accused delivered those fatal blows with that weapon, he did in fact intend to kill, or at least to cause really serious injury? Secondly – that provocation is ruled out, either because the accused himself was not provoked by the deceased so as to cause him to lose his self-control and do what he did, or because a reasonable man would not have been so far provoked?' If the jury were satisfied on *both* counts, said the judge, they should find Vanags guilty of murder.

After retiring for 90 minutes on 7 July the jury found Alexander Vanags not guilty of murder.

Speaking in mitigation before sentence was passed, Mr Wigoder told the judge that there were facts in the case that would enable him to reduce the sentence very substantially. He said of Vanags:

He has been of real service to this country, especially in the war. He was with the Polish resistance and the French Auxiliary Police in Berlin, and then he came to this country, where he was prepared to take work in a humble way . . . Once in a person's lifetime he is entitled to the credit for his past good services and I submit that in this case the occasion is now. This man will never offend again. He is a law-abiding citizen – he always has been and always will be. The jury have found that there was provocation – provocation that might have caused any reasonable person to lose self-control. And unfortunately in this case that weapon was at hand.

Here the judge remarked: 'I do find that a man who has been a miner in the pits could have overpowered a woman without resorting to that.'

Mr Wigoder replied that Mrs Essens was a strong woman, and that matrimonial disputes often took place in the heat of the moment. Vanags, he added, had brought punishment upon himself for the rest of his life – 'For his affections for this woman still remain . . . It would be a waste of human resources if he was imprisoned for a long time.'

In passing sentence, Mr Justice Swanwick told Vanags, who stood before him with his head bowed and showed no emotion:

I am quite satisfied that the jury have reached their verdict of manslaughter on the grounds of provocation. Nevertheless, this was a very serious assault on this lady despite the provocation. You used a terrible weapon which happened to come to hand. Had you thought about it, I am sure you could have overpowered her manually . . . I bear in mind everything so ably said on your behalf. But it is not a case I can pass over without a substantial sentence.

Vanags was jailed for three years for manslaughter.

On 2 April 1973, aged 45, he was brought from prison to the London Divorce Court and, accompanied by two prison officers, was given a decree nisi because his marriage to Ingrid Vanags had irretrievably broken down. The divorce was uncontested. He was released from prison in 1974 and is believed to have become the editor of a newspaper in South London.

DCS Peter Shemming, commended by the judge for 'the extremely efficient inquiry conducted under your supervision', retired in July 1973. He was 47 and had been a policeman for 25 years. His next job was as joint general manager of a country club, Woolston Hall, at Chigwell in Essex, owned in part by the James Bond actor, Sean Connery, and the former England soccer captain, Bobby Moore.

The Vietnam War was brought to an end in January 1973, and, after Watergate, President Nixon resigned.

CHAPTER 17

Donald Neilson

The Murder of Lesley Whittle, 1975

There was (perhaps still is) a tendency among some senior police officers to bathe in the limelight of a major murder case, and to exaggerate the quality of their efforts and that of the murderer, the more so the longer he evades being caught. The senior officer in charge is said to go without food and sleep for days in his dedicated search for the killer. He holds regular press conferences, makes dramatic announcements and instigates an excess of enquiries. Thousands of statements are taken, and paperwork and information piles up to such an extent that the trees cannot be seen for the wood. In the meantime, the murderer is attributed with demonic cunning and extraordinary powers of prescience, strength and disguise – how else could he outwit the police? He becomes a master criminal, a monster, a fiend.

In fact he is none of these things. He is just the proverbial needle in a haystack and extremely hard to find. If his connection with the victim or victims is obscure, or random, and his basic attempts to conceal his crime succeed, there is every chance he will never be captured – especially when, as is often the case, he is protected, knowingly or not, by a doting mother, girlfriend or wife. He is caught eventually through his own careless acts or talk, misjudgements or sheer bad luck, not through superior police intelligence and detection. And then he goes and confesses. Most murderers – those of whom we are aware – need others to know about the extraordinary thing they have done. They want to exhibit their kill.

Some regional police forces used to be (perhaps still are) not particularly adept at solving all but the most obvious murders – which is why the technical expertise, greater awareness and special skills of Scotland Yard's Murder Squad were brought in to assist. A few regional chiefs could become bogged down by a morass of reports, false trails and hunches, and be bedevilled by blinkered and bureaucratic thinking, as much as by a lack of understanding of murder and murderers. When more than one regional force was involved, the opportunities for blunders and bungling multiplied.

Richard Skepper, aged 18 and still at school, was fast asleep in his first-floor bedroom in his parents' home, a corner-shop sub-post office in New Park, Harrogate, on the York to Skipton road. His older sister and brother were not at home. His father, Donald, aged 54, a Methodist and much respected locally, had been at choir practice earlier that night, retiring at 11.15 pm on

Thursday, 14 February 1974. Young Richard was a heavy sleeper, and at about 4.15 am on the Friday the faint barking of boxer dogs at a public house across the road could not waken him. Nor did the man who quietly entered the bedroom and searched it, rummaging through the pockets of Richard's trousers beside the bed before shaking a shoulder of the sleeping youth. More shaking, and the switching on of the bedside lamp, succeeded in arousing him. Dazzled and startled, Richard saw the twin barrels of a sawn-off shotgun and behind it a man in black, wearing a black hood with a visor-like slit through which dark eyes stared. 'No noise,' whispered the apparition and switched off the light, adding 'Where are the safe keys?' Richard replied that his father kept them on a shelf downstairs. Told to lie face down, he obeyed, and, threatened now by a knife, let his wrists be tied with string behind his back and his ankles to the foot of the bed. A strip of sticking plaster was pressed across his mouth. 'Go to sleep,' the intruder whispered, and left the room.

Ten minutes later he returned. Talking in hoarse African-sounding pidgin English, he said, with the knife held close to Richard's face: 'Can't find keys. Where are keys? You come – show me.' The youth's ankles and wrists were untied and, still gagged, he was taken downstairs. A search was made but no keys were found. In the kitchen the hooded man ripped off the gag and Richard told him the keys might be in his parents' room, in a dressing-table drawer. 'You go get keys,' said the intruder. 'Me watch at door. No noise.' 'They'll wake up if I go into their room,' protested Richard. The shotgun was raised. 'You go,' said the hooded man.

In her bedroom Mrs Skepper was woken by movement on the stairs. Then she heard and saw someone dimly enter the bedroom and creep towards the dressing-table.

'Is that you, Richard?' asked Mrs Skepper. 'Are you all right?' 'Yes,' replied Richard. Then Donald Skepper awoke. 'What's the matter?' he demanded, sitting up and pulling the cord that switched on an overhead light. A dark figure, revealed in the doorway, sprang forward and said: 'Put that light out!' Mrs Skepper screamed. The figure backed away, flicking a switch by the door, intending to kill the bed-light. But the ceiling light came on instead. Simultaneously Mr Skepper demanded: 'What's this? What do you want?' 'He wants the safe keys, Dad!' said Richard. 'Oh, does he?' Mr Skepper exclaimed. 'Let's get him!' So saying, he swung his legs off the bed. There was a sharp explosion as the intruder's gun was fired. This done, he fled out of the house.

Donald Skepper, shot from three or four feet away, fell back on top of his wife, who did not realise at first that her husband was not only injured but fatally so. As Richard dialled 999 downstairs, Joanna Skepper tried to give Donald the kiss of life. He died in her arms, a two-and-a-half-inch hole in his chest. It was her birthday.

Exhaustive enquiries and searches were made in the area involving frogmen and soldiers, as well as the police; shotgun-owners and firearms-dealers were questioned; a £5,000 reward was offered by the Post Office for information; and some 30,000 people were interviewed over the following year. Seven months later, another sub-postmaster was killed.

It happened not in Yorkshire but in Lancashire, at Higher Baxenden near Accrington, at about 4.00 am on Friday, 6 September.

Derek Astin was 43, an ex-Royal Marine, and was recovering from an operation to amputate a big toe. He and his wife, Marion, were woken by someone moving about their bedroom in the flat above their shop. Despite his bandaged foot, Mr Astin hurled himself at the intruder, forcing him out on to the landing, into a bathroom, and blocking his escape. Mrs Astin had picked up a vacuum cleaner. 'Hit him with this!' she cried. There was a loud bang as a shotgun was fired at point-blank range, tearing a hole in Derek Astin's upper left arm and shoulder. He staggered back and the gunman pushed past. But somehow Mr Astin succeeded in grabbing and unbalancing his assailant, who tumbled down the stairs. As Mr Astin clutched the banisters at the top of the stairs, sagging against them, a second shot was fired, from below, this time from a .22 pistol. The bullet ripped through his buttocks and stomach. He collapsed on the landing, bleeding profusely. The intruder fled.

The Astins' 13-year-old daughter, Susan, tried to help her mother staunch the flow of blood, before running from the house, with her 10-year-old brother, Stephen, to summon help – the telephone wires had been cut. Derek Astin died in the ambulance taking him to Blackburn.

Another reward of £5,000 was offered by the Post Office and another major police investigation began. The Yorkshire CID chief hunting for the Harrogate killer, hearing of the Baxenden shooting, liaised with his Lancashire counterpart, and they concluded that the similarities of each murder, of time, method, weapon and costume, meant that they were after the same man. Similar descriptions of the gunman were provided by the widows and children, and his method of entry had also been the same. He had used a brace-and-bit drill to bore holes in wooden window frames, through which a piece of wire could be passed to dislodge the catch.

Details of other brace-and-bit burglaries involving sub-post offices in the region were studied by the police and 18 such raids, not all productive, and including those at Harrogate and Baxenden, were eventually attributed to Donald Neilson.

All but one, that at Harrogate, were south and west of Neilson's house on the edge of Bradford, in an area bounded by Preston, Birmingham, Mansfield and Leeds. They began in January 1971, at Jump near Barnsley, and ended in November 1974, a period of nearly four years, during which Neilson stole postal orders, cash and stamps worth a total of £30,000, his biggest haul being £4,400 from a sub-post office in Staffordshire.

An unsuccessful raid on a sub-post office in Nottingham in September 1967, when the intruder was tackled by the postmaster, routed and fled, was also pinned on Neilson. It seems most unlikely, however, that Neilson would have embarked on his first raid so far from his home and then lie low for over three years. He himself said his post-office raids began in 1971. After the raid at Jump in January that year, his profitable outings averaged three a year.

His last raid and third murder occurred on 11 November 1974 at a sub-post office at Langley, near Oldbury and west of Birmingham, which was run by Sydney Grayland, aged 56, and Peggy, his wife. They lived on a nearby council estate with Peggy's brother, Geoff. Sydney's health was not too good – he had been a prisoner-of-war of the Germans for several years. But since 1972, when his wife was appointed sub-postmistress, he had given her a hand. The post office was in a semi-derelict street which was about to be demolished. Every evening the Graylands would close the counter at 5.30 pm, after which the mailbags were collected by a van, the accounts completed and the place locked up. At about 6.00 pm Mr Grayland would make his way through a storeroom at the rear (which had no light) to fetch his car from a lean-to garage in the yard. He carried a torch.

What exactly happened that night is unclear, but it seems he came face to face with an intruder at the back door. Mrs Grayland said later: 'I heard a noise coming from the storeroom, and I thought it was caused by my husband tripping over. I went in to see what had happened . . . I saw my husband on the floor.' She also saw another man, and she saw his face. She continued: 'I was so terrified I can't say what he was wearing or what he looked like. I got down on my knees to my husband. He said: "Watch it, Peg. I've been hit." Probably I was hit afterwards. I next remember waking up in hospital.'

According to Neilson, he entered the storeroom wearing a hood and carrying a .22 gun, as well as a torch to which a small bottle of ammonia was taped. He had planned to surprise the man who worked there. But he was taken aback when this man appeared, shone a torch in his face and then grabbed *his* torch. In doing so the ammonia was squirted over Neilson's hood and into his eyes. Blinded by the other torch and the ammonia he fired the gun, lashed out with his foot and pulled the hood off his head. He turned to get out, but blundered into something and was then assailed by another person whom he struck with his gun. This person (Mrs Grayland) fell, but resisted when he tried to tie up her hands. She struggled and he hit her again and again. Having incapacitated her, he dashed into the shop and (despite the ammonia in his eyes) managed to steal £861 in cash and postal orders and get away.

Sydney Grayland was shot and killed by a single bullet that entered his right side and severed the abdominal aorta. Death was caused by haemorrhage and shock. Mrs Grayland, whose head was badly battered, suffered three depressed fractures of the skull.

The couple were not found until about 10.55 pm, when two PCs in a passing panda car noticed that the lights were still on in the shop. They investigated. Mr Grayland lay on the floor near the storeroom's back door, which was ajar: he was dead. His wife, her face a bloody mask, was discovered under a pile of cardboard boxes in a corner, her hands tied in front of her with a cord 25 yards long; a metal coat-stand lay across her. She survived the attack, but was unable to make a statement to the police for another month. On the floor the finger-tip torn from a black rubber glove was found, as well as a footprint made by a rubber boot, a chip of wood snapped off the handle of a .22 pistol, six .22 bullets, and five spent cartridges. A woman motorist would later say that she heard a series of cracks like fireworks as she drove past. Four of the missing bullets were never found: the fifth was in Mr Grayland.

When Peggy Grayland's condition improved she was told not only of her husband's death but also of that of her 45-year-old brother. Shattered by events, he had died of a heart attack.

Despite the fact that forensic tests proved that the bullets that killed Mr Astin *and* Mr Grayland came from the same .22 pistol, the three post-office murders were not linked in the press; neither did they attract much attention. This was partly because three regional police forces were now involved and because some police officers were bemused by the *modus operandi* of the Langley murder, which was different from the two earlier ones. But the National Federation of Sub-Postmasters was up in arms, demanding danger money for their 21,000 members as well as better protection and better pay, which ranged from about £8 to £19 a week. The Post Office promised some improvements and, with the Federation, upped the reward for information about the three murders to a record £25,000.

That November and over Christmas the West Midlands police were pre-occupied with the hunt for the IRA terrorists whose bombs in two Birmingham pubs had killed 21 and injured 166. Mrs Grayland was able to leave hospital just before Christmas and she compiled a Photofit picture of her assailant. Then, two weeks into 1975, in a Shropshire village called High-ley, 15 miles west of the sub-post office at Langley, a girl called Lesley Whittle disappeared.

She was born on 3 May 1957, when her mother, Dorothy, was 40 years old; she had an older brother, Ronald. Her father, George Whittle, a former bus-driver, ran a prosperous coach and rural bus firm which when he died, aged 65, in 1970, was worth some £106,000. Dorothy Whittle was not, how-ever, his legal wife. His first and only wife, Selena Whittle, had parted from him nearly 30 years ago, in 1941; and although a divorce was discussed, no action was taken. While Dorothy moved into his home, Selena Whittle moved to Coventry, where she survived on her wages and a maintenance allowance of £2 a week and, when these came to an end, she got by on her pension and social-security benefit. In 1970 Selena was aggrieved to read in a local paper that in addition to a £63,000 net estate, George had already settled gifts of £107,000 on his son, and £82,000 on his daughter, Lesley, while Dorothy, who had changed her surname to Whittle, had received three houses and £70,000. Selena Whittle received nothing in her husband's will – George had always told her he could not afford to increase her allowance. She took legal action, and in May 1972, a High Court judge awarded her £1,500 a year for life, backdated to her husband's death.

George Whittle's riches and meanness towards his wife made headlines in the *Daily Express* of 17 May. The item was read by Donald Neilson. That month he also read an article in *Reader's Digest* about the kidnapping in America of Barbara Mackle, a student heiress, who was held captive in an underground cell. The sensational kidnapping in Wimbledon in December 1969 of Mrs Muriel McKay, wife of a *News of the World* executive, was like-wise known to him. She was snatched from her Wimbledon home by the Hosein brothers, who demanded a ransom of one million pounds. Her body was never found, but the Hoseins were caught and imprisoned for life for her

murder. This particular crime was the first kidnap-and-ransom case perpetrated in Britain – and an unhappy example of muddle, mistrust and lack
of co-operation between the family, the police and the press. Neilson said
later: 'I studied the McKay kidnap closely. The police made such a balls of it,
and I worked on the principle of learning from their mistakes.'

He originally planned, he said, to kidnap Ronald Whittle, or his mother,
on a moonless night in January 1974, when the hours of darkness were also
very long. Much of 1973 was spent in lengthy and detailed preparations. But
the fuel and energy crisis that arose that winter, culminating in a three-day
working week, petrol coupons, lower speed limits and less traffic on the
roads at night, meant he would expose himself, in travelling at night, to extra
risks of detection. So he deferred his kidnap plans for a year – until January
1975, when circumstances, including maximum darkness, would again be
right.

In the meantime, he continued with his post-office raids, and in doing so
shot three men. If it had not been for the miners, Mr Heath and the three-day
working week, none of the sub-postmasters would have been killed. Nor
might Lesley Whittle have died.

'I shelved [the plan],' said Neilson later. 'And went on with the post
offices. And everything went wrong.'

Most things had gone wrong for him since he was born; little went right.
For a start his real name was Nappey.

He was a Yorkshireman and was born on 1 August 1936 in Morley, a
bleak little industrial town south-west of Leeds and south-east of Bradford
and less than eight miles from both. His father, Gilbert Nappey, worked in a
woollen mill, and his mother, Phyllis, in a textile factory. They lived in a
close, working-class community, in a one-up, one-down terraced house at
20 Henry Place, behind Morley High Street: the site is now a car-park. A
daughter, Joyce, was born when little Don was four and both grew up during
the black-outs, shortages and occasional dramas of wartime England, succeeded postwar by rationing and social austerity.

Don Nappey was a slight, short and scruffy boy, plagued with spots and
ragged at school, being derided as 'Dirty Nappey'. He often played truant
and, though protected by his mother, was periodically punished for various
misdemeanours by his strict, teetotal father. 'I always seemed to be getting
into a bother,' said Neilson. 'I used to get a fair few hidings.'

Early in 1947, when he was ten, his mother died of breast cancer. She had
been ill for several years and latterly neighbours could hear her agonised
screams. Henry Place was deep in snow when her coffin was taken from the
house, and her inconsolable son sobbed for days. Not long after this he was
caught by the police breaking into a Co-op. He was let off with a warning
and vowed never to be caught again.

Domestic drudgery was now added to his woes. For although a grannie
came in for a while to do the cooking, washing and shopping, these devolved
as a duty on the reluctant boy, who was eventually laden with all the household chores, with making breakfast for his little sister and father, as well as
the evening meal. He also baked cakes. This regime became increasingly un-
satisfactory to all, and Mr Nappey acquired a succession of housekeepers to

take the place of his teenage son. When Mr Nappey considered marrying one of them, Don left home. He was now 16, an apprentice joiner, and he became a lodger with the Corfields – a family in Tingley who had once been neighbours – sharing a room with the son, Gerry. He stayed there for over two years. Joyce went to stay with relatives when her father moved south and disappeared.

Gerry Corfield said later: 'Although he would sometimes come around with our group of youngsters, he was not one of us. He was a loner, the odd one out, and thought he had to prove himself by doing daredevil things, like jumping off high walls or riding a bike at breakneck speed. He was not very easy to get on with and girls always seemed to shy away from him.' Mrs Corfield said: 'He was a shy person, very much within himself. You could not seem to get through to him. But he never gave any trouble at home. He never shrank from hard work and would work overtime whenever he got the chance.' Neilson said of himself then: 'I never had a mate of my own age . . . People never thought the same way as I did. I never seemed to understand why.'

With the money he saved from working overtime, Don bought a 125 cc motorcycle and used it to roar into Bradford, where his main pastime – for he neither smoked nor drank – was to go ballroom dancing. He was good enough to win some medals. It was in a Bradford dance-hall that he met his only girlfriend and future wife, Irene Tate. She was a millworker and two years older than he. She had a twin sister called Hilda, who remembered: 'They would dance with different partners during the evening but always go home together . . . I never got on with Don very well. You couldn't speak to him or hold a conversation with him.' Of Irene, she said: 'Although we were twins, you couldn't say we were close. Irene went her way, I went mine. She preferred to be with the boys. She would sooner go off down the road and play football and cricket with the boys than be with me.'

In this period Don changed his job as an apprentice joiner three times, unhappy with the attitudes and demands of his bosses. Then on 6 January 1955, when he was 19 and a half, he was called up to do his National Service, serving with the King's Own Yorkshire Light Infantry for two years. But he was such an indifferent soldier, surly, scruffy and a poor shot, that he was back-squadded after eight weeks of basic training and had to repeat the whole process. At the end of this double dose of training he married Irene Tate at St Paul's in Morley, on 30 April 1955.

Neilson wore his battledress and a big white carnation; she a white wedding-dress. He was three months short of his 19th birthday; she was 20. His occupation was given as 'joiner' and his address as '20 Henry Place'. Hers was on the Leeds Road east of Bradford. There was no reception, no guests or relations, apart from an aunt and uncle of his who had been asked the day before to act as witnesses. It was several months before Irene's mother and her twin, Hilda, learned that Irene was married. Some of the Tates believed that Don married her to acquire an Army marriage allowance, which she was told to save, while living off her wages and staying at her older sister's place. A fellow-conscript said of Don: 'I never saw him buy anything, not even a cup of tea.' Even then he was money-conscious and mean.

An overseas allowance was also added to his pay, and while his bride languished in Bradford, Private Nappey was posted to Kenya, then to Aden and Cyprus. He was promoted to Lance-Corporal before being demobbed on 27 January 1957 – three months before Lesley Whittle was born.

His two years in the Army shaped his life, giving him interests and excitements unknown before: the peculiar pleasure of jungle warfare and survival skills, of the power of weapons, of fitness and self-reliance. He relished the hide-and-seek thrills of security patrols, dealing with Mau Mau gangs on Mount Kenya, EOKA guerillas in Cyprus, and Arab nationalists in Aden. A soldier in Kenya said: 'After Morley it was a bit like paradise. The sun was always shining . . . I wouldn't look any further than Kenya to work out how Nappey learned the tricks of his trade . . . In a way it's not surprising that one of our number used his training for illegal purposes in later life. The only surprising thing is that it was Nappey. He wasn't really very good at it.' Neilson said of himself: 'I never saw any blood, guts hanging out, or owt like that. I enjoyed my time in the Army. But I never admitted owt about it . . . It's possible to be afraid and at the same time to enjoy oneself.' He thought of joining the SAS. When his National Service came to an end, he cried.

Back in Bradford he joined Irene in her eldest sister's home, working for a while as a joiner, then as a door-to-door salesman, selling brushes. On 12 January 1960, the Nappeys' only child was born – Kathryn.

Soon after this, they moved to a terraced house on the main road to Leeds, the A647, to Grangefield Avenue. Various conversions were carried out on the house by Don, who was full of ideas and restless energy. He turned the roof space into an attic bedroom, paved the small front garden, concreted the back yard, constructed a garage and installed washbasins in the two front rooms, which were let to lodgers to supplement the family's income. He was always busy at something, repairing his car or repainting his home, which was smart to look at, but untidy within; his wife was also very casually dressed. Averse to anyone in authority, he never settled in any job. From 1962 he was self-employed, experimenting with several ventures, like wastepaper collecting, scrap-metal dealing and window-cleaning. He said later: 'Working for somebody else were no way to make out. The only way was being self-employed. That way you got everything – the wages, the profits, but also the losses . . . I got satisfaction out of working hard and completing a job. But then it was spoiled by people not wanting to pay for it.' In 1965 he became a mini-cab driver, using a Morris Oxford of his own and renting a radio. This lasted for three years, after which he set up as a joiner and carpenter, specialising in repairs, in building house extensions and garden sheds. He had an IQ of 119.

It was about this time that he changed his surname from Nappey to Neilson, so that Kathryn would not be teased, as he had been, when she started school.

One of the women lodgers used to act as a babysitter. She said later: 'Both Mr and Mrs Neilson used to go out in the car. Usually it was about 10 pm or 10.30 pm, and I would look in at Kathryn about 11.00 pm before I went to sleep. I have no idea what time they used to get back or where they had been

. . . I always wondered why no relatives visited them. Even Kathryn, whom they doted over, never seemed to have a friend around.'

A neighbour said: 'He always seemed rather secretive, and in the ten years I lived next door I only went into his house twice. He said nothing about himself, and if he had been working away from home and I asked him where he had been, he would just say "Here and there". He looked every inch a part-time paratrooper. We called him "Castro" because he always wore battledress and *marched* down the street. He even bought his own jeep.'

There was a reason for this. Wearing bush hats and camouflage gear, Neilson, his wife and daughter periodically carried out mock military manoeuvres and operations on moorland or in woods, armed with home-made weapons and guns. They ambushed each other and went on patrols; they pretended to shoot and kill, and to die. These war games, which seem to have faded out in 1973, were an outdoor expression of Neilson's military mania. Indoors, an attic hideaway was stuffed with all manner of military gear; and the bookcase in the lounge was full of works on warfare and tactics, survival, keep-fit and kindred topics. Kathryn, as she got older, was taken on runs and often went swimming with her father at the local baths. Her hair was kept short, as was her mother's, and she was treated and disciplined like a boy, being confined to barracks (forbidden to leave her room or the house) or punished with hard labour (cleaning paintwork or doing menial tasks) if she did anything wrong. Neilson was also very possessive and jealous, always wanting to know what she was doing, with whom and where. She was his playmate, the son he wanted but never had; Irene was more a mate than a wife. He said of her, after admitting he treated her badly: 'She isn't bad-tempered; she's rather a happy person. But I was the boss at home.' It seems they seldom had sex. His pleasures were chiefly solitary and secret, and he found that breaking and entering houses provided the greatest excitement of all.

His venture into petty crime was a considered career move. He told a Bradford psychiatrist, Dr Hugo Milne:

I've always worked hard and I thought I would have made a lot of money from my work. But I didn't. I was just banging my head against a wall. I never had enough capital for big jobs, although I've never gone bankrupt. So, there was only one thing left for me. There was no other way than crime . . . It's no fault of mine I haven't made any money. I didn't turn to crime to get a flashy sports car. I never even had a decent holiday until I turned to crime. When I thought about what I was earning and what others were getting for doing no work at all, there didn't seem to be any sense in it. There was no point in being honest.

He began burgling middle-class homes in the latter half of the 1960s, infrequently at first and during the winter months, when outdoor work and pursuits were reduced and the nights long and dark. He only took cash, so that no middlemen or 'fences' were involved, and he used public transport, as cars could be readily spotted and traced. He studied police routines and methods, as if they were the enemy in a one-man war, and varied the pattern and direction of his raids. He always had a bath beforehand and donned clean clothes which were splashed with disinfectant, so that any police dogs would be confused – as would the police themselves by his criss-crossing of district and county boundaries. If he lost control of a situation, or something went wrong, he abandoned the raid. Although he carried a gun, his maxim was: Never threaten to kill – Tell them 'Do as you're told and you won't get hurt'.

Long before he became notorious as the Black Panther, a title whose coining was claimed by the Post Office, police and the press, he was known by local police teams as the Red Shadow (sometimes he dressed all in red), the Phantom, and Handy Andy. His happiest moment was when he burgled what happened to be a policeman's house, and stole his whistle.

He told Dr Milne:

I was scared to death when I was breaking in anywhere. But I enjoyed the freedom of being out at night: the freedom to go anywhere I wanted, the thought that nobody was interfering, that nobody knew. There was a satisfaction in breaking the system . . . Having started on houses, post offices were just the same . . . No problem. The financial gain was greater. The money I took was Government money. As far as I'm concerned, I've never robbed anybody. I didn't want to rob old-age pensioners. If I'd thought like that, I could have bashed old people on the head, like some lunatics do . . . Everyone says a burglar is cowardly. But to wake somebody at night is not something cowardly. My thinking is that you've got a bloke in a detached house in bed at a psychological disadvantage – plus the time of two or three in the morning. He's only in his pyjamas or naked. He thinks of getting dressed, and you're away . . . When I put on a mask, I adopt a different personality. People saw me as the Black Panther, and I didn't speak in normal voices. It wasn't me . . . It's the same as in a play. It's an act – and I'm the principal actor. I've got to convince them I'm in control.

His decision to kidnap someone was to have been the climax of his criminal career, the greatest test of his skills and his final battle and triumph over the police. And with the large amount of money he expected to gain, he intended to set himself up with a permanent business.

The idea came to him after he read a copy of the *Daily Express* in May 1972.

Neilson later told the police:

The idea and information of victim and victim's home and reason for crime I obtained from a newspaper report on Whittle's will. From the newspaper I got the address and bought maps to enable me to find [the] address. From the amount of will and income from existing business I estimated that £50,000 would be sufficient and would not be too great a loss . . . I reckoned the mother would immediately pay a ransom of this amount for the son, or alternatively the son for the mother. From the maps I found location of business and house in summertime and also looked for a place where ransom could be collected. I pulled into the car park at Dudley Zoo and went into the Zoo. From the hill at certain places I saw a clear view over a large empty area. I reasoned that with a good pair of binoculars I would be able to see anyone walking at dusk or on a clear night . . . I would be far enough away on the hillside to make good my escape, if I saw instructions were not carried out correctly. Several routes were available through the woods to the rear of Zoo. Expecting the first collection to be in doubt, I then required a second collection point in a different area. I decided for a second collection to be dropped from a train. I needed a railway line in a large open space, with possibly a tunnel. From a map I followed the line of the railway, and went by car to a parking place at the opposite end of Bathpool Park [at Kidsgrove]. I left the vehicle and walked the footpath alongside the railway. The path went past a concrete drain area, and I came to an electricity sub-station. As I approached this I heard a roaring noise underfoot. I found the noise came from a slightly raised manhole cover. I raised the cover and saw a large ladder going down into a shaft. I returned at a later date with a torch and went into the drainage system. After exploring the full complex, I decided this would be used in some way for the collection . . . Next I found telephone boxes on a chosen route to be used in leaving instructions for deliverer of ransom. I then purchased several items of equipment . . . Over a long period of time I visited all areas mentioned earlier to familiarise myself with the areas.

It was well over two years before the kidnap plan, having been postponed for a year, was put into effect, by which time the three sub-postmasters had been killed. Although Neilson later claimed that he kidnapped Lesley in error, it is inconceivable he was unaware where Dorothy Whittle and her daughter slept and that Ronald was living elsewhere. Besides, mother and son were more likely to be troublesome, to resist, to faint or fight. Lesley was smaller than Neilson and more suitable for concealment underground. Like his own daughter, she would also be more easy to control.

On 12 January 1975, Kathryn Neilson was 15, and by now was finding life with her father increasingly restrictive and irksome, even intolerable. It is said that she had begun to hate her father. Two days after Kathryn's birthday, Lesley Whittle, who by then was 17 and a half, disappeared from her home.

Highley was a nondescript sprawl of a village on the crest of a hill. At one end of the High Street was a large white house called Beech Croft, designed in the 1930s Odeon-cinema style. Lesley lived there with her mother – Ronald Whittle, who was 28, having moved out when he married his wife, Gaynor. They lived not far away, and modestly enough, although the family firm, now run by Ron, who sported a trim beard, possessed 56 coaches and employed as many people. He said later: 'We've always ploughed our money back into the business. In terms of personal wealth, as opposed to business assets, you could almost say we are relatively poor. There must be many families richer than we are in the area.' Nor was Lesley wealthy. Her inheritance, held in trust, was not hers until she was 21. In the meantime, she was studying for three A levels, in geography and in pure and applied mathematics, at the Wulfrun College of Further Education in Wolverhampton, whither she travelled each day, via Bridgnorth, by bus.

On the night of Monday, 13 January, Dorothy Whittle went out to visit some friends. Lesley stayed at home. Small and slim – she was only 5′ 2″ – she watched TV ('Alias Smith and Jones'); made and received some phone-calls; altered a pair of jeans; washed her long brown hair, and before she went to bed opened the garage door and left the lights on downstairs. An untidy girl, she scattered her clothes on her bedroom floor. In the bathroom was £300 in cash in a leather briefcase, takings from the family business to be banked the following day.

Dorothy Whittle returned at about 12.45 am and pottered about for half an hour before turning out the lights and going upstairs. She checked that Lesley was in bed and asleep and, having taken a sleeping-pill with her Ovaltine, was soon asleep herself, despite high winds buffeting the house. She was up early the following Tuesday morning to get Lesley off to college, and took a breakfast tray up to Lesley's bedroom at 7.00 am.

The bed was empty – nor was Lesley anywhere else in the house. Could she have gone for a walk? Or gone early to college? But her clothes, both cast-off and clean, were still in her room. It was inexplicable. When Dorothy Whittle tried to phone her son Ron and found the line was dead (the wires had been cut), she began to panic. She rushed out of the house in her dressing-gown and drove to Ron's house, where he and his wife tried to calm her down. As Ron scoured the village in his car in case his sister had had an amnesiac fit or a nervous breakdown, his wife Gaynor, who was expecting a baby, went to Beech Croft to check the house for herself. A search confirmed that Lesley had disappeared and that the inner garage door that led into the house was open.

Then in the lounge she noticed something odd. A large vase had been removed from its usual place and stood on the hearthrug. On top of the vase was an open box of Turkish Delight, among which lay four curled-up strips of red plastic tape. Gaynor nearly fainted when she read the message, punched on each strip by a Dymo-tape machine:

NO POLICE £50,000 RANSOM BE READY TO DELIVER FIRST EVENING WAIT FOR TELEPHONE CALL AT SWAN SHOPPING CENTRE TELEPHONE BOX 64711 64611 63111 TO 1 AM IF NO CALL RETURN FOLLOWING EVENING WHEN YOU ANSWER CALL GIVE YOUR NAME ONLY AND LISTEN YOU MUST FOLLOW INSTRUCTIONS WITHOUT ARGUMENT FROM THE TIME YOU ANSWER THE TELEPHONE YOU ARE ON A TIME LIMIT IF POLICE OR TRICKS DEATH . . . £50,000 ALL IN USED NOTES £25,000 £1 £25,000 £5 THERE WILL BE NO EXCHANGE ONLY AFTER £50,000 HAS BEEN CLEARED WILL VICTIM BE RELEASED . . . DELIVER £50,000 IN WHITE SUITCASE . . . SWAN SHOPPING CENTRE KIDDERMINSTER.

Gaynor took the tapes to her husband before telling her mother-in-law. He was in his office. 'Lesley's been kidnapped!' she cried. At 9.45 am Ron Whittle telephoned the police.

The head of West Mercia CID, DCS Bob Booth, took charge of the kidnap inquiry, detaching himself from a murder investigation at Wellington in Shropshire – the naked body of a girl, stabbed to death, had been found in a ditch. He gave orders that the inquiry was to be very low-key and cautious: officers were to wear plain clothes and try to be unobtrusive; they were also to note the number of every car that passed Beech Croft and investigate the Whittles' lives. A news blackout was also imposed.

To begin with, the police were puzzled by various odd and amateurish aspects of the case, suspecting a hoax, or a student prank, or that Lesley had disappeared of her own volition. There were footprints outside the house and a trail of earth within; a few screws had been removed from the garage inner door although it had not been locked; and £300 lay untouched in the bathroom. Lesley's jewellery was missing, but she wore these items, her rings, bracelet, watch and a silver chain, in bed. Also missing was her long blue candlewick dressing-gown, and a pair of her mother's slippers. Presumably she had put these on before she left, as she slept in the nude.

What was also odd was the modest and casual nature of the ransom demand. Why only £50,000? And why pick on Lesley Whittle, when there were many other girls with far wealthier, better-known families and far more imposing homes? The plastic tapes were also addressed to an unspecific 'YOU' and made no mention of Lesley's name. 'KIDDERMINSTER' had apparently been added to correct an earlier omission, and 'IF POLICE OR TRICKS DEATH' seemed somewhat melodramatic, even juvenile. Could it be a student rag?

Lesley's college friends were questioned, including her rugby-playing boyfriend, who was now in his first year at Sheffield University. His alibi and his non-involvement in her disappearance were verified. He was clearly very upset at the news of what had happened. Enquiries concerning the Whittles themselves established that mother and daughter were close, but that brother Ron had had rows with his sister. He admitted that if anything happened to Lesley her money would pass to their mother and himself. His manner was too calm and businesslike, and he seemed very self-possessed. At the time, and for some weeks later, he was suspected by some of having organised his sister's disappearance.

Meanwhile, with DCS Booth's approval, Ron Whittle withdrew the required sum of money in notes from a Bridgnorth bank. But *two* suitcases were required to accommodate all the notes. Booth was willing that the Whittles should be seen to co-operate with the kidnapper's demands (if they were genuine). He knew that most kidnap victims seldom survived for more than 48 hours. He had also received an offer from Scotland Yard of the assistance of 12 'experts', some of whom had been involved in the botched hunt for the kidnappers of Mrs McKay. This was accepted, along with some surveillance equipment, and arrangements were made to reconnect and tap the Beech Croft phone, as well as the three call-boxes at the Swan Shopping

Centre. Full surveillance was also arranged. Operation Basket – 'We'll soon have him in the basket,' DCS Booth had said – was under way.

Kidderminster was about eight miles south-east of Highley and in another county, Hereford and Worcester. Ronald Whittle drove there in his Scimitar sports car, with the two suitcases on the passenger seat and DC Woodwiss, armed with a pistol, crouching on the floor behind him. They reached the shopping centre at about 6.00 pm. Ron Whittle took the suitcases out of the car and waited with them by the call-boxes, observed by about 40 police persons pretending to be anything other than what they were. Whittle and the others, including cramped DC Woodwiss, were prepared to wait, as instructed by the tapes, until 1.00 am. But now things began to go badly wrong.

Someone at Kidderminster had informed a local freelance journalist, Bill Williams, that a major police operation involving a kidnap was afoot, and where. He checked the information, and although a senior police officer at Kidderminster refused to confirm or deny the story (or say there was any embargo) Williams was sufficiently sure of his facts to feed them to the *Birmingham Post* at about 7.00 pm. He then telephoned the BBC newsroom at Pebble Mill. It seems that not one of the news editors who now became involved was told by the police officials they contacted *not* to publish the story. The news of the kidnapping of a young heiress, Lesley Whittle, was accordingly broadcast on local radio, BRMB, at 8.00 pm, and on the BBC TV News at 9.00.

From about 7.20 pm, both the Whittle homes in Highley were bombarded by telephone calls from various journalists. DCS Booth, now at Beech Croft, was furious and aghast. Operation Basket was blown. Soon after 9.00 pm Ron Whittle was recalled to Highley and his undercover back-up disbanded. It was felt that the kidnapper would make no move, now that details of the kidnap and of police involvement were known. The possibility that the kidnapper might *not* be near a radio or TV set seems to have been disregarded, and apparently the call-boxes at the Swan Shopping Centre were left unattended. Instead, Bob Booth gave a press conference at 10.30 pm at Kidderminster police station, in which he provided further details about the kidnap and remarked that it was 'just like an episode from "Kojak"'. Although he said, 'I am not too happy that someone saw fit to release information about police activities', he apparently refrained from telling the press to stay away from Highley and not imperil Lesley's life.

At midnight, as senior police officers planned their next move, the telephones in the three deserted call-boxes at Kidderminster began to ring, one after the other. The phone-tappers heard them, but no one was there to reply – although a passer-by picked up one phone and said: 'Who's this?'

Engineers traced the incoming calls to the exchange at Dudley, about 15 miles east of Highley; and on the following day, Wednesday, 15 January, DCS Bob Booth decided to comply with the kidnapper's demand – IF NO CALL RETURN FOLLOWING EVENING.

Very few people knew of this decision, and to divert the press from Kidderminster, Booth told reporters that no further contact had been made.

Unfortunately, reporters, including Bill Williams, now felt free to identify the Kidderminster call-boxes, and photos of them, plus full details, appeared in some local papers that afternoon. Part of the Dymo-tape ransom demand was also shown.

This time the press were rebuked. But there was now no holding them back as they vied for 'exclusives' and information. That night, when Ron Whittle returned to the call-boxes with a single, bigger suitcase and an armed guard in his car, reporters, photographers and a small crowd of curious spectators joined police undercover observers at the scene. Although the police tried to keep the unwanted observers away, the press and other bystanders were loth to miss the spectacle of Ron Whittle receiving the kidnapper's call. It never came, although he and his audience lingered there for six hours, until after midnight – when a man rang Beech Croft, saying that the ransom was to be taken to a subway in a park at Gloucester. If it was not delivered in 90 minutes, he said, Lesley would be killed.

Ron Whittle was diverted from Kidderminster via Highley to Gloucester, 50 miles to the south. Security was now very strict, and the reporters tailing his Scimitar car were successfully lost. Arriving at 2.15 am, he walked to the subway with the suitcase. He waited, and becoming impatient, shouted: 'Come and get it! I'm not leaving the case until I see my sister!' Nothing happened, except that a man and a woman walking their dog passed by. Frustrated and disappointed, Whittle and his attendant posse of policemen drove wearily back to their respective homes.

It later transpired that the couple with the dog, who lived near by, had made the phone call after seeing the Whittles' telephone number on TV – it had been broadcast to encourage the real kidnapper to telephone the Whittles' home. The couple were in urgent need of money, but decided not to collect the case when they caught sight of detectives hiding in bushes in the park. Although the man was never caught – he had fled – the woman was sentenced in July 1975 to four years in prison for demanding £50,000 with menaces. This setback was observed by some of the expert helpers from Scotland Yard.

Earlier that same Wednesday night, in what seemed to be an unconnected incident, a man was shot outside a Freightliner terminal at Dudley. Although he died 14 months later, the gunman, Neilson, was never charged with this murder. For if a victim does not die within a year and a day of an assault, the law is that a murder charge cannot be made.

Gerald Smith, aged 44, and married with two teenage children, was the overseer of the night-shift at the depot. He was walking across the main yard at about 10.15 pm when he noticed a suspicious-looking character lurking in an approach road near the car-park of Dudley Zoo. Concerned about his company's security and aware of recent IRA activities in the Midlands, he investigated, and suddenly encountered a man between two lorries. It was a cold, dark, murky night, but he saw that the other man, who was wearing a flat cap, a raincoat and a rucksack, was short and scruffy and carried a plastic bag. They exchanged a few words, Smith demanding to know what the stranger was doing there. Unsatisfied by muttered replies, he turned, intending to return to his office and phone the police.

As he walked away, Neilson shot him with a pistol in the left buttock. Smith began to run, but Neilson now shot him in the back. Smith shouted: 'You idiot! What are you playing at?' Neilson shot him four more times, before levelling the pistol at Smith's head – he was now on his knees. Smith stared up into the muzzle of the gun. But there was just a click – the pistol misfired. Neilson turned and ran.

Despite his wounds, Smith walked back to the depot. 'Get the police!' he said. 'A bloke out there just shot me. He emptied the gun at me from point-blank range!' It was not until he was taken to hospital that his serious internal injuries were revealed, necessitating the removal of a kidney and other operations; he nearly died. But he was able to give the police a good description of the assailant, although he inadvertently misled them by avowing that the gunman had a local accent, even ascribing it to Tipton, two miles from Dudley.

The police were mystified by this violent and unprovoked attack. They were amazed when empty .22 cartridge cases found in the Zoo car-park proved on Thursday to have been fired from the pistol that had already killed Derek Astin and Sydney Grayland. The Black Panther had struck again. But what was he doing in Dudley? And why had he tried to kill Gerald Smith?

No senior policeman, as far as it is known, connected the random shooting in Dudley with the kidnapper's phone-calls from Dudley the night before. And although lorry-drivers and others were questioned and the area searched, no one checked out a dark green Morris 1300 saloon, which stood in a car-park opposite a bus garage about 200 yards away. It had false number-plates and its tax disc number had been altered. It had been stolen from West Bromwich in October, three weeks before the murderous assault on the Graylands at Langley, and had been used in the kidnapping of Lesley Whittle in the early hours of Tuesday, 14 January.

Neilson had abandoned the car. He never returned to it or drove it away, believing the police would soon find it and be watching and waiting for his return. Journalists later surmised that if the police had found the car that Thursday, Lesley Whittle might not have died.

On the night of Thursday, 16 January – the second night after the kidnapping and the night after the shooting of Gerald Smith and the abortive journey to Gloucester – the transport manager of Whittle's Coaches, Len Rudd, was manning the Whittles' phone. The lines to their home had been put through to Mr Rudd's extension (the home and business lines were connected) and no policeman was present to monitor the calls although the lines were still being tapped. Mr Rudd was in his pyjamas. It was about 11.35 when his telephone rang.

He heard the bleeps of a coin-box call and then Lesley's voice. He tried to talk to her, and then realised that her words, repeated three times, had been recorded. He wrote down her message – 'Mum, you are to go to Kidsgrove Post Office telephone box. The instructions are inside, behind the backboard. I'm OK. But there's to be no police and no tricks. OK?' She sounded quite calm. Engineers would later trace this call to a telephone exchange in Staffordshire that included Kidsgrove.

Rudd telephoned Ron Whittle, who in turn rang the incident room at Bridgnorth. He was told to wait. This he did, with increasing impatience, until after midnight. Then he rang Bridgnorth again, and was told to report there for a briefing. He was fitted up with a one-way radio, and another was put in his car. No electronic bug, however, was put in the car or in the suit-case. Through the radio he could talk to the police in an emergency, but they could not communicate with him. He waited while lengthy arrangements were made for undercover surveillance in Kidsgrove. The Staffordshire police were told something was going on, but given no details. They were asked to stay out of the way.

It was not until 1.30 am, two hours after the one and only call the Whittles ever received from the kidnapper, that Ron Whittle set off in his Scimitar on the complicated 50-mile northward drive to Kidsgrove. This time he was without an armed guard. He was tired, alone and afraid.

Twice he lost his way, and it was 3.00 am before he found the designated call-box. But he could not find any Dymo-tape. The police listeners heard him say: 'I am searching behind the backboard . . . I am searching the ledges . . . Now I'm examining the floor . . . There's nothing here!' He went out to see if there was any other call-box near by, and in desperation rang the West Mercia police HQ. He was told to stay where he was and continue searching. Eventually he located the Dymo-tape, which had fallen down, or been pushed too far, behind the backboard. More minutes passed as he struggled to get it out. When at last he succeeded, instructions on the tape directed him to Bathpool Park.

The park, a large area reclaimed from mining wasteland, was a muddle of mounds, tracks, trees, tennis courts, football pitches and a ski-slope. Its main feature was a reservoir with an extensive overflow system underneath the park; and a railway line connecting Stoke-on-Trent and Manchester ran through a long cutting beside it.

Ron Whittle entered the park via Boathouse Lane at about 3.30 am, but failed to see the low wall where he was supposed to stop. The message had said – DRIVE PAST WALL AND FLASH HEADLIGHTS LOOK FOR TORCH LIGHT RUN TO TORCH FURTHER INSTRUCTIONS ON TORCH.

He drove about, flashing his headlights, to no avail. He left the car and shouted into the darkness: 'This is Ron Whittle! Is anyone there?'

After half an hour, during which he kept up a frustrated monologue on his radio, he left the park, met up with the police and drove back home.

According to Neilson, Lesley Whittle, held captive in the drainage system, died accidentally about half an hour before her brother reached the park.

She may, however, have still been alive when the park was searched the following day. This is said (by DCS Booth) to have been done by the few officers from Scotland Yard – who later denied that they were solely in-volved, if at all. No comprehensive search was apparently made, as the kidnapper was supposed to think that Ron Whittle was acting on his own – a strange pretence when the media had trumpeted that the police were fully aware of what was going on. If the park had been thoroughly searched, several objects that Neilson had left scattered about that night and previous-ly might have been found – in particular a torch placed at the top of a drainage shaft and bearing a Dymo-tape message DROP SUITCASE INTO HOLE. It seems unlikely that a comprehensive search was made, in view of the fact that nothing was found. To some observers it would later seem that a lack of consultation and communication, combined with inter-force suspicion, rivalry and carping contempt, may have combined to ensure that Lesley Whittle, dead or alive, was not found that day. Nor Neilson caught for nearly a year.

As a result, many months, and many man-hours of police time were wasted in fruitless enquiries and paperwork. The hunt for Neilson would become the most expensive in the annals of murder, costing the taxpayer well over £1 million.

For seven days after Ron Whittle's journey to Bathpool Park, he and the police waited for the kidnapper to make contact. He never did, although hoax calls continued to be made. The shooting of Gerald Smith in Dudley, though now attributed to the Black Panther, was still not connected with the kidnapping of Lesley. Then on Thursday, 23 January, the various police investigations meshed and merged.

A man told the police in Dudley that a green Morris 1300 had apparently been abandoned in a car-park. The police investigated and not only found that it had been stolen, but also that it contained a plethora of Black Panther clues, including 90 feet of rope; black plastic sheeting; a yellow foam-rubber mattress; a torch; batteries; a bottle of Lucozade; cooking equipment; men's clothing; four brown envelopes and a tape-recorder containing a cassette.

In the envelopes, each numbered and labelled by hand (eg – 'At 55719 for street light'), were four strips of Dymo-tape. They were the instructions, the ransom trail that Ron Whittle should have followed on the Tuesday and Wednesday nights, taking him from Kidderminster to call-boxes in Wolverhampton and Dudley, and then to a streetlight in the road leading to the Freightliner terminal.

The police were elated, astounded and dismayed – the Black Panther, their most wanted man, who had already killed three and seriously injured others, had kidnapped Lesley Whittle. They surmised that he had been laying the ransom trail when interrupted by Gerald Smith. The tape cassette, which was not played until after midnight, clinched the inescapable fact that Lesley was in the hands of the Panther. Assembled senior policemen heard her say three times, as if in an empty room: 'Go to the M6 north to junction 10 and then on to the A454 towards Walsall. Instructions are taped under the shelf in the telephone box.' She then added: 'There's no need to worry, Mum. I'm OK. I got a bit wet, but I'm quite dry now. I'm being treated very well. OK?'

This message was clearly meant to have been played, from Dudley, when the Panther telephoned the call-boxes at the Swan Shopping Centre at midnight on the Tuesday. It was also to have been used on the Wednesday night. The four Dymo-tape messages would then have led Whittle to the ransom drop. But where was that? The fourth message referred to instructions taped to a streetlight. As this fifth message was not in the car, the police assumed it was already in place, or had been dropped when the Panther fled after shooting Gerald Smith. They looked for a piece of red tape in the Freightliner terminal area, but found nothing. None of the call-boxes specified in the other messages was checked, although a watch was kept on them, as the police assumed that the tapes contained in the envelopes had not been placed. Yet some tapes must have been in position on the *Tuesday* night.

In fact, the tapes in the envelopes were *duplicates*. But this was not realised until 3 February, when a 17-year-old youth found a strip of black Dymo-tape in a call-box outside the bus garage in Dudley (where the Morris had been parked). It was the fourth message. The police then searched the other relevant call-boxes and found three more black tapes. A fifth was found on a lamp-post in the Freightliner road. Like the others, this was a strip of black Dymo-tape on black adhesive tape and was very hard to spot. Ron Whittle could never have seen it at night, and there were five lamp-posts in the road.

The message on this tape was – CROSS ROAD AND CAR PARK GO RIGHT TO GATE NUMBER 8. But it would have been impossible for Whittle to comply. There were many gates in the walls around the adjacent Zoo and none was numbered. It was not until 8 February that a policeman found a black strip of Dymo-tape by the perimeter wall near an iron-barred gate seven feet high. This one said: INSTRUCTIONS AT END OF ROPE. Two hundred and fifty feet of rope had been found near by on 18 January by a policeman on another inquiry. Although no taped instructions were ever found with this rope, the police concluded that the Panther's final instruction to Whittle had been for him to tie the suitcase to the rope. Whereupon it would have been hauled over the wall by the Panther and seized. He would then have made his escape within the Zoo.

Having abandoned this ransom trail and drop as well as the Morris car, the Panther had been forced on the Thursday to make another tape-recorded message with Lesley and improvise another ransom trail, taking Whittle to the Kidsgrove Post Office and thence to Bathpool Park.

Senior officers of the West Mercia and West Midlands police forces kept the discovery of the Morris car's contents and their knowledge that the Black Panther had kidnapped Lesley Whittle to themselves. Junior police officers and other forces were not told. A news black-out was imposed on the press on 27 January. It lasted a fortnight and ended with a press conference in Dudley, during which DCS Bob Booth revealed the identity of Lesley's kidnapper. He said: 'This man is the most dangerous criminal at large in this country today.'

The public's assistance was now officially sought, and alleged sightings of the Morris car over the previous winter, as well as of the Panther, whose Photofit pictures misled many, poured into police stations all over central England. Hoax calls continued, and for a time two men, with local regional accents, were imagined to be the Panther himself. House-to-house enquiries were made at Highley and Dudley, and Dudley Zoo was searched (Lesley's body was imagined by some to have been fed to carnivores there), as well as many acres of woodland, mine-workings and wasteland, where suspicious persons were said to have been seen. Lorry-drivers, coach employees, post-office employees and known criminals were questioned. Radio broadcasts and television appeals, involving Ron Whittle and DCS Booth, were made.

Press conferences were held every day. But it was not until Tuesday, 4 March, when the pretence that Whittle and the police were not allies was abandoned, that media and police attention concentrated on Bathpool Park.

Now some schoolboys came forward. Back in January one pair had found a Dymo-tape with the message DROP THE SUITCASE INTO HOLE. Another pair had found the torch to which the tape had been attached – within the bars of a concrete pillbox capping a deep shaft in the park.

On 6 March, DC Phil Maskery went down the shaft carrying a torch. At its foot was a five-foot-wide tunnel through which a few inches of water ran; and in rubbish below the shaft lay a Dymo-tape machine. Another shaft was inspected, and then a third, the deepest at 62 feet – but not before a safety check for dangerous gases had delayed further searching for a day.

At last, on the afternoon of Friday, 7 March, Lesley Whittle's body was found, nearly two months after she had been taken from her home.

DC Maskery descended the shaft down a steel ladder encased for 45 feet by a safety cage. The shaft was six feet across. There was a metal platform at 22 feet and another as far below, near which was the mouth of a small, dry tunnel. A third ladder, unprotected, took him down another nine feet to a third platform, five feet long and two feet wide, on which lay a yellow foam-rubber mattress and a folded maroon sleeping-bag that had been used as a pillow. By the light of his torch he saw below the platform part of a blue dressing-gown dangling from a metal projection. He also saw a piece of taut wire, clamped at one end to the ladder. The other end led over one edge of the platform, below which hung the pale, naked body of Lesley Whittle, still wearing her silver trinkets, and with a wire noose around her neck.

She had died almost immediately, and, in effect, of fright. An autopsy revealed that she had not been strangled by the wire noose, which had been clamped around her neck like a collar and padded with Elastoplast. The cause of death, given as 'vagal inhibition', meant that sudden pressure on the vagal nerve and carotid artery in her neck had caused her heart to stop. Although the pathologist could not establish an exact time or day of death, it was evident she had not eaten for two or three days – or even more. There were some minor bruises on her body, which was very thin and weighed seven stone. But there were no signs of sexual interference or violence, nor of any abrasions that might have been caused by the metal lip of the rusty platform. It seemed that she must have been enclosed in a sleeping-bag when she fell (or was pushed) off the platform. For a zipped-up sleeping-bag was discovered in an underground canal, whither it had been swept by rainwater flooding through the tunnel below the platform. It could have slid off her. Also found in the canal were her mother's bedroom slippers, a half-bottle of brandy, a flask, a polo-neck jumper, trousers, socks, strips of Elastoplast that had been used to cover her eyes and mouth and bind her wrists, and some unused Dymo-tape.

The length of steel wire used to tether her to the ladder was five feet long. It had snagged on a metal projection, like the dressing-gown. As a result, the full vertical drop had been reduced, leaving Lesley suspended below the platform with her toes about seven inches from the tunnel's floor. If the wire had *not* snagged, her feet would have touched the ground – and she might never have died.

At the time all these details were not known or understood, and the imagined manner of her death was viewed with horror. It seemed that the Panther had deliberately hanged his victim in her cold, dark tomb.

But who was he? Where was he? The answers to these questions were now being sought by Commander John Morrison, aged 55, the head of New Scotland Yard's Murder Squad, who had been brought in by the Chief Constable of Staffordshire to solve the murder of Lesley Whittle. Resentfully, DCS Booth told reporters: 'Staffordshire have got our body.' His final assertion, made before it was decreed that Morrison alone would in future make statements and hold press conferences, was that the kidnapper would be arrested within 24 hours. It took another nine months.

Meanwhile, every effort was made to trace the owner of the many items found in the green Morris, in the drainage system and in the park, where articles abandoned by Neilson continued to be discovered or returned by schoolboys and others, and not by the police. But not one of these items, most of which had been bought at chain-stores with cash, gave the police any leads. They knew the Panther's probable age, his height, his measurements, and the size of his shoes. They knew he was very fit, skilled in mechanical matters, in outdoor pursuits, and had probably undergone some military training. They surmised he was a tradesman, a loner, obsessed with details, and that he probably had a wife – for a pair of unglamorous women's panties were discovered in the Morris doing service as a duster. The police even had examples of his handwriting on the envelopes, and partial fingerprints on a notepad. But an exhaustive check of prints kept in criminal records drew a blank.

A reconstruction was staged in Bathpool Park in April, a local repertory actor posing as the Panther. Hundreds of men, suspected of being the Panther and named by workmates, neighbours and wives, were interviewed by the police, as were over 3,000 men who had been employed in the two-and-a-half-year construction of the Bathpool drainage system. And three men who resembled the Panther Photofits were arrested at other times, one in Shropshire and two in Leeds. Many theories and avenues of enquiry were tried and tested, and police forces elsewhere had to deal with three copy-cat kidnappings, all unsuccessful.

Then in Leeds, in October 1975, the Yorkshire police were faced with the hunt for a killer that would endure for over five years. His first victim was a prostitute, Wilma McCann. Thirteen women, in all, were murdered and seven maimed before the Yorkshire Ripper, Peter Sutcliffe, was caught, by chance, in January 1981.

And it was by chance that Donald Neilson was caught, on Thursday, 11 December 1975.

It happened in Mansfield Woodhouse, a Nottinghamshire mining village off the M1. PCs Tony White and Stuart Mackenzie were sitting in a parked panda car at about 11.00 pm, looking out for troublemakers and drunks, when Mackenzie, the driver, noticed a short, scruffy man, carrying a hold-all, hurrying along the other side of the road. The man averted his face as he passed. 'He looks worth a check,' said Mackenzie. They did a U-turn and stopped beside the stranger. PC White, in the passenger seat, asked for the man's personal details. He said he was a lorry-driver, John Moxon, from Chapel-en-le-Frith. White turned to write this down on a clipboard. 'Don't move!' said the man, suddenly pointing a double-barrelled sawn-off shotgun at White through the open window. 'You! Into the back! No tricks. Or you are dead.' White scrambled over his seat into the back of the car behind Mackenzie. The gunman got into the passenger seat, the barrels of his gun in Mackenzie's left armpit. 'Drive!' said the man.

Why Neilson did not shoot and run, as was his wont, is a mystery. But, taken by surprise, he had no plan and no escape route. He probably needed time to think.

He directed them southwards to a village called Blidworth. Both policemen pretended to be cowardly and obsequious, calling the gunman 'Sir' and going on about their wives and children. 'Shut up and sit still!' the gunman said. He asked for some string, obviously planning to tie them up. There was none in the car. 'Sorry, sir,' said White. They were now heading for Sherwood Forest, but first had to pass through another mining village called Rainworth. They approached a Y junction. 'Which way?' asked Mackenzie, and as the gunman looked ahead to read the signs, White lunged forward. He seized the muzzle and wrenched it upwards. Mackenzie braked hard. The gun exploded, tearing flesh from White's right hand. With his left he seized the gunman's head in a stranglehold. Mackenzie, who had dived out of the car, raced around to the other door, yelling to the customers in a fish-and-chip shop called the Junction Chippy to come and help. Four did so, including a man who had once been picked up by the police as a suspect in the Panther inquiry. After a violent struggle, in which the gunman's face and body were battered, he was overpowered and handcuffed to some railings near the chippy, where he collapsed.

A body search produced a belt of 12-bore cartridges and two knives. In the hold-all was a quantity of house-breaking equipment, including two hoods and a bottle of ammonia. It later transpired that Neilson had reverted that year to burgling people's homes.

He was taken to Mansfield police station, stripped and, garbed in a blanket, was interviewed for six hours overnight by DCS John McNaught. Neilson refused to give his real name and said very little. He had a black eye and his face was cut and bruised. When accused of being the Black Panther he replied: 'Not true. I no shoot anybody . . . I shoot dog, but no policeman. I no Black Panther. When Black Panther work, he shoot to kill . . . If you say I am Black Panther they lock me up and throw away the key.'

By Friday morning, word had spread, and the media besieged the police station. When Neilson's fingerprints were taken, they were found to match the partial print the Mansfield police had on file. McNaught rang Staffordshire CID. 'I think we've got your man!' he said. Commander Morrison and other senior officers drove to Mansfield. But it was not until Friday night that Neilson provided DCS Roy Readwin, head of the Nottinghamshire CID, with his real name and address, so that his wife could be told where he was.

He was taken at midnight under heavy guard to Kidsgrove, 70 miles away, as the police searched his home in Grangefield Avenue, Bradford. The house was up for sale – Neilson was planning to move away from his coloured neighbours and buy something cheaper, in Pudsey.

They found an arsenal of assorted weapons in the attic of the house, along with masses of survival equipment, anoraks, hoods, shoes, radios, torches, car keys, ammunition, ropes and wire. Mrs Neilson and Kathryn, in their night clothes, were in tears. A notebook containing sketches, addresses and plans of future raids was found in the living-room, and a small model of a black panther was discovered hidden in a sideboard. Mrs Neilson said it had been bought in Blackpool two years ago as a present for Kathryn.

At 7.00 am a police van arrived to transport over 500 potential exhibits that the police removed from the house. In garages in Northampton two stolen cars were later found.

Meanwhile, in an office at Kidsgrove police station, at 2.15 am, Neilson, now wearing a boiler suit and socks and handcuffed to a chair, faced John Morrison. The head of the Staffordshire CID, DCS Wright, and DCI Wally Boreham from Scotland Yard were also present. When Morrison asked Neilson if he could help them about Lesley Whittle's death, he replied, after a long silence: 'No, sir. Not me. Not Lesley Whittle.'

Every question was met with long silences, as much as 15 minutes. He explained: 'I'm thinking, sir.' When at last he revealed some details about his age, occupation and National Service, the interrogators left, returning at 5.20 am. Now Neilson began to sob, and when asked whether he had been to Highley and Bathpool Park he replied: 'I don't know, sir. I've been lots of places.' Asked directly whether he had murdered Lesley Whittle, he wept and said: 'No sir. Not me. Not murder the young girl.'

The interview was curtailed at 6.40 am on the Saturday morning and resumed at 3.15 pm. Slowly, Neilson began to admit that he had been to Highley, Bathpool and Dudley. After one 20-minute silence he said: 'I didn't murder her. I didn't even known who I was going to get from the house.' Morrison cautioned Neilson, who said: 'The papers don't tell the truth. The Black Panther, so-called – they tell lies about him. He is not like they say . . . I want to make a statement. I want everybody to know the truth.'

He was now asked about the sub-postmaster murders, and after further silences he said – of Harrogate: 'I'll tell you about it' – of Accrington: 'These look bad for me. But I must let the people know the truth. I did that' – and of Langley: 'My God, this is a bad one. You might as well know it was me.' Once again he wept. Of the shooting of Gerald Smith, he said: 'Yes, all right. I did all these things . . . I want to make statements about them all. It was not how people said.'

At 7.00 pm on 13 December, Neilson began talking about the kidnapping of Lesley Whittle. DCI Boreham, on Neilson's insistence, wrote down his exact words, some of which he corrected himself and initialled. At 8.25 pm, there was a break as he ate two sandwiches. At five to eleven he was given two bags of crisps, and an hour later the session was adjourned. It was resumed at 2.05 on the Sunday afternoon and ended at 5.50.

After beginning with an account of how he conceived and planned the kidnapping, he went on to give his version of the last three days of Lesley's life.

He said: 'One night I set off to go to Highley. I arrived late at night. I went through back door of garage to inner back door of house. I removed outer handle and turned spindle with pliers to enter.'

He later told the court that he had arrived at about 2.00 am on the night of a new moon. He was wearing a dark blue hood. On entering he went first to the kitchen to check if there was any dog food or a dog bowl – if there had been, he said, he would have left. Then he cut the telephone wires. He said that if his victim had screamed or shouted he would have abandoned the whole plan. His statement to the police continued:

I went upstairs, floorboards at top of landing made loud creaks. I went into first bedroom on right. There was someone in bed. I awoke the person and said: 'Don't make any noise. I want money.' The person replied: 'It's in the bathroom.' I said: 'You show me.' A girl got out of bed. She was naked. I said: 'Put on some clothes.' She took a light coat from the bed and put this on and led towards the bathroom. The boards on the landing creaked loudly. At the same time I heard a sound from a bedroom at the end of the passage at the top of the stairs. The door was open. I pushed the girl on to the top step, off the creaking boards, and motioned her to go down the steps quickly, as I thought someone may be coming from the bedroom at the end of the passage. We went quickly downstairs and out towards back door. I forgot to mention that she had put a pair of slippers on. I also carried a shotgun. We went out of the back door through the garage and up to near a clothes post in the garden. I then said, again: 'Where's the money? How much?' She said: 'In the bathroom. In coin, £200.' It was cold and she shivered. I said: 'You wait in car while I go fetch money.' She said: 'All right.' I put sticking-plaster to keep hands together, also a strip on her mouth. I then carried her to the car, which was parked in a lane [it was facing downhill], down some steps running along the side of the house. At the same time as I put sticking-plaster on her mouth I put sticking-plaster on her eyes. She climbed on to the back seat beside some sponge mattresses. I said: 'Don't make a sound and you OK.' She nodded. I closed the door then ran back to the house and left a Dymo-tape with instructions and ransom demand on it and ran back to the car. I sat in the driver's seat and lifted the sponge mattresses, which were rolled up. Told her to lie on back seat and rested sponge on top so she would not be seen. I then drove down the road, turned round and came back down the road and down through Highley going to Bathpool. When I pulled on to the main road I pulled off my hood which had been on since I entered the back garden for the first time. The girl could not possibly see my face, as she was laid on the back seat facing towards the back of the car with two pieces of foam mattress on top of her. I drove fast down the road, and after a short time the girl started struggling and making a noise. She could not get up because of the sponge mattresses. After we were clear of houses and streetlights I pulled on my hood. Stopped the car and pulled the sponge up. She was trying to speak behind the plaster. I removed the plaster from her mouth and said in an un-normal voice: 'You have been kidnapped. Be quiet and you will not be harmed. If you do not behave I will put you in the boot. If you good, you can stay there.' She said: 'I'll be quiet.' I said: 'Are you warm enough?' She said: 'Yes.' I checked the heater was on warm and drove off to Bathpool. We arrived at Bathpool early morning while still dark. In the car earlier I had put sponge mattresses, sleeping-bags, tape-recorders, torches, batteries, bottle of brandy, Dymo-tape, writing-pads, pens, polythene bags, paint and brush, survival blanket, black plastic sheet, length of wire, fasteners, socks, flasks and food and spanners. Leaving the girl in the car I took sponge mattress and sleeping-bag down shaft and through tunnel. I was carrying a torch. I left the mattress and sleeping-bag in the short dry tunnel. I then went back to the car for the girl and we went down the ladder and through to the sleeping-bag and mattress. I placed the mattress on the steel platform, sleeping-bag on top. Removed sticking-plaster from girl also dressing-gown which had become wet getting there. The girl dried herself with top half of dressing-gown and got into sleeping-bag. I put on hand lantern left previously. I reassured girl and went to collect other equipment from car. By the time I had got equipment below ground it was getting light. I had to move the car a short distance. Then went back to equipment and took all equipment to far end of tunnel where girl was. Put girl in another sleeping-bag on top of first. I gave her survival blanket and bottle of brandy and tape-recorder and flask of soup. Then sorted out equipment and Dymo-tapes. During the day I made all Dymo-tapes as required, and the girl taped message on tape-recorder for telephone by reading what I had written in capitals on writing-pad. During some of this time I conversed in un-normal voices, whilst she talked normally. At approximately 4.30– 5.00 pm when dark I went out and took car to Walsall to commence putting out instructions for collection of ransom. All these were taped in telephone boxes. The last telephone box was outside the bus garage at Dudley. After completing laying instructions at Dudley Zoo I went back to the telephone box at bus garage, with taped instructions on tape cassette that girl had made earlier that day with the ransom message to her mother. I dialled the three telephone boxes alternately at Swan Shopping Centre, Kidderminster, at approximately midnight. As near as I can remember. At first the telephones rang at the other end normally, but with no reply. After a few times dialling, all three dialling tones at other end went different, a kind of discontinued or engaged signal. Then I dialled for last time and someone answered and said: 'Who is this?' I then rang off . . . I suspected a trap and returned to Bathpool, parking on estate road at top of footpath down to Bathpool. I returned to girl and made soup, using stove from car, and we had some. I explained there would be delay.

The following evening I left to phone again from Dudley. I left the car

abandoned in the car park [after he had shot Gerald Smith] . . . I made
my way back to Bathpool. It was dark when I got back. I went back to
the girl and explained that there would be a delay, as the tape-recorder
had broken down and I couldn't send the message. During the period
from then until the time I left to make final telephone call, we made new
instruction tapes on the Phillips tape-recorder, and new Dymo instructions. I left to make final telephone call, arriving at telephone box
at approximately midnight. I made the call and played the tape into the
telephone. I thought at the time it was a male member of the Whittle
family, and the voice stated positively there would be no tricks. From
the sincere tone of the voice I fully believed that the instructions would
be carried out . . . I walked back through the woods. On the path going
through the woods, I broke up the Phillips tape and left it in the mud. As
I got to the top of the hill overlooking Bathpool I saw a police car
approach from the far end of Bathpool and check a courting couple
parked in the car park. As this was only approximately 20 minutes from
the time I had made the call I did not suspect a police trap. The police car
and the other car left almost immediately and I could see no other vehicles near the area. I returned to the girl and told her they were bringing
the money and it would take about two hours for them to get there, then
she would be going home. She wanted to come with me then, but I explained she would be better waiting there just a little while longer, until
everything was finalised. I explained I had to go get ready to collect the
money, so that no one would be seen and they would not be able to set a
trap. I then went up and removed a metal grill to enable me to descend
into the drainage system without anyone being able to follow. I had presumed it possible they would have put a bug in with the money.

The depth of the drain underground would have made it not possible
for them to follow the bug. The tunnel runs into a disused canal system.
There is also a disused rail tunnel approximately on top of the drainage
system. I reckoned with the many different entrances to all these tunnels
and they not knowing location of same, this would give me ample time
to return with the money to the girl, smash the bug, and take out the girl
with me and for her to wait for them to find her. Alternately, there is a
telephone box a short distance away up the path . . . At no time did the
girl see me. She could not possibly have recognised me by sight, description, or from voice. There was positively no reason that the girl could
not return to her family and give her family and the entire British police
force every co-operation in trying to find me. So there was positively no
reason to do the girl any harm, even if the ransom was not paid . . . The
girl could have been left where she was, or left at the top of the drainage
system, whether or not the ransom had been paid, and I would have
made my escape to safety, leaving the girl to be found in a very short
time by her family or the police.

I went and removed the grill on the top of the shaft. It was a cold,
slightly frosty, clear night. There was no fog or mist, and visibility
through my binoculars was excellent. From the top of the drainage

cover I could see the point where the instructions said the car had to stop. I could also see if there had been anyone on foot. From memory I waited approximately one-and-a-quarter hours. Then a car drove into Bathpool from the direction of the instructions. The car stopped and turned lights out. From the time-lapse it could have been a car sent by the police if there had been a phone-tap on the Whittle phone. Or it could have been a courting couple, whom I have seen on other nights come into Bathpool as late as 4.15 am . . . On this night the car that entered could have been either police or a courting couple, either of which did not disturb me. I waited, and a few minutes later a car came into Bathpool Park and drove in the direction of the instructions I had phoned. It did not, however, carry out the instructions. It then reversed quickly and went past the first car that had pulled in and drove along a dead-end track which runs parallel to the railway. At this point I had a doubt as to if a police trap was in progress. From my position I fully believed I had no cause for alarm. My safety was not threatened in any way. I waited, and began to doubt the sincerity of the man who answered the phone-call.

Approximately 45 minutes later a helicopter passed overhead, nearly directly over me. It approached from the opposite side of Bathpool to the ski-slope, travelling at right angles to the railway line . . . It must have gone some distance, then turned south. It came round in half a circle and hovered some miles to the south of me. Its lights were in plain sight to the naked eye, as there is total blackness and could be identified with binoculars. It seemed obvious from this there was a police trap in operation. I was not panicked. In the next few minutes the car that had driven along the dead-end track returned and went out of Bathpool. At this point I realised the money was not going to be paid. Minutes later the first car that entered Bathpool followed the dead-end track car out of Bathpool. I decided there was no point in waiting further. I entered the shaft through the grill opening and went along the tunnel. After climbing into the short pipe leading to the platform, I saw the light from the other side, as the girl had on her torch. As I came down out of the short tunnel on to the platform, the girl moved to her right, to allow me on to the platform beside her. As I stood on the platform she went over the side and was suspended from the wire . . .

I moved to the side of the platform that she had gone over. Her head was below the level of the platform. I saw her face. Her eyes seemed to be half closed and stopped moving. I froze, then panicked. The next thing I remember is shoving the cover up to get out. I then closed the cover. I stopped there for some moments unable to think what to do. A car came up the road and into Bathpool. I started to dash from the top of the mound down towards a disused railway line. I fell, and a bag I had in my hand spilt its contents. I lay still for some moments. Then along a track which runs near the bottom of the ski-slope I saw the lights of a vehicle slowly moving towards this end of Bathpool. A car drove out of Bathpool down the road towards Kidsgrove. I think the same car came back seconds later with no lights on. At this point I thought I was near to being surrounded. I started to collect the things and put them back into the bag. I heard the sound of dogs coming from as near as I could tell the dead-end track. I panicked and fled in the opposite direction.

After this statement, Neilson made others, more briefly, about the sub-post office shootings. The police later denied that a helicopter had flown over the park, or that any police cars drove into it. However, a courting couple noticed a panda car, with lights on – also someone (Neilson) flashing a torch.

Neilson was charged on Monday, 15 December at Newcastle-under-Lyme magistrates' court with the murder of Lesley Whittle. Other charges, of murder and attempted murder, followed on the Friday. He was remanded in custody 18 times.

Gerald Smith died on 25 March 1976, and on the day of his funeral, Neilson was committed for trial on nine charges at Stafford Crown Court: 245 statements were formally entered as well as 848 exhibits. At a pre-trial review in Birmingham in May, the venue was moved to Oxford, where an unprejudiced jury was more likely to be found than in the Midlands.

The trial began on Monday, 14 June in Oxford Crown Court, a hot, sweltering day in a summer that would become the hottest in Britain for 250 years.

The judge, Mr Justice Mars-Jones, decreed that jurymen could remove their jackets and ties and counsel their wigs. Neilson, tense and tight-lipped, wore a black tie and dark green suit. He was defended by Gilbert Gray, QC, a skilled and humorous orator. The prosecution was led by Philip Cox, QC, whose chambers were in Birmingham. Before the jury was chosen, Mr Gray succeeded in getting the charges relating to the shootings at Dudley and Rainworth removed from the indictment. They would be dealt with separately, as would the sub-post office charges. Donald Neilson would now only be tried on three charges relating to the kidnapping and murder of Lesley Whittle. This trial lasted until 1 July.

He pleaded guilty to the kidnapping and blackmail charges and not guilty to murder. The prosecution had earlier refused to consider the defence's proposition that the murder charge should be reduced to manslaughter. The central issue was whether Lesley *fell* off the platform – or was pushed – and Mr Cox contended that she was killed because she would have been able to identify her kidnapper. Mr Cox asked: 'Was he hooded *all* the time he was in that drain? Or did he relax his precautions of attempting to keep his identity from the girl?'

When a tape of Lesley's voice was played, Neilson sobbed into a large white handkerchief. He also tended to weep when his wife and daughter were mentioned. Most of the evidence of witnesses, including Neilson's statement, was read out in court. But Ron Whittle and DCS Bob Booth both made an appearance, the latter being openly critical about alleged procedural failings committed by the Staffordshire police and the team from New Scotland Yard. 'I was disgusted,' he said. For this he was later rebuked by the judge, who remarked: 'I do deplore the fact that he took advantage of the opportunity of appearing in the witness box to launch a bitter attack . . . on fellow-officers.'

Neilson himself gave evidence, standing at attention and gazing straight ahead as if he were at a court martial. In prison he had been doing 200 finger-tip press-ups and running round the exercise yard every day. He addressed the judge and counsel as 'Sir' and was both precise and prolix in his replies. He seemed determined that the court should know all about his plans and applaud his commitment, fitness and skill. He spoke for 20 hours over a period of four days, fascinating his audience by the most detailed account ever heard in a court of the genesis, preparation and execution of a crime.

He told Mr Gray: 'I needed somewhere which was soundproof. In that way the person didn't have to be gagged. I needed somewhere that a person would be able to move about. In that way they would not have to be bound. I needed somewhere where there could be light that wouldn't show out when I wasn't there.' He had thought of building a soundproof room in a garage, or of using a boat in a disused canal tunnel. 'Eventually I realised that the ideal place to cover any eventuality would be at the bottom of the main shaft at Bathpool, where there was an ample supply of fresh air.' Still maintaining that Ron Whittle was one of his main targets, he said of the wire tether: 'The only way to guarantee that he could not leave was to put steel cord round his neck . . . If I put it round the ankle, wrists or waist, he could work it with both hands on the edge of the concrete, chafing it. It was also possible to slip if off a wrist or ankle made soft and slippery by water.' He told how he coaxed, assisted and carried the blindfolded girl in the drainage system. He said: 'I lifted her by one hand under her bottom into the dry pipe.' On the platform he removed the wet dressing-gown so that she could dry herself. He said: 'I didn't look at her in the sense of what is meant when you say to look at somebody. I saw what there was to see . . . My feelings throughout the time I was with her were feelings of professional detachment.' Of his disguise he said: 'To me, having gloves and hood on were the same as wearing trousers and boots.' But at one point, when explaining how he was worried by something that had occurred, he said: 'There must have been something in my face, in my expression.' This seemed like an admission that Lesley *had* seen his face. Mr Gray tried to correct this error. He asked: 'But did you not have your hood on at the time?' To which Neilson replied, nodding: 'It must have been my manner.'

He went on to reveal that the script of the messages Lesley recorded had been written out on an 8″ × 5″ card which was taped on to his chest and under his shirt. He said her hands and feet were free, and that when he secured the wire with clips around her neck 'she made no protest and showed no signs of fear', and that she was then in the sleeping-bag with her head against the ladder. When Ron Whittle failed to appear in Bathpool Park in the early hours of 17 January, he said he decided to abandon the kidnap operation, to 'release the girl and make good my escape . . . It was obvious to me that there would be a thorough police search at Bathpool at first light . . . My last act would be to ensure that she understood fully what was happening and make sure she was on my side . . . Throughout the plan she was my ace, because when she was released she would have to tell them of my be-haviour.' As she had not been ill-treated, he expected the subsequent hunt for him to be less hostile. He said: 'It was essential for the plan that my conduct should be proper and correct at all times, and hers certainly was.'

Neilson now gave the court a more detailed account of Lesley's death:

> I descended the ladder about three rungs at a time. The time to stop, the time to rest, was after I got to the bottom of the ladder. As I came out of the dry culvert, I looked down and saw she was there in the normal position. At a glance down I saw she started to move, as she normally did, to allow me to get on to the platform beside her. She moved away from the ladder and to her right. As I took my foot off the ladder and turned to face the front, I look round and she went over. The lantern was still lit, and I grabbed this and stepped across the other side of the landing and put my foot down on the concrete ledge and went down, as it were, into a crouching position . . . I held my left hand down and towards her with the intention of pulling her back up . . . Her right hand was stretched out behind her, moving. Her other arm was bent at the elbow. Her fists were clenched . . . The torch was pointing into her face. Her eyes flickered and stopped. Everything stopped . . . It was then I realised she was dead . . . She was dead. There was absolutely nothing I could do . . . She did *not* take minutes to die. She was dead in seconds. She was dead before I left.

There were tears in his eyes and his voice had risen as he spoke.

His cross-examination took two days. Mr Cox's questions were aimed at discomfiting Neilson and implied he always had Lesley's murder in mind: 'You had planned her death, hadn't you?' – 'You did not care whether she saw your face or not, because you knew from the beginning you were going to kill her?' – 'If she had seen your face, she would be able to recognise you on a subsequent occasion?' – 'You couldn't allow her to live?' Neilson was emphatic in his replies, though he often paused to think. He was also indignant, even angered. He said 'Rubbish!' more than once.

Mr Gray, in his final speech for the defence, argued that if Neilson had meant to kill Lesley Whittle, he need never have taken so many precautions about disguise or about her well-being and comfort. He said that her death was an 'unlooked-for misadventure'. It was 'unplanned and undesired' – 'Neilson started something which went hideously wrong.'

The judge pointed out that Lesley died after Neilson abandoned the kidnap plan, believing the police were closing in. But he went on to say: 'There is no direct evidence that Neilson pushed her over the side. There is a lot of evidence to show that he did not. Otherwise you would have expected certain results, which do not appear . . . He has always denied any such thing . . . The prosecution's case depends very largely on circumstantial evidence.' It seemed he favoured a verdict of manslaughter, rather than one of murder.

But the jury, who were out for less than two hours, returned a verdict of 'Guilty'. There was some applause in the court and cries of 'Good!' Sentence was deferred. Taken below, Neilson burst into tears.

On Monday, 5 July, the same judge, counsel, and accused assembled in the same court for Neilson's second trial – on nine charges connected with burglary, the sub-post office murders, and the attempted murders of Mrs Grayland and PC Mackenzie. The three widows were among those who gave evidence, as did Neilson, who again gave the court a detailed dissertation on his criminal operations and plans. He maintained that all three deaths were accidental, that he never intended to use violence or to kill. He said: 'Violence never has been part of my plan.'

The trial lasted 12 days. The jury were out for over five hours, returning with verdicts of guilty to the three murder charges. But the attempted murder charges were reduced to one of inflicting grievous body harm in the case of Mrs Grayland, and of possessing a firearm with intent to endanger life in the case of PC Mackenzie.

Before passing sentence, the judge told Neilson:

> The enormity of your crimes puts you in a class apart from almost all convicted murderers in recent years ... You were never without a loaded shotgun or other loaded weapons when you went out on your criminal expeditions. And you never hesitated to kill whenever you thought you were in danger of arrest or detection. You showed no mercy whatsoever ... In my judgement such is the gravity and the number of offences, and the danger to the public when you are at large, that no minimum period of years would be suitable. In your case, life must mean life.

Neilson was given five life sentences, plus one of 21 years in prison, and four of ten years.

His appeal, against his conviction for murdering Lesley Whittle, was heard in July 1977 and dismissed. Lord Justice Lane said: 'If ever there was a proper decision by a jury, it was this.'

However, it now seems more than probable that Neilson never murdered Lesley Whittle – and that he should never have been convicted of murder, or even of manslaughter. There was no proof to substantiate either charge and the circumstantial evidence was very thin. The Bradford psychiatrist, Dr Milne, who interviewed Neilson for 16 hours and deemed that he was a 'classic obsessional personality with paranoid attitudes', concluded: 'What Neilson told me, as far as Lesley was concerned, I felt rang true. His version of what took place during the post office shootings did *not* ring true ... Even though he is obsessional, with an aggressive character, this is under a very considerable degree of rigid control. I found him to be most likeable and easy to talk to.'

Neilson only killed when his immediate escape was threatened, when he had no time to think. The four men he shot were also total strangers. Killing Lesley, whom he treated with comparative consideration for three days, almost like his daughter, would have been a coldly premeditated act. When things went wrong, his maxim was: Leave at once.

It is likely that he abandoned Lesley as he abandoned the Morris 1300 –

that he never went back down the shaft when his plans went awry on the night of the 16th, that he panicked, and fled.

Commander Morrison, who referred to Neilson as a 'diabolical genius', said: 'I am convinced Neilson pushed Lesley off.' But in *The Capture of the Black Panther*, Harry Hawkes concludes:

> The probability is that Neilson was not even present when Lesley died, and never saw her hanging there. For a man obsessed by detail, his statement, when analysed, is suspiciously vague and lacking in actual facts about her death. His scant account mentioned nothing about the girl being inside the sleeping-bag when she went over the side and – even more telling – there is no reference to the crucial snagging of the wire . . . Had he been there it would have been simple to unsnag the wire.

Neilson evidently expected, as he did with the Morris, that the police would find Lesley the day after he abandoned her. He might also have suspected that the police, having found her, would keep quiet about it and set up a trap. Perhaps he *did* go back down the shaft – but not for a few days or weeks – only to discover that she was dead.

It is possible that Lesley Whittle, alone at the bottom of that cold, dark shaft, imagined that Neilson would never return, and in her panic and terror, while trying to free herself from the wire, rolled off the platform to her death. She must have been inside the sleeping-bag at the time, for her body was unmarked. Or did she roll off in her sleep, during a nightmare?

Or was Neilson, in this one respect, telling the truth?

PCs White and Mackenzie were each given the Queen's Gallantry Medal, and two of the men who helped to subdue Neilson received £250. But the Post Office's £25,000 reward was never paid, as no actual information was received leading to Neilson's arrest. Kathryn Neilson is reported to have been paid a large sum of money by the *Sunday People* for her exclusive story. This sum, it seems, was originally offered to Irene Neilson. She, however, had been charged with dishonestly cashing postal orders, stolen by Neilson, along with a date stamp, from Tittensor Post Office in Staffordshire in March 1974. When the police searched the Neilson home on 13 December 1975 they discovered that Mrs Neilson had burnt about 50 postal orders from Tittensor. In August 1976, a month after Neilson was sentenced, his wife pleaded guilty at Eccleshall magistrates' court to six charges of cashing stolen postal orders and asked for 76 similar offences to be taken into consideration. Using false names and driven about by Neilson, she had cashed the postal orders in several northern towns between October 1974 and March 1975, netting £580. It was in November 1974 that the Graylands were attacked in Langley and Mr Grayland shot and killed. Although Neilson had been raiding post offices since January 1971, and burgling homes for several years, disappearing from home for many hours overnight, Irene Neilson said she knew nothing about his criminal activities until 1975.

She was sentenced in September 1976 to a year in jail; she served eight months in Strangeways Prison.

Donald Neilson, 57 in August 1993, is still in prison and 'unlikely to be released in the foreseeable future'.

The summer of 1976 was the hottest in Britain for 250 years. It was also a year of leadership changes. Harold Wilson resigned as Prime Minister and was replaced by James Callaghan; and Jeremy Thorpe, who resigned as leader of the Liberals in May, was replaced by David Steel. In September, Mao-Tse-tung, the leader of Communist China, died, and in November, when the Sex Pistols hit the charts, Jimmy Carter was elected as President of the USA.

1977 was notable in Britain for the celebrations of the 25th anniversary of the accession of Elizabeth II. Red Rum also won the Grand National for the third time; Virginia Wade won the women's singles at Wimbledon; and in August Elvis Presley died.

In 1978 two Popes died; Paul VI and John Paul I, who was succeeded by the first non-Italian Pope for 400 years, the Polish John Paul II. In Iran, millions demanded the abdication of the Shah and his replacement by the Ayatollah Khomeini. Mrs Thatcher, the Conservative leader since 1975, was about to cash in on an industrial winter of discontent.

CHAPTER 18

The Murder of Georgi Markov, 1978

Political figures, statesmen and kings, have been the objects of assassination since civilisation began. But it is only recently, with the spread of terrorism and effective armaments, that less distinguished, ordinary persons have been pointlessly slaughtered for the sake of some manic, misguided ideal, or in revenge. Terrorism has become the blind reaper of the last quarter of the twentieth century, and terrorists the most pitiless, callous and calculating of all killers. For they mainly kill and maim unprotected, innocent strangers, from afar, with steely premeditation and ice in their hearts.

In 1971, there were 17 known political assassinations of individuals throughout the world. In 1980 there were well over 1,000. The 1970s were in fact disfigured by over 3,600 terrorist actions – bomb explosions, firebombs, kidnaps and hijacks – one for every day of the year. These were caused by a tiny minority, belonging to about 140 terrorist groups. Meanwhile, hundreds of thousands, even millions, of other people died through the actions of military regimes and dictatorships, of counter-revolutionaries and the secret police, in Communist countries and elsewhere. The order for the murder of Georgi Markov came from over a thousand miles away, and was as much an act of fear and loathing, as of political retribution and spite.

Georgi Markov was a Bulgarian. A popular and successful novelist and playwright, he defected from Bulgaria in 1969. His brother, Nikolai, had defected a few years before this and settled in Italy, to where Georgi fled before coming to London in 1971. Like many other talented emigrés, he obtained work as a radio presenter and newsreader with the BBC World Service, based in Bush House and situated at the foot of Kingsway between the Aldwych and the Strand. In 1974 he met Annabel Dilke, who was also working in Bush House. She came from Dorset. They married the following year.

In Bulgaria, Markov had been for a while the 'cultural representative' of the Communist regime and was esteemed by the nation's despotic president, Todor Zhivkov – to such an extent that the two men would walk and talk together in the countryside, and on one occasion Markov spent a weekend at Zhivkov's hunting-lodge on Mount Vitosha, outside Sofia, where he was also welcomed at the country retreats of other party leaders. Originally a chemical engineer, his first literary success was a book of short stories published in 1961. His writings were received with official approval while they dealt with non-contentious matters and were agreeably full of Eastern European introspection, artistic expression and angst. But increasingly he found it difficult to conceal his impatience with the regime, and his talent for satire found ample fodder. The Bulgarian army was targeted in one of his plays and a general portrayed as a clown. It was called, ironically, *The Assassins*.

Zhivkov's regime became even more corrupt and oppressive after the Russians and other Warsaw Pact forces entered Czechoslovakia in August 1968: the country was taken over and divided into a two-state federation, and in April 1969 the First Secretary, Mr Dubček, was replaced by a Soviet dependent, Dr Husák. That year Markov, now an unabashed dissident, wrote a play *The Man Who Was I*, which displeased the cultural committee when they were given the obligatory preview in the Satire Theatre, Sofia. During the performance Markov was told he was 'in trouble'.

Being one of the Communist Party's literary élite in Sofia, he not only had a passport but superior accommodation and highly privileged transport – a BMW. He went home, packed a suitcase, gave a cousin some money to drink his health, and drove across the frontier into Yugoslavia. From then on, as far as the Bulgarian regime was concerned, he was a non-person. His name was deleted from records, his writings banned, and in his absence he was charged with fraud.

But in England he continued to write, producing three novels: *The Great Roof*, *Women of Warsaw*, and *Portrait of my Double* (none of which was apparently published here), and two plays (one of which, *Let's Go Under the Rainbow*, won an award at the Edinburgh Festival Fringe). A former colleague in the Bulgarian Writers' Union later claimed that Markov was 'a very ambitious man' and thought that by going to England he would become 'another Joseph Conrad'.

In the meantime, through the medium of the BBC's World Service, he began to exercise his new-found freedom by mocking the mediocrity of President Zhivkov and his subservience to Moscow. These broadcasts, which were transmitted to Bulgaria by the BBC, further antagonised the Communist authorities, and when he tried to re-enter Bulgaria to see his dying father, permission was refused. This added an edge of bitterness to his views and he became a more outspoken and constant critic of President Zhivkov and his regime.

Markov also provided weekly scripts for Radio Free Europe, based in Munich. These were also highly critical of Zhivkov – as were his memoirs, which were serialised chapter by chapter from Munich and transmitted to Bulgaria. They were not vituperative. But his wife, Annabel Markov, said later she believed the memoirs led to his death – although she admitted: 'When you read them now, they are so mild you cannot believe that they were enough to get someone killed. They are not a polemic against Zhivkov . . . It wasn't that he was attacking Zhivkov, but that he was laughing at him. That was what was unforgivable.'

Markov had also written a political satire with another author, David

Phillips. Called *The Right Honourable Chimpanzee*, it was about to be published, under a pseudonym, by Secker & Warburg, towards the end of 1978.

This constant verbal and impenitent assault must have irritated and angered Zhivkov and other Communist party leaders. But authors are very seldom murder victims and writers are seldom killed on account of what they write. There may have been an additional and more potent political reason for Markov's death.

In June 1977, the head of the Paris bureau of the Bulgarian Radio and Television network, Vladimir Kostov, aged 48, defected and sought political asylum in France. With his wife and two grown-up children he disappeared from Paris and sought a safe and secret lodging with friends in the South of France. His defection alarmed the Zhivkov regime much more than that of Georgi Markov. Kostov, a television commentator of some repute and great popularity – he is said to have been the Robin Day of Bulgaria – had an intimate knowledge of the inner circles of the regime, and how it worked, at home and abroad. As a senior television journalist he had also travelled widely in Europe, Russia and the Middle East. The information he had was much more extensive and up-to-date than Markov's and his defection a much greater and more dangerous loss. The Bulgarians tried to persuade the Kostovs to return by flying both their mothers to Paris. But they suspected a trap and no meeting of the families took place.

In August, Nikolai Markov, Georgi's brother, who was a stamp-dealer in Bologna, telephoned London to tell Georgi that he had been visited by a Bulgarian official and told to pass on a warning – Georgi was being blamed by party chiefs for Kostov's defection and they were bent on revenge.

Markov later denied that he played any role, let alone a crucial one, in Kostov's decision. But he was sufficiently concerned to tell some Bush House colleagues of the threat and postpone a trip to Munich. Then a Bulgarian in West Germany warned him of a plot to kill him, and it is said that while on holiday in Italy he used to stand with his back to the sea. Nothing sinister occurred, however, for nearly a year.

Then on 24 August 1978, as Kostov was ascending an escalator in the Paris Metro, he felt a stinging sensation in the lower right of his back. Later, he said he also heard a muffled crack, like an air-gun report. The wound was slight, somewhat like a bee-sting, and hurt as much. So he and his wife went to a clinic near their home in Nanterre and a male orderly tended the 'sting'. It had produced a small swelling and was exuding what looked like microscopic 'metallic crumbs'. The orderly bathed the area, wiping the crumbs away. He applied a dressing and Kostov departed, soon none the worse. He never knew what hit him – not for another two weeks, when something similar happened to Georgi Markov, on Thursday, 7 September 1978, Zhivkov's birthday.

Markov was a thick-set man, six foot, nearly 14 stone, and 49 years old. What happened to him about 6.35 that Thursday evening is uncorroborated and relies only on his own reported accounts; and there is some confusion about *where* he was attacked.

According to the *Sunday Times* Insight team:

Markov was a man of habit. Once a week, in the early afternoon, he would drive from his home in Clapham to a car park on the south side of the River Thames near Waterloo Station; he would walk the half mile across Waterloo Bridge to Aldwych and the Bush House headquarters of the BBC External Services, to begin a 12-hour shift; at 6.30, when parking restrictions in Central London end – and after reading the early evening news – Markov would go back across the river, pick up his van, drive it to Aldwych, park and then stroll back to his office in ample time to prepare the 9.30 news bulletin.

The Insight team, writing on 17 September 1978, implied that Markov was attacked as he was 'walking down the south side of Aldwych' past a bus-stop.

Mrs Markov, appearing before the inquest three-and-a-half months later, told a different story. She said her husband told her that

while waiting for a bus on the south side of Waterloo Bridge he had felt a jab in the back of his right thigh and, looking around, saw a man drop an umbrella. [She continued:] The man said he was sorry, and Georgi said he got the impression that he was trying to cover his face as he rushed off and hailed a taxi. Georgi told me he thought the man must have been a foreigner, because the taxi-driver seemed to have difficulty in understanding him.

If Markov was waiting for a bus on the *south* side of Waterloo Bridge, he was clearly heading, without his van, for the north side, for the Aldwych and Bush House. For he was in Bush House at about 7.00 pm, talking for an hour with the head of the BBC's Bulgarian Service, David Buckley. They discussed folk music. When Markov got up to leave, he complained that his leg was stiff. He told Buckley: 'I must have bumped into something. Or perhaps it was the chap who bumped into me.'

He then, it seems, asked a friend in the office, Ted Lirkoff, another Bulgarian exile, to have a look at the back of his leg and see if it was marked. Markov undid his jeans and Lirkoff peered at his thigh. He later told the inquest: 'On his leg was a little red spot, like a puncture, about one-and-a-half millimetres across. He told me there was some pain. But I got the impression that it was not a very big pain at the moment.'

Lirkoff had been much vaguer when talking to the Insight team three months earlier. Understandably apprehensive at the time, he had told them he could remember little about that Thursday night, except that Markov had said he had been 'stabbed with an umbrella while passing a bus queue, by a well-built man who had apologised in a heavy foreign accent and then fled'.

Later on that night, Markov returned to his home in Lynette Avenue, on the south side of Clapham Common, at about half-past ten. He said nothing to his wife about the umbrella attack and bedded down in his study, as he was on an early-morning shift and did not want to disturb her when he got up. But at about 2.00 am Annabel Markov was aroused by sounds of him moving about.

She later said: 'I was worried and called out to him. I got out of bed, and when I saw him he had been sick and was lying on the floor. I took his temperature, and it was 104°.' She telephoned her doctor and he told her it could be influenza and advised her to keep her husband cool. 'I stayed with him all night,' she said later. 'And it was then he told me about the attack. He said: "I have a horrible suspicion that it might be connected with something that happened today." . . . He showed me some blood on his jeans and a mark like a puncture, about the size of the tip of a ball-point pen, on the back of his right thigh.'

The next morning she went to work at 10.30, taking their two-year-old daughter, Sasha, with her, so that her husband could sleep. She told the inquest: 'I don't think either of us believed this could be what we feared – that he had actually been attacked by members of the Bulgarian Secret police.' When the doctor called that afternoon he recommended that Markov enter a hospital, and about 24 hours after Markov was attacked he was admitted to St James's Hospital, Balham, suffering from an unexplained high fever.

The house physician, Dr Bernard Riley, found a circular area of inflammation on the rear of Markov's right thigh, with a central puncture mark about two millimetres wide. He doubted whether the puncture had been caused by an umbrella, as he thought it was too small.

By Saturday, 9 September, Markov's white blood-cell count had risen from 10,600 cells on admission to 26,300 – 'astonishingly high'. It reached 33,000 – the normal count ranges from 5,000 to 10,000 – and Markov's condition continued to deteriorate, despite massive injections of antibiotics. When his temperature and blood pressure plunged, Dr Riley diagnosed septicaemia. By the morning of Monday, 11 September Markov had become 'violent and confused'. He died before mid-day of cardiac arrest, apparently caused by acute toxaemia (blood-poisoning).

It was then no more than a 'suspicious death'. But Markov's background and assertions that he had somehow been poisoned by an umbrella, attracted some high-level police interest, and his autopsy was attended by the head of the Anti-Terrorist Squad, Commander Jim Neville.

X-rays showed that a speck of 'high metallic density' like a pin-head, lay beneath the skin of Markov's thigh. Extracted, it was found to be a tiny metal sphere, 1.52 millimetres in diameter. It had two holes, .35mm wide, bored into it, which met in the middle and crossed, and it was made of an alloy composed of 90 per cent platinum and 10 per cent iridium. But what had it contained?

The pellet was sent, with some of Markov's skin from both of his legs, to the government's Chemical Defence Establishment at Porton Down, a few miles from Salisbury in Wiltshire, where highly secret research into biological warfare was carried out. The pathologist there who examined the pellet, Dr David Gall, concluded that the quantity of poison contained within the pellet (which would then have been coated and sealed with some substance that would dissolve on entering the skin) must have been so small that it would have to have been exceedingly toxic – more so than the majority of poisons produced by chemicals, reptiles, sea creatures, or plants.

In narrowing down the field of possibilities, Dr Gall injected a poison called ricin into a pig – a slightly larger dose than Markov would have received. The pig developed a fever, like Markov, and symptoms almost identical to his. A day later it died.

Meanwhile a minor operation was carried out, at Scotland Yard's request, on Vladimir Kostov in Paris, and a small metallic sphere, identical to the one found in Markov's thigh, was discovered in Kostov's back. It was thought he survived the attack on him because the encapsulated poison had somehow escaped and not entered his body. Or that the pellet had been fired from too far away and had not penetrated deeply enough. Experts concluded that the umbrella used to kill Markov had either injected the pellet when he was stabbed with its point, or had been converted into a gas-gun which, when fired at point-blank range, would send a pellet into his flesh.

All this was sensational stuff to the press. It was better than James Bond or any spy-fiction – this was real. The police were also very intrigued with the case, and detectives travelled to France, Italy and West Germany in pursuit of their investigations. Enquiries were also made in America. Although the Bulgarians offered their assistance, this was not taken up. *Their* view was that Markov had been killed by Western agents, to discredit Bulgaria's international image, and to get rid of an agent for whom they no longer had any use. The Bulgarians said it was absurd to suggest that *they* had had a hand in killing Markov ten years after his defection.

Georgi Markov was buried on Saturday, 14 October, in the ancient churchyard of Whitchurch Canonicorum, a Dorset village near Lyme Regis, far from his Bulgarian home. Sea-fog swirled around the mourners, who included Markov's mother, Raika, his brother Nikolai, and several colleagues from Bush House and Radio Free Europe; many wept. Scotland Yard detectives stood apart, and one took photographs of the mourners. Among the wreaths was one from Vladimir Kostov. It bore the message: 'In honour of Georgi's cause and sacrifice.'

Later, Annabel Markov had an inscription written in Bulgarian on one side of his gravestone and in English on the other: *He died in the cause of freedom.*

The inquest was held in Battersea on Tuesday, 2 January 1979, before the Inner West London coroner, Gavin Thurston. More snow was forecast for London that night after one of the worst winters in parts of northern Europe for 80 years. The day before, most train services in the south and east of England were curtailed or cancelled. The temperature at Linton-on-Ouse in Yorkshire fell to minus 17° Centigrade on Monday night.

Mrs Markov, described by the *Daily Telegraph* as 'dark-haired and attractive', was the first witness. She said that her husband had defected from Bulgaria 'because it was intolerable for him to remain any longer', and she described what happened on the five days before his death.

Dr Riley, the house physician at St James's Hospital, told the coroner that the fatal pellet might possibly have been pushed into Markov's thigh by the tip of the umbrella. The pathologist who carried out the post-mortem, Dr Crompton, said that ricin was a vegetable toxin and extremely rare. It was extracted from castor-oil plants, and there were some cases of people being poisoned after handling these plants. He agreed that a modified air pistol or gas-gun might have been used to fire the pellet and that Markov was unlikely to have inserted the pellet himself. 'It was in an awkward place,' he said. Asked who might have made the pellet, he replied: 'Somebody with precision tooling equipment. I would hazard a guess at a watchmaker or a surgical instrument maker.'

Dr Keeley, of the Metropolitan Police laboratory, said that a high-temperature furnace and special drilling equipment, as well as specialist skills, would have been needed to make the pellet. The two pellets found in both Markov and Kostov were identical, he said.

Dr Gall, of Porton Down, stated that ricin was twice as poisonous as the venom of a cobra. Combined with human tissue, it could be broken down by the body's natural protein-making cells and was very difficult to detect. It came from the seed of the castor-oil plant, he said, and a toxic residue was left after the oil had been extracted. The plant was grown in a number of countries, particularly in India and Italy. It also grew freely in Bulgaria. Much of the world research into ricin had been carried out in Czechoslovakia and Hungary, he said. There was no known antidote. The coroner asked: 'Does ricin have any legitimate use?' Dr Gall replied: 'There is no legitimate use for it.'

After two hours of question and answer, the coroner recorded a verdict that Georgi Markov died of toxaemia caused by the implantation of a metal pellet containing ricin. He said: 'I have no doubt it is a case of ricin poisoning, and that he was killed unlawfully.'

Although some of the investigators working on the case believed that an umbrella had been converted into a lethal weapon, others thought the umbrella had been employed as a diversion, and that, as with Kostov, someone shot at Markov with a gas-gun.

The following month (February), one of Markov's plays, *The Archangel Michael*, was given a series of rehearsed readings at the Royal Court's Theatre Upstairs in London. It was later staged at the Crucible Theatre, Sheffield, in March. In April, his life and death were the subject of a 'Panorama' TV Programme on BBC1.

His memoirs, *The Truth That Killed*, were eventually published by Weidenfeld & Nicolson in 1983. But it never seemed as if the truth would ever be known about who killed him – not until the Soviet leader, Mikhail Gorbachev, announced a wide range of domestic reforms and the Iron Curtain began to lift. A pent-up flood of democratic feeling and ideas swept across the Soviet Union and its satellite states. Peace broke out in the nuclear arms race; the Russians withdrew from Afghanistan; Germany was united; the Berlin Wall was brought down and the Cold War came to an end with the cataclysmic collapse of Communist regimes in Eastern Europe and the USSR.

In Bulgaria, President Zhivkov was ousted from power in November 1989. A few months later, in January 1990, Annabel Markov, now 47, flew to Sofia for a week, the first of several visits. Bulgaria was still a Communist state, but the new leader, Petar Mladenov, had agreed to an inquiry being made into the death of Georgi Markov, and the rehabilitation of his name and works had begun. His widow met Alexander Lilov, secretary of the general committee. She said later:

> Lilov told me that he was a great admirer of Georgi's work, and that he had read all of it and that the inquiry should take place as soon as possible. He told me it was very important that people should read Georgi's memoirs and his record of the awful years of the Zhivkov regime. He said that if Bulgaria were really to have a democracy, people ought to know the truth. I was absolutely astonished. It's more than I ever dreamed of. Perhaps they will find out the truth about his death and perhaps not. But at least now his work will be available again.

Suddenly Markov was transformed in Bulgaria from a traitorous dissident to a national hero. He and his writings were praised by the newspapers that had once denounced them. His plays and novels were to be revived. Mrs Markov met members of the Bulgarian Writers' Union. She said: 'I went to lunch at the Writers' Union and all they wanted to know about was Georgi's death. I had to tell the story again and again. They knew nothing. I couldn't believe it. In the West, the manner of Georgi's death had become a *cause célèbre*. Yet here, in his own country, they were completely ignorant.'

She returned to England on 13 January after what she called 'the most extraordinary week of my life'. She said: 'I am not embittered . . . I don't suppose I will ever get an explanation of what happened. But I am grateful that it is out in the open, that people are beginning to realise who Georgi was, what he did, and what he stood for.'

By 1991, the Communist Government had resigned. All Markov's works were again in print, his memoirs published, and his name restored to the Writers' Union. As if in recognition of all this, the new head of state, President Zhelev, on a visit to England, laid a floral tribute on Markov's grave at Whitchurch Canonicorum on 21 February 1991.

The brief ceremony was attended by Annabel Markov and her 14-year-old daughter Sasha, who as a baby had been christened in the church. Mrs Markov said: 'President Zhelev was a dissident writer himself and he deeply admires Georgi's works. He suggested that he make the visit . . . It's a kind of recognition of what was done by the old regime. It's a political and at the same time a very personal gesture by the President of Bulgaria, who is saying in effect – "The bad old days are over."'

It seemed so when in June 1991, the Bulgarian Interior Minister, Khristo Danov, admitted that the country's secret police had been involved in the murder of Georgi Markov. But the relevant files had been destroyed. The man charged with being responsible for this, General Savov, who was the former deputy minister in charge of foreign intelligence in 1978, was found shot dead in January 1992, the day before he was due to go on trial. His body lay in front of a memorial to anti-Nazi resistance fighters in his village. No bullet was found, and a villager claimed later that no pistol lay beside him – although a Colt was later produced by the police. A suicide note was said to be strangely impersonal and possibly forged.

There were other deaths in suspicious circumstances of some of those who had worked with Savov, like General Kotsev (in a car-crash), and it seemed that the real perpetrators of Markov's murder were still trying to cover their tracks. But they could not gain access to the KGB archives.

In Moscow, a former KGB general, Oleg Kallugin, bluntly declared: 'Todor Zhivkov was the organiser of the murder of Georgi Markov. No doubt about it.' He and his Interior Minister, Dimiter Stayanov, were said to have sanctioned a plan to 'neutralise enemy emigrés'. This was accomplished by the Bulgarian secret police in collaboration with the KGB. According to a KGB defector, Oleg Gordievsky, the umbrella was obtained by the KGB in Washington and converted into a weapon by the Moscow KGB, who also manufactured the pellet.

Meanwhile, in Bulgaria, two journalists identified the man who actually assassinated Markov as a retired Bulgarian diplomat, now living on a pension in Sofia. They also claimed that before he defected, Markov had been a womaniser and gambler – and worked for the secret police.

It was also revealed, in 1992, that General Kotsev, who in 1978 was in the Interior Ministry at the same time as General Savov, came to London to see the head of the Bulgarian intelligence service there – just before Markov died.

Did Kotsev bring an umbrella with him? And did he give it to someone in the intelligence service to use – someone who now lives comfortably in Sofia, 15 years after he shot or stabbed Georgi Markov on Waterloo Bridge?

Zhivkov, now aged 80, was put on trial on corruption charges in 1992. 'How can you imagine,' he protested, 'that I, Todor Zhivkov, would hand out cars to his colleagues?' He was convicted in September 1992 and sentenced to ten years in jail.

No charges relating to the murder of Georgi Markov have, so far, ever been made.

In May 1981, a Turkish gunman among the crowds in St Peter's Square in Rome, fired five bullets into Pope John Paul as he was carried across the square. The Pope survived. His assailant had spent a month in Bulgaria before the assassination attempt. President Reagan also escaped an attempted assassination. Other assassins succeeded in killing the Presidents of Bangladesh, Iran and Egypt that year. Even the Queen was shot at in the Mall, as she rode to Trooping the Colour in June. But this gun only had blanks. The most cheerful national event that year was the wedding, in July, of Lady Diana Spencer and Prince Charles.

CHAPTER 19

The Murders of Lt. Daly, SQMC Bright, L/Cpl. Young and Trooper Tipper, 1982

The IRA is a segment of the oldest terrorist organisation in the world. Nationalists opposed to English rule in Ireland began a long war of underground resistance when the English invaded Ireland in 1169 and took possession of the whole island for over 800 years. In the 1850s that resistance found expression in the Fenian Society, an Irish-American movement aimed at the overthrow of British rule and the establishment of a republic. The Fenians' ideas, centred on independence and unity for Ireland, were largely adopted by the radical nationalist party, Sinn Fein, founded in 1902. A more extreme group, the Irish Republican Volunteers, refused to fight for the British in the First World War and organised the Easter Week Rising in 1916 and proclaimed an Irish Republic. This did not in fact become reality until 1922, when the Irish Free State was born. Its name was later changed to Eire. The six counties of Northern Ireland, or Ulster, predominantly Protestant, chose to remain part of the UK, though with their own Parliament. The IRA, as the IRV had now become, refused to accept this partition of the island and of continuing British rule in Ulster and, though declared illegal, began a series of campaigns to oust the British from Northern Ireland and unite the North and South.

The present 'Troubles' began in 1969, when British troops were deployed in Northern Ireland after severe sectarian fighting. Further outbreaks of violence and rioting occurred in Londonderry and Armagh in 1970, and in August rubber bullets were first used by British soldiers in Belfast. The first British soldier was killed in February 1971. Suspected IRA terrorists were then interned without trial, and murders and bombings increased. After Bloody Sunday in January 1972 – when 13 people were killed by the Paras in Londonderry – direct rule from London was imposed on Ulster, in March 1972. A bomb explosion at the Parachute Brigade headquarters in Aldershot in February, which killed seven people, including five women and a priest, was the prelude to a bombing campaign in England that lasted for two years. Letters and parcel bombs damaged and maimed, while car-bombs and time-bombs killed and injured. In March 1973 one person was killed and 244 injured by car-bombs in the Old Bailey and Whitehall; and 72 were injured by seven explosions in the week before Christmas. In January 1974 there were further explosions: 12 people were killed when a suitcase bomb blew up on a coach on the M62, which was carrying servicemen and their families, and six *people died when two pubs in Guildford, used by soldiers, were wrecked by bomb blasts in October. A bomb explosion killed two near Woolwich barracks in November. Then 21 people died when bombs exploded in two crowded Birmingham pubs.*

In 1975, when Mrs Thatcher became the Tories' leader, a bomb blast at a pub in Caterham injured 33. In September, there was a series of explosions in or near restaurants and hotels in London: five died and 100 were injured. In October, a cancer surgeon, Gordon Hamilton Fairley, was killed by mistake by a car-bomb; and in November Ross McWhirter was shot dead outside his home. The Peace Movement launched in Ulster in 1976 coincided with comparative quiet on the English mainland for the next five years, during which, in 1977, the Queen celebrated her Silver Jubilee. Mrs Thatcher won the General Election in May 1979, and in August that year Earl Mountbatten, holidaying on a boat off north-west Ireland, was killed, along with three others, when the boat was blown up by a bomb.

The next bombing campaign began in October 1981, when a laundry-van packed with explosive, nails and bolts was detonated by remote control as a coach containing Irish Guards returned to Chelsea barracks: 37 guardsmen and civilians were injured and two civilians were killed. A week later, the Commandant General of the Royal Marines, Lieutenant-General Sir Steuart Pringle, was maimed by a car-bomb; and an explosives expert, Kenneth Howarth, died trying to defuse a bomb in Oxford Street. The Wimbledon home of the Attorney-General, Sir Michael Havers, was blasted in November. There were other, minor bomb blasts in December and January. Then there was a six-month lull.

Meanwhile, in Ulster, some of the IRA were on hunger-strike in prison: ten, including Bobby Sands, were to die as a result. A hiatus was caused by the IRA's attacks in London by increased police activity and by the Falklands War, which ended in June 1982. But a renewal of the bombing campaign was being planned – a special double event for central London on 20 July. A week before this, Gerard Tuite was jailed for ten years in Dublin for possessing explosives in London between 1978 and 1979. During his trial a cassette tape was played in court outlining IRA surveillance carried out in London on various Army barracks.

Since 1969, over 60 people had been killed in England by the IRA and hundreds injured, and 33 alleged members of the IRA had been given prison sentences ranging from 20 years to life – although nearly half of these sentences were eventually quashed. Many more had died in Ulster. From 1969 to August 1992, over 3,000 people – soldiers, policemen, civilians, and members of sectarian factions – have been killed by bullet and bomb: an average for those 23 years of over 130 a year.

Sunrise was at 5.08 on the morning of Tuesday, 20 July but, concealed by thin cloud, the sun was not apparent at first. It was bright and sunny later, with a slight breeze, and the temperature rose to 23°C.

At 6.51 am, a blue four-door Morris Marina, which had been left for two nights in a car-park under the Royal Garden Hotel, at the western end of

Hyde Park, was picked up and driven away. The car had been bought by a man at an auction at Enfield in north London on 13 July. Its registration number was LMD 657P. Some four hours after the blue Marina was collected from the hotel, at about 10.00 am, it was seen being parked by a man on the South Carriage Drive in Hyde Park. The driver was lucky to find a space in the line of vehicles on the right-hand side of the road, left there by shoppers and office workers in nearby Knightsbridge. Perhaps he had tried, and failed, to park the car outside or near the Hyde Park barracks, home of the Household Cavalry and further up the road.

The car faced west; on its left a grassy bank topped by a large plane tree sloped down to the start of Knightsbridge; on its right was the south-eastern section of Hyde Park and Rotten Row. A few hundred yards away, behind the blue Marina, was Hyde Park Corner, Park Lane and the Hilton Hotel. In front of it stretched the South Carriage Drive, a wide avenue skirting the park, passing a tall red-brick block of mansion flats and the French Embassy at Albert Gate, beyond which were the Royal Thames Yacht Club, the Hyde Park Hotel, the huge office block of Bowater House straddling Edinburgh Gate, and the long red-brick and concrete monoliths of Hyde Park barracks, dominated by an ugly, 28-storey tower of flats for married NCOs and troopers. Designed by Sir Basil Spence, the barracks was formally opened by Field-Marshal Sir Gerald Templer and Admiral of the Fleet, Earl Mountbatten, in October 1970.

The blue Marina had been parked half a mile from the barracks' main gate. In its boot – on the right-hand side nearest to the road – was a 25 lb gelignite bomb, radio-controlled. Packed around it were 30 lbs of six- and four-inch nails.

It had not been entirely abandoned. Someone watched and waited in the park – perhaps near the bandstand, not far from a statue of St George on his steed, triumphing over a slaughtered dragon, which served as a memorial to 'the Cavalry of the Empire'. Perhaps he sat on a park bench, keyed up and ready to kill, and keeping the blue car in view through the trees. He held or carried a remote-control device that would be triggered as the standard-bearer of the mounted Queen's Life Guard crossed the line of sight between him and the car.

Men of the Household Cavalry had gone on guard at Horse Guards in Whitehall since 1751, apart from a brief interval during the Second World War. These duties now alternated between mounted squadrons of the Life Guards and the Blues and Royals, both based at Hyde Park barracks. Every morning, at about half-past ten, a ceremonial unit of mounted soldiers would set off from the barracks, via Hyde Park Corner, Constitution Hill and the Mall, to Horse Guards Parade, timing themselves en route so that they arrived at the central arch of Horse Guards as the clock above it struck eleven. It was a 24-hour guard duty, and the ceremony of Changing the Guard took place every weekday at 11.00 am. If the Queen, their Colonel-in-Chief, was residing in London, the Guard was 16-strong; if she was away, it numbered 12, and was without a trumpeter, standard-bearer and officer. On Tuesday, 20 July the Queen was at Buckingham Palace, so a full Guard was mounted that morning; and that morning it was the turn of the Blues and Royals to relieve the detachment of the Life Guards on duty at Whitehall.

The Blues and Royals had been formed 13 years earlier by the amalgamation of the Royal Horse Guards (the Blues) and the Royal Dragoons (First Royal Dragoons). They were an armoured-car regiment (their main military role), and had served in Northern Ireland. Twenty-one of them had recently returned from the Falklands War and paraded through Windsor, their regimental home.

The Household Cavalry's Commanding Officer was Lt.-Col. Andrew Parker Bowles, aged 42, who had served with the Blues and Royals. The previous November, the managing director of a small security firm in London, Mr Wynne, had written to him, drawing attention to the vulnerability of the barracks' mess and advocating the installation of certain safeguards. Wynne wrote: 'The real risk to my mind is the way in which large groups of your horses walk or trot along the same route on an almost daily basis. If I were the IRA, I would only require a shovel, explosives and remote detonation facilities to wreak desperate havoc with little or no risk involved.' Lt.-Col. Parker Bowles replied: 'We are very aware of our vulnerable position.' Action to improve security, he said, was taken 'within financial restrictions'. He later told reporters:

> Without taking the cavalry through even busier streets than now, and by very roundabout routes, there is very little more that we can do. There are very few variations. If you think about it, there is a maximum of three routes by which you can get from the barracks to Horse Guards Parade. We do change the route every so often. But if you want to have a Queen's Life Guard, then I'm afraid we are vulnerable to a bomb or even to anyone who carries a gun. There are certain risks we have to take.

On that Tuesday morning the troopers and NCOs of the Blues and Royals were up early, preparing their uniforms and horses for inspection by the Adjutant at 10.00 am. Some of them had never ridden a horse before they volunteered for this three-year tour of ceremonial duty, which was prefaced by five months of riding instruction. The horses were also intensively trained and carefully chosen. Geldings or mares, most of them came from Ireland, and were selected in accordance with certain requirements: they had to have the right colour (black), the right height (16.2 hands minimum), and the right temperament. The troopers were encouraged to form strong bonds of care and understanding for their horses, which were almost as well housed as the men, with central-heating, spacious stalls, good feed and clay-brick floors.

Men and horses began lining up in the yard for inspection at 9.50 am, the men wearing black thigh-boots, white breeches, blue tunics, gleaming cuirasses (breast- and backplates), white gauntlets and silver-plated helmets with red horsehair plumes. The red and gold tasselled standard was to be borne by SQMC (Squadron Quarter-Master Corporal) Roy Bright, aged 36, who had joined the Blues in 1964. A keen sportsman, fencer and pentathlete, he had met his wife in Germany when they were both 20 and she was a military nurse. They now had two teenage children. Every weekend he drove the 150 miles to his Shropshire home to be with his family, leaving at 4.00 am every Monday morning for the long drive back to work.

Some of the troopers were very young: the trumpeter, Stephen Sullivan, the only one to ride a grey horse, was 18. Simon Tipper was 19; he had only been married for two weeks and was now living in Putney with his young wife and mother-in-law. L/Cpl. Jeffrey Young was also 19. Married at the age of 17, he already had two children, aged three and 22 months. Corporal of Horse, James Pitt, a Scot, aged 28, was soon to be married; his horse was called Eclipse. Lance-Corporal Michael Pedersen's horse, Sefton, aged 19, was the oldest horse on the parade.

Two of those in the Guard that day should not have been there. Trooper Ian Smith, aged 23, whose fiancée was expecting twins, had stood in at the last minute for a sick friend. And the officer in charge of the new Guard, Lt. Anthony Daly, also aged 23, was likewise standing in for a friend. He had then tried to exchange his duty with a senior officer, Major Henry Hayward. But the Major had engagements that afternoon and was unable to comply.

In view of the fact that Lt. Daly would definitely be Captain of the Guard, his mother had arranged to bring an Australian friend to watch the Changing of the Guard at Horse Guards Parade that morning. She was now waiting there in the officers' quarters for her son and the Guard to arrive.

Anthony Daly, born on 27 January 1959 and educated at Eton, had followed his grandfather and father into the regiment and joined the Blues and Royals in January 1977. In 1979 he served in Northern Ireland for four months. He excelled at several sports and captained regimental rugby teams, playing alongside Bright and Young. He had also run in the London marathon earlier that year. Earlier that month he had returned to London from his honeymoon in Bermuda, having married Nichola Barcilon, the daughter of an RAF group captain, at the RAF church, St Clement's Danes, in the Strand less than four weeks before.

The full Guard, once the inspection was over, formed themselves into a processional column and as the trumpeter sounded the advance they moved out of the yard just after half-past ten. With a clatter of hooves, swords at the slope, and harnesses jingling they passed through the main gate into the road and turned right. Two mounted policemen attached themselves to the column, one at the front, the other at the rear, and the sun flared over them briefly as they set off down the road towards Hyde Park Corner – at the trot, as their inspection had delayed their departure by a minute or so.

Major Hayward, aged 34 and HQ Squadron Leader, had been exercising his charger, Yukon, in the park. He returned to the barracks as the Queen's Life Guard left. Reining in his horse he saluted the standard as it passed before him. Then he rode into the yard.

The Guard trotted on down the South Carriage Drive. Lt. Daly rode on the right of the standard-bearer, SQMC Bright, with a trooper known as a 'coverer' on the standard's left. These three were in the middle of the column, which was led by the trumpeter, Trooper Sullivan, out on his own, behind a mounted policeman. Then came six troopers riding in pairs. Another six followed the standard. The position of the men in the column would in minutes be a matter of life and death, or injury – depending on whether they rode on the left, or right, and on exactly when the man who watched their approach from the park activated the bomb in the car.

The column passed Bowater House, the Hyde Park Hotel and the Royal Thames Yacht Club, opposite which, on the edge of the park, a small copse of flowering trees had been planted and dedicated by Prince Charles seven months previously, as a memorial to the former Commodore of the Yacht Club, Earl Mountbatten, killed by an IRA bomb in August 1979.

They trotted past Albert Gate and the French Embassy, and the large mansion block of apartments, the last of the buildings on their right. Now, in full view of the five-arched gate at Hyde Park Corner, through whose central arch they would ride, there was nothing on their right but a stretch of grass and some trees and a line of parked cars.

People who happened to be out walking stopped to watch and admire the colourful pageant of horses and men. Among them was a Canadian, Mrs Diane Elder, and a family with the same surname as that of Lt. Daly. Back at Albert Gate, a car driven by the *Daily Star*'s royal reporter, James Whitaker, was brought to a halt by traffic lights switching to red.

The trumpeter passed the blue Marina, and for some reason Trooper Simon Tipper, riding behind the standard carried by SQMC Bright, turned his head to the right.

The Marina exploded – and in that instant Simon Tipper died.

James Whitaker, sitting in his red Ford Cortina at the traffic lights, saw it all. He wrote later:

The moment that will haunt me for the rest of my days arrived at 10.40 and 23 seconds. I am so precise because my first, unthinking reflex was to look at my watch. Seconds before, it had been a beautiful summer day, and I had been driving to work down the South Carriage Drive. Then the traffic lights changed to red, and I slowed to a halt. Idly, I watched a detachment of the Household Cavalry clip-clopping down the road 100 yards ahead of me, plumes dancing, cuirasses gleaming in the sun, their black horses well-groomed. A ball of flame shooting into the air was the first sign of the catastrophe. This was followed almost instantaneously by an ear-splitting thud and a column of black smoke. My car shook, as if the earth trembled beneath me, and it was at that moment I looked at my watch. And at that moment everything went into slow motion. But it was what I witnessed next that will live with me forever. I saw bodies licked with flame, mis-shapen masses, tumbling down from the sky – horses, and their riders coming down after them. I drove towards the scene and got out of the car, and there was this terrible, total silence, a complete vacuum of noise. Not one horse made a single sound. No whinnying. No snorting through their nostrils. The great beasts lay on their sides or half sitting-up looking pitiful, their eyes half staring out of their sockets. One or two had somehow remained on their feet and looked around with almost human panic and shock in their dark brown eyes. One or two of the riders, their bright uniforms shattered and scorched, stood dazed, or wandered among the stricken animals. Some lay dreadfully still. A car burnt furiously by the road. Others were wrecked. The column of evil black smoke coiled into the sky, turning the sun blood red, and a woman began to scream. Now I saw more red, the glistening red of the blood that started to seep and sometimes spurt from the glossy black coats of the horses. Then the less seriously injured troopers staggered to their feet. I watched, mesmerised, as every single man who could walk began to look around for his horse, to see if it was all right, to catch the ones that had struggled up. Instinctively, the troopers cared more for their terribly wounded, muted horses, than for themselves. By now, and only a few minutes had passed, I was beginning to cry. Then two policemen ran up the road, shouting that there might be another bomb and telling me and others to move away. I ran around the corner to the Hyde Park Hotel, to phone the office and get some help. But I was not very coherent, gasping, and it was difficult to make myself understood.

The Times reported:

> The nearest soldier was about eight feet from the bomb. The force of the explosion catapulted another parked car on to the roof of a vehicle nearby. Nails and wreckage were sent flying over a 250-yard area. The windows of shops in Knightsbridge, including Barclays Bank and the National Farmers' Union, were blown out, and pieces of the booby-trapped car were found embedded in partition walls on the second and fourth floor of the NFU building . . . Hundreds of people were in the park at the time.

Bits of the car and dozens of nails had scythed through the centre and rear of the mounted column. All the Blues and Royals were injured, though some, like trumpeter Stephen Sullivan, were not seriously hurt. He said later: 'I just remember coming to and seeing soldiers and horses everywhere.' The worst injured were Lance-Corporal Young and the standard-bearer, Roy Bright. A nail had torn into Bright's neck and upwards into his brain. Trooper Ian Smith and Corporal of Horse James Pitt were also injured. Pitt said: 'It was carnage. There were horses trying to stand up, and they couldn't understand why they couldn't do so with only three legs. I never thought they would go for the animals. My horse, Eclipse, took the blast that was meant for me. That horse saved my life.' Mike Pedersen, riding Sefton, was wounded by a piece of metal that sliced into his right hip; and his little finger was transfixed by a nail. He said:

> I didn't know what had happened. I was just in a daze. There was a huge noise and I was deaf. I saw a large cloud of smoke and vaguely saw soldiers and horses on the ground. It never occurred to me it was a

bomb. Sefton's legs were outstretched and braced. He didn't try to bolt or dump me and I stayed mounted, although I didn't have any reins – they'd been blown away. I don't know if it was him or me, but between us we turned round and walked back towards the barracks. We didn't get that far before a soldier came running to meet us. He lifted me off Sefton's back, and someone else stuffed his shirt into Sefton's throat to stop the bleeding. When I found it was an IRA bomb, I couldn't believe anyone would do that to a horse.

Major Hayward was in the barracks' yard, talking to another officer. He said later:

When I heard the bang, along with everyone there, I went to the Knightsbridge side of the barracks. The sound seemed to come from there. For some reason I then turned round and saw a woman at the Ceremonial Gate. She had got out of a taxi. She was hysterical and saying something to the guard at the gate. He signalled to me to come over and I did. She was in tears and said something like: 'It's terrible! There are horses everywhere! Why aren't you doing anything about it? They need help.' It was difficult to understand what she was saying. I stepped out into the road, looked and saw the smoke. The traffic had stopped. I realised it was the Guard. I ran back into the yard, shouting at the veterinary officer, Major Carding, telling him what had happened. I ran upstairs to Andrew's office and barged in. He was in conference. I said: 'Colonel – that bomb was the Guard!' We rushed down to the yard, where we got a staff car to take us to the scene. Troopers ran down the road. Quite a few people were there already, including an ambulance and the police. We could do little. There was this mass of bodies, horses and men, in the middle of the road. Blood everywhere. The wounded horses were being shot. Some of the men were standing up, holding their heads. Cpl. Pitt's face was covered in blood. I remember seeing L/Cpl. Young lying in the road, bleeding and badly injured – he had been crushed by his horse. Anthony Daly seemed unmarked. But he was dead. It could have been me.

A policeman on diplomatic duty outside the French Embassy had run up. Armed with a revolver, he began shooting the injured horses. One was already dead. But as he aimed at their chests, intending to hit their hearts, he failed to kill them straight away. They reared as he shot them, and lunged. He managed to kill two or three before a farrier from the barracks took the gun off him and shot the remaining injured horses in their foreheads, between their eyes. Six horses were shot.

One of the mounted policemen, John Davies, aged 24, was injured, as was Echo, his horse. Of the civilians in the area, five were hit by flying metal, nails and broken glass.

Thomas Daly, a milkman, was further up the road with his wife, Pauline, and their two-year-old son, Thomas, who was in a push-chair. Mr Daly pulled the chair back off the road between two cars as the Guard approached. His wife remained on the road. Mrs Daly said later: 'There was a tremendous bang. I was aware of something hitting my leg. I must have passed out. The next thing I knew I was lying in the road. I couldn't hear any-thing at first, because of the bang.' She was also unable to hear herself screaming. But she was out of hospital in 24 hours. Her son was not hurt.

Mrs Elder, standing on the grass near the plane tree, was less fortunate. Peter Anderson, aged 22, was working in Knightsbridge. He said: 'I ran out-side and saw a fireball. I got up the bank and all I could see was devastation and carnage. The first thing I saw was a middle-aged lady. She was on her hands and knees screaming, with part of her foot blown away.' Kelly Scales, a waitress, said: 'It was horrific. I've never seen anything like it. One woman was sitting on the bank bleeding, with half her foot hanging off.'

A hairdresser, Tony Tenconi, said:

There was this massive noise and a great heat. Glass was falling from the flats above, and I thought it might be a gas explosion, until I saw a ball of flame over in the park. I ran across and it was just a carnage of horses, with blood spurting from their wounds. I ran back to the shop, grabbed a handful of towels and screamed to the girls to wet them with cold water. As I ran back there was a woman screaming 'Help me!' There was also this soldier with blood pouring out of his head. I pressed his wound together until the ambulance men arrived. I saw a soldier walk away and then just collapse. Horses lying around were twisted with pain, some trying to get up. They were slithering about and sliding into the helpers. A policeman produced a revolver and began shooting the horses around me. They were still writhing after they were shot. An officer shouted: 'Shoot them again!'

'It was a scene of sheer horror,' said a businessman, John Marriott, who lived near by. 'I saw one trooper with his head blown off. A horse was lying on top of one of the injured men and a mounted policeman covered in blood climbed on to the horse to stop it moving about and causing the soldier more harm.' Ray Ashley, a workman, said: 'There were two troopers trapped under the bodies of their horses. A policeman was shooting injured horses as they tried to get up. I had to look away. I saw one horse trying to get up on the one leg it had left. It was dreadful.' Another workman, John Marshall, said: 'One of the soldiers got up off the ground. The metal on his uniform was all twisted out of shape and his helmet was battered. He took it off and kicked it down the road.'

James Whitaker, returning to the South Carriage Drive, encountered two young troopers, in tears, leading an injured horse back to the barracks. He wept himself as from the park (the road had been cordoned off) he saw the last of the horses being shot. He wrote later: 'I have seen men die like animals, and animals die like men. And nothing, ever again, will seem the same.'

No responsibilities were greater, graver, or lasted longer than those of Lt.-

Col. Parker Bowles and his 2IC, Major Hayward, who had to deal with the effects of the bomb explosion on the men under their command, on those who survived, on the families of the dead and injured, as well as with the police, security officers and the press. The Life Guards on duty at Horse Guards Parade remained there without a change of guard for another 24 hours.

Major Hayward commandeered the staff car of a senior officer in the Royal Green Jackets who had happened to stop in South Carriage Drive. With a police escort he drove to St James's Street, while Parker Bowles returned to the barracks. Hayward said:

> I knew where Lt. Daly's wife worked. It was in an optician's. When I saw her I said: 'Something has happened,' and asked her to accompany me back to the barracks. I didn't tell her Anthony was dead. I just kept her talking. When we arrived, using the Knightsbridge entrance, I took her up to Andrew's office. The regimental medical officer was already there, with his wife . . . I then had to find Trooper Tipper's wife, and tell his father that his son had just got married – he didn't know – and now was dead.

Anthony Daly's mother, at Horse Guards Parade, heard the bang of the explosion. But it was not until eleven o'clock struck, when the Guard failed to arrive, that she realised something was dreadfully amiss. She was told of her son's death by the major-general commanding the Household Division.

The injured were taken to Westminster Hospital. Ten wounded horses, including Eclipse, aged 7, Copenhagen, aged 10, and the police horse, Echo, were brought back to the barracks, leaving a bloody trail for 400 yards down South Carriage Drive.

Major Noel Carding, the regimental vet, said of 19-year-old Sefton: 'These are the worst, the saddest, most dreadful injuries I have ever seen inflicted on a horse.' Sefton had sustained 38 wounds caused by shrapnel and nails; his jugular vein had been severed; his right eye and face were also scorched. Major Carding said: 'He has lost a great deal of blood and is in deep shock. He is deadly quiet. I've not been able to get all the lead out of him, but I hope he will survive . . . These are magnificent horses, so stouthearted. They bear their suffering in silence.'

The horses which died were Cedric, Epaulette, Falcon, Rochester, Waterford, Yeastvite and Lara. Their nameplates were removed from their empty stalls the following day.

Their bodies, however, remained out on the road that Tuesday afternoon for two hours, covered by tarpaulins, as transport was organised to take them away. The area had been cleared by the police, who feared that a second bomb might have been placed in another parked car. They were right about the second bomb. But it was not in Hyde Park.

At 12.55, as the dead horses were being removed, a distant boom was heard coming from Regent's Park.

The band of the 1st Battalion Royal Green Jackets were giving a lunchtime concert on a bandstand in the park. It was thought to be safe for them to perform in London rather than in Ulster, where their battalion was currently based. The band, numbering 30 in all, had left Winchester that morning by coach, arriving in London at half-past eleven, some 50 minutes after the car-bomb explosion in Hyde Park. The bandmaster, David Little, heard about the bomb attack on a radio as he drank before the concert with other bandsmen in a pub. He then checked the bandstand himself.

He later told an inquest: 'I walked round the bandstand and checked the floorboards. The band would have checked the bandstand earlier anyway, as we've done over the years since another band nearly got it in Brussels. I found nothing out of place. I asked a colleague to make a further check.'

The bandstand was situated on the south-western rim of Regent's Park, by a lake full of ducks, geese and swans and not far from the top of Baker Street. About 100 people listening to the music reclined in deckchairs all around the bandstand or sat on the grass. Hidden under the floorboards was an IRA bomb. There had apparently not been enough space to include a briefcase full of nails, which was found later by divers dumped in the lake. If the nails had been packed beside the bomb, the casualties would have been much greater. At 12.30 the band began to play.

At 12.55, as the band played a selection from the musical *Oliver*, the bomb exploded, triggered by remote control or by a timing device. A sheet of flame shot upwards, as did the blast, hurling bandsmen, their instruments, music stands and spears of wood into the air. The bandstand's iron cupola and supporting pillars withstood the blast.

'I remember the explosion,' said Bandmaster Little. 'And the whistling in my ears. The next thing I knew I was facing the audience with my back to the bandstand.' Cpl. John Mitchell said: 'We were playing away and bang – that was it. People were mutilated. There were bodies everywhere. They were all my friends. I've been working with them for ten years.'

Simon Braidman, a student, was sitting on the grass with his sister and another girl. He said: 'There was an enormous explosion. The sky was full of debris. I was hit by a piece of wood. I saw it falling, but I was so shocked I just couldn't move out of the way.' A pensioner, Benjamin Morris, said: 'I saw a lot of soldiers blown out of the bandstand like dummies. It was like wartime. Some were dead, lying on the grass. One soldier came up to me crying, with blood pouring down his face.' Another pensioner, Miriam Sheridan, said: 'I saw the soldiers lying on the grass with some of their intestines hanging out. Two soldiers were walking around with blood pouring from their heads. I stroked one of the soldiers' heads. He was very young, and I held his hand and I told him help would soon arrive.' A building worker, Donald McCulloch, said: 'One soldier reached out his hand for help, but his body had been blown in half. He was completely cut in two. He was still alive.'

The bandsmen's injuries were horrific: one was grossly mutilated, some lost limbs, or suffered compound fractures and burns. One bandsman died of cerebral lacerations and a fractured skull; another had both an arm and a leg torn off.

Six bandsmen died in the park, and a seventh would die later of pneumonia brought on by his multiple injuries. They were: Warrant Officer Graham Barker; Sgt. Robert Livingstone; Cpl. John McKnight; Bandsmen John Heritage, George Mesure, Keith Powell and Laurence Smith. Thirty bandsmen and civilians were injured by the bomb. Since 1969, 28 men of the Royal Green Jackets, including two officers, had been killed in Northern Ireland, five dying there in 1981.

There were shocked gasps in the House of Commons later that afternoon when the Home Secretary, William Whitelaw, revealed that in addition to the two Blues and Royals who had died in Hyde Park, six Green Jackets had now been killed in Regent's Park. The leader of the opposition, Michael Foot, declared that no political question would be settled in democratic Britain by a resort to 'pitiless barbarity'. Mrs Thatcher denounced the bomb explosions as 'these callous and cowardly crimes, committed by evil and brutal men'.

A garden party at Buckingham Palace that afternoon went ahead, amid unprecedented security checks, including the closure of the Mall. The Queen was said to be visibly distressed when she spoke of the bombings to some of the guests. It had already been a stressful month for her: an intruder, Michael Fagan, had entered the palace on 9 July and found his way to the Queen's bedroom before he was arrested. Then the senior policeman on the Palace staff, Michael Trestrail, resigned after confessing to a relationship with a male prostitute. And the Falklands War had only ended a month before.

The Queen sent a telegram to Lt.-Col. Parker Bowles which said: 'I was deeply shocked and distressed to hear of the dreadful tragedy suffered by the Queen's Life Guard today. The Duke of Edinburgh and I send our heartfelt sympathy to the families of those who died, to the injured and to the Mounted Regiment itself. Elizabeth R.'

That night, during the Royal Tournament at Earl's Court, which was attended by Prince Charles, there was a minute's silence for the victims of both bomb explosions and a trumpeter played the Last Post.

An hour before the sun set on that Tuesday there was a partial eclipse of the sun.

The following morning, Wednesday, 21 July, the newspapers carried headlines like – 'IRA MASSACRE – THE IRA BOMBERS ARE BACK'. The *Mirror* said: 'The IRA returned to London yesterday, killing without warning and without pity. They bombed not only soldiers but innocent passers-by. Year in and year out, they are the most consistently wicked gang of killers in the Western world.'

The IRA had already issued a statement in Dublin and Belfast, admitting responsibility for the bombings and comparing their situation to Britain's against Argentina in the Falklands War. They said: 'Now it is our turn to properly invoke Article 51 of the UN Charter and properly quote all Thatcher's fine phrases on the right to self-determination of a people. The Irish people have sovereign and national rights, which no task or occupational force can put down.' They justified the bombings as acts of self-defence.

A headline in the pro-IRA weekly, the *Republican News*, said: 'IRA ROCK

ENEMY MORALE'. The bomb operations in London were said to have been 'brilliantly executed', although 'regrettably there were injuries to several civilians'.

On that Wednesday morning the Duke of Edinburgh visited the Hyde Park barracks before a detachment of the Life Guards set out for Horse Guards Parade to relieve the unit from their own regiment who had now been on duty for nearly 48 hours. As Lt.-Col. Parker Bowles explained later: 'It will take more than a cowardly attack like yesterday's to stop us doing our duty. We are all determined to carry on and will continue to mount a guard as we have done for 300 years. My men would be most disappointed if we did not. I know it is what my men expect and want to do.'

The Duke inspected the new Guard and spoke to five survivors of the bomb-blast who were out of hospital and on their feet. Among them were Cpl. of Horse James Pitt and Trooper Sullivan, both of whom, with Lt.-Col. Parker Bowles and Major Carding, talked later to the press.

Reporters were also allowed to view the injured horses in the stables, and pictures of Sefton soon featured prominently in local and national papers. Major Carding said: 'Everyone is disgusted and horrified at this cowardly attack on both men and horses.' A Corporal of Horse was quoted as saying: 'Those horses are the pride of Ireland. The men who injured them are its shame.'

The new Guard of 16 men left the barracks a few minutes late and trotted up the South Carriage Drive, now cleared of cars, towards the scene of the explosion. Spectators applauded; some cheered. As the Life Guards approached the scorched and riven plane tree and passed over the patches of sand spread over the blood-stained road, they held their swords erect, at the carry, and the Captain lowered his, in honour of their dead and injured colleagues in the Blues and Royals. The spectators were silent here. Below the tree someone had left a posy of pink carnations, with a message that said: 'In loving memory. Father forgive.'

L/Cpl. Jeffrey Young died in hospital that day: he would have been 20 the following week.

Messages of sympathy, good wishes and greeting cards had already begun to arrive at the barracks, including bags of sugar lumps and carrots for the injured horses, for Sefton in particular. Eventually, one side of his stall was covered in Get Well cards. Lt.-Col. Parker Bowles received a telegram from the Prince and Princess of Wales, whose first son, Prince William, had been born in June. It said: 'We were both utterly appalled and sickened by what happened in Hyde Park yesterday and felt heavy at heart throughout the rest of the day. Please would you convey our very deepest sympathy to the families of those who lost their lives so tragically and to the troopers who looked after the horses that were killed – Charles and Diana.'

On the morning of Thursday, 22 July, the Blues and Royals rode out of the barracks once again, bearing the torn and bloodied standard that had been torn from the grasp of SQMC Bright. The sun shone, and all along the route people applauded and cheered at windows and in the street. Among them was Nichola Daly. She stood with her younger sister opposite the place where her husband had died. Her sister, Rae-Louise, who had been a bridesmaid at the Dalys' wedding, wept as the Guard rode past. Mrs Daly called out: 'Well done, Guard! Well done!'

Roy Bright died in Westminster Hospital the following night. Brain-dead since the explosion, he had been kept alive for three days by a life-support machine, until, with the approval of his wife, Marion, arrangements to transplant his kidneys to save the lives of two middle-aged women could be made.

'He would have been the first to applaud that decision,' said Mrs Bright weeks later – she had been with her husband, as was his widowed mother, when he was allowed to die. She said:

> With his brain gone, there was no sense in denying a chance of life to others . . . Doctors had told me that early tests had shown no sign of brain activity, and these tests had to be repeated before any final decisions were taken. I'll never forget Roy's face as he lay there. Once the second tests proved negative, I didn't want him to be kept alive. I couldn't imagine him living as a vegetable. Not Roy. He was always so full of life . . . Everything he did, he did with enthusiasm. We went walking, camping, caravanning, boating. He was always an outdoor man and had loved horse-riding ever since he was a boy. Apart from his family, the men and horses in his regiment were the great love of his life. He'd do anything for them. If any horse was awkward or difficult to manage they'd say 'Give it to Roy – he won't fail.' And he never did . . . He was such a strong, fit man. I didn't believe that anything could destroy him.

The biggest security operation in central London since the wedding of Prince Charles and Lady Diana Spencer took place on Monday, 26 July, when the nation paid homage in St Paul's Cathedral to those who had died in the Falklands War. The Last Post and Reveille, which were played during the service, would be heard in eleven churches elsewhere, as the Blues and Royals and Royal Green Jackets who had died on 20 July were buried over the next two weeks.

On 27 July, L/Cpl. Jeffrey Young was buried, on his birthday, at Tonyrefail, a mining village in South Wales. The funeral of Lt. Anthony Daly was held in the Garrison Church at Windsor the following day. His flag-draped coffin was carried by ten men from the Blues and Royals, including some who had been part of his last Guard. His father, Lt.-Col. Dennis Daly, was there, as well as his mother, sister and younger brother, Christopher, aged 18, who joined the Blues and Royals in 1987. During the service, Nichola Daly wept silently on the shoulder of her uniformed father, Group Captain Barcilon.

Simon Tipper was buried at Swinford, near Stourbridge in the West Midlands, and Roy Bright at Broseley in Shropshire.

By then, the death toll from both bomb explosions had reached eleven, with the death on 1 August in St Mary's Hospital of Bandsman John Heritage, a 29-year-old drummer from Banbury, who was married with two young children. By then only one of the wounded Blues and Royals was still in hospital, although ten bandsmen were still receiving hospital treatment.

In the middle of August the injured horses were put out to grass at the Army Veterinary Centre at Melton Mowbray in Leicestershire. But it was not until 28 September that Sefton was reunited with his rider, Mike Pedersen, and returned to work for another two years, retiring in August 1984. A painting of Sefton, auctioned in London, had raised £12,500 for the appeal funds set up for the dependants of the victims of the bombs, and £50,000 was donated by people in the Irish Republic. Each of the four widows of the Blues and Royals eventually received about £25,000.

The inquest into the deaths of the eleven soldiers was held at Westminster on Thursday, 21 October, the coroner recording a verdict of unlawful killing on all of the men. The head of the anti-terrorist squad at Scotland Yard, Commander Bill Hucklesby, said afterwards: 'The police are very grateful to numerous members of the public who offered information concerning these crimes.' He said 6,000 telephone calls and 400 letters had been received, and 1,200 statements taken. He added: 'I am hopeful and determined that our investigations will result in the prosecution of the criminals responsible for these bomb outrages.'

These investigations were not brought to a conclusion for five years, until 27 October 1987, when Gilbert McNamee, aged 27, was convicted on fingerprint evidence of conspiring, between January 1982 and January 1984, to cause explosions likely to endanger life or cause serious injury to property.

McNamee, known as Danny, came from Crossmaglen in County Armagh. He was one of eight children. His mother died when he was five, and when he was 14 his father was killed by an IRA bomb, meant for a passing patrol, which exploded in a Crossmaglen pub. Two of his cousins were shot by the IRA who thought they were police informants. Despite all this he went on to achieve eleven GCE 'O' Levels and three 'A' Levels and studied physics at Queen's University in Belfast. He graduated in 1982 with a pass degree, and went to work in Dundalk in Ireland as an electrician at a factory which made parts for CB radios and gaming machines. The brothers who ran the business, George and James McCann, were both members of the IRA. George McCann was later arrested in France and jailed for smuggling arms for the Irish National Liberation Army. In 1984, McNamee was himself arrested by the Irish police and charged with possessing micro-circuitry for use in explosive devices. But an Irish jury concluded that the circuits were for use in anti-theft devices in gaming machines. He was released, and returned to Crossmaglen. In January 1986, his fingerprints were routinely taken by an RUC patrol in Northern Ireland. Later that year they were found to match prints on two IRA arms caches discovered in England. He was arrested at his home in Crossmaglen in August 1986.

The trial of Danny McNamee – 'a slightly built man with thick-lensed glasses', according to the *Daily Telegraph* – began at the Central Criminal Court in London on 12 October 1987. He pleaded not guilty. The judge was

Mr Justice McCowan, who was provided with a bodyguard throughout the two-week trial. The prosecution was led by Roy Amlot, QC, and the defence by Richard Ferguson, QC.

Mr Amlot claimed that McNamee's fingerprints were on a Duracell battery attached to a bomb defused in London in December 1983, as well as on tape on two encoders, components of radio-controlled bomb mechanisms, found in two large arms caches, one of which was unearthed in an Oxfordshire wood in October 1983, and the other in Salcey Forest in Northamptonshire in January 1984. According to the prosecution, McNamee made the bombs that IRA units used in England. He was linked to the Hyde Park bombing, it was said, by fragments of a circuit board that matched similar components in one of the arms caches. 'It is not suggested,' said Mr Amlot, 'that McNamee was present in Hyde Park when the bomb went off. The crown's case is that he was the bomb-maker . . . who worked in Ireland for the Provisional IRA.'

He went on to tell the court that McNamee's alleged co-conspirators, Paul Kavanagh, Thomas Quigley, and Natalino Vella, had already been convicted, in 1985, of explosives offences. Kavanagh and Quigley had each been jailed for 35 years.

McNamee was also said, after his arrest, to have offered the police an innocent explanation for the presence of his fingerprints on the battery and encoders – 'I work with electrical equipment a lot and repair many things. If my fingerprints are on it, it must have been that I was repairing something.'

During the trial he gave evidence in his own defence and denied being involved in any way in bombings. He said that although he was an Irish nationalist, he abhorred violence. Members of his own family had been killed by the IRA, he said, and it was unthinkable that he would be one of their number or work for them.

Danny McNamee was found guilty of conspiring to cause explosions and sentenced on 27 October 1987 to 25 years in prison. He was sent to Parkhurst Prison on the Isle of Wight.

The police believed that he was 'the IRA's master-bomber' and responsible in part for the murders of at least 30 soldiers, policemen and civilians in Northern Ireland and England from 1981 to 1986, a period which included the Hyde Park and Regent's Park bombings, the bomb explosion by Harrods in December 1983, which killed six people, and the explosion that killed five in the Grand Hotel in Brighton, where Mrs Thatcher and her ministers were staying during the Conservative Party Conference in October 1984. Some policemen believed that McNamee had a hand in the manufacture of up to 80 bombs and the consequent deaths of as many people. If so, he would be the biggest mass-murderer in British criminal history. But murder is not something with which terrorists are usually charged. Their offences come under the Prevention of Terrorism Act.

An appeal against McNamee's conviction was heard before the Lord Chief Justice, Lord Lane, Mr Justice Kennedy and Mr Justice Judge in December 1990. Richard Ferguson, QC, told the court that there was not a shred of evidence to link McNamee to the Hyde Park bombing, which had only been included at the last minute in the charges against him. The indictment had been altered twice, he said – ten days before the trial and again at the end of the trial after the closing speeches, when the charge was amended to 'within the UK and elsewhere'. Mr Ferguson claimed that the judge had also misdirected the jury and misrepresented McNamee's defence. The Old Bailey trial was 'unfair', he said. He cast doubt on the validity of the forensic and fingerprint evidence, and protested at the way the police had used the press to vilify McNamee.

Lord Lane and his two Appeal Court judges dismissed the appeal; also dismissed was a later application to appeal to the House of Lords. McNamee is still in a high-security prison and unlikely to be released for several years.

A small memorial stone to the four Blues and Royals who died in the Hyde Park bombing was dedicated in the presence of the Queen Mother in October 1983. It lies on the north side of South Carriage Drive opposite the scene of the explosion, which is marked now only by a kerbstone with a chipped and damaged edge. But when the road is wet with rain or damp with dew, a scorchmark like a black stain still appears.

The bombings did not cease with McNamee's arrest, although there was a long lull, punctuated by a bomb blast at the Mill Hill barracks in north-west London in August 1988, in which a man was killed, and by a large explosion a year later at the Royal Marines School of Music at Deal in Kent, when ten soldiers died. But in the first six months of 1990 there was a series of explosions at military offices and establishments in and around London, caused by parcel-bombs and car-bombs. These culminated in blasts at the Carlton Club, at the Stock Exchange, and in the death of MP Ian Gow.

Two bombs were directed at the band of the Blues and Royals in 1991. A bomb found outside the Beck Theatre at Hayes in West London in June, where the band was playing, was defused. In November, another small bomb, outside a concert-hall in St Albans where the band was due to play, blew up accidentally and killed the man and woman who had brought it there.

In April 1992, a 200-lb car-bomb exploded in the City of London, devastating the Baltic Exchange and several buildings, including two office tower-blocks, and causing damage costing billions of pounds. It was the worst single explosion in London since the Second World War: three people were killed and 91 injured. A few hours later another car-bomb wrecked a fly-over at Staples Corner on the M25.

The bombers were back once again with another double event. The murderous war being waged by the IRA to achieve the unification of all Ireland still goes on.

CHAPTER 20

Dennis Nilsen

The Murder of Stephen Sinclair, 1983

The disintegration of modern life, of the controlling influence of the family, religion and social standards, along with the general excesses of sexual expression, the wide availability of guns and drugs, and the everyday unsettling television images of affluence, disaster and death – all these have contributed in some way to an increase in murder, and especially to the modern phenomenon of the mass murderer known as the serial killer. There have always been mass murderers, like William Palmer, the poisoner. But they were very rare, and their victims rarely exceeded seven or eight. Since the 1970s, this kind of killer has increased, exacting a bloody revenge on society; some effecting a massacre of total strangers by gun, and others killing strangers to satisfy perverted sexual desires.

One of the first killing sprees of this sort, involving guns, occurred in August 1966 in Austin, Texas, when Charles Whitman, aged 25, stabbed and shot to death 21 people in less than 12 hours, killing most by sniping at them from a university tower. More recently, another 21 people were shot and killed by a gunman in and near a McDonald's in San Ysidro, California, in July 1984; and 22 were shot, again in Texas, in 1991. In England, Michael Ryan, aged 27, shot and killed 15 people and then himself in Hungerford, Berkshire in August 1987.

A more discriminate kind of slaughter, that of the sexual murder of young women, men and boys, escalated in America in the 1970s, prefaced by the murders committed by Charles Manson and his Family: he himself claimed to have murdered 35. Dean Corll, aged 33, together with two younger associates, raped and killed at least 27 boys in Houston, Texas, before he was shot and killed by one of those associates in 1973. In Florida, Ted Bundy was sentenced to death in 1979 for raping and killing at least 18 girls. In 1980 John Wayne Gacy, a twice-married contractor in Illinois, was sentenced to life imprisonment for the rape and murder of at least 32 young men and boys.

Also in that year, in England, Peter Dinsdale, known as Bruce Lee, was charged with the manslaughter by arson of 26 people in Hull; and another arsonist, John (Punch) Thompson, aged 42, caused the deaths of 37 people in two Soho drinking-clubs at 22 Denmark Place in August 1980 – when Dennis Nilsen was working around the corner in Denmark Street. The clubs were mainly used by Spaniards and South Americans. Thompson, the biggest mass murderer in British criminal history, was said to have argued with a barman about being overcharged, then obtained a can of petrol and set the house alight.

Dennis Nilsen, the first known homosexual serial killer in the UK, murdered and attempted to murder 22 young men in London in just over four years. His first victim died on New Year's Eve 1979, almost two years before Peter Sutcliffe, the Yorkshire Ripper, killed his last, in November 1980. Sutcliffe was arrested on 2 January 1981. Nilsen was arrested two years later, a fortnight after he had killed and dismembered his fifteenth victim, and his last.

Stephen Neil Sinclair was Scottish, like Nilsen, and like him a psychopath. In later years, if he had lived, he might have become a murderer himself. His real surname was Guild. Born in Perth on 20 February 1962, he was less than a month from his twenty-first birthday when he met the tall, stooping, studious-looking, bespectacled 37-year-old man, who called himself Des, on Wednesday, 26 January 1983. Des had grey-blue eyes and was 5' 10". They coincided in a Soho pub called the Royal George in Goslett Yard, near the Jobcentre in Denmark Street where Nilsen used to work as a clerical officer, finding jobs for the unemployed. Nilsen probably told Sinclair about this, and about his childhood in the north-east of Scotland, his years in the Army, mostly in the ACC (Army Catering Corps), and his year as a police constable with the Metropolitan Police. He now worked at the Jobcentre in Kentish Town.

Sinclair was about 5' 5", with ginger hair bleached blond. He was wearing a leather jacket, jersey, a blue and white football scarf and black jeans. A drug addict, who had attempted suicide more than once by slashing his arms and wrists, he had been destitute in London for several years, sleeping rough, usually in squats or derelict buildings, easing the pain of his existence with punk music, barbiturates, drugs and drink. A social worker who knew Sinclair, said: 'He was a very lonely, depressed and isolated guy, who could only get on with people on the surface . . . As far as I know, he had no friends whatsoever . . . Exactly a year before he was killed, his only friend, another punk, was stabbed in Green Park, near Piccadilly . . . He didn't have much to live for.'

Rejected as a baby by his parents, Stephen was fostered and then adopted, aged two, by the Sinclairs of St Martins, a small village in the heather-clad hills north of Perth. The father, Neil Sinclair, was a former Army officer and a driving instructor; his wife was a domestic science teacher; they already had three daughters. The little boy became uncontrollable, destroying all his toys, thieving, lying, setting things on fire, causing trouble every day, and every night wetting his bed until he was well into his teens. He had seizures, was violent, and showed no feeling for animals, the young or old. Mr Sinclair said: 'There was absolutely no love in him: he never cried at night . . . It was no use spanking him . . . Morally, he was like a one-and-a-half year old, even in his teens. He couldn't discern right from wrong.'

The Sinclairs gave their adopted son to the social services when he was about 13. After a spell in an approved school, whither he was sent for stealing, he was fostered by a Mr and Mrs Donald. He continued to steal, to lie, to misbehave and to wet his bed. His strangeness and moods began to alarm the Donalds, who returned him to the social workers within a year. He was soon in prison; he came to London; he contracted hepatitis B. The one night he spent with Dennis Nilsen was the end of the road for them both.

There are two main accounts of what happened that night and thereafter. Both are by Nilsen. Even so, the details within them do not tally. For it seems that Nilsen sought to conceal, as much as wished to reveal what he did. He wanted to share, to proclaim his terrible secrets, but not what was really in his mind and not what he really did.

He told the police, a fortnight after the event: 'We were having a good drink at the George and later I said: "You don't mind coming back to High-gate?" And he said: "Okay." We went to an off-licence in Greek Street, and I got a bottle of whisky and about six bottles of lager. It must have been after 9.00 pm when we got to my flat at Cranley Gardens.' In another, later account Nilsen said that he bought Sinclair a hamburger at a McDonald's in Oxford Street and that the drinks were purchased at a Shaftesbury Avenue off-licence.

They would then have taken the Northern line tube to Highgate and walked the half mile from there to Nilsen's flat up Muswell Hill Road, passing between Highgate Wood and Queen's Wood.

The flat was in the attic of 23 Cranley Gardens in Muswell Hill, a leafy North London suburb. The semi-detached house, owned by an Asian woman, was shabby and in need of repair: all the woodwork, painted pale blue, was peeling; roof tiles had slipped. Three flights of stairs led to Nilsen's door, which opened on to a cramped space containing a gas-cooker, water-heater, sink and kitchen cupboards. The bathroom was beyond. Another door led to a messy, foul-smelling front room, containing two wardrobes, two armchairs, a tea-chest, heaps of belongings and bits of brown carpet; the windows were wide open. Nilsen slept and ate in the back room, which was furnished with a low double-bed, tables, an upright chair, a sofa, TV set, stereo system, posters and some plants. The rooms were cold and squalid and every ceiling sloped. They were also occupied by Nilsen's only regular companion, a shaggy black and white mongrel bitch called Bleep, who had a bad eye. She had already witnessed 14 murders, and the dismembered remains of Nilsen's two most recent victims were packed in the tea-chest and in one of the wardrobes in the chill front room.

Bleep greeted her master enthusiastically when he and young Sinclair entered the flat. Nilsen later told the police:

I remember the 9.25 episode of 'Boys from the Blackstuff' was on TV. I let the dog out straight away. Right away. I said: 'This is a fantastic pro-gramme – we've got to watch this.' We started to drink. Whisky and then lager. I then let the dog into the front room and she curled up by a chair. He [Sinclair] went out of the door at one stage and into the bath-room. I realized afterwards he was probably injecting himself with drugs. I saw a tin in his hand. He was later sitting in the lounge and started to nod off. I sat with the headphones on listening to music, to the rock opera, *Tommy*. I heard the whole of it. God knows what time it was. I can't remember anything else until I woke up the next morning. He was still in the armchair and he was dead. On the floor was a piece of string with a tie attached to it . . . I know I must have killed him . . . I must have made up the piece of string that night. I don't know if he struggled. I would have thought it was quick . . . After I found him in the chair, I listened to LBC radio . . . I left him in the chair. [That] morning I was slightly late getting in to work. When I came home in the evening I examined him and rigor mortis had set in.

That is what he guardedly told the police after his arrest, and that is what was read out later in court. What Nilsen wrote about that night in an exercise-book *after* his trial paints a different, detailed and more terrible picture, indicating premeditation and what thrills and pleasures he derived from killing and then caressing a corpse.

I am sitting cross-legged on the carpet, drinking and listening to music. It finished with the theme from *Harry's Game*. I drain my glass and take the phones off. Behind me sits Stephen Sinclair on the lazy chair. He was crashed out with drink and drugs. I sit and look at him. I stand up and approach him. My heart is pounding. I kneel down in front of him. I touch his leg and say: 'Are you awake?' There is no response. 'Oh Stephen,' I think. 'Here I go again.' I get up and go slowly and casually through to the kitchen. I take some thick string from the drawer and put it on the stainless steel draining-board. 'Not long enough,' I think. I go to the cupboard in the front room and search inside. On the floor therein I find an old tie. I cut a bit off and throw the rest away. I go back to the kitchen and make up the ligature. I look into the back room and Stephen has not stirred. Bleep comes in and I speak to her and scratch her head. 'Leave me just now, Bleep. Get your head down. Everything's all right.' She wags her tail and slinks off into the front room. Her favourite place is on one of the armchairs in there, where she curls up. Looking back, I think she knew what was to happen. Even she became resigned to it. If there was a violent struggle, she would always become excited and start barking . . . I walked back into the room. I draped the ligature over one of his knees and poured myself another drink. My heart was pounding very fast. I sat on the edge of the bed and looked at Stephen. I thought to myself: 'All that potential, all that beauty, and all that pain that is his life. I have to stop him. It will soon be over' . . . I did not feel bad. I did not feel evil. I walked over to him. I removed the scarf. I picked up one of his wrists and let go. His limp arm flopped back onto his lap. I opened one of his eyes and there was no reflex. He was deeply unconscious. I took the ligature and put it around his neck. I knelt by the side of the chair and faced the wall. I took each loose end of the ligature and pulled it tight. He stopped breathing. His hands slowly reached for his neck as I held my grip. His legs stretched out in front of him. There was a very feeble struggle. Then his arms fell limp down in front of him.

I held him there for a couple of minutes. He was limp and stayed that way . . . I spoke to him: 'Stephen, that didn't hurt at all. Nothing can touch you now.' I ran my fingers through his bleached blond hair. His face looked peaceful. He was dead. The front of his jeans was wet with urine. I wondered if he had defecated as well. I got up and had a drink and a cigarette . . . I had to wash his soiled body. I ran a bath. I kept the water in it hand-warm and poured in some lemon washing-up liquid. I returned and began to undress him. I took off his leather jacket, jersey and T-shirt. Then his running shoes and socks. I had difficulty with his tight wet jeans. He still sat there, now naked, in the armchair. He had only urinated. He obviously had not had a square meal in a couple of days. I had not really known that his hair had been bleached until I stripped him. I discovered that he had ginger pubic hair. Otherwise his body was pale and hairless. He had crepe bandages on both forearms. I removed these to reveal deep, still open, recent razor cuts. He had very recently tried to commit suicide . . . I picked up his limp body in my arms and carried it into the bathroom. I put it into the half-filled bath. I washed the body. Putting my hands under his arms I turned him over and washed the back of his body. I pulled him out. He was very slippery with all that soap. I sat him on the loo and towelled the body and his hair as best as I could. I threw him over my shoulder and took him into the back room. I sat him on the white and blue dining-chair. I sat down, took a cigarette and a drink and looked at him. His head hung back, with his mouth slightly open. His eyes were not quite closed. 'Stephen,' I thought. 'You're another problem for me. What am I going to do with you? I've run out of room.' . . . I laid him on top of the double bed. It must have been well into the next morning of 27 January. I lay beside him and placed the large mirror at the end of the bed. I stripped my own tie, shirt and grey cords off, and lay there staring at both our naked bodies in the mirror. He looked paler than I did. Being ginger-haired, he would anyway. I put talcum powder on myself and lay down again. We looked similar now. I spoke to him as if he were still alive. I was telling him how lucky he was to be out of it all. I thought how beautiful he looked, and how beautiful I looked. He looked sexy, but I had no erection. He just looked fabulous . . . Soon I felt tired. I got in between the sheets, as I was starting to become cold. He still lay there beside me on top of the bedclothes. I knew he would become cold very soon, and I did not want to feel his coldness actually in bed with me. The coldness of a corpse has nothing endearing in it. Bleep came into the room and jumped up on the bed beside me. 'Come on, old girl. Get your head down. Stephen is all right now. He's okay.' She settled down at the end of the bed, stopping only to sniff once near Stephen's leg. She knew that the warm, friendly Stephen was no more, and ignored his body completely. I turned his head towards me and kissed him on the forehead. 'Goodnight, Stephen,' I said.*

* This and all the ensuing quotations from Nilsen's journals are reproduced by the special permission of Brian Masters, author of *Killing for Company*, who retains the copyright of these journals.

In a third account, written *before* the trial, in which the murder is not even mentioned, details vary: the body is dried on the edge of the bath, not on the loo; talcum powder is put on the corpse, not on Nilsen, who now has an erection. In this account, his tendency to sanctify horrific scenes is given rhapsodic expression: 'A great peace came over me. I felt that this was it, the meaning of life, death, everything. No fear, no pain, no guilt . . . No sex, just a feeling of oneness.'

The reality was probably even more gross. For Nilsen clearly exalted in the possession of the young man's completely helpless, naked body. He told a psychiatrist that he masturbated beside, or on, Stephen Sinclair's corpse. He probably did so more than once. What else he did with it over the next eight days we do not know, though Nilsen wrote: 'Afterwards, I dressed him in my clothes.' After what? And when? He told the police: 'I put the body in the cupboard.' But when was that?

The probability is that during the nights and the weekend following Sinclair's murder his body was taken out and used and abused as Nilsen wished – until it was rendered obnoxious by decomposition and became offensive as a plaything. Now it had to be destroyed, although its parts would be kept, as were those of his two other broken and rotting male toys, crammed in black plastic bags.

Although Nilsen was apparently outspoken about his murders, and unusually so, his memory was very selective, and erratic, and very little could be verified about what he said. He probably hid much more than he revealed, as had been his habit for much of his life. For years he had lied to his family and friends, and to himself, about himself and his homosexuality (he told the police he was bisexual), and acquaintances were told things about his past life which were not true. He was inured to deceive others, and especially his victims and himself. He also, as with other murderers and most of humanity, wished people to think well of him, to be socially acceptable, despite what he had done. At the same time, he needed people to know just how unique, how special he was, how different from the rest – but not that he was a necrophiliac, indulging in vile and unnatural deeds.

He was not ashamed, however, to tell the police about his dismemberment and disposal of the bodies. After all, this showed some expertise, as well as enterprise and resolve. As a former Army cook he was used to chopping, carving and gutting meat, and when dealing with humans, was unconcerned by any concept of desecration or violation. 'I can never understand a traditional and largely superstitious fear of the dead and corpses,' he wrote. Killing, he thought, was a much more dreadful act than cutting up a corpse. That was merely distasteful and hard work. He wrote: 'The victim is the dirty platter after the feast, and the washing-up is a clinically ordinary task.'

He told the police:

'On Friday night [eight days after Sinclair was killed] I thought I might as well start doing what I had to do . . . I took a plastic bag and sliced it into a sheet. I put it in the middle part of the front room and took the body from the cupboard and laid it on the plastic sheet, face up, and got the long kitchen knife with the brown handle and sharpened it with the sharpener. I cut the head off and got the pot out of the bathroom. There was a fair amount of blood, and some of it spilled out on to the carpet. I put the head in the pot and filled it with water. I put the lid on, lit the stove, and lit the front and rear burners and one at the side. I thought – I've got the whole weekend – and got fed up. I thought I'd go and get a bottle. Then I moved the body on to another sheet, which I laid beside the original one because there was a sizeable pool of blood on the first sheet. I tried to pick up the sheet and moved through the door, and a big drop of blood splashed on to the white carpet by the bathroom door. I got a couple of paper kitchen towels and tried to soak it up. But it had soaked right into the carpet. When ʳhe head was coming to the boil, I turned the gas down to simmer, and I said: 'Come on, dog.'

He took Bleep on a lead to a supermarket in Muswell Hill Broadway, where he bought some Marlboro cigarettes, a bottle of Bacardi and some Coca-Cola. Back in the attic flat, Nilsen listened to music on his headphones and watched TV, while Sinclair's head continued to simmer in the pot. He drank most of the bottle of rum, diluted with Coke, and then went to bed, having switched off the gaslights on the stove. Overnight the head cooled in the pot and the headless corpse lay in the front room, the windows open wide.

'I did not get up until 11.00 am on the Saturday,' Nilsen said. 'The place was looking untidy, and I thought I would clean it up. I took the dog out. There was a note on my banisters – *The plumber has been. Don't flush the loo.* On the way back I saw one of the girls. She asked me if I had got the note.'

This was a barmaid, Fiona Bridges, who lived with her boyfriend, Jim All-cock, on the ground floor. They, and the two girls who shared another ground-floor room (the first-floor rooms were empty), had been inconvenienced since Thursday, 3 February, by toilets which would not flush. At this time there was a water-workers' strike in England: many areas were without any water; stand-pipes for public supplies were in use; and mains pipes had burst. The cold spell made it worse. On the Friday, Jim had contacted a plumber and Fiona had asked Nilsen, when he returned that evening from the Jobcentre at Kentish Town, if there was anything wrong with his toilet. He replied in the negative and proceeded upstairs, where a few hours later he cut off Sinclair's head. The plumber arrived on Saturday morning, while Nilsen was still in bed. But his efforts failed to solve the problem and the landlord agreed to call in Dyno-rod – but not until the Monday. Allcock left a note for Nilsen, whom the other tenants knew as Des, and Fiona explained the situation to him when he left the house to take his dog for a walk. 'I began to realise that it could be something to do with my activities,' he told the police.

His activities, apart from the stench they caused in his flat (which, however, he was used to), had alarmed him earlier that afternoon, when a friend, Martyn Hunter-Craig, visited him unexpectedly and knocked on his door. According to Nilsen, he silenced the TV and his dog, and said nothing.

According to Hunter-Craig, Des shouted something like: 'You can't come in! I'm tied up with someone.'

Though advised about the visit on Monday of the Dyno-rod man, who might require to examine the bathroom in the attic flat, Nilsen did nothing about the severed body of Stephen Sinclair, nor anything about the other remains, until the Sunday. He might have removed the stinking contents of the tea-chest and the wardrobe later that night and dumped them elsewhere, in Highgate Wood, or in any of the other woods, parks and playing-fields that lay within half a mile of Cranley Gardens. Instead he stayed in and watched TV, with the headless, naked corpse on the front-room floor. When he took some action, it was only to hide Sinclair's body and head. 'I anticipated that on Monday somebody in authority might be coming round to ask questions. I got the knife out again, I sharpened it, and I dismembered the body.'

This operation occurred on Sunday afternoon. He cut the body in half at the waist, and then separated the two arms from the torso. All the various sections, including the parboiled head, were stuffed into two black plastic sacks and put in the bigger wardrobe – apart from Sinclair's packaged lower half, which was jammed into the wall-space at the foot of the bath. To do so, Nilsen first had to move another black sack containing other remains – those of Graham Allen, slaughtered five months before – and transfer them to the wardrobe. This done, he put a deodorant block on top of one of the bags and locked the wardrobe's doors. Another deodorant stick already stood on a table in the bathroom. On Monday morning, 7 February, Nilsen set off as usual for his place of work.

He was short-tempered at work that Monday, excusing himself by saying he was under great pressure. When he returned to Cranley Gardens he was probably relieved to learn that no one from Dyno-rod had called. Again he did nothing about disposing of the remains of three young men in his flat, and on Tuesday morning he again went to work.

Dyno-rod, in the person of 30-year-old Mike Cattran, turned up at 23 Cranley Gardens at 6.15 pm on Tuesday, 8 February. Accompanied by Jim Allcock, who held a torch, Cattran investigated the manhole by the side of the house that led to a sewer and into which the waste from the household drained. A nauseating, cloying stench assailed them as the manhole cover was raised. Using the iron rungs in the manhole wall, Cattran climbed down the 12-foot shaft, until he stood at its base, where his torch spotlighted the soggy pile of over 30 pieces of grey, rotting flesh on which he now stood. He moved and another piece flopped out of the exit-pipe from the house.

He told reporters later: 'I was formerly a lifeguard in Cornwall, and I'm well aware of what decomposing flesh is like . . . It wasn't a carcass, but bits of chopped-up flesh. Enough to fill two four-gallon buckets.'

He told the *Daily Mirror*:

When I got down there I couldn't believe it. I pulled out lumps of flesh the size of my fist, and strips of flesh that looked as though they'd been cut from an arm. After a few minutes I came up for a rest and to get some fresh air. Then I went down again with a plunger. As I pushed it down towards the mains, the whole lot moved and my bottle went. There was a bit with hair on it . . . I was trying to think what sort of animal it could be . . . Eventually I got to thinking that it had to be a body.

Saying nothing of his fearful thoughts to the tenants, Cattran went inside the house and asked them if any of them had flushed meat from a freezer or dog-meat down their toilets. Nilsen said he had a dog, but fed it on tinned meat. He expressed his concern about the situation and left the house with Cattran to examine the shaft and its contents for himself. As Cattran shone his torch down the shaft on the pale porridge of flesh, Nilsen questioned him about how the drain would be cleared (with a machine), and when. 'Tomorrow morning,' said Cattran, and at 7.00 pm he telephoned his boss, who was at home, about his difficulty, using a pay-phone on the first-floor landing of the house. Then he left.

Nilsen went back upstairs and wrote a letter to the landlord, complaining about standards of maintenance, about the state of the roof, the poor lighting on the stairs, and the drains. He wrote: 'When I flush my toilet the lavatory pans in the lower flats overflow (since Friday 4 Feb 83). Obviously the drains are blocked and unpleasant odours permeate the building.' Alone with his corpses, with Bleep by his side and a rum and coke in his hand, he then wrote a poem and considered what to do.

He thought of replacing the pieces of flesh in the manhole with pieces of chicken. He thought of running away, of suicide. But he felt he had to face up to what he had done, and that what he had done should be known – 'Someone's got to know the truth about what happened to them.' He wrote later: 'I could not guarantee that another death would not occur at some future time. I was sickened by the past, the present, and a doubtful future . . . I thought of dumping the remains left in my flat, but decided to leave everything where it was.'

None the less, after midnight, he went downstairs with a torch and a large plastic carrier bag. He entered the manhole, climbed down the shaft and put all the pieces of flesh he could find in the bag, which he dumped over the back garden hedge. As he re-entered the house, with his sleeves rolled up, he encountered Jim Allcock, who had been shaken awake by a frightened Fiona and urged to investigate the sounds and movement near their bedroom window. 'There's somebody having a go at the manhole,' she had whispered. 'I bet it's him upstairs.' Nilsen looked at Allcock. 'Just went out to have a pee,' he explained, and went back up to his flat.

On the cold and frosty morning of Wednesday, 9 February, about 8.30, Nilsen and Allcock went separately to work. Nilsen was wearing Sinclair's blue and white football scarf. At 9.15 Cattran returned to No. 23 with his boss, Gary Wheeler. Cattran saw that the oblong manhole cover behind the wooden passageway gate had been moved. He lifted the cover, shone his torch down the shaft. 'It's all gone!' he cried. He scrambled inside, and poking about with his hands, retrieved a pallid chunk of flesh from inside one of the drains. Then he discovered four small bones. He laid his finds on the rough path by Wheeler's feet. The two men were joined by a nervous Fiona

Bridges, clutching her dressing-gown about her. She told them what she and Allcock had seen and heard that night. Wheeler made up his mind. He told her: 'Call the police!'

DCI Peter Jay, the tall chief of Hornsey police station's CID, arrived at Cranley Gardens at 11.00 am. The flesh and bones were taken in a plastic bag to the Hornsey Mortuary and thence to Charing Cross Hospital, where they were examined that afternoon by a pathologist, Professor Bowen. He pronounced the flesh to be human, and that the bones came from a man's hand. DCI Jay headed back to Cranley Gardens at about 4.30, with DI Steve McCusker and DC Jeff Butler, to await Nilsen's return.

At work, Nilsen tidied up his desk and left a note in a desk drawer, saying that if he was arrested the police were not to be believed should they claim he committed suicide in his cell. He told an assistant: 'If I'm not in tomorrow, I'll be either ill, dead or in jail.' About 5.15 he left the Jobcentre in Kentish Town (since closed) and, wearing Sinclair's scarf, set off home by Tube. He wrote later:

I was sure I would be arrested when I came home, or sometime that evening ... I was totally resigned to this inevitability. I was worried about what was going to happen to Bleep ... My heart began to beat very fast as I walked down Cranley Gardens. I approached the house and knew instinctively that something was out of place, ie, that nothing seemed out of place. The house was almost in total darkness. I opened the front door and stepped into the dark hallway. On my left the front room door opened and I could see three large men in plain clothes. That's it! My mind began to race in all directions ...

'Mr Nilsen?' Jay enquired. 'Yes,' replied Nilsen, and Jay said, after introducing himself: 'I've come about your drains.' 'Why should my drains be of interest to the police?' demanded Nilsen and asked if the other two were health inspectors. Jay said they were police officers and provided their ranks and names. All four then ascended the stairs to the attic flat. Nilsen led them into the back room. Jay said: 'This morning, Mr Nilsen, we found a piece of flesh in your drains. It's been identified as part of a human body.' 'Good grief!' said Nilsen. 'How awful!' 'Don't mess about,' warned Jay. 'Where's the rest of it?' 'In two plastic bags in the wardrobe next door. I'll show you.' They all moved into the front room overlooking the street. The smell made the policemen grimace. 'In there,' said Nilsen, indicating the larger wardrobe and offering his keys. Taking them, Jay said he would open the wardrobe later. 'Is there anything else?' he asked. 'It's a long story,' said Nilsen and suggested that he would tell them everything at the police station, not in his flat. Whereupon he was formally cautioned and arrested on suspicion of murder, although the police had no idea of the victim's identity – or that more than one body was involved.

DC Butler was left to guard the flat, while DCI Jay and DI McCusker took Nilsen to Hornsey police station by car. Nilsen sat in the back with McCusker, who enquired as they left Cranley Gardens: 'Are we talking about one body or two?' Nilsen, looking straight ahead, replied: 'Fifteen or sixteen. Since 1978.'

The two policemen were stunned into silence until they reached the police station in Hornsey Road. There Jay, still incredulous, asked: 'Are you telling us that since 1978 you've killed 16 people?' 'Yes,' replied Nilsen, without any sign of emotion. 'Three at Cranley Gardens, and about 13 at my previous address, 195 Melrose Avenue, Cricklewood.' He wrote later: 'That was the end of the beginning, and the end of the killing . . . It was all out.' It was also 'the day help arrived'.

But it would take 30 hours, in interviews spread over the next ten days, before Nilsen finished telling his story. In the meantime, DCS Geoff Chambers, head of Y District CID, took charge of the case.

That night the two plastic sacks in the wardrobe were removed and examined by Professor Bowen. They were stuffed with smaller shopping-bags, which contained the three upper sections, innards and the almost featureless and hairless head of Stephen Sinclair, as well as another boiled head, and a gutted male torso with arms but no hands or legs. These were some of the parts of Graham Allen, killed five months ago. The sack containing Sinclair's lower half was retrieved the following day, Thursday, as was the tea-chest in which, under a velvet curtain, sheets, newspapers, air fresheners and mothballs, were the remnants, bones and skull of John Howlett, killed in March the previous year. Bleep was taken to Battersea Dogs' Home (she died in March) and that evening it began to snow.

On Friday, 11 February, the five severed sections of Stephen Sinclair were assembled on the mortuary floor, and when Nilsen supplied the police with the victim's name, they were able to confirm his identity from his fingerprints, which were in police records. Later that day, Nilsen accompanied DCS Chambers and DCI Jay to Melrose Avenue, and indicated where the police might discover the burnt remains of 12 or 13 other men whose bodies had been consumed in bonfires at the rear of the house over the past three years. In some cases he remembered very little about his victims, and eight, in fact, would never be identified or named. Seven other young men, he said, had for varying reasons escaped his murderous assaults.

That evening, at 5.40 pm, Dennis Nilsen was charged with the murder of Stephen Sinclair, and the following morning he appeared at Highgate magistrates' court.

Since Thursday, newspaper reporters had been rabid in pursuit of stories and facts, flocking to both scenes of the crimes and harrying anyone who might have something to say. On the Friday morning, front-page headlines proclaimed: 17 BODIES IN MURDER HORROR (*Daily Mirror*) – SIXTEEN MURDERS (*Daily Express*) – MASS MURDER INQUIRY STARTS (*The Times*). Later headlines declaimed: HOUSE OF HORROR – HOUSE OF DEATH.

Neighbours at Cranley Gardens were questioned about No. 23. Mrs Peggy Macpherson, 68, said: 'None of the people who lived there seemed to stay very long.' 'Down-and-outs and tramps often visited the house,' another neighbour divulged. 'It was impossible to say who lived there and who was just staying overnight.' A third neighbour added: 'There were lots of parties there . . . Squatters who lived in the middle-floor flat used to have the parties . . . Mainly loud music and getting stoned.' Some had complained about dogs and foul smells emanating the previous summer from the drains.

About 60 reporters, spectators and TV crewmen gathered outside 195 Melrose Avenue, where a squad of policemen in green boiler suits arrived on Friday to pull apart the ground-floor flat and sift through every inch of the rear garden and wasteland. A large blue plastic tent was erected to conceal operations and protect the searchers from the snow. But two young builders, who had been completing the restoration of the flats within the house, were seized on by the press.

Mark Tekinalp, 22, said: 'We've been working on the house since last year, when it was damaged by fire. We've just discovered from the police there was a body stowed under the floorboards in the back room. Apparently it was removed later and buried in the garden along with other bodies. We used to eat out in the garden during the summer. We were apparently sitting on corpses.'

Two of the renovated flats had been sold, but not yet occupied. Diana Keating, aged 27, had bought the ground-floor flat, formerly Nilsen's, for £31,000. She said: 'I just can't believe it's happened. Believe it or not, I had wanted a flat with a garden. I didn't sense anything wrong at all, and I've visited the flat many times. I don't know when I'll be going to the flat again.'

Nilsen's family and schoolfriends in Scotland were sought out. His mother, Mrs Betty Scott (she had remarried), said: 'This has come as a great shock. I've not seen my son for about ten years.' Weeping, she fetched photographs of Dennis and trustingly gave them to a reporter. His older brother, Olav, in Fraserburgh, said: 'I've not seen my brother for about nine years. We had a silly family row.'

Much about Nilsen's background was unearthed by the press. But within a week, any revelations that might prejudice the trial were muzzled by the Attorney-General and the DPP (Director of Public Prosecutions). Nilsen himself could not stop talking. Once a lonely man, with low self-esteem, he was now the awful focus of everyone's attention. He talked at length to everyone he met. He wrote wordy and pretentious letters to all and sundry, explaining, excusing, accusing, complaining. Politics was his chief topic after himself. In Brixton Prison he began filling exercise-books with his partial, consciously literary remembrances and thoughts – writing, as he wrote his letters, from edge to edge of every page. Sometimes he wrote and spoke with wit and a certain graveyard humour. But a police officer, when asked why Nilsen had no friends, replied: 'Because he's a fucking bore.'

None the less, Nilsen's ready co-operation was required if his victims were ever to be traced, his story confirmed, and a strong case against him sustained. So his interviewers, Chambers and Jay, were chatty and matter-of-fact, communing with Des over cups of coffee, tea and packets of cigarettes, and letting him lapse into monologues without interrupting him too much. But the more he said, the less, it seemed, they were able to understand. They found out about the who, and where, and when – but not the reasons *why*.

Nilsen himself said: 'I've killed people. But I can't understand why those people. There's no common factor.' Chambers stated: 'I think you went out looking for these people with the express intention of luring them back to your flat, plying them with drink, and then killing them.' To which Nilsen replied: 'I do go out in search of company. When I voluntarily go out to drink I don't have the intention at that time to do these things. Things may happen afterwards drinkwise. But they're not foreplanned ... I seek company first, and hope everything will be all right.' He wrote later:

> In none of these cases am I conscious of feeling any hate towards any of the victims ... I remember going out to seek company and companionship, which perhaps would lead to a personal sexual and social relationship being established ... I would invite some people back with me, others would invite themselves. Sex was always a secondary consideration. I wanted a warm relationship and someone to talk to ... Because of the effects of drinking, sex would (or would not) happen the next morning ... I would never plan to kill anyone ... I would be a bit dazed, shocked and shaking all over afterwards ... I suppose I could lie and say they refused to have sex and I killed them. No, that's not true ... The only similarity was a need not to be alone ... They were not all homeless tramps, etc. Not all young, homeless men who came to my flat were attacked or killed. Not all were homosexual or bisexual. The reason that some were homosexual was mainly because they would come to the pubs which I frequented. I was approached marginally more often by those liaisons than I approached them ... I sometimes imagine that I may have felt that I applied a relieving pressure on a life as a benevolent act, in that the subjects were ultimately free from life's pain.

His first solicitor, Ronald Moss, after listening to the detailed catalogue of horrific acts that Nilsen outlined to the police, asked: 'Why?' Nilsen answered: 'I'm hoping you'll tell me that.'

Dennis Andrew Nilsen was born in the north-east of Scotland, in Fraserburgh, a fishing town, on 23 November 1945. His mother, Betty, was the pretty daughter of a fisherman, Andrew Whyte. She had married a Norwegian soldier, Olav Magnus Nilsen, in May 1942. He came to Scotland after the Germans invaded Norway in 1940 and was one of the thousands of servicemen quartered in the district to repel an imagined German invasion of Britain. The marriage was a mistake, although it produced three children, two boys and a girl. The Nilsens never had a home of their own. Betty Nilsen continued to live with her parents, sharing a room with little Olav, Dennis and Sylvia, in the Whytes' cold flat at 47 Academy Road, where drinking, smoking, cinema-going and even the radio were frowned upon; every Sunday everyone went to church. Olav Nilsen was an increasingly infrequent visitor. After the war he drifted away and the couple were divorced in 1948. Dennis was very attached to his grandfather, who died of a heart attack at sea in October 1951 when he was 62; Dennis was almost six. The sight of his grandfather in a coffin was traumatic, according to Nilsen. He wrote later: 'My troubles started here. [His death] blighted my personality permanently. I have spent all my emotional life searching for my grandfather . . . He took the real me with him under the ground.'

Other traumatic events were the drowning of a friend of his brother and, when he was about eight, his own alleged near-drowning (he walked into the sea) and rescue by an older boy, who then masturbated over his unconscious, naked body on the beach. Then when he was nine, the pigeons he kept in fish-boxes on an air-raid shelter were strangled by another small boy. Later, he and a school friend found the body of an old man who had drowned in a river. All these events, Nilsen would later infer, caused him to have an unusual preoccupation with dead bodies and confuse images of death and love.

The young Dennis was kind to animals, caring for any stray dogs and fledglings he found. He had a pet rabbit of his own, Snowy, but one winter it died. Wild rabbits infected by myxomatosis horrified him. To put them out of their misery he killed them himself. As a child he was quiet, shy, introverted, sensitive, secretive, brooding and solitary, tending to wander off on his own.

He became difficult when his mother, after a divorce was obtained, married a builder, Adam Scott. In time they had four children, three boys and a girl. Dennis was bitterly resentful, and he came to the attention of the local police more than once for minor misdemeanours. But in 1955, when he was ten, the family moved seven miles inland to the village of Strichen, to 16 Baird Road, and the discipline of Strichen School helped to sort him out, as well as the rigours of an early morning paper-round. A skinny boy, he was hospitalised with pneumonia and pleurisy when he was eleven or twelve.

It was through an uncle that he acquired interests in argumentative and radical socialism, in classical music and in the making of amateur films. His best subjects at school, where he was an above-average pupil, attentive, hard-working and neat, were art and English; he had little interest in team games or sport. At school he concealed his silent adoration for a younger boy, Adrian, a minister's son, and for a boy pictured in a French book, Pierre Duval. But his actual sexual experience by the time he left school, aged 15, was nil, although he once explored the body of his brother, with whom he shared a bed at home, while Olav was asleep.

Having joined the local Army Cadet Force when he was 14 (he liked the uniform and the acceptable, conformist image it gave him – 'I felt proud and useful'), he enlisted in the Army in August 1961, intending to train as a chef. In September he took an overnight express from Aberdeen to King's Cross Station in London and then made his way to Aldershot.

His next three years as a boy soldier were 'the happiest of my life'. In September 1964 he completed his training and catering courses and joined the ACC (Army Catering Corps). He was posted to Osnabrück in Germany. On leave in Scotland before he went overseas, he was driving a scooter in the rain when he skidded and crashed. He banged his head – but was otherwise uninjured, though bruised. Similar accidental head injuries were also sustained early in their lives by other multiple murderers, like Christie and Haigh. Perhaps there is some connection. Certainly, Nilsen then began the heavy drinking that marked the next 18 years.

From Germany, he went to Norway and then to Aden in 1967, when he was 21. He was attached to the military staff at a prison where terrorists were detained. In June he was posted as a L/Cpl. to Sharjah on the Persian Gulf, where he had his own room and achieved his first sexual experiences, with an Arab boy. He also began admiring his own body, naked, reflected in a mirror by his bed. 'The image in the mirror becomes your only friend and true lover,' he later wrote. In January 1968 he was attached to the Argyll and Sutherland Highlanders, catering for them in Plymouth, then in Cyprus and in Berlin, where he had a series of one-night encounters with male civilians, as well as one session with a female prostitute. Esteemed for his talents as a chef and his capacity for drink, he had several mates, who thought he was eccentric, a bit moody and a bit of an oddball, a loner, rather than 'queer'. Because of his initials, he was known as Dan. Now Corporal Nilsen, he went with the Argylls in 1970 to Fort George near Inverness, and in August he cooked for the Queen's Royal Guard at Ballater, near Balmoral. He spent most of his leave periods in Strichen, parading his uniform, visiting friends and the scenes of his childhood, reading and writing poetry, and devising culinary treats for his half-brothers and sister. He showed an interest in a local girl and sent off a computer-dating questionnaire. But, as his married brother Olav remarked after Dennis's arrest: 'He would have been bored back home. Strichen is no place for a poof on holiday.'

In January 1971, when Nilsen was 25, he was posted to a Signals Squadron in the Shetland Islands. Here he took part in Scottish country-dancing at socials and bought a cine-camera to record the scenery and local life. Here he also fell hopelessly in love with an 18-year-old soldier in the summer of 1972. Nothing sexual apparently occurred. But the intensity of Nilsen's feelings confused the youth and he began to distance himself, causing Nilsen much distress. Nilsen wrote later: 'I knew I was leaving the Army in a few weeks, and would probably not see him again. Every kind of deep emotional pain in those last weeks sorely afflicted me. I wished I were dead.' Before he left the Shetlands he burned all the films he had made, some of which featured the young soldier, and in which he was encouraged by Nilsen to pose as if he were dead or asleep.

After serving for eleven years in the Army, Nilsen left in November 1972. He returned to Strichen, wondering what to do next; he was now 27. There was a bitter row with Olav, after which they never spoke again, and having considered other uniformed, institutionalised careers, as a prison officer or a policeman, he opted for the latter.

In December he joined the Metropolitan Police in London, and after 16 weeks' training at Hendon, he was sent, as PC Q287, to Willesden Green police station – half a mile from Melrose Avenue where, six years later, he committed his first murder and where he would kill a total of 12 young men.

Although he worked hard and well, making several arrests and appearing in court, his left-wing opinions made him uncomfortable with the authoritarian attitudes of the police, and he missed the more relaxed camaraderie of the Army. After duty he frequently found himself on his own, isolated because of his secret homosexuality and consequent indifference to most of his colleagues' diversions. He began frequenting pubs where homosexuals were known to meet. In 1973, while still at Hendon, he had sex with a man he met at The Coleherne in Earls Court. In August, in the Section House where he and other unmarried policemen lived, he had sex with a younger man met in the King William IV. They had anal sex – the only time, according to Nilsen, this ever occurred. He wished to make this relationship more permanent. But the young man, the son of a former colonel, was more interested in sleeping around.

The pressures of his double life and dissenting views caused him to resign from the police after a year, in December 1973. He remained in London, working as a security guard and lodging in a room in Manstone Road, off Cricklewood Broadway. Then in May 1974 he began working for the Department of Employment at the Jobcentre in Denmark Street, off Charing Cross Road. He was there for eight years, interviewing the unemployed and advising them about jobs. Eventually, he became involved with the civil-service union, the CPSA, becoming the branch secretary at his place of work. Over-zealous and outspoken, he attended every union meeting, conference and anti-government demonstration, upsetting his employers and even some of his comrades by his aggressive, barrack-room style. One of his colleagues called him Des, and from then on that was what he called himself.

When not at work he increasingly visited London's gay pubs, picking up young men and boys and taking them home to his new lodging, a room at 80 Teignmouth Road, not far from Melrose Avenue. But this way of life depressed him. He wrote later: 'Anonymous sex only deepens one's sense of loneliness and solves nothing. Promiscuity is a disease.' He also wrote: 'My most fulfilling sexual feasts were savoured with the image of myself in the mirror.' None the less, disapproving and prudish though he was, he continued to search for some loving companion or friend in such pubs as The Coleherne, the King William IV, The Salisbury in St Martin's Lane, the Golden Lion in Soho, the Black Cap in Camden, and The Champion in Bayswater Road.

One 17-year-old, who had called at the Jobcentre, was invited back to Teignmouth Road. Frightened by some act or remark or look of Nilsen, he panicked, causing a scene and cutting himself on some glass. An ambulance and the police were called, and Nilsen was questioned at Willesden Green police station, where he had served for a year in 1973. No charges were brought.

Nilsen was 30 in November 1975, the month in which he met David Gallichan, aged 20, outside The Champion. Gallichan was short, fair-haired, wore ear-rings, was unemployed and rather camp. He went back to Teignmouth Road with Nilsen, stayed the night and was easily persuaded by Nilsen, desperate for some permanent relationship, to move in with him. He stayed for a year and a half. Before Christmas, Nilsen rented a rear ground-floor flat for them both at 195 Melrose Avenue, not far from Teignmouth Road.

He was able to afford the additional expense and the cost of furnishings as his father, after marrying three more times and dying in Ghana, had left him a legacy of £1,000. At the same time Nilsen learned that the real name of his father, whom he had never known, was Moksheim – as should have been his own.

Gallichan, whom Nilsen called Twinkle, came from Weston-super-Mare in Somerset. He was a passive person, seemingly content to be kept, to do the decorating, the domestic chores and tend the back garden, which Nilsen had commandeered for their exclusive use. A high fence was put around it, a plastic fish-pond and path installed, and trees and shrubs, as well as vegetables, were planted. A puppy bought in a pet-shop, which Nilsen called Bleep, and a stray kitten, called Dee-Dee, enhanced the domestic scene, as did reproductions of paintings by Canaletto which hung on the walls. They had separate beds, and sex was sporadic. But they went out to pubs and bars together and Nilsen did his best to keep Twinkle amused, by telling him jokes and playing pranks. Most evenings they stayed in.

> We got as close as anyone could [said Gallichan later]. He was like a teacher to me. He would correct me if I said something wrong or mis-pronounced a word . . . But he wasn't domineering. I had my life and he had his. He wouldn't go out often, and he never celebrated anything special, apart from Christmas. You could forget birthdays. He never got any cards . . . He never lost control when I was with him. He liked keg beer and whisky and bacardi and vodka. But he didn't drink to excess . . . He had some regrets about leaving the Army, wondering whether he should have signed up for a second term . . . He was neat and tidy in appearance. He mostly wore a tie and always polished his shoes, and took great care of personal hygiene. He had a bath in the morning and a shower in the evening when he came home, and then would have a bath before he went to bed.

In April 1976, Nilsen had a gallstone operation, and at Christmas he boldly took Twinkle to his office party in Denmark Street. But the association was becoming strained. Gallichan, who now had a job in a station buffet, began drifting back to gay bars, oppressed by the older man's autocratic manner and by London itself. Both began bringing different partners back to the flat. According to Nilsen, he once brought a Swiss girl home and they had sex.

Twinkle moved out in the summer of 1977. He said later:

> I told Dennis I was moving out . . . It was the only time I saw a different side of him. He was cold and dismissive. It was as though I had insulted him . . . He said: 'I want you to move out as soon as possible' . . . About six months after I'd moved out, I had drinks with him. He was a lot quieter. There was someone there at the flat at the time. I asked him if he wanted my address, but he said: 'No.' I was a little bit hurt.

Twinkle's new protector, with whom he went to live, was an antique-dealer in Somerset.

Nilsen, rejected, filled his empty days with work and his nights with music, drink and casual sex. He drank for hours on his own, listening to pop and classical music on his headphones. The beds, converted into a raised, double platform-bed, were occupied by occasional pick-ups, one of whom, Steve Martin, moved in for about four months. There were others. But sooner or later, they all walked out on him. On his own, Nilsen's masturbatory fantasies involving his mirror-image and death increased. Once, while three strangers slept, he filled the room with smoke. Their asphyxiation seems to have been Nilsen's intention, for he left the room. When they awoke in some alarm, he made some excuse.

Paul Dermody stayed with Nilsen for two weeks in November 1978. 'He talked at me, not to me,' said Dermody. Soon after he left, the killings began.

Towards the end of 1978, Nilsen's feelings of demoralisation and despair had reached their peak: he had achieved nothing of any importance at work and had no meaningful relationships with anyone – no one on whom to call if in need of help. He felt lonely, unloved, unwanted and no one would care if he died. He spent Christmas alone in his flat with Bleep, drowning his desolation in immoderate drinking, listening to music and watching TV.

On 30 December, full of self-pity and loathing, he forced himself to leave the flat and seek some company in an Irish pub in Cricklewood Broadway, the Cricklewood Arms. After downing several pints of draught Guinness, he began conversing with an Irish lad, aged about 17. 'That night,' he wrote later, 'things began to go terribly and horribly wrong.' He told the police:

He was much shorter than I was. About 5 feet 6 inches. He was southern Irish and had short, dark brown curly hair. His hands were rough. At closing time he indicated to me that he had too far to travel. We went back to Melrose Avenue and we started drinking. We had a damn good old drink, and later on I remember thinking: 'He'll probably be going soon – another ship passing in the night.' The next morning I had a corpse on my hands. He was dead. I believed I had killed him. Strangled him. I got the impression that he wanted to go and I wanted him to stay. I wanted company over the New Year. There was a desperation for company. My tie was around his neck. I think I started off with about 15 ties.

Nilsen, writing after his trial, revealed much more about what happened that night and thereafter. He and the Irish boy had eventually undressed and passed out in the double bed. Nothing sexual occurred. Nilsen was the first to wake, at dawn that New Year's Eve. He wrote:

The fire had been on all night, so it was quite warm. I snuggled up to him and put my arm around him. He was still fast asleep . . . I ran my hand over him, exploring him. I remember thinking because it was morning he would wake and leave me. I became extremely aroused and I could feel my heart pounding and I began to sweat. He was still sound asleep. I looked down on the floor where our clothes lay and my eyes fixed on my tie. I remember thinking that I wanted him to stay with me over the New Year, whether he wanted to or not. I reached out and got the neck-tie. I raised myself and slipped it on under his neck. I quickly straddled him and pulled tight for all I was worth. His body came alive immediately. We struggled off the bed on to the floor.

With Nilsen on top of him, the Irish boy tried to push himself away, using his feet and knocking over a coffee table, until he backed against a wall. After half a minute his struggling diminished and his arms flopped on to the floor. Trembling, exhausted, Nilsen staggered to his feet. But the boy was not dead. Unconscious, he began breathing in harsh gasps. Nilsen, panicking, filled a plastic bucket with water in the kitchen. He seized the naked boy, draped him face-down over a dining-room chair, raised his head by the hair and then pushed it into the bucket, which overflowed. There was no resistance this time. After two or three minutes the bubbles in the water ceased to rise.

Nilsen picked up the body and deposited it in an armchair. He sat down himself and recovered some of his composure, staring at his now permanent guest and reviewing what he had done and what he would do. He made himself a cup of coffee, smoked several cigarettes and removed the tie from the corpse. He then tidied the room and let Bleep in from the garden. She sniffed at the dead boy's legs. Nilsen dragged her aside and told her to keep out of the way. He decided to give the body a bath. Picking it up over his right shoulder he carried it into the bathroom, washed it thoroughly in washing-up liquid, and having dried it while floppily propped up on the loo, he carried it back to the bed, where he examined and stroked the still-warm, loose-limbed corpse. Then he covered it with the bedclothes, so that the boy seemed as if he were asleep. For a while Nilsen sat and looked at him and thought. Then he dressed and went for a walk. People had seen them together in the pub and then leave together. He expected the police would call. But when he returned to his flat he felt hungover and very tired and wanted to sleep. After dressing the boy in clean Y-fronts, vest and socks from his wardrobe, Nilsen had a bath and went to bed, where he embraced the boy, and removed his pants, caressing him as and where he wished. Sexually aroused, he attempted to penetrate the corpse. But his erection subsided: the body was cooling. He laid the dead youth on the floor, covered him with a piece of curtain, lay down in his bed and fell asleep. He slept all day. Waking that evening, he fed Bleep and the cat, made himself a meal and watched TV, with the curtained corpse on the floor. Deciding now to hide the body in case anyone called, he took up some of the living-room floorboards and tried to push the body underneath. But it had stiffened and was intractable. So Nilsen propped it against a wall: he had read somewhere that rigor mortis was temporary. The corpse stood there all night as Nilsen slept. The following morning, New Year's Day, he succeeded in laying the body in the freezing space under the floorboards, after carefully loosening its limbs and once again closely inspecting and touching every part of the corpse, from head to toe. The cat slipped under the floor and it took ten minutes to coax her out.

Nilsen then ripped up the dead boy's clothes and threw them into a dustbin. A week went by and meanwhile Nilsen went back to work. Then curiosity as much as desire prompted him to play once more with his guest. Nilsen wrote:

I disinterred him, and pulled the dirt-stained youth up onto the floor. His skin was very dirty. I stripped myself naked and carried him into the bathroom and washed the body. There was practically no discoloration and he was pale white. His limbs were more limp and relaxed than when I had put him down. I got him out of the bath and washed myself clean in the water. I carried the still wet youth into the room and laid him on the carpet. Under the orange side-lights his body aroused me sexually. I knelt over him and masturbated onto his bare stomach. Before I went to bed, I suspended him by the ankles from the high wooden platform. He hung there all night, his fingers just touching the carpet. The next day, while he was still hanging there upside-down, I stood beside him and masturbated again. I wiped him and took him down. I laid him on the kitchen floor and decided to cut him up. But I just couldn't do anything to spoil that marvellous body.

He encased the body in plastic bags and replaced it under the floorboards, where it remained for nearly eight months, until it began to smell too much. The corpse of the teenage Irish boy was burnt in the back garden on 11 August 1979.

Nilsen told the police: 'I did not dismember his body. When I took it up it was remarkable. There was very little decomposition . . . I had built a bonfire the day before. I burnt him at the bottom of the garden about three feet from the fence. It was a relief to be rid of the body. Burnt meat smells. But I had made sure to burn rubber on the fire – it cancelled out the smell.'

Afterwards, he pulverised the bones and raked them into the ground. He would build two more bonfires and kill eleven other boys and young men in 195 Melrose Avenue before he left the house in October 1981. But for nearly a year, he refrained from killing any of his visitors and from having sex with any of them (according to him), although on 13 October 1979, a small Chinese student, whom Nilsen met in a pub near Leicester Square, The Salisbury, had a narrow escape. His name was Andrew Ho.

Nilsen told the police:

He said he was very short of money and gave me a hard-luck story. He asked me if he could come back to my place and I said: 'Yes.' On getting back to Melrose Avenue I wasn't drunk and he said: 'What are you into?' I said I didn't want to have sex with him – just give him £10 and he could sod off in the Tube. He laid some emphasis on the fact that he could tie me up, and I thought his main emphasis was robbery. I was getting a bit agitated and said: 'I'll tie *you* up.' He said: 'I'm not so keen on that.' I said: 'I'll tie your legs anyway, and see what happens.' I said: 'This is a terrible way of making a living. Fraught with danger.' He lay there with this tie around his legs – his arms were free. What I did was use my tie and put it around his neck, and pulled it. I said: 'This is the sort of thing that could happen in your way of life.' I relaxed my hold and he struggled. He was in a hell of a state . . . He threw a brass candlestick at me and hit me right on the head. He picked up a letter opener and said he wanted to get out. He got out and left and I said: 'Let that be a lesson to you.'

Half an hour later the police arrived at the flat. Nilsen denied trying to strangle Ho, and the matter was dropped. He chose to make no charges although *he* was injured, and in the end no charges were brought by Ho. If they had been, another 14 men and boys might have lived. But two months later, Nilsen killed again.

His second victim was a 23-year-old Canadian, Kenneth Ockenden, who had come to London, after completing a welding course in Toronto, to visit some relatives and see something of Britain. He is said not to have been homosexual. Short, fair-haired and likeable, he had toured the Lake District with a former school friend called Larry before returning to London on his own. On Monday, 3 December he telephoned an uncle to say that he was in a hotel at King's Cross and would meet up with him on the 5th. No one ever heard from him again.

That Monday he met Nilsen at lunchtime in a pub in High Holborn, the Princess Louise. Nilsen had the afternoon off and according to him they spent the afternoon sightseeing, walking from Trafalgar Square, where they fed the pigeons, down Whitehall to Westminster Abbey. Ockenden took several photos. He agreed to go back to Melrose Avenue with Nilsen, where they had a meal of ham, egg and chips. As there were some good programmes on TV, they stocked up with rum, whisky, coke and beer at an off-licence – Ockenden insisting on paying half the bill – and returned to the flat, where they settled down to drink, watch TV and listen to music. Nilsen liked Ken Ockenden and brooded over the fact that Ken would be flying to Canada very soon and disappear from his life. He was also now listening to an LSO record through Nilsen's earphones and seemed oblivious of him. Nilsen told the police:

I was still drinking and he was drinking. I indicated: 'All right?' And he said: 'Bloody good! Fantastic!' He got engrossed in the records, and I was sitting in the corner, drinking, and I thought: 'Bloody good guest this.' I thought he'd be there all night. He was enjoying it. I turned the TV up loud. I watched TV and was drinking. He kept on listening to his music. It must have been well after midnight. Maybe one or two in the morning. I was dragging him across the floor with a flex around his neck. I was saying: 'Let me listen to the music as well.' He didn't struggle. I was dragging him across the floor. The dog was barking frantically in the kitchen, trying to get in the door. I put the dog out in the garden and said: 'Get out! This has fuck all to do with you!' He was lying on the floor. I untangled the earphones. I must have put half a glass of Bacardi in the glass. I put the earphones on and listened to the whole sequence of the records. He was dead. I kept on drinking . . . In the morning the record-player was still going round. The earphones were on the floor and I was in the armchair. I had been asleep.

Ockenden was strangled with the headphones flex. Although Nilsen provided the police with apparently helpful and detailed statements, there are many discrepancies, large and small, between what he told them and what he wrote in his exercise-books. Only the latter contain some descriptions of sexual acts with the corpses. Nowhere, however, does he describe the act of strangulation: the staring eyes, the sounds his victims made; nor what he felt. He could not admit to others that he *enjoyed* killing, and having sex with a corpse.

But in his written account of the killing of Ken Ockenden he felt able to reveal that after stripping Ockenden, who had 'completely messed himself', he cleaned him up with paper kitchen towels, gave him a bath and took the body to bed – 'No sex, only caressing, etc.' Ockenden's clothes, money, passport and films were destroyed (although his camera was kept for a while), and the body was jammed into a cupboard for a night, sitting on the floor, knees up, until rigor mortis had passed. Nilsen then loosened the corpse's limbs and took colour photographs of it with a polaroid camera he had bought specially, after clothing it in underpants, vest and socks.

He wrote:

I arranged the body in various positions and took several photos (which I destroyed with the last burning). I lay in bed fully clothed, with him lying spreadeagled on top of me as I watched television. I would sometimes speak to him, as though he were still listening. I would compliment him on his looks and anatomy. By crossing his legs I had sex between his bare thighs (although no penetration of the body occurred). I wrapped him well before putting him under the floorboards. I took him up on about four occasions in the next two weeks. It was cold down there and he was still very fresh . . . I would sit him in the other armchair next to me, as I watched an evening's TV, drinking . . . Before he returned to his 'bed' I would sit him on my knee and strip off the underwear and socks, wrap him in curtain material and put him down (actually saying: 'Goodnight, Ken').

Nilsen expected, as with the Irish boy, that someone would remember seeing him with Ockenden, at the Princess Louise, or in the off-licence. But although Ockenden's disappearance was reported in the papers, on posters and on 'Police 5' on TV (Nilsen saw the programme), no one came knocking at his door. Ockenden's parents came to London to look for their son, but no trace of him could be found – not for another three years.

None of Nilsen's 14 other victims was given as much official and public attention as Ockenden, although some were reported as missing. The Salvation Army attempts to trace 5,000 missing persons every year, following up *half* the requests it receives, and succeeds with as many as 70 per cent of its enquiries. Every year, in London alone, about 7,000 people, mainly girls and boys between the ages of 14 and 18, are registered as missing, and as many as 6,000 people can be sleeping outdoors every week. Although most of the missing are found, or return home, some totally disappear. By the end of 1990, the number of persons still missing in the Metropolitan Police District was nearly 2,000, of whom over half were male. Of this 2,000, 1,700 had been missing for more than a year, 151 for more than five years, and 48 for more than ten years.

The sorrow of Nilsen's victims was that society had little interest in them. They were generally unemployed, destitute, homeless, homosexual, friendless, with problem childhoods and mentally and emotionally disturbed. If they had been middle-class, or girls, more official concern would have been shown for them. As it was, few cared about them when they went missing, nor when their fates were known.

Such a one was Nilsen's third victim, Martyn Duffey, aged 16. Nilsen told the police that Duffey was '19 to 20 years old'. Soon after 13 May 1980, Duffey left Merseyside and came to London, carrying a suitcase in which reposed the kitchen knives he had used on a catering course. They were etched with his name. He was about 5′ 6″, had been in care, had been seen by social workers and psychiatrists about his propensities for thieving, drugs, gay clubs, and running away from home. On a Saturday (it is not known precisely where or when) he encountered Nilsen, who had been attending a CPSA conference in Southport. They went back to Melrose Avenue where, after drinking two cans of lager, Duffey went to bed. Nilsen said later, talking to the police: 'I was out on the piss that night drinking heavily. We came back to my flat. I remember the next morning he was dead on the floor. I don't remember any violence at all. He had my tie around his neck . . . I put Duffey straight under the floorboards.'

Later he wrote: 'I remember sitting astride him (his arms must have been trapped by the quilt). I strangled him with great force . . . As I sat on him I could feel my bottom becoming wet. His urine had come through the bedding and my jeans.' Duffey, unconscious, was then drowned head-down in the water-filled kitchen sink. He was stripped and washed in the bath, which Nilsen also entered, lying under Duffey. Then Duffey was dried, parked on a kitchen chair, and Nilsen dried himself. He then took the naked boy to bed. Nilsen wrote: 'I talked to him and mentioned that his body was the youngest-looking I had ever seen. I kissed him all over and held him close to me. I sat on his stomach and masturbated. I kept him temporarily in the cupboard. Two days later I found him bloated in the cupboard. He went straight under the floorboards.'

Nilsen used a luggage ticket he found on Duffey to collect the boy's suitcase from Euston Station. He disposed of all its contents, but kept the suitcase and Duffey's glasses, and remembered to leave Duffey's catering knives in the garden to rust before throwing them away – but not until he had used them himself. 'You can't put a brand new set of knives into the dustbin,' he told the police. 'Someone would have got suspicious.' He also said: 'I knew this would happen again. The killing would happen again. I was resigned to this, and I was also resigned that I would be caught eventually. But I would do as best as I could to dispose of the evidence. I wasn't talking at that stage of turning over a new leaf. If I had been arrested at 65 years of age, there might have been thousands of bodies behind me.'

That summer he disposed of the corpses of Ockenden and Duffey because of the smell. One night he dismembered them both on the kitchen floor, using Duffey's knives. He wrapped the pieces of both young men in plastic bags and packed them into two suitcases. The two heads were put in separate carrier bags. These and the suitcases were stored in a garden shed that Nilsen had built for Bleep and then encased in a makeshift tomb of bricks, which he also filled with newspapers and magazines. The shed was not locked. Periodically he sprayed it with disinfectants and aerosols. As there was no room in the suitcases for Duffey's arms and hands Nilsen buried them by a bush.

Billy Sutherland was the next to die. The third of eight children, he was brought up on a rough council estate in Edinburgh. His father was a merchant seaman. Billy was good fun, but wild. He was often in trouble, and had been in prison, as well as at an approved school. On his knuckles were tattooed LOVE and HATE. An eagle was tattooed on his chest, and swallows on his hands; on his arms were tattoos commemorating his family, and there was a dagger on his leg. Although he had several girlfriends and had sired a child, he also had sex with men, usually for money, on his sprees in London, whither he escaped when evading his responsibilities and the police. He had trained as a chef. It was probably around 12 August, Billy's 26th birthday, that he was killed.

Nilsen was vague about Billy's death. He said they met in a West End pub and that the young Scot invited himself back to Melrose Avenue. He said: 'We started drinking. I remember he had some food. We had a great binge and I killed Billy Sutherland. I remember having a tie around his neck and pulling the tie . . . I did it from the front . . . I always felt I was two or three times as strong when I had drink. I felt I had amazing strength . . . I don't remember when I put Billy under the floor.'

He was also curiously vague about his next seven victims, remembering little about them and what he did to them. Perhaps what he did with their bodies made him want to forget. On the other hand, he was killing now at the rate of about one a month.

The fifth victim, after Billy Sutherland, was a Mexican or Philippino, met in The Salisbury, who accosted Nilsen and followed him outside. He was 'probably' strangled and put under the floorboards. At some stage he was dissected and packed in a suitcase and put in the shed. The sixth to die was Irish, possibly a building worker in his late twenties, who wore an old suit jacket and old shoes; they might have met in the Cricklewood Arms. The seventh was a vagrant, encountered while Nilsen was looking for a taxi at the top of Charing Cross Road, by Oxford Street. Nilsen said:

His features were pale, hollow, withdrawn. He had a general appearance of looking grossly undernourished. He wore a long ragged trench-coat, ridiculously outsize trousers . . . He was carrying an old plastic carrier bag with bits and pieces . . . We got a taxi eventually, and we got back to Melrose Avenue. He said he wanted something to eat – he was starving. I fixed some food and coffee. He said he was tired and ate the food completely. He was not interested in alcohol at all. He was sitting there and dozed off to sleep. I started drinking.

After drinking most of a bottle of Bacardi and listening to Rick Wakeman's *Incantations*, high on drink and the music, Nilsen strangled his guest with a tie. 'There was a weak struggle. There was no sound. His legs were lifting and separating in slow motion, rather like riding a bicycle. I kept on for about a minute and a half before his legs stopped . . . It was as easy as taking candy from a baby . . . I remember thinking to myself: "You've got no more trouble now, squire" . . . I couldn't cut him up. He was so thin.'

By the end of 1980, of the many young men and boys who had entered Nilsen's flat, seven had not departed. The body of one had been burnt, but those of six others still remained, under the floorboards or in the garden shed. On a cold weekday in December, these six were consumed in a large bonfire on wasteland at the rear of the garden. He tended the fire all day, to the sound of *Tubular Bells*. He said:

I managed to get off work . . . I woke about 6.45 am. I went out into the garden and checked that nobody was about. I pulled up the floorboards and put each bundle into huge pieces of carpeting and tied them up. I dragged these onto the pile by removing palings from the back fence and keeping fairly low . . . I managed to drag the heavy suitcases through the hole in the fence and into the hollow of the bonfire . . . The fabric and structure crumbled, exposing mostly brown-coloured bones and bits of flesh . . . There were thousands of fly chrysalis. Maggots and dead flies were everywhere . . . I put an old car tyre on top of the bonfire to disguise the smell . . . I put bits of wood on from time to time. Kids from a nearby house attracted by the fire gathered around and started throwing things in. I strongly reminded them to keep well out of the way . . . Near the end of the day there was only a pile of ash. I crushed a skull with a rake.

He would write more poetically later, seeing the bonfire as 'a great visual display of living natural forces', and comparing it to 'some Viking ship glowing westwards to Valhalla'. He wrote: 'I thought on those who now magnified my empty life, seeing their sweetness pervading the London air. I stood like an obedient usher . . . They were not in the flames but in me . . . Not for them the insulting monotony of a uniform and anonymous corporation cemetery . . . The sun is setting on the glowing embers and I, weeping, drink the bottle dry.'

Such was the corporeal end of Ockenden, Duffey, Sutherland and three other young men. Douglas Stewart might also have joined them. But he was the second of those (seven, according to Nilsen) who escaped with his life.

Stewart, a sandy-haired Scot, about 5' 9", was an unemployed barman, aged 26, from Thurso, who came south to see football matches and his mother – his parents were divorced. He was in the Golden Lion in Dean Street, Soho, when Nilsen, whom he had noticed there before, approached him. It was a Wednesday in mid-November 1980. After closing-time Stewart went in a taxi with Nilsen to Melrose Avenue, where the pair of them watched TV and drank. Nilsen was very attentive, though a tedious talker, and plied his guest with spirits and beer. But Stewart was a slow drinker and seldom drank spirits, and he refused much of what was offered. He also refused to share Nilsen's bed: he said he would sleep in the chair. He dozed off as the older man lay on the bed, listening to the record-player. He awoke to find Nilsen, wearing only jeans, standing astride him and trying to strangle him with a tie. In a choking panic his fingers clawed Nilsen's cheek. For a moment the tie round his neck slackened as Nilsen turned, enabling Stewart to smash his fist into Nilsen's face. Nilsen fell back, and Stewart then fell as he heaved himself out of the chair – to which his feet had been tied. None the less he flung himself on Nilsen, pinning him down. 'What the fuck were you trying to do?' he gasped. Nilsen calmly replied: 'I could kill you now, if I wanted to.' 'Go on!' said Stewart. 'Go ahead!' 'Don't be silly,' said Nilsen. 'I wasn't trying to kill you. I never even touched you.' 'You must think I'm an idiot!' Stewart said. He got to his feet. He said he was leaving and would go to the police. 'They'll never believe you,' Nilsen said. 'Take my money,' he added. 'Go on! Take my money!' 'I don't want your money!' said Stewart, and when he tried to leave Nilsen threatened him with a knife. Stewart succeeded in pacifying Nilsen and fled. He ran to a call-box and telephoned the police. But he was so overwrought by the time a patrol car from Kilburn police station arrived that they believed the older man's cool and positive assurances that there had been a drunken row, a lovers' quarrel. They asked Stewart to make an official complaint when he was sober. He never did. And when the police checked on the London address Stewart gave them, they found it was unoccupied. If Douglas Stewart (as with Andrew Ho) had brought charges and made a statement to the police, eight others might not have died.

The eighth victim, a long-haired hippy, aged about 25 and wearing a bleached denim jacket and jeans, was killed in December 1980. His severed remains were packaged and stuffed under the floorboards. Three others were killed in the first three months of 1981. The ninth victim was a fair-haired, blue-eyed Scot, about 18 years old, who wore a green shirt, a track-suit top, and black and white football socks. Picked up in the Golden Lion, he was strangled on the platform-bed and stored under the floorboards intact. The tenth to die was 'a Billy Sutherland type' but from Belfast – 'slimmish' and 'very ordinary'. Nilsen told the police: 'I don't remember putting anything around his neck. He was just wrapped up in material, tied, and put under the floorboards. At that point there were two intact bodies and one dismembered one down there. That was it. Floorboards back, carpet replaced, and back to work at Denmark Street.'

He felt invincible, as if he were 'a quasi-god'. He told the police: 'I thought

I could do anything I wanted while this was going on. There were people upstairs, people next door. But nobody knew.'

In May 1981 the eleventh of Nilsen's victims, and the last of the eight who were never identified and named, was killed. Aged about 19 and about 5′ 5″, he was a skinhead. He wore a black leather, studded belt and black bovver boots. He was also tattooed with a Union Jack and *England Rules OK*. Around his neck was a row of dots and the legend *Cut Here*. Later, Nilsen would do just that.

They met in Leicester Square. Of the skinhead, Nilsen said:

He boasted about his toughness. How hard he was. All the bundles he had been in, and so on. How much he could drink as well. He could drink anyone under the table, he said, and I said, comparatively speaking, I was an old man – under-exercised, clerical pen-pusher – and that I would have no objection matching him drink for drink. We would drink straight whisky ... Eventually he flaked out in his armchair, where he was sitting. He was dribbling a vomit-like substance down his clothing. I remember thinking he wasn't very hard. I put a tie around his neck and strangled him. After killing him, I went to bed. End of the day, end of a drink, end of a person.

The skinhead was stripped, washed and taken to bed, where Nilsen achieved orgasm between the corpse's thighs. He was later wrapped up in a bundle and rammed under the living-room floor.

Soon after this, his flat was vandalised – as was the flat above. Everything was wrecked and creosote splashed about. Nilsen called in the police, who stood on floorboards concealing four bodies. The wreckers were never caught.

Although Nilsen's remembrance was avowedly uncertain about his fifth to eleventh victims, all unnamed, he was able to write a very exact account, after the trial, of the death of one of them, probably the ninth – the fair-haired, teenage Scot.

We climbed our drunken way naked up to the wooden platform-bed. Later, I remember being straddled over him, my knees each side of him, with the back of my head pressed against the ceiling. I was squeezing his neck and remember wanting to see more clearly what he looked like ... I got up shaking and nearly fell down the ladder. I put all the room-lights on and comforted Bleep to go back to sleep. I put a chair beside the ladder and climbed up. I pulled aside the bedding and pulled his ankles until he half hung off the platform. I got onto the chair and pulled his warm, limp, naked body into my arms. I got down from the chair and saw my reflection in a full-length mirror. I just stood there and looked at myself with the lad's naked body in my arms ... I washed him in the bath and sat him dripping wet on the loo, and bathed myself in the water. It was an act to purify him and apparently (with hindsight) me also ... I dried his body carefully with a bath towel, and the steam rose from him in the cold air. When I moved or carried him a deep sigh would come from his throat . . . Putting him again over my shoulder I carried him up the ladder and laid him on the bed . . . A tape was playing of Copeland's *Fanfare for the Common Man*. I was crying. I got into bed and held him close to me. I was whispering to him: 'Don't worry. Everything's fine. Sleep.' I explored his body . . . I held him so close in my arms that my erect penis was held between his thighs. I stripped off his pants and pulled the bedding back. I took his genitals in my hand and masturbated myself with the other hand . . . I remember first thing in the morning thinking: 'This is absolutely ridiculous.'

Nilsen went to work. On his return he fed the cat and Bleep, turned on the TV and made himself a meal. He took the body from the cupboard where it had been stored, dressed it and sat it in an armchair.

I took his hand and talked to him – my comments for the day, with cynical remarks about the TV programmes . . . I placed him on the table and slowly stripped him. I would always remove his socks last. I would closely examine (slowly) every part of his anatomy . . . his naked body fascinated me. I remember being thrilled that I had full control and ownership of this beautiful body. I would fondle his buttocks, and it amazed me that there was no reaction from him to this . . . I was fascinated by the mystery of death. I whispered to him, because I believed he was still really in there . . . I would hold him close often, and think that he had never been so appreciated in his life before . . . After a week, I stuck him under the floor . . . I wanted him to lie there underneath in a bed of white roses.

It was far from that. Despite the disinfectant that Nilsen daily sprayed under the floorboards, the 'slight smell problem' from four rotting corpses could not be dispelled. So one Friday evening in August 1981 he reluctantly decided to dismember the three that were intact and repackage them. Before he did so he sent the dog and cat into the garden and removed all his clothes. He said:

I deliberated this task reluctantly. I fortified myself with about half a bottle of drink before I lifted up the floorboards. The whole task took till after midnight. I removed the intact bundles one at a time, placed them on the kitchen floor . . . I put the wrapping to one side. I removed the clothing from the bodies and set about dissecting them. The smell was grossly unpleasant, and in some cases there existed large colonies of maggots.

He wrote later: 'The flesh looked just like any meat one would see in a butcher's shop, and having been trained in butchery I was not subject to any traumatic shocks.'

He poured salt on the maggots and at one stage was violently sick. More than once he went naked into the garden for some fresh air. Using a kitchen knife, he first cut off the head, then the hands and feet, all of which were washed in the kitchen sink, then dried, wrapped in paper towels, and put in plastic carrier bags, as were the internal organs. Each body was then cut in half; the arms were severed and the legs below the knee. These parts and the others were packed in large black plastic bags, to which deodorants were added, before being wedged under the floor. The internal organs were spilled between the garden's double fencing. Nilsen then took the dog for a walk.

The last of those who were murdered at Melrose Avenue, and the twelfth to die, was Malcolm Barlow, an epileptic, aged 23, from Sheffield. He was without parents, friends, morals or much hope and had been in and out of care and mental institutions for much of his life. On the morning of 17 September 1981, he happened to collapse in Melrose Avenue. Nilsen, on his way to work, came to Barlow's aid. Being the Good Samaritan was, after all, his job, helping the underprivileged, deprived and unemployed. He helped Barlow back to No. 195, gave him a coffee and went out again to phone for an ambulance. The following evening, when Nilsen returned from work, Barlow was outside No. 195. 'You're supposed to be in hospital,' Nilsen said. Barlow replied that he had been discharged. 'Well, you'd better come in,' said Nilsen. He made Barlow a meal. They watched TV and drank, despite the fact that Nilsen had warned his guest about drinking and taking some pills. 'Be it on your own head,' said Nilsen.

He told the police:

Much later . . . I let the dog out. On returning, I said: 'Are you still awake?' I tried to rouse him, but he was deeply unconscious. I thought: 'Not an ambulance again.' I got halfway to the phone-box and came back . . . I was slapping his face to wake him up. There was no response. I sat there for a full 20 minutes, wondering what to do. I got up and put my hands around his throat and squeezed tightly. I held that position for two or three minutes and released my hold. I didn't check, but I believed him now to be dead. I didn't have to call an ambulance . . . The next morning, not feeling much like prising up the floorboards, I dragged him through into the kitchen, put him under the sink and closed the doors. I went to work.

There Barlow's body remained for two weeks, until it was destroyed with four others in a bonfire in the rear garden, which Nilsen lit on 4 October, the day before he left Melrose Avenue. The landlord, who wished to redecorate the flats in the house and sell them off, had offered Nilsen alternative accommodation in an attic flat near Muswell Hill.

The day before the move [he said], I made preparations for the burning of the human remains at 195. I made a huge, well-constructed bonfire, using furnishings, and cabinets and things from the house. I left a sizeable hollow in the centre of the structure. This I did the day before. Early in the morning, I lifted the floorboards and started to pack the packages into the centre of the wooden structure, the base of which was two large doors on house bricks . . . Going into the kitchen, I opened the doors of the cupboard under the sink. I noticed that the body had become bloated. I removed the body and dragged it through the house and laid it inside the structure . . . The fire burned fiercely, extraordinarily fiercely. There were spurts, bangs, cracks and hisses and a continual hissing and sizzling coming from the fire. This I took to be fat and other parts of the bodies burning . . . The next morning I packed . . . I replaced the floor-boards before I went and checked there was nothing I had left, no evidence . . . I waited out front for the removal van [his belongings were partly contained in two tea-chests] . . . Driving away from 195 Melrose Avenue was a great relief.

Seven weeks later, on 23 November (Nilsen's 36th birthday), a university student, aged 19 and called Paul Nobbs, was strangled in Cranley Gardens, but allowed to live – apparently because Nilsen suddenly remembered, while strangling Nobbs, that the student had earlier phoned his mother about his plans that night.

They met in the Golden Lion. Nobbs later told the police:

I took off all my clothes and went to bed. Nilsen did the same. We kissed, cuddled and fondled each other, and I attempted to have sex, but was unable because of my state . . . I woke up between two and three in the morning with a splitting headache and felt very ill. I got out of bed, still naked, and went to the kitchen . . . I got a glass of water . . . At about 7.30, I woke again, and I noticed my face was very, very red. I had no whites of the eyes. They were completely red . . . I felt sick and had a sore throat and a pain in the head. I thought it was from the drink. Nil-sen told me I looked bloody awful. I said: 'Thank you very much.' We parted on good terms and he offered me his address and telephone num-ber. He seemed no different from the night before.

Nobbs's tutor sent him to a hospital, where doctors concluded that someone had tried to strangle him. But Nobbs was reluctant, because of his homo-sexuality, to go to the police: he told the doctor he had been mugged. As a result, another three men died.

John Howlett was killed in March 1982; Graham Allen in September; and Stephen Sinclair in January 1983. In between, Martyn Hunter-Craig and others came, and went, and two more potential victims escaped.

One was Carl Stottor, aged 21, whom Nilsen met in the Black Cap in Cam-den Town on 5 May 1982. Stottor was unhappy because he had recently broken up with a boyfriend in Blackpool. He said he wished he was dead. To which Nilsen replied: 'Don't be so silly. You've got your whole life in front of you.'

Stottor later told the court: 'I remember hearing the bell for last orders and he invited me back to his flat. I think he said how pretty I was.' Nilsen held his hand in the cab taking them to Cranley Gardens. In the attic flat Stottor had two glasses of whisky before they both went to bed. No sexual activity took place. Stottor said later:

I fell asleep and woke up feeling something around my neck, and I couldn't breathe properly. I put my hands up to this thing around my neck and couldn't release it . . . He was behind me as this was happening. He didn't shout, but in a whispered voice said: 'Keep still' . . . I then became semi-conscious. There was an increasing pressure and I couldn't breathe. I vaguely remember being carried and then I felt very cold. I knew I was in water and he was trying to drown me. He kept pushing me into the water. The third time I came out of the water I said: 'No more! Please – no more!' He pushed me back in again. I felt this man is trying to kill me, and this is what it feels like to die. I felt very relaxed and then passed out . . . The next thing I knew the dog was licking my face. Then I passed out again . . . Next I woke up in bed, and Des was in bed with me and his arm was around me. I couldn't stay awake for very long . . . When I finally came round and could get up, my face was bloated, and my neck was sore with cuts and burns. My tongue was swollen. He said I had had a nightmare . . . He said he had to throw cold water over me because I was in a state of shock . . . He asked me if I would meet him again.

Stottor went to a hospital and was told that he had probably been strangled. But, as with Nobbs, he was reluctant to go to the police. There were no witnesses and he still wondered whether it had all been a dream.

In June 1982, Nilsen was promoted and transferred to the Jobcentre at Kentish Town. He was now earning £7,000 a year.

In September, Graham Allen, from Glasgow and aged 28, was killed. He had been in a fight in Soho and was very drunk. Nilsen took him home, made him a large omelette, which Allen began to eat and then passed out, with a piece of omelette hanging out of his mouth. Nilsen removed the plate from Allen's lap and strangled him. His naked body was kept in the bath, full of cold water, for several days. He was eventually dismembered in the bath, and his head, hands and feet were boiled, and pieces of flesh flushed down the loo. Said Nilsen later: 'What was left of him was put into two black plastic sacks. One was placed in a secret cubby-hole at the end of the bath, the other was put into a tea-chest.' Allen was identified later through dental records.

For seven days, over Christmas, Trevor Simpson, an ex-prisoner, aged 20, from Derbyshire, stayed with Nilsen in the flat despite the sickly smell in the front room and the bathroom. Nothing special happened on Christmas Day: there were no presents; nor were there any decorations or cards. Nilsen scolded Simpson for reading the *Sun* and suggested they visit the tomb of Karl Marx in Highgate Cemetery. They generally ate in, with daily excursions to cinemas and pubs. Simpson was not a heavy drinker, which seemed to annoy Nilsen. One night Simpson awoke to find the room was full of smoke. Nilsen was in the kitchen and behaved very calmly, blaming Simpson for dropping a lit cigarette on to a pair of Nilsen's jeans which smouldered on the floor. Simpson left the following day.

A few days later, after midnight on New Year's Eve, a Japanese student,

Toshimitsu Ozawa, was assailed in the flat by Nilsen, who approached him (while Ozawa was wide awake) with a tie held taut in his hands. He seemed calm and Ozawa thought that his host was joking, even when the tie was put around his neck. Ozawa pushed Nilsen away. But the performance was repeated. Ozawa panicked, kicked out and fled, causing such a commotion – the dog was barking also – that the girls in the ground-floor room emerged to check on Nilsen's safety. He appeared on the stairs, holding a torch; he was very drunk.

Four weeks later Stephen Sinclair, the fifteenth of Nilsen's victims to die, was killed.

It seems clear that Nilsen originally killed to acquire, to own and to keep the bodies of young men and use them as he wished. He killed them all at night, when both he and they had drunk a good deal, and when they were insensible, defenceless and asleep. They were strangled so that their bodies would barely be marked, and probably because he enjoyed the extreme pleasure of holding life or death in his hands. Drowning was another means of suffocation, as was attempted asphyxiation by smoke. Those he killed were deliberately chosen: they were smaller than him, and much younger, generally social misfits and down-and-outs, without homes, with few friends and whose absence would not be missed. It seems that as the killings continued, Nilsen became increasingly indifferent to the physical quality of his victims, and killed because he felt he had been angered, offended or slighted in some way – and because he wanted to kill again.

The most gruesome, cold-blooded and protracted of Nilsen's murders was the thirteenth, that of John Howlett, aged 23, known to Nilsen as John the Guardsman.

He was the first to die in Cranley Gardens, in March 1982. They had met in a pub the previous December. In March they met again in The Salisbury in St Martin's Lane. It seems that Howlett, who came from High Wycombe, was after a bed for the night. They walked to Cranley Gardens from the Highgate Underground station, and once in the attic flat of No. 23, Nilsen made a meal and they watched TV and drank. After midnight Howlett announced he was tired. He said: 'I wouldn't mind getting my head down.' He left Nilsen on his own, watching TV, and went to sleep next door – the bed was then in the front room. At about 1.00 am Nilsen, displeased and drunk, put the lights out and went into the other room.

He was in the bed [said Nilsen later]. I think I said: 'I thought you were getting your head down. I didn't know you were moving in.' I roused him and he mumbled a reply. He indicated to me that he didn't feel like moving. I went into the back room, got the bottle of Bacardi, and sat on the bed. I noticed he'd taken most of his clothes off . . . I didn't feel like getting into the bed with him in it. I remember it was getting a bit cold. I remember finishing the bottle. I went to the armchair and under the cushion there was a length of loose upholstery strap. I approached to where he was lying in bed under the blankets. I wound this material round his neck. I think I said: 'It's about time you went.' I was astride him and I tightened my grip on the material. He fought back furiously and partially raised himself up. I thought I'd be overpowered. He was a very fit person. Summoning up all my strength I forced him back down and his head struck the rim of the head-rest on the bed. He still struggled fiercely, so that now he was half off the bed. In about a minute he had gone limp. There was blood on the bedding, and I assumed it was from his head. I checked if he was still breathing and he was – deep rasping breaths. I tightened my grip on him again around his neck for another minute or so. I let go my grip again, and he appeared to be dead. I stood up. The dog was barking in the next room. I went through to pacify it. I was shaking all over with the stress of the struggle . . . I returned to the front room and was shocked to see that he had started breathing again. I looped the material round his neck again, pulled it as tight as I could, and held on for what must have been two or three minutes. When I released my grip he had stopped breathing. But I noticed as he lay there on his back his heart was still beating quite strongly. I couldn't believe it. I dragged him off the bed and into the bathroom. I pulled him over the rim of the bath, so his head was hanging into the bath, put the plug in, still holding him, and ran the cold water full on. His head was on the bottom of the bath. In a minute or so the water reached his nose. The rasping breath came on again. The water rose higher and I held him under. He was struggling against it. There were bubbles coming from his mouth or nose, and he stopped struggling. I held him in that position for four or five minutes. The water had become bloody, and a substance, as well as particles of food, was coming from his mouth. Because of the blood, I emptied the bath. Having emptied the bath I put him in with his knees bent . . . I left him there all night. I washed my hands, changed the bedding and went to bed. I was smoking and shaking. I called the dog, and it came through looking a bit sheepish. I tapped the bed, saying 'Come up here', and it curled up by my feet . . . Before going to work and before dressing I pulled him out of the bath and put him into the cupboard. I got some blood on my hands and my legs. I bathed and went to work . . . For a week afterwards, I had his finger-marks on my neck.

A few days later, as a friend of Nilsen from Scotland was coming to stay, John Howlett was dissected in the bath. His internal organs, in 'half-pound lots' were flushed down the loo, as were lumps of flesh. His head, hands and feet were boiled, as were his ribs. The severed remnants of his arms, legs and pelvis, were packaged in several plastic bags and sacks and put in a tea-chest in the front room. There they remained for nearly a year.

On 10 and 11 February 1983, the foul relics of Howlett, Allen and Sinclair were retrieved from 23 Cranley Gardens by the police.

Dennis Nilsen was transferred to Brixton Prison in March, where he was confined in a single cell, as a Category A prisoner, for 23 and a half hours a day. Resentful of the way he was treated, he became alternately awkward, angry, frustrated, depressed, rebellious and paranoid. He went on hunger-strike twice, tore up depositions, refused to wear prison uniform, assaulted warders by throwing his chamber-pot contents at them and was banned from attending church services as his presence 'disturbed' the other prisoners. Curiously, he was never given any kind of medical examination, although he was questioned by psychiatrists. In April, Nilsen decided to dispense with his solicitor, Ronald Moss, and with legal aid and defend himself. A few weeks later he reapplied. This happened twice more. In September Moss was finally dismissed, five weeks before the trial, and another solicitor, Ralph Haeems, took his place. Haeems, who had been involved in the trials of the Great Train Robbers and the Krays, had been recommended by David Martin, a young gunman, convicted in September of malicious wounding and other offences, and with whom Nilsen fell in love in prison, although apparently nothing sexual occurred. On Haeems's advice, Nilsen changed his plea from guilty to not guilty, thus prolonging his trial.

While in Brixton Prison Nilsen wrote nearly 200 letters and filled 49 exercise-books with his specious, egocentric and contradictory thoughts, seeking to self-dramatise, elevate and excuse what he had done. None of these writings, which revealed much more than his police statements, was used in evidence at his trial. The author, Brian Masters, who had acquired Nilsen's trust when writing his account of the man and the murders, offered to make the journals available – Nilsen had assigned all 49 to him. But the offer was never taken up by the lawyers or the police.

Nilsen wrote: 'Killing is wrong, and I have reduced my own principles to ashes . . . My murders were for no useful end as murders never are' – 'I look back with shame that the small space on that living-room floor could have witnessed 12 deaths' – 'I have always believed they are, in a sense, living on within me' – 'I sometimes wondered if anyone cared for me or them. That could easily be me lying there. In fact a lot of the time it was. It may be that when I was killing these men, I was killing myself' – 'We are not dealing with murder here, although I have killed.'

The trial of Dennis Nilsen began at the Central Criminal Court on Monday, 24 October 1983 – a month before his 38th birthday. He was defended by Ivan Lawrence, QC, MP. The prosecution was led by Allan Green, and the judge was Mr Justice Croom-Johnson. Allan Green became Director of Public Prosecutions in 1987 and was knighted. He resigned as DPP in 1991, following a police allegation that he had been kerb-crawling and approaching prostitutes near King's Cross.

Nilsen was charged with the murders of Ken Ockenden, Martyn Duffey, Billy Sutherland, Malcolm Barlow, John Howlett and Stephen Sinclair, and with attempting to murder Douglas Stewart and Paul Nobbs. Nilsen wore gold-rimmed glasses, a grey-green jacket, pale blue shirt, and a dark blue tie with white spots. The *Daily Express* reported: 'There is a primness of the fussy clerk about him, a nervy respectability.' The *Daily Mirror* commented on his pale blue eyes and his large hands 'very still in his lap'.

It was not disputed that Nilsen had killed. The question was whether, as the defence alleged, his abnormality of mind was such that it substantially reduced his responsibility for what he had done. The prosecution claimed that the accused was fully aware of his acts, and that they were deliberately done. Oddly, the prosecution conceded in advance that neither the murders nor the victims were homosexual by nature, and the very essence and cause of the murders, the homosexuality of the accused, and of most if not all of his victims, was played down in court. Mr Green, who also wore glasses, said that Nilsen had admitted that he was bisexual and emotionally homosexual, but denied that any homosexual activity had occurred before his victims' deaths.

After Mr Green had paraphrased and quoted at length from Nilsen's detailed statements to the police, three witnesses for the prosecution were called. They were: Douglas Stewart, Paul Nobbs and Carl Stottor. The thickness of Stewart's Scottish accent and his jaunty self-assurance made a poor impression, as did the revelation that his story had been bought by the *Sunday Mirror*. The defence cast doubts on his reliability as a witness. Although Stewart denied being homosexual and said he had married two years before, the sexual proclivities of Nobbs and Stottor were not in doubt. Both were very nervous and spoke so quietly they could hardly be heard. Both testified that Nilsen's behaviour before and after each attempted murder was calm and concerned. 'How odd that was,' said Mr Lawrence.

DCI Peter Jay, after agreeing that Nilsen had been very co-operative and had no previous criminal record, read various self-analytical statements made by Nilsen and a letter to the police. One document, written on 25 February, was entitled 'Unscrambling Behaviour'. In it Nilsen wrote:

> I guess I may be a creative psychopath who, when in a loss of rationality situation, lapses temporarily into a destructive psychopath, a condition induced by rapid and heavy ingestion of alcohol. At the subconscious root lies a sense of total social isolation and a desperate search for a sexual identity . . . God only knows what thoughts go through my mind when it's captive within a destructive binge . . . It may be the perverted overkill of my need to help people . . . There is no disputing the fact that I am a violent killer under certain circumstances . . . It amazes me that I have no tears for these victims. I have no tears for myself or for those bereaved by my actions. Am I a wicked person, constantly under pressure, who just cannot cope with it, who escapes to reap revenge against society through the haze of a bottle of spirits? Maybe it's because I was just born an evil man.

DCS Chambers read out the whole of Nilsen's statements about the murders. The recitation took four hours, during which the jury of eight men and four women gazed at the impassive bespectacled person hunched in the dock with varying degrees of shock, incredulity, horror and disgust, which were heightened when the cooking-pot, wherein three heads had been boiled, was produced along with some other exhibits, in court. As Chambers spoke, Nilsen scanned a transcript of his confession, to make sure that what Chambers said was correct.

Two psychiatrists, Dr MacKeith and Dr Gallwey, were called by the defence. Dr MacKeith contended that the accused suffered from a severe personality disorder and had difficulty expressing any feelings apart from anger.

He was suspicious, paranoid, schizoid and craved attention. His problem was depersonalisation, which meant he regarded people as components of his fantasies. Allan Green, in cross-examination, maintained that Nilsen was cunning, resourceful, articulate, plausible, 'a jolly good actor', and frequently lied. Dr Gallwey said Nilsen had a False Self problem, which was magnified when he was socially and emotionally isolated. The killings were motiveless, but they prevented Nilsen from going insane or committing suicide: his self-loathing and urge for self-destruction were directed elsewhere. Gallwey agreed with Green that Nilsen knew what he was doing intellectually but was not emotionally aware. 'Did he know the nature and quality of his acts?' demanded Mr Green. 'No,' replied Gallwey. 'He knew the nature of the acts only. He did not know the quality of them.'

The prosecution was allowed a rebuttal witness, another psychiatrist, Dr Bowden, who declared that Nilsen, though abnormal, had no mental disorder, that his feelings of guilt about being homosexual had been redirected into doing something really bad, that he was not especially lonely or without friends, that he had shown remorse, was rational, purposeful, manipulative and had simply wanted to kill. Dr Bowden said: 'In my experience, the vast majority of people who kill have to regard their victims as objects – otherwise they cannot kill them.'

Mr Green summarised his and the defence's closing speeches with the words: 'The defence says: "He couldn't help it." The Crown says: "Oh yes, he could."' Mr Lawrence insisted that Nilsen was 'out of his mind', and in cataloguing a list of his horrific acts, repeatedly asked: 'Is there nothing substantially wrong with a mind like that?'

In his summing-up, Mr Justice Croom-Johnson said: 'There are evil people, who do evil things. Committing murder is one of them . . . What is meant by "substantial"? It doesn't mean *total* . . . You may legitimately differ from the doctors and use your common sense. If you found there was some impairment, but not enough, you would be allowed to find him guilty of murder.'

The jury were evidently divided about this, and having retired on Thursday, 3 November, they were unable to return with a unanimous verdict. But at 4.25 on the Friday they concluded, by a majority of ten to two, that Dennis Nilsen was guilty on the six counts of murder and one count of attempted murder (that of Stewart). They were unanimous in their guilty verdict on the attempted murder of Paul Nobbs.

Nilsen was sentenced to life imprisonment, with a recommendation that he should serve no less than 25 years.

He was sent to Wormwood Scrubs, where a prisoner slashed his face with a razor, causing a four-inch cut across his left cheek. In March 1984 he was moved to Parkhurst Prison on the Isle of Wight, and in June he was transferred to Wakefield Prison. In 1992 he was in Albany Prison, back on the Isle of Wight.

He has a cell to himself, but he mixes with others at meal-times. He is cheerful and far from morose, and still resolute about his rights. In his cell he reads a lot, writes and paints, listens to the radio, and has as his cellmate a budgerigar, called Hamish. For over a year in Wakefield he is said to have enjoyed a physical relationship with an armed robber, called Jimmy, aged 32.

Meanwhile, there were other deaths: David Martin committed suicide in Parkhurst Prison in March 1984, before Nilsen's arrival there; Nilsen's brother, Olav, died of a heart attack (like their grandfather) in 1990; David Gallichan committed suicide in December 1991; and DCS Geoff Chambers died in July 1992.

A few days after his trial Nilsen wrote in his prison journal what amounted at last to a true confession, which confirmed the prosecution's case.

I had always wished to kill, but the opportunity never really presented itself in safe conditions . . . [This was] substituted by fantasies which had *me* killed in the mirrored images. I had been killing this way for years, killing my own image. The kill was only part of the whole. The whole experience, which thrilled me intensely, was the drink, the chase, the social seduction, the getting the 'friend' back, the decision to kill, the body and its disposal. The pressure needed release. I took release through spirits and music. On that high I had a loss of morality and danger feeling . . . If the conditions were right, I would completely follow through to the death . . . I had no other thrill or happiness.

He had also written, months before: 'Am I mad? I don't feel mad. Maybe I am mad.'

The Nilsen murders, in number and kind, were repeated by tall, fair-haired, nice-looking Jeffrey Dahmer in Wisconsin, in the late 1980s. He was charged in August 1991, when he was 31, with killing 15 non-white young men and boys. He claimed to have killed 17 – there may have been more. Like Nilsen, drink played a significant part in the execution of the murders. Dahmer was a heavy drinker (rum and coke) and drugged his victims with a special potion before strangling them with a strap. The bodies were also dismembered, some heads and skulls, painted grey, being kept in a fridge. Necrophilia (oral sex in his case) was a feature of Dahmer's crimes, as was cannibalism. And he took Polaroid photos of his victims, before and after they were killed, and as he cut them up.

A few weeks after Dahmer was arrested, a Texan, Donald Evans, confessed to the killing of a ten-year-old girl in Mississippi. He also claimed to have killed about 60 other people in the past 14 years. Meanwhile, in New York, Julio Gonzales was convicted of the murder of 87 people, who died in 1990 when, after a row with his girlfriend, he set fire to a social club in the Bronx.

In southern Russia, in April 1992, a 56-year-old former teacher, Andrei Chikatilo, was charged with killing and eating at least 52 young women and children over a period of a dozen years. He was sentenced to death in October 1992 and executed by firing squad.

And so it goes on — a reflective echo of the slaughter of people that occurs increasingly around the world in fatal spasms of civil, tribal, racial and religious strife.

Epilogue

Albert Pierrepoint's own account of his first execution, as head executioner, follows. It took place at Pentonville Prison in 1940, the victim being a professional criminal sentenced to death for a gangland killing. Pierrepoint's assistant was Steve Wade.

At five minutes to nine we were given the signal that the Sheriff had gone to the Governor's office. Wade and I walked across the Prison yard with an officer who led us up to the corridor outside the condemned cell. I think the next minutes of waiting were the worst, not only then but on every occasion. It is impossible not to feel apprehension and even fear at the prospect of the responsibility of the moment, but with me the frailty passed as soon as there was action. At half a minute to nine a small group came down the corridor. There was the Sheriff, the Governor, the doctor and some senior prison officers. I suddenly had a strange realisation. I was the youngest man there, and the eyes of everyone were on me. The party paused at the next door to that of the condemned cell, the door of the execution chamber. A finger was raised and they passed in. The chief opened the door of the cell and I went forward with a strap in my hand.

The prisoner was standing, facing me, smiling. In his civilian clothes he looked as smart as I had already registered him. In my civilian clothes, amid all those uniforms, we might have been meeting for a chat in a club in Leicester Square – but who would have foreseen a robed priest in the room? I quickly strapped his wrists and said 'Follow me.'

The door in the side wall of the cell had been opened as I came in, and I walked through it into the execution chamber. He followed me, walking seven paces with the noose straight ahead of him, and the escorting officers mounting the cross-planks gently stopped him as he stood on the T. I had turned in time to face him. Eye to eye, that last look. Wade was stooping behind him, swiftly fastening the ankle strap. I pulled from my breast pocket the white cap, folded as carefully as a parachute, and drew it down over his head. 'Cheerio,' he said. I reached for the noose, pulled it down over the cap, tightened it to my right, pulled a rubber washer along the rope to hold it, and darted to my left, crouching towards the cotter pin at the base of the lever. I was in the position of a sprinter at the start of a race as I went over the cross-plank, pulled the pin with one hand, and pushed the lever with the other, instinctively looking back as I did so. There was a snap as the falling doors were bitten and held by the rubber clips, and the rope stood straight and still. The broken twine spooned down in a falling leaf, passed through a little eddy of dust, and floated into the pit.

I went to the side of the scaffold and walked down into the pit. I undid the prisoner's shirt for the stethoscope, and the doctor followed me. I came up again and waited. The doctor came back to the scaffold. 'Everything is all right,' he said. It was a curious way for a doctor to pronounce death . . . I suppose his intention was to reassure the Governor and possibly me . . .

At ten o'clock Wade and I returned to the execution chamber. He went down into the pit and, kneeling on the scaffold floor, I complied with a strange requirement. By regulation, I had to measure from the heels of the hanging man to the level of the scaffold from which he had dropped. This measurement was longer than the drop I had given him. The extra length was made up by the stretch of the man's body after death . . . He had been hanging for an hour, and the stretch was considerable . . .

I put the tape measure away, and went below. I stared at the flesh I had stilled. I had further duties to perform, but no longer as executioner. I had been nearest to this man in death, and I prepared him for burial. As he hung, I stripped him. Piece by piece I removed his clothes. It was not callous, but the best rough dignity I could give him, as he swung to the touch, still hooded in the noose. He yielded his garments without the resistance of limbs. If it had been in a prison outside London, I should have left him his shirt for a shroud, and put him in his coffin. In London there was always a post-mortem, and he had to be stripped entirely and placed on a mortuary stretcher. But in common courtesy I tied his empty shirt around his hips.

Wade had fixed the tackle above. I passed a rope under the armpits of my charge, and the body was hauled up a few feet. Standing on the scaffold, with the body now drooping, I removed the noose and the cap, and took his head between my hands, inclining it from side to side to assure myself that the break had been clean. Then I went below, and Wade lowered the rope. A dead man, being taken down from execution, is a uniquely broken body whether he is a criminal or Christ, and I received this flesh, leaning helplessly into my arms, with the linen round the loins, gently with the reverence I thought due to the shell of any man who has sinned and suffered.

Acknowledgements

In the writing of this book I have been greatly assisted by the work of writers and journalists in times long past, particularly those in the nineteenth and early twentieth centuries who wrote with such care and accuracy for *The Times*, the *Morning Advertiser*, the *Illustrated Police News*, and for local newspapers like the *Surrey Advertiser*, the *Tonbridge Free Press*, the *Essex County Chronicle*, the *Western Morning News*, and the *Torquay Times*. Other and more contemporary newspapers were also useful sources of information, in particular *The Times*, the *Sunday Times*, the *Independent*, the *Daily Telegraph*, the *Daily Mail*, the *Daily Express*, the *Daily Mirror*, the *Sun*, the *People*, the *News of the World*, the London *Evening Standard* and the *Evening News*.

I also owe a large debt of gratitude to the librarians, archivists and local historians who provided me with photocopies, advice and information: to those at the Battersea District Library, the Rugeley Central Library, the Leatherhead Central Library, the Central Library, Torquay, the Devon Record Office, the Essex Record Office, and Westminster Libraries.

My thanks to them, and chiefly to the ever-helpful staff of the Marylebone Library in London, and to Mary Clucas, Eva Wade and the staff of the Commissioner's Library in New Scotland Yard.

Thanks also to the Home Office, the Met Office, the Public Record Office at Kew, the Records Office at the Old Bailey, the Court of Appeal, Madame Tussaud's and Tonbridge School; and to Joyce Bailey, Francis Cazalet, Clare Colvin, Lt.-Col. Dennis Daly, Bernie Davis, Louise Douglas, Stewart Goodwin, Henry Hayward, Jane Herbert, Paul Mallender, Brian Masters, John Miller, Brigadier Andrew Parker Bowles, Sheila Reid, Bryan Rostron, Anthony Seldon, David Thorogood, Marjorie Waddell and Andy Wright.

Special thanks to the new Curator of the Black Museum, John Ross, and above all to his predecessor, Bill Waddell, without whose unstinting assistance, advice and co-operation this book could not have been written.

Some of the photographs in the book are reproduced by kind permission of the Metropolitan Police. These photos, of Museum exhibits, were taken by Alan Chandler.

The author and publishers also wish to thank the following: Her Majesty's

Stationery Office for permission to reproduce the 1990 criminal statistics (p. ix); Times Newspapers for permission to quote from trial reports; Harrap Ltd for permission to quote from *Executioner: Pierrepoint* by Albert Pierrepoint (pp. 358–60).